SOCIAL SECURITY LAW AND PRACTICE

CASES AND MATERIALS

■ ■ ■

By

Frank S. Bloch

Professor of Law Emeritus
Vanderbilt University Law School

Available to students as an Online Book at
www.store.westlaw.com

AMERICAN CASEBOOK SERIES®

A Thomson Reuters business

Mat # 41030916

American Casebook Series is a trademark registered in the U.S. Patent and Trademark Office.

© 2012 Thomson Reuters

610 Opperman Drive
St. Paul, MN 55123
1-800-313-9378

Printed in the United States of America

ISBN: 978-0-314-26495-4

PREFACE

This book is intended to enhance the law school curriculum in two ways: by offering materials for a course on a topic not covered fully in other courses—the Social Security Act and its major benefit programs—and by focusing the course not only on the relevant substantive law but also on specific areas of practice and procedure that are critically important to lawyers practicing in the field. Thus the deliberate title of the book and the course it supports: Social Security Law and Practice. Not surprisingly, I began developing this approach to a classroom course on Social Security after more than twenty years of experience handling Social Security cases with my students in a clinical course.

In setting out the substantive content for the course I knew that I had to expand the coverage of the Social Security Act beyond that which clinic students typically have to face. I also sought to open for discussion and reflection broader issues that students usually do not have time to address in a clinic setting. At the same time, I wanted to preserve at least some of the exposure to Social Security practice that lies at the heart of the clinical experience so that classroom students could gain a sense of the important role that lawyers play in the administration of the Social Security programs. In other words, I wrote this book expressly for a classroom course while mindful of the different opportunities and challenges that are inherent when teaching similar material in a classroom and in a clinic. As a result, these materials are not really suited for a clinical course; instead, as part of the same project, I wrote a separate shorter volume for use in a clinical course where students handle Social Security Cases. FRANK S. BLOCH, SOCIAL SECURITY LAW AND PRACTICE: A HANDBOOK FOR A LIVE-CLIENT CLINICAL COURSE (West 2012).

The basic structure of the book tracks the goals set out above by alternating between broad coverage and coverage focused on the most commonly contested issues related to disability benefits that make up the great majority of a Social Security practice. Chapter 1 offers some historical background leading up to and including the passage of the original Social Security Act in 1935, as well as an overview of the major amendments to the Act from shortly after its passage to the present. Chapter 2 then describes the basic coverage of the Act's major benefit programs, followed by more detailed discussion of the eligibility requirements for old age and survivors benefits (Chapter 3) and disability benefits (Chapter 4). The next two chapters focus specifically on the statutory disability standard and, more particularly, how that standard is implemented in practice; Chapter 5 includes a lengthy discussion and analysis of the Social Security Administration's process for determining disability, while Chapter 6 covers selected disability issues that arise frequently in contested claims for disability benefits. Chapter 7 returns to the Act in general with an explanation of the calculation and payment of benefits. The book then concludes with two chapters on practice and procedure, again with a special emphasis on those aspects of Social Security practice (Chapter 8) and administrative advocacy (Chapter 9) most important when representing a client for disability benefits.

I began to prepare the manuscript for this book after teaching the course for a few years with loosely organized photocopied materials. Rather than revise those materials for use as a draft version of the course book, I offered the course to a small number of students in a workshop-like format in which—after the students read a mildly updated version of the earlier materials—most of the class discussion was on how the materials would work, or would not work, for the classroom course I had in mind. Each student also prepared specific revisions to a part of the materials based on the class discussion and their own independent ideas for that part of the book. Much of what I learned from those students during that class—Ashley Bassel, Kevin Brunner, Cory Ridenour, Laura Robinson, John Shoaf, Stephen Smith, and Nancy Zeronda—found its way into the book manuscript. At times I also drew on portions of my electronic treatise, BLOCH ON SOCIAL SECURITY DISABILITY (Thomson Reuters, available on Westlaw, West's Social Security Excellence, and West's CD-ROM Library). I was helped in the final phases of the project by Marissa Cwik, Erica Deray, Chelsea Journigan, Sarah Payne-Jarboe and Melissa Sifferman, who provided valuable research assistance.

FSB
Nashville, Tennessee

SUMMARY OF CONTENTS

TABLE OF CONTENTS

TABLE OF CASES

The principal cases are in bold type. Cases cited or discussed in the text are in roman type. References are to pages. Cases cited in principal cases and within other quoted materials are not included.

SOCIAL SECURITY LAW AND PRACTICE

CASES AND MATERIALS

CHAPTER 1

INTRODUCTION AND HISTORICAL BACKGROUND

■ ■ ■

A. INTRODUCTION

This is a course book on Social Security law and practice, and as such it covers the key areas of substantive law and the most important and commonly encountered aspects of Social Security practice relevant to a lawyer representing clients seeking Social Security benefits. The central legislation is, of course, the Social Security Act; however, certain provisions in the Act are more important to Social Security lawyers than others. Most cases handled by Social Security lawyers involve claims for benefits under one or both of two titles: Old Age, Survivors, and Disability Insurance (OASDI), set out in Title II of the Act, and Supplemental Security Income (SSI), set out in Title XVI. A typical Social Security practice is even more limited, as the vast majority of contested Social Security cases—that is, those that require the services of an attorney—involve claims for disability benefits. (As its name implies, OASDI provides old age and disability benefits to insured workers, as well as various benefits to certain of their survivors and dependents. SSI is a public assistance program that provides old age and disability benefits to persons with limited income and resources.)

Another way to describe the scope of this book is to describe what it does not cover. Apart from the historical material set out in the next section of this chapter on the original Social Security Act in 1935, there is no coverage of the unemployment insurance program. The administrative structure of that program and the legal issues that arise are completely different from those involved with OASDI and SSI. While certainly there are many lawyers who combine a Social Security and an unemployment insurance practice, the study of the unemployment benefits program fits more closely into the labor law curriculum. Nor is there coverage of the two medical benefit programs included in the Act, Medicare and Medicaid—apart from the fact that the basic eligibility requirements for Medicare and Medicaid coverage (as opposed to the more complicated issues of payment and covered services) more-or-less track the criteria for OASDI and SSI old age and disability benefits. Finally, this book does not cover

Temporary Assistance for Needy Families (TANF), the major joint federal-state public assistance program for low income families that replaced Aid to Families with Dependent Children (AFDC) in 1996, except for brief mention of its first formulation as Aid to Dependent Children (ADC) at the time of the enactment of the original Social Security Act. As with the unemployment insurance program, the law and various practice issues relevant to the TANF program, due in large part to its shared federal and state legal and administrative structure, are substantially different from those one encounters in a Social Security practice.

The remaining eight chapters are divided into two parts: Part I on Social Security law and Part II on Social Security practice. Both Parts focus on the OASDI and SSI programs, with special emphasis on disability benefits. Thus, while the six chapters in Part I include discussion and material on the eligibility requirements for all of the various types of benefits provided under both programs, there are three chapters that cover the eligibility requirements for disability benefits in significantly greater detail. Similarly, the first of the two chapters in Part II covers the administrative decision and appeals process as they apply to all types of claims; however, the second chapter on administrative advocacy concentrates on representing claimants for disability benefits.

B. THE SOCIAL SECURITY ACT IN HISTORICAL CONTEXT

Although this book focuses on current issues of Social Security law and practice, historical context is important in two respects. First of all, there is a rich history of social legislation in Europe that dates from long before the passage of the original Social Security Act in 1935. The European experience was widely known and often recognized in colonial and early post-independence America, and was drawn upon to some extent by individual states before the federal government entered the field. The Social Security Act is a relative newcomer among Western social security laws and, as a result, some understanding of this history and its influence on pre-1935 social legislation in the United States can provide important insight as to the broader social and economic purposes of the Social Security Act passed in 1935.

A second period of historical interest begins around the time of the passage of the Social Security Act in1935 and extends through the first few decades of the Social Security program, as it expanded beyond its original limited scope into the more comprehensive program it is today. The social, economic, and political issues at the time of the passage of the original Social Security Act and those that drove the first major amendments to the Act are important not only to understand current Social Security law, but also to help provide some perspective on various challenges to current policies and practices as well as various proposals for reform.

A full discussion of this history is, of course, beyond the scope of this book. What follows is a very brief overview of social legislation that existed in the United States before 1935, some key material from the period around the passage of the Social Security Act in 1935, and a review of the major amendments that have reshaped the Act since then. The chapter concludes with an introduction to constitutional litigation challenging the coverage and administration of Social Security benefits.

1. SOCIAL LEGISLATION BEFORE 1935

Probably the earliest economic security history relevant to the United States was the emergence in 16th-century England of guilds and other trade organizations as sources of financial and social support, at least for their members. These organizations, which came to America with the early colonies, provided the only regular mechanism at the time for food and shelter to the poor. Religious communities also played a role, but they did so piecemeal and at a less institutional level.

The early 17th century brought the first significant public involvement in welfare benefits to England in the form of the Elizabethan Poor Laws aimed at relieving the plight of widows and orphans whose misfortunes were seen as coming from external sources, not of their own making. As described by William P. Quigley,

> The Poor Law of 1601 firmly established relief of the poor as a local responsibility of the parish, which is by now a traditional unit of English local government. The parish was to raise money and administer relief directly to the poor who were unable to work and to provide work for those who were able. The state filled the vacuum left by the elimination of the Church system of poor relief and adopted many of the same structures and procedures of that prior system. The law directed the local people to annually elect two or more overseers of the poor. The overseers were to work with the justices of the peace to administer poor relief.
>
> The main part of the statute was the creation of a system of general assessment to provide a consistent source of funding for the activities of local officials in relief of the poor. Taxes could be levied on every inhabitant on a weekly or other basis for the support of the poor. Further, if the parish or locality proved unable to raise enough funds for poor support, the justices of the peace were allowed to look to other more prosperous parishes in the same locale for support. Imprisonment was the penalty for refusal to pay assessments.

There were four types of activities or support allowed to be performed by the overseers under the law. First was the "setting to work the children of all such whose parents shall not by the said church wardens and overseers, or the greater part of them, be thought able to keep and maintain their children." Second was the "setting to work of all such persons, married or unmarried, having no means to maintain them, and no ordinary daily trade of life to get their living by." Third, to levy taxes on everyone and everything of value in order to provide materials for the poor to work on such as "flax, hemp, wool, thread, iron and other necessary ware and stuff." Fourth, to levy taxes "towards the necessary relief of the lame, impotent, old, blind, and such other among them, being poor and not able to work." Lastly, "to do and execute all other things ... as to them shall seem convenient."

The local authorities were empowered to build housing "for the impotent and poor of the parish." The mutual legal responsibility of parents and children was expanded to make grandparents responsible for the support of impoverished children and grandchildren, and vice versa, by establishing the principle of primary family responsibility which stated that "[t]he father and grandfather, and the mother and grandmother, and the children of every poor, old, blind, lame and impotent person, or other poor person not able to work, being of sufficient ability, shall, at their own charge, relieve and maintain every such poor person ...." This principle of primary family responsibility became a firmly entrenched rule of law.

William P. Quigley, *Five Hundred Years of English Poor Laws, 1349-1834: Regulating the Working and Nonworking Poor*, 30 AKRON L. REV. 73, 101-02 (1996).

Similar laws were introduced in the colonies in the form of local tax authority for locally determined benefit payments to the "worthy," as opposed to the "unworthy," poor. Following independence, some states initiated broader programs of social support, always along the "deserving poor" model of the Poor Laws. Typical of this approach were state-funded "poorhouses" that would receive and house individuals and families under various conditions, often with severe restrictions and conditions.

Quite different, but also illuminating, were developments in early US history concerning retirement security. Most notable among these early developments were various pension programs for veterans, the most significant by far being a series of benefit programs for veterans of the Civil War passed by Congress in stages from the end of the war through the early 1900s. By 1910, over 90% of surviving Civil War veterans were receiving disability or old-age pension benefits; however, that group made up less than 1% of the population and most of the other 99% were not covered by any other public pension scheme. About the same time, some social planners in the United States began looking to the "social insurance" experience in Europe that began in Germany in the 19th century under Chancellor Otto van Bismarck. By the early 20th century, most European countries had social insurance programs in place as part of a broad social welfare system—usually covering disability, old age, and unemployment. The federal government did not follow through at that time to cover anyone other than veterans, although some states provided limited pension benefits during the Depression and through the years immediately before the enactment of the Social Security Act.

PATRICIA E. DILLEY, THE EVOLUTION OF ENTITLEMENT: RETIREMENT INCOME AND THE PROBLEM OF INTEGRATING PRIVATE PENSIONS AND SOCIAL SECURITY
30 Loy. L.A. L. Rev. 1063, 1085-1105 (1997)*

* * *

III. The Roots of Entitlement: Evolution of Entitlement and Retirement in America

Retirement—the extended period of leisure after the end of a working life expected by most workers in the late twentieth century—is a recent phenomenon. While every human culture has some experience of supporting older members who live past the age of productive labor, it was not until widespread industrialization and the development of industrial-laboring and middle classes in Europe and the United States in the twentieth century that retirement became a relatively common occurrence.

* * *

Social Security was hailed at its enactment as a long overdue federal undertaking to guarantee direct income support for the nation's elderly, enabling them to retire without recourse to the poor house. Yet the federal government had previously assumed responsibility for providing income support in old age for a large proportion of the northern population in the form of the Civil War veterans' pensions. This pension system was based on earned entitlement—through military service—and presumed, rather than demonstrated, need. Before that, the Revolutionary War pension system had provided a precedent for federal pensions as an antipoverty measure, breaking from the old system of locally controlled poor relief.

---

* Reprinted with permission.

Both of these systems, as well as the Social Security program that would be enacted in 1935, exemplified an American approach to dealing with poverty and old age in which the right to income was created by personal effort, not awarded based on need or status. Long before the enactment of Social Security, the Civil War pension system developed into the major federal entitlement program for the elderly just as the more direct sources of income for aged persons in pre-industrial America—principally control over income-producing land—were replaced by the uncertainties of industrial employment and economic cycles. The roots of our current earnings-based retirement entitlement system can be found in the history of these nineteenth century precursors. Their development helps to explain the cultural and political strength of retirement income entitlements.

A. Old Age and Poverty Before the Retirement Era

The most recent work on the history of retirement and the elderly in America, and elsewhere, has yielded a complex portrait of the development of the concept of retirement as the natural end of a working life. It is clear that the current generation of retirees is the first to spend its entire adulthood more or less expecting to retire at a certain age. However, the work and family patterns of the American colonial experience provided a basis for all later old-age retirement income programs—entitlement for the worthy, charity, and grudging government assistance for the unworthy.

* * *

2. Colonial American approaches to poverty and aging

In pre-industrial America—the colonial period up until about the Civil War—the family-based, largely agrarian economy required and allowed work until disability from extreme old age or death. For those without control of property or income, extreme old age in the pre-Civil War era was inextricably linked with dependency, either on family or on local charity. American colonists took the same geographic approach to poor relief as their English forebears had: the poor of the town, those known to the locality, were generally cared for if they were "of good character" and unable to provide for themselves, but the vagrant poor were a threat to social stability and were shunned, if not actively driven away.

In the context of frontier agrarian and small town center economic structure, the presumption appeared to be, as it had been in England, that persons without means and outside their own homeplace beyond the reach of their kin were suspect and not worthy of charity. Clearly it would be easier to determine whether an individual was worthy of assistance if the local authorities were familiar with that person's background and current circumstances. In effect, the geographic approach was one way of enforcing a moral test of "worthiness." Aid took the form of "outdoor relief"—aid given to those still living outside of almshouses and financed by town revenues and the proceeds of liens on, or liquidation of, the pauper's property. Local officials also solved the local poverty problem by placing indigent individuals with other families, or occasionally, selling the impoverished person, or less drastically the indigent's belongings, at public auction.

The poor elderly were not especially differentiated from the disabled. They were more likely to be considered worthy of assistance if they were unable to work and without resources or family to look to for food and shelter, so long as they were recognized as "local." In effect, colonial Americans, like their European contemporaries, used local identification as a way of separating the "deserving" from the "undeserving" poor.

3. Retirement for the propertied

While retirement, in the sense of voluntary cessation of work in old age, was not unknown before the late-nineteenth century, it was relatively uncommon and was a prerogative of the propertied. Well into the beginning of the twentieth century, most American men remained in the paid labor force after age sixty-five, presumably as long as they were physically able to work and needed the income. Indeed, for the minority who survived into old age, care and comfort beyond the point at which they could no longer work was largely ensured by control over family property, and with it, over sons and daughters. Thus, the identification of age with poverty that became part of the "social question" for reformers early in the twentieth century had not yet been made in pre-Civil War America.

Nonetheless, some elderly men and couples in the pre-Civil War era retired from their farms, usually to small towns or villages. For many small farmers and artisans, retirement may not have meant a radical change but rather simply a gradual decrease in work activity depending on the adequacy of savings or other arrangements for support in old age. A frequent pattern for the nineteenth century farmer reaching old age was to lease or give parts of the family farm to the next generation in exchange for staying on the farm and continuing to work it, producing family income for both generations. Those farmers who controlled property and assets could stop working in old age and still be assured of income from the next generation whose continued support was guaranteed by the older generation's control of the farm or business.

The elderly poor without family were treated similarly to other poor individuals who were unable to work even though extreme old age probably carried with it a presumption of inability to work. Still, there were comparatively few such elderly poor to start with before the late-nineteenth century, and certainly those few had a claim on parish or local relief institutions such as the almshouse.

In summary, throughout the pre-industrial period aged Americans apparently placed a high value on independence and control over their living arrangements; where multigenerational households existed, more often than not the older generation kept control of property and therefore income. The sentimental popular picture of respected elders living with their children in harmony was not complete mythology, but it certainly was not the rule. Even in the Puritan culture, which David Hackett Fischer and others describe as especially deferential to elders, deference was apparently based in substantial part on the older generation holding onto family land long into the adulthood of the next generation. Entitlement to comfort in old age, in this era, was based quite literally on holding the deed to the family farm.

B. The Federal Pension Model: Veterans' Entitlements

The Social Security system that emerged in the late 1930s echoed in important aspects the principles and categories of coverage provided under the Civil War pension program. A comparison of the Revolutionary War and Civil War pension systems with the benefits provided under the Social Security Act after 1939 reveals strong similarities between the programs in goals, assumptions, and themes, which have persisted for 175 years of federal income support programs.

First, it appears that aid to the elderly, veterans or not, had a strong poverty-prevention element whether or not poverty was a requirement for receipt of aid; presumptive, rather than demonstrated, need was the trigger for benefit payment. Second, we can conclude from the structure of these programs that only those who matched a consensus view of worthiness—war service, inability to work because of age or disability, or both—were viewed as entitled to public support. Citizenship or residency alone was an insufficient basis for the right to adult income support.

Finally, although there is substantial evidence of late-nineteenth and early-twentieth century patterns of individual saving for the possibility of retirement in old age, individual efforts alone were not likely to provide sufficient economic security in old age to induce retirement. Those older men who did leave the work force up until the 1920s were most likely to have based their retirement security on publicly provided pensions.

1. Revolutionary War pensions: welfare for the deserving

The first American federal antipoverty program was the Revolutionary War Pension Act, enacted in 1818 and expanded in 1820. The program provided annual lifetime benefits for Revolutionary War veterans who could demonstrate lack of income or assets at the time of initial application for benefits. While enactment of the program was probably a response to nationalism aroused by the War of 1812 and sympathy for the plight of Revolutionary War veterans in dire economic circumstances, the pensions paid under the 1820 Act had many of the characteristics of old-age pensions designed to prevent poverty in old age resulting from inability to work.

Unlike the later Civil War system, the Revolutionary War pension program required an initial demonstration that the veteran was in need to establish eligibility for benefits. In a sense, this program was based on a double test of worthiness, as service to the Republic in war as well as demonstrated poverty were required for receipt of benefits. However, once sufficient poverty was initially established, veterans received pension benefits for the rest of their lives without further inquiry into their economic status.

We can see in the Revolutionary War pension program the beginning of the prophylactic approach to poverty for those deemed socially worthy that is epitomized today by the Social Security program. The first veterans of an American war were deemed worthy by virtue of their war service, and thus, once they demonstrated need, were given a fixed pension amount, enough for a "comfortable and frugal existence," without being required to demonstrate specific needs again later in life. As a result, these pension recipients were independent of local authority supervision or control and were not subject to the degradation of being placed with families or of having their belongings sold at public auction. Because their entitlement was based as much on their service as veterans as on their poverty, receipt of the pension meant independence and insulation from the control over daily life that awaited recipients of town poor relief.

2. The Civil War pension system: precursor to social insurance

The Civil War was the first American "modern" war with participation by a large proportion of the military-age adult male population rather than primarily professional soldiers, a phenomenon that led directly to the formation of the United States' first mass-scale federal social welfare program, the Civil War pension system. By 1910 the Civil War pension system was paying benefits in some areas for up to 20% of all persons age sixty-five and over, a rate comparable to the coverage provided by German and Danish old-age social insurance programs at that time.[142] Since as late as 1900 two-thirds of men over age sixty-five were still gain-

---

[142] *See* [THEDA] SKOCPOL, PROTECTING SOLDIERS [AND MOTHERS: THE POLITICAL ORIGINS OF SOCIAL POLICY IN THE UNITED STATES (1992)] at 132. [Ed. Note: most of the statistics in the next several paragraph come from this source.]

fully employed, it is likely that Civil War pensions provided a source of income for a large portion of elderly men who were no longer working or at least not working at the level of self-support.

The Civil War democratized military participation. The entire adult male population was subject to conscription, in both the North and the Confederacy, even though most soldiers volunteered for duty until late in the conflict. It was a conflict of unprecedented scale and ferocity. Over the four years spanning 1861 to 1865, over 2.2 million men—about 37% of northern men between the ages of fifteen and forty-four in 1860—served in the Union forces. Of those, almost 365,000 died from combat, illness, or war-related misadventure. By way of comparison, only about one-third of British men—also largely nonprofessional soldiers—served in World War I. As for casualties, by the end of the Civil War, eighteen out of every one thousand northern citizens had been killed in connection with the conflict. By comparison, 3.14 soldiers per thousand Americans died in World War II. Equally important is the number of men who returned home wounded—a total of almost 300,000 soldiers—constituting about fourteen of every one thousand Northerners.

From the beginning, the Civil War pension system provided benefits for those injured or harmed as a result of military service during the war and to the widows, orphans, and certain other dependents of soldiers who died "for causes traceable to their Union military service." While benefits initially were distributed based on the severity of the disability and on military rank, eligibility was not based on demonstrated need, and pensions, once granted, were paid for life. Federal protection against a decline into poverty for families of Civil War soldiers was not extended out of detached altruism. Once it became clear that the war was going to be both lengthy and extremely bloody, it became more difficult to fill the ranks with volunteer soldiers without some assurance that families left behind would be cared for.

Nonetheless, the fact that family benefits were initially included as part of the Civil War pension scheme is evidence of their underlying purpose: to compensate soldiers and their families for losses suffered during the war, inevitably including lost or diminished capacity to earn and support those families. The paramount goals of the original legislation were prevention of destitution, avoidance of local almshouses, and aid to the poor for this class of Americans viewed as worthy of assistance but "too good" for ordinary poor relief. This goal was reiterated in the legislation's repeated expansions from 1862 through the end of the century.

The Federal Civil War pension system was initially a response to the inadequacy of local poor relief and volunteer charity to provide for dependents of current and deceased Civil War soldiers during the war. Both the scale and length of the war meant that local and voluntary efforts would prove insufficient. Even though states overrode the limits of strictly local poor relief and passed tariffs, excise taxes, and other measures to finance aid to military families, ultimately federal aid was required. The most significant aspect of this system, from the perspective of the later development of retirement entitlements, was the absence of any requirement for demonstration of need. Payment of benefits was based on a presumption of need arising from the inability to work because of injuries received in the war or, in the case of family benefits, absence of the male breadwinner.

After the war ended a series of congressional expansions of the program—both in the amount of pensions and in the categories of soldiers and dependents eligible for benefits—effectively transformed a military disability pension system into a broad-scale old-age and disability family benefit system.

> Between 1880 and 1910, the U.S. federal government devoted over a quarter of its expenditures to pensions distributed among the populace; aside from interest payments on the national debt in the early 1880s, such expenditures exceeded or nearly equaled other major categories of federal spending. By 1910, about 28 percent of all American men aged 65 or more, more than half a million of them, received federal benefits averaging $189 a year.[163]

Liberalization of benefits, along with the dual impact of gradual aging and lingering minor wounds on the ability of aging veterans to support themselves, resulted in increasingly higher numbers of beneficiaries and expenditures under the program, peaking in the mid-1890s. Congress ultimately severed the direct connection between injury and benefit eligibility and repeatedly raised benefits throughout this period. Thus, as Civil War veterans aged and their earning capacity diminished regardless of any injuries they may have received in the war, the basis for the presumption of inability to earn was broadened from physical disability to simply old age, and benefits became a more significant part of total income.

Theda Skocpol estimates that by 1910, about 18% of all United States residents aged sixty-five and over were receiving benefits. This number included 28.5% of all elderly men, plus approximately 8% of all elderly women who were receiving survivors' benefits. These percentages were comparable to northern European old-age pension systems in effect at the time. Moreover, benefits were available at younger ages—at least at age sixty-two and frequently earlier—in more substantial amounts, and for more dependent family members, than under most European sys-

---

[163] [Skocpol, *supra*,] at 65 (footnote omitted).

tems at the turn of the century. In 1910 German old-age benefits averaged about 18% of the typical worker's income, and British pensions averaged about 22%. In contrast, the average United States Civil War pension benefit in 1910 equaled about 30% of the average annual income of all employed Americans.

Thus, during the period in which the United States became an industrial nation—as millions left the farms and joined the ranks of industrial workers, disrupting the property-based family and village network of support for the elderly—a federal support system developed to provide for at least a large minority, and perhaps a majority, of older workers who could not support themselves in old age. Given the high labor force participation rates of men over sixty-five well into the twentieth century—at least 60-70% by most estimates until after 1930—it seems likely that most older men who could not or did not wish to work past age sixty-five had a federal or state veterans' pension to fall back on. Widows and orphans of those who died during the war or of war-related causes were also supported by the federal system so that a substantial support network lasted into the twentieth century, even after the war generation was gone.

The Civil War pension system was contributory only in the sense that its beneficiaries sacrificed their health, youth, and the financial security of their families in service to the Union. But in most other respects, the hallmarks of eligibility under this system resemble those of the Social Security system enacted in 1935 and 1939. The characteristics that distinguished the American approach to social welfare from that of the rest of the industrialized world were fully developed in the Civil War pension system and represent a continuum from the Revolutionary War system. Benefits to those unable to provide for themselves would only be given to those who had "earned" them—either through public or military service or later through sufficient time in the industrial work force.

The common thread running from Revolutionary War veterans' benefits through Civil War veterans' benefits to Social Security retiree benefits is the need perceived by the public and the Congress for a pension entitlement based on presumed rather than demonstrated need. Entitlement was viewed as essential in order to preserve the independence of those who had, in one way or another, earned their benefits, to insulate them from intrusive poverty programs and their overseers—whether village elders or welfare office bureaucrats. This insurance against falling from one's place, both economically and socially, became more critical as industrialization broke up older patterns of aging and family care and as industry and government considered the popularization and democratization of old-age retirement.

C. Industrialization and the Beginning of "Voluntary" Retirement

Historians differ as to the exact effects of industrialization on older workers and on the extent to which employers purposely used age and seniority to exacerbate unemployment among the old. Nonetheless, there can be no doubt that by the early-twentieth century, the nature and organization of work for most Americans and Europeans had shifted from the agrarian family economy to an urban industrial economy in which the family and the elderly had different roles than in the pre-industrial world. While most older workers were capable of continuing to work past age sixty-five, and did so at least up to the 1930s, they had to develop different strategies for survival in the industrial world when economic adversity struck, whether because of economic downturn or technological advances that made skills obsolete.

* * *

Nonetheless, while industrialization did not create old-age poverty, the transition from farm to urban wage work, combined with lengthening life spans, undoubtedly made the threat of poverty in old age more real. This appears to have been particularly true as rapid technological advances made successive sets of skills obsolete. For older workers such changes required either acquisition of new skills, or if the means were available, retirement or a shift into self-employment of one sort or another. Industrialization brought with it an inherent insecurity of wage employment in an economy marked by periods of severe economic downturn that was substantially different from the experience of most earlier generations.

This increased insecurity of employment, which accompanied industrialization, may have led to increased identification of poverty with old age even though the majority of the elderly were neither in poverty nor in the poorhouse. Although most of those over sixty continued to work and maintain households alone or with their children, the possibility of poverty and the threat of the poorhouse were the fears, if not the reality, of the majority of older workers in the early part of the century.

* * *

2. SOCIAL SECURITY ACT OF 1935

The Social Security Act arose out of the economic disaster of the Great Depression and President Franklin Delano Roosevelt's comprehensive plan to combat that disaster. As President Roosevelt began his first term in office in 1933, "[i]t was hard to understate the need for action. The national income was less than half of what it had been four short years before. Nearly thirteen million Americans—about one quarter of the labor force—were desperately seeking jobs. The machinery for sheltering and feeding the unemployed was breaking down everywhere under the growing burden. * * * It was not just a matter of staving off hunger. It was a matter of seeing whether a representative democracy could conquer economic collapse." ARTHUR M. SCHLESINGER, JR., THE AGE OF ROOSEVELT: THE COMING OF THE NEW DEAL 3 (Houghton Mifflin, 1959). That same year, Congress established the Civilian Conservation Corps, set up a national relief system, provided for the development of the Tennessee Valley, and passed the Emergency Banking Act, the Home Owners' Loan Act, the Glass-Stengall Banking Act, and the Truth in Securities Act.

The Social Security Act arose alongside other Great Depression legislation to address several of the key issues for achieving long term security. In attempting to craft the legislation, President Roosevelt had to take into account the political realities of the day. Business groups and conservative politicians opposed the concept of social security, arguing that many businesses would close. Liberal and populist politicians demanded sweeping government action that would provide for all citizens. Much of what was contained in the Social Security Act resulted from the need to balance between these two forces.

President Roosevelt came to "believe that the social security program should be striven for not piecemeal, but as a single package. In this way, he evidently believed, the program would have its maximum political effect—enough to both overcome the opposition of the right to the whole idea of social insurance and to drown out the growing clamor on the left for larger benefits than the country could presumable bear." ARTHUR M. SCHLESINGER, JR., *supra*, at 304. He thus laid out a broad concept of social security for the country in a famous message to Congress in 1934:

> You are completing a work begun in March 1933, which will be regarded for a long time as a splendid justification of the vitality of representative government. I greet you and express once more my appreciation of the cooperation which has proved so effective. Only a small number of the items of our program remain to be enacted and I am confident that you will pass on them before adjournment. Many other pending measures are sound in conception, but must, for lack of time or of adequate information, be deferred to the session of the next Congress. In the meantime, we can well seek to adjust many of these measures into certain larger plans of governmental policy for the future of the Nation.

> You and I, as the responsible directors of these policies and actions, may, with good reason, look to the future with confidence, just as we may look to the past fifteen months with reasonable satisfaction.

On the side of relief we have extended material aid to millions of our fellow citizens.

On the side of recovery we have helped to lift agriculture and industry from a condition of utter Prostration.

But, in addition to these immediate tasks of relief and of recovery we have properly, necessarily and with overwhelming approval determined to safeguard these tasks by rebuilding many of the structures of our economic life and reorganizing it in order to prevent a recurrence of collapse.

* * *

Our task of reconstruction does not require the creation of new and strange values. It is rather the finding of the way once more to known, but to some degree forgotten, ideals and values. If the means and details are in some instances new, the objectives are as permanent as human nature.

Among our objectives I place the security of the men, women and children of the Nation first.

This security for the individual and for the family concerns itself primarily with three factors. People want decent homes to live in; they want to locate them where they can engage in productive work; and they want some safeguard against misfortunes which cannot be wholly eliminated in this man-made world of ours.

* * *

The third factor relates to security against the hazards and vicissitudes of life. Fear and worry based on unknown danger contribute to social unrest and economic demoralization. If, as our Constitution tells us, our Federal Government was established among other things, "to promote the general welfare," it is our plain duty to provide for that security upon which welfare depends.

Next winter we may well undertake the great task of furthering the security of the citizen and his family through social insurance.

This is not an untried experiment. Lessons of experience are available from States, from industries and from many Nations of the civilized world. The various types of social insurance are interrelated; and I think it is difficult to attempt to solve them piecemeal. Hence, I am looking for a sound means which I can recommend to provide at once security against several of the great disturbing factors in life—especially those which relate to unemployment and old age. I believe there should be a maximum of cooperation between States and the Federal Government. I believe that the funds necessary to provide this insurance should be raised by contribution rather than by an increase in general taxation. Above all, I am convinced that social insurance should be national in scope, although the several States should meet at least a large portion of the cost of management, leaving to the Federal Government the responsibility of investing, maintaining and safeguarding the funds constituting the necessary insurance reserves. I have commenced to make, with the greatest of care, the necessary actuarial and other studies for the formulation of plans for the consideration of the 74th Congress.

* * *

Franklin D. Roosevelt, Message to Congress Reviewing the Broad Objectives and Accomplishments of the Administration (June 8, 1934).

Following up on this message, President Roosevelt appointed a Committee on Economic Security that prepared and presented a report that became the basis of the Social Security Act of 1935. The five-member Committee was chaired by the Secretary of Labor, Frances Perkins, and included the Secretary of the Treasury, the Attorney General, the Secretary of Agriculture, and the Federal Emergency Relief Administrator. The task of the committee was to create a workable means to carry out the President's broad plan for social insurance. "The result was a plan which has proved itself practical and effective and yet amenable to amendments and administrative changes as have been necessary." EDWIN WITTE, DEVELOPMENT OF THE SOCIAL SECURITY ACT vi (Univ. of Wisconsin Press, 1962). In the following brief excerpt from its 1935 report, the Committee laid out its essential reasoning and outlined its major recommendations.

REPORT OF THE COMMITTEE ON ECONOMIC SECURITY
(January 15, 1935)

NEED FOR SECURITY

The need of the people of this country for "some safeguard against misfortunes which cannot be wholly eliminated in this man-made world of ours" is tragically apparent at this time, when 18,000,000 people, including children and aged, are dependent upon emergency relief for their subsistence and approximately 10,000,000 workers have no employment other than relief work. Many millions more have lost their entire savings, and there has occurred a very great decrease in earnings. The ravages of probably the worst depression of all time have been accentuated by greater urbanization, with the consequent total dependence of a majority of our people on their earnings in industry.

As progress is made toward recovery, this insecurity will be lessened, but it is not apparent that even in the "normal times" of the prosperous twenties, a large part of our population had little security. From the best estimates which are obtainable, it appears that in the years 1922 to 1929 there was an average unemployment of 8 percent among our industrial workers. In the best year of this period, the number of the unemployed averaged somewhat less than 1,500,000.

Unemployment is but one of many misfortunes which often result in destitution. In the slack year of 1933, 14,500 persons were fatally injured in American industry and 55,000 sustained some permanent injury. Non-industrial accidents exacted a much greater toll. On the average, 2.25 percent of all industrial workers are at all times incapacitated from work by reason of illness. Each year above one eighth of all workers suffer one or more illnesses which disable them for a week, and the percentage of the families in which some member is seriously ill is much greater. In urban families of low incomes, above one-fifth each year have expenditures for medical and related care of above $100 and many have sickness bills of above one-fourth and even one-half of their entire family income. A relatively small but not insignificant number of workers are each year prematurely invalided, and 8 percent of all workers are physically handicapped.

At least one-third of all our people, upon reaching old age, are dependent upon others for support. Less than 10 percent leave an estate upon death of sufficient size to be probated.

* * *

The one almost all-embracing measure of security is an assured income. A program of economic security, as we vision it, must have as its primary aim the assurance of an adequate income to each human being in childhood, youth, middle age, or old age—in sickness or in health. It must provide safeguards against all of the hazards leading to destitution and dependency.

A piecemeal approach is dictated by practical considerations, but the broad objectives should never be forgotten. Whatever measures are deemed immediately expedient should be so designed that they can be embodied in the complete program which we must have ere long.

To delay until it is opportune to set up a complete program will probably mean holding up action until it is too late to act. A substantial beginning should be made now in the development of the safeguards which are so manifestly needed for individual security. As stated in the message of June 8, these represent not "a change in values" but "rather a return to values lost in the course of our economic development and expansion."

"The road to these values is the way to progress." We will not "rest content until we have done our utmost to move forward on that road."

SUMMARY OF MAJOR RECOMMENDATIONS

* * *

EMPLOYMENT ASSURANCE

Since most people must live by work, the first objective in a program of economic security must be maximum employment. As the major contribution of the Federal Government in providing a safeguard against unemployment we suggest employment assurance—the stimulation of private employment and the provision of public employment for those able-bodied workers whom industry cannot employ at a given time. * * *

* * *

UNEMPLOYMENT COMPENSATION

Unemployment compensation, as we conceive it, is a front line of defense, especially valuable for those who are ordinarily steadily employed, but very beneficial also in maintaining purchasing power. While it will not directly benefit those now unemployed until they are reabsorbed in industry, it should be instituted at the earliest possible date to increase the security of all who are employed.

We believe that the States should administer unemployment compensation, assisted and guided by the Federal Government. * * *

* * *

OLD-AGE SECURITY

To meet the problem of security for the aged we suggest as complementary measures non-contributory old-age pensions, compulsory contributory annuities, and voluntary contributory annuities, all to be applicable on retirement at age 65 or over.

Only non-contributory old-age pensions will meet the situation of those who are now old and have no means of support. Laws for the payment of old-age pensions on a needs basis are in force in more than half of all States and should be enacted everywhere. Because most of the dependent aged are now on relief lists and derive their support principally from the Federal Government and many of the States cannot assume the financial burden of pensions unaided, we recommend that the Federal Government pay one-half the cost of old-age pensions but not more than $15 per month for any individual.

The satisfactory way of providing for the old age of those now young is a contributory system of old-age annuities. This will enable younger workers, with matching contributions from their employers, to build up a more adequate old-age protection than it is possible to achieve with non-contributory pensions based upon a means test. To launch such a system we deem it necessary that workers who are now middle-aged or older and who, therefore, cannot in the few remaining years of their industrial life accumulate a substantial reserve be, nevertheless, paid reasonably adequate annuities upon retirement. These Government contributions to augment earned annuities may either take the form of assistance under old age pension laws on a more liberal basis than in the case of persons who have made no contributions or by a Government subsidy to the contributory annuity system itself. A portion of these particular annuities will come out of Government funds, but because receipts from contributions will in the early years greatly exceed annuity payments, it will not be necessary as a financial problem to have Government contributions until after the system has been in operation for 30 years. The combined contributory rate we recommend is 1 percent of pay roll to be divided equally between employers and employees, which is to be increased by 1 percent each 5 years, until the maximum of 5 percent is reached in 20 years.

There still remains, unprotected by either of the two above plans, professional and self-employed groups, many of whom face dependency in old age. Partially to meet their problem, we suggest the establishment of a voluntary Government annuity system, designed particularly for people of small incomes.

SECURITY FOR CHILDREN

A large group of the children at present maintained by relief will not be aided by employment or unemployment compensation. There are the fatherless and other "young" families without a breadwinner. To meet the problems of the children in these families, no less than 45 States have enacted children's aid laws, generally called "mothers' pension laws." However, due to the present financial difficulty in which many States find themselves, far more of such children are on the relief lists than are in receipt of children's aid benefits. * * * We recommend Federal grants-in-aid on the basis of one-half the State and local expenditures for this purpose (one third the entire cost).

We recommend also that the Federal Government give assistance to States in providing local services for the protection and care of homeless, neglected, and delinquent children and for child and maternal health services especially in rural areas. Special aid should be given toward meeting a part of the expenditures for transportation, hospitalization, and convalescent care of crippled and handicapped children, in order that those very necessary services may be extended for a large group of children whose only handicaps are physical.

RISKS ARISING OUT OF ILL HEALTH

As a first measure for meeting the very serious problem of sickness in families with low income we recommend a Nation-wide preventive public-health program. * * *

The second major step we believe to be the application of the principles of insurance to this problem. We are not prepared at this time to make recommendations for a system of health insurance. We have enlisted the cooperation of advisory groups representing the medical and dental professions and hospital management in the development of a plan for health insurance which will be beneficial alike to the public and the professions concerned. We have asked these groups to complete their work by March 1, 1935, and expect to make a further report on this subject at that time or shortly thereafter. * * *

* * *

CONCLUSION

The program for economic security we suggest follows no single pattern. It is broader than social insurance and does not attempt merely to copy European methods. In placing primary emphasis on employment, rather than unemployment compensation, we differ fundamentally from those who see social insurance as an all-sufficient program for economic security. We recommend wide application of the principles of social insurance, but not without deviation from European models. Where other measures seemed more appropriate to our background or present situation, we have not hesitated to recommend them in preference to the European practices. In doing so we have recommended the measures at this time which seemed best calculated under our American conditions to protect individuals in the years immediately ahead from hazards which plunge them into destitution and dependency. This, we believe, is in accord with the method of attaining the definite goal of the Government, social justice, which was outlined in the message of January 4, 1935. "We seek it through tested liberal traditions, through processes which retain all of the deep essentials of that republican form of government first given to a troubled world by the United States."

We realize that these measures we recommend will not give complete economic security. As outlined in the messages of June 8, 1934, and January 4, 1935, the safeguards to which this report relates represent but one of three major aspects of economic security for men, women, and children. Nor do we regard this report and our recommendations as exhaustive of the particular aspect which this committee was directed to study— "the major hazards and vicissitudes of life." A complete program of economic security "because of many lost years, will take many future years to fulfill."

The initial steps to bring this program into operation should be taken now. This program will involve considerable cost, but this is small as compared with the enormous cost of insecurity. The measures we suggest should result in the long run in material reduction in the cost to society of destitution and dependency, and we believe, will immediately be helpful in allaying those fears which open the door to unsound proposals. The program will promote social and industrial stability and will operate to enlarge and make steady a widely diffused purchasing power upon which depends the high American standard of living and the internal market for our mass production, industry, and agriculture.

NOTE ON PASSAGE OF THE SOCIAL SECURITY ACT

President Roosevelt endorsed the Committee's recommendations and transmitted the report to Congress without delay:

> In addressing you on June eighth, 1934, I summarized the main objectives of our American program. Among these was, and is, the security of the men, women, and children of the Nation against certain hazards and vicissitudes of life. This purpose is an essential part of our task. In my annual message to you I promised to submit a definite program of action. This I do in tile form of a report to me by a Committee on Economic Security, appointed by me for the purpose of surveying the field and of recommending the basis of legislation.
>
> * * *
>
> The detailed report of the Committee sets forth a series of proposals that will appeal to the sound sense of the American people. It has not attempted the impossible, nor has it failed to exercise sound caution and consideration of all of the factors concerned: the national credit, the rights and responsibilities of States, the capacity of industry to assume financial responsibilities and the fundamental necessity of proceeding in a manner that will merit the enthusiastic support of citizens of all sorts.
>
> It is overwhelmingly important to avoid any danger of permanently discrediting the sound and necessary policy of Federal legislation for economic security by attempting to apply it on too ambitious a scale before actual experience has provided guidance for the permanently safe direction of such efforts. The place of such a fundamental in our future civilization is too precious to be jeopardized now by extravagant action. It is a sound idea—a sound ideal. Most of the other advanced countries of the

world have already adopted it and their experience affords the knowledge that social insurance can be made a sound and workable project.

Three principles should be observed in legislation on this subject. First, the system adopted, except for the money necessary to initiate it, should be self-sustaining in the sense that funds for the payment of insurance benefits should not come from the proceeds of general taxation. Second, excepting in old-age insurance, actual management should be left to the States subject to standards established by the Federal Government. Third, sound financial management of the funds and the reserves, and protection of the credit structure of the Nation should be assured by retaining Federal control over all funds through trustees in the Treasury of the United States.

At this time, I recommend the following types of legislation looking to economic security:

1. Unemployment compensation.

2. Old-age benefits, including compulsory and voluntary annuities.

3. Federal aid to dependent children through grants to States for the support of existing mothers' pension systems and for services for the protection and care of homeless, neglected, dependent, and crippled children.

4. Additional Federal aid to State and local public health agencies and the strengthening of the Federal Public Health Service. I am not at this time recommending the adoption of so called "health insurance," although groups representing the medical profession are cooperating with the Federal Government in the further study of the subject and definite progress is being made.

With respect to unemployment compensation, I have concluded that the most practical proposal is the levy of a uniform Federal payroll tax, ninety per cent of which should be allowed as an offset to employers contributing under a compulsory State unemployment compensation act. The purpose of this is to afford a requirement of a reasonably uniform character for all States cooperating with the Federal Government and to promote and encourage the passage of unemployment compensation laws in the States. The ten per cent not thus offset should be used to cover the costs of Federal and State administration of this broad system. Thus, States will largely administer unemployment compensation, assisted and guided by the Federal Government. An unemployment compensation system should be constructed in such a way as to afford every practicable aid and incentive toward the larger purpose of employment stabilization. This can be helped by the intelligent planning of both public and private employment. It also can be helped by correlating the system with public employment so that a person who has exhausted his benefits may be eligible for some form of public work as is recommended in this report. Moreover, in order to encourage the stabilization of private employment, Federal legislation should not foreclose the States from establishing means for inducing industries to afford an even greater stabilization of employment.

In the important field of security for our old people, it seems necessary to adopt three principles: First, non-contributory old-age pensions for those who are now too old to build up their own insurance. It is, of course, clear that for perhaps thirty years to come funds will have to be provided by the States and the Federal Government to meet these pensions. Second, compulsory contributory annuities which in time will establish a self-supporting system for those now young and for future generations. Third, voluntary contributory annuities by which individual initiative can increase the annual amounts received in old age. It is proposed that the Federal Government assume one-half of the cost of the old-age pension plan, which ought ultimately to be supplanted by self-supporting annuity plans.

* * *

Franklin D. Roosevelt, Message to Congress on Social Security (January 17, 1935).

The power of the report and strength of the President's message to Congress set the stage for the passage of a new Social Security Act that included essentially all of the Committee's and the Administration's goals. Those goals were deliberately limited, leaving room for the Act and its programs to develop over time. As President Roosevelt noted in his statement upon signing the Act into law on August 14, 1935:

This social security measure gives at least some protection to thirty millions of our citizens who will reap direct benefits through unemployment compensation, through old-age pensions and through increased services for the protection of children and the prevention of ill health.

We can never insure one hundred percent of the population against one hundred percent of the hazards and vicissitudes of life, but we have tried to frame a law which will give some measure of protection to the average citizen and to his family against the loss of a job and against poverty-ridden old age.

This law, too, represents a cornerstone in a structure which is being built but is by no means complete. It is a structure intended to lessen the force of possible future depressions. It will act as a protection to future Administrations against the necessity of going deeply into debt to furnish relief to the needy. The law will flatten out the peaks and valleys of deflation and of inflation. It is, in short, a law that will take care of human needs and at the same time provide the United States an economic structure of vastly greater soundness.

Franklin D. Roosevelt, Presidential Statement upon Signing the Social Security Act (Aug. 14, 1935)

3. EARLY CONSTITUTIONAL CHALLENGES

Different aspects of the Social Security Act have been challenged over the years, beginning immediately after the legislation was enacted. The main initial challenge was that the programs it created and the mechanisms established to fund them were beyond the power of Congress and a usurpation of the powers left to the states by the Tenth Amendment to the Constitution. In two cases decided on the same day, the Supreme Court upheld the constitutionality of the Act. The Court upheld the unemployment provisions of the Act in Charles C. Steward Machine Co. v. Davis, 301 U.S. 548 (1937) and, in doing so, endorsed the use of federal taxing power to move along social welfare programs that had proved to be handled ineffectively through the states. The Court then addressed the Old Age program in the companion case.

HELVERING V. DAVIS
301 U.S. 619 (1937)

Mr. Justice Cardozo delivered the opinion of the Court.

The Social Security Act is challenged once again.

In Steward Machine Co. v. Davis, 301 U.S. 548, 57 S.Ct. 883, 81 L.Ed. 1279, decided this day, we have upheld the validity of Title IX of the act, imposing an excise upon employers of eight or more. In this case Titles VIII and II are the subject of attack. Title VIII lays another excise upon employers in addition to the one imposed by Title IX (though with different exemptions). It lays a special income tax upon employees to be deducted from their wages and paid by the employers. Title II provides for the payment of Old Age Benefits, and supplies the motive and occasion, in the view of the assailants of the statute, for the levy of the taxes imposed by Title VIII. The plan of the two titles will now be summarized more fully.

Title VIII, as we have said, lays two different types of tax, an 'income tax on employees,' and 'an excise tax on employers.' The income tax on employees is measured by wages paid during the calendar year. The excise tax on the employer is to be paid 'with respect to having individuals in his employ,' and, like the tax on employees, is measured by wages. Neither tax is applicable to certain types of employment, such as agricultural labor, domestic service, service for the national or state governments, and service performed by persons who have attained the age of 65 years. The two taxes are at the same rate. For the years 1937 to 1939, inclusive, the rate for each tax is fixed at one per cent. Thereafter the rate increases 1/2 of 1 per cent. every three years, until after December 31, 1948, the rate for each tax reaches 3 per cent. In the computation of wages all remuneration is to be included except so much as is in excess of $3,000 during the calendar year affected. The income tax on employees is to be collected by the employer, who is to deduct the amount from the wages 'as and when paid.' He is indemnified against claims and demands of any person by reason of such payment. The proceeds of both taxes are to be paid into the Treasury like internal revenue taxes generally, and are not ear-marked in any way. There are penalties for nonpayment.

Title II has the caption 'Federal Old-Age Benefits.' The benefits are of two types, first, monthly pensions, and second, lump-sum payments, the payments of the second class being relatively few and unimportant.

* * *

This suit is brought by a shareholder of the Edison Electric Illuminating Company of Boston, a Massachusetts corporation, to restrain the corporation from making payments and deductions called for by the act, which is stated to be void under the Constitution of the United States. The bill tells us that the corporation has decided to obey the statute, that it has reached this decision in the face of the complainant's protests, and that it will make the payments and deductions unless restrained by a decree. * * * The prayer is for an injunction and for a declaration that the act is void.

The corporation appeared and answered without raising any issue of fact. Later the United States Commissioner of Internal Revenue and the United States Collector for the District of Massachusetts, petitioners in this court, were allowed to intervene. * * * The District Court held that the tax upon employees was not properly at issue, and that the tax upon employers was constitutional. It thereupon denied the prayer for an injunction, and dismissed the bill. On appeal to the Circuit Court of Appeals for the First Circuit, the decree was reversed, one judge dissenting. Davis v. Edison Electric Illuminating Co., 89 F. (2d) 393. The court held that Title II was void as an invasion of powers reserved by the Tenth Amendment to the states or to the people, and that Title II in collapsing carried Title VIII along with it. * * *

A petition for certiorari followed. It was filed by the intervening defendants, the Commissioner, and the Collector, brought two questions, and two only, to our notice. We were asked to determine: (1) 'Whether the tax imposed upon employers by section 804 of the Social Security Act (42 U.S.C.A. § 1004) is within the power of Congress under the Constitution,' and (2) 'Whether the validity of the tax imposed upon employees by section 801 of the Social Security Act (42 U.S.C.A. § 1001) is properly in issue in this case, and if it is, whether that tax is within the power of Congress under the Constitution.' The defendant corporation gave notice to the clerk that it joined in the petition, but it has taken no part in any subsequent proceedings. A writ of certiorari issued.

First: Questions as to the remedy invoked by the complainant confront us at the outset.

[Justice Cardozo describes a split among the members of the Court as to whether the requirements for equitable relief had been met, particularly in light of the "general rule that constitutional questions are not to be determined in the absence of strict necessity." Since a majority found "in this case extraordinary features making it fitting in their judgment to determine whether the benefits and the taxes are valid or invalid." he proceeded to the merits.]

Second: The scheme of benefits created by the provisions of Title II is not in contravention of the limitations of the Tenth Amendment.

Congress may spend money in aid of the 'general welfare.' Constitution, art. 1, § 8; United States v. Butler, 297 U.S. 1, 65, 56 S.Ct. 312, 319, 80 L.Ed. 477, Steward Machine Co. v. Davis, supra. There have been great statesmen in our history who have stood for other views. We will not resurrect the contest. It is now settled by decision. United States v. Butler, supra. The conception of the spending power advocated by Hamilton and strongly reinforced by Story has prevailed over that of Madison, which has not been lacking in adherents. Yet difficulties are left when the power is conceded. The line must still be drawn between one welfare and another, between particular and general. Where this shall be placed cannot be known through a formula in advance of the event. There is a middle ground or certainly a penumbra in which discretion is at large. The discretion, however, is not confided to the courts. The discretion belongs to Congress, unless the choice is clearly wrong, a display of arbitrary power, not an exercise of judgment. This is now familiar law. 'When such a contention comes here we naturally require a showing that by no reasonable possibility can the challenged legislation fall within the wide range of discretion permitted to the Congress.' United States v. Butler, supra, 297 U.S. 1, at page 67, 56 S.Ct. 312, 320, 80 L.Ed. 477, 102 A.L.R. 914. Nor is the concept of the general welfare static. Needs that were narrow or parochial a century ago may be interwoven in our day with the well-being of the nation. What is critical or urgent changes with the times.

The purge of nation-wide calamity that began in 1929 has taught us many lessons. Not the least is the solidarity of interests that may once have seemed to be divided. Unemployment spreads from state to state, the hinterland now settled that in pioneer days gave an avenue of escape. Spreading from state to state, unemployment is an ill not particular but general, which may be checked, if Congress so determines, by the resources of the nation. If this can have been doubtful until now, our ruling today in the case of the Steward Machine Co., supra, has set the doubt at rest. But the ill is all one or at least not greatly different whether men are thrown out of work because there is no longer work to do or because the disabilities of age make them incapable of doing it. Rescue becomes necessary irrespective of the cause. The hope behind this statute is to save men and women from the rigors of the poor house as well as from the haunting fear that such a lot awaits them when journey's end is near.

Congress did not improvise a judgment when it found that the award of old age benefits would be conducive to the general welfare. The President's Committee on Economic Security made an investigation and report, aided by a research staff of Government officers and employees, and by an Advisory Council and seven other advisory groups. Extensive hearings followed before the House Committee on Ways and Means, and the Senate Committee on Finance. A great mass of evidence was brought together supporting the policy which finds expression in the act. Among the relevant facts are these: The number of persons in the United States 65 years of age or over is increasing proportionately as well as absolutely. What is even more important the number of such persons unable to take care of themselves is growing at a threatening pace. More and more our population is becoming urban and industrial instead of rural and agricultural. The evidence is impressive that among industrial workers the younger men and women are preferred over the older. In times of retrenchment the older are commonly the first to go, and even if retained, their wages are likely to be lowered. The plight of men and women at so low an age as 40 is hard, almost hopeless, when they are driven to seek for reemployment. Statistics are in the brief. A few illustrations will be chosen from many there collected. In 1930, out of 224 American factories investigated, 71, or almost one third, had fixed maximum hiring age limits; in 4 plants the limit was under 40; in 41 it was under 46. In the other 153 plants there were no fixed limits, but in practice few were hired if they were over 50 years of age. With the loss of savings inevitable in periods of idleness, the fate of workers over 65, when thrown out of work, is little less than desperate. A recent study of the Social Security Board informs us that 'one-fifth of the aged in the United States were receiving old-age assistance, emergency relief, institutional care, employment under the works program, or some other form of aid from public or private funds; two-fifths to one-half were dependent on friends and relatives, one-eighth had some income from earnings; and possibly one-sixth had some savings or property. Approximately three out of four persons 65 or over were probably dependent wholly or partially on others for support.' We summarize in the margin the results of other studies by state and national commissions.[8] They point the same way.

The problem is plainly national in area and dimensions. Moreover, laws of the separate states cannot deal with it effectively. Congress, at least, had a basis for that belief. States and local governments are often lacking in the resources that are necessary to finance an adequate program of security for the aged. This is brought out with a wealth of illustration in recent studies of the problem. Apart from the failure of resources, states and local governments are at times reluctant to increase so heavily the burden of taxation to be borne by their residents for fear of placing themselves in a position of economic disadvantage as compared with neighbors or competitors. We have seen this in our study of the problem of unemployment compensation. Steward Machine Co. v. Davis, supra. A system of old age pensions has special dangers of its own, if put in force in one state and rejected in another. The existence of such a system is a bait to the needy and dependent elsewhere, encouraging them to migrate and seek a haven of repose. Only a power that is national can serve the interests of all.

Whether wisdom or unwisdom resides in the scheme of benefits set forth in Title II, it is not for us to say. The answer to such inquiries must come from Congress, not the courts. Our concern here as often is with power, not with wisdom. Counsel for respondent has recalled to us the virtues of self-reliance and frugality. There is a possibility, he says, that aid from a paternal government may sap those sturdy virtues and breed a race of weaklings. If Massachusetts so believes and shapes her laws in that conviction, must her breed of sons be changed, he asks, because some

---

[8] The Senate Committee estimated, when investigating the present act, that over one half of the people in the United States over 65 years of age are dependent upon others for support. Senate Report, No. 628, 74th Congress, 1st Session, p. 4. A similar estimate was made in the Report to the President of the Committee on Economic Security, 1935, p. 24.

A Report of the Pennsylvania Commission on Old Age Pensions made in 1919 after a study of 16,281 persons and interviews with more than 3,500 persons 65 years and over showed two fifths with no income but wages and one fourth supported by children; 1.5 per cent. had savings and 11.8 per cent. had property.

A report on old age pensions by the Massachusetts Commission on Pensions showed that in 1924 two thirds of those above 65 had, alone or with a spouse, less than $5,000 of property, and one fourth had none. Two thirds of those with less than $5,000 and income of less than $1,000 were dependent in whole or in part on others for support.

A report of the New York State Commission made in 1930 showed a condition of total dependency as to 58 per cent. of those 65 and over, and 62 per cent. of those 70 and over.

The national Government has found in connection with grants to states for old age assistance under another title of the Social Security Act (Title I) that in February, 1937, 38.8 per cent. of all persons over 65 in Colorado received public assistance; in Oklahoma the percentage was 44.1, and in Texas 37.5. In 10 states out of 40 with plans approved by the Social Security Board more than 25 per cent. of those over 65 could meet the residence requirements and qualify under a means test and were actually receiving public aid.

other philosophy of government finds favor in the halls of Congress? But the answer is not doubtful. One might ask with equal reason whether the system of protective tariffs is to be set aside at will in one state or another whenever local policy prefers the rule of laissez faire. The issue is a closed one. It was fought out long ago.

When money is spent to promote the general welfare, the concept of welfare or the opposite is shaped by Congress, not the states. So the concept be not arbitrary, the locality must yield. Constitution, art. 6, par. 2.

[The Court either left open or dismissed the remaining claims.]

Decree of Court of Appeals reversed, and decree of District Court affirmed.

Mr. Justice McREYNOLDS and Mr. Justice BUTLER are of opinion that the provisions of the Act here challenged are repugnant to the Tenth Amendment, and that the decree of the Circuit Court of Appeals should be affirmed.

4. DEFINING THE NATURE OF THE BENEFIT

Many years after the Supreme Court had upheld the constitutionality of the Social Security Act and after insured workers began receiving regular benefit payments, the Court had to address the nature of the benefits awarded under the Act's social insurance programs. A key element of the social insurance programs was that benefits would be contingent on payment into the system. As President Roosevelt stated in an oft-cited remark, "We put those payroll contributions there so as to give the contributors a legal, moral, and political right to collect their pensions and their unemployment benefits. With those taxes in there, no damn politician can ever scrap my social security program." ARTHUR M. SCHLESINGER, JR., *supra*, at 308-09. *See generally* Matthew H. Hawes, *So No Damn Politician Can Ever Scrap It: The Constitutional Protection of Social Security Benefits*, 65 U. PITT. L. REV. 865 (2004). The question remained, however, of what rights, if any, would be infringed if an insured worker's benefits were taken away.

FLEMMING V. NESTOR
363 U.S. 603 (1960)

Mr. Justice HARLAN delivered the opinion of the Court.

From a decision of the District Court for the District of Columbia holding § 202(n) of the Social Security Act unconstitutional, the Secretary of Health, Education, and Welfare takes this direct appeal pursuant to . The challenged section * * * provides for the termination of old-age, survivor, and disability insurance benefits payable to, or in certain cases in respect of, an alien individual who, after September 1, 1954 (the date of enactment of the section), is deported under § 241(a) of the Immigration and Nationality Act on any one of certain grounds specified in § 202(n).

Appellee, an alien, immigrated to this country from Bulgaria in 1913, and became eligible for old-age benefits in November 1955. In July 1956 he was deported pursuant to § 241(a)(6)(C)(i) of the Immigration and Nationality Act for having been a member of the Communist Party from 1933 to 1939. This being one of the benefit-termination deportation grounds specified in § 202(n), appellee's benefits were terminated soon thereafter, and notice of the termination was given to his wife, who had remained in this country.[2] Upon his failure to obtain administrative reversal of the decision, appellee commenced this action in the District Court, pursuant to § 205(g) of the Social Security Act, to secure judicial review. On cross-motions for summary judgment, the District Court ruled for appellee, holding § 202(n) unconstitutional under the Due Process Clause of the Fifth Amendment in that it deprived appellee of an accrued property right. The Secretary prosecuted an appeal to this Court, and, subject to a jurisdictional question hereinafter discussed, we set the case down for plenary hearing.

[The Court first held that the district court properly exercised jurisdiction over the case, and then proceeded to the merits of the appeal.]

I.

We think that the District Court erred in holding that § 202(n) deprived appellee of an 'accrued property right.' Appellee's right to Social Security benefits cannot properly be considered to have been of that order.

The general purposes underlying the Social Security Act were expounded by Mr. Justice Cardozo in   The issue here, however, requires some inquiry into the statutory scheme by which those purposes are sought to be achieved. Payments under the Act are based upon the wage earner's record of earnings in employment or self-employment covered by the Act, and take the form of old-age insurance and disability insurance benefits inuring to the wage earner (known as the 'primary beneficiary'), and of benefits, including survivor benefits, payable to named dependents ('secondary beneficiaries') of a wage-earner. Of special importance in this case is the fact that eligibility for benefits, and the amount of such benefits, do not in any true sense depend on contribution to the program through the payment of taxes, but rather on the earnings record of the primary beneficiary.

---

[2] Under paragraph (1)(B) of § 202(n)), appellee's wife, because of her residence here, has remained eligible for benefits payable to her as the wife of an insured individual.

The program is financed through a payroll tax levied on employees in covered employment, and on their employers. The tax rate, which is a fixed percentage of the first $4,800 of employee annual income, is set at a scale which will increase from year to year, presumably to keep pace with rising benefit costs. The tax proceeds are paid into the Treasury 'as internal-revenue collections,' and each year an amount equal to the proceeds is appropriated to a Trust Fund, from which benefits and the expenses of the program are paid. It was evidently contemplated that receipts would greatly exceed disbursements in the early years of operation of the system, and surplus funds are invested in government obligations, and the income returned to the Trust Fund. Thus, provision is made for expected increasing costs of the program.

The Social Security system may be accurately described as a form of social insurance, enacted pursuant to Congress' power to "spend money in aid of the 'general welfare,'" whereby persons gainfully employed, and those who employ them, are taxed to permit the payment of benefits to the retired and disabled, and their dependents. Plainly the expectation is that many members of the present productive work force will in turn become beneficiaries rather than supporters of the program. But each worker's benefits, though flowing from the contributions he made to the national economy while actively employed, are not dependent on the degree to which he was called upon to support the system by taxation. It is apparent that the noncontractual interest of an employee covered by the Act cannot be soundly analogized to that of the holder of an annuity, whose right to benefits is bottomed on his contractual premium payments.

It is hardly profitable to engage in conceptualizations regarding "earned rights" and "gratuities." Cf. The "right" to Social Security benefits is in one sense "earned," for the entire scheme rests on the legislative judgment that those who in their productive years were functioning members of the economy may justly call upon that economy, in their later years, for protection from "the rigors of the poor house as well as from the haunting fear that such a lot awaits them when journey's end is near." But the practical effectuation of that judgment has of necessity called forth a highly complex and interrelated statutory structure. Integrated treatment of the manifold specific problems presented by the Social Security program demands more than a generalization. That program was designed to function into the indefinite future, and its specific provisions rest on predications as to expected economic conditions which must inevitably prove less than wholly accurate, and on judgments and preferences as to the proper allocation of the Nation's resources which evolving economic and social conditions will of necessity in some degree modify.

To engraft upon the Social Security system a concept of "accrued property rights" would deprive it of the flexibility and boldness in adjustment to everchanging conditions which it demands. It was doubtless out of an awareness of the need for such flexibility that Congress included in the original Act, and has since retained, a clause expressly reserving to it "(t)he right to alter, amend, or repeal any provision" of the Act. That provision makes express what is implicit in the institutional needs of the program. It was pursuant to that provision that § 202(n) was enacted.

We must conclude that a person covered by the Act has not such a right in benefit payments as would make every defeasance of "accrued" interests violative of the Due Process Clause of the Fifth Amendment.

II.

This is not to say, however, that Congress may exercise its power to modify the statutory scheme free of all constitutional restraint. The interest of a covered employee under the Act is of sufficient substance to fall within the protection from arbitrary governmental action afforded by the Due Process Clause. In judging the permissibility of the cut-off provisions of § 202(n) from this standpoint, it is not within our authority to determine whether the Congressional judgment expressed in that section is sound or equitable, or whether it comports well or ill with the purposes of the Act. "Whether wisdom or unwisdom resides in the scheme of benefits set forth in Title II, it is not for us to say. The answer to such inquiries must come from Congress, not the courts. Our concern here, as often, is with power, not with wisdom." Particularly when we deal with a withholding of a noncontractual benefit under a social welfare program such as this, we must recognize that the Due Process Clause can be thought to interpose a bar only if the statute manifests a patently arbitrary classification, utterly lacking in rational justification.

Such is not the case here. The fact of a beneficiary's residence abroad-in the case of a deportee, a presumably permanent residence-can be of obvious relevance to the question of eligibility. One benefit which may be thought to accrue to the economy from the Social Security system is the increased over-all national purchasing power resulting from taxation of productive elements of the economy to provide payments to the retired and disabled, who might otherwise be destitute or nearly so, and who would generally spend a comparatively large percentage of their benefit payments. This advantage would be lost as to payments made to one residing abroad. For these purposes, it is, of course, constitutionally irrelevant whether this reasoning in fact underlay the legislative decision, as it is irrelevant that the section does not extend to all to whom the postulated rationale might in logic apply. Nor, apart from this, can it be deemed irrational for Congress to have concluded that the public purse should not be utilized to contribute to the support of those deported on the grounds specified in the statute.

We need go no further to find support for our conclusion that this provision of the Act cannot be condemned as so lacking in rational justification as to offend due process.

[In the last part of the opinion, the Court rejected the argument that the termination of the appellee's benefits amounted to the imposition of punishment by legislative act, rendering § 202(n) of the Act an unconstitutional bill of attainder.]

Mr. Justice BLACK, dissenting.

* * *

I.

In Lynch v. United States, 292 U.S. 571, 54 S.Ct. 840, 78 L.Ed. 1434, this Court unanimously held that Congress was without power to repudiate and abrogate in whole or in part its promises to pay amounts claimed by soldiers under the War Risk Insurance Act of 1917, §§ 400--405, 40 Stat. 409. This Court held that such a repudiation was inconsistent with the provision of the Fifth Amendment that "No person shall be * * * deprived of life, liberty, or property, without due process of law; nor shall private property be taken for public use, without just compensation." The Court today puts the Lynch case aside on the ground that "'It is hardly profitable to engage in conceptualizations regarding 'earned rights' and 'gratuities.'" From this sound premise the Court goes on to say that while "The 'right' to Social Security benefits is in one sense 'earned,'" yet the Government's insurance scheme now before us rests not on the idea of the contributors to the fund earning something, but simply provides that they may "justly call" upon the Government "in their later years, for protection from 'the rigors of the poor house as well as from the haunting fear that such a lot awaits them when journey's end is near.'" These are nice words but they cannot conceal the fact that they simply tell the contributors to this insurance fund that despite their own and their employers' payments the Government, in paying the beneficiaries out of the fund, is merely giving them something for nothing and can stop doing so when it pleases. This, in my judgment, reveals a complete misunderstanding of the purpose Congress and the country had in passing that law. It was then generally agreed, as it is today, that it is not desirable that aged people think of the Government as giving them something for nothing. An excellent statement of this view, quoted by Mr. Justice DOUGLAS in another connection, was made by Senator George, the Chairman of the Finance Committee when the Social Security Act was passed, and one very familiar with the philosophy that brought it about:

"It comports better than any substitute we have discovered with the American concept that free men want to earn their security and not ask for doles—that what is due as a matter of earned right is far better than a gratuity. * * *"

"Social Security is not a handout; it is not charity; it is not relief. It is an earned right based upon the contributions and earnings of the individual. As an earned right, the individual is eligible to receive his benefit in dignity and self-respect." 102 Cong.Rec. 15110.

The people covered by this Act are now able to rely with complete assurance on the fact that they will be compelled to contribute regularly to this fund whenever each contribution falls due. I believe they are entitled to rely with the same assurance on getting the benefits they have paid for and have been promised, when their disability or age makes their insurance payable under the terms of the law. The Court did not permit the Government to break its plighted faith with the soldiers in the Lynch case; it said the Constitution forbade such governmental conduct. I would say precisely the same thing here.

The Court consoles those whose insurance is taken away today, and others who may suffer the same fate in the future, by saying that a decision requiring the Social Security system to keep faith "would deprive it of the flexibility and boldness in adjustment to everchanging conditions which it demands." People who pay premiums for insurance usually think they are paying for insurance, not for "flexibility and boldness." I cannot believe that any private insurance company in America would be permitted to repudiate its matured contracts with its policyholders who have regularly paid all their premiums in reliance upon the good faith of the company. It is true, as the Court says, that the original Act contained a clause, still in force, that expressly reserves to Congress "(t)he right to alter, amend, or repeal any provision" of the Act. Congress, of course, properly retained that power. It could repeal the Act so as to cease to operate its old-age insurance activities for the future. This means that it could stop covering new people, and even stop increasing its obligations to its old contributors. But that is quite different from disappointing the just expectations of the contributors to the fund which the Government has compelled them and their employers to pay its Treasury. There is nothing "conceptualistic" about saying, as this Court did in Lynch, that such a taking as this the Constitution forbids.

II.

In part II of its opinion, the Court throws out a line of hope by its suggestion that if Congress in the future cuts off some other group from the benefits they have bought from the Government, this Court might possibly hold that the future hypothetical act violates the Due Process Clause. In doing so it reads due process as affording only minimal protection, and under this reading it will protect all future groups from destruction of their rights only if Congress "manifests a patently arbitrary classification, utterly lacking in rational justification." The Due Process Clause so defined provides little protection indeed compared with the specific safeguards of the Constitution such as its prohibitions against taking private property for a public use without just compensation, passing *ex post facto* laws, and imposing bills of attainder. I cannot agree, however, that the Due Process Clause is properly interpreted when it is used to subordinate and dilute the specific safeguards of the Bill of Rights, and when "due process" itself becomes so wholly dependent upon this Court's idea of what is "arbitrary" and "rational." One reason for my belief in this respect is that I agree with what is said in the Court's quotation from Helvering v. Davis, 301 U.S. 619, 644, 57 S.Ct. 904, 910, 81 L.Ed. 1307:

> "Whether wisdom or unwisdom resides in the scheme of benefits set forth in Title II, it is not for us to say. The answer to such inquiries must come from Congress, not the courts. Our concern here, as often, is with power, not with wisdom."

And yet the Court's assumption of its power to hold Acts unconstitutional because the Court thinks they are arbitrary and irrational can be neither more nor less than a judicial foray into the field of governmental policy. By the use of this due process formula the Court does not, as its proponents frequently proclaim, abstain from interfering with the congressional policy. It actively enters that field with no standards except its own conclusion as to what is "arbitrary" and what is "rational." And this elastic formula gives the Court a further power, that of holding legislative Acts constitutional on the ground that they are neither arbitrary nor irrational, even though the Acts violate specific Bill of Rights safeguards. See my dissent in Adamson v. California, supra. Whether this Act had "rational justification" was, in my judgment, for Congress; whether it violates the Federal Constitution is for us to determine, unless we are by circumlocution to abdicate the power that this Court has been held to have ever since Marbury v. Madison, 1 Cranch 137, 2 L.Ed. 60.

* * *

[Dissenting opinions of Justices Douglas and Brennan omitted.]

C. MAJOR AMENDMENTS TO THE SOCIAL SECURITY ACT

As we have seen, the original Social Security Act of 1935 established both contributory (social insurance) and non-contributory (public assistance) programs. Benefits included a federal old age insurance program and various federal-state public assistance programs covering the elderly, blind, and dependent and crippled children. Shortly thereafter, Congress began to enact a series of amendments that have expanded significantly the scope of the Act's programs.

In 1939, Congress amended the Social Security Act to provide insurance benefits to certain dependents of recipients of old-age insurance benefits and survivors of insured workers who died—essentially their spouses and children. *See* Social Security Act Amendments of 1939, 53 Stat. 1360 (1939). By extending coverage beyond insured workers to their dependents, these amendments effectively transformed the Social Security program to a family benefits program.

In 1950, Congress enacted a new title of the Social Security Act, entitled "Grants to States for Aid to the Permanently and Totally Disabled." *See* Social Security Act Amendments of 1950, Pub. L. No. 81-734, 64 Stat. 477. The purpose of the Aid to the Permanently and Totally Disabled (APTD) program was to enable states "to furnish financial assistance, as far as practicable under the conditions in such State, to needy individuals eighteen years of age or older who are permanently and totally disabled." 42 U.S.C. § 1351 (1952). The APTD program was designed as a joint federal-state public assistance program; benefits were paid by state agencies under general federal guidelines, with funds provided by both the federal government and the states. Notwithstanding a great deal of debate over whether disability should be treated as a public assistance program or a social insurance program, Congress's reasons for adding only a public assistance program for the disabled were never made clear. *See generally*, Jacobus ten Broek & Richard B. Wilson, *Public Assistance and Social Insurance--A Normative Evaluation*, 1 U. C. L. A. L. REV. 237 (1954); Jacobus ten Broek & Floyd W. Matson, *The Disabled and the Law of Welfare*, 54 CALIF. L. REV. 809 (1966).

Six years later, in 1956, Congress added disability coverage for social insurance as well when it created the Disability Insurance Benefits program as part of the re-titled Old Age, Survivors, and Disability Insurance (OASDI) program. Social Security Act Amendments of 1956, Pub. L. No. 84-880, 70 Stat. 807. The eligibility requirements for the new program, administered by the federal Social Security Administration, were relatively strict. Only persons age 50 or over could qualify for benefits. In addition, a worker was "insured" under the program only if he or she had paid Social Security taxes for a minimum number of calendar quarters and had worked at employment covered by the program in the relatively recent past. Disability Insurance Benefits were thus limited to workers who contributed significantly to the Disability Insurance Trust Fund at or near the onset of their disability. The idea was that one could not expect to stop working while fit and later claim benefits due to a disability far removed in time from one's last employment.

The Disability Insurance Benefits program was added to the Social Security Act in the face of serious opposition in the Senate, where many had felt that physical disability did not necessarily produce economic disability and that payments therefore might be awarded to persons not truly needy. Many also felt that the Aid to the Permanently and Totally Disabled program, which was operating in 42 states, adequately met the needs of the disabled and that monthly payments to disabled workers might discourage the expansion of vocational rehabilitation programs. *See* S. Rep. No. 2133, 84th Cong., 2d Sess, reprinted in 1956 U.S. Code Cong. & Ad. News 3877, 3877-80; *cf.* Minority Views on H.R. 7225, reprinted in 1956 U.S. Code Cong. & Ad. News 3941, 3941-47. A number of the restrictive provisions were included in the new law in order to satisfy opposition in the Senate. *See generally*, Matthew Diller, *Entitlement and Exclusion: The Role of Disability in the Social Welfare System*, 44 UCLA L. REV. 361, 363 (1996). However, once this limited but workable disability insurance program was enacted, Congress passed a number of amendments in the following decade aimed at expanding and liberalizing the program.

Congress lifted some of the strict requirements that had been placed on the original disability insurance program already in 1958. Congress also addressed the lack of coverage for dependents of disabled and retired workers by adding monthly benefits for wives and dependent husbands who had reached retirement age, unmarried dependent children, including older children who had become disabled in childhood, and wives who had an eligible child in their care. *See* Social Security Amendments of 1958, Pub. L. No. 85-840, 72 Stat 1013. The next major expansion of disability insurance occurred in 1960, when Congress dropped the requirement that a disabled worker had to be at least 50 years old. Social Security Amendments of 1960, Pub. L. No. 86-778, 74 Stat. 918. Congress expanded disability coverage further in 1967, by providing benefits for disabled widows and widowers of insured workers who did not have a sufficient work record of their own, based on the earnings record of the deceased spouse. Social Security Amendments of 1967, Pub. L. No. 90-248, 81 Stat. 821.

Congress enacted the first federally funded medical programs of the Social Security Act—Medicare and Medicaid—as part of President Lyndon B. Johnson's Great Society legislation in 1965. *See* Social Security Amendments of 1965, Pub. L. No. 89-97, 79 Stat. 286. Medicare provides hospital insurance benefits for Social Security beneficiaries over the age of 65 (and some disabled beneficiaries under the age of 65), as well as optional Supplemental Health Insurance benefits that cover physician services funded in part by additional premiums. Medicaid is a federal/state program jointly funded—and administered—by the states, which provides hospital and physician coverage for all recipients of federal/state public assistance benefits and, based on subsequent amendments, optional coverage for "medically indigent" individuals not eligible for welfare benefits.

In the early 1970s, Congress began to review the status of the Social Security Act's joint federal/state public assistance programs, including the original Aid to Dependent Children program (which by then had been retitled Aid to Families with Dependent Children, or AFDC) and the later-enacted Aid to the Permanently and Totally Disabled program (APTD), also known as Aid to the Aged, Blind, and Disabled (AABD). There was a general sense that the Act's system of shared responsibility between the federal and state governments for public assistance programs had become unmanageable in terms of size and complexity of administration. *See, e.g.,* H.R. Rep. No. 231, 92nd Cong., 1st Sess. (1971), reprinted in 1972 U.S. Code Cong. & Ad. News 4987, 4991 ("The welfare system in the United States has been moving toward a state of crisis and chaos"). The debate and legislative maneuvering lasted four years. In the end, the various federal-state programs for the elderly, blind, and disabled were repealed and replaced with a federal program for the elderly, blind, and disabled called Supplemental Security income (SSI). *See generally*, DANIEL P. MOYNIHAN, THE POLITICS OF A GUARANTEED INCOME (Random House 1973). However, the larger and more controversial AFDC program— replaced in 1996 by the Temporary Assistance to Needy Families (TANF) program—remained a federal-state program.

The new SSI program, which became effective on January 1, 1974, established a uniform national system of welfare benefits for the elderly and disabled. Responsibility for administering the new program was given to the Social Security Administration. Although the age requirement for SSI benefits—65 years of age—is simpler than the early-retirement-to-full-retirement age requirement for the Old Age Insurance Benefits program, the general disability standard for Supplemental Security Income is essentially identical to the standard for Disability Insurance Benefits. (There is, however, a separate SSI disability standard for children under age 18—a group not covered by the Disability Insurance Program as they could not yet be insured.) As a public assistance program, eligibility for SSI and the amount of benefits paid are based on an evaluation of subsistence needs.

Following years of debate on the issue, Congress separated the Social Security Administration from the Department of Health and Human Services, effective March 31, 1995. A seven-member bipartisan board governs the new independent agency, which is headed by a Commissioner of Social Security appointed by the President. Although this change to independent agency status was the subject of much controversy, it has had very little impact on the substance or operation of Social Security Act programs.

Congress passed two laws in 1996 that had major impact on certain Social Security Act programs. The Contract with America Advancement Act of 1996, Pub. L. No. 104-121, 110 Stat. 847, restricted eligibility for Disability Insurance Benefits and SSI by precluding eligibility based on drug or alcohol addiction. The Personal Responsibility and Work Opportunity Reconciliation Act of 1996, Pub. L. No. 104-193, 110 Stat. 2105, ended the long-standing Aid to Families with Dependent Children (AFDC) program and replaced it with a more limited Temporary Assistance for Needy Families (TANF) program and significantly tightened the criteria for child's SSI disability benefits.

Among the more significant recent changes to the Act were three laws passed in 1999, 2000, and 2003. The Ticket to Work and Work Incentives Improvement Act of 1999, Pub. L. No. 106-70, 113 Stat. 1860, established a set of new vocational rehabilitation and other support programs intended to provide greater incentive for disability beneficiaries to return to work. The Senior Citizens' Freedom to Work Act of 2000, Pub L. No. 106-182, 114 Stat. 198 (2000), eliminated the earnings test for persons who retire at full retirement age. The Medicare Prescription Drug Improvement and Modernization Act of 2003, Pub. L. No. 108-73, 117 Stat. 2066, provides, beginning in 2006, for a new voluntary prescription drug benefit administered under private health plans for persons over the age of 65 and certain people with disabilities.

Finally, in 2000 (pursuant to legislation passed in 1983) the age at which beneficiaries can receive full retirement benefits under the Social Security Act's Old Age Insurance program began increasing gradually, from 65 to 67. *See* Social Security Amendments of 1983, Pub. L. No. 98-21, 97 Stat. 65.

D. CONSTITUTIONAL LIMITS ON DEFINING AND ALLOCATING BENEFITS

As the scope of coverage has expanded and more categories of persons have become potentially eligible for Social Security benefits, persons arguably within a covered category but excluded under the provisions of the Act began challenging statutory classifications. As we saw in *Flemming v. Nestor*, the fact that Social Security benefits are not treated as an accrued property right does not mean "that Congress may exercise its power to modify the statutory scheme free of all constitutional restraint." 363 U.S. at 611. Congress is not required to grant benefits to any particular group of persons; however, once benefits are granted they must be distributed in a manner that does not violate the Equal Protection or Due

Process clauses of the Constitution. The Supreme Court has sought to balance congressional power and constitutional restraints in this area, as seen in the following two cases.

WEINBERGER V. WIESENFELD
420 U.S. 636, 95 S.Ct. 1225 (1975)

Mr. Justice BRENNAN delivered the opinion of the Court.

Social Security Act benefits based on the earnings of a deceased husband and father covered by the Act are payable, with some limitations, both to the widow and to the couple's minor children in her care. § 202(g) of the Social Security Act, as amended, 42 U.S.C. § 402(g). Such benefits are payable on the basis of the earnings of a deceased wife and mother covered by the Act, however, only to the minor children and not to the widower. The question in this case is whether this gender-based distinction violates the Due Process Clause of the Fifth Amendment.

* * *

I

Appellee Stephen C. Wiesenfeld and Paula Polatschek were married on November 15, 1970. Paula, who worked as a teacher for five years before her marriage, continued teaching after her marriage. Each year she worked, maximum social security contributions were deducted from her salary. Paula's earnings were the couple's principal source of support during the marriage, being substantially larger than those of appellee.

On June 5, 1972, Paula died in childbirth. Appellee was left with the sole responsibility for the care of their infant son, Jason Paul. Shortly after his wife's death, Stephen Wiesenfeld applied at the Social Security office in New Brunswick, N.J., for social security survivors' benefits for himself and his son. He did obtain benefits for his son * * *. However, appellee was told that he was not eligible for benefits for himself, because § 402(g) benefits were available only to women. If he had been a woman, he would have received the same amount as his son as long as he was not working and, if working, that amount reduced by $1 for every $2 earned annually above $2,400.[7]

---

[7] Stephen Wiesenfeld was employed until October 1972. However, since he earned $2,475 for the entire year 1972, n. 4, supra, he apparently would have been eligible for benefits, were he a woman, from June 1972 until he obtained employment again on February 5, 1973, at a salary of $1,500 per month. This lawsuit was filed on February 24, 1973. On September 14, 1973, appellee was dismissed from his position, so that he was unemployed and again eligible for benefits, but for the gender-based distinction, when the lower court opinion issued on December 11, 1973. Appellee, in an affidavit filed in September 1973, ascribed his employment difficulties in large part to the difficulties of childcare. In particular, he noted that he had "encountered severe

* * *

II

The gender-based distinction made by § 402(g) is indistinguishable from that invalidated in Frontiero v. Richardson, 411 U.S. 677, 93 S.Ct. 1764, 36 L.Ed.2d 583 (1973). *Frontiero* involved statutes which provided the wife of a male serviceman with dependents' benefits but not the husband of a servicewoman unless she proved that she supplied more than one-half of her husband's support. The Court held that the statutory scheme violated the right to equal protection secured by the Fifth Amendment. Schlesinger v. Ballard, 419 U.S. 498, 95 S.Ct. 572, 42 L.Ed.2d 60 (1975), explained: "In . . . *Frontiero* the challenged (classification) based on sex (was) premised on overbroad generalizations that could not be tolerated under the Constitution. . . . (T)he assumption . . . was that female spouses of servicemen would normally be dependent upon their husbands, while male spouses of servicewomen would not." A virtually identical "archaic and overbroad" generalization "not . . . tolerated under the Constitution" underlies the distinction drawn by § 402(g), namely, that male workers' earnings are vital to the support of their families, while the earnings of female wage earners do not significantly contribute to their families' support.

Section 402(g) was added to the Social Security Act in 1939 as one of a large number of amendments designed to "afford more adequate protection to the family as a unit." H.R.Rep.No.728, 76th Cong., 1st Sess., 7 (1939). Monthly benefits were provided to wives, children, widows, orphans, and surviving dependent parents of covered workers. However, children of covered female workers were eligible for survivors' benefits only in limited circumstances, see n. 5, supra, and no benefits whatever were made available to husbands or widowers on the basis of their wives' covered employment.

Underlying the 1939 scheme was the principle that "(u)nder a social-insurance plan the primary purpose is to pay benefits in accordance with the probable needs of the beneficiaries rather than to make payments to the estate of a deceased person regardless of whether or not he leaves dependents." H.R.Rep.No.728, *supra*, at 7. (Emphasis supplied.) It was felt that "(t)he payment of these survivorship benefits and supplements for the wife of an annuitant are . . . in keeping with the principle of social insurance . . . ." Ibid. Thus, the framers of the Act legislated on the "then generally accepted presumption that a man is responsible for the support

---

difficulty in obtaining the services of a suitable housekeeper, to whom I could conscientiously entrust Jason's care. I have employed four housekeepers in the past year . . .."

of his wife and children." D. Hoskins & L. Bixby, Women and Social Security: Law and Policy in Five Countries, Social Security Administration Research Report No. 42, p. 77 (1973).

Obviously, the notion that men are more likely than women to be the primary supporters of their spouses and children is not entirely without empirical support. But such a gender-based generalization cannot suffice to justify the denigration of the efforts of women who do work and whose earnings contribute significantly to their families' support.

Section 402(g) clearly operates, as did the statutes invalidated by our judgment in *Frontiero*, to deprive women of protection for their families which men receive as a result of their employment. Indeed, the classification here is in some ways more pernicious. First, it was open to the servicewoman under the statutes invalidated in *Frontiero* to prove that her husband was in fact dependent upon her. Here, Stephen Wiesenfeld was not given the opportunity to show, as may well have been the case, that he was dependent upon his wife for his support, or that, had his wife lived, she would have remained at work while he took over care of the child. Second, in this case social security taxes were deducted from Paula's salary during the years in which she worked. Thus, she not only failed to receive for her family the same protection which a similarly situated male worker would have received, but she also was deprived of a portion of her own earnings in order to contribute to the fund out of which benefits would be paid to others. Since the Constitution forbids the gender-based differentiation premised upon assumptions as to dependency made in the statutes before us in *Frontiero*, the Constitution also forbids the gender-based differentiation that results in the efforts of female workers required to pay social security taxes producing less protection for their families than is produced by the efforts of men.

III

Appellant seeks to avoid this conclusion with two related arguments. First, he claims that because social security benefits are not compensation for work done, Congress is not obliged to provide a covered female employee with the same benefits as it provides to a male. Second, he contends that § 402(g) was "reasonably designed to offset the adverse economic situation of women by providing a widow with financial assistance to supplement or substitute for her own efforts in the marketplace," Brief for Appellant 14, and therefore does not contravene the equal protection guarantee.

A

Appellant relies for the first proposition primarily on Flemming v. Nestor, 363 U.S. 603, 80 S.Ct. 1367, 4 L.Ed.2d 1435 (1960). We held in

Flemming that the interest of a covered employee in future social security benefits is "noncontractual," because "each worker's benefits, though flowing from the contributions he made to the national economy while actively employed, are not dependent on the degree to which he was called upon to support the system by taxation." *Id.*, at 609--610, 80 S.Ct. at 1371, 1372. The appellant apparently contends that since benefits derived from the social security program do not correlate necessarily with contributions made to the program, a covered employee has no right whatever to be treated equally with other employees as regards the benefits which flow from his or her employment.

We do not see how the fact that social security benefits are "noncontractual" can sanction differential protection for covered employees which is solely gender based. From the outset, social security old age, survivors', and disability (OASDI) benefits have been "afforded as a matter of right, related to past participation in the productive processes of the county." Final Report of the Advisory Council on Social Security 17 (1938). It is true that social security benefits are not necessarily related directly to tax contributions, since the OASDI system is structured to provide benefits in part according to presumed need. For this reason, *Flemming* held that the position of a covered employee "cannot be soundly analogized to that of the holder of an annuity, whose right to benefits is bottomed on his contractual premium payments." 363 U.S., at 610, 80 S.Ct. at 1372. But the fact remains that the statutory right to benefits is directly related to years worked and amount earned by a covered employee, and not to the need of the beneficiaries directly. Since OASDI benefits do depend significantly upon the participation in the work force of a covered employee, and since only covered employees and not others are required to pay taxes toward the system, benefits must be distributed according to classifications which do not without sufficient justification differentiate among covered employees solely on the basis of sex.

B

Appellant seeks to characterize the classification here as one reasonably designed to compensate women beneficiaries as a group for the economic difficulties which still confront women who seek to support themselves and their families. The Court held in Kahn v. Shevin, 416 U.S., at 355, 94 S.Ct. at 1737, that a statute 'reasonably designed to further the state policy of cushioning the financial impact of spousal loss upon the sex for whom that loss imposes a disproportionately heavy burden' can survive an equal protection attack. But the mere recitation of a benign, compensatory purpose is not an automatic shield which protects against

any inquiry into the actual purposes underlying a statutory scheme.[16]
Here, it is apparent both from the statutory scheme itself and from the
legislative history of § 402(g) that Congress' purpose in providing benefits
to young widows with children was not to provide an income to women
who were, because of economic discrimination, unable to provide for
themselves. Rather, § 402(g), linked as it is directly to responsibility for
minor children, was intended to permit women to elect not to work and to
devote themselves to the care of children. Since this purpose in no way is
premised upon any special disadvantages of women, it cannot serve to
justify a gender-based distinction which diminishes the protection afforded to women who do work.

That the purpose behind § 402(g) is to provide children deprived of
one parent with the opportunity for the personal attention of the other
could not be more clear in the legislative history. The Advisory Council
on Social Security, which developed the 1939 amendments, said explicitly
that "(s)uch payments (under § 402(g)) are intended as supplements to
the orphans' benefits *with the purpose of enabling the widow to remain at
home and care for the children.*" Final Report of the Advisory Council on
Social Security 31 (1938). (Emphasis supplied.) In 1971, a new Advisory
Council, considering amendments to eliminate the various gender-based
distinctions in the OASDI structure, reiterated this understanding: "Present law provides benefits for the mother of young . . . children . . . if she
chooses to stay home and care for the children instead of working. In the
Council's judgment, it is desirable to allow a woman who is left with the
care of the children the choice of whether to stay at home to care for the
children or to work." 1971 Advisory Council on Social Security, Reports on
the Old-Age, Survivors, and Disability Insurance and Medicare Programs
30 (hereinafter 1971 Reports). (Emphasis supplied.)

Indeed, consideration was given in 1939 to extending benefits to all
widows regardless of whether or not there were minor children. The proposal was rejected, apparently because it was felt that young widows
without children can be expected to work, while middle-aged widows "are
likely to have more savings than younger widows and many of them have
children who are grown and able to help them." Report of the Social Security Board, H.R.Doc.No.110, 76th Cong., 1st Sess., 7--8 (1939). See also
Final Report of the Advisory Council on Social Security 31 (1938); Hearings on the Social Security Act Amendments of 1939 before the House
Committee on Ways and Means, 76th Cong., 1st Sess., 61, 1217, 2169-
2170; H.R.Rep.No.728, 76th Cong., 1st Sess., 36 (1939). Thus, Congress
decided *not* to provide benefits to all widows even though it was recog-

---

[16] This Court need not in equal protection cases accept at face value assertions of legislative
purposes, when an examination of the legislative scheme and its history demonstrates that the
asserted purpose could not have been a goal of the legislation.

nized that some of them would have serious problems in the job market. Instead, it provided benefits only to those women who had responsibility for minor children, because it believed that they should not be required to work.

The whole structure of survivors' benefits conforms to this articulated purpose. Widows without minor children obtain no benefits on the basis of their husband's earnings until they reach age 60 or, in certain instances of disability, age 50. 42 U.S.C. §§ 402(e)(1) and (5). Further, benefits under § 402(g) cease when all children of a beneficiary are no longer eligible for children's benefits. If Congress were concerned with providing women with benefits because of economic discrimination, it would be entirely irrational to except those women who had spent many years at home rearing children, since those women are most likely to be without the skills required to succeed in the job market. Similarly, the Act now provides benefits to a surviving divorced wife who is the parent of a covered employee's child, regardless of how long she was married to the deceased or of whether she or the child was dependent upon the employee for support. §§ 402(g), 416(d)(3). Yet, a divorced wife who is not the mother of a child entitled to children's benefits is eligible for benefits only if she meets other eligibility requirements and was married to the covered employee for 20 years. §§ 402(b) and (e), 416(d). Once again, this distinction among women is explicable only because Congress was not concerned in § 402(g) with the employment problems of women generally but with the principle that children of covered employees are entitled to the personal attention of the surviving parent if that parent chooses not to work.

Given the purpose of enabling the surviving parent to remain at home to care for a child, the gender-based distinction of § 402(g) is entirely irrational. The classification discriminates among surviving children solely on the basis of the sex of the surviving parent. Even in the typical family hypothesized by the Act, in which the husband is supporting the family and the mother is caring for the children, this result makes no sense. The fact that a man is working while there is a wife at home does not mean that he would, or should be required to, continue to work if his wife dies. It is no less important for a child to be cared for by its sole surviving parent when that parent is male rather than female. And a father, no less than a mother, has a constitutionally protected right to the "companionship, care, custody, and management" of "the children he has sired and raised, (which) undeniably warrants deference and, absent a powerful countervailing interest, protection." Stanley v. Illinois, 405 U.S. 645, 651, 92 S.Ct. 1208, 1212, 31 L.Ed.2d 551 (1972). Further, to the extent that women who work when they have sole responsibility for children encounter special problems, it would seem that men with sole responsibility for children will encounter the same child-care related problems. Stephen

Wiesenfeld, for example, found that providing adequate care for his infant son impeded his ability to work, see n. 7, *supra*.

Finally, to the extent that Congress legislated on the presumption that women as a group would choose to forgo work to care for children while men would not,[20] the statutory structure, independent of the gender-based classification, would deny or reduce benefits to those men who conform to the presumed norm and are not hampered by their child-care responsibilities. Benefits under § 402(g) decrease with increased earnings, see *supra*, at 1229-1230. According to the appellant, "the bulk of male workers would receive no benefits in any event" because they earn too much. Thus, the gender-based distinction is gratuitous; without it, the statutory scheme would only provide benefits to those men who are in fact similarly situated to the women the statute aids.

Since the gender-based classification of § 402(g) cannot be explained as an attempt to provide for the special problems of women, it is indistinguishable from the classification held invalid in *Frontiero*. Like the statutes there, "[b]y providing dissimilar treatment for men and women who are . . . similarly situated, the challenged section violates the (Due Process) Clause." Reed v. Reed, 404 U.S. 71, 77, 92 S.Ct. 251, 254, 30 L.Ed.2d 225 (1971).

Affirmed.

Mr. Justice DOUGLAS took no part in the consideration or decision of this case.

Mr. Justice POWELL, with whom THE CHIEF JUSTICE joins, concurring.

I concur in the judgment and generally in the opinion of the Court. But I would identify the impermissible discrimination effected by § 402(g) somewhat more narrowly than the Court does. Social Security is designed, certainly in this context, for the protection of the *family*. Although it lacks the contractual attributes of insurance or an annuity, Flemming v. Nestor, 363 U.S. 603, 80 S.Ct. 1367, 4 L.Ed.2d 1435 (1960),

---

[20] Precisely this view was expressed by the 1971 Advisory Council on Social Security, whose recommendations upon which gender-based distinctions in the OASDI system to retain and which to discard were followed in the 1972 Social Security Amendments: 'The Council believes that it is unnecessary to offer the same choice (whether to work or care for surviving children) to a man. Even though many more married women work today than in the past, so that they are both workers and homemakers, very few men adopt such a dual role; the customary and predominant role of the father is not that of a homemaker but rather that of the family breadwinner. A man generally continues to work to support himself and his children after the death or disability of his wife. The Council therefore does not recommend that benefits be provided for a young father who has children in his care.' 1971 Reports 30.

it is a contributory system and millions of wage earners depend on it to provide basic protection for their families in the event of death or disability.

Many women are the principal wage earners for their families, and they participate in the Social Security system on exactly the same basis as men. When the mother is a principal wage earner, the family may suffer as great an economic deprivation upon her death as would occur upon the death of a father wage earner. It is immaterial whether the surviving parent elects to assume primary child care responsibility rather than work, or whether other arrangements are made for child care. The statutory scheme provides benefits both to a surviving mother who remains at home and to one who works at low wages. A surviving father may have the same need for benefits as a surviving mother. The statutory scheme therefore impermissibly discriminates against a female wage earner because it provides her family less protection than it provides that of a male wage earner, even though the family needs may be identical. I find no legitimate governmental interest that supports this gender classification.

Mr. Justice REHNQUIST, concurring in the result.

Part III-B of the Court's opinion contains a thorough examination of the legislative history and statutory context which define the role and purpose of § 402(g). I believe the Court's examination convincingly demonstrates that the only purpose of § 402(g) is to make it possible for children of deceased contributing workers to have the personal care and attention of a surviving parent, should that parent desire to remain in the home with the child. Moreover, the Court's opinion establishes that the Government's proffered legislative purpose is so totally at odds with the context and history of § 402(g) that it cannot serve as a basis for judging whether the statutory distinction between men and women rationally serves a valid legislative objective.

This being the case, I see no necessity for reaching the issue of whether the statute's purported discrimination against female workers violates the Fifth Amendment as applied in Frontiero v. Richardson, 411 U.S. 677, 93 S.Ct. 1764, 36 L.Ed.2d 583 (1973). I would simply conclude, as does the Court in Part III-B of its opinion, that the restriction of § 402(g) benefits to surviving mothers does not rationally serve any valid legislative purpose, including that for which § 402(g) was obviously designed. This is so because it is irrational to distinguish between mothers and fathers when the sole question is whether a child of a deceased contributing worker should have the opportunity to receive the full-time attention of the only parent remaining to it. To my mind, that should be the end of the matter. I therefore concur in the result.

CALIFANO V. BOLES

443 U.S. 282, 99 S.Ct. 2767 (1979)

Mr. Justice REHNQUIST delivered the opinion of the Court.

Since the Depression of the 1930's, the Government has taken increasingly upon itself the task of insulating the economy at large and the individual from the buffeting of economic fortune. The federal old-age, survivors, and disability insurance provisions of the Social Security Act (SSA) are possibly the pre-eminent examples: attempts to obviate, through a program of forced savings, the economic dislocations that may otherwise accompany old age, disability, or the death of a breadwinner. As an exercise in governmental administration, the social security system is of unprecedented dimension; in fiscal year 1977 nearly 150 million claims were filed.

* * * Our cases evidence a sensitivity to the legislative and administrative problems posed in the design of such a program and in the adjudication of claims on this scale. The problems are generally of two types. The first is categorization.[3] In light of the specific dislocations Congress wishes to alleviate, it is necessary to define categories of beneficiaries. The process of categorization presents the difficulties inherent in any line-drawing exercise where the draftsman confronts a universe of potential beneficiaries with different histories and distinct needs. He strives for a level of generality that is administratively practicable with full appreciation that the included class has members whose "needs" upon a statutorily defined occurrence may not be as marked as those of isolated individuals outside the classification. "General rules are essential if a fund of this magnitude is to be administered with a modicum of efficiency, even though such rules inevitably produce seemingly arbitrary consequences in some individual cases." Califano v. Jobst, 434 U.S. 47, 53, 98

---

[3] The bulk of our cases fall under this heading. Califano v. Jobst, [434 U.S. 47, 98 S.Ct. 95, 54 L.Ed.2d 228 (1977)] (termination of dependent child's benefits upon his marriage); Califano v. Webster, [430 U.S. 313, 97 S.Ct. 1192, 51 L.Ed.2d 360 (1977)] (gender-based differences in benefit computation); Califano v. Goldfarb, [430 U.S. 199, 97 S.Ct. 1021, 51 L.Ed.2d 270 (1977)] (gender-based differences in defining dependent of deceased wage earner); Mathews v. De Castro, [429 U.S. 181, 97 S.Ct. 431, 50 L.Ed.2d 389 (1976)] (denial of "wife's insurance benefits" to divorced women under 62 years of age); Norton v. Mathews, [427 U.S. 524, 96 S.Ct. 2771, 49 L.Ed.2d 672 (1976)] (illegitimate children denied presumption of dependency enjoyed by legitimates); Mathews v. Lucas, [427 U.S. 495, 96 S.Ct. 2755, 49 L.Ed.2d 651 (1976)] (same as Norton); Weinberger v. Salfi, [422 U.S. 749, 95 S.Ct. 2457, 45 L.Ed.2d 522 (1975)] (duration-of-relationship requirements for receipt of mother's or child's insurance benefits); Weinberger v. Wiesenfeld, [420 U.S. 636, 95 S.Ct. 1225, 43 L.Ed.2d 514 (1975)] (gender-based denial of survivor's benefits to widowers); Jimenez v. Weinberger, [417 U.S. 628, 94 S.Ct. 2496, 41 L.Ed.2d 363 (1974)] (denial of disability insurance benefits to illegitimate children born after onset of wage earner's disability); Richardson v. Belcher, [404 U.S. 78, 92 S.Ct. 254, 30 L.Ed.2d 231 (1971)] (reduction in social security benefits to reflect state workmen's compensation benefits); Flemming v. Nestor, [363 U.S. 603, 80 S.Ct. 1367, 4 L.Ed.2d 1435 (1960)] (termination of insurance benefits to aliens upon their deportation).

S.Ct. 95, 99, 54 L.Ed.2d 228 (1977). A process of case-by-case adjudication that would provide a "perfect fit" in theory would increase administrative expenses to a degree that benefit levels would probably be reduced, precluding a perfect fit in fact.

The second type of problem that has been brought to this Court involves the Social Security Administration's procedures for dispute resolution where benefits have been denied, decreased, or terminated because the Administration has concluded that the claimant is not entitled to what he has requested or to what he has received in the past.[4] Again the Court has been sensitive to the special difficulties presented by the mass administration of the social security system. After the legislative task of classification is completed, the administrative goal is accuracy and promptness in the actual allocation of benefits pursuant to those classifications. The magnitude of that task is not amenable to the full trappings of the adversary process lest again benefit levels be threatened by the costs of administration. Fairness can best be assured by Congress and the Social Security Administration through sound managerial techniques and quality control designed to achieve an acceptable rate of error.

This case involves a challenge to a categorization. Appellees Norman J. Boles and Margaret Gonzales represent a nationwide class of all illegitimate children and their mothers who are allegedly ineligible for insurance benefits under the SSA because in each case the mother was never married to the wage earner who fathered her child. Section 202(g)(1) of the SSA, as amended, 42 U.S.C. § 402(g)(1), only makes "mother's insurance benefits" available to widows and divorced wives. By virtue of this Court's decision in Weinberger v. Wiesenfeld, 420 U.S. 636, 95 S.Ct. 1225, 43 L.Ed.2d 514 (1975), "mother's insurance benefits" are available to widowers, leaving the title of these benefits a misnomer. There we held that the provision of such benefits only to women violated the Due Process Clause of the Fifth Amendment.

Norman W. Boles died in 1971. He left a widow, Nancy L. Boles, and their two children, who were each promptly awarded child's insurance benefits. Nancy Boles receives mother's insurance benefits. Appellee Gonzales lived with Norman W. Boles for three years before his marriage to Nancy Boles and bore a son by him, Norman J. Boles. Gonzales sought

---

[4] Califano v. Yamasaki, [442 U.S. 682, 99 S.Ct. 2545, 61 L.Ed.2d 176 (1979)] (lack of prerecoupment oral hearing in overpayment cases); Mathews v. Eldridge, [424 U.S. 319, 96 S.Ct. 893, 47 L.Ed.2d 18 (1976)] (question whether evidentiary hearing necessary before termination of disability insurance benefits); Richardson v. Wright, [405 U.S. 208, 92 S.Ct. 788, 31 L.Ed.2d 151 (1972)] (challenge to procedures employed in suspension or termination of disability benefits); Richardson v. Perales, [402 U.S. 389, 91 S.Ct. 1420, 28 L.Ed.2d 842 (1971)] (written reports by physicians who have examined disability insurance claimants are "substantial evidence" supporting denial of benefits).

mother's insurance benefits for herself and child's benefits for her son. Her son was granted benefits, but her personal request was denied because she had never been married to the wage earner.

Gonzales exhausted her administrative remedies and then filed this suit in the United States District Court for the Western District of Texas. The District Court certified a class of "all illegitimate children and their mothers who are presently ineligible for Mother's Insurance Benefits solely because 42 U.S.C. § 402(g)(1) restricts such benefits to women who were once married to the fathers of their children."   App. to Juris. Statement 1a-2a. The District Court found that § 202(g)(1) of the SSA was unconstitutional. There were three steps in its logic.

First, it read Weinberger v. Wiesenfeld, supra, as holding that mother's insurance benefits are chiefly for the benefit of the child. It quoted from a passage in that opinion where this Court observed:

> "[Section] 402(g), linked as it is directly to responsibility for minor children, was intended to permit women to elect not to work and to devote themselves to the care of children. . . .

> "That the purpose behind § 402(g) is to provide children deprived of one parent with the opportunity for the personal attention of the other could not be more clear in the legislative history." 420 U.S., at 648-649, 95 S.Ct., at 1233.

On the basis of this language it then concluded that for purposes of equal protection analysis, the pertinent discrimination in this case is not unequal treatment of unwed mothers, but rather discrimination against illegitimate children. In its final step the District Court held that the application of § 202(g)(1) at issue here is unconstitutional, relying on cases of this Court invalidating on constitutional grounds legislation that discriminated against illegitimates solely because of their status at birth.

We noted probable jurisdiction, and now conclude that the District Court incorrectly analyzed the equal protection issue in this case. We accordingly reverse.

As this Court noted in Weinberger v. Wiesenfeld, supra, 420 U.S., at 643, 95 S.Ct., at 1231, § 202(g) "was added to the Social Security Act in 1939 as one of large number of amendments designed to 'afford more adequate protection to the family as a unit.'   H.R.Rep.No. 728, 76th Cong., 1st Sess., 7 (1939)."   The benefits created in 1939 "were intended to provide persons dependent on the wage earner with protection against the economic hardship occasioned by loss of the wage earner's support." Califano v. Jobst, 434 U.S., at 50, 98 S.Ct., at 97-98. Specifically, § 202(g) "was intended to permit women [and now men] to elect not to work and to devote themselves to care of children." 420 U.S., at 648, 95 S.Ct., at 1233. The animating concern was the economic dislocation that occurs when the wage earner dies and the surviving parent is left with the choice to stay home and care for the children or to go to work, a hardship often exacerbated by years outside the labor force. "Mother's insurance benefits" were intended to make the choice to stay home easier. But the program was not designed to be, and we think is not now, a general system for the dispensing of child-care subsidies. Instead, Congress sought to limit the category of beneficiaries to those who actually suffer economic dislocation upon the death of a wage earner and are likely to be confronted at that juncture with the choice between employment or the assumption of full-time child-care responsibilities.

In this light there is an obvious logic in the exclusion from § 202(g) of women or men who have never married the wage earner. "Both tradition and common experience support the conclusion that marriage is an event which normally marks an important change in economic status." Califano v. Jobst, supra, 434 U.S., at 53, 98 S.Ct., at 99. Congress could reasonably conclude that a woman who has never been married to the wage earner is far less likely to be dependent upon the wage earner at the time of his death. He was never legally required to support her and therefore was less likely to have been an important source of income. Thus, the possibility of severe economic dislocation upon his death is more remote.

We confronted an analogous classification in Mathews v. De Castro, supra, which involved a challenge to the exclusion of divorced women from "wife's income benefits." In concluding that the classification did not deny equal protection, we observed:

> "Divorce by its nature works a drastic change in the economic and personal relationship between a husband and wife. . . . Congress could have rationally assumed that divorced husbands and wives depend less on each other for financial and other support than do couples who stay married. The problems that a divorced wife may encounter when her former husband becomes old or disabled may well differ in kind and degree from those that a woman married to a retired or disabled husband must face. . . . She may not feel the pinch of the extra expenses accompanying her former husband's old age or disability. . . . It was not irrational for Congress to recognize this basic fact in deciding to defer monthly payments to divorced wives of retired or disabled wage earners until they reach the age of 62." 429 U.S., at 188-189, 97 S.Ct., at 436.

Likewise, Weinberger v. Salfi, 422 U.S. 749, 95 S.Ct. 2457, 45 L.Ed.2d 522 (1975), upheld a 9-month duration-of-relationship eligibility requirement for the wife and stepchildren of a deceased wage earner. The stated purpose of the requirement was "to prevent the use of sham marriages to secure Social Security payments." *Id.*, at 767, 95 S.Ct., at 2468. We found that the only relevant constitutional argument was whether "the test [appellees could not] meet [was] not so rationally related to a legitimate legislative objective that it [could] be used to deprive them of benefits available to those who [did] satisfy that test." Id., at 772, 95 S.Ct., at 2470. We recognized that the statutory requirement would deny benefits in some cases of legitimate, sincere marriage relationships.

"While it is possible to debate the wisdom of excluding legitimate claimants in order to discourage sham relationships, and of relying on a rule which may not exclude some obviously sham arrangements, we think it clear that Congress could rationally choose to adopt such a course. Large numbers of people are eligible for these programs and are potentially subject to inquiry as to the validity of their relationships to wage earners. . . . Not only does the prophylactic approach thus obviate the necessity for large numbers of individualized determinations, but it also protects large numbers of claimants who satisfy the rule from the uncertainties and delays of administrative inquiry into the circumstances of their marriages." *Id.*, at 781-782, 95 S.Ct., at 2475.

It is with this background that we must analyze what the District Court in this case perceived to be the flaw in relying on dependence as a rationale for the statutory distinction between married and unmarried persons. The District Court pointed out that in 1972 Congress lifted the requirement that divorced women seeking mother's insurance benefits show that they were in some measure dependent on the wage earner immediately before his death.[8] It seized this fact as refutation of any characterization of these benefits as an attempt to ease the dislocation of those who had been dependent on the deceased. We think the District Court is demanding a precision not warranted by our cases.

Certainly Congress did not envision such precision. The legislative history surrounding the devolution of support requirements suggests that its effect on mother's insurance benefits was an incidental and relatively minor byproduct of Congress' core concern: older women who were mar-

---

[8] Originally, nothing similar to mother's insurance benefits for divorced women was provided by the SSA. Then in 1950 these benefits, subject to limitations not relevant here, were made available to a surviving divorced wife, if she had not remarried, had a child in her care entitled to child's insurance benefits, and at the time of the wage earner's death had been receiving at least one-half of her support from him.

In 1965, the remarriage bar to mother's insurance benefits was relaxed. A woman's rights as a surviving divorced mother would be restored if her second marriage ended in divorce. Moreover, a showing that she was receiving or entitled to receive "substantial contributions" from the wage earner at the time of his death would suffice in lieu of a showing that she received at least one-half of her support from the wage earner.

Finally, in 1972 Congress made the changes discussed by the District Court.

ried to wage earners for over 20 years—women who often only knew work as housewives—and who were not eligible for surviving divorced wife's insurance benefits because state divorce laws did not permit alimony or because they had accepted a property settlement in lieu of alimony.[9] The Social Security laws have maintained uniform support requirements for divorced wife's, divorced widow's, and surviving divorced mother's benefits. Obviously administration is thereby simplified. Undoubtedly, some younger divorced wives with children of deceased wage earners in their care who could not meet the old support requirements incidentally benefit from Congress' concern that many older women were being victimized once by state divorce laws and again by the Social Security laws. However, when Congress seeks to alleviate hardship and inequity under the Social Security laws, it may quite rightly conceive its task to be analogous to painting a fence, rather than touching up an etching. We have repeatedly stated that there is no constitutional requirement that "a statutory provision . . . filte[r] out those, and only those, who are in the factual position which generated the congressional concern reflected in the statute." Weinberger v. Salfi, 422 U.S., at 777, 95 S.Ct., at 2472. In sum, we conclude that the denial of mother's insurance benefits to a woman who never married the wage earner bears a rational relation to the Government's desire to ease economic privation brought on by the wage earner's death.

But the appellees argue that to characterize the problem in this fashion is to miss the point because at root this case involves discrimination against illegitimate children. Quite naturally, those who seek benefits denied them by statute will frame the constitutional issue in a manner

---

[9] Interestingly, younger women receiving mother's benefits are not even mentioned in the Committee Reports on the 1972 amendment.

"Benefits, under present law, are payable to a divorced wife age 62 or older and a divorced widow age 60 or older if her marriage lasted at least 20 years before the divorce, and to a surviving divorced mother. In order to qualify for any of these benefits a divorced woman is required to show that: (1) she was receiving at least one-half of her support from her former husband; (2) she was receiving substantial contributions from her former husband pursuant to a written agreement; or (3) there was a court order in effect providing for substantial contributions to her support by her former husband.

"In some States the courts are prohibited from providing for alimony, and in these States a divorced woman is precluded from meeting the third support requirement. Even in States which allow alimony, the court may have decided at the time of the divorce that the wife was not in need of financial support. Moreover, a divorced woman's eligibility for social security benefits may depend on the advice she received at the time of her divorce. If a woman accepted a property settlement in lieu of alimony, she could, in effect, have disqualified herself for divorced wife's, divorced widow's, or surviving divorced mother's benefits.

"The intent of providing benefits to divorced women is to protect women whose marriages are dissolved when they are far along in years–particularly housewives who have not been able to work and earn social security protection of their own. The committee believes that the support requirements of the law have operated to deprive some divorced women of the protection they should have received and, therefore, recommends that these requirements be eliminated. The requirement that the marriage of a divorced wife or widow must have lasted for at least 20 years before the divorce would not be changed."

S.Rep. No. 92-1230, p. 142 (1972). When the 1965 Changes were made there was only passing mention of younger women receiving mother's insurance benefits.

most favorable to their claim. The proper classification for purposes of equal protection analysis is not an exact science, but scouting must begin with the statutory classification itself. Only when it is shown that the legislation has a substantial disparate impact on classes defined in a different fashion may analysis continue on the basis of the impact on those classes.

We conclude that the legislation in this case does not have the impact on illegitimates necessary to warrant further inquiry whether § 202(g) is the product of discriminatory purposes. "Mother's insurance benefits" are distinct from "child's insurance benefits." The latter are benefits paid to the minor children of the deceased wage earner and, as noted, Gonzales' son did receive child's insurance benefits. The benefit to a child as a result of the parent or guardian's receipt of mother's insurance benefits is incidental: mother's insurance benefit payments do not vary with the number of children within the recipient's care, they are not available in the foster care context, and they are lost on remarriage or if the surviving parent earns a substantial income—all despite the needs of the child. Thus, the focus of these benefits is on the economic dilemma of the surviving spouse or former spouse; the child's needs as such are addressed through the separate child's insurance benefits. Nor is it invariably true that whatever derivative benefits are enjoyed by the child whose parent or guardian receives mother's insurance benefits will not be enjoyed by illegitimate children. If the illegitimate child is cared for by the deceased wage earner's wife, she will receive mother's insurance benefits even though she has no natural children of her own and never adopted the child. And many legitimate children live in households that are not headed by individuals eligible for mother's benefits.

In order to make out a disparate impact warranting further scrutiny under the Due Process Clause of the Fifth Amendment, it is necessary to show that the class which is purportedly discriminated against consequently suffers significant deprivation of a benefit or imposition of a substantial burden. If the class of beneficiaries were expanded in the fashion pressed by appellees, the beneficiaries, in terms of those who would exercise dominion over the benefits and whose freedom of choice would be enhanced thereby, would be unwed mothers, not illegitimate children. Certainly every governmental benefit has a ripple effect through familial relationships and the economy generally, its propagation determined by the proximity and sensibilities of others. Possibly the largest class of incidental beneficiaries are those who are gratified in a nonmaterial way to see a friend or relative receive benefits. Some limits must be imposed for purposes of constitutional analysis, and we conclude that in this case the incidental and, to a large decree, speculative impact on illegitimates as a class is not sufficient to treat the denial of mother's insurance benefits to unwed mothers as discrimination against illegitimate children.

The SSA and its amendments are the product of hard choices and countervailing pressures. The desire to alleviate hardship wherever it is found is tempered by the concern that the social security system in this country remain a contributory insurance plan and not become a general welfare program. General welfare objectives are addressed through public assistance legislation. In light of the limited resources of the insurance fund, any expansion of the class of beneficiaries invariably poses the prospect of reduced benefits to individual claimants. We need look no further than the facts of this case for an illustration. The benefits available to Norman W. Boles' beneficiaries under the Act are limited by his earnings record. The effect of extending benefits to Gonzales will be to reduce benefits to Nancy Boles and her children by 20%. Thus, the end result of extending benefits to Gonzales may be to deprive Nancy Boles of a meaningful choice between full-time employment and staying home with her children, thereby undermining the express legislative purpose of mother's insurance benefits. We think Congress could rationally choose to concentrate limited funds where the need is likely to be greatest.

* * *

The judgment of the District Court is accordingly

Reversed.

Mr. Justice MARSHALL, with whom Mr. Justices BRENNAN, Mr. Justice WHITE, and Mr. Justice BLACKMUN join, dissenting.

The critical question in this dispute is whether § 202(g) of the Social Security Act, 42 U.S.C. § 402(g), discriminates against unmarried parents or against illegitimate children. The Court determines that the intended beneficiaries of § 202(g) are dependent spouses, and that the statute therefore distinguishes between categories of parents. Having thus characterized the statute, the Court concludes that the use of marital status as an index of dependency on a deceased wage earner is permissible under Califano v. Jobst, 434 U.S. 47, 50, 98 S.Ct. 95, 97, 54 L.Ed.2d 228 (1977), and Mathews v. De Castro, 429 U.S. 181, 185-186, 97 S.Ct. 431, 434-435, 50 L.Ed.2d 389 (1976). If, however, as the District Court found, the statute benefits children, then it incorporates a distinction based on legitimacy which must be tested under the more rigorous standards of Jimenez v. Weinberger, 417 U.S. 628, 94 S.Ct. 2496, 41 L.Ed.2d 363 (1974), and Weber v. Aetna Casualty & Surety Co., 406 U.S. 164, 92 S.Ct. 1400, 31 L.Ed.2d 768 (1972).

Determining the proper classification for purposes of equal protection analysis is, to be sure, not "an exact science." *Ante*, at 2775. But neither is it an exercise in statutory revision. And only by disregarding the clear legislative history, structure, and effect of the Mother's Insurance Benefits Program can the Court characterize dependent spouses, rather than children, as the intended beneficiaries of § 202(g). * * * In my judgment, the history and structure of the Act establish as "convincingly" here as they did in *Wiesenfeld* that § 202(g) was designed to aid children. And because denial of support for illegitimates bears no substantial relationship to that purpose, I respectfully dissent.

* * *

E. DUE PROCESS AND THE ADMINISTRATION OF BENEFITS

As discussed later in Chapter 8, the Social Security Administration administers Social Security programs by means of a lengthy and elaborate administrative process. The manner in which claims and appeals are processed is a critical component of Social Security law and practice. Federal courts provide oversight of the Social Security administrative process in two ways. As we will see also in Chapter 8, the Social Security Act includes specific provisions for judicial review in Social Security cases. The federal courts have construed these provisions relatively strictly, at least with respect to review of individual benefit decisions, but they have allowed systemic challenges as well. Federal courts have also recognized certain due process rights that attach to the receipt of Social Security benefits.

MATHEWS V. ELDRIDGE
424 U.S. 319, 96 S.Ct. 893 (1976)

Mr. Justice POWELL delivered the opinion of the Court.

The issue in this case is whether the Due Process Clause of the Fifth Amendment requires that prior to the termination of Social Security disability benefit payments the recipient be afforded an opportunity for an evidentiary hearing.

I

Cash benefits are provided to workers during periods in which they are completely disabled under the disability insurance benefits program created by the 1956 amendments to Title II of the Social Security Act. 70 Stat. 815, 42 U.S.C. § 423. Respondent Eldridge was first awarded benefits in June 1968. In March 1972, he received a questionnaire from the state agency charged with monitoring his medical condition. Eldridge completed the questionnaire, indicating that his condition had not improved and identifying the medical sources, including physicians, from whom he had received treatment recently. The state agency then obtained reports from his physician and a psychiatric consultant. After considering these reports and other information in his file the agency informed Eldridge by letter that it had made a tentative determination that his disability had ceased in May 1972. The letter included a statement of reasons for the proposed termination of benefits, and advised Eldridge that he might request reasonable time in which to obtain and submit additional information pertaining to his condition.

In his written response, Eldridge disputed one characterization of his medical condition and indicated that the agency already had enough evidence to establish his disability. The state agency then made its final determination that he had ceased to be disabled in May 1972. This determination was accepted by the Social Security Administration (SSA), which notified Eldridge in July that his benefits would terminate after that month. The notification also advised him of his right to seek reconsideration by the state agency of this initial determination within six months.

Instead of requesting reconsideration Eldridge commenced this action challenging the constitutional validity of the administrative procedures established by the Secretary of Health, Education, and Welfare for assessing whether there exists a continuing disability. He sought an immediate reinstatement of benefits pending a hearing on the issue of his disability. 361 F.Supp. 520 (W.D.Va.1973). The Secretary moved to dismiss on the grounds that Eldridge's benefits had been terminated in accordance with valid administrative regulations and procedures and that he had failed to exhaust available remedies. In support of his contention that due process requires a pretermination hearing, Eldridge relied exclusively upon this Court's decision in Goldberg v. Kelly, 397 U.S. 254, 90 S.Ct. 1011, 25 L.Ed.2d 287 (1970), which established a right to an "evidentiary hearing" prior to termination of welfare benefits.[4] The Secretary contended that *Goldberg* was not controlling since eligibility for disability benefits, unlike eligibility for welfare benefits, is not based on financial need and since issues of credibility and veracity do not play a significant role in the disability entitlement decision, which turns primarily on medical evidence.

The District Court concluded that the administrative procedures pursuant to which the Secretary had terminated Eldridge's benefits abridged his right to procedural due process. * * * Relying entirely upon the Dis-

---

[4] In *Goldberg* the Court held that the pretermination hearing must include the following elements: (1) "timely and adequate notice detailing the reasons for a proposed termination"; (2) "an effective opportunity (for the recipient) to defend by confronting any adverse witnesses and by presenting his own arguments and evidence orally"; (3) retained counsel, if desired; (4) an "impartial" decisionmaker; (5) a decision resting "solely on the legal rules and evidence adduced at the hearing"; (6) a statement of reasons for the decision and the evidence relied on. 397 U.S., at 266-271, 90 S.Ct., at 1019-1022. In this opinion the term "evidentiary hearing" refers to a hearing generally of the type required in Goldberg.

trict Court's opinion, the Court of Appeals for the Fourth Circuit affirmed the injunction barring termination of Eldridge's benefits prior to an evidentiary hearing. 493 F.2d 1230 (1974). We reverse.

II

[The Court first addresses the question whether the District Court had jurisdiction and concluded that the initial denial of benefits constituted a final decision of the agency and therefore the court had jurisdiction over the constitutional claim under 42 U.S.C. § 405(g).]

III

A

Procedural due process imposes constraints on governmental decisions which deprive individuals of "liberty" or "property" interests within the meaning of the Due Process Clause of the Fifth or Fourteenth Amendment. The Secretary does not contend that procedural due process is inapplicable to terminations of Social Security disability benefits. He recognizes, as has been implicit in our prior decisions, e. g., Richardson v. Belcher, 404 U.S. 78, 80-81, 92 S.Ct. 254, 256-257, 30 L.Ed.2d 231 (1971); Richardson v. Perales, 402 U.S. 389, 401-402, 91 S.Ct. 1420, 1427-1428, 28 L.Ed.2d 842 (1971); Flemming v. Nestor, 363 U.S. 603, 611, 80 S.Ct. 1367, 1372-1373, 4 L.Ed.2d 1435 (1960), that the interest of an individual in continued receipt of these benefits is a statutorily created "property" interest protected by the Fifth Amendment. Cf. Arnett v. Kennedy, 416 U.S. 134, 166, 94 S.Ct. 1633, 1650, 40 L.Ed.2d 15 (Powell, J., concurring in part) (1974); Board of Regents v. Roth, 408 U.S. 564, 576-578, 92 S.Ct. 2701, 2708-2710, 33 L.Ed.2d 548 (1972); Bell v. Burson, 402 U.S., at 539, 91 S.Ct., at 1589; Goldberg v. Kelly, 397 U.S., at 261-262, 90 S.Ct., at 1016-1017. Rather, the Secretary contends that the existing administrative procedures, detailed below, provide all the process that is constitutionally due before a recipient can be deprived of that interest.

This Court consistently has held that some form of hearing is required before an individual is finally deprived of a property interest. Wolff v. McDonnell, 418 U.S. 539, 557-558, 94 S.Ct. 2963, 2975-2976, 41 L.Ed.2d 935 (1974). See, e. g. Phillips v. Commissioner of Internal Revenue, 283 U.S. 589, 596-597, 51 S.Ct. 608, 611-612, 75 L.Ed. 1289 (1931). See also Dent v. West Virginia, 129 U.S. 114, 124-125, 9 S.Ct. 231, 234, 32 L.Ed. 623 (1889). The "right to be heard before being condemned to suffer grievous loss of any kind, even though it may not involve the stigma and hardships of a criminal conviction, is a principle basic to our society." Joint Anti-Fascist Comm. v. McGrath, 341 U.S. 123, 168, 71 S.Ct. 624, 646, 95 L.Ed. 817 (1951) (Frankfurter, J., concurring). The fundamental requirement of due process is the opportunity to be heard "at a meaningful time and in a meaningful manner." Armstrong v. Manzo, 380 U.S. 545, 552, 85 S.Ct. 1187, 1191, 14 L.Ed.2d 62 (1965). See Grannis v. Ordean, 234 U.S. 385, 394, 34 S.Ct. 779, 783, 58 L.Ed. 1363 (1914). Eldridge agrees that the review procedures available to a claimant before the initial determination of ineligibility becomes final would be adequate if disability benefits were not terminated until after the evidentiary hearing stage of the administrative process. The dispute centers upon what process is due prior to the initial termination of benefits, pending review.

In recent years this Court increasingly has had occasion to consider the extent to which due process requires an evidentiary hearing prior to the deprivation of some type of property interest even if such a hearing is provided thereafter. In only one case, Goldberg v. Kelly, 397 U.S., at 266-271, 90 S.Ct., at 1019-1022, 25 L.Ed.2d 287, has the Court held that a hearing closely approximating a judicial trial is necessary. In other cases requiring some type of pretermination hearing as a matter of constitutional right the Court has spoken sparingly about the requisite procedures. Sniadach v. Family Finance Corp., 395 U.S. 337, 89 S.Ct. 1820, 23 L.Ed.2d 349 (1969), involving garnishment of wages, was entirely silent on the matter. In Fuentes v. Shevin, 407 U.S., at 96-97, 92 S.Ct., at 2002-2003, 32 L.Ed.2d 556, the Court said only that in a replevin suit between two private parties the initial determination required something more than an *ex parte* proceeding before a court clerk. Similarly, Bell v. Burson, *supra*, at 540, 91 S.Ct., at 1590, 29 L.Ed.2d 90, held, in the context of the revocation of a state-granted driver's license, that due process required only that the prerevocation hearing involve a probable-cause determination as to the fault of the licensee, noting that the hearing "need not take the form of a full adjudication of the question of liability." See also North Georgia Finishing, Inc. v. Di-Chem, Inc., 419 U.S. 601, 607, 95 S.Ct. 719, 42 L.Ed.2d 751 (1975). More recently, in Arnett v. Kennedy, *supra*, we sustained the validity of procedures by which a federal employee could be dismissed for cause. They included notice of the action sought, a copy of the charge, reasonable time for filing a written response, and an opportunity for an oral appearance. Following dismissal, an evidentiary hearing was provided. 416 U.S., at 142-146, 94 S.Ct., at 1638-1640.

These decisions underscore the truism that "'[d]ue process,' unlike some legal rules, is not a technical conception with a fixed content unrelated to time, place and circumstances." Cafeteria Workers v. McElroy, 367 U.S. 886, 895, 81 S.Ct. 1743, 1748, 6 L.Ed.2d 1230 (1961). "(D)ue process is flexible and calls for such procedural protections as the particular situation demands." Morrissey v. Brewer, 408 U.S. 471, 481, 92 S.Ct. 2593, 2600, 33 L.Ed.2d 484 (1972). Accordingly, resolution of the issue whether the administrative procedures provided here are constitutionally sufficient requires analysis of the governmental and private interests that are affected. Arnett v. Kennedy, *supra*, 416 U.S., at 167-168, 94 S.Ct., at 1650-1651 (Powell, J., concurring in part); Goldberg v. Kelly, *supra*, 397 U.S., at 263-266, 90 S.Ct., at 1018-1020; Cafeteria Workers v. McElroy, *supra*, 367 U.S., at 895, 81 S.Ct., at 1748-1749. More precisely, our prior decisions indicate that identification of the specific dictates of due process generally requires consideration of three distinct factors: First, the private interest that will be affected by the official action; second, the risk of an erroneous deprivation of such interest through the procedures used, and the probable value, if any, of additional or substitute procedural safeguards; and finally, the Government's interest, including the function involved and the fiscal and administrative burdens that the additional or substitute procedural requirement would entail. See, *e. g.*, Goldberg v. Kelly, *supra*, 397 U.S., at 263-271, 90 S.Ct., at 1018-1022.

We turn first to a description of the procedures for the termination of Social Security disability benefits and thereafter consider the factors bearing upon the constitutional adequacy of these procedures.

B

The disability insurance program is administered jointly by state and federal agencies. State agencies make the initial determination whether a disability exists, when it began, and when it ceased. 42 U.S.C. § 421(a). (FN13) The standards applied and the procedures followed are prescribed by the Secretary, see § 421(b), who has delegated his responsibilities and powers under the Act to the SSA. See 40 Fed.Reg. 4473 (1975).

* * * The principal reasons for benefits terminations are that the worker is no longer disabled or has returned to work. As Eldridge's benefits were terminated because he was determined to be no longer disabled, we consider only the sufficiency of the procedures involved in such cases.

The continuing-eligibility investigation is made by a state agency acting through a "team" consisting of a physician and a nonmedical person trained in disability evaluation. The agency periodically communicates with the disabled worker, usually by mail in which case he is sent a detailed questionnaire or by telephone, and requests information concerning his present condition, including current medical restrictions and sources of treatment, and any additional information that he considers relevant to his continued entitlement to benefits. CM § 6705.1; Disability Insurance State Manual (DISM) § 353.3 (TL No. 137, Mar. 5, 1975).

Information regarding the recipient's current condition is also obtained from his sources of medical treatment. DISM § 353.4. If there is a conflict between the information provided by the beneficiary and that obtained from medical sources such as his physician, or between two sources of treatment, the agency may arrange for an examination by an independent consulting physician. *Ibid.* Whenever the agency's tentative assessment of the beneficiary's condition differs from his own assessment, the beneficiary is informed that benefits may be terminated, provided a summary of the evidence upon which the proposed determination to terminate is based, and afforded an opportunity to review the medical reports and other evidence in his case file. He also may respond in writing and submit additional evidence. *Id.,* § 353.6.

The state agency then makes its final determination, which is reviewed by an examiner in the SSA Bureau of Disability Insurance. 42 U.S.C. § 421(c); CM §§ 6701(b), (c). If, as is usually the case, the SSA accepts the agency determination it notifies the recipient in writing, informing him of the reasons for the decision, and of his right to seek de novo reconsideration by the state agency. 20 CFR §§ 404.907, 404.909 (1975). Upon acceptance by the SSA, benefits are terminated effective two months after the month in which medical recovery is found to have occurred. 42 U.S.C. (Supp. III) § 423(a) (1970 ed., Supp. III).

If the recipient seeks reconsideration by the state agency and the determination is adverse, the SSA reviews the reconsideration determination and notifies the recipient of the decision. He then has a right to an evidentiary hearing before an SSA administrative law judge. 20 CFR §§ 404.917, 404.927 (1975). The hearing is nonadversary, and the SSA is not represented by counsel. As at all prior and subsequent stages of the administrative process, however, the claimant may be represented by counsel or other spokesmen. § 404.934. If this hearing results in an adverse decision, the claimant is entitled to request discretionary review by the SSA Appeals Council, § 404.945, and finally may obtain judicial review. 42 U.S.C. § 405(g); 20 CFR § 404.951 (1975).

Should it be determined at any point after termination of benefits, that the claimant's disability extended beyond the date of cessation initially established, the worker is entitled to retroactive payments. 42 U.S.C. § 404. Cf. § 423(b); 20 CFR §§ 404.501, 404.503, 404.504 (1975). If, on the other hand, a beneficiary receives any payments to which he is later determined not to be entitled, the statute authorizes the Secretary to attempt to recoup these funds in specified circumstances. 42 U.S.C. § 404.

C

Despite the elaborate character of the administrative procedures provided by the Secretary, the courts below held them to be constitutionally inadequate, concluding that due process requires an evidentiary hearing prior to termination. In light of the private and governmental interests at stake here and the nature of the existing procedures, we think this was error.

Since a recipient whose benefits are terminated is awarded full retroactive relief if he ultimately prevails, his sole interest is in the uninterrupted receipt of this source of income pending final administrative decision on his claim. His potential injury is thus similar in nature to that of the welfare recipient in *Goldberg*, see 397 U.S., at 263-264, 90 S.Ct., at 1018-1019, the nonprobationary federal employee in *Arnett*, see 416 U.S., at 146, 94 S.Ct., at 1640, 1641, and the wage earner in *Sniadach*. See 395 U.S., at 341-342, 89 S.Ct., at 1822-1823.

Only in *Goldberg* has the Court held that due process requires an evidentiary hearing prior to a temporary deprivation. It was emphasized there that welfare assistance is given to persons on the very margin of subsistence:

> "The crucial factor in this context a factor not present in the case of . . . virtually anyone else whose governmental entitlements are ended is that termination of aid pending resolution of a controversy over eligibility may deprive an *eligible* recipient of the very means by which to live while he waits." 397 U.S., at 264, 90 S.Ct., at 1018 (emphasis in original).

Eligibility for disability benefits, in contrast, is not based upon financial need. Indeed, it is wholly unrelated to the worker's income or support from many other sources, such as earnings of other family members, workmen's compensation awards, tort claims awards, savings, private insurance, public or private pensions, veterans' benefits, food stamps, public assistance, or the "many other important programs, both public and private, which contain provisions for disability payments affecting a substantial portion of the work force . . . ." Richardson v. Belcher, 404 U.S., at 85-87, 92 S.Ct., at 259 (Douglas, J., dissenting). *See* Staff of the House Committee on Ways and Means, Report on the Disability Insurance Program, 93d Cong., 2d Sess., 9-10, 419-429 (1974) (hereinafter Staff Report).

As *Goldberg* illustrates, the degree of potential deprivation that may be created by a particular decision is a factor to be considered in assessing the validity of any administrative decisionmaking process. *Cf.* Morrissey v. Brewer, 408 U.S. 471, 92 S.Ct. 2593, 33 L.Ed.2d 484 (1972). The potential deprivation here is generally likely to be less than in *Goldberg*, although the degree of difference can be overstated. As the District Court emphasized, to remain eligible for benefits a recipient must be "unable to engage in substantial gainful activity." 42 U.S.C. § 423; 361 F.Supp., at 523. Thus, in contrast to the discharged federal employee in Arnett, there is little possibility that the terminated recipient will be able to find even temporary employment to ameliorate the interim loss.

As we recognized last Term in Fusari v. Steinberg, 419 U.S. 379, 389, 95 S.Ct. 533, 540, 42 L.Ed.2d 521 (1975), "the possible length of wrongful deprivation of . . . benefits (also) is an important factor in assessing the impact of official action on the private interests." The Secretary concedes that the delay between a request for a hearing before an administrative law judge and a decision on the claim is currently between 10 and 11 months. Since a terminated recipient must first obtain a reconsideration decision as a prerequisite to invoking his right to an evidentiary hearing, the delay between the actual cutoff of benefits and final decision after a hearing exceeds one year.

In view of the torpidity of this administrative review process, *cf. id.*, at 383-384, 386, 95 S.Ct., at 536-537, 538, and the typically modest resources of the family unit of the physically disabled worker, the hardship imposed upon the erroneously terminated disability recipient may be significant. Still, the disabled worker's need is likely to be less than that of a welfare recipient. In addition to the possibility of access to private resources, other forms of government assistance will become available where the termination of disability benefits places a worker or his family below the subsistence level. See Arnett v. Kennedy, *supra*, 416 U.S., at 169, 94 S.Ct., at 1651-1652 (Powell, J., concurring in part); *id.*, at 201-202, 94 S.Ct., at 1667-1668 (White, J., concurring in part and dissenting in part). In view of these potential sources of temporary income, there is less reason here than in *Goldberg* to depart from the ordinary principle, established by our decisions, that something less than an evidentiary hearing is sufficient prior to adverse administrative action.

D

An additional factor to be considered here is the fairness and reliability of the existing pretermination procedures, and the probable value, if any, of additional procedural safeguards. Central to the evaluation of any administrative process is the nature of the relevant inquiry. See Mitchell v. W. T. Grant Co., 416 U.S. 600, 617, 94 S.Ct. 1895, 1905, 40 L.Ed.2d 406 (1974); Friendly, Some Kind of Hearing, 123 U.Pa.L.Rev. 1267, 1281 (1975). In order to remain eligible for benefits the disabled worker must demonstrate by means of "medically acceptable clinical and laboratory diagnostic techniques," 42 U.S.C. § 423(d)(3), that he is unable "to engage in any substantial gainful activity by reason of any *medically determinable* physical or mental impairment . . . ." § 423(d)(1)(A) (emphasis supplied). In short, a medical assessment of the worker's physical or mental condition is required. This is a more sharply focused and easily documented decision than the typical determination of welfare entitlement. In the latter case, a wide variety of information may be deemed relevant, and issues of witness credibility and veracity often are critical to the decisionmaking process. Goldberg noted that in such circumstances "written submissions are a wholly unsatisfactory basis for decision." 397 U.S., at 269, 90 S.Ct., at 1021.

By contrast, the decision whether to discontinue disability benefits will turn, in most cases, upon "routine, standard, and unbiased medical reports by physician specialists," Richardson v. Perales, 402 U.S., at 404, 91 S.Ct., at 1428, concerning a subject whom they have personally examined. In *Richardson* the Court recognized the "reliability and probative worth of written medical reports," emphasizing that while there may be "professional disagreement with the medical conclusions" the "specter of questionable credibility and veracity is not present." *Id.*, at 405, 407, 91 S.Ct., at 1428, 1430. To be sure, credibility and veracity may be a factor in the ultimate disability assessment in some cases. But procedural due process rules are shaped by the risk of error inherent in the truthfinding process as applied to the generality of cases, not the rare exceptions. The potential value of an evidentiary hearing, or even oral presentation to the decisionmaker, is substantially less in this context than in *Goldberg*.

The decision in *Goldberg* also was based on the Court's conclusion that written submissions were an inadequate substitute for oral presentation because they did not provide an effective means for the recipient to communicate his case to the decisionmaker. Written submissions were viewed as an unrealistic option, for most recipients lacked the "educational attainment necessary to write effectively" and could not afford professional assistance. In addition, such submissions would not provide the "flexibility of oral presentations" or "permit the recipient to mold his argument to the issues the decision maker appears to regard as important." 397 U.S., at 269, 90 S.Ct., at 1021. In the context of the disability-benefits-entitlement assessment the administrative procedures under review here fully answer these objections.

The detailed questionnaire which the state agency periodically sends the recipient identifies with particularity the information relevant to the entitlement decision, and the recipient is invited to obtain assistance from the local SSA office in completing the questionnaire. More important, the information critical to the entitlement decision usually is derived from medical sources, such as the treating physician. Such sources are likely to be able to communicate more effectively through written documents than are welfare recipients or the lay witnesses supporting their cause. The conclusions of physicians often are supported by X-rays and the results of clinical or laboratory tests, information typically more amenable to written than to oral presentation. *Cf.* W. Gellhorn & C. Byse, Administrative Law Cases and Comments 860-863 (6th ed. 1974).

A further safeguard against mistake is the policy of allowing the disability recipient's representative full access to all information relied upon by the state agency. In addition, prior to the cutoff of benefits the agency informs the recipient of its tentative assessment, the reasons therefor, and provides a summary of the evidence that it considers most relevant. Opportunity is then afforded the recipient to submit additional evidence or arguments, enabling him to challenge directly the accuracy of information in his file as well as the correctness of the agency's tentative conclusions. These procedures, again as contrasted with those before the Court in *Goldberg*, enable the recipient to "mold" his argument to respond to the precise issues which the decisionmaker regards as crucial.

Despite these carefully structured procedures, *amici* point to the significant reversal rate for appealed cases as clear evidence that the current process is inadequate. Depending upon the base selected and the line of analysis followed, the relevant reversal rates urged by the contending parties vary from a high of 58.6% For appealed reconsideration decisions to an overall reversal rate of only 3.3%. Bare statistics rarely provide a satisfactory measure of the fairness of a decisionmaking process. Their adequacy is especially suspect here since the administrative review system is operated on an open-file basis. A recipient may always submit new evidence, and such submissions may result in additional medical examinations. Such fresh examinations were held in approximately 30% to 40% of the appealed cases, in fiscal 1973, either at the reconsideration or evidentiary hearing stage of the administrative process. Staff Report 238. In this context, the value of reversal rate statistics as one means of evaluating the adequacy of the pretermination process is diminished. Thus, although we view such information as relevant, it is certainly not controlling in this case.

E

In striking the appropriate due process balance the final factor to be assessed is the public interest. This includes the administrative burden and other societal costs that would be associated with requiring, as a matter of constitutional right, an evidentiary hearing upon demand in all cases prior to the termination of disability benefits. The most visible burden would be the incremental cost resulting from the increased number of hearings and the expense of providing benefits to ineligible recipients pending decision. No one can predict the extent of the increase, but the fact that full benefits would continue until after such hearings would assure the exhaustion in most cases of this attractive option. Nor would the theoretical right of the Secretary to recover undeserved benefits result, as a practical matter, in any substantial offset to the added outlay of public funds. The parties submit widely varying estimates of the probable additional financial cost. We only need say that experience with the constitutionalizing of government procedures suggests that the ultimate additional cost in terms of money and administrative burden would not be insubstantial.

Financial cost alone is not a controlling weight in determining whether due process requires a particular procedural safeguard prior to some administrative decision. But the Government's interest, and hence that of the public, in conserving scarce fiscal and administrative resources is a factor that must be weighed. At some point the benefit of an additional safeguard to the individual affected by the administrative action and to society in terms of increased assurance that the action is just, may be outweighed by the cost. Significantly, the cost of protecting those whom the preliminary administrative process has identified as likely to be found undeserving may in the end come out of the pockets of the deserving since resources available for any particular program of social welfare are not unlimited. See Friendly, supra, 123 U.Pa.L.Rev., at 1276, 1303.

But more is implicated in cases of this type than ad hoc weighing of fiscal and administrative burdens against the interests of a particular category of claimants. The ultimate balance involves a determination as to when, under our constitutional system, judicial-type procedures must be imposed upon administrative action to assure fairness. We reiterate the wise admonishment of Mr. Justice Frankfurter that differences in the origin and function of administrative agencies "preclude wholesale transplantation of the rules of procedure, trial and review which have evolved from the history and experience of courts." FCC v. Pottsville Broadcasting Co., 309 U.S. 134, 143, 60 S.Ct. 437, 441, 84 L.Ed. 656 (1940). The judicial model of an evidentiary hearing is neither a required, nor even the most effective, method of decisionmaking in all circumstances. The essence of due process is the requirement that "a person in jeopardy of serious loss (be given) notice of the case against him and opportunity to meet it." Joint Anti-Fascist Comm. v. McGrath, 341 U.S., at 171-172, 71 S.Ct., at 649. (Frankfurter, J., concurring). All that is necessary is that the procedures be tailored, in light of the decision to be made, to "the capacities and circumstances of those who are to be heard," Goldberg v. Kelly, 397 U.S., at 268-269, 90 S.Ct., at 1021 (footnote omitted), to insure that they are given a meaningful opportunity to present their case. In assessing what process is due in this case, substantial weight must be given to the good-faith judgments of the individuals charged by Congress with the administration of social welfare programs that the procedures they have provided assure fair consideration of the entitlement claims of individuals. See Arnett v. Kennedy, 416 U.S., at 202, 94 S.Ct., at 1667-1668 (White, J., concurring in part and dissenting in part). This is especially so where, as here, the prescribed procedures not only provide the claimant with an effective process for asserting his claim prior to any administrative action, but also assure a right to an evidentiary hearing, as well as to subsequent judicial review, before the denial of his claim becomes final. Cf. Boddie v. Connecticut, 401 U.S. 371, 378, 91 S.Ct. 780, 786, 28 L.Ed.2d 113 (1971).

We conclude that an evidentiary hearing is not required prior to the termination of disability benefits and that the present administrative procedures fully comport with due process.

The judgment of the Court of Appeals is

Reversed.

Mr. Justice STEVENS took no part in the consideration or decision of this case.

Mr. Justice BRENNAN, with whom Mr. Justice MARSHALL concurs, dissenting.

* * * I agree with the District Court and the Court of Appeals that, prior to termination of benefits, Eldridge must be afforded an evidentiary hearing of the type required for welfare beneficiaries under Title IV of the Social Security Act, 42 U.S.C. § 601 et seq. *See* Goldberg v. Kelly, 397 U.S. 254, 90 S.Ct. 1011, 25 L.Ed.2d 287 (1970). * * *

CHAPTER 2

OVERVIEW OF COVERAGE

■ ■ ■

The Social Security Act includes a number of separate programs set out in various titles, which together provide a broad, but limited, range of benefits. The two programs covered in this book are Old Age, Survivors, and Disability Insurance (OASDI), found in Title II of the Social Security Act, and Supplemental Security Income (SSI), found in Title XVI. Persons receiving benefits under these programs are also entitled, for the most part, to benefits under the one of the Act's two medical assistance programs: Medicare in the case of OASDI recipients, Medicaid in the case of SSI recipients. (Coverage of the various benefits provided to OASDI and SSI recipients under the Medicare and Medicaid programs is beyond the scope of this book.)

Eligibility for Social Security benefits is governed by two basic sets of criteria. Each set applies to both OASDI and SSI, but many details differ depending on whether the claim is for benefits under one program or the other. The first set of criteria relates to financial circumstances, which are based on employment for social insurance benefits and on financial need for public assistance benefits. As we saw in Chapter 1, OASDI is a social insurance program and, as such, is available only to persons who are "insured" by having paid Social Security taxes while being employed (including being self-employed). SSI, on the other hand, is a public assistance program available only to persons with limited income and resources. The first two sections of this chapter describe these financial requirements in some detail.

A second set of criteria relates to personal circumstances. In addition to the financial requirements mentioned above, a claimant for OASDI or SSI must fit within one of a limited set of categories in order to be eligible for benefits. Two key personal requirements in the Social Security Act are old age and disability. Persons who are elderly or disabled may be eligible for OASDI, SSI, or both. In addition, OASDI benefits are available to certain persons whose parent or spouse (or, in certain special situations, whose child) is (or was) insured and has died, has retired, or is disabled. The personal eligibility criteria for OASDI and SSI old age, disability, and survivors benefits are described briefly in the remaining sections of this chapter. Later chapters examine these criteria in greater detail.

The financial criteria are discussed in this chapter relative to eligibility for benefits, which is distinct from their role in the calculation of benefit amounts. The same information may, however, be relevant in determining the amount of benefits. For example, quarters of coverage (QCs) are, as discussed in greater detail below, a key component of financial eligibility for OASDI benefits. At the same time, as explained further in Chapter 7, the number of QCs and the amount of earnings recorded for certain QCs can play an important role in calculating the amount of OASDI benefits to which an individual is entitled. In effect, there are three possibilities for a claimant's QCs to apply across eligibility and the calculation of benefit amount. First, a claimant can have insufficient QCs to be eligible, so that the question of amount of benefits is never reached. Second, a claimant may have enough QCs to be eligible, and the amounts earned in certain QCs will determine the amount of benefits. Or third, a claimant may have enough QCs to be eligible, but with earnings so high that the specific amounts earned in some (or all) QCs don't matter because the claimant is entitled to the maximum benefit amount. The application of financial criteria across both eligibility and the calculation of benefits is more direct for the SSI program. The amount of a claimant's income (if any) is a key element in determining eligibility for SSI—and then the amount of benefits awarded will be reduced by the amount of any income the claimant has, subject to certain exceptions.

A. EMPLOYMENT-BASED ELIGIBILITY (OASDI)

Social Security employment records are measured in terms of quarters of coverage (QCs). QCs are periods of three calendar months ending on March 31, June 30, September 30, or December 31. Individuals are credited with one QC for each quarter during which they had at least a minimum amount of earnings on which Social Security taxes were paid, including self-employment income. For calendar years before 1978, individuals were credited for quarters in which they were paid wages of $50 or more (or credited with self-employment income of $100 or more). Beginning in 1978, employers report wages on an annual, as opposed to a quarterly, basis; therefore, for calendar years after 1977, QCs are not assigned to a specific quarter, except in special situations. Instead, individuals are credited with one QC for each part of their total income in a given year that equals the amount required for a QC in that year—up to a maximum of four QCs per year. The amount of wages and self-employment income an individual must have for each post-1977 QC depends on the year. For calendar year 1978, the amount is $250; for later years, the amount is published in the Federal Register. For example, the amount for calendar year 2000 is $900, for calendar year 2012 it is $1130. Therefore, someone who earned $4000 in calendar year 2000 would be credited with four QCs; someone who earned the same amount in calendar year 2010 would be credited with only 3 QCs.

An individual must be "fully" insured in order to be eligible for OASDI benefits, although an individual's spouse or child may, under certain circumstances, be eligible for benefits if the individual was only "currently" insured. *See* **20 C.F.R. § 404.101[APP-REGS]** Whether an individual has the required insured status depends on the number of QCs in his or her Social Security employment record, which—as noted above—are in turn based on when and how long he or she worked at a job where Social Security taxes were paid.

In most instances, a claimant needs 40 QCs to be fully insured. A person is considered fully insured as of the first day of the calendar year quarter in which he or she acquired the last-needed QC. The 40 QCs can be accumulated at any time. To be fully insured on the basis of less than 40 QCs, a claimant must have accumulated a minimum of 6 QCs, at least one of which must have been earned in each calendar year elapsing after the year in which the individual reached the age of 21 and continuing until the year the individual reached retirement age, became disabled, or (with respect to survivors benefits) died. 42 U.S.C. § 414(a); **20 C.F.R. § 404.110[APP-REGS]**.

Individuals who die or become disabled before they can become fully insured may instead be "currently" insured. Currently insured status does not entitle one to OASDI benefits; however, spouses and children of persons who are only currently insured may be entitled to certain secondary benefits. To be currently insured, one must have earned a minimum of 6 QCs within a thirteen-quarter period immediately preceding death or eligibility for old age or disability insurance benefits. 42 U.S.C. § 414(b); **20 C.F.R. § 404.120(a)[APP-REGS]**. For claimants entitled to disability insurance benefits, the thirteen-quarter period does not include any quarter any part of which was included in a period of disability, except that the first and last quarters of the period of disability may be counted if they are QCs. **20 C.F.R. § 404.120(b)[APP-REGS]**

Meeting the earnings requirement for a single QC can be critical in establishing eligibility for OASDI benefits, if that QC is needed to meet the insured status requirement. Moreover, the quarters-of-coverage requirement is applied strictly; applying a *de minimis* rule in close cases has been rejected by courts, in part to avoid the cost and subjectivity inherent in making individualized determinations regarding a claimant's insured status.

McGLOCKLIN V. CHATER

948 F. Supp. 589, 52 Soc. Sec. Rep. Serv. 527 (W.D. Va. 1996),
aff'd, 129 F.3d 1259 (4th Cir. 1997)

JONES, District Judge.

In this social security case, the claimant was denied disability coverage because she was $1.00 short in the annual earnings required by the regulations. Unfortunately, I am constrained to find that there is no de minimis rule which would allow me to direct that she be granted insured status.

I

Nancy B. McGlocklin filed this action seeking review of the final decision of the Commissioner of Social Security ("Commissioner") denying her claim for a period of disability and disability insurance benefits ("DIB") under the Social Security Act. * * *

* * *

II

A claimant must establish that he or she meets the "fully insured" and "insured status" requirements of the Act before the question of disability may be considered. 42 U.S.C. §§ 416(i)(1), 416(i)(2)(c), 416(i)(3). A claimant is a "fully insured individual" if he or she has forty quarters of coverage. Further, a claimant gains "insured status" when he or she has at least twenty quarters of coverage during the forty-quarter period that ends with the quarter in which the claimant alleges that he or she became disabled. 42 U.S.C. § 423(c)(1)(B) (1988), 20 C.F.R. § 404.130 (1996). These prerequisites to a finding of disability are at the heart of the claimant's appeal to this court. Everyone agrees that McGlocklin is fully insured—she has forty-seven quarters of coverage. However, in the forty-quarter period ending December 31, 1991 (the end of the quarter in which she claims her disability began), McGlocklin has only nineteen quarters of coverage, one too few under the Act. Moreover, for the year 1985, while McGlocklin earned one quarter of coverage, she was $1.00 short of gaining an extra quarter of coverage. Had she one more dollar of earnings in 1985, McGlocklin would have insured status under the Act.

After a hearing on February 10, 1994, the ALJ issued his decision on March 22, 1995, finding that McGlocklin was entitled to an extra quarter of coverage for the year 1985 because he found her earnings shortfall to be "de minimis."

The Appeals Council issued a letter to McGlocklin on August 18, 1995, in which it informed her that it had decided it had good cause to reopen the decision of the ALJ pursuant to 20 C.F.R. § 404.988 because "the evidence which was considered by the Administrative Law Judge in reaching his decision clearly shows on its face that an error was made." The Appeals Council advised McGlocklin that an individual "must have" the amount determined to earn a quarter of coverage under the regulations. Further, the Appeals Council rejected the argument that a claimant is entitled to "round" up earnings even though the Social Security Administration "rounds" up to the nearest $10.00 increment when determining amounts required to gain a quarter of coverage. The Appeals Council notified McGlocklin of her opportunity to submit additional materials and to request a hearing. McGlocklin did not submit additional evidence or ask for a hearing. On October 24, 1995, the Appeals Council issued its decision denying McGlocklin benefits because she had only nineteen quarters of coverage rather than twenty.

      * * *

IV

I must also rule against the claimant on the merits. Her attorney understandably argues on her behalf that her work history of over eleven years should not be disregarded because of a "mere trifle"—$1.00. It is contended that the legal maxim of de minimis ought to be applied to her situation to allow her the government benefits to which she would otherwise be entitled.

While the doctrine of de minimis may be a valuable one in some areas of law, it is unavailable here. The Act and its regulations draw bright lines of eligibility which I am not authorized to forgive. Moreover, a vast administrative system such as social security depends upon maintaining such strict categories. If de minimis were the rule, how would the Commissioner's discretion ever be properly exercised? If $1.00 is de minimis, what about $5.00 or $10.00, or even $100.00?

In Weinberger v. Salfi, 422 U.S. 749, 95 S.Ct. 2457, 45 L.Ed.2d 522 (1975), the Supreme Court rejected a challenge to the Act's requirement that a widow and stepchild are eligible for coverage only if their relationship with the wage earner endures at least nine months. While the Court recognized that such an arbitrary rule might "undoubtedly exclude some surviving wives who married with no anticipation of shortly becoming widows," 422 U.S. at 781, 95 S.Ct. at 2474, it reflected a legitimate policy determination that "limited resources would not be well spent in making individual determinations." *Id*. at 784, 95 S.Ct. at 2476.

As in Salfi, the claimant's failure here to qualify because she was a dollar short undoubtedly appears unjust to her. Greater injustices would occur, however, if the strict categories of the Act were not maintained.

An appropriate judgment will be entered.

1. SPECIAL INSURED STATUS FOR DISABILITY-BASED BENEFITS

In order to qualify for Disability Insurance Benefits, a claimant must achieve "disability insured status" in addition to being "fully insured." For most claimants, this is done by meeting the requirements of what is known as the "20/40" rule. Thus, a claimant is insured for purposes of Disability Insurance Benefits if he or she has at least 20 QCs in the 40-quarter period ending with the quarter during which his or her disability began. *See* **42 U.S.C. § 423(c)[APP-STAT]; 20 C.F.R. § 404.130[APP-REGS].** As a practical matter, this means that a claimant must have worked at covered employment for at least 5 years during the 10 years preceding the onset of disability.

The 20/40 rule operates to screen out persons who do not have a substantial and relatively recent attachment to the workforce. Depending on the regularity of a claimant's work history, the time between stopping work and becoming disabled can be limited to as little as one quarter. For example, if someone worked for 10 years but only every other quarter, coverage under the 20/40 rule would lapse after only two quarters of not working. The more quarters one works in a row (and for which one receives QC credit), the more quarters can pass in which one remains insured after stopping work. However, in no event can there be a lapse of more than 20 quarters, or five years, between stopping work at covered employment and becoming disabled.

Because the disability insured status period is limited, the disability onset date can be a critical factor in determining eligibility. For claimants who worked off-and-on and then stop working before becoming disabled, a subsequently developed disability may not be covered because it began after his or her disability insured status expired. If the evidence of the onset date is ambiguous and must be inferred, an administrative law judge must consult a medical advisor on this issue. *See, e.g.*, Armstrong v. Comm'r of Soc. Sec. Admin., 160 F.3d 587, 589-90 (9th Cir.1998) ("If the 'medical evidence is not definite concerning the onset date and medical inferences need to be made, [Social Security Ruling] 83-20 requires the administrative law judge to call upon the services of a medical advisor and to obtain all evidence which is available to make the determination.'") (quoting DeLorme v. Sullivan, 924 F.2d 841, 848 (9th Cir.1991)).

A separate rule for achieving disability insured status applies to persons who become disabled before age 31. In such cases, a claimant is insured for purposes of Disability Insurance Benefits so long as he or she has QCs for at least six quarters and for at least one-half of the quarters that passed between reaching the age of 21 and becoming disabled. However, if the number of quarters during this period is an odd number, the number is reduced by one; and if the number is less than 12 QCs, the claimant must have at least six QCs in the 12-quarter period ending with that quarter. 42 U.S.C. § 423(c)(1)((B)(ii); 20 C.F.R. § 404.130(c). Additionally, under certain circumstances an individual who had a period of disability before age 31 can qualify if he or she becomes disabled again before the 20/40 requirement could be met. See 42 U.S.C. § 423(c)(1)((B)(iii); 20 C.F.R. § 404.130(d).

The additional disability insured status requirement does not apply to persons who are statutorily blind. 42 U.S.C. § 423(c)(1); 20 C.F.R. § 404.130(c). Thus, claimants who are disabled by blindness, as defined in the Act and regulations, need show only that they are fully or currently insured in order to qualify for Disability Insurance Benefits.

NOTE AND PROBLEMS

1. The separate and additional 20/40 requirement for disability benefits—applicable to otherwise "fully insured" claimants—has survived constitutional challenge. In Harvell v. Chater, 87 F.3d 371, 51 Soc. Sec. Rep. Serv. 144 (9th Cir. 1996), the claimant contended that the 20/40 requirement was unconstitutional because it denied him disability insurance benefits even though he was fully insured based on his earnings record. (Harvell had worked at covered employment and paid his payroll taxes from 1953 to 1969, and the Social Security Administration agreed that he satisfied the "fully insured" requirement. However, he did not earn any QCs during the relevant 40-quarter period, because he worked in non-covered employment for 21 years prior to the onset of his disability and did not pay social security taxes during that period.) In a *per curiam* option, the court addressed his argument as follows:

> Harvell's [sic] also contends that the so-called "20/40" rule violates the Due Process Clause of the Fifth Amendment because it denies a person disability benefits even though that person is "fully insured" under the Act. His contention is without merit. A statutory classification in the area of social welfare is consistent with the Due Process Clause of the Fifth Amendment if it is rationally based and free from invidious discrimination. Richardson v. Belcher, 404 U.S. 78, 81, 92 S.Ct. 254, 257, 30 L.Ed.2d 231 (1971) (citing Dandridge v. Williams, 397 U.S. 471, 487, 90 S.Ct. 1153, 1162-63, 25 L.Ed.2d 491 (1970)). "[T]he Due Process clause can be thought to interpose a bar only if a statute manifests a patently arbitrary classification, utterly lacking in rational justification." Flemming v. Nestor, 363 U.S. 603, 611, 80 S.Ct. 1367, 1373, 4 L.Ed.2d 1435 (1960).

> In Tuttle v. Secretary of HEW, 504 F.2d 61, 63 (10th Cir.1974), the Tenth Circuit held that the 20/40 rule as applied by the Social Security Act is not unconstitutional. The Tuttle court found that the 20/40 re-

quirements under the Social Security Act were rationally based and free of invidious discrimination, and thus must survive a constitutional challenge alleging a violation of the Due Process Clause. *Id.*

The court in *Tuttle* noted that Congress, through the Social Security Act's 20/40 rule, intended to fulfil two goals. Id. at 62. The first goal was making the social security system self-supporting by assuring that beneficiaries made some substantial contribution to the system before the onset of disability. The second goal was the provision of benefits to those who have depended on their employment income. Specifically, Congress decided that "it is reasonable and desirable that there be reliable means of limiting ... protection to those persons who have had sufficiently long and sufficiently recent covered employment to indicate that they probably have been dependent upon their earnings." S.Rep. No. 2388, 85th Cong., 2d Sess. 12 (1958), *reprinted in* 1958 U.S.C.C.A.N. 4218, 4229.

Given Congress's stated objectives as articulated in *Tuttle*, we cannot say that the 20/40 rule is a "patently arbitrary classification, utterly lacking in rational justification." *See* Flemming, 363 U.S. at 611, 80 S.Ct. at 1373. Accordingly, we follow the Tenth Circuit in holding that the 20/40 rule does not violate the Due Process Clause of the Fifth Amendment.

87 F.3d at 373.

2. Problem: Claimant A is fully insured, but stopped working on December 31, 2010. Her Social Security earnings record shows that she had 4 QCs each year for calendar years 1970-2009 and 2 QCs for calendar year 2010. Up until what date would she have disability insured status?

3. Problem: Claimant B is also fully insured and stopped working on December 31, 2010. His Social Security earnings record shows that he had 4 QCs each year for calendar years 1990-95, no QCs in calendar years 1996 and 1997, 4 QCs each year for calendar years 1998-2006, 3 QCs each year for calendar years 2006-08, no QCs in calendar year 2009, and 2 QCs 2010. Up until what date would he have disability insured status?

2. CORRECTING AN EARNINGS RECORD

Earnings information used to determine an individual's QCs is based on employment records reported to the Internal Revenue Service when Social Security taxes are paid. These records are presumed to be correct; however, where there are no such records, earnings sufficient to establish a QC can be proved by a preponderance of the evidence. Earnings records must be corrected within three years, three months, and 15 days after the earnings were received, with ten exceptions to the time limit. 42 U.S.C. §405(c)(5)(A)-(J); **20 C.F.R. §** 404.822[APP-REGS]. As seen in the following case, the time limit can also be extended in extraordinary circumstances on equitable grounds.

SMITH V. SHALALA

910 F. Supp. 152, 49 Soc. Sec. Rep. Serv. 857 (D.N.J. 1995)

LECHNER, District Judge

This is an action brought under section 205(g) of the Social Security Act (the "Act"), as amended, 42 U.S.C. § 405(g), to appeal the final determination of the Secretary of Health and Human Services (the "Secretary") denying the application of plaintiff Mary Smith ("Smith") for disability insurance benefits. * * * For the reasons set forth below, this matter is remanded for further proceedings consistent with this opinion.

* * *

The issue in this case is whether Smith, who alleges she signed under duress inaccurate tax returns filed jointly with her husband, may submit to the Secretary proof of self-employment income in the form of amended tax returns filed after the deadlines promulgated by Congress and the Secretary. If the Secretary accepts such untimely-submitted amended tax returns as proof of Smith's income, she would have the opportunity to meet the insured status requirements under the Act and, if successful, could then receive disability insurance benefits upon a showing that she was "disabled," as that term is defined in the Act.

Facts

A. Background and Hearing Testimony of Smith

Smith is a forty-nine year old mother of three children. In 1971, at the age of twenty-five, she became a registered nurse and married. After the birth of her three children Smith stopped working to raise her children.

Smith stated that two or three years into her marriage it became apparent to her that her "husband ha[d] a drinking problem." Her husband began to behave in an emotionally abusive manner. This emotional abuse included "verbal abuses, ... put downs and ... humiliations and ... degrading remarks and everything." She stated her husband first became physically violent in 1974, about three or four years after they were married. * * *

* * *

Smith stated that she returned to nursing in 1981. She continued working as a self-employed nurse until late 1983, when the onset of multiple sclerosis began to cause her difficulty working. Smith worked intermittently from late 1983 until May 1986, when her multiple sclerosis became too acute for her to work.

Smith and her husband jointly filed tax returns for the years 1983 and 1984 (the "Original Returns"). They did not report any of Smith's self-employment income on the Original Returns. On 5 October 1988, Smith and her husband jointly filed 1040X Amended Income Tax Returns which reflected Smith's self-employment income for 1983 and 1984 (the "Amended Returns"). As Smith concedes, the Amended Returns were filed after the limitations period set out by Congress in the United States Code and by the Secretary in the Code of Federal Regulations.

Smith alleges that her husband forced her to sign the Original Returns. Smith stated that her husband exercised economic control over her by physical and emotional abuse. "The economic control [was] unbelievable." "[She] wasn't allowed to touch the [Original Returns].... The only time [she] got to touch the paper was when [her husband] would bring it, stick it under [her] face, and say--bang his finger into the table or wherever, 'sign it, sign it'." Smith told her husband that "[she] want[ed] to look through [the Original Returns]," but he did not allow her to do so. He told her that she was "numb from the neck up" and "wouldn't understand it." Id. Smith testified that "[she was] not even allowed to use the checkbook [at that time]."

Smith explained that she needs to obtain disability insurance benefits in order to leave her husband. She has become physically dependent upon him as her multiple sclerosis has grown more severe. "[She is] physically dependent upon him because [she] ha[s] to have an adult with [her]. [She] cannot stand at this point.... And so [she is] stuck." In her request for a hearing before an ALJ, Smith stated that she is unable to eat by herself because she cannot hold a knife or fork. Smith also stated that she needs help getting in and out of bed. Counsel stated that her husband " 'throws' her from the chair to the bed or from the bed to the chair." In fear of reprisal from her husband, Smith has requested that all correspondence relating to the instant matter be sent directly to her attorney.

Smith stated that she first learned that she did not meet the insured status requirements of the Act when the Application was rejected.

* * *

Discussion

A. Applicable Law

* * *

An individual must be insured to qualify for disability insurance benefits under the Act. 42 U.S.C. § 423(a)(1)(A). A claimant has disability insured status under the act if she is "fully insured" and also has "at least 20 [quarters of coverage] in the 40 quarter period ... [preceding a disability]." 20 C.F.R. § 404.130(b); see 42 U.S.C. § 423(c)(1)(B)(i). * * * The criteria for determining whether a self-employed individual has earned Quarters of Coverage are different than the criteria for determining whether a wage-earner has earned Quarters of Coverage. The instant matter does not turn on the definition of a Quarter of Coverage; at issue is the deadline for submitting proof of self-employment earnings in order to be credited with sufficient Quarters of Coverage to qualify for disability insurance benefits.

The Secretary is required to maintain records indicating wages and self-employment income earned by claimants. During the limitations period of three years, three months and fifteen days following the end of any calendar year, a claimant may submit material to correct any errors in the Secretary's records concerning wages or self-employment, whether of inclusion or omission. Following the end of the limitation period, the Secretary's records as to an individual's wages or self-employment income for a given year "shall be conclusive...." 42 U.S.C. § 405(c)(4)(A). "[T]he absence of an entry" in the Secretary's records "as to the wages alleged to have been paid by an employer to an individual during any period in such year shall be presumptive evidence ... that no such alleged wages were paid to such individual in such period." 42 U.S.C. § 405(c)(4)(B).

> [T]he absence of an entry in the [Secretary's] records as to the self-employment income alleged to have been derived by an individual in such year shall be conclusive ... that no such alleged self-employment income was derived by such individual in such year unless it is shown that he [or she] filed a tax return of his [or her] self-employment income for such year before the expiration of the time limitation following such year....

42 U.S.C. § 405(c)(4)(C); see also 20 C.F.R. § 404.822(b)(2)(ii). Although there are ten exceptions to these limitations, none applies in the instant matter.

The limitations period has been characterized as a "'statute[ ] of limitation[s] ... to guard against false claims after contradictory evidence is unavailable.'" Shore v. Califano, 589 F.2d 1232, 1237 n. 11 (3d Cir.1978) (quoting Breeden v. Weinberger, 493 F.2d 1002, 1006 (4th Cir.1974)); see Rand v. Sullivan, 924 F.2d 159, 162 (9th Cir.1990). Congress adopted a more rigorous standard of proof for the self-employed than for wage-earners because it was concerned that self-employed claimants might be tempted to submit stale or manufactured evidence of their incomes.

The conclusive presumption protects the government from spurious or merely inaccurate and unverifiable claims based on after-the-fact evidence.... Because self-employed workers control the reporting of their income without the check of employers' also reporting their wages to IRS, Congress saw fit to impose a stricter standard for amendment of their [Social Security] records.

Hollman v. HHS, 696 F.2d 13, 17 (2d Cir.1982). There is an additional reason that the Secretary subjects wage-earners to a less rigorous standard of proof than the self-employed. Wage-earners must rely upon their employers to report their income. Congress and the Secretary sought to ensure that employees are not penalized for the "negligence of their employers who had failed to report wage payments." Shore, 589 F.2d at 1237. "This concern is not relevant to self-employed claimants, however, inasmuch as self-employed claimants control and are responsible for their own income tax and social security reporting." Id.

***

B. Findings of ALJ Fliegler

ALJ Fliegler observed that, to meet the insured status requirements under 20 C.F.R. § 404.130, a claimant must earn at least twenty Quarters of Coverage in a forty-quarter period. ALJ Fliegler concluded that Smith had earned only fifteen Quarters of Coverage during the forty-quarter period ending on the date she alleges she became disabled. Accordingly, ALJ Fliegler denied the Application for failure to meet the insured status requirements of the Act.

ALJ Fliegler found that the Amended Returns were not timely filed. ALJ Fliegler also determined that Smith's "failure to report her self-employment income on a timely basis resulted from extenuating circumstances well beyond her control." Although ALJ Fliegler was "sympathetic to [Smith's] situation ... [he determined he was] bound by the provisions of the Social Security Act and its attendant regulations" and he denied the Application.

C. Analysis of ALJ Fliegler's Decision

After a review of facts and the law in the instant matter, it appears ALJ Fliegler correctly interpreted the relevant statutes and Federal regulations. Smith seeks to use the Amended Returns as evidence. The Amended Returns are dated 5 October 1988. Smith had three years, three months and fifteen days after the end of calendar years 1983 and 1984 to correct the Secretary's records of her income for those years. Because the Amended Returns were submitted after that deadline, a conclusive presumption arose that the Secretary's records of Smith's income, as reflected in the Original Returns, filed in 1983 and 1984, were correct.

Smith seeks an equitable remedy. "The Plaintiff begs ... that this court exercise its equitable powers and reverse the decision of the defendant...." Reply Brief at 3. "The issue is not whether the Plaintiff submitted the appropriate forms and payment within the time limit. She did not. She did not because she could not."

D. Equitable Remedies

Smith argues that "[a] District Court is vested with equity powers and, while it may not intrude upon the administrative process, it may adjust its relief to the demands of the case in accordance with the equitable principles governing judicial action."

The time limit on filing tax returns as evidence of self-employment income in 42 U.S.C. § 405(c)(4)(C) is a "'statute[ ] of limitation[s].'" Shore, 589 F.2d at 1237 n. 11 (quoting Breeden, 493 F.2d at 1006).

"Federal statutes of limitations are generally subject to equitable tolling." Doherty v. Teamsters Pension Trust Fund, 16 F.3d 1386, 1393 (3d Cir.1994) (citing Irwin v. Department of Veterans Affairs, 498 U.S. 89, 95-96, 111 S.Ct. 453, 457-58, 112 L.Ed.2d 435 (1990). The Supreme Court has specifically authorized equitable tolling of statutes of limitations in exigent circumstances in the Social Security context. Bowen v. City of New York, 476 U.S. 467, 480, 106 S.Ct. 2022, 2030, 90 L.Ed.2d 462 (1986). Bowen was a class-action lawsuit against the Secretary, alleging that plaintiffs had been denied benefits under an illegal internal policy of the Secretary.

In *Bowen*, some members of the plaintiff-class had filed for judicial review more than sixty days after final decisions of the Secretary, notwithstanding the deadline set out in 42 U.S.C. § 405(g). The *Bowen* Court characterized the sixty-day deadline under 42 U.S.C. § 405(g) as a statute of limitations. 476 U.S. at 478, 106 S.Ct. at 2029 (citing Mathews v. Eldridge, 424 U.S. 319, 328 n. 9, 96 S.Ct. 893, 899 n. 9, 47 L.Ed.2d 18 (1976); Weinberger v. Salfi, 422 U.S. 749, 764, 95 S.Ct. 2457, 2466, 45 L.Ed.2d 522 (1975)). The Court concluded that "the equities in favor of tolling [the sixty-day limitation] are compelling," id., 476 U.S. at 480, 106 S.Ct. at 2030, because "'the Government's secretive conduct prevent[ed] plaintiffs from knowing of a violation of [their] rights.'" Id. at 481, 106 S.Ct. at 2030 (quoting City of New York v. Heckler, 742 F.2d 729, 738 (2d Cir.1984)).

The equitable concerns that motivated the *Bowen* Court to toll the sixty-day limitations period under 42 U.S.C. § 405(g) justify tolling the limitations period set out in 42 U.S.C. § 405(c)(4)(C). The failure of Smith to report her self-employment income was a consequence of circumstances beyond her control. While the Bowen Court considered the sixty-day requirement in § 405(g) as a statute of limitations, it observed that it was contained "in a statute that Congress designed to be 'unusually protective' of claimants." 476 U.S. at 467, 106 S.Ct. at 2022 (citation omitted). It further observed that Congress expressed a clear intention to allow tolling in some cases. Id. The Court noted that "the Secretary may grant an extension where a suit was not timely filed because of an illness, accident, destruction of records, or mistake." Id. at n. 12. This reasoning is equally applicable in a § 405(c)(4)(C) situation, as presented by Smith.

The Amended Returns were not filed in a timely manner because of the inability of Smith to do so as a consequence of spousal abuse. This conduct prevented her from reviewing the Original Returns and justifies tolling of the limitation period until such time as she had a reasonable opportunity to learn of the facts and take corrective action. Tolling in this case best effects the purposes of the Act.

As discussed, the records of the self-employed are conclusively deemed correct because the self-employed usually are solely responsible for the reporting of their income. In this case, although self-employed, Smith lacked control over the completion and filing of the Original Returns. In these circumstances, it is inappropriate for the Secretary to presume conclusively that her records of income for Smith, based upon the Original Returns, are correct.

On the facts in this case, the equities favoring tolling are compelling. This matter is remanded and the Secretary is instructed to consider the facts surrounding Smith's circumstances, and the abuse she suffered, to determine the period appropriate for tolling the statute of limitations. If the Secretary determines, after tolling the statute, that the Amended Returns were timely filed, she is to then consider the Amended Returns in determining Smith's Quarters of Coverage and eligibility for disability benefits.

Conclusion

For the foregoing reasons, the decision of ALJ Fliegler is remanded for further proceedings consistent with this opinion.

B. NEED-BASED ELIGIBILITY (SSI)

In contrast to the OASDI program, Supplemental Security Income (SSI) is a need-based public assistance program. As such, benefits are available only to persons with limited income and resources. An applicant's income, if any, is a major factor in deciding both eligibility for and the amount of SSI benefits. Resource limitations, on the other hand, apply only to determinations of eligibility. In other words, a claimant's income must be below a certain level in order to be financially eligible for benefits; if eligible, any income will also affect the amount of benefits awarded. A claimant's resources also cannot exceed the maximum limits; however, once eligible, the actual amount of resources that a claimant has is irrelevant (so long as the amount remains below the maximum amount allowed).

1. INCOME REQUIREMENTS

Federal regulations define income as "anything you receive in cash or in kind that you can use to meet your needs for food and shelter"; in-kind income is distinguished from cash as "food or shelter, or something you can use to get one of these." **20 C.F.R. § 416.1102[APP-REGS]**. Certain items are excluded from being counted as income because they cannot be used as food or shelter, or cannot be used to obtain food or shelter. **20 C.F.R. § 416.1103[APP-REGS]**. Examples of other items that are not counted as income include certain types of medical care and services, such as those provided free of charge, certain types of social services, income tax refunds, and bills paid by someone else. 20 C.F.R. § 416.1103 (a)-(j). Additionally, anything received from the sale or exchange of one's own property is considered a "resource" as opposed to income.

Income limits for SSI eligibility are set annually, based on the prior year amount plus, depending on the national rate of inflation, a cost-of-living increase. The amounts effective in 2012 are $698 per month for an individual and $1048 per month for an eligible couple (meaning a couple where both are eligible for and receiving assistance). Having an income that is low enough to make an individual eligible for SSI does not necessarily mean that the individual will receive "full" SSI benefits; as discussed further in Chapter 7, any income that an SSI applicant/claimant has will be taken into account in determining the amount of benefits.

Income is counted differently depending on the source, and some income is not counted at all. (These rules for counting different types of income apply equally to eligibility and to the calculation of the amount of benefits.) There are two different kinds of income—earned and unearned—and the method for counting each differs. Earned income includes wages and net earnings from self-employment, and may be in the form of cash or in-kind. However, not all of an individual's earned income is counted in determining benefit eligibility and amount. Social Security laws exclude certain earned income, as do various other federal laws. Earned income is most important with respect to SSI claims based on old age; earnings, if any, are usually insignificant for claims based on disability.

Unearned income is all income that is not earned, whether in cash or in-kind, and includes most types of periodic payments such as annuities, pensions, Social Security benefits, veterans' benefits, workers' compensation payments, railroad retirement benefits, and unemployment insurance benefits. Unearned income also includes alimony and support payments, dividends, interest, and rents.

In-kind support and maintenance are covered in great detail in the regulations. Of particular importance is the "one-third reduction rule," by which—instead of determining the actual dollar value of in-kind support—there is a flat reduction of the federal benefit rate by one-third if the beneficiary lives in another person's household and receives both food and shelter from that person. This and other rules on calculating in-kind support and maintenance are discussed further below.

A) EARNED INCOME

Earned income consists of wages received for working as an employee, earnings from self-employment, federal tax refunds and advance payments by employers pursuant to the earned income credit provisions of the Internal Revenue Code, payments for services at sheltered workshops or work activities centers, and certain royalties and honoraria. **20 C.F.R. § 416.1110**[APP-REGS]. Earned income can be in cash or in-kind; however, in-kind pay is not counted as earned income for domestic or agricultural workers.

Earned income is counted in different ways depending on the type of income that is at issue. **See 20 C.F.R. § 416.1111**[APP-REGS] Wages are determined on a monthly basis and are counted when they are received or when they are credited to an individual's account or set aside for use, whichever is earliest. 20 C.F.R. § 416.1111(a). Any deductions taken from wages are also counted as earned income. Net earnings from self-employment are counted on a taxable year basis, but are calculated to determine monthly earnings. Thus, the total amount of self-employment earnings is divided equally among the months of the taxable year to determine how much is received in each month. If an individual has net losses from self-employment, the losses are divided over the taxable year in the same way and are deducted from the individual's other earned income. 20 C.F.R. § 416.1111(b). In-kind earned income is calculated based on the current market value in the individual's locality. 20 C.F.R. §416.1111(d). If an individual receives an item not fully paid for and is responsible for the unpaid balance, then only the paid-up value is considered as income. *Id.* For example, if an individual is given an automobile valued at $1500 but must pay $1000 that is due, only $500 is counted as income.

Although claimants must disclose the source and amount of all of their earned income, certain earned income is excluded when determining eligibility and benefit amount. **20 C.F.R. §** 416.1112**(a) [APP-REGS]**. However, earned income is never reduced below zero and unused earned income exclusions are never applied to unearned income. *Id.* The following types of earned income is excluded; when a claimants has income of this type, it is excluded in the following order: as authorized by other federal laws; refunds of federal income taxes and to earned income tax credit payments; up to $30 of earned income per month, if received irregularly or infrequently; up to certain monthly and yearly maximum amounts of earned income for children under the age of 22 and regularly attending school; any portion of the $20 monthly unearned income exclusion that has not been excluded from unearned income in the same month; $65 of earned income per month; earned income used to pay "impairment-related work expenses" if the individual is disabled but not blind and under age 65 or received Supplement Security Income as a disabled person for the month preceding age 65; one-half of any remaining earned income in a month; earned income used to pay expenses "reasonably attributable" to earning the income, if the individual is blind and under age 65 or received Supplemental Security Income as a blind person for the month preceding age 65; any earned income received and spent on an approved plan to achieve self-support, if the individual is blind or disabled and under age 65; and payments made to participants in certain AmeriCorps programs. **20 C.F.R. §** 416.1112**(b)-(c)[APP-REGS]**.

B) UNEARNED INCOME

Unearned income, which can also be received in cash or in kind, is defined as all income that is not earned income. **20 C.F.R. §** 416.1120**[APP-REGS]**. Types of unearned income include annuities, pensions, and other periodic payments; alimony and support payments; dividends, interest, and certain royalties; rents (minus expenses) incurred in the taxable year that are ordinary and "necessary for the production or collection of the rental income"; death benefits, including payments received as a result of the death of another person "except for the amount of such payments that [one] spend[s] on the deceased person's last illness and burial expenses"; prizes and awards; gifts and inheritances, except those used to pay the expenses of another person's last illness and burial; and in-kind support and maintenance, including food or shelter. **20 C.F.R. §** 416.1121**(a)-(h)[APP-REGS]**. In-kind support and maintenance is discussed in greater detail below.

Unearned income is counted for each month, either when the individual receives it, when it is credited to his or her account, or when it is set aside for his or her use, whichever is earliest. **20 C.F.R. §** 416.1123**(a) [APP-REGS]**. Similar to earned income, in-kind unearned income is typically calculated based on the current market value, less any balance due. 20 C.F.R § 416.1123(c). However, calculation of in-kind support and maintenance that an individual receives is subject to special treatment, as is discussed further below.

In some situations, SSA will count more unearned income than an individual actually receives. 20 C.F.R § 416.1123(b). One such situation is when another benefit payment, such as a Social Security payment, has been reduced to recover a previous overpayment. This does not apply, however, if the individual received both SSI benefits and the other benefit at the time the overpayment occurred, and the overpaid amount was included in calculating the SSI benefit at that time. The following example is provided at 20 C.F.R § 416.1123(b)(1):

> Joe, an SSI beneficiary, is also entitled to social security insurance benefits in the amount of $200 per month. However, because of a prior overpayment of his social security insurance benefits, $20 per month is being withheld to recover the overpayment. In figuring the amount of his SSI benefits, the full monthly social security insurance benefit of $200 is included in Joe's unearned income. However, if Joe was receiving both benefits when the overpayment of the social security insurance benefit occurred and we then included the overpaid amount as income, we will compute his SSI benefit on the basis of receiving $180 as a social security insurance benefit. This is because we recognize that we computed his SSI benefit on the basis of the higher amount when he was overpaid.

SSA will also include more than an individual actually received if amounts were withheld from unearned income "because of a garnishment, or to pay a debt or other legal obligation, or to make any other payment such as payment of . . . Medicare premiums." 20 C.F.R § 416.1123(b)(2). On the other hand, SSA will include less than an individual actually received if the individual incurred expenses in getting the payment. "For example, if you are paid for damages you receive in an accident, we subtract from the amount of the payment your medical, legal, or other expenses connected with the accident." 20 C.F.R § 416.1123(b)(3). Additionally, SSA may consider someone' else's income to be available to the individual in certain situations. 20 C.F.R § 416.1123(b)(4). This is discussed further below in the section on deeming of income.

As with earned income, SSA does not count all of a person's unearned income in determining benefit eligibility and amount, **20 C.F.R. § 416.1124(a) [APP-REGS]**, unearned income is never reduced below zero, and unused unearned income exclusions are not applied to earned income—except for the $20 general exclusion discussed below. Also as with earned income, there are types of unearned income that are excluded under other federal laws. 20 C.F.R. § 416.1124(b). Additional exclusions are applied in the following order: any public agency's refund of taxes on real property or food; need-based assistance that is wholly funded by a state; grants, scholarships, or fellowships used for paying tuition, fees, and educational expenses; food raised by the individual or the individual's spouse if consumed by his or her household; federal emergency assistance; up to $60 of unearned income per month if received irregularly or infrequently; payments for providing foster care to an ineligible child placed in an individual's home; certain support and maintenance assistance; one-third of support payments made to or for a child applicant by an absent parent; the first $20 of any unearned income received in a month other than income based on need; and all unearned income spent on an approved plan for achieving self-support, if the individual is blind or disabled; the value of certain assistance paid with respect to a dwelling unit; the value of any commercial transportation ticket received as a gift for travel and not converted to cash; and payments received from a State fund to aid victims of crime. **20 C.F.R. § 416.1124(c)[APP-REGS]**. Certain veterans benefits are also treated differently for purposes of counting unearned income. 20 C.F.R. § 416.1123(e).

The most commonly used of these income exclusions in disability cases is the $20 per month of unearned income not based on need, which includes Disability Insurance Benefits. Thus, an individual who is eligible for both Disability Insurance Benefits and Supplemental Security Income because the amount of Disability Insurance Benefits he or she receives is relatively small, can have $20 per month of the Disability Insurance Benefits excluded in determining SSI eligibility and payments. As a result, the combined amount of the benefits will be $20 per month more than the base rate for SSI.

NOTE ON RETROACTIVE SOCIAL SECURITY BENEFIT PAYMENTS

Payments of retroactive monthly Social Security benefits are treated as unearned income, but the amount is calculated as if the retroactive benefits were received on a regular, monthly basis. 42 U.S.C. § 1320a-6; 20 C.F.R § 416.1123(d). The idea is to prevent potential windfalls to an individual who may qualify for both OASDI and SSI benefits. Thus, the retroactive benefits are reduced by an amount equal to the amount of SSI payments that would not have been paid if the Social Security benefits had been paid when regularly due, rather than retroactively. 20 C.F.R § 416.1123(d)(1). Since the amount of the reduction is calculated based on the receipt of Social Security benefits, if a balance is owed after the reduction is made, that balance will not count as unearned income for SSI purposes in a subsequent month in which it is received.

C) IN-KIND SUPPORT AND MAINTENANCE

As noted above, both earned and unearned income can include items received in kind. **20 C.F.R. § 416.1130[APP-REGS]** Regulations define in-kind support and maintenance as "any food or shelter that is given to you or that you receive because someone else pays for it," with shelter defined further as including "room, rent, mortgage payments, real property taxes, heating fuel, gas, electricity, water, sewerage, and garbage collection services." 20 C.F.R § 416.1130(b). In-kind support and maintenance received as unearned income is calculated in one of two ways: by the "one-third reduction rule" or the "presumed value rule," depending on whether the individual is living in the household of the person providing the support and maintenance, and whether food or shelter are also provided. 20 C.F.R. § 416.1121(h); §§ 416.1130 – 416.1147. An individual is considered to be "living in another person's household" if the other person supplying the support lives in the same household and is not the individual's spouse, a minor child, or "an ineligible person whose income may be deemed" as described below. 20 C.F.R § 416.1132(b). However, an individual is not considered to be living in another person's household if the individual (or his or her spouse or any person whose income is deemed to him or her) has an ownership interest or life estate interest in the home, is liable to the landlord for payment of any part of the rental charges, lives in a non-institutional care situation, pays at least a pro rata share of household and operating expenses, or all members of the household receive public income-maintenance payments. 20 C.F.R § 416.1132(c).

The "one-third reduction rule" is used to count in-kind support provided for individuals and eligible couples that live in another person's household for a full calendar month and also receive food and shelter from that person. Instead of determining the actual dollar value of the in-kind support, SSA uses a flat rate of one-third of the federal benefit rate. **20 C.F.R. § 416.1131[APP-REGS]**. The one-third reduction rule applies in whole or not at all, so when it applies no other in-kind support or maintenance received is counted.

If the individual does not receive *both* food and shelter, the "presumed value rule" applies instead of the one-third reduction rule. **20 C.F.R. § 416.1140[APP-REGS]**. The presumed value rule also applies if in-kind support and maintenance is received as unearned income and the individual is living in his or her own household or in a non-medical institution, such as a public or private nonprofit educational or vocational training institution or a private nonprofit retirement home. **20 C.F.R. § 416.1141(a)-(b)[APP-REGS]**. Under the "presumed value rule," SSA presumes that any food or shelter received is worth a maximum value, as opposed to making a determination about the actual dollar value. This maximum value is equal to one-third of the individual's federal benefit rate plus $20 (the general income exclusion described in 20 C.F.R. § 416.1124(c)(12)). 20 C.F.R. § 416.1140(a). The presumed value rule is a rebuttable presumption, so an individual receiving in-kind support can show that either the actual amount paid or the current market value of food or shelter received is less than the presumed value.

Until the early 1990s, SSA treated any in-kind contributions of food and shelter as income, even if provided as a loan (despite the fact that proceeds of a loan were typically not counted as income. 20 C.F.R. § 416.1103(f)). This was due to the Secretary's narrow interpretation that the regulation was only intended to pertain to loans given in the form of cash. That policy was challenged successfully in the courts and, since 1992, SSA no longer considers in-kind contributions loaned to claimants as income.

In Ceguerra v. Secretary, 933 F.2d 735, 33 Soc.Sec.Rep.Ser. 482 (9th Cir. 1991), an elderly, indigent woman received food and shelter in kind from her son while she awaited a decision regarding the wrongful termination of her SSI benefits. Prior to the termination of her benefits, Ms. Ceguerra had paid her share of the household expenses by making monthly payments to her son with part of the money from her SSI payments. "Before awarding Ceguerra's retroactive payments, * * * [t]he Secretary reduced Ceguerra's payment because she received food and shelter in her son's home while her appeal was pending. Accepting food and shelter in another's household without contributing to expenses can prompt the one-third reduction in the level of benefits." 933 F.2d at 737. The court addressed whether the transfer or provision of goods or services in kind could qualify as a loan, and held that Social Security Ruling 78-26 erroneously construed the administrative regulations and the intent of Congress. "In determining eligibility for benefits under the SSI program, the Secretary properly excludes from the calculation of income the value of loans that must be repaid. For this purpose, loans include valid and enforceable agreements to repay the value of goods and services transferred in kind." *Id.* at 742. The court also noted that SSA

> applies too narrow an interpretation of the regulation that excludes loans from income. In *Hickman* [*v. Bowen*, 803 F.2d 1377 (5th Cir.1986)], the court noted that when Congress defined "income," it made no distinction between cash and in-kind income. 803 F.2d at 1381. Similarly, [SSA] defines income to include both cash and the value of goods received in kind * * * 20 C.F.R. § 416.1102 (1990). Indeed, the *Hickman* court noted that throughout the statute and the regulations, income is consistently defined to include both cash income and in-kind income. In interpreting the regulation that defines what is a loan, the *Hickman* court saw no reason to distinguish between an obligation to repay what was received in the form of cash

and the obligation to repay what was received in the form of goods or services in kind. 803 F.2d at 1381-82. Neither do we.

When arguing before this court, the government suggested that Ceguerra could easily have avoided the operation of the rule that reduced her benefits by one-third. According to the government, Ceguerra could have arranged to accept her loan in cash instead of in kind. If Napoleon Ceguerra had given his mother a check for $250 each month, and if she had immediately endorsed the check back to her son to cover her share of the household expenses, [SSA] would have regarded the arrangement as a valid loan of cash. We do not believe that Congress intended that eligible recipients of SSI benefits be forced to conduct such a senseless charade. Moreover, when an administrative agency interprets its governing statute to require such an absurd result, we owe that interpretation no deference.

We hold that Social Security Ruling 78-26 erroneously construes the administrative regulations and the intent of Congress. In determining eligibility for benefits under the SSI program, [SSA] properly excludes from the calculation of income the value of loans that must be repaid. For this purpose, loans include valid and enforceable agreements to repay the value of goods and services transferred in kind.

Because Ceguerra entered into a valid and enforceable agreement to repay her son for her share of the household expenses, the shelter and maintenance she received did not constitute income. We therefore reverse the Secretary's decision to reduce Ceguerra's retroactive benefits by one-third.

Ceguerra, 933 F.2d at 742.

The finding that there was, in fact, a loan was supported by a signed statement from Ms. Ceguerra saying that she was expected to repay her share of the household expenses and oral statements from her son indicating that he expected to be repaid for the expenses. "Moreover, Ceguerra points out that the ALJ's conclusion that the amount of the loan was uncertain was not supported by substantial evidence. Ceguerra paid $250 per month as her pro rata share of household expenses until her SSI payments were cut off. The custom of the parties is a sufficiently clear and objective guide for determining the extent of Ceguerra's contractual obligation." *Ceguerra*, 933 F.2d at 739.

One year after the decision in *Ceguerra*, the Social Security Administration issued the following Ruling expanding the definition of a loan:

SOCIAL SECURITY RULING SSR 92-8P

(1992)

TITLE XVI: SSI LOAN POLICY, INCLUDING ITS
APPLICABILITY TO ADVANCES OF FOOD AND/OR
SHELTER

Purpose: This Ruling defines a loan for SSI purposes. It also explains when the proceeds of a loan count as resources under the SSI program, when they do not count as income, and how SSA treats a loan agreement when the lender is an SSI applicant or recipient. Social Security Ruling (SSR) 78-26 previously addressed these issues.

In addition, this Ruling reinterprets SSI regulations to permit treating, as the basis for a loan, food or shelter that an SSI applicant or recipient receives from someone in whose household he or she lives and has an obligation to pay for at a future date.

[Ruling presents relevant background, including decisions in *Ceguerra* and Hickman v. Bowen, 803 F.2d 1377 (5th Cir.1986) (cited in *Ceguerra*).]

In view of these recent court decisions, SSA has decided to reinterpret its regulations on the treatment in the SSI program of advances of food and shelter to an SSI applicant or recipient by an individual in whose household he or she is residing.

Policy Interpretation: For purposes of determining when a loan is not considered income and when a loan is considered a countable resource under the SSI program, the following policies apply:

1. A loan means an advance from lender to borrower that the borrower must repay, with or without interest. A loan can be cash or an in-kind advance in lieu of cash. For example, an advance of food or shelter can represent a loan of the pro rata share of household operating expenses. This applies to any commercial or noncommercial loan (between relatives, friends or others) that is recognized as enforceable under State law. The loan agreement may be oral or written, as long as it is enforceable under State law.

2. Any advance an SSI applicant or recipient receives that meets the above definition of a loan is not income for SSI purposes since it is subject to repayment. Any portion of borrowed funds that the borrower does not spend is a countable resource to the borrower if retained into the month following the month of receipt.

3. When money or an in-kind advance in lieu of cash is given and accepted based on any understanding other than that it is to be repaid by the receiver, there is no loan involved for SSI purposes. It could be

a gift, support payments, in-kind support and maintenance, etc., and must be treated as provided for in the rules applicable to such items.

4. If there is a bona fide loan as defined in (1) above, there is a rebuttable presumption that the loan agreement is a resource of the lender for SSI purposes.

For example, an SSI applicant or recipient reports making a loan to a relative. The loan agreement is oral. The oral agreement is found to be binding under State law. Accordingly, the loan is presumed to be a resource of the lender because it can be converted to cash if the lender calls for repayment from the borrower. The lender can rebut this presumption by showing that the loan cannot be converted to cash-- for example, because the borrower died without leaving an estate.

5. Money a lender receives as repayment of a loan (which meets the definition of a resource) reduces the outstanding loan balance and is considered a countable resource to the lender inasmuch as the repayment amount represents a return of part of the loan principal; i.e., the total value of the resource, which is the repayment amount plus the outstanding loan balance, remains unchanged.

6. Interest on a loan is counted as unearned income to the lender in the month of receipt and, if retained, is a resource as in (2) above.

Documentation: Evidence must be obtained with respect to the existence of a bona fide loan agreement. The burden of proof with respect to the bona fide nature of the loan is with the applicant or recipient.

* * *

NOTE

Courts have typically held that, although a loan agreement does not need to be in writing, it must be demonstrated with sufficient specificity, and an ALJ can decline to recognize the existence of a loan if the evidence presented is too vague. *See, e.g.*, Wagman v. Chater, No. 94 CIV. 7243, 1996 WL 219646 (S.D.N.Y. May 01, 1996). The type of evidence presented can include a written agreement or statements specifying the amount loaned, the period of time covered, or the terms of repayment. *See*, e.g., Hassbrock v. Astrue, No. H-08-2606, 2009 WL 2007147 (S.D.Tex. July 1, 2009).

D) DEEMING OF INCOME

Probably the most controversial aspect of income determinations in SSI cases is the "deeming" of income. *See* **20 C.F.R. §** 416.1160**[APP-REGS]** Deeming is the term used by SSA when it considers another person's income—such as the income of a claimant's spouse or, if the claimant is a child, the income of the child's parent—to be the claimant's income. Deemed income is considered both to determine whether an individual is eligible for a benefit and to determine the amount of the benefit. 20 C.F.R. § 416.1160(b). The rules for deeming income from spouses and parents not eligible for SSI are discussed in detail below. Rules also exist for deeming income from "essential persons" who have lived with an SSI recipient since the program was enacted, 20 C.F.R. in § 416.222, or from a recipient's sponsor, if the recipient is an alien. 42 U.S.C. § 1382c(f)(3)-(4); 20 C.F.R. § 416.1160(a)(3)-(4).

The theory behind the deeming of income is that it does not matter whether the "deemed" income is actually available to the claimant because the ineligible spouse or parent is expected to use part of his or her income toward the claimant's care. 20 C.F.R. § 416.1160(a). Deeming rules used in the federal Medicaid program, which are similar to those used in the SSI program, have been upheld as constitutional where the person whose income is deemed is legally obligated by state law to support the person for whom the income is assumed to be available, or if the deemed income is in fact available. *See* Schweiker v. Gray Panthers, 453 U.S. 34 (1981).

Generally, three steps are followed in deeming income. First, an accounting is made of the earned and unearned income of the person whose income is being deemed, applying various exclusions similar to those used with regard to a claimant's income. Second, an amount is allocated for each ineligible child in the household before deeming income to the claimant from either an ineligible spouse or ineligible parent. Finally, there are additional deeming rules applicable to each category of individual from whom income is to be deemed. 20 C.F.R. § 416.1160(c). The regulations also address situations where the one-third reduction and presumed value rules interact with the deeming rules. 20 C.F.R. § 416.1148(b)

Note and Problem on Deeming Income from Ineligible Spouses

1. If an individual is married and living in the same household as his or her ineligible spouse (that is, a spouse who is not also eligible for SSI benefits), the individual's income and resources will be deemed to include any income and resources of that spouse. 42 U.S.C. § 1382c(f)(1); 20 C.F.R. § 416.1160(a)(1). The Commissioner of Social Security may, however, determine that deeming the income would be inequitable under the circumstances and choose not to apply the deeming rules.

After following the steps described generally above for deeming income, the individual's eligibility for SSI is determined based on the amount of the ineligible spouse's income that remains after the appropriate allocations have been made. If the income that remains is less than the difference between the federal benefit rate for an eligible couple and the federal benefit rate for an eligible individual, no income will be deemed from the spouse. If, however, the income is greater than that difference, the individual and his or her spouse are treated as an "eligible couple." For an eligible couple, the individual's earned and unearned income will be combined with the remainder of his or her spouse's earned and unearned income, respectively. After any necessary income exclusions are applied (see §§ 416.1112 and 416.1124), the couple's countable income is then subtracted from the federal benefit rate for an eligible couple. The individual's SSI benefit is then equal to either the amount that results from the above calculations, or the amount remaining after the individual's own countable income is subtracted from an individual's federal benefit rate, whichever is less. **20 C.F.R. § 416.1163[APP-REGS]**

The following example is provided in the regulations for deeming income from an ineligible spouse. *See* 20 C.F.R. § 416.1163(g). The example uses the benefit rate effective January 1, 1986.

> Example 2. In September 1986, Mr. Jones, a disabled individual, lives with his ineligible spouse, Mrs. Jones, and ineligible child, Christine. Mr. Jones and Christine have no income. Mrs. Jones has earned income of $401 a month and unearned income of $252 a month. Before we deem any income, we allocate $168 to Christine. We take the $168 allocation from Mrs. Jones' $252 unearned income, leaving $84 in unearned income. Since Mrs. Jones' total remaining income ($84 unearned plus $401 earned) is more than $168, which is the difference between the September Federal benefit rate for an eligible couple and the September Federal benefit rate for an eligible individual, we compute the combined countable income as we do for a couple. We apply the $20 general income exclusion to the unearned income, reducing it further to $64. We then apply the earned income exclusion ($65 plus one-half the remainder) to Mrs. Jones' earned income of $401, leaving $168. We combine the $64 countable unearned income and $168 countable earned income, and compare it ($232) with the $504 September Federal benefit rate for a couple, and determine that Mr. Jones is eligible. Since Mr. Jones is eligible, we determine the amount of his benefit by subtracting his countable income in July (including any deemed from Mrs. Jones) from September's Federal benefit rate for a couple.

2. Problem: Mr. Smith is an SSI recipient who lives with his ineligible spouse, Mrs. Smith. Mrs. Smith earns $201 per month; Mr. Smith receives a pension (unearned income) of $100 a month. Using the procedure for deeming income from an ineligible spouse outlined above (and assuming the same benefit levels apply), calculate the amount of Mrs. Smith's income that would be deemed available to Mr. Smith.

NOTE AND PROBLEM ON DEEMING INCOME FROM INELIGIBLE PARENTS

1. The income and resources of any child under the age of 18 who is living in the same household as a parent who is not eligible for SSI will be deemed to include any income and resources of that parent (or the spouse of the parent). 42 U.S.C. § 1382c(f)(2)(A); 20 C.F.R. § 416.1160(a)(2). Income may not be deemed, however, if the child is disabled, hospitalized in a medical treatment facility, or in certain other circumstances. 42 U.S.C. § 1382c(f)(2)(B). In addition, the Commissioner of Social Security may determine that it would be inequitable under the circumstances to deem income from a parent. 42 U.S.C. § 1382c(f)(2)(A).

The same general steps are followed for deeming income from an ineligible parent as with income from an ineligible spouse. *See* **20 C.F.R. § 416.1165[APP-REGS].** However, there are specific rules regarding deducting allocations for parents. For example, allocations are not deducted for a parent who is receiving public income maintenance payments. Otherwise, allocations are calculated as set out in 20 C.F.R. § 416.1165(d):

(1) We first deduct $20 from the parents' combined unearned income, if any. If they have less than $20 in unearned income, we subtract the balance of the $20 from their combined earned income.

(2) Next, we subtract $65 plus one-half the remainder of their earned income.

(3) We total the remaining earned and unearned income and subtract—

(i) The Federal benefit rate for the month for a couple if both parents live with you; or

(ii) The Federal benefit rate for the month for an individual if only one parent lives with you.

If there is only one eligible child, any of the parents' remaining current monthly income will be deemed to be the child's unearned income. 20 C.F.R. § 416.1165(e)(1). If there is more than one eligible child, the parental income will be divided and deemed equally among the eligible children. 20 C.F.R. § 416.1165(e)(2).

After the income has been deemed to the child, the SSI benefits will then be calculated in the same manner as described with ineligible spouses. 20 C.F.R. § 416.1165(f). In the event that deeming income to an eligible child would reduce his or her benefits to zero (and effectively make the child ineligible), the income will be deemed only to other eligible children. 20 C.F.R. § 416.1165(e)(3).

The regulations also provide the following example for deeming income from an ineligible parent and calculating benefits to a disabled child. *See* 20 C.F.R. § 416.1165(h) The benefit rates used in the example are those effective January 1, 1992.

> Example 1.　Henry, a disabled child, lives with his mother and father and a 12-year-old ineligible brother.　His mother receives a pension (unearned income) of $365 per month and his father earns $1,165 per month.　Henry and his brother have no income.　First we deduct an allocation of $211 for Henry's brother from the unearned income.　This leaves $154 in unearned income.　We reduce the remaining unearned income further by the $20 general income exclusion, leaving $134.　We then reduce the earned income of $1,165 by $65 leaving $1,100.　Then we subtract one-half of the remainder, leaving $550.　To this we add the remaining unearned income of $134 resulting in $684.　From this, we subtract the parent allocation of $633 (the Federal benefit rate [effective January 1, 1992] for a couple) leaving $51 to be deemed as Henry's unearned income.　Henry has no other income.　We apply Henry's $20 general income exclusion which reduces his countable income to $31.　Since that amount is less than the $422 Federal benefit rate for an individual, Henry is eligible.　We determine his benefit amount by subtracting his countable income (including deemed income) in a prior month from the Federal benefit rate for an individual for the current month.

2. Problem: Serene, a disabled child eligible for SSI, lives with her two ineligible parents. Serene's mother has no income; her father, Mr. Hamilton, receives $3,200 per month in earned income from his job at the Postal Service. Mr. Hamilton also pays $450 per month in child support from a prior marriage. Using the formula set out in 20 C.F.R. §§ 416.1165(a)-(d) and the 2012 benefit amounts of $698 for an individual and $1048 for a couple, calculate the amount of income that should be deemed available to Serene from her parents. Then, calculate her benefit amount as per 20 C.F.R. § 416.1165(e).

2. RESOURCES REQUIREMENTS

Supplemental Security Income resource limits serve to restrict eligibility to persons with effectively no disposable assets, with certain specific exceptions. Thus, an applicant or recipient is limited to non-excludable resources that do not exceed $2,000 in value; a couple can have non-excludable resources of up to $3,000 in value. **20 C.F.R. § 416.1205[APP-REGS]**. An individual who satisfies this limit is eligible for SSI, assuming all other eligibility requirements are met, and the amount of resources he or she has below that maximum value has no effect on the amount of benefits awarded.

Resources are defined as cash or other liquid assets, or any real or personal property that an individual or his or her spouse owns and could convert to cash to be used for support and maintenance. **20 C.F.R. §** 416.1201**(a)[APP-REGS]**. Liquid resources include cash and financial instruments convertible to cash within 20 days; they are evaluated according to their equity value. 20 C.F.R. § 416.1201(b). Some items such as support and maintenance assistance, certain cash received for medical or social services, and death benefits received are not considered resources. These exceptions are described more extensively in the regulations. **20 C.F.R. §** 416.1201**(a)(2)-(4)[APP-REGS]**. Non-liquid resources include all other personal and real property that is not cash and cannot be converted to cash within 20 days. For the most part, they are evaluated according to their equity value. 20 C.F.R. § 416.1201(b). Among items excluded, subject to various limits and exceptions, are a home, personal effects, an automobile, certain property essential to means of self-support, loan agreements, household goods, burial spaces and funds for burial expenses. **20 C.F.R. §** 416.1210**[APP-REGS]** Funds held in financial institution accounts, such as savings, checking, or certificates of deposit, are also considered to be a resource if the funds can be used for the individual's support and maintenance. Determinations about whether the funds can be used in this way depend upon whether the account is individually or jointly held. **20 C.F.R. §** 416.1208**[APP-REGS]**.

Determinations about the availability, value, and excludability of resources are made at the beginning of the month. Changes in the value of resources that occur during a month will not be counted until the beginning of the next month. Similarly, if an individual receives an item in cash or in kind during a month, it will be evaluated under the income-counting rules during that month but will not be subject to the rules for counting resources until the beginning of the next month. Receipts from the sale, exchange, or replacement of a resource continue to be counted as a resource and are not considered income, regardless of when the change takes place. *See* **20 C.F.R. §** 416.1207**[APP-REGS]**. Where resources exceed the limits set forth in the regulations, an individual may dispose of a limited amount of resources in particular circumstances and under certain conditions in order to become eligible for benefits. 20 C.F.R. § 416.1207(e). Generally, resources must be sold at fair market value.

The following are examples of items typically excluded from determinations regarding an individual's resources: a home that serves as the individual's principal place of residence; most household goods and personal effects; an automobile, if used for transportation; resources necessary for a blind or disabled person to fulfill an approved plan for achieving self-support; disaster relief assistance; and burial spaces and certain funds up to $1,500 for burial expenses. 20 C.F.R. §§ 416.1210, 416.1216.

The value of property essential to self-support is also typically not counted towards the value of an individual's resources. This includes real and personal property used in a trade or business; non-business income-producing property (houses or apartments for rent, land other than home property, etc.); and property used to produce goods or services essential to an individual's daily activities. Resources, other than those used as part of a trade or business, must be non-liquid in order to be considered essential to self-support. **20 C.F.R. § 416.1220[APP-REGS]**. There are detailed rules for counting income-producing property that is essential to self-support, as well as nonbusiness property used to produce goods or services. **20 C.F.R. § 416.1222[APP-REGS]**; **20 C.F.R. § 416.1224[APP-REGS]**.

Similar to the ways in which income from a spouse or parent is deemed to an individual, the resources of a married individual or a child may be deemed to include the resources of his or her ineligible spouse or parent. **20 C.F.R. § 416.1202[APP-REGS]**. Like income, the resources will be deemed regardless of whether they are actually available to the individual. Resources of the spouse or parent are subject to the same exclusions as those of individuals. For a child, the resource limits previously described also apply: exceed $2,000 in value if the child is living with one parent; or $3,000, if the child is living with both parents (or with the parent and a spouse. 20 C.F.R. § 416.1202(b).

NOTE AND PROBLEM ON RESOURCE EXCLUSION CALCULATIONS ON SALE OF A HOME

1. The proceeds from the sale of a home which is excluded from the individual's resources will also be excluded from resources to the extent they are intended to be used and are, in fact, used to purchase another home. The new home must be similarly excluded and purchased within 3 months of the date of receipt of the proceeds. **20 C.F.R. § 416.1212[APP-REGS]** Thus, the value of a promissory note or similar installment sales contract constitutes a "proceed" which can be excluded, provided that the individual purchases a replacement home within 3 months of receipt (execution) of the note and all note-generated proceeds are reinvested in the replacement home within 3 months of receipt.

2. Problem: On April 10, an SSI recipient received a payment of $250 from the buyer of his former home under an installment sales contract. On May 3, he reinvested $200 of the payment in the purchase of a new home. On May 10, the recipient received another $250 payment, and reinvested the full amount on June 3. Determine how much of the proceeds from the sale qualify as excludable resource.

C. OLD AGE COVERAGE

As we saw in Chapter 1, old age was a major part of the original coverage of the Social Security Act of 1935 for both social insurance and public assistance benefits. Old age benefits have remained a central part of what has become the Old Age, Survivors, and Disability Insurance program (OASDI). Moreover, old age was one of the two categories of public assistance coverage (along with disability) that was taken over by the Social Security Administration when Supplemental Security Income replaced the federal-state Aid to the Aged, Blind, and Disabled (AABD) program in the early 1970s. As a result, benefits are available today on the basis of old age under both OASDI and SSI.

As explained in more detail in Chapter 3, there are two separate age requirements in the OASDI program for persons fully insured on the basis of their own earnings—one for early retirement and the other for full retirement. The age for full retirement has been undergoing a gradual extension from the traditional age of 65 to 67. *See* 42 U.S.C. § 402(a). There is no similar change underway for the early retirement age, which remains at 62. *See* 42 U.S.C. § 416(l)(2). The old age threshold for SSI has always been the traditional retirement age of 65. 42 U.S.C. § 1382c(a)(1)(A).

D. DISABILITY COVERAGE

1. BASIC ELIGIBILITY REQUIREMENTS

Disability benefits are available through the Old Age, Survivors, and Disability Insurance (OASDI) program and the Supplemental Security Income (SSI) program. The OASDI program covers not only persons who are insured on the basis of their own work record (often referred to as "wage earners"), but also their spouses (after they reach a certain age) and their adult children (so long as they became disabled before a certain age). The SSI program covers both adults and children under the age of 18. Persons seeking OASDI disability benefits as a wage earner's dependent must meet—in addition to the insured-status requirements for the wage earner—certain relationship-to-wage-earner requirements, as explained later in this chapter and also in Chapter 3.

The disability requirement is the same for all claimants under both programs, except for children under the age of 18 applying for SSI benefits:. Persons seeking disability benefits under the OASDI program and adults seeking disability benefits under the SSI program must show that they are unable to engage in "substantial gainful activity" as the result of a "medically determinable" physical or mental impairment that has lasted for, or is expected to last, at least one year (or expected to result in death), taking into account the claimant's age, level of education, and prior work experience. 42 USCA §423(d)(1). There is a separate SSI disability standard for children under the age of 18, which is intended to measure "disability" in the special context of younger age. (Until 1991, there was a separate, more restrictive disability standard for spouses of insured wage earners under the OASDI program.) These disability standards are discussed at length in Chapters 4-7.

2. CONTINUING ELIGIBILITY

Once an individual has been found to be disabled and entitled to benefits, payments continue unless and until SSA makes a determination that the recipient is no longer eligible. There are a number of special circumstances that can trigger ineligibility, including fraud or having provided incomplete or incorrect information. *See* 20 CFR § 404.1594(e); 42 U.S.C. § 423(f); 42 U.S.C. § 405(u)(1). In addition, SSI recipients can become ineligible if they come to have income or resources above the maximum allowable amount. The most important basis for finding that a recipient is no longer eligible for disability benefits—and the one most often contested by the recipient—is that he or she is no longer disabled. The standard for terminating benefits is discussed in detail in Chapter 4.

There are, of course, circumstances where the recipient obviously is no longer disabled, either because the disabling condition improved or— regardless of his or her condition—the recipient returned to work. This may come to SSA's attention when reported by the recipient, as required under 20 CFR §§ 404.1588, 416.988, or in the course of a "continuing disability review" (CDR). Even recipients who have returned to work may remain eligible if the return to work qualifies as a "trial work period"

A) CONTINUING DISABILITY REVIEWS (CDR)

The Social Security Act mandates review of on-going disability cases in order to determine continuing eligibility for benefits. **42 U.S.C.A. § 421(i)[APP-STAT]**. *See also* **20 C.F.R. §§ 404.1589-.1590, 416.989-.990[APP-REGS]**. The Social Security Administration has had statutory authority to conduct what are commonly referred to as "continuing disability reviews" (CDRs) since the 1960s; however, until 1981 the Administration reviewed only certain limited types of disability cases in significant numbers. But then in 1980, Congress amended the Act to require that CDRs be conducted every three years for all beneficiaries, except for those whose disabilities were determined to be permanent. *See* 42 U.S.C.A. § 421(i)(1). Although the 1980 Amendments were not effective until January, 1982, SSA began conducting these periodic reviews in March, 1981 amidst a great deal of controversy.

SSA was encouraged to undertake these accelerated reviews aggressively in order to ameliorate the dramatic increase in the SSA's caseload that had begun to threaten the "fiscal integretity of the disability program" in the 1970s. *See* Richard E. Levy, *Social Security Disability Determinations: Recommendations for Reform*, 1990 BYU L. REV. 461, 477-78 (1990). With respect to the early CDR programs, one senator noted that "the message perceived by the State agencies, swamped with cases, was to deny, deny, deny, and, I might add, to process cases faster and faster and faster. In the name of efficiency, we have scanned our computer terminals, rounded up the disabled workers in the country, pushed the discharge button, and let them go into a free [f]all toward economic chaos." Schweiker v. Chilicky, 487 U.S. 412, 416 (1988) (quoting 130 Cong. Rec. 26000, at 13218 (daily ed. May 22, 1984) (remarks of Sen. Cohen, cosponsor of the Social Security Disability Benefits Reform Act).

Some critics have argued that "[t]he SSA's restrictive policies exacerbated rather than improved caseload pressures by creating a caseload explosion in the review process at both the administrative and judicial level. The explosion resulted from dramatic increases in the denials and terminations of disability benefits which led to a similarly dramatic increase in the number of claimants seeking review." Levy at 479. Particularly problematic was the fact that, although large number of individuals were removed from the disability rolls, many of these individuals were truly disabled and unable to work, leading to a large number of appeals. *See* Schweiker v. Chilicky, 487 U.S. at 416 (discussing reports by legislators and the SSA documenting wrongful terminations).

The Social Security Act was amended again in 1984 to require SSA to issue regulations governing the frequency of CDRs for both Disability Insurance Benefits and Supplemental Security Income. These regulations require review at least every three years when a disability is considered permanent. In addition, the regulations authorize "diaried" reviews within six to eighteen months in cases where the claimant's condition is expected to improve. *See* 20 C.F.R. §§ 404.1590(d), 416.990(d). A "permanent" impairment is "an extremely severe condition determined ... to be at least static, but more likely to be progressively disabling." A claimant's age and work history can also be considered in determining whether an impairment is permanent. *See* 20 C.F.R. §§ 404.1590(c), 416.990(c). The regulations also provide for notice to claimants prior to review, and for a waiver of the frequency-of-review requirement to assure careful and accurate review of cases included in the continuing disability review process. 20 C.F.R. §§ 404.1589, 404.1590(g), 416.989, 416.990(g).

Since mid-1984, the Social Security Administration's policy has been to review administrative hearing decisions on an essentially random basis. Although the Administration's earlier policy was challenged and criticized by some courts, its present policy has been upheld:

Plaintiffs have made more than a colorable showing that the [CDR] program was in its initial stages a potentially prejudicial one in its effect on the impartiality of ALJs. We are not persuaded, however, that plaintiffs have made a similar showing, much less demonstrated a likelihood of succeeding on the merits, with respect to the [CDR] program as it currently exists. While we recognize that changes to the program have been made on an "interim" basis, the present policy simply does not create the dangers of bias or lack of impartiality in the ALJ decisionmaking process which the original program may have entailed. Plaintiffs have failed to show why the present policy does not achieve the legitimate purposes of agency review and supervision in a lawful manner.

Stieberger v. Heckler, 615 F. Supp. 1315, 1386-98, 11 Soc. Sec. Rep. Serv. 383 (S.D. N.Y. 1985), vacated on other grounds, 801 F.2d 29, 15 Soc. Sec. Rep. Serv. 104 (2d Cir. 1986)

Congress increased funding for CDRs in 1996. Along with this increase in funding, Congress enacted legislation adding mandates for the performance of CDRs, including reporting requirements for the Commissioner of Social Security and regular reviews to evaluate the continuing eligibility of children receiving SSI benefits. Despite some initial success, by 2003 a backlog in CDR cases had reappeared, and the SSA has continued to experience significant increases in its CDR workload. "SSA has reported that . . . the overall number of CDRs conducted annually had decreased by approximately 65 percent between fiscal years 2004 and 2008. As a result, the number of pending CDRs has increased. SSA's OIG reported in March 2010 that at the end of fiscal year 2009, SSA had a backlog of almost 1.5 million CDRs. Even with the increase in performance that SSA expects to achieve in fiscal years 2010 and 2011, the OIG estimated a CDR pending workload of over 1.5 million through 2011." Social Security Disability: Management of Disability Claims Workload Will Require Comprehensive Planning, GAO-10-667T April 27, 2010 (citing Social Security Administration, Office of the Inspector General, Full Medical Continuing Disability Reviews: Evaluation Report, A-07-09-29147 (Mar. 30, 2010)).

After a case is chosen for review, the file is sent by SSA to the state Disability Determination Section, which then notifies the recipient that a review has been undertaken. The notice includes a form requesting information on the recipient's current ability to work and about doctors he or she has seen recently. *See generally* **20 C.F.R. §§ <u>404.1589</u>, <u>416.989</u>[APP-REGS]**. If the information is not detailed enough or if the recipient has not had recent medical treatment, a consultative examination may be ordered. *See* 20 C.F.R. §§ 404.1593(c), 416.993(c). In termination of disability proceedings based on medical improvement, the regulations establish an eight-step procedure that must be followed. *See* 20 C.F.R. §§ 404.1594(f). *See also* 20 C.F.R. § 416.994(b)(5) (set out in seven steps). If SSA decides, on the basis of the record prepared for the review, that a recipient is no longer disabled, it sends a notice to the recipient that benefits will be terminated unless additional information establishing continuing disability is sent within the next 10 days. *See* 20 C.F.R. §§ 404.1594, 404.1595, 416.995, 416.1331(b). The notice must include a statement of the evidence upon which the decision to terminate was based. 20 C.F.R. §§ 404.1595(a), 416.995. A claimant's benefits can be suspended for failure to cooperate with a request for additional information, and can be terminated after twelve months of suspension if the claimant continues not to cooperate. 20 C.F.R. §§ 404.1587, 416.992.

B) TRIAL WORK PERIOD

Some recipients of Disability Insurance Benefits are entitled to a nine-month "trial work period" during which they can test their ability to work without losing their eligibility for benefits or having their payments suspended. *See generally* 42 U.S.C. §§ 422(c), 423(a); **20 C.F.R. §** 404.1592**[APP-REGS]**. The regulations also extend the trial work period to surviving spouses, widows and widowers, and disabled adult children who are receiving Disability Insurance benefits on their spouse's or parent's earnings record. 20 C.F.R. § 404.1592(d). Trial work periods are intended "to encourage persons whose statutory disability is in issue to try to rehabilitate themselves so that they may again engage in gainful activity." Sigmon v. Califano, 617 F.2d 41, 43 (4th Cir. 1980). *See also* Fabel v. Shalala, 891 F.Supp. 202, 204 (D.N.J. 1995). Recipients are entitled to only a single trial work period during any one period of eligibility for benefits. 20 C.F.R. § 404.1592(c).

There is no similar provision in the Supplemental Security Income program. The trial work period provision for SSI, 42 U.S.C. § 1382c, was amended in 1986 by the Employment Opportunities for Disabled Americans Act to eliminate the availability of trial work periods for SSI benefit recipients. *See* Employment Opportunities for Disabled Americans Act, Pub.L. No. 99-643, 100 Stat. 3574 (1986). However, SSI recipients who work despite a disabling impairment may be eligible for special cash benefits and continuing Medicaid coverage if their gross income exceeds the amount that ordinarily represents substantial gainful activity. *See* 42 U.S.C.A. § 1382h(a)(1). *See also* 20 C.F.R. § 416.260-.269; Employment Opportunities for Disabled Americans Act, S. Rep. No. 466, 99th Cong., 2nd Sess. 1986, 1986 U.S.C.C.A.N. 6087 (Sept. 22, 1986) (noting that "[w]hile this, in effect, means that an individual loses SSI eligibility in any month in which he demonstrates the ability to engage in substantial gainful activity, there is no actual loss to the individual since he automatically moves into special benefit status (unless his earnings are high enough to raise his total countable income above the level of eligibility for that status.)"). The Social Security Adiministration makes determinations regarding receipt of such benefits automatically, without requiring application by claimants. 20 C.F.R. § 416.263. SSA has adopted regulations describing the rules for determining eligibility for special SSI cash benefits and for special SSI eligibility status for an individual who works despite a disabling impairment. 20 C.F.R. § 416.260-.269. The legislative history suggests that a different program was put into place for SSI recipients because SSI deals with individuals who are particularly vulnerable to financial hardships. "On the other hand, terminating benefits in such circumstances can be a powerful disincentive to the work efforts which these severely disabled individuals are otherwise motivated to attempt. This is particularly a problem where supplemental security income eligibility (with its concomitant eligibility for Medicaid) is concerned. By definition, these programs deal with individuals who have limited resources to fall back on should their work attempts fail or prove insufficient to meet their medical and other needs." Employment Opportunities for Disabled Americans Act, S. Rep. No. 466, *supra*. Thus, the special eligibility status for SSI recipients operates much like the trial work period rules to remove disincentives to work efforts by benefit recipients.

According to Social Security Administration policy, the trial work period rules apply only after the beneficiary becomes entitled to benefits. *See* 20 C.F.R. § 404.1592(e); SSR 82-52 (1982). The Administration published final regulations in 2000 consistent with this policy, which state that an individual is not entitled to a trial work period if he or she "perform[s] work demonstrating the ability to engage in substantial gainful activity within 12 months of the onset of the impairment(s) that prevented [the claimant] from performing substantial gainful activity and before the date of any notice of determination or decision finding that [the claimant is] disabled." 20 C.F.R. § 404.1592(d)(2)(iii); *see also* Bindley v. Callahan, 962 F. Supp. 1372, 1379, 53 Soc. Sec. Rep. Serv. 440 (D. Kan. 1997) (trial work period not applicable because claimant "was not, at the time of her employment, receiving disability insurance benefits"). Similarly, a trial work period does not apply to employment that occurred before the claimant applied for benefits. *See* 20 C.F.R. § 404.1592(e); Ziff v. Chater, 930 F. Supp. 1356, 1358-59, 51 Soc. Sec. Rep. Serv. 369 (N.D. Cal. 1996). Current policy has been upheld by the Supreme Court in the face of challenges arguing that the trial work period should be available earlier. *See* Barnhart v. Walton, 535 U.S. 212 79 Soc. Sec. Rep. Serv. 1 (2002):

> For purposes of making [his] claim, Walton [the claimant] assumes what we have just decided, namely, that the statute's "12 month" duration requirements apply to both the "impairment" and the "inability" to work requirements. Walton also concedes that he returned to work after 11 months. But Walton claims that his work from month 11 to month 12 does not count against him because it is part of a "trial work" period that the statute grants to those "entitled" to Title II benefits. See 42 U.S.C. § 422(c). And Walton adds, he was "entitle[d]" to benefits because—even though he returned to work after 11

months—his "impairment" and his "inability" to work were nonetheless *"expected* to last" for at least "12 months" *before* he returned to work.

To illustrate Walton's argument, we simplify the actual circumstances. We imagine: (1) On January 1, Year One, Walton developed (a) a severe impairment, which (b) made him unable to work; (2) Eleven (not twelve) months later, on December 1, Year One, Walton returned to work; (3) On July 1, Year Two, the Agency adjudicated, and denied, Walton's claim for benefits. Walton argues that, even though he returned to work after 11 months, had the Agency looked at the matter, not *ex post*, but as if it were looking *prior* to his return to work, the Agency would have had to conclude that both his "impairment" and his "inability" to work *"can be expected* to last for a continuous period of not less than 12 months." § 423(d)(1)(A). * * *

The Agency's regulations plainly reject this view of the statute. They say, "You are *not entitled* to a trial work period" if "you perform work ... within 12 months of the onset of the impairment(s) ... *and before* the date of *any* notice of determination *or decision finding ... you ... disabled.*" 20 CFR § 404.1592(d)(2) (2001). This regulation means that the Agency, deciding before the end of Year One, might have found that Walton's impairment (or inability to work) *"can be* expected to last" for 12 months. But the Agency, deciding after Year One in which Walton in fact returned to work, would not ask whether his impairment (or inability to work) *could have been* expected to last 12 months.

* * *

Nonetheless, we believe that Agency regulation is lawful.

Barnhart v. Walton, 535 U.S. at 222-24.

As mentioned above, the purpose of trial work periods is to give disabled recipients a period of time in which to test their ability to work. The trial work period extends for up to nine months, which do not have to be consecutive. 20 C.F.R. §§ 404.1592(a); *see also* Love v. Heckler, 564 F. Supp. 195, 197-98, 2 Soc. Sec. Rep. Serv. 789 (W.D. N.C. 1983) (two periods of three and five months). In Castillo v. Bowen, 645 F. Supp. 501, 504, 15 Soc. Sec. Rep. Serv. 569 (D. Or. 1986), for example, the court affirmed an ALJ's findings that the claimant had completed a nine-month trial work period that consisted of six one-month and one three-month periods:

The ALJ noted that the Secretary's regulations specify that services earning at least $50.00 per month prior to 1979 should be considered in determining whether an individual had completed a nine month trial work period. 20 C.F.R. § 404.1592. After 1979, services earning at least $75.00 per month were to be considered.

When an individual completes nine months of work earning at least these amounts, then he has completed a trial work period. The months need not be consecutive. Id. In determining whether plaintiff had completed a nine month trial work period the ALJ noted that he had earned $100.00 in November 1975; $135.00 in December 1975; $87.45 in January 1976; $875.00 in June 1978; $188.00 in October 1978; $1,704.00 in December 1978; and that he averaged in excess of $350.00 for the first three months of 1979. These earnings, the ALJ found, constituted plaintiff's trial work period. This finding is supported by the evidence presented at the hearing and contained in the record. I therefore affirm the ALJ's finding that plaintiff completed a nine month trial work period in March 1979.

Although SSA may not consider any work performed during the trial work period as evidence that a recipient's disability has ended, it may use proof of work during a trial work period as evidence that the disability ended after the end of the trial work period. 20 C.F.R. § 404.1592(a). Benefits may be terminated during the trial work period, however, if other evidence not related to work done during the trial work period shows that a disability has ended. 20 C.F.R. §§ 404.1592(a), 404.1592(e)(3). *But see* Wilson v. Shalala, 841 F. Supp. 1491, 1497, 43 Soc. Sec. Rep. Serv. 554 (E.D. Wash. 1994) ("record does not reflect any 'medical or other' evidence that plaintiff was no longer disabled" during the trial work period) (quoting 20 C.F.R. § 404.1592(e)(2), now at 20 C.F.R. § 404.1592(e)(3)). Such evidence must be separate from proof that the recipient actually engaged in substantial gainful activity during the work period. *See* Hancock v. Barnhart, 206 F. Supp. 2d 757, 766, 81 Soc. Sec. Rep. Serv. 561 (W.D. Va. 2002) (claimant's own testimony concerning his ability to work during trial work period can be considered, as opposed to "evidence of work itself"). *Cf.* Love v. Heckler, 564 F. Supp. 195, 198, 2 Soc. Sec. Rep. Serv. 789 (W.D. N.C. 1983) (administrative law judge based decision on eight months of employment during trial work period and not on independent medical evidence).

Services that trigger the trial work period include any activity done for pay or profit, whether legal or illegal, that produce earnings of a certain amount. The earnings threshold is based on set amounts for certain years and a formula for years after 2002. 20 C.F.R. § 404.1592(b). The amount set for 2012 is $720 per month. The work must have been performed with reasonable regularity and over a reasonable period of time. *See* White v. Heckler, 740 F.2d 390, 395, 6 Soc. Sec. Rep. Serv. 170 (5th Cir. 1984) (three-day job and "abortive two-month attempt to return to work" not counted as part of trial work period); LaPierre v. Callahan, 982

F. Supp. 789, 791-92, 54 Soc. Sec. Rep. Serv. 742 (W.D. Wash. 1997) (short-term job that claimant could not perform safely or consistently did not start trial work period). Moreover, the work activity must itself be substantial gainful employment. *See, e.g.,* Scott v. Commissioner, 899 F. Supp. 275, 279, 49 Soc. Sec. Rep. Serv. 271 (S.D. W. Va. 1995) (earnings from job created for claimant by relatives and required little work may constitute a subsidy, and therefore not trial work). Services do not include volunteer work, therapy, training, daily household chores, or self-care. 20 C.F.R. § 404.1592(b); *see also* Lamkin v. Bowen, 721 F. Supp. 263, 265-70, 27 Soc. Sec. Rep. Serv. 407 (D. Colo. 1989) (on-the-job training not trial work).

C) RE-ENTITLEMENT PERIOD

As further encouragement for disabled persons to work, regulations authorize a 36-month "reentitlement period" for beneficiaries who have completed their nine-month trial work period. *See generally* **20 C.F.R. § 404.1592a[APP-REGS]**. The idea is to allow beneficiaries to try to work without losing their eligibility if they cannot continue working. SSA will determine that a beneficiary's disability ceased if he or she engages in substantial gainful employment during the reentitlement period, but benefits will be paid for the first three months regardless of whether the person is working or not. After those three months, benefits will continue to be paid for any other months during which the beneficiary does not engage in substantial gainful activity. Moreover, beneficiaries who stop working altogether during that period can be reinstated without having to reapply.

3. PERIOD OF DISABILITY

Closely related to, but separate from, eligibility for disability benefits is a "period of disability," often referred to as a "disability freeze." A period of disability is simply a continuous period of time during which an individual is disabled according to the Social Security disability standard. 42 U.S.C. § 416(i)(2)(A); 20 C.F.R. § 404.320(a). In order to be entitled to a period of disability, one must also be insured for disability during that time and it must last at least five months. See 20 C.F.R. § 404.320(b); *see also* 42 U.S.C. § 416(i)(2). An application for a period of disability must be filed within 12 months after the period ended. *See* 20 C.F.R. §404.320(b).

The purpose of a period of disability is to establish, for various administrative purposes, that the claimant was indeed disabled at that time—regardless of whether he or she was eligible to receive benefits. 20 C.F.R. § 404.320(a). A period of disability can be used, for example, to toll the 20/40 requirement, which has the effect of extending a claimant's disability insured status. *See* 20 C.F.R. §404.131(a). As the court stated in

George v. Chater, 76 F.3d 675, 677, 50 Soc. Sec. Rep. Serv. 152 (5th Cir. 1996), 20 C.F.R. §404.320(a) "contemplates applications [for a period of disability] by individuals . . . who file only to extend their insured status." A period of disability can also be helpful when calculating the amount of benefits. As explained further in Chapter 7, the primary insurance amount (PIA) formula on which benefit amounts are based removes periods of disability from the calculation, rather than treating that period as including potentially harmful no-work quarters. And the five-month waiting period—applicable to most claims for Disability Insurance Benefits—does not apply to anyone who was entitled to Disability Insurance Benefits or to a "period of disability" during the five years prior to the month the claimant again became disabled. 20 C.F.R. §404.315(a)(4).

NOTES

1. As noted earlier, Congress amended the Social Security Act in 1990 to conform the disability standard for Spouses Insurance Benefits to that applied to Disability Insurance Benefits and Supplemental Security Income. However, the change is effective only with respect to periods of disability after January 1, 1991. Therefore, for any claim filed by a surviving spouse that includes an alleged period of disability prior to 1991, the claimant's disability during the period prior to 1991 is evaluated according to the pre-1991 standard. 20 C.F.R. §404.1577.

2. Administrative res judicata can apply to any alleged period of disability that was adjudicated fully before, if the same period is included in a subsequent application for benefits. *See, e.g.*, Macera v. Barnhart, 305 F. Supp. 2d 410, 412, 95 Soc. Sec. Rep. Serv. 529 (D. Del. 2004); Higgins v. Apfel, 136 F. Supp. 2d 971, 973, 73 Soc. Sec. Rep. Serv. 510 (E.D. Mo. 2001).

E. DEPENDENT AND SURVIVORS COVERAGE

When the Social Security Act was enacted in 1935, benefits were payable under the social insurance title only to retired wage earners. Benefits for wage earners' spouses were added to the Act in 1939, as the first part of an expansion of coverage that was designed to break away from the original goal of providing benefits only to wage earners based on their own earnings record. Today, the Old Age, Survivors, and Disability Insurance (OASDI) program provides a wide variety of secondary benefit payments to spouses, children, and even parents of wage earners, all based on the wage earner's earnings record. The overriding purpose of these secondary benefits is to provide a source of income to those people most likely to have relied on the wage earner for support. Eligibility requirements for these programs are discussed further in Chapter 3.

As we saw in Chapter 1, the expansion of secondary benefits began in the context of social policy that assumed the male as breadwinner and his wife as the dependent—but has since accommodated cultural shifts to provide benefits for dependent husbands and widowers as well. Thus, subject to certain conditions, spouses (and divorced spouses), surviving spouses (and surviving divorced spouses), parents, and children of insured wage earners may be eligible for old age or disability benefits on the basis of the worker's earnings record. The spouse of someone entitled to old age benefits can also receive OASDI old age benefits on the basis of the spouse's earnings, starting at the age of 62, and disability benefits starting at age 50; surviving spouses can receive benefits at the age of 60. See 42 U.S.C. §§ 402 (b), (c), (e), (f). Surviving parents may be eligible, under certain special circumstances, from the age of 62. See 42 U.S.C. §§ 402 (h). In addition, secondary benefits are available for a wage earner's surviving children and, so long as the child is eligible for benefits, the child's surviving caretaker parent.

There is no "survivors" concept in the Supplemental Security Income (SSI) program. Surviving spouses, children, and divorced spouses who meet the income and resources requirements will qualify for SSI on the same basis as any other person, without regard to their relationship to, or the earnings record of, their deceased spouse, former spouse, or parent.

CHAPTER 3

ELIGIBILITY CRITERIA FOR OLD AGE AND SURVIVORS BENEFITS

■ ■ ■

As noted in Chapter 2, eligibility requirements for benefits under the two key benefit titles of the Social Security Act—Title II, governing the Old Age, Survivors, and Disability Insurance Program (OASDI), and Title XVI, governing the Supplemental Security Income Program (SSI)—include both financial and personal criteria. The financial criteria for OASDI and SSI eligibility—insurance status for the former program, limited income and resources for the latter—were covered in some detail in that chapter. This chapter covers the personal criteria for the old-age programs under both titles and the survivors benefit programs under Title II. The personal criteria for the disability programs under both titles are covered separately and in significantly more detail in Chapters 4-6.

The rest of this chapter is divided into two sections. The chapter begins with old age programs, including OASDI benefits for wage earners and SSI benefits for financially qualified individuals. It also covers issues relating to proof of age for purposes of both types of old age benefits.

The second section focuses on the eligibility criteria for OASDI survivors benefits. As noted in Chapter 1, during the first four years of the Social Security program, benefits were available only to primary wage earners. But in 1939, Congress expanded the program to include some of a covered wage earner's family members as beneficiaries. These secondary benefits, referred to formally as "survivors benefits," are paid to certain survivors and dependents of covered workers. Those eligible for survivors benefits can include a wage earner's spouse (including some former spouses), children, and parents. The section on survivors benefits is divided into subsections on spouses' and widow(er)s' benefits, including coverage of who qualifies as a spouse or widow(er) and the evidentiary requirements for proving marriage; on children's insurance benefits, exploring the types of relationships that qualify for entitlement in this category, the requirement that the child be dependent on the insured, and the evidence that is required to prove the parent-child relationship and dependency; and on benefits based on one's status as a parent, including "mother's and father's benefits" for caretaker parents of a wage earner's child and "parent's benefits" for a wage earner's parents.

A. OLD AGE BENEFITS

While both OASDI and SSI provide benefits on the basis of old age, the two programs differ in substantial ways that reflect the differences between social insurance and public assistance. Thus, OASDI benefits are available only to persons who worked and paid Social Security taxes in a sufficient amount and over a sufficiently long period of time to become "insured"; SSI benefits, by contrast, are available to persons with limited income and resources, independent of any work history. (These requirements are explained in detail in Chapter 2.) Consistent with this difference, the amount of an OASDI benefit is determined by a formula that is based in part on the amount of Social Security taxes paid; SSI benefits, on the other hand, are calculated to meet basic financial needs. (The methods for calculating OASDI and SSI benefits are discussed in detail in Chapter 7.)

Insured wage earners and properly qualified low income individuals are thus eligible for benefits based on their age. Because OASDI old age benefits are designed to insure against wage loss due to old age, the age requirement is based on the concept of retirement age. There is a similar, but simpler, age requirement for SSI old age benefits.

1. OASDI RETIREMENT AGE

The OASDI age requirement for insured wage earners is in two parts: early and full retirement. Until recently, the full retirement age was 65—the same age established for old age benefits in the original Social Security Act (which was based, in turn, on the age set in the nineteenth century by Chancellor Otto von Bismarck for the first modern Social Security system in Germany). However, beginning in 2003, the full retirement age began increasing gradually to 66, and beginning in 2020 it will begin increasing again from 66 to 67. The Act sets out the following schedule for when full retirement benefits may be received, based on the year a claimant reaches the age of 62 (which is, as explained below, the youngest age that qualifies for early retirement):

Year an individual reaches age 62:	The individual's full retirement age is:
1999 or earlier	65
2000	65 and 2 months
2001	65 and 4 months

2002	65 and 6 months
2003	65 and 8 months
2004	65 and 10 months
2005-2016	66
2017	66 and 2 months
2018	66 and 4 months
2019	66 and 6 months
2020	66 and 8 months
2021	66 and 10 months
2022 and after	67

See 42 U.S.C. § 402(a); 20 C.F.R. § 404.2(c)(4).

Thus, as a practical matter, the full retirement age has been 66 since 2009 (that is, for persons who reached the age of 62 in 2005); starting in 2021 (that is, for persons who reached the age of 62 in 2017), the full retirement age will begin to creep up to 67; and by 2027 (that is, for persons who reached the age of 62 in 2022), the full retirement age will be 67. The Social Security Administration has published a chart that shows the full retirement age according to one's year of birth:

Year of Birth	*Full Retirement Ages*:
1937 or earlier	65
1938	65 and 2 months
1939	65 and 4 months
1940	65 and 6 months
1941	65 and 8 months
1942	65 and 10 months
1943-1954	66
1955	66 and 2 months

1956	66 and 4 months
1957	66 and 6 months
1958	66 and 8 months
1959	66 and 10 months
1960 and later	67

See http://www.ssa.gov/pubs/retirechart.htm.

A second option is to receive early retirement benefits. Regardless of wage earners' full retirement age, they can start receiving benefits as early as age 62. 42 U.S.C. § 402(a); 20 C.F.R. § 404.2(c)(4). However, if the choice is made to retire before one's full retirement age, benefits are reduced by a fraction of a percent for each month of retirement before full retirement age. On the other hand, if an individual retires after their full retirement age, the monthly payments will be larger (to make up for the months when the individual was not receiving benefits). These rules and others are explained in detail in Chapter 7.

2. SSI AGE REQUIREMENT

SSI old age benefits are available at age 65. 42 U.S.C. § 1381. Congress has not increased the age requirement for SSI benefits and there is no option to receive a lesser amount at an earlier age.

3. PROOF OF AGE

An individual applying for old age benefits will be asked for proof that shows the claimant's date of birth. 20 C.F.R. §§ 404.715(a), 416.801. The rules governing the type of evidence required are somewhat different, however, for OASDI and SSI. The OASDI regulations distinguish between "preferred" and "other" evidence, while the SSI regulations are more detailed and complete. For OASDI, preferred evidence includes a birth certificate, hospital birth record, or a religious record showing the claimant's date of birth. In order for these records to constitute "preferred evidence," they must be recorded before age 5. If such records are not available, the claimant will be asked to provide other evidence of age, such as an original family bible or family record, school records, census records, a statement signed by the physician or midwife who was present at the claimant's birth, insurance policies, a marriage record, a passport, an employment record, a delayed birth certificate, or an immigration or naturalization record. *See* **20 C.F.R. § 404.716[APP-REGS]**.

For SSI, the requirements are more comprehensive. When determining whether an SSI applicant has reached the requisite age, SSA will give the highest probative value to a public record of birth or a religious record of birth or baptism established or recorded before the claimant reached age 5. If this is unavailable, the claimant must submit other evidence of age similar to those allowed for OASDI, such as a school record, bible or other family record, church record of baptism or confirmation while a child or young adult, marriage record, military record, delayed birth certificate, physician's or midwife's record of birth, immigration or naturalization record, or passport. In addition, SSI regulations provide explicitly that in determining the probative value of these other forms of evidence, consideration will be given to when the documents were established or recorded and the circumstances under which they were established or recorded. *See* **20 C.F.R. §§** 416.802, 416.803**[APP-REGS]**. The SSI regulations also provide for expedited adjudication of certain old age benefit claims. If an applicant alleges that he or she is at least 68 years old and submits any documentation supporting this allegation that is at least 3 years old—and if there is no evidence to the contrary—no further evidence of age will be required. *See* **20 C.F.R. §** 416.801, 416.806**[APP-REGS]**.

In most instances, proof of age is straightforward and uncontested. Nonetheless, in some cases the usual simple forms of documentation are not available and a claimant's age can be in dispute. In both of the following cases, the court confronted situations in which there was evidence to support two different birthdates. In addition to highlighting the way in which age may be disputed, these cases also show how the evidentiary requirements for proof of age are applied differently for OASDI and SSI claims. (The legal context of the SSI case was somewhat unusual; it involved an application for attorney's fees under the Equal Access to Justice Act—discussed in Chapter 8—which required the court to look at whether the government's position on the claim was "substantially justified.")

COLLIER V. APFEL

91 F.Supp.2d 904, 68 Soc. Sec. Rep. Ser. 463 (W.D.Va. 2000)

MICHAEL, Senior District Judge.

* * *

I.

In plaintiff's application for retirement benefits filed July 15, 1993 he stated that he was born on February 20, 1927. The defendant contests this assertion on the basis of the 1940 Census in Greene County, Virginia, which indicated that the plaintiff was a child in the family of Little Collier and was seven years old at the time. That would make his birth year

1932 or 1933. However, on March 25, 1980, the Circuit Court of the County of Albemarle entered an Order showing that the court considered evidence and decreed that the plaintiff was indeed born on February 20, 1927. As a consequence of the Circuit Court's Order, the Virginia Department of Health, Bureau of Vital Records and Health Statistics changed the plaintiff's birth records to reflect this judicially determined birth date. The record further contains, *inter alia*, affidavits by various relatives or friends of the plaintiff's who testified under oath that his birthday was February 20, 1927. Additionally, the plaintiff's drivers license issued on February 16, 1993 shows a date of birth of February 20, 1927.

On May 16, 1995, an Administrative Law Judge entered a decision declaring that the evidence of record best supports a February 20, 1927 date of birth, and that the plaintiff was entitled to retirement benefits. However, on June 30, 1998, the Appeals Council reversed the ALJ's decision, relying on the 1940 Federal Census.

II.

Judicial review here is limited to determining whether substantial evidence supported the administrative decision. See Estep v. Richardson, 459 F.2d 1015, 1016 (4th Cir.1972) (recognizing that the administrative decision, "if supported by substantial evidence, must be affirmed even though the reviewing court believes that substantial evidence also supports a contrary result"); Lowrey v. Chater, No. 96-2832, 1997 WL 467523, *1 (4th Cir. Aug.15, 1997) ("It is the [agency's] responsibility to resolve conflicts in the evidence; not the reviewing court's"). Substantial evidence is "more than a mere scintilla" of evidence, but only such evidence "as a reasonable mind might accept as adequate to support a conclusion." See Stroup v. Apfel, No. 96-1722, 2000 WL 216620 (4th Cir. Feb.24, 2000) (quoting Richardson v. Perales, 402 U.S. 389, 401, 91 S.Ct. 1420, 28 L.Ed.2d 842 (1971)).

In order to establish age, a claimant may produce preferred evidence which consists of: "a birth certificate or hospital birth record recorded before age of 5; or a religious record which shows [the plaintiff's] date of birth and was recorded before age 5." 20 C.F.R. § 404.716(a)(West 2000). Preferred evidence is conclusive absent substantial evidence casting doubt as to its accuracy. The Magistrate Judge placed great weight in the state judicial proceeding determining February 20, 1927 as the date the plaintiff was born. The Magistrate stated "whether the birth official certificate contains the birth date actually recorded at the time of birth or one judicially ordered to be reflected on the certificate issued by the state statistical agency, both constitute preferred evidence under the Commissioner's regulation." This court agrees with the fundamental notion of

the Magistrate's statement; however, evidence is only preferred if the judicially ordered date is recorded within the five year limit set forth in the
regulations. In the present case, the court-ordered date was not determined until 1980, undisputably several decades after the plaintiff's date
of birth. As such, the plaintiff's delayed birth certificate does not qualify
as preferred evidence.

When a plaintiff is unable to establish preferred evidence, other evidence of age has to be considered. Other convincing evidence could include: "an original family bible or family record; school records; census
records; a statement signed by the physician or midwife who was present
at your birth; insurance policies; a marriage record; a passport; an employment record; a delayed birth certificate; your child's birth certificate;
or an immigration or naturalization record." § 404.716(b). The Appeals
Council gave controlling import to the 1940 Census information rather
than the abundance of other evidence establishing the birth year to be
1927, including the delayed birth certificate. The court found that the
1940 Census was the oldest document recorded closest to the plaintiff's
birth and that the information on this document was provided by his
mother. Whereas, the affidavits of friends, family and doctors were based
on the memory of individuals. It was similar memory testimony that was
produced before the Circuit Court when it determined that the plaintiff's
correct birthday was February 20, 1927. The Appeals Council rational-
ized that older recorded evidence is more valuable than more recent
statements based on memory. Though this court agrees with the Magistrate Judge that the pre-war census information was more than likely not
as accurate as the Appeals Council supposes, the census does provide
substantial evidence that the plaintiff was not born until 1932 or 1933.
As a reviewing court is unable to reweigh the evidence before it, this court
finds that it must sustain the defendant's objection.

III.

The Appeals Council analyzed the relevant evidence in this case and
sufficiently explained its rationale in crediting certain evidence. A reasonable mind might accept such rationale as adequate in supporting the
Appeals Council's conclusion that the plaintiff was born in 1932 or 1933,
even if the court determines that the contrary result is also supported by
substantial evidence. As such, this court must sustain the defendant's
objection to the Magistrate Judge's Report and Recommendation.

An appropriate order this day shall issue.

* * *

YANG V. SHALALA

22 F.3d 213, 44 Soc. Sec. Rep. Ser. 337 (9th Cir. 1994)

WIGGINS, Circuit Judge:

Lia Yang moved for attorneys' fees under the Equal Access to Justice Act (EAJA). The district court denied her motion, finding that the position of the Secretary of Health and Human Services (Secretary) was substantially justified. Yang appeals. * * * We reverse and remand.

I.

Yang was born in Laos, apparently on September 24, 1919. She is a member of the Hmong tribe, an ethnic and language minority indigenous to remote areas within Laos. No birth certificate was prepared at the time of her birth. According to Yang, a birth record was prepared for her in 1962 pursuant to a law passed by the Laotian government in 1955. This birth record shows a September 24, 1919 date of birth.

Yang fled Laos after the Vietnamese invaded. In the process of fleeing, she left behind all of her possessions, including the birth record prepared in 1962. She entered a refugee camp in Thailand where her year of birth was recorded as 1929.

Yang was granted entry into the United States and arrived in December of 1979. Her original immigration papers recorded her year of birth as 1929. Her initial Social Security Number application apparently also marked her year of birth as 1929. This initial Social Security Number application is not in the administrative record, nor has it ever been produced by the Social Security Administration (SSA). Later, her son mailed to her the Laotian birth record prepared in 1962. Yang had her immigration papers and Social Security record amended to reflect her apparently correct year of birth, 1919.

On September 10, 1984, Yang applied for supplemental security income (SSI) benefits based on age under Title XVI of the Social Security Act (the Act). Her claim for SSI benefits was granted and she began receiving payments. Yang then moved from Washington to California, and applied for a replacement social security card. Questioning her Laotian birth record, the California office sent it with a translation request to the SSA's Central Translation Services office. The translation was completed and returned, and made no note of any irregularity. Nevertheless, the California office rejected the Laotian birth record. Yang's SSI benefits were terminated because the SSA decided that she was not yet 65 years of age.

Yang moved for reconsideration, which was denied. Yang requested de novo review by an administrative law judge (ALJ). She offered five forms of evidence in support of her 1919 birth date: (1) her Laotian birth record prepared in 1962; (2) an order of the California Superior Court establishing her date of birth as September 14, 1919; (3) the declaration of a former Laotian judge supporting the authenticity of the Laotian birth record; (4) her own testimony that she arrived in the United States as a refugee, having left behind all of her possessions, including her Laotian birth record, when she fled Laos during the Vietnamese invasion; and (5) testimony from two of her sons corroborating her testimony. Nonetheless, the ALJ affirmed. The ALJ held that the evidence that she was born in 1919 was insufficient to offset the evidence that she was born in 1929. Specifically, the ALJ found that the initial Social Security Number application was determinative. * * *

Yang challenged the Secretary's decision in the district court. The district court referred to Magistrate Christensen the cross-motions for summary judgment. The magistrate issued his recommendation that the case be remanded for further proceedings. The magistrate concluded that the ALJ should have given "full faith and credit" to the state court order. The magistrate explained, "While such state court order is not binding and does not preclude the Secretary from an independent weighing of the evidence, the Secretary, however, must start the weighing process by presuming that claimant was born on September 14, 1919." The magistrate found that the ALJ further erred by placing so much weight on the initial Social Security Number application because it did not appear in the administrative record. The district court adopted the magistrate's recommendation on July 25, 1988.

On remand, the ALJ determined that there was no evidence to rebut the presumption that Yang's year of birth is 1919. The Appeals Council agreed that her SSI benefits should be reinstated. On May 11, 1989, the district court adopted the Appeals Council decision and entered judgment in Yang's favor.

On June 9, 1989, Yang filed her application for attorneys' fees under the EAJA, 28 U.S.C. § 2412(d)(1)(A). The Secretary opposed the EAJA application on the ground that the Secretary's position was substantially justified. On July 28, 1989, the district court denied Yang's application for attorneys' fees on the ground that the motion was not timely filed.

* * *

II.

A. Was Yang's Application for EAJA attorneys' fees timely filed?

[The court found that the motion was timely filed.]

B. Was the Secretary's Position Substantially Justified?

* * *

* * * The Secretary's position was not supported by a reasonable basis in law. First, she failed to make her determination on the basis of evidence adduced at the hearing. Specifically, the Secretary assigned great probative weight to the initial Social Security Number application, which did not appear in the administrative record. Furthermore, the Secretary declined to give any weight to the state court order, which did appear in the record. This failure by the Secretary to make her determination on the basis of evidence adduced at the hearing deprived Yang of her due process rights. In addition, the Secretary's failure to make her determination on the basis of evidence adduced at the hearing also violated the Act and a SSA regulation.

Second, the Secretary violated other SSA regulations. See 20 C.F.R. § 416.801-806 (evaluating the probativeness of different types of evidence of age). For example, the Secretary failed to require that evidence other than a public or religious record established before the claimant's fifth birthday be corroborated by other evidence in the administrative record. See 20 C.F.R. § 416.802. Specifically, the Secretary found determinative the initial Social Security Number application, which was not corroborated. Indeed, the evidence itself was not even in the record. (Moreover, the Secretary ignored the Laotian birth record prepared in 1962, which was corroborated by several sources. And, the Laotian birth record had been accepted as authentic by a California state court and the Immigration and Naturalization Service.) Similarly, the Secretary failed to accept a "delayed birth certificate" as evidence of age. See 20 C.F.R. § 416.803. Specifically, the Secretary rejected Yang's Laotian birth record prepared in 1962 as evidence that she was born in 1919.

Thus, the Secretary's position was based on violations of the Constitution, the Act, and several SSA regulations. Accordingly, we find that the district court abused its discretion by finding that the Secretary's position was reasonably based in law. Most importantly, the Secretary violated Yang's due process rights by not making the determination based on evidence adduced at the hearing. This denial of Yang's due process rights precludes a finding that the Secretary's position was substantially justified. * * *

CONCLUSION

For the foregoing reasons, we reverse. * * * We remand for a determination of the amount of EAJA attorneys' fees owed to Yang.

REVERSED and REMANDED.

B. SURVIVORS BENEFITS

As noted at the beginning of this chapter, eligibility for OASDI survivors benefits always begins with a "wage earner" upon whose earnings record—and insured status—other members of his or her family may, under certain circumstances, claim benefits as well. Benefits provided to wage earners' survivors and dependents include retirement and disability benefits for dependent and surviving spouses, retirement benefits for surviving parents, disability benefits for dependent and surviving children, and general allowances for dependent and surviving children and their caretaking parents. This section discusses the basic eligibility requirements for dependent and survivor benefits, apart from the insured status of the wage earner on whose earnings record the claim is based (discussed already in Chapter 2) and the requirements for establishing disability (which are discussed in Chapters 4-6). It is divided into sub-sections based on the family relationship to the wage earner: wage earners' dependent and surviving spouses, their children, and their parents.

1. SPOUSES AND WIDOW(ER)S BENEFITS

In general terms, the Social Security Act provides benefits to spouses or widow(er)s of insured workers who retire, become disabled, or die. Spouses constitute the largest number of secondary benefit recipients; in December, 2009, approximately 7 million people received OASDI benefits based on their status as a spouse or surviving spouse of a wage earner. Social Security Administration, Annual Statistical Supplement, 2009, Table 5.A4 (2011).

Unlike with other family relationships providing the basis for secondary OASDI benefits, independent proof of dependency is not required to receive spouses benefits. Instead, dependency is presumed—and then addressed in the structure of the entitlement: a spouse's secondary benefit is 50% of the wage earner's benefit; a widow(er)'s secondary benefit is the wage earner's full benefit. However, a spouse of a wage earner is entitled to OASDI secondary benefits only if the spouse is not entitled to primary benefits based on his or her own earnings record or, if the spouse is entitled to primary benefits, only when those benefits would be less than any secondary benefits the spouse would be entitled to based on the wage earner's earnings record. Thus, a spouse of a retired wage earner can receive secondary benefits only if the spouse's primary benefits are less than 50% of the retired wage earner's benefits, and a widow or widower can receive secondary benefits only if the spouse's primary benefits would be less than the amount that would be paid based on the now-deceased wage earner's earning record. Thus, if the spouse's primary OASDI benefits equal or exceed her or his secondary benefits, the spouse receives only the primary benefit. *See* 42 U.S.C. §§ 402(b), (c), (e), (f). As a result, individuals who are not dependent on their spouses—as evidenced by the benefits they are entitled to based on their own earnings records—are disqualified from receiving dependent spouses benefits.

This section looks first at the eligibility requirements for dependent spouses of retired or disabled workers. Next, it discusses the requirements for widows and widowers of insured workers. Finally, it examines the evidence required to prove the existence of a marriage or other spousal relationship between the wage earner and a claimant for secondary benefits based on the wage earner's earnings record.

A) ELIGIBILITY REQUIREMENTS FOR SPOUSES

Generally, the wife or husband of a wage earner is considered to be a "spouse" for purposes of receiving secondary benefits if he or she is the parent of the wage earner's child or was married to the wage earner for at least one year at the time the application was filed. In addition to current spouses, former spouses who are divorced from the wage earner may be entitled to benefits, if the marriage to the wage earner lasted at least ten years and the divorced spouse-claimant is unmarried. **42 U.S.C. § 416(b), (f)[APP-STAT].**

In addition, in order to qualify for spouses benefits the spouse must have reached a specified age. A spouse can receive OASDI old age benefits on the basis of his or her spouse's earnings starting at the age of 62—except that a spouse can begin receiving benefits at any age if he or she is caring for the wage earner's child who is younger than 16 or disabled and entitled to child's disability benefits based on the wage earner's earnings record. **42 U.S.C. § 402(b), (c)[APP-STAT].** However, eligibility for benefits as the parent caretaker of a wage earner's child does not extend to divorced spouses. In the following Supreme Court case, the claimant argued that this distinction arbitrarily discriminates against divorced spouses. The Court's decision not only rejects this claim but also discusses the policy behind the provision of benefits to dependent and surviving spouses.

MATHEWS V. DE CASTRO

429 U.S. 181 (1976)

Mr. Justice STEWART delivered the opinion of the Court.

Under the Social Security Act a married woman whose husband retires or becomes disabled is granted benefits if she has a minor or other dependent child in her care. A divorced woman whose former husband retires or becomes disabled does not receive such benefits. The issue in the present case is whether this difference in the statutory treatment of married and divorced women is permissible under the Fifth Amendment to the United States Constitution.

I

Section 202(b)(1) of the Social Security Act, 49 Stat. 623, as added and amended, 42 U.S.C. § 402(b)(1) (1970 ed. and Supp. V), provides for the payment of "wife's insurance benefits." To qualify under this section a woman must be the wife or "divorced wife" of an individual entitled to old-age or disability benefits. Then, assuming that she meets the other statutory requirements, the woman is eligible to receive a monthly payment if she "has attained age 62 or (in the case of a wife) has in her care (individually or jointly with (her husband)) at the time of filing such application a child entitled to a child's insurance benefit . . . ." 42 U.S.C. § 402(b)(1)(B) (emphasis supplied). As the italicized phrase indicates, a woman under 62 who has in her care an entitled child must currently be married to the wage earner in order to be eligible to receive benefits. A divorced woman receives monthly payments if she is 62 or over and her ex-husband retires or becomes disabled, but if she is under 62, she receives no benefits even if she has a young or disabled child in her care.

The appellee, Helen de Castro, was divorced from her husband in 1968, after more than 20 years of marriage. She cares for a disabled child who is eligible for and receives child's insurance benefits under the Act. In May 1971 her former husband applied for and later was granted old-age insurance benefits. Mrs. de Castro applied for wife's insurance benefits shortly thereafter. At the time of her application she was 56 years old. Her application was denied by the Secretary of Health, Education, and Welfare because no wife's benefits are payable to a divorced wife under 62 years of age.

Mrs. de Castro then filed suit in the United States District Court for the Northern District of Illinois, seeking judicial review of the Secretary's decision. Her complaint alleged that s 202(b)(1)(B) of the Social Security Act "operates to arbitrarily discriminate against divorced wives," and prayed for an order directing the Secretary to pay benefits to her, a declaration that s 202(b)(1)(B) is unconstitutional, and an injunction against that section's application.

A three-judge court was convened pursuant to 28 U.S.C. §§ 2281, 2282. The court considered the parties' cross-motions for summary judgment and granted the relief prayed for in the complaint, holding that the wife's benefits provision "invidiously discriminates against divorced wives . . . in violation of the Fifth Amendment." de Castro v. Weinberger, 403 F.Supp. 23, 30. Central to the court's ruling was its determination that "there is no rational basis for concluding that a married wife having a dependent child in her care has a greater economic need than a divorced wife caring for such a child." Id., at 28. The Secretary appealed directly to this Court under 28 U.S.C. s 1252, and we noted probable jurisdiction.

II

The basic principle that must govern an assessment of any constitutional challenge to a law providing for governmental payments of monetary benefits is well established. Governmental decisions to spend money to improve the general public welfare in one way and not another are "not confided to the courts. The discretion belongs to Congress, unless the choice is clearly wrong, a display of arbitrary power, not an exercise of judgment." Helvering v. Davis, 301 U.S. 619, 640, 57 S.Ct. 904, 908, 81 L.Ed. 1307. In enacting legislation of this kind a government does not deny equal protection "merely because the classifications made by its laws are imperfect. If the classification has some 'reasonable basis,' it does not offend the Constitution simply because the classification 'is not made with mathematical nicety or because in practice it results in some inequality.'" Dandridge v. Williams, 397 U.S. 471, 485, 90 S.Ct. 1153, 1161, 25 L.Ed.2d 491.

To be sure, the standard by which legislation such as this must be judged "is not a toothless one," Mathews v. Lucas, 427 U.S. 495, 510, 96 S.Ct. 2755, 49 L.Ed.2d 651. But the challenged statute is entitled to a strong presumption of constitutionality. "So long as its judgments are rational, and not invidious, the legislature's efforts to tackle the problems of the poor and the needy are not subject to a constitutional straitjacket." Jefferson v. Hackney, 406 U.S. 535, 546, 92 S.Ct. 1724, 1731, 32 L.Ed.2d 285. It is with this principle in mind that we consider the specific constitutional issue presented by this litigation.

The old-age and disability insurance aspects of the Social Security system do not purport to be general public assistance laws that simply pay money to those who need it most. That was not the predominant purpose of these benefit provisions when they were enacted or when they were amended. Rather, the primary objective was to provide workers and their families with basic protection against hardships created by the loss of earnings due to illness or old age.

The wife's insurance benefit at issue here is consistent with this overriding legislative aim: It enables a married woman already burdened with dependent children to meet the additional need created when her husband reaches old age or becomes disabled. Accordingly, the District

Court's observation that many divorced women receive inadequate child-support payments, while undoubtedly true, is hardly in point. The same can be said of the District Court's statement that "there is no rational basis for concluding that a married wife having a dependent child in her care has a greater economic need than a divorced wife caring for such a child." For whatever relevance these observations might have in a case involving a constitutional attack on a statute that gave monetary benefits to women based on their general overall need, that is not this case.

Section 202(b)(1)(B) of the Act addresses the particular consequences for his family of a wage earner's old age or disability. Congress could rationally have decided that the resultant loss of family income, the extra expense that often attends illness and old age, and the consequent disruption in the family's economic well-being that may occur when the husband stops working justify monthly payments to a wife who together with her husband must still care for a dependent child.

Indeed, Congress took note of exactly these kind of factors when it amended the Social Security Act in 1958. Between 1950 and 1958 wives under retirement age with dependent children received benefits only when their husbands became entitled to old-age insurance payments. Social Security Act Amendments of 1950, s 101(a), 64 Stat. 482. Congress then amended the Act to provide the same benefits when the wage earner becomes disabled.[7] Social Security Amendments of 1958, § 205(b)(1), 72 Stat. 1021. Both the House and Senate Committee reports accompanying the proposed legislation explained that the purpose of the monthly payments was to give "recognition to the problems confronting families whose bread winners" stop work. The focus was specifically on "adequate protection for (the husband's) family," and the reports mentioned the high medical expenses often associated with disability and the possibility that the wife might have to forgo work in order to care for her disabled husband. H.R.Rep. No. 2288, 85th Cong., 2d Sess., 12-13 (1958); S.Rep. No. 2388, 85th Cong., 2d Sess., 10-11 (1958), U.S.Code Cong. & Admin.News 1958, p. 4218.

In view of the legislative purpose, it is hardly surprising that the congressional judgment evidently was a different one with respect to divorced women. Divorce by its nature works a drastic change in the economic and personal relationship between a husband and wife. Ordinarily it means that they will go their separate ways. Congress could have ra-

---

[7] Certainly the sole purpose could not have been to allow the wife to remain at home to take care of the child, as the appellee suggests, because the presence of the retired husband at home ordinarily would ensure parental supervision. Similarly, when Congress provided benefits in 1958 to wives with disabled husbands, it had purposes beyond the mere encouragement of the wife to stay home and take care of the children. See H.R.Rep. No. 2288, 85th Cong., 2d Sess., 12-13 (1958); S.Rep. No. 2388, 85th Cong., 2d Sess., 10-11 (1958), U.S.Code Cong. & Admin.News 1958, p. 4218.

tionally assumed that divorced husbands and wives depend less on each other for financial and other support than do couples who stay married. The problems that a divorced wife may encounter when her former husband becomes old or disabled may well differ in kind and degree from those that a woman married to a retired or disabled husband must face. For instance, a divorced wife need not forgo work in order to stay at home to care for her disabled husband. She may not feel the pinch of the extra expenses accompanying her former husband's old age or disability. In short, divorced couples typically live separate lives. It was not irrational for Congress to recognize this basic fact in deciding to defer monthly payments to divorced wives of retired or disabled wage earners until they reach the age of 62.

This is not to say that a husband's old age or disability may never affect his divorced wife. Many women receive alimony or child support after divorce that their former husbands might not be able to pay when they stop work. But even for this group which does not include the appellee in the present case Congress was not constitutionally obligated to use the Social Security Act to subsidize support payments. It could rationally decide that the problems created for divorced women remained less pressing than those faced by women who continue to live with their husbands.

In any event, the constitutional question "is not whether a statutory provision precisely filters out those, and only those, who are in the factual position which generated the congressional concern reflected in the statute." Weinberger v. Salfi, 422 U.S. 749, 777, 95 S.Ct. 2457, 2472, 45 L.Ed.2d 522. We conclude, accordingly, that the statutory classifications involved in this case are not of such an order as to infringe upon the Due Process Clause of the Fifth Amendment.

The judgment is reversed.

[Justice Marshall concurred in the result.]

B) ELIGIBILITY REQUIREMENTS FOR WIDOW(ER)S

As with spouses of retired wage earners, spouses of deceased wage earners must meet certain statutory requirements in order to qualify for widow(er)'s secondary benefits. Surviving spouses qualify if they were married to the wage earner for at least nine months before the wage earner died or, if married less than nine months, they are the parent—or, with some qualifications, the adopted parent—of the wage earner's child (or if the deceased wage earner adopted the surviving spouse's child before the child turned 18). **42 U.S.C. § 416(c), (g)[APP-STAT]**. In addition, the spouse must not be married and must have reached the age of 60. Surviving spouses are also eligible for disability benefits, which they can start receiving at age 50. **42 U.S.C. § 402(3), (f)[APP-STAT]**. The disability requirement for these and other Social Security disability benefits are discussed in Chapter 4.

When survivors benefits were first included in the Social Security Act, there were separate dependency requirements for widower benefits that did not apply to widow benefits. As we saw in Chapter 1, that distinction was declared unconstitutional in Weinberger v. Wiesenfeld, 420 U.S. 636 (1975). *See also* Califano v. Goldfarb, 430 U.S. 199 (1977) (invalidating requirement that widowers—but not widows—prove dependency in order to receive surviving spouses benefits). Congress eventually removed the Act's gender-based distinctions. *See* Social Security Amendments of 1977, Pub. L. No. 95-216, § 334, 91 Stat. 1509, 1544; Social Security Amendments of 1983, Pub. L. No 98-21 §§ 301-310, 97 Stat. 65, 109-18.

C) PROOF OF MARRIAGE

The Social Security Administration determines spousal relationships based on whether the courts of the state in which the wage earner is domiciled at the time an application for benefits is filed would find that the claimant and the wage earner were validly married, either at the time the claim was filed or at the time the wage earner died. Even if this requirement is not met, an individual will be deemed a wage earner's spouse if he or she would have the same status as spouses with respect to the taking of personal property under the intestate law in the state in which the insured individual was domiciled at the time of the application or the wage earner's death. In addition, 1960 amendments assured that a purported marriage will be accepted when it can be established that the claimant in good faith went through a marriage ceremony that would have been valid but for a legal impediment not known to the claimant at the time. **42 U.S.C. § 416(h)(1)(A)-(B)[APP-STAT]**.

Federal regulations provide more detailed guidance regarding the types of evidence used to establish a spousal relationship and when such evidence is required. An individual who applies for spouses benefits will be asked to provide evidence of the marriage, including where and when the marriage took place. The type of evidence requested will depend upon whether the insured person's marriage was a ceremonial marriage, a common-law marriage, or a marriage "deemed to be valid." **20 C.F.R. § 404.723[APP-REGS]**.

The first type of marriage, a "ceremonial marriage," is one that follows procedures set by law in the state or foreign country where it took place. This can include a marriage that follows certain tribal or foreign customs. If a ceremonial marriage is claimed, SSA will request signed statements from the spouse and the insured regarding the time and location of the marriage. If other evidence creates doubt as to whether a ceremonial marriage took place, SSA may request other documentation, including copies of the public or religious marriage records, certified statements as to the marriage, or the original marriage certificate. If these types of "preferred evidence" are not obtainable, the claimant will be asked for an explanation why this is the case, a signed statement of the individual who conducted the marriage ceremony, and any other probative evidence of the marriage. **20 C.F.R. §** 404.725**[APP-REGS]**.

Another type of marriage is "common-law marriage," which is a marriage considered valid under certain state laws even though no formal ceremony took place. It is a marriage between two persons who are free to marry, who consider themselves married, live together, and in some states, meet certain other requirements. Preferred evidence of this type of marriage includes signed statements of the husband and wife, if they are still alive, or of blood relatives, explaining why the person who signed the statement believes that a marriage existed. If this preferred evidence cannot be obtained, SSA will request an explanation why this is the case as well as any other convincing evidence of the marriage. **20 C.F.R. §** 404.726**[APP-REGS]**.

Finally, a "deemed valid marriage" is one that, as mentioned earlier, would have been valid but for a legal impediment not known to the claimant at the time. If this is asserted, the regulations specify certain types of preferred evidence, including documentary evidence of the ceremonial marriage or signed statements by the wage earner or purported spouse stating that he or she went through the marriage ceremony in good faith and his or her reasons for believing the marriage was valid. In addition, if reasonable doubt exists as to the marriage, the claimant may be asked to produce signed statements from others showing how the purported marriage took place in good faith or evidence that the parties were living together when the application for benefits was filed or when the wage earner died. **20 C.F.R. §** 404.727**[APP-REGS]**.

AYUSO-MORALES V. SECRETARY OF HEALTH AND HUMAN SERVICES

677 F.2d 146 (1st Cir. 1982)

BREYER, Circuit Judge.

Appellant Esther Ayuso Morales sought Social Security disability benefits based upon her status as the "widow" of the insured employee Honorio Montanez Figueroa. Under 42 U.S.C. § 416(c) to qualify as a "widow" a woman must have been married for at least nine months at the time of her husband's death. Appellant's marriage took place within the nine-month period. Benefits were denied.

On appeal, she urges that she is nonetheless eligible because she co-habited with her husband for twenty years prior to their marriage. She argues that cohabitation transformed her relationship into a legal mar-riage well before the nine-month period. She adds that, in any event, un-der 42 U.S.C. § 416(h)(1)(A) an applicant is a widow if she would, "under the laws . . . (of Puerto Rico) determining the devolution of intestate per-sonal property, have the same status . . . as a wife . . . (or) widow. . . ." She claims that the concubinage law of Puerto Rico gives her such status.

We cannot accept appellant's first argument. We realize that some common law jurisdictions recognize non-ceremonial or "common law mar-riages." These marriages are created by the consent of the parties as any other contract. But common law marriages are not recognized in Puerto Rico. The requisites of a valid marriage in Puerto Rico are set forth in Ar-ticle 69 of the Civil Code, 31 L.P.R.A. § 231. Included among these requi-sites is the "(a)uthorization and celebration of a matrimonial contract ac-cording to the forms and solemnities prescribed by law." In the absence of these forms and solemnities, there can be no marriage. Rivera v. District Court of San Juan, 58 P.R.R. 352, 354 (1941); Vazquez Bote, Notas sobre el matrimonio en derecho puertoriqueno, 49-56 Rev. P.R. 491, 493-94, 510-12 (1973-75). E. Lalaguana Dominguez, Estudios de derecho matri-monial 244-45 (1962).

It is clear that the requirements of Article 69 were not met nine months before appellant husband's death. And it is equally clear that Ar-ticle 69 does not contemplate exceptions. In fact, when the Puerto Rico Legislative Assembly once sought to recognize some common-law type marriages, it felt it had to enact a special law for that purpose. That law, the Act of March 12, 1903, defined "natural marriage" and established a procedure to legitimize and register such unions. But it was short-lived. The law of 1903 was repealed on March 7, 1906. And no other similar statute has been enacted in the Commonwealth since then. Consequently, we believe the Commonwealth courts would conclude that appellant was not legally married to Mr. Montanez Figueroa, the deceased employee, nine months before his death.

We turn next to appellant's second argument—that under the law of Puerto Rico she, as a "concubine," has the status of a widow for purposes of disposition of intestate property. She asserts that she lived together with the insured employee "for more than twenty years as husband and wife." And, this fact, she claims, is sufficient.

We do not doubt that appellant has asserted sufficient facts to invoke the civil law relationship of "concubinage more uxorio." That relationship exists whcn a man and a woman lead a common life together permanent-ly, as in an ordinary marriage—when only the formalities of marriage are missing. See Puig Pena, Las uniones maritales de hecho, 33 Revista de Derecho Privado 1086-89 (1949). Nor do we doubt that, after a long period of hostility to this relationship stemming from the Council of Trent (1545-63), the Hispanic and other civil law systems have treated this relationship with increasing liberality. Both in Europe and in Latin America provisions have been enacted to remove some of the severe inequities previously suffered. Thus, for example, Puerto Rico's Workmen's Accident Compensation Act specifically allows a "concubine" to receive certain benefits. 11 L.P.R.A. § 3 ¶ 5(2). See Ortega v. Industrial Commission of Puerto Rico, 73 P.R.R. 184 (1952); Calderon v. Industrial Commission of Puerto Rico, 64 P.R.R. 702 (1945). Its auto accident compensation law (Automobile Accident Social Protection Act) makes her eligible for other benefits. 9 L.P.R.A. § 2052(3). Her family may well be eligible for public housing as if it were legally constituted through marriage. 17 R.R.P.R. § 22a-9(a)(1) (1971). The law governing social security for chauffeurs provides death benefits for "concubines." 29 L.P.R.A. § 687. And, in 1947, the Supreme Court of Puerto Rico, reversing an earlier decision, guaranteed a "concubine" rights in the property acquired during "concubinage." Torres v. Roldan, 67 P.R.R. 342 (1947), overruling Morales v. Cruz Velez, 34 P.R.R. 796 (1926). Given the increasing legal recognition of the "concubinage" relation, we suspect there is no important policy reason for depriving the appellant of a widow's federal social security benefits.

Nonetheless, we do not believe that appellant can qualify under 42 U.S.C. § 416(h)(1)(A), for Puerto Rico's law does not treat a "concubine" like a "widow" for purposes of "determining the devolution of intestate personal property." A "concubine" is now entitled to a share of all property acquired during the concubinage, Torres v. Roldan, 67 P.R.R. at 345-46. But, those rights flow from ordinary principles of property and equity, not of inheritance. That is to say, a concubine's rights over the property acquired during the concubinage can be established by proving that such property was acquired following "(1) an express" or "(2) an implied agreement" among the partners or (3) as a way "to prevent an unjust enrichment" of one of the parties. Danz v. Suau, 82 P.R.R. 591, 598-99 (1961); Cruz v. Heirs of Landrau Diaz, 97 P.R.R. 563, 570-71 (1969); Caraballo Ramirez v. Acosta, 104 P.R.R. 474, 480-81 (1975). Her rights are typical of those governing property relationships among partners, see, e.g., Civil Code, Art. 1580, 31 L.P.R.A. § 4351, or among "co-owners," Civil Code, Arts. 326 et seq., 31 L.P.R.A. §§ 1271 et seq. Similar rules of property also account for the fact that a widow ordinarily obtains a half interest in the property acquired during marriage. Civil Code, Arts. 1895 et seq., 31 L.P.R.A. §§ 3621 et seq.

The inheritance rights of a widow, however, concern the other portion of the property acquired during marriage; in fact they concern all that property that under the law of property belongs not to her, but to the deceased. A widow inherits a life estate in that property, Civil Code, Art. 761, 31 L.P.R.A. § 2411, or, inherits an absolute title if the deceased spouse left no descendants, ascendants or collaterals up to the fourth degree, Civil Code, Arts. 903-9, 31 L.P.R.A. §§ 2671-7. The "concubine," however, inherits nothing. She has no such interest in her partner's estate. In order to be a spouse entitled to an interest in the deceased spouse's property (including the deceased spouse's half of the property acquired during marriage)

> *"there must exist a valid marriage producing civil effects"* (emphasis in the original).

Ex parte Tormes, 53 P.R.R. 396, 399 (1938) (quoting J. Ma. Manresa Y Navarro, Comentarious al Codigo civil espanol, vol. 6, 501). The "concubinage more uxorio" is clearly excluded. See Sanabria v. Secretary of Health, Education and Welfare, 390 F.Supp. 538 (D.P.R.), aff'd, 530 F.2d 961 (1st Cir. 1976); Barbosa de Rosario, Consideraciones en torno al concubinato, las comunas y el derecho de familia, 42 Rev.Jur.U.P.R. 345, 360-63, 367 (1973).

This difference in treatment for purposes of property devolution is significant enough to deprive appellant of the benefits of 42 U.S.C. § 416(h)(1)(A). Nor can the fact that appellant was a widow at death bring her back within that section for nine months of lawful marriage are required. Her constitutional "equal protection" attack on the nine-month requirement is invalid under Weinberger v. Salfi, 422 U.S. 749, 95 S.Ct. 2457, 45 L.Ed.2d 522 (1975), and Matthews v. De Castro, 429 U.S. 181, 97 S.Ct. 431, 50 L.Ed.2d 389 (1976) which upheld similar distinctions. Thus, we cannot, under the social security statutes, allow recovery.

Affirmed.

2. CHILD'S BENEFITS

In addition to spouses, certain dependent and surviving children of insured wage earner's are entitled to secondary OASDI benefits. Wage earners' children who may be entitled to benefits include dependent natural children, legally adopted children, stepchildren, grandchildren, and stepgrandchildren. This section looks first at how various qualifying parent-child relationships are defined. Next, it discusses age limits and dependency requirements for different categories of child's benefits. Finally, it examines the types of evidence needed to prove qualifying parent-child relationships and, when required, the child's dependence on the wage earner.

A) PARENT-CHILD RELATIONSHIP

Most children who qualify for OASDI secondary benefits are "natural children" of the wage earner, which includes any child with the same inheritance rights as the wage earner's natural child. In making this determination, SSA looks to the law on inheritance rights that the state courts would use to determine the devolution of intestate personal property. If the wage earner is living, it will use the law of the state where the wage earner is domiciled at the time the application is filed; if deceased, it will look to the laws of the state where the wage earner was domiciled at the time of death. **20 C.F.R. §§ 404.355(a)(1), (b)(1)[APP-REGS].**

There are also other ways to qualify as a wage earner's natural child. First, one is considered a natural child if the wage earner and the child's mother or father went through a ceremony that would have resulted in a valid marriage but for a legal impediment. Even if the child's mother or father had not married the wage earner, the child will be deemed the wage earner's natural child if the wage earner had acknowledged the child in writing, had been decreed by a court as the parent of the child, or had been ordered by a court to contribute to the support of the child. Finally, an applicant can submit other forms of evidence to show that the wage earner is his or her natural mother or father, including evidence that the wage earner was either living with the child or contributing to the child's support at the time the application was filed (or, if the insured is deceased, at the time he or she died). **20 C.F.R. § 404.355(a)(2)-(a)(4)[APP-REGS].**

In addition to natural children, other individuals may be entitled to receive children's secondary benefits. These categories include the insured's legally adopted children, stepchildren, grandchildren, stepgrandchildren, and equitably adopted children. The requirements for eligibility based on these categories are defined by statute and set out in detail in the regulations. *See* **42 U.S.C. § 416(e)[APP-STAT]; 20 C.F.R. §§ 404.356-.359[APP-REGS]**.

B) AGE LIMITS

Children of insured wage earners who have died or are receiving old age or disability benefits are entitled to benefits up to the age of 18, or 19 if still "a full-time elementary or secondary school student." 42 U.S.C. § 404(d)(1)(B). A student attending a traditional school, receiving instruction through home school, or participating in an independent study education program will be eligible, so long as the educational program is in accordance with state law where the child resides. The student must be attending school full-time carrying a full-time subject load (according to the institution's standards or those set by the state), for at least 13 weeks. A student will remain eligible during a period of nonattendance or part-time attendance if this period lasts no more than 4 consecutive months, is not due to expulsion or suspension from school, and the student shows an intention to resume studies full-time at the end of the period. Finally, a student is not eligible for benefits if he or she is being paid by an employer who has requested or required the student to attend school. **20 C.F.R. §§ 404.367, .368[APP-REGS]**.

During the time that the child is eligible for benefits, his or her caretaker parent is entitled to a parent's benefit if the wage earner is deceased. These "mother's and father's insurance benefits" are available only if the widow(er)-parent is otherwise not entitled to a surviving spouses insurance benefit. Parent benefits are discussed in greater detail later in this chapter.

The requirements for extended child's benefits beyond the age of 18 have changed over the years. The following case, involving a claim under prior law that allowed benefits through the age of 21, discusses the requirement of full-time school attendance and its relationship to the more general requirement of dependency. The opinion also includes references to various other dependency-related requirements for these benefits in effect both before and at the time the case was decided. The current dependency requirements will be discussed in greater detail in the next section of this chapter.

THERRIEN V. SCHWEIKER
795 F.2d 2, 14 Soc. Sec. Rep. Ser. 162 (2d Cir. 1986)

Before WINTER and PRATT, Circuit Judges, and MALETZ, Judge.

WINTER, Circuit Judge:

Steven W. Therrien appeals from an order of Judge Blumenfeld that upheld the denial by the Secretary of Health and Human Services (the "Secretary") of surviving-child insurance benefits under 42 U.S.C. § 402(d)(1). * * *

Therrien has been incarcerated at the Connecticut Correctional Institution at Somers since February 13, 1979. On May 8, 1979, he applied for child's insurance benefits, stating that he intended to enroll in Western Illinois University, a correspondence school. His claim was denied by the Social Security Administration ("SSA") on July 17, 1979, because he did not qualify as a full-time student according to SSA's standards. His failure to qualify was based both on the fact that he had not actually enrolled in the educational institution, and on a regulation, 20 C.F.R. § 404.367 (1980) (formerly 20 C.F.R. § 404.320 (1979)), that excluded correspondence school students from the class of persons eligible for benefits. Therrien claims that this regulation is inconsistent with the statute, and that the enrollment requirement contained in the regulation and the statute impermissibly discriminates on the basis of indigency.

At the time of Therrien's application, Section 202(d)(1) of the Social Security Act (the "Act"), 42 U.S.C. § 402(d)(1)(B)(i) (1976) (amended 1981), provided that the children of persons who died while insured by Social Security were eligible for benefits if they were unmarried and either younger than 18 years old, or a full-time student and younger than 22 years old.[1] Section 202(d) of the Act, 42 U.S.C. § 402(d)(7)(A) (1976), defined a "full-time student" as "an individual who is in full-time attendance as a student at an educational institution, as determined by the Secretary (in accordance with regulations prescribed by him) in the light of the standards and practices of the institutions involved...."

Finally, the challenged regulation provided:

You may be eligible for child's benefits if you are a full-time student. A full-time student means a person who is in full-time attendance at an educational institution. You will be considered a full-time student if all the following conditions are met; ...

(b) You are enrolled in a noncorrespondence course and carrying a subject load that is considered full-time for day students under the practices and standards of the educational institution.... If you are enrolled in any other educational institution, your course of study must last at least 13 weeks and your scheduled attendance must be at least 20 hours a week....

20 C.F.R. § 404.367 (1980).

Therrien argues in effect that the definition of a full-time student found in the regulation was inconsistent with the statute. However, because the statute explicitly delegated to the Secretary the task of prescribing regulations to effectuate the statute, the nature of our review is extremely limited. The Supreme Court has held that where there is an

explicit delegation of substantive authority [to define terms], the Secretary's definition of [a term] is 'entitled to more than mere deference or weight.' ... Rather, the Secretary's definition is entitled to 'legislative effect' because, '[i]n a situation of this kind, Congress entrusts to the Secretary, rather than to the courts, the primary responsibility for interpreting the statutory term.' ... [O]ur task is the limited one of ensuring that the Secretary did not 'excee[d] his statutory authority' and that the regulation is not arbitrary or capricious.

---

[1] Student benefits are no longer available beyond age 19. Omnibus Budget Reconciliation Act of 1981, Pub.L. No. 97-35, § 2210(a)(5)(A), 95 Stat. 357, 841.

Schweiker v. Gray Panthers, 453 U.S. 34, 44, 101 S.Ct. 2633, 2640, 69 L.Ed.2d 460 (1981) (quoting Batterton v. Francis, 432 U.S. 416, 425-26, 97 S.Ct. 2399, 2405-06, 53 L.Ed.2d 448 (1977)). Thus, Therrien must demonstrate that the regulation either was so inconsistent with the statute as to be outside the legitimate exercise of authority delegated to the Secretary, or was arbitrary or capricious.

In enacting Section 402(d)(1), Congress sought to aid dependent children of deceased or disabled insureds in completing their education. Prior to the 1965 Amendments to the Act, eligibility terminated at age 18. The Senate report that accompanied the 1965 Amendments stated:

> The committee believes that a child over age 18 who is attending school full time is dependent just as a child under 18 or a disabled older child is dependent, and that it is not realistic to stop such a child's benefit at age 18....

> The committee believes it is now appropriate and desirable to provide social security benefits for children between the ages of 18 and 22 who are full-time students and who have suffered a loss of parental support.

S.Rep. No. 404, 89th Cong., 1st Sess., reprinted in 1965 U.S.Code Cong. & Ad.News 1943, 2036-37.

Thus, Congress's concern seems to have been with dependency. The Secretary, in promulgating the regulation, was entitled to believe that full-time students attending class were less likely to be able to support themselves through employment than were part-time or correspondence students. This estimation was consistent with the statute and neither arbitrary nor capricious.

Therrien's reliance on our decision in Haberman v. Finch, 418 F.2d 664 (2d Cir.1969), is misplaced. In that case, we directed the Secretary to provide benefits to a student who had been forced by illness to reduce her weekly credit hours to 16 1/2, below the 20-hour minimum contained in the regulation. We concluded that the student was obviously within the class sought to be covered by the statute, and that she had "done her level best" to comply with the regulation. Id. at 667. In addition, we noted that the Secretary had conceded that the student's course of study was considered by the school to be "equivalent to its full-time day program." Id. at 666. Therefore, we directed the Secretary to except the student from the regulation and provide benefits.

We do not view Therrien's incarceration in the same way we viewed the physical incapacity of the student in Haberman.[2] Also, we cannot conclude that Therrien's intended course of study is the equivalent of a full-time program. Haberman is thus inapposite.

Therrien's second argument, which we discuss briefly, is a constitutional attack on the enrollment requirement of the regulation. He claims to be caught in a Catch-22 predicament, because he must be enrolled in order to receive benefits but must receive the benefits in order to enroll. However, this predicament is created not by the Secretary, but by the "cash in advance" enrollment policy of Therrien's chosen academic institution. Moreover, he is now enrolled, notwithstanding the lack of benefits and the supposed Catch-22 circumstances.

We have examined appellant's other claims and found them to be without merit.

Affirmed.

C) DEPENDENCY REQUIREMENT

As the court pointed out in *Theirrien v. Schweiker*, Congress sought to aid *dependent* children of deceased or disabled wage earners when it added children's benefits to the OASDI program. If the primary wage earner is living, the child must be dependent on the wage earner at the time that the application was filed. If the primary wage earner has died, the child must have been dependent at the time of the wage earner's death. One way that the statute implements the dependency requirement is by requiring that the claimant be unmarried in order to receive children's benefits, with certain limited exceptions. 42 U.S.C. § 402(d).

In addition, regulations provide specific guidance regarding the conditions that must be met to be considered dependent on the wage earner. These conditions vary depending upon how the claimant is related to the wage earner. Dependency is assumed once a claimant shows that he or she is the wage earner's "natural child." However, claimants with other types of relationships to the wage earner—including legally or equitably adopted children, stepchildren, grandchildren, and stepgrandchildren—are required to satisfy additional conditions. Depending on the type of relationship, the child may be asked to show that he or she lived with the wage earner at a specific time, that the child received "contributions for

---

[2] 1980 Amendments to the Act, which do not govern appellant's claim, explicitly exclude individuals "confined in a jail, prison, or other penal institution or correctional facility, pursuant to his conviction of an offense ... which constituted a felony under applicable law." Act of October 19, 1980, Pub.L. No. 96-473, § 5(b), 94 Stat. 2263, 2265 (codified at 2 U.S.C. § 402(d)(8)(A)). Although the district court noted this amendment in its discussion of the intent of Congress in enacting the 1965 Amendments, it clearly did not, as appellant claims, give the 1980 amendment retroactive effect.

support" from the wage earner, or that the wage earner provided at least "one-half support" to the child. **20 C.F.R. §** 404.360-404.365**[APP-REGS]**. All of these terms are defined by regulation. *See* **20 C.F.R. §** 404.366**[APP-REGS]**.

D) PROOF OF PARENT-CHILD RELATIONSHIP AND PROOF OF DEPENDENCY

An application for children's secondary benefits must be supported by evidence of the child's qualifying relationship to the wage earner-parent. **20 C.F.R.§** 404.730**[APP-REGS]**. If the claimant is the natural child of the wage earner, a copy of the child's public or religious birth record made before age 5 will be requested; if it shows the same last name for the child and the parent, the record will be convincing evidence of the parent-child relationship. However, more evidence must be presented if such a record is unobtainable or if other evidence calls into question whether the claimant is the wage earner's natural child. If this is the case, the child may be asked to provide evidence that he or she would be able to inherit the wage earner's personal property under the applicable state's intestacy laws, a statement signed by the wage earner attesting to the relationship, or copies of any court orders declaring that the claimant is the natural wage earner's child or requiring the wage earner to provide child support. **20 C.F.R. §** 404.731**[APP-REGS]**.

If the claimant is the wage earner's stepchild, regulations require proof of the relevant parent-child relationship as well as the child's parent's marriage to the wage earner. *See* **20 C.F.R.§** 404.732**[APP-REGS]**. Regulations provide more specific guidance on the type of evidence required where the child was adopted, either legally or equitably. **20 C.F.R.§§** 404.733, .734**[APP-REGS]**.

In addition to proving the parent-child relationship, SSA may request evidence of dependency. Again, the proof required is determined by the type of relationship between the claimant-child and the insured wage earner. If the claimant is adopted, SSA may require a signed statement "by someone who knows the facts" that confirms the relationship. The claimant may also be asked to produce a signed statement "by someone in a position to know" showing when and where the child lived with the wage earner, as well as information regarding the support that the child received. Similar regulatory provisions govern the evidentiary requirements for establishing dependency in other types of relationships. See **20 C.F.R. §** 404.736**[APP-REGS]**.

Disputed claims for survivors benefits typically involve questions about the existence (or non-existence) of the relevant family relationship—as required for eligibility under the Social Security Act—between the claimant and the wage earner. Most often, the critical relationship is that between a claimant child and his or her wage-earner father. The most common questions are paternity and the extent of the father's support for the child, both of which were at issue in the first of the following two cases. The second case also touches on these questions, but in a unique context.

JONES FOR JONES V. CHATER

101 F.3d 509, 52 Soc.Sec.Rep.Ser. 244 (7th Cir. 1996)

Before POSNER, Chief Judge, and BAUER and RIPPLE, Circuit Judges

POSNER, Chief Judge

A dependent child of a wage earner is entitled to "child's insurance benefits" under the Social Security Act if the wage earner is insured under the Act and dies, becomes disabled, or reaches the age of 65. 42 U.S.C. § 402(d). Problems of determining entitlement sometimes arise when, as in the present case, the wage earner (Ivory Claxton) dies and was not married to the child's mother (Cynthia Jones). The Act contains an exhaustive list of methods of establishing entitlement to child insurance benefits in such a case: proof that the wage earner would have been married to the child's mother but for a technical deficiency in the marriage; a written acknowledgment of paternity by the wage earner; a judicial decree that the wage earner was the child's father, provided the decree was issued before the wage earner died; a court order that the wage earner contribute to the support of the child because the wage earner was the child's parent; a determination by the Social Security Administration, based on satisfactory evidence, that the wage earner was the parent of the child and was living with or contributing to the child's support when the wage earner died; or proof that the child was entitled to inherit from the wage earner under the law of intestate succession of the wage earner's state of domicile. 42 U.S.C. §§ 416(h)(2)(A), (C). Jones sought to establish an entitlement to benefits for her 11-year-old son, Brandon Jones, by the last two of these methods--proof of paternity under state intestate statute, and paternity plus support. The Social Security Administration turned down her application on the ground that she had proved neither paternity nor support. The district court upheld the denial of benefits.

Claxton was domiciled in Missouri, and Missouri's intestate succession statute requires, so far as bears on this case, clear and convincing evidence of paternity. Mo.Ann.Stat. § 474.060(2). But that is all that the statute requires; unlike the method of establishing entitlement that we are calling "paternity plus support," there is no requirement of proving that the father ever provided any support to the child. Proof of paternity is easier under the "paternity plus support" method than under the Missouri statute, because proof by a preponderance of evidence is all that is required under the former method, and that is, of course, a lesser burden than proof by clear and convincing evidence. Oddly, we cannot find a case that holds that a preponderance of the evidence is all that the paternity plus support method requires; nor does the Social Security Act, or the regulations under it, prescribe a standard of proof, although the Act does make clear that the claimant for benefits bears the burden of persuasion. 42 U.S.C. § 405(g). But we have no doubt that preponderance of the evidence is the proper standard, as it is the default standard in civil and administrative proceedings, and no reason for a different standard in paternity-plus-support cases has been suggested or occurs to us. On the contrary, the fact that proof of support is required as well as proof of paternity is an argument for a lower standard of proof than under statutes that require proof of paternity by clear and convincing evidence but require no evidence at all of support.

The administrative law judge got this wrong; he required proof of paternity by clear and convincing evidence under both the paternity and the paternity-plus-support methods. He compounded his error by equating "clear and convincing" to "beyond a reasonable doubt." These are serious errors. While Jones indeed failed to prove Claxton's paternity beyond a reasonable doubt, the evidence of his paternity is very strong and might well be found to have satisfied the clear and convincing standard, and, all the more, the preponderance standard. It is undisputed that Claxton (who was married to, and had children by, another woman) was having an affair with Jones when she became pregnant with Brandon. In 1981, after she became pregnant, she moved to California to be with her mother. Brandon was born, and shortly afterward Claxton visited him and the mother in California and bought clothes, groceries, and other items for him. At Claxton's urging, the mother moved with the baby back to St. Louis and the two of them lived in an apartment over Claxton's grocery store. Claxton saw Brandon, and bought him clothes and toys, from time to time. In 1989 or 1990, Cynthia Jones moved with her son to Illinois. Claxton died in 1991 without having seen either Cynthia or Brandon, or provided any financial or other tangible assistance to Brandon, after their move to Illinois. Brandon testified at the benefits hearing that Claxton had told him that he was his father and that he believed it.

Claxton's widow, testifying against paternity, speculated that if her husband had given money or goods to Brandon it was purely because of the disinterested generosity for which he was known. She did not testify that her husband was not Brandon's father—only that he didn't know whether he was or not, and speculated that her husband's brother, or perhaps one of the employees of the grocery store, might be Brandon's father—might have impregnated Jones when they were living in the apartment above the store. But Brandon had already been born when he and his mother returned from California and moved into the apartment.

Although the administrative law judge's determination that Claxton was not the father cannot stand, because he applied the wrong standard of proof and the error is not harmless, we cannot reverse the determination that Jones has failed to establish entitlement by the state intestate statute method. The reason is that she has abandoned her reliance on this method in this court. Although her main brief contains a couple of references to the administrative law judge's having applied the wrong standard to determining paternity under the state intestate statute, the statute is not cited in either of her briefs; the statement of the issues presented does not mention the statute; and the only request for relief is that we remand for a redetermination of paternity under the preponderance of the evidence standard, a standard applicable to the "paternity plus support" method of establishing entitlement to child insurance benefits but not to the state intestate statute method. At argument, one of the judges said that he had a problem with the administrative law judge's handling of the state intestate method, even though Jones's lawyer did not: "I know you don't [have a problem with it], I do," the judge said. Jones's lawyer agreed that the administrative law judge had misapplied the Missouri statute, but she did not request relief from that error. The appellee's lawyer, when his turn to speak came, stated that the state intestate method was not involved in the appeal, and Jones's lawyer did not challenge this statement in her rebuttal.

Although an argument that an appellant has waived an issue can itself be waived, that did not happen here. On the contrary, the government stated in its appellee's brief (and repeated, as we have noted, at the argument) that Jones "concedes that the 'state alternative' [what we are calling the state intestate statute method of establishing entitlement to child insurance benefits] does not apply" and "instead" is claiming entitlement under the "paternity plus support" section of the child insurance benefits statute. Jones filed a reply brief but did not take issue with these statements in the government's brief, just as she did not at argument. It is true that the government's brief defends the administrative law judge's finding that Jones had not established that Claxton was her son's father, but the issue of paternity is relevant to paternity plus support as well as to the state intestate statute, so the government's discussing it cannot be taken as a tacit acknowledgment that the intestate statute method was still in the case.

Jones's lawyer may have made a tactical decision to confine her appeal to the paternity plus support method because it is easier to prove paternity under that method. She may have believed that even if she could obtain a fresh determination of paternity under the Missouri statute, the administrative law judge would not have found paternity established by clear and convincing evidence. Whatever the lawyer was thinking, we cannot grant relief on a ground so thoroughly waived, since none of the exceptions to the waiver doctrine are applicable. The government had no reason to think that the Missouri statute was still in the case, and therefore made no effort to meet an argument based on that statute—an argument not made.

Under the paternity plus support method of establishing entitlement to child insurance benefits, Jones had to prove not only that Claxton was Brandon's father, but also that Claxton was contributing to the child's support when he died, 42 U.S.C. § 416(h)(3)(C)(ii), and that the support was "regular and substantial." 20 C.F.R. § 404.366(a)(2). She cannot prove either. Until a year or two before his death, Claxton provided intermittent support to Brandon, but it could hardly be described as regular and substantial. It was not regular; and no effort was made to establish that it was substantial. After Brandon and his mother moved to Illinois, at least one year and possibly two years before Claxton's death, Claxton provided zero support to Brandon. Jones says that it was not his fault; that he wanted to; that he tried but failed to find out where she and Brandon were living. This would be relevant to a temporary interruption, see 20 C.F.R. § 404.366(a)(2), but we do not think that the statute can reasonably be interpreted to be satisfied by zero support. Remember that there are many different methods of establishing entitlement to child insurance benefits; if each is to be watered down to nothing, the statute will place no limitations on such entitlements.

Some courts relativize "substantial" to the resources of the putative father. E.g., Parker v. Schweiker, 673 F.2d 160 (6th Cir.1982); Jones v. Harris, 629 F.2d 334 (4th Cir.1980) (per curiam). None, however, has gone so far as to equate substantial to zero because the father's resources are zero or, as in this case, because circumstances beyond his control prevent him from devoting any of his resources to his child's support. Even the Sixth Circuit, the leader in relativizing, has held that the father must provide some support. Chester v. Secretary of Health & Human Services, 808 F.2d 473, 476 (6th Cir.1987); Young v. Secretary of Health & Human Services, 787 F.2d 1064, 1070 (6th Cir.1986). Our court has held the same thing, Schaefer v. Heckler, 792 F.2d 81, 86-87 (7th Cir.1986), emphasizing that the statute is not to be gutted by reference to the financial wherewithal of the father. Bennemon v. Sullivan, 914 F.2d 987 (7th Cir.1990). Sporadic support will not do, however exiguous the father's resources, because the purpose of federal child insurance benefits is not to benefit minor children as such but, as the Supreme Court pointed out in Mathews v. Lucas, 427 U.S. 495, 507-08, 514-15, 96 S.Ct. 2755, 2763-64, 49 L.Ed.2d 651 (1976), to replace the support that the child would have received from his father had the father not died. Every father whose parental rights have not been terminated (as by the lawful adoption of the child by another person) has a legal duty to support his child, Ind.Code § 35-46-1-5; 1 Homer H. Clark, Jr., The Law of Domestic Relations in the

United States § 5.4, p. 317 (2d ed. 1987), but the reality is of course different and many fathers, especially of children born out of wedlock, do not support their children. The fact that Brandon Jones is probably the child of Ivory Claxton is not by itself proof or even strong evidence that if Claxton had lived he would have supported the child. He had terminated support, at best intermittent, well before he died.

Because Jones has failed to satisfy the "support" requirement of the "paternity plus support" method of establishing entitlement, and has waived the issue whether she proved paternity under the Missouri intestacy statute, we must affirm the denial of benefits despite the administrative law judge's erroneous handling of the paternity issue.

AFFIRMED.

GILLETT-NETTING V. BARNHART
371 F.3d 593 (9th Cir. 2004)

Before: B. FLETCHER, REINHARDT, Circuit Judges, and RESTANI, Judge.

Betty B. FLETCHER, Circuit Judge:

Plaintiff-Appellant Rhonda Gillett-Netting ("Gillett-Netting"), on her own behalf and on behalf of her minor children Juliet O. Netting and Piers W. Netting, appeals the district court's grant of summary judgment for the Commissioner of Social Security ("Commissioner"). The district court affirmed the Commissioner's decision holding that Juliet and Piers are not entitled to child's insurance benefits based on the earnings of their deceased father, Robert Netting ("Netting"). Ten months after Netting died, his wife conceived Juliet and Piers using sperm that he deposited before undergoing chemotherapy for cancer. Gillett-Netting argues that the district court erred in holding that Juliet and Piers are not eligible for child's insurance benefits because they are not Netting's children under the Social Security Act ("Act") and were not dependent on Netting at the time of his death. Because Juliet and Piers are Netting's legitimate children under Arizona law, and therefore are deemed dependent on Netting for child's insurance benefits, we reverse the decision of the district court and remand to the district court with instructions to further remand to the Commissioner for an award of benefits.

I. BACKGROUND

In December 1994, Netting was diagnosed with cancer. At the time, he and his wife, Gillett-Netting, were trying to have a baby together, but Gillett-Netting suffered from fertility problems that had caused her to miscarry twice. Because doctors advised Netting that chemotherapy might render him sterile, he delayed the start of his treatment for several days so that he could deposit his semen at the University of Arizona Health Sciences Center, where it was frozen and stored for later use by his wife. Netting quickly lost his battle with cancer. He died on February 4, 1995, before his wife was able to conceive. Earlier, Netting confirmed that he wanted Gillett-Netting to have their child after his death using his frozen sperm. In-vitro fertilization of Gillett-Netting's eggs with Netting's sperm was undertaken successfully on December 19, 1995. The resulting embryos were transferred to Gillett-Netting on December 21, 1995, and Juliet and Piers Netting were born on August 6, 1996.

On August 19, 1996, Gillett-Netting filed an application on behalf of Juliet and Piers for Social Security child's insurance benefits based on Netting's earnings. The Social Security Administration (SSA) denied the claim initially and upon reconsideration, and Gillett-Netting timely filed a request for a hearing before an Administrative Law Judge (ALJ). Because neither the material facts nor the claimants' credibility were disputed, the parties agreed to submit the case to the ALJ without an administrative hearing.

The ALJ denied Gillett-Netting's claim, holding that Juliet and Piers are not entitled to benefits because they were not dependent on Netting at the time of his death. The ALJ held that "the last possible time to determine dependents [sic] on the wage earner's account is the date of the death of the wage earner." Therefore, children conceived after the wage earner's death cannot be deemed dependent on the wage earner. The Social Security Appeals Council denied Gillett-Netting's request for review, and the ALJ's decision became the final decision of the Commissioner.

Gillett-Netting filed a complaint in district court, alleging that the decision denying Juliet and Piers benefits was not supported by substantial evidence, was not in accordance with the law, and denied them equal protection of the laws. The parties filed cross-motions for summary judgment, and the district court granted summary judgment for the Commissioner. The district court held that Juliet and Piers do not qualify for child's insurance benefits because they are not Netting's "children" under the Act and they were not dependent on Netting at the time of his death. See Gillett-Netting v. Barnhart, 231 F.Supp.2d 961, 965-69 (D.Ariz.2002). Additionally, the district court held that Juliet's and Piers's right to equal protection of the laws was not violated by applying the Act to deny them child's insurance benefits. Id. at 969-70. After the district court denied Gillett-Netting's motion for reconsideration, she timely filed an appeal to this Court.

* * *

III. DISCUSSION

Developing reproductive technology has outpaced federal and state laws, which currently do not address directly the legal issues created by posthumous conception. Neither the Social Security Act nor the Arizona family law that is relevant to determining whether Juliet and Piers have a right to child's insurance benefits makes clear the rights of children conceived posthumously. Our task is to determine whether Juliet and Piers have a right to child's insurance benefits under the law as currently formulated.[3]

A. Demonstrating Entitlement to Child's Insurance Benefits

Under the Act, every child is entitled to benefits if the claimant is the child, as defined in 42 U.S.C. § 416(e), of an individual who dies fully or currently insured; the child or the child's representative files an application for benefits; the child is unmarried and a minor (or meets disability requirements) at the time of application; and the child was dependent on the insured wage earner at the time of his death. 42 U.S.C. § 402(d)(1). It is undisputed that Netting was fully insured under the Act when he died, that Juliet and Piers are his biological children and are unmarried minors, and that Gillett-Netting filed an application for child's insurance benefits on their behalf. Because we conclude that Juliet and Piers are Netting's legitimate children, they are considered to have been dependent under the Act and are entitled to benefits.

B. Juliet and Piers are Netting's Natural, Biological Children

The Act defines "child" broadly to include any "child or legally adopted child of an individual," as well as a stepchild who was the insured person's stepchild for at least nine months before the insured person died, and a grandchild or stepgrandchild of the insured person under certain circumstances. See 42 U.S.C. § 416(e). Courts and the SSA have interpreted the word "child" used in the definition of "child" to mean the natural, or biological, child of the insured. See, e.g., Weinberger v. Salfi, 422 U.S. 749, 781 n. 12, 95 S.Ct. 2457, 45 L.Ed.2d 522 (1975) (noting that a "natural or adopted child" of a wage earner need not meet the nine-month time requirement to which stepchildren are subject); Tsosie v. Califano, 630 F.2d 1328, 1333 (9th Cir.1980) ("Under § 416(e), the term 'child' in-

---

[3] Although no circuit court has previously considered the novel issue presented in this case, a well-reasoned opinion of the Massachusetts Supreme Judicial Court recently addressed related state law questions. See Woodward v. Comm'r of Soc. Sec., 435 Mass. 536, 760 N.E.2d 257 (2002) (holding that a posthumously conceived child could inherit from a deceased sperm donor under Massachusetts intestacy law where parentage is established and the donor consented both to reproduce posthumously and to support any resulting child).

cludes a person's natural children and his legally adopted children."); 20 C.F.R. § 404.354 (stating that a claimant may be "entitled to benefits as [an insured person's] child, i.e., as a natural child, legally adopted child, stepchild, grandchild, stepgrandchild, or equitably adopted child").

The Commissioner argues and the district court held that "child" is further defined by 42 U.S.C. §§ 416(h)(2), (3), and that Juliet and Piers cannot be considered the children of Netting unless they meet the requirements of one of these provisions.

These sections were added to the Act to provide various ways in which children could be entitled to benefits even if their parents were not married or their parentage was in dispute. They have no relevance to the issue before us. As the Fourth Circuit explained "[a]n *illegitimate* claimant may establish that he is a 'child' for eligibility purposes under either of three critical provisions of the Act" in § 416(h). McMillian by McMillian v. Heckler, 759 F.2d 1147, 1150(4th Cir.1985) (emphasis added).

> Until 1965, § 416(h)(2) provided the sole means by which illegitimates could establish entitlement to benefits as dependent children, with § (h)(2)(A) the primary vehicle. Under that provision, an illegitimate claimant could establish entitlement to benefits by proving his entitlement to inherit from the insured wage earner as a "child" under the intestate succession law of the state of the insured's domicile. In 1965, § (h)(3)(C) was added specifically to provide other means by which entitlement might be established.

Id. at 1152.

Under the current version of § 416(h), a claimant whose parentage is disputed is deemed to be the child of an insured individual if: (1) the child would be entitled to take an intestate share of the individual's property under the laws of the state in which the individual resided at death; (2) the child's parents went through a marriage ceremony resulting in a purported marriage between them that, but for a legal impediment unknown to them at the time, would have been a valid marriage; (3) the deceased wage earner acknowledged the claimant as his or her child in writing; (4) the deceased wage earner, before dying, had been decreed by a court to be the parent of the claimant; (5) the deceased wage earner, before dying, had been ordered by a court to contribute to the support of the claimant because the claimant was his or her child; or (6) the insured individual is shown by evidence satisfactory to the Commissioner to have been the parent of the claimant and to have been living with or contributing to the support of the claimant at the time that he died. See 42 U.S.C. §§ 416(h)(2), (3).

Although these provisions offer means of "determining whether an applicant is the child ... of a fully or currently insured individual," id. at § 416(h)(2)(A), when parentage is disputed, nothing in the statute suggests that a child must prove parentage under § 416(h) if it is not disputed. We conclude that these provisions do not come into play for the purposes of determining whether a claimant is the "child" of a deceased wage earner unless parentage is disputed. In this case, the Commissioner concedes that Juliet and Piers are Netting's biological children. Therefore, we conclude that the district court erred by holding that Juliet and Piers are not Netting's children for the purposes of the Act. See, e.g., Tsosie, 630 F.2d at 1333 (noting that "child" includes any biological child of the insured wage earner).

C. Dependency

As the district court stated, "[b]ecause Juliet and Piers were not in existence at the time of Robert's death, they cannot demonstrate actual dependency" on him at the time of his death. Gillett-Netting, 231 F.Supp.2d at 967. The only remaining issue is whether Juliet and Piers, the undisputed biological children of a deceased, insured individual, are statutorily deemed dependent on Netting without proof of actual dependency.

Under the Act, a claimant must show dependency on an insured wage earner in order to be entitled to child's insurance benefits. 42 U.S.C. § 402(d)(1). However, the Act statutorily deems broad categories of children to have been dependent on a deceased, insured parent without demonstrating actual dependency. It is well-settled that all legitimate children automatically are considered to have been dependent on the insured individual, absent narrow circumstances not present in this case. 42 U.S.C. § 402(d)(3).

Similarly, "illegitimate" children who prove parentage under 42 U.S.C. §§ 416(h)(2), (3) are "deemed to be the legitimate child of such individual" and, therefore, are deemed to have been dependent on the insured wage earner. 42 U.S.C. § 402(d)(3). Thus, the provisions of § 416(h) described above typically come into play to prove dependency rather than parentage. In summary, through the Act's statutorily deemed dependency, any

> legitimate child, a child entitled under the intestacy laws of the insured parent's domicile to inherit personal property from the parent, a child whose illegitimacy results from a formal defect in the parents' purported marriage ceremony, and a child acknowledged in writing by the insured father as his son or daughter or judicially decreed (during the father's lifetime) to be such, are all deemed under the Act to be dependent upon the parent, unless the child has been adopted

by some other individual, and thus are relieved of otherwise proving actual dependency.[6]

Norton v. Mathews, 427 U.S. 524, 527 n. 1, 96 S.Ct. 2771, 49 L.Ed.2d 672 (1976). Dependency is a broad concept under the Act, whereby the vast majority of children are statutorily deemed dependent on their deceased parents, and only completely unacknowledged, illegitimate children must prove actual dependency in order to be entitled to child's insurance benefits. Moreover, the Act is construed liberally to ensure that children are provided for financially after the death of a parent.

Juliet and Piers are indisputably Netting's legitimate children under the law of the state in which they reside. "Arizona has eliminated the status of illegitimacy[.]" State v. Mejia, 97 Ariz. 215, 399 P.2d 116 (1965). In Arizona,"[e]very child is the legitimate child of its natural parents and is entitled to support and education as if born in lawful wedlock." Ariz.Rev.Stat. § 8-601. "It has long been the policy of th[e] state to protect innocent children from the omissions of their parents" by abolishing legal distinctions based on legitimacy. Hurt v. Superior Court, 124 Ariz. *599(Cite as: 371 F.3d 593, *599) 45, 601 P.2d 1329, 1331 (1979). Under Arizona law, Netting would be treated as the natural parent of Juliet and Piers and would have a legal obligation to support them if he were alive, although they were conceived using in-vitro fertilization, because he is their biological father and was married to the mother of the children. See Ariz.Rev.Stat. § 25-501(providing that children have a right to support from their natural parents; the biological father of a child born using artificial insemination is considered a natural parent if the father is married to the mother). Although Arizona law does not deal specifically with post-humously-conceived children, *every* child in Arizona, which necessarily includes Juliet and Piers, is the legitimate child of her or his natural parents.[7]

The Commissioner nevertheless argues that Juliet and Piers do not satisfy the "legitimate child" requirement, and therefore cannot be deemed dependent under § 402(d)(3), unless they also are able to inherit from Netting under state intestacy laws or meet one of the other provisions of § 416(h). This is not the case. Legitimacy in § 402(d)(3) is deter-

---

[6] An illegitimate child who does not meet one of these requirements can be deemed legitimate and dependent if she demonstrates both parentage and actual dependency, that is, that the "insured individual was living with or contributing to the support of the applicant at the time such insured individual died." See 42 U.S.C. §§ 402(d)(3), 416(h)(3)(C).

[7] This is not to say that every posthumously-conceived child in Arizona would be eligible for survivorship benefits on the basis of the earnings of the deceased sperm donor. If the sperm donor had not been married to the mother, Arizona would not treat him as the child's natural parent, and he likely would have no obligation to support the child if he were alive. In such circumstances, no eligibility for benefits would exist unless the Commissioner made a determination that the claimant was the dependent child of the deceased wage earner for purposes of the Act by virtue of satisfying one of the requirements in § 416(h).

mined in accordance with state law. See Jimenez v. Weinberger, 417 U.S. 628, 635-36, 94 S.Ct. 2496, 41 L.Ed.2d 363 (1974) (noting that children who are considered legitimate under state law are entitled to child's insurance benefits without proving dependency). While § 416(h) provides alternative avenues for children to be deemed legitimate, nothing in the Act suggests that a child who is legitimate under state law separately must prove legitimacy under the Act. It would make little sense to require a child whose parents were married to demonstrate legitimacy by showing she meets a test set forth in § 416(h), for example by showing that her parent acknowledged her in writing or that a court determined her parentage prior to the parent's death.

Because Juliet and Piers are Netting's legitimate children under Arizona law, they are deemed dependent under § 402(d)(3) and need not demonstrate actual dependency nor deemed dependency under the provisions of § 416(h).

IV. CONCLUSION

As Netting's legitimate children, Juliet and Piers are conclusively deemed dependent on Netting under the Act and are entitled to child's insurance benefits based on his earnings. Accordingly, we **REVERSE** the decision of the district court and **REMAND** with instructions to further remand to the Commissioner of Social Security for an award of benefits.

NOTES

1. *Gillett-Netting* was distinguished in Stephen v. Commissioner, 386 F.Supp.2d 1257 (M.D. Fla. 2005). In that case, the child claimant was conceived through in vitro fertilization three years after his father (who was married to his mother) died, using sperm that was extracted (and cryopreserved) the day after the father died. Although the court acknowledged that the claimant is the wage earners' "legitimate child," it looked to whether he was dependent on the father at the time of the father's death. Citing Florida law concerning children conceived from the sperm of a person who died before the transfer of the sperm to a woman's body — and noting that under such circumstances the child is not eligible for a claim against the father's estate unless the father provided for the child in his will (which was not done in that case) — the court distinguished *Getting-Nettle* as follows:

> The Ninth Circuit decision on which claimant relies, Gillett-Netting v. Barnhart, 371 F.3d 593, 596 (9th Cir.2004), does not require a different result. In that case, the Court of Appeals held that two children who had been post-humously conceived from frozen sperm were entitled to survivor benefits under Arizona law and federal law. Arizona law did not deal specifically with posthumously-conceived children. 371 F.3d at 599. Because the children were "legitimate" children under Arizona law, the Ninth Circuit saw no need to consider whether the children could inherit

property from their deceased father under Arizona intestacy law. Id. Florida law, however, does deal specifically with posthumously-conceived children. See Fla. Stat. § 742.17 (pertaining to "Disposition of eggs, sperm, or preembryos; rights of inheritance"). Congress directs the Commissioner to apply that Florida statute in this case. See 42 U.S.C. § 416(h)(2)(A), accord, 20 C.F.R. § 404.355(b)(1).

386 F.Supp.2d 1257, at 1264-65

2. SSA issued an Acquiescence Ruling in response to *Gillett-Netting*, but it is limited to claims within the Ninth Circuit. *See* SSR 05-1(9) (2005) (explaining how SSA's interpretation of the Social Security Act differs from that set out in *Gillett-Netting*). The issue came up again in Capato ex rel. B.N.C. v. Commissioner, 631 F.3d 626, 163 Soc. Sec. Rep. Serv. 35 (3rd Cir 2011), where twin children conceived through artificial insemination after the death of their father—who was married to the mother—applied for benefits. SSA argued the Ninth Circuit's reasoning in *Gillett-Netting* was "indisputably mistaken" and that all children, even if their parents were married and parentage was not in dispute, must satisfy at least one of the provisions of 42 U.S.C. § 416(h). The Third Circuit disagreed, holding that under 42 U.S.C. § 416(3) no such proof is required when everyone agrees that a claimant is "the biological offspring" of a wage earner. *See* 631 F.3d at 631 ("we do not read §§ 402(d) or 416(e) as requiring reference to § 416(h) to establish child status under the facts of this case") (remanding for a determination whether the children were dependent). The Supreme Court has granted SSA's petition for certiorari. Astrue v. Capato ex rel. B.N.C., 132 S. Ct. 576 (2011).

E) DEPENDENCY AND DISABLED ADULT CHILDREN

Although dependency is measured most often according to specific circumstances existing at the time a claimant applies for benefits, certain standard external conditions come into play as well. The most obvious is age; after a certain age, children are considered independent and therefore are no longer eligible for child's benefits. Dependency is more open-ended for disabled children. As we will see in Chapter 4, if a child of a wage earner becomes disabled before reaching the age of 22, the "child" can continue to receive child's disability benefits as a dependent of the wage earner for so long as he or she remains disabled. However, as shown in the following case, a wage earner's disabled child is not always considered a dependent child.

CRANE V. SULLIVAN
993 F.2d 1335, 41 Soc. Sec. Rep. Ser. 214 (8th Cir. 1993)

Before FAGG and MAGILL, Circuit Judges, and PECK, Senior Circuit Judge.

JOHN W. PECK, Senior Circuit Judge

* * *

I.

Fay Crane filed her application for adult child's insurance benefits on July 27, 1989, at age 45, alleging disability due to depression, a low I.Q., glaucoma, and other physical and emotional limitations. She filed on the account of her father, Dawson Ray Spaulding, who at the time the application was filed, was a fully insured individual receiving Social Security retirement benefits.

Plaintiff Crane was married on December 28, 1968 and her marriage has not ended. Mr. Charles E. Crane, her husband, applied for SSI disability benefits on December 1, 1978 and became entitled to benefits effective on that date. Mr. Crane also applied for and began receiving Title II Social Security disability benefits effective February 1979.

* * *

II.

The issue for review is a question of statutory interpretation which is reviewed de novo. Department of Social Services v. Bowen, 804 F.2d 1035, 1037 (8th Cir.1986). On cross-motions for summary judgment, the district court reviewed two key provisions of the Social Security Act and interpreted them as entitling Crane to benefits if she can prove her claim of disability. We reverse the district court because the court failed to give appropriate deference to the Secretary's longstanding interpretation of the statutory provisions at issue. See Bowen, 804 F.2d at 1037. In reviewing an agency interpretation of a statutory provision, the Supreme Court has said that if a

> statute is silent or ambiguous with respect to the specific issue, the question for the court is whether the agency's answer is based on a permissible construction of the statute.... [A] court may not substitute its own construction of a statutory provision for a reasonable interpretation made by the administrator of an agency.

Young v. Community Nutrition Institute, 476 U.S. 974, 980, 106 S.Ct. 2360, 2364, 90 L.Ed.2d 959 (1986) (quoting Chevron U.S.A., Inc. v. Natural Resources Defense Council, Inc., 467 U.S. 837, 843-44, 104 S.Ct. 2778, 2782, 81 L.Ed.2d 694 (1984)). In this case, we find the Secretary's interpretation to be both reasonable and based upon a permissible construction of the statutes at issue.

The key provisions are sections 202(d)(1) and 202(d)(5) of the Social Security Act, 42 U.S.C. §§ 402(d)(1), 402(d)(5). Section 402(d)(1) provides, in relevant part, that a child of an individual entitled to retirement or disability benefits is also entitled to "child's insurance benefits" if the child:

(A) has filed [an] application for child insurance benefits,

(B) *at the time such application was filed was unmarried* and

　　(i) either had not attained the age of 18 or was a full-time elementary or secondary school student and had not attained the age of 19, or

　　(ii) *is under a disability ... which began before he attained the age of 22*, and

(C) was dependent upon such individual—

　　(i) if such individual is living, at the time such application was filed, [or]

　　(ii) if such individual has died, at the time of such death....

(emphasis added). Entitlement to such benefits ends when "such child dies, or marries." 42 U.S.C. § 402(d)(1)(D). Section 402(d)(5) further provides in relevant part:

In the case of a child who has attained the age of eighteen and who marries—

(A) an individual entitled to benefits [under specific subsections of the Act] ... or

(B) another individual who has attained the age of eighteen and is entitled to benefits under this subsection,

such child's entitlement to benefits under this subsection shall, notwithstanding the provisions of paragraph (1) of this subsection but subject to subsection (s) of this section, not be terminated by reason of such marriage.

(Emphasis added). An accompanying regulation, 20 C.F.R. § 404.350(d), also states that to be entitled to benefits, the claimant must be unmarried.

The district court held that § 402(d)(1)'s prohibition against married applicants is limited by § 402(d)(5). Thus, the court held that Crane would be eligible for benefits, assuming proof of disability, even though she was married at the time of her application. By contrast, the Secretary asserts that § 402(d)(5) applies only to those applicants who are already receiving child's insurance benefits, to prevent the termination of those benefits if the claimant marries another disabled person. According to the Secretary, § 402(d)(5) does not operate to create an entitlement to benefits if a person marries prior to applying for benefits. Thus, the Secretary concludes that child's insurance benefits are available to an otherwise eligible applicant only if he or she applies prior to marriage.

The Secretary's interpretation is based upon a permissible construction of the two provisions, and is supported by legislative history. Congressional reports indicate that the purpose of § 402(d)(5) is to prevent termination of benefits to a secondary beneficiary when he or she marries another beneficiary in order to prevent undue hardship, even though ordinarily child's insurance benefits are to be cut off once a dependant child marries. See S.Rep. No. 2133, 84th Cong., 2d Sess. (1956), reprinted in 1956 U.S.C.C.A.N. 3877, 3909; S.Rep. No. 2388, 85th Cong., 2d Sess. (1958), reprinted in 1958 U.S.C.C.A.N. 4218, 4233; H.R.Rep. No. 2288, 85th Cong., 2d Sess., 18 (1958), reprinted in 1958 U.S.C.C.A.N. 4218, 4233. In this case, there would be no undue hardship caused by the Secretary's interpretation because Crane has never received child's insurance benefits and has not been relying on them for support.

Not only is the Secretary's interpretation a reasonable one, it is a longstanding one. The Secretary's interpretation is consistent with Social Security Ruling 73-18c, which is based upon Judkins v. Richardson, No. 72-62 (D.Oregon 1972), Unemployment Insurance Reporter (CCH) 16,903, 1972 WL 3966. In *Judkins*, the court held that the claimant was not protected by the exception set out in § 202(d)(5) because it applies only to termination of benefits, rather than initial entitlement. A similar conclusion was reached by the district court in Sanches v. Sullivan, 735 F.Supp. 286 (N.D.Ill.1990). In that case, the court held that the claimant's marriage cut off her *eligibility* for benefits under (d)(1), even though the marriage would not have terminated any pre-existing *entitlement* to benefits under (d)(5). The court further held that (d)(5) only permits the continuation of an already-existing entitlement and does not create any entitlement to benefits where none previously existed.

Because we find the Secretary's longstanding interpretation to be reasonable and entitled to deference, we REVERSE the judgment of the district court and remand the case to the district court for entry of judgment in favor of the Secretary in accordance with this opinion.

3. PARENTS BENEFITS

There are two instances in which a parent can be eligible as such for OASDI benefits on the basis of another person's earning record. First, as noted above, a widow(er) of an insured wage earner may qualify for "mother's and father's insurance benefits" if he or she is the caretaker parent of a deceased wage earner's child under the age of 16. *See* 42 U.S.C. § 402(g). (As we saw earlier, the children themselves are entitled to child's benefits until they reach the age of 18, or 19 if they are in school full-time.)

Under certain limited circumstances, a deceased wage earner's parent may be entitled to secondary benefits. In order to qualify for this type of benefit, the parent must be at least 62 years old and must be able to show that he or she was receiving one-half of his or her financial support from the wage earner at the time of death. Parent's benefits may also be available to a wage earner's stepparents (if the marriage to the wage earner's natural parent took place before the wage earner turned 16) and adopting parents (if the wage earner was adopted before the age of 16). *See* **42 U.S.C. §§ 402 (h)(1), (h)(3)[APP-STAT]**.

CHAPTER 4

ELIGIBILITY CRITERIA FOR DISABILITY BENEFITS

■ ■ ■

The Social Security Act sets out two different disability standards that apply to current claims for benefits. There is also a third standard that applies only to claims dating back to prior to 1991. Each of these three disability standards is discussed generally in this chapter. The standards used for current claims are discussed in more detail in Chapters 5 and 6.

The most important disability standard—by far—is the standard that applies to all current claims for disability benefits under the Old Age, Survivors, and Disability Insurance (OASDI) program, including claims by wage earners and their surviving spouses and disabled children 18 years of age or older, and all claims for Supplemental Security Income (SSI) disability benefits by adults. The Social Security Act defines "disability" for all of those programs as the "inability to engage in any substantial gainful activity by reason of any medically determinable physical or mental impairment which can be expected to result in death or which has lasted or can be expected to last for a continuous period of not less than 12 months." 42 U.S.C. §423(d)(1)(A); *see also* 42 U.S.C. § 1382c(a)(3)(A).

A second, separate disability standard applies to SSI claims on behalf of children under the age of 18. The definition of disability for the purposes of child's SSI benefits differs from the general standard noted above in that it focuses on whether a child "has a medically determinable physical or mental impairment, which results in marked and severe functional limitations," 42 U.S.C. §1382c(a)(3)(C)(i), as opposed to the "inability to engage in substantial gainful activity."

The difference between these two standards—the general standard that applies to all OASDI claims and to SSI claims by adults and the special SSI standard that applies only to claims by children under the age of 18—is seen most dramatically in how they are implemented by the Social Security Administration. Claims for benefits under the general standard are evaluated by SSA's 5-step "sequential evaluation process," which includes at one point the use of a listing of qualified impairments but also allows an individualized assessment of the claimant's medical and vocational capacity to work.   Claims by children under the special SSI child's disability benefits standard are evaluated by means of a shorter version of the sequential evaluation process that lays greater emphasis on the claimant's condition meeting or equaling the requirements of a similar listing of qualified impairments.   The two disability standards are alike, however, in a number of respects: both require that the disability result from a medically determinable physical or mental impairment, and both require that the impairment be expected to result in death, or have lasted, or be expected to last, at least 12 months.   The implementation of both standards and the operation of the sequential evaluation process are discussed in detail in Chapter 5.   Special issues of disability determination under both standards are covered in Chapter 6.

A third, more restrictive disability standard defines disability as the inability to engage in "any gainful activity," as opposed to "any substantial gainful activity," and expressly excludes consideration of vocational factors such as age, education, and prior work experience. *See* 42 U.S.C. §423(d)(2)(B) (1989).   That standard applied for many years to all claims by wage earners' surviving spouses; however, it applies now only to claims for spouses benefits covering periods prior to 1991. (Thus, except for periods prior to 1991, claims by disabled spouses are now measured according to the same disability standard used for claims by wage earners, wage earners' children 18 years of age and older, and adult claimants for Supplemental Security Income.)   SSA implements this more restrictive standard for disabled spouses' claims by using only the first three steps of the 5-step sequential evaluation process, effectively requiring that that a claimant's condition meets or equals the criteria set out in the listing of qualified impairments.   The rules for implementing this standard are discussed briefly in Chapter 5.

A. DISABILITY STANDARD FOR ADULTS

As mentioned above, the general disability standard applicable to OASDI claims by wage earners, their surviving spouses, and their children 18 years of age or older, and by adults under the SSI program, is stated in the Social Security Act as the "inability to engage in any substantial gainful activity" resulting from a medically determinable physical or mental impairment that has lasted or can be expected to last for at least a year, or can be expected to result in death.   **42 U.S.C. § 423(d)(1)(A)[APP-STAT]**.   The disability standard for SSI adult claims has slightly different introductory language, with the standard phrased in terms of an individual who is "unable to engage in substantial gainful activity."   **42 U.S.C. § 1382c(a)(3)(A)[APP-STAT]**.   The substance of the two standards is the same, however, and they are interpreted consistently as being essentially identical. *See, e.g.*, Bowen v. Yuckert, 482 U.S. 137, 140 (1987) (stating that both titles of the Social Security Act define "disability" as the inability to engage in substantial gainful activity); Perez v. Chater, 77 F.3d 41, 46 (2d Cir. 1996).

The general disability standard thus has three separate components: first, a severity requirement, defined as the "inability to engage in any substantial gainful activity"; second, an origin requirement, in that the disability must be based on a "medically determinable physical or mental impairment"; and third, a duration requirement, which limits eligibility to cases where the disability "can be expected to result in death or . . . has lasted or can be expected to last for a continuous period of not less than 12 months." Each of these requirements must be met; for example, a short-term disability, no matter how severe, is not sufficient to establish eligibility for benefits.

The severity requirement is defined further in the Social Security Act. Thus, an individual meets the standard for disability "only if his physical or mental impairment or impairments are of such severity that he is not only unable to do his previous work but cannot, considering his age, education, and work experience, engage in any other kind of substantial gainful work which exists in the national economy." **42 U.S.C. §§423(d)(2)(A)[APP-STAT]**, **1382c(a)(3)(B)[APP-STAT]**. This does not change the fact that the determination of disability under the Act is predominately a medical assessment, not a vocational assessment. As explained by both Senate and House reports accompanying the 1967 amendments to the Act that added the language quoted above:

> The bill would provide that ... an individual would be disabled only if it is shown that he has a severe medically determinable physical or mental impairment or impairments; that if, despite his impairment or impairments, an individual still can do his previous work, he is not under a disability; and that if, considering the severity of his impairment together with his age, education, and experience, he has the ability to engage in some other type of substantial gainful work that exists in the national economy even though he can no longer do his previous work, he also is not under a disability * * *.

S.Rep. No. 744, 90th Cong., 1st Sess. 48-49 (1967); *See also* H.R.Rep. No. 544, 90th Cong., 1st Sess. 30 (1967).

Moreover, the disability standard focuses on a claimant's ability to perform work, not on the ability to obtain employment. Thus, the Social Security Act specifies further that the ability to perform substantial gainful activity is to be determined "regardless of whether such work exists in the immediate area in which [the claimant] lives, or whether a specific job vacancy exists * * *, or whether [the claimant] would be hired." *See* **42 U.S.C. §§423(d)(2)(A)[APP-STAT]**, **1382c(a)(3)(B)[APP-STAT]**. The ultimate question is whether there is any employment available in the "national economy"—defined as "work which exists in significant numbers either in the region where [the claimant] lives or in several regions of the country"—that the claimant can perform. (The Act sets out a more generous interpretation of the "inability to engage in substantial gainful activity" for persons over the age of 55 whose disability is based on blindness. *See* 42 U.S.C. § 423(d)(1)(B) ("requiring skills or abilities comparable to those of any gainful activity in which he has previously engaged with some regularity and over a substantial period of time"), 20 C.F.R. § 404.1583.

In 1984, Congress clarified a long-standing controversy concerning the issue of whether the severity requirement applies to individual impairments or all of a claimant's impairments in combination. The Act now states clearly that a combination of impairments can satisfy the severity requirement. *See* Social Security Disability Benefits Reform Act of 1984, Pub. L. No. 98-460 §4(a)(1), 98 Stat. 1794 (1984); 42 U.S.C. § 423(d)(2)(B).

1. STANDARD FOR FINDING A BENEFICIARY IS NO LONGER DISABLED

Closely tied to the disability standard is a provision in the Social Security Act that specifies the basis for determining that someone who once met the standard is no longer disabled. Essentially, there are two ways to approach the question of whether someone should continue to receive disability benefits: look to see whether the person's situation changed so that he or she is no longer disabled, or decide whether the person would be found disabled if he or she reapplied for benefits. In 1980, the Social Security Administration promulgated regulations that specifically disavowed the first of those approaches by discontinuing the use of a "medical improvement" standard for terminations that it had used until 1977. The new policy contained in the regulations adopted the second approach by allowing benefits to be terminated whenever a recipient no longer met the statutory definition of disability. In other words, the regulations based continuing disability on whether or not the beneficiary was unable to perform substantial gainful activity—the same standard used for initial applicants.

Recipients whose benefits were terminated under the new policy argued that their benefits could not be terminated without substantial evidence that they were no longer disabled. Sometimes the issue was phrased in terms of presumptions and burdens of proof, sometimes in terms of a different standard for terminations, and sometimes in terms of both. By 1983, a "medical improvement" standard had been adopted for terminations in eight circuits, and had been recognized or approved tacitly by three others. *See, e.g.,* Dotson v. Schweiker, 719 F.2d 80, 81-83, 3 Soc. Sec. Rep. Serv. 124 (4th Cir. 1983); Kuzmin v. Schweiker, 714 F.2d

1233, 1237, 2 Soc. Sec. Rep. Serv. 437 (3d Cir. 1983); Simpson v. Schweiker, 691 F.2d 966, 969 (11th Cir. 1982); Patti v. Schweiker, 669 F.2d 582, 587, 10 Fed. R. Evid. Serv. (LCP) 123 (9th Cir. 1982); Cassiday v. Schweiker, 663 F.2d 745, 747 (7th Cir. 1981); Crosby v. Schweiker, 650 F.2d 777, 778 (5th Cir. 1981).

Congress resolved the conflict between SSA's standard for terminating benefits and that used by the courts by adopting a "medical improvement" standard for terminating disability benefits in the 1984 amendments to the Act. Social Security Disability Benefits Reform Act of 1984, Pub L. No. 98-460 § 2, 98 Stat. 1794 (1984). Under the Act as amended, disability benefits can be terminated if "there has been any medical improvement in the [claimant's] impairment or combination of impairments (other than medical improvement which is not related to the [claimant's] ability to work)" and the claimant can engage in substantial gainful activity. 42 U.S.C. § 423 (f)(1)[APP-STAT]. There are, however, three exceptions that allow termination—assuming the claimant can engage in substantial gainful activity—without a showing of medical improvement: if there is new medical evidence and a new assessment of the claimant's residual functional capacity that shows the claimant has benefited from medical or vocational therapy or technology related to his or her ability to work; if the claimant has, in fact, undergone vocational therapy related to his or her ability to work; or if new or improved diagnostic techniques or evaluations establish that the claimant's impairment or combination of impairments was not as disabling as had been found at the last disability determination. 42 U.S.C. § 423(f)(2), (3)[APP-STAT]. Finally, benefits can be terminated without a showing of medical improvement or proof of the claimant's ability to engage in substantial gainful activity if the claimant is, in fact, engaging in substantial gainful activity, if the prior determination of disability was obtained fraudulently, or if substantial evidence from the record of the prior determination—or new evidence relating to that determination—establishes that it was made in error. 42 U.S.C. §§ 423(f)(4), 42 U.S.C. § 1382c(a)(4)[APP-STAT]. *See also* 20 C.F.R. §§ 404.1594, 20 C.F.R. 416.994[APP-REGS].

The following case, which discusses the standard for determining that a disability has ended in the particular context of a "closed period" of disability, illustrates the connection between the general eligibility standard and the special standard for termination of benefits.

SHEPHERD V. APFEL

184 F.3d 1196, 63 Soc. Sec. Rep. Ser. 125 (10th Cir. 1999)

Lucero, Circuit Judge

In this case, we join the majority of other circuits in concluding that the medical improvement standard, as created in 42 U.S.C. § 423(f) and defined by 20 C.F.R. § 404.1594(b)(1), applies in "closed period" cases in which a disability claimant is found to have been disabled for a finite period of time. Exercising jurisdiction pursuant to 28 U.S.C. § 1291, we affirm in part, reverse in part, and remand for further proceedings consistent with this opinion.

I

Appellant is a disability claimant who filed an application for disability benefits in April 1993, which was approved for a closed period of disability spanning from December 8, 1991, through December 31, 1992. A request for reconsideration was denied on July 19, 1993. Following this denial, claimant requested a hearing before an ALJ. The ALJ agreed with the earlier determination that claimant was only eligible for benefits for the closed period noted above because he was not disabled after December 31, 1992. The Appeals Council denied review, and claimant filed a complaint in federal district court. The district court affirmed the commissioner's decision.

* * *

On appeal, claimant asserts that the district court erred in holding that the medical improvement standard does not apply to closed period cases; that the ALJ's determination of his residual functional capacity was flawed; and that a proper hypothetical question was not asked of the vocational expert. We address each claim in turn.

II

A

After a claimant has been receiving disability benefits for some period, the Social Security Administration is required to review his case periodically to determine whether there has been any medical improvement in the claimant's condition and whether that improvement affects his ability to work. See 20 C.F.R. § 404.1594. If the benefit recipient's condition has improved, his eligibility to receive those benefits may terminate.

The following standard of review informs the decision to terminate benefits:

> A recipient of benefits ... may be determined not to be entitled to such benefits on the basis of a finding that the physical or mental impairment on the basis of which such benefits are provided has ceased, does not exist, or is not disabling only if such a finding is supported by

> (1) substantial evidence which demonstrates that—

(A) there has been any medical improvement in the individual's impairment or combination of impairments (other than medical improvement which is not related to the individual's ability to work), and

(B) the individual is now able to engage in substantial gainful activity....

42 U.S.C. § 423(f). The Social Security Administration's regulations define medical improvement as

any decrease in the medical severity of [the] impairment(s) which was present at the time of the most recent favorable medical decision that [the claimant was] disabled or continued to be disabled. A determination that there has been a decrease in medical severity must be based on changes (improvements) in the symptoms, signs and/or laboratory findings associated with [the] impairment(s).

20 C.F.R. § 404.1594(b)(1). The medical improvement standard clearly applies when a disability award has become final and the commissioner brings an action to terminate those benefits. The issue here, however, is whether the medical improvement standard applies in closed period cases, such as this one.[2]

B

We begin with a brief review of the statutory and regulatory development of the medical improvement standard. After a period in which the Social Security Administration had abandoned the medical evidence standard in favor of a current evidence standard, Congress enacted the Social Security Disability Benefits Reform Act of 1984 ("Reform Act"). The Reform Act adopted the medical improvement standard, which now appears at 42 U.S.C. § 423(f), and defined it in this way:

[T]he term "action relating to medical improvement" means an action raising the issue of whether an individual who has had his entitlement to benefits ... based on disability terminated (or period of disability ended) should not have had such entitlement terminated (or period of disability ended) without consideration of whether there has

---

[2] "In a 'closed period' case, the decision maker determines that a new applicant for disability benefits was disabled for a finite period of time which started and stopped prior to the date of his decision." Pickett v. Bowen, 833 F.2d 288, 289 n. 1 (11th Cir.1987). In claimant's case, the ALJ determined in a single document dated September 27, 1995, that claimant had been disabled from December 8, 1991 through December 31, 1992, but not thereafter. "Typically, both the disability decision and the cessation decision [in a closed period case] are rendered in the same document." Id.

been medical improvement in the condition of such individual ... since the time of a prior determination that the individual was under a disability.

See 42 U.S.C. § 423 note (1984 Acts) (Pub.L. No. 98-460 Sec. 2(d)(6)).

The issue of whether claimants involved in closed period cases could have their cases remanded for consideration under the medical improvement standard was not clearly resolved in the Reform Act, however, and the circuits that have considered the issue have disagreed. The Eighth Circuit has held that a closed period case was not an "action relating to medical improvement" for purposes of the Reform Act, and read the remand provisions of the Reform Act to apply only to cases " 'of a prior determination that the individual was under a disability.' " Camp v. Heckler, 780 F.2d 721, 721-22 (8th Cir.1986) (quoting 42 U.S.C. § 423 note (1984 Acts) (Pub.L. No. 98-460 Sec. 2(d)(6))). "Prior determination," the court held, "is more naturally read as referring to a previous decision in favor of disability, followed by the claimant's receipt of benefits, further followed by a new proceeding resulting in cessation or termination on the ground of medical improvement." *Id.* at 722. In a later case, the Eighth Circuit followed *Camp* in refusing to apply the medical improvement test to a closed period case. See Ness v. Sullivan, 904 F.2d 432, 435 n. 4 (8th Cir.1990). More recently, however, the circuit applied the medical improvement standard to a closed period case without discussing or citing *Camp. See* Burress v. Apfel, 141 F.3d 875, 878-880 (8th Cir.1998). Thus, the law in the Eighth Circuit regarding this issue seems presently unsettled.

Other circuits have rejected the Eighth Circuit's approach in *Camp.* The Eleventh Circuit, for example, explicitly criticized Camp for ignoring the legislative history of the Reform Act and "the broad remedial policies underlying the Disability Amendments," in which it discerned that Congress intended to reach closed period claimants. *Pickett*, 833 F.2d at 292 & 293 n. 4. *See also* Jones v. Shalala, 10 F.3d 522, 523-24 (7th Cir.1993) (applying medical improvement standard in its review of closed period case); Chrupcala v. Heckler, 829 F.2d 1269, 1274 (3d Cir.1987) ("Fairness would certainly seem to require an adequate showing of medical improvement whenever an ALJ determines that disability should be limited to a specified period."); *cf.* Bowling v. Shalala, 36 F.3d 431, 435 (5th Cir.1994) (applying traditional five-step sequential analysis to claimant's evidence in a closed period case). We are persuaded by these other circuits that applying the medical improvement standard to cases involving a closed period of disability is consistent with the language and legislative purpose in the Reform Act.[4]

C

In the case before us, the magistrate judge whose order the district court adopted assumed that the medical improvement standard did not apply in closed period cases. Furthermore, the magistrate found that even if the medical improvement did apply, the ALJ's findings support the conclusion that claimant experienced medical improvement and was able to work after that improvement. Having concluded that the medical improvement standard does apply, we must now determine whether the ALJ, who referred to the standard in his decision, applied it correctly in claimant's case. As explained below, we conclude that although the Administrative Law Judge ("ALJ") at least implicitly applied the proper standard in awarding appellant-claimant Dwayne Shepherd only a closed period of disability benefits for impairments sustained as the result of a motorcycle accident, the record lacks substantial evidence to support the ALJ's conclusion that claimant's disability ceased by December 31, 1992. Instead, the record demonstrates that claimant had achieved medical improvement and could perform substantial work by July 7, 1993.

In order to determine whether disability continues or ends, the commissioner must determine "if there has been any medical improvement in [a claimant's] impairment(s) and, if so, whether this medical improvement is related to [the claimant's] ability to work." 20 C.F.R. § 404.1594(a). The regulations contain definitions and examples of when medical improvement is related to the ability to do work, and when it is not so related. See id. at § 404.1594(b)(2) and (b)(3).

To apply the medical improvement test, the ALJ must first compare the medical severity of the current impairment(s) to the severity of the impairment(s) which was present at the time of the most recent favorable medical decision finding the claimant disabled. See id., § 404.1594(b)(7). Then, in order to determine that medical improvement is related to ability to work, the ALJ must reassess a claimant's residual functional capacity (RFC) based on the current severity of the impairment(s) which was

---

[4] We are aware of language in Brown v. Sullivan, 912 F.2d 1194,1196 (10th Cir.1990), indicating that the medical improvement standard applies only in termination cases ("The medical improvement standard applies only in termination cases, not in later applications for benefits."). See also Richardson v. Bowen, 807 F.2d 444, 445-46 (5th Cir.1987) ("The plain language of the [Reform Act] indicates that the Secretary must make a finding of medical improvement only in termination cases."). Neither Brown nor Richardson, however, involved a closed period of disability. In Brown, the claimant had filed a new application for benefits after previous benefits were terminated. Similarly, in Richardson, the claimant's closed period case had already become final, and the Secretary had refused to reopen it after the claimant had filed a new application for benefits. Because the issue of the applicability of the medical improvement standard to closed period cases was not before the court in either of these cases, we are not bound by language limiting the medical improvement standard to termination cases.

present at claimant's last favorable medical decision. *See id.*, §
404.1594(c)(2). The ALJ must then compare the new RFC with the RFC
before the putative medical improvements. The ALJ may find medical
improvement related to an ability to do work only if an increase in the
current RFC is based on objective medical evidence. *See id.*

In this case, the ALJ was asked to review a determination, made at
an earlier stage in the administrative process, that claimant was only
disabled from December 8, 1991, through December 31, 1992. The ALJ
agreed that claimant was disabled by December 8, 1991, because of a
nonunion of a fracture of the tibia, an impairment meeting the listing at
20 C.F.R., Pt. 404, Subpt. P., App. 1 § 1.11. The ALJ also found, however, that claimant was no longer disabled after December 31, 1992. As
support for this conclusion, the ALJ cited the opinions of consultative examiners who found limitation primarily in the lower extremities and none
of consequence in the upper extremities. These examinations, however,
occurred in 1993 and 1994.

The ALJ points to no evidence tied to December 31, 1992, to support
his conclusion that claimant's disability ended as of that date. There is
no evidence in the record of medical improvement of the fractured tibia,
substantiated by changes in signs, symptoms, or laboratory findings,
which took place by December 31, 1992, sufficient to support a conclusion
that disability had ceased. Nor is there an evidentiary basis upon which
the ALJ could have compared the severity of claimant's leg injury on December 31, 1992, with the same condition as it existed on December 8,
1991. Similarly, no evidence allows a comparison of claimant's RFC on
those two dates. Although the ALJ correctly recognized that the medical
improvement test applied in this closed period case, insufficient evidence
supports his conclusion that such improvement had occurred by December 31, 1992.

The same cannot be said, however, of claimant's condition in July
1993. By that date, a consultative examination revealed normal upper
extremities except for slight stiffness in the right elbow, normal range of
motion of the joints of the lower extremities except for the right ankle,
normal peripheral pulses, no ankle swelling, joints not tender to palpita-
tion, full range of motion of the knees (albeit accompanied by crackling
noises), some rotation of the knees, and evident deformities of the legs
from the fractured tibias but no tenderness. Muscle strength in the
hands, forearms, arms, and legs were normal and equal bilaterally.
Claimant could walk at a normal pace and with good stability, although
he required a leg brace on his right leg. Claimant expressed an interest
in retraining to become a motorcycle mechanic, and the consultative physician believed he could be motivated to seek alternative occupation and
training. Furthermore, Dr. Luther Woodcock had concluded that by July

1993, claimant had the residual functional capacity to perform sedentary work because he could occasionally lift ten pounds, frequently lift five to ten pounds, stand at least two hours in an eight-hour workday, sit about six hours in an eight-hour workday and had unlimited ability to push and/or pull.

Thus, there was a period between December 1992 and July 1993 during which claimant may have been eligible for benefits. Because the record is unclear, however, regarding what portion of this period saw claimant incarcerated and thus ineligible for benefits, we must remand to the district court for further development of this factual issue.

* * *

[T]he judgment is AFFIRMED in part and REVERSED in part, and the case is REMANDED for further proceedings.

B. DISABILITY STANDARD FOR CHILDREN

There are two categories of disability benefits available to "children" in the Social Security Act: Child's Insurance Benefits under the OASDI program for disabled children of insured wage earners and SSI benefits for children under the age of 18. The disability standard for Child's Insurance Benefits is the same as the standard discussed in the previous section for adults. *See* **42 U.S.C. § 1382c(a)(3)(B)[APP-STAT]**. By contrast, there is an entirely different disability standard for children under the SSI program.

The adult disability standard is applied for Child Insurance Benefits claims because the concept of "child" in that program—with respect to the awarding of disability benefits—is based on dependency and the parent-child relationship, not the age of the child. As explained in Chapter 3, dependent children of wage earners are eligible for Disability Insurance Benefits up to the age of 18 or 19 (if enrolled full-time in school) without regard to disability; therefore, the question of disability does not arise for children below the age of 18. The disability part of the Child Insurance Benefit program comes into play only after the child reaches the age of 18; in other words, only once the "child" is an adult. *See* **42 U.S.C. § 402(d)(1)(B)[APP-STAT]**.

Under the SSI program, benefits are paid to persons with limited income and resources who are at least 65 years old or disabled. Because SSI disability benefits are available at any age, the SSI program uses a separate child's disability standard for claimants under the age of 18. Thus, the current operative language in the Act, revised in 1996, provides that a child is considered disabled for purposes of SSI if he or she has "marked and severe functional limitations," as opposed to being unable to engage in substantial gainful activity. Consistent with the adult disability standard, a child SSI claimant must show that the these functional limitations are due to medically determinable physical or mental impairments that have lasted or can be expected to last for at least 12 months (or can be expected to result in death). *See* **42 U.S.C. § 1382c(a)(3)(C)[APP-STAT]; 20 C.F.R. § 416.906[APP-REGS]**.

1. SSI CHILD'S BENEFITS: DISABILITY STANDARD FOR CHILDREN UNDER THE AGE OF 18

Over the years, there has been a substantial amount of difficulty and controversy regarding the implementation of the disability standard for SSI child's benefits, in part because the base notion of disability under the Social Security Act—the inability to work at a job—does not adapt well to the special circumstances of disabled children (and particularly so for very young children). The pre-1996 history of the program and its relevance to current claims are discussed in the following case. The separate processes that SSA uses to implement the disability standards for adult and child SSI claims are discussed in detail in Chapter 5.

ENCARNACION V. ASTRUE
568 F.3d 72, 143 Soc. Sec. Rep. Serv. 33 (2nd Cir. 2009)

Before: McLAUGHLIN, WESLEY, and HALL, Circuit Judges.

McLAUGHLIN, Circuit Judge:

The plaintiffs represent a putative class of children whose parents claim that the Commissioner of Social Security (the "Commissioner") has implemented a policy (the "Policy") that excludes some children from eligibility for Supplemental Security Income Benefits ("SSI Benefits") in a manner that violates the Social Security Act (the "Act") and the Commissioner's own regulations. Pursuant to those regulations, childhood disability is determined by evaluating applicants within six domains of functioning, such as the child's ability to acquire and use information. Children are eligible for benefits if they have at least two "marked" limitations on their functioning within these domains or at least one "extreme" limitation. Under the Policy, the combined effect of a child's multiple mental or physical impairments may be deemed a marked or extreme limitation if the limitation occurs within a single domain. But the Policy prohibits the Social Security Administration (the "SSA") from considering the combined effects of limitations in different domains. Thus, the SSA will not adjust a less-than-marked limitation in one domain based on limitations in other domains.

The plaintiffs maintain that the Policy violates the Act's command that the SSA consider the combined effects of a child's impairments "throughout the disability determination process." 42 U.S.C. § 1382c(a)(3)(G). They also claim that the Policy violates a nearly identical provision in the Commissioner's regulations. The district court disagreed and granted summary judgment to the Commissioner. We AFFIRM.

BACKGROUND

This is the second time we have addressed the plaintiffs' claims. We provide an abbreviated version of the extensive background, including the relevant statutory and regulatory history, recounted in our prior decision, Encarnacion ex rel. George v. Barnhart, 331 F.3d 78, 80-86 (2d Cir.2003) ("*Encarnacion I*").

The Act provides for SSI Benefits to disabled children as well as adults. The Commissioner has authority to promulgate regulations to determine eligibility for SSI Benefits. See 42 U.S.C. § 405(a). In 1984, Congress added to the Act a provision that applies to all disability determinations (whether for children or adults), which instructs:

In determining whether an individual's physical or mental impairment or impairments are of a sufficient medical severity that such impairment or impairments could be the basis of eligibility [for SSI Benefits], the [Commissioner] shall consider the combined effect of all of the individual's impairments without regard to whether any such impairment, if considered separately, would be of such severity. If the [Commissioner] does find a medically severe combination of impairments, the combined impact of the impairments shall be considered throughout the disability determination process.

Social Security Disability Benefits Reform Act of 1984, Pub.L. No. 98-460, § 4, 98 Stat. 1794, 1800 (codified at 42 U.S.C. § 1382c(a)(3)(G)). In 1985, the SSA adopted a regulation that repeats this statute nearly verbatim. *See* 50 Fed.Reg. 8,726, 8,729 (Mar. 5, 1985)(codified at 20 C.F.R. § 416.923). These two provisions are central to the plaintiffs' claims in this case.

The Commissioner's regulations for determining a child's eligibility for SSI Benefits have undergone many amendments. One important change came as a result of the Supreme Court's decision in Sullivan v. Zebley, 493 U.S. 521, 110 S.Ct. 885, 107 L.Ed.2d 967 (1990). There, the Supreme Court held that the SSA regulations for determining whether a child is disabled, which permitted benefits to children only if their impairments matched or medically equaled specific impairments listed in an appendix to the SSA's regulations, were an impermissible implementation of the Act. *See id.* at 526, 541, 110 S.Ct. 885. The regulations did not permit a child claimant to show that "the overall functional impact of his unlisted impairment or combination of impairments is as severe as that of a listed impairment." *Id.* at 531, 110 S.Ct. 885.

In response to *Sullivan*, the SSA amended the regulations to require an "individualized functional assessment" ("IFA") for each child. *See* 56 Fed.Reg. 5,534 (Feb. 1, 1991) (codified at 20 C.F.R. § 416.924). As a result of the new regulations, a child's impairments were evaluated within six domains of childhood activity or functioning. *See Encarnacion I*, 331 F.3d at 83. The amended regulations established a hierarchy of limitations (the effect of an impairment or combination of impairments): "extreme," "marked," "moderate," and "severe." *See id.* The regulations recommended that children be deemed disabled if their impairments caused a marked limitation in one domain and a moderate limitation in another domain, or if a child had three moderate limitations. *See id.*

In 1996, the regime for children's SSI Benefits underwent more changes. Congress amended the Act to define a "disabled" child as one who "has a medically determinable physical or mental impairment, which results in marked or severe functional limitations, and which can be expected to result in death or which has lasted or can be expected to last for a continuous period of not less than 12 months." Personal Responsibility and Work Opportunity Reconciliation Act of 1996, Pub.L. No. 104-193, § 211, 110 Stat. 2105, 2188-89 (codified at 42 U.S.C. § 1382c (a)(3)(C)(i)). Congress made clear that children should not qualify for benefits under the new definition unless they have at least two marked limitations, thus making eligibility more restrictive.

The Commissioner was charged with promulgating "such regulations as may be necessary to implement" the amendment, *id.* § 215, 110 Stat. at 2196, and issued regulations pursuant to this statutory authority, *see* 20 C.F.R. § 416.924 et seq. The regulations establish a three-step process. First, the child must not be engaged in "substantial gainful activity." *Id.* § 416.924(a). Second, the child "must have a medically determinable impairment(s)" that is "severe" in that it causes "more than minimal functional limitations." *Id.* § 416.924(c). Third, the child's impairment or combination of impairments must medically or functionally equal an impairment listed in an appendix to the regulations. *See id.* § 416.924(d); 20 C.F.R. pt. 404, subpt. P, app. 1 (listing and describing impairments). The plaintiffs' challenge concerns the manner of determining functional equivalence at the third step of this process.

For a child's impairment to functionally equal a listed impairment, the impairment must "result in 'marked' limitations in two domains of functioning or an 'extreme' limitation in one domain." 20 C.F.R. § 416.926a(a). The domains that the regulations establish to determine whether impairments result in marked or extreme limitations are: (1) acquiring and using information, (2) attending and completing tasks, (3) interacting and relating with others, (4) moving about and manipulating objects, (5) caring for oneself, and (6) health and physical well-being. *Id.* § 416.926a(b)(1). The SSA must determine whether an impairment or combination of impairments causes a "marked" limitation on a child's functioning in at least two of these domains, or an "extreme" limitation in at least one domain. A "marked" limitation is "'more than moderate' but 'less than extreme'" and "interferes seriously with" a child's "ability to independently initiate, sustain, or complete activities." *Id.* § 416.926a(e)(2)(i). An "extreme" limitation is "'more than marked'" and "interferes very seriously with" a child's "ability to independently initiate, sustain, or complete activities." *Id.* § 416. 926a(e)(3). The regulations recognize that an impairment or combination of impairments may have effects in more than one domain; thus, the SSA evaluates a child's impairments in any domain in which they cause limitations. *Id.* § 416.926a(c). The question that the plaintiffs urge us to answer in the affirmative is whether the Act and the regulations require the SSA to consider the combined effects of a child's impairments across domains. In other words, must the SSA consider, for example, whether the effects of impairments that cause a moderate limitation on a child's ability to acquire and use information (domain 1) and a moderate limitation on the child's ability to complete tasks (domain 2) result in a marked limitation? The plaintiffs advocate that the SSA must consider such adjustments to limitation levels to properly take a "comprehensive look" at the applicant. Under its Policy, the SSA does not engage in this sort of analysis.

The Commissioner points to two documents to support the existence of the Policy: an SSA training manual, see SSA, Office of Disability, Publ'n No. 64-075, Childhood Disability Training: Student Manual, Tab F at 15 (1997), and commentary in the notice of the agency's final rulemaking implementing Congress's 1996 amendments, see 65 Fed.Reg. 54,747, 54,763 (Sept. 11, 2000) (codified at 20 C.F.R. pts. 404, 416). The manual provides that "[m]oderate limitations cannot be 'added up' to equal a 'marked' limitation." In the rulemaking notice, the Commissioner explained that permitting a finding of disability based on less-than-marked limitations in multiple domains would improperly reinstate the IFA process, under which a child with three moderate limitations could be considered disabled. *See id.*

In September 2000, the plaintiffs sued the Commissioner in the U.S. District Court for the Southern District of New York (Swain, J.), claiming that they were denied benefits because of the Policy and that the Policy violated the Act because it prevented the agency from considering the combined effect of impairments throughout the disability-determination process. The district court upheld the Policy, and we affirmed, reading the SSA regulations to provide sufficient flexibility to "look comprehensively at the combined effects of [a claimant's] impairments." *Encarnacion I*, 331 F.3d at 90 (internal quotation marks omitted). We left open, however, the possibility of a later suit alleging that: (1) the Commissioner did not, in fact, permit the SSA to "adjust the level of a claimant's limitation within one or two domains to 'look comprehensively' at the claimant and account for the 'interactive and cumulative effects' of limitations in other domains," or (2) the domains insufficiently account for significant aspects of childhood functioning. *See id.* at 89 & n. 7 (citations omitted).

The plaintiffs filed this case in September 2003, alleging that the Policy prevents the SSA from adding together less-than-marked limitations from separate domains and prohibits the SSA from adjusting the level of limitation in one domain to reflect the impact of limitations in other domains. In support of their claims, the plaintiffs submitted an expert declaration from Kevin P. Dwyer, a school psychologist. Dwyer opined that the Policy resulted in an "irrational and unscientific" methodology for determining disability and denied benefits to children who were as, or more, disabled than those who had two marked limitations and qualified for benefits.

The district court granted summary judgment to the Commissioner. The court concluded that *Encarnacion I* did not require the Commissioner to engage in cross-domain combination of less-than-marked limitations and that the regulations, as informed by the Policy, adequately took into account the combined effect of a child's impairments. The court also found that Dwyer's general statements, unconnected to any actual cases, were insufficient to defeat summary judgment.

The plaintiffs now appeal.

DISCUSSION

We review de novo the district court's grant of summary judgment.

I. Effect of *Encarnacion I*

The plaintiffs contend that *Encarnacion I* dictates a result in their favor. We disagree.

In *Encarnacion I*, the Court gave three reasons for rejecting the plaintiffs' challenge. First, the SSA considers impairments in each domain that they affect. 331 F.3d at 88. Second, the SSA evaluates the combined effects of impairments within each affected domain. *Id.* And third, notwithstanding the Policy, the regulations appeared to the Court to permit "the existence of sub-marked limitations in other domains [to] influence the level of impairment [the] SSA finds in any one given domain," although not in the sense that the SSA would add up less-than-marked limitations to equal a marked limitation. See id. at 88, 89. Thus, in the Court's view, the plaintiffs' challenge rested on the incorrect "assumption that after adding together limitations within domains, [the] SSA makes no further adjustments to the level of limitation in each domain." *Id.* at 88.

The Court also noted that "the flexibility to account for cumulative effects ... is likely essential to a permissible implementation of the Act" because, under Sullivan v. Zebley, 493 U.S. 521, 110 S.Ct. 885, 107 L.Ed.2d 967 (1990), and the Act's language, an impairment cannot be "assigned zero weight in the ultimate decision whether or not to award benefits." *Encarnacion I*, 331 F.3d at 89, 90. However, based on the record before it, the Court was "satisfied that the agency's policy of considering the combined impact of an impairment within every affected domain but not adding across domains is not a plainly erroneous procedure ... particularly since SSA regulations are flexible enough to allow [Administrative Law Judges] to look comprehensively at the combined effects of [a claimant's] impairments." *Id.* at 90 (internal quotation marks omitted).

Judge Raggi wrote a separate concurrence to emphasize her view that the Court's opinion permitted, but did not require, the Commissioner to adjust the limitation level within one domain based on limitations in other domains. *See id.* at 92 (Raggi, J., concurring). Judge Raggi noted that "the SSA does not presently engage in across-domain analysis in determining childhood disability," but concluded that the Commissioner's method of evaluating the combined effects of impairments within each domain they affect was a reasonable implementation of the statute. *See id.* at 92-93. With regard to the majority's statement that the flexibility it described was "likely essential to a permissible implementation of the Act," Judge Raggi understood the majority to "refer[ ] both to the flexibility available in the present SSA practice ... as well as to the flexibility afforded by the alternative across-domain adjustment process." *Id.* (internal quotation marks omitted).

We believe that *Encarnacion I* did not resolve the precise issue before us. Rather, the Court suggested what the plaintiffs assumed did not exist: the possibility of cross-domain adjustment as part of the agency's "comprehensive" look at each applicant. There is now, however, no dispute that the SSA, in practice, does not engage in the sort of cross-domain adjustment that the Court in *Encarnacion I* thought the regulations permitted. Because it believed that the regulations allowed cross-domain adjustments, the Court in *Encarnacion I* did not decide whether the Commissioner could permissibly implement the Act without such analysis.

Like Judge Raggi, we do not read the majority's statement about sufficient flexibility to require the SSA to adjust the limitation level in one domain based on limitations in other domains. *See id.* at 92. Instead, we understand the Court to have meant that the Commissioner's interpretation could not be so inflexible as to assign zero weight to an impairment in the disability-determination process.[1] We know that the Court found sufficient flexibility for the three reasons noted above. We simply do not know, because the Court was not required to decide, whether the Court would have reached the same result absent the third of those three reasons-i.e., that the agency could adjust limitation levels within a particular domain based on a comprehensive look at the claimant. We therefore must decide that issue here.

II. Deference Due the Policy

The plaintiffs allege that the Policy conflicts with both the Act and the regulations. Before addressing the substance of their challenge, we must decide the level of deference due the Commissioner.

Whether a court defers to an agency's interpretation "depends in significant part upon the interpretive method used and the nature of the question at issue." *Barnhart v. Walton*, 535 U.S. 212, 222, 122 S.Ct. 1265, 152 L.Ed.2d 330 (2002). When Congress has entrusted rulemaking authority under a statute to an administrative agency, we evaluate the agency's implementing regulations under *Chevron, U.S.A., Inc. v. Natural Resources Defense Council, Inc.*, 467 U.S. 837, 104 S.Ct. 2778, 81 L.Ed.2d 694 (1984). A similar deference applies when an agency interprets its own regulations. That interpretation, regardless of the formality of the procedures used to formulate it, is "controlling unless plainly erroneous or inconsistent with the regulation[s]." *Auer v. Robbins*, 519 U.S. 452, 461, 117 S.Ct. 905, 137 L.Ed.2d 79 (1997) (internal quotation marks omitted); *see also Encarnacion I*, 331 F.3d at 86 ("[A]n agency's interpretation of its own regulations is entitled to considerable deference, irrespective of the formality of the procedures used in formulating the interpretation."). Even if neither Chevron nor Auer applies, an agency interpretation is still entitled to " 'respect according to its persuasiveness' " under *Skidmore v. Swift & Co.*, 323 U.S. 134, 65 S.Ct. 161, 89 L.Ed. 124 (1944).

The plaintiffs argue that the Policy is not entitled to *Chevron* deference because it is not found in the regulations themselves, but is only expressed, if at all, in informal sources like the training manual.[2] The plaintiffs also argue that the Policy is not entitled to *Auer* deference to the extent that it interprets 20 C.F.R. § 416.923 because that regulation merely

---

[1] To the extent that the Court in *Encarnacion I* meant to suggest that the Act required the agency to make cross-domain adjustments, any such comments are dicta and do not free us of the obligation to decide the issue ourselves.

[2] The plaintiffs contend that the training manual and commentary to the 2000 rulemaking contain only "sparse and inconclusive references" to the Policy, and that the Commissioner has fully articulated the Policy only in this litigation.

parrots the language of 42 U.S.C. § 1382c(a)(3)(G). We need not resolve these issues because we conclude that, even applying the less deferential *Skidmore* standard, the Policy must be upheld.

III. Application of *Skidmore*

The weight we give an interpretation under *Skidmore* depends "upon the thoroughness evident in its consideration, the validity of its reasoning, its consistency with earlier and later pronouncements, and all those factors which give it power to persuade." *Skidmore*, 323 U.S. at 140, 65 S.Ct. 161. To gauge the persuasiveness of the Commissioner's interpretation, we begin with the text of the Act and regulation, both of which require the SSA to consider the combined impact of a claimant's impairments "throughout the disability determination process." 42 U.S.C. § 1382c(a)(3)(G); 20 C.F.R. § 416.923.

It is undisputed that the "disability determination process" is the sequential process that the Commissioner has established under his broad statutory authority. *See, e.g.,* 42 U.S.C. § 405(a) (authorizing the Commissioner to promulgate regulations to determine eligibility for benefits); Pub.L. No. 104-193, § 215, 110 Stat. at 2196 (authorizing the Commissioner to implement the amended definition of childhood disability). The requirement that the combination of impairments be considered throughout the process must therefore be measured with reference to the "process" the Commissioner has created. We suggested in *Encarnacion I* that "the Act appears to require that each of a claimant's impairments be given at least some effect during each step of the disability determination process." 331 F.3d at 90. The Commissioner's interpretation satisfies this test because the SSA considers all impairments within each domain, the final step of the process as the Commissioner has defined it. The SSA "will consider a single impairment in every domain it affects, no matter the degree[,][and] will assess the cumulative impact of all impairments relevant to a particular domain in assessing a child's cumulative functional limitation in that domain." *Id.* at 88. Thus, the Policy complies with the statutory language by mandating consideration of the combined impact of all impairments within each domain that the impairments affect. Contrary to the plaintiffs' argument, therefore, the Commissioner's interpretation does not assign "zero weight" to any impairment or combination of impairments.[3]

---

3 This case is unlike *Sullivan v. Zebley*, where the Supreme Court concluded that the childhood-disability regulations did not allow for consideration of all impairments throughout the process. *See* 493 U.S. at 535 n. 16, 110 S.Ct. 885. The Court explained, however, that if children were given the same level of individualized consideration as adults, the regulations would comply with the statute. See id. For adults, the agency did not merely focus on the type of impairments, but evaluated the effect of all impairments on a claimant's functioning. *See id.* at 535-36 & 535 n. 15, 110 S.Ct. 885. Within the domain system, the SSA provides an individualized assessment of the combined impact of a child's impairments; it does not merely look at the type of

We also believe that the Commissioner's interpretation is consistent with the statutory changes Congress made in 1996. As we have noted, Congress intended the changes in the definition of childhood disability to ensure that only those children with at least two marked limitations within particular domains qualified for SSI Benefits. *See id.* at 83-84. Moreover, in its efforts to tighten eligibility, Congress rejected the IFA process, which had allowed the SSA greater flexibility to award benefits to children with fewer than two marked limitations. *See id.* at 84. We find persuasive the Commissioner's view that adjusting limitations in one domain based on limitations in another domain would result in benefits to children who did not satisfy the more restrictive standard Congress sought to impose, and would be too close to the IFA process Congress eliminated.

The Commissioner's interpretation—focusing on combined impairments within each domain—is easily understood and applied in a reasonably transparent manner. In contrast, we have difficulty understanding how the plaintiffs' interpretation of the statute would function in practice.

Because the plaintiffs do not challenge the Commissioner's use of the domains to determine functional equivalence, any interpretation they offer must account for the domains. While the plaintiffs' briefs and expert declaration are replete with condemnations of the Policy, they offer nothing in the way of an alternative system that would satisfy the statute and be efficiently administered, using the domains. For example, the plaintiffs' expert opines that the Commissioner's Policy fails to consider, in the ultimate benefits determination, certain impairments that do not lead to marked limitations in any particular domain. He explains that "no competent clinician would fail to include [those impairments] as a highly relevant variable in the equation." *How* the SSA would consider impairments as a "relevant variable" outside the domains, in a system overseen by administrative law judges, not clinicians, is unexplained. The plaintiffs' briefs are similarly unenlightening. We are left with vague arguments that the Commissioner could have designed a better regulatory system to effectuate Congress's general marching orders. But "[w]here ambiguities in statutory analysis and application are presented, the agency may choose among reasonable alternatives." *Id.* at 1158.

Apart from the text, congressional purpose, and practical considerations, other factors point in favor of the Commissioner's interpretation. The SSA has substantial expertise and is charged with administering a complex statute. The agency's considerable efforts to refine the disability-determination process for children and align it with congressional purposes has led to "a body of experience and informed judgment to which

---

impairments in an objective fashion, but analyzes the effect of the impairments on the specific child claimant.

courts and litigants may properly resort for guidance." *Id.* at 1156 (internal quotation marks omitted). And the plaintiffs do not contend that the Commissioner has waffled in his interpretation of the statute or regulations; rather, his interpretation has been consistent since the agency implemented the 1996 amendments.

Finally, the plaintiffs inordinately rely on the Dwyer declaration to argue that the Policy "violates accepted clinical standards for the evaluation of children and leads to irrational results." We lack the authority and are ill-equipped, in contrast to the Commissioner, to decide the best method to determine childhood disability. Nor does the plaintiffs' expert declaration (unaccompanied by any evidence as to actual children who are adversely affected by the Policy or a concrete alternative to the Commissioner's interpretation) overcome the Commissioner's reasonable, consistent application of the statute. We will not reject the agency's otherwise persuasive interpretation on the say-so of a single expert armed only with hypotheticals.

We therefore conclude that the Commissioner's interpretation of the Act and implementing regulations, embodied in the Policy, is entitled to deference under *Skidmore*.

CONCLUSION

For the foregoing reasons, we AFFIRM the district court's judgment.

2. OASDI CHILD'S BENEFITS: PROOF OF DISABILITY BEFORE THE AGE OF 22

Although the disability standard for Child's Insurance Benefits is the same as that used for all OASDI and adult SSI disability claims, the child claimant must also prove that he or she met the standard before the age of 22. This is not a problem for claimants who apply before or shortly after they become 22 years old. Often, however, there is a substantial time lag before a child applies for benefits. In such cases, the status of the child's disability during the intervening years can be critical.

MILLER v. SHALALA

859 F.Supp. 297, 45 Soc.Sec.Rep.Ser. 457 (S.D.Ohio1994)

Holschuh, Chief Judge.

Plaintiff, James D. Miller, filed this action seeking review of a final decision of the Secretary of Health and Human Services ("Secretary") denying his application for child's insurance benefits. That application, which was filed on August 2, 1990, was based upon Miller's developmental disability, which allegedly occurred while he was the dependent child of an insured wage earner, Donald I. Miller.

* * *

Plaintiff was born on November 14, 1959, and is now 34 years old. The parties do not disagree that he is currently disabled. In fact, an application for social security disability benefits based upon his own earnings record was granted in a decision issued by an Administrative Law Judge on October 31, 1990. In that decision, the Administrative Law Judge concluded that plaintiff suffered from a severe developmental disorder with borderline intellectual functioning, and that this disorder caused marked impairment of his attention and concentration and his ability to process new information. Because of those impairments, the Administrative Law Judge did not believe that plaintiff could be expected to maintain adequate attention and concentration or demonstrate sufficient independence and reliability to perform even low stress, simple repetitive duties in unskilled entry level work in a competitive setting. The decision fixed the onset date of this disability as March 18, 1988. Thus, the issue here is not whether plaintiff is disabled, but whether he qualifies for child's disability benefits as well.

Child's disability benefits are provided for in 42 U.S.C. § 402(d)(1)(B)(ii). One of the requirements for benefits under that section is that the claimant be "under a disability ... which began before he attained the age of 22...." Thus, the focus of the inquiry in this case was whether plaintiff's existing disability began before he turned 22. The Court will discuss below the divergence in the parties' legal theories as to what, in addition to a disability commencing before age 22, must be shown in order for the plaintiff to qualify for benefits. * * *

* * *

Plaintiff has a fairly extensive work history. While in high school, and as part of the special education program, he worked as a bagger at a grocery store. After graduation, he worked in the maintenance and janitorial areas at Goodwill Industries. Through that organization, he then obtained a janitorial and maintenance job at a drug store, which he held for six months. He then went to a job training workshop and, after a period of training, obtained employment at a Ponderosa Steakhouse. He was a dishwasher, breakfast cook, and janitor. He held that job for several years, but was eventually fired because he was late for work as a result of being arrested for possession of marijuana.

Plaintiff has not held steady employment since leaving Ponderosa. He did work for a period of time as a laborer with a company that bags potting soil, and then worked at several fast food restaurants because his sister-in-law was also working there. He did light maintenance and some cooking at those restaurants. He quit the second job, however, after "getting into it" with his sister-in-law. Between the two fast food restaurant jobs, he also was a dishwasher and silver polisher with a catering service. His employment with Ponderosa ended in 1986, and he earned less than $2,000 in 1987 and 1988. It does not appear that he has had any earnings from 1989 to the present.

* * *

In his motion for summary judgment, plaintiff raises two arguments. First, he asserts that the Secretary incorrectly applied a "continuous disability" test. He asserts that his application should have been granted based upon the fact that his impairments arose prior to his twenty-second birthday, that he was under a disability at that time, and that he is now disabled from the same set of impairments. Alternatively, he argues that the Secretary's finding that he was not disabled from at least 1984 through 1986 is not supported by substantial evidence because the work he performed at Ponderosa was not truly competitive and gainful employment. * * *

The Court begins with the question of what a child must show in order to be entitled to benefits under 42 U.S.C. § 402(d). The Court of Appeals clearly answered this question in Futernick v. Richardson, 484 F.2d 647 (6th Cir.1973) (per curiam) by holding that two showings must be made: (1) that the claimant was disabled on or before the applicant's birthday (here, the twenty-second birthday); and (2) that such disability continues to the date of the application. This "continuous disability" interpretation of the statute appears to be a long-standing policy of the Secretary, and it has been accepted as an appropriate interpretation by numerous courts of appeal. This Court need not concern itself with decisions from other Courts of Appeals, however, in light of the clear holding in *Futernick*, which is, of course, binding on this Court.

Plaintiff suggests, however, that *Futernick* is not really the law of this circuit. Pointing to later decisions which, plaintiff contends, cannot be reconciled with *Futernick*, he argues that this Court must choose among conflicting precedents, and should reach a result in keeping with the liberal construction to be applied to the Social Security Act. Having reviewed the other decisions which plaintiff claims to be in conflict with *Futernick*, the Court concludes that this argument is without merit.

Plaintiff contends that Parish v. Califano, 642 F.2d 188 (6th Cir.1981) lays out a broad exception to the *Futernick* rule and leaves the Court in a position of having little guidance to determine whether the *Futernick* rule or the *Parish* exception applies. Interestingly, Parish begins by citing *Futernick* with approval. However, the Court concluded that the claimant's disability was continuous, as *Futernick* requires, because the work which the claimant had done after her twenty-second birthday was not substantial gainful activity. The Court noted that the claimant had never been employed in a competitive setting and that her work history consisted of 32 weeks of sporadic work spread out over an eight-year period. Essentially, the Court concluded that even plaintiff's lengthiest effort at employment, which came after her twenty-second birthday, was the equivalent of a "trial work period." Noting that an unsuccessful attempt to work made after an application for benefits is filed does not disqualify the applicant for benefits, the Court applied the same test to the claimant's pre-application efforts, and found they did not constitute substantial gainful activity. *Parish* was also unusual in that it involved a claimant with multiple sclerosis, which is a disorder with periods of remission. The Court concluded that the Secretary had not adequately taken into account the fact that most of the claimant's work activity occurred while her disease was in remission. Clearly, because *Parish* applied the continuous disability rule, it is not inconsistent with *Futernick*.

In keeping with *Parish*, many courts have consistently recognized that even a plaintiff who engages in what otherwise appears to be substantial gainful activity can, by presenting appropriate facts, demonstrate that his or her disability has been continuous. Thus, the inquiry in this case may be collapsed into a single question: despite the fact that plaintiff earned in excess of $300 per month for several years, which creates a rebuttable presumption that he was engaged in substantial gainful activity, was plaintiff nonetheless continuously disabled since before his twenty-second birthday?   * * *

Simply put, it is a factual question as to whether this plaintiff's work activity at Ponderosa was substantial, gainful employment. On this record, a reasonable person could conclude that it was. Nothing more is needed to sustain the Secretary's decision that plaintiff was not under a continuous disability from before his twenty-second birthday to the date of his application. Under *Futernick*, that conclusion requires that the application be denied.

Based upon the foregoing, it is ordered that:

1. The Plaintiff's motion for summary judgment is DENIED:

2. The Defendant's motion for summary judgment is GRANTED;

3. The Clerk shall enter judgment in favor of the Defendant.

NOTE

While the disability standard for children over the age of 18 is the same as for all other adult claimant, SSA has recognized that "young adults" may be evaluated somewhat differently than older adults. Basically, it evaluates disability for claimants between the ages of 18 and 25 in much the same way as it does for those considered "older adolescents" in the SSI program (between the ages of 12 and 18). *See* SSR 11-2p (2011) (setting out special rules for evaluating evidence of functioning from school programs, community experiences, psychosocial supports, structured settings, and other types of extra help and accommodations).

C. OTHER RELATED DISABILITY STANDARDS

There are a number of disability standards other than those mentioned so far that impact on Social Security disability practice. Two (really one and a group of others) relate directly to OASDI and SSI eligibility: a special disability standard for Spouses Insurance Benefits that applies only to periods of disability before 1991, and various state disability standards that apply to supplementary state payments for SSI beneficiaries. Then there are standards for other disability benefit programs—veteran's benefits is the prime example—for which a Social Security disability benefits claimant may also be eligible, and with respect to which a finding of disability may have an impact on the claimant's Social Security claim. Finally, findings relative to other disability-related legislation with different goals and objectives—the American's with Disabilities Act (ADA), for example—may also be relevant to certain Social Security claims.

1. SPECIAL DISABILITY STANDARD FOR PRE-1991 SPOUSES BENEFITS

Until 1991, the general disability standard for Spouses Insurance Benefits, applicable to claims by a wage earner's widow, widower, or surviving divorced spouse, was substantially different from the general disability standard for other OASDI and adult SSI benefits. Both standards included the requirement that the disability result from a "medically determinable" physical or mental impairment that could be expected to last at least 12 months or to result in death. However, the disability standard for spouses deviated from the general disability standard in three major respects: it required an impairment that would preclude "engaging in any gainful activity" (as opposed to "any substantial gainful activity"); it expressly authorized the Secretary of the Department of Health and Human Services—in effect, the Social Security Administration—to define that higher level of severity by regulation; and it required that a spouse's ability to engage in any gainful activity had to be determined without considering any non-medical vocational factors, such as age, education, and past work experience. *See* 42 U.S.C. § 423(d)(2)(B) (1988).

As the difference in language between "substantial gainful activity" and "any gainful activity" and the elimination of age, education, and work experience as factors in the disability standard indicate, the disability requirement for Spouse's Insurance Benefits was intended to be stricter than the disability requirement for other OASDI and adult SSI. When the Social Security Act was amended in 1967 to include coverage for disabled surviving spouses, the Senate Committee on Finance stated that these benefits were being added "under a test of disability that is somewhat more restrictive than that for disabled workers and childhood disability beneficiaries." S. Rep. No. 744, 90th Cong., 1st Sess. 49 (1967). More important as a practical matter, the standard for surviving spouses disability benefits was implemented differently by the Social Security Administration. The only basis for establishing eligibility was through proof that the claimant had an impairment that met or equaled the requirements of an impairment included in the SSA's Listing of Impairments. The Listing of Impairments and its role in the "sequential evaluation process" for determining disability are discussed in detail in Chapter 5.

Congress amended the Social Security Act in 1990 to conform the disability standard for Spouses Insurance Benefits to that applied to other AOSDI and adult SSI claims. However, the change is effective only with respect to periods of disability after January 1, 1991. Therefore, for any claim filed by a surviving spouse that includes an alleged period of disability prior to 1991, the claimant's disability during the period prior to 1991 is evaluated according to the pre-1991 standard. *See* **20 C.F.R. § 404.1577**[APP-REGS]. Implementation of the "any gainful activity" standard for pre-1991 periods of disability is discussed in Chapter 5.

2. SPECIAL SSI ELIGIBILITY FOR PERSONS RECEIVING STATE DISABILITY BENEFITS IN 1973

When the federal SSI program replaced Aid to the Aged, Blind and Disabled (AABD) in January, 1974, special provision was made for people who were receiving disability benefits under the joint federal-state program at the time the new federal program began. Recipients of benefits under the AABD program were "grandfathered" into the SSI program on the basis of the state disability standard in effect in October 1972—if they were receiving benefits for the month of December 1973 and for at least one month prior to July 1973.

Eligibility for SSI on this basis remains available so long as the recipient continues to meet the state disability standard. *See* **20 C.F.R. §**

416.907[APP-REGS]. Some state disability standards under the AABD program were more liberal than the SSI standard, so the ability to retain eligibility on the basis of a state standard can be very important. *See, e.g.,* Finnegan v. Matthews, 641 F.2d 1340, 1347 (9th Cir. 1981). A recipient of grandfathered SSI benefits is also subject to the resource limitations and rules on exclusion of resources applicable under the former state program.

3. DISABILITY DECISIONS BY OTHER AGENCIES

Quite often, an applicant for Social Security benefits will have been determined to be "disabled" by another agency in relation to a claim for a different statutory benefit. Those decisions are made on the basis of disability standards different from those used in determining disability under the Social Security Act and therefore are not be binding in a Social Security disability benefits case. Nonetheless, disability determinations by organizations and agencies other than the Social Security Administration are relevant to Social Security law and practice in two respects. First, understanding the implications of a disability finding by another organization or agency on an application for Social Security benefits helps place Social Security disability benefits in the broader context of disability law. Second, there is the very practical question of what impact, if any, a disability finding by another agency can have on a claim for Social Security disability benefits.

A) SOCIAL SECURITY DISABILITY STANDARD IN THE CONTEXT OF BROADER DISABILITY LAW AND POLICY

Disability determinations are made in a variety of contexts, ranging from providing compensation for injury to protecting civil rights. Persons claiming—on the basis of the same impairment—entitlement to income support from a Social Security disability benefit and protection against discrimination under the Americans with Disabilities Act present a classic policy conflict between disability benefits and disability rights. In *Cleveland v. Policy Management Systems Corp*, the Supreme Court ruled that an application for Social Security disability benefits does not preclude a claim under the Americans with Disabilities Act (ADA), while recognizing at the same time that statements made in the course of the disability benefits claim may have an impact on a concurrent ADA claim.

CLEVELAND V. POLICY MANAGEMENT SYSTEMS CORP.
526 U.S. 795 (1999)

Justice BREYER delivered the opinion of the Court.

The Social Security Disability Insurance (SSDI) program provides benefits to a person with a disability so severe that she is "unable to do

[her] previous work" and "cannot ... engage in any other kind of substantial gainful work which exists in the national economy." § 223(a) of the Social Security Act, as set forth in 42 U.S.C. § 423(d)(2)(A). This case asks whether the law erects a special presumption that would significantly inhibit an SSDI recipient from simultaneously pursuing an action for disability discrimination under the Americans with Disabilities Act of 1990 (ADA), claiming that "with ... reasonable accommodation" she could "perform the essential functions" of her job. § 101, 104 Stat. 331, 42 U.S.C. § 12111(8).

We believe that, in context, these two seemingly divergent statutory contentions are often consistent, each with the other. Thus pursuit, and receipt, of SSDI benefits does not automatically estop the recipient from pursuing an ADA claim. Nor does the law erect a strong presumption against the recipient's success under the ADA. Nonetheless, an ADA plaintiff cannot simply ignore her SSDI contention that she was too disabled to work. To survive a defendant's motion for summary judgment, she must explain why that SSDI contention is consistent with her ADA claim that she could "perform the essential functions" of her previous job, at least with "reasonable accommodation."

I

After suffering a disabling stroke and losing her job, Carolyn Cleveland sought and obtained SSDI benefits from the Social Security Administration (SSA). * * *

On September 22, 1995, the week before her SSDI award, Cleveland brought this ADA lawsuit. She contended that Policy Management Systems had "terminat[ed]" her employment without reasonably "accommodat[ing] her disability." She alleged that she requested, but was denied, accommodations such as training and additional time to complete her work. And she submitted a supporting affidavit from her treating physician. The District Court did not evaluate her reasonable accommodation claim on the merits, but granted summary judgment to the defendant because, in that court's view, Cleveland, by applying for and receiving SSDI benefits, had conceded that she was totally disabled. And that fact, the court concluded, now estopped Cleveland from proving an essential element of her ADA claim, namely that she could "perform the essential functions" of her job, at least with "reasonable accommodation." 42 U.S.C. § 12111(8).

* * *

II

The Social Security Act and the ADA both help individuals with disabilities, but in different ways. The Social Security Act provides monetary benefits to every insured individual who "is under a disability." 42 U.S.C. § 423(a)(1). The Act defines "disability" as an

> "inability to engage in any substantial gainful activity by reason of any ... physical or mental impairment which can be expected to result in death or which has lasted or can be expected to last for a continuous period of not less than 12 months." § 423(d)(1)(A).

The individual's impairment, as we have said, *supra*, must be

> "of such severity that [she] is not only unable to do [her] previous work but cannot, considering [her] age, education, and work experience, engage in any other kind of substantial gainful work which exists in the national economy ... ." § 423(d)(2)(A).

The ADA seeks to eliminate unwarranted discrimination against disabled individuals in order both to guarantee those individuals equal opportunity and to provide the Nation with the benefit of their consequently increased productivity. The Act prohibits covered employers from discriminating "against a qualified individual with a disability because of the disability of such individual." § 12112(a). The Act defines a "qualified individual with a disability" as a disabled person "who ... can perform the essential functions" of her job, including those who can do so only "with ... reasonable accommodation." § 12111(8).

We here consider but one of the many ways in which these two statutes might interact. This case does not involve, for example, the interaction of either of the statutes before us with other statutes, such as the Federal Employers' Liability Act, 45 U.S.C. § 51 *et seq.* Nor does it involve directly conflicting statements about purely factual matters, such as "The light was red/green," or "I can/cannot raise my arm above my head." An SSA representation of total disability differs from a purely factual statement in that it often implies a context-related legal conclusion, namely "I am disabled for purposes of the Social Security Act." And our consideration of this latter kind of statement consequently leaves the law related to the former, purely factual, kind of conflict where we found it.

The case before us concerns an ADA plaintiff who both applied for, and received, SSDI benefits. It requires us to review a Court of Appeals decision upholding the grant of summary judgment on the ground that an ADA plaintiff's "represent[ation]" to the SSA that she was totally disabled" created a "rebuttable presumption" sufficient to "judicially esto[p]" her later representation that, "for the time in question," with reasonable accommodation, she could perform the essential functions of her job. 120 F.3d 513, 518-519. The Court of Appeals thought, in essence, that claims under both Acts would incorporate two directly conflicting propositions, namely "I am too disabled to work" and "I am not too disabled to work." And in an effort to prevent two claims that would embody that kind of factual conflict, the court used a special judicial presumption, which it believed would ordinarily prevent a plaintiff like Cleveland from success- fully asserting an ADA claim.

In our view, however, despite the appearance of conflict that arises from the language of the two statutes, the two claims do not inherently conflict to the point where courts should apply a special negative pre- sumption like the one applied by the Court of Appeals here. That is be- cause there are too many situations in which an SSDI claim and an ADA claim can comfortably exist side by side.

For one thing, as we have noted, the ADA defines a "qualified indi- vidual" to include a disabled person "who ... can perform the essential functions" of her job "*with reasonable accommodation.*" Reasonable ac- commodations may include:

> "job restructuring, part-time or modified work schedules, reassign- ment to a vacant position, acquisition or modification of equipment or devices, appropriate adjustment or modifications of examinations, training materials or policies, the provision of qualified readers or in- terpreters, and other similar accommodations." 42 U.S.C. § 12111(9)(B).

By way of contrast, when the SSA determines whether an individual is disabled for SSDI purposes, it does not take the possibility of "reasonable accommodation" into account, nor need an applicant refer to the possibil- ity of reasonable accommodation when she applies for SSDI. *See* Memo- randum from Daniel L. Skoler, Associate Comm'r for Hearings and Ap- peals, SSA, to Administrative Appeals Judges, reprinted in 2 Social Secu- rity Practice Guide, App. § 15C[9], pp. 15-401 to 15-402 (1998). The omis- sion reflects the facts that the SSA receives more than 2.5 million claims for disability benefits each year; its administrative resources are limited; the matter of "reasonable accommodation" may turn on highly disputed workplace-specific matters; and an SSA misjudgment about that detailed, and often fact-specific matter would deprive a seriously disabled person of the critical financial support the statute seeks to provide. *See* Brief for United States et al. as *Amici Curiae* 10-11, and n. 2, 13. The result is that an ADA suit claiming that the plaintiff can perform her job *with* rea- sonable accommodation may well prove consistent with an SSDI claim that the plaintiff could not perform her own job (or other jobs) *without* it.

* * *

Finally, if an individual has merely applied for, but has not been awarded, SSDI benefits, any inconsistency in the theory of the claims is of the sort normally tolerated by our legal system. Our ordinary rules recognize that a person may not be sure in advance upon which legal theory she will succeed, and so permit parties to "set forth two or more statements of a claim or defense alternately or hypothetically," and to "state as many separate claims or defenses as the party has regardless of consistency." Fed. Rule Civ. Proc. 8(e)(2). We do not see why the law in respect to the assertion of SSDI and ADA claims should differ. (And, as we said, we leave the law in respect to purely factual contradictions where we found it.)

* * *

Nonetheless, in some cases an earlier SSDI claim may turn out genuinely to conflict with an ADA claim. Summary judgment for a defendant is appropriate when the plaintiff "fails to make a showing sufficient to establish the existence of an element essential to [her] case, and on which [she] will bear the burden of proof at trial." An ADA plaintiff bears the burden of proving that she is a "qualified individual with a disability"— that is, a person "who, with or without reasonable accommodation, can perform the essential functions" of her job. 42 U.S.C. § 12111(8). And a plaintiff's sworn assertion in an application for disability benefits that she is, for example, "unable to work" will appear to negate an essential element of her ADA case--at least if she does not offer a sufficient explanation. For that reason, we hold that an ADA plaintiff cannot simply ignore the apparent contradiction that arises out of the earlier SSDI total disability claim. Rather, she must proffer a sufficient explanation.

* * * When faced with a plaintiff's previous sworn statement asserting "total disability" or the like, the court should require an explanation of any apparent inconsistency with the necessary elements of an ADA claim. To defeat summary judgment, that explanation must be sufficient to warrant a reasonable juror's concluding that, assuming the truth of, or the plaintiff's good faith belief in, the earlier statement, the plaintiff could nonetheless "perform the essential functions" of her job, with or without "reasonable accommodation."

III

In her brief in this Court, Cleveland explains the discrepancy between her SSDI statements that she was "totally disabled" and her ADA claim that she could "perform the essential functions" of her job. The first statements, she says, "were made in a forum which does not consider the effect that reasonable workplace accommodations would have on the ability to work." Moreover, she claims the SSDI statements were "accurate statements" if examined "in the time period in which they were made."

The parties should have the opportunity in the trial court to present, or to contest, these explanations, in sworn form where appropriate. Accordingly, we vacate the judgment of the Court of Appeals and remand the case for further proceedings consistent with this opinion.

It is so ordered.

MITCHELL V. WASHINGTONVILLE CENTRAL SCHOOL DISTRICT

190 F.3d 1 (2nd Cir. 1999)

SACK, Circuit Judge:

* * *

I. Background

Mitchell began employment with the Washingtonville Central School District in 1987, working as Head Custodian at the Washingtonville High School. According to the job description, the Head Custodian position "involves the general supervision, care, maintenance and protection of a school building which may include the efficient performance of a variety of groundskeeping activities."

When Mitchell, whose right leg was amputated above the knee following an automobile accident in 1977 and who wears a prosthesis as a result, started as Head Custodian, his work required him to remain on his feet throughout the day except for two hours each day he spent doing desk work, a short coffee break, and a half hour lunch break. By 1989, the amount of desk work had decreased so that three days a week, aside from his breaks, Mitchell spent the entire time up and about.

Within four months of starting work at the high school, however, Mitchell experienced swelling and pain in his right leg which prevented him from wearing his prosthesis, and at times from coming to work. In addition, beginning in 1989, Mitchell suffered approximately three skin "breakdowns" on his leg each year, lasting for three to four days each time. When this happened, Mitchell was required to limit his use of his prosthesis and take occasional sick leave. These problems resulted from the extensive physical demands of the Head Custodian job, requiring prolonged use of the prosthesis.

Adding to these difficulties, according to Mitchell, the physical size of the high school doubled in 1993 and his work load substantially increased. Following a particularly strenuous day of work on November 5 of that year, Mitchell's leg began to "drain," causing him considerable discomfort. Mitchell thereafter stopped reporting to work and he notified the School District that he had been injured on the job.

* * *

In April 1994, Mitchell also applied for Social Security disability benefits. In July 1994, after his claim was initially denied, he filed a request for reconsideration, asserting: "I am totally disabled and unable to engage in any type of gainful employment due to being on my feet for long periods of time which resulted in a cyst." Again, the claim was denied and Mitchell appealed once more, this time stating in his written request for a hearing: "I am totally disabled and unable to engage in gainful employment due to being an amputee, my right leg from the knee down. This disability enables me [sic] from any type of prolonged standing or ambulation."

At a hearing on the matter in July 1995 before Administrative Law Judge Thomas P. Dorsey, in response to the question, "Why can't you work now?", Mitchell testified, "I'm not sure I can get anything where I could just sit for the entire time I'd be working." Mitchell further testified that he could stand for only five minutes at a time and that he could not carry any weight. Finally, Mitchell stated that he was in constant pain when he wore his prosthesis.

In a decision dated August 4, 1995, Judge Dorsey accepted Mitchell's representations and determined that he was disabled within the meaning of the Social Security Act, had been disabled since November 10, 1993, and would continue to be unable to work at least through December 31, 1998. The Social Security Administration thereafter began to pay Mitchell disability benefits.

Meanwhile, in November 1994, Peter M. Brenner, Sr., the Superintendent of Schools in Washingtonville, had informed Mitchell that he would recommend that the School District terminate Mitchell's employment "in light of [his] inability to perform the duties of [his] position for in excess of one year's time." Mitchell responded by sending to Superintendent Brenner a letter from Dr. Kulak, addressed "To Whom It May Concern," requesting that "due to his above knee amputation and the need for use of a prosthesis . . . [Mitchell] . . . be retrained for a job that is more sedentary . . . ." Mitchell also informed Brenner that the School District should consider his response "a request for a 'reasonable accommodation' as defined by the American Disabilities Act [sic]." Mitchell stated that Dr. Kulak's letter was "not a work release note. It is an order to secure sedentary employment and to be retrained if necessary." Mitchell advised, however, that "if the position of Head Custodian could be restructured to sedentary duties, my return [to work] may be possible."

On December 21, 1994, the School District informed Mitchell that it had terminated his employment.

Mitchell commenced this action on March 19, 1996, alleging that the School District violated the ADA by failing to provide him with a reasonable accommodation in light of his disability.

In connection with the present action, Mitchell testified at deposition that as of November 1994, after he was fitted with a new prosthesis, he could in fact remain on his feet for four hours a day, could tour the school building, and that he could walk 50 to 75 feet with his prosthesis without stopping and then only have to rest for a minute before continuing. Mitchell further testified that by June 1995, he could stand and walk for five hours a day. Mitchell's vocational expert, Edmund Provder, a certified rehabilitation counselor who examined Mitchell in November, 1996, similarly testified that Mitchell was able to perform the job of Head Custodian once he had received the new prosthesis in 1994.

Mitchell also asserts in this action that as of December, 1994, the School District should have accommodated his disability by restructuring his duties and reassigning the physical duties of the work to other custodians, transferring him to a smaller school within the School District, specifically the Round Hill School, retraining him for a more sedentary job such as courier or bus dispatcher, or granting him an extended leave of absence.

In its opinion and order of January 29, 1998, the district court granted the School District's motion for summary judgment, dismissing Mitchell's ADA claim. The district court determined that because of Mitchell's earlier statements to the Workers' Compensation Board and the Social Security Administration that he was "totally disabled," unable to work, unable to stand, unable to walk, and needed a job where he would be seated, Mitchell was judicially estopped from arguing for purposes of this ADA action that he was capable of doing work in other than a sedentary position. In light of its application of judicial estoppel, the district court held that "the ADA does not require the [School] District to restructure the Head Custodian position to a sedentary one" and that the "accommodations" suggested by Mitchell are unreasonable. As such, the court determined that Mitchell could not show that, restricted to a sedentary position, he was otherwise qualified to perform the essential functions of the position of Head Custodian with a reasonable accommodation, an element of his ADA claim. Mitchell had therefore failed to make out a prima facie case of discrimination.

The district court entered judgment in favor of the School District on February 2, 1998 and Mitchell now appeals.

II. Discussion

* * *

1. The Americans with Disabilities Act

The Americans with Disabilities Act, 42 U.S.C. § 12101 *et seq.*, prohibits covered employers from discriminating against an otherwise qualified employee "because of the disability of such individual in regard to job application procedures, the hiring, advancement, or discharge of employees, employee compensation, job training, and other terms, conditions, and privileges of employment." 42 U.S.C. § 12112(a). The statute defines "qualified individual with a disability" as "an individual with a disability who, with or without reasonable accommodation, can perform the essential functions of the employment position that such individual holds or desires." 42 U.S.C. § 12111(8).

In order to make out a prima facie case under the ADA, Mitchell was required to show (1) that he was an individual who had a disability within the meaning of the statute; (2) that the School District had notice of his disability; (3) that with reasonable accommodation he could perform the essential functions of the position sought; and (4) that the School District refused to make such accommodations. An employer can defeat a prima facie claim if it shows (1) that making a reasonable accommodation would cause it hardship, and (2) that the hardship would be undue.

The parties do not dispute that Mitchell has a disability as defined by the ADA or that the School District had notice of his disability. At issue is whether Mitchell was "otherwise qualified" for the job of Head Custodian —whether, in other words, he was able to perform the essential functions of that job, either with or without accommodation.

For reasons we explain below, we agree with the district court that because Mitchell is estopped from claiming that he could function in other than a sedentary position, he is unable to establish that with a reasonable accommodation he could perform the essential functions of Head Custodian.

2. Judicial Estoppel

     * * *

Clarifying the reach of judicial estoppel in this context, the Supreme Court has held that the pursuit and receipt of Social Security disability benefits, without more, neither estops the recipient from pursuing an ADA claim nor creates any special presumption against the recipient showing, for purposes of an ADA action, that with reasonable accommodation he or she could perform the essential functions of the job. *See* Cleveland v. Policy Management Sys. Corp, 526 U.S. 795, ___, 143 L. Ed. 2d 966, 119 S. Ct. 1597, 1599-1600 (1999). The Court reasoned that in light of the different purposes and tests of the two statutory schemes, the statement that "I am too disabled to work" made in obtaining social security benefits does not inherently conflict with a later claim under the ADA that "I am not too disabled to work." Cleveland, 526 U.S. at ___, 119 S. Ct. at 1602 (internal quotation marks omitted). Nonetheless, the Court also held that "an ADA plaintiff cannot simply ignore her SSDI contention that she was too disabled to work. To survive a defendant's motion for summary judgment, she must explain why that SSDI contention is consistent with her ADA claim that she could 'perform the essential functions' of her previous job, at least with 'reasonable accommodation.'" Cleveland, 526 U.S. at ___, 119 S. Ct. at 1600.

Mitchell argues that, contrary to these principles, in its application of judicial estoppel the district court effectively imposed a *per se* rule preventing an SSDI recipient who claims an inability to work from later asserting under the ADA that he or she is able to work. We disagree. The district court did not hold that Mitchell was estopped from arguing that he was able to work with a reasonable accommodation once he asserted, for purposes of obtaining workers' compensation and social security benefits, that he was too disabled to work. On the contrary, the lower court specifically declined to apply any such categorical rule and held Mitchell was estopped from asserting, as a factual matter, that he was capable of performing work in other than a sedentary position. Such an application of judicial estoppel is consistent with *Cleveland*. The Supreme Court emphasized that the case before it did not "involve directly conflicting statements about purely factual matters, such as . . . 'I can/cannot raise my arm above my head[,]'" and indeed that the decision "leaves the law related to . . . purely factual . . . conflicts where [the Court] found it." Cleveland, 526 U.S. at ___, 119 S. Ct. at 1601-02. Therefore, if the requirements for judicial estoppel are otherwise met, Mitchell may be prevented from claiming, as a factual matter, that he could stand and walk at work on the basis of prior factual assertions to the contrary.

Turning to those requirements, we conclude that the district court correctly held that Mitchell was estopped from asserting in the present action that he was capable of performing work that required him to stand or walk. First, it is plain that Mitchell "argued an inconsistent position in a prior proceeding," Bates [v. Long Island Railroad Co.], 997 F.2d [1028,] 1038 [(2nd Cir. 1993)]. Mitchell's prior statements, made in 1994, 1995 and 1996 to the Workers' Compensation Board and the Social Security Administration, that he was incapable of standing for any length of time or of walking and that he required work he could perform seated, clearly contradict Mitchell's position in this litigation that as of late 1994 he was able to stand and walk for a substantial portion of the work day. Second, Mitchell's earlier inconsistent statements were "adopted" by these tribunals, *see id.*, with a result favorable to Mitchell: an award of benefits. In his August 1995 decision finding that Mitchell was unable to use his prosthesis and so was "disabled" within the meaning of the Social Security Act and entitled to benefits, Administrative Law Judge Dorsey specifically credited Mitchell's testimony that he was unable to stand. Similarly, in awarding Mitchell benefits in October 1996, Workers' Compensation Judge Paksarian also found, based on the testimony and medical reports that Mitchell presented, that Mitchell "remained under permanent restriction to a sedentary job." Since Mitchell's earlier assertions as to his inability to walk or stand were accepted by these prior administrative tribunals, resulting in a determination in his favor, judicial estoppel prevents Mitchell from advancing, for purposes of this litigation, the contrary position.

3. Essential Functions of Head Custodian

We also agree with the district court that, once estopped from arguing he could walk and stand and therefore bound to the assertion that he could only do sedentary work, Mitchell could not show that he could perform the essential functions of Head Custodian with a reasonable accommodation. He therefore failed to make out a claim under the ADA.

* * *

Since Mitchell is estopped from claiming he could stand and walk at work, and he is unable to show that with a reasonable accommodation he could perform the essential functions of the Head Custodian position from a sedentary position, he fails to make out a prima facie claim of discrimination under the ADA. Summary judgment in favor of the School District was, therefore, properly granted.

* * *

NOTES

1. Before the Supreme Court decided *Cleveland*, the courts of appeal were split on the issue of how to treat a claimant who applies for Social Security disability benefits and also alleges discrimination under the ADA, resulting in three distinct approaches. One group of courts found that a claimant's application for Social Security benefits estopped the claimant from seeking ADA protection. A second group reasoned that application and receipt of Social Security benefits created a rebuttable presumption that the claimant could not be a "qualified individual" under the ADA. The last group held that an application for—and receipt of—Social Security benefits is relevant to whether the claimant could be a "qualified individual" under the ADA, but the claimant can still seek ADA protection. *See* Tory L. Lucas, *Disabling Complexity: The Americans with Disabilities Act of 1990 and its Interaction with Other Federal Laws*, 38 CREIGHTON L. REV. 871 (2005). Two years before the Court's decision in *Cleveland*, the D.C. Circuit resolved the issue consistent with the later Supreme Court opinion by stating simply: "Because the

Social Security Act and the ADA employ quite different standards and objectives—the ADA requires employers reasonably to accommodate the needs of otherwise qualified disabled individuals, while the Social Security Act awards benefits to persons who, because of their disability, cannot perform 'work which exists in the national economy,' without regard to reasonable accommodation—we hold that the receipt of Social Security disability benefits does not preclude ADA relief." Swanks v. Washington Metropolitan Area Transit Authority, 116 F.3d 582, 583 (D.C. Cir. 1997).

2. The ADA defines a "qualified individual" as:

> an individual who, with or without reasonable accommodation, can perform the essential functions of the employment position that such individual holds or desires. For the purposes of this title, consideration shall be given to the employer's judgment as to what functions of a job are essential, and if an employer has prepared a written description before advertising or interviewing applicants for the job, this description shall be considered evidence of the essential functions of the job.

42 U.S.C. § 12111(8). As the Court indicated in *Cleveland*, the Social Security Act does not include an opportunity for "reasonable accommodation." Thus, a claimant can be disabled under both the Social Security Act and the ADA if that person is unable to do his or her job without reasonable accommodation. Specifically, a request for accommodations under the ADA does not inherently conflict with an application for Social Security disability benefits because the ADA considers whether a person might be able to perform their job with reasonable accommodation, and that possibility is not taken into account in Social Security disability determinations.

3. Scholarship and advocacy separate disability policy into two discrete concepts. The first is founded on civil rights. According this concept, it is discrimination not to treat "disabled" people the same as everyone else. The goal is to eliminate discrimination against persons with disabilities in the workplace and elsewhere, thereby allowing them to participate fully in all aspects of personal and professional life. This civil rights disability policy is reflected in the ADA. The second concept is based on the conviction that disability is a basis for entitlement to public support when the "disabled" person is totally unable to work. The goal of this policy is to claim income maintenance and other social and financial support necessary for persons with disabilities to live a safe and comfortable life. This second version of disability policy is reflected in Society Security law. Unlike civil rights disability policy, which seeks to integrate persons with disabilities into the mainstream, entitlement disability policy requires a firm line of demarcation between "disabled" and "non-disabled" persons. Deborah Stone argues that "disability" is a socially constructed category of individuals rather than a common physical or mental attribute. Although doctors determine disability qualification for state purposes, "the concept of disability is fundamentally the result of political conflict about distributive criteria and the appropriate recipients of social

aid." DEBORAH A. STONE, THE DISABLED STATE 172 (Temple 1984). For further discussion of conflicting disability policies, *see* Mary Crossley, *The Disability Kaleidoscope*, 74 NOTRE DAME L. REV 621 (1999); Tory L. Lucas, *Disabling Complexity: The Americans with Disabilities Act of 1990 and its Interaction with Other Federal Laws*, 38 CREIGHTON L. REV. 871 (2005).

4. An important distinction can also be drawn between Social Security disability policy and the social policies behind another major Social Security Act program, unemployment insurance. Social Security disability benefits are limited to persons who are unable to work due to a medically determinable physical or mental impairment. As we saw earlier, the Social Security Act was amended in 1968 to clarify that eligibility is based on a claimant's capacity to work at jobs that exist in the national economy—regardless of whether such jobs are actually available. Unemployment insurance benefits are provided, by contrast, only when there are no jobs available that the claimant can perform. In other words, Social Security insures against the loss of one's capacity to work; unemployment insurance insures against the economy not providing sufficient work opportunities.

B) THE EFFECT OF DISABILITY FINDINGS BY OTHER ORGANIZATIONS AND AGENCIES

As discussed above, different agencies and organizations apply different sets of criteria to determine who is "disabled." Noting that decisions by another agency relative to whether a Social Security claimant is disabled "is based on its rules and is not our decision," Social Security regulations state clearly that "a determination made by another agency that you are disabled or blind is not binding on [the Social Security Administration]." **20 C.F.R. §§ 404.1504, 416.904[APP-REGS]**. This does not mean, however, that a finding of disability by another agency is irrelevant.

SOCIAL SECURITY RULING SSR 06-03P

(2006)

TITLES II AND XVI: CONSIDERING OPINIONS AND OTHER
EVIDENCE FROM SOURCES WHO ARE NOT "ACCEPTABLE
MEDICAL SOURCES" IN DISABILITY CLAIMS;
CONSIDERING DECISIONS ON DISABILITY BY OTHER
GOVERNMENTAL AND NONGOVERNMENTAL AGENCIES

* * *

II. Decisions on Disability by Other Governmental and Nongovernmental Agencies

The regulations at 20 CFR 404.1504 and 416.904 provide that:

[a] decision by any nongovernmental agency or any other governmental agency about whether you are disabled or blind is based on its rules and is not our decision about whether you are disabled or blind. We must make a disability or blindness determination based on social security law. Therefore, a determination made by another agency [e.g., Workers' Compensation, the Department of Veterans Affairs, or an insurance company] that you are disabled or blind is not binding on us.

Under sections 221 and 1633 of the [Social Security] Act, only a State agency or the Commissioner can make a determination based on Social Security law that you are blind or disabled. Our regulations at 20 CFR 404.1527(e) and 416.927(e) make clear that the final responsibility for deciding certain issues, such as whether you are disabled, is reserved to the Commissioner (*see also* SSR 96-5p, "Titles II and XVI: Medical Source Opinions on Issues Reserved to the Commissioner"). However, we are required to evaluate all the evidence in the case record that may have a bearing on our determination or decision of disability, including decisions by other governmental and nongovernmental agencies (20 CFR 404.1512(b)(5) and 416.912(b)(5)). Therefore, evidence of a disability decision by another governmental or nongovernmental agency cannot be ignored and must be considered.

These decisions, and the evidence used to make these decisions, may provide insight into the individual's mental and physical impairment(s) and show the degree of disability determined by these agencies based on their rules. We will evaluate the opinion evidence from medical sources, as well as "non-medical sources" who have had contact with the individual in their professional capacity, used by other agencies, that are in our case record, in accordance with 20 CFR 404.1527, 416.927, Social Security Rulings 96-2p and 96-5p, and the applicable factors listed above in the section "Factors for Weighing Opinion Evidence."

Because the ultimate responsibility for determining whether an individual is disabled under Social Security law rests with the Commissioner, we are not bound by disability decisions by other governmental and nongovernmental agencies. In addition, because other agencies may apply different rules and standards than we do for determining whether an individual is disabled, this may limit the relevance of a determination of disability made by another agency. However, the adjudicator should explain the consideration given to these decisions in the notice of decision for hearing cases and in the case record for initial and reconsideration cases.

C) DISABILITY FINDINGS FOR VETERANS BENEFITS

The most common parallel disability decision relevant to Social Security disability benefit claims are those that concern claims by veterans for disability benefits.   The United States Department of Veterans Affairs (VA) provides two types of disability benefits: Veterans Compensation and Veterans Disability Pension (often referred to as veterans disability). To receive Veterans Compensation, the claimant's disability must be service-connected. Therefore, if a claim is denied because the VA found that the disability did not result from service-related activity, the VA's decision to deny benefits would have no bearing on a claim for Social Security benefits. A finding by the VA that a claimant is not disabled may be relevant to a Social Security disability claim, but it neither mandates nor precludes eligibility for benefits—even with respect to a Veterans Disability Pension claim, where the disability standard is comparable in many respects to the Social Security disability standard.

Most cases hold that a VA finding of disability for purposes of non-service-connected disability pension benefits must be considered by SSA when determining disability. There is, however, wide variation from court to court as to how much weight they give to VA decisions, and from case to case as to the amount of weight actually given. The Fifth Circuit has stated, for example, that VA decisions are entitled to "great weight." *See* Johnson v. Sullivan, 894 F.2d 683, 686, 28 Soc. Sec. Rep. Serv. 397 (5th Cir. 1990). On the other hand, the Tenth Circuit has said that such decisions are only "entitled to weight and must be considered." Baca v. Department of Health and Human Services, 5 F.3d 476, 480, 42 Soc. Sec. Rep. Serv. 301 (10th Cir. 1993). Other courts have stated that a Veterans Administration disability decision is "critically relevant," Fowler v. Califano, 596 F.2d 600, 603 (3d Cir. 1979), "entitled to serious consideration," Champion v. Califano, 440 F. Supp. 1014, 1019 n. 9 (D.D.C. 1977), and "persuasive evidence," Williams v. Mathews, 456 F. Supp. 1125, 1129 (M.D. La. 1978).

McCARTEY v. MASSANARI
298 F.3d 1072, 82 Soc. Sec. Rep. Serv. 530 (9th Cir. 2002)

Before SCHROEDER, Chief Judge, D.W. NELSON and REINHARDT, Circuit Judges.

REINHARDT, Circuit Judge:

Thomas E. McCartey appeals from a district court judgment affirming the Commissioner's decision to deny him Social Security Disability ("SSD") benefits. One of the grounds urged by McCartey for reversal of the Commissioner's decision is that the ALJ erred in rejecting his SSD application without considering the finding of the Department of Veterans Affairs ("VA") that McCartey was unable to work due to disability. We agree and therefore reverse and remand.

I

McCartey's disability stems from a workplace accident in 1987, in which a 100 pound door fell on him and injured his lower back. Although McCartey returned to work after the accident, by 1991 his lower back pain had grown so intense that he could no longer work. Around that time, McCartey's previously extant depression worsened considerably, and he began to suffer from a host of other ailments. On June 3, 1997, the VA granted McCartey a nonservice-connected pension after finding that he was "unable to secure and follow a substantially gainful occupation" due to disability. The VA gave McCartey a total disability rating of 80%, based primarily on his depression and secondarily on his lower back injury.

At his hearing, McCartey described his disability as: "Depression, then my disk disease and joint disease and arthritis." VA medical records document that McCartey has had a history of depression since 1973, with symptoms worsening significantly in 1990. In late 1992, McCartey suffered a prolonged depressive episode in which he locked himself in his house for over a year. He left his home only to visit the doctor and tried to starve himself to death. McCartey began treatment for depression, including medication and counseling, in 1994. He continues to receive treatment today.

Medical records reveal the debilitating effect of depression on McCartey's ability to work. According to the VA rating criteria, McCartey's depression compromises his ability to function independently, appropriately, and effectively, to adapt to stressful circumstances including a work setting, and to establish and maintain effective relationships. Medical records note that McCartey has poor concentration and sometimes hears voices. He seldom sleeps more than two hours a night, so he has to rest during the day. He also experiences debilitating anxiety attacks.

McCartey's depression is complicated by the significant functional limitations caused by his back injury and other impairments. McCartey testified that because of his back problems he cannot lift more than ten pounds and must alternate sitting and standing. In addition, McCartey suffers from night sweats, which occur several times a week and significantly amplify the pain and stiffness in his joints. During the day, McCartey's main activity is pain management, which consists of alternating stretching and walking with periods of rest. Another main activity is taking medications and going to the doctor. McCartey performs limited activities of daily living, but even basic tasks like dressing or making breakfast take him a long time. Every household task must be executed slowly and carefully. McCartey cannot perform strenuous or complicated household chores. His sister drives him to the grocery store and helps him select and carry items. Overall, it is clear from the record that although McCartey is able to function minimally on a day-to-day basis, he is incapable of performing work on a sustained and continuing basis.

In a decision dated September 15, 1998, the ALJ performed a sequential evaluation analysis and found that McCartey was not disabled. At Step Two, the ALJ relied on the reports of SSA's consultative physicians to determine that McCartey's depression was "only a slight abnormality." The ALJ then disregarded McCartey's depression for the balance of his opinion. At Step 5, the ALJ relied on the testimony of a Vocational Expert to determine that there were still jobs in the national economy that McCartey could perform. In evaluating McCartey's residual functional capacity, the ALJ focused exclusively on McCartey's back injury and did not mention his depression. The ALJ's opinion contains no reference to the VA disability rating.

McCartey appealed, submitting new medical records from the VA clinic that documented his history of depression. On June 23, 2000, the Appeals Council denied the request for review, and the ALJ's decision became the final decision of the Commissioner. The Appeals Council held that the VA records documenting McCartey's history of depression were not material because they were dated after the Administrative Law Judge's decision.

McCartey sought review of the ALJ's decision in district court. The magistrate judge recommended denying the petition for review. His opinion does not mention McCartey's depression. The district judge adopted the findings of the magistrate judge and denied the petition for review.

II

* * *

The issue of the evidentiary significance of a VA disability rating is a matter of first impression in this circuit. However, the nine circuits that have considered this issue agree that a VA disability rating is entitled to evidentiary weight in a Social Security hearing. See Chambliss v. Massanari, 269 F.3d 520, 522 (5th Cir. 2001) (per curiam) (VA disability rating is generally entitled to "great weight" and "must be considered by the ALJ"); Morrison v. Apfel, 146 F.3d 625, 628 (8th Cir. 1998) ("Findings of disability by other federal agencies ... are entitled to some weight and must be considered in the ALJ's decision"); Baca v. Dept. of Health and Hum. Svcs., 5 F.3d 476, 480 (10th Cir. 1993) ("Although findings by other agencies are not binding on the Secretary, they are entitled to weight and must be considered."); Davel v. Sullivan, 902 F.2d 559, 560 n.1 (7th Cir. 1990) (VA's decision is "entitled to some weight" and should be considered by ALJ); Kane v. Heckler, 776 F.2d 1130, 1135 (3d Cir. 1985) (VA rating entitled to "substantial weight"); Stewart v. Heckler, 730 F.2d 1065, 1068 (6th Cir. 1984) (VA rating entitled to ALJ consideration); Brady v. Heckler, 724 F.2d 914, 921 (11th Cir. 1984) (per curiam) (VA rating entitled to "great weight"); De Loatche v. Heckler, 715 F.2d 148, 150 n.1 (4th Cir. 1983) (same); Hankerson v. Harris, 636 F.2d 893, 897 (2d Cir. 1980) (VA rating entitled to "some weight"); Fowler v. Califano, 596 F.2d 600, 603 (3d Cir. 1979) (same). No circuit has held that an ALJ is free to disregard a VA disability rating.

The government argues that in this circuit, unlike the others, an ALJ has no duty to consider medical opinions prepared for other benefit programs. It cites Desrosiers v. Sec'y of Health and Hum. Svcs., 846 F.2d 573, 576 (9th Cir. 1988), for this proposition. In *Desrosiers*, two doctors evaluated the claimant for the purposes of his California workers' compensation claim and determined that the claimant could no longer perform heavy work. *Id.* Because California workers' compensation rules did not require them to do so, the doctors did not opine on whether the claimant could perform other work. *Id.* The court held that the ALJ erred in relying on the doctors' reports to conclude that the claimant could still perform less than heavy work. *Id. Desrosiers* is not pertinent to the question of how much weight, if any, an ALJ should give to another federal agency's finding of disability.

We agree with all of the other circuits that have considered the question and hold that although a VA rating of disability does not necessarily compel the SSA to reach an identical result, 20 C.F.R. § 404.1504, the ALJ must consider the VA's finding in reaching his decision. The important question here is how much weight an ALJ must give the VA determination. The circuits have employed differing standards. *Compare, e.g., Kane,* 776 F.2d at 1135 ("substantial weight") *with Brady,* 724 F.2d at 921 ("great weight") *and Hankerson,* 636 F.2d at 897 ("some weight").

We agree with the approach of the Fourth, Fifth, and Eleventh Circuits and hold that in an SSD case an ALJ must ordinarily give great weight to a VA determination of disability. We so conclude because of the marked similarity between these two federal disability programs. Both programs serve the same governmental purpose — providing benefits to those unable to work because of a serious disability. Both programs evaluate a claimant's ability to perform full-time work in the national economy on a sustained and continuing basis; both focus on analyzing a claimant's functional limitations; and both require claimants to present extensive medical documentation in support of their claims. *Compare* 38 C.F.R. § 4.1 *et seq.* (VA ratings) *with* 20 C.F.R. § 404.1 *et seq* (Social Security Disability). Both programs have a detailed regulatory scheme that promotes consistency in adjudication of claims. Both are administered by the federal government, and they share a common incentive to weed out meritless claims. The VA criteria for evaluating disability are very specific and translate easily into SSA's disability framework. Because the VA and SSA criteria for determining disability are not identical, however, the ALJ may give less weight to a VA disability rating if he gives persuasive, specific, valid reasons for doing so that are supported by the record. *See Chambliss,* 269 F.3d at 522 (ALJ need not give great weight to a VA rating if he "adequately explains the valid reasons for not doing so").

III

In this case, the VA determined that McCartey was 80% disabled due to his depression and lower back injury. The ALJ failed to consider the VA finding and did not mention it in his opinion. We hold that the ALJ erred in disregarding McCartey's VA disability rating, and accordingly, the Commissioner's decision must be reversed and remanded.

We have discretion to remand a case either for additional evidence and findings or for an award of benefits. We may direct an award of benefits if the record has been fully developed and further administrative proceedings would serve no useful purpose. *Id.* Such a circumstance arises when: (1) the ALJ has failed to provide legally sufficient reasons for rejecting the claimant's evidence; (2) there are no outstanding issues that must be resolved before a determination of disability can be made; and (3) it is clear from the record that the ALJ would be required to find the claimant disabled if he considered the claimant's evidence. In this case, the VA's disability finding was supported by several hundred pages of medical records. The record is fully developed and, giving great weight to the VA disability rating, a finding of disability is clearly required. Therefore, we hold that McCartey was disabled throughout the relevant period, and we reverse and remand to the district court with instructions to remand to the ALJ for payment of benefits.

REVERSED and REMANDED.

NOTE ON NON-VA CASES

Although the majority of other-agency disability determinations involve VA claims, 20 C.F.R. § 404.1504 applies to disability determinations by all organizations and agencies other than the Social Security Administration. Another common claim is that a denial of Social Security benefits is not consistent with disability findings by state workers' compensation agencies. This argument was made in Parrish v. Commissioner of Social Security Administration, 334 Fed. Appx. 200, 2009 WL 1587791 (11th Cir. 2009), where the claimant argued, among other things, that the ALJ improperly disregarded evidence that she received state workers' compensation benefits. The court of appeals affirmed the ALJ's order, reasoning:

* * * [A]s to the workers' compensation benefits, we find that the district court committed no error. Because a decision by another agency about whether a claimant is disabled is based on its rules, and because the Commissioner must make its own determination based on social security law, a determination made by another agency that a claimant is disabled is not binding on the Commissioner. Nevertheless, "[t]he findings of disability by another agency, although not binding on the [Commissioner], are entitled to great weight." Bloodsworth v. Heckler, 703 F.2d 1233, 1241 (11th Cir. 1983). However here, the state decided to grant workers' compensation benefits to Parrish in 1990, well before the finding of medical improvement and termination of benefits in 1995. As such, the state's determination regarding benefits has little, if any, relevance to the determination of medical improvement and termination of disability.

* * *

Upon careful review of the administrative proceedings, the medical record, the proceedings in the district court, and upon consideration of the parties' briefs, we find no error. We find that the ALJ did not err in excluding these items from his evaluation of medical improvement. Accordingly, we affirm.

334 Fed. Appx. at 201-2. *See also* Turby v. Joanne Barnhart, 54 Fed. Appx. 118, 123 (3rd Cir. 2002) ("State agency determinations of disability are not binding on the Social Security Administration because the inquiries for eligibility are distinct . . . . Nonetheless, the ALJ here accorded "significant weight" to Pennsylvania's determination that [Appellant] was eligible for benefits.")

CHAPTER 5

DISABILITY DETERMINATION PROCESS

■ ■ ■

As discussed in Chapter 4, the general disability standard governing adult claims for disability benefits under both the Old Age, Survivors, and Disability Insurance (OASDI) and Supplemental Security Income (SSI) programs, although relatively sophisticated, is quite simple and straightforward: benefits are provided to people who, as the result of a physical or mental impairment, cannot perform a basic level of work activity at a job they have held in the past or at any other job that they could be expected to hold, given their age, education, and prior work history. The disability standard for SSI child's benefits is a little less concrete, but still perfectly understandable: a physical or mental impairment resulting in "marked and severe" functional limitations. (An even simpler, but stricter disability standard—the inability to engage in any gainful activity—is used for disability claims by spouses of insured wage earners for periods prior to 1991.)

There rests, however, the problem of implementing these standards. How can the Social Security Administration decide whether a 53–year old office worker with ischemic heart disease can "engage in substantial gainful activity?" What about a 37–year-old trucker with chronic lower back pain? How can SSA determine whether a three-year-old child's bronchial asthma results in "marked and severe" functional limitations? More difficult still are the many cases involving claimants—adults and children—whose disability claims are based on mental impairments.

There are millions of Social Security and SSI disability claims adjudicated each year, of which hundreds of thousands are contested to one degree or another. At a broader level, this presents serious questions of political and administrative will. What should be expected of what has been referred to as SSA's administration of "mass" justice? *See generally*, Robert G. Dixon, Jr., Social Security Disability and Mass Justice: A Problem in Welfare Adjudication (1973). *See also* Jerry L. Mashaw, Bureaucratic Justice: Managing Social Security Disability Claims 18 (1983) (describing the administration of the Social Security disability benefits program as "representative of our increasingly prevalent systems of mass justice."). The Social Security Administration has put in place an extensive administrative structure to manage this enormous caseload, which is discussed—together with other aspects of Social Security practice—in Chapters 8 and 9.

SSA has also taken substantive steps to implement the statutory standards more effectively and efficiently by promulgating a set of regulations that lay out a distinctive five-step "sequential evaluation process" for determining whether a claimant is disabled. (Earlier Social Security regulations had used the term "sequential evaluation process" and that term is still widely used.) The sequential evaluation process is used for all disability claims under the OASDI program, except for claims by wage earners' spouses for periods before 1991, and for all adult claims under the SSI program. A truncated version of the full sequential evaluation process is used for pre-1991 OASDI spouse claims and for all current claims by children for SSI benefits.

The sequential evaluation process is the subject of this chapter. The next section describes the process generally; subsequent sections discuss its component parts in greater detail. The discussion in this chapter focuses on the operation of the 5–step process used for adult claims under both OASDI and SSI; at various points where relevant, the somewhat different sequential evaluation processes for determining disability for child's SSI and pre–1991 spouse's benefits are discussed briefly as well.

A. SEQUENTIAL EVALUATION PROCESS

The full sequential evaluation process used for all disability claims under the OASDI program and for adult claims under the SSI program is designed to test a claimant's evidence of disability at five different levels, each of which raises different factual and legal issues relative to a finding of disability. The process operates somewhat like a flow chart, as seen in the figure below; at each level, depending on the facts, the claim is either resolved (depending on the level, either with a finding that the claimant is disabled or that the claimant is not disabled) or, if neither finding can be made, then the process continues to the next step. For evaluations that reach the fifth step, the process dictates finally—again, depending on the facts—whether the claimant is disabled or not. **20 C.F.R. §§ 404.1520, 416.920[APP–REGS]**. The sequential evaluation process is suspended, however, for certain claimants with particularly significant vocational limitations as set out at **20 C.F.R. §§ 404.1562, 416.962[APP–REGS]**. *See* 20 C.F.R. §§ 404.1520(g), 416.920(g).

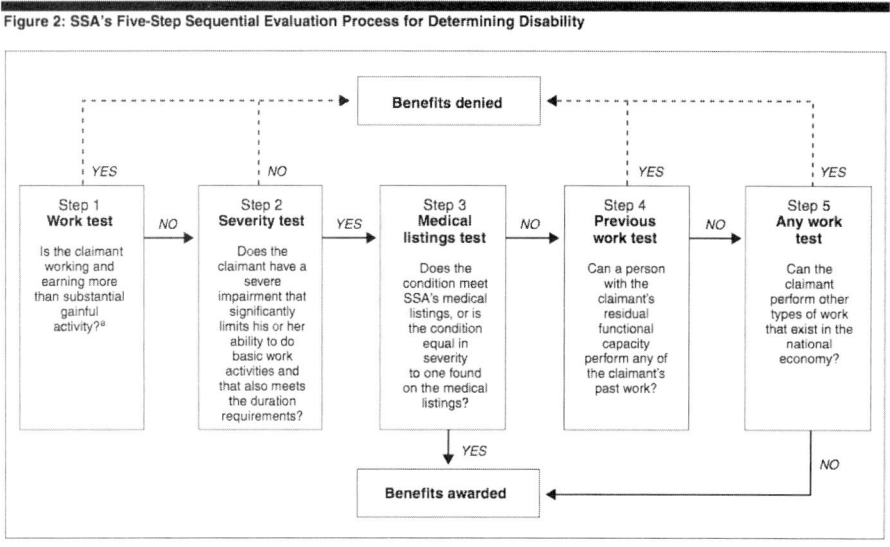

Figure 2: SSA's Five-Step Sequential Evaluation Process for Determining Disability

Source: GAO analysis of SSA data.

ᵃIn 2007 the substantial gainful activity (SGA) threshold was $1,500 per month for blind recipients and $900 per month for individuals with other disabilities.

Source: U.S. Gov't Accountability Office, Social Security Disability: Better Planning, Management, and Evaluation Could Help Address Backlogs, GAO–08–40 (2007), available at http://www.gao.gov/new.items/d0840.pdf.

In effect, the sequential evaluation process asks a series of questions. The first question is whether the claimant is performing substantial gainful activity. 20 C.F.R. §§ 404.1520(a)(4)(i), 416.920(a)(4)(i). If so, the claimant is considered not disabled regardless of his or her medical condition, and the process ends. 20 C.F.R. §§ 404.1520(b), 416.920(b). If the claimant is not currently engaging in substantial gainful activity, the process moves to the second question, which is whether the claimant has a "severe" impairment that significantly limits his or her ability to perform work. To qualify as a "severe" impairment, it must also meet the statutory duration requirement; that is, it must have lasted 12 month or be expected to last at least 12 months or to result in death. 20 C.F.R. §§ 404.1520(a)(4)(ii), .1520(c); 416.920(a)(4)(ii), .920(c). If not, the claimant is considered not disabled and the process ends there. (As discussed later in this section, SSA must consider the combined effect of claimants' impairments, if they have more than one.) If the claimant does have a severe impairment and meets the duration requirement, the evaluation process continues on to a third question, which asks whether the claimant's medical condition meets or equals the requirements of the Social Security Administration's Listing of Impairments. 20 C.F.R. §§ 404.1520(a)(4)(iii), .1520(d); 416.920(a)(4)(iii), .920(d). If so, the claimant is considered disabled and the process stops. If the claimant's impairment does not meet or equal the requirements of the Listing, the claim continues to a fourth step, which asks a medical-vocational question: is the claimant prevented from performing his or her past relevant work? 20 C.F.R. §§ 404.1520(a)(4)(iv), .1520(e)-(f); 416.920(a)(4)(iv), .920(e)-(f). If not, the claimant is considered not disabled and, once again, the process stops. If the claimant is prevented from performing his or her past relevant work, the process reaches the fifth step, which asks whether—considering the claimant's residual functional capacity, age, education, and prior work experience—he or she can perform other substantial gainful work that is available in significant numbers in the national economy. 20 C.F.R. §§ 404.1520(a)(4)(v), .1520(g); 416.920(a)(4)(v), .920(g). If such other work is available, the claimant is not disabled; if not, then the claimant is disabled.

The last two steps of the process—determining whether the claimant can perform past relevant work, and, if not, determining whether the claimant can perform other work which is available in the economy—incorporate an assessment of the claimant's "residual functional capacity" (RFC) into the analysis. A claimant's RFC is based on his or her physical and mental limitations and how they affect the claimant's ability to work; it is an evaluation of "what [the claimant] can still do despite [those] limitations." See 20 CFR §§ 404.1545(a), 416.945(a). RFC is discussed in more detail later in this chapter.

The Supreme Court described the process as follow in Bowen v. Yuckert, 482 U.S. 137, 153, 17 Soc. Sec. Rep. Serv. 661 (1987):

The [Social Security Administration] has established a five-step sequential evaluation process for determining whether a person is disabled. * * * Step one determines whether the claimant is engaged in "substantial gainful activity." If he is, disability benefits are denied. * * * If he is not, the decisionmaker proceeds to step two, which determines whether the claimant has a medically severe impairment or combination of impairments. * * * If the claimant does not have a severe impairment or combination of impairments, the disability claim is denied. If the impairment is severe, the evaluation proceeds to the third step, which determines whether the impairment is equivalent to one of a number of listed impairments that the Secretary acknowledges are so severe as to preclude substantial gainful activity. * * * If the impairment meets or equals one of the listed impairments, the claimant is conclusively presumed to be disabled. If the impairment is not one that is conclusively presumed to be disabling, the evaluation proceeds to the fourth step, which determines whether the impairment prevents the claimant from performing work he has performed in the past. If the claimant is able to perform his previous work, he is not disabled. * * * If the claimant cannot perform this work, the fifth and final step of the process determines whether he is able to perform other work in the national economy in view of his age, education, and work experience. The claimant is entitled to disability benefits only if he is not able to perform other work. * * *

Generally, claimants have the burden of proof on the issue of disability. *See* 20 CFR §§ 404.1512(a), 1649512(a); *see also* 42 U.S.C. § 423(d)(5)(A) ("An individual shall not be considered to be under a disability unless he furnishes such medical and other evidence of the existence thereof as the Commissioner of Social Security may require"). However, case law makes it clear that upon proof by the claimant that he or she cannot perform prior work at Step 4, the burden shifts to the Social Security Administration to prove that the claimant can perform other work available in the national economy at Step 5. Thus, as the Supreme Court explained in *Bowen v. Yuckert*:

> the [Social Security Administration] bears the burden of proof at step five, which determines whether the claimant is able to perform work available in the national economy. But the Secretary is required to bear this burden only if the sequential evaluation process proceeds to the fifth step. The claimant first must bear the burden at step one of showing that he is not working, at step two that he has a medically severe impairment or combination of impairments, and at step four that the impairment prevents him from performing his past work. If the process ends at step two, the burden of proof never shifts to the Secretary. Similarly, if the impairment is one that is conclusively presumed to be disabling, the claimant is not required to bear the burden of showing that he is unable to perform his prior work ... It is not unreasonable to require the claimant, who is in a better position to provide information about his own medical condition, to do so.

482 U.S. at 146 n. 5. *See also* Pass v. Chater, 65 F.3d 1200, 1203 (4th Cir. 1995) ("The applicant bears the burden of production and proof during the first four steps of the inquiry. If he or she is able to carry this burden through the fourth step, the burden shifts to the Secretary in the fifth step to show that other work is available in the national economy which the claimant could perform.") This shift in the burden of proof is covered in more detail when Steps 4 and 5 are discussed later in this chapter.

When followed fairly and correctly, the sequential evaluation process is an effective way to reach decisions in accordance with the words and goals of the statutory disability standard. The first three steps are particularly efficient to the extent that they can direct a finding of disabled or not disabled without a lengthy review of the record. Thus, claimants who are engaging in "substantial gainful activity" and those with no severe impairments are denied quickly and relatively easily at Steps 1 or 2; those with impairments that meet (or equal) the strict criteria set forth in the Social Security Administration's Listing of Impairments are granted benefits quickly and relatively objectively at Step 3. The last two steps take on the closer cases (those that cannot be resolved fully at one of the first three steps) and address the more complex medical-vocational aspects of the disability standard. Step 4 is still relatively focused; claimants who can still perform jobs that they held in the past—jobs that, by definition, they are within their vocational competence—are denied benefits on that ground. Only at step 5 does the process deal with the open-ended, ultimate question of whether the claimant can perform any jobs at all, given his or her age, education, and work experience. (As discussed later in this chapter, there are other special rules and guidelines that assist with step 5 decisions).

The sequential evaluation process is used throughout the administrative process and is fully accepted by the courts as the framework for analysis of a disability claim. As one court stated, "[i]t is important for the [administrative law judge] to follow the orderly framework set out in the [sequential evaluation regulations] to ensure uniformity and regularity in outcome as well as fairness to the claimant"). Mitchell v. Schweiker, 551 F. Supp. 1084, 1087–88 (W.D. Mo. 1982). *See also* Combs v. Commissioner of Social Security, 459 F.3d 640, 649 (6th Cir. 2006) ("The entire five-step sequential evaluation process has been designed to regulate adjudicatory conduct for the purpose of making adjudication of claims efficient and flexible."); Dugas v. Astrue, 2009 WL 1780121 (E.D.Tex. June 22, 2009) ("Administrative adjudicators of social security disability claims utilize a five-step, sequential evaluation process prescribed by regulation and approved by courts as a fair and just way for determining disability applications in conformity with the Social Security Act and as contributing to uniformity and efficiency in such determinations.").

The sequential evaluation process also provides a straightforward and effective means for courts to review individual claims for benefits. Thus, the court in Plummer v. Apfel, 186 F.3d 422, 63 Soc. Sec. Rep. Ser. 264 (3rd Cir. 1999) summarized the process and its application to the claimant as follows:

> The Social Security Administration has promulgated regulations incorporating a sequential evaluation process for determining whether a claimant is under a disability. * * * In step one, the Commissioner must determine whether the claimant is currently engaging in substantial gainful activity. * * * If a claimant is found to be engaged in substantial activity, the disability claim will be denied. * * * In step two, the Commissioner must determine whether the claimant is suffering from a severe impairment. * * * If the claimant fails to show that her impairments are "severe", she is ineligible for disability benefits.

In step three, the Commissioner compares the medical evidence of the claimant's impairment to a list of impairments presumed severe enough to preclude any gainful work. * * * If a claimant does not suffer from a listed impairment or its equivalent, the analysis proceeds to steps four and five. Step four requires the ALJ to consider whether the claimant retains the residual functional capacity to perform her past relevant work. * * * The claimant bears the burden of demonstrating an inability to return to her past relevant work. * * *

If the claimant is unable to resume her former occupation, the evaluation moves to the final step. At this stage, the burden of production shifts to the Commissioner, who must demonstrate the claimant is capable of performing other available work in order to deny a claim of disability. * * * The ALJ must show there are other jobs existing in significant numbers in the national economy which the claimant can perform, consistent with her medical impairments, age, education, past work experience, and residual functional capacity. The ALJ must analyze the cumulative effect of all the claimant's impairments in determining whether she is capable of performing work and is not disabled. * * *

In this case, the ALJ concluded Plummer is not entitled to disability benefits, finding that: (1) Plummer has not performed any substantial gainful activity since the alleged onset date of disability; (2) Plummer's wrist impairments impose significant restrictions on work-related activities, and are considered "severe" impairments; (3) Plummer does not suffer from any impairments which would meet the severity criteria listed in the relevant regulation; (4) Plummer cannot perform her past work as a clerk/typist because it involves extensive bilateral finger and hand manipulation; and (5) Plummer nonetheless has the capacity to perform a number of jobs which exist in significant numbers in the national economy. The ALJ sought the assistance of a vocational expert in making this determination. * * *

186 F.3d at 428–29.

NOTE ON THE SEQUENTIAL EVALUATION PROCESS FOR CHILD SSI CLAIMS

As noted earlier and in Chapter 4, claims for SSI benefits on behalf of disabled children under the age of 18 are assessed according to a separate disability standard. The current standard was enacted as part of 1996 reforms to the Child's SSI program; it provides that a child is disabled for purposes of SSI if the child "has a medically determinable physical or mental impairment, which results in marked and severe functional limitations, and which can be expected to result in death or which has lasted or can be expected to last for a continuous period of not less than 12 months." 42 U.S.C. §

1382c(a)(3)(C)(i). The determination of disability for Child's SSI claims follows a modified version of the sequential evaluation process designed to implement the special statutory standard for that program. Before describing that process, some background about the pre–1996 use of the sequential evaluation process for Child's SSI claims will be helpful.

Federal benefits were first provided for children with disabilities in 1974 when the federal-state public assistance for the aged, blind and disabled (AABD) was replaced by the federal SSI program and responsibility for that program was given to SSA. At that time, the Social Security Act provided that a child was disabled for purposes of the SSI program if he or she "suffer[ed] from any medically determinable physical or mental impairment of comparable severity" to an impairment that would qualify as disabling under the adult program. 42 U.S.C. § 1382c(c)(3)(A) (1974). Reasoning that the fourth and fifth steps of the sequential evaluation process, with their focus on work activity, were not applicable to claims by children, SSA simply cut off the sequential evaluation process for child SSI claims after the first three steps. As a result, children could receive SSI only if they had an impairment, or combination of impairments, that met or equaled either the requirements of the general (Part A) or special children's (Part B) Listing of Impairments. 20 C.F.R. § 416.923 (1974). (SSA added Part B to the Listing of Impairments to account for certain medical conditions unique to children that were not included in Part A, recognizing that it may not be appropriate to limit the determination of children's disabilities to the general Listing of Impairments.)

SSA's three-step process for Child SSI claims was challenged beginning in the 1980s on the ground that it was inconsistent with the comparable severity standard set out in the Social Security Act. Some courts upheld the approach, noting that SSA was entitled to deference when interpreting the statute and that adopting the three-step process was within its broad rule making power. *See, e.g.,* Powell By and Through Powell v. Schweiker, 688 F.2d 1357, 1360–61 (11th Cir. 1982); Hinckley on Behalf of Martin v. Secretary of Health and Human Services, 742 F.2d 19 (1st Cir. 1984). Other courts rejected SSA's implementation of the statutory language. The Third Circuit, for example, declined to follow Hinckley because the Listing of Impairments ignores functional consequences of impairments, yet "only impaired ability to function ... results in disability." Zebley by Zebley v. Bowen, 855 F.2d 67, 74 (3d Cir. 1988). *See generally,* Frank S. Bloch, *Three Steps And You're Out: The Misuse of the Sequential Evaluation Process in Child SSI Disability Determinations,* 37 U. Mich. J. Law Reform 39 (2003).

The Supreme Court resolved the split in Sullivan v. Zebley, 493 U.S. 521, 110 S. Ct. 885, 28 Soc. Sec. Rep. Serv. 367 (1990). The Court noted four ways in which determining disability solely on the basis of the Listing of Impairments resulted in applying a disability standard that was more restrictive than the comparable severity standard in the Act. First, the Listing does not cover all possible impairments. Second, even for medical conditions covered in the Listing, the criteria listed are stricter than anticipated under the Act; the Listings require that a claimant be precluded not just from "substantial gainful activity", but from "any gainful activity." Third, the Listing does not provide for any individualized assessment of the effects of an impairment, given the claimant's age, education, and work experience. Lastly, claimants with unlisted impairments, or a combination of impairments that do not equal the criteria set out for a listed impairment, were excluded under the "Listing-only" approach. *See* 493 U.S. at 533–534. The Court thus noted, in conclusion:

> The Secretary [of Health, Education, and Welfare] does not seriously dispute the disparity in his approach to child- and adult-disability determinations. He argues, instead, that the listings-only approach is the only practicable way to determine whether a child's impairment is "comparable" to one that would disable an adult. An individualized, functional approach to child-disability claims like that provided for adults is not feasible, the Secretary asserts, since children do not work; there is no available measure of their functional abilities analogous to an adult's ability to work, so the only way to measure "comparable severity" is to compare child claimants' medical evidence with the standard of severity set by the listings. Laying to one side the obvious point that such a comparison does not properly implement the statute because the Secretary's current listings set a level of severity higher than that prescribed by the statute, this argument still is not persuasive. Even if the listings were set at the same level of severity as the statute, and expanded to cover many more childhood impairments, *no* set of listings could ensure that child claimants would receive benefits whenever their impairments are of "comparable severity" to ones that would qualify an adult for benefits under the individualized, functional analysis contemplated by the statute and provided to adults by the Secretary. No decision process restricted to comparing claimants' medical evidence to a fixed, finite set of medical criteria can respond adequately to the infinite variety of medical conditions and combinations thereof, the varying impact of such conditions due to the claimant's individual characteristics, and the constant evolution of medical diagnostic techniques.
>
> The Secretary's claim that a functional analysis of child-disability claims is not feasible is unconvincing. The fact that a *vocational* analysis is inapplicable to children does not mean that a *functional* analysis cannot be applied to them. An inquiry into the impact of an impairment on the normal daily activities of a child of the claimant's age—speaking, walking, washing, dressing, feeding oneself, going to school, playing, etc.—is, in our view, no more amorphous or unmanageable than an inquiry into the impact of an adult's impairment on his ability to perform "any other kind of substantial gainful work which exists in the national economy," § 1382c(a)(3)(B). Moreover, the Secretary tacitly acknowledges that functional assessment of child claimants is possible, in that some of his own listings are defined in terms of functional criteria. *See, e.g.,* 20

CFR pt. 404, subpt. P, App. 1 (pt. B), § 101.03 (1989) (listing for "Deficit of musculoskeletal function" defined in terms of difficulty in walking or "[i]nability to perform age-related personal self-care activities involving feeding, dressing, and personal hygiene"); § 111.02(B) (listing for "Major motor seizures" defined in terms of "Significant interference with communication" or "Significant emotional disorder," or "Where significant adverse effects of medication interfere with major daily activities"); § 112.05(C) (mental retardation listing for claimants with IQ of 60–69 requiring "a physical or other mental impairment imposing additional and significant restriction of function or developmental progression"). Also, the Secretary's own test for cessation of disability involves an examination of a child claimant's ability to "perform age-appropriate activities." 20 CFR § 416.994(c) (1989). Finally, the Secretary's insistence that child claimants must be assessed from "a medical perspective alone, without individualized consideration of ... residual functional capacity," Brief for Petitioner 45, seems to us to make little sense in light of the fact that standard medical diagnostic techniques often include assessment of the functional impact of the disorder.

493 U.S. at 538–541.

The Social Security Administration eventually issued a complex set of regulations designed to rework the sequential evaluation process for child's SSI claims so that it that would be consistent with the ruling in *Zebley*. The post-*Zebley* process added an individualized functional assessment intended to evaluate the child claimant's ability to engage in age-appropriate activities on an age-appropriate sustained basis, which was then used to determine whether those functional limitations imposed a disability comparable to the adult standard. *See* 20 C.F.R. §§ 416.924–924e (1995). These regulations were short lived, however, as Congress revisited the disability standard for child's SSI benefits in the Personal Responsibility and Work Opportunity Reconciliation Act of 1996. Pub. L. No. 104–193, 110 Stat. 2105 (1996). In that legislation, Congress repealed the Social Security Act's "comparable severity" disability standard for children and substituted the current standard, thereby effectively reversing the Supreme Court's decision in *Zebley*.

The Social Security Administration followed up on the 1996 amendments with the current sequential evaluation process for determining disability for children, which is essentially a more flexible version of the truncated pre-*Zebley* three-step process. *See* **20 C.F.R. § 416.924[APP–REGS]** As was the case before, disability assessments for child's SSI claims are evaluated in the same manner as are adult claims through the first two steps of the sequential evaluation process. Thus, the first step asks whether the child is performing substantial gainful activity. If so, the child is considered not disabled—regardless of his or her medical condition—and the process ends. 20 C.F.R. § 416.924(b). If the child is not currently engaging in substantial gainful activity, the process moves to the second step, which asks whether the child has a severe impairment (or combination of impairments) that significantly limits his or her ability to perform work. If not, the child is considered not disabled and the process ends there. 20 C.F.R. § 416.924(c). If the child does have a severe impairment and meets the same duration requirement applied to adult claims, the evaluation process continues on to a third and final step.

While the sequential evaluation process for children does not include additional steps for claimants who are not found "disabled" at Step 3, the third step in the Child's SSI sequential evaluation process is less restrictive than Step 3 for adult claims in one important respect. A child will be found disabled at Step 3 not only if he or she has an impairment or combination of impairments that meets or equals the requirements of the Listing of Impairments, but also if the impairment(s) "functionally equals" the requirements of the Listing. 20 C.F.R. § 416.924(d).

The Child's SSI sequential evaluation process is used only for periods when child claimants are, in fact, under the age of 18. If a claimant reaches age 18 after filing his or her disability claim but before a decision is made by SSA, the process for children will be used for the period during which the claimant was under 18 and the adult process will be used for the period beginning with the day the claimant reaches age 18. 20 C.F.R. § 416.924(f).

Finally, a child's chronological age is an important factor in evaluating an impairment and there are special rules acknowledging the limits of chronological age categories when assessing the capacity of children at various steps in the Child's SSI sequential evaluation process. Typically, age is a consideration when determining the severity of an impairment and when comparing the claimant's impairment to a listing that includes specific age categories. *See* 20 C.F.R. § 416.924b. For some child claimants born prematurely (at less than 37 weeks' gestation), a corrected chronological age may be used in the evaluation to adjust for any discrepancy between developmental age and chronological age. 20 C.F.R. § 416.924b(b). Similar rules exist for adults at Step 5 of the adult process, which are discussed later in this chapter.

NOTE ON THE SEQUENTIAL EVALUATION PROCESS FOR SPOUSES' CLAIMS

The Social Security Administration also used a 3–step sequential evaluation process for claims by wage earners' spouses when benefits for disabled spouses were first provided under the Social Security Act in the late 1960s. Restricting eligibility to persons with impairments that met or equaled the criteria in the Listing was justified on the grounds that there was a different disability standard for spouses (the inability to engage in "any gainful activity") that excluded consideration of non-medical factors such as the claimant's age, education, or prior work experience. Court challenges were unsuccessful for the most part, since the statutory argument was not as strong as it was for Child SSI claims. *See, e.g.,* Sims v. Harris, 607 F.2d 1253, 1257 (9th Cir. 1979), Wokojance v. Weinberger, 513 F.2d 210, 212–13 (6th Cir. 1975); *but see* Tolany v. Heckler, 756 F.2d 268, 271–72 (2d Cir. 1985), Paris v. Schweiker,

674 F.2d 707, 710 (8th Cir. 1982). The issue became moot in 1990, when Congress amended the Act to bring spouses disability claims under that same standard as other adult claims. Omnibus Budget Reconciliation Act of 1990, Pub. L. No. 101–508 § 5103, 104 Stat. 1388, 1388–251. As a result, the 5–step sequential evaluation process is used for spouses' claims from 1991 onward; the original 3–step process is used only for claims covering periods prior to 1991. *See* 20 C.F.R. § 404.1578.

NOTE ON COMBINATION OF IMPAIRMENTS

Each of the steps of the sequential evaluation process, other than Step 1, starts with the claimant's alleged physical or mental impairment—or combination of impairments. Although the Social Security Act conditions eligibility on work incapacity resulting from "any medically determinable physical or mental impairment," the definition of disability has long been interpreted to include the inability to engage in substantial gainful activity resulting from a combination of impairments as well. There had been some controversy about combining impairments at Step 2 which was clarified in the Social Security Disability Benefits Reform Act of 1984. The Social Security Act now states clearly that a combination of impairments can satisfy the severity requirement of the sequential evaluation process. *See* PL 98–460 § 4(a)(1), 98 Stat. 1794 (1984); 42 USCA § 423(d)(2)(B). SSA then promulgated regulations implementing the 1984 Amendments which state, in part, that in determining medical severity SSA "will consider the combined effect of all of [a claimant's] impairments without regard to whether any such impairment, if considered separately, would be of sufficient severity." 20 C.F.R. §§ 404.1523, 416.923; *see also* 20 C.F.R. §§ 404.1520(a), 416.920(a); Barrett v. Barnhart, 355 F.3d 1065, 1068–69, 94 Soc. Sec. Rep. Serv. 7 (7th Cir. 2004) (evidence of arthritis, obesity, numbness and pain in arm; "all too characteristically, the administrative law judge failed to consider the applicant's medical situation as a whole"). Other issues relative to evaluating combinations of impairments at Step 2 are discussed later in this chapter.

Social Security regulations also state clearly that combining impairments is allowed at any other point in the sequential evaluation process where the claimant complains of the combined effect of more than one impairment. Thus, 20 C.F.R. §§ 404.1523, 416.923 also provide: "If we do find a medically severe combination of impairments, the combined impact of the impairments will be considered throughout the disability determination process." Combinations of impairments can present particular issues at different steps in the sequential evaluation process, which are covered later in this chapter when those steps of the process are discussed.

B. SIMPLIFIED DENIAL AT STEPS 1 AND 2: SUBSTANTIAL GAINFUL ACTIVITY, MINIMUM DURATION, AND SEVERITY

As mentioned in the previous section, the first two steps of the 5–step sequential evaluation process are designed to provide adjudicators with simple and efficient criteria for finding that, in the most obvious cases, a claimant is not disabled. Step 1 focuses on the concept of "substantial gainful activity" (often referred to as SGA); if a claimant is, at the relevant time, in fact engaging in substantial gainful activity, then obviously he or she is not unable to perform "substantial gainful activity"—the key criterion for a finding of disability under the statute—and therefore is not disabled. Step 2 goes just a little further than the first step and looks to see whether, with respect to those claimants who are not currently engaging in substantial gainful activity, they have a least a minimal medical impairment that has lasted, or is expected to last, at least one year, the minimum period set out in the Act. Claimants who do not have a severe impairment cannot possibly meet the statutory requirement and therefore are not disabled. That does not mean, however, that claimants who have a "severe impairment" are eligible for benefits; satisfying the minimal requirements at Step 2 just allows the claim to continue through the rest of the sequential evaluation process.

The first part of this section examines the concept of substantial gainful activity and how it is incorporated into Step 1 of the sequential evaluation process. (Substantial gainful activity is also discussed later in this chapter since it is used to assess a claimant's capacity to work at Steps 4 and 5 as well.) The second part of the section discusses the minimum severity and duration requirements that form the substance of Step 2.

1. STEP 1: SUBSTANTIAL GAINFUL ACTIVITY (SGA)

"Substantial gainful activity" is the measure of the minimum level of work activity that the Social Security Act considers necessary for an individual to be self-sustaining. If a claimant's capacities are such that he or she cannot perform at that minimum level—that is, cannot perform substantial gainful activity—then a finding of disability is warranted. *See* 20 C.F.R §§ 404.1571, 416.971.

Substantial gainful activity is defined as work activity that is both substantial and gainful. Substantial work activity is defined as any work activity that involves doing significant physical or mental activities, even when it is done part-time, for a lower wage, or with more limited responsibilities than work the claimant may have performed in the past. 20 C.F.R. §§ 404.1572(a), 416.972(a). Gainful work activity is defined as work activity that is done, or usually done, for pay or for profit—even if no profit actually results. 20 C.F.R. §§ 404.1572(b), 416.972(b). Activities not generally considered to be substantial gainful activity include taking care of oneself, doing household tasks, hobbies, therapy, school attendance, club activities, and social programs. *See* 20 C.F.R. §§ 404.1572(c), 416.972(c).

The Social Security Act authorizes SSA to promulgate regulations that "prescribe the criteria for determining when services performed—or earnings derived from services—demonstrate an individual's ability to engage in substantial gainful activity." 42 U.S.C. § 423(d)(4)(A). Thus, **20 C.F.R. §§ 404.1573, 416.973[APP–REGS]** set out criteria for measuring the nature of the work, how well it is done, and whether it is done under special conditions. Work that requires the use of an individual's experience, skills, supervision and responsibilities, or that contributes substantially to the operation of a business, tends to show that the individual has "the ability to work at the substantial gainful activity level." 20 C.F.R. §§ 404.1573(a), 416.973(a). On the other hand, work that involves "minimal duties that [make] little or no demands on [the claimant] and that are of little or no use to [the] employer, or to the operation of a business if [the claimant is] self-employed," tends to show that it is not substantial gainful activity. 20 C.F.R. §§ 404.1573(b), 416.973(b). In addition, SSA will look at various circumstances to determine if a claimant is working under special conditions that may indicate that the work is not substantial gainful activity, such as where the claimant is given special assistance while performing work tasks or being allowed to work "at a lower standard of productivity or efficiency." 20 C.F.R. §§ 404.1573(a), 416.973(a).

One of the key factors that SSA considers in determining whether a claimant is engaged in substantial gainful activity is the amount of his or her earnings. Social Security regulations list amounts of earnings for given years; if a claimant's earnings exceed the amount listed for the relevant period, the work activity ordinarily is considered substantial and gainful. *See generally* **20 C.F.R. §§ 404.1574, 416.974 [APP–REGS]**. The amount of earnings that will trigger this presumption is adjusted yearly to account for national average wage growth. For the year 2012, earnings of less than an average of $1,010 per month will ordinarily show that the work was not substantial gainful activity. Prior to 2001, the regulations included both a lower and an upper threshold; if an individual's earnings fell between those values, SSA would consider additional information, including work done by comparable, unimpaired individuals. 20 C.F.R. § 404.1574(b)(2)(i); (b)(6)(i); (b)(6)(iii) (2000). The lower threshold was abandoned in 2001, however, and now SSA generally will not consider information in addition to earnings unless there is other evidence indicating that the claimant, despite low earnings, may be engaged in substantial gainful activity. 20 C.F.R. §§ 404.1574(b)(2)(ii), 416.974(b)(2)(ii).

Although the value of an individual's earnings is used as a guide in determining if the work is substantial gainful activity, the key issue is whether the individual has the capacity to earn at the requisite level. The regulations thus establish a presumption that work is substantial gainful activity if the claimant earned more than the stated amount, but that presumption is rebuttable by the claimant. *See* 20 C.F.R. §§ 404.1574(a)(1), 416.974(a)(1) ("Generally, in evaluating your work activity for substantial gainful activity purposes, our primary consideration will be the earnings you derive from the work activity. We will use your earnings to determine whether you have done substantial gainful activity unless we have information from you, your employer, or others that shows that we should not count all of your earnings."). Thus, an individual who earns the listed amount or more may still be able to show that he or she is not, in fact, capable of engaging in substantial gainful activity. *But see* Dukes v. Barnhart, 436 F.3d 923, 927 (8th Cir. 2006) ("Because he is engaged in substantial gainful activity and has failed to rebut the presumption created by his earnings, Dukes is ineligible to receive SSI benefits.")

When calculating a claimant's earnings, only the amounts actually earned are considered; that is, SSA typically will consider only the reasonable value of the work performed and will exclude any earnings that exceed that value. 20 C.F.R. §§ 404.1574(a)(2), 416.974(a)(2). Therefore, the regulations detail special situations, such as when an individual's earnings are being subsidized, where SSA may determine that the full amount of an individual's earnings should not be used to determine if he or she has done substantial gainful activity. 20 C.F.R. §§ 404.1574(a)(2)-(3), 416.974(a)(2)-(3). For example, if a person does simple tasks under close and continuous supervision, SSA will look at the amount of the wages paid but it will also determine whether the individual was being paid more than the reasonable value of the actual services performed, and will then subtract the difference from the person's gross earnings to determine if the work was, in fact, substantial gainful activity. 20 C.F.R. §§ 404.1574(a)(2), 416.974(a)(2). An individual can also deduct from the earnings calculation the reasonable costs of impairment-related work expenses. These costs are deductible even if the assistance is also needed by the individual to carry out normal daily functions that are unrelated to work. *See* 42 U.S.C. § 423(d)(4)(A); 20 C.F.R. §§ 404.1576(a), 416.976(a).

ROSSELLO V. ASTRUE

529 F.3d 1181, 132 Soc.Sec.Rep.Serv. 462 (D.C. Cir. 2008)

Before: GINSBURG, BROWN, and KAVANAUGH, Circuit Judges.

KAVANAUGH, Circuit Judge:

[Joaquin Rossello applied for Social Security disability benefits on behalf of his daughter Cristina, who had a history of serious mental illness. He applied for benefits in 1993, alleging that Cristina had been continuously disabled since before the age of 22, which is the age before which a wage earner's child must become disabled in order to receive disability benefits based on the earnings record of the child's parent.]

I

* * *

The key issue before the Social Security Administration was whether Cristina Rossello has been continuously "disabled" since before the age of 22—that is, whether she has been unable since turning 22 "to engage in any substantial gainful activity by reason of any medically determinable physical or mental impairment." § 423(d)(1)(A). To determine whether an individual has been continuously disabled, the Social Security Administration first considers whether the individual's work activity since turning 22, if any, constitutes substantial gainful activity; if so, that disqualifies the claimant from benefits. 20 C.F.R. § 404.1520(a)(4)(i); see also § 404.1571 (If you are able to engage in substantial gainful activity, we will find that you are not disabled.). The Social Security Administration then considers the medical severity of the individual's impairment and whether the claimant has suffered from that impairment since before turning 22, among other factors.

The Rossellos' odyssey began in February 1993 when Joaquin Rossello applied for Social Security retirement benefits. At the same time, Joaquin also sought childhood disability benefits on behalf of his daughter Cristina, who was then 28 years old and had a history of debilitating mental illness. Joaquin submitted extensive medical evidence showing that Cristina had been diagnosed with chronic mental illness and had been hospitalized multiple times.

In 1995, the Social Security Administration denied Cristina's claim for benefits because the Rossellos had not submitted medical evidence establishing that Cristina's condition began before she turned 22 in 1986, as required by law.

The Rossellos appealed the denial to an administrative law judge and submitted additional medical evidence, including a doctor's certification that Cristina had been diagnosed with and treated for mental disorders from 1980 to 1983 (when she was 16 to 19 years old) and that she had been institutionalized for part of that time. The ALJ nonetheless denied Cristina's claim. The ALJ ruled that the record did not support Cristina's claim that she was disabled before turning 22 because the medical certificate describing her treatment from 1980 to 1983 did not constitute medical evidence of Cristina's condition during that time.

The Rossellos sought relief from the Social Security Administration's Appeals Council, which exercises discretionary review of ALJ decisions. The Appeals Council granted review but explained that Cristina's earnings in 1986 and 1987 (when she was 22 and 23 years old) suggested she had performed substantial gainful activity since turning 22–meaning she could not meet the statutory requirement that a claimant be continuously disabled since before the age of 22. The Appeals Council noted that Cristina earned an average of $334.42 per month in 1986 and $587.04 per month in 1987. Under the Social Security regulations, average monthly earnings of more than $300 in 1986 or 1987 create a presumption that an individual "engaged in substantial gainful activity." Average monthly earnings below $190 create a presumption that an individual did not engage in substantial gainful activity. As a result of Cristina's monthly earnings in 1986 and 1987, it appeared to the Appeals Council that Cristina was not continuously disabled since before the age of 22 and therefore did not qualify for childhood disability benefits.

Before making a final ruling, the Appeals Council allowed the Rossellos to submit rebuttal evidence to show that Cristina's earnings in 1986 and 1987 were "subsidized"—meaning that the work was done under special conditions because of Cristina's impairment and that her earnings exceeded the reasonable value of her work. Any portion of wages that is considered a subsidy does not count as "earnings in determining" whether an individual performed substantial gainful activity. If Cristina's earnings in 1986 and 1987 were subsidized and her average monthly unsubsidized earnings fell below the $300 threshold in the Social Security regulations, then the presumption that she had engaged in substantial gainful activity would drop out.

* * *

The Rossellos produced significant, uncontested evidence that Cristina's earnings were subsidized. They submitted multiple affidavits describing Cristina's jobs in 1986 and 1987 as provided "by the generosity and compassion of family or acquaintances that would not have hired her otherwise because of her serious mental limitations." According to the Rossellos, Cristina's primary job in 1986 and 1987 consisted of working in an office for her uncle (with whom she was living at the time). Cristina's uncle stated that Cristina was "not productive and performed only basic tasks like stuffing envelopes and elementary clerical work." Affidavit of Jorge Rossello (June 16, 2000); see also id. ("had she not been my niece, we would not have hired her"). Cristina's uncle offered her the job because he "could provide her with a sheltered environment where she could be supervised all the time." Id.

In its final ruling, the Appeals Council nonetheless denied the Rossellos' appeal. Relying on 20 C.F.R. § 404.1574(b), the Appeals Council ruled that Cristina's average monthly earnings of more than $300 in 1986 and 1987 indicated that she had performed substantial gainful activity since turning 22. The Appeals Council never expressly mentioned subsidization or analyzed Cristina's earnings under the relevant regulations; instead, it simply stated that "there is no evidence to indicate that any of [Cristina's] work activity was performed in a ... special environment." The Appeals Council held that because Cristina had performed substantial gainful activity since turning 22, she therefore was not disabled under the Act and was ineligible for childhood disability benefits. Having so concluded, the Appeals Council had no occasion to reach the ALJ's determination that Cristina's impairment did not begin before she turned 22.

* * *

II

The Rossellos argue that the record does not contain substantial evidence to justify the Appeals Council's conclusion that Cristina engaged in substantial gainful activity in 1986 and 1987. We agree with the Rossellos.

Substantial-evidence review is highly deferential to the agency factfinder, requiring only "such relevant evidence as a reasonable mind might accept as adequate to support a conclusion". Reversal of an agency decision under that standard is rare. But this is one of those rare cases. Even under the deferential, "substantial-evidence" standard of review, the Appeals Council's decision does not pass muster.

The Appeals Council initially informed the Rossellos that it had obtained Cristina's earnings record and was prepared to rule that she had not been continuously disabled since turning 22 because her average monthly earnings in 1986 and 1987 were greater than $300, thereby triggering a presumption that she had engaged in substantial gainful activity. In response, the Rossellos submitted a letter and affidavits describing Cristina's work activity in 1986 and 1987. They submitted this evidence to demonstrate that Cristina's average monthly earnings of $334.42 in 1986 and $587.04 in 1987 were "subsidized" and that her unsubsidized earnings did not indicate substantial gainful activity.

The Social Security Administration's regulations provide that earnings are subsidized if the "true value" of the work, "when compared with the same or similar work done by unimpaired persons, is less than the actual amount of earnings." § 404.1574(a)(2); see also id. ("For example, when a person with a serious impairment does simple tasks under close and continuous supervision, our determination of whether that person has done substantial gainful activity will not be based only on the amount of the wages paid."). Several circumstances "indicate the strong possibility of a subsidy," including when "[m]ental impairment is involved," when "the employee receives unusual help from others in doing the work," or when there "appears to be a marked discrepancy between the amount of pay and the value of the services." SSR 83–33.

Contrary to the conclusion of the Appeals Council that there was "no evidence" of a subsidy, the evidence indisputably establishes that Cristina's work for her uncle in 1986 and 1987—which accounts for 82 percent of her earnings during those years-was subsidized under the Social Security Administration's regulations. Cristina's work involved simple tasks performed under close supervision by her family. See Affidavit of Jorge Rossello (June 16, 2000) ("she was not productive and performed only basic tasks," such as "stuffing envelopes," in "a sheltered environment where she could be supervised all the time"). The evidence also shows that Cristina obtained the job through the kindness of her family and not based on merit. See id. ("had she not been my niece, we would not have hired her because of [her] mental disability"); see also Letter from Joaquin Rossello to Social Security Administration (July 18, 2000) (Cristina's work "provided her with a sheltered environment"). And Cristina's uncle was "President," "part owner," and "closely involved in [the] management" of the employer that accounted for 61 percent of Cristina's $334 monthly earnings in 1986 and 94 percent of her $587 monthly earnings in 1987.

The Appeals Council cited no evidence to undermine the only conclusion that the record permits-namely, that Cristina's earnings were subsidized.

If, as required by Social Security regulations, the Appeals Council had subtracted the amount of the subsidy from Cristina's earnings in those years, it presumably would have concluded that her average monthly earnings fell below the $300 threshold that triggers a presumption of substantial gainful activity. Indeed, because almost all of Cristina's earnings to appear have been subsidized to some degree, the Appeals Council presumably would have concluded that Cristina's unsubsidized earnings fell below the $190 threshold and thus triggered a presumption that she did not engage in substantial gainful activity. See SSR 83–33.[1]

---

[1]   The remainder of Cristina's earnings in 1986 came from her work at a hotel where her sister Marta was employed. The evidence suggests that Cristina's earnings there may also have been subsidized. Marta obtained the job for Cristina; Cristina's sole, very simple duty was to distribute pool towels to hotel guests; and Marta was able to directly and personally supervise her sister. The remainder of Cristina's earnings in 1987 came from work for a temporary placement agency.

We therefore agree with the Rossellos that the Social Security Administration's decision is not supported by substantial evidence.

* * *

LE V. ASTRUE

540 F.Supp.2d 1144, 131 Soc. Sec. Rep. Serv. 102 C.D. Calif. 2008)

[Editor Note: The issue in the following case was whether the claimant's work as a rice farmer was substantial gainful activity. Although the claim was denied at Step 4 of the sequential evaluation process (based on her ability to perform a prior job), the SGA analysis is the same as it would be at Step 1.]

FERNANDO M. OLGUIN, United States Magistrate Judge.

* * *

BACKGROUND AND SUMMARY OF ADMINISTRATIVE DECISION

Plaintiff, who was 61 years of age at the time of her last administrative hearing, obtained a fourth-grade education in Vietnam. Her past work experience includes employment as a rice farmer and a sewing machine operator.

Plaintiff protectively filed for SSI on March 30, 2001, alleging that she has been disabled since November 1, 1999, due to hypertension, headaches, dizziness, fainting, weakness, fatigue, and back and leg pain. Plaintiff's application was denied initially, on reconsideration, and by an Administrative Law Judge ("ALJ") in a written decision issued on April 18, 2003. Thereafter, plaintiff filed a timely request for review of the ALJ's decision by the Appeals Council ("AC"). On July 8, 2004, the AC vacated the ALJ's decision and remanded the matter for further proceedings based upon the ALJ's failure to share information with plaintiff and her counsel, the ALJ's improper evaluation of the medical evidence, and the ALJ's erroneous determination that plaintiff's past work as a sewing machine operator constituted substantial gainful activity.

On October 20, 2004, plaintiff appeared and testified at a supplemental hearing before an ALJ. The ALJ also heard testimony from Alan Boroskin, a vocational expert ("VE").

The ALJ denied plaintiff's request for benefits on April 27, 2005. Applying the five-step sequential evaluation process, the ALJ found, at step one, that plaintiff has not engaged in substantial gainful activity since her alleged onset date of disability. At step two, the ALJ found that plaintiff suffers from severe impairments consisting of "hypertension, obesity, and hyperlipidemia." At step three, the ALJ determined that the evidence does not demonstrate that plaintiffs impairments, either individually or in combination, meet or medically equal the severity of any listing set forth in the Social Security regulations.

The ALJ then assessed plaintiff's residual functional capacity ("RFC") and determined that she can perform a full range of medium work. Specifically, the ALJ found that plaintiff can:

> stand and/or walk, with normal breaks, for a total of about 6 hours during an 8–hour workday. She can sit, with normal breaks, for a total of about 6 hours during an 8–hour workday. She can lift and/or carry a maximum of 50 pounds occasionally and 25 pounds frequently.

Based on plaintiff's RFC, the ALJ determined, at step four, that "[b]ased on the [plaintiff]'s own description of her past relevant work as a rice farmer, this job did not require the performance of work-related activities precluded by her residual functional capacity.... Thus, the [plaintiff] could return to her past relevant work as a rice farmer as previously performed and as generally performed in the national economy." Accordingly, the ALJ concluded that plaintiff was not suffering from a disability as defined by the Act.

Plaintiff filed a timely request for review of the ALJ's decision, which was denied by the Appeals Council. The ALJ's decision stands as the final decision of the Commissioner.

* * *

DISCUSSION

I. THE ALJ IMPROPERLY DETERMINED THAT PLAINTIFF'S PAST WORK AS A RICE FARMER CONSTITUTED SUBSTANTIAL GAINFUL ACTIVITY.

Plaintiff contends that the ALJ erred in his step four determination that plaintiff's past employment as a rice farmer qualified as past relevant work. (See Joint Stip at 4–7 & 9–11). Specifically, plaintiff maintains that her work on a family farm in Vietnam where she grew rice and other produce for personal consumption, bartered a small portion for necessities, and was not paid a wage, does not satisfy the requirements for past relevant work because it did not constitute substantial gainful activity ("SGA"). (See id.). Further, plaintiff asserts that whether she was an employee or self-employed does not alter the determination that her work as a rice farmer does not constitute SGA. (See id.).

* * *

SGA is "work activity that is both substantial and gainful[.]" 20 C.F.R. §§ 404.1572 & 416.972. "Substantial work activity is work activity that involves doing significant physical or mental activities. [A claimant's] work may be substantial even if it is done on a part-time basis or if [the claimant] do[es] less, get[s] paid less, or ha[s] less responsibility than when [the claimant] worked before." 20 C.F.R. §§ 404.1572(a) & 416.972(a). "Gainful work activity is work activity that [a claimant] do[es] for pay or profit. Work activity is gainful if it is the kind of work usually done for pay or profit, whether or not a profit is realized." Id. at §§ 404.1572(b) & 416.972(b).

In determining whether a particular job constitutes SGA, the Social Security regulations consider two employment categories: employee and self employed. See 20 C.F.R. §§ 404.1574; 404.1575; 416.974 & 416.975. For an employee, the primary factor in determining whether his or her past work is SGA "will be the earnings [the employee] derive[d] from the work activity." Id. at §§ 404.1574(a)(1) & 416.974(a)(1). There is a rebuttable presumption that the employee either was or was not engaged in SGA if his or her average monthly earnings are above or below a certain amount established by the Commissioner's Earnings Guidelines. See id. at §§ 404.1574(b)(2)-(3) & 416.974(b)(2)-(3); see also Lewis [v Apfel, 236 F.3d 503, 515 (9th Cir. 2001)] ("Earnings can be a presumptive, but not conclusive, sign of whether a job is substantial gainful activity.").

Earnings, however, are not dispositive. For example, even where the employee's wages are not substantial, if there is other evidence indicating that the claimant was engaged in SGA or that a claimant was in the position to control the amount of wages he or she was paid, the Commissioner may consider whether the work performed is "comparable to that of unimpaired people in [the employee's] community who are doing the same or similar occupations as their means of livelihood, taking into account the time, energy, skill, and responsibility involved in the work[.]" 20 C.F.R. §§ 404.1574(b)(3)(ii)(A) & 416.974(b)(3)(ii)(A). The Commissioner may also rely upon evidence that the employee's work is clearly worth more than the SGA amounts provided for the particular calendar year in the Commissioner's Earning Guidelines based upon the prevailing pay scales in the employee's community. Id. at §§ 404.1574(b)(3)(ii)(B) & 416.974(b)(3)(ii)(B).

If a claimant is self-employed, the Commissioner will consider the work activities he or she has performed and their value to the business to determine whether the individual engaged in SGA. 20 C.F.R. §§ 404.1575(a)(2) & 416.975(a)(2). The Social Security Regulations provide three tests for determining whether self-employment qualifies as SGA:

Test one: You have engaged in substantial gainful activity if you render services that are significant to the operation of the business and receive a substantial income from the business....

Test Two: You have engaged in substantial gainful activity if your work activity, in terms of factors such as hours, skills, energy output, efficiency, duties, and responsibilities, is comparable to that of unimpaired individuals in your community who are in the same or similar businesses as their means of livelihood.

Test Three: You have engaged in substantial gainful activity if your work activity, although not comparable to that of unimpaired individuals, is clearly worth the amount shown in [the Commissioner's Earnings Guidelines] when considered in terms of its value to the business, or when compared to the salary that an owner would pay to an employee to do the work you are doing.

Id. at §§ 404.1575(a)(2)(i)-(iii) & 416.975(a)(2)(i)-(iii) (italics omitted). If the individual's work is SGA under test one, the ALJ need not apply tests two and three. See Camper v. Sullivan, 1991 WL 352422, at *2 (N.D.Cal.1991). "If, on the other hand, it is clearly established that the self-employed person is not engaging in SGA on the basis of significant services and substantial income (i.e., the first test), both the second and third tests concerning comparability and worth of work must be considered." Id. (italics in original).

Here, plaintiff described her past job as work in the fields growing rice and other produce, for which she was not paid a wage. Her work consisted of farming with hand tools and lifting bundles of food onto a cart to be carried home. It appears that plaintiff grew only enough food for personal consumption and to exchange for necessities. Finally, plaintiff indicated that she did not lead or supervise any other farm laborers.

The extent of the ALJ's analysis of whether plaintiff's past work constituted SGA was his conclusory statement that plaintiff has "past relevant work as a rice farmer." In making this determination, the ALJ relied upon plaintiff's own description of her duties as a rice farmer. (See [AR at 20].) ("Based on the [plaintiff]'s own description of her past relevant work as a rice farmer, this job did not require the performance of the work-related activities precluded by her residual functional capacity.") In his decision, the ALJ did not specify whether plaintiff's past work on the family farm was done as an employee or a self-employed individual.

Irrespective of whether plaintiff was an employee or self-employed, however, the court is persuaded that her past work as a rice farmer does not constitute SGA. If plaintiff was an employee, because she earned no wages, a presumption arose that she was not engaged in SGA. The burden then shifted to the Commissioner to point to other evidence in the record to establish that plaintiff was engaged in SGA. See Lewis, 236 F.3d at 515 ("With the presumption, the claimant has carried his or her burden [at step four] unless the ALJ points to substantial evidence, aside from earnings, that the claimant has engaged in substantial gainful activity.") (italics in original). Other than his assertion that plaintiffs work as a rice farmer constituted past relevant work, the ALJ made no effort to rebut the presumption that plaintiff was not engaged in SGA. Finally, even if the earnings presumption did not apply, plaintiff's prior work would still not be considered SGA because there is no evidence of the prevailing pay scales for rice farmers in plaintiff's community or any evidence that unimpaired people in plaintiff's community performed comparable work as rice farmers for profit.

Although defendant concedes that plaintiff was not self-employed, it is worth noting that, even assuming plaintiff was self-employed as a rice farmer, her work nevertheless did not constitute SGA. Under test one, even if plaintiff provided significant services to the rice farm, she did not receive a substantial income and thus her work cannot be considered to be SGA. Nor is there any evidence in the record that the rice and produce plaintiff grew would amount to a substantial income. Under test two, there is no evidence that plaintiff's work was comparable (considering factors such as hours, skills, energy output, efficiency, duties and responsibilities) to that of unimpaired persons in her community who earned wages or other substantial income as rice farmers or from other similar occupations. Under test three, the record contains no evidence to support a finding that plaintiff's work was clearly worth wages amounting to SGA under the Commissioner's Earning Guidelines, in terms of its value to the farm or based upon what an employer would ordinarily pay a rice farmer. See "The lack of conclusive evidence as to the comparability of the required factors" results in a finding that the work plaintiff performed was not SGA. Social Security Ruling ("SSR") 83–34. Further, "any doubt as to the comparability of the factors should be resolved in favor of" plaintiff. Id.

In sum, whether plaintiff was an employee or self-employed, the subsistence farm work she performed in Vietnam did not constitute SGA as defined by the Social Security regulations. Thus, the ALJ's determination, at step four, that plaintiff could perform her past relevant work as a rice farmer, is not supported by substantial evidence.

[The court then found that the claimant was unable to perform any other substantial gainful activity at Step 5 of the sequential evaluation process, and ordered the payment of benefits.]

NOTE ON ILLEGAL ACTIVITY

Both the Social Security Act and applicable federal regulations state directly that illegal activity can also constitute substantial gainful activity. See 42 U.S.C. §§ 423(d)(4)(B), 1382c(a)(3)(E); 20 C.F.R. §§ 404.1571, 416.971. Thus, substantial gainful activity is measured without regard to whether the activity is legal; any work activity, legal or illegal, may be evidence that an individual can work. Congress codified this policy in 1994 following a series of unsuccessful challenges to SSA's practice of considering illegal activity on a par with other work activity for these purposes. See Social Security Independence and Program Improvements Act of 1994, Pub. L. No. 103–296 § 201(a), 108 Stat. 1464 (1994). SSA considered not just the income earned in such activities, but also the claimant's ability to run an illicit operation and avoid apprehension by the authorities. See, e.g., Dotson v. Shalala, 1 F.3d 571, 575–77, 42 Soc. Sec. Rep. Serv. 17 (7th Cir. 1993); Hart v. Sullivan, 824 F. Supp. 903, 905–07, 41 Soc. Sec. Rep. Serv. 451 (N.D. Cal. 1992).

This does not mean, however, that all profitable illegal activity will count as substantial gainful activity. Corrao v. Shalala, 20 F.3d 943, 44 Soc.Sec.Rep.Ser. 150 (9th Cir. 1994) is a pre-codification case that was decided also before the Social Security Act was amended to exclude alcohol and drug addiction as a basis for disability. Corrao applied for SSI alleging disability due to mental illness, drug dependency, and lack of energy. At the administrative hearing he admitted to using heroin (1½ grams) and drinking alcohol on a daily basis (several packs of beer and a half pint of whiskey). He also testified that he had lost consciousness due to his drug and alcohol abuse, and had also lost jobs as a result. Most importantly,

> Corrao testified that he obtains the heroin he uses by purchasing heroin for others and receiving some of the purchased drugs in return. He purchases up to $600 worth of heroin daily for up to three people per day. In return, he receives approximately 1½ grams of heroin in total, worth about $150 per day. This heroin is consumed by Corrao. To obtain the heroin, Corrao has his clients pick him up and he directs them to a given location. The clients wait for him to complete his purchase and then return him home. The entire transaction takes approximately thirty to forty-five minutes.

20 F.3d at 945. Agreeing with the Seventh Circuit's decision in Dotson, supra, the court found that there is nothing to suggest that illegal activity cannot be substantial gainful activity.

> To the contrary, there clearly exist illegal activities that are both 'substantial' and 'gainful.' Tax fraud, for example, involves significant mental activity, and the completion of tax forms is an activity that normally results in a benefit to the individual completing the forms. As a matter of policy, we see no reason to prefer claimants who earn a living by illegal

means over those who survive without violating the law by suggesting that the illegal activity is neither substantial nor gainful.

Id. at 947. Corrao's "income" was above the earnings guidelines applicable to the time period in question and therefore established a presumption that he had engaged in substantial gainful activity. The court went on, however, to consider a number of additional factors, noting that "[f]or activity to constitute SGA, it still must involve 'significant physical or mental activities' and must be the type of work usually done for pay or profit." *Id.* at 948 (quoting 20 C.F.R. §§ 416.972(a), (b)).

> While the regulations clearly provide that part-time work may be considered "substantial," 20 C.F.R. § 416.972(a), substantial work must involve more time than Corrao invested. Rather than working several hours a day, Corrao's activities consumed less than an hour a day, the vast majority of which was spent riding as a passenger in a car. Such slight work performed for minimal periods of time is not substantial gainful activity.

> Even more significant to our holding is our conclusion that Corrao's activities did not require any significant mental or physical exertion. Corrao did no planning prior to these purchases, but instead was contacted by purchasers when they desired some drugs. Corrao did not organize drug dealers, nor did he have an organized or extensive clientele. Instead, the record reflects that two or three people asked him to purchase drugs for them. Corrao did not use his own money for the transactions but was provided with funds by the ultimate purchaser. Finally, although the Secretary found that Corrao received uncut heroin and used his physical and mental capacities to "cut" it (i.e., to add other substances to it), the record does not support such a finding. Corrao in fact testified that he purchased uncut heroin and gave it directly to the ultimate purchasers. There is no indication that he ever sold his portion of the drugs for cash or other items. In sum, there is no indication of initiative, organization, responsibility, or physical or mental exertion by Corrao as is required for SGA.

20 F. 3d at 948–49. *Compare* Jones v. Shalala, 21 F. 3d 191, 44 Soc. Sec. Rep. Serv. 291 (7th Cir, 1994) (petty theft earnings of $60 per day was substantial gainful activity). *See also* Speaks v. Secretary of Health and Human Services, 855 F. Supp. 1108, 1112, 45 Soc. Sec. Rep. Serv. 52 (C.D. Cal. 1994) (prostitution constitutes substantial gainful activity).

NOTE ON NON–WORK ACTIVITY

As we have seen, the ability to do a limited amount of work does not by itself establish the ability to engage in substantial gainful activity. That applies also to some, but not all, non-work activity. As one court has stated, the "[a]bility to drive an automobile, participate in some community affairs, attend school, or do some work on an intermittent basis does not necessarily establish that a person is able to engage in 'substantial gainful activity,' but such activity may be considered by SSA, along with medical testimony, in determining the right of a claimant to disability payments under the Act." Markham v. Califano, 601 F.2d 533, 534 (10th Cir. 1979).

The claimant in Cohen v. Secretary, 964 F.2d 524, 37 Soc.Sec.Rep.Ser. 341 (6th Cir. 1992) was a 50–plus year old woman with a doctorate in educational sociology who had worked as Assistant to the Dean at Wayne State School of Medicine at a salary of $45,000 per year. She applied for disability benefits because she had to stop working due to symptoms associated with Chronic Epstein–Barr virus, including chronic fatigue syndrome, memory impairment, swollen glands, and balance disorders. Her claim was denied, primarily beause of the level of activities the claimant was involved in after she stopped working. The Sixth Circuit reversed:

> The ALJ considered the fact that Cohen, a professional ballroom dancer, continued dancing over much of the period for which she now claims disability benefits. Although there is some dispute as to the frequency and duration of Cohen's ballroom dancing, Cohen's own testimony provides substantial basis for a finding that Cohen danced twice a week for three to four hours at a time from 1984 to 1987, and that she continued at a reduced schedule of approximately twice a month for an hour at a time from 1987 to March 1989, when she stopped dancing altogether. Cohen also testified, however, that she had to rest all day in order to prepare for her dancing activities, and that she was "wiped out" for a couple of days after she danced.

> In the fall of 1986, Cohen enrolled part-time at the University of Detroit Law School. Thereafter she attended that school for approximately six credit hours per semester. Cohen testified that she attended classes between the hours of 12:30 p.m. and 4:00 p.m. three days a week, and that she did homework for approximately two hours a day. Although Cohen continued dancing, on a limited basis, after she enrolled at the law school, Cohen's dancing was confined to an occasional Saturday evening, which allowed her to rest beforehand and recover afterwards.

> The ALJ also considered the fact that Cohen, in 1986, founded a national support group for persons suffering from the Epstein–Barr virus. Cohen's participation in the support group consisted primarily of talking over the telephone for approximately two to three hours per week with others suffering from the disease. Cohen withdrew from the support group in the summer of 1988.

> We believe that the level of activity maintained by Cohen since she began suffering from the Chronic Epstein–Bar virus and the associated chronic fatigue syndrome is a tribute to her courage and determination in refusing to surrender to the debilitating effects of her illness. Her activities do not, however, warrant a finding that Cohen maintained the

residual functional capacity to perform her previous work at Wayne State University or to maintain substantial gainful employment in the national economy. Cf. Wilcox v. Sullivan, 917 F.2d 272, 277 (6th Cir.1990) ("[C]laimant should not be penalized because he had the courage and determination to continue working despite his disabling condition."). The issue here is whether, despite her illness, Cohen had the residual functional capacity to maintain substantial gainful employment during the period for which she now seeks disability benefits. Residual functional capacity is defined as the "maximum degree to which the individual retains the capacity for *sustained* performance of the physical-mental requirements of jobs." 20 C.F.R. Pt. 404, Subpt. P, App. 2 § 200.00(c) (1989) (emphasis added). In determining a claimant's physical abilities, we must "assess the severity of [claimant's] impairment(s) and determine [claimant's] residual functional capacity for work activity on a *regular and continuing basis*." 20 C.F.R. § 404.1545(b) (1989) (emphasis added).

In Parish v. Califano, 642 F.2d 188 (6th Cir.1981), we recognized that "[a]ttending college on a part-time basis is not the equivalent of being able to engage in substantial gainful activity. Seven or eight classroom hours are a lot less demanding than full-time remunerative work." Id. at 191. This is so, in part, because "one may miss occasional classes without penalty, and homework may be scheduled for those times when the student feels his or her best." Id. at 192.

The logic of *Parish* is particularly apposite here, in view of the nature of Cohen's illness. Chronic fatigue syndrome is characterized by periods of exacerbation and remission. During periods of exacerbation, Cohen is confined to her bed for sixteen to eighteen hours a day, and even simple tasks such as grocery shopping can bring her near the point of collapse. Clearly, the fact that Cohen—still an intelligent woman despite the degree of cognitive dysfunction caused by her illness—has had the capacity to pass one to two law school classes per semester since the fall of 1986 does not indicate that she was capable of sustaining substantial gainful employment in the national economy. Similarly, the fact that she, a professional ballroom dancer prior to the onset of her illness, was able to continue dancing to a limited extent during the period for which she now claims disability does not warrant the conclusion that she could have engaged in substantial gainful employment. Cohen required significant rest both before and after her dance activities, and, despite her resting, over the course of the period for which she now claims disability Cohen's dance schedule was significantly decreased and ultimately terminated altogether. Cohen's efforts to continue dancing merely suggest that she was struggling to maintain some semblance of normalcy in a life otherwise turned on end by the onset of chronic fatigue syndrome.

Her activity with respect to the support group for herself and others suffering from the Chronic Epstein–Barr virus/chronic fatigue syndrome, which consisted primarily of talking on the telephone for two to three hours per week, likewise hardly suggests that she was capable of engaging in substantial gainful employment. Rather, Cohen's founding of the support group underscores the genuineness of her testimony regarding her illness.

964 F.2d at 529–31.

The court then turned to the ALJ's findings relative to the claimant's credibility based on her testimony about a recent law school exam that she had passed. When asked how she had been able to pass the exam given the cognitive dysfunction she allegedly was experiencing, she responded that she had passed by picking key words and repeating phrases that had been emphasized during class. The ALJ found that Cohen's answer undermined her credibility as a witness:

> While we recognize that the ALJ's credibility determinations are entitled to deference, we are convinced that the ALJ's emphasis on Cohen's ability to pass her law school examination was misplaced. The medical evidence, as well as her own testimony, show that Cohen maintained an above average level of intelligence despite the cognitive dysfunction that she had been experiencing. The issue, however, is not whether Cohen maintained the intelligence to continue substantial gainful employment; rather, the issue is whether Cohen has been rendered disabled by the chronic fatigue syndrome and other symptoms associated with her illness. Her ability successfully to attend law school on a part-time basis (Cohen completed one year of law school over the course of three calendar years), while probative of whether she was capable of engaging in substantial gainful activity, in view of the nature of Cohen's illness, does not provide substantial basis for the ALJ's conclusion that Cohen had the residual capacity to engage in substantial gainful employment.

Id. at 531.

NOTE ON CALCULATING EARNINGS THAT AMOUNT TO SGA

The threshold amount set out in the regulations as presumptively demonstrating the ability to engage in SGA is subject to certain deductions. In Allen v. Astrue, 2009 WL 2253815, 143 Soc. Sec. Rep. Serv. 873, (D.S.D. 2009), the issue was whether the claimant had engaged in substantial gainful activity during the period in question and thereafter was properly denied benefits at Step 1 of the sequential evaluation process. When calculating the amount earned in determining whether a claimant is engaged in SGA, SSA must deduct impairment-related work expenses (IRWE), including payments for drugs and medical services used to control the effects of a claimant's impairments. See 42 U.S.C. § 423(d)(4)(A); 20 C.F.R. § 404.1576(c)(5). The ALJ found that there was "no evidence" of IRWE to reduce the claimant's earnings and therefore denied the claim at Step 1. The court disagreed, and remanded the claim for a new hearing:

[P]laintiff submitted detailed pharmacy records showing prescriptions filled from January 5, 2006, through February 8, 2008. * * * The record also contains ample evidence connecting particular prescriptions with plaintiff's alleged impairments. For instance, plaintiff was treated on a regular basis for depression by Kay Foland, Ph.D., a certified nurse practitioner at the Manlove Psychiatric Group, beginning on December 9, 2005. Plaintiff alleged depression as a basis for disability. Plaintiff was prescribed a number of medications for her depression, including Lamictal, Remeron, Prozac, Zoloft, and Trazadone. Plaintiff's pharmacy records reflect prescriptions filled for all of these medications.

Instructive on this point is 20 C.F.R. § 404.1576(c)(5)(i), which provides that if "you must use drugs ... to control your impairment(s) the payments you make for them may be deducted [from your earnings when evaluating SGA]." 20 C.F.R. § 404.1576(c)(5)(ii) expressly notes "antidepressant medication for mental disorders" as an "example" of a drug that qualifies as an IRWE.

* * *

Based on this record, the ALJ's assertion that there was "no evidence ... that [plaintiff] had any [IRWE]" is completely inexplicable and is not supported by substantial evidence. It may be true, as defendant suggests, that some of plaintiff's prescription drugs were for ailments not asserted as a basis for disability, in which case they would not qualify as IRWE. However, what is *demonstrably* true is that many of plaintiff's drugs were prescribed for ailments asserted as a basis for disability. * * *

Defendant argues that a finding of disability is a "prerequisite" for deducting IRWE from earnings. The Court does not agree. Steps two through five of the sequential evaluation process are concerned with the substantive issue of whether or not plaintiff is actually disabled under Social Security regulations. IRWE, however, are relevant at step one, when determining SGA. To require plaintiff to prove that she is disabled prior to proving that she has not engaged in SGA would run contrary to the five-step sequential evaluation process. In effect, this would result in IRWE never being considered except in those cases where the agency has previously found an individual disabled and the claimant returns to work activity while still receiving benefits, and then benefits are ceased and administrative proceedings result.

Social Security Ruling 84–26 makes it clear that defendant's argument is without merit. This ruling provides that IRWE are to be developed and verified on both "initial claims" and in "continuing disability cases." With respect to initial claims, SSR 84–26 provides that a claimant "who is working and alleges IRWE may benefit from a deduction of IRWE from earnings in a determination as to SGA." As previously stated, SGA is determined at step one of the sequential evaluation process.

Clearly, a finding of disability is not a prerequisite for considering IRWE when computing SGA.

2009 WL 2253815 at *2–*4.

NOTE ON PART-TIME WORK

There is no doubt that part-time work can amount to substantial gainful activity at Step 1. The language at 20 C.F.R. §§ 404.1572(a), 416.972(a) applies directly to Step 1 evaluations: "Your work may be substantial even if it is done on a part-time basis." *See also* Kelley v. Apfel, 185 F.3d 1211, 1214 (11th Cir.1999) ("At Step One, there is no per se rule that part-time work cannot constitute substantial gainful activity") (citing 20 C.F.R. §§ 404.1572(a)). But part-time work may not be substantial gainful at other steps of the sequential evaluation process. As mentioned earlier, in addition to being at the heart of any Step 1 analysis—where the focus is on whether any current work, or work-like, activity amounts to substantial gainful activity—substantial gainful activity is also a key factor at the end of the sequential evaluation process. At Step 5, the question is whether the claimant can perform other work that exists in the national economy, given his or her age, education, and prior work experience. Not only must there be other jobs in the economy that the claimant can perform, but those jobs must amount to substantial gainful activity. As we will see later in this chapter when we look more closely at Step 5, part-time work is not considered to be substantial gainful activity at that point in the sequential evaluation process—and proof that a claimant whose claim reaches Step 5 could do part-time work is not sufficient to support a finding of non-disability.

2. STEP 2: MINIMUM DURATION AND SEVERITY

The Social Security Act requires not only that a claimant be unable to engage in any "substantial gainful activity," but also that this inability to work result from a "medically determinable physical or mental impairment which can be expected to result in death or which has lasted or can be expected to last for a continuous period of not less than 12 months." *See* 42 U.S.C. § 423(d)(1)(A); 20 C.F.R. §§ 404.1509, 416.909. Both components of this requirement—that the impairment be medically determinable and that it has lasted for a continuous period of 12 months (or is expected to last at least 12 months or to result in death)—have been incorporated, along with a minimum severity requirement, into Step 2 of the sequential evaluation process. Thus, in order to proceed past the second step a claimant must show that he or she has a medically determinable "severe" impairment that has lasted 12 months or can be expected to last at least 12 months or to result in death. Claimants whose impairments lack clinical evidence, are of short duration, or are "non-severe" will be denied. 20 C.F.R. §§ 404.1520(a)(4)(ii), 416.920(a)(4)(ii). The type of proof required to show that an impairment is medically determinable is discussed later in Chapter 8 on Social Security practice.

A) 12-MONTH DURATION REQUIREMENT

The duration requirement is usually not much of an issue since in many cases the impairments in question will have already lasted at least 12 months by the time the disability is evaluated. And recall that the requirement can also be met if the impairment is expected to last for at least 12 months or result in death. *See* McDonald v. Bowen, 818 F.2d 559, 562, 17 Soc. Sec. Rep. Serv. 758 (7th Cir. 1986) ("an individual may be declared disabled on the basis of an expectation of a twelve month impairment"). Although relatively rare, there are circumstances where proof that a claimant meets this threshold requirement can be critical. *See, e.g.,* Karlix v. Barnhart, 457 F.3d 742, 748, 113 Soc. Sec. Rep. Serv. 28 (8th Cir. 2006) (issue was whether an impairment met the requirement of the Listing of Impairments; impairment failed to meet the duration requirement); Hoadley v. Astrue, 503 F.Supp.2d 466, 489 123 Soc. Sec. Rep. Serv. 85 (D.Conn., 2007) (ALJ did not have to consider a mental impairment that was raised at the hearing because it failed to meet the duration requirement).

Although there is some ambiguity in the terms of the statute as to whether the duration requirement applies to both the existence of the impairment and the inability to engage in substantial gainful activity, SSA takes the position that it applies to both. *See* SSR 82–52 (1982). Some courts had ruled otherwise, finding that the duration requirement applies only to the impairment. See, e.g., Jenkins v. Heckler, 783 F. Supp. 998, 1000–02, 36 Soc. Sec. Rep. Serv. 494 (D.S.C. 1992); Goldstein v. Harris, 517 F. Supp. 1314, 1316–17 (S.D.N.Y. 1981). However, the Supreme Court approved SSA's reading in the following case.

BARNHART V. WALTON
535 U.S. 212, 79 Soc. Sec. Rep. Serv. 1 (2002)

BREYER, J., delivered the opinion of the Court, Parts I and III of which were unanimous, and Part II of which was joined by Rehnquist, C.J., and Stevens, O'Connor, Kennedy, Souter, Thomas, and Ginsburg, JJ. Scalia, J., filed an opinion concurring in part and concurring in the judgment.

Justice BREYER delivered the opinion of the Court.

The Social Security Act authorizes payment of disability insurance benefits and Supplemental Security Income to individuals with disabilities. See 42 U.S.C. § 401 et seq. (Title II disability insurance benefits); § 1381 et seq. (Title XVI supplemental security income). For both types of benefits the Act defines the key term disability as an *"inability* to engage in any substantial gainful activity by reason of any medically determinable physical or mental impairment which can be expected to result in death or *which has lasted or can be expected to last for a continuous period of not less than 12 months."* § 423(d)(1)(A) (1994 ed.) (Title II) (emphasis added); accord, § 1382c(a)(3)(A) (1994 ed., Supp. V) (Title XVI).

This case presents two questions about the Social Security Administration's interpretation of this definition.

First, the Social Security Administration (which we shall call the Agency) reads the term "inability" as including a "12 month" requirement. In its view, the "inability" (to engage in any substantial gainful activity) must last, or must be expected to last, for *at least 12 months.* Second, the Agency reads the term "expected to last" as applicable only when the "inability" has *not yet* lasted 12 months. In the case of a later Agency determination-where the "inability" *did not* last 12 months-the Agency will automatically assume that the claimant failed to meet the duration requirement. It will not look back to decide hypothetically whether, despite the claimant's actual return to work before 12 months expired, the "inability" nonetheless *might have been* expected to last that long.

The Court of Appeals for the Fourth Circuit held both these interpretations of the statute unlawful. We hold, to the contrary, that both fall within the Agency's lawful interpretive authority. See Chevron U.S.A. Inc. v. Natural Resources Defense Council, Inc., 467 U.S. 837, 104 S.Ct. 2778, 81 L.Ed.2d 694 (1984). Consequently, we reverse.

I

In 1996 Cleveland Walton, the respondent, applied for both Title II disability insurance benefits and Title XVI Supplemental Security Income. The Agency found that (1) by October 31, 1994, Walton had developed a serious mental illness involving both schizophrenia and associated depression; (2) the illness caused him then to lose his job as a full-time teacher; (3) by mid–1995 he began to work again part time as a cashier; and (4) by December 1995 he was working as a cashier full time.

The Agency concluded that Walton's mental illness had prevented him from engaging in any significant work, *i.e.,* from "engag[ing]" in any substantial gainful activity, for 11 months-from October 31, 1994 (when he lost his teaching job) until the end of September 1995 (when he earned income sufficient to rise to the level of "substantial gainful activity"). And because the statute demanded an "inability to engage in any substantial gainful activity" lasting 12, not 11, months, Walton was not entitled to benefits.

Walton sought court review. The District Court affirmed the Agency's decision, but the Court of Appeals for the Fourth Circuit reversed. The court said that the statute's 12–month duration requirement modifies the word "impairment," not the word "inability." It added that the statute's "language ... leaves no doubt" that there is no similar "duration requirement" related to an "inability" (to engage in substantial gainful activity). It concluded that, because the statute's language "speaks clearly" and is "unambiguous," Walton was entitled to receive benefits despite agency regulations restricting benefits to those unable to work for a 12–month period.

The court went on to decide that, in any event, Walton qualified because, prior to Walton's return to work, one would have "expected" his "inability" to last 12 months. It conceded that the Agency had made Walton's actual return to work determinative on this point. But it found unlawful the Agency regulations that gave the Agency the benefit of hindsight-on the ground that they conflicted with the statute's clear command.

For either reason, the Fourth Circuit concluded, Walton became "entitled" to Title II benefits no later than April 1995, five months after the onset of his illness. See 42 U.S.C. §§ 423(a)(1)(D)(i), 423(a)(1)(D)(ii) (providing for a 5–month "waiting period" before a claimant is "entitled" to benefits).

　　　* * *

II

The statutory definition of "disability" has two parts. First, it requires a certain kind of "inability," namely, an "inability to engage in any substantial gainful activity." Second it requires an "impairment", namely, a "physical or mental impairment," which provides "reason" for the "inability." The statute adds that the "impairment" must be one that "has lasted or can be expected to last ... not less than 12 months." But what about the "inability"? Must it also last (or be expected to last) for the same amount of time?

The Agency has answered this question in the affirmative. Acting pursuant to statutory rulemaking authority, it has promulgated formal regulations that state that a claimant is not disabled "regardless of [his] medical condition," if he is doing "substantial gainful activity." And the Agency has interpreted this regulation to mean that the claimant is not disabled if "within 12 months after the onset of an impairment ... the impairment no longer prevents substantial gainful activity." 65 Fed.Reg. 42774 (2000). Courts grant an agency's interpretation of its own regulations considerable legal leeway. And no one here denies that the Agency has properly interpreted its own regulation.

Consequently, the legal question before us is whether the Agency's interpretation of the statute is lawful. This Court has previously said that, if the statute speaks clearly "to the precise question at issue," we "must give effect to the unambiguously expressed intent of Congress." Chevron, 467 U.S., at 842–843, 104 S.Ct. 2778. If, however, the statute "is silent or ambiguous with respect to the specific issue," we must sustain the Agency's interpretation if it is "based on a permissible construction" of the Act. Id., at 843, 104 S.Ct. 2778. Hence we must decide (1) whether the statute unambiguously forbids the Agency's interpretation, and, if not, (2) whether the interpretation, for other reasons, exceeds the bounds of the permissible. *Ibid.*

First, the statute does not unambiguously forbid the regulation. The Fourth Circuit believed the contrary primarily for a linguistic reason. It pointed out that, linguistically speaking, the statute's "12–month" phrase modifies only the word "impairment," not the word "inability." And to that extent we agree. After all, the statute, in parallel phrasing, uses the words "which can be expected to result in death." And that structurally parallel phrase makes sense in reference to an "impairment," but makes no sense in reference to the "inability."

Nonetheless, this linguistic point is insufficient. It shows that the particular statutory provision says nothing explicitly about the "inability's" duration. But such silence, after all, normally creates ambiguity. It does not resolve it.

Moreover, a nearby provision of the statute says that an

"individual shall be determined to be under a disability only if his ... impairment ... [is] of such severity that he is not only unable to do his previous work but cannot ... engage in any other kind of substantial gainful work which exists in the national economy." 42 U.S.C. § 423(d)(2)(A) (Title II); accord § 1382c(a)(3)(B) (Title XVI).

In other words, the statute, in the two provisions, specifies that the "impairment" must last 12 months and also be severe enough to prevent the claimant from engaging in virtually any "substantial gainful work." The statute, we concede, nowhere explicitly says that the "impairment" must be *that severe* (i.e., severe enough to prevent "substantial gainful work") for 12 months. But that is a fair inference from the language. At the very least the statute is ambiguous in that respect. And, if so, then it is an equally fair inference that the "inability" must last 12 months. That is because the latter statement (i.e., that the claimant must be unable to "engage in any substantial gainful activity" for a year) is the virtual equivalent of the former statement (i.e., that the "impairment" must remain severe enough to prevent the claimant from engaging in "substantial gainful work" for a year). It simply rephrases the same point in a slightly different way.

Second, the Agency's construction is "permissible." The interpretation makes considerable sense in terms of the statute's basic objectives. The statute demands some duration requirement. No one claims that the statute would permit an individual with a chronic illness-say, high blood pressure-to qualify for benefits if that illness, while itself lasting for a year, were to permit a claimant to return to work after only a week, or perhaps even a day, away from the job. The Agency's interpretation supplies a duration requirement, which the statute demands, while doing so in a way that consistently reconciles the statutory "impairment" and "inability" language.

In addition, the Agency's regulations reflect the Agency's own longstanding interpretation. See Social Security Ruling 82–52, p. 106 (cum. ed. 1982) ("In considering 'duration,' it is the inability to engage in [substantial gainful activity] that must last the required 12–month period"); Disability Insurance State Manual § 316 (Sept. 9, 1965), Government Lodging, Tab C, § 316 ("Duration of impairment refers to that period of time during which an individual is continuously unable to engage in substantial gainful activity because of" an impairment); OASI Disability Insurance Letter No. 39 (Jan. 22, 1957), id., Tab A, p. 1 (duration requirement refers to the "expected duration of the *medical impairment*" at a level of severity sufficient to preclude substantial gainful activity). And this Court will normally accord particular deference to an agency interpretation of "longstanding" duration.

Finally, Congress has frequently amended or reenacted the relevant provisions without change. These circumstances provide further evidence-if more is needed-that Congress intended the Agency's interpretation, or at least understood the interpretation as statutorily permissible.

* * *

In this case, the interstitial nature of the legal question, the related expertise of the Agency, the importance of the question to administration of the statute, the complexity of that administration, and the careful consideration the Agency has given the question over a long period of time all indicate that Chevron provides the appropriate legal lens through which to view the legality of the Agency interpretation here at issue.

For these reasons, we find the Agency's interpretation lawful.

III

Walton's second claim is more complex. For purposes of making that claim, Walton assumes what we have just decided, namely, that the statute's "12 month" duration requirements apply to both the "impairment" and the "inability" to work requirements. Walton also concedes that he returned to work after 11 months. But Walton claims that his work from month 11 to month 12 does not count against him because it is part of a "trial work" period that the statute grants to those "entitled" to Title II benefits. See 42 U.S.C. § 422(c). And Walton adds, he was "entitle[d]" to benefits because—even though he returned to work after 11 months—his "impairment" and his "inability" to work were nonetheless *expected* to last" for at least "12 months" *before* he returned to work.

To illustrate Walton's argument, we simplify the actual circumstances. We imagine: (1) On January 1, Year One, Walton developed (a) a severe impairment, which (b) made him unable to work; (2) Eleven (not twelve) months later, on December 1, Year One, Walton returned to work; (3) On July 1, Year Two, the Agency adjudicated, and denied, Walton's claim for benefits. Walton argues that, even though he returned to work after 11 months, had the Agency looked at the matter, not ex post, but as if it were looking *prior* to his return to work, the Agency would have had to conclude that both his "impairment" and his "inability" to work "*can be expected* to last for a continuous period of not less than 12 months." § 423(d)(1)(A). He consequently satisfied the 12–month duration requirement and became "entitled" to benefits before he returned to work; he was in turn entitled to a "trial work" period; and his subsequent work as a cashier, being "trial work," should not count against him.

The Agency's regulations plainly reject this view of the statute. They say, "You are *not entitled* to a trial work period" if "you perform work ... within 12 months of the onset of the impairment(s) ... and *before* the date of *any* notice of determination or *decision finding* ... you ... *disabled*." 20 CFR § 404.1592(d)(2) (2001). This regulation means that the Agency, deciding before the end of Year One, might have found that Walton's impairment (or inability to work) "*can* be expected to last" for 12 months. But the Agency, deciding after Year One in which Walton in fact returned to work, would not ask whether his impairment (or inability to work) *could have been* expected to last 12 months.

The legal question is whether this Agency regulation is consistent with the statute. The Court of Appeals, accepting Walton's view, concluded that it is not. It said that the Agency's rules—permitting the use of hindsight when reviewing claims—are inconsistent with the statute's plain language. And, here, other courts have agreed. See Salamalekis v. Commissioner of Soc. Sec., 221 F.3d 828 (C.A.6 2000); Newton v. Chater,

92 F.3d 688 (C.A.8 1996); Walker v. Secretary of Health and Human Servs., 943 F.2d 1257 (C.A.10 1991); McDonald v. Bowen, 818 F.2d 559 (C.A.7 1986).

Nonetheless, we believe that Agency regulation is lawful. The statute is ambiguous. It says nothing about how the Agency, when it adjudicates a matter after Year One, is to treat an earlier return to work. Its language "can be expected to last" 12 months, 42 U.S.C. § 423(d)(1)(A), simply does not say as of what time the law measures the "expectation." Indeed, from a linguistic perspective, the phrase "can be expected," foresees a decisionmaker who is looking into the future, not a decisionmaker who is in the future, looking back into the past in order to see what then "was," "could be," or "could have been" expected. And read in context, the purpose of the phrase "can be expected to last" might be one of permitting the Agency to award benefits before 12 months have expired, not one of denying the Agency the benefit of hindsight.

At the same time, the Agency's regulation seems a reasonable, hence permissible, interpretation of the statute. In effect it treats a pre-Agency-decision actual return to work, e.g., Walton's return in December Year One, as if it were determinative of the expectation question. With Year Two's hindsight, Walton's "inability" to work "can" not "be expected to last 12 months." And use of that hindsight avoids the need for the Year Two decisionmaker in effect to answer a highly unwieldy question in what grammarians might call the pluperfect future tense.

Of course, administrators and judges are capable of answering hypothetical questions of this kind. But here the question concerns what must be a contrary-to-fact speculation about the future. It is a speculation that, however often raised, would rarely prove easy to resolve. And the statute's purpose does not demand its resolution. Indeed, one might ask why, other things being equal, a claimant who returns to work too early ordinarily to qualify for benefits nonetheless should qualify *if, but only if, that return was a kind of medical surprise.* Of course, as Walton says, such a rule would help encourage (or at least not discourage) a claimant's early return to work. But the statute does not demand that the Agency make of this desirable end an overriding interpretive principle. And the Agency has recognized and addressed the problem of work disincentives in other ways.

The statute's complexity, the vast number of claims that it engenders, and the consequent need for agency expertise and administrative experience lead us to read the statute as delegating to the Agency considerable authority to fill in, through interpretation, matters of detail related to its administration. The interpretation at issue here is such a matter.

The statute's language is ambiguous. And the Agency's interpretation is reasonable.

We conclude that the Agency's regulation is lawful.

* * *

[Opinion of Justice Scalia, concurring in part and concurring in the judgment, omitted.]

NOTES

1. As noted earlier, the duration requirement is met most clearly when the claimant has already been disabled for at least 12 months at the time of adjudication. A "symptom-free" period during the time preceding the adjudication does not necessarily preclude a finding that the requirement has been met. As the court said in Lebus v. Harris, 526 F.Supp. 56, 61–62 (N.D. Cal. 1981):

> While the mere existence of symptom-free periods may negate a finding of disability when a physical impairment is alleged, symptom-free intervals do not necessarily compel such a finding when a mental disorder is the basis of the claim. Unlike a physical impairment, it is extremely difficult to predict the course of mental illness. Symptom-free intervals, though sometimes indicative of a remission in the mental disorder, are generally of uncertain duration and marked by an impending possibility of relapse. Realistically, a person with a mental impairment may be unable to engage in competitive employment, as his ability to work may be sporadically interrupted by unforeseeable mental setbacks.

> * * *

> Rather, the relevant inquiry is whether a claimant can engage in any substantial gainful activity during the symptom-free intervals, given the likelihood, frequency, and severity of relapses in his mental illness. This inquiry should be evaluated in light of similar symptom-free periods in claimant's past mental history. Among the factors which the ALJ should consider are: (1) whether the claimant is engaged in the type of employment which can be interrupted and resumed unexpectedly, and (2) whether claimant is participating in a treatment program which has demonstrated past success and potential for claimant's future recovery.

Thus, the 12–month requirement can be met notwithstanding brief periods of remission. See Lester v. Chater, 81 F.3d 821, 833, 50 Soc. Sec. Rep. Serv. 536 (9th Cir. 1995) ("Occasional symptom-free periods—and even sporadic ability to work—are not inconsistent with disability."); Pagan v. Bowen, 862 F.2d 340, 346, 24 Soc. Sec. Rep. Serv. 20 (D.C. Cir. 1988) (periodic psychotic episodes without single episode lasting 12 months); Dreste v. Heckler,

741 F.2d 224, 226, 6 Soc. Sec. Rep. Serv. 208 (8th Cir. 1984) ("It is inherent in psychotic illnesses that periods of remission will occur.").

2. An unusual application of this principle is seen in a case involving Child's SSI benefits where the question was when a two-year-old child's inability to walk unassisted began for purposes of measuring the 12–month duration requirement. Reasoning that the 12–month requirement is relevant in such cases only from the time when a typical, unimpaired child would be able to walk unassisted, the court held that "child applicants for SSI disability benefits based on inability to walk should not be able to accrue time towards the durational requirement until they have reached this starting age." *See* Merrill ex rel. Merrill v. Apfel, 224 F.3d 1083, 1086, 71 Soc. Sec. Rep. Serv. 351 (9th Cir. 2000).

3. A claimant cannot combine two or more unrelated medically determinable impairments to fulfill the 12–months duration requirement. If neither of two sequentially developed impairments is alone expected to last for 12 months, then the duration requirement is not met, even though the two, in combination, would last for the 12–month period. 20 C.F.R. §§ 404.1522(a), 416.922(a). The same is true for concurrent, combined impairments; each one of a set of impairments that are claimed together to establish disability must meet the duration requirement. In Rhodes v. Barnhart, 2004 WL 856467, 96 Soc. Sec. Rep. Serv. 177 (N.D.Ill. April 20, 2004), the claimant fractured her right knee and underwent surgery to repair the fracture on October 26, 1999. Approximately one to two months later, she began to have problems with her shoulders. She attempted to return to work part-time in June or July 2000, but her leg and shoulders still bothered her. On January 25, 2001, she had surgery on her left shoulder; on April 19, 2001, she had surgery on her right shoulder. On September 10, 2001, she had surgery to repair a hernia, after which she claimed that she was unable to return to work due to knee and shoulder pain. The hardware in her knee was removed on December 11, 2001. She did not return to work after this last knee surgery due to knee and shoulder pain, and to allow the knee to heal. In affirming the denial of her claim for benefits, the court reasoned as follows:

> The relevant Social Security regulation provides:
>
> We cannot combine two or more unrelated severe impairments to meet the 12–month duration test. If you have a severe impairment(s) and then develop another unrelated severe impairment(s) but neither one is expected to last for 12 months, we cannot find you disabled, even though the two impairments in combination last for 12 months.
>
> 20 C.F.R. § 404.1522(a). The ALJ found that only plaintiff's shoulder impairment lasted for twelve months, and that plaintiff was able to perform sedentary work within twelve months after the onset of the shoulder impairment. The ALJ found that plaintiff's knee injury and

hernia did not cause plaintiff to be disabled for twelve months, and credited the medical expert's testimony that the shoulder impairment could not have been caused by using crutches while recovering from the knee injury. The ALJ characterized plaintiff's various impairments as discrete problems, and declined to consider them in combination.

Plaintiff argues that the ALJ should have considered her impairments in combination, because the medical expert testified that they all may have stemmed from her October 1999 fall. At the hearing, the medical expert testified that plaintiff's impairments all may be related to falling down with the dog. I don't know, even the hernia. However, the medical expert then reexamined the medical records relating to plaintiff's treatment after her October 1999 fall to see if plaintiff had complained about her shoulders or hernia at that time. After reviewing the records, the medical expert noted that they did not indicate any such complaint. No other evidence that plaintiff's impairments were related was presented at the hearing. Given the lack of evidence in the record that plaintiff's impairments were related, it appears that the ALJ's finding that they were not related was reasonable.

2004 WL 856467 at *6.

B) SEVERITY REQUIREMENT

By far the most important Step 2 finding is whether the claimant's impairment, or combination of impairments, is "severe". The regulations use the confusing term "severe" to describe the required finding at this step; in fact, anyone with a minimally serious impairment (or combination of impairments) passes through step two relatively easily. Correctly administered, Step 2 denials are reserved for only those claimants with the most obviously non-severe impairments; that is, claims that are so obviously unwarranted that they can and should be denied quickly and easily. *See* **20 C.F.R. §§ 404.1521, 416.921**[APP–REGS] Essentially, the claimant must have an impairment that significantly limits his or her physical or mental ability to do basic work activities, without taking into consideration of the individual's age, education, and work experience. 20 C.F.R. §§ 404.1520(c), 416.920(c). Basic work activities constitutes "the ability and aptitudes necessary to do most jobs," including physical functions such as walking, standing, sitting, or handling; capacities for seeing, hearing, and speaking; and use of judgment. 20 C.F.R. §§ 404.1521(b), 416.921(b).

When SSA originally proposed establishing a severity requirement, it expressed its view that Congress intended that predominant importance be given to medical factors when making disability determinations. *See* 43 Fed. Reg. 55350 (1978). The problem with determining severity on medical evidence alone at Step 2, however, is its potential for abuse by precluding the implementation of the full sequential evaluation process in cases where the claimant might be found to be disabled later in the process on the basis of vocational factors in combination with medical evidence. A denial on the basis of non-severity can be particularly unfair when a claimant is relatively old and has a limited amount of education and work experience. In such cases, the severity requirement can block consideration of the impact of the claimant's age, education, and work experience on his or her ability to work at Steps 4 and 5. For these reasons, there was a great deal of controversy concerning the validity and interpretation of the new severity requirement in the mid–1980s—even though it replaced a regulation that already required claimants to demonstrate that their impairment was not slight. 20 C.F.R. § 404.1502(a) (1968); *see also* Michael Diehl, *Screening Out Worthy Social Security Disability Claimants and its Effect on Homelessness*, 45 U. Miami L. Rev. 617, 631–32 (1990).

As discussed previously in Chapter 2, the early 1980s saw the implementation of an aggressive Continuing Disability Review (CDR) program, and in conjunction with those reviews Step 2 of the sequential evaluation process began to be applied much more strictly to screen out an increasing number of claims. "In particular, SSA vastly expanded the number of impairments that were regarded as non-severe, disregarded the relationship between a particular impairment and a claimant's prior work, and refused to consider the combined effects of impairments that were regarded individually as non-severe." Richard E. Levy, *Social Security Disability Determinations: Recommendations for Reform*, 1990 BYU L. Rev. 461, 490, nn. 157–159 (1990) (citations omitted). Critics noted that "[t]he impact of the heightened [severity] threshold has been reflected by the sharp rise in the proportion of denials occurring at step two, which jumped from 8.4% in 1975, to 40.3% in 1982." Diehl, *supra*, at 632, *citing* House Committee on Ways and Means, 98th Cong., 1st Sess., Background Materials and Data on Major Programs within the Jurisdiction of the Committee on Ways and Means 79 (Comm. Print) (1983); *see also* Bowen v Yuckert, 482 U.S. 137, 157 (1987) (O'Connor, J., concurring); Diehl at 624 (noting that after the sequential evaluation process was implemented in its current form, there was a rise in the number of applicants who were denied benefits, and the proportion of those denied at step two screening increased from eight to forty percent).

The impact of the heightened severity threshold was likely exacerbated by the fact that the proportion of denials under the "slight impairment" standard had already risen to almost one-third due to pressure from SSA. Diehl, *supra*, at 632 n. 85 (*citing* Theodore F. Smith, Jr., *Developments in Social Security Law*, 21 Ind. L. Rev. 367, 369–70). Referring to an 800–case study conducted by SSA in 1984 concerning implementation of the severity regulation, the court observed in Dixon v. Shalala, 54 F.3d 1019 (2d. Cir. 1995):

> The study concluded that 37 percent of denials at Step Two were erroneous. (In 22 percent of the Step Two denials studied, applicants were found in fact to have severe impairments; in the other 15 percent, documentation proved inadequate to determine severity.) The 63 percent accuracy rate fell drastically below SSA's target level of 97 percent accuracy, and almost as far below the agency's 90.6 percent accuracy 'threshold level,' representing the 'minimal acceptable level of performance.'

54 F.3d at 1027 (*citing* Dixon v. Sullivan, 792 F.Supp. 942, 950–51 (S.D.N.Y. 1992)). Commentators have argued that this response to the increase in applications unfairly denied benefits to individuals who would previously have been declared eligible. Gerald W. Heaney, *Why the High Rate of Reversals in Social Security Disability Cases?*, 7 Hamline L. Rev. 1, 2 (1984). "The most striking aspect of such cases is not merely that benefits were denied but that they were denied on the basis of a threshold requirement which was supposedly intended to screen out only frivolous claims. Not surprisingly, the application of the severity regulation created an uproar." Levy, *supra*, at 491.

In a 1985 Ruling, which was published in part to "reflect certain circuit court decisions that have taken issue with the [Social Security Administration's] previously stated definition of 'not severe' impairments," SSA indicated that a finding of non-severity could be made only when "the evidence establishes only a slight abnormality[ies] which has no more than a minimal effect on a claimant's ability to do basic work activities" and cautioned that "[g]reat care should be exercised in applying the not severe impairment concept." *See* SSR 85–28 (1985). The Ruling did not overrule the severity regulation; instead, it was intended to clarify policy.

Even following this ruling, however, there remained essentially a two-way circuit split on whether the severity regulation was consistent with the language and legislative history of the Social Security regulations governing disability determinations. The majority of circuits held that the severity regulation was valid, "but only if narrowly applied as a *de minimis* screening policy to deny frivolous claims." Scott A. O'Connor, Bowen v. Yuckert: *The Severity Regulation—A De Minimis Threshold or a More Formidable Obstacle for Disability Claimants?*, 34 Loy. L. Rev. 198, 202 n. 35 (1988); *also see* McDonald v. Secretary of Health and Human Services, 795 F.2d 1118, 1121–1126 (1st Cir. 1986); Chico v. Schweiker, 710 F.2d 947 (2d Cir. 1983); Evans v. Heckler, 734 F.2d 1012 (4th Cir. 1984); Stone v. Heckler, 752 F.2d 1099 (5th Cir. 1985); Farris v. Secretary of Health & Human Servs., 773 F.2d 85 (6th Cir. 1985); Brady v. Heckler, 724 F.2d 914 (11th Cir. 1984). In *McDonald*, for example, the First Circuit, in conjunction with its interpretation of Social Security Ruling 85–28, construed Step 2 of the sequential evaluation process as a de minimis policy intended "to do no more than screen out groundless claims." 795 F.2d at 1124. Other circuits held that the severity regulation was invalid because it "allow[ed] the Secretary to bypass a full-scale evaluation, which would consider and relate both medical and vocational factors, of an applicant who might actually be entitled to benefits were his age, education, and work experience considered." Baeder v. Heckler, 768 F.2d 547, 553 (3d. Cir. 1985); *see also* O'Connor at 202; Johnson v. Heckler, 769 F.2d 1202 (7th Cir. 1985); Brown v. Heckler, 786 F.2d 870 (8th Cir. 1986); Yuckert v. Heckler, 774 F.2d 1365 (9th Cir. 1985); Hansen v. Heckler, 783 F.2d 170 (10th Cir. 1986). The Supreme Court resolved the controversy in *Bowen v. Yuckert*.

BOWEN V. YUCKERT
482 U.S. 137, 17 Soc.Sec.Rep.Ser. 661 (1987)

POWELL, J., delivered the opinion of the Court, in which REHNQUIST, C.J., and WHITE, STEVENS, O'CONNOR, and SCALIA, JJ., joined. O'CONNOR, J., filed a concurring opinion, in which STEVENS, J., joined. BLACKMAN, J., filed a dissenting opinion, in which BRENNAN and MARSHALL, JJ., joined.

Justice POWELL delivered the opinion of the Court.

The question in this case is whether the Secretary of Health and Human Services may deny a claim for Social Security disability benefits on the basis of a determination that the claimant does not suffer from a medically severe impairment that significantly limits the claimant's ability to perform basic work activities.

I

Title II of the Social Security Act (Act) provides for the payment of insurance benefits to persons who have contributed to the program and who suffer from a physical or mental disability. Title XVI of the Act provides for the payment of disability benefits to indigent persons under the Supplemental Security Income (SSI) program. Both titles of the Act define "disability" as the "inability to engage in any substantial gainful activity by reason of any medically determinable physical or mental impairment which can be expected to result in death or which has lasted or can be expected to last for a continuous period of not less than 12 months.... " § 423(d)(1)(A). See § 1382c(a)(3)(A). The Act further provides that an individual "shall be determined to be under a disability only if his physical or mental impairment or impairments are of such severity that he is not only unable to do his previous work but cannot, considering his age, education, and work experience, engage in any other kind of substantial gainful work which exists in the national economy, regardless of whether such work exists in the immediate area in which he lives, or whether a specific job vacancy exists for him, or whether he would be hired if he applied for work." §§ 423(d)(2)(A), 1382c(a)(3)(B) (1982 ed. and Supp. III).

The Secretary has established a five-step sequential evaluation process for determining whether a person is disabled. Step one determines whether the claimant is engaged in "substantial gainful activity." If he is, disability benefits are denied. If he is not, the decisionmaker proceeds to step two, which determines whether the claimant has a medically severe impairment or combination of impairments. That determination is governed by the "severity regulation" at issue in this case. The severity regulation provides:

"If you do not have any impairment or combination of impairments which significantly limits your physical or mental ability to do basic work activities, we will find that you do not have a severe impairment and are, therefore, not disabled. We will not consider your age, education, and work experience." §§ 404.1520(c), 416.920(c).

The ability to do basic work activities is defined as "the abilities and aptitudes necessary to do most jobs." §§ 404.1521(b), 416.921(b). Such abilities and aptitudes include "[p]hysical functions such as walking, standing, sitting, lifting, pushing, pulling, reaching, carrying, or handling"; "[c]apacities for seeing, hearing, and speaking"; "[u]nderstanding, carrying out, and remembering simple instructions"; "[u]se of judgment"; "[r]esponding appropriately to supervision, co-workers, and usual work situations"; and "[d]ealing with changes in a routine work setting." *Ibid.*

* * *

II

Respondent Janet Yuckert applied for both Social Security disability insurance benefits and SSI benefits in October 1980. She alleged that she was disabled by an inner ear dysfunction, dizzy spells, headaches, an inability to focus her eyes, and flatfeet. Yuckert had been employed as a travel agent from 1963 to 1977. In 1978 and 1979, she had worked intermittently as a real estate salesperson. Yuckert was 45 years old at the time of her application. She has a high school education, two years of business college, and real estate training.

* * * [T]he ALJ found that, although Yuckert suffered from "episodes of dizziness, or vision problems," "[m]ultiple tests ... failed to divulge objective clinical findings of abnormalities that support the claimant's severity of the stated impairments." The ALJ also found that Yuckert was pursuing a "relatively difficult" 2–year course in computer programming at a community college and was able to drive her car 80 to 90 miles each week. In light of the medical evidence and the evidence of her activities, the ALJ concluded that her medically determinable impairments were not severe under 20 CFR §§ 404.1520(c) and 416.920(c) (1986). The Appeals Council denied Yuckert's request for review on the ground that the results of additional psychological tests supported the ALJ's finding that she had not suffered a significant impairment of any work-related abilities. Yuckert then sought review in the United States District Court for the Western District of Washington. The case was referred to a Magistrate, who concluded that the Secretary's determination was supported by substantial evidence. The District Court adopted the Magistrate's report and affirmed the denial of Yuckert's claim.

The United States Court of Appeals for the Ninth Circuit reversed and remanded without considering the substantiality of the evidence. The court held that the Act does not authorize the Secretary to deny benefits on the basis of a determination that the claimant is not severely impaired. The court focused on the statutory provision that a person is disabled "only if his physical or mental impairment or impairments are of such severity that he is not only unable to do his previous work but cannot, considering his age, education, and work experience, engage in any other kind of substantial gainful work.... " 42 U.S.C. § 423(d)(2)(A) (1982 ed. and Supp. III). In the court's view, this provision requires that "both medical and vocational factors [i.e., age, education, and work experience] be considered in determining disability." * * * Accordingly, the court invalidated the severity regulation, 20 CFR § 404.1520(c) (1986). Because of the importance of the issue, and because the court's decision conflicts with the holdings of other Courts of Appeals, we granted certiorari. We now reverse.

III

Our prior decisions recognize that "Congress has 'conferred on the Secretary exceptionally broad authority to prescribe standards for applying certain sections of the Act.' " Heckler v. Campbell, 461 U.S. 458, 466, 103 S.Ct. 1952, 1956, 76 L.Ed.2d 66 (1983) (quoting Schweiker v. Gray Panthers, 453 U.S. 34, 43, 101 S.Ct. 2633, 2639, 69 L.Ed.2d 460 (1981)). The Act authorizes the Secretary to "adopt reasonable and proper rules and regulations to regulate and provide for the nature and extent of the proofs and evidence and the method of taking and furnishing the same" in disability cases. 42 U.S.C. § 405(a). We have held that "[w]here, as here, the statute expressly entrusts the Secretary with the responsibility for implementing a provision by regulation, our review is limited to determining whether the regulations promulgated exceeded the Secretary's statutory authority and whether they are arbitrary and capricious." Heckler v. Campbell, supra, 461 U.S., at 466, 103 S.Ct., at 1956 (footnote and citations omitted). In our view, both the language of the Act and its legislative history support the Secretary's decision to require disability claimants to make a threshold showing that their "medically determinable" impairments are severe enough to satisfy the regulatory standards.

A

As noted above, the Social Security Amendments Act of 1954 defined "disability" as "inability to engage in any substantial gainful activity by reason of any medically determinable physical or mental impairment.... " 68 Stat. 1080, 42 U.S.C. § 423(d)(1)(A). The severity regulation requires the claimant to show that he has an "impairment or combination of impairments which significantly limits" "the abilities and aptitudes necessary to do most jobs." 20 CFR §§ 404.1520(c), 404.1521(b) (1986). On its face, the regulation is not inconsistent with the statutory definition of disability. The Act "defines 'disability' in terms of the effect a physical or mental impairment has on a person's ability to function in the workplace." See Heckler v. Campbell, supra, at 459–460, 103 S.Ct., at 1953. The regulation adopts precisely this functional approach to determining the effects of medical impairments. If the impairments are not severe enough to limit significantly the claimant's ability to perform most jobs, by definition the impairment does not prevent the claimant from engaging in any substantial gainful activity. The Secretary, moreover, has express statutory authority to place the burden of showing a medically determinable impairment on the claimant. The Act provides that "[a]n individual shall not be considered to be under a disability unless he furnishes such medical and other evidence of the existence thereof as the Secretary may require." § 423(d)(5)(A) (1982 ed. and Supp. III).

The requirement of a threshold showing of severity also is consistent with the legislative history of § 423(d)(1)(A). The Senate Report accompanying the 1954 Amendments states:

"The physical or mental impairment must be of a nature and degree of severity sufficient to justify its consideration as the cause of failure to obtain any substantial gainful work. Standards for evaluating the severity of disabling conditions will be worked out in consultation with the State agencies." S.Rep. No. 1987, 83d Cong., 2d Sess., 21 (1954), U.S.Code Cong. & Admin.News 1954, p. 3730.

House Rep. No. 1698, 83d Cong., 2d Sess., 23 (1954), contains virtually identical language. Shortly after the 1954 Amendments were enacted, the

Secretary promulgated a regulation stating that "medical considerations alone may justify a finding that the individual is not under a disability where the only impairment is a slight neurosis, slight impairment of sight or hearing, or other similar abnormality or combination of slight abnormalities." 20 CFR § 404.1502(a) (1961). This regulation, with minor revisions, remained in effect until the sequential evaluation regulations were promulgated in 1978.

B

The Court of Appeals placed little weight on § 423(d)(1)(A) or its legislative history, but concluded that the severity regulation is inconsistent with § 423(d)(2)(A). We find no basis for this holding. Section 423(d)(2)(A) was enacted as part of the Social Security Amendments of 1967. It states that "an individual ... shall be determined to be under a disability only if his physical or mental impairment or impairments are of such severity that he is not only unable to do his previous work but cannot, considering his age, education, and work experience, engage in any other kind of substantial gainful work...." *Ibid.* The words of this provision limit the Secretary's authority to grant disability benefits, not to deny them. Section 423(d)(2)(A) restricts eligibility for disability benefits to claimants whose medically severe impairments prevent them from doing their previous work and also prevent them from doing any other substantial gainful work in the national economy. If a claimant is unable to show that he has a medically severe impairment, he is not eligible for disability benefits. In such a case, there is no reason for the Secretary to consider the claimant's age, education, and work experience.

The legislative history reinforces this understanding of the statutory language. Section 423(d)(2)(A) was intended to "reemphasize the predominant importance of medical factors in the disability determination." S.Rep. No. 744, 90th Cong., 1st Sess., 48 (1967), U.S.Code Cong. & Admin.News 1967, p. 2882. The 1967 Amendments left undisturbed the longstanding regulatory provision that "medical considerations alone may justify a finding that the individual is not under a disability." 20 CFR § 404.1502(a) (1966). Indeed, it is clear that Congress contemplated a sequential evaluation process:

"The bill would provide that such an individual would be disabled [i] only if it is shown that he has a severe medically determinable physical or mental impairment or impairments; [ii] that if, despite his impairment or impairments, an individual still can do his previous work, he is not under a disability; and [iii] that if, considering the severity of his impairment together with his age, education, and experience, he has the ability to engage in some other type of substantial gainful work that exists in the national economy even though he can

no longer do his previous work, he also is not under a disability...."
S.Rep. No. 744, supra, at 48–49, U.S.Code Cong. & Admin.News
1967, at p. 2882.

See H.R.Rep. No. 544, 90th Cong., 1st Sess., 30 (1967). (FN7)

C

If there was any lingering doubt as to the Secretary's authority to require disability claimants to make a threshold showing of medical severity, we think it was removed by § 4 of the Social Security Disability Benefits Reform Act of 1984, 98 Stat. 1800. It is true that " '[t]he Reform Act is
remedial legislation, enacted principally to be of assistance to large numbers of persons whose disability benefits have been terminated.' " Bowen
v. City of New York, 476 U.S., at 486, n. 14, 106 S.Ct., at 2033, n. 14
(quoting City of New York v. Heckler, 755 F.2d 31, 33 (CA2 1985)). But
Congress nevertheless expressed its approval of the severity regulation
both in the statute and in the accompanying Reports. Sections 4(a)(1) and
(b) of the 1984 Act provides:

"In determining whether an individual's physical or mental impairment or impairments are of a sufficient medical severity that such
impairment or impairments could be the basis of eligibility under
this section, the Secretary shall consider the combined effect of all of
the individual's impairments without regard to whether any such
impairment, if considered separately, would be of such severity. If the
Secretary does find a medically severe combination of impairments,
the combined effect of the impairments shall be considered throughout the disability determination process." 42 U.S.C. §§ 423(d)(2)(C),
1382c(a)(3)(F) (1982 ed. and Supp. III).

Congress thus recognized once again that the Secretary may make an initial determination of medical severity, and that he need not consider the
claimant's age, education, and experience unless he finds "a medically
severe combination of impairments."

The Senate Report accompanying the 1984 amendments expressly
endorses the severity regulation.

"[T]he new rule [requiring consideration of the combined effects of
multiple impairments] is to be applied in accordance with the existing sequential evaluation process and is not to be interpreted as authorizing a departure from that process.... The amendment requires
the Secretary to determine first, on a strictly medical basis and without regard to vocational factors, whether the individual's impairments, considered in combination, are medically severe. If they are
not, the claim must be disallowed. Of course, if the Secretary does

find a medically severe combination of impairments, the combined impact of the impairments would also be considered during the remaining stages of the sequential evaluation process." S.Rep. No. 98–466, p. 22 (1984).

The House Report agrees:

"[I]n the interests of reasonable administrative flexibility and efficiency, a determination that a person is not disabled may be based on a judgment that the person has no impairment, or that the impairment or combination of impairments [is] slight enough to warrant a presumption that the person's work ability is not seriously affected. The current 'sequential evaluation process' allows such a determination, and the committee does not wish to eliminate or seriously impair use of that process." H.R.Rep. No. 98–618, p. 8 (1984), U.S.Code Cong. & Admin.News 1984, p. 3045.

Finally, the Conference Report stated:

"[I]n the interests of reasonable administrative flexibility and efficiency, a determination that an individual is not disabled may be based on a judgment that an individual has no impairment, or that the medical severity of his impairment or combination of impairments is slight enough to warrant a presumption, even without a full evaluation of vocational factors, that the individual's ability to perform [substantial gainful activity] is not seriously affected. The current 'sequential evaluation process' allows such a determination and the conferees do not intend to either eliminate or impair the use of that process." H.R.Conf.Rep. No. 98–1039, p. 30 (1984), U.S.Code Cong. & Admin.News 1984, p. 3088.[10]

IV

We have recognized that other aspects of the Secretary's sequential evaluation process contribute to the uniformity and efficiency of disability determinations. The need for such an evaluation process is particularly acute because the Secretary decides more than 2 million claims for disability benefits each year, of which more than 200,000 are reviewed by administrative law judges. Department of Health and Human Services,

---

[10] Senator Long, a ranking Member of the Conference Committee, observed that "[s]ome courts ... have ruled that the Secretary cannot deny claims solely on the basis that the individual has no severe medical condition but must always make an evaluation of vocational capacities." 130 Cong.Rec. 25981 (1984). Senator Long went on to state that the Senate bill, that was followed by the conference bill with only "minor language changes of a technical nature," ibid., was "carefully drawn to reaffirm the authority of the Secretary to limit benefits to only those individuals with conditions which can be shown to be severe from a strictly medical standpoint—that is, without vocational evaluation," ibid. Senator Long was one of the sponsors of the disability program when it was enacted in 1956 and also was Chairman of the Senate Finance Committee when the 1967 Amendments to the Act were enacted.

Social Security Administration 1986 Annual Report to Congress, pp. 40, 42, 46. The severity regulation increases the efficiency and reliability of the evaluation process by identifying at an early stage those claimants whose medical impairments are so slight that it is unlikely they would be found to be disabled even if their age, education, and experience were taken into account. Similarly, step three streamlines the decision process by identifying those claimants whose medical impairments are so severe that it is likely they would be found disabled regardless of their vocational background.

Respondent Yuckert has conceded that the Secretary may require claimants to make a "*de minimis*" showing that their impairment is severe enough to interfere with their ability to work. Yuckert apparently means that the Secretary may require a showing that the "impairment is so slight that it could not interfere with [the claimant's] ability to work, irrespective of age, education, and work experience." She contends that the Secretary imposed only a "*de minimis*" requirement prior to 1978, but has required a greater showing of severity since then. As we have noted, however, Congress expressly approved the facial validity of the 1978 severity regulation in the 1984 amendments to the Act. Particularly in light of those amendments and the legislative history, we conclude that the regulation is valid on its face.[12]

V

The judgment of the Court of Appeals for the Ninth Circuit is reversed. The case is remanded for the Court of Appeals to consider whether the agency's decision is supported by substantial evidence.

---

[12] As the Court of Appeals for the Ninth Circuit invalidated the regulation on its face, we have no occasion to consider whether it is valid as applied. A number of Courts of Appeals have held that the Secretary has exceeded his authority by denying large numbers of meritorious disability claims at step two. We have noted that the House Report accompanying the 1984 amendments urged the Secretary to reevaluate the severity criteria to determine whether they were too strict. Subsequent to the adjudication of Yuckert's disability claim, the Secretary issued a ruling "[t]o clarify the policy for determining when a person's impairment(s) may be found 'not severe'.... " Social Security Ruling 85–28, App. to Pet. for Cert. 37a. The ruling states:

"An impairment or combination of impairments is found 'not severe' and a finding of 'not disabled' is made at [step two] when medical evidence establishes only a slight abnormality or a combination of slight abnormalities which would have no more than a minimal effect on an individual's ability to work even if the individual's age, education, or work experience were specifically considered (i.e., the person's impairment(s) has no more than a minimal effect on his or her physical or mental ability(ies) to perform basic work activities)." Id., at 41a.

If the "evidence shows that the person cannot perform his or her past relevant work because of the unique features of that work," the decisionmaker will conduct a "further evaluation of the individual's ability to do other work considering age, education and work experience." Id., at 43a. We do not undertake to construe this ruling today.

We do, however, reject Yuckert's contention that invalidation of the regulation is an appropriate remedy for the Secretary's allegedly unlawful application of the regulation. The Court of Appeals did not invalidate the regulation on this ground. Moreover, there is no indication in the record that less drastic remedies would not have been effective.

It is so ordered.

Justice O'CONNOR, with whom Justice STEVENS joins, concurring.

The Court is, I believe, entirely correct to find that the "step two" regulation is not facially inconsistent with the Social Security Act's definition of disability. * * * Step two on its face requires only that the claimant show that he or she suffers from "an impairment or combination of impairments ... [that] significantly limit[s] ... physical or mental ability to do basic work activities." 20 CFR § 404.1521(a) (1986). "Basic work activities," the regulation says, include "walking, standing, sitting, lifting, pulling, reaching, carrying, or handling[,] ... seeing, hearing, and speaking, ... [u]nderstanding, carrying out, and remembering simple instructions[,] ... [u]se of judgment ... [r]esponding appropriately to supervision, co-workers and usual work situations[,] ... [d]ealing with changes in a routine work setting." § 404.1521(b)(1)-(6). I do not see how a claimant unable to show a significant limitation in any of these areas can possibly meet the statutory definition of disability. For the reasons set out by the Court in Part III of its opinion, I have no doubt that the Act authorizes the Secretary to weed out at an early stage of the administrative process those individuals who cannot possibly meet the statutory definition of disability. Accordingly, I concur in the Court's opinion and judgment that the regulation is not facially invalid, and that the case must be remanded so that the lower courts may determine whether or not the Secretary's conclusion that Janet Yuckert is not suffering from a sufficiently severe impairment is supported by substantial evidence.

I write separately, however, to discuss the contention of respondent and various amici (including 29 States and 5 major cities) that this facially valid regulation has been applied systematically to deny benefits to claimants who do meet the statutory definition of disability. Respondent directs our attention to the chorus of judicial criticism concerning the step two regulation, as well as to substantially unrefuted statistical evidence. Despite the heavy deference ordinarily paid to the Secretary's promulgation and application of his regulations, all 11 regional Federal Courts of Appeals have either enjoined the Secretary's use of the step two regulation or imposed a narrowing construction upon it. The frustration expressed by these courts in dealing with the Secretary's application of step two in particular cases is substantial, and no doubt in part accounts for the Court of Appeals' decision in this case to simply enjoin the regulation's further use.

Empirical evidence cited by respondent and the amici further supports the inference that the regulation has been used in a manner inconsistent with the statutory definition of disability. Before the step two regulations were promulgated approximately 8% of all claimants were denied benefits at the "not severe" stage of the administrative process; afterwards approximately 40% of all claims were denied at this stage. As the lower federal courts have enjoined use of step two and imposed narrowing constructions, the step two denial rate has fallen to about 25%. Allowance rates in Social Security disability cases have increased substantially when federal courts have demanded that the step two regulation not be used to disqualify those who are statutorily eligible. For example, in Illinois after entry of the injunction in Johnson v. Heckler, 769 F.2d 1202 (CA7 1985), cert. pending *sub nom*. Bowen v. Johnson, No. 85–1442, the approval rate for claims climbed from 34.3% to 52% at the initial screening level and from 14.8% to 34.1% at the reconsideration level.

To be sure the Secretary faces an administrative task of staggering proportions in applying the disability benefits provisions of the Social Security Act. Perfection in processing millions of such claims annually is impossible. But respondent's evidence suggests that step two has been applied systematically in a manner inconsistent with the statute. Indeed, the Secretary himself has recently acknowledged a need to "clarify" step two in light of this criticism and has attempted to do so by issuing new interpretative guidelines. See Social Security Ruling 85–28.

In my view, step two may not be used to disqualify those who meet the statutory definition of disability. The statute does not permit the Secretary to deny benefits to a claimant who may fit within the statutory definition without determining whether the impairment prevents the claimant from engaging in either his prior work or substantial gainful employment that, in light of the claimant's age, education, and experience, is available to him in the national economy. Only those claimants with slight abnormalities that do not significantly limit any "basic work activity" can be denied benefits without undertaking this vocational analysis. As the Secretary has recently admonished in his new guideline:

> "Great care should be exercised in applying the not severe impairment concept. If an adjudicator is unable to determine clearly the effect of an impairment or combination of impairments on the individual's ability to do basic work activities, the sequential evaluation process should not end with the not severe evaluation step. Rather, it should be continued. In such a circumstance, if the impairment does not meet or equal the severity level of the relevant medical listing, sequential evaluation requires that the adjudicator evaluate the individual's ability to do past work, or to do other work based on the consideration of age, education, and prior work experience." Social Security Ruling 85–28.

Applied in this manner, step two, I believe, can produce results consistent with the statute in the vast majority of cases and still facilitate the expeditious and just settlement of claims.

[Dissenting opinion of Justice Blackmum, in which Justice Brennan and Justice Marshall joined, omitted.]

NOTE ON IMPLEMENTATION OF THE SEVERITY REQUIREMENT AFTER BOWEN V. YUCKERT

Later cases have relied on both *Yuckert* and SSR 85–28 to reaffirm the *de minimis* severity requirement at Step 2 of the sequential evaluation process. "Since the Court's decision in *Yuckert*, at least seven circuits have followed Justice O'Connor's lead and held that Step 2 may do no more than screen out *de minimis* claims." Dixon v. Shalala, 54 F.3d 1019, 1030 (2d. Cir. 1995); *see also* Anthony v. Sullivan, 954 F.2d 289, 294–95 (5th Cir. 1992); Bailey v. Sullivan, 885 F.2d 52, 56–57 (3d Cir. 1989); McDonald v. Secretary of Health & Human Servs., 884 F.2d 1468, 1476–77 (1st Cir.1989); Hudson v. Bowen, 870 F.2d 1392, 1395–96 (8th Cir.1989); Higgs v. Bowen, 880 F.2d 860, 862–63 (6th Cir.1988); Yuckert v. Bowen, 841 F.2d 303, 306 (9th Cir.1988); Stratton v. Bowen, 827 F.2d 1447, 1453 (11th Cir.1987).

The Sixth Circuit has used slightly different language to make the same point, perhaps more forcefully: "The severity requirement may still be employed as an administrative convenience to screen out claims that are 'totally groundless' solely from a medical standpoint." Higgs v. Bowen, 880 F.2d 860, 863, 26 Soc. Sec. Rep. Serv. 296 (6th Cir. 1988). The Eighth Circuit similarly construed *Yuckert* to mean that a majority of the Supreme Court adopted a slight impairment standard. *See* Brown v. Bowen, 827 F.2d 311, 312 (8th Cir.1987) ("In regard to the application of that standard, however, a majority of the Court adopted a standard which provides that '[o]nly those claimants with slight abnormalities that do not significantly limit any 'basic work activity' can be denied benefits without undertaking' the subsequent steps of the sequential evaluation process." (quoting *Yuckert*, 482 U.S. at 147).

In Stratton v. Bowen, *supra*, the Eleventh Circuit imposed liability for attorney's fees on SSA under the Equal Access to Justice Act after finding that the agency lacked substantial justification for applying the Step 2 severity regulation to impose more than a "de minimis" test. Reconfirming that "the application of a threshold severity regulation that is greater than de minimis is invalid," the court noted that the Supreme Court, in *Bowen v. Yuckert*, had "observed that 'a number of courts of appeal have held that the [S]ecretary has exceeded his authority by denying large numbers of meritorious disability claims at step two.'" 827 F2d at 1453 (quoting *Yuckert*, 482 U.S. at 2297 n.12) *See also* Samuel v. Barnhart, 295 F.Supp.2d 926, 93 Soc. Sec. Rep. Serv. 453 (E.D.Wis. 2003): "In evaluating the ALJ's decision on this issue, I keep in mind that the step two requirement that the claimant have a severe impairment is generally considered to be 'a de minimis screening device to dispose of groundless claims.'" (citing Smolen v. Chater, 80 F.3d 1273, 1290 (9th Cir.1996) (citing Bowen v. Yuckert, 482 U.S. 137, 153–54 (1987) (O'Connor, J., concurring)). *But see* Anthony v. Sullivan, 954 F.2d 289, 294 (5th Cir. 1992), where the ALJ concluded that the claimant did not have a severe impairment and the Fifth Circuit agreed: *Yuckert* simply upheld the facial validity of the severity regulation as an appropriate method of streamlining the review process. "*Yuckert* did not conclude that the severity regulation properly interpreted the statutory requirements, and *Yuckert* did not purport to state the proper definition of the term 'severe impairment.'"

C. SIMPLIFIED GRANT: STEP 3 AND THE LISTING OF IMPAIRMENTS

The third step in the sequential evaluation process involves the application of the Social Security Administration's Listing of Impairments. As discussed earlier in this chapter, in order to arrive at this third step a claimant must have already demonstrated that he or she is not engaging in substantial gainful activity (Step 1) and has a medically determinable "severe" impairment—or combination of impairments—that has lasted, or is expected to last, 12 months or result in death (Step 2). If so, the claimant's impairments are compared at Step 3 to the criteria set out in the Listing. If an impairment meets the requirements of a listed impairment, then the claimant is considered to be disabled; if not, a claimant can still be found to be disabled at this step if the same or other impairments, alone or in combination, are the "medical equivalent" of a listed impairment. If the claimant has no impairment, or combination of impairments, that meet or equal the requirements of the Listing, then the sequential evaluation process continues to the final two steps, which address a claimant's ability to perform past jobs or any other jobs in the national economy. The final two steps of the sequential evaluation process are discussed later in this chapter.

Step 3 thus serves as an efficient way to decide strong claims relatively quickly, without having to consider a claimant's vocational history and capacity. The logic is simple: an impairment that meets the strict criteria of a listed impairment can be recognized and evaluated early in the disability determination process and at relatively little cost. Step 3 is most efficient when benefits can be awarded because the claimant meets the requirements of a clearly diagnosed impairment. Step 3 evaluations become somewhat more involved when a claimant's impairment does not meet the listing requirements but could be the "medical equivalent" to a listed impairment. Medical equivalence is discussed in detail later in this Section.

The Listing is used somewhat differently for OASDI and SSI disability claims, specifically with respect to claims for SSI benefits on behalf of children under the age of 18. As we saw in Chapter 4, all disability claims under the OASDI program proceed according to the adult disability standard set out in the Social Security Act, as do claims by adults under the SSI program. Claims for SSI disability benefits on behalf of children under the age of 18, on the other hand, are evaluated according to a different disability standard that relies more heavily on the Listing of Impairments. *Compare* **20 C.F.R. § 404.1525[APP–REGS]** (OASDI) *with* **20 C.F.R. § 416.925[APP–REGS] (SSI)**. For those claims, the Listing is applied first in the same manner as with adult claims at Step 3 of the sequential evaluation process. But if the medical evidence fails to show impairments that meet or equal the requirements of the Listing, then the claim proceeds to an evaluation unique to the Child SSI program: whether the child's impairments are the "functional equivalent" of a listed impairment. Functional equivalence in the Child's SSI program is discussed later in this section, after coverage of Step 3 for adult claims. The section concludes with a brief discussion of Step 3 as applied to pre–1991 spouse's disability claims.

1. APPLYING THE LISTING AT STEP 3

The Listing of Impairments, published as an appendix to the federal regulations, is divided into two parts: Part A deals with those impairments that affect adults and children in the same manner; Part B deals with impairments that only affect children. *See* 20 C.F.R. Pt. 404 Subpart P Appx. 1. Part A of the Listing is divided into 13 sections; many, but not all, of the categories of impairments are the same in Parts A and B. Each section of the Listing covers a different major body system (e.g., musculoskeletal, gastrointestinal, or cardiovascular systems), and each is divided into two parts. The first part of each section is an introduction to the body system covered in that section. The introduction defines terms used in that section, and may spell out exact medical findings necessary to meet particular listings. The second part of each section is the "Category of Impairments," which sets out individual impairments and the medical findings necessary to show that a claimant with that impairment is disabled. In a unique departure from past practice, the Social Security Administration revised Section 9 of the Listing of Impairments covering endocrine discorders to eliminate all previously listed impairments; instead, there is only an introductory section that explains how these disorders are to be evaluated, including cross-references to listing under other body systems. Reasoning that "medicial science has made significant advances in detecting endocrine disorder at earlier stages," SSA concluded that "most endocrine disorders do not reach listing-level serverity because they do not become sufficiently severe or do not remain at a sufficient level of severity long enough to meet our 12-month duration requirement." 76 Fed Reg. 19692 (April 8, 2011).

The criteria in the Listing are quite strict, as they are intended to identify persons whose medical condition alone precludes them from engaging in "any gainful activity." The "any gainful activity" standard—also referred to as "per se disability"—is a regulatory standard distinct from the general statutory disability standard that looks to the ability to engage in "substantial gainful activity" and also takes into account the claimant's age, education, and prior work experience. The distinction between these two standards was discussed by the Supreme Court in Sullivan v. Zebley, 493 U.S. 521 (1990), where the Court ruled that then-existing SSA regulations cutting off the sequential evaluation process at Step 3 for Child SSI claims were contrary to the Social Security Act. As explained earlier in this chapter, the statutory disability standard for Child SSI benefits in place until 1996 provided that—to qualify for benefits—a child had to have an impairment of "comparable severity" to an impairment that would qualify an adult under the general disability standard. In the following excerpt, the Court discussed the difference between the criteria in the Listing and the general disability standard and the implications that follow from applying the Listings criteria at Step 3 of the sequential evaluation process:

> [T]he listings in several ways are more restrictive than the statutory standard. First, the listings obviously do not cover all illnesses and abnormalities that actually can be disabling. The Secretary himself has characterized the adult listing as merely containing "over 100 *examples* of medical conditions which ordinarily prevent" a person from working, and has recognized that "it is difficult to include in the listing all the sets of medical findings which describe impairments severe enough to prevent any gainful work." SSR 83–19, at 90 (emphasis added). Second, even those medical conditions that are covered in the listings are defined by criteria setting a higher level of severity than the statutory standard, so they exclude claimants who have listed impairments in a form severe enough to preclude *substantial* gainful activity, but not quite severe enough to meet the listings level-that which would preclude *any* gainful activity. Third, the listings also exclude any claimant whose impairment would not prevent any and all persons from doing any kind of work, but which actually precludes the particular claimant from working, given its actual effects on him-such as pain, consequences of medication, and other symptoms that vary greatly with the individual and given the claimant's age, education, and work experience. Fourth, the equivalence analysis excludes claimants who have unlisted impairments, or combinations of impairments, that do not fulfill all the criteria for any one listed impairment. Thus, there are several obvious categories of claimants who would not qualify under the listings, but who nonetheless would meet the statutory standard.

493 U.S. at 533–34.

There is relatively little case law dealing with specific listed impairments, probably because close or difficult cases tend to be resolved later in the sequential evaluation process. Strong claims that should be granted at Step 3 based on the Listing are, for the most part, resolved with a finding of disability. On the other hand, if it isn't clear from readily available medical evidence that a claimant meets the requirements of one or more listed impairments, the safe approach is to pass the claim on to Steps 4 and 5. And if the claim is granted eventually at Step 5, as often is the case when an impairment is close to meeting the requirements of the Listing, the failure to find that the impairment met the listing becomes moot. But for Step 3 to fulfill its role in the sequential evaluation process, SSA must be ready to make a finding of disability whenever the medical evidence shows that a claimant has met the requirements of the Listing.

AMBERS V. HECKLER

736 F.2d 1467, 5 Soc.Sec.Rep.Ser. 383 (11th Cir. 1984

Before Roney and Johnson, Circuit Judges, and Morgan, Senior Circuit Judge.

Roney, Circuit Judge:

The interesting question on this social security appeal is whether benefits can be denied to a claimant who meets the disability listing for mental retardation but had been previously gainfully employed with that handicap. We hold that since claimant meets the listing, she is entitled to benefits regardless of the fact that she may be able to hold gainful employment as she did in the past.

Helen Ambers appeals the district court's affirmance of the denial of Social Security disability benefits. Having a performance I.Q. of 52, she meets the listing for mental retardation which would make her eligible for disability benefits pursuant to 20 C.F.R. § 404.1598, Appendix 1, Part A, Section 12.05 B. She is not presently engaged in gainful activity. She had been employed previously as a domestic.

The Secretary argues that there is substantial evidence that she can return to that kind of employment. The Secretary points to a psychological evaluation and other medical evidence to show that Ambers can return to her former work as a domestic.

At the time of the decision Ambers was 43 years old. She has a sixth grade education, but is unable to read or write on even a first grade level. Ambers has worked as a domestic, a babysitter, a waitress, and as a laborer performing yard work.

* * *

At the hearing, Dr. Mark E. Meadows, a vocational expert, testified that * * * Ambers could return to her former work as a domestic and babysitter if she had the residual functional capacity for light work. Dr. Meadows testified that Ambers functional illiteracy would not preclude her former unskilled work.

The Administrative Law Judge (ALJ) found that Ambers was able to return to her former work as a domestic and found her not disabled.

This case presents an unusual situation in that the claimant was gainfully employed in the past with her impairments and upon cessation of gainful employment meets the Secretary's disability listing in Appendix 1, Part A, Section 12.05 B. The language of the statute states that disability means "inability to engage in any substantial gainful activity by reason of medically determinable physical or mental impairment...." 42 U.S.C.A. § 423. The regulations, however, state that "[t]he Listing of Impairments describes, for each of the major body systems, impairments which are considered severe enough to prevent a person from doing any gainful activity." 20 C.F.R. § 404.1525(a); 20 C.F.R. § 416.925(a). If an individual's impairment "meets the duration requirement and is listed in Appendix 1 ... we will find (the claimant) disabled.... " 20 C.F.R. § 404.1520(d); 20 C.F.R. § 416.920(d). Therefore, upon cessation of employment, the regulations support a finding of disability if one meets the listings, even though the statute relates disability to the inability to work because of the impairment.

This is an issue of first impression for this Court. * * *

In Wright v. Schweiker, 556 F.Supp. 468 (M.D.Tenn.1983), a claimant, a former taxicab driver, having an I.Q. of 66 and physical impairments that limit him to medium or lesser work met the section 12.05 C listing of impairments. The court held that "[h]aving met the Secretary's standards for a listed impairment, no further considerations of ... vocational factors need be made prior to a finding of disability." 556 F.Supp. at 476.

Section 12.05 B was addressed in Nalley v. Schweiker, 575 F.Supp. 840 (W.D.Ky.1983). In Nalley, the district court reversed the Secretary's determination of nondisability and remanded for an award of benefits pursuant to section 12.05B where Mary E. Nalley had a verbal I.Q. of 59 on the W.A.I.S. The Court held that Nalley met "the listed impairment and should be found disabled." 575 F.Supp. at 843. Nalley had worked as a motel maid, laundress and babysitter.

This Court has held the regulations require a sequential analysis that must be followed when evaluating a disability claim. When a claimant is not engaged in substantial gainful activity, the Secretary must determine whether claimant suffers from an impairment "that significantly limits the claimants physical or mental capacity to perform basic work-related activities." Anderson v. Schweiker, 651 F.2d 306, 308 (5th Cir. Unit A 1981).

Social Security disability claims are evaluated in terms of: (1) whether a claimant is gainfully employed; (2) whether claimant's impairment meets the listing of impairments; (3) whether claimant can return to former work; and (4) whether claimant is disabled in light of age, education, and residual functional capacity. If a person is found disabled or not disabled at any point in the review, in accordance with the above delineated steps, no further review is conducted. If the claimant meets the listed impairment in Appendix 1, the claimant is determined disabled without considering age, education, and work experience.

* * *

Consideration of the fact that Ambers could return to her past work is not a relevant inquiry once she met the Listing of Impairments in Appendix 1.

REVERSED AND REMANDED.

A) OVERVIEW OF THE LISTING CRITERIA FOR MUSCULOSKELETAL SYSTEM IMPAIRMENTS

This section discusses the criteria in the Listing of Impairments for the musculoskeletal system as an example of how the Listing is structured. The next section looks more closely at how one particular listed impairment—amputation—is applied.

Musculoskeletal impairments are evaluated under Section 1 of the Listing of Impairments. *See generally* 20 C.F.R. Part 404 Subpart P Appx 1 § 1.00 (Listings). The focus is on a claimant's functional abilities—the ability to perform substantial gainful activity with limited use of hands and arms, feet and legs, or the spine—instead of an emphasis on disease classification. These functional abilities are compromised when a claimant cannot walk and/or perform fine and gross movements effectively. The impairments covered include major dysfunction of a joint, disorders of the spine, amputation, fracture, and injuries to soft tissue. Arthritis is covered within the Immune System listing. *See* 20 C.F.R. Part 404 Subpart P Appx 1 § 14.09 (Listings).

Musculoskeletal impairments are among the most commonly alleged bases for disability benefits and are also often difficult to prove. The listings for the musculoskeletal system therefore offer the possibility of resolving a large number of claims at relatively low cost, but must at the same time insist on clear and convincing proof that the listings criteria have been met. Thus, for example, the listing for major dysfunction of a joint requires "gross anatomical deformity" that inhibits motion of the affected joint(s) and goes on to require that affected joints must be major peripheral weight bearing joints (hip, knee, or ankle) limiting the ability to ambulate effectively, or major peripheral joints in each upper extremity (shoulder and elbow) which limit the ability to perform fine and gross movements. 20 C.F.R. Part 404 Subpart P Appx 1 § 1.02 (Listings). Another example is fractures, which are covered under two listings: fractures of the femur, tibia, pelvis, or one or more tarsal bones, and fracture of an upper extremity. Both are disabling if they do not heal within a 12–month period. See 20 C.F.R. Part 404 Subpart P Appx 1 §§ 1.06, 1.07 (Listings).

In order to provide a more complete picture of the musculoskeletal system listings, they are summarized below. Note that this summary includes only a brief description of the instructions in § 1.00 and only the basic requirements for meeting the individual listings, leaving out some of the more detailed criteria included in the full Listing of Impairments.

20 C.F.R. PART 404 SUBPART P APPX 1 LISTINGS § 1.00: A SUMMARY
1.00 MUSCULOSKELETAL SYSTEM

- 1.00A discusses the various causes of musculoskeletal system disorders.

- 1.00B details loss of function, including the definition of loss of function, the definition of the inability to ambulate effectively, the definition of the inability to perform fine and gross movements effectively, and symptoms associated with loss of function.

- 1.00C specifies necessary diagnosis and evaluation, including acceptable medical imaging and other diagnostic procedures.

- 1.00D sets forth the requirements of the physical examination, which must include a detailed description of the findings appropriate to the specific impairment being evaluated. This subsection also requires that such examinations be supported with objective criteria and testing methods.

- 1.00E details examination of the spine.

- 1.00F defines major joints.

- 1.00G discusses the methods for measuring joint motion.

- 1.00H details documentation required, which includes the documentation of medically prescribed treatment and the response to such treatment, the protocol for situations in which no record of ongoing treatment is available, and the necessary evaluation when the Listing criteria are not met.

- 1.00I details effects of treatment, and the documentation required for showing the response to treatment.

- 1.00J discusses orthotic, prosthetic, and assistive devices.

- 1.00K discusses disorders of the spine, and includes detailed discussions on herniated nucleus pulposus, spinal arachnoiditis, lumbar spinal stenosis, and other miscellaneous conditions.

- 1.00L covers abnormal curvatures of the spine.

- 1.00M details the meaning of under continuing surgical management.

- 1.00N discusses the necessary evaluation after fractures or soft tissue injuries if there have been no significant changes in physical findings or an appropriate medically acceptable imaging after maximum benefit from therapy has been achieved.

- 1.00O discusses major function of the face and head.

- 1.00P sets forth the necessary documentation after surgical procedures have been performed.

- 1.00Q discusses the effects of obesity on the musculoskeletal system.

1.01 Category of Impairments, Musculoskeletal

1.02 Major dysfunction of a joint(s) (due to any cause): Characterized by deformity, chronic joint pain, stiffness, limitation of motion of the affected joint(s), and applicable diagnostic findings. With:

A. Involvement of one major peripheral weight-bearing joint, resulting in the inability to ambulate effectively; or

B. Involvement of one major peripheral joint in each upper extremity, resulting in inability to perform fine and gross movements effectively.

1.03 Reconstructive surgery of a major weight-bearing joint, with inability to ambulate effectively for at least twelve months.

1.04 Disorders of the spine, resulting in compromise of a nerve root or the spinal cord. With:

A. Evidence of nerve root compression characterized by pain, limitation of spinal movement, motor loss accompanied by sensory or reflex loss; or

B. Spinal arachnoiditis, confirmed by appropriate medically testing and manifested by severe burning or pain, resulting in the need for changes in position or posture more than once every 2 hours; or

C. Lumbar spinal stenosis established by findings on appropriate medical imaging, manifested by chronic pain and weakness, and resulting in inability to ambulate effectively.

1.05 Amputation (due to any cause).

A. Both hands; or

B. One or both lower extremities at or above the ankle bones, with stump complications resulting in the inability to use a prosthetic device to ambulate effectively for at least twelve months; or

C. One hand and one lower extremity at or above the ankle bones, with inability to ambulate effectively; or

D. Pelvic amputation or hip amputation.

1.06 Fracture of the femur, tibia, pelvis, or one or more of the tarsal bones. With:

A. Solid union not evident on appropriate medically imaging and not clinically solid; and

B. Inability to ambulate effectively for at least twelve months.

1.07 Fracture of an upper extremity with nonunion of a fracture of the shaft of the humerus, radius, or ulna, under continuing surgical management, directed toward restoration of functional use of the extremity, and such function was not restored or expected to be restored within twelve months of onset.

1.08 Soft tissue injury (e.g., burns) of an upper or lower extremity, trunk, or face and head, under continuing surgical management, directed toward the restoration of major function, and such major function was not restored or expected to be restored within twelve months of onset.

B) APPLYING A PARTICULAR MUSCULOSKELETAL SYSTEM LISTING: AMPUTATION

Following up on the summary of the musculoskeletal system listings above, this section provides a more detailed look at the amputation listing together with a case that shows how courts interpret that particular listing.

20 C.F.R. Part 404 Subpart P Appx 1 § 1.05 (Listing) sets out the criteria for meeting the amputation listing as follows:

1.05 Amputation (due to any cause).

(A) Both hands; or

(B) One or both lower extremities at or above the tarsal region, with stump complications resulting in medical inability to use a prosthetic device to ambulate effectively, as defined in 1.00B2b, which have lasted or are expected to last for at least 12 months; or

(C) One hand and one lower extremity at or above the tarsal region, with inability to ambulate effectively, as defined in 1.00B2b; or

(D) Hemipelvectomy or hip disarticulation.

The amputation listing criteria focus, for the most part, on functional ability due to the advancement of technology, although the amputation of two hands is disabling without the need for any further evidence. *See* 20 C.F.R. Part 404 Subpart P Appx 1 § 1.05A (Listings). Thus, amputation of one or both lower extremities at or above the ankle region is disabling if stump complications cause the inability to use a prosthetic device to ambulate effectively and the complications last for at least twelve months. Amputation of one hand and one lower extremity at or above the ankle with the required inability to ambulate is also considered disabling, as is hemipelvectomy, or hip disarticulation. 20 C.F.R. Part 404 Subpart P Appx 1 § 1.05B–C (Listings).

GABRIEL v. ASTRUE
2009 WL 453372, 139 Soc. Sec. Rep. Serv. 738 (D.N.H. 2009)

STEVEN J. McAULIFFE, Chief Judge.

Pursuant to 42 U.S.C. § 405(g), claimant, Eugene M. Gabriel, moves to reverse the Commissioner's decision denying his applications for Social Security disability insurance benefits, or DIB, under Title II of the Social

Security Act, and for supplemental security income, or SSI, under Title XVI. In the alternative, Gabriel asks the court to remand the case for a new administrative determination. The Commissioner, in turn, moves for an order affirming his decision. For the reasons given, the matter is remanded to the Administrative Law Judge ("ALJ") for further proceedings consistent with this opinion.

* * *

Background

* * *

Eugene Gabriel is forty-eight years old. When he was eighteen, he was diagnosed with osteosarcoma, and his left leg was amputated above the knee. Since then, he has worn an above-the-knee prosthesis. Until approximately 1996, he had regular follow-up care, but has not had any since then. In November, 2006, he was diagnosed with diabetes, based upon a finding of a glucose HbA1C4 level of 6.4 by a laboratory which reported the normal range as 4.8–6.0.

At the time of his hearing, Gabriel was working part-time in the seafood department at a grocery store. Typically, he worked two four-hour days in a row, followed by a day off, and then worked two more four-hour days, followed by two days off. Before his job at the grocery store, Gabriel worked at a pizza restaurant that allowed him flexible hours and provided a number accommodations that permitted him to take care of his stump, which tended to blister and bleed if he wore his prosthesis for too long. Cursory examination of Gabriel's Social Security earnings record suggests that he had approximately twenty different jobs between 2002 and 2006.

* * *

After the hearing, the ALJ issued a decision which included the following findings:

3. The claimant has the following severe impairment: left leg amputation at the knee.

....

4. The claimant does not have an impairment or combination of impairments that meets or medically equals one of the listed impairments in 20 CFR Part 404 Subpart P, Appendix 1.

5. After careful consideration of the entire record, the undersigned finds that the claimant has the residual functional capacity to per-

form sedentary work except that he is unable to effectively use left foot controls.

....

10. Considering the claimant's age, education, work experience, and residual functional capacity, there are jobs that exist in significant numbers in the national economy that the claimant can perform.

The ALJ did not support his step-three determination, *i.e.*, that Gabriel's severe impairment did not meet or equal a listed impairment, with any specific fact finding or analysis. On the other hand, the ALJ supported his step-five determination, i.e., that Gabriel was capable of performing jobs that exist in significant numbers in the national economy, with a finding that "the claimant's statements concerning the intensity, persistence, and limiting effects of [his] symptoms are not entirely credible." Thus, the ALJ appears not to have credited Gabriel's statements that he suffered from pain and developed a rash when he wore his prosthesis while sitting. As a consequence, the ALJ did not explore the area of sedentary jobs that require no standing or walking, *i.e.*, jobs that an amputee could perform without using a prosthesis. The ALJ found Gabriel to be less than credible because "[t]here is no evidence that the claimant has been seen or treated for the blistering, redness, and bleeding that occurs to his stump with prolonged use of his prosthesis." In addition, the ALJ declined to give significant weight to Dr. Wolf's opinion, explaining that "there is no evidence of treatment for the skin breakdowns the claimant alleges."

Discussion

According to Gabriel, the ALJ's decision should be reversed, and the case remanded, because the ALJ: (1) incorrectly determined that he did not have a listed impairment; (2) failed properly to consider diabetes as part of his combination of impairments; and (3) gave insufficient weight to the opinion of an examining physician when determining that he had the residual functional capacity to perform sedentary work.

* * *

A. Step Three: Meeting a Listed Impairment

Gabriel argues that the ALJ erred, at step three, by determining that he did not have a listed impairment. More specifically, claimant argues that based on Dr. Wolf's findings and opinions, and his own testimony, the ALJ should have found that he was not able to ambulate effectively, which, in turn, would have required a determination that his disability met or equaled the listed musculoskeletal impairment of amputation. The

Commissioner disagrees, contending that claimant failed to carry his burden of proving that he suffered from a "medical inability to use a prosthetic device to ambulate effectively."

At step three, "if the impairment meets the conditions for one of the 'listed' impairments in the Social Security regulations, then the application is granted." Under the relevant regulations, "*[a]mputation (due to any cause)* ... [of] [o]ne or both lower extremities at or above the tarsal region, with stump complications resulting in medical inability to use a prosthetic device to ambulate effectively, as defined in 1.00B2b" is a listed impairment of the musculoskeletal system. 20 C.F.R. § 404, Subpt. P, Appx. 1, § 1.05B. Those same regulations explain that "[r]egardless of the cause(s) of a musculoskeletal impairment, functional loss for purposes of these listings is defined as the inability to ambulate effectively *on a sustained basis* for any reason, including pain associated with the underlying musculoskeletal impairment." *Id.* § 1.00B2a (emphasis added). The regulations provide the following relevant definitions:

> (1) *Definition.* Inability to ambulate effectively means an extreme limitation of the ability to walk; *i.e.*, an impairment(s) that interferes very seriously with the individual's ability to independently initiate, sustain, or complete activities. Ineffective ambulation is defined generally as having insufficient lower extremity functioning (see 1.00J) to permit independent ambulation without the use of a hand-held assistive device(s) that limits the functioning of both upper extremities....

> (2) *To ambulate effectively*, individuals must be capable of sustaining a reasonable walking pace over a sufficient distance to be able to carry out activities of daily living. They must have the ability to travel without companion assistance to and from a place of employment or school. Therefore, examples of ineffective ambulation include, but are not limited to, the inability to walk without the use of a walker, two crutches or two canes, the inability to walk a block at a reasonable pace on rough or uneven surfaces, the inability to use standard public transportation, the inability to carry out routine ambulatory activities, such as shopping and banking, and the inability to climb a few steps at a reasonable pace with the use of a single hand rail. The ability to walk independently about one's home without the use of assistive devices does not, in and of itself, constitute effective ambulation.

Id. § 1.00B2b.

At his hearing, Gabriel testified that use of his prosthesis for more than six hours at a time gave him blisters on his stump that would open and bleed, and that after wearing his prosthesis for a day, he would have to refrain from wearing it the next day, to let the blistering heal. He further testified that his problem with blistering first cropped up about fifteen years ago and has become progressively worse. He also testified that he takes his prosthesis off at home, and described how his part-time work schedule—four-hour work days, never more than two in a row—allowed him to care for his stump and keep the blistering to a minimum. And, in his opening statement, Gabriel's representative explained that Dr. Wolf conducted his examination at a time when Gabriel was not working and, as a result, was not stressing his stump.

As noted above, the ALJ presented no factfinding or analysis in support of his determination that Gabriel's amputation did not meet or equal a listed impairment. In response to claimant's appeal, however, the Commissioner contends that the evidence of record does not support a conclusion that Gabriel was not able to ambulate effectively. Specifically, he cites evidence concerning Gabriel's ability to: (1) walk three or four blocks; (2) take walks three times a week; (3) shop at a neighborhood convenience store; (4) go to a social club once a week; (5) work part-time in three-to four-hour shifts in a grocery store seafood department; (6) take a bus to work; (7) work part-time at a concession stand at the Verizon Wireless Arena. He also cites Dr. Wolf's observation that Gabriel was able to ambulate, and to a medical note—developed during an emergency room visit for abdominal pain—indicating that Gabriel was able to maneuver well. The Commissioner further notes Dr. DeBorja's residual functional capacity assessment, described above. Finally, in reliance upon Seavey [v. Barnhard], 276 F.3d [1, 10 (1st Cir. 2001)], the Commissioner points out that any conflicts in the evidence were for the ALJ to resolve.

The problem with the Commissioner's position is that the ALJ did not resolve the conflicts in the evidence on this issue because, as in *Audler v. Astrue*, "[t]he ALJ did not identify the listed impairment for which [Gabriel]'s symptoms fail[ed] to qualify, nor did [he] provide any explanation as to how [he] reached the conclusion that [Gabriel]'s symptoms are insufficiently severe to meet any listed impairment." 501 F.3d 446, 448 (5th Cir.2007). As the *Audler* court explained, "[s]uch a bare conclusion is beyond meaningful judicial review." * * *

* * *

In *Audler*, the court held that the ALJ's failure to provide findings and analysis to support a step-three determination was not harmless. Consequently, the court of appeals remanded the case to the district court with instructions to remand to the Commissioner. As in *Audler*, the ALJ's error in this case is not harmless. While the ALJ determined that Gabriel had the residual functional capacity to perform sedentary work, that determination, no matter how well founded, does not support the step-three determination that stump complications from Gabriel's amputation did not render him disabled under listing 1.05. Moreover, given the definition of "functional loss ... as the inability to ambulate effectively *on a sustained basis*," 20 C.F .R. § 404, Subpt. P, Appx. 1, § 1.00B2a (emphasis added), any determination that Gabriel was able to ambulate effectively on a sustained basis would have to take into account his testimony that six hours of prosthesis use gives him blisters and that he would have great difficulty using his prosthesis for two six-hour days in a row. *See Audler*, 501 F.3d at 448. At least on the face of it, it would not seem that a person who is able to use his prosthesis for no more than six hours out of every forty-eight is able to ambulate effectively on a sustained basis.

The ALJ did say that he found Gabriel's testimony about blistering less than credible because there was no evidence that he had ever been seen by a doctor or treated for blistering or any other side-effects of prolonged use of his prosthesis. But, on the other hand, the ALJ did not mention, much less find incredible, Gabriel's explanation that he had no blistering when he saw Dr. Wolf because he was making a concerted effort to avoid stressing his stump at the time of the examination. To make a sustainable step-three determination, the Commissioner must consider Gabriel's explanation for the lack of medical documentation of his blistering and, if appropriate, explain why he finds that explanation to lack credibility. Then, it will be necessary to make further findings concerning the circumstances under which Gabriel is subject to blistering of his stump due to prosthesis use and then determine whether, in light of those findings, Gabriel is or is not able to ambulate effectively on a sustained basis.

To conclude, because the ALJ presented no findings or analysis to support his step-three determination, this case must be remanded. Of course, it goes without saying that if Gabriel is not disabled, he should not be awarded benefits. But, on the other hand, if he is disabled, it seems unfair for him to be denied benefits simply because he has found ways to minimize the stump complications associated with wearing his prosthesis.

* * *

C) CARDIOVASCULAR SYSTEM IMPAIRMENTS

Another commonly used set of listings in the Listing of Impairments is Section 4 on cardiovascular system impairments. Those listings are described generally below, followed by a case involving the specific listing for chronic heart failure.

Cardiovascular impairment results from one or more of four consequences of heart disease: chronic heart failure, central cyanosis, syncope or near syncope due to poor cerebral perfusion, and discomfort or pain due to myocardial ischemia. *See generally* 20 C.F.R. Part 404 Subpart P Appx

1 § 4.00 (Listings). The listings place more emphasis on functional limitations, as opposed to diagnosis, which increases the importance of a claimant's response to a therapy regimen prescribed by the claimant's treating physician. Accordingly, a longitudinal record of therapy and observations over a period of at least three months will "usually" be required to make a determination. 20 C.F.R. Part 404 Subpart P Appx 1 § 4.00A (Listings).

The introduction to Section 4 covers the objective tests that SSA may require when evaluating disabilities arising from the cardiovascular system. The electrocardiogram (ECG, referred to sometimes also by the German abbreviation EKG) is perhaps the most important type of laboratory test used in examining the cardiovascular system. An ECG is an external recording of the electrical activity of the heart taken either at rest or while exercising, and should be interpreted by a physician who is thoroughly familiar with the meaning of the various abnormalities heart disease can produce in the heart's electrical activity. These tests are important enough that under certain circumstances SSA will purchase them in order to make a disability determination. 20 C.F.R. Part 404 Subpart P Appx 1 § 4.00B(5) (Listings). On the other hand, SSA will not purchase cardiac catheterization studies, an invasive test that evaluates coronary arteries by injecting contrast dye into them, but will consider the results of such tests as part of the evaluation process. *See* 20 C.F.R. Part 404 Subpart P Appx 1 § 4.00B(6) (Listings).

Specific listed impairments include ischemic heart disease, recurrent arrhythmias, cardiac transplantation, aneurysm of the aorta or its major branches, and peripheral vascular disease. Although not given its own listing, the preface to this section of the Listing recognizes obesity as a contributing factor to cardiovascular impairments. *See* 20 C.F.R. Part 404 Subpart P Appx 1 § 4.00I(1) (Listings). Among the more important listed cardiovascular system impairments is chronic heart failure. 20 C.F.R. Part 404 Subpart P Appx 1 § 4.02 (Listings). Heart failure results when the heart cannot pump enough blood to meet the body's needs. The listing includes a series of detailed tests and findings. It must be documented by appropriate imaging and must result in at least one category of functional effects, such as the inability to initiate, sustain, or complete activities of daily living.

MEJIA V. ASTRUE

719 F. Supp. 2d 328, 159 Soc. Sec. Rep. Serv. 367 (S.D.N.Y. 2010)

ANDREW J. PECK, United States Magistrate Judge:

Pro se plaintiff Joseph Mejia brings this action pursuant to § 205(g) of the Social Security Act (the "Act") challenging the final decision of the Commissioner of Social Security ("the Commissioner") denying Mejia Disability Insurance Benefits and Supplemental Security Income Benefits.

The Commissioner has moved for judgment on the pleadings pursuant to Fed. R. Civ. P. 12(c). The parties have consented to decision of this case by a Magistrate Judge pursuant to 28 U.S.C. 636(c).

For the reasons set forth below, the Commissioner's motion for judgment on the pleadings is *GRANTED.*

FACTS

Procedural Background

On November 2, 2007, Mejia applied for both Social Security Disability Insurance Benefits and Supplemental Security Income Benefits, alleging that he was disabled since October 16, 2007. In his application, Mejia claimed to suffer from "heart failure" and "high blood pressure." On March 12, 2008, the Social Security Administration ("SSA") conducted an initial review of Mejia's claim and found that he was not disabled. On May 13, 2008, Mejia requested an administrative hearing.

* * *

The issue before the Court is whether the Commissioner's decision, that Mejia was not disabled between October 16, 2007 and May 28, 2009, is supported by substantial evidence. The Court finds that it was.

* * *

ANALYSIS

* * *

II. *APPLICATION OF THE FIVE STEP SEQUENCE TO MEJIA'S CLAIMS*

* * *

C. *Mejia Did Not Have A Disability Listed in Appendix 1 of the Regulations*

The third step of the five-part test requires a determination of whether Mejia had an impairment listed in Appendix 1 of the Regulations. "These are impairments acknowledged by the [Commissioner] to be of sufficient severity to preclude gainful employment. If a claimant's condition meets or equals the 'listed' impairments, he or she is conclusively presumed to be disabled and entitled to benefits." Dixon v. Shalala, 54 F.3d 1019, 1022 (2d Cir.1995).

Based on the medical record, ALJ Arzt correctly determined that Mejia suffered from both hypertension and controlled congestive heart failure resulting from idiopathic cardiomyopathy. ALJ Arzt found, however, that while Mejia's medically determinable impairments were "severe," he did "not have an impairment or combination of impairments that meets or medically equals one of the listed impairments in 20 CFR Part 404, Subpart P, Appendix 1." The medical evidence supports that finding.

1. *Cardiomyopathy*

Cardiomyopathy is evaluated under Section 4.00 of Appendix 1, as explained in the section entitled "Evaluating Other Cardiovascular Impairments":

> Cardiomyopathy is a disease of the heart muscle. The heart loses its ability to pump blood (heart failure), and in some instances, heart rhythm is disturbed, leading to irregular heartbeats (arrhythmias). Usually, the exact cause of the muscle damage is never found (idiopathic cardiomyopathy).... We will evaluate cardiomyopathy under [§§] 4.02, 4.04, 4.05 or 11.04, depending on its effects on you.

20 C.F.R., Pt. 404, Subpt. P, App. 1, § 4.00(H)(3). Because there is no evidence in the record that Mejia was diagnosed with or suffered from any of the conditions listed in sections 4.04 (ischemic heart disease), 4.05 (recurrent arrhythmias) or 11.04 (central nervous system vascular accident), for Mejia's cardiomyopathy to qualify as listed impairment, it must satisfy section 4.02 (chronic heart failure). Section 4.02 requires the following:

> 4.02 Chronic heart failure while on a regimen of prescribed treatment, with symptoms and signs described in 4.00D2 [easy fatigue, weakness and shortness of breath]. The required level of severity for this impairment is met when the requirements in both A and B are satisfied.
>
> A. Medically documented presence of one of the following:
>
> 1. Systolic failure (see 4.00D1a(i)), with left ventricular end diastolic dimensions greater than 6.0 cm or ejection fraction of 30 percent or less during a period of stability (not during an episode of acute heart failure); or
>
> 2. Diastolic failure (see 4.00D 1a(ii)), with left ventricular posterior wall plus septal thickness totaling 2.5 cm or greater on imaging, with an enlarged left atrium greater than or equal to 4.5 cm, with normal or elevated ejection fraction during a period of stability (not during an episode of acute heart failure);

AND

B. Resulting in one of the following:

1. Persistent symptoms of heart failure which very seriously limit the ability to independently initiate, sustain, or complete activities of daily living in an individual for whom an MC, preferably one experienced in the care of patients with cardiovascular disease, has concluded that the performance of an exercise test would present a significant risk to the individual; or

2. Three or more separate episodes of acute congestive heart failure within a consecutive 12–month period (see 4.00A3e), with evidence of fluid retention (see 4.00D2b(ii)) from clinical and imaging assessments at the time of the episodes, requiring acute extended physician intervention such as hospitalization or emergency room treatment for 12 hours or more, separated by periods of stabilization (see 4.00D4c); or

3. Inability to perform on an exercise tolerance test at a workload equivalent to 5 METs or less due to:

a. Dyspnea, fatigue, palpitations, or chest discomfort; or

b. Three or more consecutive premature ventricular contractions (ventricular tachycardia), or increasing frequency of ventricular ectopy with at least 6 premature ventricular contractions per minute; or

c. Decrease of 10 mm Hg or more in systolic pressure below the baseline systolic blood pressure or the preceding systolic pressure measured during exercise (see 4.00D4d) due to left ventricular dysfunction, despite an increase in workload; or

d. Signs attributable to inadequate cerebral perfusion, such as ataxic gait or mental confusion.

20 C.F.R., Pt. 404, Subpt. P, App. 1, § 4.02.

Even if the chronic shortness of breath and easy fatigue that Mejia claims to suffer satisfies § 4.00(D)(2)(i)'s list of signs and symptoms, Mejia's condition does not satisfy subsections 4.02(A) or (B), much less satisfy both of those subsections.

As to subsection 4.02(A), the medical record does not support a finding of either systolic or diastolic failure.[1] With regard to § 4.02(A)(1), sys-

---

[1] Systolic failure, the inability of the heart to contract normally and expel sufficient blood is characterized by a dilated, poorly contracting left ventricle and reduced ejection fraction. 20

tolic failure, the medical record must evidence left ventricular end diastolic dimensions greater than 6.0 cm or ejection fraction of 30 percent or less. 20 C.F.R., Pt. 404, Subpt. P, App. 1, § 4.02(A)(1). Mejia's October 2007 echocardiogram, however, revealed a left ventricular end diastolic measurement of 5.6 cm, which is less than § 4.02(A)(1)'s 6 cm threshold, and Mejia had an ejection fraction of 35 to 40 percent, which is above § 4.02(A)(1)'s requisite 30 percent or less.

As to § 4.02(A)(2), although Mejia's combined left ventricular posterior and septal wall thickness totals 3.4 cm, placing him in § 4.02(A)(2)'s 2.5 cm or greater range, his left atrium measurement of 3.8 cm is less than the 4.5 cm or greater needed to qualify for diastolic failure under § 4.02(A)(2). Moreover, Mejia's 35 to 40 percent ejection fraction is below the requisite normal range.[2] Accordingly, Mejia does not satisfy subsection 4.02(A).

In addition, Mejia does not meet subsection 4.02(B)'s requirements. With respect to § 4.02(B)(1), Mejia's NYHA Class II symptoms, which place only mild limitation[s] on [his daily] activit[ies], do not rise to the level of [p]ersistent symptoms of heart failure which very seriously limit the ability to independently initiate, sustain, or complete activities of daily living. 20 C.F.R., Pt. 404, Subpt. P, App. 1, § 4.02(B)(1). Indeed, Mejia reported that he engaged in a range of daily activities, including shopping, household chores, cooking and socializing. Also, § 4.02(B)(1) applies where a doctor concludes the patient cannot safely perform an "exercise test," and Mejia had such a stress exercise test.

As to subsection 4.02(B)(2)'s requirement that the patient have at least three documented occurrences of acute congestive heart failure requiring extensive hospitalization or treatment, Mejia's record is devoid of any such instances. Likewise, Mejia did not satisfy subsection 4.02(B)(3)'s requirement that the patient have an "inability to perform on an exercise tolerance test at a workload equivalent to 5 METs or less," because Mejia exercised to a maximum of 13.5 METs during his November 2007 stress test.

Accordingly, substantial evidence supports ALJ Arzt's determination that Mejia's controlled congestive heart failure resulting from an idiopathic cardiomyopathy does not meet the Listing requirements.

C.F.R., Pt. 404, Subpt. P, App. 1, § 4.00(D)(1)(i). Diastolic failure, by contrast, is the inability of the heart to relax and fill normally and is characterized by a thickened ventricular muscle, poor ability of the left ventricle to distend, increased ventricular filling pressure, and a normal or increased EF [ejection fraction]. Id., § 4.00(D)(1)(ii).

[2] A normal ejection fraction is greater than 55%. By contrast, an ejection fraction between 30% and 40% indicates moderate systolic dysfunction and an ejection fraction below 30% demonstrates severe systolic dysfunction. American Medical Association, Guides to the Evaluation of Permanent Impairment at 170; see also Sheehan v. Metro. Life Ins. Co., 368 F.Supp.2d 228, 248 n. 12 (S.D.N.Y.2005).

* * *

[The court then found that while the claimant could not perform his past relevant work (thereby moving past Step 4), there was substantial evidence to support SSA's conclusion that he was able to perform other work in the national economy and therefore was properly denied benefits at Step 5 of the sequential evaluation process.]

2. MEDICAL EQUIVALENCE TO A LISTED IMPAIRMENT

Related to simplified findings of disability made possible by meeting the requirements of the Listing of Impairments are findings of "medical equivalence" to a listed impairment. Medical equivalence findings are also made at Step 3 of the sequential evaluation process and range from being almost as straightforward as a finding that an impairment meets the requirements of a listing to being far more complex and obscure. Because of the separate disability standard for SSI claims on behalf of children under the age of 18—and in particular the introduction of the concept of "functional equivalence" for those claims—the regulations governing medical equivalence for the SSI program differ somewhat from those governing the OASDI program. *See generally* **20 C.F.R. § 404.1526[APP–REGS]** (OASDI); **20 C.F.R. §§ 416.926, 416.926a[APP–REGS]** (SSI). Most significantly, for OASDI and adult SSI claims a finding that a claimant does not meet or equal the requirements in the Listing of Impairments results in the claim moving on to an evaluation of the impact of various vocational factors at the fourth and fifth steps of the sequential evaluation process. For child SSI claims, on the other hand, the claim will be denied unless the child can show that his or her impairment either meets the requirements of the Listing or is the medical or functional equivalent of a listed impairment. Functional equivalence for Child SSI claims is discussed later in this section.

For both programs, medical equivalence can be found in one of three ways. If the claimant has an impairment included in the Listing of Impairments but the medical evidence does not match the criteria set out in the listing for that particular impairment, the impairment will be considered medically equivalent if other medical findings related to the impairment are at least of equal medical significance to those set out for the listed impairment. If a claimant has an impairment that is not included in the Listing of Impairments, medical findings relative to the unlisted impairment will be compared to those required for a similar listed impairment to determine whether the medical findings relative to the unlisted impairment are at least of equal medical significance to those set out for the selected listed impairment. And finally, if the claimant has a number of impairments, none of which meet or equal the requirements of any listed impairment, the medical findings for all of the claimant's impairments will be combined to determine whether the combined medical findings are at least of equal medical significance to those set out for a "closely analogous" listed impairment. 20 C.F.R. §§ 404.1526(a), 416.926(a).

As with findings that an impairment meets the requirements of a listing, medical equivalence findings are based exclusively on medical evidence. This evidence, which includes symptoms, signs, and laboratory findings, must be supported by medically acceptable diagnostic techniques. When assessing a claim for medical equivalence, SSA will also consider the medical opinion of its medical or psychological consultants. 20 C.F.R. §§ 404.1526(b), 416.926(b).

The most common—and most difficult—medical equivalence claims are those that involve a combination of impairments, especially when pain and subjective complaints are involved. First of all, one must pull together a variety of otherwise insufficient medical findings relating to what are often quite different types of medical conditions. And then those findings must not only be shown to establish listings-level severity (that is, preclude engaging in "any gainful activity"), but they must also be tied somehow to a "closely analogous" listed impairment. A certain amount of precision is required to present this proof effectively and, as shown in the next case, a medical expert can be particularly helpful. As illustrated in the second of the following two cases, additional pain—even an extraordinary amount—cannot be considered separately when pain is already one of the criteria for the listed impairment relative to which a claimant wishes to show medical equivalence.

AUBUCHON V. BARNHART

403 F. Supp.2d 152, 108 Soc. Sec. Rep. Serv. 438 (D. Mass. 2005)

NIEMAN, United States Magistrate Judge.

This matter is before the court pursuant to 42 U.S.C. §§ 405(g) and 1383(c)(3) which provide for judicial review of a final decision by the defendant, the Commissioner of the Social Security Administration (the "Commissioner"), regarding an individual's entitlement to Supplemental Security Income ("SSI") and Social Security Disability Insurance ("SSDI") benefits. The action is brought by Roger Aubuchon (hereinafter "Plaintiff") on behalf of his son, David Aubuchon (hereinafter "Aubuchon"), who died on October 8, 2004. Plaintiff alleges that the Commissioner's decision denying Aubuchon SSI and SSDI benefits for a closed period of time between December 31, 1999, and August 16, 2001—memorialized in a May 28, 2004 decision by an administrative law judge—is not supported by substantial evidence and is predicated on errors of law. Plaintiff, via a motion for judgment on the pleadings, has moved to reverse or remand the decision and the Commissioner has moved to affirm.

* * *

II. Background

Aubuchon, born on March 24, 1959, completed high school and thereafter trained to be a machine operator. His prior relevant work included unskilled manual labor requiring medium to heavy exertion levels. He had also served as a maintenance man in the apartment complex where he lived prior to moving in with his parents in 1999.

Aubuchon initially claimed to be disabled beginning September 2, 1997, the day he stopped working. He later amended that onset date to December 31, 1999, his last insured date for SSDI purposes. Further procedural background follows a brief description of Aubuchon's medical history.

A. *Aubuchon's Medical History*

In 1997, Aubuchon fell from a ladder at work and injured his back. He did not suffer any broken bones and continued to work. Two years later, in June of 1999, Aubuchon visited the emergency room complaining of chronic low back pain radiating down his left leg. He was referred to doctors at Baystate Medical Center's Internal Medicine Clinic.

Aubuchon visited his primary care physician, Dr. Claudia Martorel, on September 7, 1999, and reported leg and back complaints as well as occasional urinary incontinence. Dr. Martorel, detecting alcohol on Aubuchon's breath and noting his reported alcohol abuse, ordered liver testing. That testing showed elevated liver functioning indicative of liver disease. In addition, Aubuchon was found to be anemic with a hematocrit of 29.9%.

On January 12, 2000, Dr. Marc Linson, a spinal surgeon, examined Aubuchon, who had reported that his back and leg pain worsened when he sat, stood, walked, coughed and sneezed. Dr. Linson noted that Aubuchon had a significantly decreased range of spinal motion as well as sensory loss in his left leg and foot.

On April 21, 2000, Aubuchon was examined by Dr. John Daly at Baystate's Pain Management Clinic. Dr. Daly diagnosed Aubuchon with lumbar discogenic pain secondary to a lumbar annular tear. A follow-up examination on May 17, 2000, showed no change in Aubuchon's condition. Dr. Daly described Aubuchon as having a persistent, antalgic gait, i.e., movements adapted to reduce pain, along with restricted range of motion, flexion, and extension. In addition, Aubuchon's lower back muscles were found to be tender.

During the summer of 2000, Aubuchon attended physical therapy sessions at Mercy Hospital's Weldon Center. Staff there prescribed a cane, which Aubuchon began using on July 26, 2000.

On January 19, 2001, Aubuchon again visited Dr. Martorel who noted his chronic back pain and anemia. Dr. Martorel cautioned Aubuchon about continued alcohol use and referred him to a neurosurgeon, Dr. Christopher Comey. When Aubuchon declined surgery, Dr. Comey referred him back to the Pain Management Clinic.

Dr. Arul Verghis examined Aubuchon at the Pain Management Clinic on February 9, 2001. Dr. Verghis noted that Aubuchon exhibited pain upon straight leg raising on the left side as well as decreased ankle reflexes, decreased sensation and decreased strength in all muscles of his left lower extremity. In addition, Aubuchon continued to walk with an antalgic gait. Dr. Verghis prescribed spinal steroid injections and the first injection was given during that visit. The second and last injection was given on March 26, 2001. Four days later, Dr. Martorel prescribed a megadose of Neurontin for pain control plus other medications.

On August 17, 2001, Aubuchon was hospitalized at Baystate Medical Center with acute liver disease-chronic hepatitis C and cirrhosis of the liver. Upon admission, Aubuchon exhibited "huge esophageal varices" that required extensive banding to stop the bleeding. He remained at the hospital for over two weeks. The banding procedure needed to be repeated in January of 2002 as he continued to be notably anemic. As indicated, Aubuchon died from liver disease in October of 2004.

* * *

III. *Discussion*

* * *

B. *Plaintiff's Challenge to the ALJ's Decision*

Plaintiff claims that the ALJ's decision is not based on substantial evidence of record and is predicated on errors of law. In the court's view, two of Plaintiff's more specific arguments carry weight sufficient to warrant reversal: (1) that the ALJ failed at step two of the sequential analysis to consider Aubuchon's liver disease as a "severe" impairment, and (2) that the ALJ should have deemed Aubuchon's impairments, in combination, to be medically equivalent to a listed impairment at step three.

* * *

2. Step Three

As described, a claimant will be deemed "automatically disabled" if he has "an impairment equivalent to a specific list of impairments in the regulations' Appendix 1." Thus, it is not necessary that an impairment actually be listed, only that it be deemed "medically equivalent." See 20 C.F.R. §§ 404.1526(a), 416.926(a) (2005). In the court's view, the ALJ failed to conclude that Aubuchon met the medical equivalency test at step three.

In determining medical equivalence, the SSDI and SSI regulations provide that the Commissioner will compare the listed impairments with "the symptoms, signs, and laboratory findings" exhibited by the impairment which the claimant, in fact, possesses. 20 C.F.R. §§ 404.1526(a), 416.926(a) (2005). Under SSDI, if a claimant has "more than one impairment, and none of them meets or equals a listed impairment," the Commissioner is required to review the claimant's impairments together "to determine whether the combination of [his] impairments" demonstrates medically equivalency. 20 C.F.R. § 404.1526(a) (2005) (emphasis added). Similar language is used in the SSI regulations:

> If you have an impairment that is not described in the Listing of Impairments in appendix 1, or you have a combination of impairments, no one of which meets or is medically equivalent to a listing, we will compare your medical findings with those for closely analogous listed impairments. If the medical findings related to your impairment(s) are at least of equal medical significance to those of a listed impairment, we will find that your impairment(s) is medically equivalent to the analogous listing.

20 C.F.R. § 416.926(a)(2) (2005).

In the instant case, Dr. Solomon provided uncontroverted testimony that Aubuchon's impairments, when viewed in combination, were medically equivalent to a listed impairment, most notably Listing 5.05 which applies to chronic liver disease. See 20 C.F.R. Pt. 404, Subpt. P, App. 1 § 5.05 (2005). It is significant that Dr. Solomon was called as a medical expert by the ALJ himself, that no other physician testified at the hearing, and that Dr. Solomon affirmed that he was able to review all of Aubuchon's medical records. To be sure, Dr. Solomon opined that Aubuchon did not meet a listed impairment during the relevant time frame. However, Dr. Solomon did testify about equivalency, in particular, that "the combination" of Aubuchon's impairments medically equaled a listed impairment. This testimony appears to have been ignored by the ALJ.

Dr. Solomon repeatedly testified in response to questions posed by the ALJ that Aubuchon's liver disease, in combination with his back problems, was medically equivalent to a listed impairment, even though neither may have been a listed impairment:

Q....[H]ow would [Aubuchon's] back problem supplement that portion of the [liver disease] listing which is not met? How does it—

A. Well, my view of it is that they both contribute to his—to a, a physical impairment. So while it doesn't meet the particular listing, it's *the combination is of a severity—*

.....

A.... *[T] hey both contribute to his global impairment.*

.....

Q. Was that your understanding of what equaling a listing would be? Looking at, at a global situation, but without being able to relate to a specific—

A.... My, my impression is that it's—can be multiple systems that would equal an impairment and not-doesn't have to be a particular system that's, that's been made equal by another disorder. *My impression was that the two would affect his ability to function in combination that would be equal to this list-to a listing.*

([Administrative Record] at 450, 451–52 (emphasis added).) This testimony was clear, undisputed and in line with the regulations. Granted, as the ALJ noted, Aubuchon struggled with alcohol abuse. But Dr. Solomon limited himself to the impairments for which a disability may be determined via the listings, i.e., Aubuchon's back impairments in combination with his liver disease.

Like Plaintiff, the court is somewhat perplexed that the ALJ did not grasp the concept of equivalency which Dr. Solomon applied. For example, during his questioning, the ALJ seemed to imply that Aubuchon's impairments were to be viewed in isolation or had to correspond exactly with a listed impairment:

Q. So I'm a little bit confused. What listing is met then?

A. What you say—

Q. What listing is met?

A. None is met at this time.

Q. Did you say he did meet a list oh, none is met? Oh, I'm sorry.

A. None is met as far as I can tell. But the combination equals

Q. Okay. Now, that, I guess I—and which listing would you say it would be equal?

A. Yeah. I think it equals 5.05. In-not because of the—I mean, it's clear that he does have the chronic liver disease. But he, at the time, he did, he did have abnormalities of his enzymes. But he doesn't meet all the listings. And I don't—we don't have any information what his albumin was.

Q. Oh, I guess what I'm not clear on is—

A. But would—

Q.—how would [his] back problem supplement that portion of the listing which is not met? How does it—

A. Well, my view of it is that they both contribute to his—to a, a physical impairment. So while it doesn't meet the particular listing, it's the combination is of a severity—

(A.R. at 450–51. See also id. at 24 (ALJ opining that Dr. Solomon "somehow tried to contort the back problems in with the liver problems for the equivalent of subsection 3 under Listing Section 5.05F").) Whatever uncertainty the ALJ expressed, the regulations, as described, allow medical equivalency to be established by the combination of non-listed impairments. That is exactly the situation here.

In short, Dr. Solomon testified and concluded that the combination of Aubuchon's impairments constituted medical equivalency. Since his testimony was unrebutted, Aubuchon should have been deemed automatically disabled at step three. As a result, the court has no choice but to find Aubuchon eligible for SSI and SSDI benefits for the period between December 31, 1999, and August 16, 2001.

* * *

MARCINIAK v. SHALALA

49 F.3d 1350, 47 Soc.Sec.Rep.Ser. 146 (8th Cir. 1995)

Before Hansen, Circuit Judge, John R. Gibson, Senior Circuit Judge, Morris Sheppard Arnold, Circuit Judge.

Hansen, Circuit Judge.

Carol A. Marciniak appeals from the district court's grant of summary judgment in favor of the Secretary of Health and Human Services

(Secretary), affirming the Secretary's decision to deny her application for disability insurance benefits. For the reasons discussed below, we affirm.

At the time of the hearing before the Administrative Law Judge (ALJ), Marciniak was a 43–year-old woman with a high school education who had worked for the past ten years as a library aide in the public schools. The job coincided with the school calendar year, and on May 31, 1990, Marciniak was laid off due to staff reductions. Marciniak's application for benefits claims that her disability began on May 31, 1990, because she would not have been able to work the following school year due to her medical condition.

Marciniak has a history of scoliosis (curvature of the spine). She wore a back brace as a teenager and lived for many years thereafter without serious pain or significant medical treatment. In 1987, Marciniak began to experience increased pain in her back and neck. She then sought medical treatment and was diagnosed with adult idiopathic scoliosis, for which corrective surgery was necessary. Marciniak underwent surgery in June 1988, for spinal fusion and insertion of a system of metal hooks and rods into her spine (a procedure called Harrington rod instrumentation). After several months off of work for recovery from surgery, Marciniak began a gradual return to work.

In April 1990, Marciniak was injured at work from a fall in which she twisted her neck and back. She returned to work two days after the incident and continued working until laid off on May 31, 1990.

In October 1990, a small disc herniation was discovered when Marciniak sought treatment for increased back pain. She was advised to continue a general exercise program and to return to work, avoiding activity that would require repeated neck movements or maintaining her neck in a fixed period for an extended period of time (however, her job had already been terminated).

In April 1991, Marciniak was examined by Dr. Person in connection with a worker's compensation eligibility claim. She complained of headaches, shoulder pain, back pain, spinal pain, and numbness in her fingers. Dr. Person noted that she had been taking primarily aspirin for pain, Hydrocordon for severe pain, and she was walking two miles a day for exercise. Dr. Person diagnosed Marciniak with thoracolumbar scoliosis with multiple-level arthritis and a degenerative disc disease. In his opinion, Marciniak "qualified as having a disability as set forth in the listing of impairments from May 1990 to the present." In the same breath, however, Dr. Person also indicated that Marciniak could perform sedentary work on a sustained and competitive basis from May 1990 through the date of his examination with a ten pound weight restriction and further restrictions on bending and rotating due to decreased flexibility of her spine.

Marciniak testified at the hearing that her work activities as a library aide, which required a good deal of walking, bending, and lifting, made her very sore. She testified that she can infrequently lift two to three pounds, that she can stand only 15 minutes in one place but up to an hour if allowed to move around, that she has trouble sitting for long periods of time, and that she has constant pain in her back which sometimes radiates into her legs and arms, causing anxiety, "grumpiness," and problems concentrating. Marciniak testified that she lays down as often as three times a day to manage her pain. Marciniak can no longer go grocery shopping without help, and her ability to drive a car is limited due to difficulty turning her head from side to side. She stated that she does not regularly take pain medications because she does not want to become dependent on drugs.

* * *

The ALJ found that Marciniak had severe impairments consisting of a severe small disc herniation and status post internal Harrington rod fixation but that she does not have an impairment or combination of impairments listed or medically equal to a listed impairment. The ALJ found Marciniak's subjective complaints and limitations were "[f]or the most part" credible and supported by the objective medical evidence. However, the ALJ discounted the extent of her pain, i.e., her need to sleep or rest during the day due to pain and her complaints of anxiety, irritability, and forgetfulness due to pain, because of a lack of documentation concerning these complaints. The ALJ denied benefits, concluding that Marciniak was not disabled because, although she could not perform her past relevant work, she retained the residual functional capacity to perform a significant number of sedentary jobs in the national economy.

Marciniak sought judicial review. The district court concluded that the Secretary's decision to deny benefits was supported by substantial evidence on the whole record. Marciniak appeals, contending (1) that her impairments are medically equal to a listed impairment and (2) that the ALJ improperly discredited her testimony concerning the extent of her pain and functional limitations.

* * *

"For a claimant to show that [her] impairment matches a listing, it must meet all of the specified medical criteria." Sullivan v. Zebley, 493 U.S. 521, 530, 110 S.Ct. 885, 891, 107 L.Ed.2d 967 (1990). Marciniak concedes that her impairment does not meet all of the medical criteria for any listed impairment but contends that in combination, her impairments are medically equal to the "Disorders of the Spine" impairment listed at section 1.05(C), which is described as follows:

> C. Other vertebrogenic disorders (e.g., herniated nucleus puplosus, spinal stenosis) with the following persisting for at least 3 months despite prescribed therapy and expected to last 12 months. With both 1 and 2:
>
>> 1. Pain, muscle spasm, and significant limitation of motion in the spine; and
>>
>> 2. Appropriate radicular distribution of significant motor loss with muscle weakness and sensory and reflex loss.

20 C.F.R. pt. 404, subpt. P, app. 1, § 1.05(C). "For a claimant to qualify for benefits by showing that [her] unlisted impairment, or combination of impairments, is 'equivalent' to a listed impairment, [s]he must present medical findings equal in severity to all the criteria for the one most similar listed impairment." Zebley, 493 U.S. at 531, 110 S.Ct. at 891. See also 20 C.F.R. § 404.1526. Thus, the question is whether Marciniak's combined impairments present medical findings equal in severity to all the criteria for section 1.05(C).

[Editor's note: The equivalent of the listing described in this case as listing 1.05C is found in the current Listing of Impairments at listing 1.04.]

The ALJ found that Marciniak did not meet or equal the second criteria for this listed spinal disorder because medical evidence indicated no significant motor loss with muscle weakness and no significant sensory and reflex loss. Marciniak undoubtedly suffers pain and spinal impairments, but there is substantial evidence to support the ALJ's conclusion that her medical impairments do not equal the listing because there are no medical findings comparable in kind or severity to the second criteria. Marciniak's medical records indicate that her doctors noted "[no] obvious motor or sensory deficit and deep tendon reflexes were brisk and symmetrical." Thus, even if Marciniak's complaints of pain were sufficient to equal the first medical criteria under the listing, the absence of medical findings similar and equal in severity to the second criteria is fatal to her claim of medical equivalency.

Marciniak argues that the additional pain and muscle spasms from her other spinal impairments are equivalent to the second medical criteria of the listed impairment. The Seventh Circuit, however, has said that "[when] pain is one of the listed criteria, ... it cannot be used to substitute for others not satisfied." Pope v. Shalala, 998 F.2d 473, 481 (7th Cir.1993). Marciniak contends her situation is distinguishable because her allegations of additional pain originate from other spinal impair ments; she is not merely contending that her pain is so severe that it alone should substitute for other listed criteria. We remain unconvinced. We find that Marciniak's argument is indistinguishable in substance from the argument rejected in *Pope*, and we likewise reject the argument here. When pain is a criteria for a listed impairment, additional pain alone cannot substitute for other criteria which are not satisfied, regardless of its origin.

[In the remainder of opinion, the court rejects the claimant's argument that the ALJ improperly discredited her subjective complaints of pain.]

NOTE ON MEDICAL EQUIVALENCE AND OBESITY

Until 2000, obesity was a listed impairment measure by a combination of the claimants height and weight. As noted in the following excerpt from Diaz v. Commissioner, 577 F.3d 500, 145 Soc. Sec. Rep. Serv. 486 (3rd Cir. 2009), SSA made it clear when it removed obesity as a listed impairment that a claimant's height and weight could be considered in determining medical equivalence.

The claimant in *Diaz* was 40 years old, last employed as a babysitter. Her medical conditions included scoliosis, diabetes, cholesterol, asthma, high arterial blood pressure, and arthritis, which she alleged prevented her from standing for long periods of time and contributed to her having headaches, asthma attacks, and chest pains. In addition, at 4' 11'' and 252 lbs. she had been diagnosed as morbidly obese. The ALJ failed to consider her obesity in combination with her other impairments, ignoring the directive in Social Security Ruling (SSR) 00–3p (2000). The Third Circuit reversed.

* * * In 2000, the Commissioner rescinded Paragraph 9.09 of the Listing of impairments, which dealt exclusively with obesity; however, this did not eliminate obesity as a cause of disability. To the contrary, the Commissioner promulgated SSR 00–3p, indicating how obesity is to be considered. This SSR replaced an automatic designation of obesity as a Listed impairment, based on a claimant's height and weight, with an individualized inquiry, focused on the combined effect of obesity and other severe impairments afflicting the claimant: "We will also find equivalence if an individual has multiple impairments, including obesity, no one of which meets or equals the requirements of a listing, but the combination of impairments is equivalent in severity to a listed impairment." Although SSR 00–3p was superseded by SSR 02–1p (2002), SSR 02–1p did not materially amend SSR 00–3p. *See* Rutherford v. Barnhart, 399 F.3d 546, 552 n. 4 (3d Cir.2005). SSR 00–3p instructs that "obesity may increase the severity of coexisting or related impairments to the extent that the combination of impairments meets the requirements of a listing. This is especially true of musculoskeletal, respiratory, and cardiovascular impairments. It may also be true for other coexisting or related impairments, including mental disorders." Hence, an ALJ must meaning-

fully consider the effect of a claimant's obesity, individually and in combination with her impairments, on her workplace function at step three and at every subsequent step.

In *Burnett* [v. Commissioner, 220 F.3d 112 (3d Cir.2000)], we held that an ALJ must clearly set forth the reasons for his decision. 220 F.3d at 119. Conclusory statements that a condition does not constitute the medical equivalent of a listed impairment are insufficient. The ALJ must provide a "discussion of the evidence" and an "explanation of reasoning" for his conclusion sufficient to enable meaningful judicial review. Id. at 120; *see Jones v. Barnhart,* 364 F.3d 501, 505 & n. 3 (3d Cir.2004). The ALJ, of course, need not employ particular "magic" words: "*Burnett* does not require the ALJ to use particular language or adhere to a particular format in conducting his analysis." *Jones,* 364 F.3d at 505.

Citing *Rutherford v. Barnhart,* the government urges that the "ALJ's adoption of their [Drs. Merlin, Potashnik, Tiersten, and Fechner's] conclusions constitutes a satisfactory, if indirect, consideration of that condition [obesity]." [S]ee 399 F.3d at 552. Significantly, however, in Rutherford, the claimant did not assert obesity as an impairment, nor did the ALJ note, or discuss, it. On appeal, Rutherford urged that the ALJ was required to consider her obesity explicitly and, therefore, remand of the case was required. We noted that the references to obesity in the doctors' reports were sufficient to put the ALJ on notice of the impairment, which was factored indirectly, although not explicitly, in the ALJ's determination. We then concluded that Rutherford's claim would fail in any event, because Rutherford never argued that her obesity impacted her job performance.

Here, by contrast, Diaz asserted-and the ALJ specifically determined-that Diaz's obesity constituted a severe impairment. Further, we cannot conclude, as we did in Rutherford, that Diaz's obesity had no impact, alone or in combination with her other impairments, on her workplace performance. To the contrary, Diaz's morbid obesity would seem to have exacerbated her joint dysfunction as a matter of common sense, if not medical diagnosis. SSR 02–1p also underscores the interplay between obesity and joint dysfunction, mobility, and musculoskeletal function. Although in *Rutherford* we expressed some willingness to view the reference to the reports of the claimant's examining physicians as constituting adequate, implicit treatment of the issue by the ALJ, we decline to do so here, where Diaz's obesity was urged, and acknowledged by the ALJ, as a severe impairment that was required to be considered alone and in combination with her other impairments at step three.

Accordingly, the District Court's critical determination—that the ALJ's citation of reports by doctors who were aware of Diaz's obesity sufficed—was error. Were there *any* discussion of the combined effect of Diaz's impairments, we might agree with the District Court. However, absent analysis of the cumulative impact of Diaz's obesity and other impairments on her functional capabilities, we are at a loss in our reviewing function. In Burnett, we remanded to the ALJ where his summary conclusion omitted any explanation or reasoning. 220 F.3d at 119–20. We must vacate and remand here as well. Surely the ALJ, having recognized obesity as an impairment, should determine in the first instance whether, and to what extent, Diaz's obesity, in combination with her asthma, diabetes, arthritis, back pain, and hypertension, impacted her workplace performance.

577 F.3d at 503–05.

3. FUNCTIONAL EQUIVALENCE TO A LISTED IMPAIRMENT (FOR CHILD SSI CLAIMS ONLY)

As noted earlier, Child SSI claims will be denied if the requirements of the Listing of Impairments are not met, unless the claimant can show that his or her impairment (or combination of impairments) is the medical equivalent of a listed impairment—or, according to special rules for only Child SSI claims, is the "functional equivalent" of a listed impairment. In other words, the disability determination process for child SSI claims ends with the Listing of Impairments—supplemented by the possibility of finding medical equivalence or functional equivalence. As we saw in Chapter 4 and earlier in this chapter, this more limited approach to determining disability results from the different statutory standard and different sequential evaluation process used for Child SSI claims. A similar approach, but without functional equivalence, was applied to disabled spouse claims under the OASDI program before 1990 amendments to the Social Security Act and is still applied to current claims under that program for periods of disability prior to 1991. Medical equivalence under the pre–1991 standard for disabled spouse benefits is discussed briefly at the end of this chapter.

The process for determining functional equivalence is set out in detail in the federal regulations. *See* **20 C.F.R. § 416.926a[APP–REGS]**. The process calls for assessing a child's functional limitations resulting from physical or mental impairments, including impairments that are not considered to be severe. Functional limitations may include what the child cannot do—or has difficulty doing—at home, at school, and in the community. 20 C.F.R. § 416.926a(a). The child's functioning is assessed according to six domains: "(i) acquiring and using information; (ii) attending and completing tasks; (iii) interacting and relating with others; (iv) moving about and manipulating objects; (v) caring for yourself; and, (vi) health and physical well being." 20 C.F.R. § 416.926a(b)(1). Subsections (g) through (l) of the regulations describe each domain, provide examples of the activities that are assessed within each domain, and provide examples of functional limitations within each domain.

An impairment or combination of impairments will be deemed to functionally equal the listings if they result in "marked" limitations in two domains of functioning or an "extreme" limitation in one domain of functioning. 20 C.F.R. § 416.926a(a). A "marked" limitation is "a limitation that is 'more than moderate' but 'less than extreme'"; the impairment must "seriously interfere" with the child's "ability to independently initiate, sustain, or complete activities." 20 C.F.R. § 416.926a(e)(2)(i). An "extreme" limitation is "a limitation that is 'more than marked'"; the impairment must "very seriously" interfere with the child's "ability to independently initiate, sustain, or complete activities." 20 C.F.R. § 416.926a(e)(3)(i). When assessing both marked and extreme limitations, standardized test scores are used to compare the child's functioning in a specified domain with the functioning of other children in the same domain. However, the regulations state specifically that SSA "will not rely on any test score alone" and that the agency "will consider [a child's] test scores together with the other information we have about [the child's] functioning, including reports of classroom performance and the observations of school personnel and others." *See* 20 C.F.R. § 416.926a(e)(4). Finally, subsection (m) of the regulations provides some examples of impairments that functionally equal the listings.

The following two cases involve appeals on the issue of functional equivalence. The first case examines both the claimant's circumstances and the applicable regulations in all their complexity. However, not every equivalence case is complex; the second case demonstrates a relatively simpler review of functional equivalence.

ROELANDT EX REL. ROELANDT V. APFEL

125 F.Supp.2d 1138, 72 Soc.Sec.Rep.Ser. 168 (S.D.Iowa 2001)

Pratt, District Judge.

Plaintiff, William Roelandt, on behalf of his son William J. Roelandt, filed a Complaint in this Court on March 9, 2000, seeking review of the Commissioner's decision to deny his claim for Social Security benefits under Title XVI of the Social Security Act, 42 U.S.C. §§ 1381 et seq. * * *

BACKGROUND

Plaintiff filed his application for benefits on June 16, 1996. After the application was denied initially and upon reconsideration, Plaintiff requested a hearing before an Administrative Law Judge. A hearing was held before Administrative Law Judge Andrew T. Palestini (ALJ) on March 17, 1998. The ALJ issued a Notice of Decision—Unfavorable August 10, 1998. The ALJ's decision was affirmed by the Appeals Council of the Social Security Administration on January 6, 2000. Plaintiff filed his Complaint in this Court on March 9, 2000.

EVIDENCE BEFORE THE ALJ

Plaintiff's treating physician is Barry S. Barudin, M.D. whose practice is limited to pediatrics. In a letter dated September 26, 1994, to Mrs. Gray of Hoover School in Davenport, Iowa, Dr. Barudin wrote that after an examination which revealed findings consistent with [Attention deficit hyperactivity disorder], and a conversation with the school nurse and Plaintiff's father, the doctor wrote a prescription for Ritalin.

On August 19, 1996, psychiatrist Cynthia E. Hoover, M.D., wrote a report regarding Plaintiff's treatment at Vera French Community Mental Health Center between 1995 and the date of the report. Plaintiff was seen for an intake evaluation on March 29, 1995, at which time he was eight years old. It was noted that Plaintiff's mother was drug dependent and living on the streets. Plaintiff told Dr. Hoover that he was worried about his mother and about his inability to see her. Plaintiff's father described the child "as violent, and said he talked about killing himself. He went on to say that William had been fighting in school and was wetting the bed about three times a week. He was taking Ritalin SR, 20 mgs daily and Ritalin, 5 mgs at noon." Dr. Hoover wrote:

> I saw William for a psychiatric evaluation on March 29, 1995. I noted that he was on Ritalin prescribed by his family physician. It seemed his mother was drug dependent and living on the streets. He'd been switched from one elementary school to another because his behavior was out of control, and no major behavior problems were noted subsequent to the change. It seemed his behavior deteriorated markedly when he didn't take his Ritalin. Otherwise, he was noted to be compliant, calm, and conscientious. Diagnoses were:
>
> 1. Adjustment disorder with mixed disturbance of emotions and conduct;
>
> 2. Attention deficit hyperactivity disorder, controlled;
>
> 3. Fetal alcohol exposure.

On April 11, 1995, Dr. Barudin prescribed an extra 5 mg of Ritalin, "in the PM", at the advice of Dr. Hoover. On October 9, 1995, Dr. Barudin described Plaintiff as "a cooperative young man who is doing extremely well on his current dose of Ritalin."

A Mississippi Bend Area Education Agency Multidisciplinary Team Evaluation Comprehensive Assessment Summary dated March 20, 1996, when Plaintiff was in the fourth grade and was nine years and three months old, shows that on the Wechsler Intelligence Scale for Children–III Plaintiff scored a verbal IQ of 97, a performance IQ of 112, and a full scale IQ of 104. Because Plaintiff's teacher reported that Plaintiff was having difficulty completing reading and written assignments, Plaintiff was administered the Woodcock Johnson Achievement Test Revised, the Test of Written Language, and Curriculum Based Assessments to evaluate his skills. In the area of written language, Plaintiff demonstrated difficulty expressing his thoughts in a written format. His sentence structure was very simple and he made numerous spelling errors. In the area of reading, Plaintiff was below grade level. While an average student of Plaintiff's grade level was reading approximately 100 correct words per minute, Plaintiff's was able to read 43 words per minute with seven errors. Plaintiff's math teacher reported that Plaintiff does a very nice job in math class and can complete assignments at grade level.

On April 12, 1996, it was reported to Dr. Barudin that Plaintiff was having problems with his medication, especially in the afternoon, so an additional dosage was prescribed to be given at noon each day.

Plaintiff was seen for a psychiatric Evaluation by Gretchen L. Cromer, M.D. on October 11, 1996, at the request of Disability Determination Services. It was reported to Dr. Cromer that during the previous school year, Plaintiff's father was called by the school 2 to 3 times per week because Plaintiff was verbally abusive to teachers and other students. Dr. Cromer wrote: "It is notable that after starting a stimulant medication, he was described as being a 'new person.' The father believes that the medication has been helpful for the most part, although there have been some periods where the medicine did not work." Describing his son on medication, Plaintiff's father said: "The majority of time he is close to normal," but added that there were days the medicine did not seem to work. Dr. Cromer wrote that Plaintiff's mother was hospitalized for a major depressive disorder and was "said to be drug dependent with the drug of choice being Crack as well as alcohol difficulties." Plaintiff's father said that he believed that his ex-wife had used alcohol during pregnancy. On mental status examination, there was mild fidgeting, particularly with his fingers and feet and there was no evidence of homicidal or suicidal ideation. Dr. Cromer's impression was: Adjustment reaction; attention deficit disorder; and, primary nocturnal enureasis.

Records from the Davenport Community School District dated April 22, 1997, indicate that a major area of difficulty is behavior due to attention deficit disorder. Plaintiff was using Ritalin but it was necessary for him to miss the majority of his first period classes because the medication did not take effect until then. Prior to the medication taking effect, Plaintiff was highly disruptive. During the hour and a half that it takes the medication to become effective, Plaintiff was unable to concentrate on his work and was either very silly or extremely easy to anger. It was the recommendation of the staff that Plaintiff begin his school day in a special education classroom while the medication takes effect. It was also recommended that he return to the special education classroom for a time after lunch.

The record contains several pages of Detention And Supervised Study Referral Forms from Wilson Elementary School between the dates September 12, 1996 and May 8, 1997. These forms document incidents wherein Plaintiff was disruptive and aggressive. Disciplinary reports beginning with September 12, 1997 begin on page 159 of the record. These records indicate that Plaintiff was becoming more aggressive and more difficult to handle. On September 15, 1997, Roger Keester wrote: "Can't be quiet—have talked to him today, also moved his seat, still interrupts during class—distracts other students—can't be quiet—told other student he would make a welt on his face." Other reports are dated 9/15/97 & 9/19/97 (can't be quiet, disturbing other students), 9/19/97 (shoving another student after coming to class late) & 9/20/97 (refused to work and refused to report to detention room), 9/26/97 (Running and pushing students when coming inside yelling his head off, would not listen to me or calm down), 9/30/97 (I can't deal with it any longer—he is yelling, destroying his project, doing the opposite of everything I ask.), 10/3/97 (He hit a student in a conflict at breakfast. Plus sent out of music for insubordination and disruption.), 10/6/97 (fighting), 11/25/97 (sexually harassed a girl in PE class.), 12/2/97 (fighting), 12/12/97 (could not gain control and "get on task and quit talking."), 1/6/97 (refusing to follow directions and cannot control his behavior. Starting fights with other students.), 1/9/98 (pushing girls), 1/13/98 (refusing to do work, threatening teacher and other students), 2/3/98 (fighting and threatening staff), 2/2/98 and 2/5/98 (fighting with another student. "This started when William walked to Greg's desk and threw Greg's folder on the floor."). On April 29, 1998, Gina Miller wrote:

> William was a complete disruption in study hall. I began talking to him about it. He walked out of the room and began making very serious threatening statements towards me. "Fucking bitch, I'm going to kill her, I'm going to stab her and her whole family, I'm going to trash her van, I want her neck broken, her head broken, her legs broken. She deserves to be 6 feet under. I want her lungs to fill up so she can't breath." He also kicked over a chair and threw his books on the floor.

> William is receiving a 5 day suspension for his actions. We, therefore, need to reevaluate William by doing a new IEP. When a student exceeds 10 days of being suspended in a year, a new IEP needs to be done.

On the same day another teacher wrote: "William was soooo bad. Wouldn't do work. I tried to give him a pencil he refused. He wouldn't stay seated, and he wouldn't stop talking. Whistling and everything. Put paper in recycle box and part of it on the floor. The more the kids laughed at him the worse he act. He tore my attendance up and then said oops." On March 26, Gina Miller wrote that the frequency of Plaintiff's disruptions had greatly increased and that "William is making my room non-functional. He is a constant disruption!" Ms. Miller also wrote: "At this point, William's medication has not helped him in any way during school hours." On May 7, 1998, when Plaintiff returned to school after a suspension, he refused to give the teacher his pass to readmit him, walked out of the classroom and spent 11/2 hours walking the school grounds and smearing clay on the teacher's car windows. On May 8, 1998, after Plaintiff could not control himself, his father was called to take him home for the afternoon. A report dated May 15, 1998, states that Plaintiff's behavior had become worse. "The frequency of William's inappropriate behaviors has increased to the point that when he is in school, he occupies most, if not all, of my time."

Plaintiff was seen for a psychiatric evaluation by Daniel J. Huesgen, M.D. of Vera French Community Mental Health Center, on May 21, 1997. It was noted that Dr. Barudin was closing his practice and leaving the area. Plaintiff's dose of Ritalin was 5 mgs in the morning; 20 mgs of Ritalin SR at 8:30 a.m.; 10 mgs of Ritalin at 1:00 p.m., and 5 mgs of Ritalin at 4:00 p.m. With the increased dosage, "the symptoms stabilized; however, he became more irritable, perhaps depressed, and withdrawn. He was displaying more temper outbursts, and although he had not harmed anyone, the outbursts were escalating in severity and frequency." Plaintiff was still enuretic although no organic cause had been identified. It was noted that Plaintiff's mother had used drugs and alcohol throughout the pregnancy. Dr. Huesgen wrote:

> During the examination, William presented as older than his stated age. He had several dysmorphic features, including narrow bifrontal diameter grossly, nail hypoplasia, narrow palpebral fissure, ptosis, thin upper lip, flat mid-face, smooth filtrum, short nose, and unruly scalp hair. He was able to sit still through much of the interview. Affect was irritable. Eye contact was poor. Mood was slightly depressed. His speech was of regular rate. Language was normal in comprehension and fluency. Intelligence appeared average. Attention and concentration were fair to good. No suicidal ideation, hallucinations, delusions, or paranoia were elicited.

In addition to ADHD and functional enuresis, Dr. Huesgen diagnosed oppositional defiant disorder and fetal alcohol syndrome as well as "reading disorder (per AEA report)". The sustained release Ritalin was discontinued and Ritalin, 15 mgs. three times per day was pre-scribed. Because it was reported that Plaintiff's father often forgot to give him the morning dose, it was recommended that the morning dose be given at school. When Plaintiff was seen for a follow up examination on June 11, 1997, Dexedrine was substituted for Ritalin because it was reported that the effects of Ritalin tended to "wear off" resulting in significant increases in Plaintiff's impulsivity and activity. On July 21, 1997, Plaintiff's father reported that the Dexedrine was ineffective and that the father had re-started the Ritalin at the previous dose and that Plaintiff's had responded to the Ritalin and had been doing fine. Dr. Huesgen wrote:

> Regarding his functional abilities, William does not appear significantly limited in the areas of communicative, motor and social development and functioning. However, mild to moderate limitations are noted in the areas of personal/behavioral and cognitive development and functioning. Further moderate limitations are noted in the areas of concentration, persistence and pace.

Dr. Huesgen's clinical notes are in the record at pages 260 to 83. On April 27, 1998, the doctor wrote:

> As seen in the first evaluation, William has multiple disabilities. He has fetal alcohol syndrome, his mother used alcohol during pregnancy. He has all the clinical features. He has Attention Deficit Hyperactivity Disorder, Oppositional Defiant Disorder. His symptoms of HDHD are very severe and exacerbated by the fetal alcohol exposure. He also has a Reading Disorder, by the AEA report. Medication has been partially effective in alleviating symptoms, but not yet to a satisfactory degree.

> On mental status, he is fidgety and impulsive, active, cannot sit still. He is loud, rude, irritable. No tics, no abnormal movements. His affect is sullen. He denies depressed mood.

ADMINISTRATIVE HEARING

At the hearing of March 17, 1998, three witnesses testified. The witnesses were Gina Miller and Roger Keester, a teacher and associate principal, respectively, at Plaintiff's school, and Plaintiff's father. The essence of the testimony was that while Plaintiff is a likable child, because of his illness, he is unable to keep himself from talking to the point that he disturbs the normal functioning at his school. Both Mr. Keester and Plaintiff's father testified that Plaintiff's medication does not control his illness the way that they believe it should. (Keester: " ... but the meds are not working as well as they should. I think they need to be adjusted or changed or something.") and (Father: "But, he's on, I think, the highest dosage that he can take of the Ritalin for his age and his size.... I'm going to talk to [the doctor] and see if there's a different drug that we can try.")

ADMINISTRATIVE DECISION

In his decision, dated August 10, 1998, the ALJ, stated that the adjudication of the case had been delayed because of a revision of the Regulations mandated by amendments to the Social Security Act enacted by Congress on August 22, 1996. Following the three step sequential evaluation prescribed for childhood disability claims, the ALJ first found that Plaintiff's has not engaged in substantial gainful activity during any period under adjudication. Tr. at 26. At the second step, the ALJ found that the severe impairments in this case are ADHD and an adjustment disorder. At the third step, the ALJ found that Plaintiff's impairments do not meet or equal a listed impairment, and that Plaintiff is, therefore, not disabled. The ALJ found that between the date of the application and September 24, 1997, Plaintiff did not have a "marked" or "extreme" limitation in any area of functioning. Between September 24, 1997 and the date of the decision, the ALJ found that Plaintiff had a "marked" limitation of functioning in the area of social development, but that he did not have a "marked" or "extreme" limitation of functioning in any other area. In finding that Plaintiff's social behavior has not risen to the "extreme" level, the ALJ wrote:

> The medical record indicates that some of the behavior problems have been caused by erratic taking of his prescribed medication. (Exhibits 3F, 4F, 5E, 6F, 7E, 10F) Either the claimant refuses to swallow the Ritalin (Exhibit 10F), the father forgets to give his child the morning dose of Ritalin (Exhibit 6F), or the claimant takes the Ritalin off schedule (Exhibits 3E, 5E, 7E, and 10F), delaying the ameliorative affects of the Ritalin on the child's behavior.

The ALJ found that Plaintiff was not disabled as defined in the Act, nor was he entitled to the benefits for which he had applied.

EVIDENCE SUBMITTED TO THE APPEALS COUNCIL

A school report dated September 17,1998, states that Plaintiff continued to struggle behaviorally and to be a disruption both in and out of the classroom. In class, Plaintiff needed to be told to stop talking two times every minute. Plaintiff had been suspended that school year for swinging a fist at a morning supervisor when asked to get in the back of the breakfast line. The author of the report wrote: "The frequency of Williams (sic) inappropriate behaviors has and continues to increase to the point that when he is in school, he occupies most, if not all of my time." It was noted that although Plaintiff's is capable of grade level work, it was difficult to achieve due to his impulsive and distractible behavior. The teacher noted that constant reminders to stay on task become ineffective and tend to increase Plaintiff's misbehavior. It was also noted that Plaintiff needs "more time given to complete a test due to his inability to stay on task for long periods of time." On a form entitled Functional Behavioral Assessment And Behavioral Intervention Plan Summary, it was written: "William displays extreme distractability as manifested by excessive talking, inability to sit still, listen to directions or stay on task.... These behaviors result in his inability to complete work or maintain behaviors necessary to stay in class."

On October 4, 1998, Plaintiff was admitted to Genesis Medical Center in Davenport, Iowa. Dr. Huesgen wrote that on the day of admission:

> ... evidently William had a severe anger outburst. Father also reported he was "paranoid" even more than previously. Father has used this term at baseline to describe his son. He was hanging sheets over the drapes and barricading the doors, destructive at home, kicking holes in the walls, and threatening to kill a younger brother. He tore apart father's breathing machine which father uses for his own asthma medication. He stated he was hanging up sheets because he was afraid of being kidnaped. Also he reported a fear of germs and that if someone were to sneeze or cough near him he would get their germs.
>
> During the temper outburst his father restrained him for an hour and a half. During the time of restraint he would not calm down and therefore the police were contacted. During this outburst he pushed his father down. His father could not control him. He also talked about killing his brothers in their sleep with his father.

On mental status exam, Dr. Huesgen wrote:

> He appears his stated age. He has dysmorphic features: narrow bifrontal diameter, narrow palpebral fissures, ptosis, thin upper lip, flat mid face, smooth filtrum, short nose, and unruly scalp hair. He is very active, fidgety, and impulsive. He cannot sit still. His eye contact is poor. His mood is described as "fine." His affect is irritable. His speech is increased in rate but not pressured. His intelligence appears average. His attention and concentration are fair. He denies outright hallucinations. Please see above regarding paranoia. No suicidal or homicidal ideations.

The doctor stated that Plaintiff's medication had been recently changed to dexedrine and Clonidine, and that consideration was being given to the possibility that the stimulant medication was causing paranoia. Apparently Plaintiff had been hospitalized on September 16, 1998, although those records were not submitted. Dr. Huesgen stated that at the end of the previous hospitalization, Plaintiff did not want to leave the hospital so consideration was also being given to the possibility that his behavior outburst was undertaken with the goal of readmission to the hospital, "however this is not readily apparent and it needs to be reviewed thoroughly prior to discharge because of the significant reasons for which he was admitted." Dr. Huesgen's multiaxil diagnosis was:

Axis I: Attention deficit hyperactivity disorder, combined. Enuresis. Oppositional defiant disorder.

Axis II: Reading disorder.

Axis III: Fetal alcohol syndrome.

Axis IV: Lack of maternal involvement, school problems, and poor peer relations.

Axis V. GAF score is 40.

An electroencephalographic study supported a diagnosis of a seizure disorder, but the report stated that clinical correlation was required.

The Appeals Council considered the additional evidence but concluded that the new evidence did not provide a basis for changing the ALJ's Decision.

DISCUSSION

* * *

The Personal Responsibility and Work Opportunity Act of 1996 became effective on August 22, 1996. This legislation defines childhood disability as follows:

An individual under the age of 18 shall be considered disabled for the purposes of this subchapter if that individual has a medically determinable physical or mental impairment, which results in marked and severe functional limitations, and which can be expected to result in death or which has lasted or can be expected to last for a continuous period of not less than 12 months. 42 U.S.C. § 1382c(a)(3)(C)(i).

20 C.F.R. § 416.924(a) sets out a three step sequential evaluation process for childhood disability claims. At the first step, it is determined whether or not the claimant is working. If the claimant is not working, severe impairments are identified at step two. At step three, the severe impairments are compared to the childhood listings in Appendix 1 of 20 C.F.R. Pt. 404, Subpt. P. If the impairment(s) meet or equal a listing, the child is disabled. If not, then the ALJ must find the child not disabled. In

Harper v. Apfel, 2000 WL 1369507 at *3 (S.D.Ala.2000), the Court wrote: "The current standard is more stringent than that employed prior to the effective date of Pub.L. No. 104–193, given Congress' decision, as stated in the House conference report, to confine the definition of childhood disability to the first three steps of the sequential evaluation process." *Harper* then quotes from 142 Cong.Rec. H8829, 8913 (1996 WL 428614), H.R. Conf. Rep. No. 104–725 (July 30, 1996):

> The conferees intend that only needy children with severe disabilities be eligible for SSI, and the Listing of Impairments and other current disability determination regulations as modified by these provisions properly reflect the severity of disability contemplated by the new statutory definition.... The conferees are also aware that SSA uses the term "severe" to often mean "other than minor" in an initial screening procedure for disability determination and in other places. The conferees, however, use the term "severe" in its common sense meaning.

In order to be found disabled, a child must meet, medically equal or functionally equal a listed impairment. The ALJ found that the severe impairments in this case are ADHD and an adjustment disorder. In the opinion of the Court, the medical evidence in the record that was before the ALJ also establishes that Plaintiff has a fetal alcohol syndrome. Fetal alcohol syndrome is "a brain disorder of children impaired in utero by maternal alcohol consumption, some characteristics of which are 'inappropriate social behavior, memory deficits ... lack of judgment, lack of remorse for misbehavior, lying, ... unusual aggressiveness, and wide variations in learning abilities at different times.' "Devereaux v. Perez, 218 F.3d 1045, 1057 (9th Cir.2000) quoting Barbara A. Morse, Information Processing: Identifying the Behavior Disorders of Fetal Alcohol Syndrome, in Fantastic Antone Succeeds: Experiences in Educating Children with Fetal Alcohol Syndrome 26–27 (1993, Judith S. Kleinfeld and Siobhan Wescott, editors). Evidence which was made a part of the record after the ALJ's decision indicates that it is possible that a seizure disorder is also a severe impairment. Nevertheless, the Court will limit this review to a determination of whether Plaintiff's ADHD meets, medically equals or functionally equals listing 112.11 Attention Deficit Hyperactivity Disorder. This listing, in pertinent part, requires:

> A. Medically documented findings of all three of the following:
>
> 1. Marked inattention; and
>
> 2. Marked impulsiveness; and
>
> 3. Marked hyperactivity;

AND

... for children (age 3 to attainment of age 18), resulting in at least two of the appropriate age-group criteria in paragraph B2 of 112.02.

112.02 B2. For children (age 3 to attainment of age 18), resulting in at least two of the following:

a. Marked impairment in age-appropriate cognitive/communicative function, documented by medical findings (including consideration of historical and other information from parents or other individuals who have knowledge of the child, when such information is needed and available) and including, if necessary, the results of appropriate standardized psychological tests, or for children under age 6, by appropriate tests of language and communication; or

b. Marked impairment in age-appropriate social functioning, documented by history and medical findings (including consideration of information from parents or other individuals who have knowledge of the child, when such information is needed and available) and including, if necessary, the results of appropriate standardized tests; or

c. Marked impairment in age-appropriate personal functioning, documented by history and medical findings (including consideration of information from parents or other individuals who have knowledge of the child, when such information is needed and available) and including, if necessary, appropriate standardized tests; or

d. Deficiencies of concentration, persistence, or pace resulting in frequent failure to complete tasks in a timely manner.

As evidence to support his finding that Plaintiff does not medically meet or equal the above cited listing, the ALJ relied on the opinion expressed, through the completion of Childhood Disability Evaluation Form, by two psychologists employed by Disability Determination Services. Neither of these psychologists treated or evaluated Plaintiff. Rather, the psychologists reviewed the medical and educational records provided to them. Plaintiff did not come forward with any medical evidence to refute those opinions and Plaintiff does not challenge the ALJ's finding that Plaintiff does not meet or medically equal the listed impairment. Rather, Plaintiff argues that the ALJ should have found that he functionally equals the impairment, and should, therefore, be found disabled.

20 C.F.R. § 416.926a, effective January 2, 2001, states in pertinent part:

Functional equivalence for children.

(a) General. If you have a severe impairment or combination of impairments that does not meet or medically equal any listing, we will decide whether it results in limitations that functionally equal the listings. By "functionally equal the listings," we mean that your impairment(s) must be of listing-level severity; i.e., it must result in "marked" limitations in two domains of functioning or an "extreme" limitation in one domain, as explained in this section.... When we make a finding regarding functional equivalence, we will assess the interactive and cumulative effects of all of the impairments for which we have evidence, including any impairments you have that are not "severe." (See § 416.924(c).)

* * *

(1) We will consider how you function in your activities in terms of six domains. These domains are broad areas of functioning intended to capture all of what a child can or cannot do.

* * *

The domains we use are:

(i) Acquiring and using information;

(ii) Attending and completing tasks;

(iii) Interacting and relating with others;

(iv) Moving about and manipulating objects;

(v) Caring for yourself; and,

(vi) Health and physical well-being.

In order to functionally meet a listed impairment, it must be found that two of the above domains are at the "marked" level of impairment, or that one of the domains is at the "extreme" level of impairment. The Regulation defines "marked" and "extreme" as:

(i) We will find that you have a "marked" limitation in a domain when your impairment(s) interferes seriously with your ability to independently initiate, sustain, or complete activities. Your day-to-day functioning may be seriously limited when your impairment(s) limits only one activity or when the interactive and cumulative effects of your impairment(s) limit several activities. "Marked" limitation also means a limitation that is "more than moderate" but "less than extreme." It is the equivalent of the functioning we would expect to find on standardized testing with scores that are at least two, but less than three, standard deviations below the mean.

* * *

(i) We will find that you have an "extreme" limitation in a domain when your impairment(s) interferes very seriously with your ability to independently initiate, sustain, or complete activities. Your day-to-day functioning may be very seriously limited when your impairment(s) limits only one activity or when the interactive and cumulative effects of your impairment(s) limit several activities. "Extreme" limitation also means a limitation that is "more than marked." "Extreme" limitation is the rating we give to the worst limitations. However, "extreme limitation" does not necessarily mean a total lack or loss of ability to function. It is the equivalent of the functioning we would expect to find on standardized testing with scores that are at least three standard deviations below the mean.

20 C.F.R. § 416.926a (e)(2) & (3).

In the case at bar, it is the opinion of the Court that substantial evidence on the record that was before the ALJ supports a finding that Plaintiff is limited to a marked degree, if not to an extreme degree in two of the six domains listed above—attending and completing tasks and interacting and relating with others.

Regarding the ability to attend and complete tasks, the written and oral testimony from Plaintiff's teachers and father provides substantial evidence that Plaintiff is not able to focus and maintain his attention. Plaintiff is unable to filter out distractions and remain focused on an activity at a consistent level of performance absent one on one supervision from an adult. Plaintiff repeatedly becomes sidetracked from his own activities and frequently interrupts others.

Likewise, substantial evidence in this record supports a finding that Plaintiff has serious, if not very serious, problems interacting and relating with others. According to his teachers, Plaintiff is very quick to provoke fights and other incidents, such as sexual harassment, with other students and even the school staff. Plaintiff has demonstrated a marked or extreme inability to follow social rules for interaction and conversation and to respond appropriately and meaningfully at home, school and in other social situations such as at church. Plaintiff has demonstrated a marked or extreme inability to understand and tolerate others' points of view and differences.

The ALJ was concerned that Plaintiff's medication is effective in controlling his behavior, and that it is only when the medication is not taken that Plaintiff is out of control. While there is some evidence to support that conclusion, when the record is read in its entirety it becomes clear that the medication is not effective on a consistent basis. Also, Dr.

Huesgen wrote that while an increased dosage of medication may have stabilized some symptoms, Plaintiff became more irritable, depressed and withdrawn. Both Plaintiff's father and his teachers testified that even when Plaintiff takes his medication correctly, it is not consistently effective. The records submitted to the Appeals Council indicate that some of Plaintiff's behavior problems may be due to a seizure disorder. If that is true, perhaps different medication will be effective in controlling Plaintiff's problems. That situation can be addressed when the Commissioner initiates a periodic review of Plaintiff's eligibility to continue receiving benefits. In the meantime, the evidence in this record clearly supports only one finding, namely that Plaintiff functionally meets the listings of impairments and is entitled to the benefits for which he has applied.

CONCLUSION

It is the holding of this Court that Commissioner's decision is not supported by substantial evidence on the record as a whole. The Court finds that the evidence in this record is transparently one sided against the Commissioner's decision. Using the standards articulated in the congressional record cited above, it is the holding of this Court that Plaintiff's impairments are marked and severe "in [the] common sense meaning" of those words. Plaintiff has met that definition of disability from the date of his application. Substantial evidence on the record as a whole establishes that Plaintiff functionally equals a listed impairment and that he is entitled to the benefits for which he applied. A remand to take additional evidence would only delay the receipt of benefits to which Plaintiff is entitled.

Defendant's motion to affirm the Commissioner's final decision is denied. **This cause is remanded to the Commissioner for computation and payment of benefits**. * * *

BRINDISI V. MASSANARI

2001 WL 1607485, 77 Soc.Sec.Rep.Ser. 382(N.D.Ill.2001)

Kennelly, District J.

Robert Brindisi, now nine years old, has suffered repeated and persistent ear infections since before his second birthday. By the time he turned six, he had had nine different surgeries to insert or replace tubes in his ears to help drain the fluid and allow him to hear. As a result of Robert's repeated ear problems, his speech and language abilities are delayed; he was also diagnosed with attention deficit disorder, though it is not entirely clear that that disorder arises from or is related to his speech and hearing problems. Robert also appears to suffer separation anxiety.

Tina Brindisi, Robert's mother, filed a claim for Supplemental Security Income for Robert. In that application, she alleged that Robert suffered from bad hearing, delayed speech, allergies and hyperactivity; she claimed that Robert was disabled by these injuries beginning on July 6, 1992, the day he was born. The agency denied Robert Brindisi's application initially and on reconsideration, and his mother requested a hearing before an administrative law judge. * * * ALJ Caras concluded that Robert was not disabled for purposes of entitlement to SSI. The ALJ's decision became the final agency decision when the Appeals Council denied the Brindisis' request for review. * * *

In determining whether a child is disabled within the meaning of the Social Security Act, the Commissioner employs a multi-step analysis. * * *

ALJ Caras applied this analytical framework to Robert Brindisi's case and correctly concluded, at step one, that Robert, who was only six at the time of the hearing, clearly had not engaged in any kind of gainful activity. At step two, the ALJ concluded that Robert suffered from a combination of severe impairments including speech and language delays, recurrent otitis media and attention deficit disorder. The ALJ concluded that Robert's claim failed at step three, because none of those impairments met or equaled the qualifications of any impairment listed in the regulations. The ALJ then evaluated the functional limitations Robert's impairments caused and concluded that Robert had marked limitation in the area of speech and language, no limitation in the area of motor development, less than marked limitation in the area of social development, less than marked limitation in the area of personal development, and less than marked limitation in the area of concentration, persistence and pace. The ALJ considered that Robert had no chronic illnesses, is not in a structured or highly supportive setting and does not use adaptations; he also considered that Robert is taking Ritalin, with a fair degree of success and no noted side effects. The ALJ noted that Robert was prescribed speech therapy sessions, which seemed to help, but that he was not great about adhering to the therapy schedule set for him. Id. Based on all of these factors, the ALJ concluded that Robert's impairments did not result in marked and severe functional limitations. Accordingly, the ALJ concluded that Robert was not disabled.

Judicial review of the ALJ's decision is limited to determining whether the ALJ applied the correct legal standards in reaching a decision and whether there is substantial evidence in the record to support the findings. The Brindisis do not argue the former; they argue that the ALJ's decision is not supported by substantial evidence. * * *

* * *

The Brindisis also argue that Robert's impairments met or medically equaled the requirements of the impairments listed in § 112 .06 (Anxiety Disorders) and § 112.11 (Attention Deficit Hyperactivity Disorder). Assuming Robert could satisfy the primary requirements for these disorders (excessive separation anxiety for the former and marked inattention, impulsiveness and hyperactivity for the latter), he would also have to have demonstrated at least two of the following: marked impairment in age-appropriate cognitive/communicative function, marked impairment in age-appropriate social functioning, marked impairment in age-appropriate personal functioning, or marked difficulties in maintaining concentration, persistence, or pace. See 20 C.F.R., Part 404, Subpart P, Appendix 1, §§ 112.02(B)(2), 112.06(B), 112.11(B). Although Robert arguably experienced difficulties in each of these areas, there is substantial evidence in the record to support the ALJ's findings, made in the context of the functional equivalence analysis, that Robert suffered marked impairment—i.e ., an impairment that "seriously interferes with" the child's ability to function, 20 C.F.R. § 416.926a(e)(2)(i)—in only one area, the cognitive/communicative area.

With respect to social and personal functioning and his ability to maintain concentration persistence and pace, the record reveals as follows. As of June 29, 1994, Robert "enjoy[ed] playing with cars and trucks and attempts to sing along with songs he hears on TV." He is basically able to dress himself, brush his own hair and teeth and use the bathroom on his own. A February 26, 1996 pediatric speech and language evaluation from Ravenswood Hospital stated that

> Robert demonstrates decreased social interaction behavior and increased separation anxiety. He is a shy young boy who requires ample time to "warm up" to the clinician before participating in play interaction. Robert appears to get frustrated when he can not express his wants or needs and usually acts out behaviorally by getting angry, screaming, and kicking. Overall, Roberts social and behavioral skills are approximately one year below age level.... He also demonstrates inappropriate amounts of separation anxiety and poor interactional skills.

A June 1998 speech and language evaluation stated that "Robert has a difficult time separating from his parent, and requires much coaxing to participate in activities," but noted that his "[a]ttention skills appear improved since last evaluation."

Additionally, and maybe most importantly, at the hearing before the ALJ, Robert's parents testified that Robert is able to sit and concentrate when he is taking Ritalin (though not when he is off the medication). They also testified that Robert plays well with a neighbor child, and that his motor and physical activities are not limited in any way. Both parents indicated that Ritalin, which Robert had been taking for about a year at the time of the hearing, helps and resolves many of Robert's issues. Record at 196 (Ritalin helps), 198 (Ritalin helps Robert to stay quiet so that he can listen and learn), 202 ("Right now he's not on his medication but if he was, he'd be sitting there listening to you and looking at you and he probably would have answered you."; "When he's on his medication, he's fine. He'll listen. I can talk to him once. He'll do what I say. When he's off it, I've got to keep talking loud, yelling."), 203 (the Ritalin sometimes slows Robert's speech, which makes him easier to understand). Again, although this evidence shows that Robert has some limitations (at least with respect to social functioning), it also supports the ALJ's finding that any limitation he had was less than "marked."

* * *

None of this is to say that Robert is healthy. Although, as we have concluded, Robert's impairments did not render him disabled within the meaning of the law, as of the time of the hearing before the ALJ, he unquestionably had a serious hearing impairment and serious speech and language issues as a result of his seemingly constant ear infections. But the record in this case covers a distinct and finite time period, and the Court has no way of knowing whether matters have improved or deteriorated since then. Although for Robert's sake and the sake of his family we hope for the former, if he is worse off now than he was in 1998, when the ALJ issued his decision, Robert can always reapply for benefits. The fact that substantial evidence existed in 1998 to warrant a denial of benefits does not necessarily mean that the same would be true today.

* * *

4. MEDICAL EQUIVALENCE FOR DISABLED SPOUSE CLAIMS UNDER PRE–1991 LAW

As noted in Chapter 4, prior to 1991 the Social Security Act set out a stricter "any gainful activity" standard for disability benefits for spouses of wage earners under the OASDI program. That standard was implemented with a 3–step sequential evaluation process that ended with the Listing of Impairments; claimants for disabled spouse benefits would be denied unless they met or equaled the requirements of the Listing. At the time, some courts suggested a broader definition of medical equivalence for disabled spouse cases in order to bring medical equivalence determinations in line with the statutory standard. Although there are few disabled spouse claims for a period prior to 1991, the analysis sheds an interesting light on the notion of medical equivalence and listing-level severity.

Paris v. Schweiker, 674 F.2d 707 (8th Cir. 1982) was one of the leading cases on this issue. The claimant applied for disabled widow's benefits under the OASDI program. An ALJ denied her claim, the district court affirmed the ALJ, and Paris appealed. The Eighth Circuit reversed the case with respect to the widow's benefits claim and remanded with instructions that Paris be paid widow's benefits. Following is an excerpt from the case:

> * * * The test of disability for a widow claimant is more stringent than for a person claiming under wage earner status. A widow claimant must be at least fifty years old, be the widow of a wage earner who died fully insured, and have become disabled within seven years of the wage earner's death. Here, there is no dispute that Mrs. Paris was fifty-seven years old at the time of the hearing and was the widow of Charles D. Paris, who died fully insured on March 8, 1979. The only issue is whether Mrs. Paris was disabled at the time of her claim. The ALJ concluded that she was not. We cannot agree. In our view, the record clearly establishes that in March of 1979, Mrs. Paris was disabled within the meaning of the Act.
>
> To qualify as disabled, a widow claimant must be unable to engage in any gainful activity, which is determined almost exclusively on the basis of medical conditions. Specifically, a widow must have either an impairment which has been deemed sufficiently disabling by the Secretary, or a condition which is "medically equivalent" to a listed impairment. The determination of "medical equivalence" must include consideration of laboratory findings, medically observable facts and the claimant's subjective description of impairments. Subjective symptoms alone might not be sufficient, but they must be given weight especially when corroborated by clinical or laboratory evaluations.
>
> Here, Mrs. Paris concedes that no single impairment of hers is a listed impairment under the Secretary's regulations. Her contention is that the aggregate of her impairments permanently preclude her from engaging in any gainful activity. The record clearly supports her contention.
>
> [The court then described her numerous impairments and the effects of such impairments on her overall health and her daily regimen.]
>
> [There is] overwhelming evidence that Mrs. Paris's impairments have been chronic and recurring, becoming ever more complicated and requiring ever more restrictions with respect to her activity. * * *

The fundamental flaw with the government's approach is that it isolates each condition and weighs its effects standing alone. As this Court has stated:

> In evaluating whether a claimant is capable of engaging in any gainful activity it is essential that the Secretary view the individual as a whole. It is senseless to view several disabilities as isolated from one another as the medical advisers did here. Each illness standing alone, measured in the abstract, may not be disabling. But disability claimants are not to be evaluated as having several hypothetical and isolated illnesses. These claimants are real people and entitled to have their disabilities measured in terms of their total physiological well-being.

Landess v. Weinberger, 490 F.2d 1187, 1190 (8th Cir. 1974).

Viewing Mrs. Paris's conditions as a whole, we find it impossible to reasonably conclude that she is capable of any gainful activity. This standard is the core of the medical equivalence test and we find that Mrs. Paris has met it. The case is, therefore, remanded with instructions that the Secretary be ordered to pay widow benefits to Mrs. Paris based upon her 1979 claim.

674 F2d at 708–10.

D. RESIDUAL FUNCTIONAL CAPACITY (RFC)

As we have seen, the Social Security Act's definition of disability is centered on the notion of work incapacity. The various steps of the sequential evaluation process for determining disability are designed to assess a claimant's work capacity in different contexts, but always in light of the statutory disability standard. A claimant's "residual functional capacity" (often referred to as RFC) is a measure of what—despite the existence of a severe impairment—a claimant can still do in a work setting. 20 C.F.R. §§ 404.1545(a), 416.955(a).

RFC assessments come into play in the last two steps of the sequential evaluation process: determining whether the claimant can perform past relevant work, and, if not, determining whether the claimant can perform other work available in the economy. RFC is not involved at Step 3, not only because the Listing of Impairments focuses primarily on medical factors with only limited use of functional criteria, but also because claimants that meet the strict requirements in the Listing are likely to have little or no residual capacity for work. In other words, RFC is relevant only for claimants whose impairments do not meet or equal the requirements of the Listing—and therefore the sequential evaluation process regulations incorporate RFC assessments only at the fourth and fifth steps of the process. See 20 C.F.R. §§ 404.1520(e), (f); 416.920(e), (f). The determination of a claimant's RFC is particularly important in cases decided at Step 5 according to SSA's Medical–Vocational Guidelines, which are discussed later in this chapter. In such cases, the difference between one level of RFC and another can be the difference between automatic findings of disability and non-disability.

Residual functional capacity is based on a claimant's physical and mental limitations and how they affect his or her ability to work. Although the regulations state that RFC determinations also involve consideration of environmental restrictions and other non-exertional limitations, the major emphasis is on physical exertional limitations such as sitting, standing, walking, lifting, carrying, pushing, and pulling. *See* **20 C.F.R. §§ 404.1545, 416.945[APP–REGS]**. Indeed, the various levels of RFC specified in the regulations—sedentary work, light work, medium work, heavy work, and very heavy work—are defined in the regulations in terms of "physical exertion requirements." *See* **20 C.F.R. §§ 404.1567, 416.967[APP–REGS]**. Thus, the basic requirements for sedentary work are the ability to lift a maximum of 10 pounds at one time, lift or carry light objects occasionally, such as files or small tools, and walk or stand occasionally; light work requires the ability to lift a maximum of 20 pounds at one time and the ability to carry or lift frequently objects that weigh up to 10 pounds; medium work requires the ability to lift a maximum of 50 pounds at one time, and to lift or carry frequently objects weighing up to 25 pounds; heavy work requires lifting a maximum of 100 pounds at a time and carrying or lifting frequently up to 50 pounds; very heavy work requires lifting a maximum of over 100 pounds at a time and carrying or lifting frequently over 50 pounds. Persons who can perform one of these levels of work are assumed to be able to perform all lighter work levels as well.

SOCIAL SECURITY RULING SSR 96–8P (1996)
POLICY INTERPRETATION RULING TITLES II AND XVI:
ASSESSING RESIDUAL FUNCTIONAL CAPACITY IN
INITIAL CLAIMS

   * * *

POLICY INTERPRETATION:

GENERAL

When an individual is not engaging in substantial gainful activity and a determination or decision cannot be made on the basis of medical factors alone (i.e., when the impairment is severe because it has more than a minimal effect on the ability to do basic work activities yet does not meet or equal in severity the requirements of any impairment in the Listing of

Impairments), the sequential evaluation process generally must continue with an identification of the individual's functional limitations and restrictions and an assessment of his or her remaining capacities for work-related activities. This assessment of RFC is used at step 4 of the sequential evaluation process to determine whether an individual is able to do past relevant work, and at step 5 to determine whether an individual is able to do other work, considering his or her age, education, and work experience.

Definition of RFC. RFC is what an individual can still do despite his or her limitations. RFC is an administrative assessment of the extent to which an individual's medically determinable impairment(s), including any related symptoms, such as pain, may cause physical or mental limitations or restrictions that may affect his or her capacity to do work-related physical and mental activities. (See SSR 96–4p, "Titles II and XVI: Symptoms, Medically Determinable Physical and Mental Impairments, and Exertional and Nonexertional Limitations.") Ordinarily, RFC is the individual's *maximum* remaining ability to do sustained work activities in an ordinary work setting on a **regular and continuing** basis, and the RFC assessment must include a discussion of the individual's abilities on that basis. A "regular and continuing basis" means 8 hours a day, for 5 days a week, or an equivalent work schedule.[2] RFC does not represent the *least* an individual can do despite his or her limitations or restrictions, but the *most*.[3] * * *

The RFC Assessment Must be Based Solely on the Individual's Impairment(s). The Act requires that an individual's inability to work must result from the individual's physical or mental impairment(s). Therefore, in assessing RFC, the adjudicator must consider only limitations and restrictions attributable to medically determinable impairments. **It is incorrect to find that an individual has limitations or restrictions beyond those caused by his or her medical impairment(s) including any related symptoms, such as pain, due to factors such as age or height, or whether the individual had ever engaged in certain activities in his or her past relevant work (e.g., lifting heavy weights.)** Age and body habitus (i.e., natural body build, physique, constitution, size, and weight, insofar as they are unrelated to the individu-

---

[2]   The ability to work 8 hours a day for 5 days a week is not always required when evaluating an individual's ability to do past relevant work at step 4 of the sequential evaluation process. Part-time work that was substantial gainful activity, performed within the past 15 years, and lasted long enough for the person to learn to do it constitutes past relevant work, and an individual who retains the RFC to perform such work must be found not disabled.

[3]   See SSR 83–10, "itles II and XVI: Determining Capability to Do Other Work—The Medical Vocational Rules of Appendix 2" (C.E. 1981–1985, p. 516). SSR 83–10 states that "(T)he RFC determines a work capability that is exertionally sufficient to allow performance of at least substantially all of the activities of work at a particular level (e.g., sedentary, light, or medium), but is also insufficient to allow substantial performance of work at greater exertional levels."

al's medically determinable impairment(s) and related symptoms) are not factors in assessing RFC in initial claims.[5]

Likewise, when there is no allegation of a physical or mental limitation or restriction of a specific functional capacity, and no information in the case record that there is such a limitation or restriction, the adjudicator must consider the individual to have no limitation or restriction with respect to that functional capacity.

* * *

EXERTIONAL AND NONEXERTIONAL FUNCTIONS

The RFC assessment must address both the remaining exertional and nonexertional capacities of the individual.

Exertional capacity

Exertional capacity addresses an individual's limitations and restrictions of physical strength and defines the individual's remaining abilities to perform each of seven strength demands: Sitting, standing, walking, lifting, carrying, pushing, and pulling. Each function must be considered separately (e.g., "the individual can walk for 5 out of 8 hours and stand for 6 out of 8 hours"), even if the final RFC assessment will combine activities (e.g., "walk/stand, lift/carry, push/pull"). Although the regulations describing the exertional levels of work and the *Dictionary of Occupational Titles* and its related volumes pair some functions, it is not invariably the case that treating the activities together will result in the same decisional outcome as treating them separately.

It is especially important that adjudicators consider the capacities separately when deciding whether an individual can do past relevant work. However, separate consideration may also influence decisionmaking at step 5 of the sequential evaluation process, for reasons already given in the section on "RFC and Sequential Evaluation."

Nonexertional capacity

Nonexertional capacity considers all work-related limitations and restrictions that do not depend on an individual's physical strength; i.e., all physical limitations and restrictions that are not reflected in the seven strength demands, and mental limitations and restrictions. It assesses an individual's abilities to perform physical activities such as postural (e.g.,

---

[5] The definition of disability in the Act requires that an individual's inability to work must be due to a medically determinable physical or mental impairment(s). The assessment of RFC must therefore be concerned with the impact of a disease process or injury on the individual. In determining a person's maximum RFC for sustained activity, factors of age or body habitus must not be allowed to influence the assessment.

stooping, climbing), manipulative (e.g., reaching, handling), visual (seeing), communicative (hearing, speaking), and mental (e.g., understanding and remembering instructions and responding appropriately to supervision). In addition to these activities, it also considers the ability to tolerate various environmental factors (e.g., tolerance of temperature extremes).

As with exertional capacity, nonexertional capacity must be expressed in terms of work-related functions. For example, in assessing RFC for an individual with a visual impairment, the adjudicator must consider the individual's residual capacity to perform such work-related functions as working with large or small objects, following instructions, or avoiding ordinary hazards in the workplace. In assessing RFC with impairments affecting hearing or speech, the adjudicator must explain how the individual's limitations would affect his or her ability to communicate in the workplace. Work-related mental activities generally required by competitive, remunerative work include the abilities to: understand, carry out, and remember instructions; use judgment in making work-related decisions; respond appropriately to supervision, co-workers and work situations; and deal with changes in a routine work setting.

Consider the nature of the activity affected

It is the nature of an individual's limitations or restrictions that determines whether the individual will have only exertional limitations or restrictions, only nonexertional limitations or restrictions, or a combination of exertional and nonexertional limitations or restrictions. For example, symptoms, including pain, are not intrinsically exertional or nonexertional. Symptoms often affect the capacity to perform one of the seven strength demands and may or may not have effects on the demands of occupations other than the strength demands. If the only limitations or restrictions caused by symptoms, such as pain, are in one or more of the seven strength demands (e.g., lifting) the limitations or restrictions will be exertional. On the other hand, if an individual's symptoms cause a limitation or restriction that affects the individual's ability to meet the demands of occupations other than their strength demands (e.g., manipulation or concentration), the limitation or restriction will be classified as nonexertional. Symptoms may also cause both exertional and nonexertional limitations.

Likewise, even though mental impairments usually affect nonexertional functions, they may also limit exertional capacity by affecting one or more of the seven strength demands. For example, a mental impairment may cause fatigue or hysterical paralysis.

* * *

NOTE ON PERFORMING THE FULL RANGE OF WORK ACTIVITY

RFC assessments are quite easy when the facts correspond exactly to the specific exertional requirements for sedentary, light, medium, heavy, and very heavy work. The more difficult cases involve questions as to whether the claimant can perform the full range jobs at the relevant RFC level, especially when multiple functional requirements are at issue. Shiner v. Heckler, 608 F.Supp. 481, 9 Soc. Sec. Rep. Ser. 878 (D.Mass.1985) involved the common situation where a claimant alleges difficulty in either sitting or standing for prolonged periods of time. Mr. Shiner complained of pain in the lumbar spine and down his left thigh to the knee, as well as abdominal pain radiating from his back. Dr. Pierce, his orthopedic surgeon, diagnosed the condition as a probable lumbar compression fracture. He then referred Mr. Shiner to a neurologist and an internist to determine the cause of his abdominal pain, but no abnormalities were found. Further examinations by Dr. Pierce revealed a healing fracture at L2 and evidence of an L5 root irritation, leading Dr. Pierce to conclude that Mr. Shiner had trouble sitting or standing for any length of time." He also stated that Mr. Shiner would be able to sit and stand for a total of 1/2 hour each over a consecutive 8–hour period, and that he could not lift any amount of weight frequently during 6 hours of an 8–hour work shift. After noting that the only other relevant medical evidence consisted of a one-page form with only one box checked indicating that Mr. Shiner suffered "no significant restriction of basic work-related functions," the court concluded as follows:

> The substance of the claimant's testimony at the hearing is as follows. Mr. Shiner is able to stand only one-half hour before he feels pain and discomfort. He is able to sit only for a shorter period, it being his worst position. During questioning by the ALJ Shiner was asked if he could lift a 20 pound turkey. He responded, "If I had to, I probably could." Mr. Shiner reported that he often has the television on during the day but is unable to sit through a show without developing stomach pain.

> Sedentary work is defined in the Secretary's own regulations as work "which involves sitting, a certain amount of walking and standing...." 20 C.F.R. § 404.1567(a). Where a person is unable to sit for long periods of time he may not have the capacity to do sedentary work. 20 C.F.R. § 404.1567(b). Similarly, where a claimant has to interrupt work done in a sitting position with periods of prone rest, a finding that he can perform sedentary work is not supported by substantial evidence. Hence, a determination that a claimant is able to perform sedentary work "must be predicated upon a finding that the claimant can sit most of the day, with occasional interruptions of short duration." [Benko v. Schweiker, 551 F. Supp. 698, 704 (D.N.H. 1982)].

> By this standard, the facts in the record do not constitute substantial evidence in support of the ALJ's finding that Shiner is able to per-

form sedentary work. Aside from the medical consult form checked by Dr. Goulding who appears never to have treated or examined plaintiff, there is not a scintilla of evidence which indicates that Shiner could sit in a chair for more than one-half hour during an eight-hour shift. * * *

* * *

Furthermore, sedentary work often involves some lifting. 20 C.F.R. § 404.1567(a). The pertinent medical evidence is that Shiner has very limited lifting capability and should, in fact, refrain from any lifting at all. Shiner's statement that he could "probably" lift 20 pounds once, if he "had to" is only marginally probative of his ability to lift and carry throughout the workday.

Thus, the record necessitates a conclusion that the ALJ's finding of residual functional capacity to perform sedentary work is not supported by substantial evidence.

608 F. Supp. 484–85.

E. STEP 4: ABILITY TO PERFORM PAST RELEVANT WORK

Step 4 is the first of the final two steps of the Social Security Administration's sequential evaluation process that address two related questions. Step 4 asks whether the claimant can perform past relevant work; if the claimant can perform past relevant work, he or she is not disabled. If not, the process moves to Step 5, which asks whether the claimant can perform other work available in the national economy. If the claimant can perform other work, he or she is not disabled. Only claimants who cannot perform both their past relevant work and any other work in the national economy will be found to be disabled. *See* 20 C.F.R §§ 404.1560(b), (c), 416.960(b), (c).

Step 4 thus leads to a finding of non-disability if a claimant can perform "past relevant work." The logic behind this step in the sequential evaluation process is that a claimant's ability to perform a prior job demonstrates that the claimant can still hold a job within his or her vocational range. Of course, this makes sense as a proxy for the "inability to perform substantial gainful activity" only if the prior job amounts to "substantial gainful activity" and the claimant has retained the vocational capacity to perform the requirements of the job. Social Security regulations therefore provide that while work that a claimant has done in the past "shows the kind of work" that the claimant "may be expected to do," the agency will deny a claim at Step 4 only if the past work that the claimant can still do was "done within the last 15 years, lasted long enough for [the claimant] to learn to do it, and was substantial gainful activity." 20 **C.F.R. §§ 404.1565(a), 416.965(a)[APP–REGS]**.

1. PAST RELEVANT WORK DEFINED

In most instances, there is no disagreement about which of a claimant's prior jobs qualify as past relevant work for purposes of a Step 4 analysis. The Rulings and cases that follow address the three main issues relative to what constitutes past relevant work that deserve special consideration: first, whether the inquiry should focus on the requirements of a particular job, as opposed to the general type of work involved; second, how far into a claimant's vocational past the Administration can go before the job is no longer relevant; and third, whether work a claimant performed for only a short period of time should be considered at all.

SOCIAL SECURITY RULING SSR 82–62, 1975–1982
Soc. Sec. Rep. Ser. 809 (1982)

TITLES II AND XVI: A DISABILITY CLAIMANT'S CAPACITY TO DO PAST RELEVANT WORK, IN GENERAL

* * *

POLICY STATEMENT:

The Relevance of Past Work

The term "work experience" means skills and abilities acquired through work previously performed by the individual which indicates the type of work the individual may be expected to perform. Work for which the individual has demonstrated a capability is the best indicator of the kind of work that the individual can be expected to do. Sections 404.1565(a) and 416.965(a) of the regulations state as follows: "We consider that your work experience applies [i.e., is relevant] when it was done within the last 15 years, lasted long enough for you to learn to do it, and was substantial gainful activity [SGA]."

* * * [W]ork performed 15 years or more prior to the time of adjudication of the claim (or 15 years or more prior to the date the title II disability insured status requirement was last met, if earlier) is ordinarily not considered relevant.

An individual who has worked only sporadically or for brief periods of time during the 15–year period, may be considered to have no relevant work experience.

Capacity to do past work may be indicative of the capacity to engage in SGA when that work experience constituted SGA and has current relevance considering duration and recency.

1. SGA

The adjudicative criteria for determining whether a person has done "substantial" and "gainful" work activity are explained in sections 404.1571–404.1575 and 416.971–416.975 of the regulations.

2. Duration

Duration refers to the length of time during which the person gained job experience. It should have been sufficient for the worker to have learned the techniques, acquired information, and developed the facility needed for average performance in the job situation. The length of time this would take depends on the nature and complexity of the work.

3. Recency

Recency refers to the time which has elapsed since the work was performed. A gradual change occurs in most jobs in our national economy so that after 15 years it is no longer realistic to expect that skills (or proficiencies) and abilities acquired in these jobs continue to apply. The 15–year guide is intended to insure that remote work experience which could not reasonably be expected to be of current relevance is not applied.

While the regulations provide that a claimant/beneficiary's work experience is usually relevant when the work "was done within the last 15 years," in some cases worked performed prior to the 15–year period may be considered as relevant when a continuity of skills, knowledge, and processes can be established between such work and the individual's more recent occupations.

* * *

What the Claimant Can Now Do Physically and Mentally—RFC

Evaluation under sections 404.1520(e) and 416.920(e) of the regulations requires careful consideration of the interaction of the limiting effects of the person's impairment(s) and the physical and mental demands of his or her PRW to determine whether the individual can still do that work.

Since the severity of the impairment(s) must be the primary basis for a finding of disability, evaluation begins with a determination of the claimant's functional limitations and capacities to sit, stand, walk, lift, carry, etc. * * *

Comparing RFC with the Physical and Mental Demands of Past
Relevant Occupations

The RFC to meet the physical and mental demands of jobs a claimant has performed in the past (either the specific job a claimant performed or the same kind of work as it is customarily performed throughout the economy) is generally a sufficient basis for a finding of not disabled. Past work experience must be considered carefully to assure that the available facts support a conclusion regarding the claimant's ability or inability to perform the functional activities required in this work. * * *

* * *

SOCIAL SECURITY RULING SSR 82–61 1975–1982
Soc. Sec. Rep. Ser. 836 (1982)

TITLES II AND XVI: PAST RELEVANT WORK—THE PARTICULAR JOB OR THE OCCUPATION AS GENERALLY PERFORMED

* * *

Three possible tests for determining whether or not a claimant retains the capacity to perform his or her past relevant work are as follows:

1. Whether the claimant retains the capacity to perform a past relevant job based on a broad generic, occupational classification of that job, e.g., "delivery job", "packaging job," etc.

Finding that a claimant has the capacity to do past relevant work on the basis of a generic occupational classification of the work is likely to be fallacious and unsupportable.

While "delivery jobs", or "packaging jobs," etc., may have a common characteristic, they often involve quite different functional demands and duties requiring varying abilities and job knowledge.

2. Whether the claimant retains the capacity to perform the particular functional demands and job duties peculiar to an individual job as he or she actually performed it.

Under this test, where the evidence shows that a claimant retains the RFC to perform the functional demands and job duties of a particular past relevant job as he or she actually performed it, the claimant should be found to be "not disabled."

3. Whether the claimant retains the capacity to perform the functional demands and job duties of the job as ordinarily required by employers throughout the national economy. (*The Dictionary of Occupational Titles* (DOT) descriptions can be relied upon—for jobs that are listed in the DOT—to define the job as it is *usually* performed in the national economy.) It is understood that some individual jobs may require somewhat more or less exertion than the DOT description.

A former job performed in by the claimant may have involved functional demands and job duties significantly in excess of those generally required for the job by other employers throughout the national economy. Under this test, if the claimant cannot perform the excessive functional demands and/or job duties actually required in the former job but can perform the functional demands and job duties as generally required by employers throughout the economy, the claimant should be found to be "not disabled."

POLICY STATEMENT: Under sections 404.1520(e) and 416.920(e) of the regulations, a claimant will be found to be "not disabled" when it is determined that he or she retains the RFC to perform:

1. The actual functional demands and job duties of a particular past relevant job; *or*

2. The functional demands and job duties of the occupation as generally required by employers throughout the national economy.

* * *

ARMSTRONG V. SULLIVAN

814 F. Supp. 1364, 40 Soc. Sec. Rep. Ser. 404 (W.D.Tex. 1993)

Sparks, District Judge.

Before the Court is Plaintiff's cause of action against Louis W. Sullivan, Secretary of Health and Human Services. Plaintiff seeks to have the Secretary's decision to deny her disability and supplemental security income benefits reversed or, at least, to have the case remanded.

* * *

I. BACKGROUND

Plaintiff is a 58 year old woman, who was 55 years old at the time of the hearing before the administrative law judge (ALJ). On October 18, 1988, Plaintiff filed applications with the Department of Health and Human Services (DHHS) for disability insurance benefits and supplemental security income under the Social Security Act. At that time, Plaintiff contended she was disabled due to bursitis in her left arm, arthritis, dizzy spells, bleeding ulcers, and diabetes. On January 5, 1989, DHHS notified Plaintiff of their determination that she was not entitled to either disability benefits or supplemental security income benefits. DHHS subsequently declined to grant Plaintiff's February 21, 1989, request for reconsideration, and, on May 10, 1989, Plaintiff requested a hearing before an administrative law judge.

The hearing took place before Administrative Law Judge Harold G. Adams in Austin, Texas, on August 30, 1989. On January 10, 1990, the ALJ issued his decision that Plaintiff was not entitled to either disability or supplemental security income benefits as her impairments were not so severe that she could not perform her prior work as a cashier.

Accordingly, on June 13, 1991, Plaintiff filed this action under Section 205(g) of the Social Security Act, 42 U.S.C. § 405(g), for judicial review of the Secretary's final decision.

II. EVIDENCE BEFORE THE ADMINISTRATIVE LAW JUDGE

During the August 30, 1989 hearing, Plaintiff and a vocational expert testified. In addition, the ALJ considered a significant number of exhibits, including Plaintiff's medical records dating back to 1982.

* * * As the ALJ found Plaintiff able to perform only sedentary work, the only possibly relevant prior job is Plaintiff's prior job as a cook (medium) and cashier (sedentary) at a barbecue restaurant, which she held for nine months in late 1979 and 1980.[1]

* * *

During the August 30, 1989 hearing, the ALJ posed several hypothetical questions to the vocational expert. First, he asked if Plaintiff could perform any of the work she had done in the past fifteen years if she was limited to the extent she alleged, and considering her age, education, and previous work experience. The vocational expert answered "no" because she would be too restricted while recovering from the recent surgery. Second, the ALJ asked if he found the Plaintiff could do a full range of sedentary activities, considering her transferable skills, could she perform any semi-skilled or skilled jobs in the area or national economy. The vocational expert answered, "yes, she could perform work as a cashier, her previous employment," but not until she had recovered from her shoulder surgery. Finally, the ALJ asked if Plaintiff could do any job, light or sed-

---

[1]   Ignoring the "cook" portion of the job, which is considered medium work, the ALJ concluded Plaintiff could still work as a cashier, which is considered sedentary work.

entary, considering her transferable skills, with her current limitations. The vocational expert answered he "would say she is excluded from reasonable competitive employment, given her age ... and that limitation, in addition to the neck problem, and the lack of educational background." The vocational expert did not consider Plaintiff's psychological limitations described by Dr. Bell, as Plaintiff did not see Dr. Bell until after the August 30, 1989 hearing.

* * *

V. LEGAL ANALYSIS

* * *

In Plaintiff's case, the ALJ determined that although Plaintiff did suffer from several severe impairments, she was not disabled because she was capable of performing her prior work as a cashier. Plaintiff challenges the ALJ's fact findings as well as the legal standards he employed to make those findings. Thus, this Court must examine the record to determine if substantial evidence existed to support the ALJ's findings and must review, de novo, the ALJ's application of legal principles.

A. Exertional Demands and Limitations

1. Plaintiff's Relevant Past Work

Plaintiff's first attack is on the ALJ's decision that Plaintiff can meet the exertional demands of her "alleged" past relevant[4] work. Plaintiff contends that the ALJ erred in applying the law by separating the cook and cashier portions of her job at the barbecue restaurant and finding that her past relevant work included the job of cashier. Plaintiff also maintains that, even if the job of cashier is a past relevant job, substantial evidence does not support her ability to perform that job.

With regard to Plaintiff's contention that her job at the barbecue restaurant cannot be divided into two different jobs and that, therefore, Plaintiff would be required to meet the exertional demands of the more strenuous cook duties, the Court finds the Plaintiff is correct. Past relevant work is defined as "[t]he actual functional demands and job duties of a particular past relevant job" or "[t]he functional demands and job duties of the occupation as generally required by employers throughout the national economy." *Bowers v. Railroad Retirement Bd.*, 977 F.2d 1485, 1489 (D.C.Cir.1992); *Cowan v. Sullivan*, 1992 WL 300767, at *2 (E.D.La. Oct. 5, 1992) (quoting Soc.Sec.Rul. 82–61 (1982)). Generally, ALJs look to the

---

4   "Relevant" work is work the claimant has done in the past fifteen years and which qualifies as substantial gainful activity. See 20 C.F.R. § 404.1565(a); see also id. § 404.1510 (definition of substantial gainful activity).

Dictionary of Occupational Titles ("DOT") to determine the general duties of a particular job nationwide. According to the vocational expert, "cook" is classified as a medium strength requirement and semi-skilled position, and "cashier" (DOT code 211.462–010) is classified as a sedentary and unskilled position, although the vocational expert believes a cashier's job is also a semi-skilled position.

Generally, an ALJ may not find a claimant capable of performing his or her past relevant job, if the claimant is not capable of performing *all* of the duties of that job. See e.g., *Valencia v. Heckler*, 751 F.2d 1082, 1086–87 (9th Cir.1985) (tomato sorting was merely one of plaintiff's duties as an agricultural worker and, thus, was not her past relevant work). As stated by the Ninth Circuit Court of Appeals,

> [e]very occupation consists of a myriad of tasks, each involving different degrees of physical exertion. To classify an applicant's "past relevant work" according to the least demanding function of the claimant's past occupations is contrary to the letter and spirit of the Social Security Act.

Valencia, 751 F.2d at 1086. Plaintiff argues that the ALJ did just this and impermissibly determined she could return to her past relevant work, considering only her ability to perform the less demanding duties of a cashier and ignoring her duties as a cook. The Secretary, on the other hand, appears to argue that the cashier portion of Plaintiff's job was not merely a duty, but can be considered as an independent type of work and, therefore, considered separately from the cook portion of the job.

Although there are no circuit court cases precisely on point, two district courts faced with a plaintiff who held a "composite" job support Plaintiff's position. In *Taylor v. Bowen*, [664 F. Supp. 19 (D. Me. 1987], the plaintiff's past position was that of office worker/receptionist. *Taylor*, 664 F.Supp. at 22 n. 3. The Court held the ALJ could not find the plaintiff capable of performing her past relevant type of work on the basis she could meet the demands of a receptionist job when she could not meet the demands of a job as an office worker. Id. at 23. Similarly, in *Paige v. Bowen*, [695 F. Supp. 975 (N.D. Ill. 1988], the Court recognized that a claimant's job may not adequately correspond to the DOT's description of the job title because it entails additional duties not listed in the DOT's description, but which match those duties of other DOT listed jobs with higher exertional demands. *Paige*, 695 F.Supp. at 980–81. The Court quoted that portion of Social Security Ruling 82–61 which states:

> [c]omposite jobs have *significant elements of two or more occupations* and, as such, have no counterpart in the DOT. Such situations will be evaluated according to the particular facts of each individual case.

Id. at 981 (quoting Soc.Sec.Rul. 82–61).

Plaintiff's cook/cashier position at the barbecue restaurant is clearly such a "composite" job.[7] As the ALJ has found Plaintiff capable of sedentary work only, and there is no dispute that the "cook" portion of Plaintiff's job would be classified as medium in level even by the DOT, on remand the ALJ must determine if Plaintiff has the residual functional capacity to perform other types of work.

* * *

VI. CONCLUSION

Having found a lack of substantial evidence to support the Secretary's decision in this case, and having found application of improper legal standards, the Court ORDERS that Plaintiff's Motion for Summary Judgment is DENIED and Plaintiff's Motion for Remand is GRANTED.

The Court further ORDERS that the above-styled and numbered cause is REMANDED to the Secretary of Health and Human Services for reevaluation of the evidence, further development of the facts, and a decision in accordance with the above opinion.

NOTE

In Bechtold v. Massanari, 152 F.Supp.2d 1340 75 Soc. Sec. Rep. Ser. 216 (M.D. Fla. 2001), a vocational expert identified the prior jobs as including three separate positions: sales clerk, file clerk, and receptionist, but then re-characterized the receptionist position as telephone clerk. Noting that the position of telephone clerk involves "slightly different skills and responsibilities," the court continued:

> Whether denominated "receptionist" or "telephone clerk," however, the vocational expert's past relevant work summary, which isolated and focused on one of a number of tasks Bechtold performed as part of her prior work—answering phones—from her other duties, violates the Social Security Act.

> The bifurcation of Bechtold's prior work was necessitated by the finding of the administrative law judge that Bechtold did not retain the residual functional capacity to work as a file clerk. See Tr. 18. Thus, by treating Bechtold's occasional responsibility for answering phones as a separate position, the administrative law judge was able to conclude, at step four of the analysis, that Bechtold had the residual functional capacity to perform her past work. Such separation of Bechtold's duties is impermissible, however. Where it is clear that a claimant's past employment was a

---

[7]   In fact, from the Plaintiff's description of the job in her vocational report, it appears she also did a great deal of cleaning, which is certainly not a sedentary job.

"composite job," an administrative law judge may not find a claimant capable of performing her past relevant work on the basis that she can meet some of the demands of her previous position, but not all of them.

152 F. Supp 2d at 1345.

BARNES V. SULLIVAN
932 F.2d 1356, 33 Soc.Sec.Rep.Ser. 399 (11th Cir. 1991)

Before Fay, Johnson and Hatchett, Circuit Judges.

Per Curiam:

In this social security case, claimant Maxine Barnes appeals from the denial of disability benefits under the Social Security Act (the "Act"). After exhausting her administrative remedies, she appealed to the district court, claiming that the Administrative Law Judge improperly determined her previous work experience as a sewing machine operator to constitute "past relevant work," as defined in 20 C.F.R. § 404.1565 (1990). Because we find that the record contained substantial evidence to support the Administrative Law Judge's determination that such work did constitute "past relevant work," we AFFIRM.

Facts.

* * *

Ms. Barnes is a forty-one-year-old woman who has the equivalent of a high school education. She has also received some vocational training in mechanics. Ms. Barnes has held several jobs over the preceding years. Her experience included work as a heavy equipment operator, a construction laborer, a machinist, and a sewing machine operator. Ms. Barnes testified that her disability began in August 1982 when she hurt her back while moving scaffolding boards. She met the disability insured status requirements on the alleged disability onset date and continued to meet them through September 30, 1986.

Discussion.

* * *

Ms. Barnes contends her previous experience as a sewing machine operator is not "past relevant work" as defined in the regulations, and therefore that the Secretary's determination that she is not disabled is not supported by substantial evidence. We find, upon a review of the record, that the ALJ's determination is supported by substantial evidence.

If a claimant for disability benefits is determined to retain the ability to perform her "past relevant work," she will not be found to be disabled. 20 C.F.R. § 404.1520(e) (1990). The regulations provide that:

> We consider that your work experience applies when it was done within the last 15 years, lasted long enough for you to learn to do it, and was substantial gainful activity. We do not *usually* consider that work you did 15 years or more before the time we are deciding whether you are disabled (or when the disability insured status requirement was last met, if earlier) applies. A gradual change occurs in most jobs so that after 15 years it is no longer realistic to expect that skills and abilities acquired in a job done then continue to apply. The 15 year *guide* is intended to insure that remote work experience is not currently applied.

20 C.F.R. § 404.1565(a) (1990) (emphasis added). As applied to Ms. Barnes, Social Security Ruling [82-62] provides that the fifteen year period is the fifteen year period preceding the date the claimant's disability insured status was last met.[2] Ms. Barnes last met the disability insured status on September 30, 1986. Therefore, work performed on or after September 30, 1971, would fall within the relevant fifteen year period. Ms. Barnes claims that her job as a sewing machine operator terminated more than fifteen years ago. She therefore objects to the ALJ's use of that job as past relevant work. She claims that 20 C.F.R. § 404.1565 prohibits consideration of work done more than fifteen years ago as past relevant work.

At this point, we note that the fifteen year limitation described by the regulations does not create a prohibition against considering work outside that period. Rather, our circuit has held that the limitation merely creates a "presumption of inapplicability" of skills and abilities acquired in work performed outside the fifteen year period. *Macia v. Bowen*, 829 F.2d 1009, 1012 (11th Cir.1987). *But see Diorio v. Heckler*, 721 F.2d 726, 728 (11th Cir.1983) (ALJ considered past work "in contravention of the regulations that *prohibit* consideration of any job held more than fifteen years

---

[2] According to Social Security Ruling [82-62]:

1. When deciding whether a claimant is disabled under title II or title XVI, the 15-year period is generally the 15 years prior to the time of adjudication at the initial, reconsideration or higher appellate level.

2. In those title II cases in which the claimant's disability insured status was last met prior to adjudication, the work performed for the 15-year period preceding the date the title II disability insured status requirement was last met would generally be considered relevant, since the claimant's capacity for SGA [substantial gainful activity] as of that date represents a critical disability issue.

3. When deciding whether a title II or a title XVI beneficiary continues to be disabled, relevant past work is work he or she performed in the 15 year period prior to adjudication of the issue of continuing disability.

ago." (emphasis added)).[3] However, we need not reach this issue in this case. The record in this case supports a finding that the prior work occurred within the fifteen year period.

The record provides evidence which would allow a reasonable mind to conclude that Ms. Barnes's work as a sewing machine operator is past relevant work. In the initial administrative hearing, Ms. Barnes testified that she worked as a sewing machine operator for three years following the birth of one of her children. At the time of her testimony on February 28, 1986, she testified that she had three children, ages 17, 14, and 11. She did not provide the dates of their births. She later testified at the second administrative hearing that she worked at that job for two or three years. She was unable to remember the exact dates either time she testified.

The ALJ did not specifically analyze the applicability of Ms. Barnes's sewing experience in light of 20 C.F.R. § 404.1565(a). Nevertheless, the ALJ's finding that her sewing job was past relevant work was reasonable. Ms. Barnes's eldest child was seventeen in 1986. Presumably, she was born in 1969, perhaps as early as 1968. If Ms. Barnes did work two to three years beginning in 1968, the ALJ could have reasonably found that such work continued beyond September 30, 1971. If so, such work automatically qualifies as past relevant work under the regulations.[5] The ALJ reasonably could have concluded that Ms. Barnes was employed as a sewing machine operator through 1971. * * *

We therefore conclude that the ALJ had substantial evidence to support his conclusion that Ms. Barnes's experience as a sewing machine operator constituted past relevant work. Accordingly, we AFFIRM.

---

[3] The Fifth and Sixth Circuits have ruled that the fifteen year cutoff is not mandatory.

By the very terms of this regulation, fifteen years is not a bright-line rule but a "guide" intended to help the Secretary avoid concluding that a claimant who has worked in a job requiring certain marketable skills after the workplace has changed in its requirements. The regulation states that the Secretary does not "usually" consider work beyond the 15-year period to be applicable: giving the conventional meaning to the word "usually" means that the Secretary sometimes does look to work done before the 15-year period.

Smith v. Secretary of Health and Human Services, 893 F.2d 106, 109 (6th Cir.1989). See also Bowman v. Heckler, 706 F.2d 564, 567 (5th Cir.1983) ("In deciding whether to pretermit such dated work experience, ... the Secretary is entitled to consider the particular kind of work involved and the extent to which the skills and abilities required have in fact changed over the years").

[5] Ms. Barnes did not specify after which child's birth she began to work as a sewing machine operator. Conceivably, she could have begun her work after the birth of her second child in 1972, well within the fifteen year period.

STAHOVICH V. ASTRUE

524 F.Supp.2d 95, 126 Soc. Sec. Rep. Serv. 153 (D. Mass. 2007)

NEIMAN, United States Chief Magistrate Judge.

* * *

II. Background

Plaintiff, born on September 13, 1948, has a high school education and an Associates Degree in environmental technology. His work experience includes jobs as a dishwasher, utility worker, residential counselor, waste water operator, gas station attendant, retail clerk and landscaper.

A. Medical History

Plaintiff claims that his disability began on February 1, 2000, due to two ruptured discs and depression. There appears to be little dispute with regard to the medical record. * * *

* * *

B. Procedural History

Plaintiff applied for both SSDI and SSI benefits on November 6, 2000. His applications were denied initially and on reconsideration.

Plaintiff then requested a hearing before an administrative law judge ("ALJ"). The hearing was held on April 3, 2002; both Plaintiff and a vocational expert testified. In a decision dated June 5, 2002, the ALJ found that Plaintiff was not disabled. The Appeals Council denied Plaintiff's subsequent request for review, after which Plaintiff sought judicial review.

On May 6, 2003, this court, endorsing the Commissioner's assented-to motion, remanded the case for the ALJ to further evaluate the opinions of Plaintiff's physicians, reassess Plaintiff's residual functional capacity (particularly his mental residual functional capacity), and obtain supplemental evidence from a vocational expert. After holding a second hearing on April 7, 2004, the ALJ, in a decision dated May 27, 2004, again determined that Plaintiff was not disabled. The Appeals Council denied review, thereby rendering the ALJ's second decision final for present purposes.

III. Discussion

* * *

B. *Disability Standard and the ALJ's Decision*

* * *

In determining disability, the Commissioner follows the five-step protocol described by the First Circuit as follows: * * *

In the instant case, the ALJ found as follows with respect to these questions: Plaintiff had not engaged in substantial gainful activity since the alleged onset of his disability (question one); Plaintiff has impairments that are "severe," but which do not meet or medically equal one of the listed impairments in Appendix 1 (questions two and three); and Plaintiff is able to perform his past relevant work as a gas station attendant (question four). Accordingly, the ALJ concluded that Plaintiff does not suffer from a disability and had no reason to reach question five.

C. *Plaintiff's Challenge to the ALJ's Decision*

* * *

Three preliminary matters need to be noted before the court addresses the parties' underlying dispute. First, despite the fact that the regulations, given their context in the regulatory scheme, address the vocational components of a claimant's residual functional capacity—a determination usually made at step five of the analysis—they have been applied at step four as well.

Second, the court will accept for present purposes the vocational expert's opinion that the job of a gas station attendant involves "light, unskilled work," despite the fact that the Commissioner now acknowledges that the job is classified by the Dictionary of Occupational Titles ("DOT") as "medium." To be sure, the Commissioner maintains that the vocational expert's classification of the job as "light" is more consistent with Plaintiff's testimony. But this issue was never addressed by the ALJ and, as will become evident, need not be resolved at this time.

Third, if applied to Plaintiff at the time of the second hearing, the fifteen-year period mentioned in the regulation would go back as far as 1989. There was no substantial evidence before the ALJ, however, that Plaintiff had performed the job of gas station attendant within that time period, the Commissioner's present suggestion to the contrary notwithstanding. In any event, this issue, too, can be sorted out on remand.

As to the heart of the parties' dispute, the fifteen-year time period has not been interpreted as an absolute rule and, in appropriate cases, past work which falls outside that time frame has been deemed relevant. For example, the job at issue in *Lopez-Diaz [v. Secretary*, 673 F.2d 13 (1st Cir.1982)] concerned unskilled work performed seventeen years earlier. The regulations make clear, however, that the process of determining the relevance of such prior work entails a number of subsidiary inquiries, *e.g.*, when the particular job was done, whether it lasted long enough for a claimant to know how to do it, whether the work skills acquired continue to apply, whether the work was only "off and on" or for brief periods of time. *See* 20 C.F.R. §§ 404.1565(a), 416.965(a) (2007). As the regulations state, the fifteen-year reference is simply "intended to insure that remote experience is not currently applied." *Id.*

The instant record, however, contains no searching inquiry as to any of these questions. This is in stark contrast to other similar situations. See, e.g., *Pickner v. Sullivan*, 985 F.2d 401, 403-04 (8th Cir.1993) (work performed prior to the fifteen-year period may be considered relevant if there is a "continuity in job skills" between that work and claimant's more recent work); *Dudley v. Sec'y of Health & Human Servs.*, 816 F.2d 792, 794 (1st Cir.1987) (three months work as a labeller sufficient to constitute past relevant work); *Bowman v. Heckler*, 706 F.2d 564, 567 (5th Cir.1983) (prior work as a domestic more than fifteen years prior applicable where evidence showed that claimant continued performing own housecleaning in interim).

Indeed, there was virtually nothing in the record upon which the ALJ could have based the required analysis. Plaintiff's testimony concerning his work as a gas attendant was, to say the least, sparse. When asked by the ALJ about other jobs he may have done, Plaintiff testified as follows:

A. Yeah, pumping gas, bakery truck, odd jobs that I've always done, you know, around our neighborhood like cutting the grass and painting and we had a cottage. Everybody knew me, you know—

Q. All—

A. —and trusted me and, you know, I'd open their camp for the season and—

Q. For how long—

A. —paint their boats and—

Q. For how long a period did you do these jobs such as pumping gas and I think you mentioned department stores and cutting laws. I mean, what you we talking a year or five years or

A. No, quite some time. I mean, I always kept busy, you one way or another. You know, about, I mean, most, a lot of it under the table but, you know, that's how I got paid. I mean, didn't really, didn't really matter.

Q. Well, let's just take pumping gas. Would—

A. Well—

Q.—did you do that for any length of time or was it

A. No.

Q. —a week here and a week there?

A. Well, it was always like a couple of months and, you

Q. All right. Well, let's take one time.

A. Well, then that—

Q. Couple of months.

A. Coup—, yeah, there.

Q. Were you the guy in the booth that handled the money or you, would you—

A. Do, no. I pumped the gas and handled—

Q. You were out by the pumps.

A. Both, you know.

Q. So if somebody—

A. I had to run in and out, you know.

Q. So if somebody came in said I want $10 worth of gas. You go open their tank and you put the hose in. You pump it. They give you a 20, you go inside and get change and bring it back to them.

A. Right.

Q. Okay. You did that a couple of different times for a couple of months at a time?

A. Yeah.

As is obvious, this testimony hardly touched upon the inquiries called for by the regulation, let alone clarified when Plaintiff engaged in such work.

Similarly, the record does not reveal, as was true in *Lopez-Diaz*, the "undisputed testimony of a vocational expert" concerning the skills needed for work as a gas station attendant. Granted, the Commissioner now offers an excerpt from the DOT in support of his argument that the job does not involve climbing as exposure to hazards, and only occasional stooping, kneeling and crawling. But, as noted, the DOT was not invoked by either the vocational expert or the ALJ. At most, as indicated, the vocational expert described the job as "unskilled, light." And, when asked whether an individual like Plaintiff could do any of his past work, the vocational expert answered as follows:

> No, Your Honor, not in considering the age of this gentlemen placing him at the advanced age level and, therefore, only considering transferable skills and limitations of carrying out and following simple instructions would limit him to unskilled jobs. And although his past job as a gas station attendant would be at the light level, I don't believe that I would consider that based on the grid rules for his age, there would be no transferability.[5]

The vocational expert went on to testify that his answers would be no different if the individual were fifty-two to fifty-four years of age rather than fifty-five. Only when the ALJ told the vocational expert to "forget all about the grid rules" did he opine that Plaintiff could do his past work, and only such work, as a gas station attendant.

In the end, there was insubstantial evidence for the ALJ's apparent assumption that Plaintiff's job as a gas station attendant fell within the fifteen-year limit or was anything other than "off and on." *See Lanes v. Harris*, 656 F.2d 285, 287 (8th Cir.1981) (five weeks as a water meter checker not past relevant work); *Ruperto Torres v. Sec'y of Health & Human Servs.*, 791 F.Supp. 342, 343 (D.P.R.1992) (work performed on an "off-and-on" basis not generally part of past relevant work calculation); *Love v. Heckler*, 564 F.Supp. 195, 198 (W.D.N.C.1983) (three months as a cone grader insufficient under 20 C.F.R. § 404.1565(a)). Indeed, Plaintiff did not even include the job in his work history report. That omission, of course, is not binding on the Commissioner, but it obviously indicates that the job was either so remote in time or so sporadic as to be practically meaningless for analytical purposes.

---

[5] The "grid" is a matrix of factors for determining at step five of the analysis whether an individual disabled from doing his previous work is able to do other work.

IV. Conclusion

The ALJ did not have substantial evidence to conclude that Plaintiff could do work as a gas station attendant, even if it were to be considered past relevant work. Accordingly, the Commissioner's motion to affirm will be denied and Plaintiff's motion, to the extent it seeks remand, will be allowed. On remand, the administrative law judge shall hold a new hearing so that step four, and possibly step five, of the analysis can be re-addressed in accord herewith.

NOTES

1. In Ruperto Torres v. Secretary, 791 F. Supp. 342, 37 Soc. Sec. Rep. Ser. 549 (D.P.R. 1992), the claimant was a 37-year old high school graduate with two years of vocational courses in accounting and dress design. She alleged disability due to arthritis, hypertension, ulcer, angina, pain, Addison's disease, and neuropathy. A major issue in the case was the characterization of her past work as a secretary:

> The ALJ found that the plaintiff was still capable of performing her past relevant work as a *secretary*. This conclusion is ill founded for a number of reasons. The first error stems from the ALJ's conclusion that the plaintiff had a past relevant work history of a secretary, when in fact the plaintiff's past relevant work history was as an assistant librarian. Past relevant work is a claimant's "usual work or other *applicable* past work." 20 C.F.R. § 404.1561 (1991) (emphasis added). For the purposes of determining past relevant work, it logically follows that the ALJ should evaluate the skills and abilities which have been acquired from work the claimant has performed, just as is done when evaluating other work which a claimant can perform. 20 C.F.R. § 404.1565 (1991). Work which was performed on an "off-and-on" basis is generally not part of the past relevant work calculation. Id. In the instant case, the plaintiff spent the last seven years of her working career as an assistant librarian cataloging, shelving and lifting books of 10-15 pounds. Before working as an assistant librarian, the plaintiff spent three months typing documents and preparing payroll records for a cousin. It was error for the ALJ to extrapolate from the three month experience of working for her cousin, that the plaintiff had acquired all the administrative, organizational, and operational skills of a secretary, because "off-and-on" positions are not considered pursuant to the regulations. The Court considers a three month position to be as temporal as any other "off-and-on" position. Consequently, with the erroneous conclusion that the plaintiff had the past relevant work history of a secretary as a starting point, all further conclusions by the ALJ were also erroneous.

791 S. Supp. at 343-44.

2. In Baker v. Secretary, 955 F.2d 552, 557, 36 Soc. Sec. Rep. Ser. 280 (8th Cir. 1992), the court referred to the Department of Labor's Selected Characteristics of Occupations Defined in the Dictionary of Occupational Titles in determining the amount of time necessary to acquire the vocational skills for a particular job: "According to the Department of Labor, the preparation time required to learn the job of meter reader or repairer (Titles 209.567-010 and 710.684-034) is three to six months. Thus, Baker's two-month tenure on the job would not have been long enough to be considered prior work experience. Secondly, the CETA job was a training program."

2. TREATMENT OF FOREIGN AND OUT-OF-DATE JOBS

In most instances, a claimant's work history consists of jobs held while living in the United States—and those jobs continue to exist (in other words, the prior work "exists" in the "national" economy). Special issues arise, however, where a claimant's most relevant recent employment was either in a foreign country or has since become obsolete.

SOCIAL SECURITY RULING SSR 82-40, 1975-1982
Soc.Sec.Rep.Ser. 845 (1982)

TITLES II AND XVI: THE VOCATIONAL RELEVANCE OF THE PAST WORK PERFORMED IN A FOREIGN COUNTRY

* * *

When the claimant's past work was performed within the U.S. national economy, the "kind of work" the claimant did and its physical and mental demands are ordinarily verifiable with employers and can usually be identified in such publications as the U.S. Department of Labor's *Dictionary of Occupational* Titles (DOT) and its supplements. The *DOT* provides information about the tools and machines used in an occupation; the raw materials, products, processes or services involved; the physical demands and environmental conditions; and the training time needed to achieve at least average performance. However, there is sometimes no ready and authoritative means to verify or supplement claimants' descriptions of their past jobs outside the U.S. when they are applying for disability benefits after arrival in this country.

In answer to questions about the relevance of past work performed in a foreign country, a view commonly expressed is that a foreign job is not "relevant" unless substantially similar work can be found in the U.S. economy. This view has been strongly influenced by the practice of verifying or supplementing a claimant's description of his or her past jobs with available information about work in the U.S. economy.

Such a view, however, creates some problems. It interposes a requirement that similar work must be found in the U.S. economy as a condition for determining a claimant able to do past relevant work performed in a foreign country. This elevates an element of the fifth step of the sequential evaluation process, availability of work in the national economy, to the fourth step which only deals with the claimant's ability to do his or her past work. The law does not qualify "previous work" but does specify that "other ... work" must exist in significant numbers in the national economy. The legislative history of the statutory provisions also does not qualify "previous work," but clearly indicates that the provisions were enacted to provide guidelines "to reemphasize the predominant importance of medical factors in the disability determination."

POLICY STATEMENT: An individual is found to be under a disability only if his or her physical or mental impairment(s) is the primary reason for inability to engage in substantial gainful work activity. Factors including change of residence from one geographical area to another, lack of job openings, and employers' hiring practices are not pertinent to the decision. The proper test in the fourth step of the sequential evaluation process is whether the individual can do his or her previous work, whether in the U.S. or in a foreign economy. A job in a foreign economy need not have a counterpart in the U.S. economy, and the lack of authoritative occupational reference materials for foreign economies is not a barrier to the decision that a claimant can or cannot meet the physical and mental demands of a formerly held foreign job as he or she described it.

The relevance of past work in a foreign economy for purposes of regulations sections 404.1520(e) and 416.920(e) is no different from the relevance of past work in the U.S. economy with respect to the physical and mental demands of the particular past job. If a claimant can meet the sitting, standing, walking, lifting, manipulative, intellectual, emotional and other physical and mental requirements of a past job, he or she is still functionally capable of performing that job regardless of the fact that the individual no longer resides in the country where the past work was performed. It is only after a claimant proves that he or she is not able to do his or her previous work that the burden shifts to the Secretary to show that there is work available in the U.S. national economy which the claimant can do (the fifth and last step of the sequential evaluation process).

BARNHART V. THOMAS
540 U.S. 20, 124 S. Ct. 376 (2003).

Justice SCALIA delivered the opinion of the Court.

Under the Social Security Act, the Social Security Administration (SSA) is authorized to pay disability insurance benefits and Supplemental

Security Income to persons who have a "disability." A person qualifies as disabled, and thereby eligible for such benefits, "only if his physical or mental impairment or impairments are of such severity that he is not only unable to do his previous work but cannot, considering his age, education, and work experience, engage in any other kind of substantial gainful work which exists in the national economy." 42 U.S.C. §§ 423(d)(2)(A), 1382c(a)(3)(B). The issue we must decide is whether the SSA may determine that a claimant is not disabled because she remains physically and mentally able to do her previous work, without investigating whether that previous work exists in significant numbers in the national economy.

I

Pauline Thomas worked as an elevator operator for six years until her job was eliminated in August 1995. In June 1996, at age 53, Thomas applied for disability insurance benefits under Title II and Supplemental Security Income under Title XVI of the Social Security Act. She claimed that she suffered from, and was disabled by, heart disease and cervical and lumbar radiculopathy.

After the SSA denied Thomas's application initially and on reconsideration, she requested a hearing before an Administrative Law Judge (ALJ). The ALJ found that Thomas had "hypertension, cardiac arrythmia, [and] cervical and lumbar strain/sprain." He concluded, however, that Thomas was not under a "disability" because her "impairments do not prevent [her] from performing her past relevant work as an elevator operator." He rejected Thomas's argument that she is unable to do her previous work because that work no longer exists in significant numbers in the national economy. The SSA's Appeals Council denied Thomas's request for review.

Thomas then challenged the ALJ's ruling in the United States District Court for the District of New Jersey, renewing her argument that she is unable to do her previous work due to its scarcity. The District Court affirmed the ALJ, concluding that whether Thomas's old job exists is irrelevant under the SSA's regulations. The Court of Appeals for the Third Circuit, sitting en banc, reversed and remanded. Over the dissent of three of its members, it held that the statute unambiguously provides that the ability to perform prior work disqualifies from benefits only if it is "substantial gainful work which exists in the national economy." 294 F.3d 568, 572 (2002). That holding conflicts with the decisions of four other Courts of Appeals. See *Quang Van Han v. Bowen*, 882 F.2d 1453, 1457 (CA9 1989); *Garcia v. Secretary of Health and Human Services*, 46 F.3d 552, 558 (CA6 1995); *Pass v. Chater*, 65 F.3d 1200, 1206-1207 (CA4 1995); *Rater v. Chater*, 73 F.3d 796, 799 (CA8 1996). We granted the SSA's petition for certiorari.

II

As relevant to the present case, Title II of the Act defines "disability" as the "inability to engage in any substantial gainful activity by reason of any medically determinable physical or mental impairment which can be expected to result in death or which has lasted or can be expected to last for a continuous period of not less than 12 months." 42 U.S.C. § 423(d)(1)(A). That definition is qualified, however, as follows:

> "An individual shall be determined to be under a disability only if his physical or mental impairment or impairments are of such severity that *he is not only unable to do his previous work but cannot*, considering his age, education, and work experience, *engage in any other kind of substantial gainful work which exists in the national economy.* . . ." § 423(d)(2)(A) (emphasis added).

"[W]ork which exists in the national economy" is defined to mean "work which exists in significant numbers either in the region where such individual lives or in several regions of the country." *Ibid.* Title XVI of the Act, which governs Supplemental Security Income benefits for disabled indigent persons, employs the same definition of "disability" used in Title II, including a qualification that is verbatim the same as § 423(d)(2)(A). See 42 U.S.C. § 1382c(a)(3)(B). For simplicity's sake, we will refer only to the Title II provisions, but our analysis applies equally to Title XVI.

Section 423(d)(2)(A) establishes two requirements for disability. First, an individual's physical or mental impairment must render him "unable to do his previous work." Second, the impairment must also preclude him from "engag[ing] in any other kind of substantial gainful work." The parties agree that the *latter* requirement is qualified by the clause that immediately follows it--"which exists in the national economy." The issue in this case is whether that clause also qualifies "previous work."

The SSA has answered this question in the negative. Acting pursuant to its statutory rulemaking authority, the agency has promulgated regulations establishing a five-step sequential evaluation process to determine disability. * * *

As the above description shows, step four can result in a determination of no disability without inquiry into whether the claimant's previous work exists in the national economy; the regulations explicitly reserve inquiry into the national economy for step five. Thus, the SSA has made it perfectly clear that it does not interpret the clause "which exists in the national economy" in § 423(d)(2)(A) as applying to "previous work." The issue presented is whether this agency interpretation must be accorded deference.

As we held in *Chevron U.S.A. Inc. v. Natural Resources Defense Council*, 467 U.S. 837, 843, 104 S. Ct. 2778, 81 L. Ed. 2d 694 (1984), when a statute speaks clearly to the issue at hand we "must give effect to the unambiguously expressed intent of Congress," but when the statute "is silent or ambiguous" we must defer to a reasonable construction by the agency charged with its implementation. The Third Circuit held that, by referring first to "previous work" and then to "*any other* kind of substantial gainful work which exists in the national economy," 42 U.S.C. § 423(d)(2)(A) (emphasis added), the statute unambiguously indicates that the former is a species of the *latter*. "When," it said, "a sentence sets out one or more specific items followed by 'any other' and a description, the specific items must fall within the description." 294 F.3d at 572. We disagree. For the reasons discussed below the interpretation adopted by SSA is at least a reasonable construction of the text and must therefore be given effect.

The Third Circuit's reading disregards—indeed, is precisely contrary to—the grammatical "rule of the last antecedent," according to which a limiting clause or phrase (here, the relative clause "which exists in the national economy") should ordinarily be read as modifying only the noun or phrase that it immediately follows (here, "any other kind of substantial gainful work"). While this rule is not an absolute and can assuredly be overcome by other indicia of meaning, we have said that construing a statute in accord with the rule is "quite sensible as a matter of grammar." In *FTC v. Mandel Brothers, Inc.*, 359 U.S. 385, 3 L. Ed. 2d 893, 79 S. Ct. 818 (1959), this Court employed the rule to interpret a statute strikingly similar in structure to § 423(d)(2)(A)—a provision of the Fur Products Labeling Act, 15 USC § 69 [15 USCS § 69], which defined "'invoice'" as "'a written account, memorandum, list, or catalog . . . transported or delivered to a purchaser, consignee, factor, bailee, correspondent, or agent, or *any other person who is engaged in dealing commercially in fur products or furs*.'" 359 U.S., at 386, 3 L. Ed. 2d 893, 79 S. Ct. 818 (quoting 15 U.S.C. § 69(f)) (emphasis added). Like the Third Circuit here, the Court of Appeals in *Mandel Brothers* had interpreted the phrase "'any other'" as rendering the relative clause ("'who is engaged in dealing commercially'") applicable to all the specifically listed categories. This Court unanimously reversed, concluding that the "limiting clause is to be applied only to the last antecedent." *Id.*, at 389, and n. 4, 3 L. Ed. 2d 893, 79 S. Ct. 818 (citing 2 J. Sutherland, Statutory Construction § 4921 (3d ed. 1943)).

An example will illustrate the error of the Third Circuit's perception that the specifically enumerated "previous work" "must" be treated the same as the more general reference to "any other kind of substantial gainful work." 294 F.3d at 572. Consider, for example, the case of parents who, before leaving their teenage son alone in the house for the weekend, warn him, "You will be punished if you throw a party or engage in any other activity that damages the house." If the son nevertheless throws a party and is caught, he should hardly be able to avoid punishment by arguing that the house was not damaged. The parents proscribed (1) a party, and (2) any other activity that damages the house. As far as appears from what they said, their reasons for prohibiting the home-alone party may have had nothing to do with damage to the house—for instance, the risk that underage drinking or sexual activity would occur. And even if their only concern was to prevent damage, it does not follow from the fact that the same interest underlay both the specific and the general prohibition that proof of impairment of that interest is required for both. The parents, foreseeing that assessment of whether an activity had in fact "damaged" the house could be disputed by their son, might have wished to preclude all argument by specifying and categorically prohibiting the one activity—hosting a party—that was most likely to cause damage and most likely to occur.

The Third Circuit suggested that interpreting the statute as does the SSA would lead to "absurd results." *Ibid.* See also *Kolman v. Sullivan*, 925 F.2d 212, 213 (CA7 1991) (the fact that a claimant could perform a past job that no longer exists would not be "a rational ground for denying benefits"). The court could conceive of "no plausible reason why Congress might have wanted to deny benefits to an otherwise qualified person simply because that person, although unable to perform any job that actually exists in the national economy, could perform a previous job that no longer exists." 294 F.3d at 572-573. But on the very next page the Third Circuit conceived of *just* such a plausible reason, namely, that "in the vast majority of cases, a claimant who is found to have the capacity to perform her past work also will have the capacity to perform other types of work." *Id.*, at 574, n. 5. The conclusion which follows is that Congress could have determined that an analysis of a claimant's physical and mental capacity to do his previous work would "in the vast majority of cases" serve as an effective and efficient administrative proxy for the claimant's ability to do some work that does exist in the national economy. Such a proxy is useful because the step-five inquiry into whether the claimant's cumulative impairments preclude him from finding "other" work is very difficult, requiring consideration of "each of th[e] [vocational] factors and . . . an individual assessment of each claimant's abilities and limitations," *Heckler v. Campbell*, 461 U.S. 458, 460-461, n. 1, 76 L. Ed. 2d 66, 103 S. Ct. 1952 (1983) (citing 20 CFR §§ 404.1545-404.1565 (1982)). There is good reason to use a workable proxy that avoids the more expansive and individualized step-five analysis. As we have observed, "[t]he Social Security hearing system is 'probably the largest adjudicative agency in the western world.' . . . The need for efficiency is self-evident." 461 U.S., at 461, n. 2, 76 L. Ed. 2d 66, 103 S. Ct. 1952 (citation omitted).

Third Circuit rejected this proxy rationale because it would produce results that "may not always be true, and . . . may not be true in this case." 294 F.3d at 576. That logic would invalidate a vast number of the procedures employed by the administrative state. To generalize is to be imprecise. Virtually *every* legal (or other) rule has imperfect applications in particular circumstances. Cf. *Bowen v. Yuckert*, 482 U.S. 137, 157, 96 L. Ed. 2d 119, 107 S. Ct. 2287 (1987) (O'Connor, J., concurring) ("To be sure the Secretary faces an administrative task of staggering proportions in applying the disability benefits provisions of the Social Security Act. Perfection in processing millions of such claims annually is impossible"). It is true that, under the SSA's interpretation, a worker with severely limited capacity who has managed to find easy work in a declining industry could be penalized for his troubles if the job later disappears. It is also true, however, that under the Third Circuit's interpretation, impaired workers in declining or marginal industries who cannot do "other" work could simply refuse to return to their jobs—even though the jobs remain open and available--and nonetheless draw disability benefits. The proper Chevron inquiry is not whether the agency construction can give rise to undesirable results in some instances (as here *both* constructions can), but rather whether, in light of the alternatives, the agency construction is reasonable. In the present case, the SSA's authoritative interpretation certainly satisfies that test.

We have considered respondent's other arguments and find them to be without merit.

* * *

We need not decide today whether § 423(d)(2)(A) compels the interpretation given it by the SSA. It suffices to conclude, as we do, that § 423(d)(2)(A) does not unambiguously require a different interpretation, and that the SSA's regulation is an entirely reasonable interpretation of the text. The judgment of the Court of Appeals is reversed.

F. STEP 5: ABILITY TO PERFORM OTHER WORK

1. GENERALLY

Disability claims reach the fifth and final step of the sequential evaluation process only after passing through the first four, which means that the claimant is not working (engaging in "substantial gainful activity") and has a "severe" impairment (or combination of impairments) that does not meet or equal the requirements of the Listing of Impairments but does preclude the claimant for performing any of his or her "past relevant work." As the final step of the sequential evaluation process, Step 5 addresses directly the operative language of the statutory disability standard: the inability to engage in "any substantial gainful activity" due to one or more medically determinable physical or mental impairments that "are of such severity that [the claimant] is not only unable to do his [or her] previous work but cannot, considering his [or her] age, education, and work experience, engage in any other kind of substantial gainful work which exists in the national economy." *See* 42 U.S.C. §423(d)(1)(A), (2)(A).

As discussed already in Chapter 4, Congress has specified that the disability standard looks to the existence of work that the claimant can perform and not the likelihood that the claimant will be hired to perform that work. The Social Security Act was amended to its present form in 1967 because, as explained in a House committee report on the amendments, Congress "expressed concern over . . . [the] increasing tendency to put the burden of proof on the government to identify jobs for which the individual might have a reasonable opportunity to be hired, rather than ascertaining whether jobs exist in the economy which he can do." H.R. Rep. No. 544, 90th Cong., 1st Sess. 29 (1967)); *see also* S. Rep. No. 744, 90th Cong., 1st Sess. 48 (1967), reprinted in 1967 U.S. Code Cong. & Ad. News 2834, 2881.

In its simplest form, Step 5 looks at a claimant's residual functional capacity (RFC), age, education, and past work experience to determine if he or she can do any work that exists in the national economy. If so, the claimant will be found to be not disabled; if not, the claimant will be found to be disabled. 20 C.F.R. §§ 404.1520(f)(1), 416.920(f)(1). In practice, however, Step 5 determinations are considerably more complicated. First of all, as we saw in Chapter 4, the Social Security Act defines the phrase "work which exists in the national economy" as "work which exists in significant numbers either in the region where [the claimant] lives or in several regions of the country." 42 U.S.C. §423(d)(2)(A). *See also* 20 C.F.R. §§ 404.1560(c), 416.960(c). And then there is the question of the burden of proof. As noted earlier in this chapter, if a claimant cannot perform past relevant work and thereby passes through Step 4, the burden shifts to the Social Security Administration at Step 5 to prove that the claimant can perform other work in the national economy. Moreover, the burden shifts with respect to all aspects of the question whether the claimant can perform other work existing in the national economy. Thus, Step 5 places the burden on SSA to show that there are jobs in the national economy that the claimant can perform—and that those jobs are substantial and gainful, exist in "significant" numbers, and exist "either in the region where [the claimant] lives or in several regions of the country."

A) ABILITY TO PERFORM PART-TIME WORK

The measure of work incapacity assessed at Step 5 is, in one sense, fundamentally similar to the measure used at the first step of the sequential evaluation process. Step 1 provides that a claimant cannot be disabled if he or she is actually performing substantial gainful activity; Step 5 provides that a claimant who can perform substantial gainful activity that exists in the national economy is also not disabled. For most purposes, Social Security regulations do not distinguish between the meaning of substantial gainful activity as used in these two different contexts because in both the purpose is to determine if the claimant meets the same statutory standard. In other words, both steps aim to determine whether the clamant is able to engage in substantial gainful activity. There is, however, a substantial difference between the two steps with respect to how they treat part-time work.

KELLEY V. APFEL

185 F.3d 1211, 62 Soc. Sec. Rep. Ser. 602 (11th Cir. 1999)

Before Anderson, Chief Judge, and Carnes and Hull, Circuit Judges.

Per Curiam:

We VACATE our earlier opinion in this matter, published at 173 F.3d 814, and substitute in its place the following, thus granting the government's motion for clarification. Stephen A. Kelley, Jr. appeals the district court's order affirming the Commissioner of Social Security's ("Commissioner") denial of his application for disability benefits under the Social Security Act. On appeal, Kelley asserts that the administrative law judge ("ALJ") erred in finding him not disabled. He contends that the ALJ incorrectly (1) assumed that part-time employment could constitute substantial gainful work; (2) discredited his subjective complaints of pain; and (3) used the testimony of a vocational expert, in lieu of the Medical-Vocational Guidelines, 20 C.F.R. pt. 404, subpt. P, app. 2 (also known as the "Grids"), to determine his ability to engage in substantial gainful activity.

* * *

I. KELLEY'S FIRST ARGUMENT-PART-TIME WORK

A. Resolution of this Issue in Light of the Clarification that the ALJ did not Rely on the Ability to Work Part-Time

The government's motion for clarification has now demonstrated that—contrary to our erroneous assumption in our prior, now-vacated opinion—the ALJ did not rely on an ability to do part-time work in finding that Kelley had the residual functional capacity to perform jobs existing in significant numbers in the national economy. We note that the ALJ found that Kelley had the residual functional capacity to stand and/or walk for up to 2 hours during an 8-hour workday, and to sit for up to 6 hours during an 8-hour workday. These findings, coupled with other findings—e.g., that Kelley retained the capacity to lift 10 pounds occasionally, and to frequently lift and carry objects such as docket files, ledgers, and small tools—equate to a finding of capacity to perform full-time sedentary work. All of the ALJ's determinations in this regard are supported by substantial evidence. Thus, we reject Kelley's first argument because it erroneously assumes that the ALJ's finding of capacity to perform sedentary work depends upon an ability to do part-time work, and because the ALJ's finding of capacity to perform full-time sedentary work is supported by substantial evidence. Accordingly, there is no need for us to address the relevance of part-time work.

B. The Confusion in our Prior, Now-Vacated Opinion, and a Note as to the Relevance of Part-Time Work at Steps One and Five of the Sequential Analysis

As indicated above, our prior, now-vacated opinion erroneously assumed that the ALJ had relied on an ability on Kelley's part to do part-time work. Our prior opinion directly confronted Kelley's first argument—i.e., that the ALJ incorrectly assumed that part-time work could constitute substantial gainful employment. We rejected that argument and held that part-time employment may constitute substantial gainful work. We distinguished some of our case law that may appear to suggest the contrary. In so holding, we relied on 20 C.F.R. § 404.1572(a), which provides that "[y]our work may be substantial even if it is done on a part-time basis." In a motion for clarification of our prior opinion, the government now apologizes that its panel brief to this Court was misleading,[3] and concedes that the above-cited regulation does not apply to Step Five. The government also concedes, based on certain Social Security Rulings, that the ability to perform part-time work does not preclude a finding of disability at Step Five of the sequential analysis.

---

[3] In the panel brief, the government argued that part-time work was relevant at Step Five of the sequential analysis (i.e., the step that is relevant in the instant case, see infra) and cited § 404.1572(a) (which it now acknowledges is applicable only at Step One, not at Step Five) for this proposition. The thrust of the government's prior argument was that an ability to work part-time may preclude a finding of disability. The government failed to cite the authorities upon which it now relies for the distinction between Step One and Step Five in this regard. The government's panel brief was also misleading as follows. Instead of demonstrating that the ALJ never assumed that part-time employment could constitute substantial gainful employment at Step Five, the government responded to appellant's argument that the ALJ erred by relying on the ability to perform part-time work—by arguing that the ability to work part-time could preclude a finding of disability.

The confusion over the role of part-time work in this regard stems from the fact that work, or the ability to work, is relevant in at least two distinct steps of the sequential analysis for determining entitlement to disability benefits, i.e., Steps One and Five. Step One asks whether the claimant is currently engaging in "substantial gainful activity." *See* 20 C.F.R. § 404.1520(a). If the claimant is so engaged, he is not disabled. *Id.* At Step One, there is no per se rule that part-time work cannot constitute substantial gainful activity. The regulation upon which we relied in our prior opinion (and which was cited by the government in its brief), 20 C.F.R. § 404.1572(a) ("Substantial work activity is work activity that involves doing significant physical or mental activities. Your work may be substantial even if it is done on a part-time basis ...."), pertains specifically to Step One.

The *ability* to work is relevant at Step Five, which "considers [the claimant's] residual functional capacity and [his] age, education, and past work experience to see if [he] can do other work [besides his past work]." 20 C.F.R. § 404.1520(f)(1). If the claimant can do other work in this regard, he is not disabled. *Id.* Although the issue is not totally clear, according to the government's present stance, an ability to do part-time work does not preclude a finding of disability at Step Five. In other words, at Step Five, the government's present representation is that only an ability to do full-time work will permit the ALJ to render a decision of not disabled. The government extracts this interpretation from Social Security Ruling 96-8p. That ruling provides that the relevant concept at Step Five is the residual functional capacity to perform work on a "regular and continuing basis." Social Security Ruling 96-8p. "A 'regular and continuing basis' means 8 hours a day, for 5 days a week, or an equivalent work schedule." *Id.* Thus, if the government is correct in its interpretation, a claimant could pass Step Five and be entitled to benefits even though capable of working on a part-time basis.

We emphasize that the instant case was a Step Five case, not a Step One case. Kelley did not work during the relevant time period. Rather, the sequential analysis proceeded to the question of whether Kelley had the residual functional capacity to perform jobs existing in significant numbers in the national economy, i.e., Step Five. The government's motion for clarification has now made clear that the ALJ never found that Kelley had the residual functional capacity to do only part-time work; rather, his findings equated to a finding that Kelley had the ability to do full-time sedentary work. Thus, it is not necessary for us to confront the issue of whether part-time work, as opposed to full-time work, will prevent a claimant from being found disabled at Step Five of the sequential analysis. For the same reason, the Former Fifth Circuit case upon which Kelley relies so heavily for the proposition that the capability to do only part-time work is insufficient to disqualify a claimant from receiving benefits, Johnson v. Harris, 612 F.2d 993, 998 (5th Cir.1980), is distinguishable on its facts.[4] Accordingly, in light of the government's motion for clarification, we reject Kelley's first argument without the need to address the legal issue raised regarding part-time work.

[In the remainder of opinion the court rejected Kelley's arguments concerning his subjective complaints pain and the use of a vocational expert, and affirmed the decision to deny benefits.]

BLADOW V. APFEL

205 F.3d 356, 67 Soc. Sec. Rep. Ser. 283 (8th Cir. 2000)

Before Wollman, Chief Judge, Lay and Bowman, Circuit Judges.

Lay, Circuit Judge

I. Introduction

Tony L. Bladow (Bladow) appeals an administrative law judge's (ALJ's) denial of disability benefits under Title II of the Social Security Act, 42 U.S.C. §§ 401-433. In view of the intervening case of *Kelley v. Apfel*, 185 F.3d 1211 (11th Cir.1999) (per curiam), we remand.

Bladow seeks disability benefits for a back condition that he claims prevents him from engaging in any substantial gainful activity. He complains of constant radiating pain from his right hip to ankle and occasional weakness in the right arm. The alleged onset date of this condition is March 15, 1992.

After being denied benefits initially and on reconsideration, Bladow sought an administrative hearing. Among the evidence presented to the ALJ was a Functional Capacities Evaluation (FCE) administered by an occupational therapist on October 11 and 12, 1994. The FCE tested factors such as muscle strength, body coordination, endurance, and range of body motion. The therapist concluded that Bladow could perform medi-

---

[4] We note that this situation—the possibly different roles of part-time work at Step One and Step Five, the statement in § 404.1572(a) that part-time work can be substantial gainful activity, and the language of Johnson v. Harris—has engendered substantial confusion in the courts. See, e.g., Conn v. Secretary of Health & Human Services, 51 F.3d 607 (6th Cir.1995) (taking the position that "the claimant need not be found capable of full-time work to be found capable of working" at Step Five and citing § 404.1572(a) as support for this assertion); Wood v. Callahan, 977 F.Supp. 1447 (N.D.Fla.1997) (taking the position that § 404.1572(a) applies at Step Five, and disregarding the Johnson v. Harris holding as dicta). Cf. Wright v. Sullivan, 900 F.2d 675, 679-80 (3d Cir.1990) (blurring the distinction between Step One and Step Five and engaging in substantial criticism of Johnson v. Harris even though only Step One was at issue); Burkhalter v. Schweiker, 711 F.2d 841 (8th Cir.1983) (holding that actual performance of part-time work during the disability disqualified the claimant from receiving benefits (i.e., Step One) and criticizing Johnson v. Harris which it saw as inconsistent with this rule). We save for another day the question of the relevance of part-time work at Step Five, but encourage the Commissioner to make his regulations more clear and understandable in this regard.

um level work[2] if given a more diminished schedule such as two hours a day with a gradual increase to four. The therapist further stated, however, that Bladow "may tolerate the four-hour work day and gradually increase his work hours" if returned to a light level position.[3]

The Commissioner introduced the testimony of a Vocational Expert (VE) to show that other work existed that Bladow was capable of performing. The ALJ asked the VE whether an individual with Bladow's age, education, work experience, and FCE could perform his past relevant work. Bladow's past relevant work primarily involved performing jobs requiring manual labor. He responded that such an individual could not perform Bladow's past work because he read the FCE as limiting Bladow's work schedule to four hours a day even in a light level position. The ALJ later asked whether other work exists in the national or regional economy that such a person could perform if limited to six hours a day. The VE responded that such a person could work as a bench assembler, sorter, or telemarketer, and well over 100,000 of each of these jobs exist nationally and approximately 5,000 exist regionally. The VE later admitted on cross-examination by the claimant's counsel that less than half of these jobs were available on a part-time basis. Later, the ALJ asked the VE whether light level jobs would be available to an individual with Bladow's FCE who could work eight hours a day. The VE replied in the affirmative. The ALJ then asked "[a]nd if we were limited to a six hour day— would that again limit the numbers?" Again, the VE responded in the affirmative.

Based on the testimony of the VE, the ALJ upheld the denial, finding Bladow failed the fifth step of the disability inquiry under 20 C.F.R. § 404.1520 (1999). The ALJ felt the Commissioner had satisfied its burden at step five by presenting the testimony of the VE, upon which the ALJ substantially relied. * * * The district court * * * granted the Commissioner's motion for summary judgment. Bladow now appeals the district court's ruling.

---

[2] The FCE defines "medium work" as:

[e]xerting 20 to 50 pounds [of] force occasionally, and/or 10 to 25 pounds of force frequently, and/or greater than negligible up to 10 pounds of force constantly to move objects. Physical Demand requirements are in excess of those for light work.

[3] "Light work" is defined as:

lifting no more than 20 pounds at a time with frequent lifting or carrying of objects weighing up to 10 pounds. Even though the weight lifted may be very little, a job is in this category when it requires a good deal of walking or standing, or when it involves sitting most of the time with some pushing and pulling of arm or leg controls. To be considered capable of performing a full or wide range of light work, you must have the ability to do substantially all of these activities.

20 C.F.R. § 404.1567 (1999).

II. Discussion

Bladow argues that the ALJ improperly found him not disabled based on his ability to perform other work *part-time*. Bladow feels such a finding is in violation of the Commissioner's position in *Kelley*, 185 F.3d at 1213-15, which was handed down between the district court's order and the submission of this appeal. In that case, the Commissioner explained that, at step five of the disability determination, "only an ability [on the part of the claimant] to do full-time work will permit the ALJ to render a decision of not disabled." *Id.* at 1214. The Commissioner based this policy interpretation on Social Security Ruling (SSR) 96-8p, which provides that "RFC [residual functional capacity] is an assessment of an individual's ability to do sustained work-related physical and mental activities in a work setting on a regular and continuing basis. A *'regular and continuing basis' means 8 hours a day, for 5 days a week, or an equivalent work schedule.*"[6] SSR 96-8p, 1996 WL 374184, at *1 (Social Security Administration, July 2, 1996) (emphasis added).

At oral argument in this case, the Commissioner conceded that the interpretation offered in *Kelley* is the official policy on determining RFC at step five. Nonetheless, the Commissioner argues that *Kelley* and SSR 96-8p do not mandate an award of disability benefits in this case. First, the Commissioner interprets the ALJ's finding that Bladow is not disabled as based on Bladow's ability to perform other work *full-time*. Secondly, even if the ALJ did find Bladow limited to part-time work, the government avers that limitation was a function of Bladow's deconditioning and, as such, should not be taken into consideration when determining Bladow's residual functional capacity. SSR 96-8p states that "[a]ge and body habitus (i.e., natural body build, physique, constitution, size, and weight, insofar as they are unrelated to the individual's medically determinable impairment(s) and related symptoms) are not factors in assessing RFC in initial claims." Hence, the Commissioner opines the ALJ should have ignored Bladow's part-time limitations (allegedly due to deconditioning) when determining his RFC.

---

[6] *Kelley* vacated the court's previous opinion in the same case. The court previously upheld the ALJ's alleged finding of no disability based on the claimant's capacity to perform part-time work because part-time work could be considered substantial gainful activity under 20 C.F.R. § 404.1572(a). The government subsequently moved to clarify *Kelley*, stating that the ALJ had come to the right result for the wrong reason. The government argued that unlike steps one and four where an ability to perform part-time work could prevent a finding of disability, SSR 96-8p barred part-time work from entering into the equation at step five. Thus, it urged "a final decision of the Commissioner that based a denial of benefits at step five of the sequential evaluation process on an RFC to perform only part-time work ... would not be correct under SSR 96-8p." (Mem. in Supp. of Mot. for Clarification at 9.) While the Eleventh Circuit did not seem opposed to this policy interpretation, it did not officially adopt it as law. The ALJ in *Kelley* was found to have denied the benefits based on the claimant's ability to perform other work *full-time*. Thus, SSR 96-8p was not violated and there was no need to confront the issue of whether an ability to perform part-time work could prevent a finding of no disability at step five.

In order to evaluate the Commissioner's arguments we must review the language of the ALJ's decision. The ALJ rejected the argument that the FCE reflects Bladow's inability to work at any level for more than four hours a day. In the realm of light work, which the ALJ found Bladow could perform, the ALJ stated the FCE "impl[ies] the claimant is able to work more than four hours ...." More importantly, the ALJ explained in Finding Number 12:

> Although the claimant's limitations do not allow him to perform the full range of light work, ... there are a significant number of jobs in the national economy which [he] could perform. Examples of such jobs are: telemarketer, jobs in assembly, and sorter. A vocational expert testified these jobs exist in significant numbers in the national and regional economies and would only be reduced by half *if the claimant was limited to working 6 hours a day.*

(emphasis added). Thus, while the ALJ rejected the contention that Bladow was unable to work more than four hours a day, the ALJ did not specifically find he was able to work full-time, either.

This court feels the best and most prudent option in this case is to remand for clarification of Bladow's RFC in light of *Kelley* and its treatment of SSR 96-8p. We read Finding Number 12 to be written in the alternative: if Bladow can perform full-time light level work, there are a significant number of jobs available to him in the national and regional economy; and if he can only work in a light level position part-time, the number of jobs available is only reduced by half. This language does not give us a sufficient basis to decide the issue raised in *Kelley* regarding part-time work and step five of the disability analysis. Thus, the sensible solution is to remand for clarification of Bladow's RFC in light of *Kelley*.

Before we remand, however, we address the government's body habitus argument. If the six-hour limitation is due solely to Bladow's body habitus, there is no reason to remand the case. Our analysis would then focus on whether the finding of no disability is supported by substantial evidence in the record as a whole.

The Commissioner relies largely on the language of the FCE in making its body habitus argument. The FCE forges a link of uncertain strength between Bladow's limited work hours and his "general deconditioning," stating that:

> [Bladow] would do best with a return to work of more diminished hours such as two hours and gradually increase to a four-hour position. *This is due to his decreased general conditioning and decreased functional endurance with activities* If [Bladow] is returned to a

light level position, he may tolerate the four-hour work day and gradually increase his work hours.

The FCE also suggests that Bladow engage in a general conditioning home program. The occupational therapist specifically noted in the FCE that Bladow did not have a specific home program of exercises at the time of testing. Both the ALJ and the magistrate took notice of Bladow's lack of conditioning, as well.

* * *

Under the government's argument, the FCE links Bladow's decreased work capacity to his general deconditioning, and there is other evidence that arguably supports that connection. However, we are troubled by the fact that the FCE never defines "general deconditioning," nor does it give concrete examples of Bladow's specific deconditioning in terms of its physical manifestations. * * * [W]e feel the best option is to remand on this issue, as well. On remand, the ALJ should seek to focus the blurry connection between Bladow's general deconditioning and his work limitations.

III. Conclusion

While we recognize that this application for benefits has been in progress for over five years, we believe the record is too sketchy to decide these pivotal issues at this juncture. We therefore remand this case for further administrative proceedings consistent with this opinion.

B) JOBS THAT EXIST IN THE NATIONAL ECONOMY

In most cases, Step 5 determinations turn on the extent of functional loss due to the claimant's physical and mental impairments, as well as the impact of vocational factors—age, education, prior work experience—on his or her ability to work. There may be a dispute as to whether the claimant can, in fact, perform jobs that SSA identifies as within the claimant's medical and vocational capacity, but usually the jobs identified are common and available in large numbers throughout the country. There are, however, instances where SSA must struggle to show that the jobs the claimant can do exist in certain regions and in significant numbers in the economy.

HARMON V. APFEL
168 F.3d 289, 60 Soc.Sec.Rep.Ser. 267 (6th Cir. 1999)

Before: Merritt and Moore, Circuit Judges; Duggan, District Judge.

Merritt, Circuit Judge.

Plaintiff appeals the judgment of the district court affirming the denial of supplemental security benefits. Claimant is not requesting review of the factual findings relating to her vocational profile or her residual functional capacity. Instead, the question presented is whether there are a significant number of jobs that the claimant can be expected to perform given the claimant's limitations and the distance she would be required to travel to find work. Because we find that the denial is supported by substantial evidence on the record as a whole, we affirm.

Plaintiff Shirley Harmon lives in Cumberland, Kentucky, a rural area. She applied for benefits in June 1994. Her primary complaint was debilitating back pain that necessitated that she sit or lie down most of the time. The ALJ found, and plaintiff does not dispute in this appeal, that plaintiff has the residual functional capacity to perform light work that allows her to alternate between sitting and standing every thirty minutes. Jobs such as retail receiving clerk, gasket inspector, shoe packer, gate tender, hardware assembler and switchbox assembler would be suitable with plaintiff's limitations. The vocational expert testified at plaintiff's hearing that there are about 900,000 jobs of this kind nationwide, *id.* at 6,[1] and about 700 similar jobs within a 75-mile radius of plaintiff's home.

* * *

To be entitled to disability benefits, claimant must establish a physical or mental impairment, lasting at least twelve months, that prevents her from engaging in any gainful activity. Plaintiff has the burden to establish an entitlement to benefits by proving the existence of a disability as defined in the Act. A claimant establishes a *prima facie* case by showing that she is unable to perform her former work. The burden then shifts to the Secretary to show that claimant, considering her age, education, and work experience, can perform other work existing in significant numbers in the national economy. We must affirm the Commissioner's determination if it is supported by substantial evidence on the record as a whole.

On appeal, plaintiff contends that the district court erred in finding that substantial evidence supported the determination that she was not entitled to benefits because the ALJ erred in finding that there are a significant number of jobs in the local area that she could perform. Based on the vocational expert's testimony, the ALJ determined that there were about 700 jobs within a 75-mile radius of plaintiff's home that plaintiff

---

[1] We note that the hearing transcript reflects that the vocational expert testified that there were 900,000 of these kinds of jobs available nationwide. However, the number cited by the ALJ in his decision was 700,000 ALJ Decision at 6. Although the difference in figures has no impact on our decision herein, we will rely on the lower number cited by the ALJ.

would be able to perform. Plaintiff does not dispute this number but contends that her disability prevents her from traveling to most of those jobs and that inability to travel is a factor in determining whether plaintiff is disabled within the meaning of the Social Security Act. Plaintiff contends that the vast majority of the 700 jobs identified by the vocational expert were in the Kingsport, Tennessee tri-city area, about 70 miles from plaintiff's home. The commute to these jobs would take plaintiff about an hour and one-half each way by car over hilly mountain roads. Plaintiff contends that because the restrictions used by the ALJ in the hypothetical recognized that she can stand or sit for only thirty minutes at a time, that restriction precludes her from driving to jobs in the tri-city area. In essence, plaintiff contends that when jobs in the tri-city area are eliminated from the "pool" of jobs that she could perform, there is not the requisite "significant number of jobs" that plaintiff could perform and she should therefore be eligible for benefits.

Plaintiff's argument suffers from two fatal flaws. First, the number of jobs that contributes to the "significant number of jobs" standard looks to the national economy—not just a local area. Second, while plaintiff is correct when she contends that travel to and from work is a factor to be considered, it refers to intrinsic factors concerning plaintiff's condition, not extrinsic factors such as where plaintiff has chosen to live in relation to any identified regional jobs.

The ALJ determined that 700,000 jobs constitutes a significant number in the national economy. The Social Security Act, as amended, provides that "work which exists in the national economy means work which exists in significant numbers *either* in the region where such individual lives or in several regions of the country." 42 U.S.C. § 423(d)(2)(A) (emphasis added). The Commissioner is not required to show that job opportunities exist within the local area.

The regulations implementing the Social Security Act clarify this point: "It does not matter whether ... [w]ork exists in the immediate area in which you live...." 20 C.F.R. § 416.966(a)(1)(1997). However, the regulations also state that jobs "existing in the national economy" do not include "[i]solated jobs that exist only in very limited numbers in relatively few locations outside of the region where [plaintiff] live[s]...." 20 C.F.R. § 404.1566(b). In determining whether the jobs identified are limited and isolated, the factors to be considered include the level of claimant's disability; the reliability of the vocational expert's testimony; the reliability of the claimant's testimony; the distance the claimant is capable of traveling to engage in the assigned work; the isolated nature of the jobs; the types and availability of such work and so on. *Hall v. Bowen*, 837 F.2d 272, 275 (6th Cir.1988); *Stewart v. Sullivan*, No. 89-6242, 1990 WL 75248, at *4 (6th Cir.1990), (125 jobs in local geographic area and 400,000 jobs nationwide constituted "significant number of jobs" within the meaning of 42 U.S.C. § 423(d)(2)(A)). *Hall* went on to state that these factors were suggestions only—the ALJ need not explicitly consider each factor. The Act, its legislative history and the regulations make it clear that the test is whether work exists in the national economy, not in plaintiff's neighborhood. Certainly 700,000 jobs, with no indication of gross concentration in a few areas, is a "significant number of jobs in the national economy."

Furthermore, the fact that plaintiff lives 70 miles from the nearest metropolitan area is a factor extrinsic to her disability and is not to be considered. Congress intended to "provide a definition of disability which can be applied with uniformity and consistency throughout the Nation, without regard to where a particular individual may reside...." H.R.Rep. No. 544, 90th Cong., 1st Sess. 29, 30 (1967). As the First Circuit stated 20 years ago:

> Congress, tightening the definition of disability, eliminated consideration of travel difficulties when those difficulties were extrinsic to the claimed disability; the length and expense of commuting and the resulting inconveniences were no longer to influence a disability determination. A person, otherwise able to work, is in effect offered a choice: he can choose either to commute the distance to his job or he can move closer and avoid the expense and inconvenience. Disability insurance is not available to fund his decision to live far from his job.

Lopez Diaz v. Secretary of Health, Educ. and Welfare, 585 F.2d 1137, 1140 (1st Cir.1978); see also Meeks v. Apfel, 993 F.Supp. 1265 (W.D.Mo.1997)(fact that jobs exist in metropolitan area 90 miles from plaintiff's home satisfies statutory test that jobs exist in "significant numbers"). In *Lopez Diaz* the question to be decided was whether the physical capacity to transport oneself to a job is relevant to a determination of "disability" as defined in the Act. Ms. Lopez Diaz stated that she had not worked for five years because her foot and leg pain prevented her from traveling to the city two hours away by public transportation, which included waiting for two or three buses each way. The Court held that individual considerations extrinsic to the disability itself cannot enter into a finding of disability.

Plaintiff here presents the same question as that in *Lopez Diaz*. By her own admission plaintiff can and does drive her automobile to transport herself, at least to some extent. The travel factor that plaintiff contends is relevant to her disability determination is therefore an extrinsic factor—that is, the long distance she must travel to the nearest metropolitan area and not simply a physical problem. Although we recognize and are sympathetic to plaintiff's plight, the law is clear that we may not base our decision on plaintiff's argument.

For the foregoing reasons, we affirm the judgment of the district court.

DELORME v. SULLIVAN

924 F.2d 841, 32 Soc. Sec. Rep. Ser. 285 (9th Cir. 1991)

Before Fletcher, Ferguson and Fernandez, Circuit Judges.

Ferguson, Circuit Judge:

Ronald DeLorme injured his back repeatedly during and after his employment as an interstate bus driver. He appeals from the district court's grant of summary judgment in favor of the Secretary, Department of Health and Human Services ("the Secretary") rejecting his application for disability benefits. We reverse and remand.

I. FACTS

* * *

A vocational expert testified regarding DeLorme's capacity to work. The ALJ posed the following hypothetical for the vocational expert:

> Considering the Exhibits and the testimony and considering that Mr. DeLorme can lift no more than 25 pounds—can sit at one time no longer than 45 minutes, can walk no longer than 45 minutes and cannot walk on rock or extruded ground and must use at least for an extensive walking a prosthesis or a walking stick. Also considering a background of high school plus two years of college in traffic management and one year in business systems repair. And considering the medical disability.... Would there be any positions in the economy that would be available in work that he could do?

The vocational expert said he had "found one sedentary job in a related area that I could consider," and described the position of "taxicab starter" (dispatcher). There were less than five such positions in the metropolitan area and four to five thousand such positions in the national economy. The taxicab starter position was sedentary and met the specified limitations on lifting. On further questioning by DeLorme's attorney, however, the expert said it would be "very difficult" for DeLorme to work at this position. His references to the hypothetical demonstrated some uncertainty regarding DeLorme's limitations;[8] however, he emphasized the limitations imposed by the need to alternately sit and stand.

---

[8] The vocational expert said: "[T]hat particular job ... is listed as sedentary. There are some restrictions in reaching and in fingering and in feeling. There is a question in my mind as to whether you spoke to that issue and about that p[a]rticular job. But, it is sedentary."

When asked about additional positions which might be possible for DeLorme, the vocational expert stated that the position of cashier was sedentary in nature, but that he was unsure of its suitability because De-Lorme required "a lot of leeway ... to stand up from the job and walk around.... [T]here are many cashier positions where they are not allowed that freedom—to stand and sit. That would limit it." Although there were many cashier jobs in the national economy, there were only three to four hundred such positions in the area of Idaho where DeLorme lived, a number which would be additionally limited by DeLorme's restrictions on standing and sitting to "a much smaller [number] ... really not very many, in my opinion." Further questions by DeLorme's attorney focused on difficulties with manual dexterity, which had not been part of the ALJ's hypothetical. The vocational expert testified that this would also make it extremely difficult for DeLorme to perform a cashier's work.

The ALJ found that DeLorme was not disabled. He summarized part of DeLorme's testimony regarding his training program incorrectly, stating that claimant "anticipates completing course work in the near future in electronics and expects to find employment, although he has difficulty because of his limitations." The ALJ noted DeLorme's testimony indicated he could not lift objects heavier than 20 pounds or stand longer than an hour; however, because of DeLorme's ability to continue the business machine training program, the ALJ concluded he could perform a wide range of sedentary work. * * *

* * *

V. JOBS IN THE NATIONAL ECONOMY

* * *

There is an additional dispute regarding the testimony of the vocational expert. DeLorme argues on appeal that the vocational expert actually held that there were *not* jobs in the national economy which he could perform. The vocational expert named only two jobs, taxicab dispatcher (four or five positions in the area where DeLorme lived, and four to five thousand in the national economy), and cashier (hundreds of thousands in the national economy, hundreds in the area where DeLorme lived). However, DeLorme's impairments affected his ability to perform these jobs. Although the taxicab starter position was sedentary and met the limitations on lifting, the expert said it would be "very difficult" for De-Lorme because of both restrictions on reaching and fingering, and, with somewhat greater emphasis, restrictions on sitting and standing. Regarding the position of cashier, the vocational expert stated that few such positions would give DeLorme the requisite leeway to alternately stand and sit. The three to four hundred such positions in the area of Idaho where DeLorme lived would be additionally limited by DeLorme's restrictions on standing and sitting to "a much smaller [number] ... really not very many, in my opinion."

In *Walker v. Mathews*, 546 F.2d 814 (9th Cir.1976), the vocational expert had testified that two jobs were open to an individual with the claimant's capacities. One was very rare, and the claimant's "future in [the other job] is limited to finding one of the few [such] jobs that allow him to sit and stand at will." *Id.* at 820. We held that "[i]n looking toward the pool of jobs existing in the national economy, Congress did not intend to foreclose a claimant from disability benefits on the basis of the existence of a few isolated jobs." *Id.* at 819. On the other hand, when vocational experts identify several job categories and thousands of jobs performable in the state by the claimant, we have repeatedly found substantial evidence of performable jobs. *Swenson v. Sullivan*, 876 F.2d 683, 689 (9th Cir.1989); *Martinez v. Heckler*, 807 F.2d 771, 775 (9th Cir.1986).

Here, the position of taxicab starter is comparable to the "rare" position of carton stenciling in *Walker*, 546 F.2d at 820. The position of cashier may be more widely available than the machine packaging job with similar standing and sitting limitations in *Walker*, although the vocational expert's testimony tends to show that DeLorme can hold "very few" such jobs because of his limitations. The confusion regarding DeLorme's limitations makes it difficult to evaluate the vocational expert's testimony regarding the availability of jobs suitable for DeLorme.

[The court then remanded the case, noting that "the ALJ must fully develop the record regarding DeLorme's mental and physical impairments." The court also cautioned that if, on remand, the case proceeds again to Step 5, "[t]he hypothetical posed for the vocational expert must then fully reflect all the limitations on DeLorme's activity, including his mental condition."]

2. STEP 5 AND THE MEDICAL-VOCATIONAL GUIDELINES ("GRIDS")

As noted above, Step 5 determinations require an assessment of not only a claimant's physical and mental impairments but also his or her age, education, prior work experience—and how all of those factors affect the claimant's ability to work. The Social Security Administration uses a two-part analysis in order to decide, as required at Step 5, whether a claimant can perform other work in the national economy. The first part is an evaluation of the work limitations caused by the claimant's medical condition, by means of the same residual functional capacity (RFC) assessment described earlier in relation to Step 4. Then the vocational factors of age, education, and prior work experience are brought in to decide whether, given the claimant's RFC, a significant number of jobs exist in the national economy that the claimant could perform.   20 C.F.R. §§ 404.1560(c), 416.960(c).

With the shift in burden of proof after Step 4, SSA faces the formidable task of showing that claimants who reach Step 5 can perform particular jobs that exist in significant numbers in the national economy in either the claimant's region or several regions of the country. In order to relieve that burden, SSA published a special set of rules and tables in 1979—known as the Medical-Vocational Guidelines—as an appendix to the Social Security regulations. *See* 20 C.F.R. Part 404 Subpart P Appx 2.

At the heart of the Medical-Vocational Guidelines are the so-called "grids," which consist of three tables. A claimant's RFC determines which table of the Medical-Vocational Guidelines is to be used: Table 1 applies to individuals whose RFC limits them to sedentary work; Table 2 to those limited to light work; and Table 3 to those limited to medium work. There are no tables for individuals still able to perform heavy or very heavy work because the Guidelines state, in effect, that regardless of their age, education, or work experience, sufficient jobs exist in the national economy for such individuals to pursue substantial gainful activity. There are also some regulations that dictate a finding of disability for claimants with particularly significant vocational limitations. *See* **20 C.F.R. §§ 404.1562, 416.962[APP-REGS]**. *See also* 20 C.F.R. §§ 404.1520(g), 416.920(g). On the other hand, if it is found that an individual is unable to perform work at even a sedentary level, he or she will be assumed to be disabled, absent specific evidence to the contrary. A copy of the grids is available at http://www.ssa.gov/OP_Home/cfr20/404/404-ap11.htm. (Note that the term ".....Do" found in the grid tables is intended to be synonymous with "Ditto.")

The "grids" were developed by taking notice of the numbers of unskilled jobs that exist throughout the national economy at the different functional levels, as supported by various government publications, such as the Dictionary of Occupational Titles and the Occupation Outlook Handbook published by the U.S. Department of Labor. Based on this information, each table has a set of "rules" with component parts consisting of three columns that account for a claimant's age, education, and previous work experience, and a fourth column that directs a decision of disabled or not disabled.

Provided a claimant's vocational factors and RFC coincide with all of the criteria of a particular rule, that rule directs a conclusion that the claimant is or is not disabled. For example, if a claimant is limited to light work, is closely approaching advanced age (defined as between the ages of 50 and 54), is illiterate or unable to communicate in English, and has either no previous work experience or previous work experience limited to unskilled labor, then 20 C.F.R. Part 404 Subpart P Appx 2 §200.09 would direct a finding that the claimant is disabled. On the other hand, if that same individual were at least literate and able to communicate in English, then Rule 202.10 would direct a finding of not disabled. Ultimately, claims that fall within the grids lead to a relatively straightforward disability determination at Step 5. However, as discussed in more detail at the end of this chapter, some cases do not fit neatly within the grids and therefore still require an individualized determination. *See* **20 C.F.R. §§ 404.1569, 416.969[APP-REGS]**. *See also* **20 C.F.R. §§ 404.1569a, 416.969a[APP-REGS]**.

Prior to the adoption of the Guidelines, SSA regulations provided only general guidance in making determinations concerning a claimant's ability to perform other substantial gainful activity. Moreover, those guidelines were not binding on administrative law judges. Therefore, for SSA to meet its burden of proof at an administrative hearing, testimony of a vocational expert usually had to be provided. As a result, often similarly situated claimants were treated differently. The Medical-Vocational Guidelines were developed in part to overcome this problem. As stated by SSA at the time they were first proposed, the Guidelines were intended to "consolidate and elaborate upon long standing medical-vocational evaluation policies"; to "make clearer to claimants and their representatives how disability is determined where vocational factors must be considered"; to "better assure the soundness and consistency of disability determinations in all claims filed regardless of the level at which adjudicated"; and to "promote better understanding and acceptance by the public and the courts of disability determinations that are made." 43 Fed. Reg. 55349 (1978).

After the Guidelines took effect, many claimants sought to challenge them on constitutional and statutory grounds. The major challenges put forth by claimants were that the Guidelines were beyond the rule-making power of the Secretary of Health and Human Services under the Social Security Act, that the use of the Guidelines constituted a denial of due process, and that case law still required the testimony of a vocational expert. Other related arguments were that specific jobs that the claimant could perform must still be cited, that the Guidelines create an invalid irrebuttable presumption, and that the Guidelines improperly shifted the burden of proof back to claimants. *See generally* John J. Capowski, *Accuracy and Consistency in Categorical Decision-Making: A Study of Social Security's Medical-Vocational Guidelines—Two Birds With One Stone or Pigeon-Holing Claimants?*, 42 MD. L. REV. 329 (1983). The Supreme Court addressed these and other arguments in the following case.

HECKLER V. CAMPBELL

461 U.S. 458, 1 Soc.Sec.Rep.Ser. 3 (1983)

Justice POWELL delivered the opinion of the Court.

The issue is whether the Secretary of Health and Human Services may rely on published medical-vocational guidelines to determine a claimant's right to Social Security disability benefits.

I

The Social Security Act defines "disability" in terms of the effect a physical or mental impairment has on a person's ability to function in the work place. It provides disability benefits only to persons who are unable "to engage in any substantial gainful activity by reason of any medically determinable physical or mental impairment." 42 U.S.C. § 423(d)(1)(A). And it specifies that a person must "not only [be] unable to do his previous work but [must be unable], considering his age, education, and work experience, [to] engage in any other kind of substantial gainful work which exists in the national economy, regardless of whether such work exists in the immediate area in which he lives, or whether a specific job vacancy exists for him, or whether he would be hired if he applied for work." 42 U.S.C. § 423(d)(2)(A).

In 1978, the Secretary of Health and Human Services promulgated regulations implementing this definition. The regulations recognize that certain impairments are so severe that they prevent a person from pursuing any gainful work. See 20 CFR § 404.1520(d) (1982) (referring to impairments listed at 20 CFR pt. 404, subpt. P, app. 1). A claimant who establishes that he suffers from one of these impairments will be considered disabled without further inquiry. If a claimant suffers from a less severe impairment, the Secretary must determine whether the claimant retains the ability to perform either his former work or some less demanding employment. If a claimant can pursue his former occupation, he is not entitled to disability benefits. If he cannot, the Secretary must determine whether the claimant retains the capacity to pursue less demanding work.

The regulations divide this last inquiry into two stages. First, the Secretary must assess each claimant's present job qualifications. The regulations direct the Secretary to consider the factors Congress has identified as relevant: physical ability, age, education and work experience.[1]

---

[1] The regulations state that the Secretary will inquire into each of these factors and make an individual assessment of each claimant's abilities and limitations. See 20 CFR §§ 404.1545-404.1565 (1982); cf. 20 CFR § 404.944. In determining a person's physical ability, she will consider, for example, the extent to which his capacity for performing tasks such as lifting objects or his ability to stand for long periods of time has been impaired. See § 404.1545.

Second, she must consider whether jobs exist in the national economy that a person having the claimant's qualifications could perform.

Prior to 1978, the Secretary relied on vocational experts to establish the existence of suitable jobs in the national economy. After a claimant's limitations and abilities had been determined at a hearing, a vocational expert ordinarily would testify whether work existed that the claimant could perform. Although this testimony often was based on standardized guides, vocational experts frequently were criticized for their inconsistent treatment of similarly situated claimants. To improve both the uniformity and efficiency of this determination, the Secretary promulgated medical-vocational guidelines as part of the 1978 regulations. See 20 CFR pt. 404, subpt. P, app. 2 (1982).

These guidelines relieve the Secretary of the need to rely on vocational experts by establishing through rulemaking the types and numbers of jobs that exist in the national economy. They consist of a matrix of the four factors identified by Congress—physical ability, age, education, and work experience[3]—and set forth rules that identify whether jobs requiring specific combinations of these factors exist in significant numbers in the national economy.[4] Where a claimant's qualifications correspond to the job requirements identified by a rule,[5] the guidelines direct a conclusion as to whether work exists that the claimant could perform. If such work exists, the claimant is not considered disabled.

II

In 1979, Carmen Campbell applied for disability benefits because a back condition and hypertension prevented her from continuing her work as a hotel maid. After her application was denied, she requested a hearing *de novo* before an Administrative Law Judge. He determined that her

---

[3] Each of these four factors is divided into defined categories. A person's ability to perform physical tasks, for example, is categorized according to the physical exertion requirements necessary to perform varying classes of jobs–i.e., whether a claimant can perform sedentary, light, medium, heavy, or very heavy work. 20 CFR § 404.1567. Each of these work categories is defined in terms of the physical demands it places on a worker, such as the weight of objects he must lift and whether extensive movement or use of arm and leg controls is required. *Ibid.*

[4] For example, rule 202.10 provides that a significant number of jobs exist for a person who can perform light work, is closely approaching advanced age, has a limited education but who is literate and can communicate in English, and whose previous work has been unskilled.

[5] The regulations recognize that the rules only describe "major functional and vocational patterns." 20 CFR pt. 404, subpt. P, app. 2, § 200.00(a). If an individual's capabilities are not described accurately by a rule, the regulations make clear that the individual's particular limitations must be considered. See app. 2, §§ 200.00(a), (d). Additionally, the regulations declare that the Administrative Law Judge will not apply the age categories "mechanically in a borderline situation," 20 CFR § 404.1563(a), and recognize that some claimants may possess limitations that are not factored into the guidelines, see app. 2, § 200.00(e). Thus, the regulations provide that the rules will be applied only when they describe a claimant's abilities and limitations accurately.

back problem was not severe enough to find her disabled without further inquiry, and accordingly considered whether she retained the ability to perform either her past work or some less strenuous job. He concluded that even though Campbell's back condition prevented her from returning to her work as a maid, she retained the physical capacity to do light work. *Ibid.* In accordance with the regulations, he found that Campbell was 52-years old, that her previous employment consisted of unskilled jobs and that she had a limited education. *Id.,* at 28a-29a. He noted that Campbell, who had been born in Panama, experienced difficulty in speaking and writing English. She was able, however, to understand and read English fairly well. App. 42. Relying on the medical-vocational guidelines, the Administrative Law Judge found that a significant number of jobs existed that a person of Campbell's qualifications could perform. Accordingly, he concluded that she was not disabled.

This determination was upheld by both the Social Security Appeals Council and the District Court for the Eastern District of New York. The Court of Appeals for the Second Circuit reversed. It accepted the Administrative Law Judge's determination that Campbell retained the ability to do light work. And it did not suggest that he had classified Campbell's age, education, or work experience incorrectly. The court noted, however, that it

> "has consistently required that 'the Secretary identify specific alternative occupations available in the national economy that would be suitable for the claimant' and that 'these jobs be supported by "a job description clarifying the nature of the job, [and] demonstrating that the job does not require" exertion or skills not possessed by the claimant.' "

The court found that the medical-vocational guidelines did not provide the specific evidence that it previously had required. It explained that in the absence of such a showing, "the claimant is deprived of any real chance to present evidence showing that she cannot in fact perform the types of jobs that are administratively noticed by the guidelines." *Ibid.* The court concluded that because the Secretary had failed to introduce evidence that specific alternative jobs existed, the determination that Campbell was not disabled was not supported by substantial evidence.

We granted certiorari to resolve a conflict among the Courts of Appeals.[8]

---

[8] Every other Court of Appeals addressing the question has upheld the Secretary's use of the guidelines. See *Rivers v. Schweiker,* 684 F.2d 1144, 1157-1158 (CA5 1982); *McCoy v. Schweiker,* 683 F.2d 1138, 1144-1146 (CA8 1982); *Torres v. Secretary of HHS,* 677 F.2d 167, 169 (CA1 1982); *Santise v. Schweiker,* 676 F.2d 925, 934-936 (CA3 1982); *Cummins v. Schweiker,* 670 F.2d 81, 82-83 (CA7 1982); *Kirk v. Secretary of HHS,* 667 F.2d 524, 529-535 (CA6 1981); *Frady v. Harris,*

III

The Secretary argues that the Court of Appeals' holding effectively prevents the use of the medical-vocational guidelines. By requiring her to identify specific alternative jobs in every disability hearing, the court has rendered the guidelines useless. An examination of both the language of the Social Security Act and its legislative history clearly demonstrates that the Secretary may proceed by regulation to determine whether substantial gainful work exists in the national economy. Campbell argues in response that the Secretary has misperceived the Court of Appeals' holding. Campbell reads the decision as requiring only that the Secretary give disability claimants concrete examples of the kinds of factual determinations that the Administrative Law Judge will be making. This requirement does not defeat the guidelines' purpose; it ensures that they will be applied only where appropriate. Accordingly, respondent argues that we need not address the guidelines' validity.

A

The Court of Appeals held that "[i]n failing to show suitable available alternative jobs for Ms. Campbell, the Secretary's finding of 'not disabled' is not supported by substantial evidence." It thus rejected the proposition that "the guidelines provide adequate evidence of a claimant's ability to perform a specific alternative occupation" and remanded for the Secretary to put into evidence "particular types of jobs suitable to the capabilities of Ms. Campbell". The court's requirement that additional evidence be introduced on this issue prevents the Secretary from putting the guidelines to their intended use and implicitly calls their validity into question. Accordingly, we think the decision below requires us to consider whether the Secretary may rely on medical-vocational guidelines in appropriate cases.

The Social Security Act directs the Secretary to "adopt reasonable and proper rules and regulations to regulate and provide for the nature and extent of the proofs and evidence and the method of taking and furnishing the same" in disability cases. 42 U.S.C. § 405(a). As we previously have recognized, Congress has "conferred on the Secretary exceptionally broad authority to prescribe standards for applying certain sections of the [Social Security] Act." *Schweiker v. Gray Panthers*, 453 U.S. 34, 43, 101 S.Ct. 2633, 2640, 69 L.Ed.2d 460 (1981); see *Batterton v. Francis*, 432 U.S. 416, 425, 97 S.Ct. 2399, 2405, 53 L.Ed.2d 448 (1977). Where, as here, the statute expressly entrusts the Secretary with the responsibility

---

646 F.2d 143, 145 (CA4 1981). One Court of Appeals has agreed that the Secretary may use medical-vocational guidelines but has found that with respect to age the guidelines are arbitrary. See *Broz v. Schweiker*, 677 F.2d 1351, 1359-1361 (CA11 1982), cert. pending, No. 82-816. The instant case does not present the issue addressed in Broz.

for implementing a provision by regulation,[10] our review is limited to determining whether the regulations promulgated exceeded the Secretary's statutory authority and whether they are arbitrary and capricious.

We do not think that the Secretary's reliance on medical-vocational guidelines is inconsistent with the Social Security Act. It is true that the statutory scheme contemplates that disability hearings will be individualized determinations based on evidence adduced at a hearing. See 42 U.S.C. § 423(d)(2)(A) (specifying consideration of each individual's condition); 42 U.S.C. § 405(b) (1976 ed., Supp. V) (disability determination to be based on evidence adduced at hearing). But this does not bar the Secretary from relying on rulemaking to resolve certain classes of issues. The Court has recognized that even where an agency's enabling statute expressly requires it to hold a hearing, the agency may rely on its rulemaking authority to determine issues that do not require case-by-case consideration. A contrary holding would require the agency continually to relitigate issues that may be established fairly and efficiently in a single rulemaking proceeding.

The Secretary's decision to rely on medical-vocational guidelines is consistent with *Texaco* and *Storer*. As noted above, in determining whether a claimant can perform less strenuous work, the Secretary must make two determinations. She must assess each claimant's individual abilities and then determine whether jobs exist that a person having the claimant's qualifications could perform. The first inquiry involves a determination of historic facts, and the regulations properly require the Secretary to make these findings on the basis of evidence adduced at a hearing. We note that the regulations afford claimants ample opportunity both to present evidence relating to their own abilities and to offer evidence that the guidelines do not apply to them. The second inquiry requires the Secretary to determine an issue that is not unique to each claimant--the types and numbers of jobs that exist in the national economy. This type of general factual issue may be resolved as fairly through

---

[10] Since Congress amended the Social Security Act in 1954 to provide for disability benefits, Pub.L. 761, § 106, 68 Stat. 1079, it repeatedly has suggested that the Secretary promulgate regulations defining the criteria for evaluating disability. See, e.g., Subcommittee on the Administration of the Social Security Laws of the House Committee on Ways and Means, 86th Cong., 2d Sess., Administration of Social Security Disability Insurance Program: Preliminary Report 17-18 (Comm.Print 1960) (requesting Secretary to develop "specific criteria for the weight to be given nonmedical factors in the evaluation of disability"); House Committee on Ways and Means, 93d Cong., 2d Sess., Committee Staff Report on the Disability Insurance Program 6 (1974) (recommending that the Secretary promulgate regulations defining disability to ease accelerating case load); Hearings on H.R. 8076 before the Subcommittee on Social Security of the House Committee on Ways and Means, 95th Cong., 1st Sess. 7 (Comm.Print 1977) (comments of Rep. Burke) (noting with approval that the Secretary had promised to promulgate medical-vocational guidelines to define disability). While these sources do not establish the original congressional intent, they indicate that later Congresses perceived that regulations such as the guidelines would be consistent with the statute.

rulemaking as by introducing the testimony of vocational experts at each disability hearing.

As the Secretary has argued, the use of published guidelines brings with it a uniformity that previously had been perceived as lacking. To require the Secretary to relitigate the existence of jobs in the national economy at each hearing would hinder needlessly an already overburdened agency. We conclude that the Secretary's use of medical-vocational guidelines does not conflict with the statute, nor can we say on the record before us that they are arbitrary and capricious.

B

We now consider Campbell's argument that the Court of Appeals properly required the Secretary to specify alternative available jobs. Campbell contends that such a showing informs claimants of the type of issues to be established at the hearing and is required by both the Secretary's regulation, 20 CFR § 404.944 (1980), and the Due Process Clause.

By referring to notice and an opportunity to respond, the decision below invites the interpretation given it by respondent. But we do not think that the decision fairly can be said to present the issues she raises. The Court of Appeals did not find that the Secretary failed to give sufficient notice in violation of the Due Process Clause or any statutory provision designed to implement it. Nor did it find that the Secretary violated any duty imposed by regulation. Rather the court's reference to notice and an opportunity to respond appears to be based on a principle of administrative law—that when an agency takes official or administrative notice of facts, a litigant must be given an adequate opportunity to respond.

This principle is inapplicable, however, when the agency has promulgated valid regulations. Its purpose is to provide a procedural safeguard: to ensure the accuracy of the facts of which an agency takes notice. But when the accuracy of those facts already has been tested fairly during rulemaking, the rulemaking proceeding itself provides sufficient procedural protection.[14]

IV

The Court of Appeals' decision would require the Secretary to introduce evidence of specific available jobs that respondent could perform. It would limit severely her ability to rely on the medical-vocational guidelines. We think the Secretary reasonably could choose to rely on these

---

[14] Respondent does not challenge the rulemaking itself, and, as noted above, respondent was accorded a de novo hearing to introduce evidence on issues, such as physical and mental limitations, that require individualized consideration.

guidelines in appropriate cases rather than on the testimony of a vocational expert in each case. Accordingly, the judgment of the Court of Appeals is

Reversed.

Concurring opinions of Justice Brennan and Justice Marshall, in which he also dissented in part, are omitted.

NOTES ON AGE CATEGORY AND THE GRIDS

1. *Campbell* made it clear that the Medical-Vocational Guidelines, when applicable, can be used to meet SSA's burden of proof at Step 5 and therefore, in such cases, the testimony of a vocational expert is not required and SSA does not have to cite specific jobs which the claimant can perform. *Campbell* did reserve one question, however, for future consideration: the legality of the age classification in the grids. The Eleventh Circuit took the question up in Broz v. Heckler, 721 F.2d 1297, 3 Soc. Sec. Rep. Ser. 264 (11th Cir. 1983), a case in which its decision striking down the use of the grids to deny claims at Step 5—and the application of age categories in particular—had been vacated and remanded by the Supreme Court following the decision in *Campbell*. In Broz v. Heckler, 711 F.2d 957 (11th Cir.1983) ("*Broz II*"), the Eleventh Circuit had already reconsidered—and adhered to—its original decision, Broz v. Schweiker, 677 F.2d 1351 (11th Cir.1982) ("*Broz I*"). SSA then sought a rehearing, but the Eleventh Circuit stood by its earlier rulings that age must be considered on a case-by-case basis. The court did recognize, however, that "some of our language in Broz I and Broz II swept too broadly" and therefore issued a slightly modified decision that reasoned as follows:

> [W]e swept too broadly in *Broz I* and *II* when we said that the effect of age could never be a legislative fact. *Broz I*, 677 F.2d at 1360; *Broz II*, 711 F.2d at 959. However, this recognition does not require reversal of our determination that in disability hearings the effect of age on an individual's ability to work should be determined on a case-by-case basis. We believe that Congress's intent in adding the language "considering age, education, and work experience" was that there should be an individualized determination of the effect of each of these factors on an individual's ability to work. Congress added this language to the statute when it adopted the Social Security Amendments of 1967, an omnibus bill with far-reaching changes in both welfare and social security laws. The redefinition of disability was only a minor part of the bill, and the specific language we are seeking to construe was only a minor aspect of that minor part. Consequently, there is no detailed discussion of this language in the congressional debates. However, the language is specifically mentioned in the context of explaining the need for a redefinition of disability. These statements, while not conclusive, suggest that Congress intended that there be an individualized determination of the factor of age.

Reflecting your committee's concern about the rising cost of the disability insurance program and the way the statutory definition of disability has been interpreted in some court jurisdictions, and the effect this has had and may have in the future on the administration of the disability program, the bill provides specific guidelines in the law for determining when an individual is disabled to the degree required under the definition in the law. The language added to the basic definition specifies, first, that where an individual has the ability, considering his age, education, and work experience, to engage in substantial gainful activity that exists in the national economy, he is not disabled regardless of whether a specific job is available to him or exists in the general area in which he lives.

113 Cong.Rec. 23049 (1967) (statement of Rep. Mills, chairman of House Committee on Ways and Means).

The language proposed to be added to the statute specifies the requirements that must be met in order to establish inability to engage in any substantial gainful activity for insured workers (and certain adults disabled in childhood) whose impairments are not of the level of severity that such a presumption can be made regardless of the age, education, and previous experience of the particular individual. The language added by the bill would provide: that such an individual would be disabled only if it is shown that he has a severe medically determinable physical or medical (sic) impairment or impairments; that if, despite his impairment or impairments, an individual still can do his previous work, he is not under a disability; and that if, considering the severity of his impairment together with his age, education, and experience, he has the ability to engage in some other type of substantial gainful work that exists in the national economy even though he can no longer do his previous work, he also is not under a disability regardless of whether or not such work exists in the general area in which he lives or whether he would be hired to do such work.

H.R.Rep. No. 544, 90th Cong., 1st Sess. 30 (1967).

From these explanations of the bill we infer that Congress intended that in the disability context the effect of age be determined on a case-by-case basis. Furthermore, HHS has interpreted the other two factors to require individualized determination; it suggests no reason to treat age differently; and we perceive none. We therefore reaffirm our prior holding that in the context of disability hearings the effect of age must be treated on a case-by-case basis.

721 F.2d at 1299.

2. In Daniels v. Apfel, 154 F.3d 1129, 154 A.L.R. Fed. 793, 58 Soc.Sec.Rep.Ser. 170 (10th Cir. 1998), the claimant was denied benefits based on an application of the grids in which his age—65 days short of 55 years—

dictated a finding of not disabled. Had he been 55 years of age, he would have been found disabled. The court reversed and remanded the case, relying in part on SSA's own regulations:

> The Commissioner has established three age categories: younger person (under age fifty), person approaching advanced age (age fifty to fifty-four), and person of advanced age (age fifty-five and over). See 20 C.F.R. § 404.1563. For this case, the relevant categories are approaching advanced age and advanced age. Mr. Daniels was nearly fifty-five years old at the time his insured status ended, and thus falls near the cutoff between the two categories. The difference between the two categories is subtle but critical. The regulations provide that "[i]f you are closely approaching advanced age (50-54), we will consider that *your age,* along with a severe impairment and limited work experience, *may seriously affect your ability to adjust* to a significant number of jobs in the national economy." § 404.1563(c) (emphasis added). In contrast, "[w]e consider that advanced age (55 or over) *is the point where age significantly affects a person's ability to do substantial gainful activity.*" § 404.1563(d) (emphasis added).

> By necessity, the lines drawn between the categories may be arbitrary, but that does not make the categorization impermissible. * * * Moreover, in an attempt to alleviate some of the arbitrariness of the age categories, § 404.1563(a) provides a means of softening the edges of those categories:

>> We explain in detail how we consider your age as a vocational factor in appendix 2. However, we will not apply these age categories mechanically in a borderline situation.

See Kirk v. Secretary of Health & Human Servs., 667 F.2d 524, 532 (6th Cir.1981) (noting that "[i]n line with the Secretary's acknowledgement [of the inherent difficulty in drawing precise age classifications], the regulations specifically provide that age cut-off lines are not to be applied mechanistically").

> In the comments accompanying the promulgation of this regulation's predecessor, the Commissioner explained that agency " 'practice over the years, in fact, has been in agreement with the comment that the passage of a few days or months before the attainment of a certain age should not preclude a favorable disability determination.' " *Kane v. Heckler,* 776 F.2d 1130, 1133 (3d Cir.1985) (quoting 43 Fed.Reg. 55349, 55359 (1978)). As we noted in *Lambert v. Chater,* 96 F.3d 469, 470 (10th Cir.1996), the Commissioner later repeated this notion when explaining what a borderline situation is: "A 'borderline situation' exists when there would be a shift in results caused by the passage of a few days or months."

154 F.3d at 1132-33. While noting that SSA had not defined further what constitutes a "borderline situation," the court continued: "Whatever the full extent of that range may be, we conclude that claimant here, who was only sixty-five days short of the advanced age category, does fall within the borderline situation." *Id.* at 1133. For a more recent discussion of "borderline situations," see *Crawford v. Barnhart*, 556 F.Supp.2d 49, 53-54, 133 Soc. Sec. Rep. Serv. 361 (D.D.C. 2008):

> The plaintiff claims that despite the fact that he was only 46 days shy of his 55th birthday on the date of the ALJ's decision, the ALJ failed to recognize this as a borderline case. Thus, the plaintiff argues, the ALJ improperly applied the law by mechanically using the grids. The defendant retorts that the ALJ has total discretion to decide whether to place a claimant in a higher age category in a borderline situation and, therefore, that the plaintiff cannot prevail.

> As a threshold concern, the court must first determine whether this is a borderline case, *i.e.*, whether the plaintiff is "within a few days to a few months of reaching an older age category." 20 C.F.R. § 416.963(b) (instructing an ALJ to "not apply the age categories mechanically in a borderline situation"). Although the exact parameters of a borderline case remain unclear, 46 days is certainly within a "few months." *See Daniels v. Apfel*, 154 F.3d 1129, 1131 (10th Cir.1998) (remanding for a determination of the appropriate age category when the ALJ's decision came 65 days before the plaintiff's birthday); *Kane v. Heckler*, 776 F.2d 1130, 1133 (3d Cir.1985) (remanding for application of § 416.963 when the plaintiff was 48 days short of her birthday); *Metaxotos v. Barnhart*, 2005 WL 2899851, at *8 (S.D.N.Y. Nov. 3, 2005) (remanding for consideration of the borderline situation where the plaintiff was 6 months shy of an older age category); *France v. Apfel*, 87 F.Supp.2d 484, 491 (D.Md.2000) (granting summary judgment for the plaintiff where the difference was 5 months). *But see Crady v. Sect'y of Health & Human Serv.*, 835 F.2d 617, 622 (6th Cir.1987) (applying the substantial evidence rule to determine that the ALJ has discretion to decide if a case is borderline where the claimant was one month shy of his 55th birthday). Therefore, this is a borderline case.

3. *Daniels v. Apfel* also involved the question of the burden of proof in this context. SSA argued that the claimant had the burden of showing that he should be classified in the higher age bracket, citing Reeves v. Heckler, 734 F.2d 519 (11th Cir.1984). The court saw it differently, returning ultimately to its broader view of how the age category should be applied with the grids:

> * * * Under *Reeves* and its progeny, regardless of whether a claimant is in a borderline situation, he may show that his chronological age category should not apply:

In discharging [the step-five] burden the Secretary may use the age factor as applied in the grids as evidence of the claimant's ability to adapt to a new work environment, but this age factor shall not be conclusive. If the claimant then proffers substantial credible evidence that his ability to adapt is less than the level established under the grids for persons his age, the Secretary cannot rely on the age factor of the grids and must instead establish the claimant's ability to adapt to a new work environment by independent evidence. Applied specifically to this case, this burden of production scheme allows the Secretary to rely in the first instance on the age grids, but, if Reeves introduces evidence that his ability to adapt is more limited than that presumed by the grids for 37 year-olds, the Secretary must prove Reeves's ability to adapt by other evidence.

Reeves, 734 F.2d at 525-26.

Whatever the merits of this position outside the borderline area, we find it inapplicable to borderline situations because it ignores [20 C.F.R.] § 404.1563(a). Applied to borderline situations, this position essentially places the burden on a claimant to prove why the grids should not be applied mechanically. Nothing in § 404.1563(a) supports this position. The regulation provides that once it is determined that a claimant is in a borderline situation, which, as noted earlier, the Commissioner has defined solely in terms of age relative to the next category, "We"—meaning the Social Security Administration—"will not apply these age categories mechanically." The Commissioner's argument rewrites the regulation to say essentially that "in borderline situations, we will allow you—the claimant—to prove why the grids should not be applied mechanically." The plain language of the regulation does not allow this interpretation.

Moreover, placing the burden on the Commissioner of determining in the first instance what age category to apply is consistent with the Commissioner's existing burdens. Application of § 404.1563(a) is a step-five issue, and the burden generally is on the Commissioner at step five. Additionally, as the Third Circuit has emphasized in this context, it is the Commissioner's burden to show that a claimant's characteristics precisely match those of the grids. See *Kane* [*v. Heckler*, 776 F.2d 1130, 1132-34 (3d Cir. 1985]. Kane noted that in upholding a challenge to the grids on the basis that they were arbitrary and capricious and inconsistent with the Social Security Act's assurance of individual consideration, the Supreme Court "relied on the guarantee that '[i]f an individual's capabilities are not described accurately by a rule, the regulations make clear that the individual's particular limitations must be considered.'" *Id.* at 1133-34 (quoting *Campbell*, 461 U.S. at 462 n. 5, 103 S.Ct. 1952). The court also recognized Campbell 's reference to § 404.1563(a) and its statement that " '[t]hus, the regulations provide that the rules will be applied only when they describe a claimant's abilities and limitations accurately.'" *Id.* at 1134 (quoting *Campbell*, 461 U.S. at 462 n. 5, 103 S.Ct. 1952). Kane then concluded that

> [i]n sum, courts recognize that the grids provide useful standards and allow for consistent, less complex decision-making. But judicial approval of these standards is premised on the assurance that [the Social Security Administration] will not employ them to produce arbitrary results in individual cases. Where a procrustean application of the grids results in a case that, but for the passage of a few days, would be decided differently, such an application would appear to be inappropriate. Section 404.1563(a) therefore serves an important purpose in the regulatory scheme, and ALJs should adhere to its clear language.

776 F.2d at 1134. Whether the existence of § 404.1563(a) was critical to judicial approval of the grids is of no moment for present purposes.[7] What is critical is the fact that in a borderline situation, such as we have here, § 404.1563(a) plainly precludes mechanical application of the age categories, that is, simply considering the chronological age of the claimant at the relevant time. Failing to consider the effect of a borderline situation in turn precludes application of the grids as a basis for finding no disability, because the Commissioner will not have shown that "the claimant's characteristics precisely match the criteria of a particular rule." *Channel*, 747 F.2d at 579. The ALJ here failed to do that, and therefore should not have relied on the grids for his decision. As a result, we conclude that the Commissioner misapplied the law and that the case must be remanded for further consideration of this issue.

154 F.3d at 1134-35.

3. STEP 5 WHEN THE GRIDS DO NOT APPLY

As the Court noted in *Campbell*, claimants always have the opportunity to argue that the grids do not apply to them. When a claimant's vocational factors or residual functional capacity is different from those reflected in a particular rule, that rule is not substantial evidence of the claimant's ability toperform jobs that exist in the national economy. In such cases, therefore, the Guidelines are not sufficient to meet SSA's burden of proof.

One of the most common situations taking a claim outside the Guidelines is where the claimant has non-exertional impairments. The grids

---

[7] Campbell indicated that one circuit, the Eleventh in Broz v. Schweiker, 677 F.2d 1351 (11th Cir.1982), had found the age categories arbitrary, but the Court noted that it did not have to address that issue. 461 U.S. at 464 n. 8, 103 S.Ct. 1952. The Court subsequently vacated Broz in light of Campbell, see Heckler v. Broz, 461 U.S. 952, 103 S.Ct. 2421, 77 L.Ed.2d 1311 (1983), and the Eleventh Circuit then reaffirmed it, 711 F.2d 957, and modified it, 721 F.2d 1297 (11th Cir.1983). Reeves was the Eleventh Circuit's first decision dealing with the age factor in light of Broz. See Reeves, 734 F.2d at 525-26.

take into account only exertional impairments; therefore, if a claimant suffers from a non-exertional impairment use of the Guidelines may not be appropriate.

SYKES V. APFEL

228 F.3d 259, 71 Soc.Sec.Rep.Ser. 135 (3ᵈ Cir. 2000)

Before: Becker, Chief Judge, Weis, and Oakes,[*] Circuit Judges.

Becker, Chief Judge.

In this appeal, Clifton Sykes, Sr. challenges the judgment of the District Court affirming the Social Security Administration's final decision denying him disability benefits. The case compels us to revisit the use of the medical-vocational guidelines in the regulations promulgated under the Social Security Act to establish that there are jobs in the national economy that a claimant can perform when the claimant has both exertional and nonexertional impairments.

After suffering several job-related injuries, Sykes filed for Disability Insurance Benefits with the Social Security Administration. The Commissioner of Social Security ("Commissioner") found Sykes to be not disabled within the meaning of the Social Security Act. Sykes then requested a hearing before an Administrative Law Judge ("ALJ"). The ALJ concluded that Sykes had several severe impairments, at least one of which (left-eye blindness) is a nonexertional impairment under the regulations. The ALJ nevertheless denied Sykes's application. Applying the medical-vocational guidelines "as a framework" (and without referring to a vocational expert or other evidence), the ALJ concluded that Sykes's exertional impairments left him able to perform light work, and that the exclusion of jobs requiring binocular vision from light work positions in consideration of his nonexertional impairment did not significantly compromise Sykes's broad occupational base under the guidelines. The denial became a final decision when the Social Security Administration Appeals Council denied Sykes's request for a review of the ALJ's decision.

We conclude that, under *Heckler v. Campbell*, 461 U.S. 458, 103 S.Ct. 1952, 76 L.Ed.2d 66 (1983) (construing the Social Security Act and upholding regulations promulgated thereunder), and in the absence of a rulemaking establishing the fact of an undiminished occupational base, the Commissioner cannot determine that a claimant's nonexertional impairments do not significantly erode his occupational base under the medical-vocational guidelines without either taking additional vocational evidence establishing as much or providing notice to the claimant of his intention to take official notice of this fact (and providing the claimant with

[*] Honorable James L. Oakes, United States Circuit Judge for the Second Circuit, sitting by designation.

an opportunity to counter the conclusion). Accordingly, we will reverse the order of the District Court and remand the case with instructions to return the case to the Commissioner for further proceedings. We reject Sykes's claim that the Social Security Administration has failed to acquiesce in this Court's prior decisions.

* * *

II.

* * *

Sykes's appeal requires us to decide whether, under Campbell, and in the absence of a rulemaking establishing the fact of an undiminished occupational base, the Commissioner can determine that a claimant's nonexertional impairments do not significantly erode his occupational base under the grids without either taking additional vocational evidence establishing as much or providing notice to the claimant of his intention to take official notice of this fact (and providing the claimant with an opportunity to counter the conclusion). If the Commissioner cannot make such a determination consistent with Campbell and the Social Security Act, then the District Court order affirming the ALJ's decision must be reversed.

III.

Applying the five-step [sequential evaluation process], the ALJ concluded that (1) Sykes was not currently employed in substantial gainful activity; (2) that he had the following severe impairments (exertional and nonexertional): left-eye blindness, the residual effects of a torn rotator cuff, angina, and obstructive pulmonary disease; (3) that these impairments did not meet the criteria for listed impairments in 20 C.F.R. Part 404, Subpart P, Appendix 1 (1999), and that Sykes retained the capacity to perform light work; (4) that Sykes lacked the residual functional capacity to perform his past work; and (5) that there were other jobs in the national economy that Sykes could perform.

In the fifth step of the test (for which the government bears the burden of proof), the ALJ did not consider any evidence in addition to the grids in making his determination that there were jobs in the national economy that Sykes could perform. Instead, applying the grids "as a framework" (and without referring to a vocational expert or other evidence), the ALJ concluded that there were jobs in the national economy that Sykes could perform because the exclusion of jobs requiring binocular vision from light work positions did not, in his view, significantly compromise Sykes's broad occupational base for light work. The ALJ's decision states that "using medical-vocational 'grid' rule 202.11, Table 1, Subpart P, Appendix 2, as a framework for decision-making, I find that jobs exist in significant numbers in the national economy that he has had the capacity to perform. The exclusion of jobs requiring binocular vision does not significantly compromise the broad base of light work."

* * *

The remaining (and key) question raised by Sykes's appeal is whether the Commissioner met his burden of proof for the step-five inquiry of establishing that there are jobs in the national economy that Sykes can perform given the impairments that the ALJ did accept. In *Burnam v. Schweiker*, 682 F.2d 456, 458 (3d Cir.1982), we held that the Commissioner cannot meet this burden by relying exclusively on the grids when the claimant has both exertional and nonexertional impairments. At issue in this case is the scope of this limitation.

The government argues that the ALJ appropriately used the grids in this case "as a framework." According to the government, the ALJ properly looked to the jobs listed under light work and made an independent determination that Sykes's lack of binocular vision did not significantly diminish his residual functional capacity. The government argues that, under the Social Security Act and the regulations interpreting it, the ALJ can make the determination regarding disability and need not take additional vocational evidence if he determines that the nonexertional impairment does not significantly erode the occupational base of the category of work that the claimant can perform given his exertional impairments.

A. The Grids and Nonexertional Impairments

The Social Security Administration has promulgated regulations governing the determination of disability when the claimant has an impairment or combination of impairments resulting in both exertional limitations and nonexertional limitations. The regulation governing the assessment of nonexertional limitations provides that, if a finding of disability is not possible based on exertional limitations alone,

> the rule(s) reflecting the individual's maximum residual strength capabilities, age, education, and work experience provide a framework for consideration of how much the individual's work capability is further diminished in terms of any types of jobs that would be contraindicated by the nonexertional limitations. Also, in these combinations of nonexertional and exertional limitations which cannot be wholly determined under the rules in this appendix 2, full consideration must be given to all of the relevant facts in the case in accordance with the definitions and discussions of each factor in the appropriate

sections of the regulations, which will provide insight into the adjudicative weight to be accorded each factor.

20 C.F.R. pt. 404, subpt. P, app. 2, § 200.00(e)(2) (1999). The government argues that, under this regulation, the ALJ need not refer to any additional evidence in determining whether a nonexertional impairment erodes residual functional capacity.

The courts of appeals agree at a general level that the grids cannot automatically establish that there are jobs in the national economy when a claimant has severe exertional and nonexertional impairments. In Burnam v. Schweiker, 682 F.2d 456 (3d Cir.1982), we rejected reliance on the grids in this situation because the medical-vocational grids do not "purport to establish the existence of jobs for persons ... with both exertional and nonexertional impairments." Id. at 458.

There is, however, considerable variety among the courts of appeals regarding the scope of the limitation on the use of the grids when a claimant has exertional and nonexertional impairments. Some cases from the other circuits have held that the bar on exclusive reliance on the grids in this situation is limited by the requirement that the nonexertional impairment invoked must be significant enough to limit further the range of work permitted by the exertional limitations (the residual functional capacity) before it precludes application of the grids. See, e.g., Heggarty v. Sullivan, 947 F.2d 990, 996 (1st Cir.1991) (per curiam) (noting law of circuit that the Commissioner may rely on the grids if the claimant's nonexertional impairment does not "significantly" affect his or her ability to perform the full range of jobs at the appropriate exertional level); Bapp v. Bowen, 802 F.2d 601, 605 (2d Cir.1986) (holding that if the guidelines adequately reflect a claimant's condition, using them to determine disability status is appropriate, "[b]ut if a claimant's nonexertional impairments significantly limit the range of work permitted by his exertional limitations then the grids obviously will not accurately determine disability status because they fail to take into account claimant's nonexertional impairments" (internal quotation marks omitted)); Fraga v. Bowen, 810 F.2d 1296, 1304 (5th Cir.1987) (when the claimant's nonexertional impairments do not significantly affect his residual functional capacity, the ALJ may rely exclusively on the guidelines in determining whether there is other work available that the claimant can perform); Warmoth v. Bowen, 798 F.2d 1109, 1112 (7th Cir.1986) (per curiam) ("While a vocational expert's specialized knowledge undoubtedly would be helpful in the present case, this is not to say that testimony from such an expert is required in this and every other case involving a non-exertional impairment; rather, we only require that there be reliable evidence of some kind that would persuade a reasonable person that the limitations in question do not significantly diminish the employment opportunities otherwise available." (citation omitted)); *Channel v. Heckler*, 747 F.2d 577, 582 n. 6 (10th Cir.1984) (per curiam) (holding that "the mere presence of a nonexertional impairment does not automatically preclude reliance on the grids"; rather, reliance on the grids is foreclosed only when the nonexertional impairment poses an additional limitation on the claimant's ability to perform a range of available jobs.).[12]

This described limitation on the rule against exclusive reliance on the grids when the claimant has exertional and nonexertional impairments significantly narrows the rule. It leaves the ALJ free to assess whether there is credible evidence that the nonexertional impairment limits residual functional capacity before going off the grids, in effect allowing the ALJ to refer to the grids (and consider the medical evidence) to determine whether the nonexertional impairment is severe enough to make the grids inapplicable before considering any evidence in addition to the grids. *See, e.g., Bapp*, 802 F.2d at 606 ("Upon remand the ALJ must reevaluate whether the Secretary has shown that plaintiff's capability to perform the full range of light work was not significantly diminished [by his nonexertional impairments]. That initial determination can be made without resort to a vocational expert.").

The government's interpretation of 20 C.F.R. Part 404, Subpart P, Appendix 2, § 200.00(e)(2) (1999) in effect adopts this limitation on the rule barring exclusive reliance on the grids when the claimant has exertional and nonexertional impairments. In *Washington v. Heckler*, 756 F.2d 959 (3d Cir.1985), we left open the possibility that the Commissioner could use the grids as a "framework" for determining the extent to which a nonexertional limitation may further diminish work capacity. See id. at 967-68. But the framework approach does not comport with *Heckler v. Campbell*, 461 U.S. 458, 103 S.Ct. 1952, 76 L.Ed.2d 66 (1983), when it is defined as broadly as it is here.

The regulation provides that, where an individual has an impairment or a combination of impairments resulting in both exertional and nonexertional limitations, if a finding of disability is not possible based on exertional limitations alone, the grids "provide a framework for consideration of how much the individual's work capability is further diminished in terms of any types of jobs that would be contraindicated by the nonexer-

---

[12] A finding under step two of the regulations that a claimant has a "severe" nonexertional limitation is not the same as a finding that the nonexertional limitation affects residual functional capacity. The cases cited above do not rely on the "severity" determination, but rather impose an additional requirement that the nonexertional impairment limit the capacity for work beyond the claimant's residual functional capacity, given the limitations imposed by the exertional impairment. *See, e.g., Bapp*, 802 F.2d at 606 ("By the use of the phrase 'significantly diminish' we mean the additional loss of work capacity beyond a negligible one or, in other words, one that so narrows a claimant's possible range of work as to deprive him of a meaningful employment opportunity.").

tional limitations." 20 C.F.R. pt. 404, subpt. P, app. 2, § 200.00(e)(2) (1999). By comparison, the regulations governing a determination of disability when the claimant has solely exertional impairments direct a finding of disability without reference to additional evidence when the factors of the claimant's particular impairments coincide with the criteria of a rule:

> The existence of jobs in the national economy is reflected in the "Decisions" shown in the rules; i.e., in promulgating the rules, administrative notice has been taken of the numbers of unskilled jobs that exist throughout the national economy at the various functional levels (sedentary, light, medium, heavy, and very heavy) as supported by the "Dictionary of Occupational Titles" and the "Occupational Outlook Handbook," published by the Department of Labor; the "County Business Patterns" and "Census Surveys" published by the Bureau of the Census; and occupational surveys of light and sedentary jobs prepared for the Social Security Administration by various State employment agencies. Thus, when all factors coincide with the criteria of a rule, the existence of such jobs is established. However, the existence of such jobs for individuals whose remaining functional capacity or other factors do not coincide with the criteria of a rule must be further considered in terms of what kinds of jobs or types of work may be either additionally indicated or precluded.

20 C.F.R. pt. 404, subpt. P, app. 2, § 200.00(b) (1999).

As this comparison between the regulations makes clear, the only facts established in the grids are of unskilled jobs in the national economy for claimants with exertional impairments who fit the criteria of the rule at the various functional levels. The regulations do not purport to establish jobs that exist in the national economy at the various functional levels when a claimant has a nonexertional impairment (or does not meet the criteria of the rule for other reasons).

The Supreme Court upheld reliance on the grids to determine whether there are jobs in the national economy for claimants who have only exertional impairments because, even though the Social Security Act requires an individualized determination regarding disability, the agency had promulgated valid regulations identifying these jobs and the availability of jobs was an issue that did not require case-by-case determination. *See Campbell*, 461 U.S. at 467, 103 S.Ct. 1952 (1983) ("[E]ven where an agency's enabling statute expressly requires it to hold a hearing, the agency may rely on its rulemaking authority to determine issues that do not require case-by-case determination."). The regulations still require an individualized hearing in which the claimant has an opportunity to present evidence regarding his particular disabilities; the grids only apply to "an issue that is not unique to each claimant—the types and numbers of jobs that exist in the national economy. This type of general factual issue may be resolved as fairly through rulemaking as by introducing the testimony of vocational experts at each disability hearing." *Id.* at 468, 103 S.Ct. 1952 (citations omitted).

Like the availability of jobs for claimants with exertional impairments, the availability of jobs for claimants with exertional and nonexertional impairments may well be an issue that does not require case-by-case determination and may be fairly resolved through rulemaking. But the Social Security Administration has not promulgated regulations identifying jobs in the national economy for claimants with combined exertional and nonexertional limitations or identifying nonexertional impairments that are not significant enough to diminish a claimant's occupation base considering his exertional impairment alone. *Campbell*, by force of implication, requires such a regulation (or similar procedure establishing general facts) in order to direct a determination of disability without reference to individualized evidence that there are jobs in the national economy that the claimant can perform. Until the government takes steps to establish such general facts for claimants with exertional and nonexertional impairments, the government cannot satisfy its burden under the Act by reference to the grids alone.

* * *

The Social Security Administration has not conducted a rulemaking establishing either that the lack of binocular vision does not significantly diminish the occupational base for light work or more generally establishing common facts applicable to individuals with Sykes's set of impairments. The grids establish, for exertional impairments only, that jobs exist in the national economy that people with those impairments can perform. When a claimant has an additional nonexertional impairment, the question whether that impairment diminishes his residual functional capacity is functionally the same as the question whether there are jobs in the national economy that he can perform given his combination of impairments. The grids do not purport to answer this question, and thus under *Campbell* the practice of the ALJ determining without taking additional evidence the effect of the nonexertional impairment on residual functional capacity cannot stand.

* * *

* * *

D. Conclusion

The government argues that the rule we adopt today is "rigid and burdensome." We emphasize that it need not be. The Commissioner frequently relies on vocational expert testimony; he appears to have arrangements with many such experts. But, as we have held, the Commissioner can rely on evidence other than vocational expert testimony to establish that a claimant's nonexertional limitation does not diminish residual functional capacity. * * *

The flaw in the government's argument is simple. *Campbell* permits the government to establish through a rulemaking rather than an individualized fact-finding the fact that there are jobs in the economy for claimants with particular types of impairments. But it does not permit the government to avoid its burden to establish this fact. To hold otherwise would be to eviscerate the requirement that disability hearings will be individualized determinations based on evidence adduced at a hearing.

* * *

A) RFC AND THE CAPACITY TO PERFORM THE FULL RANGE OF WORK ACTIVITY

The grids are also inapplicable when a claimant cannot perform the full range of work activity contemplated for the appropriate residual functional capacity (FRC), usually an FRC for sedentary work.

SOCIAL SECURITY RULING SSR 96-9P
(1996)

POLICY INTERPRETATION RULING TITLES II AND XVI: DETERMINING CAPABILITY TO DO OTHER WORK—IMPLICATIONS OF A RESIDUAL FUNCTIONAL CAPACITY FOR LESS THAN A FULL RANGE OF SEDENTARY WORK

PURPOSE: To explain the Social Security Administration's policies regarding the impact of a residual functional capacity (RFC) assessment for less than a full range of sedentary work on an individual's ability to do other work. In particular, to emphasize that:

1. An RFC for less than a full range of sedentary work reflects very serious limitations resulting from an individual's medical impairment(s) and is expected to be relatively rare.

2. However, a finding that an individual has the ability to do less than a full range of sedentary work does not necessarily equate with a decision of "disabled." If the performance of past relevant work is precluded by an RFC for less than the full range of sedentary work, consideration must still be given to whether there is other work in the national economy that the individual is able to do, considering age, education, and work experience.

* * *

INTRODUCTION: Under the sequential evaluation process, once it has been determined that an individual is not engaging in substantial gainful activity and has a "severe" medically determinable impairment(s) which, though not meeting or equaling the criteria of any listing, prevents the individual from performing past relevant work (PRW), it must be determined whether the individual can do any other work, considering the individual's RFC, age, education, and work experience.

* * *

Initially, the RFC assessment is a function-by-function assessment based upon all of the relevant evidence of an individual's ability to perform work-related activities. This RFC assessment is first used for a function-by-function comparison with the functional demands of an individual's PRW as he or she actually performed it and then, if necessary, as the work is generally performed in the national economy.

However, at the last step of the sequential evaluation process, the RFC assessment is used to determine an individual's "maximum sustained work capability" and, where solely non-exertional impairments are not involved, must be expressed in terms of the exertional classifications of work: sedentary, light, medium, heavy, and very heavy work. The rules of appendix 2 of subpart P of Regulations No. 4 take administrative notice of the existence of numerous unskilled occupations within each of these exertional levels. The rules are then used to direct decisions about whether an individual is disabled or, when the individual is unable to perform the full range of work contemplated by an exertional level(s), as a framework for decisionmaking considering the individual's RFC, age, education, and work experience.

The impact of an RFC for less than a full range of sedentary work is especially critical for individuals who have not yet attained age 50. Since age, education, and work experience are not usually significant factors in limiting the ability of individuals under age 50 to make an adjustment to other work, the conclusion whether such individuals who are limited to less than the full range of sedentary work are disabled will depend primarily on the nature and extent of their functional limitations or restrictions. On the other hand, since the rules in Table No. 1 of appendix 2, "Residual Functional Capacity: Maximum Sustained Work Capability Limited to Sedentary Work as a Result of Severe Medically Determinable Impairment(s)," direct a decision of "disabled" for individuals age 50 and over who are limited to a full range of sedentary work, unless the individual has transferable skills or education that provides for direct entry into skilled sedentary work, the impact of an RFC for less than the full range of sedentary work in such individuals is less critical.

POLICY INTERPRETATION: Under the regulations, "sedentary work" represents a significantly restricted range of work. Individuals who are limited to no more than sedentary work by their medical impairments have very serious functional limitations. For the majority of individuals who are age 50 or older and who are limited to the full range of sedentary work by their medical impairments, the rules and guidelines in appendix 2 require a conclusion of "disabled."

Nevertheless, the rules in Table No. 1 in appendix 2 take administrative notice that there are approximately 200 separate unskilled sedentary occupations, each representing numerous jobs, in the national economy. Therefore, even though "sedentary work" represents a significantly restricted range of work, this range in itself is not so prohibitively restricted as to negate work capability for substantial gainful activity in all individuals.

Moreover, since each occupation administratively noticed by Table No. 1 represents numerous jobs, the ability to do even a limited range of sedentary work does not in itself establish disability in all individuals, although a finding of "disabled" usually applies when the full range of sedentary work is significantly eroded (*see Using the Rules in Table No. 1 as a Framework: "Erosion" of the Occupational Base* below). In deciding whether an individual who is *limited* to a partial range of sedentary work is able to make an adjustment to work other than any PRW, the adjudicator is required to make an individualized determination, considering age, education, and work experience, including any skills the individual may have that are transferable to other work, or education that provides for direct entry into skilled work, under the rules and guidelines in the regulations.

* * *

The Occupational Base for Sedentary Work

The term "occupational base" means the approximate number of occupations that an individual has the RFC to perform considering all exertional and nonexertional limitations and restrictions. A full range of sedentary work includes all or substantially all of the approximately 200 unskilled sedentary occupations administratively noticed in Table No. 1.

Thus, the RFC addressed by a particular rule in Table No. 1 establishes an occupational base that at a minimum includes the full range of unskilled sedentary occupations administratively noticed. The base may be broadened by the addition of specific skilled or semiskilled occupations that an individual with an RFC limited to sedentary work can perform by reason of his or her education or work experience. However, if the individual has no transferable skills or no education or training that provides for direct entry into skilled work, the occupational base represented by the rules in Table No. 1 comprises only the sedentary unskilled occupations in the national economy that such an individual can perform.

The rules in Table No. 1 direct conclusions as to disability where the findings of fact coincide with all of the criteria of a particular rule; i.e., RFC (a maximum sustained work capability for sedentary work) and the vocational factors of age, education, and work experience. In order for a rule in Table No. 1 to direct a conclusion of "not disabled," the individual must be able to perform the full range of work administratively noticed by a rule. This means that the individual must be able to perform substantially all of the strength demands defining the sedentary level of exertion, as well as the physical and mental nonexertional demands that are also required for the performance of substantially all of the unskilled work considered at the sedentary level. Therefore, in order for a rule to direct a conclusion of "not disabled," an individual must also have no impairment that restricts the nonexertional capabilities to a level below those needed to perform unskilled work, in this case, at the sedentary level.

Using the Rules in Table No. 1 as a Framework: "Erosion" of the Occupational Base

Where any one of the findings of fact does not coincide with the corresponding criterion of a rule in Table No. 1 (except in those cases where the concept of borderline age applies), the rule does not direct a decision. In cases such as the following, the medical-vocational rules must be used as a framework for considering the extent of any erosion of the sedentary occupational base:

    * Any one of an individual's exertional capacities is determined to be less than that required to perform a full range of sedentary work; or

    * Based on an individual's exertional capacities, a rule in Table No. 1 would direct a decision of "not disabled," but the individual also has a nonexertional limitation(s) that narrows the potential range of sedentary work to which he or she might be able to adjust (i.e., the individual has the exertional capacity to do the full range of sedentary

work, but the sedentary occupational base is reduced because of at least one nonexertional limitation).

When there is a reduction in an individual's exertional or nonexertional capacity so that he or she is unable to perform substantially all of the occupations administratively noticed in Table No. 1, the individual will be unable to perform the full range of sedentary work: the occupational base will be "eroded" by the additional limitations or restrictions. However, the mere inability to perform substantially all sedentary unskilled occupations does not equate with a finding of disability. There may be a number of occupations from the approximately 200 occupations administratively noticed, and jobs that exist in significant numbers, that an individual may still be able to perform even with a sedentary occupational base that has been eroded.

Whether the individual will be able to make an adjustment to other work requires adjudicative judgment regarding factors such as the type and extent of the individual's limitations or restrictions and the extent of the erosion of the occupational base; i.e., the impact of the limitations or restrictions on the number of sedentary unskilled occupations or the total number of jobs to which the individual may be able to adjust, considering his or her age, education, and work experience, including any transferable skills or education providing for direct entry into skilled work. Where there is more than a slight impact on the individual's ability to perform the full range of sedentary work, if the adjudicator finds that the individual is able to do other work, the adjudicator must cite examples of occupations or jobs the individual can do and provide a statement of the incidence of such work in the region where the individual resides or in several regions of the country.

* * *

Use of Vocational Resources

When the extent of erosion of the unskilled sedentary occupational base is not clear, the adjudicator may consult various authoritative written resources, such as the DOT, the SCO, the **Occupational Outlook Handbook**, or **County Business Patterns**.

In more complex cases, the adjudicator may use the resources of a vocational specialist or vocational expert.[8] The vocational resource may be

---

[8] At the hearings and appeals levels, vocational experts (VEs) are vocational professionals who provide impartial expert opinion during the hearings and appeals process either by testifying or by providing written responses to interrogatories. A VE may be used before, during, or after a hearing. Whenever a VE is used, the individual has the right to review and respond to the VE evidence prior to the issuance of a decision. The VE's opinion is not binding on an adjudicator, but must be weighed along with all other evidence.

asked to provide any or all of the following: An analysis of the impact of the RFC upon the full range of sedentary work, which the adjudicator may consider in determining the extent of the erosion of the occupational base, examples of occupations the individual may be able to perform, and citations of the existence and number of jobs in such occupations in the national economy.

* * *

HADDOCK V. APFEL

196 F.3d 1084, 65 Soc.Sec.Rep.Ser. 168 (10th Cir. 1999)

Before BALDOCK, EBEL, and MURPHY, Circuit Judges.

EBEL, Circuit Judge.

* * *

Disability Claim

Robert Haddock was born on January 6, 1942. He completed ten years of school. His past jobs included lead carpenter, school bus driver, school janitor, and lift-dump operator. He filed his claim for disability benefits on January 19, 1995, alleging that he became disabled in November 1992 due to hip problems, shortness of breath related to heart and lung problems, lack of strength, and residual chest pains resulting from a heart attack in May 1992.

The ALJ denied Mr. Haddock's claim at step five of the evaluation sequence. He decided at step four that Mr. Haddock did not have the residual functional capacity (RFC) to return to either of his relevant past jobs-the skilled, heavy job of lead carpenter or the unskilled, medium job of school janitor. At step five, the ALJ found that Mr. Haddock nevertheless retained the RFC to perform sedentary work if he could alternate sitting and standing. He further found that Mr. Haddock had skills transferable to semi-skilled work, had a limited or less education, and was closely approaching advanced age (as Mr. Haddock was just over fifty years old at the time his insured status expired). The VE testified that Mr. Haddock could perform four jobs: payroll clerk, parts clerk, materials lister, and inventory clerk. The VE did not volunteer the source of his information, nor did anyone at the hearing ask him to identify or discuss it. Lumping all four jobs together, the VE said that there were many thousands of these jobs in the regional and national economies. The ALJ decided that Mr. Haddock was not disabled in light of this expert vocational testimony and Rule 201.11 from the medical-vocational guidelines (the "grids"). * * * Mr. Haddock passed away on December 2, 1997. Mrs. Haddock appeals from the denial of his claim for disability benefits.

* * *

* * *

Discussion

* * *

At step four, the ALJ must "'assess the nature and extent of [the claimant's] physical limitations and then determine [the claimant's] residual functional capacity for work activity on a regular and continuing basis.'" *Winfrey v. Chater*, 92 F.3d 1017, 1023 (10th Cir.1996) (quoting 20 C.F.R. § 404.1545(b)). If the ALJ concludes that the claimant cannot perform any of his past work with his remaining RFC, the ALJ bears the burden at step five to show that there are jobs in the regional or national economies that the claimant can perform with the limitations the ALJ has found him to have. It is not the claimant's burden to produce or develop vocational evidence at step five.

When a claimant's exertional level, age, education, and skill level (i.e., work experience) fit precisely within the criteria of a grid rule, an ALJ may base a determination of nondisability conclusively on the grids. When a requirement to alternate sitting and standing limits a claimant's ability to do the full range of sedentary work, as in this case, an ALJ may not rely on this shortcut method. *See Thompson* [*v. Sullivan*, 987 F.2d 1482, 1488 (10th Cir. 1993)]; 20 C.F.R. pt. 404, subpt. P, app. 2, § 200.00(e). In a case like this one, the ALJ "must cite examples of occupations or jobs the individual can do and provide a statement of the incidence of such work in the region where the individual lives or in several regions of the country." Social Security Ruling 96-9p, 1996 WL 374185, at *5; *see also* Social Security Ruling 83-14, 1983 WL 31254, at *6; Social Security Ruling 83-12, 1983 WL 31253, at *5. The requirement to identify specific jobs the claimant can perform with the limitations the ALJ has found him to have also pertains when the ALJ finds that the claimant has acquired skills which will transfer to other work, as in this case. *See* Social Security Ruling 96-9p, 1996 WL 374185, at *4; Social Security Ruling 82-41, 1982 WL 31389, at *7. Identified jobs must be shown to exist in "significant numbers" in the regional or national economies. 42 U.S.C. § 423(d)(2)(A). To summarize, in a case like this one, the ALJ must find that the claimant retains a particular exertional capacity, decide whether the claimant has acquired transferable skills, identify specific jobs that the claimant can perform with the restrictions the ALJ has found the claimant to have, and verify that the jobs the claimant can do exist in significant numbers in the regional or national economies. All of these findings must be supported by substantial evidence.

* * *

In this case, the ALJ found that Mr. Haddock was limited to sedentary, semi-skilled work that would allow him to alternate sitting and standing. The case must be remanded for the ALJ to investigate whether there is a significant number of specific jobs Mr. Haddock could have done with his limitations.

The judgment of the United States District Court for the Eastern District of Oklahoma is REVERSED, and the case is REMANDED with instructions for the district court to remand to the agency for additional proceedings.

CHAPTER 6

SPECIAL ELIGIBILITY ISSUES FOR DISABILITY BENEFITS

■ ■ ■

As noted already in Chapter 4, the Social Security Act disability standard includes—in addition to general medical and vocational criteria for eligibility—a number of special provisions covering certain special circumstances or types of claims. Typically, these statutory provisions were enacted in order to clarify policies in areas that had proven to be problematic; disability based on pain (and other subjective symptoms) and disability based on drug addiction or alcoholism are two prominent examples. Special rules governing certain difficult issues are set out in federal regulations and federal case law as well. Indeed, these special statutory or regulatory rules often were promulgated in response to litigation challenging SSA policy in the particular area, followed sometimes by public policy debate in Congress and at the Social Security Administration.

This chapter examines five such special eligibility issues that are relevant to many disability claims: pain and other subjective symptoms, mental impairments, stress, drug addiction and alcoholism, and remediable impairments and the side effects of medication.

A. PAIN AND OTHER SUBJECTIVE SYMPTOMS

1. 1984 AMENDMENTS: CLARIFYING THE STANDARD FOR DISABILITY BASED ON PAIN AND OTHER SUBJECTIVE SYMPTOMS

Although the Social Security Administration has long recognized that disability can result from pain and other subjective symptoms, the standard against which pain-based claims would be measured remained unclear through the early 1980s. Ambiguous agency policy led some adjudicators—and some federal courts—to require objective medical proof of subjective symptoms, including pain. Congress eventually responded by establishing a special statutory standard in 1984 amendments to the Social Security Act that embraced a two-step process for establishing pain-based disability. *See* Social Security Disability Benefits Reform Act of

1984, P. L. 98-460 §3, 98 Stat. 1794 (1984) (codified at 42 U.S.C. §423(d)(5)(A)). Thus, **42 U.S.C. § 423(d)(5)(A)[APP-STATS]** requires objective proof of a medical impairment that "could reasonably be expected to produce" the claimant's alleged (subjective) symptoms, including pain. (Although technically an "interim" standard that governs only claims decided before January 1, 1987, it remains in the United States Code and has been effectively re-codified in the Code of Federal Regulations, as described later in this section.)

Under this formulation, the first step in evaluating a claim based on pain or other subjective symptoms is to determine whether objective medical evidence exists that can confirm an underlying impairment that "could reasonably be expected" to result in the intensity and severity of pain or other subjective symptoms alleged by the claimant. Once such a showing is made, the second step is to determine the actual extent of the claimant's pain (or other symptoms) and whether those symptoms—which must be reasonably consistent with the medical signs and findings establishing the underlying impairment—are sufficiently severe to qualify as disabling under the Act. In effect, these types of claims present two interrelated questions:

1. Is there objective proof of an underlying medical impairment that could produce the claimant's subjective symptoms, including pain?

2. Are the claimant's symptoms, supported by subjective (and other relevant) evidence, consistent with what could be reasonably expected from the underlying impairment?

The requirement that there be proof of an objective underlying medical impairment that could produce the alleged pain serves to preclude claims based on purely subjective statements. But even claimants who have the required proof of an underlying medical impairment can still be denied benefits if they fail to show, through subjective statements and other proof, that the underlying impairment has, in fact, produced the degree of pain alleged (and that that degree of pain is disabling within the terms of the Act).

Federal courts around the country had weighed in on the issue of objective vs. subjective proof of pain and other symptoms during the early 1980s. *See, e.g.,* Wiggins v. Schweiker, 679 F.2d 1387 (11th Cir. 1982); Ware v. Schweiker, 651 F.2d 408 (5th Cir. 1981). A few months prior to the enactment of the 1984 Amendments, the Eighth Circuit entered an order that had been agreed to by the plaintiffs and the Social Security Administration in a class action seeking enforcement of that circuit's case law regarding the use of subjective evidence of pain. Polaski v. Heckler, 739 F.2d 1320, 6 Soc.Sec.Rep.Ser. 123 (8th Cir. 1984). The court in *Polaski* held—along with courts in other circuits around the country—that

1) objective medical evidence of the severity of pain was not necessary, and 2) adjudicators must fully consider all evidence and testimony relevant to subjective complaints, and not accept or reject subjective complaints based solely on their own personal observations. In a later decision in the same case, the Eighth Circuit addressed the question of whether the Act, as amended in 1984, negated the *Polaski* settlement order.

POLASKI V. HECKLER

751 F.2d 943, 8 Soc.Sec.Rep.Ser. 178 (8th Cir. 1984)

Before HEANEY, JOHN R. GIBSON and FAGG, Circuit Judges.

HEANEY, Circuit Judge.

The Secretary of Health and Human Services appeals from a district court order granting a preliminary injunction to a class of plaintiffs seeking social security disability benefits. For the reasons set forth below, we remand for further proceedings.

I. BACKGROUND.

For several months a dispute has raged in this and other Circuits on the question of whether the Secretary of Health and Human Services (Secretary) has been properly construing the Social Security Act, particularly with respect to persons who claim to be disabled because of pain and with respect to persons whose disability benefits have been terminated. * * *

* * *

* * *

III. PAIN CASES.

The July 11, 1984, stipulation signed by the Secretary and the plaintiffs with respect to evaluation of pain read as follows:

A claimant has the burden of proving that the disability results from a medically determinable physical or mental impairment. Symptoms such as pain, shortness of breath, weakness, or nervousness are the individual's own perceptions of the effects of a physical or mental impairment(s). Because of their subjective characteristics and the absence of any reliable techniques for measurement, symptoms (especially pain) are difficult to prove, disprove, or quantify. *As a result of this difficulty, some adjudicators have misinterpreted the Secretary's policies as enunciated in SSR-82-58.* [Emphasis added.]

In particular, some adjudicators may have misinterpreted Example No. 2 in SSR-82-58 to allow allegations of pain to be disregarded solely because the allegations are not fully corroborated by objective medical findings typically associated with pain. The example should not be construed to be inconsistent with the text of SSR-82-58 which states in part:

> The effects of symptoms must be considered in terms of any additional physical or mental restrictions they may impose beyond those clearly demonstrated by the objective physical manifestations of disorders. Symptoms can sometimes suggest a greater severity of impairment than is demonstrated by objective and medical findings alone.

> While the claimant has the burden of proving that the disability results from a medically determinable physical or mental impairment, direct medical evidence of the cause and effect relationship between the impairment and the degree of claimant's subjective complaints need not be produced. The adjudicator may not disregard a claimant's subjective complaints solely because the objective medical evidence does not fully support them.

> The absence of an objective medical basis which supports the degree of severity of subjective complaints alleged is just one factor to be considered in evaluating the credibility of the testimony and complaints. The adjudicator must give full consideration to all of the evidence presented relating to subjective complaints, including the claimant's prior work record, and observations by third parties and treating and examining physicians relating to such matters as:

> 1. the claimant's daily activities;

> 2. the duration, frequency and intensity of the pain;

> 3. precipitating and aggravating factors;

> 4. dosage, effectiveness and side effects of medication;

> 5. functional restrictions.

The adjudicator is not free to accept or reject the claimant's subjective complaints *solely* on the basis of personal observations. Subjective complaints may be discounted if there are inconsistencies in the evidence as a whole. [Emphasis in original.]

Polaski v. Heckler, 739 F.2d 1320, 1321-22 (8th Cir.1984).

On July 17, 1984, this Court issued an order approving the language as a correct statement of the law under the Social Security Act and of the case law in the Eighth Circuit. On July 18, 1984, the Secretary disseminated the approved language to all adjudicators--state district offices, state DDS offices, and ALJs in the Eighth Circuit. It disseminated the same information to the Appeals Council.

Thereafter, this Court permitted the parties to file supplemental briefs to explain how the agreement on the pain standard, as approved by this Court, affected this litigation. The government's brief stated:

> The approved language is simply a clarification of SSR 82-58, which is the Secretary's instructional ruling on the evaluation of pain and other subjective complaints. This point is made clear by the specific reference in the approved language to SSR 82-58 *and the fact that errors in cases involving pain may have been the result of misinterpretations of the SSR and specifically Example No. 2 in the SSR.* * * * ("[S]ome adjudicators have misinterpreted the Secretary's policies enunciated in SSR-82-58"; and "some adjudicators may have misinterpreted Example No. 2 in SSR-82-58").
>
> That the approved language is a clarification of SSR 82-58 is further reinforced by the fact that the Secretary's regulations and SSR 82-58 require that pain and other subjective complaints be evaluated according to the following factors:
>
>   1. the claimant's daily activities;
>
>   2. the duration, frequency and intensity of the pain;
>
>   3. precipitating and aggravating factors;
>
>   4. dosage, effectiveness and side effects of medication;
>
>   5. functional restrictions.
>
> See SSR 82-58. The approved language identifies the same factors and similarly requires their consideration in the evaluation of subjective complaints of pain. * * *
>
> In sum, the approved language is merely a restatement of the standard which the Secretary has been following all along. [Emphasis added, citations omitted.]

On September 19, 1984, Congress passed the Social Security Disability Benefits Reform Act of 1984.[2] That Act amended the existing law with respect to evaluation of pain. It provides:

EVALUATION OF PAIN

SEC. 3.   (a)(1)[.]   Section 223(d)(5) of the Social Security Act is amended by inserting after the first sentence the following new sentences: "An individual's statement as to pain or other symptoms shall not alone be conclusive evidence of disability as defined in this section; there must be medical signs and findings established by medically acceptable clinical or laboratory diagnostic techniques, which show the existence of a medical impairment that results from anatomical, physiological, or psychological abnormalities which could reasonably be expected to produce the pain or other symptoms alleged and which, when considered with all evidence required to be furnished under this paragraph (including statements of the individual or his physician as to the intensity and persistence of such pain or other symptoms which may reasonably be accepted as consistent with the medical signs and findings), would lead to a conclusion that the individual is under a disability.   Objective medical evidence of pain or other symptoms established by medically acceptable clinical or laboratory techniques (for example, deteriorating nerve or muscle tissue) must be considered in reaching a conclusion as to whether the individual is under a disability."

* * *

The conference report summarized Congress's understanding of present law with respect to evaluation of pain as follows:

There is no statutory provision concerning the evaluation of pain (or the use of subjective allegations of pain) in determining eligibility for disability benefits.   The definition of disability requires that the person be unable to work by reason of a "medically determinable impairment"—one which results from "anatomical, physiological, or psychological abnormalities which are demonstrable by medically acceptable clinical and laboratory diagnostic techniques."

By regulation, subjective allegations of symptoms of impairments, such as pain, cannot alone be evidence of disability.   There must be medical signs or other findings which show there is a medi-

---

[2] The existing statute stated only that: "An individual shall not be considered to be under a disability unless he furnishes such medical and other evidence of the existence thereof as the Secretary may require." 42 U.S.C. § 423(d)(5).

cal condition that could be reasonably expected to produce those symptoms and that is severe enough to be disabling.

130 Cong.Rec. H9828-29 (daily ed. Sept. 19, 1984).

The conference report then stated:

The statutory language providing for an interim standard for evaluation of pain is amended to more accurately reflect current policies.

Id. at H9829.

The Chairman of the Social Security Subcommittee, Congressman J.J. Pickle, commenting on the statutory provisions concerning pain, stated:

With reference to pain, the conference agreement puts present regulatory policy into statute until January 1, 1987, and mandates that in the meantime, a study be conducted so that we might better deal with this very difficult issue. I know that many Members in both bodies are concerned about the fairness of our present policies and I would expect that as we continue to benefit from the progress of medical science, we will improve our laws in this regard.

Id. at H9836.

No other House member commented on the statutory provision with respect to pain.

It seems clear from the conference report and the statement of Congressman Pickle, a House manager of the bill, that it was the intent of Congress to write the regulation dealing with pain into the statute. That this result was accomplished is evidenced by the fact that the amended statute closely tracks the regulations.

The question, then, is does the amended statute negate the settlement agreement approved by this Court. We conclude it does not. The Secretary's supplemental brief of August 1, 1984, quoted above, provides the rationale for this conclusion.

Our understanding is simply this: The amended statute on pain evaluation requires the Secretary and adjudicators to follow regulation § 404.1529 and ruling SSR 82-58 in evaluating pain until January 1, 1987. Adjudicators are to do so, however, in light of the settlement agreement which recognized that some adjudicators had misinterpreted SSR 82-58. It follows that all pain cases in the Eighth Circuit currently under evaluation at the administrative or judicial level will be evaluated on the basis of the amended statute, regulation § 404.1529, and ruling SSR 82-58 as clarified by the settlement agreement. Cases filed after this date will be evaluated on the same basis. As we stated in our opinion of July 17, 1984, the settlement agreement is "a correct statement of the law concerning evaluation of pain and other subjective complaints for determining disability." It would thus seem that any differences between the Secretary and this Circuit with respect to the law relating to the evaluation of pain have been resolved * * * although questions as to the substantiality of evidence in pain cases will undoubtedly continue to arise in the future.

* * *

IV. CONCLUSION.

This case is remanded to the district court with directions to proceed in a manner consistent with this opinion.

[Concurring opinion of Judge John R. Gibson omitted.]

NOTE ON SOCIAL SECURITY RULINGS ON PAIN

The court in *Polaski* referred to Social Security Ruling SSR 82-58 (1982), which was one of a number of Rulings that SSA issued as policy statements to aid in guiding the evaluation of claims based on pain. The problem was that SSR 82-58 seemed to require objective medical evidence to prove both the existence of an underlying impairment and the severity of alleged pain. SSR 82-58 was superseded in 1988 by SSR 88-13, which, after noting that SSA policy is consistent with the pain standard set out in the 1984 Amendments, explained:

> There are situations in which an individual's alleged or reported symptoms, such as pain, suggest the possibility of a greater restriction of the individual's ability to function than can be demonstrated by objective medical evidence alone. In such cases, reasonable conclusions as to any limitations on the individual's ability to do basic work activities can be derived from the consideration of other information in conjunction with medical evidence. This is consistent with court decisions which require that statements of the claimant or his/her physician as to the intensity and persistence of pain or other symptoms which may reasonably be accepted as consistent with the medical signs and laboratory findings are to be included in the evidence to be considered in making a disability determination.

SSR 88-13 was itself superseded—but only for cases in the Fourth Circuit—to comply with the decision in Hyatt v. Sullivan, 899 F.2d 329 (4th Cir.1990). As explained in the superseding Ruling, SSR 90-1p (1990):

In a recent decision in *Hyatt v. Sullivan*, the Court of Appeals for the Fourth Circuit found that SSR 88-13 was consistent with Fourth Circuit law. However, the court was concerned that some adjudicators could have read SSR 88-13 in a manner inconsistent with circuit precedent, because the instruction not only contained some language from the obsoleted SSR 82-58 (which in part had been earlier held invalid by the court) but also because it was a reiteration of certain aspects of the policy on the evaluation of pain and other symptoms that the court previously had invalidated.

Therefore, the Court of Appeals held that in order to conform with Fourth Circuit law, the Social Security Administration (SSA) must issue instructions clearly expressing the circuit rule regarding pain (i.e., that objective findings of the pain's intensity, persistence and effect on an individual's work capacity are not required to find disability) to eliminate possible confusion on the part of adjudicators. To this end, the court held that SSA could amend SSR 88-13, 'to make it clear that it is not a reiteration of previous policy and that it has a more current effective date.' This Ruling, which simply amends the purpose and effective date sections of SSR 88-13, is designed to comply with the court's order in the *Hyatt* case.

SSR 88-13 and SSR 90-1p were in turn superseded by SSR 95-5p (1995), which was then superseded two years later by the current Ruling on the subject set out below. SSR 96-7p (1996) not only clarifies SSA policy relative to the implementation of the 1984 pain standard and subsequent regulations, but also addresses the role of credibility findings relative to subjective statements of pain and other symptoms.

SOCIAL SECURITY RULING SSR 96-7P
(1996)

POLICY INTERPRETATION RULING TITLES II AND XVI: EVALUATION OF SYMPTOMS IN DISABILITY CLAIMS: ASSESSING THE CREDIBILITY OF AN INDIVIDUAL'S STATEMENTS

PURPOSE: The purpose of this Ruling is to clarify when the evaluation of symptoms, including pain, under 20 CFR 404.1529 and 416.929 requires a finding about the credibility of an individual's statements about pain or other symptom(s) and its functional effects; to explain the factors to be considered in assessing the credibility of the individual's statements about symptoms; and to state the importance of explaining the reasons for the finding about the credibility of the individual's statements in the disability determination or decision. In particular, this Ruling emphasizes that:

1. No symptom or combination of symptoms can be the basis for a finding of disability, no matter how genuine the individual's com-

plaints may appear to be, unless there are medical signs and laboratory findings demonstrating the existence of a medically determinable physical or mental impairment(s) that could reasonably be expected to produce the symptoms.

2. When the existence of a medically determinable physical or mental impairment(s) that could reasonably be expected to produce the symptoms has been established, the intensity, persistence, and functionally limiting effects of the symptoms must be evaluated to determine the extent to which the symptoms affect the individual's ability to do basic work activities. This requires the adjudicator to make a finding about the credibility of the individual's statements about the symptom(s) and its functional effects.

3. Because symptoms, such as pain, sometimes suggest a greater severity of impairment than can be shown by objective medical evidence alone, the adjudicator must carefully consider the individual's statements about symptoms with the rest of the relevant evidence in the case record in reaching a conclusion about the credibility of the individual's statements if a disability determination or decision that is fully favorable to the individual cannot be made solely on the basis of objective medical evidence.

4. In determining the credibility of the individual's statements, the adjudicator must consider the entire case record, including the objective medical evidence, the individual's own statements about symptoms, statements and other information provided by treating or examining physicians or psychologists and other persons about the symptoms and how they affect the individual, and any other relevant evidence in the case record. An individual's statements about the intensity and persistence of pain or other symptoms or about the effect the symptoms have on his or her ability to work may not be disregarded solely because they are not substantiated by objective medical evidence.

5. It is not sufficient for the adjudicator to make a single, conclusory statement that "the individual's allegations have been considered" or that "the allegations are (or are not) credible." It is also not enough for the adjudicator simply to recite the factors that are described in the regulations for evaluating symptoms. The determination or decision must contain specific reasons for the finding on credibility, supported by the evidence in the case record, and must be sufficiently specific to make clear to the individual and to any subsequent reviewers the weight the adjudicator gave to the individual's statements and the reasons for that weight.

* * *

POLICY INTERPRETATION: A symptom is an individual's own description of his or her physical or mental impairment(s). Once the existence of a medically determinable physical or mental impairment(s) that could reasonably be expected to produce pain or other symptoms has been established, adjudicators must recognize that individuals may experience their symptoms differently and may be limited by their symptoms to a greater or lesser extent than other individuals with the same medical impairments and the same medical signs and laboratory findings. Because symptoms, such as pain, sometimes suggest a greater severity of impairment than can be shown by objective medical evidence alone, any statements of the individual concerning his or her symptoms must be carefully considered if a fully favorable determination or decision cannot be made solely on the basis of objective medical evidence.

If an individual's statements about pain or other symptoms are not substantiated by the objective medical evidence, the adjudicator must consider all of the evidence in the case record, including any statements by the individual and other persons concerning the individual's symptoms. The adjudicator must then make a finding on the credibility of the individual's statements about symptoms and their functional effects.

Credibility

In general, the extent to which an individual's statements about symptoms can be relied upon as probative evidence in determining whether the individual is disabled depends on the credibility of the statements. In basic terms, the credibility of an individual's statements about pain or other symptoms and their functional effects is the degree to which the statements can be believed and accepted as true. When evaluating the credibility of an individual's statements, the adjudicator must consider the entire case record and give specific reasons for the weight given to the individual's statements.

The finding on the credibility of the individual's statements cannot be based on an intangible or intuitive notion about an individual's credibility. The reasons for the credibility finding must be grounded in the evidence and articulated in the determination or decision. It is not sufficient to make a conclusory statement that "the individual's allegations have been considered" or that "the allegations are (or are not) credible." It is also not enough for the adjudicator simply to recite the factors that are described in the regulations for evaluating symptoms. The determination or decision must contain specific reasons for the finding on credibility, supported by the evidence in the case record, and must be sufficiently specific to make clear to the individual and to any subsequent reviewers the weight the adjudicator gave to the individual's statements and the reasons for that weight. This documentation is necessary in order to give the individual a full and fair review of his or her claim, and in order to ensure a well- reasoned determination or decision.

In making a finding about the credibility of an individual's statements, the adjudicator need not totally accept or totally reject the individual's statements. Based on a consideration of all of the evidence in the case record, the adjudicator may find all, only some, or none of an individual's allegations to be credible. The adjudicator may also find an individual's statements, such as statements about the extent of functional limitations or restrictions due to pain or other symptoms, to be credible to a certain degree. For example, an adjudicator may find credible an individual's statement that the abilities to lift and carry are affected by symptoms, but find only partially credible the individual's statements as to the extent of the functional limitations or restrictions due to symptoms; i.e., that the individual's abilities to lift and carry are compromised, but not to the degree alleged. Conversely, an adjudicator may find credible an individual's statement that symptoms limit his or her ability to concentrate, but find that the limitation is greater than that stated by the individual.

Moreover, a finding that an individual's statements are not credible, or not wholly credible, is not in itself sufficient to establish that the individual is not disabled. All of the evidence in the case record, including the individual's statements, must be considered before a conclusion can be made about disability.

Factors in Evaluating Credibility

Assessment of the credibility of an individual's statements about pain or other symptoms and about the effect the symptoms have on his or her ability to function must be based on a consideration of all of the evidence in the case record. This includes, but is not limited to:

* The medical signs and laboratory findings;

* Diagnosis, prognosis, and other medical opinions provided by treating or examining physicians or psychologists and other medical sources; and

* Statements and reports from the individual and from treating or examining physicians or psychologists and other persons about the individual's medical history, treatment and response, prior work record and efforts to work, daily activities, and other information concerning the individual's symptoms and how the symptoms affect the individual's ability to work.

The adjudicator must also consider any observations about the individual recorded by Social Security Administration (SSA) employees during interviews, whether in person or by telephone. In instances where the individual attends an administrative proceeding conducted by the adjudicator, the adjudicator may also consider his or her own recorded observations of the individual as part of the overall evaluation of the credibility of the individual's statements.

Consideration of the individual's statements and the statements and reports of medical sources and other persons with regard to the seven factors listed [20 C.F.R. §§ 404.1529(c), 416.929(c)], along with any other relevant information in the case record, including the information described above, will provide the adjudicator with an overview of the individual's subjective complaints. The adjudicator must then evaluate all of this information and draw appropriate inferences and conclusions about the credibility of the individual's statements.

* * *

2. EVALUATING PAIN-BASED DISABILITY UNDER CURRENT REGULATIONS

The majority of pain-based claims involve general allegations of pain, such as those supported by proof of musculoskeletal disorders resulting in back, neck, or shoulder pain. (Another smaller group of claims that involve largely subjective impairments and diseases, such as fibromyalgia and complex regional pain syndrome, are discussed in the next section.) Evaluating claims based on musculoskeletal disorders and other impairments diagnosed through accepted clinical testing has become relatively routine following the passage of the Social Security Disability Reform Act of 1984 and the various Social Security Rulings that followed. Moreover, the Social Security Administration issued regulations on evaluating pain-based claims in 1991 in an effort to clarify once and for all SSA's interpretation of the statutory mandate. These regulations state unequivocally that the agency will consider all of a claimant's symptoms, including pain, to the extent that those symptoms are reasonably consistent with the other evidence in the record—while at the same time caution that statements of pain or other symptoms alone will not be sufficient and that there must be medical proof of an underlying impairment that could reasonably be expected to have produced the alleged pain. *See* **20 C.F.R. §§ 404.1529(a), 416.929(a)[APP-REGS]**. *See also* **20 C.F.R. §§ 404.1529(b), 416.929(b)[APP-REGS].**

The 1991 regulations also clarify that "[t]he finding that [a claimant's] impairment(s) could reasonably be expected to produce [his or her] pain or other symptoms does not involve a determination as to the intensity, persistence, or functionally limiting effects of [those] symptoms." *Id.* In other words, evaluating the intensity and persistence of symptoms and how those symptoms limit a claimant's capacity for work is a separate, second step once a qualifying underlying medical impairment has been shown. The regulations then set out guidelines for evaluating the intensity, persistence, and functionally limiting effects of symptoms with both "objective medical evidence" and "other evidence" including: the claimant's daily activities; the location, duration, frequency, and intensity of the pain or other symptoms; any precipitating and aggravating factors; the type, dosage, effectiveness, and side effects of any medication for pain or other symptoms; other treatment for pain or other symptoms; any other measures to relieve pain or other symptoms; and any other factors related to functional limitations and restrictions due to pain or other symptoms. **20 C.F.R. §§** 404.1529**(c),** 416.929**(c)[APP-REGS]**.

Finally, **20 C.F.R. §§** 404.1529**(d),** 416.929**(d)[APP-REGS]** confirm that SSA will consider a claimant's symptoms, including pain, throughout the sequential evaluation process. As noted earlier, while it is now clear that pain and other subjective symptoms must be considered in evaluating a claim for disability benefits, the record must still show that the claimant is disabled within the meaning of the Social Security Act. As the court noted in affirming the denial of benefits in Michaels v. Apfel, 46 F.Supp.2d 126, 138, 62 Soc. Sec. Rep. Serv. 36 (D. Conn. 1999): "Disability requires more than a mere inability to work without pain. The ALJ did not discredit Plaintiff's complaints of pain entirely. He found instead that the medical evidence did not 'corroborate' his allegations of 'disabling pain.'"

The 1991 regulations thus not only track the mandates of the 1984 Amendments, but they also set out detailed guidelines for implementing the disability standard for claims based on pain and other subjective symptoms. The following case reviews the lead-up to the 1984 amendments and elaborates on the application of current regulations.

CRAIG V. CHATER

76 F.3d 585, 50 Soc. Sec. Rep. Ser. 140 (4th Cir. 1996)

Before WILKINS, LUTTIG, and WILLIAMS, Circuit Judges.

LUTTIG, Circuit Judge:

Ronda S. Craig appeals from a judgment of the district court upholding the determination of the Secretary of Health and Human Services that she was ineligible for disability insurance and Supplemental Security Income. For the reasons that follow, we remand the case to the ALJ for further consideration.

I.

Craig, currently 34, began seeing Dr. David Keller, a family practitioner, in 1986. She complained of headaches, back pain, leg pain, and hip pain. Between May 1986 and December 1992, Craig visited Dr. Keller some 31 times, complaining of similar pains, as well as cramping, dizziness, fatigue, and swelling of the face, feet, and legs. In that time, plaintiff's various diagnoses included chronic back pain, chronic tension headache, lumbrosacral strain, possible carpal tunnel syndrome, probable myofacial pain syndrome, fibrocytis syndrome, epigastric pain, and possible depression. In January 1990, Craig underwent an x-ray of the cervical spine which revealed degenerative arthritic change anteriorly at C3-4, C4-5, and C5-6 and that there was very early disk space narrowing. J.A. at 118. At the same time, a CT brain scan showed "normal." *Id.* In September of 1991, Dr. Keller performed MRI scans of the cervical and lumbrosacral spines, both of which were "normal."

On June 18, 1992, Dr. Keller wrote a letter stating that Craig was disabled as of June 1, 1992, and that she would be disabled "indefinitely" because of "aching all over." On that same day, June 18, Dr. Keller wrote Dr. Doug Lemley, a rheumatologist, a letter of referral for Craig, in which he stated that she had "no objective evidence of any joint symptoms" and that her lab work was "normal" except for high cholesterol and triglyceride levels. He made no mention of any disability in this letter. Dr. Lemley examined Craig and concluded that there were "[n]o signs of active inflammation about any of the joints at this time" and "adequate range of motion at all sites." He also noted that she had complained of "occasional" swelling of the hands, feet, and knees.

On September 23, 1992, Craig had a session with Robert Madtes, a physical therapist to whom she was referred by Dr. Keller. Madtes found that she had "multiple muscle involvement with pain and decreased flexibility," but he did not declare her disabled or suggest that she be restricted in her activities.

Craig is still able to sweep occasionally, mop once a month, do some dusting, sometimes mend clothes, do laundry once a week, go grocery shopping once a month, cook twice a week, wash dishes once a week, attend church occasionally, sometimes teach Sunday School, and drive occasionally. Nevertheless, Craig alleges that she has cramps in her whole body, her joints hurt constantly (specifically her knees, legs, feet, and hands), and she experiences severe headaches. She also testified that she cannot sleep very much, that she has trouble lifting a plate with her right arm, that lifting a two-liter bottle with her left arm causes pain, and that she can only blow dry the front of her hair because she cannot hold the blow dryer long enough to do the back.

* * *

II.

* * *

E.

Finally, Craig contends that the ALJ applied the wrong standard in evaluating her subjective complaints of pain. Although Craig's argument on this point is difficult to follow, it appears that she believes that the law forbids the ALJ finding her testimony not credible. Instead, presumably, the ALJ was obliged to accept, without more, her subjective assertions of disabling pain and her subjective assessment of the degree of that pain. Of course, that is not and has never been the law in this circuit. As was observed in *Mickles v. Shalala*, 29 F.3d 918, 922 (4th Cir.1994) (Luttig, J., concurring in the judgment), and as we hold today, subjective claims of pain must be supported by objective medical evidence showing the existence of a medical impairment which could reasonably be expected to produce the actual pain, in the amount and degree, alleged by the claimant.

The reasoning for such a holding was explained in *Mickles*, essentially verbatim, as follows. A person is "disabled" under the Social Security Act, and therefore potentially eligible for SSI benefits, if he is unable "to engage in any substantial gainful activity by reason of any medically determinable physical or mental impairment which ... has lasted or can be expected to last for a continuous period of not less than twelve months." 42 U.S.C. §§ 1382c(a)(3)(A) & 423(d)(1)(A). A "physical or mental impairment" is further defined as "an impairment that results from anatomical, physiological, or psychological abnormalities which are demonstrable by medically accepted clinical and laboratory diagnostic techniques." 42 U.S.C. §§ 1382c(a)(3)(C) & 423(d)(3). Thus, for disability to be found, an underlying medically determinable impairment resulting from some demonstrable abnormality must be established. While the pain caused by an impairment, independent from any physical limitations imposed by that impairment, may of course render an individual incapable of working, allegations of pain and other subjective symptoms, without more, are insufficient. As we said in *Gross v. Heckler*, "[p]ain is not disabling per se, and subjective evidence of pain cannot take precedence over objective medical evidence or the lack thereof." 785 F.2d 1163, 1166 (4th Cir.1986) (quoting *Parris v. Heckler*, 733 F.2d 324, 327 (4th Cir.1984)); *see also* 20 C.F.R. §§ 416.928(a) & 404.1528(a) ("[A claimant's] statements ... alone ... are not enough to establish that there is a physical or mental impairment.").

In order to make this statutory requirement even more plain, Congress in 1984 amended Title II of the Social Security Act, purportedly to codify the regulatory standard for evaluating pain. The amendment, in language which closely paralleled the Secretary's 1980 regulations, *see* 20 C.F.R. §§ 416.929 & 404.1529 (1983), provided that

> [a]n individual's statement as to pain or other symptoms shall not alone be conclusive evidence of disability as defined in this section; *there must be medical signs and findings*, established by medically acceptable clinical or laboratory diagnostic techniques, *which show the existence of a medical impairment* that results from anatomical, physiological, or psychological abnormalities *which could reasonably be expected to produce the pain or other symptoms alleged* and which, when considered with all the evidence required to be furnished under this paragraph (including statements of the individual or his physician as to the intensity and persistence of such pain or other symptoms which may reasonably be accepted as consistent with the medical signs and findings), would lead to a conclusion that the individual is under a disability. Objective medical evidence of pain or other symptoms established by medically acceptable clinical or laboratory diagnostic techniques (for example, deteriorating nerve or muscle tissue) must be considered in reaching a conclusion as to whether the individual is under a disability.

42 U.S.C. § 423(d)(5)(A) (emphasis added). This standard was made applicable to SSI determinations as well by an amendment to Title XVI incorporating section 423(d)(5) by reference. *See* 42 U.S.C. § 1382c(a)(3)(G).

Interpreting section 423(d)(5)(A), this court held that in order for pain to be found disabling, there must be objective medical evidence establishing some condition that could reasonably be expected to produce the pain alleged. *Foster v. Heckler*, 780 F.2d 1125, 1129 (4th Cir.1986).[5] However, while a claimant must show by objective evidence the existence of an underlying impairment that could cause the pain alleged, "there need not be objective evidence of the pain itself." *Id.* (quoting *Green v. Schweiker*, 749 F.2d 1066, 1070-71 (3d Cir.1984)); *accord Jenkins v. Sullivan*, 906 F.2d 107, 108 (4th Cir.1990) (explaining that § 423(d)(5)(A) requires "a claimant to show objective medical evidence of some condition

---

[5] In *Foster*, we also found that § 423(d)(5)(A) was consistent with our prior precedents. *Id.* at 1129 n. 7; *see also Thompson v. Sullivan*, 980 F.2d 280, 282 (4th Cir.1992) ("[Section 423(d)(5)(A)] adopted the substance of our prior rule."); *Hyatt v. Sullivan*, 899 F.2d 329, 333 n. 4 (4th Cir.1990) (*Hyatt III*) ("[Section 423(d)(5)(A)] and Fourth Circuit pain law are not inconsistent."). *Compare Shively v. Heckler*, 739 F.2d 987, 990 (4th Cir.1984) *with* 42 U.S.C. § 423(d)(5)(A). One of those prior precedents, *Myers*, could be read to be in conflict with § 423(d)(5)(A)'s requirement of objective proof of an underlying impairment which could reasonably be expected to cause the disabling pain a claimant alleges, *see* 611 F.2d at 983, and has at least once been so read, *see Thompson*, 980 F.2d at 283 (characterizing Myers as holding "that pain itself is an impairment that can render a person disabled"). However, given the rather plain requirements expressed in the statutory language, the terms of which have since been incorporated into the governing regulations, and our consistent interpretation of those terms, we have previously declined to so construe *Myer, see, e.g., Foster*, 780 F.2d at 1129 n. 7, and we again decline to do so today.

that could reasonably be expected to produce the pain alleged, not objective evidence of the pain itself"); *Hyatt III*, 899 F.2d at 332 (stating that § 423(d)(5)(A) "requires objective medical evidence of an underlying condition that could reasonably produce the pain alleged"); *Hatcher v. Secretary, Dept. of Health & Human Serv.*, 898 F.2d 21, 24 (4th Cir.1989) ("[Section 423(d)(5)(A)] ... requires medical evidence of an impairment 'which could reasonably be expected to produce the pain or other symptoms alleged.' "); *Walker v. Bowen*, 889 F.2d 47, 49 (4th Cir.1989) ("[W]hile there must be medical evidence of some condition that could reasonably produce the pain, there need not be objective evidence of the pain itself or its intensity."); *Gross*, 785 F.2d at 1166 (upholding denial of benefits where evidence failed to show any abnormality which would explain claimant's pains). Under these cases, once objective medical evidence establishes a condition which could reasonably be expected to cause pain of the severity a claimant alleges, those allegations may not be discredited simply because they are not confirmed by objective evidence of the severity of the pain, such as heat, swelling, redness, and effusion. *See Jenkins*, 906 F.2d at 109.

Although it still appears in the statutory codification and decisions have continued to be rendered under it, section 423(d)(5)(A) is applicable only to SSDI and SSI eligibility determinations made prior to January 1, 1987. The statute is thus no longer effective, but its standard for the evaluation of pain has recently been incorporated almost *in haec verba* into the Social Security regulations.

On November 14, 1991, the Secretary, acting pursuant to the rulemaking authority delegated by Congress in 42 U.S.C. § 1302, substantially revised the regulations governing the evaluation of pain in SSDI and SSI disability determinations. *See* 20 C.F.R. §§ 404.1529, 416.929. These regulations provide the authoritative standard for the evaluation of pain in disability determinations, *see Pope v. Shalala*, 998 F.2d 473, 485-86 (7th Cir.1993), and control all determinations made since their effective date, including the instant case.

Sections 416.929 and 404.1529, governing disability determinations, incorporate the standard set forth in section 423(d)(5)(A) and explain that standard each with more than three and one half pages of small type. These lengthy regulations begin by emphasizing the importance of objective evidence in determining whether a claimant is disabled by pain:

> In determining whether you are disabled, we consider all your symptoms, including pain, and the extent to which your symptoms can reasonably be accepted as consistent with the objective medical evidence and other evidence.... However, statements about your pain or other symptoms will not alone establish that you are disabled; there

must be medical signs and laboratory findings which establish that you have a medical impairment(s) which could reasonably be expected to produce the pain or other symptoms alleged and which, when considered with all of the other evidence (including statements about the intensity and persistence of your pain or other symptoms which may reasonably be accepted as consistent with the medical signs and laboratory findings), would lead to a conclusion that you are disabled. In evaluating the intensity and persistence of your symptoms, including pain, we will consider all of the available evidence, including your medical history, the medical signs and laboratory findings and statements about how your symptoms affect you.... *We will then determine the extent to which your alleged functional limitations and restrictions due to pain or other symptoms can reasonably be accepted as consistent with the medical signs and laboratory findings and other evidence to decide how your symptoms affect your ability to work ....*

20 C.F.R. §§ 416.929(a) & 404.1529(a) (emphasis added).

Under these regulations, the determination of whether a person is disabled by pain or other symptoms is a two-step process. First, there must be objective medical evidence showing

the existence of a medical impairment(s) which results from anatomical, physiological, or psychological abnormalities and *which could reasonably be expected to produce the pain or other symptoms alleged.*

20 C.F.R. §§ 416.929(b) & 404.1529(b) (emphasis added); cf. 42 U.S.C. § 423(d)(5)(A) ("[T]here must be medical signs and findings ... which show the existence of a medical impairment ... which could reasonably be expected to produce the pain or other symptoms alleged...."). It is significant that the current regulations, like the statute upon which they were based, *see* 42 U.S.C. § 423(d)(5)(A), and paralleling the regulations which that statute purported to codify, *see* 20 C.F.R. §§ 416.929, 404.1529 (1983), were drafted using the definite article "the" and the adjective "alleged."[6] Therefore, for pain to be found to be disabling, there *must* be

---

[6] 20 C.F.R. §§ 416.929(b) & 404.1529(b) (emphasis added) both provide that,

[y]our symptoms ... will not be found to affect your ability to do basic work activities unless medical signs or laboratory findings show that a medically determinable impairment(s) is present. Medical signs and laboratory findings ... must show the existence of a medical impairment(s) which results from anatomical, physiological, or psychological abnormalities and *which could reasonably be expected to produce the pain or other symptoms alleged.*

See also Jenkins, 906 F.2d at 108 ("[T]his court has interpreted [42 U.S.C. § 423(d)(5)(A)] as requiring a claimant to show objective medical evidence of some condition *that could reasonably be expected to produce the pain alleged*, not objective evidence of the pain itself." (emphasis added)). Even if our precedents were contrary to this regulation, which they are not, these regulations would be controlling. *See Pope*, 998 F.2d at 485-86.

shown a medically determinable impairment which could reasonably be expected to cause not just pain, or some pain, or pain of some kind or severity, *but the pain the claimant alleges she suffers*. The regulation thus requires at the threshold a showing by objective evidence of the existence of a medical impairment "which could reasonably be expected to produce" the actual pain, in the amount and degree, alleged by the claimant.

This threshold test does not, as the regulation is careful to emphasize, entail a determination of the "intensity, persistence, or functionally limiting effects" of the claimant's asserted pain. See 20 C.F.R. §§ 416.929(b) & 404.1529(b). At this stage of the inquiry, the pain claimed is not directly at issue; the focus is instead on establishing a determinable underlying impairment--a statutory requirement for entitlement to benefits, see 42 U.S.C § 1382c(a)(3)(A)--which could reasonably be expected to be the cause of the disabling pain asserted by the claimant.

There is, of course, a fundamental difference between objective evidence of pain (which is not required) and objective evidence of a medical condition which could cause the pain alleged (which is). Requirement of the former is obviously not the law, for the simple reason that pain, a subjective phenomenon, although sometimes objectively verifiable, often will not be. Objective evidence of the pain the claimant feels is thus, quite sensibly, *not* required for entitlement to benefits. 20 C.F.R. §§ 416.929(c) & 404.1529(c). However, the latter--objective evidence of a condition "which could reasonably be expected to produce the pain or other symptoms alleged"—equally sensibly, *is* required by the Secretary's regulation. 20 C.F.R. §§ 416.929(b) & 404.1529(b).

Indeed, that such a requirement is part of the regulatory scheme is confirmed by the portions of the regulations providing that, in the disability hearing process, before the ALJ, and before Appeals Council, expert medical advice may be sought and considered in determining whether an "impairment[ ] could reasonably be expected to produce [the claimant's] alleged symptoms." *Id.*

It is only *after* a claimant has met her threshold obligation of showing by objective medical evidence a medical impairment reasonably likely to cause the pain claimed, that the intensity and persistence of the claimant's pain, and the extent to which it affects her ability to work, must be evaluated. *See* 20 C.F.R. §§ 416.929(c)(1) & 404.1529(c)(1). Under the regulations, this evaluation must take into account not only the claimant's statements about her pain, but also "all the available evidence," including the claimant's medical history, medical signs, and laboratory findings, *see id.*; any objective medical evidence of pain (such as evidence of reduced joint motion, muscle spasms, deteriorating tissues, redness, etc.), *see* 20 C.F.R. §§ 416.929(c)(2) & 404.1529(c)(2); and any other evidence relevant to the severity of the impairment, such as evidence of the claimant's daily activities, specific descriptions of the pain, and any medical treatment taken to alleviate it, *see* 20 C.F.R. §§ 416.929(c)(3) & 404.1529(c)(3).

The regulations, as did the statute, specifically provide for the consideration of objective medical evidence of the pain (if any such evidence exists) in the evaluation of its intensity and persistence. However, because pain is subjective and cannot always be confirmed by objective indicia, claims of disabling pain may not be rejected "*solely* because the available objective evidence does not substantiate [the claimant's] statements" as to the severity and persistence of her pain. 20 C.F.R. §§ 416.929(c)(2) & 404.1529(c)(2) (emphasis added); *see also Walker*, 889 F.2d at 49 ("[T]here need not be objective evidence of the pain itself or its intensity."); *Foster*, 780 F.2d at 1129 (same). That is, once a medically determinable impairment which could reasonably be expected to produce the pain alleged by the claimant is shown by objective evidence, the claimant's allegations as to the severity and persistence of her pain may not be dismissed merely because objective evidence of the pain itself (as opposed to the existence of an impairment that could produce the pain alleged), such as inflamed tissues or spasming muscles, are not present to corroborate the existence of pain.

This is not to say, however, that objective medical evidence and other objective evidence are not crucial to evaluating the intensity and persistence of a claimant's pain and the extent to which it impairs her ability to work. They most certainly are. Although a claimant's allegations about her pain may not be discredited solely because they are not substantiated by objective evidence of the pain itself or its severity, they need not be accepted to the extent they are inconsistent with the available evidence, including objective evidence of the underlying impairment, and the extent to which that impairment can reasonably be expected to cause the pain the claimant alleges she suffers:

> We will consider your statements about the intensity, persistence, and limiting effects of your symptoms, and we will evaluate your statements in relation to the objective medical evidence and other evidence, in reaching a conclusion as to whether you are disabled. We will consider whether there are any inconsistencies in the evidence and the extent to which there are any conflicts between your statements and the rest of the evidence, including your medical history, the medical signs and laboratory findings, and statements by your treating or examining physician or psychologist or other persons about how your symptoms affect you. *Your symptoms, including pain, will be determined to diminish your capacity for basic work activities ... to the extent that your alleged functional limitations and re-*

strictions due to symptoms, such as pain, can reasonably be accepted as consistent with the objective medical evidence and other evidence.

20 C.F.R. §§ 416.929(c)(4) & 404.1529(c)(4) (emphasis added); *cf.* 42 U.S.C. § 423(d)(5)(A) ("[T]here must be ... a medical impairment ... which, when considered with all the evidence ... (including statements of the individual or his physician as to the intensity and persistence of such pain or other symptoms which may reasonably be accepted as consistent with the medical signs and findings), would lead to a conclusion that the individual is under a disability."); *Gross*, 785 F.2d at 1166 (affirming finding that allegations of pain were incredible where medical evidence did not show an underlying impairment).

In the instant case, the ALJ did not expressly consider the threshold question of whether Craig had demonstrated by objective medical evidence an impairment capable of causing the degree and type of pain she alleges. Instead, the ALJ proceeded directly to considering the credibility of her subjective allegations of pain. J.A. at 16. Accordingly, we remand to the ALJ to determine whether Craig has an objectively identifiable medical impairment that could reasonably cause the pain of which she complains. If the ALJ concludes that she does, then, and only then, should it undertake an assessment into the credibility of Craig's subjective claims of pain.

NOTES ON CREDIBILITY AND SUBJECTIVE SYMPTOMS

1. Recall that SSR 96-7p states that "the extent to which an individual's statements about symptoms can be relied upon as probative evidence in determining whether the individual is disabled depends on the credibility of those statements." In Morris v. Barnhart, 78 Fed. Appx. 820, 91 Soc. Sec. Rep. Serv. 220, 2003 WL 22436040 (3rd Cir. 2003), the ALJ found that the claimant (Morris) was "less than credible" and thus assigned limited weight to those aspects of the opinion of her treating physician (Dr. Picciotto) based on Morris's subjective complaints. While Morris did not challenge the credibility finding, she argued that the ALJ improperly discounted Dr. Picciotto's medical opinion because it was based on her subjective complaints. The court disagreed, noting that "the mere memorialization of a claimant's subjective statements in a medical report does not elevate those statements to a medical opinion." 78 Fed. Appx. At 824. The court linked credibility findings relative to subjective symptoms with medical opinions based on claimants' statements about those symptoms as follows: "An ALJ may discredit a physician's opinion on disability that was premised largely on the claimant's own accounts of her symptoms and limitations when the claimant's complaints are properly discounted." 78 Fed. Appx. at 825 (Citing Fair v. Bowen, 885 F.2d 597, 605 (9th Cir.1989) ("The ALJ thus disregarded Dr. Bliss' opinion because it was premised on Fair's own subjective complaints, which the ALJ had already

properly discounted. This constitutes a specific, legitimate reason for rejecting the opinion of a treating physician.").

2. Consider the following exchange between an ALJ and a claimant who had alleged that he could not sit for any length of time due to radiating back pain:

ALJ: What's the furthest would you say you've driven in the last month or two? You say you have to go to the hospital.

ANS: Running back and forth to the hospital. Of course, my wife is going to Boston Medical for treatment and I didn't go with her because I just couldn't handle that trip. Her girlfriend would go up with her.

ALJ: How far did you, how far did you — have you travelled though by, by car to —

ANS: Well now I go up to — from Portsmouth to Dover. I don't know how many miles that is, but it's —

ALJ: How long does it take you?

ANS: It takes me —

ALJ: What, is it less than 20 miles?

ANS: I really don't know what the mileage is.

ALJ: Counsel, any —

ATTY: It's — the way he would be going to Dover would be approximately 10 to 12 miles.

ALJ: Oh, all right.

ANS: It takes me a half hour to 40 minutes. I, I just —

St. Pierre v. Shalala, 1995 WL 515515, *3 (D.N.H. 1995)

The ALJ included the fact that the claimant was able to sit in a car from 30 to 40 minutes among several findings to support his conclusion that the claimant's allegations of pain were not credible. The claimant argued that this was an improper basis for the ALJ's credibility ruling. What do you think? *See St. Pierre v. Shalala*, 1995 WL 515515 at *3-*4:

> When evaluating the subjective claims of pain it is proper and, indeed, required that the ALJ consider daily activities such as driving, walking and household chores. This allows the Secretary to juxtapose the claimant's subjective allegations of pain with the relative intensity of his daily regimen. However, implicit in this inquiry is that the daily ac-

tivities used in the credibility calculus are activities which reasonably reflect the claimant's condition. Conversely, activities necessarily undertaken in response to extraordinary circumstances—particularly when performed inadequately or with extreme pain—cannot be considered reliable barometers * * *. The Second Circuit addressed this issue in , and held that a claimant's ability to withstand extreme discomfort while sitting on a four-hour long bus trip to attend college is an impermissible basis upon which to negate subjective allegations of pain. The Second Circuit reasoned that

> [w]hen a disabled person gamely chooses to endure pain in order to pursue important goals, it would be a shame to hold this endurance against him in determining benefits *unless his conduct truly showed that he is capable of working.*

Id. at 49 (emphasis supplied). * * *

3. ALJs are given great deference when making credibility determinations and will not be reversed unless there was an abuse of discretion. As the court explained in Herron v. Shalala, 19 F.3d 329, 335, 44 Soc. Sec. Rep. Ser. 51 (7th Cir. 1994), "[s]ince the ALJ is in the best position to observe witnesses, we usually do not upset credibility determinations on appeal so long as they find some support in the record and are not patently wrong." At the same time, "the ALJ may not summarily discount subjective complaints of pain." Goldthrite v. Astrue, 535 F.Supp.2d 329, 337, 129 Soc. Sec. Rep. Serv. 676 (W.D.N.Y. 2008). In *Goldthrite*, the ALJ had noted that the claimant had been on welfare for seven years, was still receiving Medicaid, and had just begun receiving food stamps—all in apparent support of his conclusion that the claimant was not credible, after noting further that she had not undertaken vocational rehabilitation or looked for work on her own, and that she was not "an individual well motivated to work within her limitations when other sources of income are available." 535 F.Supp 2d at 337. The reviewing court concluded that "on the issue of [claimant's] credibility, the ALJ showed 'a shocking distrust of the plaintiff and her motivations.' * * * The fact that the [claimant] was receiving other income from public assistance does not, by itself, mean that she is less credible when testifying about her pain." 535 F.Supp 2d at 337-39.

3. CLAIMS BASED ON CHRONIC PAIN CONDITIONS

The second broad category of pain-based claims is those involving chronic pain conditions. Fibromyalgia, also known as fibrositis, is a relatively common chronic musculoskeletal pain syndrome characterized by widespread muscle pain and fatigue—without noticeable structural or inflammatory musculoskeletal abnormalities. *See generally,* Aimee E. Bierman, *Note: The Medico-Legal Enigma of Fibromyalgia: Social Security Disability Determinations and Subjective Complaints of Pain,* 44

WAYNE L. REV. 259, 259 (1998). As described by Judge Posner in Sarchet v. Chart, 78 F.3d 305, 306 (7th Cir. 1996):

> Its cause or causes are unknown, there is no cure, and, of greatest importance to disability law, its symptoms are entirely subjective. There are no laboratory tests for the presence or severity of fibromyalgia. The principal symptoms are "pain all over," fatigue, disturbed sleep, stiffness, and--the only symptom that discriminates between it and other diseases of a rheumatic character--multiple tender spots, more precisely 18 fixed locations on the body (and the rule of thumb is that the patient must have at least 11 of them to be diagnosed as having fibromyalgia) that when pressed firmly cause the patient to flinch. All these symptoms are easy to fake, although few applicants for disability benefits may yet be aware of the specific locations that if palpated will cause the patient who really has fibromyalgia to flinch.

Other chronic pain conditions that have posed difficulties when presented as the basis for a Social Security disability claim include Chronic Fatigue Syndrome (CFS) and Complex Regional Pain Syndrome (CRPS).

Since there are no objective diagnostic techniques to prove or disprove the existence of these conditions, the first step of requiring objective proof of an underlying medical impairment cannot be satisfied. On the other hand, certain subjective symptoms have been identified as indicative of the presence of these and other similar conditions and, when documented by medical sources (particularly a claimant's treating physician), eligibility for benefits can be shown. (Special rules for evaluating and weighing the opinions of a claimant's treating physician, which are applied often in cases involving subjective symptoms, are discussed in detail in Chapter 9.)

GREEN-YOUNGER V. BARNHART
335 F.3d 99, 89 Soc. Sec. Rep. Serv. 256 (2nd Cir. 2003)

Before: FEINBERG, VAN GRAAFEILAND and F.I. PARKER, Circuit Judges.

FEINBERG, Circuit Judge.

Plaintiff Green-Younger appeals from a judgment of the United States District Court for the District of Connecticut (Christopher F. Droney, J.), accepting the recommended ruling of Magistrate Judge William I. Garfinkel to affirm the decision of the Administrative Law Judge (ALJ) denying Green-Younger's application for social security disability benefits. On appeal, Green-Younger argues that the ALJ and the district court erred by failing to give controlling weight to the opinion of her treating physician that she suffers from fibromyalgia[1] and cannot work because of severe pain. For reasons stated below, we reverse and remand to the district court with instructions to remand the matter to the Commissioner of the Social Security Administration (SSA) for a calculation of disability benefits.

I. Background

At the time of her SSA hearing, Nina Green-Younger was 38 years old, and married with three children. After completing two years of college, Green-Younger worked full-time as a long-distance telephone operator for Southern New England Telephone (SNET) from 1978 to 1995. She also worked part-time as a mail sorter from 1985 to 1988. From 1988 to 1995, Green-Younger took seven disability leaves from her job, which lasted between one month and one year * * *. Green-Younger avers that she became totally disabled in May 1995, when she last worked.

A. Medical History

According to medical records and her testimony, Green-Younger's difficulties began in 1982 when she injured her back in a motor vehicle accident in the eighth month of her last pregnancy. To treat her back pain, she tried various anti-inflammatory and pain medications, physical therapy and chiropractic treatment. In April 1991, Green-Younger consulted an orthopedist who diagnosed degenerative disc disease. * * *

Beginning February 1994, Green-Younger began regular treatments with osteopath Dr. Jeffrey Helfand, a rheumatologist. After an initial consultation and examination, Dr. Helfand reported that Green-Younger complained of

> pain in her right leg and low back which she states goes down into her coccyx area associated with tingling and weakness in her right arm which has been present intermittently since 1982. She states that the pain is always present but can be more severe at sometimes than at others.... She states she has difficulty sitting or standing for any prolonged time and complains of frequent sleep difficulty. The most recent prolonged episode of low back and leg pain began around October 1993 after approximately a six-month period when she was relatively symptom free.

Dr. Helfand documented that "[m]usculoskeletal and extremity exams reveal multiple tender points in the distribution characteristic of fibromyalgia." He noted the results of a 1993 MRI showing minimal disc bulging at the L4-L5 and L5-S1 regions, but no disc herniation. Dr.

---

[1] A syndrome of chronic pain of musculoskeletal origin but uncertain cause. Stedman's Medical Dictionary 671 (27th ed.2000). This disorder is also commonly referred to as fibrositis.

Helfand found no reflex, sensory, or motor deficits, but he noted the presence of paresthesias;[2] significant spasm with limitation of lateral flexion and rotation in the lumbar paravertebral muscles; and marked tenderness over the posterior superior iliac spines bilaterally. Dr. Helfand eventually diagnosed Green-Younger as having fibromyalgia, as well as other illnesses—such as degenerative disc disease, chronic low back syndrome, and peroneal neuropathy[3]—associated with her back pain.

* * *

In July 1995, Dr. Helfand wrote several letters describing Green-Younger's current limitations. In one letter requesting a medical exemption from jury service, Dr. Helfand explained that it was "difficult for [Green-Younger] to sit in any one position for more than 30 minutes without needing to get up and walk around." In other letters, he described her current limitations to include "sitting and/or standing for 4 hours or less daily," or "continuous sitting/and or sitting for no more than 60 minutes without a rest period," and no lifting, pulling or pushing.

In August 1995, physical therapist Jill Tomasello performed a two-day work fitness evaluation of Green-Younger for SNET. Tomasello found that "test results did not meet the criteria for consistent or maximum effort," explaining that "[t]his is not unusual for the initial test" and that "repeat testing is needed to verify the results." Tomasello nevertheless concluded that Green-Younger "has demonstrated the ability to work at a sedentary work level," and recommended a work hardening program if she is "unable to tolerate a return to work." However, a subsequent evaluation performed in July 1996 suggested that Green-Younger "was able to tolerate seated activity at a work site for a maximum of 30 minutes before she would need to get up and move around freely."

In October 1995, Dr. Helfand informed SNET that Green-Younger could not return to work because of fibromyalgia, peroneal neuropathy, and chronic low back syndrome. Dr. Helfand explained in his progress notes that he had elected to consider her permanently disabled because "she has not had any dramatic improvement with any of the measures we have tried."

Dr. Helfand referred Green-Younger to a number of other doctors. Dr. Don Goldenberg, Chief of Rheumatology at the Newton-Wellesley Hospital in Massachusetts and a fibromyalgia specialist, confirmed Dr. Helfand's diagnosis of fibromyalgia. Dr. Robert Goldring, who was providing chiropractic treatment at this time to alleviate pain and spasms, stat-

---

[2] An abnormal sensation such as burning, prickling, tingling or tickling. Stedman's Medical Dictionary 1316.

[3] A disorder affecting the nerve extending along the fibula. *Id.* at 1211, 1354.

ed that Green-Younger's "long term pain" was "essentially due to her fibromyalgia." Green-Younger also consulted with orthopedist Dr. Ramon Batson. On a physical exam, he found "diffuse tenderness to palpation along the axial spine and in the SI joints bilaterally" and "trigger points present in the right trapezius muscles and in the right glutei." Dr. Batson noted Green-Younger's history of disc disease but not disc herniation, and recommended treatment for myofascial pain syndrome[6] if studies proved negative for surgical pathology.

A number of tests were ordered, apparently in part to rule out surgical pathology. Plain films did not reveal any abnormal movement or osseous lesions, but an MRI of the lumbar spine taken in 1995 again revealed bulging at the L3-L4 and L4-L5 regions. Green-Younger underwent a full body scan in July 1996. The scan revealed "one significant abnormality: there is increased activity in the right sacroiliac joint which may represent sacroiliitis[7] or a consequence of previous trauma." Dr. Helfand pursued the possibility of implanting a spinal cord stimulator, but abandoned this option after neurosurgeon Dr. Charles Needham "excluded any significant nerve compression disease and any surgical approach to management."

In July 1996, Dr. Helfand again diagnosed Green-Younger with "severe fibromyalgia." He explained that fibromyalgia is "typically characterized by severe fatigue, diffuse muscular soreness and tenderness which in certain instances can be debilitating." He noted the difficulty of proving disability on this basis because of the absence of objective evidence to quantify the severity of the pain. He reported that "her pain is frequently overwhelming and the associated fatigue can cause a significant limitation in her ability to function on a daily basis." Dr. Helfand opined that "her ability to function at a normal level because of the persistent, severe pain is markedly limited." In a December 1998 letter to Green-Younger's attorney, Dr. Helfand explained that "she continues to experience significant difficulty with her activities of daily living," and noted a "relatively acute onset of severe tenderness and stiffness ... with multiple tender points." He concluded that "it should probably be obvious that she continues to have significant disability and at this time will most likely be unable to retain any significant gainful employment."

B. Procedural History

In August 1995, Green-Younger filed an application for disability benefits. The SSA denied her application initially in October 1995 and

---

[6] According to the medical articles included in Green-Younger's brief, myofascial pain syndrome is a disorder closely related to fibromyalgia.

[7] An inflammation of the sacroiliac joint, which connects the sacrum, or lower back forming part of the pelvis, to the ilium, or hip bone. Stedman's Medical Dictionary at 1587-88, 875.

upon reconsideration in December 1995. The SSA consulting physicians disagreed with Dr. Helfand's conclusion that Green-Younger was "limited to sitting and/or standing for four hours or less," because "[e]vidence does not show deficits of motor function or significant arthritis to severely limit standing or sitting." Green-Younger sought a review before an ALJ of the SSA Office of Hearings and Appeals. A hearing was conducted in August 1997. * * *

In September 1997, the ALJ issued a decision denying Green-Younger's application. Although the ALJ found that the "medical evidence of record documents that the claimant has fibromyalgia and degenerative disc disease" and that these impairments were severe, the ALJ also found that Green-Younger retained the residual functional capacity to occasionally lift and carry up to 10 pounds, sit for six hours a day and walk or stand for two hours a day. The ALJ concluded that Green-Younger could perform her past work as a mail clerk and therefore was not disabled within the meaning of the Social Security Act. Specifically, the ALJ found that "[c]ontrary to the claimant's persistent complaints of pain, there are no objective medical findings." He noted in this regard that there was no "evidence of radiculopathy," "signs of sacroilitis," "abnormal chest examinations," or "abnormal movement or osseous lesions." As a result, the ALJ found that (1) the opinions of Dr. Helfand regarding Green-Younger's limitations "cannot be afforded extra weight because they are not well-supported by medically acceptable clinical and laboratory diagnostic techniques, and are inconsistent with the other substantial evidence of record," namely physical therapist Tomasello's work capacity evaluation; and (2) Green-Younger's "allegations of pain and functional limitations are ... not entirely credible in light of the minimal objective medical findings." In total, the ALJ's six-page opinion referred five times to a lack of objective evidence. * * *

The SSA Appeals Council affirmed the ALJ's decision and Green-Younger timely appealed to the United States District Court for the District of Connecticut, asserting numerous grounds for remand. In August 2001, Magistrate Judge William Garfinkel issued a lengthy ruling recommending affirmance of the ALJ's decision. In March 2002, the district court entered a brief order accepting the recommended ruling in its entirety.

This appeal followed.

II. Discussion

In this court, Green-Younger argues that the ALJ misapplied SSA regulations by failing to give controlling weight to the opinion of her treating physician that she suffers from fibromyalgia and that the attendant pain and fatigue severely limit her ability to function and work on a daily level. She argues that the ALJ, as well as the district court, misunderstood the nature of fibromyalgia in requiring "objective" evidence beyond those clinical signs and symptoms necessary for a diagnosis. The government notes that the ALJ did credit Dr. Helfand's diagnosis of fibromyalgia, but argues that his conclusion on the ultimate issue of legal disability was not entitled to controlling weight and that substantial evidence supports the ALJ's decision.

* * *

B. Merits

   * * *

The SSA recognizes a "treating physician" rule of deference to the views of the physician who has engaged in the primary treatment of the claimant. "A treating physician's statement that the claimant is disabled cannot itself be determinative." *Snell v. Apfel*, 177 F.3d 128, 133 (2d Cir.1999). However, SSA regulations advise claimants that "a treating source's opinion on the issue(s) of the nature and severity of your impairment(s) " will be given "controlling weight" if the opinion is "well supported by medically acceptable clinical and laboratory diagnostic techniques and is not inconsistent with the other substantial evidence in your case record." 20 C.F.R. § 404.1527(d)(2) (emphasis added).

We conclude from the record before us that the ALJ erred by failing to give controlling weight to the treating physician's opinion and effectively requiring objective evidence beyond the clinical findings necessary for a diagnosis of fibromyalgia under established medical guidelines. Dr. Helfand's opinion regarding Green-Younger's impairments meets the standard under the SSA regulations and should have been accorded controlling weight. Contrary to the government's contention, Dr. Helfand was not offering an opinion on the ultimate issue of legal disability, but rather on the "nature and severity of [Green-Younger's] impairment(s)." He opined that "her ability to function at a normal level because of the persistent, severe pain is markedly limited," noting specifically that she could not sit or stand for more than four hours a day, that she could not continuously sit or stand for 60 minutes without a rest period, and that it was difficult for her to sit for more than 30 minutes at a time.

At the time of the hearing in 1997, Dr. Helfand had coordinated Green-Younger's care for over three years, during which time she underwent numerous physical examinations and diagnostic procedures. Dr. Helfand's diagnosis of severe fibromyalgia and degenerative disc disease are "well supported by medically acceptable clinical and laboratory diagnostic techniques." Green-Younger exhibited the clinical signs and symptoms to support a fibromyalgia diagnosis under the American College of

Rheumatology (ACR) guidelines, including primarily widespread pain in all four quadrants of the body and at least 11 of the 18 specified tender points on the body. See SSA Memorandum, Fibromyalgia, Chronic Fatigue Syndrome, and Objective Medical Evidence Requirements for Disability Adjudication, at 5 (May 11, 1998) (explaining that the signs for fibromyalgia, according to the ACR, "are primarily the tender points"); see also *Sarchet v. Chater*, 78 F.3d 305, 306 (7th Cir.1996); *Lisa v. Sec. of the Dep't of Health and Human Servs.*, 940 F.2d 40, 43 (2d Cir.1991). As noted earlier, Dr. Helfand documented that "[m]usculo-skeletal and extremity exams reveal multiple tender points in the distribution characteristic of fibromyalgia." A number of other doctors, including a fibromyalgia specialist, concurred in that diagnosis, presumably using proper diagnostic techniques. In addition, several MRIs showed some bulging in her discs and several doctors concurred that Green-Younger had a history of degenerative disc disease.

The fact that Dr. Helfand also relied on Green-Younger's subjective complaints hardly undermines his opinion as to her functional limitations, as "[a] patient's report of complaints, or history, is an essential diagnostic tool." *Flanery v. Chater*, 112 F.3d 346, 350 (8th Cir.1997). Partly in an effort to avoid long-term disability status for Green-Younger, Dr. Helfand ordered various treatments, including medication, trigger point steroid injections and epidural blocks, and physical and chiropractic therapy. He personally monitored the effectiveness of various therapies and found that they failed to provide any significant improvement in Green-Younger's condition.

By contrast, the only evidence which might be inconsistent with Dr. Helfand's opinion is not substantial-that is, it cannot reasonably support the conclusion that appellant can work. The ALJ relied on the 1995 work fitness evaluation conducted by physical therapist Tomasello. Given that Tomasello was not a physician, that she stated that her conclusion was based on inconsistent results and required verification, and that a subsequent evaluation produced contrary results, Tomasello's one-shot evaluation is not substantial evidence. Similarly, the reports of two SSA consulting physicians, who did not examine Green-Younger, are also not substantial evidence. The first appears to rely entirely on Tomasello's report, whereas the second found that Green-Younger could perform sedentary work because "[e]vidence does not show deficits of motor function or significant arthritis to severely limit sitting or standing." However, Green-Younger was not complaining of deficits in motor functioning or arthritis, she was complaining of debilitating pain from fibromyalgia.

It also appears to us that the ALJ, like the SSA consulting physicians, did not actually credit Dr. Helfand's diagnosis of fibromyalgia or misunderstood its nature. The ALJ effectively required "objective" evidence for a disease that eludes such measurement. As a general matter, "objective" findings are not required in order to find that an applicant is disabled.[13]

Moreover, a growing number of courts, including our own, see *Lisa*, 940 F.2d at 44-45, have recognized that fibromyalgia is a disabling impairment and that "there are no objective tests which can conclusively confirm the disease." *Preston v. Sec. of Health and Human Servs.*, 854 F.2d 815, 818 (6th Cir.1988); see *Sarchet*, 78 F.3d at 306; see also *Harman v. Apfel*, 211 F.3d 1172, 1179-80 (9th Cir.2000); *Kelley v. Callahan*, 133 F.3d 583, 585 n. 2 (8th Cir.1998). Yet each of the ALJ's determinations turned on a perceived lack of objective evidence. First, the ALJ determined that Dr. Helfand's opinion was not "well supported by medically acceptable clinical and laboratory diagnostic techniques" because of a lack of "objective" findings.[14] Second, the ALJ determined that Dr. Helfand's opinion was "inconsistent with other substantial evidence," namely Tomasello's work fitness evaluation, because it was not supported by "objective" findings. Finally, the ALJ also found that Green-Younger's "allegations of pain and functional limitations are found not to be entirely credible, particularly in light of the minimal objective findings."

As we have discussed, the ALJ erred in not giving controlling weight to Dr. Helfand's opinions. With regard to the issue of Green-Younger's credibility, her complaints of pain in her back, legs, and upper body, fatigue, and disturbed sleep are internally consistent and consistent with common symptoms of fibromyalgia. Dr. Helfand's diagnosis of fibromyalgia bolsters the credibility of Green-Younger's complaints. See *Lisa*, 940 F.2d at 44. By comparison, the reasons suggested by the ALJ simply do not undermine her credibility. First, the ALJ found that the relative lack of physical abnormalities undercut her credibility.[15] However, we have recognized that "[i]n stark contrast to the unremitting pain of which fibrositis patients complain, physical examinations will usually yield normal results-a full range of motion, no joint swelling, as well as normal muscle strength and neurological reactions." *Id.* at 45 (quoting *Preston*, 854 F.2d at 818). Hence, the absence of swelling joints or other orthopedic and neurologic deficits "is no more indicative that the patient's fibromyalgia is not disabling than the absence of a headache is an indication that a patient's prostate cancer is not advanced." *Sarchet*, 78 F.3d at 307. Ra-

---

[13] In concluding otherwise, the magistrate judge cited a case from the Eastern District of Illinois, *May v. Apfel*, 1999 WL 1011927, at 14 (N.D.Ill.1999), which both misstated the underlying law and appears to be contrary to Seventh Circuit precedent that allows fibromyalgia to be the basis for a disability determination even though "its symptoms are entirely subjective." *Sarchet*, 78 F.3d at 306.

[14] Notably, the ALJ did not mention the presence of tender points, the primary diagnostic technique for fibromyalgia.

[15] Moreover, the ALJ's evaluation of the medical evidence understates the degree to which laboratory tests revealed the presence of physical abnormalities.

ther, these negative findings simply confirm a diagnosis of fibromyalgia by a process of exclusion, eliminating "other medical conditions which may manifest fibrositis-like symptoms of musculoskeletal pain, stiffness, and fatigue." *Preston*, 854 F.2d at 819.

* * *

III. Conclusion

After a full review of the record, we conclude that the ALJ's decision that Green-Younger is not legally disabled is based on an erroneous legal standard and is not supported by substantial evidence. When Dr. Helfand's opinions regarding Green-Younger's limitations are given controlling weight, it is clear that Green-Younger would not be able to perform her past work as a mail clerk. Dr. Blanks, the only vocational expert to testify before the ALJ, admitted that a person who could sit for only 30 minutes at a time and sit or stand for only four hours a day could not work as a mail clerk, or be otherwise employed in the national economy. Cf. *Harman*, 211 F.3d at 1180 (remanding for further proceedings because "there was no testimony from the vocational expert that the limitations found by the [treating physician] would render Appellant unable to engage in any work"). Accordingly, we reverse and remand to the district court with instructions to remand the matter to the Commissioner of the SSA for a calculation of disability benefits.

SISCO V. DEPARTMENT OF HHS
10 F.3d 739, 43 Soc. Sec. Rep. Serv. 12 (10th Cir.1993)

Before McKAY, Chief Judge, SETH and BARRETT, Circuit Judges.

McKAY, Chief Judge.

I.

This is an appeal from a federal district court's ruling affirming an Administrative Law Judge's (ALJ) denial of Social Security benefits. Plaintiff is a 45-year-old mother whose health began to deteriorate in 1983 when she acquired a lymph gland infection. The infection lasted for several months. Although she suffered from symptoms suggestive of mononucleosis, her doctors were unable to diagnose the source of the infection. Despite her illness, she was able to finish her master's degree in educational counseling and psychology and in October of 1983 began work as a psychological assistant for the Oklahoma Department of Corrections. In the early months of her new job Plaintiff began experiencing extreme fatigue and severe headaches to the point where she was unable to perform her work satisfactorily. These symptoms led to the termination of her employment in January of 1984.

Plaintiff then worked in temporary jobs as a data entry operator until she enrolled at Oral Roberts University in January of 1985 for a master's degree in divinity. Soon after attempting to return to school, however, Plaintiff was forced to drop out because her physical condition had continued to deteriorate. She was suffering from severe muscle pains over her entire body, excessive fatigue, headaches, and stomach nausea. She has been unable to return to full-time employment since she left Oral Roberts in February of 1985.

During the period when her condition was worsening, Plaintiff sought medical help for her ailments. Between April of 1985 and May of 1989, she was examined by more than fifteen doctors of various specialties. None were able to diagnose a physical problem or disease that could adequately explain the severity of her symptoms. After being unable to find a physical cause, a few doctors, including one Social Security consultant, suggested personality disorders or hypochondriasis as the root of Plaintiff's problems.

In October of 1989, Plaintiff was evaluated by a team of doctors at the Mayo Clinic in Rochester, Minnesota. After performing a series of tests and reviewing Plaintiff's medical history, the reporting doctor at Mayo diagnosed tension myalgia and chronic fatigue syndrome. Chronic fatigue syndrome is a disease that did not become widely known in the medical community until 1988 when the first diagnostic article concerning it was published. It was also in 1988 that the Centers for Disease Control in Atlanta accepted chronic fatigue syndrome as a disease. It is believed to be caused by an as yet unidentifiable virus or a "chronic [i]mmunologically mediated inflammatory process of the central nervous system." Lawrence M. Tierney, Jr., M.D., *et al., Current Medical Diagnosis and Treatment* 19 (1993).

In July of 1990, Dr. Becker, Plaintiff's treating physician, reviewed plaintiff's medical history and the report from the Mayo Clinic. In response to interrogatories posed by Plaintiff's attorney, Dr. Becker stated that the Plaintiff met both the major and minor criteria for the disease as established by the National Centers for Disease Control. He also stated that the chronic fatigue syndrome rendered Plaintiff totally disabled, unable to sustain activity-or even sit upright in a chair-for more than fifteen to twenty minutes without having to lie down to resolve fatigue.

* * *

II.

* * *

Several times in his opinion the ALJ cited the symptoms from which the Plaintiff suffers and then discounted those symptoms by reiterating that "[t]he claimant's subjective complaints are not realistically supported by the medical evidence." When discussing his finding that Plaintiff is capable of returning to work full-time as an office clerk or data entry operator, for example, the ALJ cited the "medically acceptable clinical or laboratory diagnostic techniques" language in the SSA and stated:

> From a physical point of view, [I] simply can find no impairment that would interfere with the claimant's [ability] to function. There is a diagnosis, or impression, given by some doctors that she has, may have, or could have a chronic fatigue syndrome; *however, there is no documentation of record which establishes this syndrome as required by law....* [I]t [is] up to the claimant to produce such medical and other evidence of the existence of an impairment as may be required by the Secretary. Her statements as to pain and other symptoms are not alone to be considered conclusive evidence of disability. There must be medical signs and findings, established by medically acceptable clinical or laboratory diagnostic techniques, which show the existence of a medical impairment....

> The claimant, here, has been repeatedly tested and in each instance those findings have not been forthcoming.... *Those physicians that have, indicated the chronic [fatigue] syndrome as an assessment, have not supported it with any kind of objective findings or laboratory testing which would support those conclusions.*

(emphasis added).

Thus, the ALJ impeached Plaintiff's unrebutted testimony, discredited her treating physician's unchallenged diagnosis, and rebutted the findings of the Mayo Clinic solely because he was looking for some sort of conclusive "dipstick" laboratory test-such as a blood test-under his interpretation of § 223(d)(5)(A) of the SSA. The district court adopted the same interpretation as the ALJ, noting that the diagnoses were based on "literature" rather than on "objective medical findings." *Sisco v. Sullivan,* No. CIV-91-1675-C, slip op. at 4. The ALJ cited no support for his assumption that "medically acceptable clinical or laboratory diagnosis techniques" can only mean conclusive laboratory tests. Indeed, the plain meaning of the language simply indicates that a claimant's disability must be diagnosed through the use of a technique, either clinical or laboratory, that has been accepted by the medical community.

At this point there is no "dipstick" laboratory test for chronic fatigue syndrome. If there were such a test, and had it been reasonably accessible, the ALJ might have been justified in drawing inferences from Plaintiff's failure to have it administered. The ALJ's and the district court's reading of § 223(d)(5)(A) of the Social Security Act would mean that chronic fatigue syndrome, and other disabilities that cannot be diagnosed with a "dipstick," could never be recognized as disabilities under the Act. Yet the Social Security Administration's own internal operations manual, which lists chronic fatigue syndrome as a disease to be adjudicated on a case-by-case basis, defies this interpretation. *See Program Operations Manual System,* § DI 24575. 005; *Reed,* 804 F.Supp. at 918. Furthermore, since its "discovery" a few years ago, numerous cases involving chronic fatigue syndrome have been adjudicated across the country and we are unable to find any suggestion in these cases that this disease—-or any other disease—is per se excluded from coverage because it cannot be conclusively diagnosed in a laboratory setting. *See, e.g., Thaete v. Shalala,* 826 F.Supp. 1250 (D.Colo.1993); *Irey v. Sullivan,* 993 F.2d 882 (9th Cir.1993); *Cohen v. Secretary,* 964 F.2d 524 (6th Cir.1992); and Reed v. Secretary, 804 F.Supp. 914 (E.D.Mich.1992).

Plaintiff's treating physician identified the clinical technique used by the medical community to diagnose chronic fatigue syndrome. The first method of diagnosis of this type was set forth in 1988 in the *Annals of Internal Medicine,* Vol. 108, Jan.-March 1988. The "operational" diagnosis technique used by the medical community at the present time involves testing, the matching of a detailed list of symptoms, the painstaking exclusion of other possible disorders, and a thorough review of the patient's medical history. Both her treating physician and the Mayo Clinic appeared to reach their conclusions by using this type of step-by-step diagnostic procedure. Plaintiff's treating physician stated that his diagnosis was reached under the guidelines established by the National Centers for Disease Control in Atlanta. Although this type of clinical diagnostic method may not be as dramatic or impressive to a layman as a "dipstick" laboratory test, it is the technique presently used and accepted by the medical community. Section 223(d)(5)(A) of the Social Security Act does not require more. In the ALJ's mind, chronic fatigue syndrome may not be a legitimate disease until it can be diagnosed in a laboratory setting. However, he cannot substitute his lay opinion for that of Congress, the Mayo Clinic, Plaintiff's doctor, and the entire medical community.

The second major misconception held by the ALJ and the district court was that Plaintiff's early medical history somehow rebutted or contradicted the two recent diagnoses of chronic fatigue syndrome. From 1983 through 1989, Plaintiff was examined by dozens of doctors who were unable to diagnose a physical problem sufficient to explain the severity of her symptoms. After being unable to find a physical cause, a few assessed her as a hypochondriac or as suffering from personality disorders. In his opinion, the ALJ discredited the eventual diagnoses of chronic fatigue syndrome by referring to the early examinations and stating, "The claimant, here, has been repeatedly tested and in each instance those findings have not been forthcoming. Some of the physicians who have treated the claimant have been unable at all to find anything of significance wrong with her. Some have indicated either little or no disability." Similarly, the district court noted that her eventual diagnosis "is completely contradicted by the other medical evidence of record." *Sisco v. Sullivan,* No. CIV-91-1675-C, slip op. at 3.

Under the facts of this case, the early examinations cannot be considered as contradicting or rebutting her recent diagnoses. As previously mentioned, chronic fatigue syndrome was not even recognized as a disease until 1988, and the first technique to diagnose it was not published until that same year. The Mayo Clinic was finally able to provide an explanation for Plaintiff's symptoms late in 1989. It was precisely because of the Mayo Clinic's reputation for diagnosing new and rare diseases that Plaintiff's doctors referred her there. It is highly unlikely that any of the physicians who examined Plaintiff prior to the Mayo Clinic would have considered or even been aware of chronic fatigue syndrome. The government has not cited to a single physician who examined Plaintiff *after* the Mayo Clinic or in light of the medical community's new understanding of chronic fatigue syndrome who contradicted or in any way questioned the conclusions of the Mayo Clinic and her treating physician.

Moreover, because chronic fatigue syndrome is diagnosed partially through a process of elimination, an extended medical history of "nothing-wrong" diagnoses is not unusual for a patient who is ultimately found to be suffering from the disease. The Mayo Clinic and her treating physician considered Plaintiff's entire medical history-including all the failed attempts to diagnose-in making their assessments. Finally, in a purely linguistic sense, an early report that "I am unable to find the cause" does not contradict a later report that "I have now found the cause." These statements together demonstrate an evolution rather than a contradiction. None of the pre-Mayo physicians ruled out chronic fatigue syndrome; they merely expressed an inability to discover an adequate physical explanation for her symptoms. When viewed in the proper light, Plaintiff's medical history does not rebut her recent diagnoses. *See Reed,* 804 F.Supp. at 921 (holding that conclusions of specialists who examined patient before chronic fatigue syndrome became widely known could not rebut recent diagnosis of treating physician who was a generalist). Thus, Plaintiff's testimony and medical evidence stood entirely unchallenged in front of the ALJ.

* * *

Plaintiff's disability has been evaluated by an adjudicatory body no fewer than ten times over the past several years-eight of which have been at various levels in front of the Secretary. In the meantime, Plaintiff has lived on a meager income and tried to support a teenage son. As far as quantum of proof, Plaintiff has exceeded what a claimant can legitimately be expected to prove to collect benefits under the Act. Her case stands un-challenged. The record reveals that the ALJ has resented Plaintiff's per-sistence, refused to take her disease seriously, and at times treated her claim with indifference or disrespect. The Secretary is not entitled to ad-judicate a case "ad infinitum until it correctly applies the proper legal standard and gathers evidence to support its conclusion." *Thaete*, 826 F.Supp. at 1252) (citing *Sanders v. Secretary of Health and Human Ser-vices*, 649 F.Supp. 71, 73 (N.D. Ala. 1986). The judgment of the district court is reversed and the case is remanded to the district court with in-structions to remand to the Secretary for an immediate award of benefits.

NOTES ON SOCIAL SECURITY RULINGS ON CHRONIC PAIN CONDITIONS

1. Recall that the courts in *Green-Younger* and *Sisco* both cited SSA guidelines—an internal memorandum and the agency's program operations manual (POMS)—for assessing the particular chronic pain conditions in-volved in the claims under review. SSA has also issued Rulings that serve the same purpose. As the court explained in Bischof v. Apfel, 65 F.Supp.2d 140, 145, 64 Soc. Sec. Rep. Serv. 524 (E.D.N.Y. 1999), a case involving Chron-ic Fatigue Syndrome (CFS):

> Claims involving Chronic Fatigue Syndrome present something of a di-lemma to the Commissioner. On one hand, the social security regula-tions require a claimant to demonstrate an impairment on the basis of "medical evidence consisting of signs, symptoms, and laboratory find-ings, not only by [the claimant's] statement of symptoms." 20 C.F.R. § 404.1508. On the other hand, the prevailing medical definition of Chron-ic Fatigue Syndrome allows a diagnosis on the basis of "an individual's reported symptoms alone once other possible causes for the symptoms have been ruled out." Social Security Ruling SSR 99-2p (1999) (citing Annals of Internal Medicine, 121:953-9 (1994)).

> In recognition of this dilemma, the Commissioner of Social Security has issued guidelines for use in claims involving Chronic Fatigue Syndrome. See Social Security Ruling SSR 99-2p; Program Operations Manual Sys-tem, §§ DI 24515.007 (1997). * * *

The court went on to note that POMS guidelines were in effect at the time of the administrative hearing which stated that

> CFS is characterized by the presence of persistent unexplained fatigue and by the chronicity of other symptoms. The most prevalent symptoms include episodes of low-grade fever, myalgias [muscle pain], headache, painful lymph nodes, and problems with memory and concentration. These symptoms fluctuate in frequency and severity and may be seen to

continue over a period of many months. Physical examination may be within normal limits. Individual cases must be adjudicated on the basis of the totality of evidence, including the clinical course from the onset of the illness, symptoms, signs, and laboratory findings. Consideration should be given to onset, duration, severity and residual functional capacity following the sequential evaluation process.

65 F.Supp.2d at 145. Noting further that other courts had found that this POMS policy is binding on SSA, the court concluded that "[u]nder this standard, an administrative law judge may not reject the opinions of treating physicians solely because they are based on a claimant's subjective complaints rather than specific medical signs or laboratory findings." *Id*. at 145-46. *See also id*. at 146 ("An administrative law judge also may not find that a claimant's testimony regarding Chronic Fatigue Syndrome lacks credibility solely because it is unsupported by objective medical findings.").

2. **SSR** 99-2p **(1992)[APP-RULINGS]**, cited by the court in *Bischof v. Apfel* in the preceding Note, provides that CFS can be established as a "medically determinable impairment" when it is accompanied by certain medical signs or laboratory findings. The Ruling goes on to explain the nature of the required medical signs and laboratory findings as follows:

ESTABLISHING THE EXISTENCE OF A MEDICALLY DETERMINABLE IMPAIRMENT

The following medical signs and laboratory findings establish the existence of a medically determinable impairment in individuals who have CFS. Although no specific etiology or pathology has yet been established for CFS, many research initiatives continue, and some progress has been made in ameliorating symptoms in selected individuals. With continuing scientific research, new medical evidence may emerge that will further clarify the nature of CFS and provide greater specificity regarding the clinical and laboratory diagnostic techniques that should be used to document this disorder.

Because of this, the medical criteria discussed below are only examples of signs and laboratory findings that will establish the existence of a medically determinable impairment; they are not all-inclusive. As progress is made in medical research into CFS, additional signs and laboratory findings may also be found that can be used to establish that individuals with CFS have a medically determinable impairment. The existence of CFS may be documented with medical signs or laboratory findings other than those listed below, provided that such documentation is consistent with medically accepted clinical practice and is consistent with the other evidence in the case record.

Examples of medical signs that establish the existence of a medically determinable impairment

For purposes of Social Security disability evaluation, one or more of the following medical signs clinically documented over a period of at least 6 consecutive months establishes the existence of a medically determinable impairment for individuals with CFS:

- Palpably swollen or tender lymph nodes on physical examination;

- Nonexudative pharyngitis;

- Persistent, reproducible muscle tenderness on repeated examinations, including the presence of positive tender points; or,

- Any other medical signs that are consistent with medically accepted clinical practice and are consistent with the other evidence in the case record.

EXAMPLES OF LABORATORY FINDINGS THAT ESTABLISH THE EXISTENCE OF A MEDICALLY DETERMINABLE IMPAIRMENT

At this time, there are no specific laboratory findings that are widely accepted as being associated with CFS. However, the absence of a definitive test does not preclude reliance upon certain laboratory findings to establish the existence of a medically determinable impairment in persons with CFS. Therefore, the following laboratory findings establish the existence of a medically determinable impairment in individuals with CFS.[4]

- An elevated antibody titer to Epstein-Barr virus (EBV) capsid antigen equal to or greater than 1:5120, or early antigen equal to or greater than 1:640;

- An abnormal magnetic resonance imaging (MRI) brain scan;

- Neurally mediated hypotension as shown by tilt table testing or another clinically accepted form of testing; or,

Any other laboratory findings that are consistent with medically accepted clinical practice and are consistent with the other evidence in the case record; for example, an abnormal exercise stress test or abnormal sleep

---

[4] It should be noted that standard laboratory test results in the normal range are characteristic for many individuals with CFS, and should not be relied upon to the exclusion of all other clinical evidence in decisions regarding the presence and severity of a medically determinable impairment.

studies, appropriately evaluated and consistent with the other evidence in the case record.

3. **SSR** 03-2p **(2003)[APP-RULINGS]** sets out guidelines for evaluating Reflex Sympathetic Dystrophy Syndrome (RSDS), also known as Complex Regional Pain Syndrome, Type I (CRPS). The Ruling notes that RSDS/CRPS is a medically determinable impairment—if documented by appropriate medical signs, symptoms, and laboratory findings—and then sets out a list of diagnostic criteria consisting of complaints of "persistent, intense pain that results in impaired mobility of the affected region" accompanied by certain clinical findings, such as swelling or osteoporosis. Thus, while RSDS/CRPS may be the basis for a finding of disability," the Ruling also cautions that "[d]isability may not be established on the basis of an individual's statement of symptoms alone."

4. Just as with claims based on generalized pain, the credibility of the claimant's subjective symptoms can be critically important in evaluating a claim based on a chronic pain condition. Thus, SSR 99-2p provides that where "an individual's statements about the intensity, persistence, or functionally limiting effects of symptoms are not substantiated by objective medical evidence, the adjudicator must consider all of the evidence in the case record, including any statements by the individual and other persons concerning the individual's symptoms. The adjudicator must then make a finding on the credibility of the individual's statements about symptoms and their functional effects." (Citing SSR 96-7p). *See also* Bridgeman v. Astrue, 130 Soc. Sec. Rep. Serv. 190, 2008 WL 1803619 (E.D.N.C. 2008) (rejecting the claimants argument that the ALJ erroneously required objective evidence of the intensity of the claimant's pain; "The ALJ's decision followed the guidelines in SSR 03-2p and relevant case law, which states that when an individual's subjective complaints are not supported by objective medical evidence, the ALJ must make a finding about the individual's credibility based on the entire medical record.").

B. MENTAL IMPAIRMENTS

Claims for disability benefits based on mental impairments are evaluated in essentially the same manner—and following the same five-step sequential evaluation process—as are those based on physical impairments. This policy was reaffirmed in the mid-1980s, following a period during which the Social Security Administration took the position that only those mental impairments that met the requirements of the Listing of Impairments were severe enough to qualify for benefits—effectively eliminating Steps 4 and 5 for mental impairment-based claims. That policy was enjoined in a class action lawsuit, Mental Health Ass'n of Minnesota v. Schweiker, 554 F. Supp. 157, 1 Soc. Sec. Rep. Serv. 465 (D. Minn. 1982), aff'd in part, modified in part, 720 F.2d 965, 3 Soc. Sec. Rep. Serv. 183 (8th Cir. 1983), and a few years later SSA issued a Ruling that states, in part:

Medically determinable mental disorders present a variable continuum of symptoms and effects, from minor emotional problems to bizarre and dangerous behavior. However, in determining the impact of a mental disorder on an individual's capacities, essentially the same impairment-related medical and nonmedical information is considered to determine whether the mental disorder meets listing severity as is considered to determine whether the mental impairment is of lesser severity, yet diminishes the individual's RFC. For impairments of listing severity, inability to perform substantial gainful activity (SGA) is presumed from prescribed findings. However, with mental impairments of lesser severity, such inability must be demonstrated through a detailed assessment of the individual's capacity to perform and sustain mental activities which are critical to work performance. Conclusions of ability to engage in SGA are not to be inferred merely from the fact that the mental disorder is not of listing severity.

SSR 85-16 (1985)[APP-RULINGS]. *See also* **SSR 85-15 (1985)[APP-RULINGS]** ("[T]he sequential evaluation process mandated by the regulations does not end with the finding that the impairment, though severe, does not meet or equal an impairment listed in Appendix 1 of the regulations. The process must go on to consider whether the individual can meet the mental demands of past relevant work in spite of the limiting effects of his or her impairment and, if not, whether the person can do other work, considering his or her remaining mental capacities reflected in terms of the occupational base, age, education, and work experience."); 20 C.F.R. §§ 404.1520a(a), 416.920a(a) ("The steps outlined in [the sequential evaluation process regulation] apply to the evaluation of physical and mental impairments.").

There are, however, some special provisions relating to the disability determination process for claims based on mental impairments, many of which were mandated by 1984 amendments to the Social Security Act. These include a requirement that for claims involving a possible mental impairment SSA make "every reasonable effort to ensure that a qualified psychiatrist or psychologist has completed the medical portion of the case review and any applicable residual functional capacity assessment." **42 U.S.C. § 421 (h)[APP-STAT].** In addition, Congress ordered a revision of the mental impairments section of the Listing of Impairments, with the directive that "[t]he revised criteria and listings . . . be designed to realistically evaluate the ability of a mentally impaired individual to engage in substantial gainful activity in a competitive workplace environment."). *See* Social Security Disability Benefits Reform Act of 1984, Pub. L. No. 98-460, §5(a), 98 Stat. 1794, 1801. Another set of regulations include special procedures for recording evidence of mental impairments and for determining the degree of functional loss. *See* **20 C.F.R. §§ 404.1520a(b)-(e), 416.920a(b)-(e)[APP-REGS]**.

1. MENTAL IMPAIRMENTS AND RESIDUAL FUNCTIONAL CAPACITY (RFC)

Social Security Ruling 85-16, quoted in part above, also specifies the type of evidence that should be considered when determining the RFC of a claimant with mental impairments and provides examples of the types of factors that should be taken into account when analyzing the evidence, cautioning that "it is necessary to draw meaningful inferences and allow reasonable conclusions about the individual's strengths and weaknesses." Further guidance is included at **20 C.F.R. §§ 404.1545(c), 416.945(c)[APP-REGS]**.

SCHAAL V. CALLAHAN

993 F. Supp. 85, 56 Soc. Sec. Rep. Ser. 56 (D.Conn. 1997)

MARTINEZ, United States Magistrate Judge.

The plaintiff, Daniel J. Schaal, filed this action seeking review, pursuant to 42 U.S.C. § 405(g), of the decision of the Secretary denying his claim for disability insurance benefits under the Social Security Act. The defendant moved for an order affirming the decision of the Secretary. In response to the defendant's motion, the plaintiff filed two motions for judgment on the pleadings in which he seeks an immediate award of benefits or a remand for further proceedings. For the reasons that follow, the court recommends that the plaintiffs motions be granted to the extent that the case is remanded for further proceedings and the defendant's motion be denied.

BACKGROUND

The plaintiff was born on March 14, 1951. He has a college degree in business administration and has earned 39 credits toward an M.B.A. The plaintiff currently volunteers at a coffee and bagel stand in the West Hartford town hall for two hours per day, three days per week. His last employment was as a hotel desk clerk. He also has worked as a bottle return clerk, a waiter/restaurant worker and a valet parking attendant. The plaintiffs period of insured status for Title II purposes expired on June 30, 1996. The plaintiff states that he became disabled on May 30, 1991, and claims that he is entitled to disability benefits because of a schizoaffective disorder.

* * *

The plaintiff testified that for about five years he has not been able to concentrate long enough to "stay at" whatever he is doing. Although he suffers from asthma which is worse in hot weather, he has no disabling physical impairments. The plaintiff lives with his parents and receives public assistance. He consults the town social worker, who supervises his volunteer job, once a month for counseling. The plaintiff also attends weekly sessions with a therapist who has been treating him for three or four years.

* * *

* * * The ALJ also heard testimony from the town social worker who supervises the plaintiff in the volunteer position. The social worker stated that the plaintiff "generally performs well the time he is at the town hall." He noted, however, that the plaintiff frequently leaves from fifteen to thirty minutes early because he is restless. Although generally good at following instructions, the plaintiff does a cursory job when asked to clean the facilities and his hands always appear dirty. The plaintiff is friendly and presents himself well, but exhibits anxiety-related behaviors. He will not sit down and has little interaction with customers. The plaintiff often experiences an anxiety attack and will refuse to go to the shop across the street from the town hall for supplies. As another example of anxiety-related behavior, the social worker noted that when the plaintiff arrives for his monthly counseling session, the plaintiff will not sit in the waiting room. Instead he leaves his name and stands out in the main lobby until his appointment.

The social worker offered an opinion, based upon his daily observations as the plaintiffs supervisor, regarding the plaintiffs ability to engage in substantial gainful activity. The social worker stated that the plaintiff appears to respond well to criticism, but does not, or cannot, take the initiative to change the behavior that generated the criticism. He cannot carry out tasks without excessive supervision. When the plaintiff works alone, the work is "sloppy." The social worker concluded that the plaintiff could not successfully perform the volunteer job without supervision. The plaintiff cannot make simple work-related decisions and prefers to let his coworkers deal with the public. Thus, the social worker opined that the plaintiff cannot make a transition to regular employment in a competitive environment because he cannot concentrate long enough, follow through on slightly complicated directions or make immediate decisions.

The ALJ also had the personal data questionnaire completed by the plaintiff in November 1992, the daily activities questionnaire completed by the plaintiff in October 1995, and undated activities questionnaires completed by the plaintiffs parents. The plaintiff stated in November 1992, that he had no trouble sleeping at night but required more rest so he took an afternoon nap lasting from two to five hours. He needed no help grooming or caring for his personal needs. He helped his mother with food preparation and setting the table, and washed the dishes. He made his bed and cleaned and organized his room daily. He also helped with weekly housecleaning. In addition, the plaintiff raked leaves and cleaned the cellar and garage. He shopped for clothes or food every three weeks. The plaintiff read newspapers, magazines and the Bible. He watched television about three hours per day. His interests included walking, weight lifting, basketball, craft fairs and flea markets. He visited his sister every two or three weeks. A typical visit lasted approximately three hours. The plaintiff reported that he could concentrate and work for long periods of time.

In the 1995 questionnaire, the plaintiff reported that he performs household chores including: washing dishes, laundry, cleaning and organizing his room, raking leaves and shoveling snow. He walks between fifteen and twenty miles per week, attends weekly mass and enjoys going to flea markets. He cooks for himself once or twice each week (but is not permitted to use the stove) and cares for his personal needs without assistance. He reads up to two hours per day and watches television or listens to the radio for between three and four hours per day. Although the plaintiff does not drive, he is able to use public transportation.

The plaintiff's father reported that except for meals the plaintiff spends most of his time alone. Although the plaintiff used to enjoy basketball and baseball, now he just walks. The plaintiff has almost no social contact outside of his family and seldom shops. He engages in conversations with his mother and nieces but does not like questions. The plaintiff seldom communicates his feelings to his father, preferring to speak to his mother. He does not like to be criticized or repeatedly told what to do. Although the plaintiff washes dishes and cuts the lawn, usually he cannot finish alone. When he does complete a task, however, he takes about the same time as a "normal person." The plaintiff must be watched as he will not change his clothes or bathe without coaxing. Occasionally the plaintiff experiences sleeplessness.

The plaintiff's mother stated that although the plaintiff spends some time alone, he watches television with the family after dinner. He likes gatherings and will go to movies or concerts if his parents provide the necessary money. She describes the plaintiff as shy and polite, a person trying to be accepted. The plaintiff enjoys shopping, especially in bookstores. He has no difficulty asking questions or speaking his mind, although he will speak rapidly when he is upset. The plaintiff does not like anyone to show disrespect. Because the plaintiff sometimes appears not to hear when he is corrected, his mother will stress certain points in her instructions to ensure that he understands what is expected. The plaintiffs mother said that she seldom redoes the plaintiffs chores. The plaintiff can dress himself appropriately, although he sometimes asks her opinion about clothing choices. He can prepare his own breakfast and lunch and will prepare dinner if she is not at home. The plaintiff generally knows what his mother expects from him. He will perform errands if he can walk to the store and purchases the specified items if he has been given careful instruction. The plaintiff has no difficulty sleeping.

The ALJ had before him reports of psychological evaluations and treatment covering the period from 1983 through the time of the hearing. * * *

* * *

* * *

DISCUSSION

* * *

I. Severity of the Plaintiff's Impairment

The plaintiff first argues that the ALJ's finding that the plaintiffs impairment was not of listing severity is not supported by substantial evidence. More specifically, the plaintiff contends that the ALJ failed to consider the non-medical evidence of functional limitations and failed to comply with the requirements of Social Security Ruling ("SSR") 85-16 in that he did not explain his rejection of this evidence. The plaintiff also contends that his impairment satisfies the listing requirements for schizoaffective disorders.

A. Application of SSR 85-16

The determination that a claimant is disabled by a mental impairment is a two-step process. First, the ALJ must decide whether a mental impairment exists. He does this by reviewing the record to determine whether there is any evidence of signs, symptoms, findings, functional limitations or treatments indicating a mental impairment. 20 C.F.R. § 416.920a(b). In the present case, the ALJ determined that the plaintiff suffers from a severe impairment, namely schizoaffective disorder.

Second, the ALJ must examine the four areas of activity considered to be essential to the ability to work to determine what degree of functional loss is attributable to the mental impairment. 20 C.F.R. § 416.920a(b)(3). These four areas of activity are: activities of daily living; social functioning; concentration, persistence or pace; and deterioration or decompensation in work or work-like settings. *Id.* In the present case, the ALJ determined that the plaintiff exhibited no restrictions on activities of daily living, demonstrated slight difficulty maintaining social functioning, seldom experienced deficiencies of concentration, persistence or pace which resulted in failure to complete assigned tasks in a timely manner, and never exhibited episodes of deterioration or decompensation in work or work-like settings which caused him to withdraw from the situation or to experience an exacerbation of symptoms. Thus, the ALJ determined that the plaintiff did not demonstrate functional limitations of the severity required to satisfy the listing requirements for schizoaffective disorder.

SSR 85-16 explains the importance of a residual functional capacity assessment for individuals whose mental impairments are severe but do not meet the listing requirements. The evaluation of residual functional capacity in persons suffering from mental disorders "includes consideration of the ability to understand, to carry out and remember instructions, and to respond appropriately to supervision, coworkers, and customary work pressures in a work setting." SSR 85-16, 1985 WL 56855, at *1 (S.S.A.). Evidence helpful in making this determination includes:

> History, findings, and observations from medical sources (including psychological test results), regarding the presence, frequency, and intensity of hallucinations, delusions or paranoid tendencies; depression or elation; confusion or disorientation; conversion symptoms or phobias; psychophysiological symptoms; withdrawn or bizarre behavior; anxiety or tension.

> Reports of the individual's activities of daily living and work activity, as well as testimony of third parties about the individual's performance and behavior.

> * * *

> Quality of daily activities, both in occupational and social spheres....

> Ability to sustain activities, interests, and relate to others over a period of time. The frequency, appropriateness, and independence of the activities must also be considered....

> Level of intellectual functioning.

> Ability to function in a work-like situation.

Id. at *2.

Under SSR 85-16, the ALJ bears the responsibility "to identify the pertinent evidence from medical and nonmedical reports and to make findings as to the individual's ability to perform work-related activities."

Id. Non-medical evidence may be "vital" in assessing the functional limitations of a mental impairment. *Id.* at *4. Non-medical sources specifically mentioned in the ruling include social workers and family members. In addition, "[i]nformation concerning an individual's performance in any work setting (including sheltered work and volunteer or competitive work) ... may be pertinent in assessing the individual's ability to function in a competitive work environment." *Id.* If the conclusion based upon an evaluation of sheltered work differs from that based upon medical evidence, the difference must be resolved. The ALJ's decision must explain the reason for rejecting one evaluation and accepting the other. *Id.*

In the present case, the ALJ recounted all of the record medical evidence in his decision. But the ALJ failed to even mention the activities questionnaires completed by the plaintiffs parents and only briefly mentioned the social worker's testimony. (R. 42-44). Although the ALJ professes to have applied SSR 85-16 in evaluating the plaintiffs testimony, the ALJ provides no resolution of the discrepancies between the plaintiffs testimony and that of the social worker, or of the difference in the assessments of the plaintiffs ability to maintain employment provided by the social worker and psychologists. Thus, the ALJ has failed to comply with the requirements of SSR 85-16. Upon remand, the ALJ is directed to perform the analysis contemplated by SSR 85-16. He shall consider the social worker's assessment of the plaintiffs work ability, resolve any discrepancies in the evidence of the plaintiffs functional abilities and explain the reasoning which underlies his determination.

[The court also found the record deficient to rule on the questions whether the claimant could perform his past relevant work or whether his functional limitations due to his schizoaffective disorder met the requirements of the Listing of Impairments. Accordingly, the case was remanded "for further administrative proceedings to enable the ALJ to properly evaluate the evidence of the [claimant's] functional limitations."]

2. PSYCHIATRIC REVIEW TECHNIQUE FORM (PRTF)

As noted above, the regulations provide that the Social Security Administration will record pertinent information about the claimant's mental condition in any mental impairment-based evaluation on a "standard document" that outlines the special procedures to be used for these claims. *See* 20 C.F.R. §§ 404.1520a(e), 416.920a(e). The "standard document" currently used by SSA is called a Psychiatric Review Technique Form (PRTF).

KOHLER V. ASTRUE

546 F.3d 260, 137 Soc. Sec. Rep. Serv. 278 (2nd Cir. 2008)

Before: STRAUB, POOLER, and SOTOMAYOR, Circuit Judges.

SOTOMAYOR, Circuit Judge:

Plaintiff Kathy Kohler appeals from a decision of the United States District Court for the Northern District of New York (Sharpe, *J.*), dated November 3, 2006, granting the motion for judgment on the pleadings by defendant Commissioner of the Social Security Administration ("Commissioner") and affirming the Commissioner's denial of her application for Social Security Disability Insurance ("SSDI") and Supplemental Security Income ("SSI") benefits. We hold that the Administrative Law Judge ("ALJ") erred by not following the mandatory "special technique" set forth in 20 C.F.R. § 404.1520a for evaluating the severity of a mental impairment, and we cannot conclude from the current record that this error was harmless. Accordingly, we VACATE the judgment of the district court insofar as it upheld the Commissioner's decision to deny Kohler benefits and we REMAND to the district court with instructions to remand the matter to the Commissioner for further proceedings consistent with this opinion.

BACKGROUND

Kathy Kohler, who is now 51 years old, was diagnosed with bipolar disorder in 1992. She applied for SSDI and SSI benefits on March 25, 2002, asserting that her mental impairment constituted a disability preventing her from engaging in substantial gainful employment. Her application was initially denied, but that decision was vacated and remanded by the United States District Court for the Northern District of New York on October 5, 2004 because of an inaudible tape of the hearing. A second hearing on Kohler's application was held by ALJ Carl Stephan on February 15, 2005. Kohler appeals from the ALJ's decision denying benefits following this hearing.

Medical History

In 1992, Kohler was hospitalized twice within about a month. On the first occasion, she was brought to the hospital by police after she broke down the door of an acquaintance's house. Initially observed to be agitated and confused, her demeanor improved with medication and she was released after two weeks. She was returned to the hospital ten days later by her husband, who reported that she was "out of control." She again was treated with medication and was discharged after approximately two weeks.

In 1996, Kohler moved from Buffalo, N.Y. to the North Country near Plattsburgh, NY, and began receiving medical services from North Star Behavioral Health Services ("North Star").   Her treating physician at North Star at all relevant times has been Naveen Achar. In addition, she was treated at North Star (and later in private practice) by Lorna Jewell, a nurse practitioner. At Kohler's initial screening exam in 1996, Achar noted that Kohler was not in distress, appeared to have a calm mood and bright affect, and was alert and oriented, with good memory, concentration, and judgment. He observed that Kohler's lithium prescription for the prior 4 years "seems to have controlled her mania and depressive symptoms."   His notes indicate that Kohler's "global assessment of functioning (GAF)" was 60, and that its highest value during the preceding year was 75.

In April 1998, Kohler was again hospitalized, for just over a week, after the staff of a hospital at which her boyfriend was being treated for injuries from a serious head-on collision found her wandering the hallways, talking to herself and acting bizarrely. She was diagnosed with mild lithium toxicity and showed improvement within 24 hours after her dosage was reduced. She was discharged with a GAF score of 65, which reflects "[s]ome mild symptoms (e.g. depressed mood or mild insomnia) OR some difficulty in social, occupational, or school functioning ... but generally functioning pretty well, has some meaningful interpersonal relationships." Am. Psychiatric Ass'n, *Diagnostic and Statistical Manual of Mental Disorders* 34 (4th ed.2000).

Jewell's notes from appointments with Kohler in 2000 indicate that Kohler continued to take her medications with good effect, was stable, and generally able to manage the stresses of her daily life, including stresses associated with ending a relationship of six years. After an appointment on January 3, 2001, Jewell similarly noted that Kohler was taking her medication with good effect, "appear[ed] to be stable," and was enjoying her independence.

Two weeks later, however, Kohler's condition deteriorated. On January 16, 2001, she was brought to the emergency room at the direction of Jewell, after Kohler's family reported that her behavior had become increasingly bizarre over the prior two days, and that she was agitated, talking rapidly, and unable to stop running around the house. Kohler reported that she had not been sleeping well, had missed two days of her lithium, and was experiencing symptoms such as extreme irritability and obsessive cleaning. She was given the medication Haldol to help her sleep and was sent home with her brother.

Kohler's family remained concerned about her "changed and still unstable behavior" throughout the following two weeks, leading to a telephone conference with Jewell on January 23, 2001 and an in-person appointment on January 30, 2001. At the appointment, Kohler acknowledged that she was "not doing her best and that an adjustment in medication might be called for." Jewell's notes indicate that Kohler was "not manic, but [was] perhaps approaching hypomania as indicated by her unpatterned sleeping and eating." Jewell hypothesized that the episode had been triggered by emotional stress, and suggested that Kohler might need the assistance of an "intensive case manager" ("ICM") to help organize her affairs. Kohler evidently agreed, and met with an ICM regularly for at least the next year.

Medical Evaluations

Achar, Kohler's treating physician, filled out an evaluation regarding Kohler's ability to do work-related activities on October 21, 2003. He indicated that she had only slight restriction in her ability to understand, remember, and carry out detailed instructions, and to maintain socially appropriate behavior. He further indicated that Kohler had no restriction in her ability to (a) understand, remember, and carry out short, simple instructions; (b) make judgments on simple work-related decisions; and (c) adhere to basic standards of cleanliness. Achar also reported that Kohler had no more than slight restrictions in various work-related social functions, such as interacting appropriately with the public or supervisors.

Kohler was independently evaluated by Brett T. Hartman, a psychologist, on October 9, 2003. He concluded that her prognosis was "fair, given her current stabilization of symptoms." He noted that Kohler reported a history of insomnia, but not in the previous year, and that she experienced a "variety of depressive symptoms at this time." He also noted that Kohler had reported that she "has a history of manic episodes, as recently as 1 1/2 years ago, ... but she has not had such episodes since that time." With respect to Kohler's vocational and functional capacities, Hartman concluded:

> [I]t appears that Ms. Kohler is able to follow and understand simple directions and instructions. She is also able to perform a variety of simple and rote tasks. She has fair attention and concentration skills and a fair ability to learn new information. She also has a fair ability to make appropriate decisions at this time. Claimant may have mild difficulty performing tasks on a consistent basis. She also would appear to have mild to moderate problems performing a variety of complex tasks independently, given her mild intellectual deficits. It would also appear that she would have mild problems relating adequately to others and dealing appropriately with the normal stressors of life.

In addition, Terri Linden Bruni, a state agency psychological consultant, evaluated the record evidence and completed a psychiatric review of Kohler's condition on June 3, 2002. She concluded that Kohler had "bipolar syndrome with a history of episodic periods manifested by full symptomatic picture of both manic and depressive symptoms." She rated Kohler's degree of functional limitation as "slight" for restriction of daily activities and deficiencies maintaining concentration, persistence or pace; as "moderate" for difficulties in maintaining social functioning; and "never" for repeated episodes of deterioration, each of extended duration. Bruni evaluated Kohler to be "not significantly limited" for all indicators except three, in which she found Kohler "moderately limited": (1) ability to maintain attention and concentration for extended periods, (2) ability to complete a normal workday and work week without interruptions from psychologically-based symptoms and to perform at a consistent pace without an unreasonable number and length of rest periods, and (3) ability to interact appropriately with the general public. Bruni concluded that Kohler had good results controlling her manic symptoms with medication and that her recent mental status exams "ha[d] essentially been within normal limits on all parameters."

* * *

ALJ Decision

The ALJ found that, as a result of her bipolar disorder, Kohler suffers from a "severe impairment" that limits her capacity to work. He then determined, however, that her impairment "fails to meet or equal the level of severity of any disabling condition contained in Appendix 1, Subpart P of the Social Security Regulations." The ALJ provided little analysis for this conclusion, and instead moved on to evaluate Kohler's residual functional capacity ("RFC"). The ALJ examined Kohler's medical reports, including evaluations by Achar and treatment notes by Jewell, and concluded that Kohler generally "displayed mild symptoms" that "appear well controlled" when properly medicated. Based on these medical reports, the ALJ could "identify no more than occasional problems with the claimant's capacity to understand and execute detailed instructions, her capacity to handle work stressors, and her ability to deal with others." He also found "no treating reports which would suggest that the claimant experiences more than occasional problems in social and occupational functioning." He concluded that Kohler had the RFC to perform her past relevant work as a housekeeper/cleaner, and that a finding of "not disabled" was therefore required.

Kohler timely sought review of the ALJ's final determination in the district court pursuant to 42 U.S.C. § 405(g). On November 3, 2006, the district court entered judgment upholding the denial of benefits and granting the Commissioner's motion for judgment on the pleadings. Kohler timely appealed to this Court.

DISCUSSION

* * *

"Disability" is statutorily defined as the "inability to engage in any substantial gainful activity by reason of any medically determinable physical or mental impairment ... which has lasted or can be expected to last for a continuous period of not less than 12 months." 42 U.S.C. § 423(d)(1)(A). The Commissioner of Social Security has adopted regulations that provide a five-step framework for evaluating disability claims. * * *

In addition to the five-step analysis outlined in 20 C.F.R. § 404.1520, the Commissioner has promulgated additional regulations governing evaluations of the severity of mental impairments. 20 C.F.R. § 404.1520a. These regulations require application of a "special technique" at the second and third steps of the five-step framework and at each level of administrative review. 20 C.F.R.§ 404.1520a(a). This technique requires the reviewing authority to determine first whether the claimant has a "medically determinable mental impairment." § 404.1520a(b)(1). If the claimant is found to have such an impairment, the reviewing authority must "rate the degree of functional limitation resulting from the impairment(s) in accordance with paragraph (c)," § 404.1520a(b)(2), which specifies four broad functional areas: (1) activities of daily living; (2) social functioning; (3) concentration, persistence, or pace; and (4) episodes of decompensation. § 404.1520a(c)(3). According to the regulations, if the degree of limitation in each of the first three areas is rated "mild" or better, and no episodes of decompensation are identified, then the reviewing authority generally will conclude that the claimant's mental impairment is not "severe" and will deny benefits. § 404.1520a(d)(1). If the claimant's mental impairment is severe, the reviewing authority will first compare the relevant medical findings and the functional limitation ratings to the criteria of listed mental disorders in order to determine whether the impairment meets or is equivalent in severity to any listed mental disorder. § 404.1520a(d)(2). If so, the claimant will be found to be disabled. If not, the reviewing authority will then assess the claimant's residual functional capacity. § 404.1520a(d)(3).

Importantly, the regulations require application of this process to be documented. § 404.1520a(e). At the initial and reconsideration levels of administrative review, a medical or psychological consultant generally will complete a standard document, known as a Psychiatric Review Technique Form ("PRTF"). § 404.1520a(e)(1). Until 2000, the regulations also required the ALJ to complete a PRTF and attach it to his decision. While the regulations no longer require the ALJ to complete that standard form, they do require the ALJ's written decision to reflect application of the technique, and explicitly provide that the decision "*must* include a specific finding as to the degree of limitation in each of the functional areas described in paragraph (c) of this section." § 404.1520a(e)(2) (emphasis added); *see* § 404.1520a(c)(3) (specifying the four functional areas central to the special technique).

The foregoing regulations apply to the evaluation of Kohler's application, and neither party disputes that Kohler's bipolar disorder constitutes a "medically determinable mental impairment." The ALJ therefore was required to evaluate the severity of Kohler's impairment per the procedure set forth in the regulations and summarized above, and to include the necessary findings in his written decision. But the ALJ failed to adhere to the regulations, as his written decision does not reflect application of the special technique and, in particular, lacks specific findings with respect to each of the four functional areas described in § 404.1520a(c).

The consequence of noncompliance with 20 C.F.R. § 404.1520a is a matter of first impression in this Circuit. Other courts of appeals have not hesitated to remand where an ALJ's noncompliance with § 404.1520a results in an inadequately developed record with respect to the four functional categories. For example, in *Moore v. Barnhart*, 405 F.3d 1208 (11th Cir.2005) (per curiam), the Commissioner conceded that the ALJ erred by not completing a PRTF or complying with the mode of analysis set forth in 20 C.F.R. § 404.1520a, but argued that remand was inappropriate because the error was harmless. *Id*. at 1214. The Eleventh Circuit rejected that argument, observing that "[t]he ALJ failed to even analyze or document Moore['s] condition in two of the ... functional areas: social functioning and prior episodes of decompensation. Because the ALJ's decision lacks consideration of these factors and their impact on his ultimate conclusion as to Moore's RFC, we cannot even evaluate the Commissioner's contention that the error was harmless." *Id*.

Under the previous regulations that required the ALJ to append a PRTF to its written decision, the Ninth Circuit held that failure to follow § 404.1520a requires remand "where there is a colorable claim of mental impairment." *Gutierrez v. Apfel*, 199 F.3d 1048, 1051 (9th Cir.2000). In doing so, it joined several other circuits that have remanded based on noncompliance with § 404.1520a, either under a harmless error analysis or something akin to it. *See, e.g., Montgomery v. Shalala*, 30 F.3d 98, 100 (8th Cir.1994) (remanding after concluding that error was not harmless); *Hill v. Sullivan*, 924 F.2d 972, 975 (10th Cir.1991) (per curiam) ("Since the record contained evidence of a mental impairment that allegedly prevented claimant from working, the Secretary was required to follow the procedure for evaluating the potential mental impairment set forth in his regulations and document the procedure accordingly."); *Stambaugh v. Sullivan*, 929 F.2d 292, 296 (7th Cir.1991) (remanding because ALJ failed to document application of special technique, despite evidence suggesting significant mental impairment).[6]

In this case, the ALJ does not appear to have evaluated each of the four functional areas, and did not record specific findings as to Kohler's degree of limitation in any of the areas. Nor did he conduct a distinct analysis that would permit adequate review on appeal even without the requisite findings. The bulk of the ALJ's decision focused on Kohler's ability to maintain concentration, persistence or pace and her periods of decompensation (or lack thereof). It addressed how Kohler's bipolar disorder restricts her daily activities or social functioning only in general terms, despite some evidence in the record that these limitations were more than mild.[7] It did not make the findings required by the regulations, but nevertheless concluded that Kohler suffered a severe impairment prior to the date she was last insured, and that this impairment "fail[ed] to meet or equal the level of severity of any disabling condition" listed in the regulations.

Effective review by this Court is frustrated by the decision's failure to adhere to the regulations. First, because the decision contains no specific findings regarding Kohler's degree of limitation in the four functional areas by which disabling conditions are rated, the Court cannot determine whether there is substantial evidence for the ALJ's conclusion that Kohler's impairment, while severe, was not as severe as any listed disabling condition. Second, the ALJ's decision discusses much of the relevant evidence primarily in the context of Kohler's residual functional capacity to perform work and not in the context of the four functional areas identified by the regulations. Thus, it is not clear whether the ALJ adequately considered the entire record when determining the severity of Kohler's impairment, or whether he might have found it to equal the severity of a listed condition had he followed the regulations and made specific findings regarding Kohler's degree of limitation in each functional area. It also is not clear whether the ALJ would have arrived at the same conclusion regarding Kohler's residual functional capacity to perform work had he adhered to the regulations.

These deficiencies are compounded by the ALJ's tendency to overlook or mischaracterize relevant evidence, often to Kohler's disadvantage.

---

[6] Both the Ninth and the Tenth Circuits have adhered to these principles after the 2000 revisions to § 404.1520a, albeit in unpublished decisions. *See Shivel v. Astrue*, 260 Fed.Appx. 88, 90-91 (10th Cir.2008); *Selassie v. Barnhart*, 203 Fed.Appx. 174, 176 (9th Cir.2006) ("The specific documentation requirements ... are not mere technicalities that can be ignored as long as the ALJ reaches the same result that it would have if it had followed those requirements.").

[7] For example, the PRTF completed in 2002 by Bruni reports that Kohler suffered "moderate" limitations on her social functioning.

Four examples illustrate that the effects may have been material. First, the ALJ's decision does not mention the PRTF completed by Bruni in 2002. Bruni, who based her evaluation on a review of Kohler's records, rated the limitations on Kohler's social functioning as "moderate." That suggests a more negative assessment than was reached by the ALJ, who could find "no treating reports which would suggest that the claimant experiences more than occasional problems in social and occupational functioning." Second, the ALJ's decision twice emphasizes that nurse practitioner Jewell wrote in February 2002 that Kohler "had been stable for several years with but one episode of mania." Jewell's notes in fact state (as the decision elsewhere acknowledges in passing) that Kohler "has been stable for the past several years with one episode of mania *requir[ing] hospitalization in 1997.*" That modifier is important because Kohler also experienced a significant episode of mania in midJanuary 2001, but that episode did not lead to overnight hospitalization. It also is important, and not mentioned by the ALJ, that the notes from Jewell's next meeting with Kohler are significantly less enthusiastic, reporting that Kohler "has been stable for the last year or so with some hypomania presentation." Third, the ALJ consistently interprets reports that Kohler's condition has been "stable" to mean that Kohler's condition has been good, when the term could mean only that her condition has not changed, and she could be stable at a low functional level. Finally, and most notably, the ALJ's decision never mentions Jewell's opinion that "if Ms. Kohler were capable of working in a sustainable manner in a fulltime position, she would have and maintain such a job." Although the ALJ was not required to give controlling weight to Jewell's opinion, because she is not a "treating source" under 20 C.F.R. § 404.1502, he should have given her opinion some consideration, particularly because Jewell was the only medical professional available to Kohler for long stretches of time in the very rural "North Country" of New York State. *See Mongeur v. Heckler*, 722 F.2d 1033, 1039 n. 2 (2d Cir.1983) (stating opinion of nurse practitioner who treated claimant on regular basis entitled to "some extra consideration"). We have remanded in other cases where the ALJ has similarly failed to consider relevant probative evidence. *Lopez v. Sec'y of Health & Human Servs.*, 728 F.2d 148, 150-51 (2d Cir.1984).

While we leave open the possibility that an ALJ's failure to adhere to the regulations' special technique might under other facts be harmless, *cf. Montgomery*, 30 F.3d at 100 (applying harmless error analysis to failure to follow 20 C.F.R. § 404.1520a), the record in this case does not allow us to say that the ALJ's failure here was harmless. We can neither identify findings regarding the degree of Kohler's limitations in each of the four functional areas nor discern whether the ALJ properly considered all evidence relevant to those areas. We therefore cannot determine whether the ALJ's decision regarding Kohler's claim is supported by substantial evidence and reflects application of the correct legal standards.

CONCLUSION

For the reasons discussed, we VACATE the judgment of the district court insofar as it upheld the Commissioner's decision to deny Kohler benefits and we REMAND to the district court with instructions to remand the matter to the Commissioner for further proceedings consistent with this opinion.

NOTE

In its explanation of major revisions of the regulations on mental impairments published in 2000, SSA noted that the PRTF should not be confused with the evaluation technique outlined in the regulations; the form "simply documents application of the technique." 65 Fed. Reg. 50746, 50757 (2000). Accordingly, use of the PRTF itself is not required at the administrative hearing or Appeals Council levels of review, although administrative law judge and Appeals Council decisions must include all findings and conclusions called for in the PRFT form. Consider the following excerpt from Portlock v. Apfel, 150 F.Supp.2d 659, 670, 74 Soc. Sec. Rep. Serv. 387 (D.Del. 2001):

> Portlock finally contends that Judge Reddy failed to adequately explain his findings the Psychiatric Review Technique Form ("PRTF"). The agency must complete a "standard document," see 20 C.F.R. § 404.1520a(d), called a "Psychiatric Review Technique Form," which is essentially a checklist that tracks the requirements of the Listings of Mental Disorders. Id. at Pt. 404, Subpt. P, App. 1, § 12 (1987). The regulations permit an Administrative Law Judge to complete the form without the assistance of a medical adviser. Id. at § 404.1520a(d)(1)(i). However, there must be competent evidence in the record to support the conclusions recorded on the form and the Administrative Law Judge must discuss in his opinion the evidence that he considered in reaching the conclusions expressed on the form. See id. § 404.1520a(c)(4); Plummer v. Apfel, 186 F.3d 422, 433 (3d Cir.1999) (stating that in completing PRTF, "ALJ has a duty to consider all evidence of impairments in the record").

> Judge Reddy fully considered and explained Portlock's medical evidence regarding her depression and other mental impairments. Specifically, Portlock's treating physician's opinion was rejected because it was not well-supported by medically acceptable clinical and/or laboratory diagnostic techniques. Judge Reddy also pointed to Bolton's psychiatric evaluation to affirmatively demonstrate that Portlock was not severely mentally limited. Therefore, it appears that the PRTF was adequately supported by the record.

C. STRESS

Although stress cannot itself be a qualifying disabling impairment, evidence of the effect of stress on a claimant's physical or mental condition can be very important. The effects of stress are considered most often in cases involving mental conditions or a combination of physical and mental conditions. Social Security Ruling 85-15 (1985), which is discussed in the preceding section of this chapter on mental impairments, includes the following comments on stress relative to mental illness:

> Stress and Mental Illness—Since mental illness is defined and characterized by maladaptive behavior, it is not unusual that the mentally impaired have difficulty accommodating to the demands of work and work-like settings. Determining whether these individuals will be able to adapt to the demands or "stress" of the workplace is often extremely difficult. This section is not intended to set out any presumptive limitations for disorders, but to emphasize the importance of thoroughness in evaluation on an individualized basis.

> Individuals with mental disorders often adopt a highly restricted and/or inflexible lifestyle within which they appear to function well. Good mental health services and care may enable chronic patients to function adequately in the community by lowering psychological pressures, by medication, and by support from services such as outpatient facilities, day-care programs, social work programs and similar assistance.

> The reaction to the demands of work (stress) is highly individualized, and mental illness is characterized by adverse responses to seemingly trivial circumstances. The mentally impaired may cease to function effectively when facing such demands as getting to work regularly, having their performance supervised, and remaining in the workplace for a full day. A person may become panicked and develop palpitations, shortness of breath, or feel faint while riding in an elevator; another may experience terror and begin to hallucinate when approached by a stranger asking a question. Thus, the mentally impaired may have difficulty meeting the requirements of even so-called "low-stress" jobs.

See also SSR 85-16 (1985) (noting that reports from psychiatrists and other physicians, psychologists, and other mental health professionals "may also contain other observations and opinions or conclusions on such matters as the individual's ability to cope with stress, the ability to relate to other people, and the ability to function in a group or work situation.").

Ultimately, the issue is not simply the claimant's level of stress, but rather the effect that the stress has on a claimant's ability to function in a work setting. In Weiler v. Shalala, 922 F. Supp. 689, 50 Soc. Sec. Rep. Ser. 672 (D. Mass. 1996), the claimant had a long history of treatment for pain, anxiety, and depression. She applied for disability benefits after quitting her job as a medical secretary and her claim was denied through the administrative hearing level. On appeal, she argued, among other grounds, that the ALJ failed to make an individualized assessment as to her ability to handle stress, and the court agreed:

> In examining the effects of stress on her capacity to work, the ALJ primarily relied on the vocational expert's testimony. The ALJ summarized his conclusions as follows:
>
>> Vocational expert, Stephen C. Duclos, testified that the claimant's past relevant work was sedentary and at least semi-skilled in requirements. He did testify that generally unskilled jobs are less stressful, but he noted that based on Dr. Bader's 1991 evaluation, while her perception of pain could tend to adversely affect her concentration, she was able to get along with others. The vocational expert testimony supports the conclusion that the claimant could return to her past relevant work as a secretary, at least in the less stressful secretarial positions, which exist in large numbers.
>
> The ALJ's decision to focus on the amount of stress in a particular job rather than on Weiler's ability to handle stress was in error. Stress is not a characteristic of a particular job but instead "reflects individual's subjective response to a particular situation." *Lancellotta v. Secretary of Health and Human Services*, 806 F.2d 284, 285 (1st Cir.1986).
>
> The Agency has recognized the importance of examining a claimant's individual capacity to handle stress:
>
>> Determining whether [mentally impaired] individuals will be able to adapt to the demands or "stress" of the work place is often extremely difficult. This section is ... intended ... to emphasize the importance of thoroughness in evaluation on an individualized basis ... The reaction to the demands of work (stress) is highly individualized, and mental illness is characterized by adverse responses to seemingly trivial circumstances. The mentally impaired may cease to function effectively when facing such demands as getting to work regularly, having their performance supervised, and remaining in the work place for a full day.... Thus, the mentally impaired may have difficulty meeting the requirements of even so-called "low-stress" jobs.

Social Security Ruling 85-15 (Supp.1986). The Agency further stated that:

> Consideration of these factors [ability to understand, carry out, and remember simple instructions; to respond appropriately to supervision, coworkers, and usual work situations; and to deal with changes in a routine work setting] is required for the proper evaluation of the severity of mental impairments.

Social Security Ruling 85-16.

> Based on the colloquy with the vocational expert, the ALJ concluded that Weiler, although unable to perform work in high stress secretarial positions, would be able to work in a low stress secretarial positions. In doing so, the ALJ placed the focus of the inquiry on the amount of stress in a particular job rather than on Weiler's individual ability to handle stress. This was in error. The ALJ failed to adequately consider the effects of stress on Weiler's ability to perform her PRW. Specifically, the ALJ failed to make findings on the nature of Weiler's stress, the circumstances that aggravate it, or how stress affects her ability to function in a work environment. Accordingly, the court remands to the Secretary to make an assessment of Weiler's vocational capabilities in light of her mental impairments.

922 F. Supp. at 699-700.

As seen in the following case, the effects of stress can be relevant also in cases involving physical impairments alone.

MULVENNA V. SULLIVAN

796 F.Supp. 325, 38 Soc.Sec.Rep.Ser. 567 (N.D.Ill. 1992)

SHADUR, District Judge.

John Mulvenna ("Mulvenna") claims that he was permanently disabled by an acute anterior wall myocardial infarction. Secretary of Health and Human Services Louis Sullivan ("Secretary") denied Mulvenna's claim for disability insurance benefits under the Social Security Act, 42 U.S.C. §§ 416(i) and 423.

Mulvenna has appealed that decision and now moves for summary judgment under Fed.R.Civ.P. ("Rule") 56, seeking reversal or remand. Secretary cross-moves for summary judgment. For the reasons stated in this memorandum opinion and order, both motions for final disposition are denied and the case is remanded for reconsideration of Mulvenna's theory that he is disabled by the combination of his heart condition and his special vulnerability to stress

Factual and Procedural Background

Mulvenna was born on September 16, 1932 and obtained a college degree in marketing. He worked in the retailing business for 33 years, most recently as store manager for general merchandise at a Sears store on Chicago's North Side. Mulvenna supervised 600 employees at that store.

While in Florida on New Year's Day 1988, Mulvenna suffered an acute anterior wall myocardial infarction that caused him to be hospitalized for ten days. Mulvenna was also diagnosed as having a left ventricular aneurysm, atherosclerotic heart disease, acute periocarditis, mild congestive heart failure and ventricular tachycardia. Following his hospitalization Mulvenna underwent further testing and began a cardiac rehabilitation program.

> * * *

Documentary evidence presented to ALJ Lanter comprised 35 exhibits, principally doctors' reports and test results. Two of the doctors' reports were by Dr. Ronald Schreiber, Mulvenna's treating cardiologist in Chicago. Three witnesses testified: Mulvenna, Dr. David Abramson, a cardiologist who served as the ALJ's neutral medical advisor, and vocational expert Phillip Katch.

Mulvenna (through live testimony) and Dr. Schreiber (through written submissions) contended that Mulvenna was an unusually driven, high-strung person, so susceptible to stress that any work at all might trigger a devastating or even fatal renewal of the acute cardiac problems that he experienced in early 1988. Dr. Steven West, who treated Mulvenna during his initial hospitalization in Florida, also submitted a brief letter describing Mulvenna as "totally and completely disabled" by his myocardial infarction and "due to the stress associated with work".

Mulvenna described himself this way:

> But the fact is no matter what my job was, if it was toll taker or a parking lot attendant or what, I would be the best damn toll taker or parking lot attendant in the world and I can't stop from doing that. And I would do everything I could to do that job to the utmost of my capacity. I don't know how [to] work any other way.

At the same time Mulvenna acknowledged that he maintained a fairly vigorous schedule of exercise and routine household chores. He also admitted to doing a certain amount of driving around the Chicago metropolitan area at non-rush hours without encountering stress symptoms, though he recalled an instance when he "had a problem" when driving at rush hour.

Dr. Abramson testified that while the myocardial infarction had greatly reduced Mulvenna's cardiac capacity, he did not suffer from angina pectoris. Dr. Abramson thought that Mulvenna's ability to handle routine exercise and chores undercut his argument about the dangers of work-related stress. Dr. Abramson therefore opined that Mulvenna was able to lift ten pounds in a work setting, which corresponds to the definition of "sedentary work" as that term is defined in the regulations.

Katch testified that more than 30,000 low-stress sedentary jobs existed in the region, including positions such as payroll clerk, personnel clerk, bookkeeping clerk and order clerk. Katch said that Mulvenna's skills were transferable to those jobs and Mulvenna agreed, although he continued to maintain that stress disabled him.

* * *

* * *

Decision and Reasoning of ALJ Lanter

As he went through the five-step inquiry, ALJ Lanter concluded that Mulvenna:

1. is not employed;

2. suffers from a severe impairment—specifically, the limited cardiac capacity resulting from his myocardial infarction and related ailments;

3. does not meet or exceed an impairment as described in the Listing because neither angina nor any other condition is present;

4. cannot resume his former work as manager of a large retail store; and

5. retains the RFC to do sedentary work, with a significant number of sedentary jobs being available to him in the regional economy.

Mulvenna and Secretary part company at step 3. In deciding that Mulvenna does not meet or exceed a listed impairment, ALJ Lanter relied both on testimony to that effect by Dr. Abramson and on the belief that Mulvenna himself "consistently denied angina pectoris".

At step 5 ALJ Lanter credited the testimony of Dr. Abramson that Mulvenna could perform sedentary work without supervisory responsibilities. Relatedly the ALJ rejected Dr. Schreiber's opinion that Mulvenna's susceptibility to stress made any work at all a hazard to his health:

> The Administrative Law Judge attributes greater weight to Dr. Abramson's opinion than that of Dr. Schreiber's because the treating doctor's physician-patient relationship has caused him to overstate the degree to which the claimant can tolerate stress. The claimant is able to tolerate day-to-day stress and traffic conditions as evidenced by his testimony that he drove from his home in Orland Park to Loyola Hospital to obtain Exhibit 33 with no problem and has never experienced any difficulty while driving.

In that respect ALJ Lanter also discredited Mulvenna's own testimony on the likely effects of work-related stress (*id.* (emphasis in original)):

> The Administrative Law Judge does not credit the claimant's testimony that he would be unable to tolerate the stress of *any* work. This testimony is contradicted by the medical advisor's opinion, as well as the claimant's own testimony of daily activities, which includes tolerating the stress of traffic conditions.

> At step 5 ALJ Lanter also found that Secretary had satisfied his burden of demonstrating that Mulvenna could perform a significant number of "routine stress sedentary jobs" that existed in the regional economy. In support of that conclusion the ALJ cited the testimony of vocational expert Katch.

Evaluation of Secretary's Decision

Mulvenna focuses on two alleged errors by ALJ Lanter: the refusal to continue the Hearing until a time when Dr. Schreiber could testify in person, and the finding that Mulvenna does not have angina. Mulvenna may or may not also mean to argue that Secretary erred by discrediting his stress theory—on that score the briefs are ambiguous. This opinion assumes that he does intend to press that third theory, and so it discusses each of the three (rather than two) alleged errors.

[The court ruled against the claimant on the first two grounds of appeal, finding that the ALJ did not err in denying a continuance and that substantial evidence supported the ALJ's conclusion that Mulvenna's heart condition did not match the criteria for angina under the Listing of Impairments. The court then proceeded to consider his third argument: that the combination of his weakened heart and the stress related to it was the medical equivalence of a listed impairment.]

3. Stress

ALJ Lanter concluded his opinion by finding that Mulvenna could do sedentary work, rejecting his argument about the likely effects of work-related stress. It is worth observing at the outset that the combination of a weakened heart and high susceptibility to work-related stress *may* support a finding of disability.

* * *

There is no dispute that Mulvenna is *physically* capable of sedentary work: Dr. Abramson thought he could lift up to ten pounds and Dr. Schreiber actually thought he could lift up to 30. What is in dispute is whether Mulvenna is too stress-prone to handle even a sedentary job without the risk of renewal of his acute heart trouble. Dr. Schreiber, the only source of any medical evidence supporting Mulvenna's position, sent the ALJ several articles describing the relationship of stress to heart trouble, and he added in his cover letter:

> I feel that John may have the personality and the anxiety level of the individuals that are referred to in these articles. I feel it is possible if John is required to return to work that a bad medical outcome could result to him..... [S]ince I know John quite well I feel that he is at an increased risk of suffering a cardiac event in the future if he is required to return to work. There is medical evidence to support the belief that some individuals may be at risk for subsequent cardiac events if they are placed in what they feel are stressful conditions.

Mulvenna also testified that he felt he could not handle the stress of even a sedentary job. Thus ALJ Lanter was obligated to articulate his reasons for rejecting both Dr. Schreiber's opinion and Mulvenna's testimony.

ALJ Lanter discussed Mulvenna's susceptibility to stress only after having stated (R. 17):

> He does not have any impairments equalling the Listings since no other condition is present.

At that point he went on:

> Since the claimant's status post myocardial infarction condition does not meet or equal any listing, an assessment of his residual functional capacity is necessary.

That appears to be a step 5 type of approach, rather than the appropriate one under which a claimant's RFC depends entirely on the severity of his or her impairments, which are earlier determined at step 3. Ability "to respond appropriately to ... work pressures" (Reg. § 404.1545(c)) figures in the RFC analysis only when the claimant has a mental impairment. Mulvenna denied any such impairment, and ALJ Lanter agreed (R. 13).

ALJ Lanter should instead have made an explicit finding at step 3 as to whether the combination of Mulvenna's weakened heart with his susceptibility to stress formed the medical equivalent of a Listing under Reg. § 404.1526. Then and only then would it have become proper to discuss the impact of Mulvenna's stress-related "impairment" on his RFC.

[The court then considered whether the ALJ's failure to address stress in the context of medical equivalence was harmless error in light of his discussion of stress later in the sequential evaluation process and concluded that it was not. Accordingly, the court ordered the case remanded to SSA "with instructions to give full consideration to the possibility that Mulvenna's susceptibility to stress, when combined with his weakened heart, forms the medical equivalent of a listed impairment."]

NOTE

Just as stress can affect persons in different ways, there are jobs with different levels of stress. A reaction to stress that does not prevent one from performing work that is non-stressful will not be disabling. In Schmidt v. Sullivan, 914 F.2d 117, 31 Soc. Sec. Rep. Ser. 103 (7th Cir. 1990), the claimant had a mild heart attack while working as a senior vice president of Montgomery Ward, where he supervised more than a hundred retail outlets. Some years later he took early retirement from Montgomery Ward to work at less stressful jobs—first as president of a subsidiary of another retail enterprise and then operating his own consulting business—and stopped working altogether in 1986 after being hospitalized for symptoms caused by his heart problems. The record showed that he continued to be physically active—even playing handball—despite mild angina pectoris that his doctor believed "would become frequent and severe if he returned to a high-stress executive job." The court continued:

> The administrative law judge who ruled that the plaintiff is not disabled was persuaded that the plaintiff could return to the sorts of job he held before he stopped working in 1986. The fact that the plaintiff continues to play handball appears to have weighed heavily with the administrative law judge. It is indeed difficult for a lay person to understand how a person could suffer from disabling heart disease yet play handball for forty minutes every week. * * * Attacks of angina pectoris--the chest pains that are symptoms of coronary artery disease--can be brought on by psychological stress as well as by physical exertion, The Heart: Arteries and Veins 1174 (Hurst, *et al.*, eds.1978), and people's sensitivity to different forms of strain differs. *Id.* Moreover, "angina pectoris provoked by emotional tension will sometimes last longer than angina pectoris provoked by effort because one cannot control emotions as easily as one can control physical activity." *Id.* at 1175. Apparently Mr. Schmidt

reacts worse to the kind of psychological stress that he experienced when he held responsible managerial positions than he does to the physical exertion involved in a slow game of handball. So at least the evidence of his treating physician indicates, and there is no contrary evidence. The award of benefits to a person disabled because the emotional stress of working would exacerbate his heart condition would not even be novel.

So if the administrative law judge had put all his eggs in the basket labeled not disabled from doing previous work, we would have to reverse the denial of benefits. But he did not. With support from testimony given by a job expert, he made a finding, although without elaboration, that Schmidt could find employment in a less stressful white collar job. There is little doubt that this is true. Schmidt is an experienced executive with a college degree in business administration. As he is relatively little troubled by physical exertion, he can work in a variety of sedentary jobs, provided they are not stressful. Of such jobs there is no scarcity for educated people even in their sixties, at least not so acute a scarcity as would support a finding that a person was disabled from gainful employment. It is true that white collar jobs that do not involve responsibility and hence are not stressful are, by the same token, not highly remunerative. We are speaking of such jobs as cashier in a retail store, which would be quite a comedown for a former senior vice president of one of the nation's largest retail chains. But a person is not disabled within the meaning of the Social Security Act merely because the only jobs he can obtain pay much less than his former work. The job need only exist; it need not be a job that the applicant would find attractive. * * *

914 F.2d at 118-19.

D. DRUG ADDICTION AND ALCOHOLISM

The Social Security Act specifically prohibits a finding of disability based on alcoholism or drug addiction. It does so by providing—in the section defining disability—that a claimant "shall not be considered to be disabled for purposes of [obtaining disability benefits] if alcoholism or drug addiction would (but for this subparagraph) be a contributing factor material to the Commissioner's determination that the individual is disabled." **42 U.S.C. § 423(2)(C)[APP-STAT]**. The same rule also applies to SSI claims. *See* **42 U.S.C § 1382c(a)(3)(J)[APP-STAT]**.

Current policy regarding alcoholism and drug addiction dates back to 1996, when Congress enacted the Contract with America Advancement Act, Pub. L. No. 104-121 § 105 (1996). Prior to 1996, long-standing Social Security Administration policy provided that disability claims based on addiction to drugs or alcohol should be adjudicated in the same manner as claims based on any other impairment. Thus, both alcoholism and drug addiction were recognized as qualifying impairments, although at various times Congress and SSA imposed certain additional restrictions on awarding disability benefits to persons addicted to drugs or alcohol. This shift in policy reflected concerns that awarding benefits amounted to a sanctioning—and funding—of excessive drug and alcohol consumption. As Matthew Diller has noted, "[w]hen disabling conditions are thought by many to result from volitional conduct, such as alcohol and drug addiction, the provision of disability benefits has been most controversial." Matthew Diller, *Entitlement And Exclusion: The Role Of Disability In The Social Welfare System*, 44 UCLA L. REV. 361, 385 (1996).

Under the pre-1996 law, a determination of disability based on addiction to drugs or alcohol had to be based on "sufficiently detailed medical evidence" describing an impairment which "results from anatomical, physiological, or psychological abnormalities which can be shown by medically acceptable clinical and laboratory diagnostic techniques." SSR 82-60 (1982). As with all disability claims, the impairment had to be demonstrated by symptoms, signs, and laboratory findings, which meant that a diagnosis of addiction would not, by itself, be an acceptable basis for a determination of disability. At the same time, it was well settled that either chronic alcoholism or drug addiction could, by itself, be disabling. *See, e.g.*, Ferguson v. Schweiker, 641 F.2d 243, 248 (5th Cir. 1981) ("It is well-settled that alcoholism, alone or combined with other causes, can constitute a disability if it prevents a claimant from engaging in substantial gainful activity."). But again, as with all disability cases, the claimant had the burden of showing that the addiction, either alone or in combination with another impairment, prevented him or her from engaging in substantial gainful activity.

The main principles for establishing eligibility based on alcoholism under pre-1996 regulations were presented in a widely-followed Eighth Circuit case, Adams v. Weinberger, 548 F.2d 239 (8th Cir. 1977). Adams, a chronic alcoholic, sought disability benefits on the basis of disability stemming from his alcoholism and alcohol-related impairments. The ALJ concluded that he was not entitled to disability benefits because his inability to work was attributable to his drinking habits and not to his emphysema, chronic colitis, or cirrhosis. In particular, the ALJ noted that "[i]n the absence of evidence that the claimant has significant organ damage that precludes work activity, it must be found that the power and ability to remedy his plight rests solely with him. Under the circumstances, he has not established his entitlement to disability insurance benefits." 548 F.2d at 242. The court determined that the ALJ had applied the incorrect legal standard, noting that while earlier regulations (20 C.F.R. § 404.1506 (1974)) and the then-relevant listing in the Listing of Impairments (§ 12.04(G)(3)) seemed to require a finding of organ damage for alcoholism to be considered an impairing "functional nonpsychotic disorder," they had been modified to express a more general standard. *Id.*

More importantly, the ALJ placed particular emphasis on the fact that Adams "had not followed the advice of physicians 'to stop alcohol'" and that his "heavy drinking" had caused his cirrhosis. *Id.* The court disagreed with this approach and that taken by some courts asserting that alcoholics cannot be considered disabled unless they have attempted to quit drinking: "In the case of alcoholism, the emphasis should be placed on whether the claimant is addicted to alcohol and as a consequence has lost voluntary ability to control its use." *Id.* at 244. Instead the court embraced the view that "testimony [regarding quitting] may be relevant if, medically, the claimant has the power to control his alcoholism; otherwise, the statement represents the rationalizations of a sick individual who does not realize the extent of his illness." *Id.* at 245.

Thus, under the *Adams* court's approach the claimant had to establish that he or she was addicted and, as a result of that addiction, had lost the ability to control his or her intake of drugs or alcohol voluntarily. In effect, claimants had to show that they were beyond the help of rehabilitation. At the same time, the *Adams* court reinforced the notion that if a claimant is found to be entitled to benefits as a result of alcoholism, "continuing payment of those disability benefits may be conditioned upon [the] claimant's undertaking reasonable efforts to treat his affliction." Id at 245.

1. IMPLEMENTATION OF CURRENT POLICY

Under current policy, SSA must first determine whether the claimant is disabled based on all the evidence in the record, including any evidence of alcoholism or addiction to drugs; then, if there is medical evidence that the claimant is addicted to alcohol or drugs, SSA must move on to determine whether the drug addiction or alcoholism was a material, contributing factor in making the decision on disability. *See* **20 C.F.R. §§ 404.1535, 416.935[APP-REGS]**. A finding of disability is, in effect, a "condition precedent" to applying the special rule on alcoholism and drug addiction. As a practical matter, this means that a claim must work its way through the full sequential evaluation process based on all of the claimant's circumstances, including any drug addiction or alcoholism, before the materiality of the drug addiction or alcoholism is considered as a disqualifying condition.

The key question, then, is whether the claimant—already found to be disabled based on the effects of all of his or her impairments—would still be found to be disabled if the disability determination were made on the non-addiction-related mental and physical impairments alone. If not, then alcoholism or drug addiction is considered a contributing factor material to the determination of disability and benefits will be denied. In making this determination, SSA evaluates the claimant's current physical and mental limitations upon which the finding of disability was based to determine which of those limitations would remain if the claimant stopped using drugs or alcohol. If the remaining limitations would not be disabling, the drug or alcoholism is a contributing factor material to the determination of disability and the claim must be denied; if the remaining limitations would be disabling, drug or alcohol addiction is not considered a contributing factor material to the determination of disability and benefits will be awarded notwithstanding the claimant's alcoholism or drug addiction. *See* 20 C.F.R. § 404.1535(b), 416.935(b).

BUSTAMANTE V. MASSANARI
262 F.3d 949, 75 Soc.Sec.Rep.Ser. 358 (9th Cir. 2001)

Paez, Circuit Judge:

Joseph Bustamante appeals the district court's judgment affirming the Social Security Administration's ("SSA") denial of his application for disability benefits and for Supplemental Security Income under Titles II and XVI of the Social Security Act ("the Act"). We have jurisdiction under 28 U.S.C. § 1291, and we reverse and remand because (1) the Administrative Law Judge ("ALJ") prematurely evaluated the impact of Bustamante's alcoholism prior to completing the five-step sequential disability inquiry; and (2) the ALJ's conclusion that Bustamante did not have a severe mental impairment was not supported by substantial evidence.

I. BACKGROUND

Bustamante was 53 years old at the time of the alleged onset of his disability in 1994. He has an eighth-grade education and relevant work experience as a newspaper delivery person and temporary laborer. Bustamante also has at least a 20-year history of alcohol abuse and is frequently homeless.

A. Procedural History

* * *

* * * [T]he ALJ, after considering the additional post-hearing evidence, issued a written decision finding Bustamante ineligible for disability benefits.

The ALJ found that Bustamante suffered from diabetes mellitus and had a history of pulmonary tuberculosis, but that these conditions did not constitute a severe physical impairment, as defined by 20 C.F.R. §§ 404.1521, 416.921, because the former was not severe and the latter was successfully treated with medication.

The ALJ also found that Bustamante suffered from two mental impairments: a personality disorder and a substance abuse addiction disorder, that "result[ed] in moderate difficulties with activities of daily living, marked difficulties in maintaining social functioning, and seldom ... deficiencies in concentration, persistence or pace." The ALJ noted that Bustamante also had "continual episodes of deterioration or decompensation in the work place."

Nevertheless, the ALJ rejected Bustamante's mental impairments as a basis for disability eligibility on several independent grounds. First, the ALJ found that "alcohol abuse is his primary impairment" and that "any secondary behavioral and emotional conditions he may have are the product and consequence of his alcohol abuse and not an independently severe or disabling impairment." Second, the ALJ concluded that even Bustamante's alcohol abuse did "not reach a disabling level of severity." Third, the ALJ concluded, with little analysis, that Bustamante "retains the physical and mental ability to perform basic work-related functions, including his past relevant work as a newspaper delivery person or laborer." The ALJ also found that Bustamante "was not credible as to his limitations." Finally, the ALJ concluded that "alcohol abuse is a contributing factor material to a finding of disability."

* * *

II. DISCUSSION

* * *

B. Overview of the Five-Step Disability Inquiry

The SSA regulations provide a five-step sequential evaluation process for determining whether a claimant is disabled. The claimant has the burden of proof for steps one through four, and the Commissioner has the burden of proof for step five. Additionally, the ALJ has an affirmative duty to assist the claimant in developing the record at every step of the inquiry. * * *

* * *

C. Role of Alcoholism or Drug Addiction

A finding of "disabled" under the five-step inquiry does not automatically qualify a claimant for disability benefits. Under provisions added by the Contract with America Advancement Act, Pub.L. No. 104-121, 110 Stat. 847 (March 29, 1996), an "individual shall not be considered to be disabled for purposes of [benefits under Title II or XVI of the Act] if alcoholism or drug addiction would (but for this subparagraph) be a contributing factor material to the Commissioner's determination that the individual is disabled." 42 U.S.C. §§ 423(d)(2)(C), 1382c(a)(3)(J). The SSA's implementing regulations specify: "If we find that you are disabled and have medical evidence of your drug addiction or alcoholism, we must determine whether your drug addiction or alcoholism is a contributing factor material to the determination of disability." 20 C.F.R. §§ 404.1535(a), 416.935(a).

We addressed the application of 20 C.F.R. § 404.1535 in Ball v. Massanari, 254 F.3d 817 (9th Cir.2001). The claimant in Ball was diagnosed with alcoholism, dysthymia (a type of depression), and a physical impairment not relevant to the appeal. The ALJ denied benefits after refusing to consider the claimant's alcoholism as an impairment and concluding that the claimant's dysthymia was not severe. On appeal, the claimant argued, among other things, that the ALJ had erred by failing to conduct an evaluation pursuant to § 404.1535 to determine whether the claimant's alcoholism was a contributing factor to his dysthymia—i.e., whether the claimant would continue to suffer from dysthymia if he stopped using alcohol. Ball, 254 F.3d at 819-22. We held that an ALJ need not conduct a § 404.1535 evaluation when substantial evidence supported the ALJ's determination that the claimant's dysthymia was not severe in the first place. Id. at 823 ("if the claimant's ailment does not pass step 2, ipso facto it is not disabling")

Here, we must determine whether it is error for an ALJ to determine that a claimant's mental impairments are "the product and consequence of his alcohol abuse" prior to making a determination that the claimant is disabled under the five-step inquiry.

The Tenth Circuit has held this to be error in a similar case involving a claimant diagnosed with "significant depressive symptoms" and "a long history of alcohol abuse." Drapeau v. Massanari, 255 F.3d 1211, 1213 (10th Cir.2001). In Drapeau, the court held that the ALJ erred by "fail[ing] to determine whether [the claimant] was disabled prior to finding that alcoholism was a contributing material factor thereto." Id. at 1214. It noted that "[t]he implementing regulations make clear that a finding of disability is a condition precedent to an application of [42 U.S.C.] § 423(d)(2)(C)." Id. (citing 20 C.F.R. § 416.935, the parallel regulation to 20 C.F.R. § 404.1535). We agree. The implementing regulations, 20 C.F.R. §§ 404.1535 and 416.935, both begin with the conditional language "[i]f we find that you are disabled...." It follows that an ALJ should not proceed with the analysis under §§ 404.1535 or 416.935 if he or she has not yet found the claimant to be disabled under the five-step inquiry. See Drapeau, 255 F.3d 1211, 1214 ("The ALJ cannot begin to apply [42 U.S.C.] § 423(d)(2)(C) properly when, as here, he has not yet made a finding of disability.") In other words, an ALJ must first conduct the five-step inquiry without separating out the impact of alcoholism or drug addiction. If the ALJ finds that the claimant is not disabled under the five-step inquiry, then the claimant is not entitled to benefits and there is no need to proceed with the analysis under 20 C.F.R. §§ 404.1535 or 416.935. If the ALJ finds that the claimant is disabled and there is "medical evidence of [his or her] drug addiction or alcoholism," then the ALJ should proceed under §§ 404.1535 or 416.935 to determine if the claimant "would still [be found] disabled if [he or she] stopped using alcohol or drugs." 20 C.F.R. §§ 404.1535, 416.935.

Here, the ALJ erred by concluding at step two that Bustamante's "behavioral and emotional conditions" were "the product and consequence of his alcohol abuse and not an independently severe or disabling impairment." This was improper. The ALJ should have proceeded with the five-step inquiry without attempting to determine the impact of Bustamante's alcoholism on his other mental impairments. If, and only if, the ALJ found that Bustamante was disabled under the five-step inquiry, should the ALJ have evaluated whether Bustamante would still be disabled if he stopped using alcohol.

D. Severity of Mental Impairment

To the extent that the ALJ concluded that Bustamante's mental impairments were not severe regardless of the impact of alcoholism, we find that conclusion to be unsupported by substantial evidence. * * *

III. CONCLUSION

Accordingly, we reverse and remand with instructions that the ALJ proceed with step three (and four and five, if necessary) of the disability determination without attempting to separate out the impact of Bustamante's alcohol abuse. Only if the ALJ determines that Bustamante is disabled under the five-step inquiry, should the ALJ consider whether "alcoholism is a contributing factor material to" that determination, pursuant to 20 C.F.R. §§ 404.1535 and 416.935.

NOTES

1. As emphasized in *Bustamante*, every individual who seeks benefits on the basis of disability must be evaluated first under the five-step sequential evaluation process, regardless of the presence of alcoholism or drug addiction. Only then is the question of possible disqualification due to alcoholism or drug addiction taken up. Other cases have followed a similar framework. *See, e.g., Drapeau v. Massanari*, 255 F.3d 1211, 1214-15, 74 Soc. Sec. Rep. Ser. 382 (10th Cir. 2001) ("The implementing regulations make clear that a finding of disability is a condition precedent to an application of § 423(d)(2)(C). 20 C.F.R.§ 416.935(a). * * * The ALJ cannot begin to apply §

423(d)(2)(C) properly when, as here, he has not yet made a finding of disability."); *Gibson v. Astrue*, 2008 WL 906700, 129 Soc. Sec. Rep. Serv. 908 (D. Ariz. 2008) ("In substance-abuse cases, therefore, a finding of "disabled" under the five-step sequential process does not automatically result in an award of benefits; it merely overcomes the first hurdle to that end."). As the court explained it in *Brueggemann v. Barnhart*, 348 F.3d 689, 694-95 (8th Cir. 2003):

> The plain text of the relevant regulation requires the ALJ first to determine whether Brueggemann is disabled. 20 C.F.R. § 404.1535(a) ("*If we find that you are disabled* and have medical evidence of your drug addiction or alcoholism, we must determine whether your drug addiction or alcoholism is a contributing factor material to the determination of disability." (emphasis added)). The ALJ must reach this determination initially * * * using the standard five-step approach described in 20 C.F.R. § 404.1520 without segregating out any effects that might be due to substance use disorders. The ALJ must base this disability determination on substantial evidence of Brueggemann's medical limitations without deductions for the assumed effects of substance use disorders. The inquiry here concerns strictly symptoms, not causes, and the rules for how to weigh evidence of symptoms remain well established. Substance use disorders are simply not among the evidentiary factors our precedents and the regulations identify as probative when an ALJ evaluates a physician's expert opinion in the initial determination of the claimant's disability.

> If the gross total of a claimant's limitations, including the effects of substance use disorders, suffices to show disability, then the ALJ must next consider which limitations would remain when the effects of the substance use disorders are absent. We have previously noted that when the claimant is actively abusing alcohol or drugs, this determination will necessarily be hypothetical and therefore more difficult than the same task when the claimant has stopped. Even though the task is difficult, the ALJ must develop a full and fair record and support his conclusion with substantial evidence on this point just as he would on any other.

2. In Kangail v. Barnhart, 454 F.3d 627, 112 Soc. Sec. Rep. Serv. 513 (7th Cir. 2006), the claimant had been diagnosed with bipolar disorder for more than a decade. She also had a history of alcohol and drug abuse. The ALJ ruled that she was not entitled to benefits because she was able to work when she stopped abusing alcohol and drugs, at least when she took her prescribed psychotropic medications. After noting that "[w]hen an applicant for disability benefits both has a potentially disabling illness and is a substance abuser, the issue for the administrative law judge is whether, were the applicant not a substance abuser, she would still be disabled" (citing *Brueggemann*, *Bustamante*, and *Drapeau*), the court addressed the difficult relationship between addiction and mental illness:

* * *The administrative law judge inferred from the improvement in the plaintiff's condition after she got "clean" that her only problem was substance abuse, but in so concluding he rejected abundant medical testimony without giving adequate reasons for doing so; he "played doctor," as the cases say.

He thought the medical witnesses had contradicted themselves when they said the plaintiff's mental illness was severe yet observed that she was behaving pretty normally during her office visits. There was no contradiction; bipolar disorder is episodic. The judge went so far as to attribute bipolar disorder to substance abuse, although the medical literature, while noting a positive correlation between the two conditions and speculating that alcohol may trigger bipolar symptoms, does not indicate that the disorder itself can be so caused. American Psychiatric Association, Diagnostic and Statistical Manual of Mental Disorders 187, 354 (4th ed.1994); Frederick K. Goodwin & Kay Redfield Jamison, Manic-Depressive Illness 219-25 (1990); Willem A. Nolen et al., "Correlates of 1-Year Prospective Outcome in Bipolar Disorder: Results from the Stanley Foundation Bipolar Network," 161 Am. J. Psychiatry 1452 (2004); Marcia L. Verduin et al., "Health Service Use Among Persons With Comorbid Bipolar and Substance Use Disorders," 56 Psychiatric Services 475-76 (2005).

What is clear is the reverse—that bipolar disorder can precipitate substance abuse, for example as a means by which the sufferer tries to alleviate her symptoms. Goodwin & Jamison, supra, at 219-25; Li-Tzy Wu et al., "Influence of Comorbid Alcohol and Psychiatric Disorders on Utilization of Mental Health Services in the National Comorbidity Survey," 156 Am. J. Psychiatry 1235 (1999); Edward J. Khantzian, "The Self-Medication Hypothesis of Addictive Disorders: Focus on Heroin and Cocaine Dependence," 142 Am. J. Psychiatry 1259, 1263 (1985). There was medical testimony that the plaintiff has "a tendency to indiscriminately use drugs and alcohol" during her manic phases, which are frequent-about monthly. But the fact that substance abuse aggravated her mental illness does not prove that the mental illness itself is not disabling.

* * *

The administrative law judge thought the plaintiff's inability to hold a job unimportant because she could work when she took her medicine. And it is true that bipolar disorder is treatable by drugs. But mental illness in general and bipolar disorder in particular (in part because it may require a complex drug regimen to deal with both the manic and the depressive phases of the disease, Donald M. Hilty et al., "A Review of Bipolar Disorder Among Adults," 50 Psychiatric Services 205-08 (1999); Mark Oflson et al., "Bipolar Depression in a Low-Income Primary Care Clinic," 162 Am. J. Psychiatry 2150 (2005)) may prevent the sufferer from taking her prescribed medicines or otherwise submitting to treatment. American Psychiatric Association, Diagnostic and Statistical Manual of Mental Disorders, supra, at 683; Goodwin & Jamison, supra, at 746-62; Annette Zygmunt, "Interventions to Improve Medication Adherence in Schizophrenia," 159 Am. J. Psychiatry 1653, 1662 (2002); Stephen Magura et al., "Adherence to Medication Regimens and Participation in Dual-Focus Self-Help Groups," 53 Psychiatric Services 310, 313 (2002). The administrative law judge did not consider this possibility.

454 F.3d at 629-32. The court thus concluded that the ALJ did not "provide a rational basis for the denial of disability benefits to the plaintiff" and therefore remanded the case for further proceedings at SSA.

2. ALLOCATION OF THE BURDEN OF PROOF

As noted previously in Chapter 5, the ultimate burden of proof on the question of disability rests with the claimant. While it is true that in applying the 5-step sequential evaluation process SSA must come forward with proof of jobs the claimant could perform after a finding at Step 4 that the claimant cannot perform his or her past relevant work, the claimant is responsible for providing the proof of work capacity used at Step 5. Given the fact that claims involving alcoholism or drug addiction involve an evaluation of the materiality of the claimants addiction only after a five-step finding of disability has been made, the question comes up as to which party bears the burden of proof on this post-sequential evaluation process step. And what happens if the relative responsibility between addition-related and non-addiction-related impairments for the claimant's inability to work cannot be allocated?

PARRA V. ASTRUE
481 F.3d 742 (9th Cir. 2007)

Before HALL, O'SCANNLAIN, and CALLAHAN, Circuit Judges.

CYNTHIA HOLCOMB HALL, Senior Circuit Judge.

In 1996, Congress amended the Social Security Act to preclude an award of disability benefits if drug or alcohol abuse is "a contributing factor material to the Commissioner's determination that the individual is disabled." 42 U.S.C. § 423(d)(2)(C). In this appeal, we confront an issue explicitly left open by our prior opinions, namely which party bears the burden of proof on this substance abuse issue. Consistent with other circuits that have considered this question, we hold that when evidence exists of a claimant's drug or alcohol abuse, the claimant bears the burden of proving that his substance abuse is not a material contributing factor to his disability. Because this claimant failed to carry that burden, we affirm the Commissioner's denial of benefits.

I. Background

On April 15, 1994, Joseph Parra ("Parra") applied for Disability and Supplemental Security Income benefits under Titles II and XVI of the Social Security Act. Parra alleged disability since November 1, 1992 due to alcoholism and bursitis. Following a hearing, an Administrative Law Judge ("ALJ") denied Parra's application. The ALJ found that Parra's testimony regarding his physical ailments was neither credible nor medically supported. He also found that 42 U.S.C. § 423(d)(2)(C) barred Parra from receiving benefits because Parra's alcoholism was a material contributing factor to his disability. Parra appealed this decision to the district court, which remanded the case to the ALJ under 42 U.S.C. § 405(g) with instructions to consider a medical examination performed upon Parra following the ALJ's decision.

Parra died on September 8, 2000 from cardiovascular collapse, hepatorenal syndrome, hepatocellular carcinoma, and liver cirrhosis. Parra's daughter, Cathleen, was substituted as plaintiff and testified at a hearing the following month. Subsequently, the ALJ issued a decision finding that Parra's alcoholism was a material contributing factor to any disability incurred before July 1, 1999. Because Parra's disability insurance coverage lapsed on December 31, 1995, he was entitled to no relief. Cathleen again sought review by the district court, and the parties stipulated to a second 42 U.S.C. § 405(g) remand to reconsider her testimony and the weight it should be given.

A third hearing was held before a different ALJ on January 3, 2003. At the hearing, Cathleen testified that, during his insured period, her father experienced pain in his hands and knees and also suffered from hearing difficulties, confusion, and paranoia. She also testified that he drank to the point of intoxication "occasionally" and that his alcohol use was not "excessive," although when pressed for details she explained that he often consumed twenty-four beers in a three-day period and became intoxicated at least weekly. The ALJ also heard testimony from Dr. Jerome Marmorstein, a medical expert who reviewed Parra's medical history. Dr. Marmorstein testified that Parra's medical records showed severe complications due to cirrhosis from July 1999 forward, although the disease had undoubtedly "come on over many years" and could have been "moderately well advanced" or "moderately severe" before Parra's insurance lapsed in 1995. Following Dr. Marmorstein's testimony, the ALJ stated orally that the evidence clearly indicated that Parra was disabled due to alcohol-induced cirrhosis by 1995, and that the operative question was whether the disease would have resolved itself had he quit drinking before his insurance lapsed.

The ALJ issued his final decision on April 4, 2003. He rejected Parra's bursitis claim because the medical evidence failed to show a severe physical impairment prior to December 31, 1995. Turning to the substance abuse claim, the ALJ found that "by the summer of 1994 the claimant was disabled primarily due to heavy alcohol consumption and intoxication" and also had "moderately severe but curable cirrhosis of the liver." But he further found that prior to July 1999, it was likely that Parra would have recovered had he quit drinking. Therefore Parra's cirrhosis was irreversible only after that date. The ALJ also explicitly ruled that the claimant bore the burden of proving that his alcoholism was not a contributing factor material to his disability. Because his disability likely would have resolved had Parra ceased using alcohol during his insured period, the ALJ found him ineligible for disability benefits under 42 U.S.C. § 423(d)(2)(C). The district court affirmed this ruling.

* * *

III. Discussion

Cathleen Parra appeals the ALJ's 2003 decision on three grounds. She alleges that (1) the ALJ erred by failing to perform the full five-step analysis to determine Parra's disability, (2) the ALJ erred in finding that alcoholism was material to Parra's disability, and (3) the ALJ improperly discredited Joseph and Cathleen Parra's testimony. We address each claim in turn.

A. The Five-Step Analysis

* * *

Appellant asserts that the ALJ erred by failing to conduct the full five-step analysis to determine that Parra's cirrhosis was disabling before conducting the DAA Analysis to determine if Parra's alcoholism was material. See Bustamante, 262 F.3d at 955 (holding ALJ must identify disability under five-step procedure before conducting DAA Analysis to determine whether substance abuse was material to disability). * * *

* * * Although the decision does not explicitly label Parra's cirrhosis as disabling, the ALJ gave Parra the benefit of the doubt: the DAA Analysis assumed that Parra's cirrhosis was disabling and focused correctly upon whether abstinence would have cured this disability before his insurance lapsed. Because the DAA Analysis assumed Parra's cirrhosis was disabling, any error in arriving at that initial conclusion would not affect the ALJ's ultimate decision that Parra's alcoholism was material to his cirrhosis. We therefore reject this proffered ground for reversal.

B. The DAA Analysis

Appellant next argues that the ALJ erred in finding Parra ineligible for benefits because his alcoholism was a contributing factor material to his disability under 42 U.S.C. § 423(d)(2)(C). Once medical evidence of Parra's alcoholism surfaced, the ALJ placed the burden of proof upon the claimant to establish that Parra's alcoholism was not a contributing factor material to his disability, by showing he would have remained disabled had he stopped drinking in 1995. Appellant asserts that this holding was erroneous. Once a claimant satisfies the five-step analysis, she argues, the Commissioner should bear the burden of proving that benefits should be denied. Appellant analogizes to cases involving termination of benefits, wherein the Commissioner must prove that a claimant previously adjudged disabled has recovered sufficiently to return to work. *See, e.g., Bellamy v. Sec'y of Health & Human Servs.*, 755 F.2d 1380, 1381 (9th Cir.1985).

Our prior opinions have explicitly left open the issue of which party bears the burden of proof under 42 U.S.C. § 423(d)(2)(C). We placed the burden upon the claimant in Ball [*v. Massanari*, 254 F.3d 817, 821 (9th Cir.2001)], although a later opinion correctly described this language as dicta. *See Bustamante*, 262 F.3d at 955 n. 1. We note that each circuit to have considered the issue has placed the burden squarely upon the claimant. *See, e.g., Doughty v. Apfel*, 245 F.3d 1274, 1276 (11th Cir.2001); *Mittlestedt v. Apfel*, 204 F.3d 847, 852 (8th Cir.2000); *Brown v. Apfel*, 192 F.3d 492, 498 (5th Cir.1999). Our own case law has suggested the same. *See Sousa v. Callahan*, 143 F.3d 1240, 1245 (9th Cir.1998) (remanding to allow claimant "an opportunity to present evidence as to whether claimant's disability would have continued if she stopped using drugs or alcohol"). This approach is consistent with the general rule that "[a]t all times, the burden is on the claimant to establish [his] entitlement to disability insurance benefits." *Tidwell*, 161 F.3d at 601. Moreover, placing the burden on the claimant is practical because the claimant "is the party best suited to demonstrate whether [he] would still be disabled in the absence of drug or alcohol addiction." *Brown*, 192 F.3d at 498.

Appellant's reliance on cases involving the termination of benefits is misplaced. As *Bellamy* makes clear, the Commissioner's burden in termination cases stems from the notion that "[o]nce a claimant has been found to be disabled [ ] a presumption of continuing disability arises in [his] favor." *Bellamy*, 755 F.2d at 1381 (emphasis added). But the CAAA amended the definition of "disability" under the Social Security Act, such that an individual "shall not be considered disabled" if drug or alcohol use is material to his disability. In other words, the presumption driving *Bellamy* has not yet attached when the DAA Analysis is performed because the agency has yet to determine whether the claimant is disabled. "Unquestionably, proving disability is [claimant's] burden, and any amendment to the definition of disability logically impacts [his] burden." *Brown*, 192 F.3d at 498; *see also Bellamy*, 755 F.2d at 1381 ("Social Security disability benefits claimants have the burden of proving disability."). We thus make explicit what was intimated by our earlier cases, that the claimant bears the burden of proving that drug or alcohol addiction is not a contributing factor material to his disability.

Appellant failed to carry this burden. The record offers no evidence supporting the notion that the disabling effects of Parra's cirrhosis would have remained had he stopped drinking before December 31, 1995. Dr. Marmorstein testified that cirrhosis, caused by alcohol abuse, is generally reversible and that the medical records support a finding that Parra's cirrhosis was irreversible only after July 1, 1999. Dr. Marmorstein explained that he had no reason to believe that Parra's condition would not have improved had Parra quit drinking in 1995. When pressed by Parra's counsel, he reiterated several times that "there is no way for me to know" whether Parra's cirrhosis was irreversible in 1994 or 1995 because the record was insufficient to support a conclusion either way. * * *

Appellant argues that Dr. Marmorstein's testimony was inconclusive on this point, and that inconclusive testimony is sufficient to satisfy the claimant's burden of proof under the statute. To support this claim, she relies upon two internal agency documents, HALLEX I-5-3-14A[4] and Emergency Teletype No. EM-96-94.[5] These documents, she argues, preclude a finding of materiality unless the medical evidence affirmatively shows that a disability will resolve with abstinence. We reject this argument, which effectively shifts the burden to the Commissioner to prove materiality. Assuming without deciding that the HALLEX and Teletype provisions apply to this situation, we have previously explained that internal agency documents such as these do not carry the force of law and are not binding upon the agency. Therefore, they do not create judicially enforceable duties, and we will not review allegations of noncompliance with their provisions.

---

[4] HALLEX is the Hearing, Appeals, and Litigation Law Manual, an internal agency guidebook. HALLEX I-5-3-14A states that a finding that DAA is material is appropriate "only when ... there is sufficient and appropriate medical evidence to establish ... the individual would not be considered to be disabled if he/she stopped using drugs and/or alcohol."

[5] On August 30, 1996, the SSA's Office of Disability sent this teletype to all hearing offices, responding to initial questions posed by the adoption of the CAAA. The relevant portion of the teletype explains that "a finding that DAA is material will be made only when the evidence establishes that the individual would not be disabled if he/she stopped using drugs/ alcohol." Therefore in "cases in which the evidence demonstrates multiple impairments, especially cases involving multiple mental impairments, where the MC/PC cannot project what limitations would remain if the individuals stopped using drugs/alcohol," the MC/PC "should record his/ her findings to that effect" and "the DE will find that DAA is not a contributing material factor to the determination of disability."

At most, these sources may represent the agency's unpromulgated interpretation of the statute's phrase "contributing factor material to the determination of disability." Such an interpretation is "'entitled to respect'" but only to the extent that it has the "'power to persuade.'" *Christensen v. Harris County*, 529 U.S. 576, 587, 120 S.Ct. 1655, 146 L.Ed.2d 621 (2000) (quoting *Skidmore v. Swift & Co.*, 323 U.S. 134, 140, 65 S.Ct. 161, 89 L.Ed. 124 (1944)). In this case, such an interpretation is unpersuasive because it contradicts the purpose of the statute. As noted above, Congress sought through the CAAA "to discourage alcohol and drug abuse, or at least not to encourage it with a permanent government subsidy." *Ball*, 254 F.3d at 824.[6] Appellant's proposed rule provides the opposite incentive. An alcoholic claimant who presents inconclusive evidence of materiality has no incentive to stop drinking, because abstinence may resolve his disabling limitations and cause his claim to be rejected or his benefits terminated. His claim would be guaranteed only as long as his substance abuse continues-a scheme that effectively subsidizes substance abuse in contravention of the statute's purpose.[7]

In sum, we find that Parra bore the burden of proving that his alcoholism was not a contributing factor material to his cirrhosis-related disability. Dr. Marmorstein testified that abstinence generally ameliorates the effects of cirrhosis and that the record fails to show that Parra's cirrhosis was irreversible when his disability insurance lapsed. Therefore we conclude that the ALJ's denial of benefits under 42 U.S.C. § 423(d)(2)(C) was supported by substantial evidence and free of material error.

* * *

NOTE

In Brown v. Apfel, 192 F.3d 492, 64 Soc. Sec. Rep. Ser. 128 (5th Cir. 1999), the claimant, who had held jobs as a laundry worker and a table busser for a total of five years, ceased working after suffering two back injuries. She applied for SSI benefits, alleging that she was disabled due to lower back pain. Because diagnostic tests failed to show any physiological abnormalities, Brown never had an operation but she claimed that she experienced difficulties sitting and sleeping as a result of her back pain. Her claim was denied, and following an administrative hearing the ALJ found that Brown could not work in the national economy because of "non-exertional limitations stemming from her alcoholism." 192 F.3d at 496. But the ALJ also found

---

[6] See also H.R.Rep. No. 104-379, at 17 (1995) (explaining that the amendment eliminates "a perverse incentive that affronts working taxpayers and fails to serve the interests of addicts and alcoholics, many of whom use their disability checks to purchase drugs and alcohol, thereby maintaining their addictions").

[7] The teletype elsewhere explains that a period of abstinence of one month or more is useful to test whether a claimant's substance abuse is material to his disability. Under appellant's interpretation of the teletype, the claimant has no incentive to undergo this period of abstinence, as doing so would only jeopardize his claim.

that alcohol abuse was a contributing factor material to Brown's disability, and therefore concluded that she was not disabled.

Ms. Brown also had a history of major depression with suicidal ideations and had recently been released from a psychiatric unit, where she had spent three weeks after voluntarily admitting herself. Records indicated that her depression was exacerbated by a substance abuse problem. "Brown divulged that she smokes 3 or 4 packs of cigarettes a day. She also confessed to drinking a six pack every day and two 1/2 pints of alcohol on Fridays; she admits that she has been drinking alcoholic beverages every day since she was 16. Brown additionally conceded that she began using powdered cocaine in her cigarettes for about a year when she was 36, and then started using crack cocaine two years later." *Id.* at 495.

The court ultimately held that the claimant bears the burden of proving that drug or alcohol addiction is not a contributing factor material to her disability, and that Ms. Brown failed to carry that burden. The court rejected Brown's argument suggesting that the drug and alcoholism rules essentially created a "sixth step" in the sequential evaluation process at which the burden shifts to require that SSA show that the claimant would still be disabled if he or she stopped using drugs or alcohol. After reviewing the relevant statutory and regulatory provisions, the court concluded: "Finally, and most pragmatically, Brown is the party best suited to demonstrate whether she would still be disabled in the absence of drug or alcohol addiction . . . We thus hold, for the first time, that Brown bears the burden of proving that drug or alcohol addiction is not a contributing factor material to her disability." *Id.* at 498.

In the end, the court remanded the case because Ms. Brown had not been advised that she had to carry the burden of proof. Noting that exactly how a claimant could meet this burden was itself a question of first impression in the circuit, the court went on to provide the following guidance:

> "Materiality," for purposes of this inquiry, has a very precise definition. Specifically, drug or alcohol abuse is material to a disability if the ALJ would not "find [the claimant] disabled if [the claimant] stopped using drugs or alcohol." 20 C.F.R. § 416.935(b)(1). Of course, evidence sufficient to support an ALJ finding on this issue will be strongly dependent upon the facts in each case. In this instance, the bare record itself provides no guidance as to Brown's prognosis, with respect to depression, if she ceased her chemical dependency. Though the record suggests that Brown's abuse of narcotics both exacerbated and was itself fueled by her depression, that fact is not sufficient to imply the inverse: i.e., that cessation of narcotic and alcohol usage would abate the depression. The record simply contains too many other possible reasons for Brown's depression. Therefore, assuming that Brown is still addicted to drugs and alcohol at the time of her hearing on remand, she must introduce evidence that supports a finding in her favor that she would still be disa-

bled by depression even if she stopped using drugs and alcohol. Of course, the ALJ has the option of ordering a consultative examination to guide his determination on remand.

192 F.3d at 499. *See also* Doughty v. Apfel, 245 F.3d 1274, 1280, 73 Soc. Sec. Rep. Ser. 288 (11ᵗʰ Cir. 2001) ("We agree with the Fifth Circuit's reasoning [in *Brown*] and hold that in materiality determinations pursuant to 42 U.S.C. § 423(d)(2)(C), the claimant bears the burden of proving that his alcoholism or drug addiction is not a contributing factor material to his disability determination.") (citing Mittlestedt v. Apfel, 204 F.3d 847 (8th Cir. 2000), noting that the court in *Mittlestedt* cited *Brown* on the issue of burden of proof).

NOTE ON EMERGENCY TELETYPE EM 96200

The emergency teletype discussed near the end of the opinion in *Parra v. Astrue* has a peculiar status, as its directive—that a finding of "not material" is appropriate when it is not possible to separate mental restrictions and limitations resulting from the claimant's drug or alcohol addiction from those caused by various other mental disorders shown by the evidence—has not been codified or otherwise included in any formal ruling. Indeed, it lacked even a formal designation when first issued on August 30, 1996. As explained on the Social Security Administration's website, where it is available as "EM 96200": "This EM was originally issued as EM 96-? dated August 30, 1996. The original EM 96-? was never assigned a number or posted to PolicyNet. It has been given a number and posted for the convenience of adjudicators who need to see these questions and answers." *See* https://secure.ssa.gov/apps10/public/reference.nsf/links/04292003041931PM. As a result, various courts have viewed the teletype differently.

A number of courts have followed the teletype and held a finding of "not material" is appropriate when, after having made an initial determination that a claimant is disabled, it is not possible to separate mental restrictions and limitations imposed by the drug and alcohol addiction from other mental disorders shown by the evidence. For a recent court of appeals case applying the directive of the teletype, see Salazar v. Barnhart, 468 F.3d 615, 622-24, 115 Soc. Sec. Rep. Serv. 136 (10th Cir. 2006). *See also* Brueggemann v. Barnhart, 348 F.3d 689, 693, 92 Soc. Sec. Rep. Serv. 153 (8th Cir. 2003) ("In colloquial terms, on the issue of the materiality of alcoholism, a tie goes to [the claimant]"); Hudson v. Astrue, 2010 WL 3940985 (M.D. Tenn 2010) ("If the ALJ is not able to distinguish the effects of the plaintiff's alcohol abuse from his mental impairments by looking at the record medical evidence, then the 'tie goes to [the plaintiff]' and his claim for [disability benefits] should be granted.") (quoting *Brueggemann*); Dalton v. Astrue, 2010 WL 936703, 151 Soc. Sec. Rep. Serv. 297 (W.D. Ark. 2010) ("If, on remand, the ALJ is unable to determine whether substance use disorders are a contributing factor material to the claimant's otherwise-acknowledged disability, the claimant's burden has been met and an award of benefits must follow.")(Clark v. Apfel, 98 F.Supp.2d 1182, 1185 (D. Or. 2000) (denial reversed where ALJ found that "[i]t is impossible to separate the effects of the claimant's long term polysubstance dependence and abuse from other possible mental disorders").

Other courts, however, have agreed with the Parra court and reject the teletype approach. *See, e.g.,* Brown v. Apfel, 192 F.3d 492 (5th Cir. 1999) ("We thus hold, for the first time, that Brown bears the burden of proving that drug or alcohol addiction is not a contributing factor material to her disability."); *see also* Sousa v. Chater, 945 F.Supp 1312 (E.D. Cal. 1996) (benefits denied because it was impossible to separate DA&A from mental illness). And some have simply noted its ambiguous status. In Mitchell v. Astrue, 2009 WL 3096717 (S.D.N.Y. 2009), the court described the teletype as supporting the holdings of a number of courts and went on to say that "[u]pon remand, I recommend that the ALJ be directed to consider whether this rule is still extant and, if so, to give it appropriate consideration. *See also* Ostrowski v. Barnhart, 2003 WL 22439585, 91 Soc. Sec. Rep. Serv. 565 (D. Conn. 2003) ("It seems, regardless of whether the Teletype is binding, that it represents the sound judgment of the Agency and would be persuasive in that respect."); Brown v. Apfel, 71 F.Supp.2d 28, 36. 65 Soc. Sec. Rep. Ser. 252 (D.R.I. 1999) ("Whether such a teletype is even binding on the Social Security Administration is questionable").

The Emergency Teletype has also been cited on the question of what type of proof is required on materiality. In Doughty v. Apfel, 245 F.3d 1274, 73 Soc. Sec. Rep. Ser. 288 (11th Cir. 2001), the claimant argued that the teletype requires the ALJ to call a medical or psychological consultant or a disability examiner to testify on the materiality of drug or alcohol abuse relative to a disability decision. The court disagreed:

> We do not find, however, that the Emergency Teletype imposes a new requirement upon the ALJ to seek a consultant's opinion when making a materiality determination. Rather, the regulations laid out in 20 C.F.R. § 404.1512(d)-(f) state that the ALJ may ask the claimant to attend a consultative examination at the Commissioner's expense, but only after the Commissioner (through the ALJ) has given 'full consideration to whether the additional information needed ... is readily available from the records of [the claimant's] medical sources.' 20 C.F.R. § 404.1519a(a)(1). The regulations 'normally require' a consultative examination only when necessary information is not in the record and cannot be obtained from the claimant's treating medical sources or other medical sources. 20 C.F.R. § 404.1519a(b).

245 F.3d at 1280-81. On the other hand, courts have upheld the teletypes directive requiring inquiry into the effect of periods of abstinence. *See* Fahy v. Astrue, 2008 WL 2550594, 132 Soc. Sec. Rep. Serv. 231 (E.D. Pa. 2008): "The ALJ's failure to discuss these significant periods of abstinence contravenes the Teletype's directive that 'consideration must be given to the length of the period of abstinence' as well as the directive contained in 20 C.F.R. § 416.935 requiring the ALJ to 'evaluate which of [Plaintiff's] current physical

and mental limitations ... would remain if [Plaintiff] stopped using drugs or alcohol.' 20 C.F.R. § 416.935(b)(2). *See also* 468 F.3d 615, 624, 115 Soc. Sec. Rep. Serv. 136 (10th Cir. 2006).

NOTE ON USE OF REPRESENTATIVE PAYEES

As we have seen, claimants who can show that drug addiction or alcoholism is not a contributing factor material to a determination that they are disabled may be eligible for benefits based on other impairments. In such cases, the recipient may be required to have his or her benefits paid through a representative payee. SSA will appoint a representative payee when it is in the "interest" of the beneficiary to do so. This is most commonly the case when beneficiaries are under the age of 18, or are unable to manage their benefits due to mental or physical conditions. 20 C.F.R. §§ 404.2001(b)(1), 416.601(b)(1). Moreover, SSA has reserved the right "to appoint a representative payee even if the beneficiary is a legally competent individual." 20 C.F.R. §§ 404.2001(b)(2), 416.601(b)(2); 20 C.F.R. §§ 404.2010(a), 416.610(a). The use of representative payees is discussed more generally in Chapter 7.

SSA regulations concerning the appointment of representative payees distinguish between SSI disability benefit recipients who are also addicted to drugs or alcohol and those receiving benefits under the OASDI program. *Compare* 20 C.F.R. § 404.2010(a) (SSA will pay benefits to representative payees on behalf of OASDI beneficiaries when it has information that the beneficiary is "legally incompetent or mentally incapable of managing benefit payments" or "physically incapable of managing or directing the management of his or her benefit payments") *with* 20 C.F.R. § 416.610(a) (for SSI recipients, will also pay benefits to representative payees when it has information that the beneficiary is "eligible for benefits solely on the basis of disability and drug addiction or alcoholism is a contributing factor material to the determination of disability").

In Smith v. Chater, 99 F.3d 635, 52 Soc. Sec. Rep. Serv. 65 (4th Cir. 1996), the court addressed what it termed "two collateral consequences" presented by SSA's position that while the claimant—who denied that she was an alcoholic but was found eligible based in part on her addiction to alcohol—could not be paid until she found a suitable representative payee, she could nonetheless remain as the representative payee for SSI benefits owed to her children:

> The Commissioner defends the fact that no representative payee has ever been found for Smith by relying on the Ninth Circuit case of *Briggs v. Sullivan*, 954 F.2d 534 (9th Cir.1992). After analyzing the language of 42 U.S.C.A. § 1383(a)(2)(A) and 20 C.F.R. § 416.650, the Ninth Circuit concluded that the Commissioner has no statutory duty to find a representative payee for recipients of Title XVI benefits whose disability is related to alcohol abuse. *Id.* at 540-41. Even if we were to adopt the Ninth Circuit's reasoning, we find the Commissioner's desire to wipe her

hands of Smith's case deserving of some reproach. In the face of Smith's moderate difficulty encountered when trying to locate a representative payee, the Commissioner has apparently abandoned all efforts to assist Smith by finding some willing organization or individual to serve in a representative capacity.

Apparently, the Commissioner feels that her only obligation is to screen the applicants submitted by Smith according to [42 U.S.C.] § 1383. Such a stance flies directly in the face of the Social Security Administration's entire purpose, which is to make sure that disabled persons receive public assistance. The Social Security Administration's role in insuring that disabled persons receive benefit checks is underscored by the permissive language of 20 C.F.R. § 416.650, which indicates that the Commissioner will at least *try* to find a representative payee. With that in mind, leaving Smith to languish, completely deprived of her entitled SSI payments, without offering her any aid whatsoever in securing a suitable representative payee, cannot be what Congress envisioned as the Commissioner's proper role in this regard.

The Commissioner's incongruous position of allowing Smith to remain a representative payee for her children's SSI checks, while Smith herself has been found to need a representative payee in her own right, makes even less sense. Although not apparently violative of any specific provision of 42 U.S.C.A. §§ 405(j), or 1383, the general tenor of the statute and accompanying regulations bears out the proposition that a medically determined alcoholic or drug addict cannot act in a representative capacity for the receipt of another's benefits. *See e.g.*, 20 C.F.R. § 416.620(e) ("In making our selection [for representative payee status] we consider [w]hether the potential payee is in a position to know of and look after the needs of the beneficiary."). In short, Smith could misdirect her children's money just as easily as her own.

99 F. 3d at 639.

NOTE ON TREATMENT REQUIREMENTS

An individual who qualifies for disability benefits where alcohol or drugs are involved but were not a material factor in determining disability may be required to undergo treatment for his or her alcoholism or drug addiction. SSA regulations provide, with respect to all claims, that the failure to follow prescribed medical treatment can be grounds for denial of benefits if following the prescribed treatment can restore the claimant's ability to engage in substantial gainful activity. 20 CFR 404.1530; 416.930. (The requirement to follow prescribed treatment is discussed generally in the next section of this chapter.) In addition, there are special treatment requirements that apply to beneficiaries of SSI disability benefits who are addicted to alcohol or drugs. *See* 20 C.F.R. § 416.214(a) ("If you receive benefits because you are disabled and drug addiction or alcoholism is a contributing factor material to the determination of disability, you must avail yourself of any appropriate treatment for your drug addiction or alcoholism at an approved institution or facility when this treatment is available and make progress in your treatment."); *see also* 20 C.F.R § 416.1326(a) (providing for referral to a treatment facility and for suspension of benefits for failure to "comply with the terms, conditions and requirements of treatment prescribed by the institution or facility.")

Moreover, a claimant's record in following treatment for alcoholism or addiction to drugs can be a factor when assessing the claimant's credibility. *See, e.g.*, Rey v. Astrue, 2010 WL 1222158 (C.D. Cal. 2010) (citing Fair v. Bowen, 885 F.2d 597, 603 (9th Cir.1989); Bunnell v. Sullivan, 947 F.2d 341, 346 (9th Cir. 1991)). But the connection between the claimant's treatment record and the credibility finding must have a firm factual basis. Thus, the court in *Rey* concluded that there was insufficient evidence to support the ALJ's discrediting of the claimant's testimony: "With respect to Plaintiff's continued alcohol use, the record reflects an attempt by Plaintiff to quit that is consistent with his claims of debilitating symptoms. Plaintiff testified that he has reduced his alcohol consumption for health reasons. The record also shows that Plaintiff has completed many alcohol treatment programs in an effort to cease his alcohol use entirely." 2010 WL 1222158 at *4.

NOTE ON ALCOHOLISM AND DRUG ADDICTION AND THE AMERICANS WITH DISABILITIES ACT

The Americans with Disabilities Act (ADA) takes a more lenient approach to addiction, extending protection to all alcoholics and to some drug addicts. While current drug users are expressly excluded from statutory protection, the statutes provide a "safe harbor" for recovering addicts. Under Section 104(a) of the ADA, protected individuals "shall not include any employee or applicant who is currently engaging in the illegal use of drugs, when the covered entity acts on the basis of such use." 42 U.S.C. § 12114(a). However, this exclusion does not apply to individuals who have successfully completed a supervised drug rehabilitation program, or who are currently in such a program and not engaged in drug use, or are "erroneously regarded as engaged in such use." *Id.* § 12144(b). Although Congress did not define "current" or "currently engaging," the EEOC's Interpretive Guidance states that the "term 'currently engaging' is not intended to be limited to the use of drugs on the day of, or within a matter of days or weeks before, the employment action in question. Rather the provision is intended to apply to the illegal use of drugs that has occurred recently enough to indicate that the individual is actively engaged in such conduct." 29 C.F.R. Part 1630, App. (interpreting 29 C.F.R. § 1630.3(a)-(c) on the illegal use of drugs). *See also* Shafer v. Preston Memorial Hosp. Corp., 107 F.3d 274, 277-79 (4th Cir. 1997) (rejecting a narrow reading of the word "currently" and noting that "[h]ere, "currently" means a periodic or ongoing activity in which a person engages (even if doing something else at the precise moment) that has not yet permanently ended.") Under this definition, an individual must have refrained from drug use for a longer period of time in order to be protect under the statute. *See, e.g.*,

Baustian v. Louisiana, 910 F.Supp. 274, 276 (E.D.La.1996) (holding that the ADA's safe harbor provision applies only to a long-term recovery program and requires that the individual be drug-free for a considerable period).

Moreover, alcoholics are not excluded from coverage under the ADA so long as they do not consume alcohol while on the job. *See* 42 U.S.C. § 12114(c)(2)(allowing employers to "require that employees shall not be under the influence of alcohol or be engaging in the illegal use of drugs at the workplace"). *See also* 29 U.S.C. § 705(20)(C)(v) (Rehabilitation Act of 1973, specifying that "the term 'individual with a disability' does not include any individual who is an alcoholic whose current use of alcohol prevents such individual from performing the duties of the job in question or whose employment, by reason of such current alcohol abuse, would constitute a direct threat to property or the safety of others"). At the same times, courts have not treated alcoholism as a per se disability. *See, e.g.*, Bailey v. Georgia-Pacific Corp., 306 F.3d 1162, 1167-68 (1st Cir. 2002) ("An ADA plaintiff must offer evidence demonstrating that the limitation caused by the impairment is substantial in terms of his or her own experience. Alcoholism is no exception; courts have generally refused to recognize alcoholism as a *per se* disability under the ADA . . . Evidence that alcoholics, in general, are impaired is inadequate to show a substantial limitation of one or more major life activities.") (internal citations omitted).

E. REMEDIABLE DISABILITY AND EFFECTS OF PRESCRIBED MEDICATION

Ordinarily, persons with disabilities are under some sort of medical treatment. A Social Security disability benefit claimant's treatment can have an impact on his or her eligibility in two related ways. First, there is the possibility that a course of treatment could remove or reduce limitations resulting from the claimant's impairments and allow the claimant to work. Second, there is the question of the extent to which side effects of treatment can be the basis for a finding of disability. Issues raised by both of these questions are discussed in this Section.

In some circumstances, as discussed in Section D with respect to alcoholism and drug addiction, undergoing treatment can be effectively a condition for eligibility. Such a requirement is not limited to drug addiction and alcoholism; the Listing of Impairments, for example, includes some listings that require proof of certain symptoms "despite treatment." *See, for example*, 20 C.F.R. Part 404 Subpart P Appx 1 (Listings) §§ 11.02, 11.03 (requiring proof that major motor seizures occur more frequently than once a month, or minor motor seizures occur more frequently than once per week, "in spite of at least 3 months of prescribed treatment."). *See also* SSR 87-6 (1987) ("If an individual does not have an ongoing treatment relationship, it would be unreasonable to assume that the seizures cannot be controlled with medication, at least to the level at which the listing would not be met or equaled. Therefore, in the absence of an ongoing treatment relationship, the individual's impairment cannot be found to meet or equal the listings for epilepsy.").

1. REMEDIABLE DISABILITY

Generally, claimants must follow treatment prescribed by their physicians in order to obtain benefits—if the treatment can restore their ability to perform substantial gainful activity. *See* **20 C.F.R. §§ 404.1530, 416.930[APP-REGS]**. When a claimant fails to follow prescribed treatment without a good reason, benefits will be denied or terminated. 20 C.F.R. §§ 404.1530(b), 416.930(b). Acceptable reasons for failing to follow prescribed treatment include, but are not limited to, the following: prescribed treatment is "contrary to the established teaching and tenets of [the claimant's] religion"; the same surgery was previously performed unsuccessfully; or because of its magnitude, unusual nature, or other reason, the treatment is "very risky" for the claimant. *See* 20 C.F.R. §§ 404.1530(c), 416.930(c); *see also* SSR 82-59, 1975-1982 Soc. Sec. Rep. Ser. 793 (1982) (noting that an individual does not have to present documentation to develop church teachings in Christian Science cases, because it is well established that the religion proscribes acceptance of medical treatment). Moreover, SSA will consider an individual's physical, mental, educational, and linguistic limitations (including any lack of facility with the English language) when determining if he or she has an acceptable reason for refusing treatment. 20 C.F.R. §§ 404.1530(c), 416.930(c).

Social Security Administration policy and procedures relative to the prescribed treatment requirement are detailed in **SSR 82-59, 1975-1982 Soc. Sec. Rep. Ser. 793 (1982)[APP-RULINGS]**. This Ruling provides that in some extreme cases, an individual's intense and unrelenting fear of surgery may effectively be a contraindication to surgery. However, the lack of "guaranteed success" of a surgical procedure or the fact that a third party experienced negative surgical results may not be sufficient. If a claimant cannot afford prescribed treatment, the claimant's financial circumstances and contacts with all possible free or subsidized sources of treatment must be documented and then a lack of financial resources can be a justifiable cause for failing to follow prescribed treatments. (When treatment is not reasonably available, a referral to the state vocational rehabilitation agency should be made.) Finally, the determination as to whether a prescribed treatment can be expected to restore an individual's ability to work must made by SSA based on the medical evidence in the record, and "if . . . SSA determines that ability to engage in SGA may not reasonably be expected to be restored, there is no issue of failure to follow prescribed treatment." *Id.*

A failure to follow treatment results in denial of benefits only if the treatment is "prescribed." See 20 C.F.R. §§ 404.1530, 416.930. Treatment that is merely recommended or suggested need not be followed. *See, e.g.* Schena v. Secretary, HHS, 635 F.2d 15, 19 (1st Cir. 1980) ("the denial of benefits because of Schena's alleged 'willful refusal to follow a recommended course of treatment' disregards the language of the regulation which specifically speaks in terms of the willful failure to follow 'prescribed' treatment. That various physicians suggested the operation does not necessarily mean that they prescribed it.") Moreover, the treatment must have been prescribed by a treating source; a prescription by a consultative physician does not meet this requirement. If any treating source of the claimant advises against treatment prescribed by another treating source, the claimant's failure to follow the treatment is justified. This is also the case if the claimant chooses alternative treatment prescribed by a second treating source. SSR 82-59. This issue often arises in situations where a doctor advises a claimant to lose weight or to stop smoking.

RUSS V. BARNHART

363 F.Supp.2d 1345, 103 Soc. Sec. Rep. Serv. 614 (M.D. Fla. 2005)

SNYDER, United States Magistrate Judge.

* * *

Rachele Russ filed applications for DIB and SSI in 1999. After the applications were denied initially and on reconsideration, Administrative Law Judge John Marshall Meisburg Jr. (ALJ) conducted a hearing on March 28, 2001. At the hearing, testimony was given by Claimant, who was represented by counsel.

In a Decision dated May 20, 2002, the ALJ found Ms. Russ was not entitled to benefits. The Appeals Council determined no basis existed for granting review and the Commissioner's decision became final.

* * *

II. Analysis

Plaintiff argues "[t]he ALJ erred in failing to apply the correct legal standards under 20 C.F.R. § 404.1530 and Social Security Ruling 82-59 and his decision is not supported by substantial evidence." She contends the judge incorrectly determined that she "failed to follow prescribed treatment and that if she had followed such treatment her ability to work would have been restored[.]"

Where prescribed medical treatment would restore the ability to work, a claimant's "'refusal to follow [that] treatment without a good reason will preclude a finding of disability[.]'" *Ellison [v. Barnhart,* 355 F.3d

1272, 1275 11th Cir. 2003)] (quoting *Dawkins v. Bowen*, 848 F.2d 1211, 1213 (11th Cir.1988)); see 20 C.F.R. §§ 404.1530, 416.930. An ALJ must make explicit findings in this regard if benefits are to be denied.

In cases involving obesity, "[a] physician's recommendation to lose weight does not necessarily constitute a prescribed course of treatment, nor does a claimant's failure to accomplish the recommended change constitute a refusal to undertake such treatment." *McCall v. Bowen*, 846 F.2d 1317, 1319 (11th Cir.1988) (per curiam). "[L]osing weight is a task which is not equivalent to taking pills or following a prescription." *Hammock v. Bowen*, 879 F.2d 498, 504 (9th Cir.1989).

Here, the ALJ determined "[t]he claimant was disabled as of the alleged onset date of April 29, 1997." Tr. at 42 (Finding 13). Nevertheless, he concluded the duration requirement had not been met because "failure to follow prescribed treatment has occurred and it is not justifiable[.]" *Id.*; *see also id.* (Finding 12) ("If the claimant had followed said prescribed treatment at the time of the alleged onset date, [she] would have been restored to substantial gainful activity[.]").

The judge's basis for denying benefits is not supported by substantial evidence. Concerning failure to follow prescribed treatment, he stated a physician had "urged [her] to continue losing weight[,] but [she] failed to do so." *Id.* at 39. While he also mentioned Plaintiff was placed on a diet, *id.*, the ALJ apparently equated compliance with success. He acknowledged—and did not discredit—her testimony "that she tried to follow the diet and that she did not eat very much. However, she said that she was still not able to lose weight." *Id.; see also id.* at 245 (report of "no weight loss" despite reduced food intake post-surgery). Given the nature of obesity as acknowledged by the legal system, Ms. Russ's mere "failure to accomplish the recommended change" does not establish a refusal of prescribed treatment.

The ALJ's application of the law was flawed in another respect as well. Even assuming Claimant refused to comply with prescribed treatment, the judge lacked a sufficient basis to decide treatment compliance would have restored Plaintiff's ability to work. His conclusion in this regard is based on responses to interrogatories sent to a treating physician. This evidence falls short of showing even flawless adherence to a diet and exercise program would have resulted in an ability to maintain gainful employment. The physician opined simply that Plaintiff's condition may have improved were such treatment undertaken when first prescribed,[3] and that tardy compliance would result in improvement. *Id.* at 380. A potential for non-quantified improvement is too amorphous to justify con-

---

[3] It is noted the doctor did not state a belief about whether Plaintiff complied with his advice. Rather, he indicated he did not know if such had occurred. * * *

crete functional capacity findings. Accordingly, as has been observed, "[i]mprovement does not equal an ability to work." *Seals v. Barnhart*, 308 F.Supp.2d 1241, 1252 (N.D.Ala.2004). Since the ALJ marshaled no other support for his conclusion, he must be considered to have erred in applying the relevant standard. Though the ALJ's decision about disability may have been a fairly close one, *see id.* at 40, in view of the errors discussed herein this case must be remanded.

* * *

NOTE ON FOLLOWING TREATMENT AND CREDIBILITY

A claimant's history in following prescribed treatment aimed at alleviating disabling symptom, such as pain, can be taken into account—one way or another—when assessing the credibility of a claimant's subjective complaints. As set out in SSR 96-7p (1996):

> In general, a longitudinal medical record demonstrating an individual's attempts to seek medical treatment for pain or other symptoms and to follow that treatment once it is prescribed lends support to an individual's allegations of intense and persistent pain or other symptoms for the purposes of judging the credibility of the individual's statements. Persistent attempts by the individual to obtain relief of pain or other symptoms, such as by increasing medications, trials of a variety of treatment modalities in an attempt to find one that works or that does not have side effects, referrals to specialists, or changing treatment sources may be a strong indication that the symptoms are a source of distress to the individual and generally lend support to an individual's allegations of intense and persistent symptoms.

> On the other hand, the individual's statements may be less credible if the level or frequency of treatment is inconsistent with the level of complaints, or if the medical reports or records show that the individual is not following the treatment as prescribed and there are no good reasons for this failure. However, the adjudicator must not draw any inferences about an individual's symptoms and their functional effects from a failure to seek or pursue regular medical treatment without first considering any explanations that the individual may provide, or other information in the case record, that may explain infrequent or irregular medical visits or failure to seek medical treatment. The adjudicator may need to recontact the individual or question the individual at the administrative proceeding in order to determine whether there are good reasons the individual does not seek medical treatment or does not pursue treatment in a consistent manner. The explanations provided by the individual may provide insight into the individual's credibility. For example:

* The individual's daily activities may be structured so as to minimize symptoms to a tolerable level or eliminate them entirely, avoiding physical or mental stressors that would exacerbate the symptoms. The individual may be living with the symptoms, seeing a medical source only as needed for periodic evaluation and renewal of medications.

* The individual's symptoms may not be severe enough to prompt the individual to seek ongoing medical attention or may be relieved with over-the-counter medications.

* The individual may not take prescription medication because the side effects are less tolerable than the symptoms.

* The individual may be unable to afford treatment and may not have access to free or low-cost medical services.

* The individual may have been advised by a medical source that there is no further, effective treatment that can be prescribed and undertaken that would benefit the individual.

* Medical treatment may be contrary to the teaching and tenets of the individual's religion.

See also Myles v. Astrue, 582 F.3d 672, 677, 147 Soc. Sec. Rep. Serv. 48, (7th Cir. 2009) ("ALJ was required by [SSR 96-7p] to consider explanations for instances where Myles did not keep up with her treatment, and he did not do so").

2. DISABILITY DUE TO EFFECTS OF PRESCRIBED MEDICATION

Social Security regulations do not speak generally to the evaluation of side effects; however, the regulations reflect SSA's policy to consider all of an individual's symptoms, including pain. 20 C.F.R. §§ 404.1529(a), 416.929(a). As we saw earlier in this chapter, those regulations acknowledge that subjective symptoms can demonstrate that an impairment is more severe than can be shown by objective medical evidence alone and that SSA will evaluate any other information that an individual submits about his or her symptoms. *See* 20 C.F.R. § 404.1529(c)(3), 416.929(c)(3). Among the factors that are considered as potentially relevant to an assessment of an individual's symptoms, such as pain, include the type, dosage, effectiveness, and side effects of any medication taken to alleviate those symptoms. 20 C.F.R. § 404.1529(c)(3)(iv), 416.929(c)(3)(iv).

Strictly speaking, disability cannot be based on the effects of prescribed medication alone. There must also be an underlying physical or mental impairment for which the drug treatment has been prescribed.

Thus, this is better understood as a combination-of-impairments issue, involving a primary impairment for which medications have been prescribed and a secondary set of limitations due to the side effects of the medications.

As with all disability determinations, the burden of proof is on the claimant to show that there is, in fact, an impairment or combination of impairments which prevents him or her from engaging in substantial gainful activity. In the case of disabling side effects from prescribed drugs, the claimant must show that there are disabling side effects caused by a particular drug. In French v. Massanari, 152 F. Supp. 2d 1329, 75 Soc. Sec. Rep. Serv. 227 (M.D. Fla. 2001), the claimant argued that the ALJ should have developed the record relative to the side effects of his medications. The court disagreed:

> French * * * [asserted] that the administrative law judge should have determined whether French's medications themselves render French disabled, or at least contribute to his disability. In *Cowart v. Schweiker*, 662 F.2d 731 (11th Cir.1981), the Eleventh Circuit recognized that an administrative law judge may have a duty to investigate the possible side effects of medications taken by a social security claimant as an element of her disability analysis. In Cowart, the claimant, who was unrepresented and had not waived her right to counsel, asserted that the side effects of her medications contributed to her disability and testified that as a result of taking her drugs, she was "kind of zonked most of the time." In contrast, French was represented at the hearing and did not allege at that time that the side effects of his medications contribute to his disability. *See, e.g., Bowen v. Yuckert*, 482 U.S. 137, 146 n. 5, 107 S.Ct. 2287, 96 L.Ed.2d 119 (1987) ("It is not unreasonable to require the claimant, who is in a better position to provide information about his own medical condition, to do so."). Moreover, the only indication in the entire record of the side effects of French's medications is his statement before the administrative law judge implying that his pain medication makes him "groggy." The determination by the administrative law judge of how much weight to accord this assertion was colored by other evidence, such as French's testimony that he has an alternate medication that he can use while driving, and the notable absence in French's medical records of any complaints by French about side effects of his medications. Nor does the record indicate that any of the many doctors that examined and treated French was concerned about the potential side effects of his medications. Under the circumstances, the failure of the administrative law judge to inquire further into possible side effects did not deprive French of a meaningful opportunity to be heard.

152 F. Supp. 2d at 1337-38.

On the other hand, SSA is obligated to consider adverse side effects where the claimant does present proof that medication has a negative impact on his or her ability to work. The claimant in Hung Thanh Le v. Astrue, 2010 WL 1854081, 152 Soc. Sec. Rep. Serv. 199 (C.D. Cal. 2010), argued that the ALJ failed to address properly the side effects of Vicodin, which he testified "made him sleepy all the time [and] caused him to lay down two or three times a day for one to two hours." The court agreed:

> When the ALJ is evaluating Plaintiff's limitations, she must consider the side effects of medication. Social Security Ruling 96-7p specifically requires consideration of the "type, dosage, effectiveness, and side effects of any medication the individual takes or has taken to alleviate pain or other symptoms." 20 C.F.R. § 404.1529(c)(3)(iv); 416.929(c)(3)(iv). The Ninth Circuit has observed that an ALJ must "consider all factors that might have a significant impact on an individual's ability to work." *Erickson v. Shalala*, 9 F.3d 813, 817 (9th Cir.1993) (citing *Varney v. Secretary of HHS*, 846 F.2d 581, 585 (9th Cir.1988)). Such factors "may include side effects of medications as well as subjective evidence of pain." *Erickson*, 9 F.3d at 818.

> In her decision, the ALJ does discuss Plaintiff's allegations of side effects caused by his Vicodin use. Specifically, the ALJ states that "there [wa]s no credible evidence of regular usage of strong medication to alleviate pain that would significantly impair the claimant's ability to do basic work activities and no documented evidence in the medical record of any significant side effects." This conclusion is contradicted by the record.

> Plaintiff's medical records indicate that he had been taking Vicodin very regularly to alleviate his pain since 1997. Vicodin qualifies as strong medication to alleviate pain. Although the medical records do not show evidence of severe side effects, Plaintiff testified that his Vicodin use had increased by almost double his past dosage. It is this increase in pain medication and its side effects that the ALJ failed to consider in her assessment of Plaintiff's ability to work.

> During the hearing, Plaintiff's counsel asked Plaintiff, "after the latest rounds of surgery, did they have to change the amount of Vicodin you're taking?" (Plaintiff responded, "because I had to take it for quite a long time since I had the surgery from 1996[to] now ... the medication doesn't do any good. So the doctor ha[d] to increase it from 325 milligram[s] to 625 milligram[s]." Plaintiff's counsel then asked, "how does the Vicodin affect you?" to which Plaintiff respond-

ed that "it's helped me with the pain but [I] cannot do anything because I feel sleepy all the time."

2010 WL 1854081 at *5-*6.

Noting that the record was unclear as to when the claimant's Vicodin
use increased and that she testified that because of increased use she
could not drive and needed help with her basic daily activities, the *Hung
Thanh Le* court concluded: "Because Plaintiff's increased usage and dosage of pain medication could cause significant side effects, it was error for
the ALJ not to expressly consider those side effects in her evaluation of
Plaintiff's disability claim. The case must be remanded to remedy this
defect. On remand, if necessary, the ALJ should utilize a medical expert
to testify about the effect of Plaintiff's increased medication usage on his
ability to work." 2010 WL 1854081at *6. *Compare* Osenbrock v. Apfel,
240 F.3d 1157, 1164, 72 Soc. Sec. Rep. Ser. 433 (9th Cir. 2001) (ALJ did
not have to include alleged side effects of medication when questioning
vocational expert because, while "[t]here were passing mentions of the
side effects of Mr. Osenbrock's medication in some of the medical records,
but there was no evidence of side effects severe enough to interfere with
Osenbrock's ability to work.").

The side effects of medication should be taken into account at all
steps of the sequential evaluation process, including certain listings in
the Listing of Impairments. *See, e.g.*, 20 C.F.R. Part 404 Subpart P Appx
1 (Listings) § 11.00(A) (epilepsy listings; "Where adequate seizure control
is obtained only with unusually large doses, the possibility of impairment
resulting from the side effects of this medication must also be assessed.").
See also Kennedy v. Heckler, 602 F. Supp. 709, 712, 8 Soc. Sec. Rep. Serv.
807 (W.D.N.C. 1985) ("the ALJ failed to take into account the ... disabling
effects of taking from ten to forty mg. of stellazine [sic] a day. [The claimant's] 'stability' is clearly attributable to her heavy medication and artifi-
cially stabilized environment") (citing listing for mental impairments).
Side effects of medication must be considered as well in determining
whether a claimant retains the ability to perform past relevant work, or
any other work in the national economy. *See, e.g.*, McDevitt v. Commissioner, 241 Fed. Appx. 615, 616 (11th Cir. July 18, 2007) ("While the ALJ
found McDevitt's testimony "somewhat exaggerated," the ALJ made no
finding, as to credibility or otherwise, regarding McDevitt's claim that his
medications caused severe concentration problems and made him drowsy.
Since the ALJ failed to make a finding as to this claim, the ALJ's determination that McDevitt could perform the duties of a telemarketer was
not based on substantial evidence in the record.").

CHAPTER 7

CALCULATION AND PAYMENT OF BENEFITS

■ ■ ■

The method for determining the amount of benefit payments depends first on whether the benefits are paid through the Social Security Act's social insurance program (Old Age, Survivors, and Disability Insurance, or OASDI) or its public assistance program (Supplemental Security Income, or SSI). The difference—consistent with the basic financial eligibility requirements for the two types of programs discussed in Chapter 2—is that social insurance payments are tied more or less to the amount of the worker's earnings subject to Social Security taxes, while public assistance payments are tied to a fixed standard of financial need. Thus, OASDI benefit payments are calculated by using a formula that includes in the calculation the number of years the beneficiary worked at covered employment and the amount of his or her covered earnings; SSI payments are calculated on the basis of a federally established standard of need, less any non-exempt income the beneficiary receives. These two different methods for calculating benefit payments are discussed in the next two sections of this chapter.

There are a number of other provisions that affect the amount of benefit payments, particularly with respect to the OASDI program. Although a detailed review of all of the factors that go into benefit computations is beyond the scope of this book, two related rules for reducing benefit payments deserve special attention: the treatment of certain other benefits received by the beneficiary, and the calculation of OASDI benefit payments to multiple beneficiaries on the basis of a single wage earner's earnings record. These rules are discussed immediately following the sections on OASDI and SSI benefit computations. The chapter then concludes with a discussion of adjustments for overpayments and underpayments, rules governing the suspension of benefits, and payments made to representative payees.

A. OASDI INSURANCE FORMULA

Consistent with its purposes as a contribution-based social insurance program, the amount of benefits that an OASDI recipient is entitled to receive depends to a certain extent on the earnings record of the claimant—or the wage earner on the basis of whose earnings record a spouse's or child's claim is based. As described in greater detail in Chapters 2 and 3, the eligibility requirements for the various social insurance programs under OASDI include a number of personal and financial criteria. Generally, one must have worked and paid Social Security taxes in a sufficient amount over a specified period of time in order to be "insured" under the program. For instance, in order to receive old age benefits under OASDI, a potential recipient (or the wage earner on whose earnings record benefits are claimed) must have paid Social Security taxes while working at covered employment for at least forty quarters. The rationale for this requirement is to ensure that the Social Security Administration pays benefits only to those wage earners who have done their part in contributing to the fiscal integrity of the Social Security system. As noted in Lerner v. Richardson, 393 F. Supp. 1387, 1391 (E.D. Pa. 1975), "[t]he entire social welfare scheme embodied in the [Social Security] Act rests on the Congressional determination 'that those who in their productive years were functioning members of the economy may justly call upon that economy, in their later years, for protection from the 'rigors of the poor house.'" 393 F. Supp. at 1391 (quoting Helvering v. Davis, 301 U.S. 619, 641 (1937)). *Lerner v. Richardson* involved a physician who claimed that the benefit formula used by the SSA resulted in much lower benefit payments than he should have been receiving. In determining the physician's benefit amount, SSA excluded from his earnings record self-employment income on which, pursuant to a subsequently amended portion of the Social Security Act, he had not been required to pay Social Security taxes. In ruling that the physician was not entitled to include in the calculation of his benefit payment earnings on which he had not paid Social Security taxes, the court also noted that "it is reasonable for Congress to build into the system a safeguard against disproportionately high payments to those who have made the smallest contributions." *Id.*

The percentage of a worker's paycheck that is taken out for Social Security taxes has increased markedly over the years—from 1 percent of a covered worker's paycheck in 1937 to today's 6.2 percent—as the OASDI program has grown larger and its funding needs have increased. The average benefit in 2010 for a single retired worker was $1,175; $752 for a child of a deceased worker; and $1,134 for a wage earner's elderly widow or widower. *See* Social Security Administration, Fact Sheet on the Old-Age, Survivors, and Disability Insurance Program, Dec. 31, 2010, http://www.ssa.gov/OACT/FACTS/index.html. The scale of the various OASDI programs is immense: as of December 31, 2010 there were over 54 million beneficiaries under the various OASDI programs receiving a total of more than $58 billion each month. *Id.* It is against this backdrop that the Social Security Act integrates workers' earnings records into the calculation of their and their survivors' and dependents' benefit payments.

1. PRIMARY INSURANCE AMOUNT (PIA)

The amount of monthly OASDI benefits paid to a beneficiary is based on a figure known as the Primary Insurance Amount (PIA), which in turn is based on the earnings record of the beneficiary or the person on whose earnings record the beneficiary is claiming benefits. (Earnings records and related issues of dependency and eligibility are covered in Chapter 2.) The basic PIA calculation is the same for all types of benefits under the program, although the amount actually paid may differ.

SSA uses two primary methods to calculate a wage earner's PIA. *See generally* **20 C.F.R. § 404.204[APP-REGS]**. The proper method to use depends on the year the claimant turns 62 (the earliest age at which one can claim old age benefits) or the year he or she becomes eligible for disability benefits, whichever is earlier. *See* 20 C.F.R. § 404.204(b). If this year is before 1979, the PIA is based on the beneficiary's average monthly wage (AMW). 20 C.F.R. § 404.204(b)(2). If it is after 1978, the PIA is based on a figure called the average indexed monthly earnings (AIME). 20 C.F.R. §§ 404.204(b)(1), 404.210(a). In addition, there are several other methods used to calculate the PIA for beneficiaries in special situations, including those who did most of their eligible work prior to 1951 and those who had a prior period of disability. 20 C.F.R. § 404.204(c). If a beneficiary's PIA could be determined using more than one method, SSA uses the highest figure of those calculated under all possible methods. 20 C.F.R. § 404.204(a). There is a special minimum PIA for some beneficiaries, including certain individuals with long periods of relatively low earnings.

The calculation of PIAs under the AMW method is described in 20 C.F.R. § 404.221. The process begins with determining the number of years of earnings to include and which of those years will be used in the calculation. 20 C.F.R. § 404.221(c). Up to five years are deducted from the number of earnings years to arrive at the number of "benefit computation years." 20 C.F.R. § 404.221(c)(3). The "benefit computation years" are the years of highest earnings, up to the proper number. The AMW is then calculated by totaling the creditable earnings in the benefit computation years, dividing that total by the number of months in the benefit computation years, and rounding to the next lower whole dollar. 20 C.F.R. § 404.221(d). The AMW is then converted to PIA through the use of a table, which is weighted in favor of lower AMW amounts by using a higher percentage multiplier for low AMWs than for higher AMWs. 20 C.F.R. § 404.222; *see also* 20 C.F.R. Pt. 404, Subpart C, Appendix III.

The method of calculating a PIA under the AIME method takes a somewhat different route by indexing earnings to adjust for the upward trend in wages over the intervening years. *See generally* **20 C.F.R. §**

404.210[APP-REGS]; *see also* **20 C.F.R. §** 404.211[APP-REGS]. SSA uses an individual's wages, compensation, self-employment income, and deemed military wage credits that are creditable to the individual for Social Security purposes for years after 1950. 20 C.F.R. § 404.211(b)(1). The determination of computation base years is the same under both methods, 20 C.F.R. § 404.211(b)(2), but the earnings for those years are indexed by comparing the claimant's earnings in each year with the average earnings in that year and then adjusting the beneficiary's earnings to reflect average increases in earnings in the relevant time period. *See* 20 C.F.R. § 404.211(d). There is a similar rule for removing certain years from the calculations which results in using the years of highest indexed earnings from the computation base years. The AIME is then calculated by adding together the indexed earnings in the benefit computation years; dividing by the number of months in those years; and rounding down to the next dollar. 20 C.F.R. § 404.212(f).

The first step in indexing an individual's Social Security earnings is to divide the average wages for the individual's indexing year, in turn, by the average wages for each year beginning with 1951 and ending with that indexing year. 20 C.F.R. § 404.211(d)(1)-(2). The second step is to multiply the actual year-by-year dollar amounts of the individual's earnings (up to the maximum amounts creditable) by the quotients found in step one for each of those years, and rounding the results to the nearest penny. 20 C.F.R. § 404.211(d)(3). The quotient for an individual's indexing year is 1.0, meaning that his or her earnings in that year are used in their actual dollar amount; any earnings after the indexing year that may be used in computing your average indexed monthly earnings are also used in their actual dollar amount. The AIME is then converted to the PIA through the use of a formula that changes for each year. *See* 20 C.F.R. § 404.212(b).

The following example of the indexing of a worker's earnings is provided in the regulations at 20 C.F.R. § 404.211(d):

Ms. A reaches age 62 in July 1979. Her year-by-year social security earnings since 1950 are as follows:

Year	Earnings
1951	$3,200
1952	$3,400
1953	$3,300
1954	$3,600
1955	$3,700
1956	$3,700
1957	$4,000
1958	$4,200
1959	$4,400

1960	$4,500
1961	$2,800
1962	$2,200
1963	$0
1964	$0
1965	$3,700
1966	$4,500
1967	$5,400
1968	$6,200
1969	$6,900
1970	$7,300
1971	$7,500
1972	$7,800
1973	$8,200
1974	$9,000
1975	$9,900
1976	$11,100
1977	$9,900
1978	$11,000

Step 1. The first step in indexing Ms. A's earnings is to find the relationship between the general wage level in Ms. A's indexing year (1977) and the general wage level in each of the years 1951-1976. We refer to Appendix I for average wage figures, and perform the following computations:

Year	I. 1977 general wage level	II. Nationwide average of the total wages	III. Column I divided by column II equals relationship
1951	9,779.44	$2,799.16	3.4937053
1952	9,779.44	2,973.32	3.2890641
1953	9,779.44	3,139.44	3.1150269
1954	9,779.44	3,155.64	3.0990354
1955	9,779.44	3,301.44	2.9621741
1956	9,779.44	3,532.36	2.7685287
1957	9,779.44	3,641.72	2.6853904
1958	9,779.44	3,673.80	2.6619413
1959	9,779.44	3,855.80	2.5362934
1960	9,779.44	4,007.12	2.4405159
1961	9,779.44	4,086.76	2.3929568
1962	9,779.44	4,291.40	2.2788461
1963	9,779.44	4,396.64	2.2242986
1964	9,779.44	4,576.32	2.1369659
1965	9,779.44	4,658.72	2.0991689
1966	9,779.44	4,938.36	1.9803012
1967	9,779.44	5,213.44	1.8758133
1968	9,779.44	5,571.76	1.7551797
1969	9,779.44	5,893.76	1.6592871
1970	9,779.44	6,186.24	1.5808375
1971	9,779.44	6,497.08	1.5052054

1972	9,779.44	7,133.80	1.3708599
1973	9,779.44	7,580.16	1.2901364
1974	9,779.44	8,030.76	1.2177478
1975	9,779.44	8,630.92	1.1330704
1976	9,779.44	9,226.48	1.0599318
1977	9,779.44	9,779.44	1.0000000

Step 2. After we have found these indexing quotients, we multiply Ms. A's actual year-by-year earnings by them to find her indexed earnings, as shown below:

Year	I. Actual earnings	II. Indexing quotient	III. Column I multiplied by column II equals indexed earnings
1951	$3,200	3.4937053	$11,179.86
1952	$3,400	3.2890641	11,182.82
1953	$3,300	3.1150269	10,279.59
1954	$3,600	3.0990354	11,156.53
1955	$3,700	2.9621741	10,960.04
1956	$3,700	2.7685287	10,243.56
1957	$4,000	2.6853904	10,741.56
1958	$4,200	2.6619413	11,180.15
1959	$4,400	2.5362934	11,159.69
1960	$4,500	2.4405159	10,982.32
1961	$2,800	2.3929568	6,700.28
1962	$2,200	2.2788461	5,013.46
1963	$0	2.2242986	
1964	$0	2.1369659	
1965	$3,700	2.0991689	7,766.92
1966	$4,500	1.9803012	8,911.36
1967	$5,400	1.8758133	10,129.39
1968	$6,200	1.7551797	10,882.11
1969	$6,900	1.6592871	11,449.08
1970	$7,300	1.5808375	11,540.11
1971	$7,500	1.5052054	11,289.04
1972	$7,800	1.3708599	10,692.71
1973	$8,200	1.2901364	10,579.12
1974	$9,000	1.2177478	10,959.73
1975	$9,900	1.1330704	11,217.40
1976	$11,100	1.0599318	11,765.24
1977	$9,900	1.0000000	9,900.00
1978	$11,000	N/A	11,000.00

The regulations go on to describe the procedure for calculating Ms. A's AIME based on the indexed earnings as set out in the tables above:

[W]e see that Ms. A reaches age 62 in 1979. Her elapsed years are 1951-1978 (28 years). We subtract 5 from her 28 elapsed years to find that we must use 23 benefit computation years. This means that we will use her 23 highest computation base years to find her average indexed monthly earnings. We exclude the 5 years 1961-1965 and total her indexed earnings for the remaining years, i.e., the benefit computation years (including her unindexed earnings in 1977 and 1978) and get $249,381.41. We then divide that amount by the 276 months in her 23 benefit computation years and find her average indexed monthly earnings to be $903.56, which is rounded down to $903.

20 C.F.R. § 404.211(f).

2. FORMULA FOR CALCULATING WAGE EARNERS' OASDI BENEFITS

The Social Security Administration has set up a "Benefit Calculator" on its website that allows individuals to estimate the amount of their retirement benefits based on their actual earnings record. *See* http://www.ssa.gov/estimator. Therefore, it might not seem important for a wage earner's attorney—or anyone other than the Social Security Administration, for that matter—to be able to calculate the amount of benefits that a wage earner will receive. Nonetheless, attorneys who practice in the area of Social Security should know at least the mechanics of the calculations that SSA uses to determine monthly benefit amounts. This section sets out in plain English the process that SSA goes through in determining the amount of benefits that an eligible wage earner is entitled to under the OASDI program. The first seven steps retrace the calculation of AIME described more generally above.

Step 1: The Social Security Administration picks the wage earner's indexing year. In the case of old age retirement benefits, this is the second year before the year in which the wage earner first becomes eligible for benefits, which is 62 for most wage earners; therefore, normally the indexing year will be the year in which the wage earner turns 60. In the case of disability benefits, the indexing year is the second year before the year in which the disability occurred.

Step 2: The indexing quotient for each year in the wage earner's earnings record is produced. This is done by dividing the average monthly wage for the indexing year by the respective average monthly wage for each individual year in the wage earner's earnings record. The average monthly wages for each year are released annually by the Social Security Administration.

Step 3: The wage earner's nominal wages for each year are multiplied by the respective indexing quotient for each year in the wage earner's earnings record to produce the wage earner's indexed earnings for each year in his or her earnings record.

Step 4: The wage earner's base computation years are then determined by removing the lowest five years of the wage earner's indexed earnings for retirement benefits and up to five years in the event that the wage earner is eligible for disability benefits (*see* 20 C.F.R. 404.211(e)(3)-(4) for the actual mechanics of calculating the dropout years for disability benefits). Once the appropriate number of years with the lowest indexed earnings have been removed then all remaining years are referred to as the wage earner's base computation years. These base computation years will form the basis upon which the wage earner's monthly benefit is calculated.

Step 5: The wage earner's indexed earnings from all base computation years are added up in order to figure out the wage earner's total indexed earnings over the course of his or her career.

Step 6: The number of base computation years from step 4 is multiplied by 12 in order to figure out the number of total months in the base computation years. Then the wage earner's aggregate indexed earnings over all base computation years in his or her earnings record from step 5 are divided by the number of total months in the base computation years.

Step 7: The number from step 6 is rounded down to the nearest dollar. This amount is the wage earner's Average Indexed Monthly Earnings or AIME. This number is not actually the amount of benefits that the wage earner will receive. Some further adjustments need to be made to the AIME in order to determine the wage earner's Primary Insurance Amount or PIA, the actual number that will constitute the wage earner's monthly benefit.

Step 8: In order to determine the amount of the wage earner's AIME that will actually be included in the wage earner's monthly benefit check, SSA then applies a formula to the AIME. This formula revolves around the use of certain "bend points," which are dollar thresholds set annually by SSA. These bend points are important because they determine how much of a wage earner's AIME he or she will actually be entitled to in monthly OASDI benefits. The bend points operate by paying x percent of a first prescribed amount of the AIME, y percent of a next prescribed amount of the AIME, and so on. (NOTE: The practical reality of these bend points is to favor wage earners with lower AIME amounts. This can be seen by looking at the percentage of the amount of the AIME above each bend point that actually ends up being included in the wage earner's PIA, and thus actually is paid out to the wage earner in benefits. For example, in the year 2010, wage earners kept 90 percent of the amount of their AIME equal to or less than $761, while they kept only 32 percent above $761 and below $4,586, and only 15 percent over $4,586. As a result, wage earners with an AIME over $761 take home a smaller percentage of their AIME than wage earners with an AIME at or under $761. Moreover, the higher a wage earner's AIME, the less the percentage of that amount is included in the wage earner's PIA—and thus in the wage earner's benefit checks when he or she retires or becomes disabled.)

The actual process of turning an AIME into a PIA through use of the bend points works as follows:

a) The AIME figure from step 7 is compared with the first bend point amount. If the AIME is over the first bend point amount, then the first bend point amount is multiplied by 0.90; if the AIME is under the first bend point amount, then the entire AIME is multiplied by 0.90.

b) The AIME figure from step 7 is then compared with the second bend point amount. If the AIME is over that second bend point amount, then the second bend point amount is subtracted from the first bend point amount. That number is then multiplied by 0.32. If the AIME is not over the second bend point amount, then the AIME is subtracted from the first bend point amount. That number is then multiplied by 0.32.

c) If the AIME is over the second bend point amount, then one further step is necessary. The second bend point amount is subtracted from the AIME from step 7 and that number is then multiplied by 0.15.

d) Next, the numbers from (a), (b) and (c) are added together. This number is then rounded down to the nearest dime, so the last digit of that number is essentially replaced with a zero. This amount is the wage earner's Primary Insurance Amount or PIA. However, this is not the end of the process, as the wage earner's PIA still might need another adjustment before the process is over, depending on whether the wage earner is receiving retirement benefits and is either waiting until full retirement age to receive benefits or else taking early retirement.

Step 9: The PIA must be reduced to account for early retirement reductions, if the wage earner is retiring before achieving his or her full retirement age. The reduction is 5/9% for each of the first 36 months of early retirement and 5/12% for each month beyond 36 months. (NOTE: This step is performed only if the worker is retiring at less than his or her full retirement age.)

The process of adjusting the PIA in case of early retirement works as follows:

a) Figure out how many months of early retirement the worker has taken. Take the worker's full retirement age and subtract that number from the age at which the worker is actually retiring. Then multiply that figure by 12 in order to express this figure in months.

b) If the number in a) is greater than 36, then subtract that number from 36 and multiply it by 5/12; multiply 36 by 5/9; then add the two sums together to determine the total percentage reduction.

c) If the number in a) is less than or equal to 36, then multiply that number by 5/9 to determine the total percentage reduction.

d) Multiply the PIA from step 8 by the percentage reduction calculated at b) or c) above, as applicable.

e) Round the reduced PIA from (d) to the nearest lowest dime to determine the amount that the wage earner will actually receive if he or she retired early.

Step 10: If the wage earner is retiring at full retirement age, then the number from step 8 must be adjusted for any cost of living increases since the wage earner turned 62. This adjustment is necessary to account for any inflation that has occurred since the time that the wage earner turned 62. This process works as follows:

a) First subtract 62 from the age at retirement (in years). This will tell you how many Cost of Living Adjustments (or COLAs) will need to be done.

b) Look up the COLA for the year that the wage earner turned 63. This will be expressed in a decimal. Add one to that decimal and then multiply the PIA from step 8 by that number.

c) Repeat the process at b) using the revised PIA from b) and the COLA for the year the wage earner turned 64.

d) Redo the same process for each year up until the wage earner hits retirement age.

3. THE OASDI BENEFIT CALCULATION PROCESS: EXAMPLE

This example walks through the wage benefit calculation described above for a wage earner born in 1948 with a full retirement age of 66 and the following earnings record:

	Nominal earnings	Step 2 Calculation	Indexing factor	Indexed earnings
1970	$5,784	41,334.97/6,186.24	6.6818	$38,647
1971	6,094	41,334.97/6,497.08	6.3621	38,771
1972	6,712	41,334.97/7,133.80	5.7942	38,891
1973	7,155	41,334.97/7,580.16	5.4530	39,017
1974	7,603	41,334.97/8,030.76	5.1471	39,133
1975	8,197	41,334.97/8,630.92	4.7892	39,257
1976	8,790	41,334.97/9,226.48	4.4800	39,380
1977	9,346	41,334.97/9,779.44	4.2267	39,503
1978	10,119	41,334.97/10,556.03	3.9158	39,624
1979	11,038	41,334.97/11,479.46	3.6008	39,745
1980	12,069	41,334.97/12,513.46	3.3032	39,867
1981	13,325	41,334.97/13,773.10	3.0011	39,990
1982	14,101	41,334.97/14,531.34	2.8445	40,111
1983	14,833	41,334.97/15,239.24	2.7124	40,233
1984	15,752	41,334.97/16,135.07	2.5618	40,354
1985	16,473	41,334.97/16,822.51	2.4571	40,476
1986	17,013	41,334.97/17,321.82	2.3863	40,598
1987	18,152	41,334.97/18,426.51	2.2432	40,719
1988	19,104	41,334.97/19,334.04	2.1379	40,843
1989	19,919	41,334.97/20,099.55	2.0565	40,964
1990	20,901	41,334.97/21,027.98	1.9657	41,085
1991	21,744	41,334.97/21,811.60	1.8951	41,207
1992	22,932	41,334.97/22,935.42	1.8022	41,329
1993	23,198	41,334.97/23,132.67	1.7869	41,452
1994	23,891	41,334.97/23,753.53	1.7402	41,574
1995	24,921	41,334.97/24,705.66	1.6731	41,695
1996	26,216	41,334.97/25,913.90	1.5951	41,817
1997	27,827	41,334.97/27,426.00	1.5071	41,939
1998	29,368	41,334.97/28,861.44	1.4322	42,060
1999	31,095	41,334.97/20,469.84	1.3566	42,183
2000	32,909	41,334.97/32,154.82	1.2855	42,304
2001	33,791	41,334.97/32,921.92	1.2555	42,426
2002	34,228	41,334.97/33,252.09	1.2431	42,548
2003	35,166	41,334.97/34,064.95	1.2134	42,671
2004	36,905	41,334.97/35,648.55	1.1595	42,792
2005	38,365	41,334.97/36,952.94	1.1186	42,914
2006	40,242	41,334.97/38,651.41	1.0694	43,036
2007	42,187	41,344.97/40,405.48	1.0230	43,157
2008	43,280	41,334.97/41,344.97	1.0000	43,280
2009	44,144	None[1]	1.0000	44,144

NOTE: Each step is described first generally, then (*in italics*) by applying the particular facts from the example. The third column of the table ("In-

---

[1] The indexing factor is not calculated for 2009 because it falls after the indexing year of 2008, which eliminates the need to adjust the wage earner's 2009 wages for inflation.

dexing factor") is used at Step 2; the fourth column ("Indexed earnings") is used at Step 3.

Step 1: Pick the wage earner's indexing year. In the case of old age retirement benefits, this is the second year before the year in which the wage earner first becomes eligible for benefits, which is 62 for most wage earners, and so normally the indexing year will be the year in which the wage earner turns 60. In the case of disability benefits, this is the second year before the year in which the disability occurred. *Here, the indexing year is 2008, which is two years before the wage earner turned 62 and became eligible for retirement benefits.*

Step 2: Calculate the indexing quotient for each year in the wage earner's earnings record. This is done by dividing the average monthly wage for the indexing year by the average monthly wage for each year in the wage earner's earnings record. *Since 2008 is the baseline year, the average monthly wages for 2008 are used to calculate the indexing factor for each year in the wage earner's earnings record. The average monthly wages for 2008 ($41,334.97) are divided by the average monthly wage for each year, as shown in the third column of the table. The indexing factor for each year of the wage earner's earnings record is found in the fourth column of the table.*

Step 3: Multiply the wage earner's nominal wages for each year by the respective indexing factor for that year. *This step is performed by multiplying the wage earner's nominal earnings for each year (listed in the second column) by the indexing factor for that year (listed in the fourth column). The resulting indexed earnings for each year in this wage earner's earnings record are listed in the final column of the table.*

Step 4: Determine the wage earner's base computation years by removing the lowest 5 years of the wage earner's indexed earnings (up to five years in the event that the wage earner is eligible for disability benefits). *Five years are subtracted from the wage earner's earnings record in this example since the wage earner is entitled to retirement benefits. Those years are 1970, 1971, 1972, 1973 and 1974, the five years in the earnings record in which the wage earner's indexed earnings were the lowest.*

Step 5: Add up the indexed earnings from all base computation years in order to figure out the wage earner's total indexed earnings. *The entries in the last column of the table are added together for all base computation years (1975 through 2009) for a grand total of $1,447,278.00.*

Step 6: Multiply the number of base computation years from step 4 by 12 to determine the number of months in the base computation years. Then divide the aggregate indexed earnings from step 5 by the number of months in the base computation years. *There are 35 base computation* *years in this wage earner's earnings records, resulting in a total of 420 months (35 x 12). The $1,447,278.00 of total indexed earnings from step 5 divided by the 420 total months in the base computation years results in a monthly total of $3,445.90.*

Step 7: Round the number from Step 6 down to the nearest dollar to determine the wage earner's Average Indexed Monthly Earnings or AIME. This number is not actually the amount of benefits that the wage earner will receive, but instead some further adjustments need to be made to the AIME in order to determine the wage earner's AIME. *This wage earner's AIME is $3,445.00 ($3,445.90 rounded down to the nearest dollar).*

Step 8: Determine the amount of the wage earner's Primary Insurance Amount, or PIA, using the following steps:

a) Compare the AIME from step 7 with the first bend point amount. The first bend point is $761 and the AIME from step 7 ($3,445.00) is over that amount, so we proceed to (i) below.

(i) If the AIME is over the first bend point amount, then multiply that first bend point amount by 0.90. *$761 x 0.90 = 684.90.*

(ii) If the AIME is under the first bend point amount, then multiply the entire AIME by 0.90. *Not Applicable.*

b) Compare the AIME from step 7 with the second bend point amount. The AIME of $3,445.00 is under the second bend point amount of $4,586, so we proceed to (ii) below.

(i) If the AIME is over that second bend point amount, then subtract the second bend point amount from the first bend point amount. Multiply that number by 0.32. *Not Applicable.*

(ii) If the AIME is not over the second bend point amount, then subtract the AIME from the first bend point amount and multiply that number by 0.32. *$3,445.00 - $761 = $2,684.00; $2,684.00 x 0.32 = $858.88.*

c) If the AIME is over the second bend point amount, then one further step is necessary (the second bend point amount is subtracted from the AIME and then multiplied by 0.15). *The AIME of $3,445.00 is not over the second bend point amount of $4,586, so we do not have to perform this step.*

d) Next, add up the numbers from a), b), and c) and then round this number down to the nearest dime to determine the PIA. *$684.90 + $858.88 = $1,543.78; rounded down to the nearest dime, the PIA is*

$1,543.70 (before any adjustments are made for early retirement and any applicable COLAs are applied).

Step 9: Reduce the PIA if the wage earner is retiring before his or her full retirement age. Since this wage earner is retiring at 62 instead of 66, this step must be performed using the following steps:

a) Figure out how many months of early retirement are being taken by the worker, if any. Subtract the early retirement age from the worker's full retirement age and multiply that figure by 12 to calculate the number in months. *This worker's full retirement age is 66, so the number of early retirement years is 4 (66 – 61); 4 years of early retirement multiplied by 12 months for each year results in 48 months of early retirement, so we need to proceed to b) below.*

b) If the number in a) is greater than 36, then:

(i) Subtract 36 from the number in a) and multiply it by 5/12. *48 - 36 = 12; 12 x 5/12= 5.*

(ii) Then multiply 36 by 5/9. *36 x 5/9 = 20.*

(iii) Add your answers from (i) and (ii) to determine the total percentage reduction for early retirement. *5 + 20 = 25%.*

c) If the number in a) is less than or equal to 36, then multiply that number by 5/9. *Not Applicable.*

d) Take the percentage from (b)(iii) or (c), whichever is applicable, and multiply it by the PIA from step 8. Then subtract that amount from the PIA from step 8 to determine the adjusted PIA. *The PIA from step 8 is $1,543.70; $1,543.70 x 25% = $385.92; $1,543.70 - $385.92 = $1,157.78.*

e) Round the amount from d) to the nearest lowest dollar to determine the revised PIA and the amount that the wage earner will actually receive when retiring early at age 62. *$1,157.78 rounded down to the nearest dollar is $1,157.00, which will be the amount of this wage earner's monthly benefit check.*

Step 10: If the wage earner is retiring at full retirement age, then the number from step 8 must be adjusted for any cost of living increases that have been promulgated by the Social Security Administration since the wage earner turned 62. *This step is not applicable since this wage earner is taking early retirement.*

NOTE: The charts below show the steps followed in the example above for calculating the AIME and the PIA and then reducing the PIA to account for early retirement in a simpler form:

AIME calculation

Years that Drop Out	1970, 1971, 1972, 1973, 1974
Highest 35 total	$1,447,278.00
Highest 35 total/420 months in those 35 years	$3,445.90
Rounded down to the nearest dollar	$3,445.00
AIME	**$3,445.00**

PIA calculation

90% of first $761 of AIME	$761x.90% = $684.90
32% of AIME over $761 up to and including $4,586	$3445 - $761 = $2684; $2684 x 32% = $858.88
15% of AIME over $4,586	$0
Total:	$684.90 + $858.88 = $1543.78
Reduce to nearest lower dime	$1543.70
PIA	**$1,543.70**

Reductions for early retirement

For first three years of early retirement, reduce by 5/9% for each month	36 x 5/9% = 20%
For any additional months of early retirement, reduce by 5/12% for each month	12 x (5/12% = 5%
Total Reductions for Early Retirement	20% + 5% = 25%
PIA	$1,543.70 x 25% = $385.92; $1,543.70 - $385.92 = $1,157.78
Round PIA down to the nearest dollar	$1,157.00
Monthly Benefit	**$1,157.00**

NOTE ON CALCULATING EARLY- AND DELAYED-RETIREMENT
BENEFITS AND DEPENDENT BENEFITS

As we saw in the example set out above, Social Security old age benefits are reduced when the beneficiary begins receiving them before full retirement age. Typically, the amount of reduced benefits represents the amount that the beneficiary would have received at full retirement age less a percentage that reflects the number of months prior to full retirement age at which the beneficiary began receiving benefits. *See* 20 C.F.R. § 404.312; § 404.410. Thus, there is a reduction of 5/9% for each of the first 36 months of early retirement and 5/12% for each month in excess of 36. 20 C.F.R. § 404.410(a). In other words, someone who retires three years before full retirement age receives 20% (36 months x 5/9%) less per month than he or she would have received if benefits began only at full retirement age. For every month over 36 months in which the wage earner retires early, he or she receives an additional 5/12% reduction for each additional month of early retirement. Therefore, wage earners who retire four years before full retirement—the earliest retirement date for persons with the current full retirement age of 66—receive 25 percent (36 months x 5/9% plus 12 months x 5/12%) less per month than they would receive if they had retired at full retirement age.

One also has the option of delaying retirement up to the age of 70, either by continuing to work beyond full retirement age or by simply waiting to receive benefits. The amount of delayed-retirement benefits is calculated by increasing the amount paid on one's PIA. For individuals born after January 1, 1943, the rate of increase is 2/3% per month, or up to 8% per year. *See* 20 C.F.R. § 404.313.

When a dependent—usually a spouse or a child—of an insured wage earner receives benefits under the wage earner's account, the benefits formula begins with the insured wage earner's Primary Insurance Amount (PIA), calculated as discussed above. Then, depending on the type of benefits involved, the basic benefit amount can be a percentage of—or the full amount of—the wage earner's PIA. In the case of Child's benefits, for example, the amount is 75% of the wage earner's PIA if the wage earner has died and 50% if he or she is retired or disabled (42 U.S.C. § 402(d)(2), 20 C.F.R. § 404.353); in the case of widow(er)'s benefits, the basic amount is 100% of the insured wage earner's PIA, unless the wage earner had been receiving old age benefits that were reduced because he or she began receiving those benefits before reaching full retirement age (42 U.S.C. §§ 402(e)(2)(A), (f)(2)(A), 20 C.F.R. § 404.338). Finally, the basic benefit amount may then be reduced for a number of reasons. The two most important are the payment of secondary benefits to other persons on the same wage earner's account—the so-called family maximum—and the receipt of certain other benefits, both of which are discussed later in this chapter.

NOTE ON PAYMENT OF BENEFITS

OASDI benefits are payable beginning with the first month covered by the application in which the claimant meets all of the requirements for entitlement. 20 C.F.R. § 404.316(a). An application for old-age benefits can be effective for up to 6 months prior to the date it was filed; applications for disability benefits can be effective for up to 12 months prior to the date they were filed. These same rules apply to claims by dependent spouses and dependent children. *See, e.g.,* 20 C.F.R. § 404.621.

There is, however, a five-month waiting period before a claimant is eligible for disability benefits; in effect, claimants are eligible for benefit payments only after the first five months of disability. *See* 42 U.S.C.A. §§ 423(a)(1), 423(c)(2); 20 C.F.R. § 404.315(a)(4). *See also* 20 C.F.R. § 404.335(c)(1) (widow(er)'s disability benefits). The waiting period is a cost-saving measure designed to delay the commencement of benefit payments that would be paid to otherwise eligible beneficiaries. It is fundamentally different from the 12-month duration requirement of the general disability standard, which is an eligibility criterion related to the severity of the claimant's condition. The waiting period begins with the first full month in which the claimant is both disabled and insured for disability; it cannot begin, however, earlier than the seventeenth month before the claimant filed for benefits, no matter how long the claimant may have been disabled before then. 42 U.S.C.A. § 423(c)(2)(B), 20 C.F.R. § 404.315(a)(4). The waiting period does not apply to persons who were previously entitled to disability benefits or to a period of disability any time within five years of the month they again became disabled. 20 C.F.R. § 404.315(a)(4). SSA's practice of starting the waiting period on the first day of the month following the month in which an individual becomes disabled has been upheld. *See* Robbins v. Schweiker, 708 F.2d 340, 342, 2 Soc. Sec. Rep. Serv. 116 (8th Cir. 1983). The constitutionality of the five-month waiting period has been upheld as well. *See* Price v. Heckler, 733 F.2d 699, 701, 5 Soc. Sec. Rep. Serv. 122 (9th Cir. 1984).

B. SSI STANDARD OF NEED

The Supplemental Security Income (SSI) program is designed to provide elderly, blind, and disabled people a certain minimum level of income. As discussed in Chapter 2, this policy is reflected in the financial requirements for eligibility; that is, the eligibility requirements apart from the personal requirements that claimants be disabled, blind, or elderly (65 or older). Unlike OASDI benefits, SSI benefits are not based on earnings records since SSI is not a contribution-based social insurance program. SSI benefits are available only to persons who are disabled, blind, or elderly and have limited resources and limited income. As a result, essentially the same income rules that are used to determine eligibility are used to calculate the amount of SSI benefit payments. When an SSI applicant has income that is—according to the applicable income rules—low enough to qualify the applicant for eligibility, then that income will be taken into consideration when calculating the amount of benefit payments. (The financial eligibility rules also take into account a claimant's resources. However, unlike the income rules, once a claimant meets the resource requirements for eligibility those rules have no effect on the amount of benefits paid—except to the extent that income produced from certain allowed resources can be considered income.)

SSI benefit calculations begin with a national standard of need, which is expressed in an initial monthly benefit rate that was set by Congress when the program was first enacted—plus various cost-of-living increases passed by Congress since then (including an automatic cost-of-living increase currently in place). When the program began on January 1, 1974, the basic Supplemental Security Income benefit amount for an individual was $157.70 per month; the monthly benefit for eligible couples (meaning couples where both are eligible for SSI) was $236.60. The 2012 benefit amount for individuals is $698 per month; the 2012 amount for an eligible couple is $1,048 per month. States may supplement the federal program with additional payments, at their option. *See* 20 C.F.R. §416.110(f) (requiring also that states supplement SSI benefits for persons who had received old age or disability benefits in 1973 under pre-SSI federal-state programs to insure that they receive at least as much as they did under the discontinued federal-state programs.).

A beneficiary with no other income will receive the full amount of the standard of need. For beneficiaries with other sources of income, the base amount is reduced dollar-for-dollar by any income received and not otherwise excluded as countable income under the regulations. The most common exclusion is the first $20 per month of other Social Security benefits. (The SSI income exclusion rules are discussed in more detail in Chapter 2, Section B.)

SSI benefits are paid from the first day of the month following the month in which the application was filed or eligibility was first established, whichever is later. 20 C.F.R. §416.501. When first found eligible for benefits, most claimants receive a "lump sum" payment of past-due benefits covering the period from the first month of eligibility to the month when the first regular payment is made. As part of 1996 amendments to the Social Security Act, past-due benefits for SSI recipients under the age of 18 must be placed in a dedicated account and spent only for limited purposes, if the amount is greater than six times the monthly amount. Expenses that may be paid with these funds include certain medical, personal, and educational needs of the child. *See* 20 C.F.R. §§ 416.546, 416.640(e).

1. CALCULATION OF THE SSI BENEFIT AMOUNT

The calculation of an SSI benefit involves two steps. First, the claimant's "countable income" is determined by applying various exemptions to any income that the claimant may have. As noted above, these exemptions are essentially the same ones used when counting an applicant's income for purposes of determining financial eligibility. *See* Chapter 2, Section B; 20 C.F.R §§ 416.420, 416.1104. Then, the claimant's countable income—if any—is subtracted from the basic SSI benefit rate to calculate the amount of the benefit payment. 20 C.F.R § 416.420. Thus, a monthly SSI benefit is calculated as follows:

1) The claimant's total income is calculated and then reduced by the amount of any of that income that SSA does not count, to arrive at the claimant's "countable income";

2) The SSI benefit rate is reduced by any countable income to determine the amount of the claimant's benefit payment.

Or, more simply, the calculation of a claimant's SSI benefit can be expressed in the following formula: SSI benefit = SSI benefit rate – (income – exclusions).

2. SSI BENEFIT CALCULATION PROCESS: EXAMPLES

NOTE: These examples use the 2012 SSI individual benefit amount of $698.

1. The claimant has no income. At Step 1, the "countable income" will be equal to $0; at Step 2, the SSI benefit rate will not be reduced, since the countable income is $0. Therefore, the claimant will receive the full benefit amount for an individual, or $698 ($698 – 0 = $698).

2. The claimant has a total monthly income consisting of $500 in Social Security disability benefits. (Note that the first $20 of other Social Security benefits is excluded.) At Step 1, the "countable income" will be $480 ($500 in Social Security benefits minus the $20 exclusion); at Step 2, the SSI benefit rate is reduced by $480 in countable income. Therefore, the claimant will receive SSI benefits in the amount of $218 ($698 - $480 = $194).

3. The claimant has a total monthly income consisting of wages of $775 from his job at the local factory, which is his only source of income. (Note that the first $65 of earned income is excluded, plus one-half of the remainder.) At Step 1, the "countable income" will be $355 ($775 in earned income minus $420 (the first $65 of $775 plus one-half of the remaining earned income of $710)); at Step 2, the SSI benefit rate is reduced by $355 in countable income. Therefore, the claimant will receive SSI benefits in the amount of $343 ($698 - $355 = $343).

C. MULTIPLE BENEFITS; FAMILY MAXIMUM

Persons eligible for OASDI or SSI often are eligible for other benefits under the Social Security Act or through other types of benefit programs. *See* **20 C.F.R. §** 404.407**[APP-REGS]**. To the extent that any such benefits are considered income by the applicable federal regulations, they will be counted as appropriate in determining the amount of benefits. There are, in addition, special income rules that apply to the treatment of certain types of other benefits.

One set of special rules applies where a claimant is eligible for benefits both on the basis of his or her own earnings and on the basis someone else's earnings, typically a spouse or parent. This occurs, for example, where someone is entitled to old age or disability benefits as an insured wage earner and also entitled to secondary benefits as a spouse or child.

In such cases, the secondary benefit is reduced by the amount of the primary benefit, but not below zero, so that the total amount of benefits will be the greater amount of the two. 20 C.F.R. § 404.407(a). Children eligible for benefits on more than one wage earner's account receive the benefits payable through the account with the largest Primary Insurance Amount. *See* 20 C.F.R. § 404.407(d). The rationale for these policies is that the social insurance goals of the Social Security program had already been achieved, at least to some extent, where a beneficiary is otherwise entitled to some form of benefits under the Social Security Act. The basic approach is to leave the beneficiary with at least the amount of the highest paying benefits to which he or she is entitled.

Certain non-Social Security benefits are covered by special rules that can affect the amount of OASDI benefits. Thus, a wage earner's Social Security benefits are reduced when the wage earner receives payments under a worker's compensation law, and that reduction is also passed on to children receiving benefits under the wage earner's account. Also, certain dependent benefits are reduced if the beneficiary is receiving a government pension not covered by the Social Security Act. *See* 20 C.F.R. §§404.408, 404.408a.

When multiple benefit eligibility includes SSI, the SSI benefit usually is reduced dollar-for-dollar to account for the other benefit payments because SSI benefits are based on need. However, as noted above, the first $20 per month of other Social Security benefits are not counted, resulting in a $20 net gain for SSI recipients receiving other Social Security benefits as well.

Finally, there are special rules where a number of persons are eligible for and receiving Social Security benefits based on a single wage earner's earnings record. As we saw in Chapter 3, a wage earner, his or her children, spouse (and possibly former spouse), and certain other dependents may all be receiving benefits on the basis of the wage earner's earnings record. Because the number of potential claimants on a single wage earner's earnings may be quite large, the Social Security Act sets a maximum amount of benefits payable in any month on any account. This amount, known as the "family maximum," is determined on the basis of the insured wage earner's Primary Insurance Amount (PIA).

There are a number of different ways to calculate the family maximum depending on the year that the wage earner died, turned 62, or became disabled—all of which set the amount somewhere between approximately 150 to approximately 175 percent of the wage earner's PIA. *See generally* **42 U.S.C.§** 403(a)[APP-STAT]; **20 C.F.R. §404.403[APP-REGS]**. The basic rule is to reduce proportionately all benefits other than those of the primary wage earner so that the total amount paid to all beneficiaries does not exceed the family maximum. **20 C.F.R. §404.404[APP-REGS]**. Thus, where the family maximum is set at 150 percent of the wage earner's PIA and assuming the wage earner is receiving 100 percent, his or her two children could receive a total of only 50 percent of the PIA, or 25 percent each. The rule is applied only relative to benefits actually paid on the basis of the wage earner's account; when a member of a wage earner's family is receiving benefits on another account, although eligible to receive benefits on the wage earner's account, the benefits received on the basis of the other account are not counted for purposes of the family maximum. Surviving divorced spouse's benefits are determined outside of the family maximum rule, presumably because these persons are considered outside of the wage earner's family. Thus, those benefits are calculated without regard to other benefits based on the insured deceased former spouse's account.

The following case discusses the manner in which SSA goes about reducing the amount of OASDI or SSI benefits when a recipient is also receiving other benefits simultaneously and the other benefit is paid in a lump sum. The case also provides valuable discussion of the rationale for allowing such reductions. The specific context, also relatively common, is where a recipient of OASDI disability benefits also receives state workers' compensation benefits. 42 U.S.C. § 424a(a)(2) provides that the combined amount of workers' compensation and disability benefits cannot exceed 80% of the recipient's average pre-disability earnings. In the event that the combined amount exceeds 80% of the recipient's average pre-disability earnings, SSA must reduce the amount of disability benefits so that the total amount of the two benefit payments will not exceed 80% of the beneficiary's pre-injury earnings, using one of three methods specified by Congress.

HARDEN V. U.S. DEPT. OF HEALTH AND HUMAN SERVICES
979 F.2d 1082 (5th Cir. 1992)

Before REYNALDO G. GARZA and GARWOOD, Circuit Judges, and WERLEIN, District Judge.

REYNALDO G. GARZA, Circuit Judge:

Appellant appeals the method used by the Secretary of the Department of Health and Human Services in calculating her Social Security Administration's ("SSA") disability benefits. Upon review we conclude the calculation was reasonable and we therefore affirm.

FACTS

Gloria Harden injured her back on September 29, 1983 while working for Levi Strauss & Co. in San Antonio, Texas. She applied for Social

Security benefits on April 30, 1984. The appellant also applied for and received state workers' compensation of $189 a week from October 3, 1983 through July 8, 1984 for a total of 40 weeks. Harden settled her workers' compensation claim for a lump sum of $20,000 on July 8, 1984. Appellant's request for disability benefits was originally denied but the district court reversed the SSA's rejection and ordered payment of benefits.

The Social Security Administration offset the amount of Harden's disability benefits by part of the workers' compensation lump sum settlement. * * *

The SSA took the amount received per week by Harden, $189, and divided it into the $20,000, giving her 105 weeks of reduction. They excluded Harden's legal fees from the reduction. The fees, $5006.84, were allocated over 105 weeks is $47.62, therefore $141.68, ($189 minus $47.62), was deducted from her benefits every week for a total of 105 weeks.

Harden appealed this calculation, arguing that the lump sum should have been prorated over the remaining 361 weeks allowed by Texas law for permanent disability benefits. The Administrative Law Judge ["ALJ"] affirmed the SSA's calculation. The Appeals Council declined to review Harden's case, thus making the ALJ's decision the Secretary's final determination. The district court granted the Secretary's motion for summary judgment.

ANALYSIS

The legislative intent of disability reduction is to prevent the receipt of duplicative benefits resulting in greater than pre-injury earnings. Congress instituted the offset because in a majority of states the combined benefits surpassed pre-injury earnings. "This was thought to cause two evils: first, it reduced a worker's incentive to return to the workplace and hence impeded rehabilitative efforts; and second, it created fears that the duplication of benefits would lead to an erosion of state workers' compensation programs." *Freeman v. Harris,* 625 F.2d 1303, 1306 (5th Cir.1980) (citing *Hearings on H.R. 6675 Before the Senate Comm. on Finance,* 89th Cong., 1st Sess. 151, 252, 259, 366, 540, 738-40, 892-97, 949, 990 (1965)). U.S.C. § 424a(b) states that if a benefit is paid in a lump sum and the Secretary deems that it is a commutation of, or a substitute for, periodic payments, then he shall prorate it to approximate the reduction prescribed by § 424a(a)(2). Statute § 424a(b) reads:

> If any periodic benefit for a total or partial disability under a law or plan described in subsection (a)(2) of this section is payable on other than a monthly basis (excluding a benefit payable as a lump sum except to the extent that it is a commutation of, or a substitute for, pe-

riodic payments), the reduction under this section shall be made at such time or times and in such amounts as the Secretary finds will approximate as nearly as practicable the reduction prescribed by subsection (a) of this section. *Id.*

The Secretary interpreted the lump sum payment made pursuant to a compromise and release settlement a "lump-sum as a commutation of or a substitute for periodic benefits...." 20 C.F.R. § 404.408(g) (1991). The Secretary's Program Operation Manual (POMS) establishes the Secretary's method for proration of lump-sum awards. POMS provides that:

The priority for establishing weekly rates is as follows:

1. The rate specified in the lump sum award. If the award specifies a rate based on life expectancy list the case under code 557.

2. The periodic rate paid prior to the lump sum (if no rate is specified in the lump-sum award).

3. If WC [workers' compensation], the State's WC maximum in effect in the year of injury. This figure can be used if no rate is specified in the award if there was no preceding periodic benefit. It can also be used pending postadjudicative development of the rates specified in 1 or 2 above.

POMS, DI 11501.235C.

The Secretary correctly chose option 2 since the settlement failed to name a rate for option 1 to apply. The previous monthly rate of $189 selected by the Secretary was reasonable. The Secretary has clearly fulfilled Congress's intent in limiting combined benefits to 80% of pre-injury earnings. The statute is silent as to which rate the Secretary must employ when it has not been specified in the compromise. This gap is left to the discretion of the agency to fill via Congresses' express delegation of authority expressed in § 424a. The "court may not substitute its own construction of a statutory provision for a reasonable interpretation made by the administrator of an agency." *Chevron U.S.A. v. Natural Res. Def. Council,* 467 U.S. 837, 844, 104 S.Ct. 2778, 2782, 81 L.Ed.2d 694 (1984). We may only review whether the Secretary applied proper legal standards and conducted the proceedings in accord with statutes and regulations. This court finds that the Secretary has done both.

* * *

D. OVERPAYMENTS AND UNDERPAYMENTS

Federal regulations provide for the adjustment of OASDI and SSI benefit payments if a recipient receives more or less than the amount due under applicable law. *See generally* **20 C.F.R. §§ 404.502[APP-REGS]**, **404.503[APP-REGS]**. When a recipient receives more than the correct amount due for any given period it is called an overpayment; when less than the correct amount of benefits is received, including when no payment is made at all, it is called an underpayment.

In the absence of a waiver (discussed below), SSA can recover overpayments by withholding all or part of a recipient's monthly or past-due benefits. *See generally* **20 C.F.R. §§404.535[APP-REGS]**, 416.573. SSA can collect the entire amount of past-due benefit payments, 20 C.F.R. §§404.535(a), 416.573(a), and up to 10 percent from monthly benefits. 20 C.F.R. §§404.535(b)(1), 416.573(b)(1). The entire amount of current benefit payments may be withheld if the recipient "willfully misrepresented or concealed material information" concerning the overpayment. 20 C.F.R. §§404.535(b)(2)(ii), 416.573(b)(2)(ii). As for repaying an underpayment, if the recipient is still living SSA will pay the amount due either through a separate lump sum payment or by increasing the recipient's monthly payment. 20 C.F.R. §§404.503(a), 416.542(a). If an underpaid OASDI recipient is dead, SSA will make payments to his or her dependents. 42 U.S.C.A. §404(d); 20 C.F.R. §404.503(b)-(e). If an SSI recipient is dead, the underpaid amount will be paid to the surviving spouse, but only if he or she was living with the underpaid recipient and eligible for SSI. 20 C.F.R. §416.542(b).

1. WAIVER OF OVERPAYMENT RECOVERY AND RIGHT TO APPEAL

An overpayment of an OASDI benefit can be waived if the recipient was "without fault" in obtaining the overpayment and if recovery would either defeat the purpose of the Social Security Act or be "against equity and good conscience." **42 U.S.C. §§ 404(b)[APP-STAT], 20 C.F.R. §§ 404.506[APP-REGS]**. Waiver of an SSI overpayment is also available if the recipient was without fault and recovery would impede the efficient or effective administration of the program because of the small amount involved. **42 U.S.C. § 1383(b)(1)(B)[APP-STAT]; 20 C.F.R. §416.550 [APP-REGS]**. SSA is required to send notice to an overpaid recipient and to anyone else from whom it intends to recover benefits or whose benefits it intends to adjust. That notice must inform them of their right to request a waiver of the recovery or adjustment. 20 C.F.R. §§ 404.502a, 416.558(a).

The Social Act does not require that SSA hold a hearing to determine whether an overpayment has occurred or if a recipient is entitled to a waiver of recovery. However, in Califano v. Yamsaki, 442 U.S. 682 (1979), the Supreme Court held that the "without fault" and other limitations on the ability of SSA to recover of overpayments contained in the

Act give benefit recipients the right to an oral hearing on overpayment findings and denials of waiver requests. The next case discusses the standard for waiver of overpayments, as well as the recipient's burden of proof. It is followed by the Supreme Court's decision in *Yamasaki*.

COULSTON V. APFEL

224 F.3d 897 (8th Cir. 2000)

Before WOLLMAN, Chief Judge, BEAM, and BYE, Circuit Judges.

PER CURIAM.

Occasionally, the Social Security Administration (the Administration) sends a benefit check to the wrong person. When this occurs, the Administration is entitled to recover the money unless the recipient of the check was without fault and recovery would subvert the purpose of social security or be against equity and good conscience.

In this case, the Administration erroneously sent a $20,658 check to Jim Coulston, a man who receives benefits because of an intellectual impairment. Coulston, who has trouble reading, thought the check was a back payment for medical expenses because he canceled his Medicare, so he cashed the check and used most of the money to pay bills and purchase Christmas presents. We must now decide whether the Administration may recoup its money. We find it may not.

Coulston returned the unspent money to the Administration, but he did not have the resources to immediately repay the money already spent. The Administration threatened to withhold any further benefit checks from Coulston until it reclaimed the remainder ($18,249) of the money. Coulston then sought a waiver from repayment to the Administration, asserting he was without fault and that recovery would subvert the purpose of social security or be against equity and good conscience. He received a hearing before an Administrative Law Judge (ALJ), who found Coulston undeserving of a waiver. Coulston then brought his case to federal district court, which upheld the ALJ's determination. So, to decide this case, we must review the ALJ opinion and the record evidence.

After receiving the check, Coulston got, in the ALJ's words, "advice from and was assisted by" his ex-wife and a friend. Basically, this assistance was in cashing and spending the check. In determining whether Coulston was without fault, the ALJ relied substantially on the role Coulston's ex-wife and friend played. The ALJ noted that, while Coulston had an intellectual impairment, there was no evidence that either his ex-wife or friend suffered from a similar disability. This led the ALJ to conclude that, before cashing and spending the check, "at least one of the three individuals involved" should have made further inquiries with the Administration. The ALJ also noted that, in deciding the case, he considered that neither Coulston's ex-wife nor friend testified at the hearing to explain why they did not question Coulston's receipt of the check. Also important to the ALJ's conclusion was the ability of Coulston's ex-wife and friend to manage their own finances and dispense advice.

The thrust of much of the ALJ's opinion is that Coulston's ex-wife and friend knew or should have suspected what was going on. This may well be true, but it is irrelevant. The Administration's regulations state that a claimant is at fault if he knew or should have known the overpayment was incorrect. *See* 20 C.F.R. § 404.507. The Administration's regulations also state that the determination of fault is only made as to the overpaid individual or any other person from whom the Administration seeks to recover. *See id.* What that means in this case is that the ALJ should have considered what Coulston himself knew or should have known. Instead, the ALJ relied substantially on what Coulston's ex-wife and friend should have known; and while Coulston's ex-wife and friend very well may have known (or should have known) what was going on, it was erroneous to impute their actions and abilities to Coulston.

We also think the ALJ did not properly account for the intellectual impairments of Coulston. When determining whether an overpaid individual is without fault, the ALJ is required by statute to "specifically take into account" the individual's mental or educational limitations. *See* 42 U.S.C. § 404(b). To be fair, the ALJ noted most of Coulston's intellectual and educational limitations, including: his difficulty with reading and writing; his attendance of special education classes at school; and his eight months of training with Goodwill Industries to learn the skill of dishwashing. But, the ALJ then basically ignored how these limitations would have affected Coulston's ability to know the check was erroneous. Instead, as related above, the ALJ relied substantially on the lack of intellectual limitations of Coulston's "advisors"—his ex-wife and friend.

The ALJ also placed significant emphasis on the events surrounding Coulston's attempts to cash the check. The ALJ found Coulston was unable to cash the check at the first bank he tried—the obvious inference being that the bank refused to cash the check because of its substantial amount. This, according to the ALJ, should have been a tip-off to Coulston and to his friend that a problem existed with the check. But, the record reveals the bank refused to cash the check because of a problem with Coulston's identification, not because of the large amount of the check. And, again, while his friend may have known the real situation, Coulston's intellectual limitations may well have prevented him from ascertaining the real situation.

The parties in this case make much of Coulston's supposed interaction or supposed non-interaction with the Administration in the month following his receipt of the erroneous check. After Coulston received the check, he received a notice from the Administration informing him he was entitled to the check and to a substantial increase in his monthly benefits. The Administration claims Coulston only received this notice after he became aware the check was an error. Coulston also claims he and his ex-wife made several phone calls to the Administration, and Administration employees said he was entitled to the $20,658. The Administration claims that, in every phone call, they informed Coulston he was not entitled to the money. But, the ALJ declined to credit either version of events, and so do we. The evidence on this issue is inconclusive, and, as an appellate court, we should not engage in fact-finding on this issue.

The Administration also calls to our attention Coulston's "history" of overpayments. Apparently, in the early 1980s, Coulston was overpaid by about $4,000. But, the ALJ made no mention of this history in his opinion, and we do not put much stock in it either, as we doubt most people, even those without an intellectual impairment, would remember an overpayment incident that occurred almost fifteen years earlier.

So, after a careful review of the record, the following evidence remains: Coulston has an intellectual impairment substantial enough to entitle him to social security benefits for the last twenty-plus years; he received a check with an overpayment; he believed the overpayment was for back medical payments because he had canceled his Medicare policy; he spent much of the check to pay off bills and buy Christmas presents until informed the check was a mistake; and he then paid back the remaining money. Is this enough for Coulston to meet his burden of proving he is without fault?

We think Coulston meets his burden; but barely. Generally, if the evidence is in equipoise, the party with the burden of proof loses. The evidence here is so close that it is almost in equipoise. But, Coulston testified he thought the overpayment was for back medical payments. The ALJ had the opportunity to discredit this testimony, and did not. So, Coulston's subjective thinking, coupled with the objective evidence of his intellectual impairment, leads us to conclude he has met his burden of proving he was without fault.

Our finding that Coulston was without fault does not automatically result in a victory for him. We must also determine whether repayment would defeat the purpose of providing social security to Coulston or would be against equity or good conscience.

Coulston is far from well-off. Coulston works on-and-off as a part-time dishwasher, and he receives about $650 a month in social security benefits. Thus, his annual income skirts the poverty line. See United States Census Bureau (visited Aug. 14, 2000) www.census.gov/hhes/poverty/threshld/thresh99.html (1999 poverty threshold is $8,667). Coulston also has no savings account, so he obviously lives from check to check. In light of these circumstances, we credit Coulston's statement at the hearing that he "has a hard time making ends meet," and, because of this, we think taking even a small amount of benefits away from Coulston would defeat the purpose of social security.

For the foregoing reasons, we reverse and remand to the district court with directions to enter judgment in favor of Coulston.

BYE, Circuit Judge, concurring.

[Judge Bye first pointed out that while the majority found that Coulston met his burden of proof on the question of fault, the proper standard of review is "substantial evidence." On that issue, he concluded "that the ALJ's decision is not supported by 'substantial evidence,' for the simple reason that the Commissioner introduced no evidence to controvert Coulston's account of events."]

II

The majority properly proceeds to examine the second step of the overpayment analysis, whether Coulston's repayment "would defeat the purpose of [Title II] or would be against equity and good conscience." 42 U.S.C. § 404(b). The majority compares Coulston's monthly income with the poverty line and determines that Coulston could not afford to repay the SSA. Yet the record suggests the possibility of a different answer. Coulston receives about $650 a month in SSA benefits, and he earns about $500 per month as a part-time dishwasher. Adding those sums together, his total monthly income exceeds $1100. Given Coulston's remarkably low estimate of his monthly expenses, he appears to have at least $500 per month in disposable income. Presumably, some portion of that income could be used to repay the SSA without defeating the purpose of social security.

These calculations are, of course, my own findings of fact. The majority's conclusion that Coulston cannot repay the SSA is equally dependent on implicit fact-finding. Our disagreement illustrates why circuit judges are properly loathe to find the facts on appeal. Faced with a fact-dependent impasse, the majority ought to remand to permit the ALJ to make "ability to repay" findings.[2]

---

[2] The ALJ never calculated Coulston's ability to repay (the second step) since he found Coulston "at fault" (the first step).

Despite the presence of this potential factual dispute, however, we need not remand. A claimant's reliance on agency representations *automatically* establishes that repayment would offend equity and good conscience. *See* Gladden [v. Callahan, 139 F.3d 1219, 1223 (8th Cir.1998)]. Much like the claimant in *Gladden*, Coulston relied upon a host of SSA representations in assuming that the lump-sum check belonged to him. I am hard-pressed to overlook *Gladden*'s clear language in favor of the majority's own calculation of Coulston's ability to repay. I deem *Gladden* controlling, and I would avoid analyzing Coulston's financial picture entirely. The majority's methodology leads ineluctably to the conclusion that this matter ought to be remanded—a conclusion in considerable tension with *Gladden*.

I respectfully concur in the judgment of the court.

CALIFANO V. YAMASAKI
442 U.S. 682 (1979)

Mr. Justice BLACKMUN delivered the opinion of the Court.

Petitioner, the Secretary of the Department of Health, Education, and Welfare (HEW), has determined that respondents, beneficiaries under the Social Security Act, have been overpaid. He seeks to recoup those overpayments by withholding future benefits to which respondents would otherwise be entitled. Respondents in turn have requested reconsideration or waiver of recoupment under § 204 of the Act, 42 U.S.C. § 404. The primary questions in this case are whether petitioner must grant respondents the opportunity for an oral hearing before recoupment begins, and whether jurisdiction under § 205(g) of the Act, 42 U.S.C. § 405(g), permits a federal district court to certify a nationwide class and grant injunctive relief.

I

Section 204(a)(1) of the Social Security Act, 53 Stat. 1368, as amended, 42 U.S.C. § 404(a)(1), authorizes the recovery of overpayments made to a beneficiary under the old-age, survivors', or disability insurance programs administered by HEW. In particular, it permits the Secretary to recoup erroneous overpayments by decreasing future payments to which the overpaid person is entitled.

Section 204(b), however, expressly limits the recoupment authority conferred by § 204(a)(1). Section 204(b), as set forth in 42 U.S.C. § 404(b), commands that

"there shall be no adjustment of payments to, or recovery by the United States from, any person who is without fault if such adjustment or recovery would defeat the purpose of this subchapter or would be against equity and good conscience."

The Secretary has undertaken to define the terms employed in § 204(b). Under his regulations, "without fault" means that the recipient neither knew nor should have known that the overpayment or the information on which it was based was incorrect. 20 C.F.R. § 404.507 (1978). For example, a recipient who justifiably relied upon erroneous information from an official source within the Social Security Administration would be "without fault." § 404.510.

The regulations say that to "defeat the purpose of the subchapter" is to "deprive a person of income required for ordinary and necessary living expenses." § 404.508(a). Those expenses are defined to include, among other things, food, rent, and medical bills. §§ 404.508(a)(1) and (2). Recoupment is "against equity and good conscience" when the recipient "because of a notice that such payment would be made or by reason of the incorrect payment, relinquished a valuable right . . . or changed his position for the worse." § 404.509. An example of detrimental reliance that would be sufficient is permitting private hospital insurance to lapse in the mistaken expectation of receiving federal hospital benefits. *Ibid.*

The Secretary's practice is to make an *ex parte* determination under § 204(a) that an overpayment has been made, to notify the recipient of that determination, and then to shift to the recipient the burden of either (i) seeking reconsideration to contest the accuracy of that determination, or (ii) asking the Secretary to forgive the debt and waive recovery in accordance with § 204(b). If a recipient files a written request for reconsideration or waiver, recoupment is deferred pending action on that request. The papers are sent to one of the seven regional offices where the request is reviewed.

If the regional office decision goes against the recipient, recoupment begins. The recipient's monthly benefits are reduced or terminated until the overpayment has been recouped. Only if the recipient continues to object is he given an opportunity to present his story in person to someone with authority to decide his case. That opportunity takes the form of an on-the-record *de novo* evidential hearing before an independent hearing examiner. The recipient may seek subsequent review by the Appeals Council and finally by a federal court. If it is decided that the Secretary's initial determination was in error, the amounts wrongfully recouped are repaid.

* * *

III

A court presented with both statutory and constitutional grounds to support the relief requested usually should pass on the statutory claim before considering the constitutional question. Due respect for the coordinate branches of government, as well as a reluctance when conscious of fallibility to speak with our utmost finality, counsels against unnecessary constitutional adjudication. And if "a construction of the statute is fairly possible by which [a serious doubt of constitutionality] may be avoided," *Crowell v. Benson*, 285 U.S. 22, 62, 52 S.Ct. 285, 296, 76 L.Ed. 598 (1932), a court should adopt that construction. In particular, this Court has been willing to assume a congressional solicitude for fair procedure, absent explicit statutory language to the contrary.

* * * We turn to the statute first, and find that it fairly may be read to require a prerecoupment decision by the Secretary. With respect to § 204(a) reconsideration as to whether overpayment occurred, we agree that the statute does not require that the decision involve a prior oral hearing, and we reject respondents' contention that the Constitution does so. With respect to § 204(b) waiver of the Secretary's right to recoup, however, because the nature of the statutory standards makes a hearing essential, we find it unnecessary to determine whether the Constitution would require a similar result.

A

On its face, § 204 requires that the Secretary make a pre-recoupment waiver decision, and that the decision, like that concerning the fact of the overpayment, be accurate. In the imperative voice, it says "there shall be no adjustment of payments to, or recovery by the United States from, any person" who qualifies for waiver. Echoing this requirement, § 204(a) says that only "proper" adjustments or recoveries are to be made. The implication is that a recoupment from a person qualifying under § 204(b) would not be "proper."

Insofar as § 204 is read to require a prerecoupment decision, the reading is in accord with the manner in which the Secretary presently administers the statute. No recoupment is made until a preliminary waiver or reconsideration decision has taken place, either by default after the recipient has received proper notice, or by review of a written request. * * *

B

The heart of the present dispute concerns not whether a prerecoupment decision should be made, but whether making the decision by regional office review of the written waiver request is sufficient to protect the recipient's right not to be subjected to an improper recoupment.

In this regard, requests for reconsideration under § 204(a), as to whether overpayment occurred, may be distinguished from requests for waiver of the Secretary's right to recoup under § 204(b). As the Court of Appeals in this case and in *Mattern* [*v. Mathews*, 582 F.2d 248, 255-256 (CA3 1978)] noted, requests under § 204(a) for reconsideration involve relatively straightforward matters of computation for which written review is ordinarily an adequate means to correct prior mistakes. Many of the named respondents were found to have been overpaid based on earnings reports they themselves had submitted. But unlike the Court of Appeals in this case, we do not think that the rare instance in which a credibility dispute is relevant to a § 204(a) claim is sufficient to require the Secretary to sift through all requests for reconsideration and grant a hearing to the few that involve credibility. The statute authorizes only "proper" recoupment, but some leeway for practical administration must be allowed. Nor do the standards of the Due Process Clause, more tolerant than the strict language here in issue, require that prerecoupment oral hearings be afforded in § 204(a) cases. The nature of a due process hearing is shaped by the "risk of error inherent in the truthfinding process as applied to the generality of cases, not the rare exceptions." *Mathews v. Eldridge*, 424 U.S. [319, 344 (1970).] It would be inconsistent with that principle to require a hearing under § 204(a) when review of a beneficiary's written submission is an adequate means of resolving all but a few § 204(a) disputes.

By contrast, written review hardly seems sufficient to discharge the Secretary's statutory duty to make an accurate determination of waiver under § 204(b). Under that subsection, the Secretary must assess the absence of "fault" and determine whether or not recoupment would be "against equity and good conscience." These standards do not apply under § 204(a). The Court previously has noted that a "broad 'fault' standard is inherently subject to factual determination and adversarial input." *Mitchell v. W. T. Grant Co.*, 416 U.S. 600, 617, 94 S.Ct. 1895, 1905, 40 L.Ed.2d 406 (1974). As the Secretary's regulations make clear, "fault" depends on an evaluation of "all pertinent circumstances" including the recipient's "intelligence . . . and physical and mental condition" as well as his good faith. 20 C.F.R. § 404.507 (1978). We do not see how these can be evaluated absent personal contact between the recipient and the person who decides his case. Evaluating fault, like judging detrimental reliance, usually requires an assessment of the recipient's credibility, and written submissions are a particularly inappropriate way to distinguish a genuine hard luck story from a fabricated tall tale.

The consequences of the injunctions entered by the District Courts confirm the reasonableness of interpreting § 204(b) to require a prerecoupment oral hearing. In compliance with those orders, the Secretary, beginning with calendar year 1977, has granted what respondents term "a short personal conference with an impartial employee of the Social Security Administration at which time the recipient presents testimony and evidence and cross-examines witnesses, and the administrative employee questions the recipient." Of the approximately 2,000 conferences held between January 1977 and October 1978, 30% resulted in a reversal of the Secretary's decision. This rate of reversal confirms the view that, without an oral hearing, the Secretary may misjudge a number of cases that he otherwise would be able to assess properly, and that the hearing requirement imposed by the Court of Appeals significantly furthers the statutory goal that "there shall be no" recoupment when waiver is appropriate. We therefore agree with the Court of Appeals that an opportunity for a pre-recoupment oral hearing is required when a recipient requests waiver under § 204(b).

* * *

[On the procedural and jurisdictional issues, the Court concluded that class certification was permissible under § 205(g) of the Act (42 U.S.C. § 405(g)), that the lower court did not abuse its discretion in certifying a nationwide class, and that § 205(g) permits an award of injunctive relief.]

2. "NETTING" OVERPAYMENTS AND UNDERPAYMENTS

Situations arise, not infrequently, where a beneficiary has been both overpaid and underpaid before neither the overpayment nor the underpayment has been accounted for, raising the question whether SSA can adjust future benefit payments resolve the underpayment and the overpayment at the same time. To do so, SSA has developed a system whereby it "nets" the overpayment and underpayment amounts—essentially by calculating the difference between an underpayment and an overpayment and treating the netted amount either as an adjusted overpayment or an adjusted underpayment, as the case may be. *See* 20 C.F.R. §§ 404.504[APP-REGS], 416.538(a)[APP-REGS]. In the face of a challenge to this practice by a group of benefit recipients, the Supreme Court upheld the "netting" system in the following case.

SULLIVAN V. EVERHART

494 U.S. 83 (1990)

Justice SCALIA delivered the opinion of the Court.

If the Secretary of Health and Human Services determines that a beneficiary has received "more or less than the correct amount of payment," the Social Security Act requires him to effect "proper adjustment or recovery," subject to certain restrictions in the case of overpayments. This case requires us to decide whether the Secretary's so-called "netting" regulations, under which he calculates the difference between past underpayments and past overpayments, are merely a permissible method of determining whether "more or less than the correct amount of payment" was made, or are instead, as to netted-out overpayments, an "adjustment or recovery" that must comply with procedures for recovery of overpayments imposed by the Act.

I

Two statutory benefit programs established by the Social Security Act (Act) are involved: the Old-Age, Survivors, and Disability Insurance program (OASDI) and the Supplemental Security Income program (SSI). Millions of Americans receive benefits under these programs; inevitably, some beneficiaries occasionally receive more than their entitlement, and others less. The OASDI program provides the following procedure for correcting such errors:

"Whenever the Secretary finds that more or less than the correct amount of payment has been made to any person under this subchapter, proper adjustment or recovery shall be made, under regulations prescribed by the Secretary, as follows:

"(A) With respect to payment to a person of more than the correct amount, the Secretary shall decrease any payment under this subchapter to which such overpaid person is entitled, or shall require such overpaid person or his estate to refund the amount in excess of the correct amount, or shall decrease any payment under this subchapter payable to his estate or to any other person on the basis of the wages and self-employment income which were the basis of the payments to such overpaid person, or shall apply any combination of the foregoing....

"(B) With respect to payment to a person of less than the correct amount, the Secretary shall make payment of the balance of the amount due such underpaid person...." Act §§ 204(a)(1)(A), (B); 42 U.S.C. §§ 404(a)(1)(A), (B) (1982 ed., Supp. V).

As to overpayments, the Act provides:

"In any case in which more than the correct amount of payment has been made, there shall be no adjustment of payments to, or recovery by the United States from, any person who is without fault if such adjustment or recovery would defeat the purpose of this subchapter or would be against equity and good conscience." Act § 204(b); 42 U.S.C. § 404(b) (1982 ed.).

The provisions regulating payment errors in the SSI program are substantially similar. *Califano v. Yamasaki,* 442 U.S. 682, 697, 99 S.Ct. 2545, 2555, 61 L.Ed.2d 176 (1979), held that the limitation on adjustment or recovery of overpayments imposed by § 204(b) of the Act gives recipients the right to an oral hearing at which they may attempt to convince the Secretary to waive recoupment.

In the provisions set forth above, the Act contemplates that the Secretary will "fin[d] [whether] more or less than the correct amount" of payment has been made. Elsewhere, it confers upon the Secretary general authority to "make rules and regulations and to establish procedures, not inconsistent with the provisions of this subchapter, which are necessary or appropriate to carry out such provisions," Act § 205(a), 42 U.S.C. § 405(a) (1982 ed.); see also Act § 1631(d)(1), 42 U.S.C. § 1383(d)(1) (1982 ed., Supp. V) (SSI). Pursuant to that authority, the Secretary promulgated the regulations at issue here. The SSI regulation provides:

"The amount of an underpayment or overpayment is the difference between the amount paid to a recipient and the amount of payment actually due such recipient for a given period. An overpayment or underpayment period begins with the first month for which there is a difference between the amount paid and the amount actually due for that month. The period ends with the month the initial determination of overpayment or underpayment is made." 20 C.F.R. § 416.538 (1989).

The OASDI regulation unhelpfully provides that "[t]he amount of an overpayment or underpayment is the difference between the amount paid to the beneficiary and the amount of the payment to which the beneficiary was actually entitled," 20 C.F.R. § 404.504 (1989), but the Secretary has interpreted this as embodying the methodology set forth in the SSI regulation. Dept. of Health and Human Services, Social Security Ruling 81-19a (cum. ed. 1981).

Two hypotheticals will illustrate the operation of the netting regulations. Mr. A, entitled to $100 per month, is erroneously paid $80 in January and erroneously paid $150 in February. In March, the Secretary determines that these payments were incorrect, nets the errors (*i.e.,* calculates the difference between the underpayment and the overpayment), and seeks to recover the net overpayment of $30. Mrs. B, also entitled to $100 per month, receives $50 in April and $110 in May. In June, the Secretary makes the incorrect payment determination, nets the errors, and pays out $40. In neither case may the beneficiary seek to have the underpayment and the overpayment treated separately: Mr. A could not demand $20 for January and seek a waiver of the recoupment of $50 for February, and Mrs. B could not demand $50 for April and seek a waiver for the $10 in May.

In the present case, the Secretary made both underpayments and overpayments to each of the respondents, and netted those errors pursuant to the regulations. He determined that three respondents (the original plaintiffs) received net underpayments, and paid that net amount. The other respondents (intervenors below) received net overpayments, and the Secretary offered them hearings to determine whether recoupment should be waived as to the net overpayment. The plaintiffs (later joined by the intervenors) filed this suit under §§ 205(g) and 1631(c)(3) of the Act, 42 U.S.C. §§ 405(g), 1383(c)(3) (1982 ed.), in the United States District Court for the District of Colorado. They claimed that the netting regulations were facially invalid because (1) they were contrary to the Act and (2) they violated beneficiaries' rights to procedural due process. The District Court granted respondents' motion for summary judgment on the former ground, and the Court of Appeals for the Tenth Circuit affirmed in all relevant respects. * * *

* * *

II

Our mode of reviewing challenges to an agency's interpretation of its governing statute is well established: We first ask "whether Congress has directly spoken to the precise question at issue. If the intent of Congress is clear, that is the end of the matter; for the court, as well as the agency, must give effect to the unambiguously expressed intent of Congress." *Chevron U.S.A. Inc. v. Natural Resources Defense Council, Inc.,* 467 U.S. 837, 842-843, 104 S.Ct. 2778, 2781, 81 L.Ed.2d 694 (1984). "In ascertaining the plain meaning of the statute, the court must look to the particular statutory language at issue, as well as the language and design of the statute as a whole." *K mart Corp. v. Cartier, Inc.,* 486 U.S. 281, 291, 108 S.Ct. 1811, 1817, 100 L.Ed.2d 313 (1988). But "if the statute is silent or ambiguous with respect to the specific issue, the question for the court is whether the agency's answer is based on a permissible construction of the statute," *Chevron, supra,* 467 U.S. at 843, 104 S.Ct., at 2781, that is, whether the agency's construction is "rational and consistent with the statute," *NLRB v. Food and Commercial Workers,* 484 U.S. 112, 123, 108

S.Ct. 413, 420, 98 L.Ed.2d 429 (1987). These principles apply fully to the Secretary's administration of the Act. See *Schweiker v. Gray Panthers,* 453 U.S. 34, 43, 101 S.Ct. 2633, 2639, 69 L.Ed.2d 460 (1981); *Batterton v. Francis,* 432 U.S. 416, 425, 97 S.Ct. 2399, 2405, 53 L.Ed.2d 448 (1977).

A

We first consider whether the Act speaks directly to the validity of the netting regulations. Two provisions are relevant: a general authorization and a specific limitation. First, the Act authorizes the Secretary to determine whether "more or less than the correct amount" has been paid. 42 U.S.C. §§ 404(a)(1), 1383(b)(1)(A) (1982 ed., Supp. V). The Act does not define the term "correct amount." It assuredly *could* be construed to refer to the amount properly owing *for a given month.* If that were the only possible interpretation, respondents would prevail, since the netting regulations ascertain the correct amount for a longer time period. But the Act does not foreclose a more expansive interpretation of "correct amount," viz., the amount properly owing *as of the date of the determination.* Although the Act elsewhere describes OASDI and SSI as monthly benefit programs, it nowhere specifies that the correctness of payments must be determined on a month-by-month basis.

The fuller context of the OASDI provisions suggests that Congress, in authorizing the Secretary to determine whether the "correct amount" was paid, did not prohibit him from making that determination for more than a monthly time period. The Act authorizes a determination of whether "the correct amount of *payment* has been made," 42 U.S.C. § 404(a)(1) (1982 ed., Supp. V), and mandates adjustments "[w]ith respect to *payment* to a person of more than the correct amount," § 404(a)(1)(A), and "[w]ith respect to *payment* to a person of less than the correct amount," § 404(a)(1)(B). If Congress had in mind only shortfalls or excesses in individual monthly payments, rather than in the overall payment balance, it would have been more natural to refer to "the correct amount of *any payment,*" and to require adjustment "with respect to *any payment* ... of less [or more] than the correct amount." This terminology is used elsewhere in § 204(a)(1)(A), whenever individual monthly payments are at issue ("the Secretary shall decrease *any payment* under this subchapter to which such overpaid person is entitled"; "shall decrease *any payment* under this subchapter payable to his estate"). 42 U.S.C. § 404(a)(1)(A) (1982 ed., Supp. V) (emphases added). Moreover, the provision governing adjustment of overpayments to a deceased beneficiary seems to contemplate computation on a multipayment basis ("[T]he Secretary ... shall decrease any payment under this subchapter payable to his estate or to any other person on the basis of the wages and self-employment income which were the basis *of the payments to such overpaid person* ") *Ibid.* (emphasis added).

The Act's provisions governing SSI are slightly different, but in no way contradict the Secretary's position. They authorize the Secretary to determine whether "more or less than the correct amount of *benefits* has been paid," 42 U.S.C. § 1383(b)(1)(A) (1982 ed., Supp. V) (emphasis added). Had this read "more or less than the correct amount of *any benefit*" it might support respondents' position, but as written it at least bears (if it does not indeed favor) the interpretation that more than a single monthly benefit is at issue.

Respondents nevertheless maintain, as did the Court of Appeals, that another provision of the Act directly precludes the Secretary from netting underpayments and overpayments. They point to § 204(b), 42 U.S.C. § 404(b) (1982 ed.), which provides: "In any case in which more than the correct amount of payment has been made, there shall be no adjustment of payments to, or recovery by the United States from, any person who is without fault if such adjustment or recovery would defeat the purpose of this subchapter or would be against equity and good conscience." See also Act § 1631(b)(1)(B), 42 U.S.C. § 1383(b)(1)(B) (1982 ed., Supp. V) (SSI). Respondents argue that by using the phrase "adjustment or recovery," Congress intended to subject to this requirement all collection methods, including the setoff effected by netting. They claim this broad meaning is given to the words "adjustment" and "recovery" by other Social Security regulations, common usage, and general legal usage. Under this interpretation, when the agency calculates the difference between, or nets, Mr. A's $20 underpayment and his $50 overpayment, see *supra,* at 963, it has engaged in "adjustment or recovery," but without complying with the restrictions on "adjustment or recovery" that the Act imposes.

In our view, however, with this provision as with those discussed earlier, respondents have established at most that the language may bear the interpretation they desire-not that it cannot bear the interpretation adopted by the Secretary. "Adjustment" *can* have the more limited meaning (which the Secretary favors) of "an increase or decrease" of payments (Webster's [Third New International Dictionary at] 27), and "recovery" *can* have the more limited meaning of "get[ting] back" payments already made (see *id.,* at 1898 ("recover")). Moreover, other provisions of the Act support this limited meaning. It is at least reasonable, if not necessary, to read the phrase "adjustment or recovery" in § 204(b) *in pari materia* with the identical phrase in § 204(a)(1). The latter section directs the Secretary, if he finds that incorrect payment has been made, to make "proper adjustment or recovery ... *as follows.*" In the case of overpayment, he shall "decrease any payment under this subchapter to which such overpaid person is entitled, or shall require such overpaid person or his estate to refund the amount in excess of the correct amount...." 42 U.S.C. § 404(a)(1)(A) (1982 ed., Supp. V). As to SSI, "adjustment or recovery shall ... be made by appropriate adjustments in future payments to such individual or by recovery from ... or by payment to such individual or his eligible spouse...." 42 U.S.C. § 1383(b)(1)(A) (1982 ed., Supp. V). Giving the terms their more limited meaning does not produce absurd policy consequences. Reducing future benefits, or requiring the beneficiary to pay over cash, will ordinarily produce more hardship than merely setting off past underpayments and overpayments. It is not at all unreasonable to think that waiver hearings were established only for the former.

As used in the Act, therefore, adjustment can be read to mean decreasing future payments, and recovery to mean obtaining a refund from the beneficiary. Under this interpretation, when the agency nets Mr. A's underpayment against his overpayment, it is not engaged in "adjustment or recovery," but only in the calculation of whether "more or less than the correct amount of payment has been made." Only *after* making that calculation does the Secretary take the additional step of rectifying any error by "adjustment" (increasing or decreasing future payments) or "recovery" (obtaining a refund from the beneficiary). And it is only this latter step that is governed by § 204(b) of the Act. We do not say this is an inevitable interpretation of the statute; but it is assuredly a permissible one.

B

Since the Act reasonably bears the Secretary's interpretation that netting is permitted, only one issue remains: Respondents contend that the manner in which the regulations provide for netting to be conducted is arbitrary and capricious, because of their definition of the netting period. Overpayments are netted with underpayments up to the "month [of] the initial determination" of error. 20 C.F.R. § 416.538 (1989). "Initial determination" is a term of art meaning the Secretary's formal determination that an error was committed. See 20 C.F.R. §§ 404.902, 416.1402 (1989). Needless to say, that formal determination will not be simultaneous with the Secretary's first discovery that something is amiss; delay is inevitable. Respondents contend that this delay is fatal. At best, they say, the period over which netting is conducted will turn on the fortuity of the time period between discovery and formal determination. At worst, the Secretary will manipulate the netting period by delaying formal determination, thus including more underpayments in the netting period and reducing the net overpayment subject to the recoupment-waiver procedures.

It seems to us not arbitrary or capricious to establish a grace period within which these determinations can be considered and formally made; they should not be spur-of-the-moment decisions. That delay will extend the netting period, and may result in the inclusion of more underpayments to be netted. But we cannot say that the alternatives-immediate determinations, or determinations within a fixed period-would not produce errors that make beneficiaries worse off on the whole.

Moreover, although the Secretary's regulations do not establish a fixed time period for the formal determination, they do establish a time limit upon the principal adverse consequence of delay: the netting-in of additional underpayments. The regulations provide:

> "Where an apparent overpayment has been detected but determination of the overpayment has not been made (see § 416.558(a)), a determination and payment of an underpayment which is otherwise due cannot be delayed unless a determination with respect to the apparent overpayment can be made before the close of the month following the month in which the underpaid amount was discovered." 20 C.F.R. § 416.538 (1989).

Respondents' fear of intentional manipulation of the netting period can be entirely dismissed if this provision is observed in good faith-as we must presume, in this facial challenge, it will be. The intentional manipulation hypothesis is in any event implausible. Deliberately protracting the netting period may indeed draw in future underpayments; but it may just as likely draw in future overpayments, which will be uncollectible until the Secretary's determination is made. The Secretary might conceivably ensure that delay works to the Government's financial advantage by *deliberately* underpaying while keeping the netting period open, but since that is an obvious violation of the Act it is again not the stuff of which a facial challenge can be constructed.

In addition to the fact that the disadvantages of the Secretary's approach are less than respondents assert, the disadvantages of respondents' approach are more. The Secretary points out that a separate accounting for each month would cause the agency great expense, in the cost of a greatly increased volume of complex recoupment-waiver proceedings, in the cost of overpayments that are simply written off because the cost of the proceedings would exceed the recovery, and in the cost of overpayments whose return will be subject to lengthy delays. These expenses "in the end come out of the pockets of the deserving since resources available for any particular program of social welfare are not unlimited." *Mathews v. Eldridge,* 424 U.S. 319, 348, 96 S.Ct. 893, 909, 47 L.Ed.2d 18 (1976).

Respondents seek to minimize the administrative burden by proposing a scheme under which the Secretary would notify the beneficiary of underpayments and overpayments, withhold reimbursement of the underpayments for a brief period during which the beneficiary may seek waiver of recoupment of overpayments, and then net the underpayments and that portion of the overpayments as to which waiver has not been sought. This scheme, however, does not at all address the problem of delay in netting that is the asserted basis for finding the regulations arbitrary and capricious. Substituting "notification" of underpayments and overpayments for "determination" of underpayments and overpayments merely gives the occasion for the delay another name. What this alternative proposal of respondents really puts forward is an alternative means of assuring that overpayments cannot be "netted out" without an opportunity for waiver hearing. As we discussed at length earlier, the statute does not require such assurance. In sum, we find no basis for holding the regulations arbitrary and capricious.

* * *

Justice STEVENS, with whom Justice BRENNAN, Justice MARSHALL, and Justice KENNEDY join, dissenting.

* * *

This is what the statutory command says about OASDI overpayments:

> "In any case in which more than the correct amount of payment has been made, there shall be no adjustment of payments to, or recovery by the United States from, any person who is without fault if such adjustment or recovery would defeat the purpose of this subchapter or would be against equity and good conscience." § 204(b) of the Act; 42 U.S.C. § 404(b) (1982 ed.).

We have previously recognized that this provision "concerning the fact of the overpayment" speaks in "the imperative voice" and requires that " 'there shall be no adjustment of payments to, or recovery by the United States from, any person' who qualifies for waiver." *Califano v. Yamasaki*, 442 U.S., at 693-694, 99 S.Ct., at 2553-2554.

As the Court of Appeals for the Tenth Circuit observed, by this provision and its SSI counterpart the "statute makes a clear differentiation" between overpayments and underpayments. *Everhart v. Bowen*, 853 F.2d 1532, 1537 (1988). "While the provisions relating to underpayments mandate payment without qualification, the recovery of overpayment provisions are qualified by the waiver of recoupment procedures." *Ibid.* The reason for this distinction is easily surmised. A needy person who unknowingly receives an overpayment may spend it, not realizing that the Government will later take back money by reducing needed benefits, or by refusing to compensate for a prior underpayment. The beneficiary may be left without money essential to pay monthly bills. Thus, as Judge Gibbons has observed, the "difference in treatment of overpayments and underpayments ... is quite consistent with the fundamental policy motivating Congress in enacting both Titles; namely assuring those most in need in our society that they will receive a monthly benefit which will from month to month provide for the necessities of life." *Lugo v. Schweiker*, 776 F.2d 1143, 1154 (CA3 1985) (dissenting opinion). The procedures at issue here, however, "treat overpayments and underpayments equally," *Everhart*, 853 F.2d, at 1537, thereby deviating from both the letter and the purpose of the statutory command.

If we use two typical cases involving a $500 overpayment as examples, we can readily see how the Secretary's "netting regulations" violate the statutory command. In the first example, we may assume that the $500 overpayment was made in 1978 and first discovered in 1988. If we further assume that the beneficiary was without fault and that it would have been against equity and good conscience to recoup that amount from him in 1988, it necessarily follows that he had a statutory right to a waiver of any such recoupment. In our second hypothetical example, we may assume the same facts with the addition that in 1988 the beneficiary's monthly checks were erroneously reduced by $250 for each of two months. Under the Secretary's reading of the statute, the beneficiary's request for payment of the balance of the amount due for those two months could be denied on the ground that neither more nor less than the correct amount of payment had been made during the period between 1978 and 1988.

In my view such a reading of the statute is intolerable. The assumption that an underpayment in 1988--whether negligent or deliberate--could extinguish a needy beneficiary's statutory right to request a waiver of recoupment of an overpayment that occurred years earlier is flatly inconsistent with the statutory command that "equity and good conscience" should determine the waiver issue. For the Secretary to pretend that neither more nor less than the correct amount had been paid--when there was not only a series of incorrect monthly payments in 1978 but also a pair of incorrect payments in 1988--is nothing short of rewriting history to destroy a citizen's valuable statutory right.

    * * *

Indeed, *Califano v. Yamasaki*, 442 U.S. 682, 99 S.Ct. 2545, 61 L.Ed.2d 176 (1979), in which we first recognized the hearing right the Secretary has denied to these respondents, itself rejected the Secretary's reading of this statute. Although the statute does not state by express terms that a hearing is essential before the Secretary makes a § 204(b) waiver decision, we nevertheless found it clear in Yamasaki that Congress intended that a hearing be held. We analyzed the statute and concluded that "the nature of the statutory standards makes a hearing essential." *Id.*, at 693, 99 S.Ct., at 2553. The import of the statutory terms in this case is, I believe, equally clear.

The majority, however, refuses to heed the direction of those standards. In so doing, the majority makes much of its conclusion that, had

Congress wished to prohibit netting, "it would have been more natural" for Congress to phrase its command in terms of "any payment." Perhaps that is so. But it is entirely possible that Congress clearly intended to prohibit any netting that diminishes waiver rights, but nonetheless did not have the netting problem in mind when drafting language relevant to overpayments and underpayments. The netting procedure here is so inconsistent with the mandatory character of the waiver provision, with the statutory terms discussed above, and with the statute's reference to "equity and good conscience," that Congress might simply have thought it unnecessary to add further language ruling out specifically any such program. In any event, the majority's argument is irrelevant. Just as we do not sit to supply statutory directives where Congress gave none, we likewise do not sit to insist that Congress express its intent as precisely as would be possible. Our duty is to ask what Congress intended, and not to assay whether Congress might have stated that intent more naturally, more artfully, or more pithily.

In this case it is clear beyond peradventure that Congress intended to ensure that needy citizens would receive their full monthly benefit checks, even if that policy sometimes means forgoing any opportunity the Government might have to recoup an earlier overpayment. The Secretary's reading of the statute puts an unreasonable strain upon both its words and its purpose. If context were ignored entirely, I suppose that a student of language could justify the Secretary's interpretation of "adjustment" and "payment," and his duty to find historical facts. Perhaps that is what the majority means when it says that the statutory language "reasonably bears," ante, at 966, the Secretary's argument. But I find it inconceivable that wise judges can conclude that regulations in which the Secretary delegates to himself the power to rewrite history are "based on a permissible construction of the statute." *Chevron U.S.A. Inc. v. Natural Resources Defense Council, Inc.*, 467 U.S., at 843, 104 S.Ct., at 2781.

I respectfully dissent.

E. SUSPENSION OF BENEFITS

The Social Security Administration may, under certain circumstances, temporarily suspend benefits awarded under both the OASDI and the SSI program. A number of the suspension provisions for the SSI program relate to financial need, such as where a beneficiary's "countable income" or "countable resources" exceed maximum amounts. *See* 20 C.F.R. §§ 416.1323(a), 416.1324(a)(1). Benefits may also be suspended if eligibility was conditioned on the beneficiary disposing of a specified resources and the beneficiary failed to do so. 20 C.F.R. § 416.1324(a)(2). Benefits can be suspended under both programs if a beneficiary fails to provide certain information, including medical information relevant to determining whether a recipient of disability benefits is still disabled. *See* 20 C.F.R. § 404.1596(b)(2), 416.1322.

SSI benefits will be suspended when a beneficiary is confined to prison or most other public institutions. 20 C.R.R. § 416.1325. OASDI benefits will also be suspended when a beneficiary is confined to prison, but not when confined to other types of public institutions unless confined by court order in civil commitment proceeding "in connection with . . . a verdict or finding that the individual is not guilty of [a criminal] offense by reason of insanity." 42 U.S.C. § 402(x)(1)(A)(ii). This provision was analyzed in Artz v. Barnhart, 330 F.3d 170, 88 Soc. Sec. Rep. Serv. 1 (3rd Cir. 2003). Artz was found not guilty of the murder of his mother by reason of insanity, determined to be a danger to himself or others, and therefore involuntarily committed to a state psychiatric hospital. At the time, benefits were payable to all persons civilly committed and he was found eligible for disability benefits. At various times he was released and re-committed, and when the current suspension rules came into effect he was notified that his benefits would be suspended as he was then confined in a public institution. Following an administrative hearing, the ALJ ruled that his benefits had been properly suspended because he was confined "in connection with" his not-guilty-by-reason-of-insanity verdict. The court of appeals agreed, based in part on its finding that state procedures applied during his most recent re-commitment differed from those applied in ordinary civil commitments:

> Artz argues that his benefits were improperly suspended because during the time in question he was not confined "in connection with" the verdict of NGRI but was instead confined as a result of a normal civil commitment proceeding. Artz argues that the only connections between the NGRI verdict and the order under which he was committed during the time in question are that "they both happened to Mr. Artz and they both had the same case number." "These connections," he adds, "are not what is contemplated in the statute."

> A. In analyzing Artz's argument, we begin with the key statutory phrase "in connection with" the NGRI verdict. In United States v. Loney, 219 F.3d 281, 284-85 (3d Cir.2000), we considered the meaning of the phrase "in connection with," and although the context was different—in Loney, we were interpreting a provision of the Sentencing Guidelines, U.S.S.G. § 2K2.1(b)(5)—our discussion there is instructive. Stating that we should interpret the phrase in accordance with "ordinary usage," we concluded that the phrase should be interpreted "'broadly,'" "'expansively,'" and "as covering a wide range of relationships." Loney, 219 F.3d at 284 (citations omitted). We observed that the phrase "expresses some relationship or association, one that

can be satisfied in a number of ways such as a causal or logical relationship." Id. We added:

> We do not attempt to provide an exhaustive list of relationships that will resolve every case. As other courts have observed, 'no simple judicial formula can adequately capture the precise contours' of the 'in connection with' requirement, particularly in light of the myriad factual contexts in which the phrase might come into play.

Id. (citation omitted).

In light of this discussion of the ordinary meaning of the phrase "in connection with," we hold that the phrase is more than broad enough to apply in the present case. Artz was confined during the months at issue (February 1995 to April 1996) pursuant to a court order that was issued on July 22, 1994, and that formed a link in a tight chain of events stretching back to the NGRI verdict. As previously noted, that verdict led immediately and directly to a period of confinement for evaluation, and as a result of that evaluation, Artz was civilly committed in August 1981. He was conditionally released from this confinement in June 1989, and one of the conditions of his release was that he take the medication that was prescribed for him. After several shorter periods of re-confinement for failure to abide by conditions of release, the July 22, 1994, commitment order was issued based on the conclusion that he posed a danger to himself and others because he was no longer taking his medication. This sequence establishes a nexus that is sufficient to satisfy the Loney Court's understanding of the ordinary meaning of the phrase "in connection with."

Moreover, when Artz was committed in July 22, 1994, his prior NGRI verdict had a significant effect on the test that the judge was required to apply. Due to the prior verdict, the judge was required to find only that a preponderance of the evidence, not clear and convincing evidence, established that he presented the requisite danger. This link too is ample to satisfy Loney.

B. Artz asks us to read the statutory language more narrowly. According to Artz, a civil commitment meets the "in connection with" requirement only if "the hospitalization ... immediately follows the NGRI verdict." In his case, he argues, the covered period was "from August of 1981 [when he was civilly committed following his criminal trial] to June of 1989 [when the Superior Court ordered his conditional release]." We find this argument unconvincing.

First, we see no basis for interpreting the broad phrase "in connection with" to mean "immediately follow[ing]." That is not what the phrase connotes in ordinary usage, and we see no basis for giving the phrase that special meaning here. Second, Artz's concession that his confinement from August 1981 to June 1989 was "in connection with" the NGRI verdict undermines his central argument that he was confined during the period at issue in this case pursuant to what was in essence an ordinary civil commitment. Artz's commitment was ordered in August 1981 pursuant to the same standard—proof of dangerousness by a preponderance of the evidence—as his reconfinement in 1994. Moreover, the 1981 order, like the 1994 order, was based on Artz's condition at the time in question. Thus, if the 1981 commitment was "in connection with" the NGRI verdict, we think that the same is true of the 1994 recommitment.

C. This interpretation of 42 U.S.C. § 402(x) is supported by the Social Security Administration's Program Operations Manual System ["POMS"], "the publicly available operating instructions for processing Social Security claims." Wash. Dept. of Social Servs. v. Keffeler, 537 U.S. 371, 123 S.Ct. 1017, 1025, 154 L.Ed.2d 972 (2003). "While these administrative interpretations are not products of formal rulemaking, they nevertheless warrant respect." Id. at 1026. POMS GN 02607.310 provides as follows:

> NOTE: Some jurisdictions have special procedures for re-confining NGRI individuals (i.e., insanity acquittees) on conditional release which differ from usual civil commitment procedures. If a court orders the individual re-confined under these special procedures, consider the NGRI individual confined "in connection with" the NGRI verdict or finding.

Because the procedures applicable when Artz was re-confined in 1994 differed from normal civil commitment procedures in the ways already explained, this provision supports the suspension of Artz's benefits.

330 F.3d at 174-76.

Finally, certain fugitives and probation and parole violators are ineligible for SSI or OASDI benefits if they are fleeing to avoid prosecution or to avoid custody or confinement after conviction for a crime, or violating a condition of probation or parole.   See 42 U.S.C. §§ 402(x)(1)(A)(iv) (OASDI), 1382(e)(4)(A) (SSI).   SSA had taken the position that the "fleeing felon" rule requires suspension when a person has an outstanding warrant for his or her arrest—even if unaware that the warrant had been issued.   However, pursuant to a class action settlement order in Martinez v. Astrue, 08-Civ-4735 CW (N.D. Cal. 2009), SSA no longer applies the "fleeing felon" rule simply on the basis that an individual has an out-standing arrest warrant. On a related issue, the Second Circuit struck down SSA's practice of suspending benefits on the grounds that a beneficiary had violated conditions of probation or parole based simply on proof of a warrant alleging that the beneficiary was violating a condition of probation or parole. Clark v. Astrue, 602 F.3d 140, 152 Soc. Sec. Rep. Serv. 347 (2d Cir. 2010).

F. REPRESENTATIVE PAYEES

Representative payees are persons or organizations selected by the Social Security Administration to receive payments on behalf of a recipient of OASDI or SSI benefits. *See generally*, 42 U.S.C.A. §§ 405(j), 1383(a)(2)(A)(ii); 20 C.F.R. §§ 404.2001-404.2065, 416.601-416.665. Thus, SSA reserves the right to certify benefit payments to a representative payee if "the interests of the beneficiary would be better served" by doing so due to the beneficiary's mental or physical condition, or their young age. 20 C.F.R. §§ 404.2001(a), 416.601(a). Although this may include a beneficiary otherwise considered to be legally competent, 20 C.F.R. §§ 404.2001(a)(2), 416. 601(a)(2), for the most part representative payees are used where the beneficiary is either "legally incompetent or mentally incapable of managing benefit payments" or is "physically incapable of managing or directing the management of his or her benefit payments." See 20 C.F.R. §§ 404.2010(a), 416.610(a). As noted earlier in Chapter 6 in the context of persons eligible for disability benefits notwithstanding an addiction to drugs or alcohol, the SSI regulations state that representative payees will be certified also where the beneficiary is "eligible for benefits solely on the basis of disability and drug addiction or alcoholism is a contributing factor material to the determination of disability." 20 C.F.R. § 416.610(a)(3).

The Social Security Administration issued a number of new regulations in 2004 intended to codify practices and procedures, including provisions in the Social Security Protection Act of 2004 aimed at institutional representative payees. *See* 69 Fed. Reg. 60224 (October 7, 2004). These include rules on notifying beneficiaries when SSA intends to appoint a representative payee, giving the beneficiary the opportunity to appeal the proposed appointment. *See* 20 C.F.R. §§ 404.2030, 416.630. Representative payees should be persons or organizations that "best serve the interest of the beneficiary," which, for individuals, should include consideration of the relationship between the beneficiary and the possible payee, the amount of interest the payee shows in the beneficiary, and any legal authority that the payee may have relative to the beneficiary—such as being the beneficiary's custodian. 20 C.F.R. §§ 404.2020, 416.620. The highest priority is given to legal guardians or spouses for beneficiaries who are at least 18 years old, and to the natural or adoptive parents or guardians for beneficiaries under the age of 18. *See* 20 C.F.R. §§ 404.2021, 416.621. The regulations set out examples of the proper use of funds on behalf of a beneficiary, such as for their current maintenance, institutional care, support of legal dependents, and claims of creditors. 20 C.F.R. §§ 404.2040, 416.640.

State agencies can become representative payees for recipients receiving state services, including foster care and institutional care, and can use the funds they receive to pay for that care. In addition, certain qualified organizations can serve as representative payees and be compensated for that service. *See* 20 C.F.R. §§ 404.2040(a)-(b), 416.640(b).

MASON V. SYBINSKI
280 F.3d 788, 78 Soc. Sec. Rep. Ser. 340 (7th Cir. 2002)

FLAUM, Chief Judge.

Ivy Mason, on behalf of herself and a class of past, present, and future mentally impaired Social Security recipients who are institutionalized in Indiana state mental health institutions, brought action against the state of Indiana. The class sought declaratory and injunctive relief to prevent the state hospitals, appointed by the Social Security Administration ("SSA" or "the Administration") as representative payees, from deducting a portion of the recipients' Social Security benefits to pay for institutional maintenance without their voluntary consent. The class contends that the state hospitals' actions violate the anti-attachment provision of the Social Security Act ("the Act") as well as procedural due process. The district court granted summary judgment in favor of the state on all claims. Mason, on behalf of the class, now appeals. For the reasons stated herein, we affirm the decision of the district court.

I. BACKGROUND

The SSA, when it determines that a recipient is unable to manage or direct management of her own Social Security benefits, appoints a representative payee to do the job for her. 42 U.S.C. § 405(j) (2001); 20 C.F.R. § 404.2001 (2000). Representative payees are subject to a number of Social Security regulations created to prevent misuse or abuse of the funds. The appointed payee must use the payments received only for the "use and benefit" of the beneficiary, "in a manner ... he or she determines, under the guidelines in this subpart, to be in the best interests of the beneficiary." 20 C.F.R. § 404.2035. The regulations define "for the use and benefit" of the recipient to include costs of current maintenance, 20 C.F.R. § 404.2040(a)(1), and define "current maintenance" to include customary charges by a state, federal, or private institution where the beneficiary is receiving care. 20 C.F.R. § 404.2040(b). The Act states, moreover, that a creditor who provides the beneficiary with goods or services for consideration cannot be that person's representative payee except, inter alia, when that creditor is a state-licensed or certified care facility. 42 U.S.C. § 405(j)(2)(C)(i)(III); 42 U.S.C.§ 405(j)(2)(C)(iii).

The regulations set forth an order of preference in selecting a representative payee for institutionalized beneficiaries. If a legal guardian, spouse, other relative, or friend who demonstrates a strong concern for the recipient exists, the SSA will generally appoint that person to be the payee. If not, however, the Administration's preference is to appoint the state institution where the recipient resides. 20 C.F.R. § 404.2021(a).

When the SSA appoints a state hospital as representative payee, it provides notice to the hospital that it must use the payments for the benefit and care of the recipient. The Administration also provides notice to the beneficiary herself that a payee has been appointed and that she has the right to appeal that appointment. The recipient is told that the representative payee will be responsible for managing her benefits. In Indiana, when a state hospital is appointed payee, it verbally informs the beneficiary that her benefits may be used to pay for the cost of their care. Also, the SSA generally informs the beneficiary (and did so, by letter, in Mason's case) that the hospital, as payee, will apply part of the money toward its bill.

After receiving a recipient's benefit payment, the hospital deposits the money into a trust account. According to guide lines and specific instruction from the SSA, the hospital provides the recipient with spending money for bills, clothing and other reasonable expenses. It also deducts a portion of the benefits to pay for institutional costs. The hospital does not obtain written consent from the beneficiary to allow the state to apply the benefits to the cost of institutionalization.

Under Indiana law, residents of hospitals and institutions are liable for the cost of their treatment and care. If a person is legally admitted to a state institution, however, she is entitled to care and maintenance there, regardless of her ability to pay. When a patient is admitted, Indiana mental health institutions generally show her a notification of liability. After the hospital is appointed as representative payee for a patient, however, it does not inform her that she will be treated at the hospital even if she does not use her Social Security benefits to pay for the cost.

Ivy Mason, the class representative, is mentally disabled and has been a resident patient at Richmond State Hospital ("RSH") from July 7, 1992 to January 14, 1993; from October 4, 1994 to June 18, 1999; and from December 4, 1999 to the present. Upon her second and third admissions, pursuant to Indiana law, she signed a "Notification of Liability for Cost and Care of Treatment." From at least January 1998 until her second release, and for the entirety of her current stay at the hospital, RSH has been the representative payee for her Social Security benefits. On January 29, 1998, the SSA awarded Mason Social Security survivor's benefits retroactive to 1989 and informed her that she would be getting both ongoing monthly benefits in the sum of $618 as well as a lump-sum check for $34,408.73 for her back benefits. The SSA told both Mason and RSH that $25,942.73 of the lump-sum check was to be applied to her outstanding hospital bill. RSH did so and, under SSA guidance, also uses a portion of her monthly benefits check (as of the time of discovery, about $518) to pay her bill (which, again at the time of discovery, was approximately $7,170 per month). As of May 31, 2000, the bill for Mason's care at RSH totaled $412,070.98.

II. DISCUSSION

* * *

a. 42 U.S.C. § 407

The class argues that, although the Social Security Act does allow state hospitals and institutions to act as representative payees, those hospitals cannot apply a resident recipient's benefits to its own costs, absent that beneficiary's consent, without violating the anti-attachment provision of the Act. That provision provides:

> The right of any person to any future payment under this subchapter will not be transferable or assignable, at law or in equity, and none of the moneys paid or payable or rights existing under this subchapter shall be subject to execution, levy, attachment, garnishment, or other legal process, or to the operation of any bankruptcy or insolvency law.

42 U.S.C. § 407

In short, the class members contend that the state's application of recipients' benefits to their cost of care without their specified consent is a form of "other legal process." In support of this argument, they attempt to extend a line of cases that interprets broadly the § 407 prohibition against attachment to include the situation where, as here, the state acts as representative payee. In *Philpott v. Essex County Welfare Bd.*, the Supreme Court held that states are not in a preferred position compared to other creditors; they cannot subject benefit payments to any legal process. 409 U.S. 413, 93 S.Ct. 590, 34 L.Ed.2d 608 (1973). Similarly, the Supreme Court in *Bennett v. Arkansas* held that the anti-attachment provision applies to state creditors, such as hospitals, that have provided the beneficiary with care and maintenance. 485 U.S. 395, 108 S.Ct. 1204, 99 L.Ed.2d 455 (1988). This Court has held that when a state hospital asked a resident Social Security recipient to sign a form allowing the state to accumulate her benefits into a trust fund it could use to pay for the cost of care and maintenance, and that form did not inform the patient that it was revocable or that she would be treated regardless of whether she signed it, the state violated the Act's anti-attachment provision. *Tidwell v. Schweiker, 677 F.2d 560, 567 (7th Cir.1982)*. If the form were signed voluntarily—that is, if the beneficiary were informed that the form was revocable and that she would receive treatment even if she did not sign it—then no violation would have occurred. *Id.; see also Crawford v. Gould*, 56 F.3d 1162 (9th Cir.1995) (holding that a state may apply a patient's benefits to the cost of her care only if she has provided consent.)

The class relies heavily on *Tidwell* to claim that Indiana, in the instant case, unlawfully subjected institutionalized recipients' Social Security benefits to legal process by taking a portion of those benefits without their voluntary consent. The holding of *Tidwell*, however, as well as those of *Philpott* and *Bennett*, did not involve the situation where the state acted as representative payee. In this case, the district court held, and we agree, that a representative payee's decision to apply benefits to the recipient's cost of care in a state institution does not amount to other legal process--even when the payee is the state itself. We decline to extend the Tidwell holding to cover such a circumstance. Moreover, the Supreme Court's decisions in *Philpott* and *Bennett*, which hold that just as other creditors do, a state creditor violates the anti-attachment provision when it attaches or subjects to other legal process a recipient's benefits-- simply do not apply here because no attachment or legal process took place. A properly appointed representative payee's responsible management of a Social Security recipient's benefits cannot amount to "other legal process," regardless of whether that payee is an arm of the state.

The Social Security Act and regulations, as outlined above, permit— in fact, encourage—state institutions to act as representative payees and, more pertinently, when acting as payees, to apply recipients' benefits to the cost of their care and maintenance at a state institution where they reside. 20 C.F.R. § 404.2021; § 404.2035; § 404.2040. "Section 407 was not intended to outlaw a procedure expressly authorized by the Social Security Administration's own regulations." *King v. Schafer*, 940 F.2d 1182, 1185 (8th Cir.1991). Generally, the Social Security Act prohibits creditors from acting as representative payees. 42 U.S.C. § 405(j)(2)(C)(i)(III). It does so for the same reason that it includes the anti-attachment provision: to protect beneficiaries' Social Security income from the reach of creditors. The Act explicitly excepts state institutions from this prohibition, 42 U.S.C. § 405(j)(2)(C)(iii), suggesting first that Congress did not intend money management by representative payees who are also creditors to be included in the ambit of the anti-attachment provision (otherwise the separate prohibition would be redundant), and second that it considered the balance of interests and decided--without noting special restrictions--that, despite the need to protect recipients' benefits from creditors, state institutions should be allowed to act as representative payees.

Tidwell announced the rule that when a state hospital, not acting as representative payee, applies the recipient's benefits to the cost of her care, that action amounts to other legal process unless the recipient gave voluntary consent to remove it from the purview of § 407. *Tidwell*, 677 F.2d at 568. We find, for the reasons stated above, that the state's actions in this case do not constitute "execution, levy, attachment, garnishment, or other legal process," and therefore are always outside the ambit of the anti-attachment provision. The question of whether the resident recipients must give voluntary consent, then, is beside the point. Because the state's actions do not amount to other legal process, the recipient's consent is unnecessary.

The rationale behind the anti-attachment provision is to "protect social security beneficiaries and their dependents from the claims of creditors." *Fetterusso v. New York*, 898 F.2d 322, 327 (2d Cir.1990). We do not deny the importance and validity of such protection, even when the "creditor" is the state hospital providing care and maintenance to the recipient. *See, e.g., Bennett*, 485. U.S. 395; Tidwell, 677 F.2d 560. But, without straying from the goal of protecting the recipients' benefits, Congress and the Social Security Administration saw fit to allow state hospitals to act as representative payees when certain safeguards were met: the payee must use the money for the use and benefit of the recipient, which may include paying for the cost of her current care and maintenance, 20 C.F.R. § 404.2035, and the SSA must provide notice to the recipient that it intends to name a representative payee, who that payee will be, and that the recipient has the right to object to and appeal the decision. U.S. Const. amend. XIV, *Tidwell*, 677 F.2d at 564. The class does not contend that the above criteria are not being met. Indiana hospitals follow carefully the SSA's guidelines regarding use of recipients' benefits. They apply a portion of the money to recipients' personal needs--clothing, spending money, and the like--and only then do they apply a portion of the benefits to institutional costs. There is no evidence that the beneficiaries' moneys are left unprotected. Congress has never indicated that representative payees need to obtain beneficiaries' consent before applying their Social Security income in any given manner, so long as that application is for the use and benefit of the recipient. We will not now narrow the discretion that Congress explicitly granted representative payees to use the money "in a manner ... he or she determines, under the guidelines in this subpart, to be in the best interests of the beneficiary." 20 C.F.R. § 404.2035.

[The court also rejected the parties' due process argument, noting that beneficiaries can appeal action taken by a representative payee and that "the notice provided by the SSA informs Social Security beneficiaries that their appointed payee will have the authority to manage their receipts so long as they do so in a manner consistent with federal law and for the use and benefit of the recipient. By accepting the appointment of a representative payee, a beneficiary, while retaining some right to her property, does not retain the right to make individual management decisions regarding her benefits unless she utilizes the SSA's appeal process."]

CHAPTER 8

INTRODUCTION TO SOCIAL SECURITY PRACTICE

■ ■ ■

As with other areas of law practice, Social Security practice involves both substantive law—the various provisions of the Social Security Act, Social Security Administration rules and regulations interpreting and implementing the Act, and federal court case law presented and discussed in previous chapters of this book—and rules of procedure. In the case of Social Security practice, the procedural rules are influenced to a large extent by the sheer volume of cases that pass through the system, especially at the administrative level. This chapter covers the basic structure for processing claims for Old Age, Survivors, and Disability Insurance (OASDI) and Supplemental Security Income (SSI) benefits, including all levels of administrative decision making and appeals. It also covers briefly judicial review and various provisions for attorney's fees.

For the most part, Social Security practice is concentrated at the administrative appeals process. And the vast majority of cases handled by lawyers involve claims for disability benefits. Accordingly, the next chapter includes more detailed discussion of selected issues of administrative advocacy that are particularly important when handling a Social Security disability benefits case.

A. ADMINISTRATIVE DECISION-MAKING PROCESS

Social Security claims pass through one of the largest administrative decision-making systems in the world. Millions of claims are filed every year and hundreds of thousands of claims are contested through three of levels of administrative review. The current Social Security decision-making process is complex not only because of the large numbers of claims and appeals, but also because the vast majority of disputed claims involve the determination of disability. Deciding whether any one claimant is unable to engage in "substantial gainful activity" in light of not only his or her physical and mental impairments, but also while taking into account any effects of age, education, and prior work experience, can be difficult; making fair and accurate disability determinations for millions of claims (and in hundreds of thousands of appeals) is a daunting task. Some of this work is reflected in the statutory disability standard and the various regulations that interpret that standard. As we saw in Chapter 5, the "sequential evaluation process" and its components, including the Listing of Impairments and the Medical-Vocational Guidelines, provide important structure for reaching a decision. The setting in which it all takes place—and which influences greatly the quality of decisions on claims for benefits—is the administrative process.

There are four levels of administrative decision-making for Social Security claims—the initial decision plus up to three stages of administrative review—and most claims must pass through each before a decision is subject to judicial review. The process begins at the local Social Security Administration district office, but the all-important disability decisions are then contracted out to state-run Disability Determination Services (DDS). SSA, together with the DDSs for disability claims, makes the initial decision and, in case of appeal, performs the first level of review known as reconsideration. The next two levels of administrative appeal are handled also by SSA, but through two separate appeal units: the Office of Disability Adjudication and Review (ODAR) (formerly known as the Office of Hearings and Appeals, or OHA), which is responsible for de novo administrative hearings conducted by independent administrative law judges; and the Appeals Council, which reviews administrative hearing decisions on appeal or on its own initiative. Each of these four parts of the Social Security administrative process—the initial decision, reconsideration, administrative hearings, and Appeals Council review—are discussed in some detail in the next two sections of this chapter.

Much has been written about the problems associated with Social Security claim processing and appeals, and SSA has attempted over the years to meet various criticisms by proposing—but usually failing to implement—broad systemic reform. Past efforts to effectuate reform in the Social Security claims and adjudication process were summed up by Milton Carrow at a point when SSA began testing new models, none of which were implemented:

> The Social Security Administration (SSA) adjudicates more cases than all the federal courts combined. Its complex processes include four levels of adjudication and appeal from which further appeals lie to the federal courts with three additional levels. The social security system serves the most vulnerable population in our society—the elderly, the disabled, and the poor. Collectively, Congress, SSA, interested organizations, and scholars have generated a myriad of studies and reports, all of which aim to reduce the complexity and stress built into the system. In recent years, reform efforts have targeted the initial decisionmaking process under the expectation that with

improvements at that level, appeal backlogs can be significantly reduced, thus saving time, anguish, and money.

Within this context, ten years ago Congress mandated SSA to conduct demonstration projects to determine the efficacy of supplanting the existing paper process with face-to-face interviews with claimants, focusing on the initial intake stage of the disability claims process. SSA was to report the project results to the House Ways and Means Committee no later than December 31, 1986. SSA undertook costly studies for several years, but to date (1994) no final report has been published and no definitive findings have been made. During this same period, a proliferation of government and nongovernment agencies conducted investigations of various aspects of SSA's initial decisionmaking process. They criticized the manner in which SSA conducted its demonstration project, sharply denounced the unfairness and ineffectiveness of the existing process, and, unlike the temporizing of the SSA, made specific recommendations for improvement. The seriousness of this situation is highlighted by the fact that in fiscal 1991, as in previous years, 68.9% of the initial decisions that were appealed were later reversed by Administrative Law Judges (ALJs).

By a Notice of Proposed Rulemaking dated October 22, 1993, SSA proposes to "test" five models revolving around the face-to-face interview process. Thus, ignoring all that has gone before, SSA again has embarked on a costly, time-consuming effort that calls to mind Santayana's warning that "those who cannot remember the past are condemned to repeat it."

Milton M. Carrow, *A Tortuous Road to Bureaucratic Fairness: Righting The Social Security Disability Claims Process*, 46 ADMIN. L. REV. 297, 297-98 (1994). For an earlier study, see JERRY L. MASHAW ET AL., SOCIAL SECURITY HEARINGS AND APPEALS: A STUDY OF THE SOCIAL SECURITY ADMINISTRATION HEARING SYSTEM (1978). Some current proposals for reform of the administrative decision-making process are discussed briefly later in this chapter; however, the bulk of the next sections on administrative decision making and appeals covers the process currently in operation.

NOTE ON REOPENING

Decisions that cannot be appealed may nonetheless be reopened. **20 C.F.R. §§ 404.987, 416.1487[APP-REGS]**. Decisions can be reopened based on one of three sets of criteria: within one year of the date of the decision involved, "for any reason"; within four years for OASDI benefits or within two years for SSI benefits, upon a showing of "good cause"; and at any time, if the decision "was obtained by fraud or similar fault" or under certain other specific, limited circumstances. *See generally* **20 C.F.R. §§** 404.988, 416.1488**[APP-REGS]**. "Good cause" is explained further at **20 C.F.R. §§** 404.989, 416.1489**[APP-REGS]**. There was some doubt a number of years ago as to whether SSA could reopen claims according to the same criteria as claimants. A few courts held that only claimants could request reopening, or that SSA's ability to do so was severely limited. However, SSA amended its regulations in 1994 to make it clear that it may reopen claims on its own initiatives according to the same criteria as those applicable to requests by claimants. *See* 59 Fed. Reg. 8,532 (1994); 20 CFR §§404.987(b), 416.1487(b).

B. APPLICATION AND INITIAL DECISION

An application for Old Age, Survivors, and Disability Insurance (OASDI) or Supplemental Security Income (SSI) benefits must be filed with the Social Security Administration. If an applicant has any doubt as to which program would be appropriate, or if eligibility may be established for both, applications for both types of benefits may be filed. Most applications are filed at a local SSA office. *See* **20 C.F.R. §§** 404.614, 416.325**[APP-REGS]**. SSA also allows applications for OASDI benefits to be filed on-line via the Internet. 20 C.F.R. § 422.505(a). *See* http://www.socialsecurity.gov/applyonline. Applications usually are considered filed on the date received; however, the postmark date will be used if the date received "would result in the loss or lessening of rights." 20 CFR § 404.614(b)(2). The same rule is used for SSI, if use of the later date would result in "a loss of benefits." 20 CFR § 416.325(b)(1).

Most SSA offices have "specialists" who deal with claims for OASDI benefits and different specialists who deal with claims for SSI. These specialists assist the claimant with the application process. The initial application form includes detailed questions relevant to program eligibility and the claimant is expected to provide full information to support his or her claim.

Not surprisingly, the greatest amount of information requested is for disability claims. A special disability report form requests information used to determine the nature of the claimant's physical and mental impairments, the date of onset of the alleged disability, and whether the claimant performed any work after the alleged date of onset. It includes space for claimants to list their medical problems and to explain how the impairments affect their ability to perform work and to participate in daily activities. It also includes a request for information about the claimant's medical records, including any medical tests performed in the past year; the name, address, and telephone number of any doctor or other medical source seen by the claimant; the reasons for the visits; and the type of treatment received. There is now an online version of the disability report form that tracks the paper version of the form. *See* https://secure.ssa.gov/apps6z/radr/radr-fe. Claimants or their representatives can save the form and return for additional sessions before submitting the form electronically; the completed form can be printed out as a file copy. Additional medical and school records can be submitted online through the "Electronic Records Express" service, found at: www.ssa.gov/ere. Congress imposed new penalties in 1999 for persons who knowingly make a false or misleading statement or who omit a material fact for use in determining eligibility for benefits. The penalties, which apply to all statements made on or after December 14, 1999, are nonpayment for six months for the first incident, 12 months for the second, and 24 months for any others. *See* 42 U.S.C. §1320a-8a; 20 C.F.R. §§404.459, 416.1340.

Only a few claims for disability benefits—those that can be resolved finally at Step 1 of the sequential evaluation process—are decided at the local office. This is because Step 1 denials can be based on relatively simple and objective vocational evidence, without having to assess any alleged physical or mental impairments. Thus, claims will be denied at the local office if the claimant is, or was, performing substantial gainful activity during the period for which he or she is seeking benefits. All other claims—those that require an assessment of medical evidence—are forwarded for further evaluation to the Disability Determination Section (DDS), a state agency with the specific responsibility for making disability determinations. *See* 20 C.F.R. §§ 404.1503(a), 416.903(a).

When a claim is received by the DDS, it is assigned to a disability examiner who works together with a member of the medical staff, known as a medical consultant, to determine whether the claimant is disabled, the date the disability began, and, in termination cases, the date the disability ended. After reviewing the file, the examiner decides whether additional medical records are needed and, if so, from which medical sources additional records should be requested. SSA regulations provide that before making a determination of disability it will develop a "complete medical history" and "make every reasonable effort" to help claimants obtain relevant evidence from their medical sources. **20 C.F.R. §§ 404.1512(d), 416.912(d)[APP-REGS]**. For claims that may involve a mental impairment, the DDS must make "every reasonable effort . . . to ensure that a qualified psychiatrist or psychologist has completed the medical portion of the case review and any applicable residual functional capacity assessment." 20 C.F.R. §§ 404.1503(e), 416.916(e). While claimants are responsible for providing sufficient evidence to prove that they are disabled, SSA can pay for existing evidence that the claimant cannot obtain. 20 C.F.R. S§ 404.1514, 416.914. Moreover, if the examiner is not able to obtain enough current medical information from the claimant's medical sources, SSA will arrange and pay for a consultative examination. See **20 C.F.R. §§ 404.1517, 416.917[APP-REGS]**. Special rules on the weight given to the reports of consultative examinations, particularly when they conflict with reports from a claimant's treating physician, are discussed in detail in Chapter 9, Section E.

Once the disability examiner has enough medical information, the examiner—together with a DDS medical consultant—evaluates the claimant's condition according to SSA's sequential evaluation process for determining disability. Disability examiners usually make the preliminary evaluation at the second and third steps of the process, which require a decision as to whether the claimant has a "severe" impairment, and, if so, whether the criteria in the Listing of Impairments have been met or equaled. The examiners must consult with the medical consultant on the issue of medical equivalence. If the claim is not granted based on the Listing of Impairments, the examiner works up the last two steps of the sequential evaluation process—on the claimants' ability to perform past work or other work in light of his or her age, education and work experience—in conjunction with the medical consultant and, in some cases, with a vocational expert. Medical consultants are charged with determining claimants' residual functional capacity (RFC); that is, whether they are able to perform sedentary, light, or medium work. 20 C.F.R. §§ 404.1546, 416.946. The final disability decision is made by the examiner and the consultant together, unless there is no medical evidence in the record—because the agency was unable to obtain any—and the claimant refused to attend a consultative examination, without good cause. **20 C.F.R. §§ 404.1615(c), 416.1015(c)[APP-REGS]**. *See also* **20 C.F.R §§ 404.1518, 416.918[APP-REGS]** (setting out the consequences of failure to appear at a consultative examination).

For many years, there were no guidelines for purchasing consultative examinations and the extent to which they were ordered varied widely. In 1991, SSA published detailed regulations that outline when it will, and when it will not, purchase a consultative examination. Basically, the regulations provide that SSA will purchase a consultative examination "when the evidence as a whole, both medical and nonmedical, is not sufficient to support a decision" on the claimant's disability, including when the "medical evidence the file does not contain such as clinical findings, laboratory tests, a diagnosis or prognosis necessary for decision." **20 C.F.R. §§ 404.1519a, 416.919a[APP-REGS]**. Generally, consultative examinations will not be purchased where non-medical evidence indicates that the claimant would not be eligible for disability benefits over the period at issue. **20 C.F.R. §§ 404.1519b, 416.919b[APP-REGS]**

Although disability decisions are made by the state DDS agencies, the final decision on eligibility for benefits is always made at the local Social Security district office. Technically, the DDS's disability decision is a recommended decision. *See* 20 CFR §§404.1503(d), 416.903(d). The reality, however, is that the DDS's recommended decision is followed in virtually all cases. But SSA does have the authority to review any decision that an individual is under a disability, either before or after any action is taken on the claim. 42 U.S.C. §421(c)(1).

Initial disability decisions that SSA does not review are implemented as recommended by the DDS; those that are reviewed are either approved for implementation or returned to the DDS for a new decision. Claims are then processed at the local SSA office, including the development of any additional nonmedical requirements, especially for SSI claims, and the awarding of auxiliary benefits to dependents, when required. If the decision is to deny the claim, the notice will explain to the claimant why the claim was denied. The claimant is also notified that a request for reconsideration must be filed within 60 days of the denial.

SSA began implementing a special process in 2006 for certain types of claims where it appears that an initial finding of disability can be made within a short period of time. Nationwide implementation of these "Quick Disability Determinations" (QDD) began in early 2008. Claims are selected for a QDD if the file indicates that there is a "high degree of probability" that the claimant is disabled and where the evidence necessary to establish disability can "be easily and quickly verified." *See generally* **20 C.F.R. §§ 404.1619, 416.1019[APP-REGS]**. Under the 2006 rules, the time limit for making a quick decision was twenty days; the twenty-day limit was removed when QDDs were extended nationwide in 2007, on the theory that most QDD decisions would be made within that time period even without a specific requirement and that the advantage of continuing the process beyond twenty days in rare cases outweighed any benefit of holding to a rigid limit. If a claim goes through the QDD procedure but cannot be approved, it continues on through the regular disability determination process. 20 C.F.R. §§ 404.1619(c), 416.1019(c). Around the same time, SSA instituted "compassionate allowances" for claimants with medical conditions that "invariably qualify under the Listing of Impairments . . . based on minimal, but sufficient, objective medical evidence." *See* 20 C.F.R. §§ 404.1602, 416.1002. The initial list of 50 conditions included amyotrophic lateral sclerosis (ALS or "Lou Gehrig disease") and various types of cancers; SSA has since added 63 new conditions including early onset Alzheimer's disease and multiple system atrophy. *See* http://www.ssa.gov/compassionateallowances/conditions.htm for the complete list.

Until recently, one could re-file a claim for benefits—that is, file a second claim after an earlier claim for the same benefit and benefit period had been denied—while the earlier claim was on appeal. If the claimant's condition had worsened significantly in the meantime, the second claim could be granted before the first claim was heard on appeal. However, SSA changed its policy in 2011 so that one can no longer have two claims for the same type of benefits pending at the same time. SSR 11-1p (2011). In effect, a claimant now has to to choose between filing a new claim and pursuing an appeal. The Ruling provides, however, that one can still report new medical conditions, or a worsening of existing medical conditions, in which case SSA will forward that information to the office handling the pending appeal.

C. ADMINISTRATIVE APPEALS

As noted earlier, there are three levels of administrative appeal from benefit decisions by the Social Security Administration: reconsideration, administrative hearing, and Appeals Council review. Generally, a claimant must pass through all three levels of appeal before an adverse decision can be reviewed in court. Although they all take place within SSA, each has its own distinctive features. Each of the three levels will be discussed in this section. Judicial review is discussed in the next section.

The following chart, provides an overview of the progression of disability claims through the initial decision and administrative appeals process:

FISCAL YEAR 2009 WORKLOAD DATA: DISABILITY DECISIONS

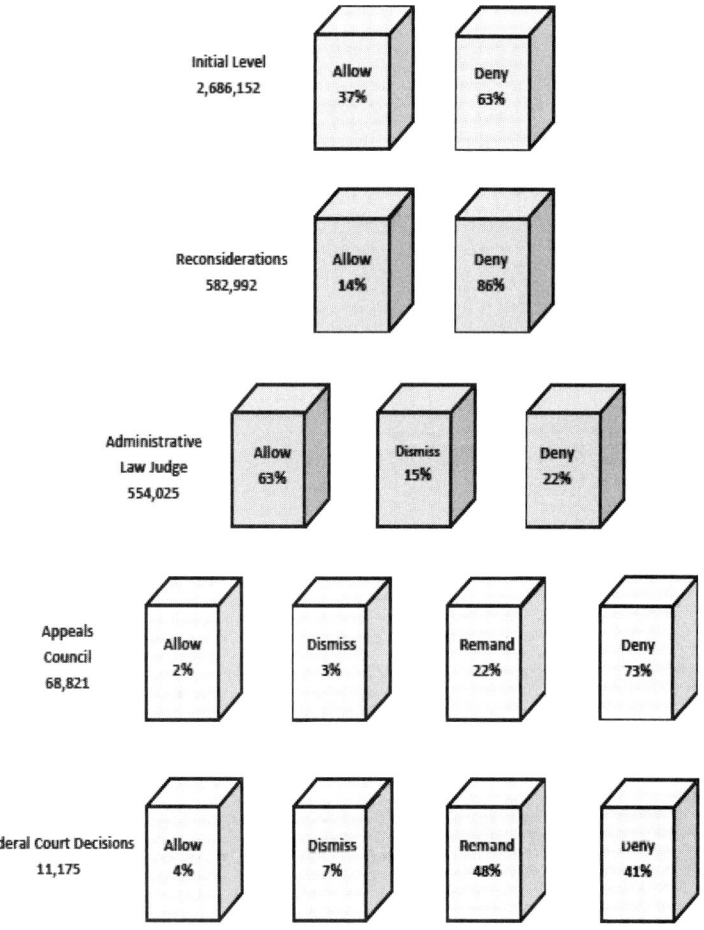

Source: Social Security Administration, Office of the Inspector General, *Disability Insurance and Supplemental Security Income Claims Allowed But Not Paid* (June, 2011) Appendix B-7, available at http://oig.ssa.gov/sites/default/files/audit/full/pdf/A-01-10-10177.pdf.

NOTE ON TIME LIMITS FOR FILING AN ADMINISTRATIVE APPEAL

The time limit for seeking review at each of the three levels of administrative appeal is the same: within 60 days following receipt of notice of the prior administrative action. *See* 20 **C.F.R. §§** 404.909, 416.1409**[APP-REGS]** (reconsideration); **20 C.F.R. §§** 404.933, 416.1433**[APP-REGS]** (administrative hearings); **20 C.F.R. §§** 404.968, 416.1468**[APP-REGS]** (Appeals Council review). The rules for extensions of time and for counting the 60-day time period are the same for all levels of administrative appeal as well. (The regulations cited in this note address requests for reconsideration; however, the substance applies equally to requests for administrative hearings and Appeals Council review.)

The 60-day time limit begins on the day after the notice of the action appealed from was received. 20 C.F.R. §§ 404.909(a)(1), 416.1409(a). SSA assumes that notices are received five days after the date of mailing shown on the notice; therefore, as a practical matter an appeal must be filed within 65 days after the decision was mailed, not counting the day of mailing. The five-day period is, however, only a presumption and can be rebutted with statements claiming non-receipt. *See* 20 C.F.R. §§ 404.901, 416.1401 ("Date you receive notice means 5 days after the date on the notice, unless you show us that you did not receive it within the 5-day period."). In Hobt v. Commissioner, 175 Fed. Appx. 709, 710-11, 2006 WL 988282 (6th Cir. 2006), the claimant's application for benefits was denied and, according to SSA, a notice upholding the denial on reconsideration was mailed on September 2, 2003. His attorney filed a request for an administrative hearing on December 5, 2003, explaining that the claimant learned of the reconsideration denial only on December 2, 2003. The ALJ denied the request on the ground that it was not timely filed, having presumed that the claimant received the notice within five days after SSA claimed it had been mailed. The court disagreed:

> The ALJ's use of a presumption of receipt with 5 days of the alleged date of mailing was contrary to the case law of this Circuit. As this Court explained in *McKentry* [*v. Secretary*, 655 F.2d 721, 724 (1981)], a presumption of receipt is inappropriate where there is no evidence that the notice was ever mailed. Additionally, the *McKentry* court expressly held that a dated copy of the notice in a claimant's file was not proof mailing. *Id.* ("The presence of a piece of paper in the Department's file is not necessarily proof of mailing.") Even if such a presumption were appropriate, however, it was effectively rebutted by claimant's uncontradicted statement that he did not receive notice of the denial until December 2, 2003.

175 Fed. Appx. at 710-11. On the other hand, most courts insist that claimants cannot simply state that they did not receive the notice within five days. *See e.g.*, Rouse v. Harris, 482 F. Supp. 766, 769 (D.N.J.1980) (requiring "a more concrete showing that the [claimant] or her attorney actually did not receive the Secretary's notice within five days of the date of mailing").

Although requests for an administrative appeal must be timely, under certain circumstances SSA will grant an extension of time to file. The appellant must show "good cause" as to why the deadline was missed, examples of which are set out in a nonexclusive list in the regulations. See **20 C.F.R. §§ 404.911, 416.1411[APP-REGS]**. SSA revised its regulations on "good cause" for extensions of time to file an appeal in 1994 in order to take into account whether the claimant had any physical, mental, educational, or linguistic limitations which prevented the claimant from filing a timely request or from understanding or knowing about the need to file a timely request for review. 20 C.F.R. §§ 404.911(a)(4), 416.1411(a)(4). These rules give the relevant person at SSA a great deal of discretion, in part because—as discussed later in this chapter—there is only very limited judicial review of a decision to deny a request for an extension.

NOTE ON APPEALS FROM TERMINATION OF BENEFITS

Generally, decisions to terminate benefits are appealed in the same way as appeals from any other decision by SSA. As noted in Chapter 4, there are separate standards for terminating benefits on the ground that the recipient is no longer disabled and, as noted later in this chapter, there is a special limited hearing at reconsideration if disability benefits were terminated on medical grounds. In addition, persons whose SSI benefits are terminated and those whose OASDI disability benefits were terminated on medical grounds can have their benefit payments continued pending an appeal—if they file a request for an appeal within 10 days. 20 C.F.R. §§ 404.1597a(f), 416.1336(b). Payment of SSI benefits pending appeal is a constitutional right for need-based programs since the Supreme Court's decision in Goldberg v. Kelly, 397 U.S. 254 (1970) (involving the former Aid to Families with Dependent Children (AFDC) program). The Court declined to extend that right to social insurance programs in Mathews v. Eldridge, 424 U.S. 319 (1976); however, Congress extended the same rights to the limited group of OASDI disability benefit recipients a few years later.

1. RECONSIDERATION

The first step in appealing an adverse decision by SSA—with respect to an application for benefits or any other decision made by the agency— is to request a "reconsideration" of the decision. **20 C.F.R. §§ 404.907, 416.1407[APP-REGS]**. A request for reconsideration must be filed with the local Social Security office within 60 days of receiving a notice of decision, unless the time to appeal has been extended for good cause. 20 C.F.R. §§ 404.909, 416.1409.

Reconsideration is an internal re-examination of all the evidence in the file at the time of the appealed-from decision, together with any subsequently submitted additional evidence. In an appeal from a disability decision, reconsideration takes place under the same procedures at the same DDS where the initial decision was made; however, the reconsideration decision is made by examiners and consultants who did not take part in the initial determination. Thus, if an initial denial was based on a finding of medical ineligibility, a different two-person team at the DDS will examine the claimant's medical condition at the reconsideration stage. This means that at this first level of administrative review, the review is still on paper only; there is no face-to-face meeting with the decision maker. However, in termination cases where a beneficiary is found to be no longer disabled for medical reasons, the beneficiary can request a face-to-face "disability hearing" as part of the reconsideration process. Disability hearings are discussed in more detail in Note 2 below.

Only a small percentage of decisions are reversed at reconsideration, and all reconsideration reversals arc reviewed at the appropriate regional SSA office. Most reversals are based on new medical evidence; sometimes, however, claims that were denied because the duration requirement was not met are reversed on reconsideration simply because of the passage of time. A reversal may also result because of a better definition or progression of the claimant's disability. A reconsideration decision is final unless appealed within 60 days.

NOTES

1. Reconsideration has been criticized for many years as an unnecessary and time-consuming repeat decision, which diverts limited resources from other stages of the disability determination process. A number of recent reform proposals have included the elimination—or significant reduction—of this level of appeal. For example, since the 1990s, some states have eliminated reconsideration on a test basis as part of the Social Security Administration's Hearing Process Improvement project (also known as "Disability Redesign"). In 2006, the Disability Service Improvement Process ("DSIP"), which was implemented in several states (most notably in the Boston region), completely eliminated the reconsideration step of the current appeals process. Instead, a new officer, known as the Federal Reviewing Official, reviewed state agency denials of benefits upon the claimant's request. However, these and most other elements of the DSIP were repealed in 2008. *See* 73 Fed. Reg. 10381 (February 27, 2008); 20 C.F.R. § 405.240.

Critics argue that by shortening the overall length of the process, eliminating reconsideration would reduce problems that arise when claimants' medical conditions change during the course of administrative review. Additionally, they argue that elimination of reconsideration would allow for the redistribution of limited resources to the two critical decision points in the administration process: the initial decision and the ALJ hearing. Reconsideration has also been criticized as being too limited, in the sense that it consists of a review of a paper record without any face-to-face contact between the claimant and the decision maker.

A second school of thought believes that the reconsideration stage has merit and should not be eliminated. Because reconsideration is limited to review of a paper record and occurs within the same DDS as the initial determination, it provides a relatively low-cost mechanism to correct errors in initial decisions. If the process catches even a small number of errors, reconsideration has value in producing more accurate decisions and ensuring fairness to claimants. The debate over reconsideration continues, but even after numerous proposals for reform and repeated criticism it remains in place—at least for the time being.

2. As noted earlier, there is one notable situation in which reconsideration is not limited to review of a paper record. In 1983, Congress amended the Social Security Act to require special reconsideration procedures for all claims where SSA terminated benefits upon a finding of nondisability, but only if the decision was based on medical factors. *See generally* 42 U.S.C. §§405(b)(2), 1383(a)(7)(A). Thus, where disability benefits are terminated because the claimant's impairment ceased, did not exist, or is no longer disabling, reconsideration includes a "disability hearing." **20 C.F.R. §§ 404.914, 416.1414[APP-REGS]**. See also 20 C.F.R. §§ 404.916, 416.1416. Disability hearings are held by disability hearing officers, who are experienced disability examiners who were not involved in the initial determination of the claim. 20 C.F.R. §§ 404.915, 416.1415. The scope of the disability hearing is limited to the initial or revised determination based on medical factors that the claimant is not disabled. All other issues must be reviewed in accordance with the reconsideration procedures described above.

2. ADMINISTRATIVE HEARING

The next level of appeal is an administrative hearing before an administrative law judge (ALJ). A claimant has 60 days from the date of receipt of a reconsideration notice to request an administrative hearing, unless the time limit is extended for good cause. 20 C.F.R. §§ 404.933, 416.1433. If the claimant requests a hearing, one will be held unless the ALJ decides to issue a fully favorable decision without a hearing, or to remand for further administrative action because the ALJ believes that a revised decision will be favorable to the claimant. The ALJ may also dismiss the appeal on certain specified grounds.

The administrative hearing record begins with the evidence compiled during the initial decision and at reconsideration, which is forwarded to the Office of Disability Adjudication and Review (ODAR) (formerly known as the Office of Hearings and Appeals, or OHA). The ALJ, working together with ODAR staff, then reviews and develops the record independently without assuming, in a case involving disability benefits, that the DDS obtained all of the information available at the time it made its decisions. They decide what additional evidence is necessary, if any, and whether a vocational expert or medical expert should be called to appear at the hearing. ODAR staff can obtain existing medical reports from treating sources or hospitals and can order consultative examinations. The case may also be referred for a prehearing case review. *See* **20 C.F.R. §§ 404.941, 416.1441[APP-REGS]**.

Once the claimant's file has been completed, the case is set for hearing unless the claimant chooses not to appear or the ALJ decides to issue a favorable decision without a hearing or to remand the claim for further evaluation at the DDS agency level. **20 C.F.R. §§ 404.948, 416.1448[APP-REGS]**. At the hearing itself, claimants, on their own or through their representatives, can present any testimony and additional documentary evidence they wish. **20 C.F.R. §§ 404.950, 416.1450[APP-REGS]**. With the exception of disability hearings at the reconsideration level where benefits were terminated on medical grounds, the ALJ is the only decision maker in the entire administrative appeals process that sees the claimant in person.

The hearing itself is informal and non-adversarial. The rules of evidence do not apply. Typically, the administrative law judge will ask a series of questions and then, if the claimant is represented, the claimant's representative will continue the questioning. The hearing is the first opportunity to take sworn testimony from outside witnesses and is typically the first stage at which the claimant obtains representation. Following the hearing, the ALJ must issue a formal written decision that includes a recitation of the evidence considered, findings of facts, and detailed reasons for the decision. An administrative hearing decision is final unless a request for review is filed with the Appeals Council within 60 days.

NOTES

1. In Butz v. Economou, 438 U.S. 478, 513-514 (1978), the Supreme Court described the role of a federal ALJ as follows:

> There can be little doubt that the role of the modern federal hearing examiner or administrative law judge within this framework is "functionally comparable" to that of a judge. His powers are often, if not generally, comparable to those of a trial judge. He may issue subpoenas, rule on proffers of evidence, regulate the course of the hearing, and make or recommend decision. More importantly, the process of agency adjudications is currently structured so as to assure that the hearing examiner exercises his independent judgment on the evidence before him, free from pressures by the parties or other officials within the agency. Prior to the Administrative Procedure Act, there was considerable concern that persons hearing administrative cases at the trial level could not exercise independent judgment because they were required to perform prosecutorial and investigative functions as well as their judicial work and because they were often subordinate to executive officials within the

agency. Since the securing of fair and competent hearing personnel was viewed as "the heart of formal administrative adjudication," the Administrative Procedure Act contains a number of provisions designed to guarantee the independence of hearing examiners. They may not perform duties inconsistent with their duties as hearing examiners. When conducting a hearing under the 5 of the APA, a hearing examiner is not responsible to, or subject to, the supervision or direction of employees or agents engaged in the performance of investigative or prosecution functions for the agency. Nor may a hearing examiner consult any person or party, including other agency officials, concerning a fact at issue in the hearing, unless on notice and opportunity for all parties to participate. Hearing examiners must be assigned to cases in rotation so far as practicable. They may be removed only for good cause established and determined by the Civil Service Commission after a hearing on the record. Their pay is also controlled by the Civil Service Commission.

The roles of the administrative law judge and the claimant's representative at Social Security administrative hearings are discussed in more detail in Chapter 9, Section D.

2. ODAR is one of the largest administrative judicial systems in the world. ODAR has ten regional offices, 146 hearing offices, and four national hearing centers. Currently, there are approximately 1,300 ALJs and 6,100 support staff in ODAR. The Social Security Administration issues more than half a million hearing and appeal decisions each year.

The following chart, based on data from SSA's 2010 Annual Statistical Supplement, Table 2.F8, sets out the total number of ALJs working at ODAR and their average workload for the years 2007-2009:

	2007	2008	2009
Number of ALJs	1,006	960	1,057
Average monthly hearing dispositions per ALJ	45	48	49
Average hearings pending per ALJ	702	643	575

3. The administrative hearing stage has been heavily criticized for substantial backlog and delays. To convey a sense of the backlog, at the end of June, 2007 there were over 745,000 cases pending at ODAR. SSA considers 400,000 a manageable level to keep workflow moving. See OFFICE OF INSPECTOR GENERAL, AUDIT REPORT: ADMINISTRATIVE LAW JUDGES' CASELOAD PERFORMANCE (February 2008), at 9. Increasing workload and limited agency resources have led to lengthy waiting periods for hearings and disability decisions.

Looking forward, this trend will only be exacerbated by the retirement of the "baby boomer" generation and increases in life expectancies. Critics argue that such delays impose significant burdens on individuals in immediate need of benefits, thereby undermining a core purpose of the Social Security program and raising questions about its efficiency. As the Inspector General stated, "It is imperative that ALJs process cases at an acceptable level to reduce the emotional and financial impact of long processing times for the thousands of claimants awaiting decisions on their appeals." *Id.*, at 11. For a discussion of the impact of backlog in social security cases more generally, see generally Jeffrey S. Wolfe, *The Times they are a Changin': A New Jurisprudence for Social Security*, 29 J. NAT'L ASS'N ADMIN. L. JUDICIARY 515 (2009).

The Social Security Administration has sought to reform the administrative hearing process on a number of occasions over the past twenty years in response to these concerns over dramatic increases in requests for ALJ hearings and unprecedented levels of cases pending in hearing offices. One of the few remaining reforms from the Disability Service Improvement Process project—Quick Disability Decisions—creates a quicker disability determination process for those claimants with obvious disabilities, as discussed earlier in this chapter. Other reform proposals have targeted at helping the Social Security Administration decide cases more efficiently and enhancing the productivity of ALJs. Such measures have included reorganizing the local hearing offices by pooling the staff attorneys and hearing assistants who had previously been assigned to specific ALJs, setting national targets for case processing speeds, providing peer counseling for low-producing ALJs, and implementing direct job discipline. However, reform proposals have met with strong resistance by ALJs who view them as attacks on the decisional independence guaranteed to them by the Administrative Procedures Act.

4. Another persistent criticism of the administrative hearing stage and the disability determination process more generally is that ALJs and other decision makers often make determinations based on incomplete evidentiary records. Two major factors contribute to the incomplete record problem. First, medical conditions may change during the many years it takes claimants to go through the various stages of the administrative process. As a result, medical records which were accurate at the time of the initial determination may no longer be accurate at later stages in the process. Second, decision makers are neither properly trained nor given sufficient resources to compile the detailed medical information needed to make a determination of disability.

Concerns that disability decisions are informed by incomplete evidentiary records have sparked many proposals for reform, including the appointment of nonadversarial "Counselors" whose main responsibility would be to ensure that ALJs have a fully developed evidentiary record when they make their decisions. *See* Frank S. Bloch, Jeffrey S. Lubbers & Paul R. Verkuil, *Developing a Full and Fair Evidentiary Record in a Nonadversarial Setting: Two Proposals for Improving Social Security Disability Adjudications*, 25 CARDOZO L. REV. 1 (2003). As part of Disability Service Improvement Process (DSIP), SSA sought to implement a Medical-Vocational Expert System comprised of a Medical-Vocational Expert unit, as well as a national network of medical, psychological, and vocational experts. This project, which was designed to enhance the expertise necessary to make disability decisions, was terminated along with other aspects of the DSIP. *See* 74 Fed. Reg. 63688 (December 4, 2009).

5. In the mid-1990s, a new attorney advisor position was added at what was then the Office of Hearings and Appeals as part of SSA's Hearing Process Improvement project. The position was created to address the increased workload at the hearing level and expedite the processing of cases pending at OHA without infringing on a claimant's right to a hearing before an ALJ. To this end, attorney advisors were authorized to conduct prehearing proceedings, such as reviewing the record and requesting additional evidence, and to issue decisions wholly favorable to the claimant. The attorney advisor program continued until 2001, at which point it was phased out in response to criticism that attorney advisers did not have a significant impact on the backlog of cases, did not produce decisions comparable in quality to those rendered by ALJs after hearing, and therefore wasted limited resources. The position was reinstated in 2007, however, and attorney advisors are now used again at ODAR. *See* 74 Fed. Reg. 33327 (July 13, 2009).

6. Regulations allow for the appearance of claimants and witnesses by video conference under certain circumstance, subject to objection by the claimant. *See* 20 C.F.R. §§ 404. 936(c), 416.1436(c); 20 C.F.R. §§ 404. 950, 416.1450. In some cases witnesses will simply call in by telephone, which is not authorized by regulation. One court noted the problem and resolved it as follows:

> It appears that the use of telephonic testimony by medical experts is on the rise across the nation. Well over half of the instances in which a federal court notes that a medical expert testified by telephone in a Social Security benefits case have occurred in the last three years. Given the growing use of medical expert telephonic testimony in Social Security Administrative hearings—which likely serves efficiency purposes and may not often disadvantage claimants—this Court will not go so far as to rule that all medical expert testimony in such hearings must be either in person or by video teleconference. However, ALJs must provide claimants with notice that a witness will be testifying telephonically, and absent a new rule, medical experts should not be allowed to testify telephonically over a claimant's timely objection. If the Commissioner wishes to receive Chevron deference when it allows such telephonic testimony without notice or over claimants' objections, the Social Security Administration must create a rule through the approved notice-and-comment process.

Edwards v. Astrue, 2011 WL 3490024, *8, 168 Soc. Sec. Rep. Serv. 361 (D.Conn. 2011).

3. APPEALS COUNCIL REVIEW

A claimant who is dissatisfied with the decision of the administrative law judge following an administrative hearing has one final opportunity for administrative review within the Social Security Administration: review of the hearing decision by the Appeals Council. *See* 20 C.F.R. §§ 404.967, 416.1467. The Appeals Council is an independent, quasi-judicial body within SSA, with exclusive jurisdiction to decide appeals from ALJ decisions. The Appeals Council was designed to oversee the administrative appeals process, promote national consistency in ALJ hearing decisions, and ensure that the Commissioner's records are adequate for judicial review. Currently, it consists of approximately 46 Administrative Appeals Judges, 51 Appeals Officers, and several hundred support personnel.

A request for review by the Appeals Council must be filed within 60 days of receipt of the hearing decision, unless the time limit is extended for good cause. **20 C.F.R. §§ 404.968, 416.1468[APP-REGS]**. The Appeals Council can grant or deny the request for review; if the petition for review is granted, the Council will either issue a decision or remand the case for further administrative action. Social Security regulations list four grounds for review: an abuse of discretion by the administrative law judge; an error of law in the administrative hearing decision; the decision is not supported by substantial evidence; and the decision presents "broad policy or procedural issues that may affect the general public interest." *See* **20 C.F.R. §§ 404.970(a), 416.1470(a)[APP-REGS]**. In practice, the Appeals Council rarely grants review. If review is granted, the claimant may request an oral argument; however, in most cases a decision or remand order is issued at the same time the Council grants review. The Council can also dismiss an appeal if not timely filed or under other limited circumstances.

The Appeals Council does not see the claimant but merely reviews the record. A claimant may submit new evidence to the Appeals Council together with a request for review, which will be considered by the Council together with the record established at the hearing. The new evidence must, however, relate to the time period relevant to the pending application, which means before the date of the administrative hearing decision.

In addition to claimant-initiated review of an adverse ALJ decision, the Appeals Council can review the decision of an administrative law judge on its own motion, through both random and selective sampling. *See generally* **20 C.F.R. §§ 404.969, 416.1469[APP-REGS]**. When the Appeals Council reviews a favorable administrative hearing decision on its own motion, the claimant is entitled interim benefits during the review process if a final decision on the review is not issued within 110 days. 20 C.F.R. §§ 404.969(d), 416.1467(d).

A decision by the Appeals Council, either to deny a request for review or, following the granting of a request for review, to affirm, modify, or reverse the hearing decision, is a final decision by SSA, subject to judicial review. However, if the case is remanded for further action by an ALJ, there is no final decision and the administrative process continues.

NOTES

1. In addition to claims heard at the review level, the Appeals Council deals with cases in two other situations. First, the Appeals Council hears claims where a civil action has been filed in federal district court and the government attorney asks the Council to conduct a supplemental review. This may happen when the attorney believes the case is indefensible in court, even if it was correctly denied initially. The attorney may recommend that the case be remanded to SSA to pay the claim, further develop the evidentiary record, or flesh out the written rationale for denial. Second, the Appeals Council hears cases after the district judge has issued a final decision or has remanded the case to the SSA with orders to conduct a new hearing or adduce new evidence. If the district court's orders are clear, the case may go directly back to the ALJ. In other cases, the Appeals Council may supplement the court's remand order with additional guidance before sending the case to an ALJ. After the new hearing, the ALJ issues a "recommended decision" which then goes back to the Appeals Council. The Appeals Council may adopt or modify the recommendation. District court remands are discussed in more detail later in this chapter.

2. Over the years, there have been a number of calls to eliminate the Appeals Council or to reduce its role to discretionary review. For instance, the Disability Services Improvement Process (DSIP) sought to replace the Appeals Council with a new reviewing body—the Decision Review Board—with the idea that it would review and correct decisional errors and ensure consistent adjudication at all stages of the process. That change was abandoned in 2008 along with most other aspects of the DSIP.

Much of the criticism comes from the fact that—with the passage of time and the ability to consider new evidence—the Appeals Council often reviews a substantially different record that that which was before the ALJ. Another common criticism is that requiring Appeals Council action before judicial review in all cases lengthens the process unnecessarily for the vast majority of claims that are denied review. Many wonder if a fourth tier of administrative review is justified given its cost when the Appeals Council reverses the ALJ decision in only five percent of the cases it reviews.

The following passage from *Salling v. Bowen*, 641 F. Supp. 1046, 1058-59 (W.D. Va. 1986), summarizes the controversy surrounding the Appeals Council:

> This court is of the opinion that money expended for the Appeals Council and its staff is unnecessary expense. Why should the ALJ not be the final arbiter in the case? If he does his duty, he is supposed to express the government's viewpoint, develop all the evidence that can be obtained for the claimant or the government, and to conduct a fair and just hearing. If an appeal is to be granted, it should after hearing be taken directly to court because the ALJ is in the best position to judge the case having seen the claimant and being in an area where he is familiar with the doctors involved. In a time when efforts are being made to save money, the abolishment of the Appeals Council and one of the two stages of state DDS review is worthy of great consideration.

On the other hand, others argue that Appeals Council serves a valuable function in screening and resolving cases before they reach the district court, thereby protecting district courts from excessive litigation and conserving judicial resources. They also contend that the Appeals Council acts as a centralized final reviewing authority to create a uniform agency position. For an early critique an detailed description of the Appeals Council, see Charles H. Koch, Jr. & David A. Koplow, *The Fourth Bite at the Apple: A Study of the Operation and Utility of the Social Security Administration's Appeals Council*, 17 FLA. ST. U. L. REV. 199 (1990). Despite continuing criticism, the Appeals Council remains in operation today essentially as it has throughout its history.

A) SCOPE OF APPEALS COUNCIL REVIEW

When a claimant seeks Appeals Council review of an administrative hearing decision, the entire claim is subject to review. This is certainly the case where the claimant requests review generally from an unfavorable decision. Full review by the Appeals Council is appropriate also where the claimant has requested review only on certain issues, at least so long as the claimant was notified that a request for review of a partially favorable decision could be subject to full-scale review.

WILLIAMS V. SULLIVAN
970 F.2d 1178, 38 Soc. Sec. Rep. Serv. 220 (3d Cir. 1992)

Robert E. Cowen, Circuit Judge.

This is an appeal from a denial of disability benefits under the Social Security Act. Following a hearing in 1989, the administrative law judge found that appellant Thomas Williams was disabled as of March 28, 1988. Williams sought review by the Appeals Council regarding the date of onset of his disability, requesting that the Council award retroactive benefits back to December 1986. Upon review, the Appeals Council determined that Williams was not disabled at all. The district court affirmed the ruling of no disability by the Appeals Council. Because the Appeals Council acted within its discretion when it reviewed the case in full, and its conclusion that Williams was not disabled was supported by substantial evidence, we will affirm.

* * *

III.

Williams first challenges the Appeals Council's authority to review his entire case. He appealed one narrow issue, the onset date of his disability, but the Appeals Council reviewed his entire record and reversed the ALJ's determination of disability altogether. Williams asserts that this policy of wide open review is fundamentally unfair and violates due process because it chills a claimant's right to appeal by implicitly threatening the potential loss of benefits already granted.

Although an ALJ's findings of fact may be taken as conclusive, the Appeals Council may review all the evidence of record to decide whether the ALJ's findings are supported by substantial evidence. In Powell v. Heckler, 789 F.2d 176 (3d Cir.1986), this court held that the Appeals Council need not limit its review to the issue appealed, but may review a claimant's entire case provided it gives sufficient notice that appeals will be subject to full review. *Id.* at 179; *see also* Hale v. Sullivan, 934 F.2d 895, 898 (7th Cir.1991) (once the Appeals Council receives a timely request for review, it is entitled to review the entirety of the case); Gronda v. Secretary of Health & Human Serv., 856 F.2d 36, 38-39 (6th Cir.1988) (Appeals Council had authority to review entire case within 60 days of ALJ's decision even though claimant only requested review of narrow aspect of case), cert. denied, 489 U.S. 1052, 109 S.Ct. 1312, 103 L.Ed.2d 581 (1989); Bivines v. Bowen, 833 F.2d 293, 297 (11th Cir.1987) (where claimant files application for review, Appeals Council may not revisit unchallenged issues unless it gives claimant notice); Kennedy v. Bowen, 814 F.2d 1523, 1524 (11th Cir.1987) (Appeals Council must give notice of its intent to re-examine issues not challenged by claimant); DeLong v. Heckler, 771 F.2d 266, 267-68 (7th Cir.1985) (application for limited review of date of onset of disability gave Appeals Council the prerogative to broaden the scope of its review).

When Williams was first notified of the results of his hearing before the ALJ, he received a letter stating he had received a favorable decision. This letter contained a paragraph which put him on notice that if he appealed he might lose those benefits:

> When you appeal, you request the Appeals Council to review the de-
> cision. If the Appeals Council grants your request, it will review the
> entire record in your case. It will review those parts of the decision
> which you think are wrong. It will also review those parts which you
> think are correct and may make them unfavorable or less favorable
> to you. You will receive a new decision.

This paragraph was sufficient to put Williams on notice that if he appealed he risked losing his award.[4] Since this means of notification was
reasonably calculated to apprise both Williams and his counsel of the risk
associated with appealing the award, no due process violation can be
found.

> "[F]undamental fairness requires that partly dissatisfied claimants ...
> be apprised of the risks inherent in their projected appeals." Powell, 789
> F.2d at 180.   Here, Williams received, along with the partially favorable
> hearing decision, a notice explaining his appeal rights.   This notice,
> mailed directly to Williams and his attorney with the hearing decision,
> plainly stated that if an appeal were taken, the Appeals Council would
> review the entire record and might make a decision different from that of
> the ALJ.

> Williams argues that the Appeals Council should have notified him
> within 60 days of the date of the hearing decision of the issues upon
> which it would review Williams' case. The 60-day limit upon which Wil-
> liams relies, however, applies only to review initiated by the Council upon
> its own motion. 20 C.F.R. § 404.969 (1991). Here, Williams himself initi-
> ated the request for review. No mandatory deadlines apply to claimant-
> initiated requests. In any event, because the notice explaining his appeal
> rights accompanied the letter notifying Williams of the favorable decision
> of the ALJ, it complies with 20 C.F.R. § 404.969. There was no violation
> of due process in the Appeals Council's review of the entire record under-
> lying the ALJ's decision.

[The court finds that there was substantial evidence to support the Appeals Council's decision that the claimant was not disabled.]

---

[4] We held in *Powell* that where a claimant makes a timely application for review of a limited
issue, the Appeals Council must give notice within sixty days of the ALJ decision if it intends to
undertake review on the merits beyond those framed by the claimant. 789 F.2d at 179. Because
the Appeals Council failed to give timely notice of its intention to make a broader review of the
record, it was limited to the onset date issue raised by Powell. Id. at 178-79.   In the present
matter, however, the letter notifying Williams of his benefits award stated not only that the Appeals Council could exercise plenary review but also that the Council had the authority to review
the decision on its own motion within 60 days. Regardless of which entity initiates review, the
Council may consider the entire case provided it gives sufficient notice to the claimant of the
scope of its review.

NOTE

Circuit courts are split as to whether the Appeals Council must notify a claimant of its decision of to review the merits of a claim when the claimant requested only review of a technical mistake. For instance, in *Ciccone v. Appel*, 38 F. Supp. 2d 224 (E.D.N.Y. 1999), the claimant requested only that the Appeals Council correct a technical mistake regarding the date of his application. Following the Eleventh Circuit approach, the court held that the Appeals Council was required to notify the claimant of its intent to review the merits of his claim:

> [T]he remaining issue is whether the Appeals Council was required to notify plaintiff of its decision to review the merits of his claim, or whether the letter accompanying the ALJ's decision provided sufficient notice that the Council could review the entire record even though plaintiff had requested a mere technical correction. 20 C.F.R. § 404.968 entitles a claimant to request that the Appeals Council review an ALJ's decision within 60 days of receiving notice of the decision. Section 404.969 grants the Appeals Council the authority to review the entire decision of an ALJ on its own motion, also within 60 days of the decision. When the Council initiates review on its own motion, Section 404.969 requires the Council to notify all parties by mail. Section 404.973 also requires written notice "[w]hen the Appeals Council decides to review a case."

> The Commissioner argues that the Appeals Council was not required under the C.F.R. to notify plaintiff of its intent to review the merits of his claim. Specifically, the Commissioner contends that the Appeals Council was entitled to review any and all issues raised in the ALJ's decision and/or to remand the case without notice to plaintiff because the letter accompanying the ALJ's decision explicitly warned plaintiff that a request for review would place the entire administrative record before the Appeals Council. The letter read:

> > If you file an appeal, the Council will consider all of my decision, even the parts with which you agree....Requesting review places the entire record of your case before the Council. Review can make any part of my decision more or less favorable or unfavorable to you. On review, the Council may itself consider the issues and decide your case. The Council may also send it back to an Administrative law Judge for a new decision.

> Plaintiff contends that it would be unjust to permit the Council to overturn an ALJ's decision without notice after a claimant had already begun to collect payments and that such a policy would have a chilling effect on a claimant's willingness to seek rightful corrections.

> The Court of Appeals for the Second Circuit has not ruled on this issue, and the circuits that have ruled are divided. The Third, Sixth, Seventh and Eighth Circuits have held that the warnings accompanying an

ALJ's decision are sufficient to put claimants on notice that they risk losing their award if they appeal even limited aspects of the ALJ's decision. See Culbertson v. Shalala, 30 F.3d 934, 937-38 (8th Cir.1994); Williams v. Sullivan, M.D., 970 F.2d 1178, 1182-83 (3rd Cir.), cert. denied, 507 U.S. 924, 113 S.Ct. 1294, 122 L.Ed.2d 685 (1993); Hale v. Sullivan, 934 F.2d 895, 898 (7th Cir.1991); Gronda v. Secretary of Health & Human Services, 856 F.2d 36, 39 (6th Cir.), cert. denied, 489 U.S. 1052, 109 S.Ct. 1312, 103 L.Ed.2d 581 (1989). The Eleventh Circuit has held, however, that, when a claimant makes a limited application for review, the Appeals Council must provide the claimant with notice of its intent to review the ALJ's entire decision, including the reasons for its review and the issues to be considered. See Baker v. Sullivan, 880 F.2d 319, 320 (11th Cir.1989); Bivines v. Bowen, 833 F.2d 293, 296 (11th Cir.1987); Kennedy v. Bowen, 814 F.2d 1523, 1527 (11th Cir.1987). See also McDonald v. Secretary of Health and Human Services, 796 F.Supp. 616 (D.Mass.1992); Everhart v. Bowen, 694 F.Supp. 1518 (D.Colo.1987). The Eleventh Circuit reasons that, "when the Appeals Council expands its scope of review in a claimant-initiated appeal, this expansion is equivalent to the Appeals Council's own motion review of the added issues, and the Council is not absolved from the notice requirement under 20 C.F.R. section 404.969." Baker, 880 F.2d at 320.

Under the facts of this case, the Eleventh Circuit's reasoning is persuasive. A reasonable claimant would not expect an ostensibly final decision to be impacted by a request for a technical correction as to the date of his application, and a "no-notice" policy would have an unreasonably chilling effect on a claimant's willingness to seek such limited review. By requesting the additional benefits guaranteed him by the regulations (which, according to plaintiff, totaled approximately $2,973), plaintiff subjected himself to a denial of benefits altogether or to a finding of overpayment. The letter accompanying the ALJ's decision did not adequately notify plaintiff that his request for a correction put him at such a risk. The letter states that a request for "review" places the entire record before the Council but it does not define "review" or explain that requests for corrections that do not go to the merits of a claim entitle the Appeals Council to engage in a full-scale evaluation of the claim. The Appeals Council's decision to review the merits of plaintiff's case was equivalent to a decision to review the claim on its own motion pursuant to Section 404.969, and, therefore, notice was required.

D. JUDICIAL REVIEW

The Social Security Act provides specifically for judicial review of adverse benefit determinations on Social Security claims in the federal district courts. Federal court appeals of Social Security administrative decisions follow, in most respects, the usual rules for judicial review of administrative action. On the other hand, there are some serious jurisdictional questions with respect to other types of cases that a Social Security claimant may want to file in federal court. The basic jurisdictional rules for individual claims and some of these other jurisdictional issues are discussed in the first part of this section. The scope of review and the standard of review applied in these cases are discussed in the second part of this section.

NOTE ON MAGISTRATE JUDGES

Magistrate judges are term-limited Article I federal trial judges appointed by life-tenured Article III federal district court judges. *See generally* 28 U.S.C. § 636. Magistrate judges play an increasingly important role in Social Security cases, as in many judicial districts Social Security appeals are referred routinely to magistrate judges to prepare a report and recommendation to the court. Moreover, parties can consent to have a magistrate judge act as a district judge in a particular case.

When a district judge assigns a case to a magistrate judge, the magistrate judge conducts a hearing and prepares proposed findings of fact and a recommended decision. The parties then have fourteen days to ask the district judge to review the magistrate judge's findings and recommendations. District judges review the cases *de novo* and may accept, reject, or modify the magistrate judge's report in whole or in part. *See id.* § 636(b)(1). When a magistrate judges hears a case with the consent of the parties, the magistrate judge's decision is the final decision of the district court. *Id.* § 636(c). For this reason, the parties' consent must be express and in writing. *See* McGinnis v. Shalala, 2 F.3d 548, 551 (5th Cir. 1993) ("A magistrate judge may act in the capacity of a federal district court under 28 U.S.C. § 636(c) only upon the express, written consent of both parties. * * * [C]onsent to trial by magistrate judge must be express; we have 'refused to 'infer this statutorily required consent from the conduct of the parties.'").

1. JURISDICTION

The Social Security Act addresses directly the matter of federal court jurisdiction over Social Security cases. Thus, **42 U.S.C. § 405(g)[APPSTAT]** provides, in part:

Any individual, after any final decision of the Commissioner of Social Security made after a hearing to which he was a party, irrespective of the amount in controversy, may obtain a review of such decision by a civil action commenced within sixty days after the mailing to him of notice of such decision or within such further time as the Commissioner of Social Security may allow. Such action shall be brought in the district court of the United States for the judicial district in which the plaintiff resides, or has his principal place of business, or, if he does not reside or have his principal place of business within any such judicial district, in the United States District Court for the District of Columbia. * * * The court shall have power to enter, upon the pleadings and transcript of the record, a judgment affirming, modifying, or reversing the decision of the Commissioner of Social Security, with or without remanding the cause for a rehearing. * * *

The Act also authorizes district courts to remand cases to SSA for further action, including taking new evidence, but only if "there is new evidence which is material and that there is good cause for the failure to incorporate such evidence into the record in a prior proceeding." *Id.* Together with this broad grant of jurisdiction to review decisions on individual claims for benefits after an administrative hearing has been held, the Act explicitly precludes other bases for federal court jurisdiction:

> The findings and decision of the Commissioner of Social Security after a hearing shall be binding upon all individuals who were parties to such hearing. No findings of fact or decision of the Commissioner of Social Security shall be reviewed by any person, tribunal, or governmental agency except as herein provided. No action against the United States, the Commissioner of Social Security, or any officer or employee thereof shall be brought under section 1331 or 1346 of Title 28 to recover on any claim arising under this subchapter.

42 U.S.C. § 405(h).

The Act thus provides a clear jurisdictional basis for federal district court review of any ordinary, individual disability claim where the issue is eligibility under applicable laws and regulations. It is equally clear that ordinary individual claims can be appealed to federal court only after all administrative remedies have been exhausted. As noted earlier, this is usually accomplished by first seeking a hearing before an administrative law judge and then appealing the decision, if it is unfavorable, to the Appeals Council. According to SSA regulations, if the Appeals Council grants review of a claim the decision of the Appeals Council is the Commissioner's final decision. If the Appeals Council denies the request for review, the ALJ's decision becomes the final decision. *See* 20 CFR §§ 404.900(a)(4)-(5), 404.955, 404.981, 422.210(a). If a claimant fails to request review from the Appeals Council, there is no final decision and the claimant is not entitled to judicial review.

Once the exhaustion requirement has been satisfied, an appeal must be filed within 60 days of the Appeal Council decision, whether on the merits or denying a request for review. This 60-day filing deadline is considered to be a waivable statute of limitations, as opposed to a jurisdictional requirement; accordingly, SSA will grant an extension of time to file an appeal upon a showing of good cause. *See* **20 C.F.R. §§ 404.982, 416.1482[APP-REGS]**.

A) EXHAUSTION OF ADMINISTRATIVE REMEDIES

Situations may arise, however, where for some reason the exhaustion requirement has not been or cannot be met. The Supreme Court has endorsed federal court review of SSA policies under certain circumstances without first exhausting administrative remedies, notwithstanding the Act's removal of general federal question jurisdiction in Social Security cases. The Court has also rejected the idea that federal courts should require "issue exhaustion" in Social Security cases, in addition to exhaustion of administrative remedies.

WEINBERGER V. SALFI
422 U.S. 749, 95 S. Ct. 2457 (1975)

Mr. Justice REHNQUIST delivered the opinion of the Court.

Appellants, the Department of Health, Education, and Welfare, its Secretary, the Social Security Administration and various of its officials, appeal from a decision of the United States District Court for the Northern District of California invalidating duration-of-relationship Social Security eligibility requirements for surviving wives and stepchildren of deceased wage earners. 373 F.Supp. 961 (1974).

That court concluded that it had jurisdiction of the action by virtue of 28 U.S.C. § 1331, and eventually certified the case as a class action. On the merits, it concluded that the nine-month requirements of §§ 216(c)(5) and (e) (2) of the Social Security Act constituted 'irrebutable presumptions' which were constitutionally invalid * * *. We hold that the District Court did not have jurisdiction of this action under 28 U.S.C. § 1331, and that while it had jurisdiction of the claims of the named appellees under the provisions of 42 U.S.C. § 405(g), it had no jurisdiction over the claims asserted on behalf of unnamed class members. We further decide that the District Court was wrong on the merits of the constitutional question tendered by the named appellees.

* * *

II

The third sentence of 42 U.S.C. § 405(h) provides in part:

> 'No action against the United States, the Secretary, or any officer or employee thereof shall be brought under (§ 1331 et seq.) of Title 28 to recover on any claim arising under (Title II of the Social Security Act).'

On its face, this provision bars district court federal-question jurisdiction over suits, such as this one, which seek to recover Social Security benefits. Yet it was § 1331 jurisdiction which appellees successfully in-voked in the District Court. That court considered this provision, but concluded that it was inapplicable because it amounted to no more than a codification of the doctrine of exhaustion of administrative remedies. The District Court's reading of § 405(h) was, we think, entirely too narrow.

That the third sentence of § 405(h) is more than a codified require-ment of administrative exhaustion is plain from its own language, which is sweeping and direct and which states that no action shall be brought under § 1331, not merely that only those actions shall be brought in which administrative remedies have been exhausted. Moreover, if the third sentence is construed to be nothing more than a requirement of ad-ministrative exhaustion, it would be superfluous. This is because the first two sentences of § 405(h) * * * assure that administrative exhaustion will be required. Specifically, they prevent review of decisions of the Secretary save as provided in the Act, which provision is made in § 405(g). The lat-ter section prescribes typical requirements for review of matters before an administrative agency, including administrative exhaustion.[6] Thus the District Court's treatment of the third sentence of § 405(h) not only ig-nored that sentence's plain language, but also relegated it to a function which is already performed by other statutory provisions.

* * *

A somewhat more substantial argument that the third sentence of § 405(h) does not deprive the District Court of federal-question jurisdiction relies on the fact that it only affects actions to recover on 'any claim aris-ing under (Title II)' of the Social Security Act.[7] The argument is that the present action arises under the Constitution and not under Title II. It would, of course, be fruitless to contend that appellees' claim is one which does not arise under the Constitution, since their constitutional argu-ments are critical to their complaint. But it is just as fruitless to argue that this action does not also arise under the Social Security Act. For not only is it Social Security benefits which appellees seek to recover, but it is the Social Security Act which provides both the standing and the sub-stantive basis for the presentation of their constitutional contentions. Ap-pellees sought, and the District Court granted, a judgment directing the Secretary to pay Social Security benefits. To contend that such an action

---

[6] Nor can it be argued that the third sentence of § 405(h) simply serves to prevent a bypass of the § 405(g) requirements by filing a district court complaint alleging entitlement prior to ap-plying for benefits through administrative channels. The entitlement sections of the Act specify the filing of an application as a prerequisite to entitlement, so a court could not in any event award benefits absent an application. * * * Once the application is filed, it is either approved, in which event any suit for benefits would be mooted, or it is denied. Even if the denial is nonfinal, it is still a 'decision of the Secretary' which, by virtue of the second sentence of § 405(h), may not be reviewed save pursuant to § 405(g).

[7] Title II contains the old-age, survivors, and disability insurance programs codified at 42 U.S.C. s 401 et seq.

does not arise under the Act whose benefits are sought is to ignore both the language and the substance of the complaint and judgment. This being so, the third sentence of § 405(h) precludes resort to federal-question jurisdiction for the adjudication of appellees' constitutional contentions.

* * *

As has been stated, the Social Security Act itself provides for district court review of the Secretary's determinations. Title 42 U.S.C. § 405(g) provides that '(a)ny individual, after any final decision of the Secretary made after a hearing to which he was a party, irrespective of the amount in controversy, may obtain a review of such decision by a civil action commenced within sixty days after the mailing to him of notice of such decision . . ..' * * * The question with which we must now deal is whether this provision could serve as a jurisdictional basis for the District Court's consideration of the present case. We conclude that it provided jurisdiction only as to the named appellees and not as to the unnamed members of the class.

Section 405(g) specifies the following requirements for judicial review: (1) a final decision of the Secretary made after a hearing; (2) commencement of a civil action within 60 days after the mailing of notice of such decision (or within such further time as the Secretary may allow); and (3) filing of the action in an appropriate district court, in general that of the plaintiff's residence or principal place of business. The second and third of these requirements specify, respectively, a statute of limitations and appropriate venue. As such, they are waivable by the parties, and not having been timely raised below, need not be considered here. We interpret the first requirement, however, to be central to the requisite grant of subject-matter jurisdiction--the statute empowers district courts to review a particular type of decision by the Secretary, that type being those which are 'final' and 'made after a hearing.'

In the present case, the complaint seeks review of the denial of benefits based on the plain wording of a statute which is alleged to be unconstitutional. That a denial on such grounds, which are beyond the power of the Secretary to affect, is nonetheless a decision of the Secretary for these purposes has been heretofore established. Flemming v. Nestor, 363 U.S. 603, 80 S.Ct. 1367, 4 L.Ed.2d 1435 (1960). As to class members, however, the complaint is deficient in that it contains no allegations that they have even filed an application with the Secretary, much less that he has rendered any decision, final or otherwise, review of which is sought. The class thus cannot satisfy the requirements for jurisdiction under 42 U.S.C. § 405(g). Other sources of jurisdiction being foreclosed by § 405(h), the District Court was without jurisdiction over so much of the complaint as concerns the class, and it should have entered by appropriate order of dismissal.

The jurisdictional issue with respect to the named appellees is somewhat more difficult. In a paragraph entitled 'Exhaustion of Remedies,' the complaint alleges that they fully presented their claims for benefits 'to their district Social Security Office and, upon denial, to the Regional Office for reconsideration.' It further alleges that they have no dispute with the Regional Office's findings of fact or applications of statutory law, and that the only issue is a matter of constitutional law which is beyond the Secretary's competence. On their face these allegations with regard to exhaustion fall short of meeting the literal requirement of § 405(g) that there shall have been a 'final decision of the Secretary made after a hearing.' They also fall short of satisfying the Secretary's regulations, which specify that the finality required for judicial review is achieved only after the further steps of a hearing before an administrative law judge and, possibly, consideration by the Appeals Council. See 20 CFR §§ 404.916, 404.940, 404.951 (1974).

We have previously recognized that the doctrine of administrative exhaustion should be applied with a regard for the particular administrative scheme at issue. Parisi v. Davidson, 405 U.S. 34, 92 S.Ct. 815, 31 L.Ed.2d 17 (1972); McKart v. United States, 395 U.S. 185, 89 S.Ct. 1657, 23 L.Ed.2d 194 (1969). Exhaustion is generally required as a matter of preventing premature interference with agency processes, so that the agency may function efficiently and so that it may have an opportunity to correct its own errors, to afford the parties and the courts the benefit of its experience and expertise, and to compile a record which is adequate for judicial review. Plainly these purposes have been served once the Secretary has satisfied himself that the only issue is the constitutionality of a statutory requirement, a matter which is beyond his jurisdiction to determine, and that the claim is neither otherwise invalid nor cognizable under a different section of the Act. Once a benefit applicant has presented his or her claim at a sufficiently high level of review to satisfy the Secretary's administrative needs, further exhaustion would not merely be futile for the applicant, but would also be a commitment of administrative resources unsupported by any administrative or judicial interest.

The present case, of course, is significantly different from McKart in that a 'final decision' is a statutorily specified jurisdictional prerequisite. The requirement is, therefore, as we have previously noted, something more than simply a codification of the judicially developed doctrine of exhaustion, and may not be dispensed with merely by a judicial conclusion of futility such as that made by the District Court here. But it is equally true that the requirement of a 'final decision' contained in § 405(g) is not precisely analogous to the more classical jurisdictional requirements contained in such sections of Title 28 as 1331 and 1332. The term 'final decision' is not only left undefined by the Act, but its meaning is left to the Secretary to flesh out by regulation. Section 405(l) accords the Secretary complete authority to delegate his statutory duties to officers and employees of the Department of Health, Education, and Welfare. The statutory scheme is thus one in which the Secretary may specify such requirements for exhaustion as he deems serve his own interests in effective and efficient administration. While a court may not substitute its conclusion as to futility for the contrary conclusion of the Secretary, we believe it would be inconsistent with the congressional scheme to bar the Secretary from determining in particular cases that full exhaustion of internal review procedures in not necessary for a decision to be 'final' within the language of § 405(g).

Much the same may be said about the statutory requirement that the Secretary's decision be made 'after a hearing.' Not only would a hearing be futile and wasteful, once the Secretary has determined that the only issue to be resolved is a matter of constitutional law concededly beyond his competence to decide, but the Secretary may, of course, award benefits without requiring a hearing. We do not understand the statute to prevent him from similarly determining in favor of the applicant, without a hearing, all issues with regard to eligibility save for one as to which he considers a hearing to be useless.

In the present case the Secretary does not raise any challenge to the sufficiency of the allegations of exhaustion in appellees' complaint. We interpret this to be a determination by him that for the purposes of this litigation the reconsideration determination is 'final.' The named appellees thus satisfy the requirements for § 405(g) judicial review, and we proceed to the merits of their claim.

[Proceeding to the merits, the Court held that the nine-month duration-of-marriage requirement is constitutional.]

[Dissenting opinion of Justice Douglas omitted, in which he agreed with Justice Brennan that "there is clearly jurisdiction."]

Mr. Justice BRENNAN, with whom Mr. Justice MARSHALL joins, dissenting.

The District Court did not err, in my view, either in holding that it had jurisdiction by virtue of 28 U.S.C. § 1331, or in holding that the nine-month requirements of 42 U.S.C. § 416(c)(5) and (e)(2) (1970 ed. and Supp. III) are constitutionally invalid.

I

Jurisdiction

The jurisdictional issue to which the Court devotes 10 pages, only to conclude that there is indeed jurisdiction over the merits of this case both here and in the District Court, was not raised in this Court by the parties before us nor argued, except most peripherally, in the briefs or at oral argument. The question involves complicated questions of legislative intent and a statutory provision, 42 U.S.C. § 405(h), which has baffled district court's and courts of appeals for years in this and other contexts.   Of course, this Court is always obliged to inquire into its own jurisdiction, when there is a substantial question about whether jurisdiction is proper either in the lower courts or in this Court. But since here there is, according to the Court, jurisdiction over the cause of action in any event, I would have thought it the wiser course merely to note that there was jurisdiction in the District Court either under 28 U.S.C. § 1331 or under 42 U.S.C. § 405(g), leaving the resolution of the question of which is applicable to a case in which the decision is of some consequence, and in which the parties have, either of their own volition or upon request of the Court, briefed and argued the issue. Surely, the Court does not intend to adopt a new policy of always on its own canvassing, with a full discussion, all jurisdictional issues lurking behind every case, whether or not the issue has any impact at all on the resolution of the case.

Because the Court nonetheless treats the question fully, I am obliged to do so as well. For, at least insofar as my own research and consideration, unaided by the help ordinarily offered by adversary consideration, is adequate, I am convinced that the Court is quite wrong about the intended reach of § 405(h), and that its construction attributes to Congress a purpose both contrary to all established notions of administrative exhaustion and absolutely without support in the clear language or legislative history of the statute.   * * *

A

The Court rejects the District Court's conclusion that § 405(h) is no more than a codified requirement of administrative exhaustion on the basis of the third sentence of the section, which it characterizes as 'sweeping and direct and (stating) that no action shall be brought under § 1331, not merely that only those actions shall be brought in which administrative remedies have been exhausted.' * * * But the sentence does not say that no action of any kind shall be brought under § 1331, or other general grants of jurisdiction, which may result in entitling someone to benefits under Title II of the Act; it says merely that no action shall be brought under § 1331 et. seq. 'to recover on any claim arising under (Title II).' (Emphasis added.) This action, I believe, does not 'arise under' Title II in the manner intended by § 405(h), and it is, at least in part, not an action to 'recover' on a claim.

Section 405(h), I believe, only bans, except under § 405(g), suits which arise under Title II in the sense that they require the application of the statute to a set of facts, and which seek nothing more than a determination of eligibility claimed to arise under the Act. Thus, I basically agree with the District Court that § 405(h), including its last sentence, merely codifies the usual requirements of administrative exhaustion. The last sentence, in particular, provides that a plaintiff cannot avoid § 405(g) and the first two sentences of § 405(h) by bringing an action under .a general grant of jurisdiction claiming that the Social Security Act itself provides him certain rights. Rather, on such a claim a plaintiff must exhaust administrative remedies, and the District Court is limited to review of the Secretary's decision, in the manner prescribed by § 405(g).

* * *

D

Finally, even if I could agree, and I do not, that § 405(g) is the exclusive route for consideration of this kind of case, I would dissent from the Court's treatment of the exhaustion requirement of § 405(g). The Court admits that the purposes of administrative exhaustion "have been served once the Secretary has satisfied himself that the only issue is the constitutionality of a statutory requirement, a matter which is beyond his jurisdiction to determine, and that the claim is neither otherwise invalid nor cognizable under a different section of the Act.' Nonetheless, the Court construes the statute so as to permit 'the *Secretary* (to) specify such requirements for exhaustion as *he deems* serve *his own* interests in effective and efficient administration. . . . (A) court may not substitute its conclusion as to futility for the contrary conclusion of the Secretary.' *Ante*, at 2467. (Emphasis supplied.)

If, as the Court holds, the finality and hearing requirements of § 405(g) are not jurisdictional,[14] then I fail to see why it is left to the Secretary to determine when the point of futility is reached, a power to be exercised, apparently, with regard only to the Secretary's needs and without taking account of the claimants' interest in not exhausting futile remedies, and in obtaining promptly benefits which have been unconstitution-

---

[14] The Court has to ignore plain language of the statute in order to avoid the absurd result of requiring full exhaustion on all claims such as this one, even after the point of futility is reached. The statute says that judicial review can be had only 'after a hearing.' § 405(g), and it is apparent that the hearing contemplated is a full, evidentiary hearing, see § 405(b). Rather than avoiding the statutory language by holding that the Secretary can nonetheless dispense with a hearing, the Court would do better to recognize that the patent inapplicability of the statutory language to this kind of case suggests that the statute was never intended to apply at all to constitutional attacks beyond the Secretary's competence.

ally denied. Further, the Court leaves the way open for a lawless application of this power, since the Secretary can evidently, once the case is in court, assert or not assert the full exhaustion requirements of § 405(g), as he pleases.

* * *

SIMS V. APFEL

530 U.S. 103, 69 Soc. Sec. Rep. Ser. 415 (2000)

Justice THOMAS announced the judgment of the Court and delivered the opinion of the Court with respect to Parts I and II-A, and an opinion with respect to Part II-B, in which Justice STEVENS, Justice SOUTER, and Justice GINSBURG join.

A person whose claim for Social Security benefits is denied by an administrative law judge (ALJ) must in most cases, before seeking judicial review of that denial, request that the Social Security Appeals Council review his claim. The question is whether a claimant pursuing judicial review has waived any issues that he did not include in that request. We hold that he has not.

I

In 1994, petitioner Juatassa Sims filed applications for disability benefits under Title II of the Social Security Act and for supplemental security income benefits under Title XVI of that Act. She alleged disability from a variety of ailments, including degenerative joint diseases and carpal tunnel syndrome. After a state agency denied her claims, she obtained a hearing before a Social Security ALJ. * * * The ALJ, in 1996, also denied her claims, concluding that, although she did have some medical impairments, she had not been and was not under a "disability," as defined in the Act. * * *

Petitioner then requested that the Social Security Appeals Council review her claims. A claimant may request such review by completing a one-page form provided by the Social Security Administration (SSA)—Form HA-520—or "by any other writing specifically requesting review." 20 CFR § 422.205(a) (1999). Petitioner, through counsel, chose the latter option, submitting to the Council a letter arguing that the ALJ had erred in several ways in analyzing the evidence. The Council denied review.

Next, petitioner filed suit in the District Court for the Northern District of Mississippi. She contended that (1) the ALJ had made selective use of the record; (2) the questions the ALJ had posed to a vocational expert to determine petitioner's ability to work were defective because they omitted several of petitioner's ailments; and (3) in light of certain peculiarities in the medical evidence, the ALJ should have ordered a consultative examination. The District Court rejected all of these contentions. App. 74-84.

The Court of Appeals for the Fifth Circuit affirmed in an unpublished opinion. 162 F.3d 1160 (1998). That court affirmed on the merits with regard to petitioner's first contention. With regard to the second and third contentions, it concluded that, under its decision in Paul v. Shalala, 29 F.3d 208, 210 (1994), it lacked jurisdiction because petitioner had not raised those contentions in her request for review by the Appeals Council. We granted certiorari to resolve a conflict among the Courts of Appeals over whether a Social Security claimant waives judicial review of an issue if he fails to exhaust that issue by presenting it to the Appeals Council in his request for review.

II

A

The Social Security Act provides that "[a]ny individual, after any final decision of the Commissioner of Social Security made after a hearing to which he was a party, ... may obtain a review of such decision by a civil action" in federal district court. 42 U.S.C. § 405(g). But the Act does not define "final decision," instead leaving it to the SSA to give meaning to that term through regulations. See § 405(a); *Weinberger v. Salfi*, 422 U.S. 749, 766, 95 S.Ct. 2457, 45 L.Ed.2d 522 (1975). SSA regulations provide that, if the Appeals Council grants review of a claim, then the decision that the Council issues is the Commissioner's final decision. But if, as here, the Council denies the request for review, the ALJ's opinion becomes the final decision. See 20 CFR §§ 404.900(a)(4)-(5), 404.955, 404.981, 422.210(a) (1999).[2] If a claimant fails to request review from the Council, there is no final decision and, as a result, no judicial review in most cases. See § 404.900(b); *Bowen v. City of New York*, 476 U.S. 467, 482-483, 106 S.Ct. 2022, 90 L.Ed.2d 462 (1986). In administrative-law parlance, such a claimant may not obtain judicial review because he has failed to exhaust administrative remedies. See *Salfi*, supra, at 765-766, 95 S.Ct. 2457.

The Commissioner rightly concedes that petitioner exhausted administrative remedies by requesting review by the Council. Petitioner thus obtained a final decision, and nothing in § 405(g) or the regulations implementing it bars judicial review of her claims.

---

[2] Part 404 of 20 CFR (1999) applies to Title II of the Act. The regulations governing Title XVI, which can be found at 20 CFR pt. 416 (1999), are, as relevant here, not materially different. We will therefore omit references to the latter regulations.

Nevertheless, the Commissioner contends that we should require issue exhaustion in addition to exhaustion of remedies. That is, he contends that a Social Security claimant, to obtain judicial review of an issue, not only must obtain a final decision on his claim for benefits, but also must specify that issue in his request for review by the Council. (Whether a claimant must exhaust issues before the ALJ is not before us.) The Commissioner argues, in particular, that an issue-exhaustion requirement is "an important corollary" of any requirement of exhaustion of remedies. We think that this is not necessarily so and that the corollary is particularly unwarranted in this case.

Initially, we note that requirements of administrative issue exhaustion are largely creatures of statute. * * * Our cases addressing issue exhaustion reflect this fact. * * * Here, the Commissioner does not contend that any statute requires issue exhaustion in the request for review.

Similarly, it is common for an agency's regulations to require issue exhaustion in administrative appeals. And when regulations do so, courts reviewing agency action regularly ensure against the bypassing of that requirement by refusing to consider unexhausted issues. Yet, SSA regulations do not require issue exhaustion. (Although the question is not before us, we think it likely that the Commissioner could adopt a regulation that did require issue exhaustion.)

It is true that we have imposed an issue-exhaustion requirement even in the absence of a statute or regulation. But the reason we have done so does not apply here. The basis for a judicially imposed issue-exhaustion requirement is an analogy to the rule that appellate courts will not consider arguments not raised before trial courts. As the Court explained in *Hormel v. Helvering*, 312 U.S. 552, 61 S.Ct. 719, 85 L.Ed. 1037 (1941):

> "Ordinarily an appellate court does not give consideration to issues not raised below. For our procedural scheme contemplates that parties shall come to issue in the trial forum vested with authority to determine questions of fact. This is essential in order that parties may have the opportunity to offer all the evidence they believe relevant to the issues which the trial tribunal is alone competent to decide; it is equally essential in order that litigants may not be surprised on appeal by final decision there of issues upon which they have had no opportunity to introduce evidence. And the basic reasons which support this general principle applicable to trial courts make it equally desirable that parties should have an opportunity to offer evidence on the general issues involved in the less formal proceedings before administrative agencies entrusted with the responsibility of fact finding." *Id.*, at 556, 61 S.Ct. 719.

As we further explained in [*United States v. L.A. Tucker Truck Lines, Inc.*, 344 U.S. 33, 73 S.Ct. 67 (1952)], courts require administrative issue exhaustion "as a general rule" because it is usually "appropriate under [an agency's] practice" for "contestants in an adversary proceeding" before it to develop fully all issues there. 344 U.S., at 36-37, 73 S.Ct. 67. (We also spoke favorably of issue exhaustion in *Unemployment Compensation Comm'n of Alaska v. Aragon*, 329 U.S. 143, 154-155, 67 S.Ct. 245, 91 L.Ed. 136 (1946), without relying on any statute or regulation, but in that case the waived issue had not been raised before the District Court, see *id.*, at 149, 155, 67 S.Ct. 245.)

But, as *Hormel* and *L.A. Tucker Truck Lines* suggest, the desirability of a court imposing a requirement of issue exhaustion depends on the degree to which the analogy to normal adversarial litigation applies in a particular administrative proceeding. Cf. *McKart v. United States*, 395 U.S. 185, 193, 89 S.Ct. 1657, 23 L.Ed.2d 194 (1969) (application of doctrine of exhaustion of administrative remedies "requires an understanding of its purposes and of the particular administrative scheme involved"); *Salfi*, 422 U.S., at 765, 95 S.Ct. 2457 (same). Where the parties are expected to develop the issues in an adversarial administrative proceeding, it seems to us that the rationale for requiring issue exhaustion is at its greatest. Where, by contrast, an administrative proceeding is not adversarial, we think the reasons for a court to require issue exhaustion are much weaker. More generally, we have observed that "it is well settled that there are wide differences between administrative agencies and courts," *Shepard v. NLRB*, 459 U.S. 344, 351, 103 S.Ct. 665, 74 L.Ed.2d 523 (1983), and we have thus warned against reflexively "assimilat[ing] the relation of ... administrative bodies and the courts to the relationship between lower and upper courts," *FCC v. Pottsville Broadcasting Co.*, 309 U.S. 134, 144, 60 S.Ct. 437, 84 L.Ed. 656 (1940).

B

The differences between courts and agencies are nowhere more pronounced than in Social Security proceedings. Although "[m]any agency systems of adjudication are based to a significant extent on the judicial model of decisionmaking," 2 K. Davis & R. Pierce, Administrative Law Treatise § 9.10, p. 103 (3d ed.1994), the SSA is "[p]erhaps the best example of an agency" that is not, B. Schwartz, Administrative Law 469-470 (4th ed.1994). See *id.*, at 470 ("The most important of [the SSA's modifications of the judicial model] is the replacement of normal adversary procedure by ... the 'investigatory model' " (quoting Friendly, Some Kind of Hearing, 123 U. Pa. L.Rev. 1267, 1290 (1975))). Social Security proceedings are inquisitorial rather than adversarial. It is the ALJ's duty to investigate the facts and develop the arguments both for and against granting benefits, and the Council's review is similarly broad. The Commis-

sioner has no representative before the ALJ to oppose the claim for benefits, and we have found no indication that he opposes claimants before the
Council.

The regulations make this nature of SSA proceedings quite clear.
They expressly provide that the SSA "conduct[s] the administrative review process in an informal, nonadversary manner." 20 CFR § 404.900(b)
(1999). They permit—but do not require—the filing of a brief with the
Council (even when the Council grants review), and the Council's review
is plenary unless it states otherwise. The Commissioner's involvement in
the Appeals Council's decision whether to grant review appears to be not
as a litigant opposing the claimant, but rather just as an advisor to the
Council regarding which cases are good candidates for the Council to review pursuant to its authority to review a case *sua sponte*. The regulations further make clear that the Council will "evaluate the entire record," including "new and material evidence," in determining whether to
grant review. § 404.970(b). Similarly, the notice of decision that ALJ's
provide unsuccessful claimants informs them that if they request review,
the Council will "consider all of [the ALJ's] decision, even the parts with
which you may agree" and that the Council might review the decision
"even if you do not ask it to do so." Finally, Form HA-520, which the
Commissioner considers adequate for the Council's purposes in determining whether to review a case, provides only three lines for the request for
review, and a notice accompanying the form estimates that it will take
only 10 minutes to "read the instructions, gather the necessary facts and
fill out the form." The form therefore strongly suggests that the Council
does not depend much, if at all, on claimants to identify issues for review.
Given that a large portion of Social Security claimants either have no
representation at all or are represented by non-attorneys, the lack of such
dependence is entirely understandable.

Thus, the *Hormel* analogy to judicial proceedings is at its weakest in
this area. The adversarial development of issues by the parties—the
"com[ing] to issue," 312 U.S., at 556, 61 S.Ct. 719—on which that analogy
depends simply does not exist. The Council, not the claimant, has primary responsibility for identifying and developing the issues. We therefore
agree with the Eighth Circuit that "the general rule [of issue exhaustion]
makes little sense in this particular context." Harwood [v. Apfel, 186 F.3d
1039, 1042 (C.A.8 1999)].

Accordingly, we hold that a judicially created issue-exhaustion requirement is inappropriate. Claimants who exhaust administrative remedies need not also exhaust issues in a request for review by the Appeals
Council in order to preserve judicial review of those issues. The judgment
of the Fifth Circuit is reversed, and the case is remanded for further proceedings consistent with this opinion.

Justice O'CONNOR, concurring in part and concurring in the judgment.

In most cases, [an] issue not presented to an administrative decisionmaker cannot be argued for the first time in federal court. On this underlying principle of administrative law, the Court is unanimous. In the absence of a specific statute or regulation requiring issue exhaustion, however, such a rule is not always appropriate. * * * I write separately because, in my view, the agency's failure to notify claimants of an issue exhaustion requirement in this context is a sufficient basis for our decision. Requiring issue exhaustion is particularly inappropriate here, where the regulation and procedures of the Social Security Administration (SSA) affirmatively suggest that specific issues need not be raised before the Appeals Council.

Although the SSA's regulations warn claimants that completely failing to request Appeals Council review will forfeit the right to seek judicial review, see 20 CFR § 404.900(b) (1999), the regulations provide no notice that claimants must also raise specific issues before the Appeals Council to reserve them for review in federal court, see ante, at 2084 (SSA regulations do not require issue exhaustion). To the contrary, the relevant regulations and procedures indicate that issue exhaustion before the Appeals Council is not required. To request Appeals Council review, a claimant need not file a brief. See § 404.975. Rather, he can file either Form HA-520, "Request for Review of Hearing Decision/Order," or "any other writing specifically requesting review." § 422.205(a). Form HA-520, the suggested means of requesting review, provides only three lines (roughly two inches) for the statement of issues and grounds for appeal, and the SSA estimates that it should take a total of 10 minutes to read the instructions, collect the relevant information, and complete the form. Moreover, Appeals Council review is plenary unless the Council informs the claimant otherwise in writing; as the notice of decision of the Administrative Law Judge (ALJ) to petitioner stated, if she requested review before the Appeals Council, "the Council will consider all of [the ALJ's] decision .... Requesting review places the entire record of your case before the Council."

Justice BREYER concedes that these factors "might mislead the Social Security claimant" to believe that issue exhaustion is not required. He nonetheless contends that this is not a problem because the SSA has assured the Court that it "has not invoked [issue exhaustion] in suits brought by claimants who were unrepresented during the Appeals Council proceedings." As a matter of past practice, the agency's statement appears to be inaccurate. But even if this stated policy were uniformly followed, I think it would be unwise to adopt a rule that imposes different issue exhaustion obligations depending on whether claimants are represented by counsel.

In this case, the SSA told petitioner (1) that she could request review by sending a letter or filling out a 1-page form that should take 10 minutes to complete, (2) only that failing to request Appeals Council review would preclude judicial review, and (3) that the Appeals Council would review her entire case for issues. She did everything that the agency asked of her. I would not impose any additional requirements, and would reverse the judgment and remand for further proceedings consistent with this opinion.

Justice BREYER, with whom THE CHIEF JUSTICE and Justices SCALIA and KENNEDY join, dissenting.

Under ordinary principles of administrative law a reviewing court will not consider arguments that a party failed to raise in timely fashion before an administrative agency. As this Court explained long ago:

> "[O]rderly procedure and good administration require that objections to the proceedings of an administrative agency be made while it has opportunity for correction in order to raise issues reviewable[*2088] by the courts. ... [C]ourts should not topple over administrative decisions unless the administrative body not only has erred but has erred against objection made at the time appropriate under its practice." [*United States v. L.A. Tucker Truck Lines, Inc.*, 344 U.S. 33, 37, 73 S.Ct. 67, 97 L.Ed. 54 (1952)]

Although the rule has exceptions, it applies with particular force where resolution of the claim significantly depends upon specialized agency knowledge or practice. In this case, petitioner asked the reviewing court to consider arguments of the kind that clearly fall within the general rule, namely, whether an administrative law judge should have ordered a further medical examination or asked different questions of a vocational expert. No one claims that any established exception to this ordinary "exhaustion" or "waiver" rule applies.

* * *

I would add that these ordinary "exhaustion of remedies" rules are particularly important in Social Security cases, where the Appeals Council is asked to process over 100,000 claims each year, where many of those cases ultimately find their way to federal court, and where the Social Security Act itself stresses their applicability.

Nor, with one exception, do I see why the nonadversarial nature of the Social Security Administration internal appellate process makes a difference. An initial ALJ proceeding is, after all, itself nonadversarial. Yet I assume the plurality would not forgive the requirement that a party ordinarily must raise all relevant issues before the ALJ.

Neither does the law in this area disfavor informal proceedings. Considerations of time and expense can favor such proceedings. And, since a Social Security claimant is permitted his own counsel or other representative if he wishes, the informality does not necessarily work to his disadvantage. Indeed, the plurality's rule, by interfering with the ordinary ALJ/Appeals Council/District Court order for presenting agency-specific arguments, threatens to complicate judicial review, thereby producing increased delay without any benefit to the agency or to the claimants themselves.

There is, however, one exception, *i.e.*, one way in which the informality of the proceedings may matter. Administrative lawyers are normally aware of the basic "exhaustion of remedies" rules, including the specific waiver principle here at issue. But the internal appellate review proceeding's informality; the absence of a clear statement in the rules or on the Appeals Council instructional form insisting upon the raising of all, not just some, issues; the presence on the instructional form of just a few lines for the listing of issues; and an attached estimate that on average an appellant can "read the instructions, gather the necessary facts and fill out the form" in 10 minutes, see Form HA-520—taken together—might mislead the Social Security claimant. That is, it might make the claimant believe he need not raise every issue before the Appeals Council.

But the Social Security Administration says that it does not apply its waiver rule where the claimant is not represented. And I cannot say it is "arbitrary, capricious, [or] an abuse of discretion" to apply the waiver rule when a claimant was represented before the Appeals Council, as was petitioner, by an attorney. Petitioner's lawyer should have known the basic legal principle: namely, that, with important exceptions, a claimant must raise his objections in an internal agency appellate proceeding or forgo the opportunity later to raise them in court. The Fifth Circuit, moreover, had precedent applying the general rule in this specific context. *Paul v. Shalala*, 29 F.3d 208, 210-211 (1994). And far from being misled by the agency's form, petitioner's lawyer followed an alternative procedure and filed 19 pages of detailed legal and factual arguments challenging the ALJ's decision. In these circumstances, petitioner is accountable for her lawyer's decision—whether neglectful or by design—to reserve some of her objections for federal court.

For these reasons, I would affirm the judgment of the Court of Appeals.

B) REVIEW OF DECISIONS MADE WITHOUT A HEARING

Another type of case that presents jurisdictional issues is where there were no administrative remedies to exhaust. Certain administrative decisions have the effect of denying a claim but are made without an opportunity for a hearing. The most important of these are refusals to reopen an application and dismissals of appeals, usually on grounds that the appeal was not filed on time or that the claim was barred by administrative res judicata. The Supreme Court held in Califano v. Sanders, 430 U.S. 99, 108, 97 S. Ct. 980, 986 (1977), that federal courts have no jurisdiction to review decisions by SSA not to reopen prior applications for benefits because such decisions are not made following a hearing. The rationale of *Sanders* has been extended regularly to preclude judicial review where claims were dismissed because administrative review was not requested within applicable time limits and an extension of time to file was not granted. The Court in *Sanders* recognized, however, that a constitutional challenge to decisions not to reopen claims may be subject to different exhaustion requirements, thereby laying the groundwork for a recognized exception to the jurisdictional bar in reopening and dismissal cases where the claimant raises a colorable constitutional issue. As in the following case, most successful arguments invoking this exception seem to be based on the mental incapacity of the claimant.

UDD V. MASSANARI

245 F.3d 1096, 73 Soc.Sec.Rep.Ser. 24 (9ᵗʰ Cir. 2001)

REINHARDT, Circuit Judge:

This is an appeal from an order of the district court upholding the refusal of the Commissioner of the Social Security Administration to reopen an adverse benefits decision made in 1976. The claimant seeks benefits retroactive to that year on the ground that the termination of his benefits violated due process because he lacked the mental capacity to understand the termination notice and the procedures for requesting review of that termination.

I.

During his military service in 1973, Kris Udd began suffering from visual and auditory hallucinations and loss of control of his arms and legs. After his discharge, he sought treatment from a Veterans Administration ("VA") hospital and was diagnosed with schizophrenia. From the time of this diagnosis to the present, he has received service-connected disability benefits from the Department of Veterans Affairs.

In March 1976, Udd applied for disability benefits from the Social Security Administration (SSA). SSA determined that he was disabled, with an onset date of May 3, 1974, and he commenced receiving benefits. The benefits were terminated as of October 31, 1976, but the reason for the termination is unknown, because SSA destroyed Udd's records pursuant to its record retention policy. At the time, Udd did not have an attorney or legal guardian responsible for pursuing his claim.

Udd did not receive disability benefits for eighteen years. In 1994, Udd filed a second application for social security disability benefits alleging disability beginning on November 1, 1976. At the reconsideration stage, SSA granted his application and determined that he was disabled from November 1, 1976 through the date of his application. However, his benefits were limited by a SSA rule providing that successful claimants may receive retroactive benefits only for the twelve months preceding the filing of an application for benefits. Udd filed a request for a hearing, asserting that the 1976 termination decision should be reopened to permit him to receive benefits retroactive to the date on which his benefits were terminated. Udd argued that his mental condition in 1976 was such that he cannot be held responsible for the failure to make a timely request for review of the termination decision.

After a hearing, the Administrative Law Judge ("ALJ") found that Udd did not lack the mental capacity on October 31, 1976 to understand the procedures for requesting review, stating, "[h]is mental impairment prevented him from working, but did not totally incapacitate him, as evidenced by his ability to live by himself and have relationships, and by his babysitting activities in December 1976." Accordingly, the ALJ refused to excuse Udd's failure to appeal or to vacate the termination decision and reinstate his benefits as of November 1, 1976.

Udd requested review of the ALJ's decision by the Appeals Council, but the Council concluded that there was no basis for granting the request for review and upheld the ALJ's determination as the final decision of the Commissioner of Social Security. Udd sought review in federal court. The district court found that the ALJ's findings were supported by substantial evidence and concluded that Udd had not established that his due process rights were violated by the Commissioner's refusal to reopen his 1976 termination of benefits. Udd timely filed this appeal.

II.

The Social Security Act limits judicial review of the Commissioner's decisions to "any final decision ... made after a hearing." 42 U.S.C. § 405(g). A decision not to reopen a prior, final benefits decision is discretionary and ordinarily does not constitute a final decision; therefore, it is not subject to judicial review. *Califano v. Sanders*, 430 U.S. 99, 107-09, 97 S.Ct. 980, 51 L.Ed.2d 192 (1977). Sanders, however, recognized an exception "where the Secretary's denial of a petition to reopen is challenged on constitutional grounds." *Id.* at 109, 97 S.Ct. 980. We have held that "the Sanders exception applies to any colorable constitutional claim of due process violation that implicates a due process right either to a meaningful opportunity to be heard or to seek reconsideration of an adverse benefits determination." *Evans v. Chater*, 110 F.3d 1480, 1483 (9th Cir.1997) (citations omitted). A challenge that is not "wholly insubstantial, immaterial, or frivolous" raises a colorable constitutional claim. *Boettcher v. Sec'y of Health & Human Serv.*, 759 F.2d 719, 722 (9th Cir.1985).

Udd argues that due process requires reopening the prior termination decision because he lacked the mental capacity to understand the Secretary's termination notice and the procedures for contesting that termination. Where a claimant alleges that a prior determination should be reopened because he suffered from a mental impairment and was not represented by counsel at the time of the denial of benefits, he has asserted a colorable constitutional claim. Accordingly, we hold that we have jurisdiction to consider the merits of Udd's due process claim.

III.

It is axiomatic that due process requires that a claimant receive meaningful notice and an opportunity to be heard before his claim for disability benefits may be denied. *Mathews v. Eldridge*, 424 U.S. 319, 333, 96 S.Ct. 893, 47 L.Ed.2d 18 (1976). Udd argues that the 1976 termination of benefits denied him due process of law because his mental impairment prevented him from understanding the order of termination and complying with the administrative review process.

In 1991, SSA issued Ruling 91-5p, which provides that if a claimant presents evidence that mental incapacity prevented him from requesting timely review of an administrative action, and the claimant had no one legally responsible for prosecuting the claim on his behalf at the time of the prior adverse action, SSA "will determine whether or not good cause exists for extending the time to request review." "The claimant will have established mental incapacity for the purpose of establishing good cause when the evidence establishes that he or she lacked the mental capacity to understand the procedures for requesting review." In making the 91-5p determination, the following four factors must be considered: (1) inability to read or write; (2) lack of facility with the English language; (3) limited education; and (4) any mental or physical condition which limits the claimant's ability to do things for him/herself. In all cases, "[t]he adjudicator will resolve any reasonable doubt in favor of the claimant."

* * *

We hold that Udd met the requirements set forth in SSR 91-5p at the time of the termination of benefits on October 31, 1976. It is undisputed that Udd had no attorney or other representative legally responsible for prosecuting his claim at the time. Udd presented overwhelming evidence from his medical records indicating that he lacked the mental capacity to understand the procedures for review. In evaluating this evidence, the ALJ applied an incorrect legal standard and failed to resolve doubts in favor of the claimant, as is required by SSR 91-5p. In sum, substantial evidence does not support the ALJ's finding in this case.

* * *

Accordingly, we hold that Udd has established that he lacked the mental capacity on October 31, 1976 to understand the cessation of his disability benefits and to take the steps necessary to pursue an appeal. The termination of his benefits without meaningful notice thus constituted a denial of due process. Ordinarily, when a due process violation requires that an application for benefits be reopened, the case is remanded to the Commissioner so that the agency can rule on the merits of the plaintiff's disability claims in the first instance. Here, however, the SSA has already made that determination. It held, in connection with Udd's second application for disability benefits, that he has been continuously disabled from November 1, 1976. There is therefore no need for further administrative adjudication beyond the calculation of benefits retroactive to November 1, 1976.

IV.

We reverse the ALJ's determination and remand to the district court with instructions to direct the Commissioner to reopen the application for disability insurance benefits filed by Udd in 1976 and to award him benefits retroactive to November 1, 1976.

NOTE ON REMANDS

As noted earlier, the Social Security Act specifically authorizes district courts to remand Social Security cases for further administrative proceedings. With respect to remands, 42 U.S.C. § 405(g) provides:

> The court shall have power to enter, upon the pleadings and transcript of the record, a judgment affirming, modifying, or reversing the decision of the Commissioner of Social Security, with or without remanding the cause for a rehearing. * * * The court may, on motion of the Commissioner of Social Security made for good cause shown before the Commissioner files the Commissioner's answer, remand the case to the Commissioner of Social Security for further action by the Commissioner of Social Security, and it may at any time order additional evidence to be taken before the Commissioner of Social Security, but only upon a showing that there is new evidence which is material and that there is good cause for the failure to incorporate such evidence into the record in a prior proceeding; and the Commissioner of Social Security shall, after the case is remanded, and after hearing such additional evidence if so ordered, modify or affirm the Commissioner's findings of fact or the Commissioner's decision, or both, and shall file with the court any such additional and modified findings of fact and decision, and a transcript of the additional

record and testimony upon which the Commissioner's action in modifying or affirming was based. Such additional or modified findings of fact and decision shall be reviewable only to the extent provided for review of the original findings of fact and decision.

The remands authorized by the first part of Section 405(g) quoted above—those ordered following a judgment either affirming, modifying, or reversing the administrative decision—are known as "sentence four" remands, so-named because that authority appears in the fourth sentence of Section 405(g). Typically, these are cases where a remand is ordered following a ruling on the merits affirming, modifying, or reversing the decision of an administrative law judge (or a lower court). Remands authorized by the second part of Section 405(g) quoted above—where the court simply orders additional evidence to be taken without reaching a judgment on the merits—are known as "sentence six" remands, as that authority appears in the sixth sentence of Section 405(g). Courts can order sentence six remands either on SSA's motion before it files an answer, upon a showing of good cause, or otherwise upon a showing that there is material new evidence and that the moving party had good cause for the failing to submit that evidence during the administrative appeal process.

Common situations where sentence four remands are ordered include cases where the administrative decision was based on an incorrect application of the law and a new assessment is required under the correct legal standard, and those where the ALJ or the Appeals Council failed to consider key evidence or failed to make required findings. Cases where the court finds that new evidences needs to be developed can be remanded under sentence four or sentence six, depending on whether the court also affirms, modifies, or reverses the appealed-from administrative decision. Basically, remands that simply call for additional evidence fall under sentence six; those where additional evidence is required due to an error of law fall under sentence four. Recall, however, that sentence six imposes additional requirements on both SSA and claimants. SSA may use sentence six to obtain a remand in advance of the court's decision, but it must show good cause as to why the case should not proceed to judgment—in effect, requiring SSA to show that it is not just trying to avoid litigating a poorly handled claim. And sentence six remands requested by claimants are limited by the requirements that new evidence be material and that there was good clause for failing to submit that evidence into the administrative record.

Special Appeals Council rules apply when a case is remanded by the court to SSA for further proceedings. In effect, the Appeals Council may either reconsider the case itself or send it back to ODAR for further action by an administrative law judge. *See* 20 C.F.R. §§ 404.983, 416.1483. If sent to ODAR, the ALJ may consider any issues regardless of whether they were raised in the initial administrative proceedings. *Id.* The procedures followed when the Appeals Council takes the case are set out in **20 C.F.R. § 404.984, 416.1484[APP-REGS]**.

Most courts order remands for additional evidence freely, with the idea the ultimate goal is to reach a decision on the basis of a full and complete record. There are instances, however, where courts interpret the requirements for a sentence six remand strictly. Consider the following reasoning in Field v. Chater, 920 F. Supp. 240, 244-45, 50 Soc. Sec. Rep. Ser. 562 (D. Me. 1995), where the claimant showed on appeal that she could not preform her past relevant work and yet SSA had not offered proof of other jobs in the economy that she could perform:

> The Social Security Act authorizes the court to enter a judgment "affirming, modifying, or reversing the decision of the Commissioner of Social Security, with or without remanding the cause for a rehearing." 42 U.S.C. § 405(g). The court may "at any time order additional evidence to be taken before the Commissioner of Social Security, but only upon a showing that there is new evidence which is material and that there is good cause for the failure to incorporate such evidence into the record in a prior proceeding." *Id.* As the Second Circuit noted more than a decade ago in *Carroll* [*v. Secretary*, 705 F.2d 638, 44 (2d Cir. 1983)], Congress added this language to the Social Security Act in 1980 as a "mandate to foreshorten the often painfully slow process by which disability determinations are made." There is simply no cause for the Commissioner's failure to adduce appropriate testimony from the vocational expert as to the transferability of the plaintiff's work skills. Accordingly, I agree with the plaintiff that the Commissioner's request for a remand "is no more than a request for a second bite at the apple," well over two years after she filed her initial request for benefits, and that to remand in these circumstances would be to countenance the notion that the Commissioner may have as many chances as she needs, *ad infinitum*, to meet her burden at Step 5. Such a possibility cannot be what Congress envisioned in light of the quoted language from section 405(g). A claimant who seeks disability benefits from the Social Security Administration, and then does all that is expected of her pursuant to the sequential evaluation process, deserves an answer from the system. In circumstances where the claimant has made out a prima facie case for benefits and the Commissioner's vocational expert does not present the required evidence of the claimant's ability to perform work that exists in the national economy, the appropriate relief is an award of benefits absent some good cause for the evidentiary gap.

920 F. Supp. at 244-45.

Finally, the distinction between remands ordered under sentence four or under sentence six can be critical to an attorney's ability to receive fees under the Equal Access to Justice Act (EAJA). The EAJA aspects of sentence four and sentence six remands are discussed at the end of this chapter.

2. SCOPE OF JUDICIAL REVIEW

The scope of judicial review in Social Security appeals is limited. Federal court review is based exclusively on the record developed at the administrative hearing or before the Appeals Council; new evidence in support of the claim cannot be introduced at the district court. As noted above, if a claimant comes across "new and material evidence" after the administrative process is complete and can show "good cause" for failing to submit it earlier, the evidence can be presented to the court as a basis for remand. *See* 42 U.S.C. § 405(g). If the court agrees to remand the case, the new evidence is developed at the administrative level and any further judicial review will be based on the new administrative record.

The scope of review is essentially the same in the courts of appeals. However, the courts of appeals may refuse to consider, or may limit its review of, an issue that was not raised at the district court. *See, e.g.,* Young v. Secretary, 925 F.2d 146, 149 (6th Cir. 1990) (Social Security claimant "cannot raise an issue before the court of appeals that was not raised before the district court"). The Fifth Circuit stated its view recently as follows: "[T]his court ordinarily does not review issues raised for the first time on appeal. In exceptional circumstances, however, the court "may, in the interests of justice, review an issue that was not raised in the district court." Castillo v. Barnhart, 325 F.3d 550, 553, 87 Soc. Sec. Rep. Serv. 10, 2003 WL 1455537 (5th Cir. 2003) (citing Kinash v. Callahan, 129 F.3d 736, 739 n. 10, 54 Soc. Sec. Rep. Ser. 491, 1997 WL 719113 (5th Cir. 1997).

3. STANDARD OF REVIEW

The question on an appeal of a claim for Social Security benefits is whether the Social Security Administration's decision comports with relevant legal standards and whether there is sufficient evidence to support the decision. Questions of law are reviewed de novo by the district court and questions of fact are reviewed under the "substantial evidence" standard. *See* 42 U.S.C. § 405 (g) ("The findings of the Commissioner of Social Security as to any fact, if supported by substantial evidence, shall be conclusive"). As the Supreme Court said in Richardson v. Perales, 402 U.S. 389, 401, 91 S. Ct. 1420 (1971) (quoting Consolidated Edison Co. v. NLRB, 305 U.S. 197, 229 (1938)), the statutory standard of "substantial evidence" set out in § 405(g) means "more than a mere scintilla. It means such relevant evidence as a reasonable mind might accept as adequate to support a conclusion." *See also* 20 C.F.R. §§ 404.901, 416.1401 ("Substantial evidence means such relevant evidence as a reasonable mind might accept as adequate to support a conclusion.").

In effect, proper application of the substantial evidence standard requires that reviewing judges not draw independent factual conclusions from the evidence. Instead, they should ask whether a reasonable mind could infer facts found by the ALJ (or the Appeals Council) from the evidence; if so, then those facts must be taken as true for purposes of determining whether the decision is supported by substantial evidence in the record as a whole. Even if a court finds that a preponderance of the evidence favors the claimant and therefore would have ruled otherwise in the first instance, administrative findings should be accepted when supported by substantial evidence.

The following case illustrates the type of inquiry a court conducts when deciding whether substantial evidence supports the Social Security Administration's decision:

YOUNG V. BARNHART

362 F.3d 995, 96 Soc. Sec. Rep. Serv. 1 (7th Cir. 2004)

ILANA DIAMOND ROVNER, Circuit Judge.

James Young applied for Social Security disability benefits, claiming that he suffered from progressively declining cognitive abilities and increasing personality problems which interfered completely with his ability to work. The Social Security Administration ("SSA") denied Young's application and upon review, the administrative law judge ("ALJ") determined that Young was not disabled. The Social Security Appeals Council denied Young's request for review. Young now appeals from the district court's judgment upholding the denial of benefits. Because we find that ALJ's residual functional capacity assessment and hypothetical question to the vocational expert were flawed, we reverse and remand for further proceedings.

I.

Young, a fifty-five year old veteran, applied to the SSA for disability insurance benefits on July 24, 1998, claiming that as of December 31, 1992, he was no longer able to work due to an adjustment disorder with mixed features, anger control, and personality problems. These problems, he asserts, stem from a 1987 motorcycle accident and the resultant extended coma which left him with residual brain injuries. At the time of the accident he was employed as a load master with the Air Force, but was discharged in 1990 after the military determined that he was disabled. Since that time, Young has worked in many different jobs with very little success at maintaining employment. He was fired from his most recent job as a mail carrier for the U.S. Postal Service because of, among other things, his inability to understand the schedule, report to work on time, relate theory to task performance, and complete his deliveries in a timely fashion. He also has had little success in maintaining employment as a bartender, lawn laborer, or airport baggage handler. In 1996 the Department of Veterans Affairs ("VA") found that although Young's injuries were seventy percent disabling, he was 100 percent unemployable. Since 1997, Young has worked approximately thirty hours a week performing custodial duties at a bar that his wife, Tamara Young, owns.

The SSA denied Young's July 24, 1998 disability benefits application and his subsequent request for reconsideration. He fared no better before the ALJ who determined, after a May 5, 2000 hearing, that Young was not disabled. The Social Security Appeals Council declined his request for rehearing and the decision of the ALJ, therefore, is the final decision of the Commissioner. On appeal to the United States District Court, Magistrate Judge Crocker affirmed the decision of the Commissioner. Young filed this appeal claiming that (1) the ALJ incorrectly dismissed the consultative examining doctor's psychological exam and medical opinion, (2) the ALJ erred by using a residual functional capacity assessment that did not incorporate all of the evidence, (3) the ALJ erred in creating the list of jobs that Young could perform, and (4) the ALJ made an improper credibility assessment.

The ALJ had a dizzying array of medical and psychological information to consider, including the opinions of no fewer than eight psychological and medical professionals who either examined or evaluated Young. Since we review the record as a whole, we briefly summarize some of the relevant evidence from the record here:

In August 1990, Dr. William Hathaway, a staff neurologist for the U.S. Air Force, examined Young and determined that he had poor visual memory abilities, relied on inefficient mnemonic strategies, was easily distracted during learning tasks, but performed within the normal range on a host of other memory tasks. He also found that Young had some impaired motor functioning in his left hand, problems in visuospatial functioning, and had deficits in concept formation and conceptual flexibility. Dr. Hathaway also noted displays of low frustration tolerance, irritability, "impulsivity" and a potential for poor social judgment, which he concluded substantially interfered with Young's daily performance. He recommended that the military consider Young for final medical retirement.

In 1996, the Department of Veterans Affairs determined that Young was seventy percent disabled (up from thirty percent prior) and 100% unemployable. The change in disability was based on a Veterans Administration psychological exam performed in March 1995. That exam confirmed mild cognitive deficits, impulsivity, poor social judgment and apathy, and a drop in IQ from the above average to normal range, irritability, and short temper. The examiner noted at the time that although neuropsychological testing showed only a mild impairment, in practice it translated into a significant impairment for Young in his social and occupational life. The Veterans Administration report indicated that Young had trouble climbing, balancing, and working in high places or places with poor ventilation. He could not perform fast-paced work or work around cluttered or slippery floors, hazardous machinery or poor lighting. He also had partial restrictions on working alone, working with others, exacting performance, repetitive work, and following instructions.

In October 1998, the state disability agency referred Young to Michael J. Ostrowski, Ph.D. for an evaluation. Dr. Ostrowski diagnosed Young with an adjustment disorder, finding that he had some symptoms of decreased mood and functioning. Dr. Ostrowski did not find pronounced memory deficiencies, but noted that he did not conduct formal memory testing. He concluded that Young would not have difficulty carrying out work-related activities such as following instructions, sustaining persistence, and adopting to change, but did note that Young's temper problems might make it difficult for Young to relate well to coworkers.

Dr. Robert Hodes, a consultative non-examining psychologist completed an SSA Mental Residual Capacity Assessment on November 6, 1998, in which he concluded that Young was moderately limited in his ability to carry out detailed instructions, to interact appropriately with the general public, to set realistic goals, and to make plans independently of others. Dr. Hodes filled out the SSA Psychiatric Review Technique Form in which he noted the presence of pathological dependence, passivity or aggressivity and moderate difficulties maintaining social functioning. Dr. Hodes concluded that Young seemed capable of performing simple routine work.

Dr. Ward Jankus, a consulting, examining physician with the Wisconsin Department of Health and Human Services examined Young in early 1999 and determined that he had higher level memory and concentration problems and "mild higher level balance deficits." His exam focused mostly on Young's physical condition, which, with the exception of the balance problems, was largely unremarkable.

In April 1999, Dr. Jack Spear, a non-examining, consultative psychologist completed a Mental Residual Functional Capacity assessment of Young. He found some mild to moderate limitations in Young's ability to understand and remember detailed directions, and in his ability to maintain attention and concentration for extended periods. He also determined that Young was slightly to moderately limited in his ability to maintain social functioning, and noted that Young had difficulties with concentration, persistence, and pace which he described as occurring seldom to often. His ultimate conclusion was that Young had an adjustment disorder and the mental residual functional capacity to perform unskilled work with objects, rather than people or data.

Dr. Timothy Howell examined Young in July 1999, and determined that he had a short-term memory impairment, and a personality change manifested by an increased tendency to become irritable. Dr. Howell noted that Young's memory problems had interfered with his past job performance. Howell gave Young a score of fifty on the Global Assessment of Functioning Scale, indicating serious symptoms or functional limitations.

Dr. Douglas Varvil-Weld, a psychologist who, in February 2000, examined Young at the request of the ALJ, found significant deficits in Young's ability to maintain attention and concentration and to understand, remember, and carry out complex job instructions. He also found some deficits in Young's ability to use judgment, function independently, cope with work stress, and in his ability to understand, remember, and carry out even simple job instructions. Dr. Varvil-Weld administered memory testing which revealed some memory deficiencies, including memory deficiencies affecting attention and concentration. He concluded that Young might have difficulty sustaining his efforts and persistence in a work environment. He also concluded that Young could be expected to have some difficulty with distractibility, with remembering and carrying out instructions, and with physically tolerating stress in the work-place. He found no evidence that he would have difficulty working effectively with others.

The medical expert, Dr. Kenneth Sherry, testified at Young's May 5, 2000 disability hearing. Although he could not explain the degradation in Young's memory functioning between the 1990, 1998, and 1999 evaluations on the one hand and Dr. Varvil-Weld's testing in March 2000, he did report that Young had problems with visual-spacial memory, higher cognitive functioning, and some visual memory problems. In addition, he was able to conclude that Young would have problems with concentration, persistence, and pace-problems that might occur frequently or often. Although Dr. Sherry noted that Young had lost two jobs due to his temper and that those behavior problems might be part of his organic mental syndrome, he had trouble evaluating whether Young would suffer from deterioration and decompensation in work or work-like settings.

The ALJ also heard the testimony of Young and his wife. Young testified that he often had trouble remembering things, and that these memory deficits have caused him great trouble in work settings. He testified that he lost his job with the post office because he could not remember the routes and procedures, and that at his wife's bar he forgets to put away cleaning supplies and sometimes triggers the security alarm. Young testified that he was fired from two jobs due to physical altercations with coworkers, and that he can no longer work as a bartender because of his temper. He also testified that he generally sticks close to home-doing housework, playing computer games, and watching television. When he does go out socially, he relies on his wife to keep him from offending others. Tamara Young corroborated her husband's testimony, noting in particular her husband's memory and temperament problems.

II.

The Commissioner has set forth a five-step evaluation process to determine whether a claimant is disabled. Following this process, the ALJ considered:

1) Whether Young was currently engaged in substantial gainful activity?

2) Whether Young had a severe impairment?

3) Whether Young's impairment met or equaled one of the impairments listed in the SSA regulations?

4) Whether Young could perform his past relevant work?

5) Whether Young could make the adjustment to other work?

20 C.F.R. § 404.1520(a)(4)(i)-(iv). The process is sequential, and if the ALJ can make a conclusive finding at any step that the claimant either is or is not disabled, then she need not progress to the next step. If the claimant makes it past step four, the burden shifts to the Commissioner to demonstrate that the claimant can successfully perform a significant number of jobs that exist in the national economy.

In this case, the ALJ proceeded through all five steps of the analysis. He concluded that (1) Young had not engaged in substantial gainful activity during the relevant time period; (2) Young's impairments were severe; (3) they did not meet or equal one of the impairments listed in the SSA regulations; (4) Young could not perform his past relevant work; and (5) Young could, in fact, make the adjustment to work at a number of jobs which exist in the national economy in significant numbers.

At the fourth and fifth steps, the ALJ must consider an assessment of the claimant's residual functional capacity ("RFC"). The RFC is an assessment of what work-related activities the claimant can perform despite her limitations. The RFC must be assessed based on all the relevant evidence in the record.

The ALJ made a determination that Young had the RFC to perform the nonexertional requirements of simple, routine, repetitive, low stress work with limited contact with coworkers and the public.

Young argues, in his initial point, that the ALJ improperly rejected the medical evidence submitted by one of the medical experts, Dr. Varvil-Weld. Had he accepted the report of Dr. Varvil-Weld, Young argues, the ALJ would have found that Young's memory and concentration difficulties were far more significant than he found. Young also argues that, had the ALJ parsed the medical evidence from the other experts, he would have found that it was not, in fact, conflicting but that it supported Young's disability claim.

In reviewing the decision of the ALJ, we cannot engage in our own analysis of whether Young is severely impaired as defined by the SSA regulations. Nor may we reweigh evidence, resolve conflicts in the record, decide questions of credibility, or, in general, substitute our own judgment for that of the Our task is limited to determining whether the ALJ's factual findings are supported by substantial evidence. 42 U.S.C. § 405(g). Evidence is substantial if a reasonable person would accept it as adequate to support the conclusion.

Young complains that "the ALJ appears to give greater weight to the earlier 1990 mental status exam conducted by the VA, than to the recent mental status exam conducted in February 2000." Weighing conflicting evidence from medical experts, however, is exactly what the ALJ is required to do. And we may not re-weigh the evidence. The ALJ did not ignore Dr. Varvil-Weld's evidence as Young maintains, but rather considered it in light of all of the other evidence before him. In considering the weight to give to the 1990 and 2000 memory examinations, the judge considered the testimony of Dr. Sherry who stated that he could not find a medical explanation for the significant drop in Young's memory function, and considered the fact that Young had "an incentive not do well" on the later evaluation since it was administered for the purpose of determining Young's eligibility for benefits. This conclusion is not an improper medical determination, but rather is the type of context consideration that judges regularly make when assessing the weight to attribute to conflicting evidence.

We cannot conclude that the ALJ's decision to disfavor the evidence submitted by Dr. Varvil-Weld regarding Young's mental status examination scores was not supported by substantial evidence. The ALJ evaluated the evidence submitted by the many medical experts in this case and where that evidence was conflicting, he resolved those conflicts by giving more weight to some evidence and less to others. Specifically, he concluded that Dr. Varvil-Weld's conclusions that Young had poor or no capacity to maintain attention and concentration was inconsistent with other medical opinions and worthy of less weight. This is not a case where a treating physicians' opinion was disregarded in favor of the opinion of a consulting physician. In this case, none of the medical experts was a treating physician. Nor was it a case where the ALJ improperly rejected an examining physician's opinion in favor of a non-examining physician's decision. But in this case one examining physician's opinion was contradicted by several other examining and non-examining physicians' opinions. After weighing the evidence, the ALJ opted to believe the latter group of experts. The ALJ's decision that the evidence presented by Drs. Hathaway, Spear, Hodes, Ostrowski, Jankus, and Howell more accurately reflected Young's cognitive and memory problems was supported by substantial evidence.

[Remainder of the opinion is omitted.]

A) SUBSTANTIAL EVIDENCE RULE IN PRACTICE

The substantial evidence rule has important implications in key areas of Social Security practice, including credibility determinations, vocational findings, and determinations of pain. Generally, it is applied strictly; however, there are many qualifications to the general rule which, together with guidelines on the weight to be given different types of medical evidence, leave claimants room to argue that SSA's findings of fact should be disregarded as not supported by substantial evidence. Although courts should not substitute their judgment for that of the Administration, courts must keep in mind the overall beneficent purposes of the Social Security Act. Moreover, "this very narrow ambit of judicial review does not release [the courts] from [their] responsibility to scrutinize the record in its entirety to determine whether substantial evidence does support [SSA's] findings." Millet v. Schweiker, 662 F.2d 1199, 1201 (5th Cir. 1981).

On the other hand, it is clear that a reviewing court need not give special deference to conclusions of law reached by an administrative law judge or the Appeals Council. Moreover, the facts in the record must have been evaluated by SSA in light of the correct legal standards in order for its findings to be protected by the substantial evidence test. Therefore, when the proper legal standard is not used, the Administration's decision will be set aside even though the findings are supported by substantial evidence. Consider the following two cases in which federal courts found that SSA's decision was not supported by substantial evidence.

ANGEL V. BARNHART

329 F.3d 1208, 88 Soc. Sec. Rep. Serv. 7 (10th Cir. 2003)

Before SEYMOUR, KELLY, and LUCERO, Circuit Judges.

PAUL KELLY, Jr., Circuit Judge.

Plaintiff-appellant Sara Angel appeals from the district court's order affirming the Commissioner's denial of her application for disability insurance benefits and supplemental security income benefits under the Social Security Act. We exercise jurisdiction under 42 U.S.C. § 405(g) and 28 U.S.C. § 1291. We review the Commissioner's decision to determine whether the factual findings are supported by substantial evidence and whether the correct legal standards were applied.

Angel claims that she has been disabled for the relevant time period of July 24, 1997, through December 31, 1999 as a result of back and bladder impairments. After Angel's application for benefits was initially denied, a de novo hearing was held before an administrative law judge (ALJ). In a decision dated January 21, 2000, the ALJ determined, at step three of the five-part sequential evaluation process for determining disability, that Angel's back impairment did not meet or equal the impairment listing for vertebrogenic disorders of the spine, listing 1.05C. The ALJ then determined at step four of the evaluation process that Angel was not disabled. First, the ALJ concluded that, while Angel suffers from severe back and bladder impairments, she has the residual functional capacity to perform a wide range of light work subject to the limitations of "lifting no more than 10 pounds on a frequent basis and no more than a maximum of 20 pounds, standing or walking for no more than 2 hours at a time, or for longer than 6 hours during an eight hour day, only occasional stooping, and a need to self catheterize her bladder for 10[to] 15 minutes every 2 to 2 1/2 hours during the work day." Second, based on the testimony of the vocational expert concerning the residual functional capacity necessary to perform her past relevant work, the ALJ determined that Angel was capable of performing her past relevant work as an insurance clerk, receptionist, accounts payable clerk, senior office assistant, convenience store clerk, and barmaid.

* * *

Having thoroughly reviewed the record and the pertinent legal authorities, we conclude that the ALJ's finding at step three that Angel's back impairment does not meet or equal listing 1.05C is supported by substantial evidence in the record. However, we agree with Angel that the ALJ erred at step four by failing to address all of the relevant evidence in the record concerning the process she must undergo to catheterize herself. We also agree with Angel that the ALJ erred at step four by failing to provide sufficient reasons for rejecting her testimony and her treating physician's opinions regarding the limitations imposed by her back pain and problems. Accordingly, we reverse the order of the district court affirming the ALJ's decision denying benefits, and we remand this matter for further proceedings before the ALJ.[4]

1. Listing 1.05C.

Listing 1.05C provides as follows:

> C. Other vertebrogenic disorders (e.g., herniated [disk], spinal stenosis) with the following persisting for at least 3 months despite prescribed therapy and expected to last 12 months. With both 1 and 2:
>
> 1. Pain, muscle spasm, and significant limitation of motion in the spine; and
>
> 2. Appropriate radicular distribution of significant motor loss with muscle weakness and sensory and reflex loss.

20 C.F.R. Pt. 404, Subpt. P, App. 1, § 1.05C (1999).[5] Although the listing does not define the term "vertebrogenic disorder," another section of the listing regulations, which specifically cross-references § 1.05C, states that it includes disorders that result in impairment "because of distortion of the bony and ligamentous architecture of the spine or impingement of a herniated [disk] or bulging annulus on a nerve root."

Angel's treating osteopath, Dr. Schneider, testified at the hearing before the ALJ that Angel met or equaled listing 1.05C. According to Dr. Schneider, "[Angel] actually meets number one. Number two on that, the bladder dysfunction and her lack of tenacity or lack of reflex there, I think she meets it or equals that criteria." As this quote makes clear, Dr. Schneider only addressed the two sub-parts of listing 1.05C, and she did not specifically address the threshold issue under the listing of whether Angel suffered from a vertebrogenic disorder of the spine during the relevant time period of July 24, 1997 through December 31, 1999. Further, there is no evidence in the record that Angel suffered from a vertebrogenic disorder of the spine during the relevant time period.

The record shows that Angel injured her back in a work-related incident in October 1994, and she underwent a right hemilaminectomy and disk excision in May 1995 to repair a herniated disk at L5-S1. An MRI subsequently taken in February 1997 showed no definite evidence of any recurrent disk herniation at L5-S1. Although the February 1997 MRI did

---

[4] Given the nature of our remand, we do not address Angel's claim that she does not have the residual functional capacity to perform her past relevant work, and we leave that issue for the ALJ to reconsider on remand.

[5] Listing 1.05C was revised in 2002, and it is now listing 1.04. *See* 20 C.F.R. Pt. 404, Subpt. P, App. 1, § 1.04 (2002).

show disk degeneration at L5-S1 and a mild bulging of the disc at L4-5, an electromyogram (EMG) performed at the same time showed no definite evidence of active lumbar radiculopathy in Angel's lower extremities. Based on the EMG results, Dr. Benner, Angel's neurosurgeon, reported to her at the time that there were "no signs of any nerve root damage or irritation" in the area of her prior surgery.

During her testimony at the hearing before the ALJ in November 1999, Dr. Schneider testified that it was her belief that Angel "probably" had a "new" herniated disk at L4-L5. Dr. Schneider admitted, however, that she did not have any objective medical evidence to support her testimony. In fact, an MRI taken in December 1998 showed no evidence of a herniated disk at L4-L5 or elsewhere on Angel's lumbar spine. On January 25, 2000, a little over a month after the hearing before the ALJ, Dr. Schneider referred Angel for another MRI, and that MRI also showed no evidence of a herniated disk in Angel's lumbar spine.

In her brief on appeal, Angel has admitted that her back problems do not satisfy listing 1.05C standing alone. To overcome this failure of proof, Angel argues that the ALJ erred by failing to consider her bladder problem in combination with her back problems in determining whether she met or equaled listing 1.05C. *Id.* at 14-15. We disagree. At most, Angel has only shown that her urologist, Dr. Forrest, has opined that her bladder problem "most likely arises from old spinal cord disease" and that the bladder problem "is more than likely associated with nerve changes present within the spinal cord causing the resulting hypotonicity of the bladder." Angel has failed, however, to put forth any specific medical evidence linking her bladder problem to a vertebrogenic disorder of the spine such as the herniated disk she sustained in October 1994. Thus, we hold that the ALJ's determination that Angel does not meet or equal listing 1.05C is supported by substantial evidence in the record.

* * *

3. ALJ's Credibility and Treating Physician Determinations.

At the hearing before the ALJ, Angel testified that, as a result of her back pain and problems, she can lift no more than a gallon of milk and she can only stand, sit, or walk for fifteen to twenty minutes at a time. This is consistent with the testimony and opinions of Dr. Schneider. However, the ALJ found that Angel's testimony was not credible and that Dr. Schneider's opinions were not supported by the medical evidence in the record. Angel argues that the reasons put forth by the ALJ for rejecting her testimony and the opinions of Dr. Schneider are not supported by the record. We agree.

With respect to the credibility of Angel's subjective complaints regarding her back pain and problems, the ALJ found that they were "not fully credible because, but not limited to, the objective findings, or the lack thereof, by treating and examining physicians, the lack of medication for severe pain, the frequency of treatments by physicians and the lack of discomfort shown by the claimant at the hearing." The ALJ also found that Angel's credibility "is diminished because the objective medical evidence shows a significant lack of continuous treatment for her back and her treating physician, Dr. Schneider, did not refer her to a specialist." With respect to Dr. Schneider's opinions, the ALJ gave them "a reduced weight because they are not supported by any objective testing, x-rays, CT scans, MRIs, or even physical examinations."

The ALJ's findings are not supported by substantial evidence in the record because the record shows that: (1) Angel had objective findings of back problems in the form of degenerative disk disease, one or more bulging disks, and scar tissue documented by the MRIs taken in 1997, 1998, and 2000, and there is no dispute that she had a herniated disk and steroid atrophy in 1995; (2) Angel has been taking prescribed pain medication for several years; (3) Angel has been seeing Dr. Schneider for treatment of her back pain and problems for several years, although, as Dr. Schneider conceded at the hearing before the ALJ, her treatment has primarily involved providing prescriptions for pain medication; and (4) Angel has seen two specialists to evaluate her continuing back pain and problems (her neurosurgeon, Dr. Benner, and an orthopedic surgeon, Dr. Bazih).

The ALJ may be correct that the level of treatment Angel has received for her back pain and problems is inconsistent with her and Dr. Schneider's claims regarding the severity of her back impairment. But, in the absence of a more thorough analysis and more specific findings by the ALJ, the ALJ cannot ignore the dispositive issue of whether Angel's objectively documented back problems were capable of producing the pain and physical limitations that she and Dr. Schneider were alleging as of the time of the hearing before the ALJ. Accordingly, we conclude that the ALJ's conclusory findings are an insufficient basis for rejecting Angel's testimony and Dr. Schneider's opinions, and we remand the step four issue of whether Angel's back impairment prevents her from performing her past relevant work to the ALJ for reconsideration. * * *

The order of the district court is REVERSED, and this case is REMANDED to the district court with instructions to remand the case to the Commissioner for further proceedings before the ALJ.

TEJADA V. APFEL

167 F.3d 770, 60 Soc. Sec. Rep. Ser. 90 (2d Cir. 1999)

TSOUCALAS, Judge:

Maria Tejada appeals from the judgment entered in the United States District Court for the Southern District of New York, granting defendant's motion for judgment on the pleadings and upholding a final determination by the Commissioner of Social Security ("Commissioner") denying Tejada's application for Supplemental Security Income ("SSI") disability benefits. For the reasons discussed below, we vacate and remand for further proceedings in accordance with this opinion.

BACKGROUND

Plaintiff-Appellant Maria Tejada was born in the Dominican Republic on October 10, 1935, and came to the United States in September 1988. The record shows that she is unable to communicate in English, that she can speak but cannot read or write Spanish, and that she has never attended school. Tejada's last job, which she held from 1990-1992, was as an assembly worker on a car parts assembly line. Tejada's position required her to stand for most of her eight-hour work day, to perform frequent bending and reaching, and occasionally to lift up to ten pounds. Appellant stopped working on December 5, 1992, because of her disability and because her daughter was in a coma.

The record below reveals that at the time of her initial application, Tejada had multiple health problems, including diabetes, from which she suffered for over 15 years. Tejada's diabetes was unpredictable and difficult to manage; in fact, she was once taken to the hospital in an ambulance because her blood sugar dropped to alarming levels. Her precarious situation forced the William Ryan Community Health Center, one of Tejada's treating facilities, to adjusted her insulin dosage several times over a three-year period (1991-1994). The Ryan Center diagnosed Tejada as having diabetes mellitus with peripheral neuropathy in November 1993. A podiatrist confirmed the diagnosis of diabetes mellitus in October 1994. In late 1994, the Ryan Center discontinued Tejada's insulin treatment and replaced it with Micronase, a medication used in the treatment of non-insulin dependent diabetes mellitus. Also, in late 1994, another doctor of the Ryan Center diagnosed Tejada with diabetic neuropathy.

Tejada's other disabling complaints included weakness, dizziness, fatigue, stomach bloating, pains in her chest, increased size of her thyroid, arthritis pain in her back, knees, hands and shoulders, hypertension, worsening vision, depression, and leg edema. Her frequent headaches and dizzy spells required her to lie down for several hours at a time. The cramping, pain, and swelling in her legs required her to keep her legs in water for at least one hour per day and to keep them elevated 2-3 hours per day. Pain relievers afforded no relief. On May 3, 1994, Tejada saw a podiatrist who diagnosed osteoarthritis.

* * *

Tejada argues that the ALJ erred in concluding that she was able to return to her past employment. Specifically, Tejada asserts that the ALJ's description of the requirements of her former employment was ambiguous and was not supported by substantial evidence. Tejada further alleges that the ALJ failed to consider most of the medical records she submitted.

DISCUSSION

* * *

When reviewing the Commissioner's denial of disability benefits, this Court's "'focus is not so much on the district court's ruling as it is on the administrative ruling.'" *Schaal v. Apfel*, 134 F.3d 496, 500-01 (2d Cir.1998) (quoting *Rivera v. Sullivan*, 923 F.2d 964, 967 (2d Cir.1991)). First, the Court reviews the Commissioner's decision to determine whether the Commissioner applied the correct legal standard.

Next, the Court examines the record to determine if the Commissioner's conclusions are supported by substantial evidence. *See Townley*, 748 F.2d at 112 ("It is not the function of a reviewing court to determine *de novo* whether a claimant is disabled. The [Commissioner's] findings of fact, if supported by substantial evidence, are binding."). Substantial evidence is "'more than a mere scintilla. It means such relevant evidence as a reasonable mind might accept as [*774] adequate to support a conclusion.'" *Richardson v. Perales*, 402 U.S. 389, 401, 91 S.Ct. 1420, 28 L.Ed.2d 842 (1971) (quoting *Consolidated Edison Co. v. NLRB*, 305 U.S. 197, 229, 59 S.Ct. 206, 83 L.Ed. 126 (1938)). The Court carefully considers the whole record, examining evidence from both sides "'because an analysis of the substantiality of the evidence must also include that which detracts from its weight.'" *Quinones v. Chater*, 117 F.3d 29, 33 (2d Cir.1997) (quoting *Williams v. Bowen*, 859 F.2d 255, 258 (2d Cir.1988)).

* * *

Here, the ALJ found that Tejada was not performing substantial gainful activity and that her condition constituted a severe impairment (although not one listed, or equivalent to the impairments listed, in Appendix 1 of the regulations). Tejada's claim therefore survived the first two steps of the Commissioner's inquiry. However, the ALJ concluded that Tejada had "the residual functional capacity to perform work-related activities except for work involving more than 20 pounds." Further, the ALJ determined that since Tejada's past relevant work did not require her to lift more than 20 pounds, she was not precluded from returning to her prior job. Although the ALJ had previously concluded that Tejada's job involved her standing a minimum of six hours in an eight-hour workday, he did not address whether her leg edema, arthralgia, diabetes mellitus, or severe hypertension would prevent her from performing a job that requires such exertion. The issue in this case is whether the Commissioner's determination-that Tejada, despite her impairments, had the residual functional capacity to perform the work-related activities (except for work that involved lifting more than 20 pounds) of her old job in a metal factory assembly line-was supported by substantial evidence.

At the outset, we are troubled by the ALJ's failure to develop the record in this case. By statute, the ALJ was required to develop Tejada's complete medical history for at least a twelve-month period if there was reason to believe that the information was necessary to reach a decision. 42 U.S.C. §§ 423(d)(5)(B), 1382c(a)(3)(G) (1994); 20 C.F.R. § 416.912(d)(2) (1998). Moreover, "[i]t is the rule in our circuit that 'the ALJ, unlike a judge in a trial, must ... affirmatively develop the record' in light of 'the essentially non-adversarial nature of a benefits proceeding,' " even if the claimant is represented by counsel. *Pratts v. Chater*, 94 F.3d 34, 37 (2d Cir.1996) (quoting *Echevarria v. Secretary of HHS*, 685 F.2d 751, 755 (2d Cir.1982)). In this case, we question the decision of the ALJ not to develop the record further concerning Tejada's arthritis or her depression, particularly since the ALJ himself referred to the fact that Tejada was under treatment for both conditions. Further, although the ALJ noted 15 visits to medical facilities in a two year period, he merely labeled these visits as "infrequent" instead of identifying what treatment was received and the purpose of these visits (there is a dispute as to how many times Tejada received medical treatment for her ailments--the record shows up to 18 documented visits in a one year period). In any event, we need not decide whether the ALJ failed to develop a complete record because, as we discuss below, we find that the record, as developed by the ALJ, does not support the ALJ's findings by substantial evidence that Tejada could perform her past relevant work.

Taken all together, the facts in the record before us do not support the ALJ's determination that Tejada could return to her prior employment. And, on these facts, we conclude that Tejada has met her burden of showing that she does not have the residual functional capacity to perform the work of her former job-that is, that she has satisfied the fourth requirement of the five-part test.

* * *

Here, the record shows that Tejada suffered from leg edema that demanded that she elevate her legs a few hours a day pursuant to a physician's advice. Moreover, although the record does not indicate whether the ALJ considered the podiatrist's report, we give some weight to the podiatrist's diagnosis that plaintiff suffers from osteoarthritis and peripheral neuropathy of the feet. In light of this evidence, the ALJ's determination that Tejada was able to continue her past employment, which required standing for prolonged periods of time, is not supported by substantial evidence.

The record reveals that the ALJ had discredited Tejada's testimony concerning certain aspects of her alleged disability. We are not disturbing these findings. Nonetheless, we must reverse on the grounds that the ALJ overlooked objective medical evidence documenting Tejada's leg edema and her arthritis. His determination that Tejada can return to her past employment is therefore both based on legal error and is not supported by substantial evidence.

For the reasons set forth above, the judgment of the district court is hereby vacated and the case is remanded to the district court with instructions that the matter be remanded to the Commissioner for a rehearing and determination confined to step five of the sequential analysis. If the Commissioner is unable to find other work under the Medical-Vocational Guidelines which the claimant could perform, the Commissioner is directed to calculate and dispense SSI benefits. Since Ms. Tejada's application for benefits has been pending for more than five years, we urge the Commissioner to expedite the proceedings on remand.

E. ATTORNEY'S FEES

There are two main sources of attorney's fees in Social Security cases. Most awards by far are paid by the claimant, usually out of past-due benefits. Another source of fees is the Equal Access to Justice Act (EAJA), a federal fee-shifting statute. Both are discussed below. For the most part, attorney's fees for OASDI and SSI claims are governed by the same or similar rules. Many of the same rules apply also to non-attorney representatives. The status of non-attorney representatives at the Social Security Administration is discussed in Chapter 9.

1. FEE FROM THE CLAIMANT

Attorney's fees paid out of the claimant's benefits are regulated by statute and regulations. *See generally* 42 U.S.C.A. § 406(a)-(b), 20 C.F.R. §§ 404.1720-.1735 (OASDI); 42 U.S.C.A. § 1383(d)(2), 20 C.F.R. §§ 416.1520-.1535 (SSI). Fees for claims resolved within SSA are authorized at the administrative level where the final decision is reached. Thus, administrative law judges approve fees in cases where a favorable hearing decision was issued, and the Appeals Council authorizes fees in cases decided finally only by the Appeals Council. The representative must file a request for fees in writing, which must include a list of services performed, the amount of the fee, and any expenses incurred. 20 C.F.R. §§ 404.1725(a), 416.1525(a). SSA considers a number of factors when evaluating a representative's request for fees, including the type and amount of services performed, the difficulty of the case (including the skill required of the representative), and the results achieved. *See* 20 C.F.R. §§ 404.1725(b)(1), 416.1525(b)(1). Although the amount of benefits received is taken into consideration, it does not control the amount of fee authorized. 20 C.F.R. §§ 404.1725(b)(2), 416.1525(b)(2).

Separate from its role in authorizing the amount of fees, which are not subject to a statutory limit and can be awarded even if no past-due benefits are due, SSA will withhold up to 25 percent of past-due benefits for direct payment to attorneys for agency-level representation. Until recently, the Social Security Act authorized withholding of past-due benefits for direct payment of fees only under the OASDI program; however, Congress extended the program to SSI claims under a 5-year demonstration project that also tested withholding and direct payments to certain non-attorney representatives. *See* 20 C.F.R. §§ 404.1720(b), 416.1520(b). The extension of fee withholding and direct payment to SSI claims and non-attorney representatives was made permanent in 2010. *See* Social Security Disability Applicants' Access to Professional Representation Act of 2010, Pub. L. No. 111-142.

As part of The Ticket to Work and Work Incentives Improvement Act of 1999, Congress imposed a "user fee" on attorneys whose fees are paid by SSA out of withheld past-due benefits. Pub. L. No. 106-170, 113 Stat 1860 (1999). The rate was set at 6.3%, with the possibility of reducing the percentage in future years if the administrative costs warrant a reduction. *See* 42 U.S.C.A. § 406(d). The rate has remained the same but the fee is capped at $83.

In order to encourage attorneys to handle Social Security cases where little or no past-due benefits can be withheld, SSA has approved the use of agreements by which claimants agree to deposit funds into a trust or escrow account that can be used to pay attorney's fees. The funds can be used only to pay fees approved by SSA and any funds in excess of the amount authorized must be refunded to the claimant. *See* SSR 82-39 (1982).

A claimant and his or her representative can also agree on a fee, which will be awarded automatically so long as the agreement was filed with SSA before the claim was approved. 42 U.S.C. §§406(a)(2)(A)(i), 1383(d)(2)(A). The amount of an agreed fee is limited to 25% of past-due benefits or $6000, whichever is less. 42 U.S.C.A. §406(a)(2)(A)(ii), 1383(d)(2)(A). These rules on agreed-upon fees apply to non-attorney representatives as well.

Finally, courts can award fees for representation in judicial proceedings in Social Security cases. The Social Security Act limits the amount of an attorney's fee in cases where the claimant prevailed in court to 25 percent of past-due benefits; in addition, as noted earlier an award up to this amount can be withheld from past-due benefits for direct payment to the attorney. The 25 percent limitation on court-awarded fees is intended as a maximum, not an amount to be awarded routinely. In awarding a fee, courts will look to many factors similar to those SSA considers when setting a fee for administrative representation, including the difficulty of the case, the amount of time involved, the level of skill required, and the result achieved. A number of courts use the "lodestar" approach, in which an hourly fee is set based on an established set of factors used in Social Security cases. Other courts focus more directly on the amount of time spent and the complexity of the case.

The Supreme Court resolved a split among the circuits on how courts should determine the amount of fees in the following case. The Court refers in its analysis to fees awarded under the Equal Access to Justice Act, which are discussed further in the next part of this section.

GISBRECHT V. BARNHART
535 U.S. 789 (2002)

Justice GINSBURG delivered the opinion of the Court.

This case concerns the fees that may be awarded attorneys who successfully represent Social Security benefits claimants in court. Under 42 U.S.C. § 406(b), a prevailing claimant's fees are payable only out of the benefits recovered; in amount, such fees may not exceed 25 percent of past-due benefits. At issue is a question that has sharply divided the Federal Courts of Appeals: What is the appropriate starting point for judicial determinations of "a reasonable fee for [representation before the court]"? Is the contingent-fee agreement between claimant and counsel, if not in excess of 25 percent of past-due benefits, presumptively reasonable? Or should courts begin with a lodestar calculation (hours reasonably spent on the case times reasonable hourly rate) of the kind we have approved under statutes that shift the obligation to pay to the loser in the litigation?

Congress, we conclude, designed § 406(b) to control, not to displace, fee agreements between Social Security benefits claimants and their counsel. Because the decision before us for review rests on lodestar calculations and rejects the primacy of lawful attorney-client fee agreements, we reverse the judgment below and remand for recalculation of counsel fees payable from the claimants' past-due benefits.

I

A

Fees for representation of individuals claiming Social Security old-age, survivor, or disability benefits, both at the administrative level and in court, are governed by prescriptions Congress originated in 1965. The statute deals with the administrative and judicial review stages discretely: [42 U.S.C.] § 406(a) governs fees for representation in administrative proceedings; § 406(b) controls fees for representation in court.

For representation of a benefits claimant at the administrative level, an attorney may file a fee petition or a fee agreement. In response to a petition, the agency may allow fees "for services performed in connection with any claim before" it; if a determination favorable to the benefits claimant has been made, however, the Commissioner of Social Security "*shall* ... fix ... a reasonable fee" for an attorney's services. § 406(a)(1) (emphasis added). In setting fees under this method, the agency takes into account, in addition to any benefits award, several other factors. Fees may be authorized, on petition, even if the benefits claimant was unsuccessful.

As an alternative to fee petitions, the Social Security Act, as amended in 1990, accommodates contingent-fee agreements filed with the agency in advance of a ruling on the claim for benefits. If the ruling on the benefits claim is favorable to the claimant, the agency will generally approve the fee agreement, subject to this limitation: Fees may not exceed the lesser of 25 percent of past-due benefits or $4,000 (increased to $5,300 effective February 2002). [Editor note: this amount has since been increased to $6000.]

For proceedings in court, Congress provided for fees on rendition of "a judgment favorable to a claimant." 42 U.S.C. § 406(b)(1)(A). The Commissioner has interpreted § 406(b) to "prohibi[t] a lawyer from charging fees when there is no award of back benefits."

As part of its judgment, a court may allow "a reasonable fee ... not in excess of 25 percent of the ... past-due benefits" awarded to the claimant. § 406(b)(1)(A). The fee is payable "out of, and not in addition to, the amount of [the] past-due benefits." *Ibid*. Because benefits amounts figuring in the fee calculation are limited to those past due, attorneys may not gain additional fees based on a claimant's continuing entitlement to benefits.

The prescriptions set out in §§ 406(a) and (b) establish the exclusive regime for obtaining fees for successful representation of Social Security benefits claimants. Collecting or even demanding from the client anything more than the authorized allocation of past-due benefits is a criminal offense.

In many cases, as in the instant case, the Equal Access to Justice Act (EAJA), enacted in 1980, effectively increases the portion of past-due benefits the successful Social Security claimant may pocket. 28 U.S.C. § 2412. Under EAJA, a party prevailing against the United States in court, including a successful Social Security benefits claimant, may be awarded fees payable by the United States if the Government's position in the litigation was not "substantially justified." § 2412(d)(1)(A). EAJA fees are determined not by a percent of the amount recovered, but by the "time expended" and the attorney's "[hourly] rate," § 2412(d)(1)(B), capped in the mine run of cases at $125 per hour.

Congress harmonized fees payable by the Government under EAJA with fees payable under § 406(b) out of the claimant's past-due Social Security benefits in this manner: Fee awards may be made under both prescriptions, but the claimant's attorney must "refun[d] to the claimant the amount of the smaller fee." Act of Aug. 5, 1985, Pub.L. 99-80, § 3, 99 Stat. 186. "Thus, an EAJA award offsets an award under Section 406(b), so that the [amount of the total past-due benefits the claimant actually receives] will be increased by the ... EAJA award up to the point the claimant receives 100 percent of the past-due benefits."

B

Petitioners Gary Gisbrecht, Barbara Miller, and Nancy Sandine brought three separate actions in the District Court for the District of Oregon under 42 U.S.C. § 405(g), seeking Social Security disability benefits under Title II of the Social Security Act. All three petitioners were represented by the same attorneys, and all three prevailed on the merits of their claims. Gisbrecht was awarded $28,366 in past-due benefits; Miller, $30,056; and Sandine, $55,952. Each petitioner then successfully sought attorneys' fees payable by the United States under EAJA: Gisbrecht was awarded $3,339.11, Miller, $5,164.75, and Sandine, $6,836.10.

Pursuant to contingent-fee agreements standard for Social Security claimant representation, Gisbrecht, Miller, and Sandine had each agreed to pay counsel 25 percent of all past-due benefits recovered. Their attorneys accordingly requested § 406(b) fees of $7,091.50 from Gisbrecht's recovery, $7,514 from Miller's, and $13,988 from Sandine's. Given the EAJA offsets, the amounts in fact payable from each client's past-due benefits recovery would have been $3,752.39 from Gisbrecht's recovery, $2,349.25 from Miller's, and $7,151.90 from Sandine's.

Following Circuit precedent, the District Court in each case declined to give effect to the attorney-client fee agreement. Instead, the court employed for the § 406(b) fee calculation a "lodestar" method, under which the number of hours reasonably devoted to each case was multiplied by a reasonable hourly fee. This method yielded as § 406(b) fees $3,135 from Gisbrecht's recovery, $5,461.50 from Miller's, and $6,550 from Sandine's. Offsetting the EAJA awards, the court determined that no portion of Gisbrecht's or Sandine's past-due benefits was payable to counsel, and that only $296.75 of Miller's recovery was payable to her counsel as a § 406(b) fee. The three claimants appealed.

Adhering to Circuit precedent applying the lodestar method to calculate fees under § 406(b), the Court of Appeals for the Ninth Circuit consolidated the cases and affirmed the District Court's fee dispositions. The Appeals Court noted that fees determined under the lodestar method could be adjusted by applying 12 further factors, one of them, "whether the fee is fixed or contingent." While "a district court must *consider* a plaintiff's request to increase a fee [based on a contingent-fee agreement]," the Ninth Circuit stated, "a court 'is not required to articulate its reasons' for accepting or rejecting such a request."

We granted certiorari in view of the division among the Circuits on the appropriate method of calculating fees under § 406(b). We now reverse the Ninth Circuit's judgment.

II

Beginning with the text, § 406(b)'s words, "a reasonable fee ... not in excess of 25 percent of ... the past-due benefits," read in isolation, could be construed to allow either the Ninth Circuit's lodestar approach or petitioners' position that the attorney-client fee agreement ordinarily should control, if not "in excess of 25 percent." The provision instructs "a reasonable fee," which could be measured by a lodestar calculation. But § 406(b)'s language does not exclude contingent-fee contracts that produce fees no higher than the 25 percent ceiling. Such contracts are the most common fee arrangement between attorneys and Social Security claimants. Looking outside the statute's inconclusive text, we next take into account, as interpretive guides, the origin and standard application of the proffered approaches.

[The Court reviews past practices relative to calculating attorney's fees and notes that "the lodestar method today holds sway in federal court adjudications of disputes over the amount of fees properly shifted to the loser in litigation."]

Fees shifted to the losing party, however, are not at issue here. Unlike 42 U.S.C. § 1988 (1994 ed. and Supp. V) and EAJA, 42 U.S.C. § 406(b) (1994 ed., Supp. V) does not authorize the prevailing party to recover fees from the losing party. Section 406(b) is of another genre: It authorizes fees payable from the successful party's recovery. * * * Characteristically in cases of the kind we confront, attorneys and clients enter into contingent-fee agreements "specifying that the fee will be 25 percent of any past-due benefits to which the claimant becomes entitled."

* * *

Before 1965, the Social Security Act imposed no limits on contingent-fee agreements drawn by counsel and signed by benefits claimants. In formulating the 1965 Social Security Act amendments that included § 406(b), Congress recognized that "attorneys have upon occasion charged ... inordinately large fees for representing claimants [in court]." S.Rep. No. 404, 89th Cong., 1st Sess., pt. 1, p. 122 (1965), U.S.Code Cong. & Admin.News 1965, pp. 1943, 2062. Arrangements yielding exorbitant fees, the Senate Report observed, reserved for the lawyer one-third to one-half of the accrued benefits. *Ibid.* Congress was mindful, too, that the longer the litigation persisted, the greater the buildup of past-due benefits and, correspondingly, of legal fees awardable from those benefits if the claimant prevailed. *Ibid.*

Attending to these realities, Congress provided for "a reasonable fee, not in excess of 25 percent of accrued benefits," as part of the court's judgment, and further specified that "no other fee would be payable." *Ibid.* Violation of the "reasonable fee" or "25 percent of accrued benefits" limitation was made subject to the same penalties as those applicable for charging a fee larger than the amount approved by the Commissioner for services at the administrative leve—a fine of up to $500, one year's imprisonment, or both. *Ibid.* "[T]o assure the payment of the fee allowed by the court," Congress authorized the agency "to certify the amount of the fee to the attorney out of the amount of the accrued benefits." *Ibid.*

Congress thus sought to protect claimants against "inordinately large fees" and also to ensure that attorneys representing successful claimants would not risk "nonpayment of [appropriate] fees. But nothing in the text or history of § 406(b) reveals a "desig[n] to prohibit or discourage attorneys and claimants from entering into contingent fee agreements." *Ibid.* Given the prevalence of contingent-fee agreements between attorneys and Social Security claimants, it is unlikely that Congress, simply by prescribing "reasonable fees," meant to outlaw, rather than to contain, such agreements.

This conclusion is bolstered by Congress' 1990 authorization of contingent-fee agreements under § 406(a), the provision governing fees for agency-level representation. Before enacting this express authorization, Congress instructed the Social Security Administration to prepare a report on attorney's fees under Title II of the Social Security Act. The report, presented to Congress in 1988, reviewed several methods of determining attorney's fees, including the lodestar method. This review led the agency to inform Congress that, although the contingency method was hardly flawless, the agency could "identify no more effective means of ensuring claimant access to attorney representation."

Congress subsequently altered § 406(a) to validate contingent-fee agreements filed with the agency prior to disposition of the claim for benefits. As petitioners observe, it would be anomalous if contract-based fees expressly authorized by § 406(a)(2) at the administrative level were disallowed for court representation under § 406(b).

* * *

Most plausibly read, we conclude, § 406(b) does not displace contingent-fee agreements as the primary means by which fees are set for successfully representing Social Security benefits claimants in court. Rather, § 406(b) calls for court review of such arrangements as an independent check, to assure that they yield reasonable results in particular cases. Congress has provided one boundary line: Agreements are unenforceable to the extent that they provide for fees exceeding 25 percent of the past-due benefits. Within the 25 percent boundary, as petitioners in this case acknowledge, the attorney for the successful claimant must show that the fee sought is reasonable for the services rendered.

Courts that approach fee determinations by looking first to the contingent-fee agreement, then testing it for reasonableness, have appropriately reduced the attorney's recovery based on the character of the representation and the results the representative achieved. If the attorney is responsible for delay, for example, a reduction is in order so that the attorney will not profit from the accumulation of benefits during the pendency of the case in court. If the benefits are large in comparison to the amount of time counsel spent on the case, a downward adjustment is similarly in order. In this regard, the court may require the claimant's attorney to submit, not as a basis for satellite litigation, but as an aid to the court's assessment of the reasonableness of the fee yielded by the fee agreement, a record of the hours spent representing the claimant and a statement of the lawyer's normal hourly billing charge for noncontingent-fee cases. Judges of our district courts are accustomed to making reasonableness determinations in a wide variety of contexts, and their assessments in such matters, in the event of an appeal, ordinarily qualify for highly respectful review.

* * *

The courts below erroneously read § 406(b) to override customary attorney-client contingent-fee agreements. We hold that § 406(b) does not displace contingent-fee agreements within the statutory ceiling; instead, §

406(b) instructs courts to review for reasonableness fees yielded by those agreements. Accordingly, we reverse the judgment of the Court of Appeals for the Ninth Circuit and remand the case for further proceedings consistent with this opinion.

Dissenting opinion of Justice SCALIA omitted.

2. FEES UNDER THE EQUAL ACCESS TO JUSTICE ACT

The Equal Access to Justice Act (EAJA), 28 U.S.C. §2412, is a fee-shifting statute that authorizes an award of attorney's fees against government agencies—including the Social Security Administration—unless the government's position was "substantially justified" or there are special circumstances that would make the award unjust. EAJA fees are awarded, however, only if the claimant is the "prevailing party" on a contested issue. They are not limited to 25 percent of past-due benefits, as are fees paid out of a claimant's award; they can be awarded in any amount, as long as the total fee is reasonable. However, if the EAJA fee amounts to more than 25% of the claimant's past-due benefits, SSA will not authorize an additional fee. If the EAJA fee is less than 25% of the claimant's past-due benefits, then the difference, up to the 25%, can be paid out of past-due benefits.

The EAJA is limited to cases where the government is a party to the proceeding, and therefore does not apply to non-adversary administrative proceedings before the Social Security Administration. There had been a great deal of debate among courts concerning the applicability of the Act to an attorney's administrative work when a claimant files an appeal in federal court and obtains a court order remanding the claim for further administrative proceedings. As discussed earlier in this chapter, there are two different types of remands authorized in 42 U.S.C. § 405(g): "sentence four" remands, in conjunction with a judgment affirming, modifying, or reversing SSA's decision; and "sentence six" remands, which merely send the matter back to SSA for collection of additional evidence. (The "sentences" referred to are those appearing in the remand provisions of § 405(g).) In Shalala v. Schaefer, 509 U.S. 292 (1993), the Supreme Court limited the authorization of EAJA fees for administrative work following a remand to "sentence six" remands; that is, EAJA fees are available for work at the agency level only when done following a remand ordered for the purpose of considering additional evidence. In "sentence-four" cases, attorney's fees are available, if allowed, only for the lawyer's work in federal court that resulted in the remand order.

The most difficult issue in EAJA fee disputes is determining whether SSA's position opposing the claimant was substantially justified. While the term "substantially justified" does not lend itself to a precise definition, the courts and Congress have set out several guidelines. As the Supreme Court stated in an early EAJA case, "as between the two commonly used connotations of the word 'substantially,' the one most naturally conveyed by ['substantially justified'] is not 'justified to a high degree,' but rather 'justified in substance or in the main'—that is, justified to a degree that could satisfy a reasonable person. * * *   To be 'substantially justified' means, of course, more than merely undeserving of sanctions for frivolousness; that is assuredly not the standard for Government litigation of which a reasonable person would approve." Pierce v. Underwood, 487 U.S. 552, 565, 108 S. Ct. 2541 (1988). *See also* 487 U.S. at 566 n.2 ("our analysis does not convert the term 'substantially justified' into 'reasonably justified.' . . . [A] position can be justified even though it is not correct, and we believe that it can be substantially (i.e., for the most part) justified if a reasonable person could think it correct, that is, if it has a reasonable basis in law and fact").

Finally, there had been a split among the circuits on the question of who is the "prevailing party" entitled to the fee, the claimant or the attorney. The Supreme Court recently resolved this split, holding that that the attorney's fee is payable to the claimant and therefore subject to an administrative offset to satisfy a pre-existing debt owed by the claimant to the government. Astrue v. Ratliff, 560 U.S. ___, 130 S. Ct. 2521, 153 Soc. Sec. Rep. Serv. 352 (June 14, 2010).

CHAPTER 9

ADMINISTRATIVE ADVOCACY

■ ■ ■

This chapter is intended to bring together some key aspects of substantive law and administrative procedure in the context of Social Security practice. Disability cases make up the bulk of any Social Security practice and as we have seen, particularly in Chapters 5, 6, and 8, the critical contested disability issues in Social Security cases are developed and resolved for the most part during the administrative process—from initial claim processing through up to three levels of administrative appeal. Although benefit decisions by the Social Security Administration are subject to judicial review, for most cases that can occur only after the administrative appeals process has been exhausted—and even then, the scope of review is limited by the "substantial evidence" rule.

Administrative advocacy is, therefore, a critical part of Social Security practice. As with other areas of practice, true competence comes only after many years of experience. Nonetheless, there are some aspects of administrative advocacy that are sufficiently central to Social Security practice that an introduction may be helpful to understanding the other material included in this book and as a foundation for possible future work in the field. Accordingly, this chapter covers selected topics of administrative advocacy central to a Social Security practice, including the role of key actors in the administrative process, the sources of Social Security law, and various standards and rules governing proof of eligibility.

A. LAWYERS AND REPRESENTATIVES

Social Security claimants are entitled to be represented at all stages of the administrative process. *See* 20 C.F.R. §§ 404.1700, 416.1500; *see also* 42 U.S.C. § 406(a). Although there is no constitutional right to appointed counsel, claimants have a constitutional right to bring a lawyer to a Social Security hearing. Mathews v. Eldridge, 424 U.S. 319, 339, 96 S. Ct. 893 (1976). Claimants can be represented by an attorney or by a non-attorney "authorized representative." *See* **20 C.F.R. §§ 404.1705, 416.1505**[APP-REGS]. An attorney must be in good standing and must not have been disqualified or suspended from acting as a representative in dealings with the Social Security Administration. 20 C.F.R. 404.1705(a). A non-attorney authorized representative must be "generally known to have a good character and reputation," "capable of giving valuable help" in connection with the claim, and neither disqualified or suspended from acting as a representative before SSA nor prohibited by law from acting as a representative. 20 C.F.R. §§ 404.1705(b), 416.1505(b).

These special rules, particularly those authorizing non-attorney representatives, apply only to administrative appeals. Only licensed attorneys can handle cases appealed to the federal courts, although some courts have held that non-attorney parents can handle their child's Social Security appeals in federal court. *See, e.g.*, Harris v. Apfel, 209 F.3d 413, 417, 68 Soc. Sec. Rep. Serv. 437 (5th Cir. 2000) ("We are persuaded that prohibiting non-attorney parents from proceeding *pro se* in appeals from administrative SSI decisions, on behalf of a minor child, would jeopardize seriously the child's statutory right to judicial review"). Most courts restrict this authority, however, to situations where the parents have "a sufficient interest in the case" to warrant the responsibility. *Compare* Machadio v. Apfel, 276 F.3d 103, 107, 77 Soc. Sec. Rep. Serv. 559 (2d Cir. 2002) (non-attorney parent serving as representative payee for his child's SSI benefits; "Where a district court, after appropriate inquiry into the particular circumstances of the matter at hand, determines that a non-attorney parent who brings an SSI appeal on behalf his or her children has a sufficient interest in the case and meets basic standards of competence, we hold that in such cases a non-attorney parent may bring an action on behalf of his or her child without representation by an attorney.") *with* Sabbia v. Commissioner, 669 F.Supp.2d 914, 917, 150 Soc. Sec. Rep. Serv. 553 (N.D. Ill. 2009) ("Both *Machadio* and *Harris* involved custodial parents who were financially responsible for their children. The courts reasoned that because the parents had a personal stake in the outcome of their children's actions, they could be trusted to represent their children's interests. Machadio, 276 F.3d at 108; Harris, 209 F.3d at 416. That rationale is clearly inapplicable here, since both Dominic Jr. and Nicole are adults.").

Once appointed, the representative can have access to all information otherwise available to the claimant, can submit evidence and advocate on behalf of the claimant, and is entitled to receive notice of all SSA action on the claim. **20 C.F.R. §§ 404.1710(a), 416.1510(a)[APP-REGS]; 20 C.F.R. §§ 404.1715, 416.1515[APP-REGS]**. Correspondence sent from SSA to an authorized representative will have the same force and effect as if it had been sent directly to the claimant. 20 C.F.R. § 404.1715. As noted in Chapter 8, both attorney and non-attorney representatives can obtain fees under conditions established by—and subject to the approval of—the Social Security Administration, although some conditions differ depending on whether the representative is an attorney or a non-attorney.

Claimants may, of course, waive their right to be represented at a hearing. However, the claimant must be competent to waive the right. In Earp v. Commissioner, 168 F.Supp.2d 628, 76 Soc. Sec. Rep. Serv. 483 (E.D. Tex. 2001), the claimant waived her right to counsel but then argued on appeal that she did not fully understand what she was doing. The court agreed and remanded the case:

> "After reviewing the record and hearing testimony, the Court has serious reservations whether Plaintiff fully understood what she was doing. The Plaintiff was illiterate. Plaintiff lacked the mental abilities to conduct a proper cross-examination of the vocational and medical experts. Since there is conflicting evidence in this record regarding whether Plaintiff is mentally retarded, the Court must find that she has not properly waived her right to counsel."

168 F.Supp.2d at 634. Simply asking if a claimant had been represented before and would like to proceed without counsel may not be sufficient to establish a knowing and competent waiver. Thus, in Lewis v. Barnhart, 201 F. Supp. 2d 918, 81 Soc. Sec. Rep. Serv. 83 (N.D. Ind. 2002), the claimant objected that "the ALJ did not elicit a valid waiver of his right to proceed with a representative" and the court agreed:

> In this case, the ALJ's discussion with Lewis about counsel was brief. He asked three questions, "Have you thought about having an attorney represent you?"; "Have you ever had an attorney represent you before in anything?"; and "So you'd like to go ahead today without an attorney?" R. at 21. The fact that Lewis had been represented by counsel in another setting does not mean that he understood the benefits of counsel in the context of a social security disability administrative hearing. Therefore, his waiver of the right to representation was invalid, and the burden shifts to the Commissioner to prove that the ALJ discharged his heightened duty to develop the record.

201 F. Supp. 2d at 938-39.

Moreover, many courts have held that a waiver is not effective at an administrative hearing unless the ALJ advises the claimant of the possibility of either obtaining free counsel or working out a contingency fee arrangement with a private lawyer. *See, e.g.*, Wilks v. Apfel, 113 F. Supp. 2d 30, 34, 71 Soc. Sec. Rep. Serv. 74 (D.D.C. 2000) ("The ALJ did not adequately inform plaintiff about his right to counsel, specifically what that right entailed."); Frank v. Chater, 924 F. Supp. 416, 421-26, 50 Soc. Sec. Rep. Serv. 790 (E.D.N.Y. 1996) (written notices to claimant did not advise him of the benefits of counsel or of the possibility of free legal services or a contingency fee arrangement); Gullett v. Chater, 973 F. Supp. 614, 621, 54 Soc. Sec. Rep. Serv. 175 (E.D. Tex. 1997) (waiver of counsel invalid where ALJ did not inform claimant of, among other things, "the opportunities for free legal services available in East Texas"). As set out by the Seventh Circuit in Binion v. Shalala, 13 F.3d 243, 245, 43 Soc. Sec. Rep. Serv. 289 (7th Cir. 1994): "To ensure a valid waiver of counsel, we require the ALJ to explain to the pro se claimant (1) the manner in which an attorney can aid in the proceedings, (2) the possibility of free counsel or a contingency arrangement, and (3) the limitation on attorney fees to 25 percent of past due benefits and required court approval of the fees." (citing Thompson v. Sullivan, 933 F.2d 581, 584 (7th Cir.1991). Consistent with this view, SSA regulations provide that where a claimant is not represented by an attorney it will include in its notice of any adverse decision information about options for obtaining an attorney, including from a legal services organization. See **20 C.F.R. §§** <u>404.1706</u>, <u>416.1506</u>**[APP-REGS]**.

1. STANDARDS OF CONDUCT FOR REPRESENTATIVES

The Social Security Administration issued comprehensive standards for the conduct of claimant representatives in 1998. *See generally* 63 Fed. Reg. 41404 (August 4, 1998); **20 C.F.R. §§** <u>404.1740</u>, <u>416.1540</u>**[APP-REGS]**. The standards require representatives to obtain promptly any evidence that the claimant wants to present, including any material medical evidence. 20 C.F.R. §§ 404.1740(b)(1), 416.1540(b)(1). The representative is also required to assist the claimant with any requests for evidence from SSA, including information about the claimant's education, work experience, and daily activities. 20 C.F.R. §§ 404.1740(b)(2), 416.1540(b)(2). Moreover, claimants' representatives must further the "efficient, fair and orderly conduct of the administrative decisionmaking process" by providing competent representation, and acting with reasonable diligence and promptness. *See* 20 C.F.R. §§ 404.1740(b)(3), 416.1540(b)(3). They are bound not to act in any way to "threaten, coerce, intimidate, deceive or knowingly mislead a claimant" or to make false statements, unreasonably delay proceedings, divulge information without the claimant's permission, or engage in other various unprofessional or illegal behavior. See 20 C.F.R. §§ 404.1740(c), 416.1540(c)

Since 2004, persons who have been disbarred or suspended from practice in any court or disqualified from participating in any federal program or from appearing before any federal agency can be refused (or disqualified from) the right to appear before SSA. *See* Social Security Protection Act of 2004, § 205, Pub. L. No. 108-203 (amending 42 U.S.C.A. § 406(a)). SSA issued regulations on the disqualification and reinstatement of claimant representatives in 2006. *See generally* 71 Fed. Reg. 2871 (January 18, 2006); **20 C.F.R. §§** <u>404.1745</u>, <u>416.1545</u>**[APP-REGS]**; **20 C.F.R. §§** <u>404.1770</u>, <u>116.1570</u>**[APP-REGS]**. Specifically, the regulations distinguish between situations where the person was disbarred or disqualified by reason of misconduct, in which case disqualification or suspension from appearing before SSA is mandatory, and where such action was taken for "solely administrative reasons," in which case the person will not be prohibited from appearing before SSA. 20 C.F.R. §§ 404.1770(a)(2), 416.1570(a)(2). The regulations also set out standards for reinstatement. 20 C.F.R. §§ 404.1799, 416.1599.

A representative may challenge a disqualification or suspension by appealing to the Appeals Council. 20 C.F.R. §§ 404.1770(b)(1), 416.1570(b)(1). As we saw in Chapter 8, federal court jurisdiction is limited where the administrative decision appealed from was other than a claim for benefits. The following case discusses the jurisdiction issues where an attorney challenged the SSA's decision to suspend him from representing claimants because he collected and retained a fee in excess of the SSA-authorized fee.

STANLEY V. ASTRUE

298 Fed. App'x 537, 2008 WL 4394251 (8th Cir. 2008)

Before MURPHY, BYE, and BENTON, Circuit Judges.

PER CURIAM.

Attorney James W. Stanley, Jr., appeals the district court's dismissal of his action challenging the Social Security Administration's (SSA's) decision to suspend him from representing claimants. Stanley previously represented Joyce Martin on her claims for disability insurance benefits (DIB) and supplemental security income (SSI). Under their contract, Martin agreed to pay Stanley the lesser of 25% of all past due benefits, or $4,000, if there was a favorable outcome on her applications. An administrative law judge (ALJ) found Martin entitled to SSI and DIB based on her mental problems and concluded that the fee agreement met statutory conditions. Soon thereafter Stanley wrote to Martin, directing her to send him 25% of her retroactive SSI benefits.

The Social Security Administration (SSA) later notified Martin that Stanley was entitled to no more than $4,000 on her DIB claim. Stanley was copied on the notice, and the SSA issued him a $4,000 check for the DIB claim. Approximately a month later, the SSA informed Martin that she was entitled to almost $20,000 in back benefits on her SSI claim, and that she would be notified later as to how much Stanley could charge. Before the allowable fee was determined, Stanley collected $4,000 from Martin on her SSI claim; he did not place the money in a trust or escrow account. After the SSA informed Martin, in a letter copied to Stanley, that she was responsible for paying Stanley only $4,000 total on both her SSI and DIB claims, Stanley moved for reconsideration arguing he was entitled to another $4,000 on the SSI claim. Meanwhile he offered to refund

Martin $2,500, and he wrote to the ALJ representing that he and Martin had compromised on the fee; Martin's contemporaneous letters to the ALJ reflected her confusion on the matter. The ALJ directed Stanley to remit the entire $4,000, because he was prohibited from collecting separate fees on the SSI and DIB claims; Stanley did not repay Martin until around six months later.

The SSA charged Stanley under specified statutes and regulations with collecting and retaining a fee in excess of the SSA-authorized fee; misleading Martin as to her benefits and other rights; and knowingly making false or misleading statements on an SSA matter. After a hearing, an ALJ found against Stanley and suspended him for five years from representing parties before the SSA; the Appeals Council affirmed. This counseled lawsuit followed, in which Stanley asserted jurisdiction under 42 U.S.C. § 405(g) and the Administrative Procedures Act (APA).

We agree with the district court that Stanley did not properly invoke jurisdiction under section 405(g), which applies to DIB claims and provides that "[a]ny individual, after any final decision of the Commissioner of Social Security made after a hearing to which he was a party ... may obtain a [judicial] review of such decision."

We find it significant that, in a prior case involving a challenge to an attorney's fees determination, this court was not persuaded that judicial review under section 405(g) is available to attorneys. Other circuit decisions support the district court's conclusion that section 405(g) did not confer jurisdiction to review the merits of Stanley's suspension. See Ezell v. Bowen, 849 F.2d 844, 845-46 (4th Cir.1988) (per curiam) (applicable regulatory provisions provide for judicial review of only "initial determinations," which do not include decisions to disqualify or suspend persons from acting as representatives); Howard v. Bowen, 823 F.2d 185, 186 (7th Cir.1987) (§ 405(g) authorizes civil actions merely to review decisions denying disability benefits); McCarthy v. Sec'y of Health & Human Servs., 793 F.2d 741, 743 (6th Cir.1986) (attorneys are not "parties" to administrative proceedings for purposes of § 405(g)). We thus reject Stanley's contention that the regulations precluding judicial review of an administrative decision to suspend a representative are contrary to section 405(g). Further, we agree with the district court that the APA is not an alternative basis for jurisdiction. See Califano v. Sanders, 430 U.S. 99, 104-07, 97 S.Ct. 980, 51 L.Ed.2d 192 (1977) (APA does not independently grant district courts subject matter jurisdiction to review SSA decision).

Although there is a basis for judicial review when colorable constitutional claims are at issue, see id. at 109, 97 S.Ct. 980, the district court correctly determined that Stanley did not raise any such claims. Stanley has taken the position throughout these proceedings that he is raising only a claim of substantive due process, but we see no basis for any colorable claim under traditional substantive due process analysis; and in any event, his specific contentions-about notice, vagueness, a chilling effect, and deprivation of a valuable property right without sworn witnesses-are more consistent with procedural due process or First Amendment claims.

Giving Stanley the benefit of the doubt by examining whether his assertions support a colorable procedural due process or First Amendment claim, as did the district court, we conclude that they do not. First, as to notice of proscribed conduct, the statute itself precludes Stanley from collecting $4,000 for the DIB claim and also for the SSI claim. Further, when Stanley agreed to represent Martin, he certified on a form he signed that he would not collect any fee unless it had been approved under the laws, regulations, and rulings cited and summarized on the form, which included that, even after the SSA approved a fee agreement, the SSA would notify the claimant of how much the representative could collect on a successful claim; that a fee could be collected in advance only if it was held in trust or escrow; and that attorneys could be suspended or disqualified from representing anyone before the SSA if they collected an unauthorized fee.

Second, we fail to see how the regulations are vague and ambiguous: they clearly provide that when there is evidence that a representative has engaged in prohibited acts-such as knowingly misleading a claimant as to her rights, or knowingly charging, collecting, or retaining a fee-the SSA may begin proceedings to disqualify or suspend the representative. See 20 C.F.R. §§ 404.1740(c), 404.1745(b), 416.1540(c), 416.1545(b). Third, we are unpersuaded by Stanley's assertion that he was deprived of a valuable property right without the use of sworn witnesses because he had an opportunity to testify at the administrative hearing, he did not challenge the evidence before the ALJ, and he declined to offer any other evidence. Fourth, as to what the district court construed as an overbreadth challenge to the regulations, Stanley was not denied the opportunity to raise a bona fide fee dispute to the SSA, which is clearly allowed under 20 C.F.R. §§ 404.1720(d), 416.1520(d) (review of fee determinations). Rather, he was sanctioned for collecting an illegal fee despite his unsupported protestations that the fee was allowed.

* * *

B. SOCIAL SECURITY RULINGS AND THE PROGRAM OPERATIONS MANUAL SYSTEM (POMS)

In addition to the Social Security Act and the various regulations promulgated by the Social Security Administration, there are a number of other important published sources of Social Security law. Two of these are described in this section: Social Security Rulings (including a sub-category of Acquiescence Rulings), which apply across the administrative process, and the Program Operations Manual System (often referred to as POMS), which is used at the local office level. There is also a special manual used at the Office of Disability Adjudication and Review (ODAR), known as the Hearings, Appeals, and Litigation Law (HALLEX).

Social Security Rulings are policy statements or interpretations of the Social Security Act and implementing regulations issued by SSA. Once a Ruling is published, it is binding at all levels of the administrative process. *See* Preface to Social Security Rulings at iii (cum. ed. 1989) ("[a]lthough Social Security rulings do not have the force and effect of law or regulation, they are binding on all components of the Social Security Administration, . . . and are to be relied on as precedents in adjudicating other cases"). Courts generally have deferred to Social Security Rulings as SSA's interpretation of the Social Security Act and implementing regulations. Most courts find that they are entitled to deference because they constitute an agency's interpretations of its own regulations and the statute that it administers. As a result, most courts will follow Social Security Rulings unless they are "plainly erroneous" or "inconsistent" with the Social Security Act. *See, e.g.,* Andrade v. Secretary, 985 F.2d 1045, 1051, 40 Soc. Sec. Rep. Serv. 117 (10th Cir. 1993). The Ninth Circuit has explained the status of Social Security Rulings within SSA and in federal court review as follows: "The Commissioner issues Social Security Rulings [('SSRs')] to clarify the Act's implementing regulations and the agency's policies. SSRs are binding on all components of the SSA. SSRs do not have the force of law. However, because they represent the Commissioner's interpretation of the agency's regulations, we give them some deference. We will not defer to SSRs if they are inconsistent with the statute or regulations." Holohan v. Massanari, 246 F.3d 1195, 1211 n. 1, 73 Soc. Sec. Rep. Serv. 243 (9th Cir. 2001) (internal citations omitted). *See also* Myers v. Apfel, 238 F.3d 617, 620, 72 Soc. Sec. Rep. Serv. 427 (5th Cir. 2001) ("The Social Security Administration's rulings are not binding on this court, but they may be consulted when the statute at issue provides little guidance.").

Acquiescence Rulings came about after SSA's "non-acquiescence" policy, under which it would neither follow nor appeal circuit court decisions it disagreed with, came under attack in the early 1980s. The catalyst for the controversy was the termination of disability benefits by SSA for hundreds of thousands of beneficiaries who could not provide affirmative proof that they were still disabled:

In 1980, Congress authorized a program of continuing disability investigations (CDIs) to combat cheating by recipients. When the

Reagan administration came to office, the SSA vigorously conducted CDI investigations, resulting in the termination of benefits of almost 500,000 people. The SSA placed the burden of proof upon disability beneficiaries, who had to show in review hearings that they were still disabled to avoid termination of their benefits. The SSA continued this policy despite repeated rulings by various federal courts of appeals that the Social Security Act required the agency to show that the recipient's medical condition had improved before terminating benefits. Vast numbers of SSA orders denying benefits were never appealed by the mostly poor, physically and mentally ill, uneducated, and uncounseled beneficiaries, despite the high likelihood that their appeals would have been successful. Most of these individuals lacked the resources to pursue litigation. Even if they had sufficient resources, relief would have been years away, due to the sudden flood of social security claims upon already crowded court dockets.

To avoid adverse Supreme Court precedents, the SSA did not seek certiorari in the cases in which it was defeated. Thus, vigorous and defiant nonacquiescence enabled the SSA to maintain its policy of denying claims even in the face of repeated court defeats. The SSA nonacquiescence policy provoked bitter criticism from all quarters: Congress, the press, state governments, and the bench. One judge compared SSA nonacquiescence with the "repudiated pre-Civil War doctrine of nullification." [*Lopez v. Heckler*, 713 F.2d 1432, 1441 (9th Cir. 1983) (Pregerson, J., concurring).]

In the end, extreme judicial measures were brought to bear against the SSA nonacquiescence policy. In the case of *Lopez v. Heckler*, [572 F. Supp. 26 (C.D. Cal.) (1984)] a class action was filed joining all Ninth Circuit SSA claimants. The class of plaintiffs sought to enjoin continued SSA nonacquiescence to Ninth Circuit precedent as a denial of due process and a violation of the separation of powers doctrine. The district court issued a preliminary injunction forbidding the SSA from ignoring Ninth Circuit precedent. Although the Ninth Circuit affirmed the preliminary injunction, the Supreme Court eventually vacated it because of congressional amendments to the Social Security Act.

In *Stieberger v. Heckler*[, 615 F. Supp. 1315 (S.D.N.Y. 1985), vacated sub nom. *Stieberger v. Bowen*, 801 F.2d 29 (2d Cir. 1986)], and *Schisler v. Heckler*[, 787 F.2d 76 (2d Cir. 1986),] a district court and a circuit court panel, both within the Second Circuit, enjoined the SSA from continuing to nonacquiesce in that Circuit. The district court in *Stieberger* held that SSA nonacquiescence "was inconsistent with the constitutionally required separation of powers." [*Stieberger*, 615 F. Supp. at 1367.] The injunction in *Schisler* merely required the SSA to publish in its relevant publications its acquiescence to the Second Circuit ruling for the purpose of informing its employees that they were required to follow this decision. [*See Schisler*, 787 F.2d at 84.] The court limited injunctive relief to this publication order.

Peter J. Rooney, *Comment, Nonacquiescence by the Securities and Exchange Commission: It's Relevance to the Nonacquiescence Debate*, 140 U. PA. L. REV. 1111, 1113-15 (1992). *See also* Ann Ruben, *Note, Social Security Administration in Crisis: Nonacquiescence and Social Insecurity*, 52 BROOK. L. REV. 89 (1986). As we saw in Chapter 4, Congress eventually enacted a separate standard for terminating disability benefits. *See* Social Security Disability Benefits Reform Act of 1984, Pub. L. No. 98-460, 98 Stat. 1794 (codified at 42 U.S.C. § 423(f)). Congress took that action in part because of SSA's non-acquiescence to court rulings on the issue.

SSA issued new regulations outlining a transparent "acquiescence" policy in 1990. Under current regulations, SSA follows circuit court decisions that are inconsistent with Administration policy at all levels of administrative appeal and judicial review within the particular circuit, unless it decides to seek further judicial review of that decision or to relitigate the relevant issue in another case. This action is formalized in an Acquiescence Ruling, which explains how SSA will apply the particular rule in the relevant circuit. *See* **20 C.F.R. §§ 404.985, 416.1485[APP-REGS]**.

SSA publishes its standard operating procedures and policies in the Program Operations Manual System (POMS). POMS is a multi-volume manual used for the processing and adjudication of all Social Security claims at SSA district and field offices and at the state Disability Determination Services (DDS). POMS is intended to fill in the substantive and procedural gaps of the Social Security Act and implementing regulations as they are applied on the ground. POMS has been reworked and reorganized repeatedly in the past and is updated frequently through various types of instructions, some of which apply only on a regional basis. Originally, POMS was published in a series of difficult-to-manage volumes; however, since 2002 a "public version" identical to the version used by SSA employees (but without certain codes and sensitive instructions) is available on the Internet at http://policy.ssa.gov/poms.nsf.

The Supreme Court addressed the legal effect of POMS in Schweiker v. Hansen, 450 U.S. 785 (1981). Noting that it is not a regulation but rather "a 13-volume handbook for internal use by thousands of SSA employees," the Court stated directly that "[i]t has no legal force, and it does not bind the SSA." 450 U.S. at 789. Later cases have cited *Hansen* for the proposition that POMS is not binding upon the agency; however, other courts have held that POMS does have some persuasive force. *See, e.g.,*

Bubnis v. Apfel, 150 F.3d 177, 181 57 Soc. Sec. Rep. Serv. 547 (2d Cir. 1998) (dispute involving worker's compensation offset; "Because these guidelines represent the Commissioner's interpretation of the statutory mandate, they deserve substantial deference, and will not be disturbed as long as they are reasonable and consistent with the statute."); Davis v. Secretary, 867 F.2d 336, 340, 24 Soc. Sec. Rep. Serv. 495 (6th Cir. 1989) ("Although the POMS is a policy and procedure manual that employees of the [Social Security Administration] use in evaluating Social Security claims and does not have the force and effect of law, it is nevertheless persuasive"); Chamberlain v. Schweiker, 518 F. Supp. 1336, 1340 (C.D. Ill. 1981) (while statements in POMS do not have the force and effect of law, "they are an indication of the [Commissioner's] interpretation of the law and should be followed, in the absence of firm law to the contrary or compelling indications that [the Commissioner] is wrong").

C. PROOF OF ELIGIBILITY

Social Security claimants have the burden of establishing eligibility for benefits. The claimant is thus responsible for obtaining the evidence necessary to prove eligibility and for providing that evidence, including necessary documents, to SSA. **20 C.F.R. §** 404.704**[APP-REGS]**; *see also* **20 C.F.R. §** 416.200**[APP-REGS]**. This is particularly true with regard to the most difficult and most often contested issue in such cases: whether the claimant is disabled according to the applicable disability standard. The Social Security Act states specifically that a claimant "shall not be considered to be under a disability unless he furnishes such medical and other evidence of the existence thereof as the [Social Security Administration] may require." **42 U.S.C. §** 423**(d)(5)(A)[APP-STAT]**. *See also* **20 C.F.R. §§**404.1512**(a),** 416.912**(a)[APP-REGS]** ("In general, [claimants] have to prove to [the Social Security Administration] that [they] are blind or disabled."). At the same time, SSA must make "reasonable efforts" to help the claimant obtain medical reports, 20 C.F.R. §§ 404.1512(d), 416.912(d), and, as discussed further in Section E of this chapter, in some cases the SSA may pay for the claimant to attend a consultative examination.

While claimants bear the burden of proof, the burden is satisfied by a simple preponderance of the evidence. *See* Mandziej v. Chater, 944 F. Supp. 121, 129, 52 Soc. Sec. Rep. Serv. 267 (D.N.H. 1996) ("The Act places a heavy initial burden on the plaintiff to establish the existence of a disabling impairment. * * * Nevertheless, the plaintiff is not required to establish a doubt-free claim; the initial burden is satisfied by the usual civil standard, a "preponderance of the evidence."). SSA codified this long-standing practice in 2009 "to clarify that we apply the preponderance of the evidence standard when we make determinations and decisions at all levels of our administrative review process." 73 Fed. Reg. 76940-41 (December 18, 2008). *See* 20 C.F.R. §§ 404.902, 416.1402 (initial determinations); 20 C.F. R. §§ 404.920, 416.1420 (reconsideration); 20 C.F.R. §§ 404.953(a), 416.1453(a) (administrative hearings). The standard is defined at 20 C.F.R. §§ 404.901, 416.1401: "Preponderance of the evidence means such relevant evidence that as a whole shows that the existence of the fact to be proven is more likely than not."

The Social Security Administration will consider virtually any relevant information in making its determination as to a claimant's disability. The regulations state that SSA will advise the claimant of what evidence is needed and how to get it, and it will consider any evidence submitted. 20 C.F.R. § 404.704. In conjunction with this, claimants are responsible for furnishing SSA with any information needed to show that they have an impairment and how severe it is. 20 C.F.R. §§ 416.200, 404.1512(c). If requested, a claimant must also provide information about his or her age, education and training, work experience, daily activities, efforts to work, and any other factors showing how the claimant's impairment affects his or her ability to work. 20 C.F.R. § 404.1512(c). If a claimant does not give SSA the necessary information, SSA will make a decision based on the information available. **20 C.F.R. §§ <u>404.1516</u>, <u>416.916</u>[APP-REGS]**. Claimants are not excused from giving evidence because they have "religious or personal reasons against medical examinations, tests, or treatment." *Id.*

Courts often list four sources of evidence for proving disability: objective medical facts; diagnoses or opinions of medical experts based on those facts; subjective statements of symptoms of disability, such as pain or fatigue, from the claimant or other lay witnesses; and information about the claimant's age, education, and prior work experience. As the court stated in Stone v. Barnhart, 332 F.Supp.2d 474, 481, 100 Soc. Sec. Rep. Serv. 76 (D. Conn. 2004):

> In determining whether the claimant has the residual functional capacity to perform other work, the Commissioner must evaluate the claimant on the basis of four factors: "(1) the objective medical facts; (2) diagnoses or medical opinions based on these facts; (3) subjective evidence of pain and disability testified to by the claimant and family or others; and (4) the claimant's educational background, age, and work experience." Gold [v. Secretary], 463 F.2d [38,] 41 n. 2 [(2d Cir. 1972)]. However, subjective reports will not alone establish a disability; objective medical evidence must also be present. 20 C.F.R. § 404.1529(a) ("... there must be medical signs and laboratory findings which show that you have a medical impairment(s) which could reasonably be expected to produce the pain or other symptoms alleged...."). "Objective evidence" is defined as "evidence obtained from the application of medically acceptable clinical and laboratory diag-

nostic techniques, such as evidence of reduced joint motion, muscle spasm, sensory deficit or motor disruption." Id. § 404.1529(c)(2).

See also Perez v. Barnhart, 415 F.3d 457, 462, 105 Soc. Sec. Rep. Serv. 399, 2005 WL 1540802 (5th Cir. 2005) ("In determining whether substantial evidence of disability exists, this court weighs four factors: (1) objective medical evidence; (2) diagnoses and opinions; (3) the claimant's subjective evidence of pain and disability; and (4) the claimant's age, education, and work history."). One or more of these sources, or perhaps other evidence such as the opinion of a vocational expert about the claimant's vocational ability and the availability of jobs, may be necessary in a particular case. The evidence required depends on where in the "sequential evaluation process" the disability decision is made.

There are no more detailed guidelines on the amount of evidence necessary to establish eligibility for benefits. The claimant must show that the relevant necessary findings are more likely than not, but the context in which decisions for Social Security benefits are made can have an influence. Thus, one court noted that although the claimant has the burden of proving disability, "due regard for the beneficent purposes of the legislation requires that a more tolerant standard be used . . . than . . . where the adversary system prevails." Hess v. Secretary, 497 F.2d 837, 840 (3d Cir. 1974). On the other hand, the claimant's burden has been described as "heavy" and "bordering on the unrealistic." Johnson v. Harris, 612 F.2d 993, 997 (5th Cir. 1980). *See also* Bazile v. Apfel, 113 F. Supp. 2d 181, 184, 71 Soc. Sec. Rep. Serv. 79 (D. Mass. 2000) (noting "heavy initial burden" of establishing disability through "credible evidence").

There are, however, some rules on medical evidence and allocating the burden of proof that help clarify what a claimant must show in order to prove eligibility for benefits. Some of these have been discussed earlier in this book in other contexts, such as the "medical improvement" requirement for terminating benefits (Chapter 4) and the shifting of the burden of proof upon a showing that the claimant is unable to perform prior relevant work at Step 4 of the "sequential evaluation process" (Chapter 5). Another important set of rules on the weight and sufficiency of different sources of medical evidence are discussed later in Section E of this chapter.

Perhaps the most important point concerning proof of eligibility in difficult Social Security cases is that a court will uphold a final decision denying a claim for benefits if it is supported by "substantial evidence." As explained in Chapter 8, the substantial evidence rule applied on judicial review is defined as "more than a mere scintilla. It means such relevant evidence as a reasonable mind might accept as adequate to support a conclusion." Richardson v. Perales, 402 U.S. 389, 401 (1971) (quoting

Consolidated Edison Co. v. NLRB, 305 U.S. 197 (1938). SSA also uses the substantial evidence rule to review ALJ factual determinations at the Appeals Council. *See* 20 C.F.R. §§ 404.901, 416.1401 (defining substantial evidence as "such relevant evidence as a reasonable mind might accept as adequate to support a conclusion."). Therefore, in order to prevail on appeal, a claimant must present sufficient evidence at the administrative hearing level to impeach or contradict any evidence supporting a possible denial. The claimant's burden of proof becomes, in effect, more than an affirmative showing of disability; the claimant must also assure that there is an absence of substantial evidence of non-disability in the record—in case the claim is denied and relief will have to come on appeal.

Evidence supporting a claim for benefits must be, of course, both competent and legitimate. Moreover, SSA regulations advise that claimants "should also be aware that Section 208 of the Social Security Act provides criminal penalties for misrepresenting the facts or for making false statements to obtain social security benefits for [the individual] or someone else." 20 C.F.R. § 404.704. The Social Security Act also provides for a redetermination of benefits if it appears that fraud or "similar fault" was involved in the claim. *See* **42 U.S.C.A. §§ 405(u)(1)(A),** <u>**1383**</u>**(e)(7)(A)[APP-STAT]**. In 2000, SSA issued a Ruling that clarifies what "similar fault" means in this context: "A 'similar fault' finding can be made only if there is reason to believe, based on a preponderance of the evidence, that the person committing the fault knew that the evidence provided was false or incomplete. A 'similar fault' finding cannot be based on speculation or suspicion." SSR 00-02p (2000).

D. ADMINISTRATIVE HEARING AND THE ROLE OF THE ADMINISTRATIVE LAW JUDGE

As we saw in Chapter 8, the purpose of Social Security administrative hearings is to allow claimants the opportunity to present all relevant evidence concerning all relevant issues to an impartial decision-maker—an independent federal administrative law judge. In most cases, this is the only time that a claimant has the opportunity to present his or her case for entitlement to benefits to someone who can both receive live testimony and make an eligibility decision. The hearing is particularly important because, as discussed above and also in Chapter 8, the ALJ's factual findings will be set aside on Appeals Council or judicial review only if not supported by substantial evidence.

The ALJ conducts a de novo review of the claim based on all evidence already in the record and any supplemental evidence, including testimony, presented at the hearing. The hearing itself is informal and the rules of evidence do not apply; however, witnesses testify under oath and a transcript is made of the hearing. The informal nature of Social Security hearings was challenged unsuccessfully in the following important case.

RICHARDSON V. PERALES
402 U.S. 389, 91 S. Ct. 1420 (1971)

Mr. Justice BLACKMUN delivered the opinion of the Court.

In 1966 Pedro Perales, a San Antonio truck driver, then aged 34, height 5 11, weight about 220 pounds, filed a claim for disability insurance benefits under the Social Security Act. Sections 216(i)(1) and 223(d)(1) of that Act both provide that the term 'disability' means 'inability to engage in any substantial gainful activity by reason of any medically determinable physical or mental impairment which * * *.' Section 205(g), 42 U.S.C. § 405(g), relating to judicial review, states, 'The findings of the Secretary as to any fact, if supported by substantial evidence, shall be conclusive * * *.'

The issue here is whether physicians' written reports of medical examinations they have made of a disability claimant may constitute 'substantial evidence' supportive of a finding of nondisability, within the § 205(g) standard, when the claimant objects to the admissibility of those reports and when the only live testimony is presented by his side and is contrary to the reports.

I

In his claim Perales asserted that on September 29, 1965, he became disabled as a result of an injury to his back sustained in lifting an object at work. He was seen by a neurosurgeon, Dr. Ralph A. Munslow, who first recommended conservative treatment. When this provided no relief, myelography was performed and surgery for a possible protruded intervertebral disc at L-5 was advised. The patient at first hesitated about surgery and appeared to improve. On recurrence of pain, however, he consented to the recommended procedure. Dr. Munslow operated on November 23. * * * No disc protrusion or other definitive pathology was identified at surgery. The post-operative diagnosis was: 'Nerve root compression syndrome, left.' The patient was discharged from Dr. Munslow's care on January 25, 1966, with a final diagnosis of 'Neuritis, lumbar, mild.'

Mr. Perales continued to complain, but Dr. Munslow and Dr. Morris H. Lampert, a neurologist called in consultation, were still unable to find any objective neurological explanation for his complaints. Dr. Munslow advised that he return to work.

In April 1966 Perales consulted Dr. Max Morales, Jr., a general practitioner of San Antonio. Dr. Morales hospitalized the patient from April 15 to May 2. [H]is final discharge diagnosis was: 'Back sprain, lumbosacral spine.'

Perales then filed his claim. As required by § 221 of the Act, 42 U.S.C. § 421, the claim was referred to the state agency for determination. The agency obtained the hospital records and a report from Dr. Morales. The report set forth no physical findings or laboratory studies, but the doctor again gave as his diagnosis: 'Back sprain-lumbosacral spine,' this time 'moderately severe,' with 'Ruptured disk not ruled out.' The agency arranged for a medical examination, at no cost to the patient, by Dr. John H. Langston, an orthopedic surgeon. This was done May 25.

Dr. Langston's ensuing report to the Division of Disability Determination was devastating from the claimant's standpoint. The doctor referred to Perales' being 'on crutches or cane' since his injury. He noted a slightly edematous condition in the legs, attributed to 'inactivity and sitting around'; slight tenderness in some of the muscles of the dorsal spine, thought to be due to poor posture; and 'a very mild sprain (of those muscles) which would resolve were he actually to get a little exercise and move.' Apart from this, and from the residuals of the pantopaque myelography and hemilaminectomy, Dr. Langston found no abnormalities of the lumbar spine. Otherwise, he described Perales as a 'big physical healthy specimen * * * obviously holding back and limiting all of his motions, intentionally. * * * His upper extremities, though they are completely uninvolved by his injury, he holds very rigidly as though he were semi-paralyzed. His reach and grasp are very limited but intentionally so. * * * Neurological examination is entirely normal to detailed sensory examination with pinwheel, vibratory sensations, and light touch. Reflexes are very active and there is no atrophy anywhere.' * * *

The state agency denied the claim. Perales requested reconsideration. Dr. Morales submitted a further report to the agency and an opinion to the claimant's attorney. This outlined the surgery and hospitalizations and his own conservative and continuing treatment of the patient, the medicines prescribed, the administration of ultrasound therapy, and the patient's constant complaints. The doctor concluded that the patient had not made a complete recovery from his surgery that he was not malingering, that his injury was permanent, and that he was totally and permanently disabled. He recommended against any further surgery.

The state agency then arranged for an examination by Dr. James M. Bailey, a board-certified psychiatrist with a sub-specialty in neurology. Dr. Bailey's report to the agency on August 30, 1966, concluded with the following diagnosis:

'Paranoid personality, manifested by hostility, feelings of persecution and long history of strained interpersonal relationships.

'I do not feel that this patient has a separate psychiatric illness at this time. It appears that his personality is conducive to anger, frustrations, etc.'

The agency again reviewed the file. The Bureau of Disability Insurance of the Social Security Administration made its independent review. The report and opinion of Dr. Morales, as the claimant's attending physician, were considered, as were those of the other examining physicians. The claim was again denied.

Perales requested a hearing before a hearing examiner. The agency then referred the claimant to Dr. Langston and to Dr. Richard H. Mattson for electromyography studies. Dr. Mattson's notes referred to 'some chronic or past disturbance of function in the nerve supply' to the left and right anterior tibialis muscles and right extensor digitorium brevis muscles that was 'strongly suggestive of lack of maximal effort' and was 'the kind of finding that is typically associated with a functional or psychogenic component to weakness.' There was no evidence of 'any active process effecting (sic) the nerves at present.' Dr. Langston advised the agency that Dr. Mattson's finding of 'very poor effort' verified what Dr. Langston had found on the earlier physical examination.

The requested hearing was set for January 12, 1967, in San Antonio. Written notice thereof was given the claimant with a copy to his attorney. The notice contained a definition of disability, advised the claimant that he should bring all medical and other evidence not already presented, afforded him an opportunity to examine all documentary evidence on file prior to the hearing, and told him that he might bring his own physician or other witnesses and be represented at the hearing by a lawyer.

The hearing took place at the time designated. A supplemental hearing was held March 31. The claimant appeared at the first hearing with his attorney and with Dr. Morales. The attorney formally objected to the introduction of the several reports of Drs. Langston, Bailey, Mattson, and Lampert, and of the hospital records. Various grounds of objection were asserted, including hearsay, absence of an opportunity for cross-examination, absence of proof the physicians were licensed to practice in Texas, failure to demonstrate that the hospital records were proved under the Business Records Act, and the conclusory nature of the reports. These objections were overruled and the reports and hospital records were introduced. The reports of Dr. Morales and of Dr. Munslow were then submitted by the claimant's counsel and admitted.

At the two hearings oral testimony was submitted by claimant Perales, by Dr. Morales, by a former fellow employee of the claimant, by a vocational expert, and by Dr. Lewis A. Leavitt, a physician board-certified in physical medicine and rehabilitation, and chief of, and professor in, the Department of Physical Medicine at Baylor University College of Medicine. Dr. Leavitt was called by the hearing examiner as an independent 'medical adviser,' that is, as an expert who does not examine the claimant but who hears and reviews the medical evidence and who may offer an opinion. The adviser is paid a fee by the Government. The claimant, through his counsel, objected to any testimony by Dr. Leavitt not based upon examination or upon a hypothetical. Dr. Leavitt testified over this objection and was cross-examined by the claimant's attorney. He stated that the consensus of the various medical reports was that Perales had a mild low-back syndrome of musculo-ligamentous origin.

The hearing examiner, in reliance upon the several medical reports and the testimony of Dr. Leavitt, observed in his written decision, 'There is objective medical evidence of impairment which the heavy preponderance of the evidence indicates to be of mild severity. * * * Taken altogether, the Hearing Examiner is of the conclusion that the claimant has not met the burden of proof.' He specifically found that the claimant 'is suffering from a low back syndrome of musculo-ligamentous origin, and of mild severity'; that while he 'has an emotional overlay to his medical impairment it does not require psychiatric treatment and is of minimal contribution, if any, to his medical impairment or to his general ability to engage in substantial gainful activity'; that '(n) either his medical impairment nor his emotional overlay, singly or in combination, constitute a disability as defined' in the Act; and that the claimant is capable of engaging as a salesman in work in which he had previously engaged, of working as a watchman or guard where strenuous activity is not required, or as a ticket-taker or janitor. The hearing examiner's decision then, was that the claimant was not entitled to a period of disability or to disability insurance benefits.

It is to be noted at this point that § 205(d) of the Act, 42 U.S.C. § 405(d), provides that the Secretary has power to issue subpoenas requiring the attendance and testimony of witnesses and the production of evidence and that the Secretary's regulations authorized by § 205(a), 42 U.S.C. § 405(a), provide that a claimant may request the issuance of subpoenas, 20 CFR § 404.926. Perales, however, who was represented by counsel, did not request subpoenas for either of the two hearings.

The claimant then made a request for review by the Appeals Council * * *. * * * The Appeals Council ruled that the decision of the hearing examiner was correct.

Upon this adverse ruling the claimant instituted the present action for review pursuant to § 205(g). Each side moved for summary judgment on the administrative transcript. The District Court stated that it was reluctant to accept as substantial evidence the opinions of medical experts submitted in the form of unsworn written reports, the admission of which would have the effect of denying the opposition an opportunity for cross-examination; that the opinion of a doctor who had never examined the claimant is entitled to little or no probative value, especially when opposed by substantial evidence including the oral testimony of an examining physician; and that what was before the court amounted to hearsay upon hearsay. The case was remanded for a new hearing before a different examiner. On appeal the Fifth Circuit noted the absence of any request by the claimant for subpoenas and held that, having this right and not exercising it, he was not in a position to complain that he had been denied the rights of confrontation and of cross-examination. It held that the hearsay evidence in the case was admissible under the Act; that, specifically, the written reports of the physicians were admissible in the administrative hearing; that Dr. Leavitt's testimony also was admissible; but that all this evidence together did not constitute substantial evidence when it was objected to and when it was contradicted by evidence from the only live witnesses.

On rehearing, the Court of Appeals observed that it did not mean by its opinion that uncorroborated hearsay could never be substantial evidence supportive of a hearing examiner's decision adverse to a claimant. It emphasized that its ruling that uncorroborated hearsay could not constitute substantial evidence was applicable only when the claimant had objected and when the hearsay was directly contradicted by the testimony of live medical witnesses and by the claimant in person. Certiorari was granted in order to review and resolve this important procedural due process issue.

II

We therefore are presented with the not uncommon situation of conflicting medical evidence. The trier of fact has the duty to resolve that conflict. We have, on the one hand, an absence of objective findings, an expressed suspicion of only functional complaints, of malingering, and of the patient's unwillingness to do anything about remedying an unprovable situation. We have, on the other hand, the claimant's and his personal physician's earnest pleas that significant and disabling residuals from the mishap of September 1965 are indeed present.

The issue revolves, however, around a system which produces a mass of medical evidence in report form. May material of that kind ever be 'substantial evidence' when it stands alone and is opposed by live medical evidence and the client's own contrary personal testimony? The courts below have held that it may not.

III

The Social Security Act has been with us since 1935. It affects nearly all of us. The system's administrative structure and procedures, with essential determinations numbering into the millions, are of a size and extent difficult to comprehend. But, as the Government's brief here accurately pronounces, 'Such a system must be fair—and it must work.'

Congress has provided that the Secretary

'shall have full power and authority to make rules and regulations and to establish procedures * * * necessary or appropriate to carry out such provisions, and shall adopt reasonable and proper rules and regulations to regulate and provide for the nature and extent of the proofs and evidence and the method of taking and furnishing the same in order to establish the right to benefits hereunder.' § 205(a), 42 U.S.C. § 405(a).

Section 205(b) directs the Secretary to make findings and decisions; on request to give reasonable notice and opportunity for a hearing; and in the course of any hearing to receive evidence. It then provides:

'Evidence may be received at any hearing before the Secretary even though inadmissible under rules of evidence applicable to court procedure.'

In carrying out these statutory duties the Secretary has adopted regulations that state, among other things:

'The hearing examiner shall inquire fully into the matters at issue and shall receive in evidence the testimony of witnesses and any documents which are relevant and material to such matters. * * * The * * * procedure at the hearing generally * * * shall be in the discretion of the hearing examiner and of such nature as to afford the parties a reasonable opportunity for a fair hearing.' 20 C.F.R. § 404.927.

From this it is apparent that (a) the Congress granted the Secretary the power by regulation to establish hearing procedures; (b) strict rules of evidence, applicable in the courtroom, are not to operate at social security hearings so as to bar the admission of evidence otherwise pertinent; and (c) the conduct of the hearing rests generally in the examiner's discretion. There emerges an emphasis upon the informal rather than the formal. This, we think, is as it should be, for this administrative procedure, and these hearings, should be understandable to the layman claimant, should not necessarily be stiff and comfortable only for the trained attorney, and should be liberal and not strict in tone and operation. This is the obvious intent of Congress so long as the procedures are fundamentally fair.

IV

With this background and this atmosphere in mind, we turn to the statutory standard of 'substantial evidence' prescribed by § 205(g). The Court has considered this very concept in other, yet similar, contexts. The National Labor Relations Act, § 10(e), in its original form, provided that the NLRB's findings of fact 'if supported by evidence, shall be conclusive.' 49 Stat. 454. The Court said this meant 'supported by substantial evidence' and that this was

> 'more than a mere scintilla. It means such relevant evidence as a reasonable mind might accept as adequate to support a conclusion.' Consolidated Edison Co. v. NLRB, 305 U.S. 197, 229, 59 S.Ct. 206, 217, 83 L.Ed. 126 (1938).

The Court has adhered to that definition in varying statutory situations. * * *

V

We may accept the propositions advanced by the claimant, some of them long established, that procedural due process is applicable to the adjudicative administrative proceeding involving 'the differing rules of fair play, which through the years, have become associated with differing types of proceedings,' Hannah v. Larche, 363 U.S. 420, 442, 80 S.Ct. 1502, 1515, 4 L.Ed.2d 1307 (1960); that "the 'right' to Social Security benefits is in one sense 'earned.'" Flemming v. Nestor, 363 U.S. 603, 610, 80 S.Ct. 1367, 1372, 4 L.Ed.2d 1435 (1960); and that the

> 'extent to which procedural due process must be afforded the recipient is influenced by the extent to which he may be 'condemned to suffer grievous loss'. * * * Accordingly * * * 'consideration of what procedures due process may require under any given set of circumstances must begin with a determination of the precise nature of the government function involved as well as of the private interest that has been affected by governmental action.' Goldberg v. Kelly, 397 U.S. 254, 262-263, 90 S.Ct. 1011, 1018, 25 L.Ed.2d 287 (1970).

The question, then, is as to what procedural due process requires with respect to examining physicians' reports in a social security disability claim hearing.

We conclude that a written report by a licensed physician who has examined the claimant and who sets forth in his report his medical findings in his area of competence may be received as evidence in a disability hearing and, despite its hearsay character and an absence of cross-examination, and despite the presence of opposing direct medical testimony and testimony by the claimant himself, may constitute substantial evidence supportive of a finding by the hearing examiner adverse to the claimant, when the claimant has not exercised his right to subpoena the reporting physician and thereby provide himself with the opportunity for cross-examination of the physician.

We are prompted to this conclusion by a number of factors that, we feel, assure underlying reliability and probative value:

1. The identity of the five reporting physicians is significant. Each report presented here was prepared by a practicing physician who had examined the claimant. A majority (Drs. Langston, Bailey, and Mattson) were called into the case by the state agency. Although each received a fee, that fee is recompense for his time and talent otherwise devoted to private practice or other professional assignment. We cannot, and do not, ascribe bias to the work of these independent physicians, or any interest on their part in the outcome of the administrative proceeding beyond the professional curiosity a dedicated medical man possesses.

2. The vast workings of the social security administrative system make for reliability and impartiality in the consultant reports. We bear in mind that the agency operates essentially, and is intended so to do, as an adjudicator and not as an advocate or adversary. This is the congressional plan. We do not presume on this record to say that it works unfairly.

3. One familiar with medical reports and the routine of the medical examination, general or specific, will recognize their elements of detail and of value. The particular reports of the physicians who examined claimant Perales were based on personal consultation and personal examination and rested on accepted medical procedures and tests. The operating neurosurgeon, Dr. Munslow, provided his pre-operative observations and diagnosis, his findings at surgery, his post-operative diagnosis, and his post-operative observations. Dr. Lampert, the neurologist, provided the history related to him by the patient, Perales' complaints, the physical examination and neurologic tests, and his professional impressions and recommendations. Dr. Langston, the orthopedist, did the same post-operatively, and described the orthopedic tests and neurologic examination he performed, the results and his impressions and prognosis. Dr. Mattson, who did the post-operative electromyography, described the results of that test, and his impressions. And Dr. Bailey, the psychiatrist,

related the history, the patient's complaints, and the psychiatric diagnosis that emerged from the typical psychiatric examination.

These are routine, standard, and unbiased medical reports by physician specialists concerning a subject whom they had seen. That the reports were adverse to Perales' claim is not in itself bias or an indication of nonprobative character.

4. The reports present the impressive range of examination to which Perales was subjected. A specialist in neurosurgery, one in neurology, one in psychiatry, one in orthopedics, and one in physical medicine and rehabilitation add up to definitive opinion in five medical specialties, all somewhat related, but different in their emphases. It is fair to say that the claimant received professional examination and opinion on a scale beyond the reach of most persons and that this case reveals a patient and careful endeavor by the state agency and the examiner to ascertain the truth.

5. So far as we can detect, there is no inconsistency whatsover in the reports of the five specialists. Yet each result was reached by independent examination in the writer's field of specialized training.

6. Although the claimant complains of the lack of opportunity to cross-examine the reporting physicians, he did not take advantage of the opportunity afforded him under 20 CFR § 404.926 to request subpoenas for the physicians. The five-day period specified by the regulation for the issuance of the subpoenas surely afforded no real obstacle to this, for he was notified that the documentary evidence on file was available for examination before the hearing and, further, a supplemental hearing could be requested. In fact, in this very case there was a supplemental hearing more than two and a half months after the initial hearings. This inaction on the claimant's part supports the Court of Appeals' view, 412 F.2d, at 50-51, that the claimant as a consequence is to be precluded from now complaining that he was denied the rights of confrontation and cross-examination.

7. Courts have recognized the reliability and probative worth of written medical reports even in formal trials and, while acknowledging their hearsay character, have admitted them as an exception to the hearsay rule. * * *

8. Past treatment by reviewing courts of written medical reports in social security disability cases is revealing. Until the decision in this case, the courts of appeals, including the Fifth Circuit, with only an occasional criticism of the medical report practice, uniformly recognized reliability and probative value in such reports. The courts have reviewed administrative determinations, and upheld many adverse ones, where the

only supporting evidence has been reports of this kind, buttressed some-times, but often not, by testimony of a medical adviser such as Dr. Leavitt. In these cases admissibility was not contested, but the decisions do demonstrate traditional and ready acceptance of the written medical report in social security disability cases.

9. There is an additional and pragmatic factor which, although not controlling, deserves mention. This is what Chief Judge Brown has de-scribed as '(t)he sheer magnitude of that administrative burden,' and the resulting necessity for written reports without 'elaboration through the traditional facility of oral testimony.' Page v. Celebrezze, 311 F.2d 757, 760 (CA5 1963). With over 20,000 disability claim hearings annually, the cost of providing live medical testimony at those hearings, where need has not been demonstrated by a request for a subpoena, over and above the cost of the examinations requested by hearing examiners, would be a substantial drain on the trust fund and on the energy of physicians al-ready in short supply.

VI

1. Perales relies heavily on the Court's holding and statements in Goldberg v. Kelly, *supra*, particularly the comment that due process re-quires notice 'and an effective opportunity to defend by confronting any adverse witnesses * * *.' 397 U.S., at 267--268, 90 S.Ct., at 1020. *Kelly*, however, had to do with termination of AFDC benefits without prior no-tice. It also concerned a situation, the Court said, 'where credibility and veracity are at issue, as they must be in many termination proceedings.' 397 U.S., at 269, 90 S.Ct., at 1021.

The Perales proceeding is not the same. We are not concerned with termination of disability benefits once granted. Neither are we concerned with a change of status without notice. Notice was given to claimant Per-ales. The physicians' reports were on file and available for inspection by the claimant and his counsel. And the authors of those reports were known and were subject to subpoena and to the very cross-examination that the claimant asserts he has not enjoyed. Further, the specter of questionable credibility and veracity is not present; there is professional disagreement with the medical conclusions, to be sure, but there is no at-tack here upon the doctors' credibility or veracity. Kelly affords little comfort to the claimant.

2. Perales also, as the Court of Appeals stated, would describe the medical reports in question as 'mere uncorroborated hearsay' and would relate this to Mr. Chief Justice Hughes' sentence in Consolidated Edison Co. v. NLRB, 305 U.S., at 230, 59 S.Ct., at 217: 'Mere uncorroborated hearsay or rumor does not constitute substantial evidence.'

Although the reports are hearsay in the technical sense, because their content is not produced live before the hearing examiner, we feel that the claimant and the Court of Appeals read too much into the single sentence from Consolidated Edison. The contrast the Chief Justice was drawing, at the very page cited, was not with material that would be deemed formally inadmissible in judicial proceedings but with material 'without a basis in evidence having rational probative force.' This was not a blanket rejection by the Court of administrative reliance on hearsay irrespective of reliability and probative value. The opposite was the case.

3. The claimant, the District Court, and the Court of Appeals also criticize the use of Dr. Leavitt as a medical adviser. Inasmuch as medical advisers are used in approximately 13% of disability claim hearings, comment as to this practice is indicated. We see nothing 'reprehensible' in the practice, as the claimant would describe it. The trial examiner is a layman; the medical adviser is a board-certified specialist. He is used primarily in complex cases for explanation of medical problems in terms understandable to the layman-examiner. He is a neutral adviser. This particular record discloses that Dr. Leavitt explained the technique and significance of electromyography. He did offer his own opinion on the claimant's condition. That opinion, however, did not differ from the medical reports. Dr. Leavitt did not vouch for the accuracy of the facts assumed in the reports. No one understood otherwise. We see nothing unconstitutional or improper in the medical adviser concept and in the presence of Dr. Leavitt in this administrative hearing.

4. Finally, the claimant complains of the system of processing disability claims. He suggests, and is joined in this by the briefs of amici, that the Administrative Procedure Act, rather than the Social Security Act, governs the processing of claims and specifically provides for cross-examination, 5 U.S.C. § 556(d). (1964 ed., Supp. V). The claimant goes on to assert that in any event the hearing procedure is invalid on due process grounds. He says that the hearing examiner has the responsibility for gathering the evidence and 'to make the Government's case as strong as possible'; that naturally he leans toward a decision in favor of the evidence he has gathered; that justice must satisfy the appearance of justice, citing Offutt v. United States, 348 U.S. 11, 14, 75 S.Ct. 11, 13, 99 L.Ed. 11 (1954), and In re Murchison, 349 U.S. 133, 136, 75 S.Ct. 623, 99 L.Ed. 942 (1955); and that an 'independent hearing examiner such as in the' Longshoremen's and Harbor Workers' Compensation Act should be provided.

We need not decide whether the APA has general application to social security disability claims, for the social security administrative procedure does not vary from that proscribed by the APA. Indeed, the latter is modeled upon the Social Security Act. The cited § 556(d) provides that any documentary evidence 'may be received' subject to the exclusion of the irrelevant, the immaterial, and the unduly repetitious. It further provides that a 'party is entitled to present his case or defense by oral or documentary evidence * * * and to conduct such cross-examination as may be required for a full and true disclosure of the facts' and in 'determining claims for money or benefits * * * an agency may, when a party will not be prejudiced thereby, adopt procedures for the submission of all or part of the evidence in written form.'

These provisions conform, and are consistent with, rather than differ from or supersede, the authority given the Secretary by the Social Security Act's §§ 205(a) and (b) 'to establish procedures,' and 'to regulate and provide for the nature and extent of the proofs and evidence and the method of taking and furnishing the same in order to establish the right to benefits,' and to receive evidence 'even though inadmissible under rules of evidence applicable to court procedure.' Hearsay, under either Act, is thus admissible up to the point of relevancy.

The matter comes down to the question of the procedure's integrity and fundamental fairness. We see nothing that works in derogation of that integrity and of that fairness in the admission of consultants' reports, subject as they are to being material and to the use of the subpoena and consequent cross-examination. This precisely fits the statutorily prescribed 'cross-examination as may be required for a full and true disclosure of the facts.' That is the standard. It is clear and workable and does not fall short of procedural due process.

Neither are we persuaded by the advocate-judge-multiple-hat suggestion. It assumes too much and would bring down too many procedures designed, and working well, for a governmental structure of great and growing complexity. The social security hearing examiner, furthermore, does not act as counsel. He acts as an examiner charged with developing the facts. The 44.2% reversal rate for all federal disability hearings in cases where the state agency does not grant benefits, attests to the fairness of the system and refutes the implication of impropriety.

We therefore reverse and remanded for further proceedings. We intimate no view as to the merits. It is for the District Court now to determine whether the Secretary's findings, in the light of all material proffered and admissible, are supported by 'substantial evidence' within the command of § 205(g).

[Dissenting opinion of Justice Douglas, joined by Justices Black and Brennan, omitted.]

1. NON-ADVERSARIAL HEARINGS

Social Security administrative hearings are non-adversarial. This means more than the fact that SSA is not represented as such at a hearing; it means that the SSA has no institutional position other than to award benefits to those persons entitled to benefits and to deny claims of those who are not. It also means that the ALJ has a greater role to play than the typical trial court judge. Social Security administrative law judges must participate actively both before and at the hearing in developing written evidence and obtaining relevant testimony from the claimant and other witnesses. The requirement that ALJs decide Social Security claims on the basis of a full and complete record means that they must be ready to participate in developing evidence and presenting witnesses whether a claimant is represented or not.

Although the claimant is responsible for providing proof of eligibility for benefits, the ALJ has the discretion to decide whether to seek out additional evidence in a particular case. Virtually all ALJs will question the claimant, at least with respect to the claimant's major impairments and past employment; most will also take an active part in questioning witnesses, together with the claimant or, if the claimant has one, the claimant's representative. The ALJ must also decide whether medical or vocational experts should testify at the hearing. Medical experts are rarely called by the judge; however, vocational experts may be necessary in certain cases, especially for those that are likely to be decided only at the fifth step of the sequential evaluation process. The role of vocational experts at the administrative hearing is discussed later in this chapter.

Concerns about the efficiency of the non-adversary hearing system led to an experiment by the Social Security Administration in the mid-1980s with the use of representatives at hearings to represent the Administration. The concept was abandoned at the end of the brief experiment, in part because of the following case:

SALLING V. BOWEN
641 F. Supp. 1046, 15 Soc. Sec. Rep. Serv. 394 (W.D. Va. 1986)

GLEN M. WILLIAMS, District Judge.

This complaint was filed on November 12, 1982 by seven applicants for Social Security benefits, seeking injunctive and declaratory relief and challenging a proposed experiment whereby a government advocate appeared at their Social Security and Supplemental Security Income (SSI) disability hearings. The challenged program began operations October 12, 1982 and was considered a demonstration project under the supervision of the Office of Hearings and Appeals (OHA) called SSA Representation Project (SSARP). The court notes initially that it is contended by the plaintiffs in this case that this is an experimental program of the Social Security Administration (SSA); whereas, the Department of Health and Human Services (HHS) in the various memoranda regarding this matter refer to it as "Adjudicatory Improvement Project" (AIP), indicating that there is a difference between an experiment and a project. Initially this program was to be conducted in the SSA's Offices of Hearings and Appeals (OHA) in Kingsport, Tennessee; Baltimore, Maryland; Columbia, South Carolina; Brentwood, Missouri; and Pasadena, California. However, for reasons which are not necessary to go into at this time, the Brentwood, Missouri Program has been discontinued. * * *

* * *

* * *

SSA REPRESENTATION PROJECT (SSARP)

Court Exhibit 1 is 20 C.F.R. Parts 404 and 416 entitled "Project to Improve the Hearing Process through the Involvement of SSA Representatives." This was published in the Federal Register Volume 47, No. 181, on August 19, 1982. This is called a project the purpose of which is to determine whether SSA representatives in disability cases at the administrative hearing level can contribute toward improving the quality and timeliness of hearing dispositions. These representatives will be able to "sharpen factual issues" and "remove the burden of case record development from ALJs." The project is listed as having a duration of at least one year and is to be instituted in five offices.

As a background for these rules, it is stated that there has been a "lack of decisional consistency within SSA's several levels of disability adjudication and among SSA's ALJs." It is further mentioned that there has been an unprecedented increase in the number of hearing requests resulting in "backlogs and delays for claimants awaiting hearings." * * * The program further provides that the [Social Security Administration representative (SSAR)] will have the power to "ask that the administrative law judge disqualify himself or herself" and that the SSAR has the power to "recommend that the administrative law judge issue a favorable decision without the need for a hearing." The SSARs are to appear at the hearing if the other side is represented by counsel. The regulations further specifically state that: "After the hearing, the SSA representative will not participate in any proceedings before the Appeals Council although the Appeals Council may exercise its own authority to review any case on its own motion." The regulations further provide that the SSARs will be employed directed by the OHA and they will be located in or near the OHAs. Thus, the SSARs are not independently employed but are under the direct control of the OHA. It is made clear that the SSARs' prehearing case activities are "outside the purview of the ALJ who will not be assigned to the case until the SSA representative has completed his or her preparation for the hearing." With regard to the relationship between the SSA representative and the Appeals Council, Section 6 provides that the SSARs shall be allowed "to bring cases to the attention of the Appeals Council for possible review on its own motion." On the other hand, "nor will the SSA representative submit arguments, comment on new evidence or otherwise participate as a party in Appeals Council proceedings." An evaluation of this program will be based on whether it has improved timeliness and quality of the disposition of cases. * * * The regulations discuss at length the question of whether the intention is to make this an adversary process. It is clearly stated that it is not the intention that the SSAR would categorically advocate affirmation of DDS decisions and therefore it would remain to be seen whether the SSAR was actually an adversary. Therefore, it would not be subject to the Equal Access for Justice Act for the purpose of providing fees because it would not be presumed that the SSAR will not be "substantially justified."

Beginning the first of April, 1986, the AIP, instead of terminating, embarked upon a new plan * * *. * * * Court Exhibit 2 reflects that the new project got underway on April 1, 1986 and the restructuring was undertaken in accordance with the existing regulations * * * which provide the project's purposes and indicate that the project purposes will remain the same and the substantive procedure set forth in these regulations are not being modified. The most significant change in the restructuring of the SSARP is the separation of SSARP offices from the participating OHAs offices, both physically and organizationally. This also results in a revision of the case processing procedures for SSARP cases, makes the SSARP offices entirely independent of the ALJs and OHAs, and greatly changes the manner in which a file is handled. * * * The SSARP offices do all the prehearing screening, case docketing, control, selection of documents to be included in the hearing exhibit, preparation of the exhibit list, preparation and release of development requests, contact with the attorney if there is one, and contact with the claimant where there is no attorney and direct intervention on the part of an SSAR where the person is not represented, by communication with the claimant. Indeed, the ALJ who will eventually try the case will not know that he is assigned to the case until the case has been received in the OHA for hearing. The SSARP, now AIP, whose employees are employed and under the direct control of the OHA will have complete control of the file without the ALJ even seeing it until the time of the hearing. This again acts as a halter on the independence of the ALJs in the handling of cases, and places the file not in the hand of an independent person but in the hands of an advocate of the government. Once the ALJ receives the file, assuming that he should decide that additional evidence is needed for development of the case, the SSAR again will be given the opportunity to review the file, including additional development prior to the case being scheduled for hearing. No such provision is made for the representative of the claimant. The SSAR, in addition to appearing, will submit written proposed findings of fact and conclusions of law to the ALJ after the case has been heard.

* * *

FINDINGS OF FACT

(1) One of the stated purposes when the project began in October 1982, was to improve timeliness of hearings, and "result in a more expeditious process." This court finds from the statistics which have been furnished from October 1982 through February 1986, from affidavits which have been submitted by attorneys, from evidence which has been presented by claimants, from personal interviews of ALJs, and from other documents presented by the government that the exact reverse has occurred and the time for hearing dispositions has greatly increased. In some instances, the time for hearing a case is three times as long; there is a longer delay between the request for a hearing and the hearing: the number of cases disposed of by the ALJs has decreased; more cases are being referred to the Appeals Council for own-motion reviews by the SSARs, many of which should not have been sent to the Appeals Council for own-motion review: which cumulatively has resulted in great harm to claimants by causing delay in their receipt of benefits.

* * *

(2) One of the goals of this program was that it was to create some uniformity of decisions. The results have shown that there is not uniformity even among the various offices participating in SSARP. In the May 1983 report directed to Louie B. Hayes, Associate Commissioner for OHA from Joy Loving, the record shows that the percentage of reversals of dispositions in the Baltimore office was 43%; Brentwood, 63%; Columbia, 36%; Kingsport, 49%; and Pasadena, 53%. Loving went on to state in this report, "I estimate that almost one fourth of the reversal decisions issued are the result of GR recommendations." There was also a great deal of difference between decisions involving unrepresented claimants and those involving represented claimants. For example, the record from October 1982 through February 1986 discloses as between represented and unrepresented claimants in the Kingsport OHA that the unrepresented claimants totaled 1,286 of which there were 412 decisions favorable to the claimants and 454 unfavorable to them and 107 dismissals, showing that nearly 60% of the claimants without counsel lost their claims. On the other hand, according to the report of Loving in May of 1983, in four of the five participating SSARP OHAs, it appears that where an SSAR was involved and there was an adversary status, there was a higher reversal rate. Remarkably, in Pasadena, California, the repre-

sented claimants were only awarded benefits 48% of the time whereas, the unrepresented claimants were granted benefits 49% of the time. Thus, in Pasadena, the people who did not have counsel won more cases than those who did have counsel whereas, in the other participating OHAs, the opposite was true, and by a large percentage. One searches in vain among the statistics which have been furnished to find anything to show that there has been uniformity in arriving at decisions nationwide even among those OHAs participating in the SSARP much less compared to those who do not participate.

(3) Has the quality of the hearing dispositions improved? The answer to this has to be a resounding no. It was pointed out in the regulations that the duty would be placed upon the SSARs to take away from the ALJs the burden of developing the cases so that the ALJs could devote their time toward making decisions and getting out opinions. The statistics which the court has been furnished up to this time show that there has been a remarkable decline in decisions, particularly in the Kingsport OHA, as compared to the period of time before October, 1982. Admittedly, these statistics are incomplete, but the court can only deal with the statistics that have been furnished. Furthermore, the attorneys who have filed affidavits in this case have remarked on the slowness of getting decisions. This court is in a good position, due to the number of appeals which come to it, to evaluate the decisions which have come out of the Kingsport OHA compared with those before the SSARP was commenced. This court has not kept statistics on the number of remands for improperly developed files, however, the court is concerned about the lack of proper development on the part of the SSARs. According to affidavits made by the attorneys in this case, the SSARs had done very little in developing the files. If the SSARs found that the claimant's case was weak, they left it alone; but if the claimant's case was strong, consultative examinations were sought. This court has issued one published opinion dealing with this problem, Darnell v. Bowen, 631 F.Supp. 96 (W.D.Va.1986). In the *Darnell* case, the court stated as follows:

> There is no contradictory evidence in the case *sub judice*, because the SSAR and the ALJ totally failed in their duty to fully and fairly develop the evidence by obtaining consultative physical and psychiatric examinations for the indigent SSI claimant, and in so doing, they defeated the intent of Congress in establishing the SSI program.

The court went on to state:

> In short, the SSAR, instead of developing the evidence for hearing, in Darnell's claim, totally failed in his duty so to do to the benefit of his client, the Secretary, and to the detriment of the indigent SSI claimant. Such disregard for the purpose of the SSI program and the pur-

ported intent of the SSARP borders on outrage. The SSAR magnanimously offered to consider additional evidence in this matter: 'by copy of this motion, statement and a copy of the list of proposed exhibits presently of record, we are advising the claimant's appointed representative of our current position in this matter.... We are not aware of the existence of any addition relevant evidence.'

Id.

Thus, in *Darnell*, the burden of developing the case was shifted to the indigent SSI claimant from the SSAR. This court went on to say:

> This case is illustrative of one of the many problems that this court has perceived since the inception of the SSARP. Under the notice of proposed rule-making and the final rule-making by the Secretary and the adoption of the SSARP regulations, it was represented that the SSARs would be non-adversary. It has become manifestly apparent to this court that the SSARs in practice have been almost totally adversative, and that their prehearing development of claims has been a one-sided development in favor of the Secretary in disregard of their duty to fairly and fully develop the claim not only for the Secretary but also for the claimant. This case just represents one bad example, among dozens of others that the court has observed since the inception of the program in October of 1982 at the Kingsport, Tennessee Office of Hearings and Appeals.

Id.

* * *

(4) In the regulations promulgated on August 19, 1982, it was stated as follows:

> After the hearing, the SSA representative will not participate in any proceedings before the Appeals Council, although the Appeals Council may exercise its authority to review any case on its own motion.

The regulations went on to say, however, that an SSAR could call the attention of the Appeals Council to the fact that a certain case might merit own-motion review. Court Exhibit No. 6 is a letter from an ALJ in the Kingsport OHA expressing his views on the restructuring of the SSARP. This letter is dated December 4, 1985 and in it, the ALJ observes as follows:

> I am particularly concerned with the practice of the SSAR referring almost any favorable decision to the Appeals Council. Claimants fall-

ing under the SSAR Project are clearly subjected to a more rigorous review.

* * *

* * *

(6) This case has been represented as one in which there is an experimental project going on in which there is no adversary proceeding involved; that it is simply a situation in which the SSAR is there to assist the ALJ. The latest action which removes the SSAR offices from the OHAs and establishes them at a different location where they can handle the cases as they see fit without supervision by ALJs shows that this program has moved at a rapid pace to become a full-fledged adversary proceeding. Let us compare a normal lawsuit which is filed in a clerk's office, an independent office. In this experimental Social Security program, the suit is brought and the file remains in the hands of one attorney (an adversary) and the other one does not have possession of the file until such time as the ALJ gets to hear it and the ALJ does not have the file until such time as he gets ready to hear the case. The ALJ is required to develop the case but is prevented from doing so because it is in the hands of an SSAR who is representing one side of the case. The SSAR is free to develop the file in any manner he sees fit. We are all aware of the unfortunate situation in which a person can be sent to enough doctors until one will find or make some different diagnosis from the others or will fail to diagnose any impairment. All that is needed is one doctor to say something contradictory and there is a factual issue which has to be resolved. The federal courts are bound by the Secretary's finding of facts even if one person says one thing and ten say another. The situation exemplified here shows jurisprudence at its worst. An ALJ can only conduct an informal hearing; he is not set up to conduct a court trial. He has no power of contempt. He has no way of maintaining order. How is he expected to carry out his function as a judge charged with developing the evidence when the file is in the possession of a person representing the government? When an attorney for the government appears before this court and says that this case does not represent a situation in which an adversary type proceeding has developed, he is refusing to admit what the facts reveal.

(7) This court finds that both the SSARP and the AIP are simply nothing more nor less than an attempt by the bureaucracy to control the independence of the ALJs. Their mission is to employ people who will have control of the files before they go to the ALJ. This program began in an announced purpose of having the representatives develop the case and permit the judge to sit and objectively hear and, if necessary, further develop and decide the case. By giving the file to the SSAR instead of to the

ALJ it permits the government a second chance to defeat the claim by new medical evidence without the claimant knowing anything about it. It affords the opportunity for the SSARs to go fishing for additional evidence to support the government's position. In essence, there are persons in the administration who do not trust judges and in particular, do not trust ALJs and who want to destroy their independence, and have used the SSARP and AIP process to aid in their efforts.

(8) The Social Security Administration, by unadvertised internal decision, radically changed the SSARP to the AIP by internal rules that do not have the force and effect of regulations duly adopted after advertisement in the Federal Register, as required by the [Administrative Procedures Act].

I.

PROCEDURAL DUE PROCESS

What is and what is not procedural due process is as varied as the various administrative proceedings in the governments of states and of the United States and what is procedural due process under one set of circumstances where governmental action is involved may not apply in an entirely different governmental action depending somewhat upon the private interests involved. In Hanna v. Larche, 363 U.S. 420, 442, 80 S.Ct. 1502, 1514, 4 L.Ed.2d 1307 (1960), the Supreme Court stated,

> [D]ue process embodies the differing rules of fair play which, through the years, have become associated with differing types of proceedings.

The particular nature of procedural due process as it applies in a Social Security context, is clearly set forth in a landmark case, Richardson v. Perales, 402 U.S. 389, 91 S.Ct. 1420, 28 L.Ed.2d 842 (1971), where the Court stated the following:

> There emerges an emphasis upon the informal rather than the formal. This, we think, is as it should be, for this administrative procedure and these hearings, should be understandable to the layman claimant, should not necessarily be stiff and comfortable only for the trained attorney, and should be liberal and not strict in tone and operation. This is the obvious intent of Congress so long as the procedures are fundamentally fair.

Id. at 400-401, 91 S.Ct. at 1427.

Citing Flemming v. Nestor, 363 U.S. 603, 80 S.Ct. 1367, 4 L.Ed.2d 1435 (1960) and Goldberg v. Kelly, 397 U.S. 254, 90 S.Ct. 1011, the *Perales* Court stated that the right to Social Security benefits is in one sense

earned and that the "extent to which procedural due process must be afforded to the recipient is influenced by the extent to which he may be
condemned to suffer grievous loss." *Perales*, 402 U.S. at 401-402, 91 S.Ct.
at 1427.   Thus, the Court noted that there was a private interest involved
which was affected by the governmental action and therefore the focus
must be upon the private interest.   *Id.* at 401-02, 91 S.Ct. at 1427-28.
Thus, procedural due process in Social Security cases requires a much
stricter standard than, for example, a Veterans Administration claim
where there is no protected property interest but, rather, a recipient of
government benefits receives them, in a sense, by way of grace.

Again, stressing that due process is a flexible concept, the Supreme
Court has further described the type of due process required in a Social
Security case in Mathews v. Eldridge, 424 U.S. 319, 96 S.Ct. 893, 47
L.Ed.2d 18 (1976), where the Court said at 334-35, 96 S.Ct. at 903:

> More precisely, our prior decisions indicate that identification of the
> specific dictates of due process generally requires consideration of
> three distinct factors: first, the private interest that will be affected
> by the official action;   second, the risk of an erroneous deprivation of
> such interests through the procedures used, and the probable value,
> if any, of additional or substitute procedural safeguards;   and finally,
> the government's interests, including the function involved and the
> fiscal and administrative burdens that the additional or substitute
> procedural requirement would entail.

The court is of the opinion that the SSARP does not meet the three-
prong standard for procedural due process of *Eldridge*, nor does it meet
the informal and fundamentally fair test of *Perales*.

With regard to the first prong of the *Eldridge* test relating to the private interest, it is obvious that, in a Social Security context, a person has
a property interest to protect.   The undisputed evidence in this case
shows that instead of meeting a standard of speeding up and facilitating
the processing of claims, this procedure has tended to lengthen and cause
delays in a person's obtaining disability benefits.   The goal to build upon
the record and to present a better record for review has had the opposite
effect and has resulted in SSARs obtaining evidence for the government
without regard to developing the cases for the claimants.   * * *

          * * *

The SSARs, using their authority to refer cases to the Appeals Council have adopted an adversary appellate process as shown by the undisputed evidence in this case.   * * *   The court, in its factual findings discussion, has set out some examples of the procedure's adverse effect on
claimants.   One had died during the appellate process and in all of the

others there was approximately an additional year before they received their Social Security benefits. Without the SSARs, it is probable that none of these cases would have been before the Appeals Council for its own-motion review.

Furthermore, as this court has pointed out in the findings of fact, the goal of the program to assist the ALJ in the development of the evidence has not been achieved. The only change in the development of the case has been to prevent the claimants from recovering and not to assist the claimant in any way. The government has not presented evidence to this court in a single case in which evidence has been produced favorable to the claimant that enabled the claimant to obtain Social Security benefits. Under the previous system, the ALJ was an independent person with judicial experience, hired by an independent agency, and he was in control of the development of the evidence. There was better development of the record than has been shown under the current procedures.

The second prong of the *Eldridge* test is whether there is a risk of an erroneous deprivation through the procedures used. An actual examination of cases showing the effect of the SSARs on the appeals process reveals that there is a risk of an erroneous deprivation as shown by those cases which have been referred to the Appeals Council by the SSARs and have resulted in the claimant eventually receiving benefits after lengthy delay. Also, the wide discrepancy in the statistics relating to claimants not represented by counsel indicates an erroneous deprivation to a large group of people through the procedures used.

With regard to the third prong of the *Eldridge* test, as to whether the government's interest would be improved either by relieving the government of administrative burdens or fiscal responsibilities, there has been no showing that the government's interest is protected in this regard. Despite the fact that numerous congressmen have requested figures on the cost of this program, there have been none presented in response to their requests and there have been none presented to this court; however, it is obvious that when an entirely new bureaucratic entity has been established, there is an extra fiscal burden upon the government. The ultimate results do not show that there is any reduction in the grant of benefits. If there is any benefit to the government, it relates only to delayed payment of benefits by the government to the detriment of claimants; however, no evidence was presented concerning this.

The greatest lack of fundamental fairness as required in the *Perales* test is that the proceedings which have heretofore been deemed to have been informal and non-adversarial are now formal, stiff, strict and adversarial. There are no rules of evidence to guide ALJs in conducting adversary proceedings. They have no power to hold one in contempt, a necessity in a formal adversary proceeding. Congress did not intend it to be an adversary proceeding, and, indeed, the regulations which were promulgated at the time the SSARP was announced do not require an adversarial proceeding. The element of fundamental unfairness is obvious in this regard. Furthermore, an essential element of fundamental fairness is notice of a hearing within a reasonable time. The statistics show that the SSARP causes delays in processing and is violative of due process in this regard.

Another requirement of due process is that administrative agencies must follow their own rules. As was stated by the Court of Appeals for the Ninth Circuit:

> When administrative bodies promulgate rules or regulations to serve as guidelines, these guidelines should be followed. Failure to follow such guidelines tends to cause unjust discrimination and deny adequate notice contrary to fundamental concepts of fair play and due process. (Citations omitted).

N.L.R.B. v. Welcome-American Fertilizer Co., 443 F.2d 19, 20 (9th Cir.1971). In *Perales*, the features which were approved as fundamentally fair included the admissibility of written reports of licensed physicians which was predicated upon five factors: (1) the doctors, although paid a consulting fee by the state agency, were independent, unbiased and disinterested; (2) the hearing was non-adversarial; (3) the reports reflected an endeavor to ascertain the truth; (4) the reports rested upon accepted medical procedures and tests; and (5) the doctor could be subpoenaed for cross-examination. Three of the five factors present in *Richardson v. Perales* are absent in the SSARP. The government advocates are not independent. They are hired by the agency which is a party and they are not unbiased and disinterested and no one even argues that they are. The mere presence of a government advocate at the hearing renders it adversarial and indeed, he proceeds so to act on through the appellate process. Finally, unlike the consultative physician in *Perales*, the government advocate is under no obligation to try to ascertain the truth, but, rather, he is there to state the SSA's position in the case. As this court noted in the opening remarks in connection with this case, the whole purpose of any proceeding should be to seek out the truth. This objective has been lost in this administrative process, and due to the fundamental unfairness inherent in the SSARP and the AIP, they violate due process.

II.

THE SSAR PROGRAM HAS VIOLATED ITS IMPLEMENTING REGULATIONS AND WAS NOT PROPERLY IMPLEMENTED FROM THE BEGINNING

It is a fundamental principle of administrative law that an agency must comply with its own regulations. Once regulations have been duly promulgated, they are as binding upon the government as they are upon the citizen. * * * In particular, the requirement that an agency is bound to follow its own rules has been applied specifically to the Secretary of HHS in Social Security cases. The regulations promulgated in this case are the SSARP, 20 C.F.R. §§ 404.965 and 416.1465 published at 47 Fed.Reg. 36,117 *et seq.* (Aug. 19, 1982). In addressing the question as to whether the program would be adversarial these regulations stated:

> It was never our intention that the SSA representative would categorically advocate affirmation of state agency decision denying benefits. On the contrary, as representatives of the SSA, these individuals will not advocate the denial of claims when the evidence presents a clear case for entitlement. To emphasize this, we have clarified the language of the regulations.... To provide that the SSA representative may, when appropriate, request that the administrative law judge allow the payment of benefits. We believe that this change will resolve any uncertainty about whether the role of the SSA representative is adversarial.

As this court has pointed out, all of the evidence in this case shows that the SSARP is an adversarial process. Without repeating the evidence that has been previously set forth, the court would particularly note the adversarial nature of the proceedings as they have recently been outlined wherein the SSARs will be located in a separate office and will have complete control of the file. They will determine when the case will be assigned to an ALJ for a hearing and will be comparable to any other attorney except that he is an advocate on one side of the case who has complete control of the case file until the time of trial.

* * *

THE SSAR VIOLATES THE SOCIAL SECURITY ACT

The legislative history of the disability program, which was added by the Social Security amendments of 1956, 70 Stat. 818, shows that the Social Security Administration was designed to function as an impartial adjudicator of the claims and not as an advocate. In *Richardson v. Perales, supra,* the Supreme Court, in reviewing the legislative history of the Act, noted as follows:

We bear in mind that the agency operates essentially, and is intended so to do, as an adjudicator and not as an advocate or adversary. This is the congressional plan. We do not presume on this record to say that it works unfairly.

402 U.S. at 403, 91 S.Ct. at 1428. In 1979, citing *Perales* and *Eldridge*, the Supreme Court stated as follows:

Again, the Court has been sensitive to the special difficulties presented by the mass administration of the Social Security system. After the legislative task of classification is completed, the administrative goal is accuracy and promptness in the actual allocation of benefits pursuant to those classifications. The magnitude of that task is not amenable to the full trappings of the adversary process lest again benefit levels be threatened by the cost of administration. Fairness can best be assured by Congress and the Social Security Administration, through sound managerial techniques and quality control designed to achieve an acceptable rate of error. (Citations Omitted).

Califano v. Boles, 443 U.S. 282, 285, 99 S.Ct. 2767, 2770, 61 L.Ed.2d 541 (1979).

There can be no better expression of the intention of Congress on the issue of Social Security ALJ hearings being non-adversarial than that by Judge Winter in Adams v. Harris, 643 F.2d 995, 1003, n. 8 (4th Cir.1981) (Winter, C.J. dissenting):

I agree with the Secretary's contention that the disability determination process was designed by Congress to be non-adversarial. I would emphasize that the Social Security Administration misconceives its role when it casts itself as adversary to the claimant by erecting unnecessary barriers to the truthfinding process.

This court has recognized that if regulations are adopted by the administration which are in contradiction to the statute, they are "simply void" because the Secretary has no power to promulgate regulations contrary to the Act itself. Clements v. Celebrezze, 216 F.Supp. 78 (W.D.Va.1963).

＊ ＊ ＊

＊ ＊ ＊ If there is any doubt as to the ALJs' views regarding the adversative nature of the proceedings involved, one need only to review the remarks of the Honorable Barry M. Wesker, Hearing Officer and Chief ALJ of OHA, Pasadena, California, which is one of the OHAs under the plan. In his remarks dated November 27, 1985, addressed to Frank V. Smith,

III, Associate Commissioner, OHA, Court exhibit # 8, he states, in part, as follows:

> I frankly cannot see that any portion of this restructuring dealing with delivery and caseload can be accomplished without the publication of new regulations. 20 C.F.R. § 404.900 and its companion in Title XVI state clearly that the first four stages of administrative review shall be informal and non-adversary. While it is true that 404.965 and 404.1465 [sic] have a 'notwithstanding' clause, the fact that the regulations provide that the claimant shall continue to have all the rights set out in this section make clear that these regulations do not intend for these proceedings to be adversarial. If the SSARP were to receive the potential evidence first, it seems axiomatic that this procedure goes beyond traditional adversary proceedings in that the claimant has no discovery rights to assert and is entirely at the mercy of the SSARP.

In another part of this same memorandum under a heading "Adjudication under the Act," Chief Judge Wesker goes on to state as follows:

> While § 205 of the Act provides the general authority for the Secretary to carry out the SSARP, the language of Part B-1 makes it clear that the Secretary must give the individual 'reasonable notice and opportunity for a hearing' and in pertinent part 'to hold such hearings and conduct such investigations and other proceedings as he may deem necessary or proper for the administration of this title. In the course of any hearing, investigation, or other proceeding, he may administer oaths and affirmations, examine witnesses, and receive evidence. Evidence may be received at any hearing before the Secretary, even though inadmissible under Rules of Evidence applicable to court procedure.' The last sentence quoted makes it clear that the Act intends for this to be a non-adversary procedure. The previous phrases as worded made it clear that it is a hearing which has primacy and the investigation which is secondary. To the extent that the SSARP's development of the case is an investigation, that development is secondary to the primary duties of the Secretary to the claimant; that is, to hold a hearing. Since it is only the administrative law judge who can hold such a hearing, the result should be obvious.

Chief Judge Wesker goes on to say under a heading of Court Cases:

> In all circuits, it is a fundamental tenet that an administrative law judge has the responsibility for development. This fundamental jurisprudential concept is inextricably interwoven with the burden of proof as enunciated heretofore, to-wit: the claimant must first make a prima facie case before the burden of going forward with the evi-

dence shifts to the government.... Further it is clear by this attempt to remove that developmental burden from the administrative law judge that the administration is curtailing the administrative law judge's authority without curtailing his responsibility ... however, when the administrative law judge who has been given this responsibility in no uncertain terms, allows that responsibility and statutory duty to be diminished in this fashion, we are coming very close to violations of a number of Canon of Ethics. One that comes to mind immediately would be number 2 of the Canon of Judicial Ethics dealing with public interest. The last sentence of that Canon of Ethics is particularly instructive: 'He should avoid unconsciously falling into the attitude of mind that the litigants are made for the courts instead of the courts for the litigants.'

CONCLUSION

We have seen that the administrative procedures used in making Social Security disability determinations are a cumbersome "Rube Goldberg" process at best, which have been further encumbered by a threat to the independence of the ALJs who are the only people in the entire system who are oriented toward the main goal which should be the seeking of truth and ultimate triumph of justice. This experimental administrative program has been improperly implemented from its inception in violation of the Secretary's published regulations, in that it was advertised to be non-adversarial but has been adversarial from the beginning; has not achieved its goal of aiding in the development of cases but has, at best, maintained the present system or, at worst, tended to cause the ALJs to rely upon the SSARs to the detriment of claimants; has not achieved its goal of improving quality of decisions or expediting cases; has not achieved its goal of increasing productivity; has not achieved its goal of uniformity; is in violation of the intention of the Social Security Act itself; the regulations have not been implemented as required, in that SSARs have continued to participate after the hearing level by filing briefs with the Appeals Council; the AIP, as it is being implemented effective April 1, 1986, is in violation of the APA because the changes were not advertised by notice in the Federal Register as required; and the entire concept, as it has been implemented in both the SSARP and the AIP, is in violation of the fundamental principles of procedural due process as prescribed by the Fifth Amendment and as determined by the courts to be applicable in social security cases.

For the reasons stated herein, a permanent injunction shall be granted enjoining any further proceedings using the SSARP or the AIP in any of the remaining five participating OHAs throughout the United States. An appropriate order will be entered this day.

2. ROLE OF THE ADMINISTRATIVE LAW JUDGE

The non-adversarial nature of Social Security administrative hearings places the ALJ conducting those hearings in a difficult position. As the court stated in Buccheri v. Astrue, 586 F. Supp. 2d 54, 60, 138 Soc. Sec. Rep. Serv. 855 (D. Conn. 2008), "[b]ecause a hearing on disability benefits is a non-adversarial proceeding, it is well-settled that the ALJ has an affirmative obligation to develop the administrative record, even in cases in which the claimant is represented by counsel." The court in *Buccheri* cited Pratts v. Chater, 94 F.3d 34, 37, 51 Soc. Sec. Rep. Serv. 549 (2d Cir. 1996), in which the Second Circuit explained further:

> It is the rule in our circuit that "the ALJ, unlike a judge in a trial, must [her]self affirmatively develop the record" in light of "the essentially non-adversarial nature of a benefits proceeding." Echevarria v. Secretary of HHS, 685 F.2d 751, 755 (2d Cir.1982). This duty arises from the Commissioner's regulatory obligations to develop a complete medical record before making a disability determination, 20 C.F.R. § 404.1512(d)-(f) (1995), and exists even when, as here, the claimant is represented by counsel.

94 F.3d at 37. Thus, ALJs must balance their responsibility to assure that they decide claims on the basis of a complete record following a full and fair hearing with the potentially conflicting responsibilities of assuring not only that all evidence relevant to the position of an unrepresented Social Security Administration is included in the record, but also assuring that the claimant's position, presented either by the claimant or a representative, is fully documented as well. This situation has been described as a "three hats" dilemma for Social Security ALJs.

BATTLES V. SHALALA
36 F.3d 43, 45 Soc. Sec. Rep. Serv. 604 (8th Cir. 1994)

HENLEY, Senior Circuit Judge.

Prentis Battles, Jr. appeals from a judgment of the district court upholding a decision of the Secretary of Health and Human Services denying his claim for supplemental security income benefits. We reverse and remand.

In December 1991, Battles filed an application for benefits, alleging a disability due to back and "right side" problems. In a disability questionnaire, Battles, who was born in 1940, stated he had a seventh grade education, had not worked in fifteen years, and was homeless. He described a reclusive social life, indicating that he did not visit with people and that his relatives had nothing to do with him. In July 1992, Battles, who was represented by an attorney, appeared at a hearing before an administrative law judge (ALJ), claiming he could not work because of back pain, a "bad kidney," and breathing problems. In response to questions from his attorney, Battles stated that he could not "read or write too good," spent his days scavenging dumpsters for food and objects to sell, and spent nights sleeping in other people's cars.

The only evidence submitted in connection with the hearing was a February 1992 report of a consultative physician. Lumbar spine and chest x-rays were normal. The doctor diagnosed pain of unknown origin in the rib region and chronic obstructive lung disease.

The ALJ found that Battles' allegations of disabling pain were not credible and denied his claim for benefits.

Battles appealed the decision to the Appeals Council and submitted an additional medical report of an orthopedist, who found "no musculo-skeletal condition to explain the patient's symptoms." The doctor, however, diagnosed chronic obstructive lung disease and advised a pulmonology evaluation. The Appeals Council upheld the ALJ's decision.

Battles then sought review in the district court, alleging that he was disabled by a combination of physical and mental impairments. He also filed a motion to remand under 42 U.S.C. § 405(g) based on a report of Dr. William Wilkins, a psychologist who evaluated Battles in June 1993. Intelligence tests revealed that Battles had borderline intellectual functioning, with a full scale IQ score of 72, a verbal IQ of 80, and a performance IQ of 63. Psychological tests, coupled with social history, indicated that Battles had a "fairly well entrenched pattern of a schizotypal personality disorder," which was characterized by inappropriate behaviors, and suffered from "an almost lifelong history of significant alcohol abuse." He also suffered from severe dyslexia.

The district court upheld the denial of benefits and denied the motion to remand.

On appeal Battles challenges the district court's denial of his motion to remand. He, however, suggests that the motion to remand probably would have been unnecessary had the ALJ fulfilled his duty to fully and fairly develop the record as to a mental impairment. We agree. The Secretary acknowledges that it is her " 'duty to develop the record fully and fairly, even if ... the claimant is represented by counsel.' " Boyd v. Sullivan, 960 F.2d 733, 736 (8th Cir.1992) (quoting Warner v. Heckler, 722 F.2d 428, 431 (8th Cir.1983)). This is so because an administrative hearing is not an adversarial proceeding. Henrie v. Dept. of Health & Human Serv., 13 F.3d 359, 361 (10th Cir.1993). "[T]he goals of the Secretary and the advocates should be the same: that deserving claimants who apply for benefits receive justice." Sears v. Bowen, 840 F.2d 394, 402 (7th

Cir.1988). Moreover, "[a]n adequate hearing is indispensable because a reviewing court may consider only the Secretary's final decision [and] the evidence in the administrative transcript on which the decision was based." Higbee v. Sullivan, 975 F.2d 558, 562 (9th Cir.1992) (per curiam).

While the Secretary is correct that she is in under no duty to "go to inordinate lengths to develop a claimant's case[,]" Thompson v. Califano, 556 F.2d 616, 618 (1st Cir.1977), it is also true that she must "make an investigation that is not wholly inadequate under the circumstances." Miranda v. Secretary of Health, Educ. & Welfare, 514 F.2d 996, 998 (1st Cir.1975). "There is no bright line test for determining when the [Secretary] has ... failed to develop the record. The determination in each case must be made on a case by case basis." Lashley v. Secretary of Health & Human Serv., 708 F.2d 1048, 1052 (6th Cir.1983).

In the circumstances of this case, we believe that the ALJ failed to fully and fairly develop the record. Although length of a hearing is not dispositive, it is a consideration. Thompson v. Sullivan, 987 F.2d 1482, 1492 (10th Cir.1993). Here, the hearing "lasted a mere [ten] minutes, and was fully transcribed in approximately eleven pages." Lashley, 708 F.2d at 1052. The ALJ asked no questions and counsel's questions failed to shed light on Battles' mental capacity to work. "Superficial questioning of inarticulate claimants or claimants with limited education is likely to elicit responses which fail to portray accurately the extent of their limitations." *Id.* We believe that Battles' testimony that he was virtually illiterate, had not worked in fifteen years, ate out of garbage cans, slept in other people's cars, and had no relationships with other persons was "sufficient to raise an issue as to [his] mental and psychological capacity to engage in substantial gainful activity."[2] Cannon v. Harris, 651 F.2d 513, 519 (7th Cir.1981). The Secretary's own rules provide that "mental illness is defined and characterized by maladaptive behavior." Social Security Ruling (SSR) 85-15. The rules recognize that "[i]ndividuals with mental disorders often adopt a highly restricted and/or inflexible lifestyle" and "emphasize the importance of thoroughness in evaluation on an individualized basis." *Id.* Indeed, the regulations provide a mandatory procedure to evaluate mental impairments, 20 C.F.R. § 416.920a, and for ex-

---

[2] We are aware that this court has held that as a general rule an ALJ has no "obligation to investigate a claim not presented at the time of the application for benefits and not offered at the hearing as a basis for disability[,]" Brockman v. Sullivan, 987 F.2d 1344, 1348 (8th Cir.1993), but this case is an exception to the rule. "Unfairness or prejudice resulting from an incomplete record—whether because of lack of counsel or lack of diligence on the ALJ's part—requires a remand." Highfill v. Bowen, 832 F.2d 112, 115 (8th Cir.1987) (evidence "put the ALJ on notice of the need for further inquiry"). Even if Battles had not raised an issue concerning the fairness of his hearing, we might well have raised it sua sponte.

amination by a psychiatrist or psychologist when there is "evidence which indicates the existence of a mental impairment." *Id.* at § 416.903(e).[3]

* * *

Accordingly, we reverse the judgment of the district court and remand this case with instructions to remand to the Secretary for further proceedings.

3. THE ALJ'S ROLE WHEN A CLAIMANT IS UNREPRESENTED

A Social Security ALJ's responsibility is far greater when a claimant is unrepresented. As stated in an often-quoted passage from an early Second Circuit case (when appeals were heard by hearing examiners rather than administrative law judges), at a hearing where the claimant is not represented "a duty devolves on the hearing examiner to scrupulously and conscientiously probe into, inquire of, and explore for all of the relevant facts." Gold v. Secretary of Health & Human Services, 463 F.2d 38, 43 (2d Cir. 1972). Moreover, ALJs must be "especially diligent in ensuring that favorable as well as unfavorable facts and circumstances are elicited." Cox v. Califano, 587 F.2d 988, 991 (9th Cir. 1978) (quoting Rosa v. Weinberger, 381 F. Supp. 377, 381 (E.D.N.Y.1974)). This responsibility is taken seriously by reviewing courts. *See, e.g.*, Jozefick v. Shalala, 854 F. Supp. 342, 344, 44 Soc. Sec. Rep. Serv. 677 (M.D. Pa. 1994) ("Absence of counsel at the administrative hearing not only increases the responsibility of the ALJ, but also requires the court to undertake a searching review of the record to determine that the claimant has received a full and fair hearing.").

The ALJ's role when a claimant is unrepresented is still that of a judge, however, not the claimant's lawyer. "The ALJ does not act as counsel for claimant, but as an examiner who thoroughly develops the facts. The special duty assigned to the ALJ 'requires, essentially, a record which shows that the claimant was not prejudiced by lack of counsel.'" Thompson v. Sullivan, 933 F.2d 581, 586, 33 Soc. Sec. Rep. Serv. 407 (7th Cir. 1991) (quoting Smith v. Schweiker, 677 F.2d 826, 829 (11th Cir. 1982)).

---

[3] The rules also provide that "[r]eports from psychiatrists ... and other professionals working in the field of mental health should contain the individual's medical history, mental status evaluation, psychological testing, diagnosis, ... a description of the individual's daily activities, and a medical assessment describing ability to do work-related activities." SSR 85-16. Here, the doctor who conducted a consultative "general physical examination" in February 1992 concluded that Battles had the ability "to respond appropriately to supervision, co-workers, and work pressure in a work setting," even though Battles had told the doctor he had not worked in fifteen years. Based on the report in the record, it does not appear that the doctor worked in the mental health field or conducted a mental status evaluation. Nor does the report contain a description of Battles' daily activities, social history, or any basis upon which the doctor based his conclusions.

TONAPETYAN V. HALTER

242 F.3d 1144, 72 Soc. Sec. Rep. Serv. 509 (9th Cir. 2001)

Before: PREGERSON, CANBY and DAVID R. THOMPSON, Circuit Judges.

CANBY, Circuit Judge:

Silva Tonapetyan appeals from the district court's summary judgment affirming the decision of the Commissioner of Social Security denying her supplemental security income disability benefits under Title XVI of the Social Security Act, 42 U.S.C. § 1381 *et seq.* Tonapetyan asserted that she was disabled as the result of a number of physical and mental impairments. She contends that the administrative law judge (ALJ) improperly: (1) determined that she lacked credibility; (2) rejected the opinions of her treating physicians in favor of the opinions of examining physicians and non-examining medical experts; and (3) failed to develop the record fully and fairly. We have jurisdiction under 28 U.S.C. § 1291. Because we hold that the ALJ failed to develop fully the record with respect to Tonapetyan's mental impairment, we reverse the judgment of the district court and remand with instructions to remand the case to the Commissioner for further proceedings.

* * *

* * *

II. Conflicting Medical Evidence

* * *

B. Mental Impairment

The ALJ determined that Tonapetyan suffers from the medically-determinable mental impairment of non-severe dysthymia, which restricts her to unskilled work. In reaching this conclusion, the ALJ relied on the opinion of examining psychiatrist, Dr. Greenleaf, who concluded that Tonapetyan's cognitive skills are intact and that she can handle complex instructions, and on the opinion of non-examining psychological expert, Dr. Walter, who concluded that Tonapetyan suffers from mild depression. The ALJ rejected the opinions of two physicians as unsupported by objective clinical findings and heavily reliant on Tonapetyan's subjective statements; they were her treating psychiatrist, Dr. Trabulus, who had diagnosed her with chronic schizophrenia, and her examining psychiatrist, Dr. Grant, who diagnosed her with depressive disorder with psychotic features.

The Commissioner contends that, on the record as it stands, the ALJ properly resolved these conflicting opinions, just as he resolved to our satisfaction the similarly conflicting evidence of Tonapetyan's physical impairment. On the basis of Dr. Walter's equivocal testimony with respect to Tonapetyan's alleged mental impairment of schizophrenia, however, we find the current record incomplete.

III. Full and Fair Hearing

The ALJ in a social security case has an independent " 'duty to fully and fairly develop the record and to assure that the claimant's interests are considered.' " Smolen, 80 F.3d at 1288 (quoting Brown v. Heckler, 713 F.2d 441, 443 (9th Cir.1983)). This duty extends to the represented as well as to the unrepresented claimant. When the claimant is unrepresented, however, the ALJ must be especially diligent in exploring for all the relevant facts. In this case, Tonapetyan was represented, but by a lay person rather than an attorney. The ALJ's duty to develop the record fully is also heightened where the claimant may be mentally ill and thus unable to protect her own interests. Ambiguous evidence, or the ALJ's own finding that the record is inadequate to allow for proper evaluation of the evidence, triggers the ALJ's duty to "conduct an appropriate inquiry." Smolen, 80 F.3d at 1288. The ALJ may discharge this duty in several ways, including: subpoenaing the claimant's physicians, submitting questions to the claimant's physicians, continuing the hearing, or keeping the record open after the hearing to allow supplementation of the record.

Although the ALJ here did not specifically find that the evidence of Tonapetyan's mental impairment was ambiguous, or that he lacked sufficient evidence to render a decision, he relied heavily upon the testimony of the medical expert, Dr. Walter, who found just that. Dr. Walter began his testimony by describing Dr. Trabulus's lack of anecdotal records as "confusing," and by recommending that a more detailed report be obtained. He found it "difficult to say" whether the medical record was complete enough to allow the ALJ to reach a conclusion in the case. When asked for his diagnosis, he noted that Tonapetyan was unquestionably "somewhat depressed." He resisted concluding that she did or did not suffer from schizophrenia, however, suggesting that he would "have to see more evidence of that and a more detailed explanation" from Dr. Trabulus. Only when pressed by the ALJ for a diagnosis "based upon what's in the record" did he give his diagnosis of mild depressive affective disorder, or "dysthymia." Yet, he remained equivocal throughout his testimony. For example, when asked about Tonapetyan's restrictions of daily activities, he responded: "Well, we have a dichotomy here between the two reports [of Drs. Trabulus and Greenleaf].... I have no way of just saying let's divide them. I would say—I guess, I guess I have a difficult time with it." Finally, when asked by Tonapetyan's lay representative whether a complete report from Dr. Trabulus would change his opinion regarding Tonapetyan's mental impairment, Dr. Walter responded: "Yes. If you clarified her symptoms that she's telling him."

The ALJ clearly relied heavily on Dr. Walter's testimony, adopting his "dysthymia" diagnosis as well as his criticisms of Drs. Grant and Trabulus. Given this reliance, the ALJ was not free to ignore Dr. Walter's equivocations and his concern over the lack of a complete record upon which to assess Tonapetyan's mental impairment. Moreover, he was not free to ignore Dr. Walter's specific recommendation that a more detailed report from Dr. Trabulus be obtained. That he did so constitutes reversible error. We therefore direct a remand for further development of the record with regard to Tonapetyan's mental impairment, and for further appropriate proceedings in light of that additional development.

IV. Conclusion

We conclude that the ALJ failed to develop the record fully and fairly with respect to Tonapetyan's possible mental impairment, including schizophrenia or other disorders with psychotic features. Accordingly, we reverse the district court's summary judgment and remand with instructions to remand to the Commissioner for further administrative proceedings consistent with this disposition.

YOUNGER V. SHALALA
30 F.3d 1265, 45 Soc. Sec. Rep. Serv. 176 (10th Cir. 1994)

Before ANDERSON and KELLY, Circuit Judges, and LUNGSTRUM, District Judge.

LUNGSTRUM, District Judge.

Plaintiff Sherilyn Younger, on behalf of her children, claimants Kia R. and Tia L. Younger, appeals the district court's decision affirming the Secretary's ruling denying her request for children's benefits under the Social Security Act. Claimants' applications were denied both initially and upon reconsideration. After a de novo hearing, the administrative law judge (ALJ) also denied their request. The Appeals Council denied review, and claimants filed a complaint in the district court. The district court affirmed the ALJ's decision following its review of the magistrate judge's findings and recommendations and claimants' objections. Appellant's Br. at 2-3. We affirm.

The Social Security Act provides insurance benefits to dependent children of a deceased, fully insured, wage earner. If dependency cannot be presumed under the Act, a claimant can show that he or she is the child of a deceased wage earner under other provisions of the Act. Here,

Ms. Younger alleged that, although she was never married to their father, claimants are the children of Charles L. Costello, a deceased insured wage earner. She contends on appeal that 1) the record evidence tends to support the children's claim to benefits under 42 U.S.C. § 416(h)(2)(A) and the intestacy laws of Oklahoma, and 2) the ALJ failed in his duty to fully develop the record.

Our review of the district court's decision is limited to determining whether the record as a whole contains substantial evidence to support the Secretary's decision and whether the Secretary applied the proper legal standards. In child benefit cases, the claimant bears the burden of proving entitlement as the child of a deceased insured wage earner. Where, as here, a claimant appears before the ALJ pro se, the ALJ has a heightened duty to investigate all issues presented, and to develop the record as to those issues.

I

The statutory provision on which claimants rely, 42 U.S.C. § 416(h)(2)(A), entitles an applicant to child's benefits if the applicant can show entitlement to a share of the wage earner's estate under applicable state law. Review of this claim therefore requires a review of Oklahoma's law of intestate succession, found at Okla.Stat. tit. 84, § 215.

On appeal, claimants rest their claim on § 215(c), which requires that "the father publicly acknowledged such child as his own, receiving it as such, with the consent of his wife, if he is married, into his family and otherwise treating it as if it were a child born in wedlock."   * * * Claimants' evidence consists of affidavit testimony from various persons that the wage earner publicly acknowledged claimants as his own children, and that he took them to his wife's home in Wichita for a two-month period.

Responding to claimants' arguments on appeal, appellee is correct in her assertion that public acknowledgment alone does not satisfy the requirements of § 215(c). The wage earner must have also received the children into his family with the consent of his wife and otherwise treated them as his legitimate children. Therefore, even if claimants are deemed to have shown that the wage earner publicly acknowledged them as his own children, we must conclude that substantial evidence supports the ALJ's decision that claimants have not satisfied the requirements of Oklahoma's intestate succession law and, therefore, have not met the requirements of 42 U.S.C. § 416(h)(2)(A).

II

Claimants' second argument is a legal one, requiring a review of the standards applicable to an ALJ's duty to develop the record under the circumstances of this case. It is well established that "[t]he ALJ has a basic obligation in every social security case to ensure that an adequate record is developed during the ... hearing consistent with the issues raised." Henrie v. United States Dep't of Health & Human Servs., 13 F.3d 359, 360-61 (10th Cir.1993) (disability case). That duty is heightened where a claimant is unrepresented. The duty is one of inquiry, to inform the ALJ of the relevant facts and to hear the claimant's version of those facts. We find this standard equally applicable in a child benefit case such as this one.

In the applications for benefits, plaintiff, on behalf of her children, stated her belief that the wage earner listed the children on his tax returns, that he may have listed them on an employment application, and that he took one of the children for emergency hospital treatment in 1981. The hearing transcript reveals that the ALJ solicited testimony from plaintiff in the following areas: a) the times during which the wage earner lived with plaintiff, b) the times during which the wage earner saw the children, c) the existence of any documentary evidence that the wage earner was the children's father, including birth certificates, Aid For Dependent Children (AFDC) applications, child support orders, tax returns, and probation reports, d) the wage earner's public acknowledgments that the children were his, including affidavits to that effect, e) his wife's statements that she did not know the children were her husband's until his funeral, f) the lack of any written acknowledgment by the wage earner that the children were his, and g) the wage earner's monetary support of the children.

None of the submitted documentation, which included the wage earner's obituary, birth records for the children from the state Vital Statistics division, and hospital birth certificates, provide support for claimants' case. Additionally, before the hearing, the agency followed up on the allegations in their applications for benefits. The agency contacted a case worker who filed AFDC applications for the children. The case worker's files included notes that the wage earner had picked up the children from day care and had once threatened plaintiff that he would get custody of the children. Other than these statements made by plaintiff, however, the files revealed no paternity affidavits or other documents signed by the wage earner.

The agency contacted the Internal Revenue Service regarding the wage earner's tax records, and was told that the information they wanted (evidence of paternity) was not on the computer system. The agency also contacted Diane Stone, with whom the wage earner lived before his death. She said that the wage earner was the children's father, but that she could find no acknowledgment of paternity among his papers. The agency contacted the wage earner's wife, who said he never told her the children were his. Finally, the agency contacted plaintiff herself. She stated that the hospital could find no record of the wage earner's emergency visit in 1981. She said further that she had contacted the wage earner's employer, who could find no mention of the children in his records. She stated that the wage earner had not been ordered to pay child support, and there was no court decree of paternity.

On appeal, claimants list thirteen different areas they claim the ALJ should have asked plaintiff about or inquired further through other sources. Our review indicates that these areas 1) were adequately covered by the agency's pre-hearing investigations, 2) were adequately covered by the ALJ at the hearing, 3) were never mentioned by plaintiff during proceedings before the agency, despite repeated opportunities to do so, 4) involve credibility of witnesses, which was not a factor the Secretary relied on in reaching her decision, or 5) are not relevant to the issue before the agency in this case.

Our careful study of the record leads us to conclude that the ALJ met his duty to develop the record in this case. The ALJ questioned plaintiff extensively about her relationship with the wage earner and about the possibility of any documentation of paternity. Beyond the duty to develop the record as to issues, factual matters, and avenues raised by a claimant, an ALJ need not make out a claimant's case where, as here, claimants bear the burden of demonstrating entitlement to benefits. Although the result is unfortunate for claimants, the court finds that the judgment of the United States District Court for the Northern District of Oklahoma must be AFFIRMED.

NOTES

1. For other formulations of the ALJ's heightened duty to develop the record what a claimant is unrepresented, see Smith v. Harris, 644 F.2d 985, 989 (3d Cir. 1981) ("where the claimant is unrepresented by counsel, the ALJ has a duty to exercise 'a heightened level of care' and 'assume a more active role'"); Clark v. Harris, 638 F.2d 1347, 1351 (5th Cir. 1981) (The ALJ's "'basic obligation to develop a full and fair record rises to a special duty when an unrepresented claimant unfamiliar with hearing procedures appears before him.'") (quoting Barker v. Harris, 486 F. Supp. 846 (N.D. Ga. 1980)); D'Angelo v. Commissioner, 475 F. Supp. 2d 716, 720, 119 Soc. Sec. Rep. Serv. 453 (W.D. Mich. 2007) ("The ALJ has a 'special duty' to develop the administrative record and ensure a fair hearing for claimants that are unrepresented by counsel.").

2. The usual remedy when an ALJ fails to meet his or her duty to develop the record fully is to remand the case to SSA for a supplemental hearing. *See, e.g.,* Smith v. Apfel, 231 F.3d 433, 337, 71 Soc. Sec. Rep. Serv. 627 (7th Cir. 2000) (citations omitted) ("Although a claimant has the burden to prove disability, the ALJ has a duty to develop a full and fair record. Failure to fulfill this obligation is 'good cause' to remand for gathering of additional evidence."); Fontanez ex rel. Fontanez v. Barnhart, 195 F. Supp. 2d 1333, 1338, 80 Soc. Sec. Rep. Serv. 388 (M.D. Fla. 2002) (claim turned on evidence of the claimant's functioning; "Contrary to his duty to fully develop the record, the ALJ failed to determine the significance of [the claimant]'s low scores. This requires remand."). Courts will not remand a case, however, if the evidence on file would support the denial of benefits notwithstanding the ALJ's failure to develop the record further. Thus, "[t] he ALJ's decision will be affirmed unless the claimant shows (1) that the ALJ failed to fulfill his duty to adequately develop the record and (2) that the claimant was prejudiced thereby." Wilson v. Barnhart, 129 F. App'x 912, 915, 104 Soc. Sec. Rep. Serv. 335 (5th Cir. 2005). *See also* Goodwater v. Barnhart, 579 F. Supp. 2d 746, 755, 137 Soc. Sec. Rep. Serv. 592 (D.S.C. 2007) ("An ALJ's failure to fulfill this duty to pro se claimants may result in remand where the absence of counsel results in prejudice to the claimant."). Whether the claimant was prejudiced depends on the court's expectations about the completeness of the evidentiary record at the hearing . *Compare* Luna v. Shalala, 22 F.3d 687, 692, 44 Soc. Sec. Rep. Serv. 348, 1994 WL 138107 (7th Cir. 1994) ("a significant omission is usually required before this court will find that the Secretary failed to assist *pro se* claimants in developing the record fully and fairly.") *with* Jozeflick v. Shalala, 854 F. Supp. 342, 350 n. 2, 44 Soc. Sec. Rep. Serv. 677 (M.D. Pa 1994)("A remand would not be warranted where it is clear that the claimant could not possibly establish entitlement to benefits or the "evidentiary gap" is not material to the disability determination.").

E. WEIGHT AND SUFFICIENCY OF MEDICAL EVIDENCE

Medical evidence of disability is sufficient when it establishes that the applicable disability standard has been met. Some claims are supported by consistent, probative medical evidence that lead to relatively easy decisions. However, often the supporting evidence is inconclusive or inconsistent. When that happens, the examiner at the state Disability Determination Service (DDS) or the administrative law judge may request additional evidence, possibly including one or more consultative examinations by a physician hired by SSA to evaluate the extent of the claimant's disability.

Problems concerning the weight and sufficiency of medical evidence arise most often when there is a conflict in medical opinions—often between the claimant's own doctor, referred to as a "treating physician," and an SSA-retained consulting physician. Moreover, the staff medical consultant employed by the DDS, who reviews the claim file without observing the claimant, may also have a conflicting opinion. As a result, the question whether there is sufficient medical evidence for a given claim depends to a large extent on the weight given to conflicting reports of two or three of these different types of medical sources.

1. GENERAL RULES ON WEIGHT AND SUFFICIENCY

As mentioned above, a claimant must present sufficient medical evidence to show that the applicable disability standard has been met. 20 C.F.R. §§ 404.1512(a), 416.912(a). The claimant may submit evidence that contains medical opinions, which includes "statements from physicians and psychologists or other acceptable medical sources that reflect judgments about the nature and severity of [the claimant's] impairment(s), including [his or her] symptoms, diagnosis and prognosis, what [he or she] can still do despite impairment(s), and [his or her] physical or mental restrictions. **20 C.F.R. §§ 404.1527(a)(2), 416.927(a)(2)[APP-REGS]**. SSA assumes the responsibility for reviewing the medical evidence in order to determine whether the claim can be evaluated on the basis of that evidence alone, or whether it should request additional evidence, possibly including one or more consultative examinations. 20 C.F.R. §§ 404.1527(b), (c), 416.927(b), (c). SSA's findings will vary depending upon the consistency and completeness of the information in the claimant's file, resulting essentially in one of four scenarios set out in 20 C.F.R. §§ 404.1527(c), 416.927(c):

(1) If all of the evidence we receive, including all medical opinion(s), is consistent, and there is sufficient evidence for us to decide whether you are disabled, we will make our determination or decision based on that evidence.

(2) If any of the evidence in your case record, including any medical opinion(s), is inconsistent with other evidence or is internally inconsistent, we will weigh all of the evidence and see whether we can decide whether you are disabled based on the evidence we have.

(3) If the evidence is consistent but we do not have sufficient evidence to decide whether you are disabled, or if after weighing the evidence we decide we cannot reach a conclusion about whether you are disabled, we will try to obtain additional evidence under the provisions of §§ 404.1512 and 404.1519 through 404.1519h. We will request additional existing records, recontact your treating sources or any other examining sources, ask you to undergo a consultative examination at our expense, or ask you or others for more information. We will consider any additional evidence we receive together with the evidence we already have.

(4) When there are inconsistencies in the evidence that cannot be resolved, or when despite efforts to obtain additional evidence the evidence is not complete, we will make a determination or decision based on the evidence we have.

Social Security regulations draw a distinction between "acceptable medical sources," who can offer opinions on the existence of a medical impairment, and "other sources" who can provide evidence only of severity and functional limitations. *See generally* **20 C.F.R. §§ 404.1513, 416.913[APP-REGS]**. The list of "acceptable" sources includes licensed or certified physicians or psychologists, as well as licensed optometrists (only for purposes of establishing visual disorders), licensed podiatrists, and qualified speech-language pathologists (only for purposes of establishing certain disorders). "Other" sources include medical sources not listed as acceptable, such as nurse-practitioners, physicians' assistants, naturopaths, chiropractors, audiologists, and therapists, as well educational personnel, social welfare agency personnel, and "other non-medical sources," such as spouses and other relatives, caregivers, friends, neighbors, and clergy. *See* 20 C.F.R. §§ 404.1513(a), (d), 416.913(a), (d).

Thus, in determining the overall sufficiency of medical evidence by weighing evidence from conflicting reports, the weight given a particular report will depend to a great extent on who submitted the report and how well it was written. For example, because physician's assistants and other non-physician medical professionals are not "acceptable medical sources" as defined in the regulations, their opinions are accorded less weight than the opinions of licensed physicians. But at least one court has held that a nurse practitioner's opinion was properly considered as part of a physician's opinion, although it would not be competent evidence on its own:

> According to the ALJ, the observations of Dr. Kincade and [nurse practitioner (NP)] Blaker indicated that Gomez was not disabled. The ALJ then concluded that these observations were entitled to greater weight than Dr. Aho's conclusion that Gomez was disabled and should be awarded benefits. Gomez argues that the ALJ erred in failing to distinguish between the opinions of Dr. Kincade and NP Blaker, and thus accorded NP Blaker's opinion more weight than was warranted. Gomez contends that Social Security regulations require the opinions of nurse practitioners to receive less weight than those of treating physicians or examining psychologists.

> The Code of Federal Regulations distinguishes between those opinions coming from "acceptable medical sources" and those coming from "other sources." 20 C.F.R. §§ 404.1513(a) and (e), 416.913(a) and (e). From this, 20 C.F.R. §§ 404.1527 and 416.927 each set forth simi-

lar guidelines for the Commissioner to follow when weighing conflicting opinions from acceptable medical sources, while containing no specific guidelines for the weighing of opinions from other sources. This permits the Commissioner to accord opinions from other sources less weight than opinions from acceptable medical sources.

Acceptable medical sources specifically include licensed physicians and licensed psychologists, but not nurse practitioners. 20 C.F.R. §§ 404.1513(a)(1) and (3); 416.913(a)(1) and (3). Thus, Gomez argues that NP Blaker's opinions should be separated from those of Dr. Kincade, and not given as much weight as the opinion of Dr. Aho, an acceptable medical source.

Chart notes indicate that although Dr. Kincade did not personally examine Gomez any time after July, 1990, NP Blaker consulted with Dr. Kincade regarding Gomez's treatment numerous times over the course of her relationship with Gomez. NP Blaker worked closely under the supervision of Dr. Kincade and she was acting as an agent of Dr. Kincade in her relationship with Gomez. Her opinion was properly considered as part of the opinion of Dr. Kincade, an acceptable medical source. Thus, the ALJ did accord it appropriate weight and consideration under 20 C.F.R. §§ 404.1527 and 416.927, as against the opinion of Dr. Aho, an examining, nontreating source.

Moreover, 20 C.F.R. § 416.913(a)(6) states that "[a] report of an interdisciplinary team that contains the evaluation and signature of an acceptable medical source is also considered acceptable medical evidence," while later in that section the statute designates nurse practitioners as an "other source." § 416.913(e)(3). While nowhere in the regulations is the term "interdisciplinary team" expressly defined, a plain reading of these sections taken together indicates that a nurse practitioner working in conjunction with a physician constitutes an acceptable medical source, while a nurse practitioner working on his or her own does not.

Gomez v. Chater, 74 F.3d 967, 970-71, 50 Soc. Sec. Rep. Serv. 18 (9th Cir. 1996). *Cf.* Nichols v. Commissioner, 260 F. Supp. 2d 1057, 1065-66, 88 Soc. Sec. Rep. Serv. 589 (D. Kan. 2003) (distinguishing *Gomez*; no evidence that nurse practitioner worked closely under doctor's supervision or had consulted with doctor during course of claimant's treatment).

SSA issued a Ruling in 2006 that sets out criteria for evaluating evidence from "other sources," including non-physician medical sources and lay witnesses. The Ruling draws on the criteria used to evaluate medical opinions from "acceptable medical sources" listed in 20 C.F.R. §§ 404.1527(d), 416.927(d): the nature and extent of the relationship between the claimant and the source; the quality of the source, including any relevant specialization; the extent to which the opinions are supported by relevant evidence; and whether the opinions are consistent with other evidence in the record. The Ruling makes explicit SSA policy that a strong non-physician medical source opinion, according to these criteria, can be given greater weight than a less-strong opinion from an "acceptable medical source." The Ruling also includes criteria for evaluating information from non-medical, non-professional sources, such as family members and friends; however, it does not provide that opinions from these sources can outweigh those of a medical source. SSR 06-03p (2006). In no event, however, can opinions of lay witnesses on medical matter be weighed according to the rules for medical sources. *See, e.g.*, Dewey v. Astrue, 509 F.3d 447, 125 Soc. Sec. Rep. Serv. 678 (8th Cir. 2007) (error for ALJ to weigh opinion of a lay person according to rules for weighing opinion of medical consultants).

In some instances, an ALJ may give less weight to a physician's statement than it would otherwise warrant because the claimant's attorney solicited the statement. As one court stated in the context of its practice of discounting specialized reports obtained by SSA, "[t]here is no reason to treat differently the opinion of a non-treating physician who has seen the patient only once, at the request of the patient or her lawyer." Henderson v. Sullivan, 930 F.2d 19, 21, 33 Soc. Sec. Rep. Serv. 142 (8th Cir. 1991).

The weight given to a particular medical report is affected not only by its source, but also by its quality. *See generally* **20 C.F.R. §§ 404.1527(d), 416.927(d) [APP-REGS]**. As the court noted in Wilson v. Commissioner, 378 F.3d 541, 544, 99 Soc. Sec. Rep. Serv. 11 (6th Cir. 2004), citing 20 C.F.R. §§ 404.1527(d)(2): "[i]f the opinion of a treating source is not accorded controlling weight, an ALJ must apply certain factors—namely, the length of the treatment relationship and the frequency of examination, the nature and extent of the treatment relationship, supportability of the opinion, consistency of the opinion with the record as a whole, and the specialization of the treating source—in determining what weight to give the opinion." The most persuasive reports are those that address specific limitations on the claimant's ability to work and are supported by particular medical findings and observations. On the other hand, so-called "conclusory" reports that simply state that the claimant is "totally disabled" or "unable to work" are entitled to little weight—regardless of the physician's credentials. *See, e.g.*, Bland v. Apfel, 201 F.3d 449 (Table), 1999 WL 1243120 (10th Cir. 1999) ("the record shows that the ALJ applied the correct standard in discounting Dr. Davis' conclusory opinion, unsupported by medical evidence, that plaintiff was totally disabled").

In appropriate cases, the medical opinions of specialists are entitled to greater weight than those of general practitioners. Thus, 20 C.F.R. §§ 404.1527(d)(5), 416.927(d)(5) provide that greater weight should be given "to the opinion of a specialist about medical issues related to his or her area of specialty than to the opinion of a source who is not a specialist." There is also some indication that board-certified physicians may be given more weight than non-board certified physicians. Reports of specialists or board certified physicians are entitled to special weight, however, only when there is a match between the physician's specialty or certification and the claimant's medical impairments. *See, e.g.*, Culbertson v. Barnhart, 214 F. Supp. 2d 788, 796, 83 Soc. Sec. Rep. Serv. 26 (N.D. Ohio 2002) ("Dr. Nelson is a board certified anesthesiologist; he is not certified in environment medicine or allergies. Thus, the ALJ could properly attribute much less weight to Dr. Nelson's opinions concerning Plaintiff's allergies or chemical sensitivities."). *See also* Sherrill v. Secretary, 757 F.2d 803, 805, 9 Soc. Sec. Rep. Serv. 130 (6th Cir. 1985) (opinion of an internist concerning claimant's psychiatric impairment not substantial evidence).

NOTE ON NON-EXAMINING PHYSICIANS

Medical consultants and medical advisors are both non-examining physicians (or psychologists), whose opinions may affect the outcome of Social Security disability determinations. As we have seen, the Supreme Court upheld the use of non-examining physicians in the face of a due process challenge in Richardson v. Perales, 402 U.S. 389, 408, 91 S. Ct. 1420, 1431, 28 L. Ed. 2d 842 (1971) ("[The medical advisor] is used primarily in complex cases for explanation of medical problems in terms understandable to the layman-examiner. He is a neutral adviser."). Some early cases interpreted the Court's decision in *Perales* narrowly, as authorizing the use of non-examining physicians only so long as their role was limited to explaining medical terms. Most courts, however, have read *Perales* as allowing the use of non-examining physicians generally, and have concentrated instead on what weight should be given to their opinions. Current regulations clarify that opinion evidence from non-examining state agency medical and psychological consultants and medical advisors should be considered in the same manner as opinions of other non-examining physicians and psychologists. *See* **20 C.F.R. §§404.1527(f), 416.927(f)[APP-REGS]**.

2. TREATING PHYSICIANS VS. CONSULTING PHYSICIANS

Courts have long held that opinions of treating physicians are entitled generally to greater weight than the opinions of consulting physicians. The usual reason for giving greater weight to the reports of treating physicians is that they have had more contact with the claimant, and are therefore able to make a more effective appraisal of their condition. *See, e.g.*, Bowman v. Heckler, 706 F.2d 564, 568 & n. 3, 2 Soc. Sec. Rep. Serv. 41 (5th Cir.1983) ("reliance on the opinion of the treating physician is based not only on the fact that he is employed to cure but also on his greater opportunity to observe and know the patient as an individual."); *see also* Murray v. Heckler, 722 F.2d 499, 501, 3 Soc. Sec. Rep. Serv. 288 (9th Cir. 1983). During the early and mid-1980s, however, SSA did not follow this practice and the issue of treating physician opinions came up regularly in the courts and in Congress. In 1984, as part of a broad-reaching set of policy directives aimed at regularizing the Social Security disability determination process, Congress amended the Social Security Act to require that the SSA "make every reasonable effort" to utilize reports from treating physicians in making disability determinations before relying on reports from outside consultants. *See* 42 U.S.C. §423(d)(5)(B). *See generally* Social Security Disability Benefits Reform Act of 1984, Pub. L. No. 98-460, 98 Stat. 1794.

Despite the action taken by Congress in the 1984 amendments, courts continued to announce rules for determining the weight to be given opinions of treating physicians. The Eighth, Tenth, and Eleventh Circuits followed similar rules giving substantial or considerable weight to evidence from treating physicians. *See* Frey v. Bowen, 816 F.2d 508, 513, 17 Soc. Sec. Rep. Serv. 417 (10th Cir. 1987); Turpin v. Bowen, 813 F.2d 165, 170, 17 Soc. Sec. Rep. Serv. 32 (8th Cir. 1987); Lamb v. Bowen, 847 F.2d 698, 703, 21 Soc. Sec. Rep. Serv. 581 (11th Cir. 1988). In a 1996 article, Rachel Schneider characterized other ways in which different circuits regarded the role of treating physicians:

> The circuit courts also assigned relative weight to the opinions of treating physicians depending on the circumstances. For example, in the Ninth Circuit, the treating physician's opinion constituted substantial evidence only if it rested on objective evidence; but if the treating physician's medical reports were brief, inconclusive, unsupported, or contradictory, they could be disregarded. Also, under the Ninth Circuit's rule, questions of credibility were deferred to the SSA. Still, when the ALJ was required to make findings explaining why the treating physician's opinion wase not followed.

> Courts have also considered the opinions given by non-treating physicians. Two other types of medical opinions, those from consultative examiners and those from medical consultants, may be requested by the SSA when it is evaluating a claim of disability. Therefore, when the SSA or courts define the treating physician rule, they must define the weight to be given to treating physician testimony relative to the testimony of these two other types of medical examiners, both of whom receive compensation from the SSA. * * *

In several circuits, including the Second, Sixth, Eight, and Tenth, the opinions of consultative examiners were given only "limited weight" and could not constitute the "substantial evidence" necessary to override the treating physician. The Tenth Circuit expressed outright suspicion of SSA-paid doctors, holding that "the reports of [treating] physicians . . . are given greater weight than are reports of physicians employed and paid by the government for the purpose of defending against a disability claim."

Rachel Schneider, *A Role for The Courts: Treating Physician Evidence in Social Security Disability Determinations*, 3 U. CHI. L. SCH. ROUNDTABLE 391, 397 (1996) (footnotes omitted).

The Second Circuit adopted a strongly deferential approach to the treating physician issue, as shown in the following opinion near the end of a series of decisions in a class action suit that also involved SSA's "non-acquiescence" to the court-ordered rule.

STIEBERGER V. BOWEN

801 F.2d 29, 15 Soc. Sec. Rep. Serv. 104 (2d Cir. 1986)

JON O. NEWMAN, Circuit Judge:

This appeal from the issuance of a preliminary injunction against the Secretary of Health and Human Services potentially raises far-reaching issues concerning the proper role of agencies and courts in the implementation of statutes. The issues arise in the context of adjudicating claims for disability benefits. The District Court for the Southern District of New York (Leonard B. Sand, Judge) ruled that the Secretary has violated and will violate the rights of a class of present and future claimants for disability benefits by failing to apply the law of this Circuit concerning the so-called "treating physician rule," the standard for assessing the significance of the medical testimony presented by a claimant's treating physician. The Court issued an injunction barring the Secretary from denying or terminating benefits under policies inconsistent with decisions of this Circuit and granting other relief to implement this prohibition. Stieberger v. Heckler, 615 F.Supp. 1315 (S.D.N.Y.1985). After the District Court's decision, another panel of this Court ordered a substantial but less far-reaching remedy on behalf of a class of disability claimants who had complained of the Secretary's failure to observe the treating physician rule. Schisler v. Heckler, 787 F.2d 76 (2d Cir.1986). For reasons that follow, we conclude that the Schisler remedy has removed, at least for now, the justification for the preliminary injunction issued in this case, and we therefore vacate the injunction.

BACKGROUND

* * *

The suit challenges two policies of the Secretary. The first concerns what the District Court concluded was the Secretary's *de facto* policy of non-acquiescence in the law of this Circuit concerning the treating physician rule. * * *

On the issue of non-acquiescence, the District Court initially noted that the treating physician rule has been clearly articulated in the decisions of this Circuit. In *Schisler* we summarized the rule as follows:

> The rule, which has been the law of this circuit for at least five years, provides that a treating physician's opinion on the subject of medical disability, i.e., diagnosis and nature and degree of impairment, is: (i) binding on the fact-finder unless contradicted by substantial evidence; and (ii) entitled to some extra weight because the treating physician is usually more familiar with a claimant's medical condition than are other physicians, although resolution of genuine conflicts between the opinion of the treating physician, with its extra weight, and any substantial evidence to the contrary remains the responsibility of the fact-finder.

787 F.2d at 81 (citations omitted). We also noted in *Schisler* that an additional element of the rule is "'that there is no requirement that the [treating] physician's medical testimony be supported by objective clinical or laboratory findings.'" *Id.* at 82 n. 2 (quoting Bluvband v. Heckler, 730 F.2d [886, 893 (2d Cir. 1984)].

The District Court then considered whether the Secretary was complying with the rule. The Court cited Social Security Ruling (SSR) 82-48c (1982), which provides that other things being equal, the fact that a physician treated a claimant will increase the weight accorded to that physician's opinion, but noted that this SSR does not mention that the treating physician's opinion is binding unless contradicted by substantial evidence. The Court also cited regulations suggesting that a treating physician's opinion must be supported by clinical or laboratory findings. Mention was also made of SSR 83-6c (1983), which adopted views expressed in Cummins v. Schweiker, 670 F.2d 81, 84 (7th Cir.1982), to the effect that a treating physician's views sometimes ought not to be given controlling weight because that physician "might have been leaning over backwards to support the application for disability benefits." Finally, the District Court placed major emphasis on decisions of this Court and of eighteen judges of the district courts within New York that have overturned denial or termination of disability benefits because of inadequate compliance or even disregard of the treating physician rule.

Based on these materials, Judge Sand concluded that "the preliminary showing here is virtually as strong a showing of *de facto* non-acquiescence as can be made." * * * That conclusion led the District Court squarely to face the legality of the non-acquiescence policy it was satisfied existed. * * *

The District Court noted that, prior to 1985, the Social Security Administration (SSA) had broadly asserted entitlement to disregard decisions of the courts of appeals as binding authority, except in the particular case in which a decision is rendered. * * * He concluded that the pre-1985 non-acquiescence policy of the Secretary was unlawful.

Turning to Circular 185, * * * Judge Sand recognized that the new policy represents some curtailment of the virtually unbridled non-acquiescence policy of the past. * * *

* * *

Judge Sand concluded that the new non-acquiescence policy, like its predecessor, was unlawful, even though it obviously represented some effort by SSA to promote adherence to circuit law while reserving the right to identify test cases appropriate for relitigation of circuit law with which the agency disagrees. * * *

Having concluded that the plaintiffs had shown a strong probability of success on the merits of their claim, the District Court then considered the propriety of injunctive relief. * * *

* * * The Court therefore issued the preliminary injunction challenged on this appeal.

The terms of the injunction are contained in paragraph 6 of the District Court's order, set forth as Appendix A to the Court's opinion. First, the Secretary and all his agents and employees are enjoined from denying or terminating disability benefits pursuant to policies that are inconsistent with decisions of the Second Circuit. Second, the defendants are directed to rescind, with respect to New York residents, all policies, including Interim Circular No. 185, that state a general policy of non-acquiescence or state a policy of nonacquiescence in any decision of the Second Circuit. Third, the defendants are directed to inform all agents and employees who adjudicate disability claims of all decisions of the Second Circuit that reverse decisions of the Secretary denying or terminating disability benefits and to furnish a copy of the court ruling with instructions that the ruling is to be followed. Fourth, the defendants are directed to inform all agents and employees who adjudicate disability claims that the Second Circuit's decision in *Bluvband v. Heckler, supra,* is to be followed and to furnish a copy of that decision and a copy of the District Court's phrasing of the requirements of the treating physician rule. The injunction thus imposes obligations in three categories: adjudication of claims, rescission of non-acquiescence policies, and distribution of information.

DISCUSSION

In challenging the District Court's preliminary injunction, the Secretary advances several contentions. Objection is raised to the basic approach of the injunction to the extent that it places adjudicators of disability claims at risk of contempt in the event the District Court concludes that they have denied benefits pursuant to policies inconsistent with Second Circuit case law. In addition, the Secretary contends that the injunction is not warranted because the accusation of non-acquiescence in the treating physician rule as announced in this Circuit is incorrect. Finally, the invalidation of the Secretary's general approach to non-acquiescence, as set forth in Interim Circular No. 185, is challenged as premature.

The District Court was not insensitive to the Secretary's concern that injunctive relief was inappropriate because it would place adjudicators of disability claims at risk of contempt. * * *

Thus, the District Court did not contemplate that an ALJ or any other adjudicator of a particular disability claim would risk contempt. Nevertheless, the terms of the Court's injunction understandably raise apprehensions among the defendants, and very likely among their employees and agents, that the risk of contempt will be present in the adjudication process. It is true that the injunction does not require benefits to be granted in any particular case. But the injunction does more with respect to the adjudication process than oblige the defendants to issue instructions to adjudicators. It specifically provides in paragraph 6a that all agents and employees of the defendants, which appears to mean members of the Appeals Council, all ALJs, and all state officials acting as agents of the Secretary in the initial processing of claims, are enjoined from denying or terminating benefits "pursuant to policies, procedures, rulings or regulations which are inconsistent with decisions of" the Second Circuit. 615 F.Supp. at 1400. Adjudicators will not be comforted by the District Court's assurance that they do not face contempt proceedings if they are found only to have misapplied a correct legal standard to the facts of a particular case. As the treating physician rule cases of this Court and the district courts demonstrate, courts frequently cannot tell whether the adjudicator has ignored the treating physician rule and implicitly applied some more restrictive policy of the Secretary's, or have "simply" misapplied the correct legal standard. ALJs and other adjudicators could clarify matters considerably if they would indicate in their opinions that they recognize the binding authority of the treating physician rule and that they are endeavoring to apply it to the facts of the cases before them. Courts could then readily distinguish between disregard of the rule and its mere misapplication. Unfortunately, we have already seen too many cases where ALJs make no mention of the treating physician rule and give no adequate indication that they are applying it. If such cases were to recur with the injunction in effect, there would be the distinct possibility that an adjudicator would face contempt for non-compliance with the injunction, even though his denial of benefits might have resulted only from misapplication of the correct standard. Even if actual contempt proceedings would be rare, confined to adjudicators whose disregard of relevant law was established by a pattern of non-complying decisions, all adjudicators would apprehend some risk that even their good-faith efforts to apply the correct standard would be retrospectively found to be a denial of benefits pursuant to policies inconsistent with relevant law.

* * *

The Secretary's more specific objection to the injunction is that it is not needed because in fact SSA complies with the treating physician rule. The Secretary represents that his policy is "essentially the same" as the requirements of our case law. Those instances where denials of benefits have been reversed for lack of compliance with the treating physician rule are said to be "only a tiny fraction of the thousands of disability claims in New York every year" and an inadequate basis from which to conclude that there has been a policy of non-acquiescence in the rule. Though we have characterized the quantity of such cases as "almost legion," there is some force to the Secretary's argument that many of the reversals involve a misapplication of the rule rather than an outright ignoring of it, and that even the few cases where we have said the rule was ignored do not necessarily demonstrate a policy of non-acquiescence. As the Secretary points out, published opinions of this Court and the district courts tend to occur where error is noticed. A pattern of disregard of the treating physician rule, sufficient to show a policy of non-acquiescence, would be more solidly demonstrated if the rule were shown to have been ignored in a significant fraction of a random sample of cases at the ALJ level involving the opinion of a treating physician. At the same time, it is worth pointing out that the Secretary's claim of compliance with the treating physician rule would be more persuasive if supported by an SSA survey of ALJ decisions in this area. Having failed to undertake such a survey to demonstrate its alleged compliance in the face of repeated judicial criticisms, the agency does not cover itself with glory by cavalierly dismissing the District Court's conclusion of non-acquiescence as "absurd."

* * *

As we indicated at the outset, the context in which all of the Secretary's objections to the injunction arise has been significantly altered by our decision in *Schisler v. Heckler*, supra, rendered on April 2, 1986, several months after Judge Sand issued the injunction. * * *

The injunction ordered in *Schisler* substantially reduces the need for the preliminary injunction issued by Judge Sand in the pending case. Under the supervision of Judge Elfvin in the Western District of New York, the Secretary is now obliged to formulate and issue instructions to all adjudicators, state and federal, concerning the content of the treating physician rule and the requirement of its use.[5] This remedy, when implemented, should accomplish what Judge Sand sought to accomplish in paragraph 6d of his injunction. * * *

Our decision to vacate the preliminary injunction does not, however, preclude the possibility that some form of injunctive relief may be warranted when the merits of the plaintiffs' claims have been adjudicated. * * * Any indication that the Secretary is not proceeding expeditiously to issue adequate instructions about the treating physician rule to all adjudicators will provide substantial basis for the formulation of appropriate injunctive relief at the conclusion of the pending litigation before Judge Sand. * * * Whether or not any permanent injunction should be issued will depend on what the record discloses when finally concluded.

For all of the foregoing reasons, the preliminary injunction is vacated.

3. TREATING PHYSICIAN RULES IN PRACTICE

Rules concerning the proper weight given to opinions of treating physicians remained controversial until the early 1990s, when the Social Security Administration issued regulations, as required by Congress, to establishing standards for evaluating medical opinions. According to these regulations, the Administration gives "controlling" weight to a treating physician's opinion concerning the nature and severity of a claimant's medical condition, if the opinion "is well-supported by medically acceptable clinical and laboratory diagnostic techniques and is not inconsistent with the other substantial evidence in [the] case record." *See* 20 C.F.R. §§

---

[5] The formulation of the treating physician rule that we ordered transmitted to state and federal adjudicators deliberately omitted the component, enunciated in *Bluvband v. Heckler*, *supra*, 730 F.2d at 893, "that there is no requirement that the physician's medical testimony be supported by objective clinical or laboratory findings" (citations omitted). This component was omitted because of the Secretary's contention in the pending litigation that section 3(a)(1) of the Reform Act, 42 U.S.C. § 423(d)(5)(A) Supp. II 1984), had changed the rules for evaluating a claimant's subjective symptoms. *See Schisler v. Heckler*, *supra*, 787 F.2d at 81-82 n. 2. Since we are vacating the preliminary injunction issued in the pending case, we do not decide at this stage of the litigation the bearing, if any, of the Reform Act on the above quoted statement from *Bluvband*.

404.1527(d)(2), 416.927(d)(2). If SSA does not give controlling weight to a treating physician's opinion, it must provide a good reason for making this decision and must accord the opinion the weight given to any other medical opinion. The regulations also established that medical assessments are part of the evidentiary record, but are not necessarily dispositive of a finding of disability.

Although the current regulations were promulgated to streamline the varying approaches being taken by the circuit courts, only the Second Circuit has explicitly acknowledged and responded to the regulations. The regulations were challenged in the Second Circuit on the ground that they accorded less deference to the opinions of treating physicians than required by the Second Circuit's rule in the cases described in *Stieberger v. Bowen*, and therefore should not be binding in that circuit. The court disagreed, finding that although the new regulations differed in some respects from its rule, they were consistent with the Social Security Act and therefore within the Social Security Administration's rule making authority; "[b]ecause the regulations are valid, they are binding on the Courts." *See* Schisler v. Sullivan, 3 F.3d 563, 568, 42 Soc. Sec. Rep. Serv. 184 (2d Cir. 1993). Overall, the regulations have supplanted prior court-established rules. See, e.g., Castellano v Secretary, 26 F.3d 1027, 1029, 44 Soc. Sec. Rep. Serv. 561 (10th Cir. 1994); Nelson v Sullivan, 966 F.2d 363, 367-68, 37 Soc. Sec. Rep. Serv. 489 (8th Cir. 1992); Matney v Sullivan, 981 F.2d 1016, 1019, 39 Soc. Sec. Rep. Serv. 588 (9th Cir. 1992). *See generally* Rachel Schneider, *A Role for The Courts: Treating Physician Evidence in Social Security Disability Determinations, supra,* at 402 ("The other circuits have either claimed that the 1991 regulations codified their circuit's law or have continued to follow their pre-1991 precedent, implying that they perceive no change in their circuit's law based on the regulations.").

The treating physician rule remains an important element in the assessment of medical evidence in contested cases. The force of the rule is modified significantly, however, by the fact that greater weight is not given to the opinions of treating physicians without considering the quality of their reports. Thus, a treating physician's conclusory opinion may be discounted in favor of a contrary opinion from a non-treating physician, and even a consulting physician. Similarly, form reports with check-boxes that are unaccompanied by more-detailed supporting information are not accorded much weight, even if completed by a treating physician.

ROSA V. ASTRUE

708 F. Supp. 2d 941 (E.D. Mo. 2010)

MARY ANN L. MEDLER, United States Magistrate Judge.

This is an action under Title 42 U.S.C. § 405(g) for judicial review of the final decision of Michael J. Astrue, the Commissioner of Social Security ("Defendant") denying the applications for Social Security benefits under Title II of the Social Security Act, 42 U.S.C. §§ 401 *et seq.*, and Supplemental Security Income ("SSI") under Title XVI of the Act, 42 U.S.C. §§ 1381 *et seq.*, filed by Plaintiff Kimberly J. Rosa ("Plaintiff"). * * *

I.

PROCEDURAL HISTORY

Plaintiff filed applications for benefits on June 26, 2007, alleging a disability onset date of October 1, 2006. Plaintiff's applications were denied, and she filed a request for a hearing before an administrative law judge ("ALJ"). On September 4, 2008, a hearing was held before an ALJ, who issued an decision denying Plaintiff's applications on November 7, 2008. Plaintiff filed a Request for Review with the Appeals Council, which the Appeals Council denied. As such, the decision of the ALJ stands as the final decision of the Commissioner.

* * *

III.

DISCUSSION

The issue before the court is whether substantial evidence supports the Commissioner's final determination that Plaintiff was not disabled. Thus, even if there is substantial evidence that would support a decision opposite to that of the Commissioner, the court must affirm his decision as long as there is substantial evidence in favor of the Commissioner's position.

The ALJ in the matter under consideration first noted that Plaintiff claimed she had severe impairments of headaches, stomach problems, degenerative disc disease, depression, anxiety, and a growth on her ovaries which affected her health. The ALJ found that Plaintiff's only severe impairment is degenerative disc disease; that she does not have an impairment which meets or medically equals one of the listed impairments in 20 C.F.R. Part 404, Subpart P, Appendix 1; that she can perform the full range of sedentary work; that her past relevant work as an office assistant in a real estate office does not require the performance of work-related activities precluded by her RFC; and that, therefore, Plaintiff is not disabled. Plaintiff contends that the ALJ's decision is not supported by substantial evidence because the ALJ failed to give proper weight to the opinion of Plaintiff's treating doctor, Tonya Little, M.D., regarding Plaintiff's residual functional capacity ("RFC"); because the ALJ failed to obtain the testimony from a vocational expert ("VE"); and because the ALJ failed to properly consider Plaintiff's pain.

A. The Opinion of Plaintiff's Treating Doctor:

Plaintiff contends that the ALJ did not give proper weight Dr. Little's opinion, stated in a Medical Assessment Disability Claim Form (the "Form"), completed on August 27, 2008, that Plaintiff needs to be able to change positions every ten to fifteen minutes; that she cannot lift more than ten pounds; that she cannot push, pull, stoop, squat, or bend repetitively; and that Plaintiff's pain frequently interferes with her attention and concentration. Additionally, Dr. Little reported in the Form that Plaintiff has chronic back pain from degenerative disc disease of the lumbar spine, frequent neck pain and migraines from degenerative disc disease of the cervical spine, and weakness of the right quadriceps and hamstring due to atrophy; that Plaintiff's subjective complaints were reasonably consistent with the objective findings; that Plaintiff cannot perform sedentary work because she needs to be able to change positions every ten to fifteen minutes, cannot lift more than ten pounds, and cannot push, pull, stoop, squat, or bend repetitively; and that Plaintiff's "pain levels become debilitating if she does any of the above activities [more than] 2 hrs daily on a repetitive basis."

"It is the ALJ's function to resolve conflicts among the various treating and examining physicians." *Estes v. Barnhart*, 275 F.3d 722, 725 (8th Cir.2002) (internal quotation marks omitted). The opinions and findings of the plaintiff's treating physician are entitled to "controlling weight" if that opinion is "'well-supported by medically acceptable clinical and laboratory diagnostic techniques and is not inconsistent with the other substantial evidence in [the] record.'" *Prosch v. Apfel*, 201 F.3d 1010, 1012-13 (8th Cir.2000) (quoting 20 C.F.R. § 404.1527(d)(2)(2000)). Indeed, if they are not controverted by substantial medical or other evidence, they are binding. However, while the opinion of the treating physician should be given great weight, this is true only if the treating physician's opinion is based on sufficient medical data. Although a treating physician's opinion is entitled to great weight, it does not automatically control or obviate the need to evaluate the record as a whole." Hogan v. Apfel, 239 F.3d 958, 961 (8th Cir.2001).

Where diagnoses of treating doctors are not supported by medically acceptable clinical and laboratory diagnostic techniques, the court need not accord such diagnoses great weight. An ALJ may "discount or even disregard the opinion of a treating physician where other medical assessments are supported by better or more thorough medical evidence, or where a treating physician renders inconsistent opinions that undermine the credibility of such opinions." *Prosch*, 201 F.3d at 1013. *See also Cox v.*

Barnhart, 471 F.3d 902, 907 (8th Cir.2006) (holding that an ALJ may give a treating doctor's opinion limited weight if it is inconsistent with the record).

A treating physician's checkmarks on a form are conclusory opinions which can be discounted if contradicted by other objective medical evidence. A treating physician's opinion that a claimant is not able to return to work "involves an issue reserved for the Commissioner and therefore is not the type of 'medical opinion' to which the Commissioner gives controlling weight." *Ellis v. Barnhart*, 392 F.3d 988, 994 (8th Cir.2005). Moreover, a brief, conclusory letter from a treating physician stating that the applicant is disabled is not binding on the Secretary. *Ward v. Heckler*, 786 F.2d 844, 846 (8th Cir.1986) (per curiam) ("Even statements made by a claimant's treating physician regarding the existence of a disability have been held to be properly discounted in favor of the contrary medical opinion of a consulting physician where the treating physician's statements were conclusory in nature."). On the other hand, a treating physician's observations should not necessarily be treated as conclusory where the doctor had "numerous examinations and hospital visits" with a claimant. *See Turpin v. Bowen*, 813 F.2d 165, 171 (8th Cir.1987).

Additionally, SSR 96-2p states, in its "Explanation of Terms," that it "is an error to give an opinion controlling weight simply because it is the opinion of a treating source if it is not well-supported by medically acceptable clinical and laboratory diagnostic techniques or if it is inconsistent with other substantial evidence in the case record." Additionally, SSR 96-2p clarifies that 20 C.F.R. §§ 404.1527 and 416.927 require that the ALJ provide "good reasons in the notice of the determination or decision for the weight given to a treating source's medical opinion(s)."

When considering the weight to be given the opinion of a treating doctor, the entire record must be evaluated as a whole. "'It is the ALJ's function to resolve conflicts among the various treating and examining physicians.'" *Tindell v. Barnhart*, 444 F.3d 1002, 1004 (8th Cir.2006) (quoting *Vandenboom v. Barnhart*, 421 F.3d 745, 749-50 (8th Cir.2005) (internal marks omitted)). An ALJ is entitled to give less weight to the opinion of a treating doctor where the doctor's opinion is based largely on the plaintiff's subjective complaints rather than on objective medical evidence.

"Generally, the longer a treating source has treated [a claimant] and the more times [the claimant has] been seen by a treating source, the more weight [the Commissioner] will give to the source's medical opinion." 20 C.F.R. §§ 404.1527(d)(2)(i) & 416.927(d)(2)(i). See also *Randolph v. Barnhart*, 386 F.3d 835, 840 (8th Cir.2004) (holding that a doctor's opinion stated in a checklist should not have been given controlling weight because the doctor had met with the plaintiff only three times at the time he completed the form).

In Plaintiff's case, as stated above, after considering Plaintiff's allegations, the ALJ found that the only severe impairment which Plaintiff has is degenerative disc disease and that Plaintiff has the RFC to perform the full range of sedentary work. Upon not giving controlling weight to Dr. Little's opinion as stated on the Form, the ALJ considered the objective medical evidence, including Dr. Little's own treatment notes. In particular, the ALJ considered that an electrodiagnostic study of the lower extremities and spine performed on January 20, 2006, showed no evidence of motor neuropathy or radiculopathy, and that on January 31, 2006, it was reported that Plaintiff had normal gait and station. The ALJ further considered that it was reported on March 6, 2006, that Plaintiff's neck was supple. The court notes that on January 31 and March 6, 2006, upon Plaintiff's receiving injections of facet joints to treat back pain, it was reported that Plaintiff had "[n]early 80-90% reduction to SI joint symptomology with improvement in gait, reduction in compression pain, and SI side to side mobility improved."

The ALJ considered that Plaintiff saw Dr. Little on May 22, 2006, at which time Plaintiff had "some swelling in her back" and that Dr. Little reported on this date that Plaintiff's *spine had "no tenderness"*; that she had limited range of motion in her back and extremities due to pain; and that she had *normal sensation*. The ALJ further considered a May 30, 2006 MRI report stating that *"mild spondylitic changes effect the C5 interspace without focal disc herniation or recess stenosis."* The court notes that this MRI report also states that the exam showed *"no evidence of foraminal narrowing through out the cervical column."* The ALJ also considered that a May 30, 2006 MRI report states that studies of the lumbar spine revealed flattening of the normal concave disc at L4. Tr. 20. The court notes that the MRI report regarding the lumbar spine examination states that the *"epidural spaces [were] preserved"* and that the "S 1 nerve roots [were] of equal size and signal with the thecal sac midline."

The ALJ also considered that Charles A. Wetherington, M.D., of the Microsurgery and Brain Research Institute, examined Plaintiff on June 6, 2006, and that Dr. Wetherington reported that Plaintiff "appeared to be in *good physical condition;* " that her *strength was 5/5*; that she had *intact sensation* and *negative straight leg raising* tests; that she had some midline lumbosacral tenderness with palpation of the lumbar spine; and that she had more significant tenderness with palpation over the SI joints. The court notes that Dr. Wetherington also reported that Plaintiff complained of neck pain with numbness and tingling in both arms and hands and pain in the thoracic and lumbar spine; that review of Plaintiff's *MRIs "reveal[ed] some very mild degenerative changes* at C5-6" and "some *very mild degenerative changes* at L5-S 1 with *no thecal sac and neural foraminal narrowing and compression;* " and that Dr. Wetherington reported that he did not "feel [Plaintiff] has a surgical lesion and surgical intervention would not offer relief."

[The court then reviewed reports of two other physicians who had examined the claimant that were inconsistent with Dr. Little's report, as well as additional notes written by Dr. Little after examining the claimant several times. The court also reviewed the ALJ's references to various notes and reports, noting the ALJ "discredited Dr. Little's opinion and found that [the claimant] could perform the full range of sedentary work."]

Upon discrediting Dr. Little's opinion that Plaintiff cannot perform sedentary work, consistent with the Regulations and case law, the ALJ considered the record as a whole. See Further, the ALJ resolved the conflicts between Dr. Little's opinion and the reports and records of other doctors of record. In any case, the ALJ was not bound by Dr. Little's conclusory statement that Plaintiff is unable to do even sedentary work as the ALJ identified good reasons for not accepting Dr. Little's conclusion. To the extent that Plaintiff argues that the ALJ engaged in "medical conjecture" upon discrediting Dr. Little opinion, the court finds that because the ALJ identified his reasons for doing so and because his decision in this regard is supported by substantial evidence on the record, it is apparent that the ALJ did not engage in medical conjecture. Although Plaintiff argues that, upon discrediting Dr. Little's opinion, the ALJ should not have considered medical evidence prior to Plaintiff's alleged onset date, an ALJ is "entitled to consider all of the evidence of record." *Vandenboom v. Barnhart*, 421 F.3d 745, 750 (8th Cir.2005). Moreover, "there is no valid reason to exclude consideration of medical records dated prior to [Plaintiff's] alleged date of onset." Id. The court finds, therefore, that the decision of the ALJ not to give controlling weight to the opinion of Dr. Little is supported by substantial evidence on the record as a whole and that the ALJ's decision in this regard is consistent with the case law and Regulations. Additionally, the court finds that the ALJ's finding that Plaintiff has the RFC to engage in the full range of sedentary work is supported by substantial evidence on the record.

[The court concluded that the testimony of a vocational expert was not needed and that the ALJ's findings that the claimant could perform her past relevant work was based on substantial evidence, as was the ALJ's conclusion that her allegations of pain were not credible. Accordingly, the Commissioner's decision was affirmed.]

F. VOCATIONAL EXPERTS

Vocational experts can play an important role in Social Security disability cases because a claimant's ability to engage in substantial gainful activity—the level of severity required by the statutory disability standard—must be evaluated by taking into account, in addition to any physical or mental impairments, the claimant's age, education, and prior work experience. Because this type of vocational evidence is considered at only three steps of the five-step sequential evaluation process and the vocational issues involved at two of those steps are quite narrow (Step 1, limited to current employment, and Step 4, limited to past relevant work), the use of vocational experts is concentrated at Step 5 adjudications.

ALJs often call vocational experts to testify at hearings—particularly where SSA denied the claim before reaching Step 5 and the vocational evidence was not well developed at the DDS. Vocational expert participation is relatively common at administrative hearings because by the time a case gets to the administrative hearing level a significant percentage involve the more difficult vocational issues. Yet even at Step 5, vocational expertise is not needed for every claim. While a vocational expert may be used to provide evidence as to where a claimant falls within a particular "grid" in SSA's Medical-Vocational Guidelines, vocational expertise is most useful for claims where the grids cannot be used and specific evidence is required as to whether the claimant—given his or her age, education, and prior work experience—can perform any jobs in the national economy. As we saw in Chapter 5, those types of Step 5 determinations typically require proof of a claimant's ability to perform specified jobs and vocational experts are uniquely qualified to provide that proof. Claimants can also use a vocational expert to support their case, either with a written report or through live testimony at a hearing.

Typically, vocational expert testimony is solicited by means of hypothetical questions. The hypothetical must include all limitations supported by the record, including the side effects of medication. It is also important that the role of a vocational expert not be confused with that of a medical expert. A vocational expert's conclusion, even though it may encompass both medical and vocational judgments, must be based on competent underlying medical evidence.

NALLEY V. APFEL

100 F. Supp. 2d 947, 70 Soc. Sec. Rep. Serv. 77 (S.D. Iowa 2000)

PRATT, District Judge.

Plaintiff, Kenneteh L. Nalley, Jr., filed a Complaint in this Court on February 16, 1999, seeking review of the Commissioner's decision to deny his claim for Social Security benefits under Title II and Title XVI of the

Social Security Act. This Court may review a final decision by the Commissioner. For the reasons set out herein, the decision of the Commissioner is reversed.

* * *

DISCUSSION

* * *

In the case *sub judice*, the ALJ found that Plaintiff is unable to do any of his past relevant work. The burden of proof, therefore, was shifted from Plaintiff to the Commissioner to prove with medical evidence that Plaintiff has a residual functional capacity to do other kinds of work, and that other work exists in significant numbers that Plaintiff can perform.

In the case at bar, the medical evidence establishes that Plaintiff suffered a severe head injury when he was beaten with a baseball bat by his ex-brother-in-law. The evidence establishes that this injury left him blind in one eye and deaf in one ear. We know from the medical evidence that in October of 1995, a few days after an object fell on his chest and pushed him backwards, Plaintiff lost feeling in his legs and has been confined to a wheelchair ever since. The medical evidence also tells us that Plaintiff has a history of a seizure disorder. * * *

In addition to the aforementioned, we also know from the medical evidence that the side effects of Plaintiff's medication cause drowsiness, nausea, and an inability to concentrate. When the side effects of the medication were presented to the vocational expert on cross examination, he testified that competitive work would not be possible.

In order to constitute substantial evidence upon which to base a denial of benefits, a vocational expert testimony must be in response to a hypothetical question which captures the concrete consequences of the claimants severe impairments. A hypothetical question must include the side effects of medication if, as here, such is supported by the medical evidence in the record. The side effects of Plaintiff's medication were clearly established by Dr. Friday. The ALJ's hypothetical was defective because it did not include consideration of the side effects of Plaintiff's medication. In addition to the side effects of medication, the ALJ also neglected to mention Plaintiff's inability to see in his right eye, hear in his right ear, or the occasional slurring of speech diagnosed by Dr. Fritsch. The failure to mention these limitations renders the ALJ's hypothetical defective. The response thereto, therefore, does not constitute substantial evidence supporting the ALJ's decision.

The ALJ's hypothetical is defective in another respect. The ALJ asked the vocational expert to consider the effect of Plaintiff's carpal tunnel syndrome and rotator cuff injury, based upon the ALJ's observation of Plaintiff adjusting the arm of his wheelchair and Plaintiff removing a boot from his foot. In the first place, the impairments were established by medial evidence. In the second place, neither the ALJ nor the vocational expert are medical experts. It is error for an ALJ to ask a vocational expert to interpret the medical evidence or to base testimony on the expert's own observations. Baugus v. Secretary of Health & Human Services, 717 F.2d 443, 447 (8th Cir.1983) (A vocational expert cannot be expected to assume the evidence and testimony and then state an opinion as to whether a claimant has residual skills that can be transferred to other occupations. The result of such a procedure is to require vocational experts to make credibility findings, weigh and balance conflicting evidence, and interpret often complicated medical documents and testimony.) Finally, as Judge Heaney wrote in Lanning v. Heckler, 777 F.2d 1316 (8th Cir.1985): "This Court and the United States Department of Justice have agreed that the ALJ may not reject a claimant's subjective complaints solely on the basis of personal observations."

In the case at Bar, the Commissioner did not meet his burden of proving either that Plaintiff has the residual functional capacity to work or that jobs exist that he is able to do in his impaired condition. In Gavin v. Heckler, 811 F.2d 1195, 1201 (8th Cir.1987), the Court held that where the medical evidence in the record overwhelmingly supports a finding of disability, remand is unnecessary. The vocational expert testified that the side effects of Plaintiff's medication render competitive work impossible. As in *Gavin*, a remand in this case would be a "futile gesture" which would serve only to delay the receipt of benefits to which Plaintiff is clearly entitled. An order to award benefits, therefore, is hereby entered.

1. USE OF THE DICTIONARY OF OCCUPATIONAL TITLES (DOT)

Over the years, courts have adopted different approaches when a vocational expert's opinion conflicted with the US Department of Labor's Dictionary of Occupational Titles (DOT). The problem stems in large part from the fact that the DOT has not been updated in many years and is no longer current. SSA is considering the creation and publication of its own "occupational information system" (OIS) designed specifically for use in the administration of its disability programs. That project is being run by SSA's Occupational Information Development Advisory Panel (OIDAP) established under the Federal Advisory Committee Act.

Some courts have held that when there is a conflict between the testimony of a vocational expert and the DOT, the DOT controls. Others have held that the expert's testimony "trumps" the DOT. More recently, courts have tended to follow a middle ground position allowing adjudicators to rely on a vocational expert's testimony in conflict with the DOT if the record reflects a substantial reason for deviating from the DOT. *See, e.g.,* Carey v. Apfel, 230 F.3d 131, 146, 71 Soc. Sec. Rep. Serv. 393 (5th Cir. 2000) ("To the extent that there is any implied or indirect conflict between the vocational expert's testimony and the DOT in this case, we agree with the majority of the circuits that the ALJ may rely upon the vocational expert's testimony provided that the record reflects an adequate basis for doing so.").

In the meantime, SSA issued a Ruling on this issue in late 2000. The Ruling provides that "[w]hen there is an apparent unresolved conflict between [vocational expert or vocational specialist] evidence and the DOT, the adjudicator must elicit a reasonable explanation for the conflict before relying on the [vocational expert or vocational specialist] evidence to support a determination or decision about whether the claimant is disabled." SSR 00-4p (2000). The Ruling also states explicitly that "[n]either the DOT nor the [vocational expert or vocational specialist] evidence automatically 'trumps' when there is a conflict. The adjudicator must resolve the conflict by determining if the explanation given by the [vocational expert or vocational specialist] is reasonable and provides a basis for relying on the [vocational expert or vocational specialist] testimony rather than on the DOT information." *Id.*

HACKETT V. BARNHART

395 F.3d 1168, 102 Soc. Sec. Rep. Serv. 252 (10th Cir. 2005)

Before HARTZ, and BALDOCK, Circuit Judges, and BRIMMER, District Judge.

HARTZ, Circuit Judge.

[The claimant, a 31-year-old college graduate with a variety of work experience, including as a checker/cashier, an occupational therapist, and a wedding coordinator, sought disability benefits due to various musculoskeletal impairments, depression, and migraines. On the question of her disability, the court agreed that she could not perform her past relevant work and that the case should be decided at Step 5 of the sequential evaluation process. In this appeal, she argued three grounds for reversal of SSA's decision to deny her claim: (1) the Appeals Council did not properly take into account a decision in her Colorado workers' compensation case; (2) the ALJ failed to support the finding that her testimony was not credible and did not give proper weight to her treating physicians' opinions; and (3) the ALJ misstated the vocational expert's testimony and failed to reconcile a conflict between that VE's testimony and the DOT. The court ruled for SSA on all grounds, except the ALJ's failure to reconcile the conflict between the VE's testimony and the DOT.]

* * *

Plaintiff's final contention is that the ALJ misstated the testimony of the VE and failed to reconcile the VE's actual testimony with the Dictionary of Occupational Titles (DOT), contrary to this court's decision in Haddock v. Apfel, 196 F.3d 1084 (10th Cir.1999), and Social Security Ruling 00-4p.

Haddock held that "before an ALJ may rely on expert vocational evidence as substantial evidence to support a determination of nondisability, the ALJ must ask the expert how his or her testimony as to the exertional requirement of identified jobs corresponds with the Dictionary of Occupational Titles, and elicit a reasonable explanation for any discrepancy on this point." *Id.* at 1087. Although this holding may seem to be limited to only discrepancies with respect to exertional limitations, *Haddock* itself addressed both exertional and skill-level limitations that conflicted with the DOT. Thus, whether the ALJ fulfilled his duties regarding any conflict between the DOT job descriptions and Plaintiff's nonexertional limitations is also controlled by *Haddock*. Likewise, Social Security Ruling 00-4p, which essentially codifies *Haddock*, requires a reasonable explanation for conflicts between a VE's testimony and the DOT relating to any "occupational information."

In his decision the ALJ said that the VE had admitted at the hearing that his opinions about the jobs Plaintiff could do did not directly correspond with information in the DOT. The ALJ then asserted that the VE explained this discrepancy by relying on his own "education, experience and observations of the jobs as actually performed in the economy." As Plaintiff and the district court have pointed out, however, there is no indication in the record that the VE expressly acknowledged a conflict with the DOT or that he offered any explanation for the conflict. The district court nevertheless ruled that the ALJ's assertion about the VE's explanation was unnecessary because there was no conflict between the VE's testimony and the DOT. We agree with respect to the "people" function of the designated jobs, but disagree with respect to the required reasoning level.

A. "PEOPLE" FUNCTION

Plaintiff contends that the jobs identified by the VE are not available to her because her RFC limits her to jobs that accommodate her need to "avoid direct contact with the general public and have only occasional interaction with coworkers," whereas these jobs are defined in the DOT as requiring significant work with people. We disagree.

Each job listed in the DOT is described by reference to various components. One component is "Worker Functions." The worker function labeled "People" expresses the degree of interaction with other people that the job requires. Both jobs identified for Plaintiff—call-out operator and surveillance-system monitor—have a people rating of 6, which means that they require "[t]alking with and/or signaling people to convey or exchange information [and] giving assignments and/or directions to helpers or assistants." DOT, Vol. II at 1006. The job descriptions for these two positions, however, indicate that contact with people is rather limited. The DOT description for call-out operator states:

> Compiles credit information, such as status of credit accounts, personal references, and bank accounts to fulfill subscribers' requests, using telephone. Copies information onto form to update information for credit record on file, or for computer input. Telephones subscriber to relay requested information or submits data obtained for typewritten report to subscriber.

DOT, Vol. I, 237.367-014 at 207. The description for surveillance-system monitor states:

> Monitors premises of public transportation terminals to detect crimes or disturbances, using closed circuit television monitors, and notifies authorities by telephone of need for corrective action: Observes television screens that transmit in sequence views of transportation facility sites. Pushes hold button to maintain surveillance of location where incident is developing, and telephones police or other designated agency to notify authorities of location of disruptive activity. Adjusts monitor controls when required to improve reception, and notifies repair service of equipment malfunctions.

Id. 379.367-010 at 281.

The ALJ expressly informed the VE that Plaintiff would be restricted to "no direct public contact." Yet the VE stated the two above jobs would be suitable, saying: "[The] jobs ... are fairly solitary jobs. The call-out operator being indirect contact via telephone." We see no conflict between the DOT and this testimony. Nor do we see any conflict between the DOT descriptions of the designated jobs and Plaintiff's restriction to only occasional interaction with co-workers.

B. REASONING LEVEL

The DOT states that both surveillance-system monitor and call-out operator require a reasoning level of three, defined as the ability to "[a]pply commonsense understanding to carry out instructions furnished in written, oral, or diagrammatic form[, and d]eal with problems involving several concrete variables in or from standardized situations." DOT, Vol. II at 1011; *see id.*, Vol. I at 281 (categorizing surveillance-system monitor as requiring level-three reasoning); *id.* at 207 (same with regard to call-out operator).

Plaintiff argues that her RFC, as found by the ALJ, is incompatible with jobs requiring a reasoning level of three. The ALJ's findings with regard to Plaintiff's RFC include: "Mentally, [Plaintiff] retains the attention, concentration, persistence and pace levels required for simple and routine work tasks." This limitation seems inconsistent with the demands of level-three reasoning. *See* Lucy v. Chater, 113 F.3d 905, 909 (8th Cir.1997) (rejecting contention that a claimant limited to following only simple instructions could engage in the full range of sedentary work because many unskilled jobs in that category require reasoning levels of two or higher). We note that level-two reasoning requires the worker to "[a]pply commonsense understanding to carry out detailed but uninvolved written or oral instructions [and d]eal with problems involving a few concrete variables in or from standardized situations." DOT, Vol. II at 1011. This level-two reasoning appears more consistent with Plaintiff's RFC.

We therefore must reverse this portion of the ALJ's decision and remand to allow the ALJ to address the apparent conflict between Plaintiff's inability to perform more than simple and repetitive tasks and the level-three reasoning required by the jobs identified as appropriate for her by the VE. * * *

* * *

G. CREDIBILITY OF CLAIMANTS AND LAY WITNESSES

Information from claimants and lay witnesses can be important at any stage in the administrative process. As we saw earlier, statements by claimants and their witnesses are among the types of evidence of disability specifically recognized by federal regulations. *See* **20 C.F.R. §§ 404.1512, 416.912[APP-REGS]** (defining "evidence" to include statements by claimants and others about the claimant's impairments, restrictions, daily activities, efforts to work, and "any other relevant statements [claimants] make to medical sources during the course of examination or treatment, or to us during interviews, on applications, in letters, and in testimony in our administrative proceedings."). Claimants and their witnesses must, of course, be credible and claimants'—and their witnesses'—credibility is particularly important at the administrative hearing because it is the only point in the administrative process, except for reconsideration disability hearings when benefits are terminated on the basis of nondisability, that the decision maker meets face-to-face with claimants and witnesses. An ALJ's assessment of claimant and witness credibility can be a critical factor in determining disability and other factual matter relevant to a claim for Social Security benefits.

As discussed in Chapter 6, there are special rules on proving disability based on pain and other subjective symptoms. Thus, ALJs must take into account, in addition to expert medical and vocational evidence, "subjective evidence of pain and disability as testified to by the claimant and corroborated by ... others who have observed him." DePaepe v. Richardson, 464 F.2d 92, 94 (5th Cir. 1972). *See also* Murphy v. Sullivan, 953 F.2d 383, 385, 36 Soc. Sec. Rep. Serv. 117 (8th Cir. 1992). As set out in SSR 96-7p (1996), which addresses assessing the credibility of an individual's statements about pain and other subjective symptoms:

> It is not sufficient for the adjudicator to make a single, conclusory statement that "the individual's allegations have been considered" or that "the allegations are (or are not) credible." It is also not enough for the adjudicator simply to recite the factors that are described in the regulations for evaluating symptoms. The determination or decision must contain specific reasons for the finding on credibility, supported by the evidence in the case record, and must be sufficiently specific to make clear to the individual and to any subsequent reviewers the weight the adjudicator gave to the individual's statements and the reasons for that weight.

Claimants and lay witnesses can also testify more generally about how the impairment affects a claimant's ability to work and about a wide range of other non-expert matters.

One of the most common challenges to administrative hearing decisions is the failure of the ALJ to make specific findings on the credibility of witnesses, including the claimant. The ALJ must also provide adequate reasoning for the findings. *See* Lewis v. Apfel, 236 F.3d 503, 511, 72 Soc. Sec. Rep. Serv. 263 (9th Cir. 2001) ("Lay testimony as to a claimant's symptoms is competent evidence that an ALJ must take into account, unless he or she expressly determines to disregard such testimony and gives reasons germane to each witness for doing so. One reason for which an ALJ may discount lay testimony is that it conflicts with medical evidence. The ALJ's decision in this case met these standards.") (citations omitted).

STOUT V. COMMISSIONER

454 F.3d 1050, 112 Soc. Sec. Rep. Serv. 496 (9th Cir. 2006)

Before: BROWNING, D.W. NELSON, and O'SCANNLAIN, Circuit Judges.

BROWNING, Circuit Judge:

Gordon Stout appeals the district court's judgment affirming the Social Security Commissioner's ("Commissioner") denial of his applications for Disability Insurance Benefits ("DIB") and Supplemental Security Income ("SSI") under Titles II and XVI, respectively, of the Social Security Act. Stout contends the Administrative Law Judge ("ALJ") improperly disregarded lay testimony regarding his inability to work. We have jurisdiction under 28 U.S.C. § 1291. Because the ALJ failed to discuss competent lay witness testimony favorable to Stout, we reverse the district court's judgment and remand.

I

Stout filed his current claims for DIB and SSI in February 2000, alleging disability primarily due to back and mental impairments with an onset date of April 18, 1997. The Social Security Administration denied these claims initially and upon reconsideration. Stout requested a hearing.

At his hearing in February 2002, Stout's sister, Udena Stout ("Udena"), testified that Stout's impairments negatively affect his ability to work. Additionally, the ALJ received into evidence a letter from Stout's brother-in-law, Jay Vasquez, with whom Stout worked for approximately fifteen years. Similar to Udena's testimony, Vasquez described Stout's inability to work without certain accommodations. During a supplemental hearing in March 2002, a vocational expert ("VE") testified. In response to the ALJ's hypothetical, the VE opined that Stout could perform one of his previous jobs and other jobs in the national economy.

In his decision, the ALJ found Stout able to perform his past relevant work as a vine pruner and, therefore, not disabled within the meaning of the Social Security Act. The Appeals Council denied Stout's request for review, making the ALJ's decision the Commissioner's final decision. See 20 C.F.R. § 404.981. Stout sought judicial review in the United States District Court for the District of Oregon, which affirmed the Commissioner's decision. Stout timely appeals.

* * *

III

* * *

B

On appeal, Stout challenges the ALJ's findings at steps four and five [of the sequential evaluation process]. At step four, the ALJ determined

Stout's RFC—the most Stout could still do despite his limitations. Finding that Stout had various physical restrictions and a limited capacity for teamwork and required non-complex, "two to three step tasks which are fairly repetitive," the ALJ concluded Stout could "perform a wide range of light unskilled work, and the inclusive sedentary level work."

Based upon Stout's RFC and the VE's testimony, the ALJ found Stout able to perform his past relevant work as a vine pruner. Consequently, the ALJ concluded Stout was not disabled within the meaning of the Social Security Act.

Stout contends the ALJ erred in finding he could perform his past relevant work and other work in the national economy. Specifically, he argues the ALJ erred in rejecting without comment the lay witness testimony of his sister, Udena, and brother-in-law, Jay Vasquez. The Commissioner concedes error but argues it was harmless. We disagree.

C

In determining whether a claimant is disabled, an ALJ must consider lay witness testimony concerning a claimant's ability to work. *See* Dodrill v. Shalala, 12 F.3d 915, 919 (9th Cir.1993); 20 C.F.R. §§ 404.1513(d)(4) & (e), 416.913(d)(4) & (e). Indeed, "lay testimony as to a claimant's symptoms or how an impairment affects ability to work *is* competent evidence ... and therefore *cannot* be disregarded without comment." Nguyen v. Chater, 100 F.3d 1462, 1467 (9th Cir.1996) (citations omitted). Consequently, "[i]f the ALJ wishes to discount the testimony of lay witnesses, he must give reasons that are germane to each witness." Dodrill, 12 F.3d at 919.

Here, the ALJ was required to consider and comment upon the uncontradicted lay testimony, as it concerned how Stout's impairments impact his ability to work. Both Udena and Vasquez testified, consistent with medical evidence, about Stout's inability to deal with the demands of work. After explaining Stout has "problems" accomplishing even simple tasks, Vasquez, who worked with Stout for fifteen years as both his boss and co-worker, provided the following example: "I would have [Stout] clean out the tool trailer and ask him to label nails, nuts, bolts, and screws. Ten minutes later I would come back and he would be throwing things on the ground, becoming frustrated with the simplest of tasks." Similarly, Udena testified that simple, monotonous tasks "easily frustrate[ ]" Stout, so much so that, "when something doesn't go just right[,] ... he goes into a rage, blindly throwing things and self-destruction [sic]."

Moreover, both witnesses explained Stout's uncommon need for supervision to perform uncomplicated tasks. For instance, Udena testified that for Stout to "keep focused on the job at hand," someone must "watch over him." While she stated Stout "could handle" simple jobs, such as "pick[ing] up stuff in the yard," she further clarified why he needs supervision to accomplish such jobs: "Mentally he would tend to stray [from] what he's supposed to be doing, find interest in other things, wander off, and probably explore the area." Likewise, Vasquez stated that, for Stout to accomplish even "menial labor," he requires "constant supervision." Although the VE specifically testified that a need for literal, constant supervision would not be acceptable in competitive employment, save for one passing reference to Udena's testimony about Stout's general self-destructive behaviors, the ALJ's decision wholly fails to mention Udena's or Vasquez's testimony about how Stout's impairments affect his ability to work. Therefore, the ALJ erred.

D

Conceding the ALJ's silent disregard of the lay testimony contravenes our case law and the controlling regulations, the Commissioner requests we disregard the error as harmless. The Commissioner's argument echoes, if not recites verbatim, the district court's harmless error analysis, which it began by reasoning that Udena's testimony "suggests [Stout] has always had intellectual deficits, depression, and episodes of self-destructive behavior. Yet, [Stout] has been able to engage in substantial work activity in the past." As to Vasquez's testimony, the court reasoned that he worked with Stout for fifteen years and, "[w]hile it took effort, [Stout] was able to engage in substantial gainful activity while suffering from his current impairments." Because the district court found "[t]he medical evidence establishes that nothing has changed," it concluded there was "no reason to overturn the ALJ's decision."

[The court, while recognizing that the harmless error rule can be applied in Social Security cases, concluded that "where the ALJ's error lies in a failure to properly discuss competent lay testimony favorable to the claimant, a reviewing court cannot consider the error harmless unless it can confidently conclude that no reasonable ALJ, when fully crediting the testimony, could have reached a different disability determination."]

In the present case, we cannot so conclude. If fully credited, the lay testimony supports a conclusion that Stout's mental impairments render him in need of a special working environment which, particularly when considering the VE's testimony, a reasonable ALJ could find precludes Stout from returning to gainful employment. Consequently, the ALJ's error in failing to provide reasons for rejecting it was not harmless.

* * *

Moreover, the ALJ's error did not occur during an unnecessary exercise or procedure. Numerous regulations command the ALJ to consider, throughout the sequential process, lay testimony as to how claimants' impairments affect their ability to work. *See, e.g.*, 20 C.F.R. §§ 404.1513(d)(4) & (e), 404.1529(c), 404.1545, 416.913(d)(4) & (e), 416.929(c), 416.945. And, as we have held on many occasions, if the ALJ wishes to discount such testimony in accord with this obligation, "he must give reasons that are germane to each witness." Dodrill, 12 F.3d at 919.

IV

Because the ALJ failed to provide any reasons for rejecting competent lay testimony, and because we conclude that error was not harmless, substantial evidence does not support the Commissioner's decision that Stout can perform his previous work as a vine pruner. Consequently, we reverse the district court's judgment and remand with instructions to remand to the Commissioner for further administrative proceedings consistent with this opinion.

O'SCANNLAIN, Circuit Judge, dissenting:

I respectfully dissent from the majority's conclusion that the ALJ's failure to comment properly on the lay witness testimony of Stout's sister and brother-in-law was not harmless error. I am persuaded, as was the District Court, that even if the lay witness testimony is credited, all the evidence taken as a whole overwhelmingly supports denial of Stout's application for Disability Insurance Benefits and Supplemental Security Income.

"A decision of the ALJ will not be reversed for errors that are harmless." Burch v. Barnhart, 400 F.3d 676, 679 (9th Cir.2005). Here, the lay testimony, when viewed in conjunction with the evidence the ALJ properly considered, does not undermine the ALJ's finding that Stout can engage in his prior work as a vine pruner.

The thrust of the lay testimony was that, in his past work as a roofer, Stout had difficulty working with other people without supervision. Although the letter from Stout's brother-in-law, Jay Vasquez, used the term "constant supervision" to describe the assistance Stout requires, the remainder of Vasquez's letter indicates that Vasquez did not provide Stout literal, constant supervision during the ten years Stout worked in his construction company. It also indicates that after Vasquez closed his construction company, Stout worked as a roofer for another company without supervision and support from a family member. Similarly, the testimony of Stout's sister, Udena Stout, does not stand for the proposition that Stout requires constant supervision. In fact, Udena testified that Stout's need for supervision would vary in relationship to the complexity of the task. She indicated that Stout could handle simple tasks that require minimal interaction with others, although he would have a tendency to become bored or lose focus.

All the limitations reasonably supported by the lay testimony appeared in the ALJ's RFC finding. The ALJ noted that Stout has "mild to moderate" difficulties in social functioning and in concentration, persistence, or pace. This information appeared in the ALJ's RFC, which noted that Stout "has a limited capacity for teamwork and needs to minimize repetitive public contact .... has a limited capacity for multitasking with complex instructions .... [and] ..."needs two to three step tasks which are fairly repetitive."

As the district court observed, Stout has engaged in substantial work activity in the past and there is no evidence, in the lay testimony or elsewhere, that his mental capabilities have changed. I accordingly agree with the district court's determination that the ALJ's failure to comment properly on the lay testimony is harmless error.

ALBALOS V. SULLIVAN
907 F.2d 871, 30 Soc. Sec. Rep. Serv. 451 (9th Cir. 1990)

PER CURIAM:

Plaintiff, Leonard Albalos, appeals the district court's judgment for the Secretary of Health and Human Services ("Secretary"). The Secretary refused to waive a deduction overpayment because Albalos failed to show he was "without fault" in failing to file excess earnings reports. The Secretary also imposed a penalty upon Albalos for these failures. We reverse.

FACTS

Leonard Albalos was born in the Philippines in 1909 and speaks a Philippine dialect as his native language. He completed six grades of formal education in the Philippines before immigrating to the United States. For fifty-seven years, he has performed various unskilled jobs.

In 1972, Albalos applied for Social Security benefits. Albalos was required to file annual earnings reports if he received earnings in excess of an exempt amount. If these earnings create an overpayment of benefits, the Secretary is to make deductions from monthly benefits.

In 1978, Albalos was advised of his failure to file a report for 1976. He suffered a deduction overpayment after failing to respond to the advisory notice.

Albalos also failed to file reports for 1978 and 1980. On April 26, 1984, he received a notice advising him of these failures and informing him that he would be subject to a deduction overpayment of $868.60 and a penalty of $295.50. Upon Albalos' request for reconsideration of the penalty, the penalty was doubled after a Social Security Administration representative discovered the penalty imposed for the 1976 failure.

Upon request for a hearing, the Administrative Law Judge ("ALJ") denied Albalos' claims as to the deduction overpayment and penalties for the 1978 and 1980 failures. The Appeals Council denied review. Albalos filed his complaint in the district court, pursuant to 42 U.S.C. § 405(g). The district court granted the Secretary's motion for summary judgment. Albalos filed timely notice of appeal. We have jurisdiction over the appeal.

DISCUSSION

* * *

The ALJ refused to waive the deduction overpayment because Albalos was "not without fault." Under 42 U.S.C. § 404(b), being "without fault" is one of the requirements for waiver. * * *

That standard requires consideration of "all pertinent circumstances," including "age, intelligence, education, and physical and mental condition." This determination is "highly subjective, highly individualized, and highly dependent on the interaction between the intentions and state of mind of the claimant and the peculiar circumstances of his situation." Elliott v. Weinberger, 564 F.2d 1219, 1233 (9th Cir.1977), *aff'd in part and rev'd in part sub nom.* Califano v. Yamasaki, 442 U.S. 682, 99 S.Ct. 2545, 61 L.Ed.2d 176 (1979).

Although Albalos produced evidence on each of the factors described in 20 C.F.R. § 404.507, the ALJ failed to make findings on these factors. Those findings are mandated not only by 20 C.F.R. § 404.507, but also by 20 C.F.R. § 404.511. The latter regulation requires a finding of whether a "high degree of care" has been exercised before a "without fault" determination will be made. In turn, "high degree of care" depends on a consideration of the individual's circumstances. It does appear that 20 C.F.R. § 404.511 sets a higher standard than that set by 20 C.F.R. § 404.507, but both regulations require attention to the individual characteristics of the individual. That is reasonable, since it is difficult to assess fault in the subjective sense without knowing something about the subject. Because the ALJ did not make findings regarding those circumstances, we reverse.

Furthermore, we must reverse because no explicit finding as to Albalos' credibility was made. Lewin v. Schwieker, 654 F.2d 631, 635 (9th Cir.1981). Albalos' credibility was critical to the "without fault" determination. As *Lewin* stated:

The circuit courts have consistently recognized the need for full and detailed findings of fact essential to the Secretary's conclusion.

....

The rule has been applied to credibility determinations and the courts have consistently required that there be an explicit finding whether the Secretary believed or disbelieved the claimant whenever the claimant's credibility is a critical factor in the Secretary's decision.

....

Because the ALJ's decision neither expressly discredits [the claimant's] testimony nor articulates any reasons for questioning her credibility, and fails to indicate the amount of weight given to various items of evidence, it cannot stand.

654 F.2d at 634-35. An "implicit" finding that Albalos was not credible does not satisfy this standard.

* * *

The decision of the district court is REVERSED and the case REMANDED to the district court for remand to the Secretary for further proceedings consistent with this opinion.

NOTES

1. For judicial review to function properly, the ALJ "must let the parties and the reviewing courts know, in some intelligible fashion, where they stand on the pivotal issues of fact posed by the applications they adjudicate." *See* Chiappa v. Secretary, 497 F. Supp. 356, 358 (S.D.N.Y. 1980) (describing "the repeated failure of Administrative Law Judges to make specific findings as to * * * the credibility of the applicant's testimony, particularly claims of disabling pain," as "a persistent problem that arises in disability cases."); *see also* Bray v. Commissioner, 554 F.3d 1219, 1226-27, 140 Soc. Sec. Rep. Serv. 67 (9th Cir. 2009) ("If an ALJ finds a claimant's characterization of his or her own symptoms unreliable, the ALJ must make a credibility determination backed up by specific findings."). This requirement is based as much on concerns for efficiency in the appeals process as it is based on concerns of fairness and correctness in the decisions themselves.

2. In the case of a child who is unable to describe his or her symptoms adequately, the description of those symptoms given by the person who is most familiar with the child, such as a parent, guardian, or other relative, will be accepted as a statement of the child's symptoms. *See* 20 C.F.R. § 416.928(a) ("If you are a child under age 18 and are unable to adequately de-

scribe your symptom(s), we will accept as a statement of this symptom(s) the description given by the person who is most familiar with you, such as a parent, other relative, or guardian"). As the court stated in Briggs v. Massanari, 248 F.3d 1235, 1239, 74 Soc. Sec. Rep. Serv. 48 (10th Cir. 2001): "If the child claimant is unable adequately to describe his symptoms, the ALJ must accept [the description provided by] the testimony of the person most familiar with the child's condition[, such as a parent]. In such a case, the ALJ must make specific findings concerning the credibility of the parent's testimony, just as he would if the child were testifying." (citing 20 C.F.R. § 416.928(a)).

3. Testimony of friends and family members sometimes is viewed with suspicion, especially when there is little or no corroborating evidence. *See e.g.*, Rautio v. Bowen, 862 F.2d 176, 180, 24 Soc. Sec. Rep. Serv. 7 (8th Cir. 1988) (testimony of claimant's fiancé discounted "as she lives with [the claimant] and has a financial interest in the case"); Tremblay v. Secretary, 676 F.2d 11, 13 (1st Cir. 1982) (testimony of family members "hardly neutral"). However, the mere fact that a witness is a member of the claimant's family is not a basis for rejecting his or her testimony. In Smolen v. Chater, 80 F.3d 1273, 50 Soc. Sec. Rep. Serv. 500 (9th Cir. 1996), the claimant alleged disability based on fatigue and pain. Her medical records were "sparse" so she relied on family members to testify about her symptoms at the administrative hearing, but the ALJ rejected that testimony.

> The first reason the ALJ gave for doing so was that the testimony was from "family witnesses" who were therefore "understandably advocates, and biased." This amounted to a wholesale dismissal of the testimony of all the witnesses as a group and therefore does not qualify as a reason germane to each individual who testified. Moreover, the same could be said of any family member who testified in any case. The fact that a lay witness is a family member cannot be a ground for rejecting his or her testimony. To the contrary, testimony from lay witnesses who see the claimant every day is of particular value, *see* Dodrill [v. Shalala, 12 F.3d 915, 919 (9th Cir.1993) ("[a]n eyewitness can often tell whether someone is suffering or merely malingering ... this is particularly true of witnesses who view the claimant on a daily basis ..."); such lay witnesses will often be family members.

> The second reason for rejecting the testimony of Smolen's family members was that "medical records, including chart notes made at the time, are far more reliable and entitled to more weight than recent recollections made by family members and others, made with a view toward helping their sibling in pending litigation." Contrary to the testimony of Smolen's family members, the ALJ concluded that, because Smolen's medical records through 1987 did not reflect symptoms of fatigue and severe back pain, it was "simply beyond belief that Smolen suffered such fatigue ... back pain and dysfunction during her 14-year gap between her two severe bouts of cancers...." The rejection of the testimony of Smolen's family members because Smolen's medical records did not corroborate

her fatigue and pain violates SSR 88-13, which directs the ALJ to consider the testimony of lay witnesses where the claimant's alleged symptoms are *unsupported* by her medical records. *See* SSR 88-13 (where "allegation [of subjective symptom] is not supported by objective medical evidence in the file, the adjudicator shall obtain detailed descriptions of daily activities by directing specific inquiries about the [symptom] and its effects to ... third parties who would be likely to have such knowledge.").

80 F.3d at 1288-89.

APPENDIX A

SELECTED REGULATIONS

■ ■ ■

NOTE: This appendix includes regulations in Part 404 that apply only to the OASDI program, others in Part 416 that apply only to the SSI program, and many that are the same for both programs and appear in both Parts. Where the regulations for SSI are identical—or nearly identical—to those for OASDI, only the OASDI regulations are included. (For those regulations, a *"See also"* reference for the SSI counterpart follows the heading for the OASDI regulation.)

20 C.F.R. § 404.101 Introduction.

(a) Insured status. * * * Your insured status is a basic factor in determining if you are entitled to old-age or disability insurance benefits or to a period of disability. It is also a basic factor in determining if dependents' or survivors' insurance benefits or a lump-sum death payment are payable based on your earnings record. If you are neither fully nor currently insured, no benefits are payable based on your earnings. * * *

(b) QCs. * * * In general, you are credited with QCs based on the wages you are paid and the self-employment income you derive during certain periods. * * *

20 C.F.R. § 404.110 How we determine fully insured status.

(a) General. We describe how we determine the number of quarters of coverage (QCs) you need to be fully insured in paragraphs (b), (c), and (d) of this section. * * *

(b) How many QCs you need to be fully insured.

(1) You need at least 6 QCs but not more than 40 QCs to be fully insured. A person who died before 1951 with at least 6 QCs is fully insured.

(2) You are fully insured for old-age insurance benefits if you have one QC (whenever acquired) for each calendar year elapsing af-

ter 1950 or, if later, after the year in which you became age 21, and before the year you reach retirement age, that is, before—

(i) The year you become age 62, if you are a woman;

(ii) The year you become age 62, if you are a man who becomes age 62 after 1974;

(iii) The year 1975, if you are a man who became age 62 in 1973 or 1974; or

(iv) The year you became age 65, if you are a man who became age 62 before 1973.

(3) A person who is otherwise eligible for survivor's benefits and who files an application will be entitled to benefits based on your earnings if you die fully insured. You will be fully insured if you had one QC (whenever acquired) for each calendar year elapsing after 1950 or, if later, after the year you became age 21, and before the earlier of the following years:

(i) The year you die; or

(ii) The year you reach retirement age as shown in paragraph (b)(2) of this section.

* * *

(e) When your fully insured status begins. You are fully insured as of the first day of the calendar quarter in which you acquire the last needed QC (see § 404.145).

20 C.F.R. § 404.120 How we determine currently insured status.

(a) What the period is for determining currently insured status. You are currently insured if you have at least 6 quarters of coverage (QCs) during the 13–quarter period ending with the quarter in which you—

(1) Die;

(2) Most recently became entitled to disability insurance benefits; or

(3) Became entitled to old-age insurance benefits.

(b) What quarters are not counted as part of the 13–quarter period. We do not count as part of the 13–quarter period any quarter all or part of which is included in a period of disability established for you, except that the first and last quarters of the period of disability may be counted if they are QCs (see § 404.146(d)).

20 C.F.R. § 404.130 How we determine disability insured status.

(a) General. We have four different rules for determining if you are insured for purposes of establishing a period of disability or becoming entitled to disability insurance benefits. To have disability insured status, you must meet one of these rules and you must be fully insured ***.

(b) Rule I—You must meet the 20/40 requirement. You are insured in a quarter for purposes of establishing a period of disability or becoming entitled to disability insurance benefits if in that quarter—

(1) You are fully insured; and

(2) You have at least 20 QCs in the 40–quarter period (see paragraph (f) of this section) ending with that quarter.

(c) Rule II—You become disabled before age 31. You are insured in a quarter for purposes of establishing a period of disability or becoming entitled to disability insurance benefits if in that quarter—

(1) You have not become (or would not become) age 31;

(2) You are fully insured; and

(3) You have QCs in at least one-half of the quarters during the period ending with that quarter and beginning with the quarter after the quarter you became age 21; however—

(i) If the number of quarters during this period is an odd number, we reduce the number by one; and

(ii) If the period has less than 12 quarters, you must have at least 6 QCs in the 12–quarter period ending with that quarter.

(d) Rule III—You had a period of disability before age 31. You are insured in a quarter for purposes of establishing a period of disability or becoming entitled to disability insurance benefits if in that quarter—

(1) You are disabled again at age 31 or later after having had a prior period of disability established which began before age 31 and for which you were only insured under paragraph (c) of this section; and

(2) You are fully insured and have QCs in at least one-half the calendar quarters in the period beginning with the quarter after the

quarter you became age 21 and through the quarter in which the later period of disability begins, up to a maximum of 20 QCs out of 40 calendar quarters; however—

(i) If the number of quarters during this period is an odd number, we reduce the number by one;

(ii) If the period has less than 12 quarters, you must have at least 6 QCs in the 12–quarter period ending with that quarter; and

(iii) No monthly benefits may be paid or increased under Rule III before May 1983.

(e) Rule IV—You are statutorily blind. You are insured in a quarter for purposes of establishing a period of disability or becoming entitled to disability insurance benefits if in that quarter—

(1) You are disabled by blindness as defined in § 404.1581; and

(2) You are fully insured.

(f) How we determine the 40–quarter or other period. In determining the 40–quarter period or other period in paragraph (b), (c), or (d) of this section, we do not count any quarter all or part of which is in a prior period of disability established for you, unless the quarter is the first or last quarter of this period and the quarter is a QC. However, we will count all the quarters in the prior period of disability established for you if by doing so you would be entitled to benefits or the amount of the benefit would be larger.

20 C.F.R. § 404.204 Methods of computing primary insurance amounts—general.

(a) General. We compute most workers' primary insurance amounts under one of two major methods. There are, in addition, several special methods of computing primary insurance amounts which we apply to some workers. Your primary insurance amount is the highest of all those computed under the methods for which you are eligible.

(b) Major methods.

(1) If after 1978 you reach age 62, or become disabled or die before age 62, we compute your primary insurance amount under what we call the average-indexed-monthly-earnings method, which is described in §§ 404.210–404.212. The earliest of the three dates determines the computation method we use.

(2) If before 1979 you reached age 62, become disabled, or died, we compute your primary insurance amount under what we call the "average-monthly-wage" method, described in §§ 404.220–404.222.

(c) Special methods.

(1) Your primary insurance amount, computed under any of the special methods for which you are eligible as described in this paragraph, may be substituted for your primary insurance amount computed under either major method described in paragraph (b) of this section.

* * *

(3) If you had all or substantially all of your social security earnings before 1951, we will also compute your primary insurance amount under what we call the "old-start" method.

* * *

20 C.F.R. § 404.210 Average-indexed-monthly-earnings method.

(a) Who is eligible for this method. If after 1978, you reach age 62, or become disabled or die before age 62, we will compute your primary insurance amount under the average-indexed-monthly-earnings method.

(b) Steps in computing your primary insurance amount under the average-indexed-monthly-earnings method. We follow these three major steps in computing your primary insurance amount:

(1) First, we find your average indexed monthly earnings, as described in § 404.211;

(2) Second, we find the benefit formula in effect for the year you reach age 62, or become disabled or die before age 62, as described in § 404.212; and

(3) Then, we apply that benefit formula to your average indexed monthly earnings to find your primary insurance amount, as described in § 404.212.

(4) Next, we apply any automatic cost-of-living or ad hoc increases in primary insurance amounts that became effective in or after the year you reached age 62, unless you are receiving benefits based on the minimum primary insurance amount, in which case not all the increases may be applied, as described in § 404.277.

20 C.F.R. § 404.211 Computing your average indexed monthly earnings.

(a) General. In this method, your social security earnings after 1950 are indexed, as described in paragraph (d) of this section, then averaged over the period of time you can reasonably have been expected to have worked in employment or self-employment covered by social security. (Your earnings before 1951 are not used in finding your average indexed monthly earnings.)

(b) Which earnings may be used in computing your average indexed monthly earnings—

    (1) Earnings. In computing your average indexed monthly earnings, we use wages, compensation, self-employment income, and deemed military wage credits (see §§ 404.1340 through 404.1343) that are creditable to you for social security purposes for years after 1950.

    (2) Computation base years. We use your earnings in your computation base years in finding your average indexed monthly earnings. All years after 1950 up to (but not including) the year you become entitled to old-age or disability insurance benefits, and through the year you die if you had not been entitled to old-age or disability benefits, are computation base years for you. The year you become entitled to benefits and following years may be used as computation base years in a recomputation if their use would result in a higher primary insurance amount. * * *

(c) Average of the total wages. Before we compute your average indexed monthly earnings, we must first know the average of the total wages of all workers for each year from 1951 until the second year before you become eligible. The average of the total wages for years after 1950 are shown in appendix I. * * *

(d) Indexing your earnings.

    (1) The first step in indexing your social security earnings is to find the relationship (under paragraph (d)(2)) between—

        (i) The average wage of all workers in your computation base years; and

        (ii) The average wage of all workers in your indexing year. As a general rule, your indexing year is the second year before the earliest of the year you reach age 62, or become disabled or die before age 62. * * *

(2) To find the relationship, we divide the average wages for your indexing year, in turn, by the average wages for each year beginning with 1951 and ending with your indexing year. We use the quotients found in these divisions to index your earnings as described in paragraph (d)(3) of this section.

(3) The second step in indexing your social security earnings is to multiply the actual year-by-year dollar amounts of your earnings (up to the maximum amounts creditable, as explained in §§ 404.1047 and 404.1096 of this part) by the quotients found in paragraph (d)(2) of this section for each of those years. We round the results to the nearer penny. (The quotient for your indexing year is 1.0; this means that your earnings in that year are used in their actual dollar amount; any earnings after your indexing year that may be used in computing your average indexed monthly earnings are also used in their actual dollar amount.)

Example. Ms. A reaches age 62 in July 1979. Her year-by-year social security earnings since 1950 are as follows:

Year	Earnings
1951	$3,200
1952	3,400
1953	3,300
1954	3,600
1955	3,700
1956	3,700
1957	4,000
1958	4,200
1959	4,400
1960	4,500
1961	2,800
1962	2,200
1963	0
1964	0
1965	3,700
1966	4,500
1967	5,400
1968	6,200
1969	6,900
1970	7,300
1971	7,500
1972	7,800
1973	8,200
1974	9,000
1975	9,900
1976	11,100
1977	9,900
1978	11,000

Step 1. The first step in indexing Ms. A's earnings is to find the relationship between the general wage level in Ms. A's indexing year (1977) and the general wage level in each of the years 1951–1976. We refer to Appendix I for average wage figures, and perform the following computations:

Year	I. 1977 general wage level	II. Nation wide average of the total wages	III. Column I divided by column II equals relationship
1951	$9,779.44	$2,799.16	3.4937053
1952	9,779.44	2,973.32	3.2890641
1953	9,779.44	3,139.44	3.1150269
1954	9,779.44	3,155.64	3.0990354
1955	9,779.44	3,301.44	2.9621741
1956	9,779.44	3,532.36	2.7685287
1957	9,779.44	3,641.72	2.6853904
1958	9,779.44	3,673.80	2.6619413
1959	9,779.44	3,855.80	2.5362934
1960	9,779.44	4,007.12	2.4405159
1961	9,779.44	4,086.76	2.3929568
1962	9,779.44	4,291.40	2.2788461
1963	9,779.44	4,396.64	2.2242986
1964	9,779.44	4,576.32	2.1369659
1965	9,779.44	4,658.72	2.0991689
1966	9,779.44	4,938.36	1.9803012
1967	9,779.44	5,213.44	1.8758133
1968	9,779.44	5,571.76	1.7551797
1969	9,779.44	5,893.76	1.6592871
1970	9,779.44	6,186.24	1.5808375
1971	9,779.44	6,497.08	1.5052054
1972	9,779.44	7,133.80	1.3708599
1973	9,779.44	7,580.16	1.2901364
1974	9,779.44	8,030.76	1.2177478
1975	9,779.44	8,630.92	1.1330704
1976	9,779.44	9,226.48	1.0599318
1977	9,779.44	9,779.44	1.0000000

Step 2. After we have found these indexing quotients, we multiply Ms. A's actual year-by-year earnings by them to find her indexed earnings, as shown below:

Year	I. Actual earnings	II. Indexing quotient	III. Column I multiplied by column II equals indexed earnings
1951	$3,200	3.4937053	$11,179.86
1952	3,400	3.2890641	11,182.82
1953	3,300	3.1150269	10,279.59
1954	3,600	3.0990354	11,156.53
1955	3,700	2.9621741	10,960.04
1956	3,700	2.7685287	10,243.56
1957	4,000	2.6853904	10,741.56
1958	4,200	2.6619413	11,180.15
1959	4,400	2.5362934	11,159.69
1960	4,500	2.4405159	10,982.32
1961	2,800	2.3929568	6,700.28
1962	2,200	2.2788461	5,013.46
1963	0	2.2242986	0
1964	0	2.1369659	0
1965	3,700	2.0991689	7,766.92
1966	4,500	1.9803012	8,911.36
1967	5,400	1.8758133	10,129.39
1968	6,200	1.7551797	10,882.11
1969	6,900	1.6592871	11,449.08
1970	7,300	1.5808375	11,540.11
1971	7,500	1.5052054	11,289.04
1972	7,800	1.3708599	10,692.71
1973	8,200	1.2901364	10,579.12
1974	9,000	1.2177478	10,959.73
1975	9,900	1.1330704	11,217.40
1976	11,100	1.0599318	11,765.24
1977	9,900	1.0000000	9,900.00
1978	11,000	0	11,000.00

* * *

(e) Number of years to be considered in finding your average indexed monthly earnings. To find the number of years to be used in computing your average indexed monthly earnings—

(1) We count the years beginning with 1951, or (if later) the year you reach age 22, and ending with the earliest of the year before you reach age 62, become disabled, or die. Years wholly or partially within a period of disability (as defined in § 404.1501(b) of subpart P of this part) are not counted unless your primary insurance amount would be higher. In that case, we count all the years during the period of disability, even though you had no earnings in some of those years. These are your elapsed years. From your elapsed years, we then subtract up to 5 years, the exact number depending on the kind of benefits to which you are entitled. You cannot, under this procedure, have fewer than 2 benefit computation years.

(2) For computing old-age insurance benefits and survivors insurance benefits, we subtract 5 from the number of your elapsed years. See paragraphs (e)(3) and (4) of this section for the dropout as applied to disability benefits. This is the number of your benefit computation years; we use the same number of your computation base years (see paragraph (b)(2) of this section) in computing your average indexed monthly earnings. For benefit computation years, we use the years with the highest amounts of earnings after indexing. They may include earnings from years that were not indexed, and must include years of no earnings if you do not have sufficient years with earnings. You cannot have fewer than 2 benefit computation years.

(3) Where the worker is first entitled to disability insurance benefits (DIB) after June 1980, there is an exception to the usual 5 year dropout provision explained in paragraph (e)(2) of this section. (For entitlement before July 1980, we use the usual dropout.) We call this exception the disability dropout. We divide the elapsed years by 5 and disregard any fraction. The result, which may not exceed 5, is the number of dropout years. We subtract that number from the number of elapsed years to get the number of benefit computation years, which may not be fewer than 2. After the worker dies, the disability dropout no longer applies and we use the basic 5 dropout years to compute benefits for survivors. We continue to apply the disability dropout when a person becomes entitled to old-age insurance benefits (OAIB), unless his or her entitlement to DIB ended at least 12 months before he or she became eligible for OAIB. For first DIB entitlement before July 1980, we use the rule in paragraph (e)(2) of this section.

(4) For benefits payable after June 1981, the disability dropout might be increased by the child care dropout. If the number of disability dropout years is fewer than 3, we will drop out a benefit computation year for each benefit computation year that the worker meets the child care requirement and had no earnings, until the total of all dropout years is 3. The child care requirement for any year is that the worker must have been living with his or her child (or his or her spouse's child) substantially throughout any part of any calendar year that the child was alive and under age 3. In actual practice, no more than 2 child care years may be dropped, because of the combined effect of the number of elapsed years, 1–for–5 dropout years (if any), and the computation years required for the computation.

Example. Ms. M., born August 4, 1953, became entitled to disability insurance benefits (DIB) beginning in July 1980 based on a disability which began January 15, 1980. In computing the DIB, we determined that the elapsed years are 1975 through 1979, the number of dropout years is 1 (5 elapsed years divided by 5), and the number of computation years is 4. Since Ms. M. had no earnings in 1975 and 1976, we drop out 1975 and use her earnings for the years 1977 through 1979.

Ms. M. lived with her child, who was born in 1972, in all months of 1973 and 1974 and did not have any earnings in those years. We, therefore, recompute Ms. M.'s DIB beginning with July 1981 to give her the advantage of the child care dropout. To do this, we reduce the 4 computation years by 1 child care year to get 3 computation years. Because the child care dropout cannot be applied to computation years in which the worker had earnings, we can drop only one of Ms. M.'s computation years, i.e., 1976, in addition to the year 1975 which we dropped in the initial computation.

* * *

(f) Your average indexed monthly earnings. After we have indexed your earnings and found your benefit computation years, we compute your average indexed monthly earnings by—

(1) Totalling your indexed earnings in your benefit computation years;

(2) Dividing the total by the number of months in your benefit computation years; and

(3) Rounding the quotient to the next lower whole dollar, if not already a multiple of $1.

Example. From the example in paragraph (d) of this section, we see that Ms. A reaches age 62 in 1979. Her elapsed years are 1951–1978 (28 years). We subtract 5 from her 28 elapsed years to find that we must use 23 benefit computation years. This means that we will use her 23 highest computation base years to find her average indexed monthly earnings. We exclude the 5 years 1961–1965 and total her indexed earnings for the remaining years, i.e., the benefit computation years (including her unindexed earnings in 1977 and 1978) and get $249,381.41. We then divide that amount by the 276 months in her 23 benefit computation years and find her average indexed monthly earnings to be $903.56, which is rounded down to $903.

20 C.F.R. § 404.212 Computing your primary insurance amount from your average indexed monthly earnings.

(a) General. We compute your primary insurance amount under the average-indexed-monthly-earnings method by applying a benefit formula to your average indexed monthly earnings.

(b) Benefit formula.

(1) We use the applicable benefit formula in Appendix II for the year you reach age 62, become disabled, or die whichever occurs first. If you die before age 62, and your surviving spouse or surviving divorced spouse is first eligible after 1984, we may compute the primary insurance amount, for the purpose of paying benefits to your widow(er), as if you had not died but reached age 62 in the second year after the indexing year that we computed under the provisions of § 404.211(d)(4). We will not use this primary insurance amount for computing benefit amounts for your other survivors or for computing the maximum family benefits payable on your earnings record. Further, we will only use this primary insurance amount if it results in a higher widow(er)'s benefit than would result if we did not use this special computation.

(2) The dollar amounts in the benefit formula are automatically increased each year for persons who attain age 62, or who become disabled or die before age 62 in that year, by the same percentage as the increase in the average of the total wages (see Appendix I).

(3) We will publish benefit formulas for years after 1979 in the Federal Register at the same time we publish the average of the total wage figures. We begin to use a new benefit formula as soon as it is applicable, even before we periodically update Appendix II.

(4) We may use a modified formula, as explained in § 404.213, if you are entitled to a pension based on your employment which was not covered by Social Security.

(c) Computing your primary insurance amount from the benefit formula. We compute your primary insurance amount by applying the benefit formula to your average indexed monthly earnings and adding the results for each step of the formula. For computations using the benefit formulas in effect for 1979 through 1982, we round the total amount to the next higher multiple of $0.10 if it is not a multiple of $0.10 and for computations using the benefit formulas effective for 1983 and later years, we round to the next lower multiple of $0.10. (See paragraph (e) of this section for a discussion of the minimum primary insurance amount.)

(d) Adjustment of your primary insurance amount when entitlement to benefits occurs in a year after attainment of age 62, disability or death. If you (or your survivors) do not become entitled to benefits in the same year you reach age 62, become disabled, or die before age 62, we compute your primary insurance amount by—

(1) Computing your average indexed monthly earnings as described in § 404.211;

(2) Applying to your average indexed monthly earnings the benefit formula for the year in which you reach age 62, or become disabled or die before age 62; and

(3) Applying to the primary insurance amount all automatic cost-of-living and ad hoc increases in primary insurance amounts that have gone into effect in or after the year you reached age 62, became disabled, or died before age 62. (See § 404.277 for special rules on minimum benefits, and Appendix VI for a table of percentage increases in primary insurance amounts since December 1978. Increases in primary insurance amounts are published in the Federal Register and we periodically update Appendix VI.)

(e) Minimum primary insurance amount. If you were eligible for benefits, or died without having been eligible, before 1982, your primary insurance amount computed under this method cannot be less than $122. This minimum benefit provision has been repealed effective with January 1982 for most workers and their families where the worker initially becomes eligible for benefits in that or a later month, or dies in January 1982 or a later month without having been eligible before January 1982. * * *

20 C.F.R. § 404.354 Your relationship to the insured.

You may be related to the insured person in one of several ways and be entitled to benefits as his or her child, i.e., as a natural child, legally adopted child, stepchild, grandchild, stepgrandchild, or equitably adopted child. For details on how we determine your relationship to the insured person, see §§ 404.355 through 404.359.

20 C.F.R. § 404.355 Who is the insured's natural child?

(a) Eligibility as a natural child. You may be eligible for benefits as the insured's natural child if any of the following conditions is met:

(1) You could inherit the insured's personal property as his or her natural child under State inheritance laws, as described in paragraph (b) of this section.

(2) You are the insured's natural child and the insured and your mother or father went through a ceremony which would have resulted in a valid marriage between them except for a "legal impediment" as described in § 404.346(a).

(3) You are the insured's natural child and your mother or father has not married the insured, but the insured has either acknowledged in writing that you are his or her child, been decreed by a court to be your father or mother, or been ordered by a court to contribute to your support because you are his or her child. If the insured is deceased, the acknowledgment, court decree, or court order must have been made or issued before his or her death. * * *

(4) Your mother or father has not married the insured but you have evidence other than the evidence described in paragraph (a)(3) of this section to show that the insured is your natural father or mother. Additionally, you must have evidence to show that the insured was either living with you or contributing to your support at the time you applied for benefits. If the insured is not alive at the time of your application, you must have evidence to show that the insured was either living with you or contributing to your support when he or she died. See § 404.366 for an explanation of the terms "living with" and "contributions for support."

(b) Use of State Laws—

(1) General. To decide whether you have inheritance rights as the natural child of the insured, we use the law on inheritance rights that the State courts would use to decide whether you could inherit a child's share of the insured's personal property if the insured were to

die without leaving a will. If the insured is living, we look to the laws of the State where the insured has his or her permanent home when you apply for benefits. If the insured is deceased, we look to the laws of the State where the insured had his or her permanent home when he or she died. If the insured's permanent home is not or was not in one of the 50 States, the Commonwealth of Puerto Rico, the Virgin Islands, Guam, American Samoa, or the Northern Mariana Islands, we will look to the laws of the District of Columbia. * * * If these laws would permit you to inherit the insured's personal property as his or her child, we will consider you the child of the insured.

(2) Standards. We will not apply any State inheritance law requirement that an action to establish paternity must be taken within a specified period of time measured from the worker's death or the child's birth, or that an action to establish paternity must have been started or completed before the worker's death. If applicable State inheritance law requires a court determination of paternity, we will not require that you obtain such a determination but will decide your paternity by using the standard of proof that the State court would use as the basis for a determination of paternity.

(3) Insured is living. If the insured is living, we apply the law of the State where the insured has his or her permanent home when you file your application for benefits. We apply the version of State law in effect when we make our final decision on your application for benefits. If you do not qualify as a child of the insured under that version of State law, we look at all versions of State law that were in effect from the first month for which you could be entitled to benefits up until the time of our final decision and apply the version of State law that is most beneficial to you.

(4) Insured is deceased. If the insured is deceased, we apply the law of the State where the insured had his or her permanent home when he or she died. We apply the version of State law in effect when we make our final decision on your application for benefits. If you do not qualify as a child of the insured under that version of State law, we will apply the version of State law that was in effect at the time the insured died, or any version of State law in effect from the first month for which you could be entitled to benefits up until our final decision on your application. We will apply whichever version is most beneficial to you. We use the following rules to determine the law in effect as of the date of death:

(i) If a State inheritance law enacted after the insured's death indicates that the law would be retroactive to the time of death, we will apply that law; or

(ii) If the inheritance law in effect at the time of the insured's death was later declared unconstitutional, we will apply the State law which superseded the unconstitutional law.

20 C.F.R. § 404.356 Who is the insured's legally adopted child.

You may be eligible for benefits as the insured's child if you were legally adopted by the insured. If you were legally adopted after the insured's death by his or her surviving spouse you may also be considered the insured's legally adopted child. We apply the adoption laws of the State or foreign country where the adoption took place, not the State inheritance laws described in § 404.355, to determine whether you are the insured's legally adopted child.

20 C.F.R. § 404.357 Who is the insured's stepchild.

You may be eligible for benefits as the insured's stepchild if, after your birth, your natural or adopting parent married the insured. You also may be eligible as a stepchild if you were conceived prior to the marriage of your natural parent to the insured but were born after the marriage and the insured is not your natural parent. The marriage between the insured and your parent must be a valid marriage under State law or a marriage which would be valid except for a legal impediment described in § 404.346(a). If the insured is alive when you apply, you must have been his or her stepchild for at least 1 year immediately preceding the day you apply. * * * If the insured is not alive when you apply, you must have been his or her stepchild for at least 9 months immediately preceding the day the insured died. This 9–month requirement will not have to be met if the marriage between the insured and your parent lasted less than 9 months under the conditions described in § 404.335(a)(2)(i)-(iii).

20 C.F.R. § 404.358 Who is the insured's grandchild or stepgrandchild.

(a) Grandchild and stepgrandchild defined. You may be eligible for benefits as the insured's grandchild or stepgrandchild if you are the natural child, adopted child, or stepchild of a person who is the insured's child as defined in §§ 404.355 through 404.357, or § 404.359. Additionally, for you to be eligible as a grandchild or stepgrandchild, your natural or adoptive parents must have been either deceased or under a disability, as defined in § 404.1501(a), at the time your grandparent or stepgrandparent became entitled to old-age or disability benefits or died; or if your grandparent or stepgrandparent had a period of disability that continued until he or she became entitled to benefits or died, at the time the period of disability began. * * *

(b) Legally adopted grandchild or stepgrandchild. If you are the insured's grandchild or stepgrandchild and you are legally adopted by the insured or by the insured's surviving spouse after his or her death, you are considered an adopted child and the dependency requirements of § 404.362 must be met.

20 C.F.R. § 404.359 Who is the insured's equitably adopted child.

You may be eligible for benefits as an equitably adopted child if the insured had agreed to adopt you as his or her child but the adoption did not occur. The agreement to adopt you must be one that would be recognized under State law so that you would be able to inherit a child's share of the insured's personal property if he or she were to die without leaving a will. * * *

20 C.F.R. § 404.360 When a child is dependent upon the insured person.

One of the requirements for entitlement to child's benefits is that you be dependent upon the insured. The evidence you need to prove your dependency is determined by how you are related to the insured. To prove your dependency you may be asked to show that at a specific time you lived with the insured, that you received contributions for your support from the insured, or that the insured provided at least one-half of your support. These dependency requirements, and the time at which they must be met, are explained in §§ 404.361–404.365. The terms living with, contributions for support, and one-half support are defined in § 404.366.

20 C.F.R. § 404.361 When a natural child is dependent.

(a) Dependency of natural child. If you are the insured's natural child, as defined in § 404.355, you are considered dependent upon him or her, except as stated in paragraph (b) of this section.

(b) Dependency of natural child legally adopted by someone other than the insured.

(1) Except as indicated in paragraph (b)(2) of this section, if you are legally adopted by someone other than the insured (your natural parent) during the insured's lifetime, you are considered dependent upon the insured only if the insured was either living with you or contributing to your support at one of the following times:

(i) When you applied;

(ii) When the insured died; or

(iii) If the insured had a period of disability that lasted until he or she became entitled to disability or old-age benefits or died, at the beginning of the period of disability or at the time he or she became entitled to disability or old-age benefits.

(2) You are considered dependent upon the insured (your natural parent) if:

(i) You were adopted by someone other than the insured after you applied for child's benefits; or

(ii) The insured had a period of disability that lasted until he or she became entitled to old-age or disability benefits or died, and you are adopted by someone other than the insured after the beginning of that period of disability.

20 C.F.R. § 404.362 When a legally adopted child is dependent.

(a) General. If you were legally adopted by the insured before he or she became entitled to old-age or disability benefits, you are considered dependent upon him or her. If you were legally adopted by the insured after he or she became entitled to old-age or disability benefits and you apply for child's benefits during the life of the insured, you must meet the dependency requirements stated in paragraph (b) of this section. If you were legally adopted by the insured after he or she became entitled to old-age or disability benefits and you apply for child's benefits after the death of the insured, you are considered dependent upon him or her. If you were adopted after the insured's death by his or her surviving spouse, you may be considered dependent upon the insured only under the conditions de-scribed in paragraph (c) of this section.

(b) Adoption by the insured after he or she became entitled to bene-fits—

(1) General. If you are legally adopted by the insured after he or she became entitled to benefits and you are not the insured's natural child or stepchild, you are considered dependent on the insured dur-ing his or her lifetime only if—

(i) You had not attained age 18 when adoption proceedings were started, and your adoption was issued by a court of competent juris-diction within the United States; or

(ii) You had attained age 18 before adoption proceedings were started; your adoption was issued by a court of competent jurisdiction within the United States, and you were living with or receiving at least one-half of your support from the insured for the year immediately preceding the month in which your adoption was issued.

(2) Natural child and stepchild. If you were legally adopted by the insured after he or she became entitled to benefits and you are the insured's natural child or stepchild, you are considered dependent upon the insured.

(c) Adoption by the insured's surviving spouse—

(1) General. If you are legally adopted by the insured's surviving spouse after the insured's death, you are considered dependent upon the insured as of the date of his or her death if—

(i) You were either living with or receiving at least one-half of your support from the insured at the time of his or her death; and,

(ii) The insured had started adoption proceedings before he or she died; or if the insured had not started the adoption proceedings before he or she died, his or her surviving spouse began and completed the adoption within 2 years of the insured's death.

(2) Grandchild or stepgrandchild adopted by the insured's surviving spouse. If you are the grandchild or stepgrandchild of the insured and any time after the death of the insured you are legally adopted by the insured's surviving spouse, you are considered the dependent child of the insured as of the date of his or her death if—

(i) Your adoption took place in the United States;

(ii) At the time of the insured's death, your natural, adopting or stepparent was not living in the insured's household and making regular contributions toward your support; and

(iii) You meet the dependency requirements stated in § 404.364.

20 C.F.R. § 404.363 When is a stepchild dependent?

If you are the insured's stepchild, as defined in § 404.357, we consider you dependent on him or her if you were receiving at least one-half of your support from him or her at one of these times—

(a) When you applied;

(b) When the insured died; or

(c) If the insured had a period of disability that lasted until his or her death or entitlement to disability or old-age benefits, at the beginning of the period of disability or at the time the insured became entitled to benefits.

20 C.F.R. § 404.364 When is a grandchild or stepgrandchild dependent?

If you are the insured's grandchild or stepgrandchild, as defined in § 404.358(a), you are considered dependent upon the insured if—

(a) You began living with the insured before you became 18 years old; and

(b) You were living with the insured in the United States and receiving at least one-half of your support from him or her for the year before he or she became entitled to old-age or disability benefits or died; or if the insured had a period of disability that lasted until he or she became entitled to benefits or died, for the year immediately before the month in which the period of disability began. If you were born during the 1–year period, the insured must have lived with you and provided at least one-half of your support for substantially all of the period that begins on the date of your birth. Paragraph (c) of this section explains when the substantially all requirement is met.

(c) The substantially all requirement will be met if, at one of the times described in paragraph (b) of this section, the insured was living with you and providing at least one-half of your support, and any period during which he or she was not living with you and providing one-half of your support did not exceed the lesser of 3 months or one-half of the period beginning with the month of your birth.

20 C.F.R § 404.365 When an equitably adopted child is dependent.

If you are the insured's equitably adopted child, as defined in § 404.359, you are considered dependent upon him or her if you were either living with or receiving contributions for your support from the insured at the time of his or her death. If your equitable adoption is found to have occurred after the insured became entitled to old-age or disability benefits, your dependency cannot be established during the insured's life. If your equitable adoption is found to have occurred before the insured became entitled to old-age or disability benefits, you are considered dependent upon him or her if you were either living with or receiving contributions for your support from the insured at one of these times—

(a) When you applied; or

(b) If the insured had a period of disability that lasted until he or she became entitled to old-age or disability benefits, at the beginning of the period of disability or at the time the insured became entitled to benefits.

20 C.F.R. § 404.366 "Contributions for support," "one-half support," and "living with" the insured defined—determining first month of entitlement.

To be eligible for child's or parent's benefits, * * * you must be dependent upon the insured person at a particular time or be assumed dependent upon him or her. * * * Your dependency upon the insured person may be based upon whether at a specified time you were receiving contributions for your support or one-half of your support from the insured person, or whether you were living with him or her. These terms are defined in paragraphs (a) through (c) of this section.

(a) Contributions for support. The insured makes a contribution for your support if the following conditions are met:

(1) The insured gives some of his or her own cash or goods to help support you. Support includes food, shelter, routine medical care, and other ordinary and customary items needed for your maintenance. The value of any goods the insured contributes is the same as the cost of the goods when he or she gave them for your support. If the insured provides services for you that would otherwise have to be paid for, the cash value of his or her services may be considered a contribution for your support. An example of this would be work the insured does to repair your home. The insured person is making a contribution for your support if you receive an allotment, allowance, or benefit based upon his or her military pay, veterans' pension or compensation, or social security earnings.

(2) Contributions must be made regularly and must be large enough to meet an important part of your ordinary living costs. Ordinary living costs are the costs for your food, shelter, routine medical care, and similar necessities. If the insured person only provides gifts or donations once in a while for special purposes, they will not be considered contributions for your support. Although the insured's contributions must be made on a regular basis, temporary interruptions caused by circumstances beyond the insured person's control, such as illness or unemployment, will be disregarded unless during this interruption someone else takes over responsibility for supporting you on a permanent basis.

(b) One-half support. The insured person provides one-half of your support if he or she makes regular contributions for your ordinary living costs; the amount of these contributions equals or exceeds one-half of your ordinary living costs; and any income (from sources other than the insured person) you have available for support purposes is one-half or less of your ordinary living costs. We will consider any income which is available to you for your support whether or not that income is actually used for your ordinary living costs. Ordinary living costs are the costs for your food, shelter, routine medical care, and similar necessities. A contribution may be in cash, goods, or services. The insured is not providing at least one-half of your support unless he or she has done so for a reasonable period of time. Ordinarily we consider a reasonable period to be the 12–month period immediately preceding the time when the one-half support requirement must be met under the rules in§§ 404.362(c)(1) and 404.363 (for child's benefits), in § 404.370(f) (for parent's benefits) and in § 404.408a(c) (for benefits where the Government pension offset may be applied). A shorter period will be considered reasonable under the following circumstances:

(1) At some point within the 12–month period, the insured either begins or stops providing at least one-half of your support on a permanent basis and this is a change in the way you had been supported up to then. In these circumstances, the time from the change up to the end of the 12–month period will be considered a reasonable period, unless paragraph (b)(2) of this section applies. The change in your source of support must be permanent and not temporary. Changes caused by seasonal employment or customary visits to the insured's home are considered temporary.

(2) The insured provided one-half or more of your support for at least 3 months of the 12–month period, but was forced to stop or reduce contributions because of circumstances beyond his or her control, such as illness or unemployment, and no one else took over the responsibility for providing at least one-half of your support on a permanent basis. Any support you received from a public assistance program is not considered as a taking over of responsibility for your support by someone else. Under these circumstances, a reasonable period is that part of the 12–month period before the insured was forced to reduce or stop providing at least one-half of your support.

(c) "Living with" the insured. You are living with the insured if you ordinarily live in the same home with the insured and he or she is exercising, or has the right to exercise, parental control and authority over your activities. You are living with the insured during temporary separations if you and the insured expect to live together in the same place after the separation. Temporary separations may include the insured's absence because of active military service or imprisonment if he or she still exercises parental control and authority. However, you are not considered to be living with the insured if you are in active military service or in prison.
* * *

* * *

20 C.F.R. § 404.367 When you are a "full-time elementary or secondary school student".

You may be eligible for child's benefits if you are a full-time elementary or secondary school student. * * * You are a full-time elementary or secondary school student if you meet all the following conditions:

(a) You attend a school which provides elementary or secondary education as determined under the law of the State or other jurisdiction in which it is located. Participation in the following programs also meets the requirements of this paragraph:

> (1) You are instructed in elementary or secondary education at home in accordance with a home school law of the State or other jurisdiction in which you reside; or

> (2) You are in an independent study elementary or secondary education program in accordance with the law of the State or other jurisdiction in which you reside which is administered by the local school or school district/jurisdiction.

(b) You are in full-time attendance in a day or evening noncorrespondence course of at least 13 weeks duration and you are carrying a subject load which is considered full-time for day students under the institution's standards and practices. If you are in a home schooling program as described in paragraph (a)(1) of this section, you must be carrying a subject load which is considered full-time for day students under standards and practices set by the State or other jurisdiction in which you reside;

(c) To be considered in full-time attendance, your scheduled attendance must be at the rate of at least 20 hours per week unless one of the exceptions in paragraphs (c)(1) and (2) of this section applies. If you are in an independent study program as described in paragraph (a)(2) of this section, your number of hours spent in school attendance are determined by combining the number of hours of attendance at a school facility with the agreed upon number of hours spent in independent study. You may still be considered in full-time attendance if your scheduled rate of attendance is below 20 hours per week if we find that:

> (1) The school attended does not schedule at least 20 hours per week and going to that particular school is your only reasonable alternative; or

(2) Your medical condition prevents you from having scheduled attendance of at least 20 hours per week. To prove that your medical condition prevents you from scheduling 20 hours per week, we may request that you provide appropriate medical evidence or a statement from the school.

(d) You are not being paid while attending the school by an employer who has requested or required that you attend the school;

(e) You are in grade 12 or below; and

(f) You are not subject to the provisions in § 404.468 for nonpayment of benefits to certain prisoners and certain other inmates of publicly funded institutions.

20 C.F.R § 404.368 When you are considered a full-time student during a period of nonattendance.

If you are a full-time student, your eligibility may continue during a period of nonattendance (including part-time attendance) if all the following conditions are met:

(a) The period of nonattendance is 4 consecutive months or less;

(b) You show us that you intend to resume your studies as a full-time student at the end of the period or at the end of the period you are a full-time student; and

(c) The period of nonattendance is not due to your expulsion or suspension from the school.

20 C.F.R. § 404.403 Reduction where total monthly benefits exceed maximum family benefits payable.

(a) General.

(1) The Social Security Act limits the amount of monthly benefits that can be paid for any month based on the earnings of an insured individual. If the total benefits to which all persons are entitled on one earnings record exceed a maximum amount prescribed by law, then those benefits must be reduced so that they do not exceed that maximum.

(2) The method of determining the total benefits payable (the family maximum) depends on when the insured individual died or became eligible, whichever is earlier. For purposes of this section, the year in which the insured individual becomes eligible refers generally to the year in which the individual attains age 62 or becomes disa-

bled. However, where eligibility or death is in 1979 or later, the year of death, attainment of age 62, or beginning of current disability does not control if the insured individual was entitled to a disability benefit within the 12 month period preceding current eligibility or death. Instead the year in which the individual became eligible for the former disability insurance benefit is the year of eligibility.

(3) The benefits of an individual entitled as a divorced spouse or surviving divorced spouse will not be reduced pursuant to this section. The benefits of all other individuals entitled on the same record will be determined under this section as if no such divorced spouse or surviving divorced spouse were entitled to benefits.

(4) In any case where more than one individual is entitled to benefits as the spouse or surviving spouse of a worker for the same month, and at least one of those individuals is entitled based on a marriage not valid under State law, the benefits of the individual whose entitlement is based on a valid marriage under State law will not be reduced pursuant to this section. The benefits of all other individuals entitled on the same record (unless excluded by paragraph (a)(3) of this section) will be determined under this section as if such validly married individual were not entitled to benefits.

(5) When a person entitled on a worker's earnings record is also entitled to benefits on another earnings record, we consider only the amount of benefits actually due or payable on the worker's record to the dually-entitled person when determining how much to reduce total monthly benefits payable on the worker's earnings record because of the maximum. We do not include, in total benefits payable, any amount not paid because of that person's entitlement on another earnings record (see § 404.407). The effect of this provision is to permit payment of up to the full maximum benefits to other beneficiaries who are not subject to a deduction or reduction. (See § 404.402 for other situations where we apply deductions or reductions before reducing total benefits for the maximum.)

Example 1: A wage earner, his wife and child are entitled to benefits. The wage earner's primary insurance amount is $600.00. His maximum is $900.00. Due to the maximum limit, the monthly benefits for the wife and child must be reduced to $150.00 each. Their original benefit rates are $300.00 each.

Maximum—$900.00

Subtract primary insurance amount—$600.00

Amount available for wife and child—$300.00

Divide by 2—$150.00 each for wife and child

The wife is also entitled to benefits on her own record of $120.00 monthly. This reduces her wife's benefit to $30.00. The following table illustrates this calculation.

Wife's benefit, reduced for maximum—$150.00

Subtract reduction due to dual entitlement—$120.00

Wife's benefit—$30.00

In computing the total benefits payable on the record, we disregard the $120.00 we cannot pay the wife. This allows us to increase the amount payable to the child to $270.00. The table below shows the steps in our calculation.

Amount available under maximum—$300.00

Subtract amount due wife after reduction due to entitlement to her own benefit—$30.00

Child's benefit—$270.00

* * *

* * *

20 C.F.R. § 404.404 How reduction for maximum affects insured individual and other persons entitled on his earnings record.

If a reduction of monthly benefits is required under the provisions of § 404.403, the monthly benefit amount of each of the persons entitled to a monthly benefits on the same earnings record (with the exception of the individual entitled to old-age or disability insurance benefits) is proportionately reduced so that the total benefits that can be paid in 1 month (including an amount equal to the primary insurance amount of the old-age or disability insurance beneficiary, when applicable) does not exceed the maximum family benefit (except as provided in § 404.405 where various savings clause provisions are described).

20 C.F.R § 404.407 Reduction because of entitlement to other benefits.

(a) Entitlement to old-age or disability insurance benefit and other monthly benefit. If an individual is entitled to an old-age insurance benefit or disability insurance benefit for any month after August 1958 and to any other monthly benefit payable under the provisions of title II of the

Act for the same month, such other benefit for the month * * * is reduced (but not below zero) by an amount equal to such old-age insurance benefit * * * or such disability insurance benefit, as the case may be.

(b) Entitlement to widow's or widower's benefit and other monthly benefit. If an individual is entitled for any month after August 1965 to a widow's or widower's insurance benefit under the provisions of section 202 (e)(4) or (f)(5) of the Act and to any other monthly benefit payable under the provisions of title II of the Act for the same month, except an old-age insurance benefit, such other insurance benefit for that month * * * shall be reduced, but not below zero, by an amount equal to such widow's or widower's insurance benefit after any reduction or reductions under paragraph (a) of this section * * *.

(c) Entitlement to old-age insurance benefit and disability insurance benefit. Any individual who is entitled for any month after August 1965 to both an old-age insurance benefit and a disability insurance benefit shall be entitled to only the larger of such benefits for such month, except that where the individual so elects, he or she shall instead be entitled to only the smaller of such benefits for such month. * * *

(d) Child's insurance benefits. * * * Where a child is simultaneously entitled to child's insurance benefits on more than one earnings record, the general rule is that the child will be paid an amount which is based on the record having the highest primary insurance amount. However, the child will be paid a higher amount which is based on the earnings record having a lower primary insurance amount if no other beneficiary entitled on any record would receive a lower benefit because the child is paid on the record with the lower primary insurance amount.

* * *

20 C.F.R § 404.410 How does SSA reduce my benefits when my entitlement begins before full retirement age?

Generally your old-age, wife's, husband's, widow's, or widower's benefits are reduced if entitlement begins before the month you attain full retirement age (as defined in § 404.409). However, your benefits as a wife or husband are not reduced for any month in which you have in your care a child of the worker on whose earnings record you are entitled. The child must be entitled to child's benefits. Your benefits as a widow or widower are not reduced below the benefit amount you would receive as a mother or father for any month in which you have in your care a child of the worker on whose record you are entitled. The child must be entitled to child's benefits. Subject to §§ 404.411 through 404.413, reductions in benefits are made in the amounts described.

(a) How does SSA reduce my old-age benefits? The reduction in your primary insurance amount is based on the number of months of entitlement prior to the month you attain full retirement age. The reduction is 5/9 of 1 percent for each of the first 36 months and 5/12 of 1 percent for each month in excess of 36.

Example: Alex's full retirement age for unreduced benefits is 65 years and 8 months. She elects to begin receiving benefits at age 62. Her primary insurance amount of $980.50 must be reduced because of her entitlement to benefits 44 months prior to full retirement age. The reduction is 36 months at 5/9 of 1 percent and 8 months at 5/12 of 1 percent.

980.50 x 36 x 5/9 x .01 = $196.10

980.50 x 8 x 5/12 x .01 = $32.68

The two added together equal a total reduction of $228.78. This amount is rounded to $228.80 (the next higher multiple of 10 cents) and deducted from the primary insurance amount. The resulting $751.70 is the monthly benefit payable.

(b) How does SSA reduce my wife's or husband's benefits? Your wife's or husband's benefits before any reduction (see §§ 404.304 and 404.333) are reduced first (if necessary) for the family maximum under § 404.403. They are then reduced based on the number of months of entitlement prior to the month you attain full retirement age. This does not include any month in which you have a child of the worker on whose earnings record you are entitled in your care. The child must be entitled to child benefits. The reduction is 25/36 of 1 percent for each of the first 36 months and 5/12 of 1 percent for each month in excess of 36.

Example: Sam is entitled to old-age benefits. His spouse Ashley elects to begin receiving wife's benefits at age 63. Her full retirement age for unreduced benefits is 65 and 4 months. Her benefit will be reduced for 28 months of entitlement prior to full retirement age. If her unreduced benefit is $412.40 the reduction will be $412.40 x 28 x 25/36 x .01. The resulting $80.18 is rounded to $80.20 (the next higher multiple of 10 cents) and subtracted from $412.40 to determine the monthly benefit amount of $332.20.

(c) How does SSA reduce my widow's or widower's benefits?

Your entitlement to widow's or widower's benefits may begin at age 60 based on age or at age 50 based on disability. Refer to § 404.335 for more information on the requirements for entitlement. Both types are reduced if entitlement begins prior to attainment of full retirement age (as defined in § 404.409).

(1) Widow's or widower's benefits based on age. Your widow's or widower's unreduced benefit amount (the worker's primary insurance amount after any reduction for the family maximum under § 404.403), is reduced or further reduced based on the number of months of entitlement prior to the month you attain full retirement age. This does not include any month in which you have in your care a child of the worker on whose earnings record you are entitled. The child must be entitled to child's benefits. The number of months of entitlement prior to full retirement age is multiplied by .285 and then divided by the number of months in the period beginning with the month of attainment of age 60 and ending with the month immediately before the month of attainment of full retirement age.

Example: Ms. Bogle is entitled to an unreduced widow benefit of $785.70 beginning at age 64. Her full retirement age for unreduced old-age benefits is 65 years and 4 months. She will receive benefits for 16 months prior to attainment of full retirement age. The number of months in the period from age 60 through full retirement age of 65 and 4 months is 64. The reduction in her benefit is $785.70 x 16 x .285 divided by 64 or $55.98. $55.98 is rounded to the next higher multiple of 10 cents ($56.00) and subtracted from $785.70. The result is a monthly benefit of $729.70.

(2) Widow's or widower's benefits based on disability.

(i) For months after December 1983, your widow's or widower's benefits are not reduced for months of entitlement prior to age 60. You are deemed to be age 60 in your month of entitlement to disabled widow's or widower's benefits and your benefits are reduced only under paragraph (c)(1) of this section.

(ii) For months from January 1973 through December 1983, benefits as a disabled widow or widower were reduced under paragraph (c)(1) of this section. The benefits were then subject to an additional reduction of 43/240 of one percent for each month of entitlement prior to age 60 based on disability.

* * *

* * *

20 C.F.R. § 404.502 Overpayments.

Upon determination that an overpayment has been made, adjustments will be made against monthly benefits and lump sums as follows:

(a) Individual overpaid is living.

(1) If the individual to whom an overpayment was made is at the time of a determination of such overpayment entitled to a monthly benefit or a lump sum under title II of the Act, or at any time thereafter becomes so entitled, no benefit for any month and no lump sum is payable to such individual, except as provided in paragraphs (c) and (d) of this section, until an amount equal to the amount of the overpayment has been withheld or refunded. Such adjustments will be made against any monthly benefit or lump sum under title II of the Act to which such individual is entitled whether payable on the basis of such individual's earnings or the earnings of another individual.

(2) If any other individual is entitled to benefits for any month on the basis of the same earnings as the overpaid individual, except as adjustment is to be effected pursuant to paragraphs (c) and (d) of this section by withholding a part of the monthly benefit of either the overpaid individual or any other individual entitled to benefits on the basis of the same earnings, no benefit for any month will be paid on such earnings to such other individual until an amount equal to the amount of the overpayment has been withheld or refunded.

(3) If a representative payee receives a payment on behalf of a beneficiary after that beneficiary dies, the representative payee or his estate is solely liable for repaying the overpayment. * * *

(b) Individual overpaid dies before adjustment. If an overpaid individual dies before adjustment is completed under the provisions of paragraph (a) of this section, no lump sum and no subsequent monthly benefit will be paid on the basis of earnings which were the basis of the overpayment to such deceased individual until full recovery of the overpayment has been effected, except as provided in paragraphs (c) and (d) of this section or under § 404.515. Such recovery may be effected through:

(1) Payment by the estate of the deceased overpaid individual,

(2) Withholding of amounts due the estate of such individual under title II of the Act,

(3) Withholding a lump sum or monthly benefits due any other individual on the basis of the same earnings which were the basis of the overpayment to the deceased overpaid individual, or

(4) Any combination of the amount above.

(5) The methods in paragraphs (b)(1) and (b)(2) of this section for overpayments owed by a representative payee for payments made after the beneficiary's death. We will not recover such overpayments

from any person other than the individual who was representative payee or his estate, but we may recover these overpayments from such other person under § 404.503(b).

(c) Adjustment by withholding part of a monthly benefit.

(1) Where it is determined that withholding the full amount each month would "defeat the purpose of title II," i.e., deprive the person of income required for ordinary and necessary living expenses (see § 404.508), adjustment under paragraphs (a) and (b) of this section may be effected by withholding an amount of not less than $10 of the monthly benefit payable to an individual.

(2) Adjustment as provided by this paragraph will not be available if the overpayment was caused by the individual's intentional false statement or representation, or willful concealment of, or deliberate failure to furnish, material information. In such cases, recovery of the overpayment will be accomplished as provided in paragraph (a) of this section.

* * *

20 C.F.R. § 404.502a Notice of right to waiver consideration.

Whenever an initial determination is made that more than the correct amount of payment has been made, and we seek adjustment or recovery of the overpayment, the individual from whom we are seeking adjustment or recovery is immediately notified. The notice includes:

(a) The overpayment amount and how and when it occurred;

(b) A request for full, immediate refund, unless the overpayment can be withheld from the next month's benefit;

(c) The proposed adjustment of benefits if refund is not received within 30 days after the date of the notice and adjustment of benefits is available;

(d) An explanation of the availability of a different rate of withholding when full withholding is proposed, installment payments when refund is requested and adjustment is not currently available, and/or cross-program recovery when refund is requested and the individual is receiving another type of payment from SSA (language about cross-program recovery is not included in notices sent to individuals in jurisdictions where this recovery option is not available);

(e) An explanation of the right to request waiver of adjustment or recovery and the automatic scheduling of a file review and pre-recoupment hearing (commonly referred to as a personal conference) if a request for waiver cannot be approved after initial paper review;

(f) An explanation of the right to request reconsideration of the fact and/or amount of the overpayment determination;

(g) Instructions about the availability of forms for requesting reconsideration and waiver;

(h) An explanation that if the individual does not request waiver or reconsideration within 30 days of the date of the overpayment notice, adjustment or recovery of the overpayment will begin;

(i) A statement that an SSA office will help the individual complete and submit forms for appeal or waiver requests; and

(j) A statement that the individual receiving the notice should notify SSA promptly if reconsideration, waiver, a lesser rate of withholding, repayment by installments or cross-program adjustment is wanted.

20 C.F.R. § 404.503 Underpayments.

Underpayments will be adjusted as follows:

(a) Individual underpaid is living. If an individual to whom an underpayment is due is living, the amount of such underpayment will be paid to such individual either in a single payment (if he is not entitled to a monthly benefit or a lump-sum death payment) or by increasing one or more monthly benefits or a lump-sum death payment to which such individual is or becomes entitled. However, if we determine that the individual to whom an underpayment is due also received an overpayment as defined in § 404.501(a) for a different period, we will apply any underpayment due the individual to reduce that overpayment, unless we have waived recovery of the overpayment under the provisions of §§ 404.506 through 404.512.

(b) Individual dies before adjustment of underpayment. If an individual to who has been underpaid dies before receiving payment or negotiating a check or checks representing such payment, we first apply any amounts due the deceased individual against any overpayments as defined in § 404.501(a) owed by the deceased individual, unless we have waived recovery of such overpayment under the provisions of §§ 404.506 through 404.512. We then will distribute any remaining underpayment to the living person (or persons) in the highest order of priority as follows:

(1) The deceased individual's surviving spouse * * * who was either:

(i) Living in the same household * * * with the deceased individual at the time of such individual's death, or

(ii) Entitled to a monthly benefit on the basis of the same earnings record as was the deceased individual for the month in which such individual died.

(2) The child or children of the deceased individual * * * entitled to a monthly benefit on the basis of the same earnings record as was the deceased individual for the month in which such individual died (if more than one such child, in equal shares to each such child).

(3) The parent or parents of the deceased individual, entitled to a monthly benefit on the basis of the same earnings record as was the deceased individual for the month in which such individual died (if more than one such parent, in equal shares to each such parent). * * *

(4) The surviving spouse of the deceased individual * * * who does not qualify under paragraph (b)(1) of this section.

(5) The child or children of the deceased individual * * * who do not qualify under paragraph (b)(2) of this section (if more than one such child, in equal shares to each such child).

(6) The parent or parents of the deceased individual, who do not qualify under paragraph (b)(3) of this section (if more than one such parent, in equal shares to each such parent). * * *

(7) The legal representative of the estate of the deceased individual as defined in paragraph (d) of this section.

* * *

20 C.F.R. § 404.504 Relation to provisions for reductions and increases.

The amount of an overpayment or underpayment is the difference between the amount paid to the beneficiary and the amount of the payment to which the beneficiary was actually entitled. Such payment, for example, would be equal to the difference between the amount of a benefit in fact paid to the beneficiary and the amount of such benefit as reduced under section 202(j)(1), 202(k)(3), 203(a), or 224(a), or as increased under section 202(d)(2), 202(m), or 215(f) and (g). In effecting an adjustment with respect to an overpayment, no amount can be considered as having been withheld from a particular benefit which is in excess of the amount of such benefit as so decreased.

20 C.F.R. § 404.506 When waiver may be applied and how to process the request.

(a) Section 204(b) of the Act provides that there shall be no adjustment or recovery in any case where an overpayment under title II has been made to an individual who is without fault if adjustment or recovery would either defeat the purpose of title II of the Act, or be against equity and good conscience.

(b) If an individual requests waiver of adjustment or recovery of a title II overpayment within 30 days after receiving a notice of overpayment that contains the information in § 404.502a, no adjustment or recovery action will be taken until after the initial waiver determination is made. If the individual requests waiver more than 30 days after receiving the notice of overpayment, SSA will stop any adjustment or recovery actions until after the initial waiver determination is made.

(c) When waiver is requested, the individual gives SSA information to support his/her contention that he/she is without fault in causing the overpayment (see § 404.507) and that adjustment or recovery would either defeat the purpose of title II of the Act (see § 404.508) or be against equity and good conscience (see § 404.509). That information, along with supporting documentation, is reviewed to determine if waiver can be approved. If waiver cannot be approved after this review, the individual is notified in writing and given the dates, times and place of the file review and personal conference; the procedure for reviewing the claims file prior to the personal conference; the procedure for seeking a change in the scheduled dates, times, and/or place; and all other information necessary to fully inform the individual about the personal conference. The file review is always scheduled at least 5 days before the personal conference. We will offer to the individual the option of conducting the personal conference face-to-face at a place we designate, by telephone, or by video teleconference. The notice will advise the individual of the date and time of the personal conference.

(d) At the file review, the individual and the individual's representative have the right to review the claims file and applicable law and regulations with the decisionmaker or another SSA representative who is prepared to answer questions. We will provide copies of material related to the overpayment and/or waiver from the claims file or pertinent sections of the law or regulations that are requested by the individual or the individual's representative.

(e) At the personal conference, the individual is given the opportunity to:

(1) Appear personally, testify, cross-examine any witnesses, and make arguments;

(2) Be represented by an attorney or other representative (see § 404.1700), although the individual must be present at the conference; and

(3) Submit documents for consideration by the decisionmaker.

* * *

(g) SSA issues a written decision to the individual (and his/her representative, if any) specifying the findings of fact and conclusions in support of the decision to approve or deny waiver and advising of the individual's right to appeal the decision. If waiver is denied, adjustment or recovery of the overpayment begins even if the individual appeals.

(h) If it appears that the waiver cannot be approved, and the individual declines a personal conference or fails to appear for a second scheduled personal conference, a decision regarding the waiver will be made based on the written evidence of record. Reconsideration is then the next step in the appeals process (but see § 404.930(a)(7)).

20 C.F.R. § 404.507 Fault.

"Fault" as used in "without fault" (see § 404.506 and 42 CFR 405.355) applies only to the individual. Although the Administration may have been at fault in making the overpayment, that fact does not relieve the overpaid individual or any other individual from whom the Administration seeks to recover the overpayment from liability for repayment if such individual is not without fault. In determining whether an individual is at fault, the Social Security Administration will consider all pertinent circumstances, including the individual's age and intelligence, and any physical, mental, educational, or linguistic limitations (including any lack of facility with the English language) the individual has. What constitutes fault (except for deduction overpayments—see § 404.510) on the part of the overpaid individual or on the part of any other individual from whom the Administration seeks to recover the overpayment depends upon whether the facts show that the incorrect payment to the individual or to a provider of services or other person, or an incorrect payment made under section 1814(e) of the Act, resulted from:

(a) An incorrect statement made by the individual which he knew or should have known to be incorrect; or

(b) Failure to furnish information which he knew or should have known to be material; or

(c) With respect to the overpaid individual only, acceptance of a payment which he either knew or could have been expected to know was incorrect.

20 C.F.R § 404.508 Defeat the purpose of Title II.

(a) General. Defeat the purpose of title II, for purposes of this subpart, means defeat the purpose of benefits under this title, i.e., to deprive a person of income required for ordinary and necessary living expenses. This depends upon whether the person has an income or financial resources sufficient for more than ordinary and necessary needs, or is dependent upon all of his current benefits for such needs. An individual's ordinary and necessary expenses include:

(1) Fixed living expenses, such as food and clothing, rent, mortgage payments, utilities, maintenance, insurance (e.g., life, accident, and health insurance including premiums for supplementary medical insurance benefits under title XVIII), taxes, installment payments, etc.;

(2) Medical, hospitalization, and other similar expenses;

(3) Expenses for the support of others for whom the individual is legally responsible; and

(4) Other miscellaneous expenses which may reasonably be considered as part of the individual's standard of living.

(b) When adjustment or recovery will defeat the purpose of title II. Adjustment or recovery will defeat the purposes of title II in (but is not limited to) situations where the person from whom recovery is sought needs substantially all of his current income (including social security monthly benefits) to meet current ordinary and necessary living expenses.

20 C.F.R. § 404.509 Against equity and good conscience; defined.

(a) Recovery of an overpayment is "against equity and good conscience" (under title II and title XVIII) if an individual—

(1) Changed his or her position for the worse (Example 1) or relinquished a valuable right (Example 2) because of reliance upon a notice that a payment would be made or because of the overpayment itself; or

(2) Was living in a separate household from the overpaid person at the time of the overpayment and did not receive the overpayment (Examples 3 and 4).

(b) The individual's financial circumstances are not material to a finding of against equity and good conscience.

Example 1. A widow, having been awarded benefits for herself and daughter, entered her daughter in private school because the monthly benefits made this possible. After the widow and her daughter received payments for almost a year, the deceased worker was found to be not insured and all payments to the widow and child were incorrect. The widow has no other funds with which to pay the daughter's private school expenses. Having entered the daughter in private school and thus incurred a financial obligation toward which the benefits had been applied, she was in a worse position financially than if she and her daughter had never been entitled to benefits. In this situation, the recovery of the payments would be "against equity and good conscience."

Example 2. After being awarded old-age insurance benefits, an individual resigned from employment on the assumption he would receive regular monthly benefit payments. It was discovered 3 years later that (due to a Social Security Administration error) his award was erroneous because he did not have the required insured status. Due to his age, the individual was unable to get his job back and could not get any other employment. In this situation, recovery of the overpayments would be "against equity and good conscience" because the individual gave up a valuable right.

Example 3. M divorced K and married L. M died a few years later. When K files for benefits as a surviving divorced wife, she learns that L had been overpaid $3,200 on M's earnings record. Because K and L are both entitled to benefits on M's record of earnings and we could not recover the overpayment from L, we sought recovery from K. K was living in a separate household from L at the time of the overpayment and did not receive the overpayment. K requests waiver of recovery of the $3,200 overpayment from benefits due her as a surviving divorced wife of M. In this situation, it would be "against equity and good conscience" to recover the overpayment from K.

Example 4. G filed for and was awarded benefits. His daughter, T, also filed for student benefits on G's earnings record. Since T was an independent, full-time student living in another State, she filed for benefits on her own behalf. Later, after T received 12 monthly benefits, the school reported that T had been a full-time student only 2 months and had withdrawn from school. Since T was overpaid 10 monthly benefits, she was requested to return the overpayment to SSA. T did not return the overpayment and further attempts to collect the overpayment were unsuccessful. G was asked to repay the overpayment because he was receiving benefits on the same earnings record. G requested waiver. To support his waiver request G established that he was not at fault in causing the over-payment because he did not know that T was receiving benefits. Since G is without fault and, in addition, meets the requirements of not living in the same household at the time of the overpayment and did not receive the overpayment, it would be "against equity and good conscience" to re-cover the overpayment from G.

20 C.F.R. § 404.535 How much will we withhold from your title VIII and title XVI benefits to recover a title II overpayment?

(a) If past-due benefits are payable to you, we will withhold the lesser of the entire overpayment balance or the entire amount of past-due bene-fits.

(b)(1) We will collect the overpayment from current monthly benefits due in a month under title VIII and title XVI by withholding the lesser of the amount of the entire overpayment balance or:

(i) 10 percent of the monthly title VIII benefits payable for that month and

(ii) in the case of title XVI benefits, an amount no greater than the lesser of the benefit payable for that month or an amount equal to 10 percent of your income for that month (including such monthly benefit but excluding payments under title II when recovery is also made from title II benefits and excluding income excluded pursuant to §§ 416.1112 and 416.1124 of this chapter).

(2) Paragraph (b)(1) of this section does not apply if:

(i) You request and we approve a different rate of withholding, or

(ii) You or your spouse willfully misrepresented or concealed ma-terial information in connection with the overpayment.

(c) In determining whether to grant your request that we withhold less than the amount described in paragraph (b)(1) of this section, we will use the criteria applied under § 404.508 to similar requests about with-holding from title II benefits.

(d) If you or your spouse willfully misrepresented or concealed mate-rial information in connection with the overpayment, we will collect the overpayment by withholding the lesser of the overpayment balance or the entire amount of title VIII and title XVI benefits payable to you. We will not collect at a lesser rate. (See § 416.571 of this chapter for what we mean by concealment of material information.)

20 C.F.R. § 404.614 When an application or other form is considered filed.

(a) *General rule.* Except as otherwise provided in paragraph (b) of this section and in §§ 404.630 through 404.633 which relate to the filing date of an application, an application for benefits, or a written statement, request, or notice is filed on the day it is received by an SSA employee at one of our offices or by an SSA employee who is authorized to receive it at a place other than one of our offices.

(b) *Other places and dates of filing.* We will also accept as the date of filing—

(1) The date an application for benefits, or a written statement, request or notice is received by any office of the U.S. Foreign Service or by the Veterans Administration Regional Office in the Philippines;

(2) The date an application for benefits or a written statement, request or notice is mailed to us by the U.S. mail, if using the date we receive it would result in the loss or lessening of rights. The date shown by a U.S. postmark will be used as the date of mailing. If the postmark is unreadable, or there is no postmark, we will consider other evidence of when you mailed it to us; or

(3) The date an application for benefits is filed with the Railroad Retirement Board or the Veterans Administration. See § 404.611 (b) and (c) for an explanation of when an application for benefits filed with the Railroad Retirement Board or the Veterans Administration is considered an application for social security benefits.

20 C.F.R. § 404.704 Your responsibility for giving evidence.

When evidence is needed to prove your eligibility or your right to continue to receive benefit payments, you will be responsible for obtaining and giving the evidence to us. We will be glad to advise you what is needed and how to get it and we will consider any evidence you give us. If your evidence is a foreign-language record or document, we can have it translated for you. Evidence given to us will be kept confidential and not disclosed to anyone but you except under the rules set out in Part 401. You should also be aware that Section 208 of the Social Security Act provides criminal penalties for misrepresenting the facts or for making false statements to obtain social security benefits for yourself or someone else.

20 C.F.R. § 404.716 Type of evidence of age to be given.

(a) *Preferred evidence.* The best evidence of your age, if you can obtain it, is either: a birth certificate or hospital birth record recorded before age 5; or a religious record which shows your date of birth and was recorded before age 5.

(b) Other evidence of age. If you cannot obtain the preferred evidence of your age, you will be asked for other convincing evidence that shows your date of birth or age at a certain time such as: an original family bible or family record; school records; census records; a statement signed by the physician or midwife who was present at your birth; insurance policies; a marriage record; a passport; an employment record; a delayed birth certificate, your child's birth certificate; or an immigration or naturalization record.

20 C.F.R. § 404.723 When evidence of marriage is required.

If you apply for benefits as the insured person's husband or wife, widow or widower, divorced wife or divorced husband, we will ask for evidence of the marriage and where and when it took place. We may also ask for this evidence if you apply for child's benefits or for the lump-sum death payment as the widow or widower. If you are a widow, widower, or divorced wife who remarried after your marriage to the insured person ended, we may also ask for evidence of the remarriage. You may be asked for evidence of someone else's marriage if this is necessary to prove your marriage to the insured person was valid. In deciding whether the marriage to the insured person is valid or not, we will follow the law of the State where the insured person had his or her permanent home when you applied or, if earlier, when he or she died ** *. What evidence we will ask for depends upon whether the insured person's marriage was a ceremonial marriage, a common-law marriage, or a marriage we will deem to be valid.

20 C.F.R. § 404.725 Evidence of a valid ceremonial marriage.

(a) General. A valid ceremonial marriage is one that follows procedures set by law in the State or foreign country where it takes place. These procedures cover who may perform the marriage ceremony, what licenses or witnesses are needed, and similar rules. A ceremonial marriage can be one that follows certain tribal Indian custom, Chinese custom, or similar traditional procedures. We will ask for the evidence described in this section.

(b) Preferred evidence. Preferred evidence of a ceremonial marriage is—

(1) If you are applying for wife's or husband's benefits, signed statements from you and the insured about when and where the marriage took place. If you are applying for the lump-sum death

payment as the widow or widower, your signed statement about when and where the marriage took place; or

(2) If you are applying for any other benefits or there is evidence causing some doubt about whether there was a ceremonial marriage: a copy of the public record of marriage or a certified statement as to the marriage; a copy of the religious record of marriage or a certified statement as to what the record shows; or the original marriage certificate.

(c) Other evidence of a ceremonial marriage. If preferred evidence of a ceremonial marriage cannot be obtained, we will ask you to explain why and to give us a signed statement of the clergyman or official who held the marriage ceremony, or other convincing evidence of the marriage.

20 C.F.R. § 404.726 Evidence of common-law marriage.

(a) General. A common-law marriage is one considered valid under certain State laws even though there was no formal ceremony. It is a marriage between two persons free to marry, who consider themselves married, live together as man and wife, and, in some States, meet certain other requirements. We will ask for the evidence described in this section.

(b) Preferred evidence. Preferred evidence of a common-law marriage is—

(1) If both the husband and wife are alive, their signed statements and those of two blood relatives;

(2) If either the husband or wife is dead, the signed statements of the one who is alive and those of two blood relatives of the deceased person; or

(3) If both the husband and wife are dead, the signed statements of one blood relative of each;

Note: All signed statements should show why the signer believes there was a marriage between the two persons. If a written statement cannot be gotten from a blood relative, one from another person can be used instead.

(c) Other evidence of common-law marriage. If you cannot get preferred evidence of a common-law marriage, we will ask you to explain why and to give us other convincing evidence of the marriage. We may not ask you for statements from a blood relative or other person if we believe other evidence presented to us proves the common-law marriage.

20 C.F.R. § 404.727 Evidence of a deemed valid marriage

(a) General. A deemed valid marriage is a ceremonial marriage we consider valid even though the correct procedures set by State law were not strictly followed or a former marriage had not yet ended. We will ask for the evidence described in this section.

(b) Preferred evidence. Preferred evidence of a deemed valid marriage is—

(1) Evidence of the ceremonial marriage as described in § 404.725(b)(2);

(2) If the insured person is alive, his or her signed statement that the other party to the marriage went through the ceremony in good faith and his or her reasons for believing the marriage was valid or believing the other party thought it was valid;

(3) The other party's signed statement that he or she went through the marriage ceremony in good faith and his or her reasons for believing it was valid;

(4) If needed to remove a reasonable doubt, the signed statements of others who might have information about what the other party knew about any previous marriage or other facts showing whether he or she went through the marriage in good faith; and

(5) Evidence the parties to the marriage were living in the same household when you applied for benefits or, if earlier, when the insured person died * * *.

(c) Other evidence of a deemed valid marriage. If you cannot obtain preferred evidence of a deemed valid marriage, we will ask you to explain why and to give us other convincing evidence of the marriage.

20 C.F.R.§ 404.730 When evidence of a parent or child relationship is needed.

If you apply for parent's or child's benefits, we will ask for evidence showing your relationship to the insured person. What evidence we will ask for depends on whether you are the insured person's natural parent or child; or whether you are the stepparent, stepchild, grandchild, stepgrandchild, adopting parent or adopted child.

20 C.F.R. § 404.731 Evidence you are a natural parent or child.

If you are the natural parent of the insured person, we will ask for a copy of his or her public or religious birth record made before age 5. If you are the natural child of the insured person, we will ask for a copy of your public or religious birth record made before age 5. In either case, if this record shows the same last name for the insured and the parent or child, we will accept it as convincing evidence of the relationship. However, if other evidence raises some doubt about this record or if the record cannot be gotten, we will ask for other evidence of the relationship. We may also ask for evidence of marriage of the insured person or of his or her parent if this is needed to remove any reasonable doubt about the relationship. To show you are the child of the insured person, you may be asked for evidence you would be able to inherit his or her personal property under State law where he or she had a permanent home * * *. In addition, we may ask for the insured persons signed statement that you are his or her natural child, or for a copy of any court order showing the insured has been declared to be your natural parent or any court order requiring the insured to contribute to you support because you are his or her son or daughter.

20 C.F.R.§ 404.732 Evidence you are a stepparent or stepchild.

If you are the stepparent or stepchild of the insured person, we will ask for the evidence described in § 404.731 or § 404.733 that which shows your natural or adoptive relationship to the insured person's husband, wife, widow, or widower. We will also ask for evidence of the husband's, wife's, widow's, or widower's marriage to the insured person * * *.

20 C.F.R. § 404.733 Evidence you are the legally adopting parent or legally adopted child.

If you are the adopting parent or adopted child, we will ask for the following evidence:

(a) A copy of the birth certificate made following the adoption; or if this cannot be gotten, other evidence of the adoption; and, if needed, evidence of the date of adoption;

(b) If the widow or widower adopted the child after the insured person died, the evidence described in paragraph (a) of this section; your written statement whether the insured person was living in the same household with the child when he or she died * * *; what support the child was getting from any other person or organization; and if the widow or widower had a deemed valid marriage with the insured person, evidence of that marriage * * *;

(c) If you are the insured's stepchild, grandchild, or stepgrandchild as well as his or her adopted child, we may also ask you for evidence to show how you were related to the insured before the adoption.

20 C.F.R. § 404.734 Evidence you are an equitably adopted child.

In many States, the law will treat someone as a child of another if he or she agreed to adopt the child, the natural parents or the person caring for the child were parties to the agreement, he or she and the child then lived together as parent and child, and certain other requirements are met. If you are a child who had this kind or relationship to the insured person (or to the insured persons's wife, widow, or husband), we will ask for evidence of the agreement if it is in writing. If it is not in writing or cannot be gotten, other evidence may be accepted. Also, the following evidence will be asked for: Written statements of your natural parents and the adopting parents and other evidence of the child's relationship to the adopting parents.

20 C.F.R § 404.735 Evidence you are the grandchild or stepgrandchild.

If you are the grandchild or stepgrandchild of the insured person, we will ask you for the kind of evidence described in §§ 404.731 through 404.733 that shows your relationship to your parent and your parent's relationship to the insured.

20 C.F.R § 404.736 Evidence of a child's dependency.

(a) When evidence of a child's dependency is needed. If you apply for child's benefit's we may ask for evidence you were the insured person's dependent at a specific time—usually the time you applied or the time the insured died or became disabled. What evidence we ask for depends upon how you are related to the insured person.

(b) Natural or adopted child. If you are the insured person's natural or adopted child, we may ask for the following evidence:

(1) A signed statement by someone who knows the facts that confirms this relationship and which shows whether you were legally adopted by someone other than the insured. If you were adopted by someone else while the insured person was alive, but the adoption was annulled, we may ask for a certified copy of the annulment decree or other convincing evidence of the annulment.

(2) A signed statement by someone in a position to know showing when and where you lived with the insured and when and why you may have lived apart; and showing what contributions the insured made to your support and when and how they were made.

(c) Stepchild. If you are the insured person's stepchild, we will ask for the following evidence:

(1) A signed statement by someone in a position to know—showing when and where you lived with the insured and when and why you may have lived apart.

(2) A signed statement by someone in a position to know showing you received at least one-half of your support from the insured for the one-year period ending at one of the times mentioned in paragraph (a) of this section; and the income end support you had in this period from any other source.

(d) *Grandchild or Stepgrandchild.* If you are the insured person's grandchild or stepgrandchild, we will ask for evidence described in paragraph (c) of this section showing that you were living together with the insured and receiving one-half of your support from him or her for the year before the insured became entitled to benefits or to a period of disability, or died. We will also ask for evidence of your parent's death or disability.

20 C.F.R § 404.822 Correction of the record of your earnings after the time limit ends.

(a) *Generally.* After the time limit for any year ends, we may correct the record of your earnings for that year if satisfactory evidence shows SSA records are incorrect and any of the circumstances in paragraphs (b) through (e) of this section applies.

(b) *Correcting SSA records to agree with tax returns.* We will correct SSA records to agree with a tax return of wages or self-employment income to the extent that the amount of earnings shown in the return is correct.

* * *

(c) *Written request for correction or application for benefits filed before the time limit ends*—

* * *

(d) *Transfer of wages to or from the Railroad Retirement Board*—

* * *

(e) *Other circumstances permitting correction*—

(1) *Investigation started before time limit ends.* * * *

(2) *Error apparent on face of records.* * * *

(3) Fraud. * * *

(4) Entries for wrong person or period. * * *

(5) Less than correct wages on SSA records. * * *

(6) Wage payments under a statute. * * *

20 C.F.R § 404.907 Reconsideration—general. (*See also* 20 C.F.R. 416.1407)

If you are dissatisfied with the initial determination, reconsideration is the first step in the administrative review process that we provide, except that we provide the opportunity for a hearing before an administrative law judge as the first step for those situations described in § 404.930(a)(6) and (a)(7), where you appeal an initial determination denying your request for waiver of adjustment or recovery of an overpayment (see § 404.506). If you are dissatisfied with our reconsidered determination, you may request a hearing before an administrative law judge.

20 C.F.R. § 404.909 How to request reconsideration. (*See also* 20 C.F.R. 416.1409)

(a) We shall reconsider an initial determination if you or any other party to the reconsideration files a written request—

    (1) Within 60 days after the date you receive notice of the initial determination (or within the extended time period if we extend the time as provided in paragraph (b) of this section);

    (2) At one of our offices, the Veterans Administration Regional Office in the Philippines, or an office of the Railroad Retirement Board if you have 10 or more years of service in the railroad industry.

(b) Extension of time to request a reconsideration. If you want a reconsideration of the initial determination but do not request one in time, you may ask us for more time to request a reconsideration. Your request for an extension of time must be in writing and must give the reasons why the request for reconsideration was not filed within the stated time period. If you show us that you had good cause for missing the deadline, we will extend the time period. To determine whether good cause exists, we use the standards explained in § 404.911.

20 C.F.R. § 404.911 Good cause for missing the deadline to request review. (*See also* 20 C.F.R. 416.1411)

(a) In determining whether you have shown that you had good cause for missing a deadline to request review we consider—

(1) What circumstances kept you from making the request on time;

(2) Whether our action misled you;

(3) Whether you did not understand the requirements of the Act resulting from amendments to the Act, other legislation, or court decisions; and

(4) Whether you had any physical, mental, educational, or linguistic limitations (including any lack of facility with the English language) which prevented you from filing a timely request or from understanding or knowing about the need to file a timely request for review.

(b) Examples of circumstances where good cause may exist include, but are not limited to, the following situations:

(1) You were seriously ill and were prevented from contacting us in person, in writing, or through a friend, relative, or other person.

(2) There was a death or serious illness in your immediate family.

(3) Important records were destroyed or damaged by fire or other accidental cause.

(4) You were trying very hard to find necessary information to support your claim but did not find the information within the stated time periods.

(5) You asked us for additional information explaining our action within the time limit, and within 60 days of receiving the explanation you requested reconsideration or a hearing, or within 30 days of receiving the explanation you requested Appeal Council review or filed a civil suit.

(6) We gave you incorrect or incomplete information about when and how to request administrative review or to file a civil suit.

(7) You did not receive notice of the determination or decision.

(8) You sent the request to another Government agency in good faith within the time limit and the request did not reach us until after the time period had expired.

(9) Unusual or unavoidable circumstances exist, including the circumstances described in paragraph (a)(4) of this section, which

show that you could not have known of the need to file timely, or which prevented you from filing timely.

20 C.F.R. § 404.913 Reconsideration procedures. (*See also* 20 C.F.R. 416.1413)

(a) Case review. With the exception of the type of case described in paragraph (b) of this section, the reconsideration process consists of a case review. Under a case review procedure, we will give you and the other parties to the reconsideration an opportunity to present additional evidence to us. The official who reviews your case will then make a reconsidered determination based on all of this evidence.

(b) Disability hearing. If you have been receiving benefits based on disability and you request reconsideration of an initial or revised determination that, based on medical factors, you are not now disabled, we will give you and the other parties to the reconsideration an opportunity for a disability hearing. (See §§ 404.914 through 404.918.)

20 C.F.R. § 404.914 Disability hearing—general. (*See also* 20 C.F.R. 416.1414)

(a) Availability. We will provide you with an opportunity for a disability hearing if:

(1) You have been receiving benefits based on a medical impairment that renders you disabled;

(2) We have made an initial or revised determination based on medical factors that you are not now disabled because your impairment:

(i) Has ceased;

(ii) Did not exist; or

(iii) Is no longer disabling; and

(3) You make a timely request for reconsideration of the initial or revised determination.

(b) Scope. The disability hearing will address only the initial or revised determination, based on medical factors, that you are not now disabled. Any other issues which arise in connection with your request for reconsideration will be reviewed in accordance with the reconsideration procedures described in§ 404.913(a).

* * *

20 C.F.R. § 404.915 Disability hearing—disability hearing officers. (*See also* 20 C.F.R. 416.1415)

(a) General. Your disability hearing will be conducted by a disability hearing officer who was not involved in making the determination you are appealing. The disability hearing officer will be an experienced disability examiner * * *

* * *

20 C.F.R. § 404.916 Disability hearing—procedures. (*See also* 20 C.F.R. 416.1416)

(a) General. The disability hearing will enable you to introduce evidence and present your views to a disability hearing officer if you are dissatisfied with an initial or revised initial determination, based on medical factors, that you are not now disabled as described in § 404.914(a)(2).

(b) Your procedural rights. We will advise you that you have the following procedural rights in connection with the disability hearing process:

(1) You may request that we assist you in obtaining pertinent evidence for your disability hearing and, if necessary, that we issue a subpoena to compel the production of certain evidence or testimony. We will follow subpoena procedures similar to those described in § 404.950(d) for the administrative law judge hearing process;

(2) You may have a representative at the hearing appointed under Subpart R of this Part, or you may represent yourself;

(3) You or your representative may review the evidence in your case file, either or the date of you hearing or at an earlier time at your request, and present additional evidence;

(4) You may present witnesses and question any witnesses at the hearing;

(5) You may waive your right to appear at the hearing. If you do not appear at the hearing, the disability hearing officer will prepare and issue a written reconsidered determination based on the information in your case file.

(c) Case preparation. After you request reconsideration, your case file will be reviewed and prepared for the hearing. This review will be conducted in the component of our office (including a State agency) that made the initial or revised determination, by personnel who were not involved in making the initial or revised determination. Any new evidence you submit in connection with your request for reconsideration will be included in this review. If necessary, further development of the evidence, including arrangements for medical examinations, will be undertaken by this component. After the case file is prepared for the hearing, it will be forwarded by this component to the disability hearing officer for a hearing. If necessary, the case file may be sent back to this component at any time prior to the issuance of the reconsidered determination for additional development. Under paragraph (d) of this section, this component has the authority to issue a favorable reconsidered determination at any time in its development process.

(d) *Favorable reconsideration determination without a hearing.* If all the evidence in your case file supports a finding that you are now disabled, either the component that prepares your case for hearing under paragraph (c) or the disability hearing officer will issue a written favorable reconsideration determination, even if a disability hearing has not yet been held.

(e) *Opportunity to submit additional evidence after the hearing.* At your request, the disability hearing officer may allow up to 15 days after your disability hearing for receipt of evidence which is not available at the hearing, if:

(1) The disability hearing officer determines that the evidence has a direct bearing on the outcome of the hearing; and

(2) The evidence could not have been obtained before the hearing.

(f) *Opportunity to review and comment on evidence obtained or developed by us after the hearing.* If, for any reason, additional evidence is obtained or developed by us after your disability hearing, and all evidence taken together can be used to support a reconsidered determination that is unfavorable to you with regard to the medical factors of eligibility, we will notify you, in writing, and give you an opportunity to review and comment on the additional evidence. You will be given 10 days from the date you receive our notice to submit your comments (in writing or, in appropriate cases, by telephone), unless there is good cause for granting you additional time, as illustrated by the examples in § 404.911(b). Your comments will be considered before a reconsidered determination is issued. If you believe that it is necessary to have further opportunity for a hearing with respect to the additional evidence, a supplementary hearing may be scheduled at your request. Otherwise, we will ask for your written comments on the additional evidence, or, in appropriate cases, for your telephone comments.

20 C.F.R. § 404.922 Notice of a reconsidered determination. (*See also* 20 C.F.R. 416.1422)

We shall mail a written notice of the reconsidered determination to the parties at their last known address. We shall state the specific reasons for the determination and tell you and any other parties of the right to a hearing. If it is appropriate, we will also tell you and any other parties how to use the expedited appeals process.

20 C.F.R. § 404.933 How to request a hearing before an administrative law judge. (*See also* 20 CFR § 416.1433)

(a) Written request. You may request a hearing by filing a written request. You should include in your request—

(1) The name and social security number of the wage earner;

(2) The reasons you disagree with the previous determination or decision;

(3) A statement of additional evidence to be submitted and the date you will submit it; and

(4) The name and address of any designated representative.

(b) When and where to file. The request must be filed—

(1) Within 60 days after the date you receive notice of the previous determination or decision (or within the extended time period if we extend the time as provided in paragraph (c) of this section);

(2) At one of our offices, the Veterans Administration Regional Office in the Philippines, or an office of the Railroad Retirement Board for persons having 10 or more years of service in the railroad industry.

(c) Extension of time to request a hearing. If you have a right to a hearing but do not request one in time, you may ask for more time to make your request. The request for an extension of time must be in writing and it must give the reasons why the request for a hearing was not filed within the stated time period. You may file your request for an extension of time at one of our offices. If you show that you had good cause for missing the deadline, the time period will be extended. To determine whether good cause exists, we use the standards explained in § 404.911.

20 C.F.R. § 404.941 Prehearing case review (*See also* 20 C.FR.R. § 416.1441)

(a) General. After a hearing is requested but before it is held, we may, for the purposes of a prehearing case review, forward the case to the component of our office (including a State agency) that issued the determination being reviewed. That component will decide whether the determination may be revised. A revised determination may be wholly or partially favorable to you. A prehearing case review will not delay the scheduling of a hearing unless you agree to continue the review and delay the hearing. If the prehearing case review is not completed before the date of the hearing, the case will be sent to the administrative law judge unless a favorable revised determination is in process or you and the other parties to the hearing agree in writing to delay the hearing until the review is completed.

(b) When a prehearing case review may be conducted. We may conduct a prehearing case review if—

(1) Additional evidence is submitted;

(2) There is an indication that additional evidence is available;

(3) There is a change in the law or regulation; or

(4) There is an error in the file or some other indication that the prior determination may be revised.

(c) Notice of a prehearing revised determination. If we revise the determination in a prehearing case review, we shall mail written notice of the revised determination to all parties at their last known address. We shall state the basis for the revised determination and advise all parties of their right to request a hearing on the revised determination within 60 days after the date or receiving this notice.

(d) Revised determination wholly favorable. If the revised determination is wholly favorable to you, we shall tell you in the notice that the administrative law judge will dismiss the hearing request unless a party requests that the hearing proceed. A request to continue must be made in writing within 30 days after the date the notice of the revised determination is mailed.

(e) Revised determination partially favorable. If the revised determination is partially favorable to you, we shall tell you in the notice what was not favorable. We shall also tell you that the hearing you requested will be held unless you, the parties to the revised determination and the parties to the hearing tell us that all parties agree to dismiss the hearing request.

20 C.F.R. § 404.944 Administrative law judge hearing procedures—general. (*See also* 20 C.FR.R. § 416.1444)

A hearing is open to the parties and to other persons the administrative law judge considers necessary and proper. At the hearing, the administrative law judge looks fully into the issues, questions you and the other witnesses, and accepts as evidence any documents that are material to the issues. The administrative law judge may stop the hearing temporarily and continue it at a later date if he or she believes that there is material evidence missing at the hearing. The administrative law judge may also reopen the hearing at any time before he or she mails a notice of the decision in order to receive new and material evidence. The administrative law judge may decide when the evidence will be presented and when the issues will be discussed.

20 C.F.R. § 404.946 Issues before an administrative law judge. (*See also* 20 C.FR.R. § 416.1446)

(a) General. The issues before the administrative law judge include all the issues brought out in the initial, reconsidered or revised determination that were not decided entirely in your favor. However, if evidence presented before or during the hearing causes the administrative law judge to question a fully favorable determination, he or she will notify you and will consider it an issue at the hearing.

(b) New issues—

(1) General. The administrative law judge may consider a new issue at the hearing if he or she notifies you and all the parties about the new issue any time after receiving the hearing request and before mailing notice of the hearing decision. The administrative law judge or any party may raise a new issue; an issue may be raised even though it arose after the request for a hearing and even though it has not been considered in an initial or reconsidered determination. However, it may not be raised if it involves a claim that is within the jurisdiction of a State agency under a Federal–State agreement concerning the determination of disability.

(2) Notice of a new issue. The administrative law judge shall notify you and any other party if he or she will consider any new issue. * * *

20 C.F.R. § 404.948 Deciding a case without an oral hearing before an administrative law judge. (*See also* 20 C.FR.R. § 416.1448)

(a) Decision wholly favorable. If the evidence in the hearing record supports a finding in favor of you and all the parties on every issue, the administrative law judge may issue a hearing decision without holding an oral hearing. However, the notice of the decision will inform you that you have the right to an oral hearing and that you have a right to examine the evidence on which the decision is based.

(b) Parties do not wish to appear.

(1) The administrative law judge may decide a case on the record and not conduct an oral hearing if—

(i) You and all the parties indicate in writing that you do not wish to appear before the administrative law judge at an oral hearing; or

(ii) You live outside the United States and you do not inform us that you want to appear and there are no other parties who wish to appear.

(2) When an oral hearing is not held, the administrative law judge shall make a record of the material evidence. The record will include the applications, written statements, certificates, reports, affidavits, and other documents that were used in making the determination under review and any additional evidence you or any other party to the hearing present in writing. The decision of the administrative law judge must be based on this record.

(c) Case remanded for a revised determination.

(1) The administrative law judge may remand a case to the appropriate component of our office for a revised determination if there is reason to believe that the revised determination would be fully favorable to you. This could happen if the administrative law judge receives new and material evidence or if there is a change in the law that permits the favorable determination.

(2) Unless you request the remand, the administrative law judge shall notify you that your case has been remanded and tell you that if you object, you must notify him or her of your objections within 10 days of the date the case is remanded or we will assume that you agree to the remand. If you object to the remand, the administrative law judge will consider the objection and rule on it in writing.

20 C.F.R. § 404.949 Presenting written statements and oral arguments. (*See also* 20 C.F.R. § 416.1449)

You or a person you designate to act as your representative may appear before the administrative law judge to state your case, to present a written summary of your case, or to enter written statements about the facts and law material to your case in the record. A copy of your written statements should be filed for each party.

20 C.F.R. § 404.950 Presenting evidence at a hearing before an administrative law judge. (*See also* 20 C.FR.R. § 416.1450)

(a) The right to appear and present evidence. Any party to a hearing has the right to appear before the administrative law judge, either in person or, when the conditions in § 404.936(c) exist, by video teleconferencing, to present evidence and to state his or her position. A party may also make his or her appearance by means of a designated representative, who may make the appearance in person or by video teleconferencing.

(b) Waiver of the right to appear. You may send the administrative law judge a waiver or a written statement indicating that you do not wish to appear at the hearing. You may withdraw this waiver any time before a notice of the hearing decision is mailed to you. Even if all of the parties waive their right to appear at a hearing, the administrative law judge may notify them of a time and a place for an oral hearing, if he or she believes that a personal appearance and testimony by you or any other party is necessary to decide the case.

(c) What evidence is admissible at a hearing. The administrative law judge may receive evidence at the hearing even though the evidence would not be admissible in court under the rules of evidence used by the court.

(d) Subpoenas.

(1) When it is reasonably necessary for the full presentation of a case, an administrative law judge or a member of the Appeals Council may, on his or her own initiative or at the request of a party, issue subpoenas for the appearance and testimony of witnesses and for the production of books, records, correspondence, papers, or other documents that are material to an issue at the hearing.

(2) Parties to a hearing who wish to subpoena documents or witnesses must file a written request for the issuance of a subpoena with the administrative law judge or at one of our offices at least 5 days before the hearing date. The written request must give the names of the witnesses or documents to be produced; describe the address or

location of the witnesses or documents with sufficient detail to find them; state the important facts that the witness or document is expected to prove; and indicate why these facts could not be proven without issuing a subpoena.

(3) We will pay the cost of issuing the subpoena.

(4) We will pay subpoenaed witnesses the same fees and mileage they would receive if they had been subpoenaed by a Federal district court.

(e) *Witnesses at a hearing.* Witnesses may appear at a hearing. They shall testify under oath or affirmation, unless the administrative law judge finds an important reason to excuse them from taking an oath or affirmation. The administrative law judge may ask the witnesses any questions material to the issues and shall allow the parties or their designated representatives to do so.

(f) *Collateral estoppel—issues previously decided.* An issue at your hearing may be a fact that has already been decided in one of our previous determinations or decisions in a claim involving the same parties, but arising under a different title of the Act or under the Federal Coal Mine Health and Safety Act. If this happens, the administrative law judge will not consider the issue again, but will accept the factual finding made in the previous determination or decision unless there are reasons to believe that it was wrong.

20 C.F.R. § 404.967 Appeals Council review—general. (*See also* 20 C.F.R. § 416.1467)

If you or any other party is dissatisfied with the hearing decision or with the dismissal of a hearing request, you may request that the Appeals Council review that action. The Appeals Council may deny or dismiss the request for review, or it may grant the request and either issue a decision or remand the case to an administrative law judge. The Appeals Council shall notify the parties at their last known address of the action it takes.

20 C.F.R. § 404.968 How to request Appeals Council review. (*See also* 20 C.F.R. § 416.1468)

(a) *Time and place to request Appeals Council review.* You may request Appeals Council review by filing a written request. Any documents or other evidence you wish to have considered by the Appeals Council should be submitted with your request for review. You may file your request—

(1) Within 60 days after the date you receive notice of the hearing decision or dismissal (or within the extended time period if we extend the time as provided in paragraph (b) of this section);

(2) At one of our offices, the Veterans Administration Regional Office in the Philippines, or an office of the Railroad Retirement Board if you have 10 or more years of service in the railroad industry.

(b) Extension of time to request review. You or any party to a hearing decision may ask that the time for filing a request for the review be extended. The request for an extension of time must be in writing. It must be filed with the Appeals Council, and it must give the reasons why the request for review was not filed within the stated time period. If you show that you had good cause for missing the deadline, the time period will be extended. To determine whether good cause exists, we use the standards explained in § 404.911.

20 C.F.R. § 404.969 Appeals Council initiates review. (*See also* 20 C.F.R. § 416.1469)

(a) General. Anytime within 60 days after the date of a decision or dismissal that is subject to review under this section, the Appeals Council may decide on its own motion to review the action that was taken in your case. We may refer your case to the Appeals Council for it to consider reviewing under this authority.

(b) Identification of cases. We will identify a case for referral to the Appeals Council for possible review under its own-motion authority before we effectuate a decision in the case. We will identify cases for referral to the Appeals Council through random and selective sampling techniques, which we may use in association with examination of the cases identified by sampling. We will also identify cases for referral to the Appeals Council through the evaluation of cases we conduct in order to effectuate decisions.

(1) Random and selective sampling and case examinations. We may use random and selective sampling to identify cases involving any type of action (i.e., wholly or partially favorable decisions, unfavorable decisions, or dismissals) and any type of benefits (i.e., benefits based on disability and benefits not based on disability). We will use selective sampling to identify cases that exhibit problematic issues or fact patterns that increase the likelihood of error. Neither our random sampling procedures nor our selective sampling procedures will identify cases based on the identity of the decisionmaker or the identity of the office issuing the decision. We may examine cases that have been identified through random or selective sampling to refine

the identification of cases that may meet the criteria for review by the Appeals Council.

(2) Identification as a result of the effectuation process. We may refer a case requiring effectuation to the Appeals Council if, in the view of the effectuating component, the decision cannot be effectuated because it contains a clerical error affecting the outcome of the claim; the decision is clearly inconsistent with the Social Security Act, the regulations, or a published ruling; or the decision is unclear regarding a matter that affects the claim's outcome.

(c) Referral of cases. We will make referrals that occur as the result of a case examination or the effectuation process in writing. The written referral based on the results of such a case examination or the effectuation process will state the referring component's reasons for believing that the Appeals Council should review the case on its own motion. Referrals that result from selective sampling without a case examination may be accompanied by a written statement identifying the issue(s) or fact pattern that caused the referral. Referrals that result from random sampling without a case examination will only identify the case as a random sample case.

(d) Appeals Council's action. If the Appeals Council decides to review a decision or dismissal on its own motion, it will mail a notice of review to all the parties as provided in § 404.973. The Appeals Council will include with that notice a copy of any written referral it has received under paragraph (c) of this section. The Appeals Council's decision to review a case is established by its issuance of the notice of review. If it is unable to decide within the applicable 60–day period whether to review a decision or dismissal, the Appeals Council may consider the case to determine if the decision or dismissal should be reopened pursuant to §§ 404.987 and 404.988. If the Appeals Council decides to review a decision on its own motion or to reopen a decision as provided in §§ 404.987 and 404.988, the notice of review or the notice of reopening issued by the Appeals Council will advise, where appropriate, that interim benefits will be payable if a final decision has not been issued within 110 days after the date of the decision that is reviewed or reopened, and that any interim benefits paid will not be considered overpayments unless the benefits are fraudulently obtained.

20 C.F.R. § 404.970 Cases the Appeals Council will review. (*See also* 20 C.F.R. § 416.1470)

(a) The Appeals Council will review a case if—

(1) There appears to be an abuse of discretion by the administrative law judge;

(2) There is an error of law;

(3) The action, findings or conclusions of the administrative law judge are not supported by substantial evidence; or

(4) There is a broad policy or procedural issue that may affect the general public interest.

(b) If new and material evidence is submitted, the Appeals Council shall consider the additional evidence only where it relates to the period on or before the date of the administrative law judge hearing decision. The Appeals Council shall evaluate the entire record including the new and material evidence submitted if it relates to the period on or before the date of the administrative law judge hearing decision. It will then review the case if it finds that the administrative law judge's action, findings, or conclusion is contrary to the weight of the evidence currently of record.

20 C.F.R. § 404.977 Case remanded by Appeals Council. (*See also* 20 C.F.R. § 416.1477)

(a) When the Appeals Council may remand a case. The Appeals Council may remand a case to an administrative law judge so that he or she may hold a hearing and issue a decision or a recommended decision. The Appeals Council may also remand a case in which additional evidence is needed or additional action by the administrative law judge is required.

(b) Action by administrative law judge on remand. The administrative law judge shall take any action that is ordered by the Appeals Council and may take any additional action that is not inconsistent with the Appeals Council's remand order.

(c) Notice when case is returned with a recommended decision. When the administrative law judge sends a case to the Appeals Council with a recommended decision, a notice is mailed to the parties at their last known address. The notice tells them that the case has been sent to the Appeals Council, explains the rules for filing briefs or other written statements with the Appeals Council, and includes a copy of the recommended decision.

* * *

20 C.F. R § 404.982 Extension of time to file action in Federal district court. (*See also* 20 C.F.R. § 416.1482)

Any party to the Appeals Council's decision or denial of review, or to an expedited appeals process agreement, may request that the time for filing an action in a Federal district court be extended. The request must be in writing and it must give the reasons why the action was not filed within the stated time period. The request must be filed with the Appeals Council, or if it concerns an expedited appeals process agreement, with one of our offices. If you show that you had good cause for missing the deadline, the time period will be extended. To determine whether good cause exists, we use the standards explained in § 404.911.

20 C.F.R. § 404.983 Case remanded by a Federal court. (*See also* 20 C.F.R. § 416.1483)

When a Federal court remands a case to the Commissioner for further consideration, the Appeals Council, acting on behalf of the Commissioner, may make a decision, or it may remand the case to an administrative law judge with instructions to take action and issue a decision or return the case to the Appeals Council with a recommended decision. If the case is remanded by the Appeals Council, the procedures explained in § 404.977 will be followed. Any issues relating to your claim may be considered by the administrative law judge whether or not they were raised in the administrative proceedings leading to the final decision in your case.

20 C.F.R. § 404.984 Appeals Council review of administrative law judge decision in a case remanded by a Federal court. (*See also* 20 C.F.R. § 416.1484)

(a) General. In accordance with § 404.983, when a case is remanded by a Federal court for further consideration, the decision of the administrative law judge will become the final decision of the Commissioner after remand on your case unless the Appeals Council assumes jurisdiction of the case. The Appeals Council may assume jurisdiction based on written exceptions to the decision of the administrative law judge which you file with the Appeals Council or based on its authority pursuant to paragraph (c) of this section. If the Appeals Council assumes jurisdiction of your case, any issues relating to your claim may be considered by the Appeals Council whether or not they were raised in the administrative proceedings leading to the final decision in your case or subsequently considered by the administrative law judge in the administrative proceedings following the court's remand order. The Appeals Council will either make a new, independent decision based on the entire record that will be the final decision of the Commissioner after remand or remand the case to an administrative law judge for further proceedings.

(b) You file exceptions disagreeing with the decision of the administrative law judge.

(1) If you disagree with the decision of the administrative law judge, in whole or in part, you may file exceptions to the decision with the Appeals Council. Exceptions may be filed by submitting a

written statement to the Appeals Council setting forth your reasons for disagreeing with the decision of the administrative law judge. The exceptions must be filed within 30 days of the date you receive the decision of the administrative law judge or an extension of time in which to submit exceptions must be requested in writing within the 30–day period. A timely request for a 30–day extension will be granted by the Appeals Council. A request for an extension of more than 30 days should include a statement of reasons as to why you need the additional time.

(2) If written exceptions are timely filed, the Appeals Council will consider your reasons for disagreeing with the decision of the administrative law judge and all the issues presented by your case. If the Appeals Council concludes that there is no reason to change the decision of the administrative law judge, it will issue a notice to you addressing your exceptions and explaining why no change in the decision of the administrative law judge is warranted. In this instance, the decision of the administrative law judge is the final decision of the Commissioner after remand.

(3) When you file written exceptions to the decision of the administrative law judge, the Appeals Council may assume jurisdiction at any time, even after the 60–day time period which applies when you do not file exceptions. If the Appeals Council assumes jurisdiction, it will make a new, independent decision based on its consideration of the entire record affirming, modifying, or reversing the decision of the administrative law judge or remand the case to an administrative law judge for further proceedings, including a new decision. The new decision of the Appeals Council is the final decision of the Commissioner after remand.

(c) Appeals Council assumes jurisdiction without exceptions being filed. Any time within 60 days after the date of the decision of the administrative law judge, the Appeals Council may decide to assume jurisdiction of your case even though no written exceptions have been filed. Notice of this action will be mailed to all parties at their last known address. You will be provided with the opportunity to file briefs or other written statements with the Appeals Council about the facts and law relevant to your case. After the briefs or other written statements have been received or the time allowed (usually 30 days) for submitting them has expired, the Appeals Council will either issue a final decision of the Commissioner affirming, modifying, or reversing the decision of the administrative law judge, or remand the case to an administrative law judge for further proceedings, including a new decision.

(d) Exceptions are not filed and the Appeals Council does not otherwise assume jurisdiction. If no exceptions are filed and the Appeals Council does not assume jurisdiction of your case, the decision of the administrative law judge becomes the final decision of the Commissioner after remand.

20 C.F.R. § 404.985 Application of circuit court law. (*See also* 20 C.F.R. § 416.1485)

The procedures which follow apply to administrative determinations or decisions on claims involving the application of circuit court law.

(a) General. We will apply a holding in a United States Court of Appeals decision that we determine conflicts with our interpretation of a provision of the Social Security Act or regulations unless the Government seeks further judicial review of that decision or we relitigate the issue presented in the decision in accordance with paragraphs (c) and (d) of this section. We will apply the holding to claims at all levels of the administrative review process within the applicable circuit unless the holding, by its nature, applies only at certain levels of adjudication.

(b) Issuance of an Acquiescence Ruling. When we determine that a United States Court of Appeals holding conflicts with our interpretation of a provision of the Social Security Act or regulations and the Government does not seek further judicial review or is unsuccessful on further review, we will issue a Social Security Acquiescence Ruling. The Acquiescence Ruling will describe the administrative case and the court decision, identify the issue(s) involved, and explain how we will apply the holding, including, as necessary, how the holding relates to other decisions within the applicable circuit. These Acquiescence Rulings will generally be effective on the date of their publication in the Federal Register and will apply to all determinations and decisions made on or after that date unless an Acquiescence Ruling is rescinded as stated in paragraph (e) of this section. The process we will use when issuing an Acquiescence Ruling follows:

(1) We will release an Acquiescence Ruling for publication in the Federal Register for any precedential circuit court decision that we determine contains a holding that conflicts with our interpretation of a provision of the Social Security Act or regulations no later than 120 days from the receipt of the court's decision. This timeframe will not apply when we decide to seek further judicial review of the circuit court decision or when coordination with the Department of Justice and/or other Federal agencies makes this timeframe no longer feasible.

(2) If we make a determination or decision on your claim between the date of a circuit court decision and the date we publish an Acquiescence Ruling, you may request application of the published Acquiescence Ruling to the prior determination or decision. You must demonstrate that application of the Acquiescence Ruling could change the prior determination or decision in your case. You may demonstrate this by submitting a statement that cites the Acquiescence Ruling or the holding or portion of a circuit court decision which could change the prior determination or decision in your case. If you can so demonstrate, we will readjudicate the claim in accordance with the Acquiescence Ruling at the level at which it was last adjudicated. Any readjudication will be limited to consideration of the issue(s) covered by the Acquiescence Ruling and any new determination or decision on readjudication will be subject to administrative and judicial review in accordance with this subpart. Our denial of a request for readjudication will not be subject to further administrative or judicial review. If you file a request for readjudication within the 60–day appeal period and we deny that request, we shall extend the time to file an appeal on the merits of the claim to 60 days after the date that we deny the request for readjudication.

(3) After we receive a precedential circuit court decision and determine that an Acquiescence Ruling may be required, we will begin to identify those claims that are pending before us within the circuit and that might be subject to readjudication if an Acquiescence Ruling is subsequently issued. When an Acquiescence Ruling is published, we will send a notice to those individuals whose cases we have identified which may be affected by the Acquiescence Ruling. The notice will provide information about the Acquiescence Ruling and the right to request readjudication under that Acquiescence Ruling, as described in paragraph (b)(2) of this section. It is not necessary for an individual to receive a notice in order to request application of an Acquiescence Ruling to his or her claim, as described in paragraph (b)(2) of this section.

(c) Relitigation of court's holding after publication of an Acquiescence Ruling. After we have published an Acquiescence Ruling to reflect a holding of a United States Court of Appeals on an issue, we may decide under certain conditions to relitigate that issue within the same circuit. We may relitigate only when the conditions specified in paragraphs (c)(2) and (3) of this section are met, and, in general, one of the events specified in paragraph (c)(1) of this section occurs.

(1) Activating events:

(i) An action by both Houses of Congress indicates that a circuit court decision on which an Acquiescence Ruling was based was decided inconsistently with congressional intent, such as may be expressed in a joint resolution, an appropriations restriction, or enactment of legislation which affects a closely analogous body of law;

(ii) A statement in a majority opinion of the same circuit indicates that the court might no longer follow its previous decision if a particular issue were presented again;

(iii) Subsequent circuit court precedent in other circuits supports our interpretation of the Social Security Act or regulations on the issue(s) in question; or

(iv) A subsequent Supreme Court decision presents a reasonable legal basis for questioning a circuit court holding upon which we base an Acquiescence Ruling.

(2) The General Counsel of the Social Security Administration, after consulting with the Department of Justice, concurs that relitigation of an issue and application of our interpretation of the Social Security Act or regulations to selected claims in the administrative review process within the circuit would be appropriate.

(3) We publish a notice in the Federal Register that we intend to relitigate an Acquiescence Ruling issue and that we will apply our interpretation of the Social Security Act or regulations within the circuit to claims in the administrative review process selected for relitigation. The notice will explain why we made this decision.

(d) Notice of relitigation. When we decide to relitigate an issue, we will provide a notice explaining our action to all affected claimants. In adjudicating claims subject to relitigation, decisionmakers throughout the SSA administrative review process will apply our interpretation of the Social Security Act and regulations, but will also state in written determinations or decisions how the claims would have been decided under the circuit standard. Claims not subject to relitigation will continue to be decided under the Acquiescence Ruling in accordance with the circuit standard. So that affected claimants can be readily identified and any subsequent decision of the circuit court or the Supreme Court can be implemented quickly and efficiently, we will maintain a listing of all claimants who receive this notice and will provide them with the relief ordered by the court.

(e) Rescission of an Acquiescence Ruling. We will rescind as obsolete an Acquiescence Ruling and apply our interpretation of the Social Security Act or regulations by publishing a notice in the Federal Register when any of the following events occurs:

(1) The Supreme Court overrules or limits a circuit court holding that was the basis of an Acquiescence Ruling;

(2) A circuit court overrules or limits itself on an issue that was the basis of an Acquiescence Ruling;

(3) A Federal law is enacted that removes the basis for the holding in a decision of a circuit court that was the subject of an Acquiescence Ruling; or

(4) We subsequently clarify, modify or revoke the regulation or ruling that was the subject of a circuit court holding that we determined conflicts with our interpretation of the Social Security Act or regulations, or we subsequently publish a new regulation(s) addressing an issue(s) not previously included in our regulations when that issue(s) was the subject of a circuit court holding that conflicted with our interpretation of the Social Security Act or regulations and that holding was not compelled by the statute or Constitution.

20 C.F.R. § 404.987 Reopening and revising determinations and decisions. (*See also* 20 C.F.R. § 416.1487)

(a) General. Generally, if you are dissatisfied with a determination or decision made in the administrative review process, but do not request further review within the stated time period, you lose your right to further review and that determination or decision becomes final. However, a determination or a decision made in your case which is otherwise final and binding may be reopened and revised by us.

(b) Procedure for reopening and revision. We may reopen a final determination or decision on our own initiative, or you may ask that a final determination or a decision to which you were a party be reopened. In either instance, if we reopen the determination or decision, we may revise that determination or decision. The conditions under which we may reopen a previous determination or decision, either on our own initiative or at your request, are explained in § 404.988.

20 C.F.R. § 404.988 Conditions for reopening. (*See also* 20 C.F.R. § 416.1488)

A determination, revised determination, decision, or revised decision may be reopened—

(a) Within 12 months of the date of the notice of the initial determination, for any reason;

(b) Within four years of the date of the notice of the initial determination if we find good cause, as defined in § 404.989, to reopen the case; or

(c) At any time if—

(1) It was obtained by fraud or similar fault (see § 416.1488(c) of this chapter for factors which we take into account in determining fraud or similar fault);

(2) Another person files a claim on the same earnings record and allowance of the claim adversely affects your claim;

(3) A person previously determined to be dead, and on whose earnings record your entitlement is based, is later found to be alive;

(4) Your claim was denied because you did not prove that a person died, and the death is later established—

(i) By a presumption of death under § 404.721(b); or

(ii) By location or identification of his or her body;

* * *

20 C.F.R § 404.989 Good cause for reopening. (*See also* 20 C.F.R. § 416.1489)

(a) We will find that there is good cause to reopen a determination or decision if—

(1) New and material evidence is furnished;

(2) A clerical error in the computation or recomputation of benefits was made; or

(3) The evidence that was considered in making the determination or decision clearly shows on its face that an error was made.

(b) We will not find good cause to reopen your case if the only reason for reopening is a change of legal interpretation or administrative ruling upon which the determination or decision was made.

20 C.F.R. § 404.990 Finality of determinations and decisions on revision of an earnings record. (*See also* 20 C.F.R. § 416.1489)

A determination or a decision on a revision of an earnings record may be reopened only within the time period and under the conditions provided in section 205(c)(4) or (5) of the Act, or within 60 days after the date you receive notice of the determination or decision, whichever is later.

20 C.F.R. § 404.1504 Determinations by other organizations and agencies. (*See also* 20 C.F.R § 416.904)

A decision by any nongovernmental agency or any other governmental agency about whether you are disabled or blind is based on its rules and is not our decision about whether you are disabled or blind. We must make a disability or blindness determination based on social security law. Therefore, a determination made by another agency that you are disabled or blind is not binding on us.

20 C.F.R. § 404.1512 Evidence. (*See also* 20 C.F.R § 416.912)

(a) General. In general, you have to prove to us that you are blind or disabled. Therefore, you must bring to our attention everything that shows that you are blind or disabled. This means that you must furnish medical and other evidence that we can use to reach conclusions about your medical impairment(s) and, if material to the determination of whether you are blind or disabled, its effect on your ability to work on a sustained basis. We will consider only impairment(s) you say you have or about which we receive evidence.

(b) What we mean by "evidence." Evidence is anything you or anyone else submits to us or that we obtain that relates to your claim. This includes, but is not limited to:

(1) Objective medical evidence, that is, medical signs and laboratory findings as defined in § 404.1528 (b) and (c);

(2) Other evidence from medical sources, such as medical history, opinions, and statements about treatment you have received;

(3) Statements you or others make about your impairment(s), your restrictions, your daily activities, your efforts to work, or any other relevant statements you make to medical sources during the course of examination or treatment, or to us during interviews, on applications, in letters, and in testimony in our administrative proceedings;

(4) Information from other sources * * *;

(5) Decisions by any governmental or nongovernmental agency about whether you are disabled or blind; and

(6) At the initial level of the administrative review process, when a State agency disability examiner makes the initial determination alone (see § 404.1615(c)(3)), opinions provided by State agency medical and psychological consultants based on their review of the evidence in your case record (see § 404.1527(f)(1)(ii));

(7) At the reconsideration level of the administrative review process, when a State agency disability examiner makes the determination alone (see § 404.1615(c)(3)), findings, other than the ultimate determination about whether you are disabled, made by State agency medical or psychological consultants and other program physicians, psychologists, or other medical specialists at the initial level of the administrative review process, and other opinions they provide based on their review of the evidence in your case record at the initial and reconsideration levels (see § 404.1527(f)(1)(iii)); and

(8) At the administrative law judge and Appeals Council levels, findings, other than the ultimate determination about whether you are disabled, made by State agency medical or psychological consultants and other program physicians or psychologists, or other medical specialists, and opinions expressed by medical experts or psychological experts that we consult based on their review of the evidence in your case record. See §§ 404.1527(f)(2)–(3).

(c) Your responsibility. You must provide medical evidence showing that you have an impairment(s) and how severe it is during the time you say that you are disabled. You must provide evidence, without redaction, showing how your impairment(s) affects your functioning during the time you say that you are disabled, and any other information that we need to decide your claim. If we ask you, you must provide evidence about:

(1) Your age;

(2) Your education and training;

(3) Your work experience;

(4) Your daily activities both before and after the date you say that you became disabled;

(5) Your efforts to work; and

(6) Any other factors showing how your impairment(s) affects your ability to work. * * *

(d) Our responsibility. Before we make a determination that you are not disabled, we will develop your complete medical history for at least the 12 months preceding the month in which you file your application unless there is a reason to believe that development of an earlier period is necessary or unless you say that your disability began less than 12 months before you filed your application. We will make every reasonable effort to help you get medical reports from your own medical sources when you give us permission to request the reports.

(1) "Every reasonable effort" means that we will make an initial request for evidence from your medical source and, at any time between 10 and 20 calendar days after the initial request, if the evidence has not been received, we will make one followup request to obtain the medical evidence necessary to make a determination. The medical source will have a minimum of 10 calendar days from the date of our followup request to reply, unless our experience with that source indicates that a longer period is advisable in a particular case.

(2) By "complete medical history," we mean the records of your medical source(s) covering at least the 12 months preceding the month in which you file your application. If you say that your disability began less than 12 months before you filed your application, we will develop your complete medical history beginning with the month you say your disability began unless we have reason to believe your disability began earlier. If applicable, we will develop your complete medical history for the 12–month period prior to (1) the month you were last insured for disability insurance benefits * * *, (2) the month ending the 7–year period you may have to establish your disability and you are applying for widow's or widower's benefits based on disability * * *, or (3) the month you attain age 22 and you are applying for child's benefits based on disability * * *.

(e) Recontacting medical sources. When the evidence we receive from your treating physician or psychologist or other medical source is inadequate for us to determine whether you are disabled, we will need additional information to reach a determination or a decision. To obtain the information, we will take the following actions.

(1) We will first recontact your treating physician or psychologist or other medical source to determine whether the additional information we need is readily available. We will seek additional evidence or clarification from your medical source when the report from your medical source contains a conflict or ambiguity that must be resolved, the report does not contain all the necessary information, or does not appear to be based on medically acceptable clinical and laboratory diagnostic techniques. We may do this by requesting copies of your medical source's records, a new report, or a more detailed report from your medical source, including your treating source, or by telephoning your medical source. In every instance where medical evidence is obtained over the telephone, the telephone report will be sent to the source for review, signature and return.

(2) We may not seek additional evidence or clarification from a medical source when we know from past experience that the source either cannot or will not provide the necessary findings.

(f) Need for consultative examination. If the information we need is not readily available from the records of your medical treatment source, or we are unable to seek clarification from your medical source, we will ask you to attend one or more consultative examinations at our expense. * * * Generally, we will not request a consultative examination until we have made every reasonable effort to obtain evidence from your own medical sources. However, in some instances, such as when a source is known to be unable to provide certain tests or procedures or is known to be non-productive or uncooperative, we may order a consultative examination while awaiting receipt of medical source evidence. We will not evaluate this evidence until we have made every reasonable effort to obtain evidence from your medical sources.

(g) Other work. In order to determine under § 404.1520(g) that you are able to make an adjustment to other work, we must provide evidence about the existence of work in the national economy that you can do * * *, given your residual functional capacity * * *, age, education, and work experience.

20 C.F.R. § 404.1513 Medical and other evidence of your impairment(s). (*See also* 20 C.F.R. § 416.913)

(a) Sources who can provide evidence to establish an impairment. We need evidence from acceptable medical sources to establish whether you have a medically determinable impairment(s). See § 404.1508. Acceptable medical sources are—

(1) Licensed physicians (medical or osteopathic doctors);

(2) Licensed or certified psychologists. Included are school psychologists, or other licensed or certified individuals with other titles who perform the same function as a school psychologist in a school setting, for purposes of establishing mental retardation, learning disabilities, and borderline intellectual functioning only;

(3) Licensed optometrists, for purposes of establishing visual disorders only (except, in the U.S. Virgin Islands, licensed optometrists, for the measurement of visual acuity and visual fields only);

(4) Licensed podiatrists, for purposes of establishing impairments of the foot, or foot and ankle only, depending on whether the State in which the podiatrist practices permits the practice of podiatry on the foot only, or the foot and ankle; and

(5) Qualified speech-language pathologists, for purposes of establishing speech or language impairments only. For this source, "qualified" means that the speech-language pathologist must be licensed by

the State professional licensing agency, or be fully certified by the State education agency in the State in which he or she practices, or hold a Certificate of Clinical Competence from the American Speech–Language–Hearing Association.

(b) Medical reports. Medical reports should include—

(1) Medical history;

(2) Clinical findings (such as the results of physical or mental status examinations);

(3) Laboratory findings (such as blood pressure, x-rays);

(4) Diagnosis (statement of disease or injury based on its signs and symptoms);

(5) Treatment prescribed with response, and prognosis; and

(6) A statement about what you can still do despite your impairment(s) based on the acceptable medical source's findings on the factors under paragraphs (b)(1) through (b)(5) of this section (except in statutory blindness claims). Although we will request a medical source statement about what you can still do despite your impairment(s), the lack of the medical source statement will not make the report incomplete. See § 404.1527.

(c) Statements about what you can still do. At the administrative law judge and Appeals Council levels, we will consider residual functional capacity assessments made by State agency medical and psychological consultants and other program physicians and psychologists to be "statements about what you can still do" made by nonexamining physicians and psychologists based on their review of the evidence in the case record. Statements about what you can still do (based on the acceptable medical source's findings on the factors under paragraphs (b)(1) through (b)(5) of this section) should describe, but are not limited to, the kinds of physical and mental capabilities listed as follows (See §§ 404.1527 and 404.1545(c)):

(1) The acceptable medical source's opinion about your ability, despite your impairment(s), to do work-related activities such as sitting, standing, walking, lifting, carrying, handling objects, hearing, speaking, and traveling; and

(2) In cases of mental impairment(s), the acceptable medical source's opinion about your ability to understand, to carry out and remember instructions, and to respond appropriately to supervision, coworkers, and work pressures in a work setting.

(d) Other sources. In addition to evidence from the acceptable medical sources listed in paragraph (a) of this section, we may also use evidence from other sources to show the severity of your impairment(s) and how it affects your ability to work. Other sources include, but are not limited to—

(1) Medical sources not listed in paragraph (a) of this section (for example, nurse-practitioners, physicians' assistants, naturopaths, chiropractors, audiologists, and therapists);

(2) Educational personnel (for example, school teachers, counselors, early intervention team members, developmental center workers, and daycare center workers);

(3) Public and private social welfare agency personnel; and

(4) Other non-medical sources (for example, spouses, parents and other caregivers, siblings, other relatives, friends, neighbors, and clergy).

(e) Completeness. The evidence in your case record, including the medical evidence from acceptable medical sources (containing the clinical and laboratory findings) and other medical sources not listed in paragraph (a) of this section, information you give us about your medical condition(s) and how it affects you, and other evidence from other sources, must be complete and detailed enough to allow us to make a determination or decision about whether you are disabled or blind. It must allow us to determine—

(1) The nature and severity of your impairment(s) for any period in question;

(2) Whether the duration requirement described in § 404.1509 is met; and

(3) Your residual functional capacity to do work-related physical and mental activities, when the evaluation steps described in § 404.1520(e) or (f)(1) apply.

20 C.F.R. § 404.1514 When we will purchase existing evidence. (*See also* 20 C.F.R § 416.914)

We need specific medical evidence to determine whether you are disabled or blind. You are responsible for providing that evidence. However, we will pay physicians not employed by the Federal government and other non-Federal providers of medical services for the reasonable cost of providing us with existing medical evidence that we need and ask for after November 30, 1980.

20 C.F.R. § 404.1516 If you fail to submit medical and other evidence. (*See also* 20 C.F.R § 416.916)

If you do not give us the medical and other evidence that we need and request, we will have to make a decision based on information available in your case. We will not excuse you from giving us evidence because you have religious or personal reasons against medical examinations, tests, or treatment.

20 C.F.R. § 404.1517 Consultative examination at our expense. (*See also* 20 C.F.R. § 416.917)

If your medical sources cannot or will not give us sufficient medical evidence about your impairment for us to determine whether you are disabled or blind, we may ask you to have one or more physical or mental examinations or tests. We will pay for these examinations. However, we will not pay for any medical examination arranged by you or your representative without our advance approval. If we arrange for the examination or test, we will give you reasonable notice of the date, time, and place the examination or test will be given, and the name of the person or facility who will do it. We will also give the examiner any necessary background information about your condition.

20 C.F.R. § 404.1518 If you do not appear at a consultative examination. (*See also* 20. C.F.R. § 416.018)

(a) General. If you are applying for benefits and do not have a good reason for failing or refusing to take part in a consultative examination or test which we arrange for you to get information we need to determine your disability or blindness, we may find that you are not disabled or blind. If you are already receiving benefits and do not have a good reason for failing or refusing to take part in a consultative examination or test which we arranged for you, we may determine that your disability or blindness has stopped because of your failure or refusal. Therefore, if you have any reason why you cannot go for the scheduled appointment, you should tell us about this as soon as possible before the examination date. If you have a good reason, we will schedule another examination. We will consider your physical, mental, educational, and linguistic limitations (including any lack of facility with the English language) when determining if you have a good reason for failing to attend a consultative examination.

(b) Examples of good reasons for failure to appear. Some examples of what we consider good reasons for not going to a scheduled examination include—

(1) Illness on the date of the scheduled examination or test;

(2) Not receiving timely notice of the scheduled examination or test, or receiving no notice at all;

(3) Being furnished incorrect or incomplete information, or being given incorrect information about the physician involved or the time or place of the examination or test, or;

(4) Having had death or serious illness occur in your immediate family.

(c) Objections by your physician. If any of your treating physicians tell you that you should not take the examination or test, you should tell us at once. In many cases, we may be able to get the information we need in another way. Your physician may agree to another type of examination for the same purpose.

20 C.F.R. § 404.1519 The consultative examination. (*See also* 20 C.F.R. § 416.919)

A consultative examination is a physical or mental examination or test purchased for you at our request and expense from a treating source or another medical source, including a pediatrician when appropriate. The decision to purchase a consultative examination will be made on an individual case basis in accordance with the provisions of §§ 404.1519a through 404.1519f. Selection of the source for the examination will be consistent with the provisions of § 404.1503a and §§ 404.1519g through 404.1519j. The rules and procedures for requesting consultative examinations set forth in §§ 404.1519a and 404.1519b are applicable at the reconsideration and hearing levels of review, as well as the initial level of determination.

20 C.F.R. § 404.1519a When we will purchase a consultative examination and how we will use it. (*See also* 20 C.F.R. § 416.919a)

(a)(1) General. The decision to purchase a consultative examination for you will be made after we have given full consideration to whether the additional information needed (e.g., clinical findings, laboratory tests, diagnosis, and prognosis) is readily available from the records of your medical sources. See § 404.1512 for the procedures we will follow to obtain evidence from your medical sources. Before purchasing a consultative examination, we will consider not only existing medical reports, but also the disability interview form containing your allegations as well as other pertinent evidence in your file.

(2) When we purchase a consultative examination, we will use the report from the consultative examination to try to resolve a conflict or ambiguity if one exists. We will also use a consultative exami-

nation to secure needed medical evidence the file does not contain such as clinical findings, laboratory tests, a diagnosis or prognosis necessary for decision.

(b) Situations requiring a consultative examination. A consultative examination may be purchased when the evidence as a whole, both medical and nonmedical, is not sufficient to support a decision on your claim. Other situations, including but not limited to the situations listed below, will normally require a consultative examination:

(1) The additional evidence needed is not contained in the records of your medical sources;

(2) The evidence that may have been available from your treating or other medical sources cannot be obtained for reasons beyond your control, such as death or noncooperation of a medical source;

(3) Highly technical or specialized medical evidence that we need is not available from your treating or other medical sources;

(4) A conflict, inconsistency, ambiguity or insufficiency in the evidence must be resolved, and we are unable to do so by recontacting your medical source; or

(5) There is an indication of a change in your condition that is likely to affect your ability to work, but the current severity of your impairment is not established.

20 C.F.R. § 404.1519b When we will not purchase a consultative examination. (*See also* 20 C.F.R. § 416.919b)

We will not purchase a consultative examination in situations including, but not limited to, the following situations:

(a) In period of disability and disability insurance benefit claims, when you do not meet the insured status requirement in the calendar quarter you allege you became disabled or later and there is no possibility of establishing an earlier onset;

(b) In claims for widow's or widower's benefits based on disability, when your alleged month of disability is after the end of the 7–year period specified in§ 404.335(c)(1) and there is no possibility of establishing an earlier onset date, or when the 7–year period expired in the past and there is no possibility of establishing an onset date prior to the date the 7–year period expired;

(c) In disability insurance benefit claims, when your insured status expired in the past and there is no possibility of establishing an onset date prior to the date your insured status expired;

(d) When any issues about your actual performance of substantial gainful activity or gainful activity have not been resolved;

(e) In claims for child's benefits based on disability, when it is determined that your alleged disability did not begin before the month you attained age 22, and there is no possibility of establishing an onset date earlier than the month in which you attained age 22;

(f) In claims for child's benefits based on disability that are filed concurrently with the insured individual's claim and entitlement cannot be established for the insured individual;

(g) In claims for child's benefits based on disability where entitlement is precluded based on other nondisability factors.

20 C.F.R. § 404.1519g Who we will select to perform a consultative examination. (*See also* 20 C.F.R. § 416.919g)

(a) We will purchase a consultative examination only from a qualified medical source. The medical source may be your own physician or psychologist, or another source. If you are a child, the medical source we choose may be a pediatrician. For a more complete list of medical sources, see § 404.1513.

(b) By qualified, we mean that the medical source must be currently licensed in the State and have the training and experience to perform the type of examination or test we will request; the medical source must not be barred from participation in our programs under the provisions of § 404.1503a. The medical source must also have the equipment required to provide an adequate assessment and record of the existence and level of severity of your alleged impairments.

(c) The medical source we choose may use support staff to help perform the consultative examination. Any such support staff (e.g., X-ray technician, nurse) must meet appropriate licensing or certification requirements of the State. See § 404.1503a.

20 C.F.R. § 404.1519h Your treating source. (*See also* 20 C.F.R. § 416.919h)

When in our judgment your treating source is qualified, equipped, and willing to perform the additional examination or tests for the fee schedule payment, and generally furnishes complete and timely reports, your treating source will be the preferred source to do the purchased examination. Even if only a supplemental test is required, your treating source is ordinarily the preferred source.

20 C.F.R. § 404.1519i Other sources for consultative examinations. (*See also* 20 C.F.R. § 416.919i)

We will use a medical source other than your treating source for a purchased examination or test in situations including, but not limited to, the following situations:

(a) Your treating source prefers not to perform such an examination or does not have the equipment to provide the specific data needed;

(b) There are conflicts or inconsistencies in your file that cannot be resolved by going back to your treating source;

(c) You prefer a source other than your treating source and have a good reason for your preference;

(d) We know from prior experience that your treating source may not be a productive source, e.g., he or she has consistently failed to provide complete or timely reports.

20 C.F.R § 404.1519p Reviewing reports of consultative examinations. (*See also* 20 C.F.R. § 416.919p)

(a) We will review the report of the consultative examination to determine whether the specific information requested has been furnished. We will consider the following factors in reviewing the report:

(1) Whether the report provides evidence which serves as an adequate basis for decisionmaking in terms of the impairment it assesses;

(2) Whether the report is internally consistent; Whether all the diseases, impairments and complaints described in the history are adequately assessed and reported in the clinical findings; Whether the conclusions correlate the findings from your medical history, clinical examination and laboratory tests and explain all abnormalities;

(3) Whether the report is consistent with the other information available to us within the specialty of the examination requested; Whether the report fails to mention an important or relevant complaint within that specialty that is noted in other evidence in the file (e.g., your blindness in one eye, amputations, pain, alcoholism, depression);

(4) Whether this is an adequate report of examination as compared to standards set out in the course of a medical education; and

(5) Whether the report is properly signed.

(b) If the report is inadequate or incomplete, we will contact the medical source who performed the consultative examination, give an explanation of our evidentiary needs, and ask that the medical source furnish the missing information or prepare a revised report.

(c) With your permission, or when the examination discloses new diagnostic information or test results that reveal a potentially life-threatening situation, we will refer the consultative examination report to your treating source. When we refer the consultative examination report to your treating source without your permission, we will notify you that we have done so.

(d) We will perform ongoing special management studies on the quality of consultative examinations purchased from major medical sources and the appropriateness of the examinations authorized.

(e) We will take steps to ensure that consultative examinations are scheduled only with medical sources who have access to the equipment required to provide an adequate assessment and record of the existence and level of severity of your alleged impairments.

20 C.F.R. § 404.1520 Evaluation of disability in general. (*See also* 20 C.F.R § 416.920)

(a) General—

(1) Purpose of this section. This section explains the five-step sequential evaluation process we use to decide whether you are disabled, as defined in § 404.1505.

(2) Applicability of these rules. These rules apply to you if you file an application for a period of disability or disability insurance benefits (or both) or for child's insurance benefits based on disability. They also apply if you file an application for widow's or widower's benefits based on disability for months after December 1990. (See § 404.1505(a).)

(3) Evidence considered. We will consider all evidence in your case record when we make a determination or decision whether you are disabled.

(4) The five-step sequential evaluation process. The sequential evaluation process is a series of five steps that we follow in a set or-

der. If we can find that you are disabled or not disabled at a step, we make our determination or decision and we do not go on to the next step. If we cannot find that you are disabled or not disabled at a step, we go on to the next step. Before we go from step three to step four, we assess your residual functional capacity. (See paragraph (e) of this section.) We use this residual functional capacity assessment at both step four and step five when we evaluate your claim at these steps. These are the five steps we follow:

(i) At the first step, we consider your work activity, if any. If you are doing substantial gainful activity, we will find that you are not disabled. (See paragraph (b) of this section.)

(ii) At the second step, we consider the medical severity of your impairment(s). If you do not have a severe medically determinable physical or mental impairment that meets the duration requirement in § 404.1509, or a combination of impairments that is severe and meets the duration requirement, we will find that you are not disabled. (See paragraph (c) of this section.)

(iii) At the third step, we also consider the medical severity of your impairment(s). If you have an impairment(s) that meets or equals one of our listings in appendix 1 of this subpart and meets the duration requirement, we will find that you are disabled. (See paragraph (d) of this section.)

(iv) At the fourth step, we consider our assessment of your residual functional capacity and your past relevant work. If you can still do your past relevant work, we will find that you are not disabled. (See paragraph (f) of this section and § 404.1560(b).)

(v) At the fifth and last step, we consider our assessment of your residual functional capacity and your age, education, and work experience to see if you can make an adjustment to other work. If you can make an adjustment to other work, we will find that you are not disabled. If you cannot make an adjustment to other work, we will find that you are disabled. (See paragraph (g) of this section and § 404.1560(c).)

(5) When you are already receiving disability benefits. If you are already receiving disability benefits, we will use a different sequential evaluation process to decide whether you continue to be disabled. We explain this process in § 404.1594(f).

(b) If you are working. If you are working and the work you are doing is substantial gainful activity, we will find that you are not disabled regardless of your medical condition or your age, education, and work experience.

(c) You must have a severe impairment. If you do not have any impairment or combination of impairments which significantly limits your physical or mental ability to do basic work activities, we will find that you do not have a severe impairment and are, therefore, not disabled. We will not consider your age, education, and work experience. * * *

(d) When your impairment(s) meets or equals a listed impairment in Appendix 1. If you have an impairment(s) which meets the duration requirement and is listed in Appendix 1 or is equal to a listed impairment(s), we will find you disabled without considering your age, education, and work experience.

(e) When your impairment(s) does not meet or equal a listed impairment. If your impairment(s) does not meet or equal a listed impairment, we will assess and make a finding about your residual functional capacity based on all the relevant medical and other evidence in your case record, as explained in § 404.1545. (See paragraph (g)(2) of this section and § 404.1562 for an exception to this rule.) We use our residual functional capacity assessment at the fourth step of the sequential evaluation process to determine if you can do your past relevant work (paragraph (f) of this section) and at the fifth step of the sequential evaluation process (if the evaluation proceeds to this step) to determine if you can adjust to other work (paragraph (g) of this section)

(f) Your impairment(s) must prevent you from doing your past relevant work. If we cannot make a determination or decision at the first three steps of the sequential evaluation process, we will compare our residual functional capacity assessment, which we made under paragraph (e) of this section, with the physical and mental demands of your past relevant work. (See § 404.1560(b).) If you can still do this kind of work, we will find that you are not disabled.

(g) Your impairment(s) must prevent you from making an adjustment to any other work.

(1) If we find that you cannot do your past relevant work because you have a severe impairment(s) (or you do not have any past relevant work), we will consider the same residual functional capacity assessment we made under paragraph (e) of this section, together with your vocational factors (your age, education, and work experience) to determine if you can make an adjustment to other work. * * * If you can make an adjustment to other work, we will find you not disabled. If you cannot, we will find you disabled.

(2) We use different rules if you meet one of the two special medical-vocational profiles described in § 404.1562. If you meet one of those profiles, we will find that you cannot make an adjustment to other work, and that you are disabled.

20 C.F.R § 404.1520a Evaluation of mental impairments. (*See also* 20 C.F.R. § 416.920a)

(a) General. The steps outlined in § 404.1520 apply to the evaluation of physical and mental impairments. In addition, when we evaluate the severity of mental impairments for adults (persons age 18 and over) and in persons under age 18 when Part A of the Listing of Impairments is used, we must follow a special technique at each level in the administrative review process. We describe this special technique in paragraphs (b) through (e) of this section. Using the technique helps us:

(1) Identify the need for additional evidence to determine impairment severity;

(2) Consider and evaluate functional consequences of the mental disorder(s) relevant to your ability to work; and

(3) Organize and present our findings in a clear, concise, and consistent manner.

(b) Use of the technique.

(1) Under the special technique, we must first evaluate your pertinent symptoms, signs, and laboratory findings to determine whether you have a medically determinable mental impairment(s). See § 404.1508 for more information about what is needed to show a medically determinable impairment. If we determine that you have a medically determinable mental impairment(s), we must specify the symptoms, signs, and laboratory findings that substantiate the presence of the impairment(s) and document our findings in accordance with paragraph (e) of this section.

(2) We must then rate the degree of functional limitation resulting from the impairment(s) in accordance with paragraph (c) of this section and record our findings as set out in paragraph (e) of this section.

(c) Rating the degree of functional limitation.

(1) Assessment of functional limitations is a complex and highly individualized process that requires us to consider multiple issues and all relevant evidence to obtain a longitudinal picture of your overall degree of functional limitation. We will consider all relevant

and available clinical signs and laboratory findings, the effects of your symptoms, and how your functioning may be affected by factors including, but not limited to, chronic mental disorders, structured settings, medication, and other treatment.

(2) We will rate the degree of your functional limitation based on the extent to which your impairment(s) interferes with your ability to function independently, appropriately, effectively, and on a sustained basis. Thus, we will consider such factors as the quality and level of your overall functional performance, any episodic limitations, the amount of supervision or assistance you require, and the settings in which you are able to function. See 12.00C through 12.00H of the Listing of Impairments in appendix 1 to this subpart for more information about the factors we consider when we rate the degree of your functional limitation.

(3) We have identified four broad functional areas in which we will rate the degree of your functional limitation: Activities of daily living; social functioning; concentration, persistence, or pace; and episodes of decompensation. See 12.00C of the Listing of Impairments.

(4) When we rate the degree of limitation in the first three functional areas (activities of daily living; social functioning; and concentration, persistence, or pace), we will use the following five-point scale: None, mild, moderate, marked, and extreme. When we rate the degree of limitation in the fourth functional area (episodes of decompensation), we will use the following four-point scale: None, one or two, three, four or more. The last point on each scale represents a degree of limitation that is incompatible with the ability to do any gainful activity.

(d) *Use of the technique to evaluate mental impairments.* After we rate the degree of functional limitation resulting from your impairment(s), we will determine the severity of your mental impairment(s).

(1) If we rate the degree of your limitation in the first three functional areas as "none" or "mild" and "none" in the fourth area, we will generally conclude that your impairment(s) is not severe, unless the evidence otherwise indicates that there is more than a minimal limitation in your ability to do basic work activities (see § 404.1521).

(2) If your mental impairment(s) is severe, we will then determine if it meets or is equivalent in severity to a listed mental disorder. We do this by comparing the medical findings about your impairment(s) and the rating of the degree of functional limitation to the criteria of the appropriate listed mental disorder. We will record the presence or absence of the criteria and the rating of the degree of

functional limitation on a standard document at the initial and re-consideration levels of the administrative review process, or in the decision at the administrative law judge hearing and Appeals Council levels (in cases in which the Appeals Council issues a decision). See paragraph (e) of this section.

(3) If we find that you have a severe mental impairment(s) that neither meets nor is equivalent in severity to any listing, we will then assess your residual functional capacity.

(e) Documenting application of the technique. At the initial and re-consideration levels of the administrative review process, we will complete a standard document to record how we applied the technique. At the administrative law judge hearing and Appeals Council levels (in cases in which the Appeals Council issues a decision), we will document application of the technique in the decision. The following rules apply:

(1) When a State agency medical or psychological consultant makes the determination together with a State agency disability examiner at the initial or reconsideration level of the administrative review process as provided in § 404.1615(c)(1) of this part, the State agency medical or psychological consultant has overall responsibility for assessing medical severity. A State agency disability examiner may assist in preparing the standard document. However, our medical or psychological consultant must review and sign the document to attest that it is complete and that he or she is responsible for its content, including the findings of fact and any discussion of supporting evidence.

(2) When a State agency disability examiner makes the determination alone as provided in § 404.1615(c)(3), the State agency disability examiner has overall responsibility for assessing medical severity and for completing and signing the standard document.

(3) When a disability hearing officer makes a reconsideration determination as provided in § 404.1615(c)(4), the determination must document application of the technique, incorporating the disability hearing officer's pertinent findings and conclusions based on this technique.

(4) At the administrative law judge hearing and Appeals Council levels, the written decision must incorporate the pertinent findings and conclusions based on the technique. The decision must show the significant history, including examination and laboratory findings, and the functional limitations that were considered in reaching a conclusion about the severity of the mental impairment(s). The deci-

sion must include a specific finding as to the degree of limitation in each of the functional areas described in paragraph (c) of this section.

(5) If the administrative law judge requires the services of a medical expert to assist in applying the technique but such services are unavailable, the administrative law judge may return the case to the State agency or the appropriate Federal component, using the rules in § 404.941 of this part, for completion of the standard document. If, after reviewing the case file and completing the standard document, the State agency or Federal component concludes that a determination favorable to you is warranted, it will process the case using the rules found in § 404.941(d) or (e) of this part. If, after reviewing the case file and completing the standard document, the State agency or Federal component concludes that a determination favorable to you is not warranted, it will send the completed standard document and the case to the administrative law judge for further proceedings and a decision.

20 C.F.R. § 404.1521 What we mean by an impairment(s) that is not severe. (*See also* 20 C.F.R § 416.921)

(a) Non-severe impairment(s). An impairment or combination of impairments is not severe if it does not significantly limit your physical or mental ability to do basic work activities.

(b) Basic work activities. When we talk about basic work activities, we mean the abilities and aptitudes necessary to do most jobs. Examples of these include—

(1) Physical functions such as walking, standing, sitting, lifting, pushing, pulling, reaching, carrying, or handling;

(2) Capacities for seeing, hearing, and speaking;

(3) Understanding, carrying out, and remembering simple instructions;

(4) Use of judgment;

(5) Responding appropriately to supervision, co-workers and usual work situations; and

(6) Dealing with changes in a routine work setting.

20 C.F.R. § 404.1523 Multiple impairments. (*See also* 20 C.F.R §
  416.923)

In determining whether your physical or mental impairment or impairments are of a sufficient medical severity that such impairment or
impairments could be the basis of eligibility under the law, we will consider the combined effect of all of your impairments without regard to
whether any such impairment, if considered separately, would be of sufficient severity. If we do find a medically severe combination of impairments, the combined impact of the impairments will be considered
throughout the disability determination process. If we do not find that
you have a medically severe combination of impairments, we will determine that you are not disabled (see 404.1520).

20 C.F.R. § 404.1525 Listing of Impairments in appendix 1.

(a) What is the purpose of the Listing of Impairments? The Listing of
Impairments (the listings) is in appendix 1 of this subpart. It describes for
each of the major body systems impairments that we consider to be severe
enough to prevent an individual from doing any gainful activity, regardless of his or her age, education, or work experience.

(b) How is appendix 1 organized? There are two parts in appendix 1:

(1) Part A contains criteria that apply to individuals age 18 and
over. We may also use part A for individuals who are under age 18 if
the disease processes have a similar effect on adults and children.

(2) Part B contains criteria that apply only to individuals who
are under age 18; we never use the listings in part B to evaluate individuals who are age 18 or older. In evaluating disability for a person under age 18, we use part B first. If the criteria in part B do not
apply, we may use the criteria in part A when those criteria give appropriate consideration to the effects of the impairment(s) in children. To the extent possible, we number the provisions in part B to
maintain a relationship with their counterparts in part A.

(c) How do we use the listings?

(1) Most body system sections in parts A and B of appendix 1 are
in two parts: an introduction, followed by the specific listings.

(2) The introduction to each body system contains information
relevant to the use of the listings in that body system; for example,
examples of common impairments in the body system and definitions
used in the listings for that body system. We may also include specific criteria for establishing a diagnosis, confirming the existence of an

impairment, or establishing that your impairment(s) satisfies the criteria of a particular listing in the body system. Even if we do not include specific criteria for establishing a diagnosis or confirming the existence of your impairment, you must still show that you have a severe medically determinable impairment(s), as defined in §§ 404.1508 and 404.1520(c).

(3) In most cases, the specific listings follow the introduction in each body system, after the heading, Category of Impairments. Within each listing, we specify the objective medical and other findings needed to satisfy the criteria of that listing. We will find that your impairment(s) meets the requirements of a listing when it satisfies all of the criteria of that listing, including any relevant criteria in the introduction, and meets the duration requirement (see § 404.1509).

(4) Most of the listed impairments are permanent or expected to result in death. For some listings, we state a specific period of time for which your impairment(s) will meet the listing. For all others, the evidence must show that your impairment(s) has lasted or can be expected to last for a continuous period of at least 12 months.

(5) If your impairment(s) does not meet the criteria of a listing, it can medically equal the criteria of a listing. We explain our rules for medical equivalence in § 404.1526. We use the listings only to find that you are disabled or still disabled. If your impairment(s) does not meet or medically equal the criteria of a listing, we may find that you are disabled or still disabled at a later step in the sequential evaluation process.

(d) Can your impairment(s) meet a listing based only on a diagnosis? No. Your impairment(s) cannot meet the criteria of a listing based only on a diagnosis. To meet the requirements of a listing, you must have a medically determinable impairment(s) that satisfies all of the criteria in the listing.

(c) How do we consider your symptoms when we determine whether your impairment(s) meets a listing? Some listed impairments include symptoms, such as pain, as criteria. Section 404.1529(d)(2) explains how we consider your symptoms when your symptoms are included as criteria in a listing.

20 C.F.R. § 404.1526 Medical equivalence. (*See also* 20 C.F.R. § 416.926)

(a) What is medical equivalence? Your impairment(s) is medically equivalent to a listed impairment in appendix 1 if it is at least equal in severity and duration to the criteria of any listed impairment.

(b) How do we determine medical equivalence? We can find medical equivalence in three ways.

(1)(i) If you have an impairment that is described in appendix 1, but—

(A) You do not exhibit one or more of the findings specified in the particular listing, or

(B) You exhibit all of the findings, but one or more of the findings is not as severe as specified in the particular listing,

(ii) We will find that your impairment is medically equivalent to that listing if you have other findings related to your impairment that are at least of equal medical significance to the required criteria.

(2) If you have an impairment(s) that is not described in appendix 1, we will compare your findings with those for closely analogous listed impairments. If the findings related to your impairment(s) are at least of equal medical significance to those of a listed impairment, we will find that your impairment(s) is medically equivalent to the analogous listing.

(3) If you have a combination of impairments, no one of which meets a listing (see § 404.1525(c)(3)), we will compare your findings with those for closely analogous listed impairments. If the findings related to your impairments are at least of equal medical significance to those of a listed impairment, we will find that your combination of impairments is medically equivalent to that listing.

* * *

(c) What evidence do we consider when we determine if your impairment(s) medically equals a listing? When we determine if your impairment medically equals a listing, we consider all evidence in your case record about your impairment(s) and its effects on you that is relevant to this finding. We do not consider your vocational factors of age, education, and work experience (see, for example, § 404.1560(c)(1)). We also consider the opinion given by one or more medical or psychological consultants designated by the Commissioner. (See § 404.1616.)

(d) Who is a designated medical or psychological consultant? A medical or psychological consultant designated by the Commissioner includes any medical or psychological consultant employed or engaged to make medical judgments by the Social Security Administration, the Railroad Retirement Board, or a State agency authorized to make disability determinations. A medical consultant must be an acceptable medical source identified in § 404.1513(a)(1) or (a)(3) through (a)(5). A psychological consultant used in cases where there is evidence of a mental impairment must be a qualified psychologist. (See § 404.1616 for limitations on what medical consultants who are not physicians can evaluate and the qualifications we consider necessary for a psychologist to be a consultant.)

(e) Who is responsible for determining medical equivalence? In cases where the State agency or other designee of the Commissioner makes the initial or reconsideration disability determination, a State agency medical or psychological consultant or other designee of the Commissioner (see § 404.1616 of this part) has the overall responsibility for determining medical equivalence. For cases in the disability hearing process or otherwise decided by a disability hearing officer, the responsibility for determining medical equivalence rests with either the disability hearing officer or, if the disability hearing officer's reconsideration determination is changed under § 404.918 of this part, with the Associate Commissioner for Disability Determinations or his or her delegate. For cases at the administrative law judge or Appeals Council level, the responsibility for deciding medical equivalence rests with the administrative law judge or Appeals Council.

20 C.F.R. § 404.1527 Evaluating opinion evidence. (*See also* 20 C.F.R. § 416.927)

(a) General.

* * *

(2) Evidence that you submit or that we obtain may contain medical opinions. Medical opinions are statements from physicians and psychologists or other acceptable medical sources that reflect judgments about the nature and severity of your impairment(s), including your symptoms, diagnosis and prognosis, what you can still do despite impairment(s), and your physical or mental restrictions.

* * *

(c) Making disability determinations. After we review all of the evidence relevant to your claim, including medical opinions, we make findings about what the evidence shows.

(1) If all of the evidence we receive, including all medical opinion(s), is consistent, and there is sufficient evidence for us to decide whether you are disabled, we will make our determination or decision based on that evidence.

(2) If any of the evidence in your case record, including any medical opinion(s), is inconsistent with other evidence or is internally in-

consistent, we will weigh all of the evidence and see whether we can decide whether you are disabled based on the evidence we have.

(3) If the evidence is consistent but we do not have sufficient evidence to decide whether you are disabled, or if after weighing the evidence we decide we cannot reach a conclusion about whether you are disabled, we will try to obtain additional evidence under the provisions of §§ 404.1512 and 404.1519 through 404.1519h. We will request additional existing records, recontact your treating sources or any other examining sources, ask you to undergo a consultative examination at our expense, or ask you or others for more information. We will consider any additional evidence we receive together with the evidence we already have.

(4) When there are inconsistencies in the evidence that cannot be resolved, or when despite efforts to obtain additional evidence the evidence is not complete, we will make a determination or decision based on the evidence we have.

(d) How we weigh medical opinions. Regardless of its source, we will evaluate every medical opinion we receive. Unless we give a treating source's opinion controlling weight under paragraph (d)(2) of this section, we consider all of the following factors in deciding the weight we give to any medical opinion.

(1) Examining relationship. Generally, we give more weight to the opinion of a source who has examined you than to the opinion of a source who has not examined you.

(2) Treatment relationship. Generally, we give more weight to opinions from your treating sources, since these sources are likely to be the medical professionals most able to provide a detailed, longitudinal picture of your medical impairment(s) and may bring a unique perspective to the medical evidence that cannot be obtained from the objective medical findings alone or from reports of individual examinations, such as consultative examinations or brief hospitalizations. If we find that a treating source's opinion on the issue(s) of the nature and severity of your impairment(s) is well-supported by medically acceptable clinical and laboratory diagnostic techniques and is not inconsistent with the other substantial evidence in your case record, we will give it controlling weight. When we do not give the treating source's opinion controlling weight, we apply the factors listed in paragraphs (d)(2)(i) and (d)(2)(ii) of this section, as well as the factors in paragraphs (d)(3) through (d)(6) of this section in determining the weight to give the opinion. We will always give good reasons in our notice of determination or decision for the weight we give your treating source's opinion.

(i) Length of the treatment relationship and the frequency of examination. Generally, the longer a treating source has treated you and the more times you have been seen by a treating source, the more weight we will give to the source's medical opinion. When the treating source has seen you a number of times and long enough to have obtained a longitudinal picture of your impairment, we will give the source's opinion more weight than we would give it if it were from a nontreating source.

(ii) Nature and extent of the treatment relationship. Generally, the more knowledge a treating source has about your impairment(s) the more weight we will give to the source's medical opinion. We will look at the treatment the source has provided and at the kinds and extent of examinations and testing the source has performed or ordered from specialists and independent laboratories. For example, if your ophthalmologist notices that you have complained of neck pain during your eye examinations, we will consider his or her opinion with respect to your neck pain, but we will give it less weight than that of another physician who has treated you for the neck pain. When the treating source has reasonable knowledge of your impairment(s), we will give the source's opinion more weight than we would give it if it were from a nontreating source.

(3) Supportability. The more a medical source presents relevant evidence to support an opinion, particularly medical signs and laboratory findings, the more weight we will give that opinion. The better an explanation a source provides for an opinion, the more weight we will give that opinion. Furthermore, because nonexamining sources have no examining or treating relationship with you, the weight we will give their opinions will depend on the degree to which they provide supporting explanations for their opinions. We will evaluate the degree to which these opinions consider all of the pertinent evidence in your claim, including opinions of treating and other examining sources.

(4) Consistency. Generally, the more consistent an opinion is with the record as a whole, the more weight we will give to that opinion.

(5) Specialization. We generally give more weight to the opinion of a specialist about medical issues related to his or her area of specialty than to the opinion of a source who is not a specialist.

(6) Other factors. When we consider how much weight to give to a medical opinion, we will also consider any factors you or others bring to our attention, or of which we are aware, which tend to sup-

port or contradict the opinion. For example, the amount of under-standing of our disability programs and their evidentiary require-ments that an acceptable medical source has, regardless of the source of that understanding, and the extent to which an acceptable medical source is familiar with the other information in your case record are relevant factors that we will consider in deciding the weight to give to a medical opinion.

(e) Medical source opinions on issues reserved to the Commissioner. Opinions on some issues, such as the examples that follow, are not medi-cal opinions, as described in paragraph (a)(2) of this section, but are, in-stead, opinions on issues reserved to the Commissioner because they are administrative findings that are dispositive of a case; i.e., that would di-rect the determination or decision of disability.

(1) Opinions that you are disabled. We are responsible for mak-ing the determination or decision about whether you meet the statu-tory definition of disability. In so doing, we review all of the medical findings and other evidence that support a medical source's state-ment that you are disabled. A statement by a medical source that you are "disabled" or "unable to work" does not mean that we will deter-mine that you are disabled.

(2) Other opinions on issues reserved to the Commissioner. We use medical sources, including your treating source, to provide evi-dence, including opinions, on the nature and severity of your im-pairment(s). Although we consider opinions from medical sources on issues such as whether your impairment(s) meets or equals the re-quirements of any impairment(s) in the Listing of Impairments in appendix 1 to this subpart, your residual functional capacity (see §§ 404.1545 and 404.1546), or the application of vocational factors, the final responsibility for deciding these issues is reserved to the Com-missioner.

(3) We will not give any special significance to the source of an opinion on issues reserved to the Commissioner described in para-graphs (e)(1) and (e)(2) of this section.

(f) Opinions of nonexamining sources. We consider all evidence from nonexamining sources to be opinion evidence. When we consider the opin-ions of nonexamining sources, we apply the rules in paragraphs (a) through (e) of this section. In addition, the following rules apply to State agency medical and psychological consultants, other program physicians and psychologists, and medical experts we consult in connection with ad-ministrative law judge hearings and Appeals Council review:

(1) In claims adjudicated by the State agency, a State agency medical or psychological consultant (or a medical or psychological expert (as defined in § 405.5 of this chapter) in claims adjudicated under the procedures in part 405 of this chapter) may make the determination of disability together with a State agency disability examiner or provide one or more medical opinions to a State agency disability examiner when the disability examiner makes the initial or reconsideration determination alone (see § 404.1615(c)). The following rules apply:

(i) When a State agency medical or psychological consultant makes the determination together with a State agency disability examiner at the initial or reconsideration level of the administrative review process as provided in § 404.1615(c)(1), he or she will consider the evidence in your case record and make findings of fact about the medical issues, including, but not limited to, the existence and severity of your impairment(s), the existence and severity of your symptoms, whether your impairment(s) meets or medically equals the requirements for any impairment listed in appendix 1 to this subpart, and your residual functional capacity. These administrative findings of fact are based on the evidence in your case but are not in themselves evidence at the level of the administrative review process at which they are made.

(ii) When a State agency disability examiner makes the initial determination alone as provided in § 404.1615(c)(3), he or she may obtain the opinion of a State agency medical or psychological consultant about one or more of the medical issues listed in paragraph (f)(1)(i) of this section. In these cases, the State agency disability examiner will consider the opinion of the State agency medical or psychological consultant as opinion evidence and weigh this evidence using the relevant factors in paragraphs (a) through (e) of this section.

(iii) When a State agency disability examiner makes a reconsideration determination alone as provided in § 404.1615(c)(3), he or she will consider findings made by a State agency medical or psychological consultant at the initial level of the administrative review process and any opinions provided by such consultants at the initial and reconsideration levels as opinion evidence and weigh this evidence using the relevant factors in paragraphs (a) through (e) of this section.

(2) Administrative law judges are responsible for reviewing the evidence and making findings of fact and conclusions of law. They will consider opinions of State agency medical or psychological consultants, other program physicians and psychologists, and medical experts as follows:

(i) Administrative law judges are not bound by any findings made by State agency medical or psychological consultants, or other program physicians or psychologists. State agency medical and psychological consultants and other program physicians, psychologists, and other medical specialists are highly qualified physicians, psychologists, and other medical specialists who are also experts in Social Security disability evaluation. Therefore, administrative law judges must consider findings and other opinions of State agency medical and psychological consultants and other program physicians, psychologists, and other medical specialists as opinion evidence, except for the ultimate determination about whether you are disabled (see § 404.1512(b)(8)).

(ii) When an administrative law judge considers findings of a State agency medical or psychological consultant or other program physician, psychologist, or other medical specialists, the administrative law judge will evaluate the findings using relevant factors in paragraphs (a) through (e) of this section, such as the consultant's medical specialty and expertise in our rules, the supporting evidence in the case record, supporting explanations the medical or psychological consultant provides, and any other factors relevant to the weighing of the opinions. Unless a treating source's opinion is given controlling weight, the administrative law judge must explain in the decision the weight given to the opinions of a State agency medical or psychological consultant or other program physician, psychologist, or other medical specialists, as the administrative law judge must do for any opinions from treating sources, nontreating sources, and other nonexamining sources who do not work for us.

(iii) Administrative law judges may also ask for and consider opinions from medical experts on the nature and severity of your impairment(s) and on whether your impairment(s) equals the requirements of any impairment listed in appendix 1 to this subpart. When administrative law judges consider these opinions, they will evaluate them using the rules in paragraphs (a) through (e) of this section.

(3) When the Appeals Council makes a decision, it will follow the same rules for considering opinion evidence as administrative law judges follow.

(4) In claims adjudicated under the procedures in part 405 of this chapter at the Federal reviewing official, administrative law judge, and the Decision Review Board levels of the administrative review process, we will follow the same rules for considering opinion evidence that administrative law judges follow under this section.

20 C.F.R. § 404.1528 Symptoms, signs, and laboratory findings. (*See also* 20 C.F.R § 416.928)

(a) Symptoms are your own description of your physical or mental impairment. Your statements alone are not enough to establish that there is a physical or mental impairment.

(b) Signs are anatomical, physiological, or psychological abnormalities which can be observed, apart from your statements (symptoms). Signs must be shown by medically acceptable clinical diagnostic techniques. Psychiatric signs are medically demonstrable phenomena that indicate specific psychological abnormalities, e.g., abnormalities of behavior, mood, thought, memory, orientation, development, or perception. They must also be shown by observable facts that can be medically described and evaluated.

(c) Laboratory findings are anatomical, physiological, or psychological phenomena which can be shown by the use of medically acceptable laboratory diagnostic techniques. Some of these diagnostic techniques include chemical tests, electrophysiological studies (electrocardiogram, electroencephalogram, etc.), roentgenological studies (X-rays), and psychological tests.

20 C.F.R. § 404.1529 How we evaluate symptoms, including pain. (*See also* 20 C.F.R § 416.929)

(a) General. In determining whether you are disabled, we consider all your symptoms, including pain, and the extent to which your symptoms can reasonably be accepted as consistent with the objective medical evidence and other evidence. * * * We will consider all of your statements about your symptoms, such as pain, and any description you, your treating source or nontreating source, or other persons may provide about how the symptoms affect your activities of daily living and your ability to work. However, statements about your pain or other symptoms will not alone establish that you are disabled; there must be medical signs and laboratory findings which show that you have a medical impairment(s) which could reasonably be expected to produce the pain or other symptoms alleged and which, when considered with all of the other evidence (including statements about the intensity and persistence of your pain or other symptoms which may reasonably be accepted as consistent with the medical signs and laboratory findings), would lead to a conclusion that you are disabled. In evaluating the intensity and persistence of your symptoms, including pain, we will consider all of the available evidence, including your medical history, the medical signs and laboratory findings and statements about how your symptoms affect you. * * * We will then determine the extent to which your alleged functional limitations and restrictions due to pain or other symptoms can reasonably be accepted as consistent with the medical signs and laboratory findings and other evidence to decide how your symptoms affect your ability to work.

(b) Need for medically determinable impairment that could reasonably be expected to produce your symptoms, such as pain. Your symptoms, such as pain, fatigue, shortness of breath, weakness, or nervousness, will not be found to affect your ability to do basic work activities unless medical signs or laboratory findings show that a medically determinable impairment(s) is present. * * * The finding that your impairment(s) could reasonably be expected to produce your pain or other symptoms does not involve a determination as to the intensity, persistence, or functionally limiting effects of your symptoms. We will develop evidence regarding the possibility of a medically determinable mental impairment when we have information to suggest that such an impairment exists, and you allege pain or other symptoms but the medical signs and laboratory findings do not substantiate any physical impairment(s) capable of producing the pain or other symptoms.

(c) Evaluating the intensity and persistence of your symptoms, such as pain, and determining the extent to which your symptoms limit your capacity for work—

(1) General. When the medical signs or laboratory findings show that you have a medically determinable impairment(s) that could reasonably be expected to produce your symptoms, such as pain, we must then evaluate the intensity and persistence of your symptoms so that we can determine how your symptoms limit your capacity for work. In evaluating the intensity and persistence of your symptoms, we consider all of the available evidence, including your history, the signs and laboratory findings, and statements from you, your treating or nontreating source, or other persons about how your symptoms affect you. We also consider the medical opinions of your treating source and other medical opinions * * *. * * *

(2) Consideration of objective medical evidence. Objective medical evidence is evidence obtained from the application of medically acceptable clinical and laboratory diagnostic techniques, such as evidence of reduced joint motion, muscle spasm, sensory deficit or motor disruption. Objective medical evidence of this type is a useful indicator to assist us in making reasonable conclusions about the intensity and persistence of your symptoms and the effect those symptoms, such as pain, may have on your ability to work. We must always attempt to obtain objective medical evidence and, when it is obtained, we will consider it in reaching a conclusion as to whether you are disabled. However, we will not reject your statements about the intensity and persistence of your pain or other symptoms or about the

effect your symptoms have on your ability to work solely because the available objective medical evidence does not substantiate your statements.

(3) Consideration of other evidence. Since symptoms sometimes suggest a greater severity of impairment than can be shown by objective medical evidence alone, we will carefully consider any other information you may submit about your symptoms. The information that you, your treating or nontreating source, or other persons provide about your pain or other symptoms (e.g., what may precipitate or aggravate your symptoms, what medications, treatments or other methods you use to alleviate them, and how the symptoms may affect your pattern of daily living) is also an important indicator of the intensity and persistence of your symptoms. Because symptoms, such as pain, are subjective and difficult to quantify, any symptom-related functional limitations and restrictions which you, your treating or nontreating source, or other persons report, which can reasonably be accepted as consistent with the objective medical evidence and other evidence, will be taken into account as explained in paragraph (c)(4) of this section in reaching a conclusion as to whether you are disabled. We will consider all of the evidence presented, including information about your prior work record, your statements about your symptoms, evidence submitted by your treating or nontreating source, and observations by our employees and other persons. * * * Factors relevant to your symptoms, such as pain, which we will consider include:

(i) Your daily activities;

(ii) The location, duration, frequency, and intensity of your pain or other symptoms;

(iii) Precipitating and aggravating factors;

(iv) The type, dosage, effectiveness, and side effects of any medication you take or have taken to alleviate your pain or other symptoms;

(v) Treatment, other than medication, you receive or have received for relief of your pain or other symptoms;

(vi) Any measures you use or have used to relieve your pain or other symptoms (e.g., lying flat on your back, standing for 15 to 20 minutes every hour, sleeping on a board, etc.); and

(vii) Other factors concerning your functional limitations and restrictions due to pain or other symptoms.

(4) How we determine the extent to which symptoms, such as pain, affect your capacity to perform basic work activities. In determining the extent to which your symptoms, such as pain, affect your capacity to perform basic work activities, we consider all of the available evidence described in paragraphs (c)(1) through (c)(3) of this section. We will consider your statements about the intensity, persistence, and limiting effects of your symptoms, and we will evaluate your statements in relation to the objective medical evidence and other evidence, in reaching a conclusion as to whether you are disabled. We will consider whether there are any inconsistencies in the evidence and the extent to which there are any conflicts between your statements and the rest of the evidence, including your history, the signs and laboratory findings, and statements by your treating or nontreating source or other persons about how your symptoms affect you. Your symptoms, including pain, will be determined to diminish your capacity for basic work activities to the extent that your alleged functional limitations and restrictions due to symptoms, such as pain, can reasonably be accepted as consistent with the objective medical evidence and other evidence.

(d) Consideration of symptoms in the disability determination process. We follow a set order of steps to determine whether you are disabled. If you are not doing substantial gainful activity, we consider your symptoms, such as pain, to evaluate whether you have a severe physical or mental impairment(s), and at each of the remaining steps in the process. * * * We also consider your symptoms, such as pain, at the appropriate steps in our review when we consider whether your disability continues. * * *

(1) Need to establish a severe medically determinable impairment(s). Your symptoms, such as pain, fatigue, shortness of breath, weakness, or nervousness, are considered in making a determination as to whether your impairment or combination of impairment(s) is severe. * * *

(2) Decision whether the Listing of Impairments is met. Some listed impairments include symptoms usually associated with those impairments as criteria. Generally, when a symptom is one of the criteria in a listing, it is only necessary that the symptom be present in combination with the other criteria. It is not necessary, unless the listing specifically states otherwise, to provide information about the intensity, persistence, or limiting effects of the symptom as long as all other findings required by the specific listing are present.

(3) Decision whether the Listing of Impairments is medically equaled. If your impairment is not the same as a listed impairment,

we must determine whether your impairment(s) is medically equivalent to a listed impairment. * * * In considering whether your symptoms, signs, and laboratory findings are medically equal to the symptoms, signs, and laboratory findings of a listed impairment, we will look to see whether your symptoms, signs, and laboratory findings are at least equal in severity to the listed criteria. However, we will not substitute your allegations of pain or other symptoms for a missing or deficient sign or laboratory finding to raise the severity of your impairment(s) to that of a listed impairment. If the symptoms, signs, and laboratory findings of your impairment(s) are equivalent in severity to those of a listed impairment, we will find you disabled. If it does not, we will consider the impact of your symptoms on your residual functional capacity. * * *

(4) Impact of symptoms (including pain) on residual functional capacity. If you have a medically determinable severe physical or mental impairment(s), but your impairment(s) does not meet or equal an impairment listed in Appendix 1 of this subpart, we will consider the impact of your impairment(s) and any related symptoms, including pain, on your residual functional capacity. * * *

20 C.F.R § 404.1530 Need to follow prescribed treatment. (*See also* 20 C.F.R § 416.930)

(a) What treatment you must follow. In order to get benefits, you must follow treatment prescribed by your physician if this treatment can restore your ability to work.

(b) When you do not follow prescribed treatment. If you do not follow the prescribed treatment without a good reason, we will not find you disabled or, if you are already receiving benefits, we will stop paying you benefits.

(c) Acceptable reasons for failure to follow prescribed treatment. We will consider your physical, mental, educational, and linguistic limitations (including any lack of facility with the English language) when determining if you have an acceptable reason for failure to follow prescribed treatment. The following are examples of a good reason for not following treatment:

(1) The specific medical treatment is contrary to the established teaching and tenets of your religion.

(2) The prescribed treatment would be cataract surgery for one eye, when there is an impairment of the other eye resulting in a severe loss of vision and is not subject to improvement through treatment.

(3) Surgery was previously performed with unsuccessful results and the same surgery is again being recommended for the same impairment.

(4) The treatment because of its magnitude (e.g. open heart surgery), unusual nature (e.g., organ transplant), or other reason is very risky for you; or

(5) The treatment involves amputation of an extremity, or a major part of an extremity.

20 C.F.R. § 404.1535 How we will determine whether your drug addiction or alcoholism is a contributing factor material to the determination of disability. (*See also* 20 C.F.R § 416.929)

(a) General. If we find that you are disabled and have medical evidence of your drug addiction or alcoholism, we must determine whether your drug addiction or alcoholism is a contributing factor material to the determination of disability.

(b) Process we will follow when we have medical evidence of your drug addiction or alcoholism.

(1) The key factor we will examine in determining whether drug addiction or alcoholism is a contributing factor material to the determination of disability is whether we would still find you disabled if you stopped using drugs or alcohol.

(2) In making this determination, we will evaluate which of your current physical and mental limitations, upon which we based our current disability determination, would remain if you stopped using drugs or alcohol and then determine whether any or all of your remaining limitations would be disabling.

(i) If we determine that your remaining limitations would not be disabling, we will find that your drug addiction or alcoholism is a contributing factor material to the determination of disability.

(ii) If we determine that your remaining limitations are disabling, you are disabled independent of your drug addiction or alcoholism and we will find that your drug addiction or alcoholism is not a contributing factor material to the determination of disability.

20 C.F.R § 404.1545 Your residual functional capacity. (*See also* 20 C.F.R § 416.945)

(a) General—

(1) Residual functional capacity assessment. Your impairment(s), and any related symptoms, such as pain, may cause physical and mental limitations that affect what you can do in a work setting. Your residual functional capacity is the most you can still do despite your limitations. We will assess your residual functional capacity based on all the relevant evidence in your case record. (See § 404.1546.)

(2) If you have more than one impairment. We will consider all of your medically determinable impairments of which we are aware, including your medically determinable impairments that are not severe, as explained in §§ 404.1520(c), 404.1521, and 404.1523, when we assess your residual functional capacity. (See paragraph (e) of this section.)

(3) Evidence we use to assess your residual functional capacity. We will assess your residual functional capacity based on all of the relevant medical and other evidence. In general, you are responsible for providing the evidence we will use to make a finding about your residual functional capacity. (See § 404.1512(c).) However, before we make a determination that you are not disabled, we are responsible for developing your complete medical history, including arranging for a consultative examination(s) if necessary, and making every reasonable effort to help you get medical reports from your own medical sources. (See §§ 404.1512(d) through (f).) We will consider any statements about what you can still do that have been provided by medical sources, whether or not they are based on formal medical examinations. (See § 404.1513.) We will also consider descriptions and observations of your limitations from your impairment(s), including limitations that result from your symptoms, such as pain, provided by you, your family, neighbors, friends, or other persons. (See paragraph (e) of this section and § 404.1529.)

(4) What we will consider in assessing residual functional capacity. When we assess your residual functional capacity, we will consider your ability to meet the physical, mental, sensory, and other requirements of work, as described in paragraphs (b), (c), and (d) of this section.

(5) How we will use our residual functional capacity assessment.

(i) We will first use our residual functional capacity assessment at step four of the sequential evaluation process to decide if you can do your past relevant work. (See §§ 404.1520(f) and 404.1560(b).)

(ii) If we find that you cannot do your past relevant work (or you do not have any past relevant work), we will use the same assessment of your residual functional capacity at step five of the sequential evaluation process to decide if you can make an adjustment to any other work that exists in the national economy. (See §§ 404.1520(g) and 404.1566.) At this step, we will not use our assessment of your residual functional capacity alone to decide if you are disabled. We will use the guidelines in §§ 404.1560 through 404.1569a, and consider our residual functional capacity assessment together with the information about your vocational background to make our disability determination or decision. For our rules on residual functional capacity assessment in deciding whether your disability continues or ends, see § 404.1594.

(b) Physical abilities. When we assess your physical abilities, we first assess the nature and extent of your physical limitations and then determine your residual functional capacity for work activity on a regular and continuing basis. A limited ability to perform certain physical demands of work activity, such as sitting, standing, walking, lifting, carrying, pushing, pulling, or other physical functions (including manipulative or postural functions, such as reaching, handling, stooping or crouching), may reduce your ability to do past work and other work.

(c) Mental abilities. When we assess your mental abilities, we first assess the nature and extent of your mental limitations and restrictions and then determine your residual functional capacity for work activity on a regular and continuing basis. A limited ability to carry out certain mental activities, such as limitations in understanding, remembering, and carrying out instructions, and in responding appropriately to supervision, co-workers, and work pressures in a work setting, may reduce your ability to do past work and other work.

(d) Other abilities affected by impairment(s). Some medically determinable impairment(s), such as skin impairment(s), epilepsy, impairment(s) of vision, hearing or other senses, and impairment(s) which impose environmental restrictions, may cause limitations and restrictions which affect other work-related abilities. If you have this type of impairment(s), we consider any resulting limitations and restrictions which may reduce your ability to do past work and other work in deciding your residual functional capacity.

(e) Total limiting effects. When you have a severe impairment(s), but your symptoms, signs, and laboratory findings do not meet or equal those of a listed impairment in Appendix 1 of this subpart, we will consider the limiting effects of all your impairment(s), even those that are not severe, in determining your residual functional capacity. Pain or other symptoms may cause a limitation of function beyond that which can be determined on the basis of the anatomical, physiological or psychological abnormalities considered alone; e.g., someone with a low back disorder may be fully capable of the physical demands consistent with those of sustained medium work activity, but another person with the same disorder, because of pain, may not be capable of more than the physical demands consistent with those of light work activity on a sustained basis. In assessing the total limiting effects of your impairment(s) and any related symptoms, we will consider all of the medical and nonmedical evidence * * *.

20 C.F.R.§ 404.1560 When your vocational background will be considered. (*See also* 20 C.F.R § 416.960)

(a) General. If you are applying for a period of disability, or disability insurance benefits as a disabled worker, or child's insurance benefits based on disability which began before age 22, or widow's or widower's benefits based on disability for months after December 1990, and we cannot decide whether you are disabledat one of the first three steps of the sequential evaluation process (see § 404.1520), we will consider your residual functional capacity together with your vocational background, as discussed in paragraphs (b) and (c) of this section.

(b) Past relevant work. We will first compare our assessment of your residual functional capacity with the physical and mental demands of your past relevant work.

(1) Definition of past relevant work. Past relevant work is work that you have done within the past 15 years, that was substantial gainful activity, and that lasted long enough for you to learn to do it. (See § 404.1565(a).)

(2) Determining whether you can do your past relevant work. We will ask you for information about work you have done in the past. We may also ask other people who know about your work. (See § 404.1565(b).) We may use the services of vocational experts or vocational specialists, or other resources, such as the Dictionary of Occupational Titles and its companion volumes and supplements, published by the Department of Labor, to obtain evidence we need to help us determine whether you can do your past relevant work, given your residual functional capacity. A vocational expert or specialist may offer relevant evidence within his or her expertise or knowledge concerning the physical and mental demands of a claimant's past relevant work, either as the claimant actually performed it or as generally performed in the national economy. Such evidence may be helpful in supplementing or evaluating the accuracy of the claimant's description of his past work. In addition, a vocational expert or specialist may offer expert opinion testimony in response to a hypothetical question about whether a person with the physical and mental limitations imposed by the claimant's medical impairment(s) can meet

the demands of the claimant's previous work, either as the claimant actually performed it or as generally performed in the national economy.

(3) If you can do your past relevant work. If we find that you have the residual functional capacity to do your past relevant work, we will determine that you can still do your past work and are not disabled. We will not consider your vocational factors of age, education, and work experience or whether your past relevant work exists in significant numbers in the national economy.

(c) Other work.

(1) If we find that your residual functional capacity is not enough to enable you to do any of your past relevant work, we will use the same residual functional capacity assessment we used to decide if you could do your past relevant work when we decide if you can adjust to any other work. We will look at your ability to adjust to other work by considering your residual functional capacity and your vocational factors of age, education, and work experience. Any other work (jobs) that you can adjust to must exist in significant numbers in the national economy (either in the region where you live or in several regions in the country).

(2) In order to support a finding that you are not disabled at this fifth step of the sequential evaluation process, we are responsible for providing evidence that demonstrates that other work exists in significant numbers in the national economy that you can do, given your residual functional capacity and vocational factors. We are not responsible for providing additional evidence about your residual functional capacity because we will use the same residual functional capacity assessment that we used to determine if you can do your past relevant work.

20 C.F.R. § 404.1562 Medical-vocational profiles showing an inability to make an adjustment to other work. (*See also* 20 C.F.R § 416.962)

(a) If you have done only arduous unskilled physical labor. If you have no more than a marginal education (see § 404.1564) and work experience of 35 years or more during which you did only arduous unskilled physical labor, and you are not working and are no longer able to do this kind of work because of a severe impairment(s) (see §§ 404.1520(c), 404.1521, and 404.1523), we will consider you unable to do lighter work, and therefore, disabled.

Example to paragraph (a): B is a 58–year-old miner's helper with a fourth grade education who has a lifelong history of unskilled arduous physical labor. B says that he is disabled because of arthritis of the spine, hips, and knees, and other impairments. Medical evidence shows a "severe" combination of impairments that prevents B from performing his past relevant work. Under these circumstances, we will find that B is disabled.

(b) If you are at least 55 years old, have no more than a limited education, and have no past relevant work experience. If you have a severe, medically determinable impairment(s) (see §§ 404.1520(c), 404.1521, and 404.1523), are of advanced age (age 55 or older, see § 404.1563), have a limited education or less (see § 404.1564), and have no past relevant work experience (see § 404.1565), we will find you disabled. If the evidence shows that you meet this profile, we will not need to assess your residual functional capacity or consider the rules in appendix 2 to this subpart.

20 C.F.R. § 404.1563 Your age as a vocational factor. (*See also* 20 C.F.R § 416.96)

(a) General. "Age" means your chronological age. When we decide whether you are disabled under § 404.1520(f)(1), we will consider your chronological age in combination with your residual functional capacity, education, and work experience; we will not consider your ability to adjust to other work on the basis of your age alone. In determining the extent to which age affects a person's ability to adjust to other work, we consider advancing age to be an increasingly limiting factor in the person's ability to make such an adjustment, as we explain in paragraphs (c) through (e) of this section. If you are unemployed but you still have the ability to adjust to other work, we will find that you are not disabled. In paragraphs (b) through (e) of this section and in appendix 2 to this subpart, we explain in more detail how we consider your age as a vocational factor.

(b) How we apply the age categories. When we make a finding about your ability to do other work under § 404.1520(f)(1), we will use the age categories in paragraphs (c) through (e) of this section. We will use each of the age categories that applies to you during the period for which we must determine if you are disabled. We will not apply the age categories mechanically in a borderline situation. If you are within a few days to a few months of reaching an older age category, and using the older age category would result in a determination or decision that you are disabled, we will consider whether to use the older age category after evaluating the overall impact of all the factors of your case.

(c) Younger person. If you are a younger person (under age 50), we generally do not consider that your age will seriously affect your ability to adjust to other work. However, in some circumstances, we consider that persons age 45–49 are more limited in their ability to adjust to other work than persons who have not attained age 45. See Rule 201.17 in appendix 2.

(d) *Person closely approaching advanced age.* If you are closely approaching advanced age (age 50–54), we will consider that your age along with a severe impairment(s) and limited work experience may seriously affect your ability to adjust to other work.

(e) *Person of advanced age.* We consider that at advanced age (age 55 or older) age significantly affects a person's ability to adjust to other work. We have special rules for persons of advanced age and for persons in this category who are closely approaching retirement age (age 60–64). See § 404.1568(d)(4).

(f) *Information about your age.* We will usually not ask you to prove your age. However, if we need to know your exact age to determine whether you get disability benefits or if the amount of your benefit will be affected, we will ask you for evidence of your age.

20 C.F.R. § 404.1564 Your education as a vocational factor. (*See also* 20 C.F.R § 416.964)

(a) *General.* Education is primarily used to mean formal schooling or other training which contributes to your ability to meet vocational requirements, for example, reasoning ability, communication skills, and arithmetical ability. However, if you do not have formal schooling, this does not necessarily mean that you are uneducated or lack these abilities. Past work experience and the kinds of responsibilities you had when you were working may show that you have intellectual abilities, although you may have little formal education. Your daily activities, hobbies, or the results of testing may also show that you have significant intellectual ability that can be used to work.

(b) *How we evaluate your education.* The importance of your educational background may depend upon how much time has passed between the completion of your formal education and the beginning of your physical or mental impairment(s) and by what you have done with your education in a work or other setting. Formal education that you completed many years before your impairment began, or unused skills and knowledge that were a part of your formal education, may no longer be useful or meaningful in terms of your ability to work. Therefore, the numerical grade level that you completed in school may not represent your actual educational abilities. These may be higher or lower. However, if there is no other evidence to contradict it, we will use your numerical grade level to determine your educational abilities. The term education also includes how well you are able to communicate in English since this ability is often acquired or improved by education. In evaluating your educational level, we use the following categories:

(1) Illiteracy. Illiteracy means the inability to read or write. We consider someone illiterate if the person cannot read or write a simple message such as instructions or inventory lists even though the person can sign his or her name. Generally, an illiterate person has had little or no formal schooling.

(2) Marginal education. Marginal education means ability in reasoning, arithmetic, and language skills which are needed to do simple, unskilled types of jobs. We generally consider that formal schooling at a 6th grade level or less is a marginal education.

(3) Limited education. Limited education means ability in reasoning, arithmetic, and language skills, but not enough to allow a person with these educational qualifications to do most of the more complex job duties needed in semi-skilled or skilled jobs. We generally consider that a 7th grade through the 11th grade level of formal education is a limited education.

(4) High school education and above. High school education and above means abilities in reasoning, arithmetic, and language skills acquired through formal schooling at a 12th grade level or above. We generally consider that someone with these educational abilities can do semi-skilled through skilled work.

(5) Inability to communicate in English. Since the ability to speak, read and understand English is generally learned or increased at school, we may consider this an educational factor. Because English is the dominant language of the country, it may be difficult for someone who doesn't speak and understand English to do a job, regardless of the amount of education the person may have in another language. Therefore, we consider a person's ability to communicate in English when we evaluate what work, if any, he or she can do. It generally doesn't matter what other language a person may be fluent in.

(6) Information about your education. We will ask you how long you attended school and whether you are able to speak, understand, read and write in English and do at least simple calculations in arithmetic. We will also consider other information about how much formal or informal education you may have had through your previous work, community projects, hobbies, and any other activities which might help you to work.

20 C.F.R. § 404.1565 Your work experience as a vocational factor. (*See also* 20 C.F.R § 416.965)

(a) General. Work experience means skills and abilities you have acquired through work you have done which show the type of work you may be expected to do. Work you have already been able to do shows the kind of work that you may be expected to do. We consider that your work experience applies when it was done within the last 15 years, lasted long enough for you to learn to do it, and was substantial gainful activity. We do not usually consider that work you did 15 years or more before the time we are deciding whether you are disabled (or when the disability insured status requirement was last met, if earlier) applies. A gradual change occurs in most jobs so that after 15 years it is no longer realistic to expect that skills and abilities acquired in a job done then continue to apply. The 15–year guide is intended to insure that remote work experience is not currently applied. If you have no work experience or worked only "off-and-on" or for brief periods of time during the 15–year period, we generally consider that these do not apply. If you have acquired skills through your past work, we consider you to have these work skills unless you cannot use them in other skilled or semi-skilled work that you can now do. If you cannot use your skills in other skilled or semi-skilled work, we will consider your work background the same as unskilled. However, even if you have no work experience, we may consider that you are able to do unskilled work because it requires little or no judgment and can be learned in a short period of time.

* * *

20 C.F.R. § 404.1566 Work which exists in the national economy. (*See also* 20 C.F.R § 416.966)

(a) General. We consider that work exists in the national economy when it exists in significant numbers either in the region where you live or in several other regions of the country. It does not matter whether—

    (1) Work exists in the immediate area in which you live;

    (2) A specific job vacancy exists for you; or

    (3) You would be hired if you applied for work.

(b) How we determine the existence of work. Work exists in the national economy when there is a significant number of jobs (in one or more occupations) having requirements which you are able to meet with your physical or mental abilities and vocational qualifications. Isolated jobs that exist only in very limited numbers in relatively few locations outside of the region where you live are not considered "work which exists in the national economy". We will not deny you disability benefits on the basis of the existence of these kinds of jobs. If work that you can do does not exist in the national economy, we will determine that you are disabled. However, if work that you can do does exist in the national economy, we will determine that you are not disabled.

(c) Inability to obtain work. We will determine that you are not disabled if your residual functional capacity and vocational abilities make it possible for you to do work which exists in the national economy, but you remain unemployed because of—

(1) Your inability to get work;

(2) Lack of work in your local area;

(3) The hiring practices of employers;

(4) Technological changes in the industry in which you have worked;

(5) Cyclical economic conditions;

(6) No job openings for you;

(7) You would not actually be hired to do work you could otherwise do; or

(8) You do not wish to do a particular type of work.

(d) Administrative notice of job data. When we determine that unskilled, sedentary, light, and medium jobs exist in the national economy (in significant numbers either in the region where you live or in several regions of the country), we will take administrative notice of reliable job information available from various governmental and other publications. For example, we will take notice of—

(1) Dictionary of Occupational Titles, published by the Department of Labor;

(2) County Business Patterns, published by the Bureau of the Census;

(3) Census Reports, also published by the Bureau of the Census;

(4) Occupational Analyses, prepared for the Social Security Administration by various State employment agencies; and

(5) Occupational Outlook Handbook, published by the Bureau of Labor Statistics.

(e) Use of vocational experts and other specialists. If the issue in determining whether you are disabled is whether your work skills can be used in other work and the specific occupations in which they can be used, or there is a similarly complex issue, we may use the services of a vocational expert or other specialist. We will decide whether to use a vocational expert or other specialist.

20 C.F.R. § 404.1567 Physical exertion requirements. (*See also* 20 C.F.R § 416.967)

To determine the physical exertion requirements of work in the national economy, we classify jobs as sedentary, light, medium, heavy, and very heavy. These terms have the same meaning as they have in the Dictionary of Occupational Titles, published by the Department of Labor. In making disability determinations under this subpart, we use the following definitions:

(a) Sedentary work. Sedentary work involves lifting no more than 10 pounds at a time and occasionally lifting or carrying articles like docket files, ledgers, and small tools. Although a sedentary job is defined as one which involves sitting, a certain amount of walking and standing is often necessary in carrying out job duties. Jobs are sedentary if walking and standing are required occasionally and other sedentary criteria are met.

(b) Light work. Light work involves lifting no more than 20 pounds at a time with frequent lifting or carrying of objects weighing up to 10 pounds. Even though the weight lifted may be very little, a job is in this category when it requires a good deal of walking or standing, or when it involves sitting most of the time with some pushing and pulling of arm or leg controls. To be considered capable of performing a full or wide range of light work, you must have the ability to do substantially all of these activities. If someone can do light work, we determine that he or she can also do sedentary work, unless there are additional limiting factors such as loss of fine dexterity or inability to sit for long periods of time.

(c) Medium work. Medium work involves lifting no more than 50 pounds at a time with frequent lifting or carrying of objects weighing up to 25 pounds. If someone can do medium work, we determine that he or she can also do sedentary and light work.

(d) Heavy work. Heavy work involves lifting no more than 100 pounds at a time with frequent lifting or carrying of objects weighing up to 50 pounds. If someone can do heavy work, we determine that he or she can also do medium, light, and sedentary work.

(e) Very heavy work. Very heavy work involves lifting objects weighing more than 100 pounds at a time with frequent lifting or carrying of objects weighing 50 pounds or more. If someone can do very heavy work, we determine that he or she can also do heavy, medium, light and sedentary work.

20 C.F.R. § 404.1568 Skill requirements. (*See also* 20 C.F.R § 416.968)

In order to evaluate your skills and to help determine the existence in the national economy of work you are able to do, occupations are classified as unskilled, semi-skilled, and skilled. In classifying these occupations, we use materials published by the Department of Labor. When we make disability determinations under this subpart, we use the following definitions:

(a) Unskilled work. Unskilled work is work which needs little or no judgment to do simple duties that can be learned on the job in a short period of time. The job may or may not require considerable strength. For example, we consider jobs unskilled if the primary work duties are handling, feeding and offbearing (that is, placing or removing materials from machines which are automatic or operated by others), or machine tending, and a person can usually learn to do the job in 30 days, and little specific vocational preparation and judgment are needed. A person does not gain work skills by doing unskilled jobs.

(b) Semi-skilled work. Semi-skilled work is work which needs some skills but does not require doing the more complex work duties. Semi-skilled jobs may require alertness and close attention to watching machine processes; or inspecting, testing or otherwise looking for irregularities; or tending or guarding equipment, property, materials, or persons against loss, damage or injury; or other types of activities which are similarly less complex than skilled work, but more complex than unskilled work. A job may be classified as semi-skilled where coordination and dexterity are necessary, as when hands or feet must be moved quickly to do repetitive tasks.

(c) Skilled work. Skilled work requires qualifications in which a person uses judgment to determine the machine and manual operations to be performed in order to obtain the proper form, quality, or quantity of material to be produced. Skilled work may require laying out work, estimating quality, determining the suitability and needed quantities of materials, making precise measurements, reading blueprints or other specifications, or making necessary computations or mechanical adjustments to control or regulate the work. Other skilled jobs may require dealing with people, facts, or figures or abstract ideas at a high level of complexity.

(d) Skills that can be used in other work (transferability).

(1) What we mean by transferable skills. We consider you to have skills that can be used in other jobs, when the skilled or semi-skilled work activities you did in past work can be used to meet the requirements of skilled or semi-skilled work activities of other jobs or kinds of work. This depends largely on the similarity of occupationally significant work activities among different jobs.

(2) How we determine skills that can be transferred to other jobs. Transferability is most probable and meaningful among jobs in which—

(i) The same or a lesser degree of skill is required;

(ii) The same or similar tools and machines are used; and

(iii) The same or similar raw materials, products, processes, or services are involved.

(3) Degrees of transferability. There are degrees of transferability of skills ranging from very close similarities to remote and incidental similarities among jobs. A complete similarity of all three factors is not necessary for transferability. However, when skills are so specialized or have been acquired in such an isolated vocational setting (like many jobs in mining, agriculture, or fishing) that they are not readily usable in other industries, jobs, and work settings, we consider that they are not transferable.

(4) Transferability of skills for individuals of advanced age. If you are of advanced age (age 55 or older), and you have a severe impairment(s) that limits you to sedentary or light work, we will find that you cannot make an adjustment to other work unless you have skills that you can transfer to other skilled or semiskilled work (or you have recently completed education which provides for direct entry into skilled work) that you can do despite your impairment(s). We will decide if you have transferable skills as follows. If you are of advanced age and you have a severe impairment(s) that limits you to no more than sedentary work, we will find that you have skills that are transferable to skilled or semiskilled sedentary work only if the sedentary work is so similar to your previous work that you would need to make very little, if any, vocational adjustment in terms of tools, work processes, work settings, or the industry. (See § 404.1567(a) and § 201.00(f) of appendix 2.) If you are of advanced age but have not attained age 60, and you have a severe impairment(s) that limits you to no more than light work, we will apply the rules in paragraphs (d)(1) through (d)(3) of this section to decide if you have skills that are transferable to skilled or semiskilled light work (see § 404.1567(b)). If you are closely approaching retirement age (age 60 or

older) and you have a severe impairment(s) that limits you to no more than light work, we will find that you have skills that are transferable to skilled or semiskilled light work only if the light work is so similar to your previous work that you would need to make very little, if any, vocational adjustment in terms of tools, work processes, work settings, or the industry. (See § 404.1567(b) and Rule 202.00(f) of appendix 2 to this subpart.)

20 C.F.R. § 404.1569 Listing of Medical–Vocational Guidelines in Appendix 2. (*See also* 20 C.F.R § 416.969)

The Dictionary of Occupational Titles includes information about jobs (classified by their exertional and skill requirements) that exist in the national economy. Appendix 2 provides rules using this data reflecting major functional and vocational patterns. We apply these rules in cases where a person is not doing substantial gainful activity and is prevented by a severe medically determinable impairment from doing vocationally relevant past work. The rules in appendix 2 do not cover all possible variations of factors. Also, as we explain in § 200.00 of appendix 2, we do not apply these rules if one of the findings of fact about the person's vocational factors and residual functional capacity is not the same as the corresponding criterion of a rule. In these instances, we give full consideration to all relevant facts in accordance with the definitions and discussions under vocational considerations. However, if the findings of fact made about all factors are the same as the rule, we use that rule to decide whether a person is disabled.

20 C.F.R. § 404.1569a Exertional and nonexertional limitations. (*See also* 20 C.F.R § 416.969a)

(a) General. Your impairment(s) and related symptoms, such as pain, may cause limitations of function or restrictions which limit your ability to meet certain demands of jobs. These limitations may be exertional, nonexertional, or a combination of both. Limitations are classified as exertional if they affect your ability to meet the strength demands of jobs. The classification of a limitation as exertional is related to the United States Department of Labor's classification of jobs by various exertional levels (sedentary, light, medium, heavy, and very heavy) in terms of the strength demands for sitting, standing, walking, lifting, carrying, pushing, and pulling. * * * Limitations or restrictions which affect your ability to meet the demands of jobs other than the strength demands, that is, demands other than sitting, standing, walking, lifting, carrying, pushing or pulling, are considered nonexertional. * * * [I]f you can no longer do your past relevant work because of a severe medically determinable impairment(s), we must determine whether your impairment(s), when considered along with your age, education, and work experience, prevents you from doing any other work which exists in the national economy in order to decide whether you are disabled * * * or continue to be disabled * * *. Paragraphs (b), (c), and (d) of this section explain how we apply the medical-vocational guidelines in appendix 2 of this subpart in making this determination, depending on whether the limitations or restrictions imposed by your impairment(s) and related symptoms, such as pain, are exertional, nonexertional, or a combination of both.

(b) Exertional limitations. When the limitations and restrictions imposed by your impairment(s) and related symptoms, such as pain, affect only your ability to meet the strength demands of jobs (sitting, standing, walking, lifting, carrying, pushing, and pulling), we consider that you have only exertional limitations. When your impairment(s) and related symptoms only impose exertional limitations and your specific vocational profile is listed in a rule contained in appendix 2 of this subpart, we will directly apply that rule to decide whether you are disabled.

(c) Nonexertional limitations.

(1) When the limitations and restrictions imposed by your impairment(s) and related symptoms, such as pain, affect only your ability to meet the demands of jobs other than the strength demands, we consider that you have only nonexertional limitations or restrictions. Some examples of nonexertional limitations or restrictions include the following:

(i) You have difficulty functioning because you are nervous, anxious, or depressed;

(ii) You have difficulty maintaining attention or concentrating;

(iii) You have difficulty understanding or remembering detailed instructions;

(iv) You have difficulty in seeing or hearing;

(v) You have difficulty tolerating some physical feature(s) of certain work settings, e.g., you cannot tolerate dust or fumes; or

(vi) You have difficulty performing the manipulative or postural functions of some work such as reaching, handling, stooping, climbing, crawling, or crouching.

(2) If your impairment(s) and related symptoms, such as pain, only affect your ability to perform the nonexertional aspects of work-related activities, the rules in appendix 2 do not direct factual conclusions of disabled or not disabled. The determination as to whether disability exists will be based on the principles in the appropriate

sections of the regulations, giving consideration to the rules for specific case situations in appendix 2.

(d) Combined exertional and nonexertional limitations. When the limitations and restrictions imposed by your impairment(s) and related symptoms, such as pain, affect your ability to meet both the strength and demands of jobs other than the strength demands, we consider that you have a combination of exertional and nonexertional limitations or restrictions. If your impairment(s) and related symptoms, such as pain, affect your ability to meet both the strength and demands of jobs other than the strength demands, we will not directly apply the rules in appendix 2 unless there is a rule that directs a conclusion that you are disabled based upon your strength limitations; otherwise the rules provide a framework to guide our decision.

20 C.F.R. § 404.1573 General information about work activity. (*See also* 20 C.F.R § 416.973)

(a) The nature of your work. If your duties require use of your experience, skills, supervision and responsibilities, or contribute substantially to the operation of a business, this tends to show that you have the ability to work at the substantial gainful activity level.

(b) How well you perform. We consider how well you do your work when we determine whether or not you are doing substantial gainful activity. If you do your work satisfactorily, this may show that you are working at the substantial gainful activity level. If you are unable, because of your impairments, to do ordinary or simple tasks satisfactorily without more supervision or assistance than is usually given other people doing similar work, this may show that you are not working at the substantial gainful activity level. If you are doing work that involves minimal duties that make little or no demands on you and that are of little or no use to your employer, or to the operation of a business if you are self-employed, this does not show that you are working at the substantial gainful activity level.

(c) If your work is done under special conditions. The work you are doing may be done under special conditions that take into account your impairment, such as work done in a sheltered workshop or as a patient in a hospital. If your work is done under special conditions, we may find that it does not show that you have the ability to do substantial gainful activity. Also, if you are forced to stop or reduce your work because of the removal of special conditions that were related to your impairment and essential to your work, we may find that your work does not show that you are able to do substantial gainful activity. However, work done under special conditions may show that you have the necessary skills and ability to work at the substantial gainful activity level. Examples of the special conditions that may relate to your impairment include, but are not limited to, situations in which—

    (1) You required and received special assistance from other employees in performing your work;

    (2) You were allowed to work irregular hours or take frequent rest periods;

    (3) You were provided with special equipment or were assigned work especially suited to your impairment;

    (4) You were able to work only because of specially arranged circumstances, for example, other persons helped you prepare for or get to and from your work;

    (5) You were permitted to work at a lower standard of productivity or efficiency than other employees; or

    (6) You were given the opportunity to work despite your impairment because of family relationship, past association with your employer, or your employer's concern for your welfare.

    (d) *If you are self-employed.* Supervisory, managerial, advisory or other significant personal services that you perform as a self-employed individual may show that you are able to do substantial gainful activity.

    (e) *Time spent in work.* While the time you spend in work is important, we will not decide whether or not you are doing substantial gainful activity only on that basis. We will still evaluate the work to decide whether it is substantial and gainful regardless of whether you spend more time or less time at the job than workers who are not impaired and who are doing similar work as a regular means of their livelihood.

20 C.F.R. § 404.1574 Evaluation guides if you are an employee. (*See also* 20 C.F.R § 416.974)

    (a) We use several guides to decide whether the work you have done shows that you are able to do substantial gainful activity. If you are working or have worked as an employee, we will use the provisions in paragraphs (a) through (d) of this section that are relevant to your work activity. We will use these provisions whenever they are appropriate, whether in connection with your application for disability benefits (when we make an initial determination on your application and throughout any appeals you may request), after you have become entitled to a period of disability or to disability benefits, or both.

(1) Your earnings may show you have done substantial gainful activity. Generally, in evaluating your work activity for substantial gainful activity purposes, our primary consideration will be the earnings you derive from the work activity. We will use your earnings to determine whether you have done substantial gainful activity unless we have information from you, your employer, or others that shows that we should not count all of your earnings. The amount of your earnings from work you have done (regardless of whether it is unsheltered or sheltered work) may show that you have engaged in substantial gainful activity. Generally, if you worked for substantial earnings, we will find that you are able to do substantial gainful activity. However, the fact that your earnings were not substantial will not necessarily show that you are not able to do substantial gainful activity. We generally consider work that you are forced to stop or to reduce below the substantial gainful activity level after a short time because of your impairment to be an unsuccessful work attempt. Your earnings from an unsuccessful work attempt will not show that you are able to do substantial gainful activity. We will use the criteria in paragraph (c) of this section to determine if the work you did was an unsuccessful work attempt.

(2) We consider only the amounts you earn. When we decide whether your earnings show that you have done substantial gainful activity, we do not consider any income that is not directly related to your productivity. When your earnings exceed the reasonable value of the work you perform, we consider only that part of your pay which you actually earn. If your earnings are being subsidized, we do not consider the amount of the subsidy when we determine if your earnings show that you have done substantial gainful activity. We consider your work to be subsidized if the true value of your work, when compared with the same or similar work done by unimpaired persons, is less than the actual amount of earnings paid to you for your work. For example, when a person with a serious impairment does simple tasks under close and continuous supervision, our determination of whether that person has done substantial gainful activity will not be based only on the amount of the wages paid. We will first determine whether the person received a subsidy; that is, we will determine whether the person was being paid more than the reasonable value of the actual services performed. We will then subtract the value of the subsidy from the person's gross earnings to determine the earnings we will use to determine if he or she has done substantial gainful activity.

(3) If you are working in a sheltered or special environment. If you are working in a sheltered workshop, you may or may not be earning the amounts you are being paid. The fact that the sheltered

workshop or similar facility is operating at a loss or is receiving some charitable contributions or governmental aid does not establish that you are not earning all you are being paid. Since persons in military service being treated for severe impairments usually continue to receive full pay, we evaluate work activity in a therapy program or while on limited duty by comparing it with similar work in the civilian work force or on the basis of reasonable worth of the work, rather than on the actual amount of the earnings.

(b) Earnings guidelines—

(1) General. If you are an employee, we first consider the criteria in paragraph (a) of this section and § 404.1576, and then the guides in paragraphs (b)(2) and of this section. When we review your earnings to determine if you have been performing substantial gainful activity, we will subtract the value of any subsidized earnings (see paragraph (a)(2) of this section) and the reasonable cost of any impairment-related work expenses from your gross earnings (see § 404.1576). The resulting amount is the amount we use to determine if you have done substantial gainful activity. We will generally average your earnings for comparison with the earnings guidelines in paragraphs (b)(2) and (3) of this section. * * *

(2) Earnings that will ordinarily show that you have engaged in substantial gainful activity. We will consider that your earnings from your work activity as an employee (including earnings from sheltered work or a comparable facility especially set up for severely impaired persons) show that you engaged in substantial gainful activity if:

(i) Before January 1, 2001, they averaged more than the amount(s) in Table 1 of this section for the time(s) in which you worked.

(ii) Beginning January 1, 2001, and each year thereafter, they average more than the larger of:

(A) The amount for the previous year, or

(B) An amount adjusted for national wage growth, calculated by multiplying $700 by the ratio of the national average wage index for the year 2 calendar years before the year for which the amount is being calculated to the national average wage index for the year 1998. We will then round the resulting amount to the next higher multiple of $10 where such amount is a multiple of $5 but not of $10 and to the nearest multiple of $10 in any other case.

TABLE 1

For months:	Your monthly earnings averaged more than:
In calendar years before 1976	200
In calendar year 1976	230
In calendar year 1977	240
In calendar year 1978	260
In calendar year 1979	280
In calendar years 1980-89	300
January 1990–June 1999	500
July 1999–December 2000	700

(3) Earnings that will ordinarily show that you have not engaged in substantial gainful activity.

(i) General. If your average monthly earnings are equal to or less than the amount(s) determined under paragraph (b)(2) of this section for the year(s) in which you work, we will generally consider that the earnings from your work as an employee (including earnings from work in a sheltered workshop or comparable facility) will show that you have not engaged in substantial gainful activity. We will generally not consider other information in addition to your earnings except in the circumstances described in paragraph (b)(3)(ii) of this section.

(ii) When we will consider other information in addition to your earnings. We will generally consider other information in addition to your earnings if there is evidence indicating that you may be engaging in substantial gainful activity or that you are in a position to control when earnings are paid to you or the amount of wages paid to you (for example, if you are working for a small corporation owned by a relative). (See paragraph (b)(3)(iii) of this section for when we do not apply this rule.) Examples of other information we may consider include, whether—

(A) Your work is comparable to that of unimpaired people in your community who are doing the same or similar occupations as their means of livelihood, taking into account the time, energy, skill, and responsibility involved in the work; and

(B) Your work, although significantly less than that done by unimpaired people, is clearly worth the amounts shown in paragraph (b)(2) of this section, according to pay scales in your community.

(iii) *Special rule for considering earnings alone when evaluating the work you do after you have received social security disability benefits for at least 24 months.* Notwithstanding paragraph (b)(3)(ii) of this section, we will not consider other information in addition to your earnings to evaluate the work you are doing or have done if—

(A) At the time you do the work, you are entitled to social security disability benefits and you have received such benefits for at least 24 months (see paragraph (b)(3)(iv) of this section); and

(B) We are evaluating that work to consider whether you have engaged in substantial gainful activity or demonstrated the ability to engage in substantial gainful activity for the purpose of determining whether your disability has ceased because of your work activity (see §§ 404.1592a(a)(1) and (3)(ii) and 404.1594(d)(5) and (f)(1)).

(iv) *When we consider you to have received social security disability benefits for at least 24 months.* For purposes of paragraph (b)(3)(iii) of this section, social security disability benefits means disability insurance benefits for a disabled worker, child's insurance benefits based on disability, or widow's or widower's insurance benefits based on disability. We consider you to have received such benefits for at least 24 months beginning with the first day of the first month following the 24th month for which you actually received social security disability benefits that you were due or constructively received such benefits. The 24 months do not have to be consecutive. We will consider you to have constructively received a benefit for a month for purposes of the 24–month requirement if you were otherwise due a social security disability benefit for that month and your monthly benefit was withheld to recover an overpayment. Any months for which you were entitled to benefits but for which you did not actually or constructively receive a benefit payment will not be counted for the 24–month requirement. If you also receive supplemental security income payments based on disability or blindness under title XVI of the Social Security Act, months for which you received only supplemental security income payments will not be counted for the 24–month requirement.

(c) *The unsuccessful work attempt—*

(1) *General.* Ordinarily, work you have done will not show that you are able to do substantial gainful activity if, after working for a period of 6 months or less, your impairment forced you to stop working or to reduce the amount of work you do so that your earnings from such work fall below the substantial gainful activity earnings

level in paragraph (b)(2) of this section, and you meet the conditions described in paragraphs (c)(2), (3), (4), and (5), of this section. * * *

* * *

* * *

20 C.F.R. § 404.1575 Evaluation guides if you are self-employed. (*See also* 20 C.F.R § 416.975)

(a) If you are a self-employed person. If you are working or have worked as a self-employed person, we will use the provisions in paragraphs (a) through (e) of this section that are relevant to your work activity. We will use these provisions whenever they are appropriate, whether in connection with your application for disability benefits (when we make an initial determination on your application and throughout any appeals you may request), after you have become entitled to a period of disability or to disability benefits, or both.

(1) How we evaluate the work you do after you have become entitled to disability benefits. If you are entitled to social security disability benefits and you work as a self-employed person, the way we will evaluate your work activity will depend on whether the work activity occurs before or after you have received such benefits for at least 24 months and on the purpose of the evaluation. For purposes of paragraphs (a) and (e) of this section, social security disability benefits means disability insurance benefits for a disabled worker, child's insurance benefits based on disability, or widow's or widower's insurance benefits based on disability. We will use the rules in paragraph (e)(2) of this section to determine if you have received such benefits for at least 24 months.

(i) We will use the guides in paragraph (a)(2) of this section to evaluate any work activity you do before you have received social security disability benefits for at least 24 months to determine whether you have engaged in substantial gainful activity, regardless of the purpose of the evaluation.

(ii) We will use the guides in paragraph (e) of this section to evaluate any work activity you do after you have received social security disability benefits for at least 24 months to determine whether you have engaged in substantial gainful activity for the purpose of determining whether your disability has ceased because of your work activity.

* * *

(2) General rules for evaluating your work activity if you are self-employed. We will consider your activities and their value to your business to decide whether you have engaged in substantial gainful activity if you are self-employed. We will not consider your income alone because the amount of income you actually receive may depend on a number of different factors, such as capital investment and profit-sharing agreements. We will generally consider work that you were forced to stop or reduce to below substantial gainful activity after 6 months or less because of your impairment as an unsuccessful work attempt. See paragraph (d) of this section. We will evaluate your work activity based on the value of your services to the business regardless of whether you receive an immediate income for your services. We determine whether you have engaged in substantial gainful activity by applying three tests. If you have not engaged in substantial gainful activity under test one, then we will consider tests two and three. The tests are as follows:

(i) Test one: You have engaged in substantial gainful activity if you render services that are significant to the operation of the business and receive a substantial income from the business. Paragraphs (b) and (c) of this section explain what we mean by significant services and substantial income for purposes of this test.

(ii) Test Two: You have engaged in substantial gainful activity if your work activity, in terms of factors such as hours, skills, energy output, efficiency, duties, and responsibilities, is comparable to that of unimpaired individuals in your community who are in the same or similar businesses as their means of livelihood.

(iii) Test Three: You have engaged in substantial gainful activity if your work activity, although not comparable to that of unimpaired individuals, is clearly worth the amount shown in § 404.1574(b)(2) when considered in terms of its value to the business, or when compared to the salary that an owner would pay to an employee to do the work you are doing.

(b) What we mean by significant services.

(1) If you are not a farm landlord and you operate a business entirely by yourself, any services that you render are significant to the business. If your business involves the services of more than one person, we will consider you to be rendering significant services if you contribute more than half the total time required for the management of the business, or you render management services for more than 45 hours a month regardless of the total management time required by the business.

(2) If you are a farm landlord, that is, you rent farm land to another, we will consider you to be rendering significant services if you materially participate in the production or the management of the production of the things raised on the rented farm. * * *

(c) What we mean by substantial income.

(1) Determining countable income. We deduct your normal business expenses from your gross income to determine net income. Once we determine your net income, we deduct the reasonable value of any significant amount of unpaid help furnished by your spouse, children, or others. Miscellaneous duties that ordinarily would not have commercial value would not be considered significant. We deduct impairment-related work expenses that have not already been deducted in determining your net income. Impairment-related work expenses are explained in § 404.1576. We deduct unincurred business expenses paid for you by another individual or agency. An unincurred business expense occurs when a sponsoring agency or another person incurs responsibility for the payment of certain business expenses, e.g., rent, utilities, or purchases and repair of equipment, or provides you with equipment, stock, or other material for the operation of your business. We deduct soil bank payments if they were included as farm income. That part of your income remaining after we have made all applicable deductions represents the actual value of work performed. The resulting amount is the amount we use to determine if you have done substantial gainful activity. For purposes of this section, we refer to this amount as your countable income. We will generally average your countable income for comparison with the earnings guidelines in § 404.1574(b)(2). See § 404.1574a for our rules on averaging of earnings.

(2) When countable income is considered substantial. We will consider your countable income to be substantial if—

(i) It averages more than the amounts described in § 404.1574(b)(2); or

(ii) It averages less than the amounts described in § 404.1574(b)(2) but it is either comparable to what it was before you became seriously impaired if we had not considered your earnings or is comparable to that of unimpaired self-employed persons in your community who are in the same or a similar business as their means of livelihood.

(d) The unsuccessful work attempt—

(1) General. Ordinarily, work you have done will not show that you are able to do substantial gainful activity if, after working for a period of 6 months or less, you were forced by your impairment to stop working or to reduce the amount of work you do so that you are no longer performing substantial gainful activity and you meet the conditions described in paragraphs (d)(2), (3), (4), and (5) of this section. * * *

(2) Event that must precede an unsuccessful work attempt. There must be a significant break in the continuity of your work before we will consider you to have begun a work attempt that later proved unsuccessful. You must have stopped working or reduced your work and earnings below substantial gainful activity because of your impairment or because of the removal of special conditions which took into account your impairment and permitted you to work. Examples of such special conditions may include any significant amount of unpaid help furnished by your spouse, children, or others, or unincurred business expenses, as described in paragraph (c) of this section, paid for you by another individual or agency. We will consider your prior work to be discontinued for a significant period if you were out of work at least 30 consecutive days. We will also consider your prior work to be discontinued if, because of your impairment, you were forced to change to another type of work.

(3) If you worked 3 months or less. We will consider work of 3 months or less to be an unsuccessful work attempt if it ended, or was reduced below substantial gainful activity, because of your impairment or because of the removal of special conditions which took into account your impairment and permitted you to work.

(4) If you worked between 3 and 6 months. We will consider work that lasted longer than 3 months to be an unsuccessful work attempt if it ended, or was reduced below substantial gainful activity, within 6 months because of your impairment or because of the removal of special conditions which took into account your impairment and permitted you to work and—

(i) You were frequently unable to work because of your impairment;

(ii) Your work was unsatisfactory because of your impairment;

(iii) You worked during a period of temporary remission of your impairment; or

(iv) You worked under special conditions that were essential to your performance and these conditions were removed.

(5) If you worked more than 6 months. We will not consider work you performed at the substantial gainful activity level for more than 6 months to be an unsuccessful work attempt regardless of why it ended or was reduced below the substantial gainful activity earnings level.

(e) Special rules for evaluating the work you do after you have received social security disability benefits for at least 24 months.

(1) General. We will apply the provisions of this paragraph to evaluate the work you are doing or have done if, at the time you do the work, you are entitled to social security disability benefits and you have received such benefits for at least 24 months. * * *

20 C.F.R. § 404.1577 Disability defined for widows, widowers, and surviving divorced spouses for monthly benefits payable for months prior to January 1991.

For monthly benefits payable for months prior to January 1991, the law provides that to be entitled to a widow's or widower's benefit as a disabled widow, widower, or surviving divorced spouse, you must have a medically determinable physical or mental impairment which can be expected to result in death or has lasted or can be expected to last for a continuous period of not less than 12 months. The impairment(s) must have been of a level of severity to prevent a person from doing any gainful activity. To determine whether you were disabled, we consider only your physical or mental impairment(s). We do not consider your age, education, and work experience. * * *

20 C.F.R. § 404.1589 We may conduct a review to find out whether you continue to be disabled. (*See also* 20 C.F.R § 416.989)

After we find that you are disabled, we must evaluate your impairment(s) from time to time to determine if you are still eligible for disability cash benefits. We call this evaluation a continuing disability review. We may begin a continuing disability review for any number of reasons including your failure to follow the provisions of the Social Security Act or these regulations. When we begin such a review, we will notify you that we are reviewing your eligibility for disability benefits, why we are reviewing your eligibility, that in medical reviews the medical improvement review standard will apply, that our review could result in the termination of your benefits, and that you have the right to submit medical and other evidence for our consideration during the continuing disability review. In doing a medical review, we will develop a complete medical history of at least the preceding 12 months in any case in which a determination is made that you are no longer under a disability. If this review shows that we should stop payment of your benefits, we will notify you in writing and give you an opportunity to appeal. In § 404.1590 we describe those events that may prompt us to review whether you continue to be disabled.

20 C.F.R § 404.1590 When and how often we will conduct a continuing disability review. (*See also* 20 C.F.R § 416.990)

(a) General. We conduct continuing disability reviews to determine whether or not you continue to meet the disability requirements of the law. Payment of cash benefits or a period of disability ends if the medical or other evidence shows that you are not disabled as determined under the standards set out in section 223(f) of the Social Security Act. In paragraphs (b) through (g) of this section, we explain when and how often we conduct continuing disability reviews for most individuals. In paragraph (h) of this section, we explain special rules for some individuals who are participating in the Ticket to Work program. In paragraph (i) of this section, we explain special rules for some individuals who work.

(b) When we will conduct a continuing disability review. Except as provided in paragraphs (h) and (i) of this section, we will start a continuing disability review if—

(1) You have been scheduled for a medical improvement expected diary review;

(2) You have been scheduled for a periodic review (medical improvement possible or medical improvement not expected) in accordance with the provisions of paragraph (d) of this section;

(3) We need a current medical or other report to see if your disability continues. (This could happen when, for example, an advance in medical technology, such as improved treatment for Alzheimer's disease or a change in vocational therapy or technology raises a disability issue.);

(4) You return to work and successfully complete a period of trial work;

(5) Substantial earnings are reported to your wage record;

(6) You tell us that—

(i) You have recovered from your disability; or

(ii) You have returned to work;

(7) Your State Vocational Rehabilitation Agency tells us that—

(i) The services have been completed; or

(ii) You are now working; or

(iii) You are able to work;

(8) Someone in a position to know of your physical or mental condition tells us any of the following, and it appears that the report could be substantially correct:

(i) You are not disabled; or

(ii) You are not following prescribed treatment; or

(iii) You have returned to work; or

(iv) You are failing to follow the provisions of the Social Security Act or these regulations;

(9) Evidence we receive raises a question as to whether your disability continues; or

(10) You have been scheduled for a vocational reexamination diary review.

(c) Definitions. As used in this section—

Medical improvement expected diary—refers to a case which is scheduled for review at a later date because the individual's impairment(s) is expected to improve. Generally, the diary period is set for not less than 6 months or for not more than 18 months. Examples of cases likely to be scheduled for medical improvement expected diary are fractures and cases in which corrective surgery is planned and recovery can be anticipated.

Permanent impairment—medical improvement not expected—refers to a case in which any medical improvement in the person's impairment(s) is not expected. This means an extremely severe condition determined on the basis of our experience in administering the disability programs to be at least static, but more likely to be progressively disabling either by itself or by reason of impairment complications, and unlikely to improve so as to permit the individual to engage in substantial gainful activity. The interaction of the individual's age, impairment consequences and lack of recent attachment to the labor market may also be considered in determining whether an impairment is permanent. Improvement which is considered temporary under § 404.1579(c)(4) or § 404.1594(c)(3)(iv), as appropriate, will not be considered in deciding if an impairment is permanent. Examples of permanent impairments taken from the list contained in our other written guidelines which are available for public review are as follows and are not intended to be all inclusive:

(1) Parkinsonian Syndrome which has reached the level of severity necessary to meet the Listing in appendix 1.

(2) Amyotrophic Lateral Sclerosis which has reached the level of severity necessary to meet the Listing in appendix 1.

(3) Diffuse pulmonary fibrosis in an individual age 55 or over which has reached the level of severity necessary to meet the Listing in appendix 1.

(4) Amputation of leg at hip.

Nonpermanent impairment—refers to a case in which any medical improvement in the person's impairment(s) is possible. This means an impairment for which improvement cannot be predicted based on current experience and the facts of the particular case but which is not at the level of severity of an impairment that is considered permanent. Examples of nonpermanent impairments are: regional enteritis, hyperthyroidism, and chronic ulcerative colitis.

Vocational reexamination diary—refers to a case which is scheduled for review at a later date because the individual is undergoing vocational therapy, training or an educational program which may improve his or her ability to work so that the disability requirement of the law is no longer met. Generally, the diary period will be set for the length of the training, therapy, or program of education.

(d) Frequency of review. If your impairment is expected to improve, generally we will review your continuing eligibility for disability benefits at intervals from 6 months to 18 months following our most recent decision. Our notice to you about the review of your case will tell you more precisely when the review will be conducted. If your disability is not considered permanent but is such that any medical improvement in your impairment(s) cannot be accurately predicted, we will review your continuing eligibility for disability benefits at least once every 3 years. If your disability is considered permanent, we will review your continuing eligibility for benefits no less frequently than once every 7 years but no more frequently than once every 5 years. Regardless of your classification, we will conduct an immediate continuing disability review if a question of continuing disability is raised pursuant to paragraph (b) of this section.

(e) Change in classification of impairment. If the evidence developed during a continuing disability review demonstrates that your impairment has improved, is expected to improve, or has worsened since the last review, we may reclassify your impairment to reflect this change in severity. A change in the classification of your impairment will change the frequency with which we will review your case. We may also reclassify certain impairments because of improved tests, treatment, and other technical advances concerning those impairments.

* * *

20 C.F.R. § 404.1592 The trial work period.

(a) Definition of the trial work period. The trial work period is a period during which you may test your ability to work and still be considered disabled. It begins and ends as described in paragraph (e) of this section. During this period, you may perform services (see paragraph (b) of this section) in as many as 9 months, but these months do not have to be consecutive. We will not consider those services as showing that your disability has ended until you have performed services in at least 9 months. However, after the trial work period has ended we will consider the work you did during the trial work period in determining whether your disability ended at any time after the trial work period.

(b) What we mean by services. When used in this section, services means any activity (whether legal or illegal), even though it is not substantial gainful activity, which is done in employment or self-employment for pay or profit, or is the kind normally done for pay or profit. We generally do not consider work done without remuneration to be services if it is done merely as therapy or training or if it is work usually done in a daily routine around the house or in self-care. We will not consider work you have done as a volunteer in the federal programs described in section 404.1574(d) in determining whether you have performed services in the trial work period.

* * *

(c) Limitations on the number of trial work periods. You may have only one trial work period during a period of entitlement to cash benefits.

(d) Who is and is not entitled to a trial work period.

(1) You are generally entitled to a trial work period if you are entitled to disability insurance benefits, child's benefits based on disability, or widow's or widower's or surviving divorced spouse's benefits based on disability.

(2) You are not entitled to a trial work period—

(i) If you are entitled to a period of disability but not to disability insurance benefits, and you are not entitled to any other type of disability benefit under title II of the Social Security Act (i.e., child's benefits based on disability, or widow's or widower's benefits or surviving divorced spouse's benefits based on disability);

(ii) If you perform work demonstrating the ability to engage in substantial gainful activity during any required waiting period for benefits;

(iii) If you perform work demonstrating the ability to engage in substantial gainful activity within 12 months of the onset of the impairment(s) that prevented you from performing substantial gainful activity and before the date of any notice of determination or decision finding that you are disabled; or

(iv) For any month prior to the month of your application for disability benefits (see paragraph (e) of this section).

(e) When the trial work period begins and ends. The trial work period begins with the month in which you become entitled to disability insurance benefits, to child's benefits based on disability or to widow's, widower's, or surviving divorced spouse's benefits based on disability. It cannot begin before the month in which you file your application for benefits * * *. It ends with the close of whichever of the following calendar months is the earliest:

(1) The 9th month (whether or not the months have been consecutive) in which you have performed services if that 9th month is prior to January 1992;

(2) The 9th month (whether or not the months have been consecutive and whether or not the previous 8 months of services were prior to January 1992) in which you have performed services within a period of 60 consecutive months if that 9th month is after December 1991; or

(3) The month in which new evidence, other than evidence relating to any work you did during the trial work period, shows that you are not disabled, even though you have not worked a full 9 months. We may find that your disability has ended at any time during the trial work period if the medical or other evidence shows that you are no longer disabled. See § 404.1594 for information on how we decide whether your disability continues or ends.

20 C.F.R. § 404.1592a The reentitlement period.

(a) General. The reentitlement period is an additional period after 9 months of trial work during which you may continue to test your ability to work if you have a disabling impairment, as defined in § 404.1511. If you work during the reentitlement period, we may decide that your disability has ceased because your work is substantial gainful activity and stop your benefits. However, if, after the month for which we found that your disability ceased because you performed substantial gainful activity, you stop engaging in substantial gainful activity, we will start paying you benefits again; you will not have to file a new application. The following rules apply if you complete a trial work period and continue to have a disabling impairment:

(1) The first time you work after the end of your trial work period and engage in substantial gainful activity, we will find that your disability ceased. When we decide whether this work is substantial gainful activity, we will apply all of the relevant provisions of §§ 404.1571–404.1576 including, but not limited to, the provisions for averaging earnings, unsuccessful work attempts, and deducting impairment-related work expenses, as well as the special rules for evaluating the work you do after you have received disability benefits for at least 24 months. We will find that your disability ceased in the first month after the end of your trial work period in which you do substantial gainful activity, applying all the relevant provisions in §§ 404.1571–404.1576.

(2)(i) If we determine under paragraph (a)(1) of this section that your disability ceased during the reentitlement period because you perform substantial gainful activity, you will be paid benefits for the first month after the trial work period in which you do substantial gainful activity (i.e., the month your disability ceased) and the two succeeding months, whether or not you do substantial gainful activity in those succeeding months. After those three months, we will stop your benefits for any month in which you do substantial gainful activity. (See §§ 404.316, 404.337, 404.352 and 404.401a.) If your benefits are stopped because you do substantial gainful activity, they may be started again without a new application and a new determination of disability if you stop doing substantial gainful activity in a month during the reentitlement period. * * *

* * *

* * *

20 C.F.R § 404.1594 How we will determine whether your disability continues or ends. (*See also* 20 C.F.R. § 416.994)

(a) General. There is a statutory requirement that, if you are entitled to disability benefits, your continued entitlement to such benefits must be reviewed periodically. If you are entitled to disability benefits as a disabled worker or as a person disabled since childhood, or, for monthly benefits payable for months after December 1990, as a disabled widow, widower, or surviving divorced spouse, there are a number of factors we consider in deciding whether your disability continues. We must determine if there has been any medical improvement in your impairment(s) and, if so, whether this medical improvement is related to your ability to work. If your impairment(s) has not medically improved we must consider whether one or more of the exceptions to medical improvement applies. If medical improvement related to your ability to work has not occurred and no exception applies, your benefits will continue. Even where medical improvement related to your ability to work has occurred or an exception applies, in most cases (see paragraph (e) of this section for exceptions), we must also show that you are currently able to engage in substantial gainful activity before we can find that you are no longer disabled.

(b) Terms and definitions. There are several terms and definitions which are important to know in order to understand how we review whether your disability continues. * * *

(1) Medical improvement. Medical improvement is any decrease in the medical severity of your impairment(s) which was present at the time of the most recent favorable medical decision that you were disabled or continued to be disabled. A determination that there has been a decrease in medical severity must be based on changes (improvement) in the symptoms, signs and/or laboratory findings associated with your impairment(s) (see § 404.1528).

Example 1: You were awarded disability benefits due to a herniated nucleus pulposus. At the time of our prior decision granting you benefits you had had a laminectomy. Postoperatively, a myelogram still shows evidence of a persistent deficit in your lumbar spine. You had pain in your back, and pain and a burning sensation in your right foot and leg. There were no muscle weakness or neurological changes and a modest decrease in motion in your back and leg. When we reviewed your claim your treating physician reported that he had seen you regularly every 2 to 3 months for the past 2 years. No further myelograms had been done, complaints of pain in the back and right leg continued especially on sitting or standing for more than a short period of time. Your doctor further reported a moderately decreased range of motion in your back and right leg, but again no muscle atrophy or neurological changes were reported. Medical improvement has not occurred because there has been no decrease in the severity of your back impairment as shown by changes in symptoms, signs or laboratory findings.

* * *

(2) Medical improvement not related to ability to do work. Medical improvement is not related to your ability to work if there has been a decrease in the severity of the impairment(s) as defined in

paragraph (b)(1) of this section, present at the time of the most recent favorable medical decision, but no increase in your functional capacity to do basic work activities as defined in paragraph (b)(4) of this section. If there has been any medical improvement in your impairment(s), but it is not related to your ability to do work and none of the exceptions applies, your benefits will be continued.

Example: You are 65 inches tall and weighed 246 pounds at the time your disability was established. You had venous insufficiency and persistent edema in your legs. At the time, your ability to do basic work activities was affected because you were able to sit for 6 hours, but were able to stand or walk only occasionally. At the time of our continuing disability review, you had undergone a vein stripping operation. You now weigh 220 pounds and have intermittent edema. You are still able to sit for 6 hours at a time and to stand or walk only occasionally although you report less discomfort on walking. Medical improvement has occurred because there has been a decrease in the severity of the existing impairment as shown by your weight loss and the improvement in your edema. This medical improvement is not related to your ability to work, however, because your functional capacity to do basic work activities (i.e., the ability to sit, stand and walk) has not increased.

(3) *Medical improvement that is related to ability to do work.* Medical improvement is related to your ability to work if there has been a decrease in the severity, as defined in paragraph (b)(1) of this section, of the impairment(s) present at the time of the most recent favorable medical decision and an increase in your functional capacity to do basic work activities as discussed in paragraph (b)(4) of this section. A determination that medical improvement related to your ability to do work has occurred does not, necessarily, mean that your disability will be found to have ended unless it is also shown that you are currently able to engage in substantial gainful activity as discussed in paragraph (b)(5) of this section.

Example 1: You have a back impairment and had a laminectomy to relieve the nerve root impingement and weakness in your left leg. At the time of our prior decision, basic work activities were affected because you were able to stand less than 6 hours, and sit no more than 1/2 hour at a time. You had a successful fusion operation on your back about 1 year before our review of your entitlement. At the time of our review, the weakness in your leg has decreased. Your functional capacity to perform basic work activities now is unimpaired because you now have no limitation on your ability to sit, walk, or stand. Medical improvement has occurred because there has been a decrease in the severity of your impairment as demonstrated by the decreased weakness in your leg. This medical improvement is related to your ability to work because there has also been an increase in your functional capacity to perform basic work activities (or residual functional capacity) as shown by the absence of limitation on your ability to sit, walk, or stand. Whether or not your disability is found to have ended, however, will depend on our determination as to whether you can currently engage in substantial gainful activity.

* * *

(4) Functional capacity to do basic work activities. Under the law, disability is defined, in part, as the inability to do any substantial gainful activity by reason of any medically determinable physical or mental impairment(s). In determining whether you are disabled under the law, we must measure, therefore, how and to what extent your impairment(s) has affected your ability to do work. We do this by looking at how your functional capacity for doing basic work activities has been affected. Basic work activities means the abilities and aptitudes necessary to do most jobs. Included are exertional abilities such as walking, standing, pushing, pulling, reaching and carrying, and nonexertional abilities and aptitudes such as seeing, hearing, speaking, remembering, using judgment, dealing with changes and dealing with both supervisors and fellow workers. * * *

* * *

(5) Ability to engage in substantial gainful activity. In most instances, we must show that you are able to engage in substantial gainful activity before your benefits are stopped. When doing this, we will consider all your current impairments not just that impairment(s) present at the time of the most recent favorable determination. If we cannot determine that you are still disabled based on medical considerations alone (as discussed in §§ 404.1525 and 404.1526), we will use the new symptoms, signs and laboratory findings to make an objective assessment of your functional capacity to do basic work activities or residual functional capacity and we will consider your vocational factors. See §§ 404.1545 through 404.1569.

(6) Evidence and basis for our decision. Our decisions under this section will be made on a neutral basis without any initial inference as to the presence or absence of disability being drawn from the fact that you have previously been determined to be disabled. We will consider all evidence you submit, as well as all evidence we obtain from your treating physician(s) and other medical or nonmedical sources. * * *

(7) Point of comparison. For purposes of determining whether medical improvement has occurred, we will compare the current medical severity of that impairment(s) which was present at the time

of the most recent favorable medical decision that you were disabled or continued to be disabled to the medical severity of that impairment(s) at that time. If medical improvement has occurred, we will compare your current functional capacity to do basic work activities (i.e., your residual functional capacity) based on this previously existing impairment(s) with your prior residual functional capacity in order to determine whether the medical improvement is related to your ability to do work. The most recent favorable medical decision is the latest decision involving a consideration of the medical evidence and the issue of whether you were disabled or continued to be disabled which became final.

* * *

(d) First group of exceptions to medical improvement. The law provides for certain limited situations when your disability can be found to have ended even though medical improvement has not occurred, if you can engage in substantial gainful activity. These exceptions to medical improvement are intended to provide a way of finding that a person is no longer disabled in those limited situations where, even though there has been no decrease in severity of the impairment(s), evidence shows that the person should no longer be considered disabled or never should have been considered disabled. If one of these exceptions applies, we must also show that, taking all your current impairment(s) into account, not just those that existed at the time of our most recent favorable medical decision, you are now able to engage in substantial gainful activity before your disability can be found to have ended. As part of the review process, you will be asked about any medical or vocational therapy you received or are receiving. Your answers and the evidence gathered as a result as well as all other evidence, will serve as the basis for the finding that an exception applies.

(1) Substantial evidence shows that you are the beneficiary of advances in medical or vocational therapy or technology (related to your ability to work). * * *

(2) Substantial evidence shows that you have undergone vocational therapy (related to your ability to work). * * *

(3) Substantial evidence shows that based on new or improved diagnostic or evaluative techniques your impairment(s) is not as disabling as it was considered to be at the time of the most recent favorable decision. * * *

(4) Substantial evidence demonstrates that any prior disability decision was in error. * * *

(5) You are currently engaging in substantial gainful activity. * * *

(e) Second group of exceptions to medical improvement. In addition to the first group of exceptions to medical improvement, the following exceptions may result in a determination that you are no longer disabled. In these situations the decision will be made without a determination that you have medically improved or can engage in substantial gainful activity.

(1) A prior determination or decision was fraudulently obtained. * * *

(2) You do not cooperate with us. * * *

(3) We are unable to find you. * * *

(4) You fail to follow prescribed treatment which would be expected to restore your ability to engage in substantial gainful activity. * * *

(f) Evaluation steps. To assure that disability reviews are carried out in a uniform manner, that decisions of continuing disability can be made in the most expeditious and administratively efficient way, and that any decisions to stop disability benefits are made objectively, neutrally and are fully documented, we will follow specific steps in reviewing the question of whether your disability continues. Our review may cease and benefits may be continued at any point if we determine there is sufficient evidence to find that you are still unable to engage in substantial gainful activity. The steps are as follows. (See paragraph (i) of this section if you work during your current period of entitlement based on disability or during certain other periods.)

(1) Are you engaging in substantial gainful activity? If you are (and any applicable trial work period has been completed), we will find disability to have ended (see paragraph (d)(5) of this section).

(2) If you are not, do you have an impairment or combination of impairments which meets or equals the severity of an impairment listed in appendix 1 of this subpart? If you do, your disability will be found to continue.

(3) If you do not, has there been medical improvement as defined in paragraph (b)(1) of this section? If there has been medical improvement as shown by a decrease in medical severity, see step (4). If there has been no decrease in medical severity, there has been no medical improvement. (See step (5).)

(4) If there has been medical improvement, we must determine whether it is related to your ability to do work in accordance with paragraphs (b)(1) through (4) of this section; i.e., whether or not there has been an increase in the residual functional capacity based on the impairment(s) that was present at the time of the most recent favorable medical determination. If medical improvement is not related to your ability to do work, see step (5). If medical improvement is related to your ability to do work, see step (6).

(5) If we found at step (3) that there has been no medical improvement or if we found at step (4) that the medical improvement is not related to your ability to work, we consider whether any of the exceptions in paragraphs (d) and (e) of this section apply. If none of them apply, your disability will be found to continue. If one of the first group of exceptions to medical improvement applies, see step (6). If an exception from the second group of exceptions to medical improvement applies, your disability will be found to have ended. The second group of exceptions to medical improvement may be considered at any point in this process.

(6) If medical improvement is shown to be related to your ability to do work or if one of the first group of exceptions to medical improvement applies, we will determine whether all your current impairments in combination are severe (see § 404.1521). This determination will consider all your current impairments and the impact of the combination of those impairments on your ability to function. If the residual functional capacity assessment in step (4) above shows significant limitation of your ability to do basic work activities, see step (7). When the evidence shows that all your current impairments in combination do not significantly limit your physical or mental abilities to do basic work activities, these impairments will not be considered severe in nature. If so, you will no longer be considered to be disabled.

(7) If your impairment(s) is severe, we will assess your current ability to do substantial gainful activity in accordance with § 404.1560. That is, we will assess your residual functional capacity based on all your current impairments and consider whether you can still do work you have done in the past. If you can do such work, disability will be found to have ended.

(8) If you are not able to do work you have done in the past, we will consider one final step. Given the residual functional capacity assessment and considering your age, education and past work experience, can you do other work? If you can, disability will be found to have ended. If you cannot, disability will be found to continue.

* * *

(h) Before we stop your benefits. Before we stop your benefits or a period of disability, we will give you a chance to explain why we should not do so. Sections 404.1595 and 404.1597 describe your rights (including appeal rights) and the procedures we will follow.

* * *

20 C.F.R. § 404.1615 Making disability determinations. (*See also* 20 C.F.R. § 416.1015)

(a) When making a disability determination, the State agency will apply subpart P, part 404, of our regulations.

(b) The State agency will make disability determinations based only on the medical and nonmedical evidence in its files.

(c) Disability determinations will be made by either:

(1) A State agency medical or psychological consultant and a State agency disability examiner;

(2) A State agency disability examiner alone when there is no medical evidence to be evaluated (i.e., no medical evidence exists or we are unable, despite making every reasonable effort, to obtain any medical evidence that may exist) and the individual fails or refuses, without a good reason, to attend a consultative examination (see § 404.1518); or

(3) A State agency disability examiner alone if the claim is adjudicated under the quick disability determination process (see § 404.1619) or as a compassionate allowance (see § 404.1602), and the initial or reconsidered determination is fully favorable to you. This paragraph will no longer be effective on November 12, 2013 unless we terminate it earlier or extend it beyond that date by publication of a final rule in the Federal Register; or

(4) A State agency disability hearing officer.

* * * The State agency disability examiner and disability hearing officer must be qualified to interpret and evaluate medical reports and other evidence relating to the claimant's physical or mental impairments and as necessary to determine the capacities of the claimant to perform substantial gainful activity.

* * *

(d) An initial determination by the State agency that an individual is not disabled, in any case where there is evidence which indicates the existence of a mental impairment, will be made only after every reasonable effort has been made to ensure that a qualified psychiatrist or psychologist has completed the medical portion of the case review and any applicable residual functional capacity assessment. (See § 404.1616 for the qualifications we consider necessary for a psychologist to be a psychological consultant and § 404.1617 for what we mean by "reasonable effort".) If the services of qualified psychiatrists or psychologists cannot be obtained because of impediments at the State level, the Commissioner may contract directly for the services. In a case where there is evidence of mental and nonmental impairments and a qualified psychologist serves as a psychological consultant, the psychologist will evaluate only the mental impairment, and a physician will evaluate the nonmental impairment.

* * *

20 C.F.R. § 404.1619 Quick disability determination process. (*See also 20 C.F.R. § 416.1029*)

(a) If we identify a claim as one involving a high degree of probability that the individual is disabled, and we expect that the individual's allegations will be easily and quickly verified, we will refer the claim to the State agency for consideration under the quick disability determination process pursuant to this section and § 404.1620(c).

(b) If we refer a claim to the State agency for a quick disability determination, a designated quick disability determination examiner must do all of the following:

(1) Subject to the provisions in paragraph (c) of this section, make the disability determination after consulting with a State agency medical or psychological consultant if the State agency disability examiner determines consultation is appropriate or if consultation is required under § 404.1526(c). The State agency may certify the disability determination forms to us without the signature of the medical or psychological consultant.

(2) Make the quick disability determination based only on the medical and nonmedical evidence in the file.

(3) Subject to the provisions in paragraph (c) of this section, make the quick disability determination by applying the rules in subpart P of this part.

(c) If the quick disability determination examiner cannot make a determination that is fully favorable, or if there is an unresolved disagreement between the disability examiner and the medical or psychological consultant (except when a disability examiner makes the determination alone under § 404.1615(c)(3)), the State agency will adjudicate the claim using the regularly applicable procedures in this subpart.

20 C.F.R. § 404.1705 Who may be your representative. (*See also* 20 C.F.R. § 416.1505)

(a) Attorney. You may appoint as your representative in dealings with us, any attorney in good standing who—

(1) Has the right to practice law before a court of a State, Territory, District, or island possession of the United States, or before the Supreme Court or a lower Federal court of the United States;

(2) Is not disqualified or suspended from acting as a representative in dealings with us; and

(3) Is not prohibited by any law from acting as a representative.

(b) Person other than attorney. You may appoint any person who is not an attorney to be your representative in dealings with us if he or she—

(1) Is generally known to have a good character and reputation;

(2) Is capable of giving valuable help to you in connection with your claim;

(3) Is not disqualified or suspended from acting as a representative in dealings with us; and

(4) Is not prohibited by any law from acting as a representative.

20 C.F.R. § 404.1706 Notification of options for obtaining attorney representation. (*See also* 20 C.F.R. § 416.1506)

If you are not represented by an attorney and we make a determination or decision that is subject to the administrative review process * * * and it does not grant all of the benefits or other relief you requested or it adversely affects any entitlement to benefits that we have established or may establish for you, we will include with the notice of that determination or decision information about your options for obtaining an attorney to represent you in dealing with us. We will also tell you that a legal services organization may provide you with legal representation free of charge if you satisfy the qualifying requirements applicable to that organization.

20 C.F.R. § 404.1707 Appointing a representative. (*See also* 20 C.F.R. § 416.1507)

We will recognize a person as your representative if the following things are done:

(a) You sign a written notice stating that you want the person to be your representative in dealings with us.

(b) That person signs the notice, agreeing to be your representative, if the person is not an attorney. An attorney does not have to sign a notice of appointment.

(c) The notice is filed at one of our offices if you have initially filed a claim or have requested reconsideration; with an administrative law judge if you requested a hearing; or with the Appeals Council if you have requested a review of the administrative law judge's decision.

20 C.F.R. § 404.1710 Authority of a representative. (*See also* 20 C.F.R. § 416.1510)

(a) What a representative may do. Your representative may, on your behalf—

(1) Obtain information about your claim to the same extent that you are able to do;

(2) Submit evidence;

(3) Make statements about facts and law; and

(4) Make any request or give any notice about the proceedings before us.

(b) What a representative may not do. A representative may not sign an application on behalf of a claimant for rights or benefits under title II of the Act unless authorized to do so under § 404.612.

20 C.F.R § 404.1715 Notice or request to a representative. (*See also* 20 C.F.R. § 416.1515)

(a) We shall send your representative—

(1) Notice and a copy of any administrative action, determination, or decision; and

(2) Requests for information or evidence.

(b) A notice or request sent to your representative, will have the same force and effect as if it had been sent to you.

20 C.F.R. § 404.1740 Rules of conduct and standards of responsibility for representatives. (*See also* 20 C.F.R. § 416.1540)

(a) Purpose and scope.

(1) All attorneys or other persons acting on behalf of a party seeking a statutory right or benefit shall, in their dealings with us, faithfully execute their duties as agents and fiduciaries of a party. A representative shall provide competent assistance to the claimant and recognize the authority of the Agency to lawfully administer the process. The following provisions set forth certain affirmative duties and prohibited actions which shall govern the relationship between the representative and the Agency, including matters involving our administrative procedures and fee collections.

(2) All representatives shall be forthright in their dealings with us and with the claimant and shall comport themselves with due regard for the nonadversarial nature of the proceedings by complying with our rules and standards, which are intended to ensure orderly and fair presentation of evidence and argument.

(b) Affirmative duties. A representative shall, in conformity with the regulations setting forth our existing duties and responsibilities and those of claimants (see § 404.1512 in disability and blindness claims):

(1) Act with reasonable promptness to obtain the information and evidence that the claimant wants to submit in support of his or her claim, and forward the same to us for consideration as soon as practicable. In disability and blindness claims, this includes the obligations to assist the claimant in bringing to our attention everything that shows that the claimant is disabled or blind, and to assist the claimant in furnishing medical evidence that the claimant intends to personally provide and other evidence that we can use to reach conclusions about the claimant's medical impairment(s) and, if material to the determination of whether the claimant is blind or disabled, its effect upon the claimant's ability to work on a sustained basis, pursuant to § 404.1512(a);

(2) Assist the claimant in complying, as soon as practicable, with our requests for information or evidence at any stage of the administrative decisionmaking process in his or her claim. In disability and blindness claims, this includes the obligation pursuant to § 404.1512(c) to assist the claimant in providing, upon our request, evidence about:

(i) The claimant's age;

(ii) The claimant's education and training;

(iii) The claimant's work experience;

(iv) The claimant's daily activities both before and after the date the claimant alleges that he or she became disabled;

(v) The claimant's efforts to work; and

(vi) Any other factors showing how the claimant's impairment(s) affects his or her ability to work. * * *; and

(3) Conduct his or her dealings in a manner that furthers the efficient, fair and orderly conduct of the administrative decisionmaking process, including duties to:

(i) Provide competent representation to a claimant. Competent representation requires the knowledge, skill, thoroughness and preparation reasonably necessary for the representation. This includes knowing the significant issue(s) in a claim and having a working knowledge of the applicable provisions of the Social Security Act, as amended, the regulations and the Rulings; and

(ii) Act with reasonable diligence and promptness in representing a claimant. This includes providing prompt and responsive answers to requests from the Agency for information pertinent to processing of the claim.

(c) Prohibited actions. A representative shall not:

(1) In any manner or by any means threaten, coerce, intimidate, deceive or knowingly mislead a claimant, or prospective claimant or beneficiary, regarding benefits or other rights under the Act;

(2) Knowingly charge, collect or retain, or make any arrangement to charge, collect or retain, from any source, directly or indirectly, any fee for representational services in violation of applicable law or regulation;

(3) Knowingly make or present, or participate in the making or presentation of, false or misleading oral or written statements, assertions or representations about a material fact or law concerning a matter within our jurisdiction;

(4) Through his or her own actions or omissions, unreasonably delay or cause to be delayed, without good cause * * *, the processing of a claim at any stage of the administrative decisionmaking process;

(5) Divulge, without the claimant's consent, except as may be authorized by regulations prescribed by us or as otherwise provided by Federal law, any information we furnish or disclose about a claim or prospective claim;

(6) Attempt to influence, directly or indirectly, the outcome of a decision, determination or other administrative action by offering or granting a loan, gift, entertainment or anything of value to a presiding official, Agency employee or witness who is or may reasonably be expected to be involved in the administrative decisionmaking process, except as reimbursement for legitimately incurred expenses or lawful compensation for the services of an expert witness retained on a non-contingency basis to provide evidence; or

(7) Engage in actions or behavior prejudicial to the fair and orderly conduct of administrative proceedings, including but not limited to:

(i) Repeated absences from or persistent tardiness at scheduled proceedings without good cause * * *;

(ii) Willful behavior which has the effect of improperly disrupting proceedings or obstructing the adjudicative process; and

(iii) Threatening or intimidating language, gestures or actions directed at a presiding official, witness or Agency employee which results in a disruption of the orderly presentation and reception of evidence.

20 C.F.R. § 404.1745 Violations of our requirements, rules, or standards. (*See also* 20 C.F.R. § 416.1545)

When we have evidence that a representative fails to meet our qualification requirements or has violated the rules governing dealings with us, we may begin proceedings to suspend or disqualify that individual from acting in a representational capacity before us. We may file charges seeking such sanctions when we have evidence that a representative:

(a) Does not meet the qualifying requirements described in § 404.1705;

(b) Has violated the affirmative duties or engaged in the prohibited actions set forth in § 404.1740;

(c) Has been convicted of a violation under section 206 of the Act;

(d) Has been, by reason of misconduct, disbarred or suspended from any bar or court to which he or she was previously admitted to practice (see § 404.1770(a)); or

(e) Has been, by reason of misconduct, disqualified from participating in or appearing before any Federal program or agency (see § 404.1770(a)).

20 C.F.R. § 404.1770 Decision by hearing officer. (*See also* 20 C.F.R. § 416.1570)

(a) General.

* * *

(2) In deciding whether an individual has been, by reason of misconduct, disbarred or suspended by a court or bar, or disqualified from participating in or appearing before any Federal program or agency, the hearing officer will consider the reasons for the disbarment, suspension, or disqualification action. If the action was taken for solely administrative reasons (e.g., failure to pay dues or to complete continuing legal education requirements), that will not disqualify the individual from acting as a representative before SSA. However, this exception to disqualification does not apply if the administrative action was taken in lieu of disciplinary proceedings (e.g., acceptance of a voluntary resignation pending disciplinary action). Although the hearing officer will consider whether the disbarment, suspension, or disqualification action is based on misconduct when deciding whether an individual should be disqualified from acting as a representative before us, the hearing officer will not re-examine or revise the factual or legal conclusions that led to the disbarment, suspension or disqualification. For purposes of determining whether an individual has been, by reason of misconduct, disqualified from participating in or appearing before any Federal program or agency—

(i) Disqualified refers to any action that prohibits an individual from participating in or appearing before a Federal program or agency, regardless of how long the prohibition lasts or the specific terminology used.

(ii) Federal program refers to any program established by an Act of Congress or administered by a Federal agency.

(iii) Federal agency refers to any authority of the executive branch of the Government of the United States.

(3) If the hearing officer finds that the charges against the representative have been sustained, he or she shall either—

(i) Suspend the representative for a specified period of not less than 1 year, nor more than 5 years, from the date of the decision; or

(ii) Disqualify the representative from acting as a representative in dealings with us until he or she may be reinstated under § 404.1799. Disqualification is the sole sanction available if the charges have been sustained because the representative has been disbarred or suspended from any court or bar to which he or she was previously admitted to practice or disqualified from participating in or appearing before any Federal program or agency, or because the representative has collected or received, and retains, a fee for representational services in excess of the amount authorized.

(4) The hearing officer shall mail a copy of the decision to the parties at their last known addresses. The notice will inform the parties of the right to request the Appeals Council to review the decision.

(b) Effect of hearing officer's decision.

(1) The hearing officer's decision is final and binding unless reversed or modified by the Appeals Council upon review.

* * *

20 C.F.R. § 416.200 Introduction

You are eligible for SSI benefits if you meet all the basic requirements listed in § 416.202. * * * You must give us any information we request and show us necessary documents or other evidence to prove that you meet these requirements. * * * We determine your eligibility for each month on the basis of your countable income in that month. You continue to be eligible unless you lose your eligibility because you no longer meet the basic requirements or because of one of the reasons given in §§ 416.207 through 416.216.

20 C.F.R. § 416.202 Who may get SSI benefits.

You are eligible for SSI benefits if you meet all of the following requirements:

(a) You are—

(1) Aged 65 or older (Subpart H);

(2) Blind (Subpart I); or

(3) Disabled (Subpart I).

(b) You are a resident of the United States (§ 416.1603), and—

(1) A citizen or a national of the United States (§ 416.1610);

(2) An alien lawfully admitted for permanent residence in the United States (§ 416.1615);

(3) An alien permanently residing in the United States under color of law (§ 416.1618); or

(4) A child of armed forces personnel living overseas as described in § 416.216.

(c) You do not have more income than is permitted (Subparts K and D).

(d) You do not have more resources than are permitted (Subpart L).

(e) You are disabled, drug addiction or alcoholism is a contributing factor material to the determination of disability (see § 416.935), and you have not previously received a total of 36 months of Social Security benefit payments when appropriate treatment was available or 36 months of SSI benefits on the basis of disability where drug addiction or alcoholism was a contributing factor material to the determination of disability.

(f) You are not—

(1) Fleeing to avoid prosecution for a crime, or an attempt to commit a crime, which is a felony under the laws of the place from which you flee (or which, in the case of the State of New Jersey, is a high misdemeanor under the laws of that State);

(2) Fleeing to avoid custody or confinement after conviction for a crime, or an attempt to commit a crime, which is a felony under the laws of the place from which you flee (or which, in the case of the State of New Jersey, is a high misdemeanor under the laws of that State); or

(3) Violating a condition of probation or parole imposed under Federal or State law.

(g) You file an application for SSI benefits (Subpart C).

20 C.F.R. § 416.325 When an application is considered filed.

(a) General rule. We consider an application for SSI benefits filed on the day it is received by an employee at any social security office, by someone at another Federal or State office designated to receive applications for us, or by a person we have authorized to receive applications for us.

(b) Exceptions.

(1) When we receive an application that is mailed, we will use the date shown by the United States postmark as the filing date if using the date the application is received will result in a loss of benefits. If the postmark is unreadable or there is no postmark, we will use the date the application is signed (if dated) or 5 days before the day we receive the signed application, whichever date is later.

(2) We consider an application to be filed on the date of the filing of a written statement or the making of an oral inquiry under the conditions in §§ 416.340, 416.345 and 416.350.

(3) We will establish a "deemed" filing date of an application in a case of misinformation under the conditions described in § 416.351. The filing date of the application will be a date determined under § 416.351(b).

20 C.F.R. § 416.538 Amount of underpayment or overpayment.

(a) General. The amount of an underpayment or overpayment is the difference between the amount paid to a recipient and the amount of payment actually due such recipient for a given period. An underpayment or overpayment period begins with the first month for which there is a difference between the amount paid and the amount actually due for that month. The period ends with the month the initial determination of overpayment or underpayment is made. With respect to the period established, there can be no underpayment to a recipient or his or her eligible spouse if more than the correct amount payable under title XVI of the Act has been paid, whether or not adjustment or recovery of any overpayment for that period to the recipient or his or her eligible spouse has been waived under the provisions of §§ 416.550 through 416.556. A subsequent initial determination of overpayment will require no change with respect to a prior determination of overpayment or to the period relating to such determination to the extent that the basis of the prior overpayment remains the same.

* * *

(e) Reduction of underpaid amount. Any underpayment amount otherwise payable to a survivor on account of a deceased recipient is reduced by the amount of any outstanding penalty imposed against the benefits payable to such deceased recipient or survivor under section 1631(e) of the Act (see § 416.537(b)(2)).

20 C.F.R. § 416.542 Underpayments—to whom underpaid amount is payable.

(a) Underpaid recipient alive—underpayment payable

(1) If an underpaid recipient is alive, the amount of any underpayment due him or her will be paid to him or her in a separate payment or by increasing the amount of his or her monthly payment. If the underpaid amount meets the formula in § 416.545 and one of the exceptions does not apply, the amount of any past-due benefits will be paid in installments.

(2) If an underpaid recipient whose drug addiction or alcoholism is a contributing factor material to the determination of disability (as described in § 416.935) is alive, the amount of any underpayment due the recipient will be paid through his or her representative payee in installment payments. * * *

(3) If an underpaid individual under age 18 is alive and has a representative payee and is due past-due benefits which meet the formula in § 416.546, SSA will pay the past-due benefits into the dedicated account described in § 416.640(e). If the underpaid individual dies before the benefits have been deposited into the account, we will follow the rules which apply to underpayments for the payment of any unpaid amount due to any eligible survivor of a deceased individual as described in paragraph (b) of this section.

(b) Underpaid recipient deceased—underpaid amount payable to survivor.

(1) If a recipient dies before we have paid all benefits due or before the recipient endorses the check for the correct payment, we may pay the amount due to the deceased recipient's surviving eligible spouse or to his or her surviving spouse who was living with the underpaid recipient within the meaning of section 202(i) of the Act (see § 404.347) in the month he or she died or within 6 months immediately preceding the month of death.

(2) If the deceased underpaid recipient was a disabled or blind child when the underpayment occurred, the underpaid amount may be paid to the natural or adoptive parent(s) of the underpaid recipient who lived with the underpaid recipient in the month he or she died or within the 6 months preceding death. * * *

* * *

(4) No benefits may be paid to the estate of any underpaid recipient, the estate of the surviving spouse, the estate of a parent, or to any survivor other than those listed in * * * this section. * * *

(c) Underpaid recipient's death caused by an intentional act. No benefits due the deceased individual may be paid to a survivor found guilty by a court of competent jurisdiction of intentionally causing the underpaid recipient's death.

20 C.F.R. § 416.550 Waiver of adjustment or recovery—when applicable.

Waiver of adjustment or recovery of an overpayment of SSI benefits may be granted when (EXCEPTION: This section does not apply to a sponsor of an alien):

(a) The overpaid individual was without fault in connection with an overpayment, and

(b) Adjustment or recovery of such overpayment would either:

(1) Defeat the purpose of title XVI, or

(2) Be against equity and good conscience, or

(3) Impede efficient or effective administration of title XVI due to the small amount involved.

20 C.F.R. § 416.801 Evidence as to age—when required.

An applicant for benefits under title XVI of the Act shall file supporting evidence showing the date of his birth if his age is a condition of eligibility for benefits or is otherwise relevant to the payment of benefits pursuant to such title XVI. * * * In the absence of evidence to the contrary, if the applicant alleges that he is at least 68 years of age and submits any documentary evidence at least 3 years old which supports his allegation, no further evidence of his age is required. In the absence of evidence to the contrary, if a State required reasonably acceptable evidence of age and provides a statement as to an applicant's age, no further evidence of his age is required unless a statistically valid quality control sample has shown that a State's determination of age procedures do not yield an acceptable low rate of error.

20 C.F.R. § 416.802 Type of evidence to be submitted.

Where an individual is required to submit evidence of date of birth as indicated in § 416.801, he shall submit a public record of birth or a religious record of birth or baptism established or recorded before his fifth birthday, if available. Where no such document recorded or established before age 5 is available the individual shall submit as evidence of age another document or documents which may serve as the basis for a determination of the individual's date of birth provided such evidence is corroborated by other evidence or by information in the records of the Administration.

20 C.F.R. § 416.803 Evaluation of evidence.

Generally, the highest probative value will be accorded to a public record of birth or a religious record of birth or baptism established or recorded before age 5. Where such record is not available, and other documents are submitted as evidence of age, in determining their probative value, consideration will be given to when such other documents were established or recorded, and the circumstances attending their establishment or recordation. Among the documents which may be submitted for such purpose are: school record, census record, Bible or other family record, church record of baptism or confirmation in youth or early adult life, insurance policy, marriage record, employment record, labor union record, fraternal organization record, military record, voting record, vaccination record, delayed birth certificate, birth certificate of child of applicant, physician's or midwife's record of birth, immigration record, naturalization record, or passport.

20 C.F.R § 416.806 Expedited adjudication based on documentary evidence of age.

Where documentary evidence of age recorded at least 3 years before the application is filed, which reasonably supports an aged applicant's allegation as to his age, is submitted, payment of benefits may be initiated even though additional evidence of age may be required by §§ 416.801 through 416.805. The applicant will be advised that additional evidence is required and that, if it is subsequently established that the prior finding of age is incorrect, the applicant will be liable for refund of any overpayment he has received. If any of the evidence initially submitted tends to show that the age of the applicant or such other person does not correspond with the alleged age, no benefits will be paid until the evidence required by §§ 416.801 through 416.805 is submitted.

20 C.F.R. § 416.906 Basic definition of disability for children.

If you are under age 18, we will consider you disabled if you have a medically determinable physical or mental impairment or combination of impairments that causes marked and severe functional limitations, and that can be expected to cause death or that has lasted or can be expected to last for a continuous period of not less than 12 months. Notwithstanding the preceding sentence, if you file a new application for benefits and you are engaging in substantial gainful activity, we will not consider you disabled. * * *

20 C.F.R. § 416.907 Disability under a State plan.

You will also be considered disabled for payment of supplemental security income benefits if—

(a) You were found to be permanently and totally disabled as defined under a State plan approved under title XIV or XVI of the Social Security Act, as in effect for October 1972;

(b) You received aid under the State plan because of your disability for the month of December 1973 and for at least one month before July 1973; and

(c) You continue to be disabled as defined under the State plan.

20 C.F.R. § 416.924 How we determine disability for children.

(a) Steps in evaluating disability. We consider all relevant evidence in your case record when we make a determination or decision whether you are disabled. If you allege more than one impairment, we will evaluate all the impairments for which we have evidence. Thus, we will consider the combined effects of all your impairments upon your overall health and functioning. We will also evaluate any limitations in your functioning that result from your symptoms, including pain (see § 416.929). We will also consider all of the relevant factors in §§ 416.924a and 416.924b whenever we assess your functioning at any step of this process. We follow a set order to determine whether you are disabled. If you are doing substantial gainful activity, we will determine that you are not disabled and not review your claim further. If you are not doing substantial gainful activity, we will consider your physical or mental impairment(s) first to see if you have an impairment or combination of impairments that is severe. If your impairment(s) is not severe, we will determine that you are not disabled and not review your claim further. If your impairment(s) is severe, we will review your claim further to see if you have an impairment(s) that meets, medically equals, or functionally equals the listings. If you have such an impairment(s), and it meets the duration requirement, we will find that you are disabled. If you do not have such an impairment(s), or if it does not meet the duration requirement, we will find that you are not disabled.

(b) If you are working. If you are working and the work you are doing is substantial gainful activity, we will find that you are not disabled regardless of your medical condition or age, education, or work experience. * * *

(c) You must have a medically determinable impairment(s) that is severe. If you do not have a medically determinable impairment, or your impairment(s) is a slight abnormality or a combination of slight abnormalities that causes no more than minimal functional limitations, we will find that you do not have a severe impairment(s) and are, therefore, not disabled.

(d) Your impairment(s) must meet, medically equal, or functionally equal the listings. An impairment(s) causes marked and severe functional limitations if it meets or medically equals the severity of a set of criteria for an impairment in the listings, or if it functionally equals the listings.

(1) Therefore, if you have an impairment(s) that meets or medically equals the requirements of a listing or that functionally equals the listings, and that meets the duration requirement, we will find you disabled.

(2) If your impairment(s) does not meet the duration requirement, or does not meet, medically equal, or functionally equal the listings, we will find that you are not disabled.

* * *

20 C.F.R. § 416.925 Listing of Impairments in appendix 1 of subpart P of part 404 of this chapter.

(a) What is the purpose of the Listing of Impairments? The Listing of Impairments (the listings) is in appendix 1 of subpart P of part 404 of this chapter. For adults, it describes for each of the major body systems impairments that we consider to be severe enough to prevent an individual from doing any gainful activity, regardless of his or her age, education, or work experience. For children, it describes impairments that cause marked and severe functional limitations.

(b) How is appendix 1 organized? There are two parts in appendix 1:

(1) Part A contains criteria that apply to individuals age 18 and over. We may also use part A for individuals who are under age 18 if the disease processes have a similar effect on adults and children.

(2)(i) Part B contains criteria that apply only to individuals who are under age 18; we never use the listings in part B to evaluate individuals who are age 18 or older. In evaluating disability for a person under age 18, we use part B first. If the criteria in part B do not apply, we may use the criteria in part A when those criteria give appropriate consideration to the effects of the impairment(s) in children. To the extent possible, we number the provisions in part B to maintain a relationship with their counterparts in part A.

(ii) Although the severity criteria in part B of the listings are expressed in different ways for different impairments, "listing-level severity" generally means the level of severity described in § 416.926a(a); that is, "marked" limitations in two domains of functioning or an "extreme" limitation in one domain. (See § 416.926a(e) for the definitions of the terms marked and extreme as they apply to children.) Therefore, in general, a child's impairment(s) is of "listing-level severity" if it causes marked limitations in two domains of functioning or an extreme limitation in one. However, when we decide whether your impairment(s) meets the requirements of a listing, we will decide that your impairment is of "listing-level severity" even if it does not result in marked limitations in two domains of functioning, or an extreme limitation in one, if the listing that we apply does not require such limitations to establish that an impairment(s) is disabling.

(c) How do we use the listings?

(1) Most body system sections in parts A and B of appendix 1 of subpart P of part 404 of this chapter are in two parts: an introduction, followed by the specific listings.

(2) The introduction to each body system contains information relevant to the use of the listings in that body system; for example, examples of common impairments in the body system and definitions used in the listings for that body system. We may also include specific criteria for establishing a diagnosis, confirming the existence of an impairment, or establishing that your impairment(s) satisfies the criteria of a particular listing in the body system. Even if we do not include specific criteria for establishing a diagnosis or confirming the existence of your impairment, you must still show that you have a severe medically determinable impairment(s), as defined in §§ 416.908, 416.920(c), and 416.924(c).

(3) In most cases, the specific listings follow the introduction in each body system, after the heading, Category of Impairments. Within each listing, we specify the objective medical and other findings needed to satisfy the criteria of that listing. We will find that your

impairment(s) meets the requirements of a listing when it satisfies all of the criteria of that listing, including any relevant criteria in the introduction, and meets the duration requirement (see § 416.909).

(4) Most of the listed impairments are permanent or expected to result in death. For some listings, we state a specific period of time for which your impairment(s) will meet the listing. For all others, the evidence must show that your impairment(s) has lasted or can be expected to last for a continuous period of at least 12 months.

(5) If your impairment(s) does not meet the criteria of a listing, it can medically equal the criteria of a listing. We explain our rules for medical equivalence in § 416.926. We use the listings only to find that you are disabled or still disabled. If your impairment(s) does not meet or medically equal the criteria of a listing, we may find that you are disabled or still disabled at a later step in the sequential evaluation process.

(d) Can your impairment(s) meet a listing based only on a diagnosis? No. Your impairment(s) cannot meet the criteria of a listing based only on a diagnosis. To meet the requirements of a listing, you must have a medically determinable impairment(s) that satisfies all of the criteria of the listing.

(e) How do we consider your symptoms when we determine whether your impairment(s) meets a listing? Some listed impairments include symptoms, such as pain, as criteria. Section 416.929(d)(2) explains how we consider your symptoms when your symptoms are included as criteria in a listing.

20 C.F.R. § 416.926a Functional equivalence for children.

(a) General. If you have a severe impairment or combination of impairments that does not meet or medically equal any listing, we will decide whether it results in limitations that functionally equal the listings. By "functionally equal the listings," we mean that your impairment(s) must be of listing-level severity; i.e., it must result in "marked" limitations in two domains of functioning or an "extreme" limitation in one domain, as explained in this section. We will assess the functional limitations caused by your impairment(s); i.e., what you cannot do, have difficulty doing, need help doing, or are restricted from doing because of your impairment(s). When we make a finding regarding functional equivalence, we will assess the interactive and cumulative effects of all of the impairments for which we have evidence, including any impairments you have that are not "severe." (See § 416.924(c).) When we assess your functional limitations, we will consider all the relevant factors in §§ 416.924a, 416.924b, and 416.929 including, but not limited to:

(1) How well you can initiate and sustain activities, how much extra help you need, and the effects of structured or supportive settings (see § 416.924a(b)(5));

(2) How you function in school (see § 416.924a(b)(7)); and

(3) The effects of your medications or other treatment (see § 416.924a(b)(9)).

(b) *How we will consider your functioning.* We will look at the information we have in your case record about how your functioning is affected during all of your activities when we decide whether your impairment or combination of impairments functionally equals the listings. Your activities are everything you do at home, at school, and in your community. We will look at how appropriately, effectively, and independently you perform your activities compared to the performance of other children your age who do not have impairments.

(1) We will consider how you function in your activities in terms of six domains. These domains are broad areas of functioning intended to capture all of what a child can or cannot do. In paragraphs (g) through (l), we describe each domain in general terms. For most of the domains, we also provide examples of activities that illustrate the typical functioning of children in different age groups. For all of the domains, we also provide examples of limitations within the domains. However, we recognize that there is a range of development and functioning, and that not all children within an age category are expected to be able to do all of the activities in the examples of typical functioning. We also recognize that limitations of any of the activities in the examples do not necessarily mean that a child has a "marked" or "extreme" limitation, as defined in paragraph (e) of this section. The domains we use are:

(i) Acquiring and using information;

(ii) Attending and completing tasks;

(iii) Interacting and relating with others;

(iv) Moving about and manipulating objects;

(v) Caring for yourself; and,

(vi) Health and physical well-being.

(2) When we evaluate your ability to function in each domain, we will ask for and consider information that will help us answer the following questions about whether your impairment(s) affects your

functioning and whether your activities are typical of other children your age who do not have impairments.

(i) What activities are you able to perform?

(ii) What activities are you not able to perform?

(iii) Which of your activities are limited or restricted compared to other children your age who do not have impairments?

(iv) Where do you have difficulty with your activities-at home, in childcare, at school, or in the community?

(v) Do you have difficulty independently initiating, sustaining, or completing activities?

(vi) What kind of help do you need to do your activities, how much help do you need, and how often do you need it?

* * *

(c) The interactive and cumulative effects of an impairment or multiple impairments. When we evaluate your functioning and decide which domains may be affected by your impairment(s), we will look first at your activities and your limitations and restrictions. Any given activity may involve the integrated use of many abilities and skills; therefore, any single limitation may be the result of the interactive and cumulative effects of one or more impairments. And any given impairment may have effects in more than one domain; therefore, we will evaluate the limitations from your impairment(s) in any affected domain(s).

(d) How we will decide that your impairment(s) functionally equals the listings. We will decide that your impairment(s) functionally equals the listings if it is of listing-level severity. Your impairment(s) is of listing-level severity if you have "marked" limitations in two of the domains in paragraph (b)(1) of this section, or an "extreme" limitation in one domain. We will not compare your functioning to the requirements of any specific listing. We explain what the terms "marked" and "extreme" mean in paragraph (e) of this section. We explain how we use the domains in paragraph (f) of this section, and describe each domain in paragraphs (g)-(l). * * *

(e) How we define "marked" and "extreme" limitations—

* * *

(2) Marked limitation.

(i) We will find that you have a "marked" limitation in a domain when your impairment(s) interferes seriously with your ability to independently initiate, sustain, or complete activities. Your day-to-day functioning may be seriously limited when your impairment(s) limits only one activity or when the interactive and cumulative effects of your impairment(s) limit several activities. "Marked" limitation also means a limitation that is "more than moderate" but "less than extreme." It is the equivalent of the functioning we would expect to find on standardized testing with scores that are at least two, but less than three, standard deviations below the mean.

(ii) If you have not attained age 3, we will generally find that you have a "marked" limitation if you are functioning at a level that is more than one-half but not more than two-thirds of your chronological age when there are no standard scores from standardized tests in your case record.

(iii) If you are a child of any age (birth to the attainment of age 18), we will find that you have a "marked" limitation when you have a valid score that is two standard deviations or more below the mean, but less than three standard deviations, on a comprehensive standardized test designed to measure ability or functioning in that domain, and your day-to-day functioning in domain-related activities is consistent with that score. (See paragraph (e)(4) of this section.)

(iv) For the sixth domain of functioning, "Health and physical well-being," we may also consider you to have a "marked" limitation if you are frequently ill because of your impairment(s) or have frequent exacerbations of your impairment(s) that result in significant, documented symptoms or signs. For purposes of this domain, "frequent means that you have episodes of illness or exacerbations that occur on an average of 3 times a year, or once every 4 months, each lasting 2 weeks or more. We may also find that you have a "marked" limitation if you have episodes that occur more often than 3 times in a year or once every 4 months but do not last for 2 weeks, or occur less often than an average of 3 times a year or once every 4 months but last longer than 2 weeks, if the overall effect (based on the length of the episode(s) or its frequency) is equivalent in severity.

(3) Extreme limitation.

(i) We will find that you have an "extreme" limitation in a domain when your impairment(s) interferes very seriously with your ability to independently initiate, sustain, or complete activities. Your day-to-day functioning may be very seriously limited when your impairment(s) limits only one activity or when the interactive and cumulative effects of your impairment(s) limit several activities. "Extreme" limitation also means a limitation that is "more than marked." "Extreme" limitation is the rating we give to the worst limitations. However, "extreme limitation" does not necessarily mean a total lack or loss of ability to function. It is the equivalent of the functioning we would expect to find on standardized testing with scores that are at least three standard deviations below the mean.

(ii) If you have not attained age 3, we will generally find that you have an "extreme" limitation if you are functioning at a level that is one-half of your chronological age or less when there are no standard scores from standardized tests in your case record.

(iii) If you are a child of any age (birth to the attainment of age 18), we will find that you have an "extreme" limitation when you have a valid score that is three standard deviations or more below the mean on a comprehensive standardized test designed to measure ability or functioning in that domain, and your day-to-day functioning in domain-related activities is consistent with that score. (See paragraph (e)(4) of this section.)

(iv) For the sixth domain of functioning, "Health and physical well-being," we may also consider you to have an "extreme" limitation if you are frequently ill because of your impairment(s) or have frequent exacerbations of your impairment(s) that result in significant, documented symptoms or signs substantially in excess of the requirements for showing a "marked" limitation in paragraph (e)(2)(iv) of this section. However, if you have episodes of illness or exacerbations of your impairment(s) that we would rate as "extreme" under this definition, your impairment(s) should meet or medically equal the requirements of a listing in most cases. See §§ 416.925 and 416.926.

(4) How we will consider your test scores.

(i) As indicated in § 416.924a(a)(1)(ii), we will not rely on any test score alone. No single piece of information taken in isolation can establish whether you have a "marked" or an "extreme" limitation in a domain.

(ii) We will consider your test scores together with the other information we have about your functioning, including reports of classroom performance and the observations of school personnel and others.

(A) We may find that you have a "marked" or "extreme" limitation when you have a test score that is slightly higher than the level provided in paragraph (e)(2) or (e)(3) of this section, if other information in your case record shows that your functioning in day-to-day activities is seriously or very seriously limited because of your impairment(s). For example, you may have IQ scores above the level in paragraph (e)(2), but other evidence shows that your impairment(s) causes you to function in school, home, and the community far below your expected level of functioning based on this score.

(B) On the other hand, we may find that you do not have a "marked" or "extreme" limitation, even if your test scores are at the level provided in paragraph (e)(2) or (e)(3) of this section, if other information in your case record shows that your functioning in day-to-day activities is not seriously or very seriously limited by your impairment(s). For example, you may have a valid IQ score below the level in paragraph (e)(2), but other evidence shows that you have learned to drive a car, shop independently, and read books near your expected grade level.

(iii) If there is a material inconsistency between your test scores and other information in your case record, we will try to resolve it. The interpretation of the test is primarily the responsibility of the psychologist or other professional who administered the test. But it is also our responsibility to ensure that the evidence in your case is complete and consistent or that any material inconsistencies have been resolved. Therefore, we will use the following guidelines when we resolve concerns about your test scores:

(A) We may be able to resolve the inconsistency with the information we have. We may need to obtain additional information; e.g., by recontact with your medical source(s), by purchase of a consultative examination to provide further medical information, by recontact with a medical source who provided a consultative examination, or by questioning individuals familiar with your day-to-day functioning.

(B) Generally, we will not rely on a test score as a measurement of your functioning within a domain when the information we have about your functioning is the kind of information typically used by medical professionals to determine that the test results are not the best measure of your day-to-day functioning. When we do not rely on test scores, we will explain our reasons for doing so in your case record or in our decision.

(f) How we will use the domains to help us evaluate your functioning.

(1) When we consider whether you have "marked" or "extreme" limitations in any domain, we examine all the information we have in

your case record about how your functioning is limited because of your impairment(s), and we compare your functioning to the typical functioning of children your age who do not have impairments.

(2) The general descriptions of each domain in paragraphs (g)-(l) help us decide whether you have limitations in any given domain and whether these limitations are "marked" or "extreme."

(3) The domain descriptions also include examples of some activities typical of children in each age group and some functional limitations that we may consider. These examples also help us decide whether you have limitations in a domain because of your impairment(s). The examples are not all-inclusive, and we will not require our adjudicators to develop evidence about each specific example. When you have limitations in a given activity or activities in the examples, we may or may not decide that you have a "marked" or "extreme" limitation in the domain. We will consider the activities in which you are limited because of your impairment(s) and the extent of your limitations under the rules in paragraph (e) of this section. We will also consider all of the relevant provisions of §§ 416.924a, 416.924b, and 416.929.

(g) *Acquiring and using information.* In this domain, we consider how well you acquire or learn information, and how well you use the information you have learned.

(1) *General.*

(i) Learning and thinking begin at birth. You learn as you explore the world through sight, sound, taste, touch, and smell. As you play, you acquire concepts and learn that people, things, and activities have names. This lets you understand symbols, which prepares you to use language for learning. Using the concepts and symbols you have acquired through play and learning experiences, you should be able to learn to read, write, do arithmetic, and understand and use new information.

(ii) Thinking is the application or use of information you have learned. It involves being able to perceive relationships, reason, and make logical choices. People think in different ways. When you think in pictures, you may solve a problem by watching and imitating what another person does. When you think in words, you may solve a problem by using language to talk your way through it. You must also be able to use language to think about the world and to understand others and express yourself; e.g., to follow directions, ask for information, or explain something.

(2) Age group descriptors—

(i) Newborns and young infants (birth to attainment of age 1). At this age, you should show interest in, and explore, your environment. At first, your actions are random; for example, when you accidentally touch the mobile over your crib. Eventually, your actions should become deliberate and purposeful, as when you shake noisemaking toys like a bell or rattle. You should begin to recognize, and then anticipate, routine situations and events, as when you grin with expectation at the sight of your stroller. You should also recognize and gradually attach meaning to everyday sounds, as when you hear the telephone or your name. Eventually, you should recognize and respond to familiar words, including family names and what your favorite toys and activities are called.

(ii) Older infants and toddlers (age 1 to attainment of age 3). At this age, you are learning about the world around you. When you play, you should learn how objects go together in different ways. You should learn that by pretending, your actions can represent real things. This helps you understand that words represent things, and that words are simply symbols or names for toys, people, places, and activities. You should refer to yourself and things around you by pointing and eventually by naming. You should form concepts and solve simple problems through purposeful experimentation (e.g., taking toys apart), imitation, constructive play (e.g., building with blocks), and pretend play activities. You should begin to respond to increasingly complex instructions and questions, and to produce an increasing number of words and grammatically correct simple sentences and questions.

(iii) Preschool children (age 3 to attainment of age 6). When you are old enough to go to preschool or kindergarten, you should begin to learn and use the skills that will help you to read and write and do arithmetic when you are older. For example, listening to stories, rhyming words, and matching letters are skills needed for learning to read. Counting, sorting shapes, and building with blocks are skills needed to learn math. Painting, coloring, copying shapes, and using scissors are some of the skills needed in learning to write. Using words to ask questions, give answers, follow directions, describe things, explain what you mean, and tell stories allows you to acquire and share knowledge and experience of the world around you. All of these are called "readiness skills," and you should have them by the time you begin first grade.

(iv) School-age children (age 6 to attainment of age 12). When you are old enough to go to elementary and middle school, you should be able to learn to read, write, and do math, and discuss history and science. You will need to use these skills in academic situations to demonstrate what you have learned; e.g., by reading about various subjects and producing oral and written projects, solving mathematical problems, taking achievement tests, doing group work, and entering into class discussions. You will also need to use these skills in daily living situations at home and in the community (e.g., reading street signs, telling time, and making change). You should be able to use increasingly complex language (vocabulary and grammar) to share information and ideas with individuals or groups, by asking questions and expressing your own ideas, and by understanding and responding to the opinions of others.

(v) *Adolescents (age 12 to attainment of age 18).* In middle and high school, you should continue to demonstrate what you have learned in academic assignments (e.g., composition, classroom discussion, and laboratory experiments). You should also be able to use what you have learned in daily living situations without assistance (e.g., going to the store, using the library, and using public transportation). You should be able to comprehend and express both simple and complex ideas, using increasingly complex language (vocabulary and grammar) in learning and daily living situations (e.g., to obtain and convey information and ideas). You should also learn to apply these skills in practical ways that will help you enter the workplace after you finish school (e.g., carrying out instructions, preparing a job application, or being interviewed by a potential employer).

(3) *Examples of limited functioning in acquiring and using information.* The following examples describe some limitations we may consider in this domain. Your limitations may be different from the ones listed here. Also, the examples do not necessarily describe a "marked" or "extreme" limitation. Whether an example applies in your case may depend on your age and developmental stage; e.g., an example below may describe a limitation in an older child, but not a limitation in a younger one. As in any case, your limitations must result from your medically determinable impairment(s). However, we will consider all of the relevant information in your case record when we decide whether your medically determinable impairment(s) results in a "marked" or "extreme" limitation in this domain.

(i) You do not demonstrate understanding of words about space, size, or time; e.g., in/under, big/little, morning/night.

(ii) You cannot rhyme words or the sounds in words.

(iii) You have difficulty recalling important things you learned in school yesterday.

(iv) You have difficulty solving mathematics questions or computing arithmetic answers.

(v) You talk only in short, simple sentences and have difficulty explaining what you mean.

(h) Attending and completing tasks. In this domain, we consider how well you are able to focus and maintain your attention, and how well you begin, carry through, and finish your activities, including the pace at which you perform activities and the ease with which you change them.

* * *

(3) Examples of limited functioning in attending and completing tasks. The following examples describe some limitations we may consider in this domain. Your limitations may be different from the ones listed here. Also, the examples do not necessarily describe a "marked" or "extreme" limitation. * * *

(i) You are easily startled, distracted, or overreactive to sounds, sights, movements, or touch.

(ii) You are slow to focus on, or fail to complete activities of interest to you, e.g., games or art projects.

(iii) You repeatedly become sidetracked from your activities or you frequently interrupt others.

(iv) You are easily frustrated and give up on tasks, including ones you are capable of completing.

(v) You require extra supervision to keep you engaged in an activity.

(i) Interacting and relating with others. In this domain, we consider how well you initiate and sustain emotional connections with others, develop and use the language of your community, cooperate with others, comply with rules, respond to criticism, and respect and take care of the possessions of others.

* * *

(3) Examples of limited functioning in interacting and relating with others. * * *

(i) You do not reach out to be picked up and held by your caregiver.

(ii) You have no close friends, or your friends are all older or younger than you.

(iii) You avoid or withdraw from people you know, or you are overly anxious or fearful of meeting new people or trying new experiences.

(iv) You have difficulty playing games or sports with rules.

(v) You have difficulty communicating with others; e.g., in using verbal and nonverbal skills to express yourself, carrying on a conversation, or in asking others for assistance.

(vi) You have difficulty speaking intelligibly or with adequate fluency.

(j) Moving about and manipulating objects. In this domain, we consider how you move your body from one place to another and how you move and manipulate things. These are called gross and fine motor skills.

* * *

(3) Examples of limited functioning in moving about and manipulating objects. * * *

(i) You experience muscle weakness, joint stiffness, or sensory loss (e.g., spasticity, hypotonia, neuropathy, or paresthesia) that interferes with your motor activities (e.g., you unintentionally drop things).

(ii) You have trouble climbing up and down stairs, or have jerky or disorganized locomotion or difficulty with your balance.

(iii) You have difficulty coordinating gross motor movements (e.g., bending, kneeling, crawling, running, jumping rope, or riding a bike).

(iv) You have difficulty with sequencing hand or finger movements.

(v) You have difficulty with fine motor movement (e.g., gripping or grasping objects).

(vi) You have poor eye-hand coordination when using a pencil or scissors.

(k) Caring for yourself. In this domain, we consider how well you maintain a healthy emotional and physical state, including how well you get your physical and emotional wants and needs met in appropriate ways; how you cope with stress and changes in your environment; and whether you take care of your own health, possessions, and living area.

* * *

(3) Examples of limited functioning in caring for yourself. * * *

(i) You continue to place non-nutritive or inedible objects in your mouth.

(ii) You often use self-soothing activities showing developmental regression (e.g., thumbsucking, re-chewing food), or you have restrictive or stereotyped mannerisms (e.g., body rocking, headbanging).

(iii) You do not dress or bathe yourself appropriately for your age because you have an impairment(s) that affects this domain.

(iv) You engage in self-injurious behavior (e.g., suicidal thoughts or actions, self-inflicted injury, or refusal to take your medication), or you ignore safety rules.

(v) You do not spontaneously pursue enjoyable activities or interests.

(vi) You have disturbance in eating or sleeping patterns.

(l) Health and physical well-being. In this domain, we consider the cumulative physical effects of physical or mental impairments and their associated treatments or therapies on your functioning that we did not consider in paragraph (j) of this section. When your physical impairment(s), your mental impairment(s), or your combination of physical and mental impairments has physical effects that cause "extreme" limitation in your functioning, you will generally have an impairment(s) that "meets" or "medically equals" a listing.

* * *

(4) Examples of limitations in health and physical well-being. * * *

(i) You have generalized symptoms, such as weakness, dizziness, agitation (e.g., excitability), lethargy (e.g., fatigue or loss of energy or stamina), or psychomotor retardation because of your impairment(s).

(ii) You have somatic complaints related to your impairments (e.g., seizure or convulsive activity, headaches, incontinence, recurrent infections, allergies, changes in weight or eating habits, stomach discomfort, nausea, headaches, or insomnia).

(iii) You have limitations in your physical functioning because of your treatment (e.g., chemotherapy, multiple surgeries, chelation, pulmonary cleansing, or nebulizer treatments).

(iv) You have exacerbations from one impairment or a combination of impairments that interfere with your physical functioning.

(v) You are medically fragile and need intensive medical care to maintain your level of health and physical well-being.

(m) *Examples of impairments that functionally equal the listings.* The following are some examples of impairments and limitations that functionally equal the listings. Findings of equivalence based on the disabling functional limitations of a child's impairment(s) are not limited to the examples in this paragraph, because these examples do not describe all possible effects of impairments that might be found to functionally equal the listings. As with any disabling impairment, the duration requirement must also be met (see §§ 416.909 and 416.924(a)).

(1) Documented need for major organ transplant (e.g., liver).

(2) Any condition that is disabling at the time of onset, requiring continuing surgical management within 12 months after onset as a life-saving measure or for salvage or restoration of function, and such major function is not restored or is not expected to be restored within 12 months after onset of this condition.

(3) Effective ambulation possible only with obligatory bilateral upper limb assistance.

(4) Any physical impairment(s) or combination of physical and mental impairments causing complete inability to function independently outside the area of one's home within age-appropriate norms.

(5) Requirement for 24–hour-a-day supervision for medical (including psychological) reasons.

(6) Infants weighing less than 1200 grams at birth, until attainment of 1 year of age.

(7) Infants weighing at least 1200 but less than 2000 grams at birth, and who are small for gestational age, until attainment of 1 year of age. (Small for gestational age means a birth weight that is at

or more than 2 standard deviations below the mean or that is below the 3rd growth percentile for the gestational age of the infant.)

(8) Major congenital organ dysfunction which could be expected to result in death within the first year of life without surgical correction, and the impairment is expected to be disabling (because of residual impairment following surgery, or the recovery time required, or both) until attainment of 1 year of age.

(n) *Responsibility for determining functional equivalence.* In cases where the State agency or other designee of the Commissioner makes the initial or reconsideration disability determination, a State agency medical or psychological consultant or other designee of the Commissioner (see § 416.1016 of this part) has the overall responsibility for determining functional equivalence. For cases in the disability hearing process or otherwise decided by a disability hearing officer, the responsibility for determining functional equivalence rests with either the disability hearing officer or, if the disability hearing officer's reconsideration determination is changed under § 416.1418 of this part, with the Associate Commissioner for Disability Programs or his or her delegate. For cases at the administrative law judge or Appeals Council level, the responsibility for deciding functional equivalence rests with the administrative law judge or Appeals Council.

20 C.F.R § 416.1102 What is income.

Income is anything you receive in cash or in kind that you can use to meet your needs for food and shelter. * * * In-kind income is not cash, but is actually food or shelter, or something you can use to get one of these.

20 C.F.R. § 416.1103 What is not income.

Some things you receive are not income because you cannot use them as food or shelter, or use them to obtain food or shelter. In addition, what you receive from the sale or exchange of your own property is not income; it remains a resource. The following are some items that are not income:

(a) *Medical care and services.* Medical care and services are not income if they are any of the following:

(1) Given to you free of charge or paid for directly to the provider by someone else;

(2) Room and board you receive during a medical confinement;

(3) Assistance provided in cash or in kind (including food or shelter) under a Federal, State, or local government program, whose pur-

pose is to provide medical care or medical services (including vocational rehabilitation);

(4) In-kind assistance (except food or shelter) provided under a nongovernmental program whose purpose is to provide medical care or medical services;

(5) Cash provided by any nongovernmental medical care or medical services program or under a health insurance policy (except cash to cover food or shelter) if the cash is either:

(i) Repayment for program-approved services you have already paid for; or

(ii) A payment restricted to the future purchase of a program-approved service.

Example: If you have paid for prescription drugs and get the money back from your health insurance, the money is not income.

(6) Direct payment of your medical insurance premiums by anyone on your behalf.

(7) Payments from the Department of Veterans Affairs resulting from unusual medical expenses.

(b) Social services. Social services are not income if they are any of the following:

(1) Assistance provided in cash or in kind (but not received in return for a service you perform) under any Federal, State, or local government program whose purpose is to provide social services including vocational rehabilitation (Example: Cash given you by the Department of Veterans Affairs to purchase aid and attendance);

(2) In-kind assistance (except food or shelter) provided under a nongovernmental program whose purpose is to provide social services; or

(3) Cash provided by a nongovernmental social services program (except cash to cover food or shelter) if the cash is either:

(i) Repayment for program-approved services you already have paid for; or

(ii) A payment restricted to the future purchase of a program-approved service.

Example: If you are unable to do your own household chores and a private social services agency provides you with cash to pay a homemaker the cash is not income.

(c) Receipts from the sale, exchange, or replacement of a resource. * * *

Example: If you sell your automobile, the money you receive is not income; it is another form of a resource.

(d) Income tax refunds. * * *

(e) Payments by credit life or credit disability insurance. * * *

* * *

(f) Proceeds of a loan. * * *

(g) Bills paid for you. * * *

* * *

(h) Replacement of income you have already received. * * *

* * *

(i) Weatherization assistance. * * *

(j) Receipt of certain noncash items. * * *

* * *

20 C.F.R. § 416.1104 Income we count.

We have described generally what income is and is not for SSI purposes (§ 416.1103). There are different types of income, earned and unearned, and we have rules for counting each. The earned income rules are described in §§ 416.1110 through 416.1112 and the unearned income rules are described in §§ 416.1120 through 416.1124. One type of unearned income is in-kind support and maintenance (food or shelter). The way we value it depends on your living arrangement. These rules are described in §§ 416.1130 through 416.1148 of this part. In some situations we must consider the income of certain people with whom you live as available to you and part of your income. These rules are described in §§ 416.1160 through 416.1169. We use all of these rules to determine the amount of your countable income—the amount that is left after we subtract what is not income or is not counted.

20 C.F.R. § 416.1110 What is earned income.

Earned income may be in cash or in kind. We may include more of your earned income than you actually receive. We include more than you actually receive if amounts are withheld from earned income because of a garnishment or to pay a debt or other legal obligation, or to make any other payments. Earned income consists of the following types of payments:

(a) Wages—

(1) Wages paid in cash–general. Wages are what you receive (before any deductions) for working as someone else's employee. Wages are the same for SSI purposes as for the social security retirement program's earnings test. (See § 404.429(c) of this chapter.) Wages include salaries, commissions, bonuses, severance pay, and any other special payments received because of your employment.

(2) Wages paid in cash to uniformed service members. Wages paid in cash to uniformed service members include basic pay, some types of special pay, and some types of allowances. Allowances for on-base housing or privatized military housing are unearned income in the form of in-kind support and maintenance. Cash allowances paid to uniformed service members for private housing are wages.

(3) Wages paid in kind. Wages may also include the value of food, clothing, shelter, or other items provided instead of cash. We refer to this type of income as in-kind earned income. However, if you are a domestic or agricultural worker, the law requires us to treat your in-kind pay as unearned income.

(b) Net earnings from self-employment. Net earnings from self-employment are your gross income from any trade or business that you operate, less allowable deductions for that trade or business. Net earnings also include your share of profit or loss in any partnership to which you belong. * * *

(c) Refunds on account of earned income credits are payments made to you under the provisions of section 32 of the Internal Revenue Code of 1986, as amended. Refunds on account of earned income credits are payments made to you under the provisions of section 43 of the Internal Revenue Code of 1954, as amended. These refunds may be greater than taxes you have paid. You may receive earned income tax credit payments along with any other Federal income tax refund you receive because of overpayment of your income tax, (Federal income tax refunds made on the basis of taxes you have already paid are not income to you as stated in § 416.1103(d).) Advance payments of earned income tax credits are made by your employer under the provisions of section 3507 of the same code. You can receive earned income tax credit payments only if you meet certain requirements of family composition and income limits.

(d) Payments for services performed in a sheltered workshop or work activities center. * * *

(e) Certain royalties and honoraria. * * *

20 C.F.R. § 416.1111 How we count earned income.

(a) Wages. We count wages at the earliest of the following points: when you receive them or when they are credited to your account or set aside for your use. We determine wages for each month. We count wages for services performed as a member of a uniformed service (as defined in § 404.1330 of this chapter) as received in the month in which they are earned.

(b) Net earnings from self-employment. We count net earnings from self-employment on a taxable year basis. However, we divide the total of these earnings equally among the months in the taxable year to get your earnings for each month. For example, if your net earnings for a taxable year are $2,400, we consider that you received $200 in each month. If you have net losses from self-employment, we divide them over the taxable year in the same way, and we deduct them only from your other earned income.

* * *

(d) In-kind earned income. We use the current market value of in-kind earned income for SSI purposes. * * * If you receive an item that is not fully paid for and are responsible for the unpaid balance, only the paid-up value is income to you. * * *

* * *

20 C.F.R. § 416.1112 Earned income we do not count.

(a) General. While we must know the source and amount of all of your earned income for SSI, we do not count all of it to determine your eligibility and benefit amount. We first exclude income as authorized by other Federal laws (see paragraph (b) of this section). Then we apply the other exclusions in the order listed in paragraph (c) of this section to the rest of your income in the month. We never reduce your earned income below zero or apply any unused earned income exclusion to unearned income.

(b) Other Federal laws. Some Federal laws other than the Social Security Act provide that we cannot count some of your earned income for SSI purposes. We list the laws and exclusions in the appendix to this subpart which we update periodically.

(c) Other earned income we do not count. We do not count as earned income—

(1) Any refund of Federal income taxes you receive under section 32 of the Internal Revenue Code (relating to earned income tax credit) and any payment you receive from an employer under section 3507 of the Internal Revenue Code (relating to advance payment of earned income tax credit);

(2) The first $30 of earned income received in a calendar quarter if you receive it infrequently or irregularly. We consider income to be received infrequently if you receive it only once during a calendar quarter from a single source and you did not receive it in the month immediately preceding that month or in the month immediately subsequent to that month. We consider income to be received irregularly if you cannot reasonably expect to receive it.;

(3) If you are under age 22 and a student who is regularly attending school * * *:

(i) For earned income beginning January 1, 2002, [certain specified monthly and yearly maximum amounts] * * *

* * *

(4) Any portion of the $20 monthly exclusion in § 416.1124(c)(10) which has not been excluded from your unearned income in that same month;

(5) $65 of earned income in a month;

(6) Earned income you use to pay impairment-related work expenses, if you are disabled (but not blind) and under age 65 or you are disabled (but not blind) and received SSI as a disabled individual (or received disability payments under a former State plan) for the month before you reached age 65.

* * *

(7) One-half of remaining earned income in a month;

(8) Earned income used to meet any expenses reasonably attributable to the earning of the income if you are blind and under age

65 or if you receive SSI as a blind person for the month before you reach age 65. * * *;

(9) Any earned income you receive and use to fulfill an approved plan to achieve self-support if you are blind or disabled and under age 65 or blind or disabled and received SSI as a blind or disabled person for the month before you reached age 65. * * *; and

(10) Payments made to participants in AmeriCorps State and National and AmeriCorps National Civilian Community Corps (NCCC). Payments to participants in AmeriCorps State and National and AmeriCorps NCCC may be made in cash or in-kind and may be made directly to the AmeriCorps participant or on the AmeriCorps participant's behalf. These payments include, but are not limited to: Living allowance payments, stipends, educational awards, and payments in lieu of educational awards.

20 C.F.R. § 416.1120 What is unearned income.

Unearned income is all income that is not earned income. We describe some of the types of unearned income in § 416.1121. We consider all of these items as unearned income, whether you receive them in cash or in kind.

20 C.F.R. § 416.1121 Types of unearned income.

Some types of unearned income are—

(a) Annuities, pensions, and other periodic payments. This unearned income is usually related to prior work or service. It includes, for example, private pensions, social security benefits, disability benefits, veterans benefits, worker's compensation, railroad retirement annuities and unemployment insurance benefits.

(b) Alimony and support payments. * * *

(c) Dividends, interest, and certain royalties. * * *

(d) Rents. * * * We deduct from rental payments your ordinary and necessary expenses in the same taxable year. These include only those expenses necessary for the production or collection of the rental income and they must be deducted when paid, not when they are incurred. * * *

(e) Death benefits. We count payments you get which were occasioned by the death of another person except for the amount of such payments that you spend on the deceased person's last illness and burial expenses. Last illness and burial expenses include related hospital and medical expenses, funeral, burial plot and interment expenses, and other related costs.

* * *

(f) Prizes and awards. * * *

(g) Gifts and inheritances. * * * Gifts and inheritances occasioned by the death of another person, to the extent that they are used to pay the expenses of the deceased's last illness and burial, as defined in paragraph (e) of this section, are not considered income.

(h) Support and maintenance in kind. This is food or shelter furnished to you. Our rules for valuing this income depend on your living arrangement. We use one rule if you are living in the household of a person who provides you with both food and shelter. We use different rules for other situations where you receive food or shelter. We discuss all of the rules in §§ 416.1130 through 416.1147.

20 C.F.R § 416.1123 How we count unearned income.

(a) When we count unearned income. We count unearned income at the earliest of the following points: When you receive it or when it is credited to your account or set aside for your use. We determine your unearned income for each month. We describe exceptions to the rule on how we count unearned income in paragraphs (d), (e) and (f) of this section.

(b) Amount considered as income. We may include more or less of your unearned income than you actually receive.

(1) We include more than you actually receive where another benefit payment (such as a social security insurance benefit) (see § 416.1121) has been reduced to recover a previous overpayment. * * * Exception: We do not include more than you actually receive if you received both SSI benefits and the other benefit at the time the overpayment of the other benefit occurred and the overpaid amount was included in figuring your SSI benefit at that time.

Example: Joe, an SSI beneficiary, is also entitled to social security insurance benefits in the amount of $200 per month. However, because of a prior overpayment of his social security insurance benefits, $20 per month is being withheld to recover the overpayment. In figuring the amount of his SSI benefits, the full monthly social security insurance benefit of $200 is included in Joe's unearned income. However, if Joe was receiving both benefits when the overpayment of the social security insurance benefit occurred and we then included the overpaid amount as income, we will compute his SSI benefit on the basis of receiving $180 as a social security insurance benefit. This is because we recognize that we computed his SSI benefit on the basis of the higher amount when he was overpaid.

* * *

(4) In certain situations, we may consider someone else's income to be available to you, whether or not it actually is. (For the rules on this process, called deeming, see §§ 416.1160 through 416.1169.)

(c) In-kind income. We use the current market value (defined in § 416.1101) of in-kind unearned income to determine its value for SSI purposes. We describe some exceptions to this rule in §§ 416.1131 through 416.1147. If you receive an item that is not fully paid for and are responsible for the balance, only the paid-up value is income to you.

* * *

(d) Retroactive monthly social security benefits. We count retroactive monthly social security benefits according to the rule in paragraph (d)(1) of this section, unless the exception in paragraph (d)(2) of this section applies:

(1) Periods for which SSI payments have been made. When you file an application for social security benefits and retroactive monthly social security benefits are payable on that application for a period for which you also received SSI payments (including federally-administered State supplementary payments), we count your retroactive monthly social security benefits as unearned income received in that period. Rather than reducing your SSI payments in months prior to your receipt of a retroactive monthly social security benefit, we will reduce the retroactive social security benefits by an amount equal to the amount of SSI payments (including federally-administered State supplementary payments) that we would not have paid to you if your social security benefits had been paid when regularly due rather than retroactively (see § 404.408b(b)). If a balance is due you from your retroactive social security benefits after this reduction, for SSI purposes we will not count the balance as unearned income in a subsequent month in which you receive it. This is because your social security benefits were used to determine the amount of the reduction. This exception to the unearned income counting rule does not apply to any monthly social security benefits for a period for which you did not receive SSI.

(2) Social security disability benefits where drug addiction or alcoholism is a contributing factor material to the determination of disability. If your retroactive social security benefits must be paid in in-

stallments because of the limitations on paying lump sum retroactive benefits to disabled recipients whose drug addiction or alcoholism is a contributing factor material to the determination of disability as described in § 404.480, we will count the total of such retroactive social security benefits as unearned income in the first month such installments are paid, except to the extent the rule in paragraph (d)(1) of this section would provide that such benefits not be counted.

(e) Certain veterans benefits.

* * *

(f) Uniformed service compensation. * * *

20 C.F.R. § 416.1124 Unearned income we do not count.

(a) General. While we must know the source and amount of all of your unearned income for SSI, we do not count all of it to determine your eligibility and benefit amount. We first exclude income as authorized by other Federal laws (see paragraph (b) of this section). Then we apply the other exclusions in the order listed in paragraph (c) of this section to the rest of your unearned income in the month. We never reduce your unearned income below zero or apply any unused unearned income exclusion to earned income except for the $20 general exclusion described in paragraph (c)(12) of this section.

(b) Other Federal laws. Some Federal laws other than the Social Security Act provide that we cannot count some of your unearned income for SSI purposes. We list the laws and the exclusions in the appendix to this subpart which we update periodically.

(c) Other unearned income we do not count. We do not count as unearned income—

(1) Any public agency's refund of taxes on real property or food;

(2) Assistance based on need which is wholly funded by a State or one of its political subdivisions. (For purposes of this rule, an Indian tribe is considered a political subdivision of a State.) * * *;

(3) Any portion of a grant, scholarship, fellowship, or gift used or set aside for paying tuition, fees, or other necessary educational expenses. However, we do count any portion set aside or actually used for food or shelter;

(4) Food which you or your spouse raise if it is consumed by you or your household;

* * *

(6) The first $60 of unearned income received in a calendar quarter if you receive it infrequently or irregularly. We consider income to be received infrequently if you receive it only once during a calendar quarter from a single source and you did not receive it in the month immediately preceding that month or in the month immediately subsequent to that month. We consider income to be received irregularly if you cannot reasonably expect to receive it.

* * *

(8) Payments for providing foster care to an ineligible child who was placed in your home by a public or private nonprofit child placement or child care agency;

* * *

(10) Certain support and maintenance assistance * * *;

(11) One-third of support payments made to or for you by an absent parent if you are a child;

(12) The first $20 of any unearned income in a month other than income in the form of in-kind support and maintenance received in the household of another (see § 416.1131) and income based on need. Income based on need is a benefit that uses financial need as measured by your income as a factor to determine your eligibility. The $20 exclusion does not apply to a benefit based on need that is totally or partially funded by the Federal government or by a nongovernmental agency. However, assistance which is based on need and funded wholly by a State or one of its political subdivisions is excluded totally from income as described in § 416.1124(c)(2). If you have less than $20 of unearned income in a month and you have earned income in that month, we will use the rest of the $20 exclusion to reduce the amount of your countable earned income;

(13) Any unearned income you receive and use to fulfill an approved plan to achieve self-support if you are blind or disabled and under age 65 * * *. * * *;

(14) The value of any assistance paid with respect to a dwelling unit under—

(i) The United States Housing Act of 1937;

(ii) The National Housing Act;

(iii) Section 101 of the Housing and Urban Development Act of 1965;

(iv) Title V of the Housing Act of 1949; or

(v) Section 202(h) of the Housing Act of 1959.

* * *

(16) The value of any commercial transportation ticket, for travel by you or your spouse among the 50 States, the District of Columbia, the Commonwealth of Puerto Rico, the Virgin Islands, Guam, American Samoa, and the Northern Mariana Islands, which is received as a gift by you or your spouse and is not converted to cash. If such a ticket is converted to cash, the cash you receive is income in the month you receive the cash;

(17) Payments received by you from a fund established by a State to aid victims of crime;

* * *

(20) Interest or other earnings on a dedicated account which is excluded from resources. (See § 416.1247).

* * *

(22) Interest and dividend income from a countable resource or from a resource excluded under a Federal statute other than section 1613(a) of the Social Security Act; and

(23) AmeriCorps State and National and AmeriCorps National Civilian Community Corps cash or in-kind payments to AmeriCorps participants or on AmeriCorps participants' behalf. * * *;

(24) Any annuity paid by a State to a person (or his or her spouse) based on the State's determination that the person is:

(i) A veteran (as defined in 38 U.S.C. 101); and

(ii) Blind, disabled, or aged.

20 C.F.R § 416.1130 In-kind Support and Maintenance: Introduction.

(a) General. Both earned income and unearned income include items received in kind (§ 416.1102). Generally, we value in-kind items at their current market value and we apply the various exclusions for both earned and unearned income. However, we have special rules for valuing food or shelter that is received as unearned income (in-kind support and maintenance). * * *

* * *

(b) How we define in-kind support and maintenance. In-kind support and maintenance means any food or shelter that is given to you or that you receive because someone else pays for it. Shelter includes room, rent, mortgage payments, real property taxes, heating fuel, gas, electricity, water, sewerage, and garbage collection services.

* * *

(c) How we value in-kind support and maintenance. Essentially, we have two rules for valuing the in-kind support and maintenance which we must count. The one-third reduction rule applies if you are living in the household of a person who provides you with both food and shelter (§§ 416.1131 through 416.1133). The presumed value rule applies in all other situations where you are receiving countable in-kind support and maintenance (§§ 416.1140 through 416.1145). If certain conditions exist, we do not count in-kind support and maintenance. These are discussed in §§ 416.1141 through 416.1145.

20 C.F.R. § 416.1131 The one-third reduction rule.

(a) What the rule is. Instead of determining the actual dollar value of in-kind support and maintenance, we count one-third of the Federal benefit rate as additional income, if you (or you and your eligible spouse)—

(1) Live in another person's household (see § 416.1132) for a full calendar month except for temporary absences (see § 416.1149), and

(2) Receive both food and shelter from the person in whose household you are living. (If you do not receive both food and shelter from this person, see § 416.1140.)

(b) How we apply the one-third reduction rule. The one-third reduction applies in full or not at all. When you are living in another person's household, and the one-third reduction rule applies, we do not apply any income exclusions to the reduction amount. However, we do apply appropriate exclusions to any other earned or unearned income you receive. * * *

(c) If you receive other support and maintenance. If the one-third reduction rule applies to you, we do not count any other in-kind support and maintenance you receive.

20 C.F.R. § 416.1132 What we mean by "living in another person's household".

* * *

(b) *Another person's household.* You live in another person's household if paragraph (c) of this section does not apply and if the person who supplies the support and maintenance lives in the same household and is not—

(1) Your spouse (as defined in § 416.1806);

(2) A minor child; or

(3) An ineligible person (your spouse, parent, or essential person) whose income may be deemed to you as described in §§ 416.1160 through 416.1169.

(c) *Your own household—not another person's household.* You are not living in another person's household (you live in your own household) if—

(1) You (or your spouse who lives with you or any person whose income is deemed to you) have an ownership interest or a life estate interest in the home;

(2) You (or your spouse who lives with you or any person whose income is deemed to you) are liable to the landlord for payment of any part of the rental charges;

(3) You live in a noninstitutional care situation as described in § 416.1143;

(4) You pay at least a pro rata share of household and operating expenses (see§ 416.1133); or

(5) All members of the household receive public income—maintenance payments (§ 416.1142).

20 C.F.R. § 416.1140 The presumed value rule.

(a) *How we apply the presumed value rule.*

(1) When you receive in-kind support and maintenance and the one-third reduction rule does not apply, we use the presumed value rule. Instead of determining the actual dollar value of any food or shelter you receive, we presume that it is worth a maximum value. This maximum value is one-third of your Federal benefit rate plus

the amount of the general income exclusion described in § 416.1124(c)(12).

(2) The presumed value rule allows you to show that your in-kind support and maintenance is not equal to the presumed value. We will not use the presumed value if you show us that—

(i) The current market value of any food or shelter you receive, minus any payment you make for them, is lower than the presumed value; or

(ii) The actual amount someone else pays for your food or shelter is lower than the presumed value.

(b) How we determine the amount of your unearned income under the presumed value rule.

(1) If you choose not to question the use of the presumed value, or if the presumed value is less than the actual value of the food or shelter you receive, we use the presumed value to figure your unearned income.

(2) If you show us, as provided in paragraph (a)(2) of this section, that the presumed value is higher than the actual value of the food or shelter you receive, we use the actual amount to figure your unearned income.

20 C.F.R. § 416.1141 When the presumed value rule applies.

The presumed value rule applies whenever we must count in-kind support and maintenance as unearned income and the one-third reduction rule does not apply. This means that the presumed value rule applies if you are living—

(a) In another person's household (as described in § 416.1132(b)) but not receiving both food and shelter from that person;

(b) In your own household (as described in § 416.1132(c)). For exceptions, see § 416.1142 if you are in a public assistance household and § 416.1143 if you are in a noninstitutional care situation;

(c) In a nonmedical institution including any—

(1) Public nonmedical institution if you are there for less than a full calendar month;

(2) Public or private nonprofit educational or vocational training institution;

(3) Private nonprofit retirement home or similar institution where there is an express obligation to provide your full support and maintenance or where someone else pays for your support and maintenance. For exceptions, see § 416.1144; and

(4) For-profit institution where someone else pays for your support and maintenance. If you or the institution pay for it, see § 416.1145.

20 C.F.R. § 416.1148 If you have both in-kind support and maintenance and income that is deemed to you.

(a) The one-third reduction and deeming of income. If you live in the household of your spouse, parent, essential person, or sponsor whose income can be deemed to you, * * * the one-third reduction does not apply to you. * * * However, if you live in another person's household as described in § 416.1131, and someone whose income can be deemed to you lives in the same household, we must apply both the one-third reduction and the deeming rules to you.

(b) The presumed value rule and deeming of income.

(1) If you live in the same household with someone whose income can be deemed to you * * *, any food or shelter that person provides is not income to you. However, if you receive any food or shelter from another source, it is income and we value it under the presumed value rule (§ 416.1140). We also apply the deeming rules.

(2) If you are a child under age 18 who lives in the same household with an ineligible parent whose income may be deemed to you, and you are temporarily absent from the household to attend school * * *, any food or shelter you receive at school is income to you unless your parent purchases it. Unless otherwise excluded, we value this income under the presumed value rule (§ 416.1140). We also apply the deeming rules to you (§ 416.1165).

20 C.F.R. § 416.1160 What is deeming of income?

(a) General. We use the term deeming to identify the process of considering another person's income to be your own. When the deeming rules apply, it does not matter whether the income of the other person is actually available to you. We must apply these rules anyway. There are four categories of individuals whose income may be deemed to you.

(1) Ineligible spouse. If you live in the same household with your ineligible spouse, we look at your spouse's income to decide whether we must deem some of it to you. We do this because we expect your

spouse to use some of his or her income to take care of some of your needs.

(2) Ineligible parent. If you are a child to whom deeming rules apply (see § 416.1165), we look at your ineligible parent's income to decide whether we must deem some of it to be yours. If you live with both your parent and your parent's spouse (i.e., your stepparent), we also look at your stepparent's income to decide whether we must deem some of it to be yours. We do this because we expect your parent (and your stepparent, if living with you and your parent) to use some of his or her income to take care of your needs.

* * *

(b) When we deem. We deem income to determine whether you are eligible for a benefit and to determine the amount of your benefit. However, we may consider this income in different months for each purpose.

(1) Eligibility. We consider the income of your ineligible spouse, ineligible parent, sponsor or essential person in the current month to determine whether you are eligible for SSI benefits for that month.

(2) Amount of benefit. We consider the income of your ineligible spouse, ineligible parent, sponsor, or essential person in the second month prior to the current month to determine your benefit amount for the current month. Exceptions:

* * *

(c) Steps in deeming. Although the way we deem income varies depending upon whether you are an eligible individual, an eligible child, an alien with a sponsor, or an individual with an essential person, we follow several general steps to determine how much income to deem.

(1) We determine how much earned and unearned income your ineligible spouse, ineligible parent, sponsor, or essential person has, and we apply the appropriate exclusions. (See § 416.1161(a) for exclusions that apply to an ineligible parent or spouse, and § 416.1161(b) for those that apply to an essential person or to a sponsor.)

(2) Before we deem income to you from either your ineligible spouse or ineligible parent, we allocate an amount for each ineligible child in the household. (Allocations for ineligible children are explained in § 416.1163(b) and § 416.1165(b).) We also allocate an amount for each eligible alien who is subject to deeming from your

ineligible spouse or parent as a sponsor. (Allocations for eligible aliens are explained in § 416.1163(c).)

(3) We then follow the deeming rules which apply to you.

(i) For deeming income from your ineligible spouse, see § 416.1163.

(ii) For deeming income from your ineligible parent, see § 416.1165.

(iii) For deeming income from your ineligible spouse when you also have an eligible child, see § 416.1166.

* * *

(d) Definitions for deeming purposes. For deeming purposes—

* * *

Ineligible child means your natural child or adopted child, or the natural or adopted child of your spouse, or the natural or adopted child of your parent or of your parent's spouse (as the term child is defined in § 416.1101 and the term spouse is defined in § 416.1806), who lives in the same household with you, and is not eligible for SSI benefits.

Ineligible parent means a natural or adoptive parent, or the spouse (as defined in § 416.1101) of a natural or adoptive parent, who lives with you and is not eligible for SSI benefits. The income of ineligible parents affects your benefit only if you are a child under age 18.

Ineligible spouse means someone who lives with you as your husband or wife and is not eligible for SSI benefits.

* * *

20 C.F.R. § 416.1163 How we deem income to you from your ineligible spouse.

If you have an ineligible spouse who lives in the same household, we apply the deeming rules to your ineligible spouse's income in the following order.

(a) Determining your ineligible spouse's income. We first determine how much earned and unearned income your ineligible spouse has, using the appropriate exclusions in § 416.1161(a).

(b) Allocations for ineligible children. We then deduct an allocation for ineligible children in the household to help meet their needs. * * *

* * *

(c) Allocations for aliens sponsored by your ineligible spouse. We also deduct an allocation for eligible aliens who have been sponsored by and who have income deemed from your ineligible spouse. * * *

* * *

(d) Determining your eligibility for SSI.

(1) If the amount of your ineligible spouse's income that remains after appropriate allocations is not more than the difference between the Federal benefit rate for an eligible couple and the Federal benefit rate for an eligible individual, there is no income to deem to you from your spouse. In this situation, we subtract only your own countable income from the Federal benefit rate for an individual to determine whether you are eligible for SSI benefits.

(2) If the amount of your ineligible spouse's income that remains after appropriate allocations is more than the difference between the Federal benefit rate for an eligible couple and the Federal benefit rate for an eligible individual, we treat you and your ineligible spouse as an eligible couple. We do this by:

(i) Combining the remainder of your spouse's unearned income with your own unearned income and the remainder of your spouse's earned income with your earned income;

(ii) Applying all appropriate income exclusions in §§ 416.1112 and 416.1124; and

(iii) Subtracting the couple's countable income from the Federal benefit rate for an eligible couple. * * *

(e) Determining your SSI benefit.

(1) In determining your SSI benefit amount, we follow the procedure in paragraphs (a) through (d) of this section. * * *

(2) Your SSI benefit under the deeming rules cannot be higher than it would be if deeming did not apply. Therefore, your benefit is the lesser of the amount computed under the rules in paragraph (d)(2) of this section or the amount remaining after we subtract only your own countable income from an individual's Federal benefit rate.

* * *

(g) Examples. * * * The Federal benefit rates are those effective January 1, 1986.

* * *

Example 2. In September 1986, Mr. Jones, a disabled individual, lives with his ineligible spouse, Mrs. Jones, and ineligible child, Christine. Mr. Jones and Christine have no income. Mrs. Jones has earned income of $401 a month and unearned income of $252 a month. Before we deem any income, we allocate $168 to Christine. We take the $168 allocation from Mrs. Jones' $252 unearned income, leaving $84 in unearned income. Since Mrs. Jones' total remaining income ($84 unearned plus $401 earned) is more than $168, which is the difference between the September Federal benefit rate for an eligible couple and the September Federal benefit rate for an eligible individual, we compute the combined countable income as we do for a couple. We apply the $20 general income exclusion to the unearned income, reducing it further to $64. We then apply the earned income exclusion ($65 plus one-half the remainder) to Mrs. Jones' earned income of $401, leaving $168. We combine the $64 countable unearned income and $168 countable earned income, and compare it ($232) with the $504 September Federal benefit rate for a couple, and determine that Mr. Jones is eligible. Since Mr. Jones is eligible, we determine the amount of his benefit by subtracting his countable income in July (including any deemed from Mrs. Jones) from September's Federal benefit rate for a couple.

* * *

20 C.F.R. § 416.1165 How we deem income to you from your ineligible parent(s).

If you are a child living with your parents, we apply the deeming rules to you through the month in which you reach age 18. We follow the rules in paragraphs (a) through (e) of this section to determine your eligibility. To determine your benefit amount, we follow the rules in paragraph (f) of this section. * * *

(a) Determining your ineligible parent's income. We first determine how much current monthly earned and unearned income your ineligible parents have, using the appropriate exclusions in § 416.1161(a).

(b) Allocations for ineligible children. We next deduct an allocation for each ineligible child in the household as described in § 416.1163(b).

(c) Allocations for aliens who are sponsored by and have income deemed from your ineligible parent. We also deduct an allocation for eligible aliens who have been sponsored by and have income deemed from your ineligible parent as described in § 416.1163(c).

(d) *Allocations for your ineligible parent(s).* We next deduct allocations for your parent(s). We do not deduct an allocation for a parent who is receiving public income-maintenance payments * * *. The allocations are calculated as follows:

(1) We first deduct $20 from the parents' combined unearned income, if any. If they have less than $20 in unearned income, we subtract the balance of the $20 from their combined earned income.

(2) Next, we subtract $65 plus one-half the remainder of their earned income.

(3) We total the remaining earned and unearned income and subtract—

(i) The Federal benefit rate for the month for a couple if both parents live with you; or

(ii) The Federal benefit rate for the month for an individual if only one parent lives with you.

(e)(1) *When you are the only eligible child.* If you are the only eligible child in the household, we deem any of your parents' current monthly income that remains to be your unearned income. We combine it with your own unearned income and apply the exclusions in § 416.1124 to determine your countable unearned income in the month. We add this to any countable earned income you may have and subtract the total from the Federal benefit rate for an individual to determine whether you are eligible for benefits.

(2) *When you are not the only eligible child.* If your parents have more than one eligible child under age 18 in the household, we divide the parental income to be deemed equally among those eligible children.

(3) *When one child's income makes that child ineligible.* We do not deem more income to an eligible child than the amount which, when combined with the child's own income, reduces his or her SSI benefit to zero. * * * If the share of parental income that would be deemed to a child makes that child ineligible (reduces the amount to zero) because that child has other countable income, we deem any remaining parental income to other eligible children under age 18 in the household in the manner described in paragraph (e)(2) of this section.

(f) Determining your SSI benefit. In determining your SSI benefit amount, we follow the procedure in paragraphs (a) through (d) of this section. * * *

* * *

(h) Examples. * * * The Federal benefit rates are those effective January 1, 1992.

Example 1. Henry, a disabled child, lives with his mother and father and a 12–year-old ineligible brother. His mother receives a pension (unearned income) of $365 per month and his father earns $1,165 per month. Henry and his brother have no income. First we deduct an allocation of $211 for Henry's brother from the unearned income. This leaves $154 in unearned income. We reduce the remaining unearned income further by the $20 general income exclusion, leaving $134. We then reduce the earned income of $1,165 by $65 leaving $1,100. Then we subtract one-half of the remainder, leaving $550. To this we add the remaining unearned income of $134 resulting in $684. From this, we subtract the parent allocation of $633 (the Federal benefit rate for a couple) leaving $51 to be deemed as Henry's unearned income. Henry has no other income. We apply Henry's $20 general income exclusion which reduces his countable income to $31. Since that amount is less than the $422 Federal benefit rate for an individual, Henry is eligible. We determine his benefit amount by subtracting his countable income (including deemed income) in a prior month from the Federal benefit rate for an individual for the current month. See § 416.420.

* * *

20 C.F.R. § 416.1201 Resources; general.

(a) Resources; defined. * * * resources means cash or other liquid assets or any real or personal property that an individual (or spouse, if any) owns and could convert to cash to be used for his or her support and maintenance.

(1) If the individual has the right, authority or power to liquidate the property or his or her share of the property, it is considered a resource. If a property right cannot be liquidated, the property will not be considered a resource of the individual (or spouse).

(2) Support and maintenance assistance not counted as income under § 416.1157(c) will not be considered a resource.

(3) Except for cash reimbursement of medical or social services expenses already paid for by the individual, cash received for medical

or social services that is not income under § 416.1103(a) or (b), or a retroactive cash payment which is income that is excluded from deeming under § 416.1161(a)(16), is not a resource for the calendar month following the month of its receipt. However, cash retained until the first moment of the second calendar month following its receipt is a resource at that time.

(i) For purposes of this provision, a retroactive cash payment is one that is paid after the month in which it was due.

(ii) This provision applies only to the unspent portion of those cash payments identified in this paragraph (a)(3). Once the cash from such payments is spent, this provision does not apply to items purchased with the money, even if the period described above has not expired.

(iii) Unspent money from those cash payments identified in this paragraph (a)(3) must be identifiable from other resources for this provision to apply. The money may be commingled with other funds, but if this is done in such a fashion that an amount from such payments can no longer be separately identified, that amount will count toward the resource limit described in § 416.1205.

(4) Death benefits, including gifts and inheritances, received by an individual, to the extent that they are not income in accordance with paragraphs (e) and (g) of § 416.1121 because they are to be spent on costs resulting from the last illness and burial of the deceased, are not resources for the calendar month following the month of receipt. However, such death benefits retained until the first moment of the second calendar month following their receipt are resources at that time.

(b) Liquid resources. Liquid resources are cash or other property which can be converted to cash within 20 days, excluding certain nonwork days as explained in § 416.120(d). Examples of resources that are ordinarily liquid are stocks, bonds, mutual fund shares, promissory notes, mortgages, life insurance policies, financial institution accounts (including savings, checking, and time deposits, also known as certificates of deposit) and similar items. Liquid resources, other than cash, are evaluated according to the individual's equity in the resources. (See § 416.1208 for the treatment of funds held in individual and joint financial institution accounts.)

(c) Nonliquid resources.

(1) Nonliquid resources are property which is not cash and which cannot be converted to cash within 20 days excluding certain non-

work days as explained in§ 416.120(d). Examples of resources that are ordinarily nonliquid are loan agreements, household goods, automobiles, trucks, tractors, boats, machinery, livestock, buildings and land. Nonliquid resources are evaluated according to their equity value except as otherwise provided. (See § 416.1218 for treatment of automobiles.)

(2) * * * the "equity value" of an item is defined as:

(i) The price that item can reasonably be expected to sell for on the open market in the particular geographic area involved; minus

(ii) Any encumbrances.

20 C.F.R. § 416.1202 Deeming of resources.

(a) Married individual. In the case of an individual who is living with a person not eligible under this part and who is considered to be the husband or wife of such individual * * *, such individual's resources shall be deemed to include any resources, not otherwise excluded under this subpart, of such spouse whether or not such resources are available to such individual. In addition to the exclusions listed in § 416.1210, we also exclude the following items:

(1) Pension funds that the ineligible spouse may have. * * *

* * *

(b) Child—

(1) General. In the case of a child ** * who is under age 18, we will deem to that child any resources, not otherwise excluded under this subpart, of his or her ineligible parent who is living in the same household with him or her * * *. We also will deem to the child the resources of his or her ineligible stepparent. * * * We will deem to a child the resources of his or her parent and stepparent whether or not those resources are available to him or her. We will deem to a child the resources of his or her parent and stepparent only to the extent that those resources exceed the resource limits described in § 416.1205. * * * We will not deem to a child the resources of his or her parent or stepparent if the child is excepted from deeming under paragraph (b)(2) of this section. In addition to the exclusions listed in § 416.1210, we also exclude the following items:

(i) Pension funds of an ineligible parent (or stepparent). * * *

* * *

(2) Disabled child under age 18. In the case of a disabled child under age 18 who is living in the same household with his or her parents, the deeming provisions of paragraph (b)(1) of this section shall not apply if such child—

(i) Previously received a reduced SSI benefit while a resident of a medical treatment facility* * *;

(ii) Is eligible for medical assistance under a Medicaid State home care plan * * *; and

(iii) Would otherwise be ineligible because of the deeming of his or her parents' resources or income.

* * *

20 C.F.R. § 416.1205 Limitation on resources.

(a) Individual with no eligible spouse. An aged, blind, or disabled individual with no spouse is eligible for benefits under title XVI of the Act if his or her nonexcludable resources do not exceed $1,500 prior to January 1, 1985, and all other eligibility requirements are met. An individual who is living with an ineligible spouse is eligible for benefits under title XVI of the Act if his or her nonexcludable resources, including the resources of the spouse, do not exceed $2,250 prior to January 1, 1985, and all other eligibility requirements are met.

(b) Individual with an eligible spouse. An aged, blind, or disabled individual who has an eligible spouse is eligible for benefits under title XVI of the Act if their nonexcludable resources do not exceed $2,250 prior to January 1, 1985, and all other eligibility requirements are met.

(c) Effective January 1, 1985 and later. The resources limits and effective dates for January 1, 1985 and later are as follows:

Effective date	Individual	Individual and spouse
Jan. 1, 1985	$1,600	$2,400
Jan. 1, 1986	1,700	$2,550
Jan. 1, 1987	1,800	$2,700
Jan. 1, 1988	1,900	$2,850
Jan. 1, 1989	2,000	$3,000

20 C.F.R. § 416.1207 Resources determinations.

(a) General. Resources determinations are made as of the first moment of the month. A resource determination is based on what assets an individual has, what their values are, and whether or not they are excluded as of the first moment of the month.

(b) Increase in value of resources. If, during a month, a resource increases in value or an individual acquires an additional resource or replaces an excluded resource with one that is not excluded, the increase in the value of the resources is counted as of the first moment of the next month.

(c) Decrease in value of resources. If, during a month, a resource decreases in value or an individual spends a resource or replaces a resource that is not excluded with one that is excluded, the decrease in the value of the resources is counted as of the first moment of the next month.

(d) Treatment of items under income and resource counting rules. Items received in cash or in kind during a month are evaluated first under the income counting rules and, if retained until the first moment of the following month, are subject to the rules for counting resources at that time.

(e) Receipts from the sale, exchange, or replacement of a resource. If an individual sells, exchanges or replaces a resource, the receipts are not income. They are still considered to be a resource. This rule includes resources that have never been counted as such because they were sold, exchanged or replaced in the month in which they were received. * * *

* * *

20 C.F.R § 416.1208 How funds held in financial institution accounts are counted.

(a) General. Funds held in a financial institution account (including savings, checking, and time deposits, also known as certificates of deposit) are an individual's resource if the individual owns the account and can use the funds for his or her support and maintenance. We determine whether an individual owns the account and can use the funds for his or her support and maintenance by looking at how the individual holds the account. This is reflected in the way the account is titled.

(b) Individually-held account. If an individual is designated as sole owner by the account title and can withdraw funds and use them for his or her support and maintenance, all of the funds, regardless of their source, are that individual's resource. For as long as these conditions are met, we presume that the individual owns 100 percent of the funds in the account. This presumption is non-rebuttable.

(c) Jointly-held account—

(1) Account holders include one or more SSI claimants or recipients. If there is only one SSI claimant or recipient account holder on a jointly held account, we presume that all of the funds in the account belong to that individual. If there is more than one claimant or recipient account holder, we presume that all the funds in the account belong to those individuals in equal shares.

(2) Account holders include one or more deemors. If none of the account holders is a claimant or recipient, we presume that all of the funds in a jointly-held account belong to the deemor(s), in equal shares if there is more than one deemor. A deemor is a person whose income and resources are required to be considered when determining eligibility and computing the SSI benefit for an eligible individual (see §§ 416.1160 and 416.1202).

(3) Right to rebut presumption of ownership. If the claimant, recipient, or deemor objects or disagrees with an ownership presumption as described in paragraph (c)(1) or (c)(2) of this section, we give the individual the opportunity to rebut the presumption. * * *

* * *

20 C.F.R. § 416.1210 Exclusions from resources; general.

In determining the resources of an individual (and spouse, if any) the following items shall be excluded:

(a) The home (including the land appertaining thereto) to the extent its value does not exceed the amount set forth in § 416.1212;

(b) Household goods and personal effects as defined in § 416.1216;

(c) An automobile, if used for transportation, as provided in § 416.1218;

(d) Property of a trade or business which is essential to the means of self-support as provided in § 416.1222;

(e) Nonbusiness property which is essential to the means of self-support as provided in § 416.1224;

(f) Resources of a blind or disabled individual which are necessary to fulfill an approved plan for achieving self-support as provided in § 416.1226;

(g) Stock in regional or village corporations held by natives of Alaska during the twenty-year period in which the stock is inalienable pursuant to the Alaska Native Claims Settlement Act (see § 416.1228);

(h) Life insurance owned by an individual (and spouse, if any) to the extent provided in § 416.1230;

(i) Restricted allotted Indian lands as provided in § 416.1234;

(j) Payments or benefits provided under a Federal statute other than title XVI of the Social Security Act where exclusion is required by such statute;

(k) Disaster relief assistance as provided in § 416.1237;

(l) Burial spaces and certain funds up to $1,500 for burial expenses as provided in § 416.1231;

(m) Title XVI or title II retroactive payments as provided in § 416.1233;

(n) Housing assistance as provided in § 416.1238;

(o) Refunds of Federal income taxes and advances made by an employer relating to an earned income tax credit, as provided in § 416.1235;

(p) Payments received as compensation for expenses incurred or losses suffered as a result of a crime as provided in § 416.1229;

(q) Relocation assistance from a State or local government as provided in § 416.1239;

(r) Dedicated financial institution accounts as provided in § 416.1247.

(s) Gifts to children under age 18 with life-threatening conditions as provided in § 416.1248;

(t) Restitution of title II, title VIII or title XVI benefits because of misuse by certain representative payees as provided in § 416.1249;

(u) Any portion of a grant, scholarship, fellowship, or gift used or set aside for paying tuition, fees, or other necessary educational expenses as provided in § 416.1250;

(v) Payment of a refundable child tax credit, as provided in § 416.1235; and

(w) Any annuity paid by a State to a person (or his or her spouse) based on the State's determination that the person is:

(1) A veteran (as defined in 38 U.S.C. 101); and

(2) Blind, disabled, or aged.

20 C.F.R. § 416.1212 Exclusion of the home.

(a) Defined. A home is any property in which an individual (and spouse, if any) has an ownership interest and which serves as the individual's principal place of residence. This property includes the shelter in which an individual resides, the land on which the shelter is located and related outbuildings.

(b) Home not counted. We do not count a home regardless of its value. However, see §§ 416.1220–416.1224 when there is an income-producing property located on the home property that does not qualify under the home exclusion.

(c) If an individual changes principal place of residence. If an individual (and spouse, if any) moves out of his or her home without the intent to return, the home becomes a countable resource because it is no longer the individual's principal place of residence. If an individual leaves his or her home to live in an institution, we still consider the home to be the individual's principal place of residence, irrespective of the individual's intent to return, as long as a spouse or dependent relative of the eligible individual continues to live there. The individual's equity in the former home becomes a countable resource effective with the first day of the month following the month it is no longer his or her principal place of residence.

(d) If an individual leaves the principal place of residence due to domestic abuse. If an individual moves out of his or her home without the intent to return, but is fleeing the home as a victim of domestic abuse, we will not count the home as a resource in determining the individual's eligibility to receive, or continue to receive, SSI payments. In that situation, we will consider the home to be the individual's principal place of residence until such time as the individual establishes a new principal place of residence or otherwise takes action rendering the home no longer excludable.

(e) Proceeds from the sale of an excluded home.

(1) The proceeds from the sale of a home which is excluded from the individual's resources will also be excluded from resources to the extent they are intended to be used and are, in fact, used to purchase another home, which is similarly excluded, within 3 months of the date of receipt of the proceeds.

(2) The value of a promissory note or similar installment sales contract constitutes a "proceed" which can be excluded from resources if—

(i) The note results from the sale of an individual's home as described in § 416.1212(a);

(ii) Within 3 months of receipt (execution) of the note, the individual purchases a replacement home as described in § 416.1212(a) (see paragraph (e) of this section for an exception); and

(iii) All note-generated proceeds are reinvested in the replacement home within 3 months of receipt (see paragraph (f) of this section for an exception).

(3) In addition to excluding the value of the note itself, other proceeds from the sale of the former home are excluded resources if they are used within 3 months of receipt to make payment on the replacement home. Such proceeds, which consist of the downpayment and that portion of any installment amount constituting payment against the principal, represent a conversion of a resource.

(f) Failure to purchase another excluded home timely. If the individual does not purchase a replacement home within the 3–month period specified in paragraph (d)(2)(ii) of this section, the value of a promissory note or similar installment sales contract received from the sale of an excluded home is a countable resource effective with the first moment of the month following the month the note is executed. If the individual purchases a replacement home after the expiration of the 3–month period, the note becomes an excluded resource the month following the month of purchase of the replacement home provided that all other proceeds are fully and timely reinvested as explained in paragraph (f) of this section.

(g) Failure to reinvest proceeds timely.

(1) If the proceeds (e.g., installment amounts constituting payment against the principal) from the sale of an excluded home under a promissory note or similar installment sales contract are not reinvested fully and timely (within 3 months of receipt) in a replacement home, as of the first moment of the month following receipt of the payment, the individual's countable resources will include:

(i) The value of the note; and

(ii) That portion of the proceeds, retained by the individual, which was not timely reinvested.

(2) The note remains a countable resource until the first moment of the month following the receipt of proceeds that are fully and timely reinvested in the replacement home. Failure to reinvest proceeds for a period of time does not permanently preclude exclusion of the promissory note or installment sales contract. However, previously received proceeds that were not timely reinvested remain countable resources to the extent they are retained.

Example 1. On July 10, an SSI recipient received his quarterly payment of $200 from the buyer of his former home under an installment sales contract. As of October 31, the recipient has used only $150 of the July payment in connection with the purchase of a new home. The exclusion of the unused $50 (and of the installment contract itself) is revoked back to July 10. As a result, the $50 and the value of the contract as of August 1, are included in a revised determination of resources for August and subsequent months.

* * *

(h) Interest payments. If interest is received as part of an installment payment resulting from the sale of an excluded home under a promissory note or similar installment sales contract, the interest payments do not represent conversion of a resource. The interest is income under the provisions of §§ 416.1102, 416.1120, and 416.1121(c).

20 C.F.R. § 416.1216 Exclusion of household goods and personal effects.

a) Household goods.

(1) We do not count household goods as a resource to an individual (and spouse, if any) if they are:

(i) Items of personal property, found in or near the home, that are used on a regular basis; or

(ii) Items needed by the householder for maintenance, use and occupancy of the premises as a home.

(2) Such items include but are not limited to: Furniture, appliances, electronic equipment such as personal computers and television sets, carpets, cooking and eating utensils, and dishes.

(b) Personal effects.

(1) We do not count personal effects as resources to an individual (and spouse, if any) if they are:

(i) Items of personal property ordinarily worn or carried by the individual; or

(ii) Articles otherwise having an intimate relation to the individual.

(2) Such items include but are not limited to: Personal jewelry including wedding and engagement rings, personal care items, prosthetic devices, and educational or recreational items such as books or musical instruments. We also do not count as resources items of cultural or religious significance to an individual and items required because of an individual's impairment. However, we do count items that were acquired or are held for their value or as an investment because we do not consider these to be personal effects. Such items can include but are not limited to: Gems, jewelry that is not worn or held for family significance, or collectibles. Such items will be subject to the limits in § 416.1205.

20 C.F.R. § 416.1218 Exclusion of the automobile.

(a) Automobile; defined. As used in this section, the term automobile includes, in addition to passenger cars, other vehicles used to provide necessary transportation.

(b) Limitation on automobiles. In determining the resources of an individual (and spouse, if any), automobiles are excluded or counted as follows:

(1) Total exclusion. One automobile is totally excluded regardless of value if it is used for transportation for the individual or a member of the individual's household.

(2) Other automobiles. Any other automobiles are considered to be nonliquid resources. Your equity in the other automobiles is counted as a resource. (See § 416.1201(c).)

20 C.F.R § 416.1220 Property essential to self-support; general.

When counting the value of resources an individual (and spouse, if any) has, the value of property essential to self-support is not counted, within certain limits. There are different rules for considering this property depending on whether it is income-producing or not. Property essential to self-support can include real and personal property (for example, land, buildings, equipment and supplies, motor vehicles, and tools, etc.) used in a trade or business (as defined in § 404.1066 of Part 404), non-business income-producing property (houses or apartments for rent, land other than home property, etc.) and property used to produce goods or services essential to an individual's daily activities. Liquid resources other than those used as part of a trade or business are not property essential to self-support. If the individual's principal place of residence qualifies under the home exclusion, it is not considered in evaluating property essential to self-support.

20 C.F.R. § 416.1222 How income-producing property essential to self-support is counted.

(a) General. When deciding the value of property used in a trade or business or nonbusiness income-producing activity, only the individual's equity in the property is counted. We will exclude as essential to self-support up to $6,000 of an individual's equity in income-producing property if it produces a net annual income to the individual of at least 6 percent of the excluded equity. If the individual's equity is greater than $6,000, we count only the amount that exceeds $6,000 toward the allowable resource limit specified in § 416.1205 if the net annual income requirement of 6 percent is met on the excluded equity. If the activity produces less than a 6–percent return due to circumstances beyond the individual's control (for example, crop failure, illness, etc.), and there is a reasonable expectation that the individual's activity will again produce a 6–percent return, the property is also excluded. If the individual owns more than one piece of property and each produces income, each is looked at to see if the 6–percent rule is met and then the amounts of the individual's equity in all of those properties producing 6 percent are totaled to see if the total equity is $6,000 or less. The equity in those properties that do not meet the 6–percent rule is counted towards the allowable resource limit specified in § 416.1205. If the individual's total equity in the properties producing 6–percent income is over the $6,000 equity limit, the amount of equity exceeding $6,000 is counted as a resource towards the allowable resource limit.

* * *

Example 2. Charlotte operates a farm. She owns 3 acres of land on which her home is located. She also owns 10 acres of farm land not connected to her home. There are 2 tool sheds and 2 animal shelters located on the 10 acres. She has various pieces of farm equipment that are necessary for her farming activities. We exclude the house and the 3 acres under the home exclusion (see§ 416.1212). However, we look at the other 10 acres of land, the buildings and equipment separately to see if her total equity in them is no more than $6,000 and if the annual rate of return is

6 percent of her equity. In this case, the 10 acres and buildings are valued at $4,000 and the few items of farm equipment and other inventory are valued at $1,500. Charlotte sells produce which nets her more than 6 percent for this year. The 10 acres and other items are excluded as essential to her self-support and they continue to be excluded as long as she meets the 6–percent annual return requirement and the equity value of the 10 acres and other items remains less than $6,000.

* * *

(b) Exception. Property that represents the authority granted by a governmental agency to engage in an income-producing activity is excluded as property essential to self-support if it is:

    (1) Used in a trade or business or nonbusiness income-producing activity, or,

    (2) Not used due to circumstances beyond the individual's control, e.g., illness, and there is a reasonable expectation that the use will resume.

Example. John owns a commercial fishing permit granted by the State Commerce Commission, a boat, and fishing tackle. The boat and tackle have an equity value of $6,500. Last year, John earned $2,000 from his fishing business. The value of the fishing permit is not determined because the permit is excluded under the exception. The boat and tackle are producing in excess of a 6 percent return on the excluded equity value, so they are excluded under the general rule (see paragraph (a) of this section) up to $6,000. The $500 excess value is counted toward the resource limit as described in § 416.1205.

20 C.F.R. § 416.1224 How nonbusiness property used to produce goods or services essential to self-support is counted.

Nonbusiness property is considered to be essential for an individual's (and spouse, if any) self-support if it is used to produce goods or services necessary for his or her daily activities. This type of property includes real property such as land which is used to produce vegetables or livestock only for personal consumption in the individual's household (for example, corn, tomatoes, chicken, cattle). This type of property also includes personal property necessary to perform daily functions exclusive of passenger cars, trucks, boats, or other special vehicles. (See § 416.1218 for a discussion on how automobiles are counted.) Property used to produce goods or services or property necessary to perform daily functions is excluded if the individual's equity in the property does not exceed $6,000. Personal property which is required by the individual's employer for work is not counted, regardless of value, while the individual is employed. Examples of this type of personal property include tools, safety equipment, uniforms and similar items.

Example. Bill owns a small unimproved lot several blocks from his home. He uses the lot, which is valued at $4,800, to grow vegetables and fruit only for his own consumption. Since his equity in the property is less than $6,000, the property is excluded as necessary to self-support.

Appendix 2 To Subpart P of Part 404—Medical–Vocational Guidelines, 20 C.F.R. Pt. 404, Subpt. P, App. 2.

200.00 Introduction. (a) The following rules reflect the major functional and vocational patterns which are encountered in cases which cannot be evaluated on medical considerations alone, where an individual with a severe medically determinable physical or mental impairment(s) is not engaging in substantial gainful activity and the individual's impairment(s) prevents the performance of his or her vocationally relevant past work. They also reflect the analysis of the various vocational factors (i.e., age, education, and work experience) in combination with the individual's residual functional capacity (used to determine his or her maximum sustained work capability for sedentary, light, medium, heavy, or very heavy work) in evaluating the individual's ability to engage in substantial gainful activity in other than his or her vocationally relevant past work. Where the findings of fact made with respect to a particular individual's vocational factors and residual functional capacity coincide with all of the criteria of a particular rule, the rule directs a conclusion as to whether the individual is or is not disabled. However, each of these findings of fact is subject to rebuttal and the individual may present evidence to refute such findings. Where any one of the findings of fact does not coincide with the corresponding criterion of a rule, the rule does not apply in that particular case and, accordingly, does not direct a conclusion of disabled or not disabled. In any instance where a rule does not apply, full consideration must be given to all of the relevant facts of the case in accordance with the definitions and discussions of each factor in the appropriate sections of the regulations.

(b) The existence of jobs in the national economy is reflected in the Decisions shown in the rules; i.e., in promulgating the rules, administrative notice has been taken of the numbers of unskilled jobs that exist throughout the national economy at the various functional levels (sedentary, light, medium, heavy, and very heavy) as supported by the Dictionary of Occupational Titles and the Occupational Outlook Handbook, published by the Department of Labor; the County Business Patterns and Census Surveys published by the Bureau of the Census; and occupational surveys of light and sedentary jobs prepared for the Social Security Administration by various State employment agencies. Thus, when all factors coincide with the criteria of a rule, the existence of such jobs is established. However, the existence of such jobs for individuals whose remaining functional capacity or other factors do not coincide with the criteria of a rule must be further considered in terms of what kinds of jobs or types of work may be either additionally indicated or precluded.

(c) In the application of the rules, the individual's residual functional capacity (i.e., the maximum degree to which the individual retains the capacity for sustained performance of the physical-mental requirements of jobs), age, education, and work experience must first be determined. When assessing the person's residual functional capacity, the Board considers his or her symptoms (such as pain), signs, and laboratory findings together with other evidence the Board obtains.

(d) The correct disability decision (i.e., on the issue of ability to engage in substantial gainful activity) is found by then locating the individual's specific vocational profile. If an individual's specific profile is not listed within this Appendix 2, a conclusion of disabled or not disabled is not directed. Thus, for example, an individual's ability to engage in substantial gainful work where his or her residual functional capacity falls between the ranges of work indicated in the rules (e.g., the individual who can perform more than light but less than medium work), is decided on the basis of the principles and definitions in the regulations, giving consideration to the rules for specific case situations in this appendix 2. These rules represent various combinations of exertional capabilities, age, education and work experience and also provide an overall structure for evaluation of those cases in which the judgments as to each factor do not coincide with those of any specific rule. Thus, when the necessary judgments have been made as to each factor and it is found that no specific rule applies, the rules still provide guidance for decisionmaking, such as in cases involving combinations of impairments. For example, if strength limitations resulting from an individual's impairment(s) considered with the judgments made as to the individual's age, education and work experience correspond to (or closely approximate) the factors of a particular rule, the adjudicator then has a frame of reference for considering the jobs or types of work precluded by other, nonexertional impairments in terms of numbers of jobs remaining for a particular individual.

(e) Since the rules are predicated on an individual's having an impairment which manifests itself by limitations in meeting the strength requirements of jobs, they may not be fully applicable where the nature of an individual's impairment does not result in such limitations, e.g., certain mental, sensory, or skin impairments. In addition, some impairments may result solely in postural and manipulative limitations or environmental restrictions. Environmental restrictions are those restrictions which result in inability to tolerate some physical feature(s) of work settings that occur in certain industries or types of work, e.g., an inability to tolerate dust or fumes.

(1) In the evaluation of disability where the individual has solely a nonexertional type of impairment, determination as to whether disability exists shall be based on the principles in the appropriate sections of the regulations, giving consideration to the rules for specific case situations in this appendix 2. The rules do not direct factual conclusions of disabled or not disabled for individuals with solely nonexertional types of impairments.

(2) However, where an individual has an impairment or combination of impairments resulting in both strength limitations and nonexertional limitations, the rules in this subpart are considered in determining first whether a finding of disabled may be possible based on the strength limitations alone and, if not, the rule(s) reflecting the individual's maximum residual strength capabilities, age, education, and work experience provide a framework for consideration of how much the individual's work capability is further diminished in terms of any types of jobs that would be contraindicated by the nonexertional limitations. Also, in these combinations of nonexertional and exertional limitations which cannot be wholly determined under the rules in this appendix 2, full consideration must be given to all of the relevant facts in the case in accordance with the definitions and discussions of each factor in the appropriate sections of the regulations, which will provide insight into the adjudicative weight to be accorded each factor.

201.00 Maximum sustained work capability limited to sedentary work as a result of severe medically determinable impairment(s). (a) Most sedentary occupations fall within the skilled, semi-skilled, professional, administrative, technical, clerical, and benchwork classifications. Approximately 200 separate unskilled sedentary occupations can be identified, each representing numerous jobs in the national economy. Approximately 85 percent of these jobs are in the machine trades and benchwork occupational categories. These jobs (unskilled sedentary occupations) may be performed after a short demonstration or within 30 days.

(b) These unskilled sedentary occupations are standard within the industries in which they exist. While sedentary work represents a significantly restricted range of work, this range in itself is not so prohibitively restricted as to negate work capability for substantial gainful activity.

(c) Vocational adjustment to sedentary work may be expected where the individual has special skills or experience relevant to sedentary work or where age and basic educational competences provide sufficient occupational mobility to adapt to the major segment of unskilled sedentary work. Inability to engage in substantial gainful activity would be indicated where an individual who is restricted to sedentary work because of a severe medically determinable impairment lacks special skills or experience relevant to sedentary work, lacks educational qualifications relevant to most sedentary work (e.g., has a limited education or less) and the individual's age, though not necessarily advanced, is a factor which significantly limits vocational adaptability.

(d) The adversity of functional restrictions to sedentary work at advanced age (55 and over) for individuals with no relevant past work or who can no longer perform vocationally relevant past work and have no transferable skills, warrants a finding of disabled in the the absence of the rare situation where the individual has recently completed education which provides a basis for direct entry into skilled sedentary work. Advanced age and a history of unskilled work or no work experience would ordinarily offset any vocational advantages that might accrue by reason of any remote past education, whether it is more or less than limited education.

(e) The presence of acquired skills that are readily transferable to a significant range of skilled work within an individual's residual functional capacity would ordinarily warrant a finding of ability to engage in substantial gainful activity regardless of the adversity of age, or whether the individual's formal education is commensurate with his or her demonstrated skill level. The acquisition of work skills demonstrates the ability to perform work at the level of complexity demonstrated by the skill level attained regardless of the individual's formal educational attainments.

(f) In order to find transferability of skills to skilled sedentary work for individuals who are of advanced age (55 and over), there must be very little, if any, vocational adjustment required in terms of tools, work processes, work settings, or the industry.

(g) Individuals approaching advanced age (age 50–54) may be significantly limited in vocational adaptability if they are restricted to sedentary work. When such individuals have no past work experience or can no longer perform vocationally relevant past work and have no transferable skills, a finding of disabled ordinarily obtains. However, recently completed education which provides for direct entry into sedentary work will preclude such a finding. For this age group, even a high school education or more (ordinarily completed in the remote past) would have little impact for effecting a vocational adjustment unless relevant work experience reflects use of such education.

(h) The term younger individual is used to denote an individual age 18 through 49. For those within this group who are age 45–49, age is a less positive factor than for those who are age 18–44. Accordingly, for such individuals; (1) who are restricted to sedentary work, (2) who are unskilled or have no transferable skills, (3) who have no relevant past work or who can no longer perform vocationally relevant past work, and (4) who are either illiterate or unable to communicate in the English language, a finding of disabled is warranted. On the other hand, age is a more positive factor for those who are under age 45 and is usually not a significant factor in limiting such an individual's ability to make a vocational adjustment, even an adjustment to unskilled sedentary work, and even where the individual is illiterate or unable to communicate in English. However, a finding of disabled is not precluded for those individuals under age 45 who do not meet all of the criteria of a specific rule and who do not have the ability to perform a full range of sedentary work. The following examples are illustrative: Example 1: An individual under age 45 with a high school education can no longer do past work and is restricted to unskilled sedentary jobs because of a severe medically determinable cardiovascular impairment (which does not meet or equal the listings in appendix 1). A permanent injury of the right hand limits the individual to sedentary jobs which do not require bilateral manual dexterity. None of the rules in appendix 2 are applicable to this particular set of facts, because this individual cannot perform the full range of work defined as sedentary. Since the inability to perform jobs requiring bilateral manual dexterity significantly compromises the only range of work for which the individual is otherwise qualified (i.e., sedentary), a finding of disabled would be appropriate. Example 2: An illiterate 41 year old individual with mild mental retardation (IQ of 78) is restricted to unskilled sedentary work and cannot perform vocationally relevant past work, which had consisted of unskilled agricultural field work; his or her particular characteristics do not specifically meet any of the rules in appendix 2, because this individual cannot perform the full range of work defined as sedentary. In light of the adverse factors which further narrow the range of sedentary work for which this individual is qualified, a finding of disabled is appropriate.

(i) While illiteracy or the inability to communicate in English may significantly limit an individual's vocational scope, the primary work functions in the bulk of unskilled work relate to working with things (rather than with data or people) and in these work functions at the unskilled level, literacy or ability to communicate in English has the least significance. Similarly the lack of relevant work experience would have little significance since the bulk of unskilled jobs require no qualifying work experience. Thus, the functional capability for a full range of sedentary work represents sufficient numbers of jobs to indicate substantial vocational scope for those individuals age 18–44 even if they are illiterate or unable to communicate in English.

Table No. 1—Residual Functional Capacity: Maximum Sustained Work Capability Limited to Sedentary Work as a Result of Severe Medically Determinable Impairment(s)

Rule	Age	Education	Previous work experience	Decision
201.01	Advanced age	Limited or less	Unskilled or none	Disabled
201.02	......do	......do	Skilled or semiskilled—skills not transferable [1]	Do.
201.03	......do	......do	Skilled or semiskilled—skills transferable [1]	Not disabled
201.04	......do	High school graduate or more—does not provide for direct entry into skilled work [2]	Unskilled or none	Disabled
201.05	......do	High school graduate or more—provides for direct entry into skilled work [2]	......do	Not disabled
201.06	......do	High school graduate or more—does not provide for direct entry into skilled work [2]	Skilled or semiskilled—skills not transferable [1]	Disabled
201.07	......do	......do	Skilled or semiskilled—skills transferable [1]	Not disabled
201.08	......do	High school graduate or more—provides for direct entry into skilled work [2]	Skilled or semiskilled—skills not transferable [1]	Do.
201.09	Closely approaching advanced age	Limited or less	Unskilled or none	Disabled
201.10	......do	......do	Skilled or semiskilled—skills not transferable	Do.
201.11	......do	......do	Skilled or semiskilled—skills transferable	Not disabled
201.12	......do	High school graduate or more—does not provide for direct entry into skilled work [3]	Unskilled or none	Disabled
201.13	......do	High school graduate or more—provides for direct entry into skilled work [3]	......do	Not disabled
201.14	......do	High school graduate or more—does not provide for direct entry into skilled work [3]	Skilled or semiskilled—skills not transferable	Disabled
201.15	......do	......do	Skilled or semiskilled—skills transferable	Not disabled
201.16	......do	High school graduate or more—provides for direct entry into skilled work [3]	Skilled or semiskilled—skills not transferable	Do.
201.17	Younger individual age 45-49	Illiterate or unable to communicate in English	Unskilled or none	Disabled
201.18	......do	Limited or less—at least literate and able to communicate in English	......do	Not disabled
201.19	......do	Limited or less	Skilled or semiskilled—skills not transferable	Do.
201.20	......do	......do	Skilled or semiskilled—skills transferable	Do.
201.21	......do	High school graduate or more	Skilled or semiskilled—skills not transferable	Do.
201.22	......do	,.....do	Skilled or semiskilled—skills transferable	Do.
201.23	Younger individual	Illiterate or unable to communicate in	Unskilled or none	Do. [4]

Rule	Age	Education	Previous work experience	Decision
	age 18-44	English		
201.24	......do	Limited or less—at least literate and able to communicate in English	......do	Do.[4]
201.25	......do	Limited or less	Skilled or semiskilled—skills not transferable	Do.[4]
201.26	......do	......do	Skilled or semiskilled—skills transferable	Do.[4]
201.27	......do	High school graduate or more	Unskilled or none	Do.[4]
201.28	......do	......do	Skilled or semiskilled—skills not transferable	Do.[4]
201.29	......do	......do	Skilled or semiskilled—skills transferable	Do.[4]

202.00 Maximum sustained work capability limited to light work as a result of severe medically determinable impairment(s). (a) The functional capacity to perform a full range of light work includes the functional capacity to perform sedentary as well as light work. Approximately 1,600 separate sedentary and light unskilled occupations can be identified in eight broad occupational categories, each occupation representing numerous jobs in the national economy. These jobs can be performed after a short demonstration or within 30 days, and do not require special skills or experience.

(b) The functional capacity to perform a wide or full range of light work represents substantial work capability compatible with making a work adjustment to substantial numbers of unskilled jobs and, thus, generally provides sufficient occupational mobility even for severely impaired individuals who are not of advanced age and have sufficient educational competences for unskilled work.

(c) However, for individuals of advanced age who can no longer perform vocationally relevant past work and who have a history of unskilled work experience, or who have only skills that are not readily transferable to a significant range of semi-skilled or skilled work that is within the individual's functional capacity, or who have no work experience, the limitations in vocational adaptability represented by functional restriction to light work warrant a finding of disabled. Ordinarily, even a high school education or more which was completed in the remote past will have little positive impact on effecting a vocational adjustment unless relevant work experience reflects use of such education.

(d) Where the same factors in paragraph (c) of this section regarding education and work experience are present, but where age, though not advanced, is a factor which significantly limits vocational adaptability (i.e., closely approaching advanced age, 50–54) and an individual's vocational scope is further significantly limited by illiteracy or inability to communicate in English, a finding of disabled is warranted.

(e) The presence of acquired skills that are readily transferable to a significant range of semi-skilled or skilled work within an individual's residual functional capacity would ordinarily warrant a finding of not disabled regardless of the adversity of age, or whether the individual's formal education is commensurate with his or her demonstrated skill level. The acquisition of work skills demonstrates the ability to perform work at the level of complexity demonstrated by the skill level attained regardless of the individual's formal educational attainments.

(f) For a finding of transferability of skills to light work for individuals of advanced age who are closely approaching retirement age (age 60–64), there must be very little, if any, vocational adjustment required in terms of tools, work processes, work settings, or the industry.

(g) While illiteracy or the inability to communicate in English may significantly limit an individual's vocational scope, the primary work functions in the bulk of unskilled work relate to working with things (rather than with data or people) and in these work functions at the unskilled level, literacy or ability to communicate in English has the least significance. Similarly, the lack of relevant work experience would have little significance since the bulk of unskilled jobs require no qualifying work experience. The capability for light work, which includes the ability to do sedentary work, represents the capability for substantial numbers of such jobs. This, in turn, represents substantial vocational scope for younger individuals (age 18–49) even if illiterate or unable to communicate in English.

Table No. 2—Residual Functional Capacity: Maximum Sustained Work Capability Limited to Light Work as a Result of Severe Medically Determinable Impairment(s)

Rule	Age	Education	Previous work experience	Decision
202.01	Advanced age	Limited or less	Unskilled or none	Disabled.
202.02	......do	......do	Skilled or semiskilled—skills not transferable	Do.
202.03	......do	......do	Skilled or semiskilled—skills transferable [1]	Not disabled.
202.04	......do	High school graduate or more—does not provide for direct entry into skilled work [2]	Unskilled or none	Disabled.
202.05	......do	High school graduate or more—provides for direct entry into skilled work [2]	......do	Not disabled.
202.06	......do	High school graduate or more—does not provide for direct entry into skilled work [2]	Skilled or semiskilled—skills not transferable	Disabled.
202.07	......do	......do	Skilled or semiskilled—skills transferable [2]	Not disabled.

Rule	Age	Education	Previous work experience	Decision
202.08	......do	High school graduate or more—provides for direct entry into skilled work [2]	Skilled or semiskilled—skills not transferable	Do.
202.09	Closely approaching advanced age	Illiterate or unable to communicate in English	Unskilled or none	Disabled.
202.10	......do	Limited or less—at least literate and able to communicate in English	......do	Not disabled.
202.11	......do	Limited or less	Skilled or semiskilled—skills not transferable	Do.
202.12	......do	......do	Skilled or semiskilled—skills transferable	Do.
202.13	......do	High school graduate or more	Unskilled or none	Do.
202.14	......do	......do	Skilled or semiskilled—skills not transferable	Do.
202.15	......do	......do	Skilled or semiskilled—skills transferable	Do.
202.16	Younger individual	Illiterate or unable to communicate in English	Unskilled or none	Do.
202.17	......do	Limited or less—at least literate and able to communicate in English	......do	Do.
202.18	......do	Limited or less	Skilled or semiskilled—skills not transferable	Do.
202.19	......do	......do	Skilled or semiskilled—skills transferable	Do.
202.20	......do	High school graduate or more	Unskilled or none	Do.
202.21	......do	......do	Skilled or semiskilled—skills not transferable	Do.
202.22	......do	......do	Skilled or semiskilled—skills transferable	Do.

203.00 Maximum sustained work capability limited to medium work as a result of severe medically determinable impairment(s). (a) The functional capacity to perform medium work includes the functional capacity to perform sedentary, light, and medium work. Approximately 2,500 separate sedentary, light, and medium occupations can be identified, each occupation representing numerous jobs in the national economy which do not require skills or previous experience and which can be performed after a short demonstration or within 30 days.

(b) The functional capacity to perform medium work represents such substantial work capability at even the unskilled level that a finding of disabled is ordinarily not warranted in cases where a severely impaired individual retains the functional capacity to perform medium work. Even the adversity of advanced age (55 or over) and a work history of unskilled work may be offset by the substantial work capability represented by the functional capacity to perform medium work. However, an individual with a marginal education and long work experience (i.e., 35 years or more) limited to the performance of arduous unskilled labor, who is not working and is no longer able to perform this labor because of a severe impairment(s), may still be found disabled even though the individual is able to do medium work.

(c) However, the absence of any relevant work experience becomes a more significant adversity for individuals of advanced age (55 and over). Accordingly, this factor, in combination with a limited education or less, militates against making a vocational adjustment to even this substantial range of work and a finding of disabled is appropriate. Further, for individuals closely approaching retirement age (60–64) with a work history of unskilled work and with marginal education or less, a finding of disabled is appropriate.

Table No. 3—Residual Functional Capacity: Maximum Sustained Work Capability Limited to Medium Work as a Result of Severe Medically Determinable Impairment(s)

Rule	Age	Education	Previous work experience	Decision
203.01	Closely approaching retirement age	Marginal or none	Unskilled or none	Disabled.
203.02	......do	Limited or less	None	Do.
203.03	......do	Limited	Unskilled	Not disabled.
203.04	......do	Limited or less	Skilled or semiskilled—skills not transferable	Do.
203.05	......do	......do	Skilled or semiskilled—skills transferable	Do.
203.06	......do	High school graduate or more	Unskilled or none	Do.
203.07	......do	High school graduate or more—does not provide for direct entry into skilled work	Skilled or semiskilled—skills not transferable	Do.
203.08	......do	......do	Skilled or semiskilled—skills transferable	Do.
203.09	......do	High school graduate or more—provides for direct entry into skilled work	Skilled or semiskilled—skills not transferable	Do.
203.10	Advanced age	Limited or less	None	Disabled.
203.11	......do	......do	Unskilled	Not disabled.
203.12	......do	......do	Skilled or semiskilled—skills not transferable	Do.
203.13	......do	......do	Skilled or semiskilled—skills transferable	Do.
203.14	......do	High school graduate or more	Unskilled or none	Do.
203.15	......do	High school graduate or more—does not provide for direct entry into skilled work	Skilled or semiskilled—skills not transferable	Do.
203.16	......do	......do	Skilled or semiskilled—skills transferable	Do.
203.17	......do	High school graduate or more—provides for direct entry into skilled work	Skilled or semiskilled—skills not transferable	Do.
203.18	Closely approaching	Limited or less	Unskilled or none	Do.

Rule	Age	Education	Previous work experi-ence	Decision
	advanced age			
203.19	......do	......do	Skilled or semiskilled—skills not transferable	Do.
203.20	......do	......do	Skilled or semiskilled—skills transferable	Do.
203.21	......do	High school graduate or more	Unskilled or none	Do.
203.22	......do	High school graduate or more—does not provide for direct entry into skilled work	Skilled or semiskilled—skills not transferable	Do.
203.23	......do	......do	Skilled or semiskilled—skills transferable	Do.
203.24	......do	High school graduate or more—provides for direct entry into skilled work	Skilled or semiskilled—skills not transferable	Do.
203.25	Younger individual	Limited or less	Unskilled or none	Do.
203.26	......do	......do	Skilled or semiskilled—skills not transferable	Do.
203.27	......do	......do	Skilled or semiskilled—skills transferable	Do.
203.28	......do	High school graduate or more	Unskilled or none	Do.
203.29	......do	High school graduate or more—does not provide for direct entry into skilled work	Skilled or semiskilled—skills not transferable	Do.
203.30	......do	......do	Skilled or semiskilled—skills transferable	Do.
203.31	......do	High school graduate or more—provides for direct entry into skilled work	Skilled or semiskilled—skills not transferable	Do.

204.00 Maximum sustained work capability limited to heavy work (or very heavy work) as a result of severe medically determinable impairment(s). The residual functional capacity to perform heavy work or very heavy work includes the functional capability for work at the lesser functional levels as well, and represents substantial work capability for jobs in the national economy at all skill and physical demand levels. Individuals who retain the functional capacity to perform heavy work (or very heavy work) ordinarily will not have a severe impairment or will be able to do their past work—either of which would have already provided a basis for a decision of not disabled. Environmental restrictions ordinarily would not significantly affect the range of work existing in the national economy for individuals with the physical capability for heavy work (or very heavy work). Thus an impairment which does not preclude heavy work (or very heavy work) would not ordinarily be the primary reason for unemployment, and generally is sufficient for a finding of not disabled, even though age, education, and skill level of prior work experience may be considered adverse.

APPENDIX B

SELECTED SOCIAL SECURITY RULINGS

■ ■ ■

SOCIAL SECURITY RULING 03-2p (2003)

Policy Interpretation Ruling

TITLES II AND XVI: EVALUATING CASES INVOLVING REFLEX SYMPATHETIC DYSTROPHY SYNDROME/COMPLEX REGIONAL PAIN SYNDROME

* * *

Policy Interpretation

What Is RSDS/CRPS?

RSDS/CRPS is a chronic pain syndrome most often resulting from trauma to a single extremity. It can also result from diseases, surgery, or injury affecting other parts of the body. Even a minor injury can trigger RSDS/CRPS. The most common acute clinical manifestations include complaints of intense pain and findings indicative of autonomic dysfunction at the site of the precipitating trauma. Later, spontaneously occurring pain may be associated with abnormalities in the affected region involving the skin, subcutaneous tissue, and bone. It is characteristic of this syndrome that the degree of pain reported is out of proportion to the severity of the injury sustained by the individual. When left untreated, the signs and symptoms of the disorder may worsen over time.

* * *

What Are the Diagnostic Criteria for RSDS/CRPS?

A diagnosis of RSDS/CRPS requires the presence of complaints of persistent, intense pain that results in impaired mobility of the affected region. The complaints of pain are associated with:

- Swelling;

- Autonomic instability--seen as changes in skin color or texture, changes in sweating (decreased or excessive sweating), skin temperature changes, or abnormal pilomotor erection (gooseflesh);

- Abnormal hair or nail growth (growth can be either too slow or too fast);

- Osteoporosis; or

- Involuntary movements of the affected region of the initial injury.

* * *

How Is RSDS/CRPS Identified as a Medically Determinable Impairment?

RSDS/CRPS constitutes a medically determinable impairment when it is documented by appropriate medical signs, symptoms, and laboratory findings, as discussed above. RSDS/CRPS may be the basis for a finding of "disability." Disability may not be established on the basis of an individual's statement of symptoms alone.

For purposes of Social Security disability evaluation, RSDS/CRPS can be established in the presence of persistent complaints of pain that are typically out of proportion to the severity of any documented precipitant and one or more of the following clinically documented signs in the affected region at any time following the documented precipitant:

- Swelling;

- Autonomic instability--seen as changes in skin color or texture, changes in sweating (decreased or excessive sweating), changes in skin temperature, and abnormal pilomotor erection (gooseflesh);

- Abnormal hair or nail growth (growth can be either too slow or too fast);

- Osteoporosis; or

- Involuntary movements of the affected region of the initial injury.

When longitudinal treatment records document persistent limiting pain in an area where one or more of these abnormal signs has been documented at some point in time since the date of the precipitating injury, disability adjudicators can reliably determine that RSDS/CRPS is present and constitutes a medically determinable impairment. It may be noted in the treatment records that these signs are not present continuously, or the signs may be present at one examination and not appear at another.

Transient findings are characteristic of RSDS/CRPS, and do not affect a finding that a medically determinable impairment is present.

* * *

SOCIAL SECURITY RULING SSR 99-2p (1999)

TITLES II AND XVI: EVALUATING CASES INVOLVING CHRONIC FATIGUE SYNDROME (CFS)

* * *

This Ruling explains that CFS, when accompanied by appropriate medical signs or laboratory findings, is a medically determinable impairment that can be the basis for a finding of "disability." It also provides guidance for the evaluation of claims involving CFS.

POLICY INTERPRETATION:

CFS constitutes a medically determinable impairment when it is accompanied by medical signs or laboratory findings, as discussed below. CFS may be a disabling impairment.

DEFINITION OF CFS

CFS is a systemic disorder consisting of a complex of symptoms that may vary in incidence, duration, and severity. It is characterized in part by prolonged fatigue that lasts 6 months or more and that results in substantial reduction in previous levels of occupational, educational, social, or personal activities. In accordance with criteria established by the CDC, a physician should make a diagnosis of CFS "only after alternative medical and psychiatric causes of chronic fatiguing illness have been excluded" (Annals of Internal Medicine, 121:953-9, 1994). CFS has been diagnosed in children, particularly adolescents, as well as in adults.

Under the CDC definition, the hallmark of CFS is the presence of clinically evaluated, persistent or relapsing chronic fatigue that is of new or definite onset (i.e., has not been lifelong), cannot be explained by another physical or mental disorder, is not the result of ongoing exertion, is not substantially alleviated by rest, and results in substantial reduction in previous levels of occupational, educational, social, or personal activities. Additionally, the current CDC definition of CFS requires the concurrence of 4 or more of the following symptoms, all of which must have persisted or recurred during 6 or more consecutive months of illness and must not have pre-dated the fatigue:

Self-reported impairment in short-term memory or concentration severe enough to cause substantial reduction in previous levels of occupational, educational, social, or personal activities;

Sore throat;

Tender cervical or axillary lymph nodes;

Muscle pain;

Multi-joint pain without joint swelling or redness;

Headaches of a new type, pattern, or severity;

Unrefreshing sleep; and

Postexertional malaise lasting more than 24 hours.

Within these parameters, an individual with CFS can also exhibit a wide range of other manifestations, such as muscle weakness, swollen underarm (axillary) glands, sleep disturbances, visual difficulties (trouble focusing or severe photosensitivity), orthostatic intolerance (e.g.,light headedness or increased fatigue with prolonged standing), other neurocognitive problems (e.g., difficulty comprehending and processing information), fainting, dizziness, and mental problems (e.g., depression, irritability, anxiety).

* * *

ESTABLISHING THE EXISTENCE OF A MEDICALLY DETERMINABLE IMPAIRMENT

The following medical signs and laboratory findings establish the existence of a medically determinable impairment in individuals who have CFS. Although no specific etiology or pathology has yet been established for CFS, many research initiatives continue, and some progress has been made in ameliorating symptoms in selected individuals. With continuing scientific research, new medical evidence may emerge that will further clarify the nature of CFS and provide greater specificity regarding the clinical and laboratory diagnostic techniques that should be used to document this disorder.

Because of this, the medical criteria discussed below are only examples of signs and laboratory findings that will establish the existence of a medically determinable impairment; they are not all-inclusive. As progress is made in medical research into CFS, additional signs and laboratory findings may also be found that can be used to establish that individuals with CFS have a medically determinable impairment. The existence of CFS may be documented with medical signs or laboratory findings other than those listed below, provided that such documentation is consistent with medically accepted clinical practice and is consistent with the other evidence in the case record.

Examples of medical signs that establish the existence of a
medically determinable impairment

For purposes of Social Security disability evaluation, one or more of the following medical signs clinically documented over a period of at least 6 consecutive months establishes the existence of a medically determinable impairment for individuals with CFS:

Palpably swollen or tender lymph nodes on physical examination;

Nonexudative pharyngitis;

Persistent, reproducible muscle tenderness on repeated examinations, including the presence of positive tender points;[3] or,

Any other medical signs that are consistent with medically accepted clinical practice and are consistent with the other evidence in the case record.

Examples of laboratory findings that establish the existence of a
medically determinable impairment

At this time, there are no specific laboratory findings that are widely accepted as being associated with CFS. However, the absence of a definitive test does not preclude reliance upon certain laboratory findings to establish the existence of a medically determinable impairment in persons with CFS. Therefore, the following laboratory findings establish the existence of a medically determinable impairment in individuals with CFS:[4]

An elevated antibody titer to Epstein-Barr virus (EBV) capsid antigen equal to or greater than 1:5120, or early antigen equal to or greater than 1:640;

An abnormal magnetic resonance imaging (MRI) brain scan;

---

[3] There is considerable overlap of symptoms between CFS and Fibromyalgia Syndrome (FMS), but individuals with CFS who have tender points have a medically determinable impairment. Individuals with impairments that fulfill the American College of Rheumatology criteria for FMS (which includes a minimum number of tender points) may also fulfill the criteria for CFS. However, individuals with CFS who do not have the specified number of tender points to establish FMS, will still be found to have a medically determinable impairment.

[4] It should be noted that standard laboratory test results in the normal range are characteristic for many individuals with CFS, and should not be relied upon to the exclusion of all other clinical evidence in decisions regarding the presence and severity of a medically determinable impairment.

Neurally mediated hypotension as shown by tilt table testing or another clinically accepted form of testing; or,

Any other laboratory findings that are consistent with medically accepted clinical practice and are consistent with the other evidence in the case record; for example, an abnormal exercise stress test or abnormal sleep studies, appropriately evaluated and consistent with the other evidence in the case record.

MENTAL FINDINGS THAT ESTABLISH THE EXISTENCE OF A MEDICALLY DETERMINABLE IMPAIRMENT

Some individuals with CFS report ongoing problems with short-term memory, information processing, visual-spatial difficulties, comprehension, concentration, speech, word-finding, calculation, and other symptoms suggesting persistent neurocognitive impairment. When ongoing deficits in these areas have been documented by mental status examination or psychological testing, such findings constitute medical signs or (in the case of psychological testing) laboratory findings that establish the presence of a medically determinable impairment.

Individuals with CFS may also exhibit medical signs, such as anxiety or depression, indicative of the existence of a mental disorder. When such medical signs are present and appropriately documented, the existence of a medically determinable impairment is established.

* * *

DOCUMENTATION

General. As with all claims for disability under both title II and title XVI, documentation of medical signs or laboratory findings in cases involving CFS is critical to establishing the presence of a medically determinable impairment. In cases in which CFS is alleged, longitudinal clinical records reflecting ongoing medical evaluation and treatment from the individual's medical sources, especially treating sources, are extremely helpful in documenting the presence of any medical signs or laboratory findings, as well as the individual's functional status over time. Every reasonable effort should be made to secure all available, relevant evidence in cases involving CFS to ensure appropriate and thorough evaluation.

* * *

Assessing Credibility. In accordance with SSR 96-7p, if the existence of a medically determinable impairment that could reasonably be expected to produce the symptoms has been established, as outlined above, but an individual's statements about the intensity, persistence, or functionally limiting effects of symptoms are not substantiated by objective medical evidence, the adjudicator must consider all of the evidence in the case record, including any statements by the individual and other persons concerning the individual's symptoms. The adjudicator must then make a finding on the credibility of the individual's statements about symptoms and their functional effects. When additional information is needed to assess the credibility of the individual's statements about symptoms and their effects, the adjudicator must make every reasonable effort to obtain available information that could shed light on the credibility of the individual's statements.

Treating and other medical sources. In evaluating credibility, the adjudicator should ask the treating or other medical source(s) to provide information about the extent and duration of an individual's impairment(s), including observations and opinions about how well the individual is able to function, the effects of any treatment, including side effects, and how long the impairment(s) is expected to limit the individual's ability to function. Opinions from an individual's medical sources, especially treating sources, concerning the effects of CFS on the individual's ability to function in a sustained manner in performing work activities or in performing activities of daily living are important in enabling adjudicators to draw conclusions about the severity of the impairment(s) and the individual's RFC. In this regard, any information a medical source is able to provide contrasting the individual's impairment(s) and functional capacities since the alleged onset of CFS with the individual's status prior to the onset of CFS will be helpful in evaluating the individual's impairment(s) and its functional consequences.

Third-party information, including evidence from medical sources who are not acceptable medical sources for the purpose of establishing the existence of a medically determinable impairment, but who have provided services to the individual, may be very useful in deciding the individual's credibility. Information other than an individual's allegations and reports from the individual's treating sources helps to assess an individual's ability to function on a day-to-day basis and to depict the individual's capacities over a period of time. Such evidence includes, but is not limited to:

Information from neighbors, friends, relatives, or clergy;

Statements from such individuals as past employers, rehabilitation counselors, or school teachers about the individual's impairment(s) and the effects of the impairment(s) on the individual's functioning in the work place, rehabilitation facility, or educational institution;

Statements from other practitioners with knowledge of the individual, e.g., nurse-practitioners, physicians' assistants, naturopaths, therapists, social workers, and chiropractors;

Statements from other sources with knowledge of the individual's ability to function in daily activities; and

The individual's own record (such as a diary, journal, or notes) of his or her own impairment(s) and its impact on function over time.

The adjudicator should carefully consider this information when making findings about the credibility of the individual's allegations regarding functional limitations or restrictions.

SOCIAL SECURITY RULING 85-15, 1983-1991
Soc. Sec. Rep. Ser. 343 (1985)

TITLES II AND XVI: CAPABILITY TO DO OTHER WORK--THEMEDICAL-VOCATIONAL RULES AS A FRAMEWORK FOR EVALUATING SOLELY NONEXERTIONAL IMPAIRMENTS

* * *

PURPOSE: The original purpose of SSR 83-13 was to clarify how the regulations and the exertionally based numbered decisional rules in Appendix 2, Subpart P, Regulations No. 4, provide a framework for decisions concerning persons who have only a nonexertional limitation(s) of function or an environmental restriction(s). The purpose of this revision to SSR 83-13 and SSR 85-7 is to emphasize, in the sections relating to mental impairments: (1) that the potential job base for mentally ill claimants without adverse vocational factors is not necessarily large even for individuals who have no other impairments, unless their remaining mental capacities are sufficient to meet the intellectual and emotional demands of at least unskilled, competitive, remunerative work on a sustained basis; and (2) that a finding of disability can be appropriate for an individual who has a severe mental impairment which does not meet or equal the Listing of Impairments, even where he or she does not have adversities in age, education, or work experience.

* * *

Examples of Nonexertional Impairments and Their Effects on the Occupational Base

1. Mental Impairments

There has been some misunderstanding in the evaluation of mental impairments. Unless the claimant or beneficiary is a widow, widower, surviving divorced spouse or a disabled child under the Supplemental Security Income program, the sequential evaluation process mandated by the regulations does not end with the finding that the impairment, though severe, does not meet or equal an impairment listed in Appendix 1 of the regulations. The process must go on to consider whether the individual can meet the mental demands of past relevant work in spite of the limiting effects of his or her impairment and, if not, whether the person can do other work, considering his or her remaining mental capacities reflected in terms of the occupational base, age, education, and work experience. The decisionmaker must not assume that failure to meet or equal a listed mental impairment equates with capacity to do at least unskilled work. This decision requires careful consideration of the assessment of RFC.

In the world of work, losses of intellectual and emotional capacities are generally more serious when the job is complex. Mental impairments may or may not prevent the performance of a person's past jobs. They may or may not prevent an individual from transferring work skills. (See SSR 82-41, PPS-67, Work Skills and Their Transferability as Intended by the Expanded Vocational Factors Regulations effective February 26, 1979.)

Where a person's only impairment is mental, is not of listing severity, but does prevent the person from meeting the mental demands of past relevant work and prevents the transferability of acquired work skills, the final consideration is whether the person can be expected to perform unskilled work. The basic mental demands of competitive, remunerative, unskilled work include the abilities (on a sustained basis) to understand, carry out, and remember simple instructions; to respond appropriately to supervision, coworkers, and usual work situations; and to deal with changes in a routine work setting. A substantial loss of ability to meet any of these basic work-related activities would severely limit the potential occupational base. This, in turn, would justify a finding of disability because even favorable age, education, or work experience will not offset such a severely limited occupational base.

> Example 1: A person whose vocational factors of age, education, and work experience would ordinarily be considered favorable (i.e., very young age, university education, and highly skilled work experience) would have a severely limited occupational base if he or she has a mental impairment which causes a substantial loss of ability to respond appropriately to supervision, coworkers, and usual work situations. A finding of disability would be appropriate.

Where there is no exertional impairment, unskilled jobs at all levels of exertion constitute the potential occupational base for persons who can meet the mental demands of unskilled work. These jobs ordinarily involve dealing primarily with objects, rather than with data or people, and they generally provide substantial vocational opportunity for persons with solely mental impairments who retain the capacity to meet the intellectual and emotional demands of such jobs on a sustained basis. However, persons with this large job base may be found disabled because of adversities in age, education, and work experience. (This is illustrated in examples 2 and 3 immediately following.)

Example 2: Someone who is of advanced age, has a limited education, has no relevant work experience, and has more than a nonsevere mental impairment will generally be found disabled. (See SSR 82-63, PPS-79, Medical-Vocational Profiles Showing an Inability to Make an Adjustment to Other Work.)

Example 3: Someone who is closely approaching retirement age, has a limited education or less, worked for 30 years in a cafeteria doing an unskilled job as a "server," almost constantly dealing with the public, and now cannot, because of a severe mental impairment, frequently deal with the public. In light of the narrowed vocational opportunity in conjunction with the person's age, education, lack of skills, and long commitment to the particular type of work, a finding of disabled would be appropriate; but the decision would not necessarily be the same for a younger, better-educated, or skilled person. (Compare sections 404.1562 and 416.962 of the regulations and rule 203.01 of Appendix 2.)

Where a person has only a mental impairment but does not have extreme adversities in age, education, and work experience, and does not lack the capacity to do basic work-related activities, the potential occupational base would be reduced by his or her inability to perform certain complexities or particular kinds of work. These limitations would affect the occupational base in various ways.

Example 4: Someone who is of advanced age, has a high school education, and did skilled work as manager of a housing project can no longer, because of a severe mental impairment, develop and implement plans and procedures, prepare budget requests, schedule repairs or otherwise deal with complexities of this level and nature. Assuming that, in this case, all types of related skilled jobs are precluded but the individual can do work which is not detailed and does not require lengthy planning, the remaining related semiskilled jobs to which skills can be transferred and varied unskilled jobs, at all levels of exertion, constitute a significant vocational opportunity. A conclusion of "not disabled" would be appropriate. (Compare rules 201.07, 202.07, and 203.13 of Appendix 2.)

Example 5: Someone who is of advanced age, has a limited education, and did semiskilled work as a first-aid attendant no longer has the mental capacity to work with people who are in emergency situations and require immediate attention to cuts, burns, suffocation, etc. Although there may be very few related semiskilled occupations to which this person could transfer work skills, the large occupational base of unskilled work at all levels of exertion generally would justify a finding of not under a disability. (This is consistent with rules 203.11-203.17 of Appendix 2.)

<u>Stress and Mental Illness</u>—Since mental illness is defined and characterized by maladaptive behavior, it is not unusual that the mentally impaired have difficulty accommodating to the demands of work and work-like settings. Determining whether these individuals will be able to adapt to the demands or "stress" of the workplace is often extremely difficult. This section is not intended to set out any presumptive limitations for disorders, but to emphasize the importance of thoroughness in evaluation on an individualized basis.

Individuals with mental disorders often adopt a highly restricted and/or inflexible lifestyle within which they appear to function well. Good mental health services and care may enable chronic patients to function adequately in the community by lowering psychological pressures, by medication, and by support from services such as outpatient facilities, day-care programs, social work programs and similar assistance.

The reaction to the demands of work (stress) is highly individualized, and mental illness is characterized by adverse responses to seemingly trivial circumstances. The mentally impaired may cease to function effectively when facing such demands as getting to work regularly, having their performance supervised, and remaining in the workplace for a full day. A person may become panicked and develop palpitations, shortness of breath, or feel faint while riding in an elevator; another may experience terror and begin to hallucinate when approached by a stranger asking a question. Thus, the mentally impaired may have difficulty meeting the requirements of even so-called "low-stress" jobs.

Because response to the demands of work is highly individualized, the skill level of a position is not necessarily related to the difficulty an individual will have in meeting the demands of the job. A claimant's condition may make performance of an unskilled job as difficult as an objectively more demanding job. For example, a busboy need only clear dishes from tables. But an individual with a severe mental disorder may find unmanageable the demands of making sure that he removes all the dishes, does not drop them, and gets the table cleared promptly for the waiter or waitress. Similarly, an individual who cannot tolerate being supervised may not be able to work even in the absence of close supervision; the *knowledge* that one's work is being judged and evaluated, even when the supervision is remote or indirect, can be intolerable for some mentally impaired persons. Any impairment related limitations created by an individual's response to demands of work, however, must be reflected in the RFC assessment.

* * *

SOCIAL SECURITY RULING SSR 85-16, 1983-1991
Soc. Sec. Rep. Ser. 352 (1985)

TITLES II AND XVI: RESIDUAL FUNCTIONAL CAPACITY FOR MENTAL IMPAIRMENTS

* * *

PURPOSE: To state the policy and describe the issues to be considered when an individual with a mental impairment requires an assessment of the residual functional capacity (RFC) in order to determine the individual's capacity to engage in basic work-related activities.

* * *

INTRODUCTION: An individual whose impairment(s) meets, or is medically equivalent to, the requirements of an impairment(s) contained in the Listing of Impairments is considered unable to function adequately in work-related activities. On the other hand, an individual whose impairment is found to be not severe is considered not to be significantly restricted in the ability to engage in basic work-related activities. An individual whose impairment(s) falls between these two levels has a significant restriction in the ability to engage in some basic work-related activities. It is, therefore, necessary to determine the RFC for these individuals. This policy statement provides guides for the determination of RFC for individuals whose mental impairment(s) does not meet or equal the listing, but is more than not severe.

POLICY STATEMENT:

Importance of RFC Assessments in Mental Disorders

Medically determinable mental disorders present a variable continuum of symptoms and effects, from minor emotional problems to bizarre and dangerous behavior. However, in determining the impact of a mental disorder on an individual's capacities, essentially the same impairment-related medical and nonmedical information is considered to determine whether the mental disorder meets listing severity as is considered to determine whether the mental impairment is of lesser severity, yet diminishes the individual's RFC. For impairments of listing severity, inability to perform substantial gainful activity (SGA) is presumed from prescribed findings. However, with mental impairments of lesser severity, such inability must be demonstrated through a detailed assessment of the individual's capacity to perform and sustain mental activities which are critical to work performance. Conclusions of ability to engage in SGA are not to be inferred merely from the fact that the mental disorder is not of listing severity.

[20 C.F.R. § 404.1545(c)] presents the broad issues to be considered in the evaluation of RFC in mental disorders. It states that this evaluation includes consideration of the ability to understand, to carry out and remember instructions, and to respond appropriately to supervision, coworkers, and customary work pressures in a work setting. Consideration of these factors, which are contained in section 12.00 of the Listing of Impairments in Appendix 1, is required for the proper evaluation of the severity of mental impairments.

The determination of mental RFC involves the consideration of evidence, such as:

- History, findings, and observations from medical sources (including psychological test results), regarding the presence, frequency, and intensity of hallucinations, delusions or paranoid tendencies; depression or elation; confusion or disorientation; conversion symptoms or phobias; psychophysiological symptoms; withdrawn or bizarre behavior; anxiety or tension.

- Reports of the individual's activities of daily living and work activity, as well as testimony of third parties about the individual's performance and behavior.

- Reports from workshops, group homes, or similar assistive entities.

In analyzing the evidence, it is necessary to draw meaningful inferences and allow reasonable conclusions about the individual's strengths and weaknesses. Consideration should be given to factors such as:

- Quality of daily activities, both in occupational and social spheres (see Listing 12.00, Introduction), as well as of the individual's actions with respect to a medical examination.

- Ability to sustain activities, interests, and relate to others over a period of time. The frequency, appropriateness, and independence of the activities must also be considered (see PPS No. 96, SSR 83-15, Titles II and XVI: Evaluation of Chronic Mental Impairments).

- Level of intellectual functioning.

- Ability to function in a work-like situation.

When a case involves an individual (except disabled widow(ers) and title XVI children under 18) who has a severe impairment(s), which does not meet or equal the criteria in the Listing of Impairments, the individual's RFC must be considered in conjunction with the individual's age, education, and work experience. While some individuals will have a significant restriction of the ability to perform some work-related activities, not all such activities will be precluded by the mental impairment. However, all limits on work-related activities resulting from the mental impairment must be described in the mental RFC assessment.

* * *

Evaluation of Medical and Other Evidence

Medical evidence is critical to determinations of disability. It provides medical history, test results, examination findings, and observations, as well as conclusions of medical sources trained and knowledgeable in the diagnosis and treatment of diseases and disorders.

Reports from psychiatrists and other physicians, psychologists, and other professionals working in the field of mental health should contain the individual's medical history, mental status evaluation, psychological testing, diagnosis, treatment prescribed and response, prognosis, a description of the individual's daily activities, and a medical assessment describing ability to do work-related activities. These reports may also contain other observations and opinions or conclusions on such matters as the individual's ability to cope with stress, the ability to relate to other people, and the ability to function in a group or work situation.

Medical documentation can often give clues as to functional limitation. For example, evidence that an individual is markedly withdrawn or seclusive suggests a greatly reduced capacity for close contact and interaction with other people. The conclusion of reduced RFC in this area can then be applied to all steps of vocational assessment. For example, when the vocational assessment establishes that the claimant's past work has been limited to work requiring close contact and interaction with other people, the preceding assessment would indicate that the claimant would be unable to fulfill the requirements of his or her past work. Therefore, the determination of disability in this instance would depend on the individual's vocational capacity for other work.

Similarly, individuals with paranoid tendencies may be expected to experience moderate to moderately severe difficulties in relating to coworkers or supervisors, or in tolerating normal work pressures. The ability to respond appropriately to supervision and to coworkers under customary work pressure is a function of a number of different factors, some of which may be unique to a specific work situation.

The evaluation of intellectual functioning by a program physician, psychologist, ALJ, or AC member provides information necessary to determine the individual's ability to understand, to remember instructions, and to carry out instructions. Thus, an individual, in whom the only finding in intellectual testing is an IQ between 60 and 69, is ordinarily expected to be able to understand simple oral instructions and to be able to carry out these instructions under somewhat closer supervision than required of an individual with a higher IQ. Similarly, an individual who has an IQ between 70 and 79 should ordinarily be able to carry out these instructions under somewhat less close supervision.

Since treating medical sources often have considerable information about the development and progress of an individual's impairment, as well as information about the individual's response to treatment, evidence from treating sources should be given appropriate consideration. * * *

Other evidence also may play a vital role in the determination of the effects of impairment. To arrive at an overall assessment of the effects of mental impairment, relevant, reliable information, obtained from third party sources such as social workers, previous employers, family members, and staff members of halfway houses, mental health centers, and community centers, may be valuable in assessing an individual's level of activities of daily living. Information concerning an individual's performance in any work setting (including sheltered work and volunteer or competitive work), as well as the circumstances surrounding the termination of the work effort, may be pertinent in assessing the individual's ability to function in a competitive work environment.

Reports of workshop evaluation may also be of value in assessing the individual's ability to understand, to carry out and remember instructions, and to respond appropriately to supervisors, coworkers, and customary work pressures in a work setting. * * *

Descriptions and observations of the individual's restrictions by medical and other sources (including Social Security Administration representatives, such as district office representatives and ALJ's), in addition to those made during formal medical examinations, must also be considered in the determination of RFC. However, care must be taken not to give duplicate weight to certain findings. For example, a competent psychometric assessment of intellectual functioning provides a sample, referenced to established norms, of the individual's capabilities in various areas, including those germane to a workshop situation. Such a psychometric assessment, therefore, usually provides the same impairment-related information about functional capacity that might also be disclosed in the course of a workshop evaluation. Since the effects of the same underlying impairment(s) may be revealed in both assessment approaches, it would be incorrect to consider this duplicate representation of the same impairment to reflect separate and independent impairments. Such an approach would give the same impairment(s) double weight.

Observations and findings from a workshop evaluation may supplement the psychometric assessment or may raise some question concerning the accuracy of the psychometric assessment. Whenever a significant discrepancy in conclusions between the two arises, an explanation must be given by the program physician, psychologist, ALJ, or AC member for rejecting or modifying the conclusions of the psychometric assessment or the workshop evaluation.

* * *

SOCIAL SECURITY RULING SSR 82-59, 1975-1982
Soc. Sec. Rep. Ser. 793 (1982)

TITLES II AND XVI: FAILURE TO FOLLOW PRESCRIBED
TREATMENT

* * *

INTRODUCTION: Individuals with a disabling impairment which is amenable to treatment that could be expected to restore their ability to work must follow the prescribed treatment to be found under a disability, unless there is a justifiable cause for the failure to follow such treatment. This policy statement discusses failure to follow prescribed treatment, explains in detail the requirements necessary for such a finding, explains the consequences of such action, and illustrates examples of justifiable causes for "failure."

POLICY STATEMENT: An individual who would otherwise be found to be under a disability, but who fails without justifiable cause to follow treatment prescribed by a treating source which the Social Security Administration (SSA) determines can be expected to restore the individual's ability to work, cannot by virtue of such "failure" be found to be under a disability. (See discussion below for title XVI "blindness" cases.)

Identifying "Failure" as an Issue

SSA may make a determination that an individual has failed to follow prescribed treatment only where all of the following conditions exist:

1. The evidence establishes that the individual's impairment precludes engaging in any substantial gainful activity (SGA) or, in the case of a disabled widow(er) that the impairment meets or equals the Listing of Impairments in Appendix 1 of Regulations No. 4, Subpart P; and

2. The impairment has lasted or is expected to last for 12 continuous months from onset of disability or is expected to result in death; and

3. Treatment which is clearly expected to restore capacity to engage in any SGA (or gainful activity, as appropriate) has been prescribed by a treating source; and

4. The evidence of record discloses that there has been refusal to follow prescribed treatment.

Where SSA makes a determination of "failure," a determination must also be made as to whether or not failure to follow prescribed treatment is justifiable.

Treatment Must be Prescribed by Claimant's Treating Source

A treating source(s) is any duly licensed physician(s) who is actually attending to the claimant's or beneficiary's medical needs. Where the individual does not have an attending physician, the treating physician(s) in the hospital, clinic, or other medical facility where the individual goes for medical care will be considered the treating source.

A Disability Determination Services (DDS) staff physician is not a treating source. Similarly, a physician whose only relationship to the claimant is as a consulting examiner may not be considered a treating source. Therefore, where a consulting examiner's findings establish severity and for the first time indicate that specific treatment can be expected to restore ability to engage in any SGA (or gainful activity, as appropriate), the case should not be denied for failure to follow prescribed treatment. The DDS will refer such cases to the vocational rehabilitation (VR) agency for further action.

Treatment Expected to Restore Ability to Work

While it is a treating source who must prescribe treatment in order for the issue of "failure" to arise, the judgment as to whether prescribed treatment can be expected to restore ability to work will be made by SSA. In the event the treating source states that prescribed treatment will restore ability to work, consideration should be given to such opinion. However, if despite such opinion SSA determines that ability to engage in SGA may not reasonably be expected to be restored, there is no issue of failure to follow prescribed treatment.

Where SSA believes that treatment might restore an individual's ability to engage in any SGA (or gainful activity, as appropriate), but no treating source has prescribed such treatment, a determination of allowance will be made, and the DDS will refer the individual to VR. When a hearing or appeals council (AC) decision is issued, the administrative law judge or AC will follow established procedure to request the effectuating component to make such referral if a question of restorative treatment is involved.

* * *

Justifiable Cause for Failure to Follow Prescribed Treatment

Under circumstances such as those described below, an individual's failure to follow prescribed treatment will be generally accepted as "justifiable" and, therefore, such "failure" would not preclude a finding of "disability" or that disability continues.

1. *Acceptance of prescribed treatment would be contrary to the teachings and tenets of the claimant's or beneficiary's religion.* A finding of disability would be in order where the evidence establishes that the disabled individual rejects prescribed treatment on the grounds that he or she is a member of a church which teaches that healing may be accomplished only through faith or prayer.

In such a case, the claimant or beneficiary must be asked to identify church affiliation. In addition, a statement or other information from either church authorities or other members of the religious order must be obtained to substantiate that the individual is a member of the church. Additionally, the church's position relative to medical treatment must ordinarily be documented (see note below for exception) by obtaining either church literature or a statement from church authorities concerning the teachings and tenets of the church.

NOTE: In Christian Science cases, it is not necessary to develop church teachings since it is well established that such teachings proscribe acceptance of medical treatment. In these cases, a statement by a Christian Science practitioner or church authority verifying the individual's membership suffices.

2. *Cataract extraction for one eye is prescribed but the loss of visual efficiency in the other eye is severe and cannot be corrected through treatment.*

3. In an unusual case, a claimant's or beneficiary's fear of surgery may be so intense and unrelenting that it is, in effect, a contraindication to surgery. *If a treating source who had advised surgery later decides that the individual's fear is so great that the individual is not a satisfactory candidate for surgery, there is no issue of "failure."*

Where fear of surgery is suggested to be extreme, but the treating source has limited contact with the person and is unable to indicate the significance of the fear, an independent examination by a psychiatrist may be warranted as a means of resolving whether the fear contraindicates surgery.

Attendant to allegations of fear, it is not uncommon to see surgery refused on the grounds that the absolute success of such treatment has not been "guaranteed." No physician can guarantee the results of a major surgical procedure since any surgery generally entails some degree of risk. An individual may also attempt to justify refusal of surgery on the grounds of alleged personal or third party knowledge of persons who did not improve, or perhaps worsened, following surgery similar to that recommended to the individual by a treating physician. However, such reason(s) for nonacceptance of surgical treatment will not, in and of itself, negate a finding of "failure."

4. *The individual is unable to afford prescribed treatment which he or she is willing to accept, but for which free community resources are unavailable.* Although a free or subsidized source of treatment is often available, the claim may be allowed where such treatment is not reasonably available in the local community. All possible resources (e.g., clinics, charitable and public assistance agencies, etc.), must be explored. Contacts with such resources and the claimant's financial circumstances must be documented. Where treatment is not available, the case will be referred to VR.

5. *Any duly licensed treating medical source who has treated the claimant or beneficiary advises against the treatment prescribed for the currently disabling condition.* Thus, if a person has two treating sources who take opposing views regarding treatment, one recommending and one advising against the same treatment, failure to follow the recommended treatment was justifiable. (Where an individual chooses to follow treatment recommended by one treating source, to the exclusion of alternative treatment recommended by one or more other treating sources, the issue of "failure" does not arise.)

6. *The claimant or beneficiary is presently unable to work because of a condition for which major surgery was performed with unsuccessful results, and additional major surgery is prescribed for the same impairment.*

7. *The treatment carries a high degree of risk because of the enormity or unusual nature of the procedure* (e.g., organ transplant, open heart surgery).

8. The treatment recommended involves amputation of an extremity (e.g., amputation at or above the tarsal region).

The specific reasons listed above are not all-inclusive as acceptable justifications for refusing to accept prescribed treatment. A full evaluation must be made in each case to determine whether the individual's reason(s) for failure to follow prescribed treatment is justifiable.

* * *

APPENDIX C

SELECTED STATUTES

■ ■ ■

42 U.S.C. § 402 Old-age and survivors insurance benefit payments

(a) Old-age insurance benefits

Every individual who—

> (1) is a fully insured individual (as defined in section 414(a) of this title),
>
> (2) has attained age 62, and
>
> (3) has filed application for old-age insurance benefits or was entitled to disability insurance benefits for the month preceding the month in which he attained retirement age (as defined in section 416(l) of this title),

shall be entitled to an old-age insurance benefit for each month, beginning with—

>> (A) in the case of an individual who has attained retirement age (as defined in section 416(l) of this title), the first month in which such individual meets the criteria specified in paragraphs (1), (2), and (3), or
>>
>> (B) in the case of an individual who has attained age 62, but has not attained retirement age (as defined in section 416(l) of this title), the first month throughout which such individual meets the criteria specified in paragraphs (1) and (2) (if in that month he meets the criterion specified in paragraph (3)),

and ending with the month preceding the month in which he dies. * * *

(b) Wife's insurance benefits

(1) The wife (as defined in section 416(b) of this title) and every divorced wife (as defined in section 416(d) of this title) of an individual entitled to old-age or disability insurance benefits, if such wife or such divorced wife—

(A) has filed application for wife's insurance benefits,

(B) has attained age 62 * * *,

(C) in the case of a divorced wife, is not married, and

(D) is not entitled to old-age or disability insurance benefits, or is entitled to old-age or disability insurance benefits based on a primary insurance amount which is less than one-half of the primary insurance amount of such individual,

shall (subject to subsection (s) of this section) be entitled to a wife's insurance benefit * * *

(2) * * * such wife's insurance benefit for each month shall be equal to one-half of the primary insurance amount of her husband (or, in the case of a divorced wife, her former husband) for such month.

* * *

(c) Husband's insurance benefits

(1) The husband (as defined in section 416(f) of this title) and every divorced husband (as defined in section 416(d) of this title) of an individual entitled to old-age or disability insurance benefits, if such husband or such divorced husband—

(A) has filed application for husband's insurance benefits,

(B) has attained age 62 * * *,

(C) in the case of a divorced husband, is not married, and

(D) is not entitled to old-age or disability insurance benefits, or is entitled to old-age or disability insurance benefits based on a primary insurance amount which is less than one-half of the primary insurance amount of such individual,

shall (subject to subsection (s) of this section) be entitled to a husband's insurance benefit * * *.

(2) * * * such husband's insurance benefit for each month shall be equal to one-half of the primary insurance amount of his wife (or, in the case of a divorced husband, his former wife) for such month.

* * *

(d) Child's insurance benefits

(1) Every child (as defined in section 416(e) of this title) of an individual entitled to old-age or disability insurance benefits, or of an individual who dies a fully or currently insured, if such child—

(A) has filed application for child's insurance benefits,

(B) at the time such application was filed was unmarried and (i) either had not attained the age of 18 or was a full-time elementary or secondary school student and had not attained the age of 19, or (ii) is under a disability (as defined in section 423(d) of this title) which began before he attained the age of 22, and

(C) was dependent upon such individual—

(i) if such individual is living, at the time such application was filed,

(ii) if such individual has died, at the time of such death, or

(iii) if such individual had a period of disability which continued until he became entitled to old-age or disability insurance benefits, or (if he has died) until the month of his death, at the beginning of such period of disability or at the time he became entitled to such benefits,

shall be entitled to a child's insurance benefit * * *

* * *

(2) Such child's insurance benefit for each month shall, if the individual on the basis of whose wages and self-employment income the child is entitled to such benefit has not died prior to the end of such month, be equal to one-half of the primary insurance amount of such individual for such month. Such child's insurance benefit for each month shall, if such individual has died in or prior to such month, be equal to three-fourths of the primary insurance amount of such individual.

(3) A child shall be deemed dependent upon his father or adopting father or his mother or adopting mother at the time specified in paragraph (1)(C) of this subsection unless, at such time, such individual was not living with or contributing to the support of such child and—

(A) such child is neither the legitimate nor adopted child of such individual, or

(B) such child has been adopted by some other individual.

* * *

(4) A child shall be deemed dependent upon his stepfather or stepmother at the time specified in subparagraph (1)(C) of this subsection if, at that time, the child was receiving at least one-half of his support from such stepfather or stepmother.

* * *

(8) In the case of—

(A) an individual entitled to old-age insurance benefits (other than an individual referred to in subparagraph (B)), or

(B) an individual entitled to disability insurance benefits, or an individual entitled to old-age insurance benefits who was entitled to disability insurance benefits for the month preceding the first month for which he was entitled to old-age insurance benefits,

a child of such individual adopted after such individual became entitled to such old-age or disability insurance benefits shall be deemed not to meet the requirements of clause (i) or (iii) of paragraph (1)(C) unless such child—

(C) is the natural child or stepchild of such individual (including such a child who was legally adopted by such individual), or

(D)(i) was legally adopted by such individual in an adoption decreed by a court of competent jurisdiction within the United States, and

(ii) in the case of a child who attained the age of 18 prior to the commencement of proceedings for adoption, the child was living with or receiving at least one-half of the child's support from such individual for the year immediately preceding the month in which the adoption is decreed.

(9)(A) A child who is a child of an individual under clause (3) of the first sentence of section 416(e) of this title and is not a child of such individual under clause (1) or (2) of such first sentence shall be deemed not to be dependent on such individual at the time specified in subparagraph (1)(C) of this subsection unless (i) such child was living with such individual in the United States and receiving at least one-half of his support from such individual (I) for the year immediately before the month in which such individual became entitled to old-age insurance benefits or disability insurance benefits or died, or (II) if such individual had a period of disability which continued until he had become entitled to old-age insurance benefits, or disability insurance benefits, or died, for the year immediately before the month in which such period of disability began, and (ii) the period during which such child was living with such individual began before the child attained age 18.

> (B) In the case of a child who was born in the one-year period during which such child must have been living with and receiving at least one-half of his support from such individual, such child shall be deemed to meet such requirements for such period if, as of the close of such period, such child has lived with such individual in the United States and received at least one-half of his support from such individual for substantially all of the period which begins on the date of such child's birth.

* * *

(e) Widow's insurance benefits

(1) The widow (as defined in section 416(c) of this title) and every surviving divorced wife (as defined in section 416(d) of this title) of an individual who died a fully insured individual, if such widow or such surviving divorced wife—

> (A) is not married,

> (B) (i) has attained age 60 or (ii) has attained age 50 but has not attained age 60 and is under a disability (as defined in section 423(d) of this title) * * *,

* * *

shall be entitled to a widow's insurance benefit * * *.

* * *

(2)(A) * * * such widow's insurance benefit for each month shall be equal to the primary insurance amount * * *.

* * *

(f) Widower's insurance benefits

(1) The widower (as defined in section 416(g) of this title) and every surviving divorced husband (as defined in section 416(d) of this title) of an individual who died a fully insured individual, if such widower or such surviving divorced husband—

> (A) is not married,

(B) (i) has attained age 60 or (ii) has attained age 50 but has not attained age 60 and is under a disability (as defined in section 423(d) of this title) * * *,

* * *

* * *

shall be entitled to a widower's insurance benefit * * *.

* * *

(2)(A) * * * such widow's insurance benefit for each month shall be equal to the primary insurance amount * * *.

* * *

(g) Mother's and father's insurance benefits

(1) The surviving spouse and every surviving divorced parent (as defined in section 416(d) of this title) of an individual who died a fully or currently insured individual, if such surviving spouse or surviving divorced parent—

(A) is not married,

(B) is not entitled to a surviving spouse's insurance benefit,

(C) is not entitled to old-age insurance benefits, or is entitled to old-age insurance benefits each of which is less than three-fourths of the primary insurance amount of such individual,

(D) has filed application for mother's or father's insurance benefits, or was entitled to a spouse's insurance benefit on the basis of the wages and self-employment income of such individual for the month preceding the month in which such individual died,

(E) at the time of filing such application has in his or her care a child of such individual entitled to a child's insurance benefit, and

(F) in the case of a surviving divorced parent—

(i) the child referred to in subparagraph (E) is his or her son, daughter, or legally adopted child, and

(ii) the benefits referred to in such subparagraph are payable on the basis of such individual's wages and self-employment income, shall (subject to subsection (s) of this section) be entitled to a mother's or father's insurance benefit * * *

* * *

(h) Parent's insurance benefits

(1) Every parent (as defined in this subsection) of an individual who died a fully insured individual, if such parent—

(A) has attained age 62,

(B) (i) was receiving at least one-half of his support from such individual at the time of such individual's death or, if such individual had a period of disability which did not end prior to the month in which he died, at the time such period began or at the time of such death, and (ii) filed proof of such support within two years after the date of such death, or, if such individual had such a period of disability, within two years after the month in which such individual filed application with respect to such period of disability or two years after the date of such death, as the case may be,

(C) has not married since such individual's death,

(D) is not entitled to old-age insurance benefits, or is entitled to old-age insurance benefits each of which is less than 82 1/2 percent of the primary insurance amount of such deceased individual if the amount of the parent's insurance benefit for such month is determinable under paragraph (2)(A) (or 75 percent of such primary insurance amount in any other case), and

(E) has filed application for parent's insurance benefits,

shall be entitled to a parent's insurance benefit * * *

* * *

(3) As used in this subsection, the term "parent" means the mother or father of an individual, a stepparent of an individual by a marriage contracted before such individual attained the age of sixteen, or an adopting parent by whom an individual was adopted before he attained the age of sixteen.

* * *

(x) Limitation on payments to prisoners, certain other inmates of publicly funded institutions, fugitives, probationers, and parolees

(1)(A) Notwithstanding any other provision of this subchapter, no monthly benefits shall be paid under this section or under section 423 of this title to any individual for any month ending with or during or beginning with or during a period of more than 30 days throughout all of which such individual—

(i) is confined in a jail, prison, or other penal institution or correctional facility pursuant to his conviction of a criminal offense,

(ii) is confined by court order in an institution at public expense in connection with—

(I) a verdict or finding that the individual is guilty but insane, with respect to a criminal offense,

(II) a verdict or finding that the individual is not guilty of such an offense by reason of insanity,

(III) a finding that such individual is incompetent to stand trial under an allegation of such an offense, or

(IV) a similar verdict or finding with respect to such an offense based on similar factors (such as a mental disease, a mental defect, or mental incompetence),

(iii) immediately upon completion of confinement as described in clause (i) pursuant to conviction of a criminal offense an element of which is sexual activity, is confined by court order in an institution at public expense pursuant to a finding that the individual is a sexually dangerous person or a sexual predator or a similar finding,

(iv) is fleeing to avoid prosecution, or custody or confinement after conviction, under the laws of the place from which the person flees, for a crime, or an attempt to commit a crime, which is a felony under the laws of the place from which the person flees, or, in jurisdictions that do not define crimes as felonies, is punishable by death or imprisonment for a term exceeding 1 year regardless of the actual sentence imposed, or

(v) is violating a condition of probation or parole imposed under Federal or State law.

* * *

** *

42 U.S.C. § 403. Reduction of insurance benefits

(a) Maximum benefits

(1) In the case of an individual whose primary insurance amount has been computed or recomputed under section 415(a)(1) or (4) of this title, or section 415(d) of this title, as in effect after December 1978, the total monthly benefits to which beneficiaries may be entitled under section 402 or 423 of this title for a month on the basis of the wages and self-employment income of such individual shall, except as provided by paragraphs (3) and (6) (but prior to any increases resulting from the application of paragraph (2)(A)(ii)(III) of section 415(i) of this title), be reduced as necessary so as not to exceed—

> (A) 150 percent of such individual's primary insurance amount to the extent that it does not exceed the amount established with respect to this subparagraph by paragraph (2),

> (B) 272 percent of such individual's primary insurance amount to the extent that it exceeds the amount established with respect to subparagraph (A) but does not exceed the amount established with respect to this subparagraph by paragraph (2),

> (C) 134 percent of such individual's primary insurance amount to the extent that it exceeds the amount established with respect to subparagraph (B) but does not exceed the amount established with respect to this subparagraph by paragraph (2), and

> (D) 175 percent of such individual's primary insurance amount to the extent that it exceeds the amount established with respect to subparagraph (C).

Any such amount that is not a multiple of $0.10 shall be decreased to the next lower multiple of $0.10.

42 U.S.C. § 404 Overpayments and underpayments

(a) Procedure for adjustment or recovery

(1) Whenever the Commissioner of Social Security finds that more or less than the correct amount of payment has been made to any person under this subchapter, proper adjustment or recovery shall be made, under regulations prescribed by the Commissioner of Social Security, as follows:

> (A) With respect to payment to a person of more than the correct amount, the Commissioner of Social Security shall decrease any payment under this subchapter to which such overpaid person is entitled, or shall require such overpaid person or his estate to refund

the amount in excess of the correct amount, or shall decrease any payment under this subchapter payable to his estate or to any other person on the basis of the wages and self-employment income which were the basis of the payments to such overpaid person, or shall obtain recovery by means of reduction in tax refunds based on notice to the Secretary of the Treasury as permitted under section 3720A of Title 31, or shall apply any combination of the foregoing. * * *

(B)(i) Subject to clause (ii), with respect to payment to a person of less than the correct amount, the Commissioner of Social Security shall make payment of the balance of the amount due such underpaid person, or, if such person dies before payments are completed or before negotiating one or more checks representing correct payments, disposition of the amount due shall be made in accordance with subsection (d) of this section.

(ii) No payment shall be made under this subparagraph to any person during any period for which monthly insurance benefits of such person—

(I) are subject to nonpayment by reason of section 402(x)(1) of this title, or

(II) in the case of a person whose monthly insurance benefits have terminated for a reason other than death, would be subject to nonpayment by reason of section 402(x)(1) of this title but for the termination of such benefits,

until section 402(x)(1) of this title no longer applies, or would no longer apply in the case of benefits that have terminated.

* * *

* * *

(b) No recovery from persons without fault

In any case in which more than the correct amount of payment has been made, there shall be no adjustment of payments to, or recovery by the United States from, any person who is without fault if such adjustment or recovery would defeat the purpose of this subchapter or would be against equity and good conscience. In making for purposes of this subsection any determination of whether any individual is without fault, the Commissioner of Social Security shall specifically take into account any physical, mental, educational, or linguistic limitation such individual may have (including any lack of facility with the English language).

* * *

(d) Payment to survivors or heirs when eligible person is deceased

If an individual dies before any payment due him under this subchapter is completed, payment of the amount due (including the amount of any unnegotiated checks) shall be made—

> (1) to the person, if any, who is determined by the Commissioner of Social Security to be the surviving spouse of the deceased individual and who either (i) was living in the same household with the deceased at the time of his death or (ii) was, for the month in which the deceased individual died, entitled to a monthly benefit on the basis of the same wages and self-employment income as was the deceased individual;

> (2) if there is no person who meets the requirements of paragraph (1), or if the person who meets such requirements dies before the payment due him under this subchapter is completed, to the child or children, if any, of the deceased individual who were, for the month in which the deceased individual died, entitled to monthly benefits on the basis of the same wages and self-employment income as was the deceased individual (and, in case there is more than one such child, in equal parts to each such child);

> (3) if there is no person who meets the requirements of paragraph (1) or (2), or if each person who meets such requirements dies before the payment due him under this subchapter is completed, to the parent or parents, if any, of the deceased individual who were, for the month in which the deceased individual died, entitled to monthly benefits on the basis of the same wages and self-employment income as was the deceased individual (and, in case there is more than one such parent, in equal parts to each such parent);

> (4) if there is no person who meets the requirements of paragraph (1), (2), or (3), or if each person who meets such requirements dies before the payment due him under this subchapter is completed, to the person, if any, determined by the Commissioner of Social Security to be the surviving spouse of the deceased individual;

> (5) if there is no person who meets the requirements of paragraph (1), (2), (3), or (4), or if each person who meets such requirements dies before the payment due him under this subchapter is completed, to the person or persons, if any, determined by the Commissioner of Social Security to be the child or children of the deceased individual (and, in case there is more than one such child, in equal parts to each such child);

(6) if there is no person who meets the requirements of paragraph (1), (2), (3), (4), or (5), or if each person who meets such requirements dies before the payment due him under this subchapter is completed, to the parent or parents, if any, of the deceased individual (and, in case there is more than one such parent, in equal parts to each such parent); or

(7) if there is no person who meets the requirements of paragraph (1), (2), (3), (4), (5), or (6), or if each person who meets such requirements dies before the payment due him under this subchapter is completed, to the legal representative of the estate of the deceased individual, if any.

42 U.S.C. § 405 Evidence, procedure, and certification for payments

(a) Rules and regulations; procedures

The Commissioner of Social Security shall have full power and authority to make rules and regulations and to establish procedures, not inconsistent with the provisions of this subchapter, which are necessary or appropriate to carry out such provisions, and shall adopt reasonable and proper rules and regulations to regulate and provide for the nature and extent of the proofs and evidence and the method of taking and furnishing the same in order to establish the right to benefits hereunder.

(b) Administrative determination of entitlement to benefits; findings of fact; hearings; investigations; evidentiary hearings in reconsiderations of disability benefit terminations; subsequent applications

(1) The Commissioner of Social Security is directed to make findings of fact, and decisions as to the rights of any individual applying for a payment under this subchapter. Any such decision by the Commissioner of Social Security which involves a determination of disability and which is in whole or in part unfavorable to such individual shall contain a statement of the case, in understandable language, setting forth a discussion of the evidence, and stating the Commissioner's determination and the reason or reasons upon which it is based. Upon request by any such individual or upon request by [other interested individuals], the Commissioner shall give such applicant and such other individual reasonable notice and opportunity for a hearing with respect to such decision, and, if a hearing is held, shall, on the basis of evidence adduced at the hearing, affirm, modify, or reverse the Commissioner's findings of fact and such decision. Any such request with respect to such a decision must be filed within sixty days after notice of such decision is received by the individual making such request. The Commissioner of Social Security is further authorized, on

the Commissioner's own motion, to hold such hearings and to conduct such investigations and other proceedings as the Commissioner may deem necessary or proper for the administration of this subchapter. In the course of any hearing, investigation, or other proceeding, the Commissioner may administer oaths and affirmations, examine witnesses, and receive evidence. Evidence may be received at any hearing before the Commissioner of Social Security even though inadmissible under rules of evidence applicable to court procedure.

(2) In any case where—

> (A) an individual is a recipient of disability insurance benefits, or of child's, widow's, or widower's insurance benefits based on disability,

> (B) the physical or mental impairment on the basis of which such benefits are payable is found to have ceased, not to have existed, or to no longer be disabling, and

> (C) as a consequence of the finding described in subparagraph (B), such individual is determined by the Commissioner of Social Security not to be entitled to such benefits,

> any reconsideration of the finding described in subparagraph (B), in connection with a reconsideration by the Commissioner of Social Security (before any hearing under paragraph (1) on the issue of such entitlement) of the Commissioner's determination described in subparagraph (C), shall be made only after opportunity for an evidentiary hearing, with regard to the finding described in subparagraph (B), which is reasonably accessible to such individual. * * *

* * *

* * *

(g) Judicial review

Any individual, after any final decision of the Commissioner of Social Security made after a hearing to which he was a party, irrespective of the amount in controversy, may obtain a review of such decision by a civil action commenced within sixty days after the mailing to him of notice of such decision or within such further time as the Commissioner of Social Security may allow. Such action shall be brought in the district court of the United States for the judicial district in which the plaintiff resides, or has his principal place of business, or, if he does not reside or have his principal place of business within any such judicial district, in the United

States District Court for the District of Columbia. As part of the Commissioner's answer the Commissioner of Social Security shall file a certified copy of the transcript of the record including the evidence upon which the findings and decision complained of are based. The court shall have power to enter, upon the pleadings and transcript of the record, a judgment affirming, modifying, or reversing the decision of the Commissioner of Social Security, with or without remanding the cause for a rehearing. The findings of the Commissioner of Social Security as to any fact, if supported by substantial evidence, shall be conclusive* * *. The court may, on motion of the Commissioner of Social Security made for good cause shown before the Commissioner files the Commissioner's answer, remand the case to the Commissioner of Social Security for further action by the Commissioner of Social Security, and it may at any time order additional evidence to be taken before the Commissioner of Social Security, but only upon a showing that there is new evidence which is material and that there is good cause for the failure to incorporate such evidence into the record in a prior proceeding; and the Commissioner of Social Security shall, after the case is remanded, and after hearing such additional evidence if so ordered, modify or affirm the Commissioner's findings of fact or the Commissioner's decision, or both, and shall file with the court any such additional and modified findings of fact and decision, and a transcript of the additional record and testimony upon which the Commissioner's action in modifying or affirming was based. Such additional or modified findings of fact and decision shall be reviewable only to the extent provided for review of the original findings of fact and decision. The judgment of the court shall be final except that it shall be subject to review in the same manner as a judgment in other civil actions. Any action instituted in accordance with this subsection shall survive notwithstanding any change in the person occupying the office of Commissioner of Social Security or any vacancy in such office.

(h) Finality of Commissioner's decision

The findings and decision of the Commissioner of Social Security after a hearing shall be binding upon all individuals who were parties to such hearing. No findings of fact or decision of the Commissioner of Social Security shall be reviewed by any person, tribunal, or governmental agency except as herein provided. No action against the United States, the Commissioner of Social Security, or any officer or employee thereof shall be brought under section 1331 or 1346 of Title 28 to recover on any claim arising under this subchapter.

* * *

(j) Representative payees

(1)(A) If the Commissioner of Social Security determines that the interest of any individual under this subchapter, would be served thereby, certification of payment of such individual's benefit under this subchapter may be made, regardless of the legal competency or incompetency of the individual, either for direct payment to the individual, or for his or her use and benefit, to another individual, or an organization, with respect to whom the requirements of paragraph (2) have been met (hereinafter in this subsection referred to as the individual's "representative payee"). If the Commissioner of Social Security or a court of competent jurisdiction determines that a representative payee has misused any individual's benefit paid to such representative payee pursuant to this subsection or section 1007 or 1383(a)(2) of this title, the Commissioner of Social Security shall promptly revoke certification for payment of benefits to such representative payee pursuant to this subsection and certify payment to an alternative representative payee or, if the interest of the individual under this subchapter would be served thereby, to the individual.

(B) In the case of an individual entitled to benefits based on disability, the payment of such benefits shall be made to a representative payee if the Commissioner of Social Security determines that such payment would serve the interest of the individual because the individual also has an alcoholism or drug addiction condition (as determined by the Commissioner) and the individual is incapable of managing such benefits.

(2)(A) Any certification made under paragraph (1) for payment of benefits to an individual's representative payee shall be made on the basis of—

(i) an investigation by the Commissioner of Social Security of the person to serve as representative payee, which shall be conducted in advance of such certification and shall, to the extent practicable, include a face-to-face interview with such person, and

(ii) adequate evidence that such certification is in the interest of such individual (as determined by the Commissioner of Social Security in regulations).

* * *

* * *

(u) Redetermination of entitlement

(1)(A) The Commissioner of Social Security shall immediately redetermine the entitlement of individuals to monthly insurance benefits under this subchapter if there is reason to believe that fraud or similar fault was involved in the application of the individual for such benefits, unless a United States attorney, or equivalent State prosecutor, with jurisdiction over potential or actual related criminal cases, certifies, in writing, that there is a substantial risk that such action by the Commissioner of Social Security with regard to beneficiaries in a particular investigation would jeopardize the criminal prosecution of a person involved in a suspected fraud.

(B) When redetermining the entitlement, or making an initial determination of entitlement, of an individual under this subchapter, the Commissioner of Social Security shall disregard any evidence if there is reason to believe that fraud or similar fault was involved in the providing of such evidence.

(2) For purposes of paragraph (1), similar fault is involved with respect to a determination if—

(A) an incorrect or incomplete statement that is material to the determination is knowingly made; or

(B) information that is material to the determination is knowingly concealed.

(3) If, after redetermining pursuant to this subsection the entitlement of an individual to monthly insurance benefits, the Commissioner of Social Security determines that there is insufficient evidence to support such entitlement, the Commissioner of Social Security may terminate such entitlement and may treat benefits paid on the basis of such insufficient evidence as overpayments.

42 U.S.C. § 416 Additional definitions

For the purposes of this subchapter—

(a) Spouse; surviving spouse

(1) The term "spouse" means a wife as defined in subsection (b) of this section or a husband as defined in subsection (f) of this section.

(2) The term "surviving spouse" means a widow as defined in subsection (c) of this section or a widower as defined in subsection (g) of this section.

(b) Wife

The term "wife" means the wife of an individual, but only if she (1) is the mother of his son or daughter, (2) was married to him for a period of not less than one year immediately preceding the day on which her application is filed, or (3) in the month prior to the month of her marriage to him [she was entitled to or, if applied for would be entitled to, certain benefits]. * * *

(c) Widow

(1) The term "widow" * * * means the surviving wife of an individual, but only if (A) she is the mother of his son or daughter, (B) she legally adopted his son or daughter while she was married to him and while such son or daughter was under the age of eighteen, (C) he legally adopted her son or daughter while she was married to him and while such son or daughter was under the age of eighteen, (D) she was married to him at the time both of them legally adopted a child under the age of eighteen, (E) except as provided in paragraph (2), she was married to him for a period of not less than nine months immediately prior to the day on which he died, or (F) in the month prior to the month of her marriage to him [she was entitled to or, if applied for would be entitled to, certain benefits].

(2) The requirements of paragraph (1)(E) in connection with the surviving wife of an individual shall be treated as satisfied if—

(A) the individual had been married prior to the individual's marriage to the surviving wife,

(B) the prior wife was institutionalized during the individual's marriage to the prior wife due to mental incompetence or similar incapacity,

(C) during the period of the prior wife's institutionalization, the individual would have divorced the prior wife and married the surviving wife, but the individual did not do so because such divorce would have been unlawful, by reason of the prior wife's institutionalization, under the laws of the State in which the individual was domiciled at the time (as determined based on evidence satisfactory to the Commissioner of Social Security),

(D) the prior wife continued to remain institutionalized up to the time of her death, and

(E) the individual married the surviving wife within 60 days after the prior wife's death.

(d) Divorced spouses; divorce

(1) The term "divorced wife" means a woman divorced from an individual, but only if she had been married to such individual for a period of 10 years immediately before the date the divorce became effective.

(2) The term "surviving divorced wife" means a woman divorced from an individual who has died, but only if she had been married to the individual for a period of 10 years immediately before the date the divorce became effective.

* * *

(4) The term "divorced husband" means a man divorced from an individual, but only if he had been married to such individual for a period of 10 years immediately before the date the divorce became effective.

(5) The term "surviving divorced husband" means a man divorced from an individual who has died, but only if he had been married to the individual for a period of 10 years immediately before the divorce became effective.

* * *

(e) Child

The term "child" means (1) the child or legally adopted child of an individual, (2) a stepchild who has been such stepchild for not less than one year immediately preceding the day on which application for child's insurance benefits is filed or (if the insured individual is deceased) not less than nine months immediately preceding the day on which such individual died, and (3) a person who is the grandchild or stepgrandchild of an individual or his spouse, but only if (A) there was no natural or adoptive parent (other than such a parent who was under a disability, as defined in section 423(d) of this title) of such person living at the time (i) such individual became entitled to old-age insurance benefits or disability insurance benefits or died, or (ii) if such individual had a period of disability which continued until such individual became entitled to old-age insurance benefits or disability insurance benefits, or died, at the time such period of disability began, or (B) such person was legally adopted after the death of such individual by such individual's surviving spouse in an adoption that was decreed by a court of competent jurisdiction within the United States and such person's natural or adopting parent or stepparent was not living in such individual's household and making regular contributions toward such person's support at the time such individual died. For purposes of clause (1), a person shall be deemed, as of the date of death of an individual, to be the legally adopted child of such individual if such person was either living with or receiving at least one-half of his support from such individual at the time of such individual's death and was legally adopted by such individual's surviving spouse after such individual's death, but only if (A) proceedings for the adoption of the child had been instituted by such individual before his death, or (B) such child was adopted by such individual's surviving spouse before the end of two years after (i) the day on which such individual died or (ii) August 28, 1958. For purposes of clause (2), a person who is not the stepchild of an individual shall be deemed the stepchild of such individual if such individual was not the mother or adopting mother or the father or adopting father of such person and such individual and the mother or adopting mother, or the father or adopting father, as the case may be, of such person went through a marriage ceremony resulting in a purported marriage between them which, but for a legal impediment described in the last sentence of subsection (h)(1)(B) of this section, would have been a valid marriage. For purposes of clause (2), a child shall be deemed to have been the stepchild of an individual for a period of one year throughout the month in which occurs the expiration of such one year. For purposes of clause (3), a person shall be deemed to have no natural or adoptive parent living (other than a parent who was under a disability) throughout the most recent month in which a natural or adoptive parent (not under a disability) dies.

(f) Husband

The term "husband" means the husband of an individual, but only if (1) he is the father of her son or daughter, (2) he was married to her for a period of not less than one year immediately preceding the day on which his application is filed, or (3) in the month prior to the month of his marriage to her [he was entitled to or, if applied for would be entitled to, certain benefits].

(g) Widower

(1) The term "widower" (except when used in the first sentence of section 402(i) of this title) means the surviving husband of an individual, but only if (A) he is the father of her son or daughter, (B) he legally adopted her son or daughter while he was married to her and while such son or daughter was under the age of eighteen, (C) she legally adopted his son or daughter while he was married to her and while such son or daughter was under the age of eighteen, (D) he was married to her at the time both of them legally adopted a child under the age of eighteen, (E) except as provided in paragraph (2), he was married to her for a period of not less than nine months immediately prior to the day on which she died, or (F) in the month before the month of his marriage to her [he was entitled to or, if applied for would be entitled to, certain benefits].

(2) The requirements of paragraph (1)(E) in connection with the surviving husband of an individual shall be treated as satisfied if—

(A) the individual had been married prior to the individual's marriage to the surviving husband,

(B) the prior husband was institutionalized during the individual's marriage to the prior husband due to mental incompetence or similar incapacity,

(C) during the period of the prior husband's institutionalization, the individual would have divorced the prior husband and married the surviving husband, but the individual did not do so because such divorce would have been unlawful, by reason of the prior husband's institutionalization , under the laws of the State in which the individual was domiciled at the time (as determined based on evidence satisfactory to the Commissioner of Social Security),

(D) the prior husband continued to remain institutionalized up to the time of his death, and

(E) the individual married the surviving husband within 60 days after the prior husband's death.

(h) Determination of family status

(1)(A)(i) An applicant is the wife, husband, widow, or widower of a fully or currently insured individual for purposes of this subchapter if the courts of the State in which such insured individual is domiciled at the time such applicant files an application, or, if such insured individual is dead, the courts of the State in which he was domiciled at the time of death, or, if such insured individual is or was not so domiciled in any State, the courts of the District of Columbia, would find that such applicant and such insured individual were validly married at the time such applicant files such application or, if such insured individual is dead, at the time he died.

(ii) If such courts would not find that such applicant and such insured individual were validly married at such time, such applicant shall, nevertheless be deemed to be the wife, husband, widow, or widower, as the case may be, of such insured individual if such applicant would, under the laws applied by such courts in determining the devolution of intestate personal property, have the same status with respect to the taking of such property as a wife, husband, widow, or widower of such insured individual.

(B)(i) In any case where under subparagraph (A) an applicant is not (and is not deemed to be) the wife, widow, husband, or widower of a fully or currently insured individual, * * * but it is established to the satisfaction of the Commissioner of Social Security that such applicant in good faith went through a marriage ceremony with such individual resulting in a purported marriage between them which, but for a legal impediment not known to the applicant at the time of such ceremony, would have been a valid marriage, then * * * such purported marriage shall be deemed to be a valid marriage. * * *

(ii) The provisions of clause (i) shall not apply if the Commissioner of Social Security determines, on the basis of information brought to the Commissioner's attention, that such applicant entered into such purported marriage with such insured individual with knowledge that it would not be a valid marriage.

* * *

(iv) For purposes of this subparagraph, a legal impediment to the validity of a purported marriage includes only an impediment (I) resulting from the lack of dissolution of a previous marriage or otherwise arising out of such previous marriage or its dissolution, or (II) resulting from a defect in the procedure followed in connection with such purported marriage.

(2)(A) In determining whether an applicant is the child or parent of a fully or currently insured individual for purposes of this subchapter, the Commissioner of Social Security shall apply such law as would be applied in determining the devolution of intestate personal property by the courts of the State in which such insured individual is domiciled at the time such applicant files application, or, if such insured individual is dead, by the courts of the State in which he was domiciled at the time of his death, or, if such insured individual is or was not so domiciled in any State, by the courts of the District of Columbia. Applicants who according to such law would have the same status relative to taking intestate personal property as a child or parent shall be deemed such.

(B) If an applicant is a son or daughter of a fully or currently insured individual but is not (and is not deemed to be) the child of such insured individual under subparagraph (A), such applicant shall nevertheless be deemed to be the child of such insured individual if such insured individual and the mother or father, as the case may be, of such applicant went through a marriage ceremony resulting in a purported marriage between them which, but for a legal impediment [(I) resulting from the lack of dissolution of a previous marriage or otherwise arising out of such previous marriage or its dissolution, or (II) resulting from a defect in the procedure followed in connection with such purported marriage] would have been a valid marriage.

(3) An applicant who is the son or daughter of a fully or currently insured individual, but who is not (and is not deemed to be) the child of such insured individual under paragraph (2) of this subsection, shall nevertheless be deemed to be the child of such insured individual if:

(A) in the case of an insured individual entitled to old-age insurance benefits (who was not, in the month preceding such entitlement, entitled to disability insurance benefits)—

(i) such insured individual—

(I) has acknowledged in writing that the applicant is his or her son or daughter,

(II) has been decreed by a court to be the mother or father of the applicant, or

(III) has been ordered by a court to contribute to the support of the applicant because the applicant is his or her son or daughter, and such acknowledgment, court decree, or court order was made not less than one year before such insured individual became entitled to old-age insurance benefits or attained retirement age (as defined in subsection (l) of this section), whichever is earlier; or

(ii) such insured individual is shown by evidence satisfactory to the Commissioner of Social Security to be the mother or father of the applicant and was living with or contributing to the support of the applicant at the time such applicant's application for benefits was filed;

(B) in the case of an insured individual entitled to disability insurance benefits, or who was entitled to such benefits in the month preceding the first month for which he or she was entitled to old-age insurance benefits—

(i) such insured individual—

(I) has acknowledged in writing that the applicant is his or her son or daughter,

(II) has been decreed by a court to be the mother or father of the applicant, or

(III) has been ordered by a court to contribute to the support of the applicant because the applicant is his or her son or daughter,

and such acknowledgment, court decree, or court order was made before such insured individual's most recent period of disability began; or

(ii) such insured individual is shown by evidence satisfactory to the Commissioner of Social Security to be the mother or father of the applicant and was living with or contributing to the support of that applicant at the time such applicant's application for benefits was filed;

(C) in the case of a deceased individual—

(i) such insured individual—

(I) had acknowledged in writing that the applicant is his or her son or daughter,

(II) had been decreed by a court to be the mother or father of the applicant, or

(III) had been ordered by a court to contribute to the support of the applicant because the applicant was his or her son or daughter,

and such acknowledgment, court decree, or court order was made before the death of such insured individual, or

(ii) such insured individual is shown by evidence satisfactory to the Commissioner of Social Security to have been the mother or father of the applicant, and such insured individual was living with or contributing to the support of the applicant at the time such insured individual died.

For purposes of subparagraphs (A)(i) and (B)(i), an acknowledgment, court decree, or court order shall be deemed to have occurred on the first day of the month in which it actually occurred.

* * *

42 U.S.C. § 421 Disability determinations

(a) State agencies

(1) In the case of any individual, the determination of whether or not he is under a disability (as defined in section 416(i) or 423(d) of this title) and of the day such disability began, and the determination of the day on which such disability ceases, shall be made by a State agency * * *

(2) The disability determinations described in paragraph (1) made by a State agency shall be made in accordance with the pertinent provisions of this subchapter and the standards and criteria contained in regulations or other written guidelines of the Commissioner of Social Security per-

taining to matters such as disability determinations * * *. In addition, the Commissioner of Social Security shall promulgate regulations specifying, in such detail as the Commissioner deems appropriate, performance standards and administrative requirements and procedures to be followed in performing the disability determination function in order to assure effective and uniform administration of the disability insurance program throughout the United States. * * *

* * *

(b) Determinations by Commissioner of Social Security

(1) If the Commissioner of Social Security finds, after notice and opportunity for a hearing, that a State agency is substantially failing to make disability determinations in a manner consistent with the Commissioner's regulations and other written guidelines, the Commissioner of Social Security shall, not earlier than 180 days following the Commissioner's finding, and after the Commissioner has complied with the requirements of paragraph (3), make the disability determinations referred to in subsection (a)(1) of this section.

* * *

(3)(A) The Commissioner of Social Security shall develop and initiate all appropriate procedures to implement a plan with respect to any partial or complete assumption by the Commissioner of Social Security of the disability determination function from a State agency * * *.

* * *

(c) Review of determination by Commissioner of Social Security

(1) The Commissioner of Social Security may on the Commissioner's own motion or as required under paragraphs (2) and (3) review a determination, made by a State agency under this section, that an individual is or is not under a disability (as defined in section 416(i) or 423(d) of this title) and, as a result of such review, may modify such agency's determination and determine that such individual either is or is not under a disability (as so defined) or that such individual's disability began on a day earlier or later than that determined by such agency, or that such disability ceased on a day earlier or later than that determined by such agency. A review by the Commissioner of Social Security on the Commissioner's own motion of a State agency determination under this paragraph may be made before or after any action is taken to implement such determination.

(2) The Commissioner of Social Security (in accordance with paragraph (3)) shall review determinations, made by State agencies pursuant to this section, that individuals are under disabilities (as defined in section 416(i) or 423(d) of this title). Any review by the Commissioner of Social Security of a State agency determination under this paragraph shall be made before any action is taken to implement such determination.

(3)(A) In carrying out the provisions of paragraph (2) with respect to the review of determinations made by State agencies pursuant to this section that individuals are under disabilities (as defined in section 416(i) or 423(d) of this title), the Commissioner of Social Security shall review—

(i) at least 50 percent of all such determinations made by State agencies on applications for benefits under this subchapter, and

(ii) other determinations made by State agencies pursuant to this section to the extent necessary to assure a high level of accuracy in such other determinations.

(B) In conducting reviews pursuant to subparagraph (A), the Commissioner of Social Security shall, to the extent feasible, select for review those determinations which the Commissioner of Social Security identifies as being the most likely to be incorrect.

(C) Not later than April 1, 1992, and annually thereafter, the Commissioner of Social Security shall submit to the Committee on Ways and Means of the House of Representatives and the Committee on Finance of the Senate a written report setting forth the number of reviews conducted under subparagraph (A)(ii) during the preceding fiscal year and the findings of the Commissioner of Social Security based on such reviews of the accuracy of the determinations made by State agencies pursuant to this section.

(d) Hearings and judicial review

Any individual dissatisfied with any determination under subsection (a), (b), (c), or (g) of this section shall be entitled to a hearing thereon by the Commissioner of Social Security to the same extent as is provided in section 405(b) of this title with respect to decisions of the Commissioner of Social Security, and to judicial review of the Commissioner's final decision after such hearing as is provided in section 405(g) of this title.

* * *

(h) Evaluation of mental impairments by qualified medical professionals

An initial determination under subsection (a), (c), (g), or (i) of this section that an individual is not under a disability, in any case where there is evidence which indicates the existence of a mental impairment, shall be made only if the Commissioner of Social Security has made every reasonable effort to ensure that a qualified psychiatrist or psychologist has completed the medical portion of the case review and any applicable residual functional capacity assessment.

(i) Review of disability cases to determine continuing eligibility; permanent disability cases; appropriate number of cases reviewed; reporting requirements

(1) In any case where an individual is or has been determined to be under a disability, the case shall be reviewed by the applicable State agency or the Commissioner of Social Security (as may be appropriate), for purposes of continuing eligibility, at least once every 3 years, subject to paragraph (2); except that where a finding has been made that such disability is permanent, such reviews shall be made at such times as the Commissioner of Social Security determines to be appropriate. Reviews of cases under the preceding sentence shall be in addition to, and shall not be considered as a substitute for, any other reviews which are required or provided for under or in the administration of this subchapter.

(2) The requirement of paragraph (1) that cases be reviewed at least every 3 years shall not apply to the extent that the Commissioner of Social Security determines, on a State-by-State basis, that such requirement should be waived to insure that only the appropriate number of such cases are reviewed. The Commissioner of Social Security shall determine the appropriate number of cases to be reviewed in each State after consultation with the State agency performing such reviews, based upon the backlog of pending reviews, the projected number of new applications for disability insurance benefits, and the current and projected staffing levels of the State agency, but the Commissioner of Social Security shall provide for a waiver of such requirement only in the case of a State which makes a good faith effort to meet proper staffing requirements for the State agency and to process case reviews in a timely fashion. * * *

(3) The Commissioner of Social Security shall report annually to the Committee on Finance of the Senate and the Committee on Ways and Means of the House of Representatives with respect to the number of reviews of continuing disability carried out under paragraph (1), the number of such reviews which result in an initial termination of benefits, the number of requests for reconsideration of such initial termination or for a hearing with respect to such termination under subsection (d) of this section, or both, and the number of such initial terminations which are overturned as the result of a reconsideration or hearing.

(4) In any case in which the Commissioner of Social Security initiates a review under this subsection of the case of an individual who has been determined to be under a disability, the Commissioner of Social Security shall notify such individual of the nature of the review to be carried out, the possibility that such review could result in the termination of benefits, and the right of the individual to provide medical evidence with respect to such review.

(5) For suspension of reviews under this subsection in the case of an individual using a ticket to work and self-sufficiency, see section 1320b–19(i) of this title.

(j) Rules and regulations; consultative examinations

The Commissioner of Social Security shall prescribe regulations which set forth, in detail—

> (1) the standards to be utilized by State disability determination services and Federal personnel in determining when a consultative examination should be obtained in connection with disability determinations;

> (2) standards for the type of referral to be made; and

> (3) procedures by which the Commissioner of Social Security will monitor both the referral processes used and the product of professionals to whom cases are referred.

Nothing in this subsection shall be construed to preclude the issuance, in accordance with section 553(b)(A) of Title 5, of interpretive rules, general statements of policy, and rules of agency organization relating to consultative examinations if such rules and statements are consistent with such regulations.

(k) Establishment of uniform standards for determination of disability

(1) The Commissioner of Social Security shall establish by regulation uniform standards which shall be applied at all levels of determination, review, and adjudication in determining whether individuals are under disabilities as defined in section 416(i) or 423(d) of this title.

(2) Regulations promulgated under paragraph (1) shall be subject to the rulemaking procedures established under section 553 of Title 5.

* * *

42 U.S.C. § 423 Disability insurance benefit payments

(a) Disability insurance benefits

(1) Every individual who—

(A) is insured for disability insurance benefits,

(B) has not attained retirement age,

(C) if not a United States citizen or national—

(i) has been assigned a social security account number that was, at the time of assignment, or at any later time, consistent with the requirements of subclause (I) or (III) of section 405(c)(2)(B)(i) of this title; or

(ii) at the time any quarters of coverage are earned—

(I) is described in subparagraph (B) or (D) of section 1101(a)(15) of Title 8,

(II) is lawfully admitted temporarily to the United States for business (in the case of an individual described in such subparagraph (B)) or the performance as a crewman (in the case of an individual described in such subparagraph (D)), and

(III) the business engaged in or service as a crewman performed is within the scope of the terms of such individual's admission to the United States.

(D) has filed application for disability insurance benefits, and

(E) is under a disability (as defined in subsection (d) of this section),

shall be entitled to a disability insurance benefit * * *

* * *

(c) Definitions; insured status; waiting period

For purposes of this section—

(1) An individual shall be insured for disability insurance benefits in any month if—

(A) he would have been a fully insured individual (as defined in section 414 of this title) had he attained age 62 and filed application for benefits under section 402(a) of this title on the first day of such month, and

(B)(i) he had not less than 20 quarters of coverage during the 40–quarter period which ends with the quarter in which such month occurred, or

(ii) if such month ends before the quarter in which he attains (or would attain) age 31, not less than one-half (and not less than 6) of the quarters during the period ending with the quarter in which such month occurred and beginning after he attained the age of 21 were quarters of coverage, or (if the number of quarters in such period is less than 12) not less than 6 of the quarters in the 12–quarter period ending with such quarter were quarters of coverage, or

(iii) in the case of an individual (not otherwise insured under clause (i)) who, by reason of section 416(i)(3)(B)(ii) of this title, had a prior period of disability that began during a period before the quarter in which he or she attained age 31, not less than one-half of the quarters beginning after such individual attained age 21 and ending with the quarter in which such month occurs are quarters of coverage, or (if the number of quarters in such period is less than 12) not less than 6 of the quarters in the 12–quarter period ending with such quarter are quarters of coverage;

except that the provisions of subparagraph (B) of this paragraph shall not apply in the case of an individual who is blind (within the meaning of "blindness" as defined in section 416(i)(1) of this title). * * *

(2) The term "waiting period" means, in the case of any application for disability insurance benefits, the earliest period of five consecutive calendar months—

(A) throughout which the individual with respect to whom such application is filed has been under a disability, and

(B) (i) which begins not earlier than with the first day of the seventeenth month before the month in which such application is filed if such individual is insured for disability insurance benefits in such seventeenth month, or (ii) if he is not so insured in such month, which begins not earlier than with the first day of the first month after such seventeenth month in which he is so insured.

* * *

(d) "Disability" defined

(1) The term "disability" means—

(A) inability to engage in any substantial gainful activity by reason of any medically determinable physical or mental impairment which can be expected to result in death or which has lasted or can be expected to last for a continuous period of not less than 12 months; or

(B) in the case of an individual who has attained the age of 55 and is blind (within the meaning of "blindness" as defined in section 416(i)(1) of this title), inability by reason of such blindness to engage in substantial gainful activity requiring skills or abilities comparable to those of any gainful activity in which he has previously engaged with some regularity and over a substantial period of time.

(2) For purposes of paragraph (1)(A)—

(A) An individual shall be determined to be under a disability only if his physical or mental impairment or impairments are of such severity that he is not only unable to do his previous work but cannot, considering his age, education, and work experience, engage in any other kind of substantial gainful work which exists in the national economy, regardless of whether such work exists in the immediate area in which he lives, or whether a specific job vacancy exists for him, or whether he would be hired if he applied for work. For purposes of the preceding sentence (with respect to any individual), "work which exists in the national economy" means work which exists in significant numbers either in the region where such individual lives or in several regions of the country.

(B) In determining whether an individual's physical or mental impairment or impairments are of a sufficient medical severity that such impairment or impairments could be the basis of eligibility under this section, the Commissioner of Social Security shall consider the combined effect of all of the individual's impairments without regard to whether any such impairment, if considered separately, would be of such severity. If the Commissioner of Social Security does find a medically severe combination of impairments, the combined impact of the impairments shall be considered throughout the disability determination process.

(C) An individual shall not be considered to be disabled for purposes of this subchapter if alcoholism or drug addiction would (but for this subparagraph) be a contributing factor material to the Commissioner's determination that the individual is disabled.

(3) For purposes of this subsection, a "physical or mental impairment" is an impairment that results from anatomical, physiological, or psychological abnormalities which are demonstrable by medically acceptable clinical and laboratory diagnostic techniques.

* * *

(5)(A) An individual shall not be considered to be under a disability unless he furnishes such medical and other evidence of the existence thereof as the Commissioner of Social Security may require. An individual's statement as to pain or other symptoms shall not alone be conclusive evidence of disability as defined in this section; there must be medical signs and findings, established by medically acceptable clinical or laboratory diagnostic techniques, which show the existence of a medical impairment that results from anatomical, physiological, or psychological abnormalities which could reasonably be expected to produce the pain or other symptoms alleged and which, when considered with all evidence required to be furnished under this paragraph (including statements of the individual or his physician as to the intensity and persistence of such pain or other symptoms which may reasonably be accepted as consistent with the medical signs and findings), would lead to a conclusion that the individual is under a disability. Objective medical evidence of pain or other symptoms established by medically acceptable clinical or laboratory techniques (for example, deteriorating nerve or muscle tissue) must be considered in reaching a conclusion as to whether the individual is under a disability. Any non-Federal hospital, clinic, laboratory, or other provider of medical services, or physician not in the employ of the Federal Government, which supplies medical evidence required and requested by the Commissioner of Social Security under this paragraph shall be entitled to payment from the Commissioner of Social Security for the reasonable cost of providing such evidence.

(B) In making any determination with respect to whether an individual is under a disability or continues to be under a disability, the Commissioner of Social Security shall consider all evidence available in such individual's case record, and shall develop a complete medical history of at least the preceding twelve months for any case in which a determination is made that the individual is not under a disability. In making any determination the Commissioner of Social Security shall make every reasonable effort to obtain from the individual's treating physician (or other treating health care provider) all medical evidence, including diagnostic tests, necessary in order to properly make such determination, prior to evaluating medical evidence obtained from any other source on a consultative basis.

(6)(A) Notwithstanding any other provision of this subchapter, any physical or mental impairment which arises in connection with the commission by an individual (after October 19, 1980) of an offense which constitutes a felony under applicable law and for which such individual is subsequently convicted, or which is aggravated in connection with such an offense (but only to the extent so aggravated), shall not be considered in determining whether an individual is under a disability.

> (B) Notwithstanding any other provision of this subchapter, any physical or mental impairment which arises in connection with an individual's confinement in a jail, prison, or other penal institution or correctional facility pursuant to such individual's conviction of an offense (committed after October 19, 1980) constituting a felony under applicable law, or which is aggravated in connection with such a confinement (but only to the extent so aggravated), shall not be considered in determining whether such individual is under a disability for purposes of benefits payable for any month during which such individual is so confined.

* * *

(f) Standard of review for termination of disability benefits

A recipient of benefits under this subchapter or subchapter XVIII of this chapter based on the disability of any individual may be determined not to be entitled to such benefits on the basis of a finding that the physical or mental impairment on the basis of which such benefits are provided has ceased, does not exist, or is not disabling only if such finding is supported by—

(1) substantial evidence which demonstrates that—

> (A) there has been any medical improvement in the individual's impairment or combination of impairments (other than medical improvement which is not related to the individual's ability to work), and

> (B) the individual is now able to engage in substantial gainful activity; or

(2) substantial evidence which—

> (A) consists of new medical evidence and a new assessment of the individual's residual functional capacity, and demonstrates that—

>> (i) although the individual has not improved medically, he or she is nonetheless a beneficiary of advances in medical or vocational therapy or technology (related to the individual's ability to work), and

>> (ii) the individual is now able to engage in substantial gainful activity, or

(B) demonstrates that—

(i) although the individual has not improved medically, he or she has undergone vocational therapy (related to the individual's ability to work), and

(ii) the individual is now able to engage in substantial gainful activity; or

(3) substantial evidence which demonstrates that, as determined on the basis of new or improved diagnostic techniques or evaluations, the individual's impairment or combination of impairments is not as disabling as it was considered to be at the time of the most recent prior decision that he or she was under a disability or continued to be under a disability, and that therefore the individual is able to engage in substantial gainful activity; or

(4) substantial evidence (which may be evidence on the record at the time any prior determination of the entitlement to benefits based on disability was made, or newly obtained evidence which relates to that determination) which demonstrates that a prior determination was in error.

Nothing in this subsection shall be construed to require a determination that a recipient of benefits under this subchapter or subchapter XVIII of this chapter based on an individual's disability is entitled to such benefits if the prior determination was fraudulently obtained or if the individual is engaged in substantial gainful activity, cannot be located, or fails, without good cause, to cooperate in a review of the entitlement to such benefits or to follow prescribed treatment which would be expected to restore his or her ability to engage in substantial gainful activity. In making for purposes of the preceding sentence any determination relating to fraudulent behavior by any individual or failure by any individual without good cause to cooperate or to take any required action, the Commissioner of Social Security shall specifically take into account any physical, mental, educational, or linguistic limitation such individual may have (including any lack of facility with the English language). Any determination under this section shall be made on the basis of all the evidence available in the individual's case file, including new evidence concerning the individual's prior or current condition which is presented by the individual or secured by the Commissioner of Social Security. Any determination made under this section shall be made on the basis of the weight of the evidence and on a neutral basis with regard to the individual's condition, without any initial inference as to the presence or absence of disability being drawn from the fact that the individual has previously been determined to be disabled. * * *

* * *

42 U.S.C. § 1382c Definitions [Supplemental Security Income]

(a)(1) For purposes of this subchapter, the term "aged, blind, or disabled individual" means an individual who—

(A) is 65 years of age or older, is blind (as determined under paragraph (2)), or is disabled (as determined under paragraph (3)), and

(B)(i) is a resident of the United States, and is either (I) a citizen or (II) an alien lawfully admitted for permanent residence or otherwise permanently residing in the United States under color of law (including any alien who is lawfully present in the United States as a result of the application of the provisions of section 1182(d)(5) of Title 8), or

(ii) is a child who is a citizen of the United States, and who is living with a parent of the child who is a member of the Armed Forces of the United States assigned to permanent duty ashore outside the United States.

* * *

(3)(A) Except as provided in subparagraph (C), an individual shall be considered to be disabled for purposes of this subchapter if he is unable to engage in any substantial gainful activity by reason of any medically determinable physical or mental impairment which can be expected to result in death or which has lasted or can be expected to last for a continuous period of not less than twelve months.

(B) For purposes of subparagraph (A), an individual shall be determined to be under a disability only if his physical or mental impairment or impairments are of such severity that he is not only unable to do his previous work but cannot, considering his age, education, and work experience, engage in any other kind of substantial gainful work which exists in the national economy, regardless of whether such work exists in the immediate area in which he lives, or whether a specific job vacancy exists for him, or whether he would be hired if he applied for work. For purposes of the preceding sentence (with respect to any individual), "work which exists in the national economy" means work which exists in significant numbers either in the region where such individual lives or in several regions of the country.

(C)(i) An individual under the age of 18 shall be considered disabled for the purposes of this subchapter if that individual has a medically determinable physical or mental impairment, which results in marked and severe functional limitations, and which can be expected to result in death or which has lasted or can be expected to last for a continuous period of not less than 12 months.

(ii) Notwithstanding clause (i), no individual under the age of 18 who engages in substantial gainful activity (determined in accordance with regulations prescribed pursuant to subparagraph (E)) may be considered to be disabled.

(D) For purposes of this paragraph, a physical or mental impairment is an impairment that results from anatomical, physiological, or psychological abnormalities which are demonstrable by medically acceptable clinical and laboratory diagnostic techniques.

(E) The Commissioner of Social Security shall by regulations prescribe the criteria for determining when services performed or earnings derived from services demonstrate an individual's ability to engage in substantial gainful activity. In determining whether an individual is able to engage in substantial gainful activity by reason of his earnings, where his disability is sufficiently severe to result in a functional limitation requiring assistance in order for him to work, there shall be excluded from such earnings an amount equal to the cost (to such individual) of any attendant care services, medical devices, equipment, prostheses, and similar items and services (not including routine drugs or routine medical services unless such drugs or services are necessary for the control of the disabling condition) which are necessary (as determined by the Commissioner of Social Security in regulations) for that purpose, whether or not such assistance is also needed to enable him to carry out his normal daily functions; except that the amounts to be excluded shall be subject to such reasonable limits as the Commissioner of Social Security may prescribe. Notwithstanding the provisions of subparagraph (B), an individual whose services or earnings meet such criteria shall be found not to be disabled. The Commissioner of Social Security shall make determinations under this subchapter with respect to substantial gainful activity, without regard to the legality of the activity.

(F) Notwithstanding the provisions of subparagraph (A) through (E), an individual shall also be considered to be disabled for purposes of this subchapter if he is permanently and totally disabled as defined under a State plan approved under subchapter XIV or XVI of this chapter as in effect for October 1972 and received aid under such plan (on the basis of disability) for December 1973 (and for at least one month prior to July 1973), so long as he is continuously disabled as so defined.

(G) In determining whether an individual's physical or mental impairment or impairments are of a sufficient medical severity that such impairment or impairments could be the basis of eligibility under this section, the Commissioner of Social Security shall consider the combined effect of all of the individual's impairments without regard to whether any such impairment, if considered separately, would be of such severity. If the Commissioner of Social Security does find a medically severe combination of impairments, the combined impact of the impairments shall be considered throughout the disability determination process.

* * *

(I) In making any determination under this subchapter with respect to the disability of an individual who has not attained the age of 18 years and to whom section 421(h) of this title does not apply, the Commissioner of Social Security shall make reasonable efforts to ensure that a qualified pediatrician or other individual who specializes in a field of medicine appropriate to the disability of the individual (as determined by the Commissioner of Social Security) evaluates the case of such individual.

(J) Notwithstanding subparagraph (A), an individual shall not be considered to be disabled for purposes of this subchapter if alcoholism or drug addiction would (but for this subparagraph) be a contributing factor material to the Commissioner's determination that the individual is disabled.

(4) A recipient of benefits based on disability under this subchapter may be determined not to be entitled to such benefits on the basis of a finding that the physical or mental impairment on the basis of which such benefits are provided has ceased, does not exist, or is not disabling only if such finding is supported by—

(A) in the case of an individual who is age 18 or older—

(i) substantial evidence which demonstrates that—

(I) there has been any medical improvement in the individual's impairment or combination of impairments (other than medical improvement which is not related to the individual's ability to work), and

(II) the individual is now able to engage in substantial gainful activity; or

(ii) substantial evidence (except in the case of an individual eligible to receive benefits under section 1382h of this title) which—

(I) consists of new medical evidence and a new assessment of the individual's residual functional capacity, and demonstrates that—

(aa) although the individual has not improved medically, he or she is nonetheless a beneficiary of advances in medical or vocational therapy or technology (related to the individual's ability to work), and

(bb) the individual is now able to engage in substantial gainful activity, or

(II) demonstrates that—

(aa) although the individual has not improved medically, he or she has undergone vocational therapy (related to the individual's ability to work), and

(bb) the individual is now able to engage in substantial gainful activity; or

(iii) substantial evidence which demonstrates that, as determined on the basis of new or improved diagnostic techniques or evaluations, the individual's impairment or combination of impairments is not as disabling as it was considered to be at the time of the most recent prior decision that he or she was under a disability or continued to be under a disability, and that therefore the individual is able to engage in substantial gainful activity; or

(B) in the case of an individual who is under the age of 18—

(i) substantial evidence which demonstrates that there has been medical improvement in the individual's impairment or combination of impairments, and that such impairment or combination of impairments no longer results in marked and severe functional limitations; or

(ii) substantial evidence which demonstrates that, as determined on the basis of new or improved diagnostic techniques or evaluations, the individual's impairment or combination of impairments, is not as disabling as it was considered to be at the time of the most recent prior decision that the individual was under a disability or continued to be under a disability, and such impairment or combination of impairments does not result in marked and severe functional limitations; or

(C) in the case of any individual, substantial evidence (which may be evidence on the record at the time any prior determination of the entitlement to benefits based on disability was made, or newly obtained evidence which relates to that determination) which demonstrates that a prior determination was in error.

Nothing in this paragraph shall be construed to require a determination that an individual receiving benefits based on disability under this subchapter is entitled to such benefits if the prior determination was fraudulently obtained or if the individual is engaged in substantial gainful activity, cannot be located, or fails, without good cause, to cooperate in a review of his or her entitlement or to follow prescribed treatment which would be expected (i) to restore his or her ability to engage in substantial gainful activity, or (ii) in the case of an individual under the age of 18, to eliminate or improve the individual's impairment or combination of impairments so that it no longer results in marked and severe functional limitations. Any determination under this paragraph shall be made on the basis of all the evidence available in the individual's case file, including new evidence concerning the individual's prior or current condition which is presented by the individual or secured by the Commissioner of Social Security. Any determination made under this paragraph shall be made on the basis of the weight of the evidence and on a neutral basis with regard to the individual's condition, without any initial inference as to the presence or absence of disability being drawn from the fact that the individual has previously been determined to be disabled.

* * *

(f)(1) For purposes of determining eligibility for and the amount of benefits for any individual who is married and whose spouse is living with him in the same household but is not an eligible spouse, such individual's income and resources shall be deemed to include any income and resources of such spouse, whether or not available to such individual, except to the extent determined by the Commissioner of Social Security to be inequitable under the circumstances.

(2)(A) For purposes of determining eligibility for and the amount of benefits for any individual who is a child under age 18, such individual's income and resources shall be deemed to include any income and resources of a parent of such individual (or the spouse of such a parent) who is living in the same household as such individual, whether or not available to such individual, except to the extent determined by the Commissioner of Social Security to be inequitable under the circumstances.

(B) Subparagraph (A) shall not apply in the case of any child who has not attained the age of 18 years who—

(i) is disabled;

(ii) received benefits under this subchapter, pursuant to section 1382(e)(1)(B) of this title, while in an institution described in section 1382(e)(1)(B) of this title;

(iii) is eligible for medical assistance under a State home care plan approved by the Secretary under the provisions of section 1396n(c) of this title relating to waivers, or authorized under section 1396a(e)(3) of this title; and

(iv) but for this subparagraph, would not be eligible for benefits under this subchapter.

(3) For purposes of determining eligibility for and the amount of benefits for any individual who is an alien, such individual's income and resources shall be deemed to include the income and resources of his sponsor and such sponsor's spouse (if such alien has a sponsor) as provided in section 1382j of this title. Any such income deemed to be income of such individual shall be treated as unearned income of such individual.

(4) For purposes of paragraphs (1) and (2), a spouse or parent (or spouse of such a parent) who is absent from the household in which the individual lives due solely to a duty assignment as a member of the Armed Forces on active duty shall, in the absence of evidence to the contrary, be deemed to be living in the same household as the individual.

* * *

42 U.S.C. § 1383. Procedure for payment of benefits

* * *

(b) Overpayments and underpayments; adjustment, recovery, or payment of amounts by Commissioner

(1)(A) Whenever the Commissioner of Social Security finds that more or less than the correct amount of benefits has been paid with respect to any individual, proper adjustment or recovery shall, subject to the succeeding provisions of this subsection, be made by appropriate adjustments in future payments to such individual or by recovery from such individual or his eligible spouse (or from the estate of either) or by payment to such individual or his eligible spouse, or, if such individual is deceased, by payment—

(i) to any surviving spouse of such individual, whether or not the individual's eligible spouse, if * * * such surviving husband or wife was living in the same household with the individual at the time of his death or within the 6 months immediately preceding the month of such death, or

(ii) if such individual was a disabled or blind child who was living with his parent or parents at the time of his death or within the 6 months immediately preceding the month of such death, to such parent or parents.

(B) The Commissioner of Social Security (i) shall make such provision as the Commissioner finds appropriate in the case of payment of more than the correct amount of benefits with respect to an individual with a view to avoiding penalizing such individual or his eligible spouse who was without fault in connection with the overpayment, if adjustment or recovery on account of such overpayment in such case would defeat the purposes of this subchapter, or be against equity and good conscience, or (because of the small amount involved) impede efficient or effective administration of this subchapter, and (ii) shall in any event make the adjustment or recovery (in the case of payment of more than the correct amount of benefits), in the case of an individual or eligible spouse receiving monthly benefit payments under this subchapter * * *, in amounts which in the aggregate do not exceed (for any month) the lesser of (I) the amount of his or their benefit under this subchapter for that month or (II) an amount equal to 10 percent of his or their income for that month * * *, and in the case of an individual or eligible spouse to whom a lump sum is payable under this subchapter * * * shall, as at least one means of recovering such overpayment, make the adjustment or recovery from the lump sum payment in an amount equal to not less than the lesser of the amount of the overpayment or the lump sum payment, unless fraud, willful misrepresentation, or concealment of material information was involved on the part of the individual or spouse in connection with the overpayment, or unless the individual requests that such adjustment or recovery be made at a higher or lower rate and the Commissioner of Social Security determines that adjustment or recovery at such rate is justified and appropriate. The availability (in the case of an individual who has been paid more than the correct amount of benefits) of procedures for adjustment or recovery at a limited rate under clause (ii) of the preceding sentence shall not, in and of itself, prevent or restrict the provision (in such case) of more substantial relief under clause (i) of such sentence.

* * *

(e) Administrative requirements prescribed by Commissioner; criteria; reduction of benefits to individual for noncompliance with requirements; payment to homeless

    * * *

(7)(A)(i) The Commissioner of Social Security shall immediately redetermine the eligibility of an individual for benefits under this subchapter if there is reason to believe that fraud or similar fault was involved in the application of the individual for such benefits, unless a United States attorney, or equivalent State prosecutor, with jurisdiction over potential or actual related criminal cases, certifies, in writing, that there is a substantial risk that such action by the Commissioner of Social Security with regard to recipients in a particular investigation would jeopardize the criminal prosecution of a person involved in a suspected fraud.

(ii) When redetermining the eligibility, or making an initial determination of eligibility, of an individual for benefits under this subchapter, the Commissioner of Social Security shall disregard any evidence if there is reason to believe that fraud or similar fault was involved in the providing of such evidence.

(B) For purposes of subparagraph (A), similar fault is involved with respect to a determination if—

(i) an incorrect or incomplete statement that is material to the determination is knowingly made; or

(ii) information that is material to the determination is knowingly concealed.

(C) If, after redetermining the eligibility of an individual for benefits under this subchapter, the Commissioner of Social Security determines that there is insufficient evidence to support such eligibility, the Commissioner of Social Security may terminate such eligibility and may treat benefits paid on the basis of such insufficient evidence as overpayments.

* * *

* * *